COLLINS

GERMAN ★ ENGLISH
ENGLISH ★ GERMAN
DICTIONARY

BERKLEY BOOKS, NEW YORK

General Editor
R. H. Thomas

The text of this dictionary has been
adapted from the Collins Gem
German-English, English-German
Dictionary

First published in this edition 1982

Editors
Veronika Schnoor, Ute Nicol, Peter Terrell

Assistant Editor
Anne Dickinson

This Berkley book contains the complete
text of the original edition.
It has been completely reset in a typeface
designed for easy reading and was printed
from new film.

COLLINS GERMAN/ENGLISH · ENGLISH/GERMAN
DICTIONARY

A Berkley Book / published by arrangement with
Collins Publishers

PRINTING HISTORY
Collins Gem edition published 1982
Berkley edition / August 1982

ISBN: 0-425-10272-6

A BERKLEY BOOK " TM 757,375
Berkley Books are published by The Berkley Publishing Group,
200 Madison Avenue, New York, New York 10016.
The name "BERKLEY" and the "B" logo
are trademarks belonging to Berkley Publishing Corporation.
PRINTED IN THE UNITED STATES OF AMERICA

10   9   8   7

VORWORT

Der Wörterbuchbenutzer, dem es darum geht, Englisch zu lesen und zu verstehen, findet in diesem Wörterbuch eine ausführliche Erfassung der englischen Gegenwartssprache mit zahlreichen gebräuchlichen Wendungen und Anwendungsbeispielen. Er findet in alphabetischen Listen auch die häufigsten geläufigen Abkürzungen, Kurzwörter und Ortsnamen.

Der Benutzer, der sich verständigen, also auf Englisch ausdrücken will, findet eine klare und ausführliche Behandlung aller Grundwörter mit zahlreichen Hinweisen für eine angebrachte Übersetzung und den korrekten Gebrauch.

INTRODUCTION

The user whose aim is to read and understand German will find a comprehensive and up-to-date wordlist including numerous phrases in current use. He will also find listed alphabetically the main irregular forms with a cross-reference to the basic form where a translation is given, as well as some of the most common abbreviations, acronyms and geographical names in separate alphabetical lists.

The user who wishes to communicate and to express himself in the foreign language will find clear and detailed treatment of all the basic words, with numerous indicators pointing to the appropriate translation, and helping him to use it correctly.

Adjektiv	**a**	adjective
Abkürzung	**abbr**	abbreviation
Akkusativ	**acc**	accusative
Adverb	**ad**	adverb
Landwirtschaft	**Agr**	agriculture
Anatomie	**Anat**	anatomy
Architektur	**Archit**	architecture
Artikel	**art**	article
Kunst	**Art**	art
Astrologie	**Astrol**	astrology
Astronomie	**Astron**	astronomy
attributiv	**attr**	attributive
Kraftfahrzeuge	**Aut**	automobiles
Hilfsverb	**aux**	auxiliary
Luftfahrt	**Aviat**	aviation
Biologie	**Biol**	biology
Botanik	**Bot**	botany
britisch	**Brit**	British
Kartenspiel	**Cards**	
Chemie	**Chem**	chemistry
Film	**Cine**	cinema
Konjunktion	**cj**	conjunction
umgangssprachlich	**col**	colloquial
Handel	**Comm**	commerce
Komparativ	**comp**	comparative
Kochen und Backen	**Cook**	cooking
zusammengesetztes Wort	**cpd**	compound
Dativ	**dat**	dative
kirchlich	**Eccl**	ecclesiastical
Elektrizität	**Elec**	electricity
besonders	**esp**	especially
und so weiter	**etc**	et cetera
etwas	**etw**	something
Euphemismus, Hüllwort	**euph**	euphemism
Femininum	**f**	feminine
übertragen	**fig**	figurative
Finanzwesen	**Fin**	finance
Genitiv	**gen**	genitive
Geographie	**Geog**	geography
Grammatik	**Gram**	grammar
Geschichte	**Hist**	history
unpersönlich	**impers**	impersonal
unbestimmt	**indef**	indefinite
nicht getrennt gebraucht	**insep**	inseparable
Interjektion, Ausruf	**interj**	interjection
interrogativ, fragend	**interrog**	interrogative
unveränderlich	**inv**	invariable
unregelmäßig	**irreg**	irregular
jemand	**jd**	somebody
jemandem	**jdm**	(to) somebody
jemanden	**jdn**	somebody
jemandes	**jds**	somebody's
Rechtswesen	**Jur**	law
Sprachwissenschaft	**Ling**	linguistics
wörtlich	**lit**	literal
literarisch	**liter**	literary

Literatur	Liter	of literature
Maskulinum	m	masculine
Mathematik	Math	mathematics
Medizin	Med	medicine
Meteorologie	Met	meteorology
militärisch	Mil	military
Bergbau	Min	mining
Musik	Mus	music
Substantiv, Hauptwort	n	noun
nautisch, Seefahrt	Naut	nautical, naval
Nominativ	nom	nominative
Neutrum	nt	neuter
Zahlwort	num	numeral
Objekt	obj	object
veraltet	old	
sich	o.s.	oneself
Parlament	Parl	parliament
abschätzig	pej	pejorative
Photographie	Phot	photography
Physik	Phys	physics
Plural	pl	plural
Politik	Pol	politics
besitzanzeigend	poss	possessive
Präfix, Vorsilbe	pref	prefix
Präposition	prep	preposition
Presse	Press	
Typographie	Print	printing
Pronomen, Fürwort	pron	pronoun
Psychologie	Psych	psychology
1. Vergangenheit, Imperfekt	pt	past
Partizip Perfekt	ptp	past participle
Radio	Rad	radio
Eisenbahn	Rail	railways
Relativ-	rel	relative
Religion	Rel	religion
jemand (−en, −em)	sb	someone, somebody
Schulwesen	Sch	school
Naturwissenschaft	Sci	science
schottisch	Scot	Scottish
Singular, Einzahl	sing	singular
Skisport	Ski	skiing
etwas	sth	something
Suffix, Nachsilbe	suff	suffix
Superlativ	superl	superlative
Technik	Tech	technology
Nachrichtentechnik	Tel	telecommunications
Theater	Theat	theatre
Fernsehen	TV	television
Hochschulwesen	Univ	university
(nord)amerikanisch	US	(North) America
gewöhnlich	usu	usually
Verb	v	verb
intransitives Verb	vi	intransitive verb
reflexives Verb	vr	reflexive verb
transitives Verb	vt	transitive verb
Zoologie	Zool	zoology
zwischen zwei Sprechern	~	change of speaker
ungefähre Entsprechung	≈	cultural equivalent
eingetragenes Warenzeichen	®	registered trademark

Regular German noun endings

nom		gen	pl	nom		gen	pl
-ant	m	-anten	-anten	-ion	f	-ion	-ionen
-anz	f	-anz	-anzen	-ist	m	-isten	-isten
-ar	m	-ar(e)s	-are	-ium	nt	-iums	-ien
-chen	nt	-chens	-chen	-ius	m	-ius	-iusse
-ei	f	-ei	-eien	-ive	f	-ive	-iven
-elle	f	-elle	-ellen	-keit	f	-keit	-keiten
-ent	m	-enten	-enten	-lein	nt	-leins	-lein
-enz	f	-enz	-enzen	-ling	m	-lings	-linge
-ette	f	-ette	-etten	-ment	nt	-ments	-mente
-eur	m	-eurs	-eure	-mus	m	-mus	-men
-euse	f	-euse	-eusen	-schaft	f	-schaft	-schaften
-heit	f	-heit	-heiten	-tät	f	-tät	-täten
-ie	f	-ie	-ien	-tor	m	-tors	-toren
-ik	f	-ik	-iken	-ung	f	-ung	-ungen
-in	f	-in	-innen	-ur	f	-ur	-uren
-ine	f	-ine	-inen				

Phonetic symbols
Lautschrift

[:] length mark Längezeichen   ['] stress mark Betonung
['] glottal stop Knacklaut

all vowel sounds are approximate only
alle Vokallaute sind nur ungefähre Entsprechungen

lie	[aɪ]	weit	day	[eɪ]	
now	[aʊ]	Haut	girl	[ɜ:]	
above	[ə]	bitte	board	[ɔ:]	
green	[i:]	viel	root	[u:]	Hut
pity	[ɪ]	Bischof	come	[ʌ]	Butler
rot	[ɒ,ɔ]	Post	salon	[ɔ̃]	Champignon
full	[ʊ]	Pult	avant (garde)	[ɑ̃]	Ensemble
			fair	[ɛə]	mehr
bet	[b]	Ball	beer	[ɪə]	Bier
dim	[d]	dann	toy	[ɔɪ]	Heu
face	[f]	Faß	pure	[ʊə]	
go	[g]	Gast	wine	[w]	
hit	[h]	Herr	thin	[θ]	
you	[j]	ja	this	[ð]	
cat	[k]	kalt			
lick	[l]	Last	Hast	[a]	mash
must	[m]	Mast	Ensemble	[ã]	avant (garde)
nut	[n]	Nuß	Metall	[e]	meths
bang	[ŋ]	lang	häßlich	[ɛ]	
pepper	[p]	Pakt	Cousin	[ɛ̃]	
sit	[s]	Rasse	vital	[i]	
shame	[ʃ]	Schal	Moral	[o]	
tell	[t]	Tal	Champignon	[õ]	salon
vine	[v]	was	ökonomisch	[ø]	
loch	[x]	Bach	gönnen	[œ]	
zero	[z]	Hase	Heu	[ɔy]	toy
leisure	[ʒ]	Genie	kulant	[u]	
bat	[æ]		physisch	[y]	
farm	[ɑ:]	Bahn	Müll	[ʏ]	
set	[e]	Kette	ich	[ç]	

[*]   r can be pronounced before a vowel; Bindungs–R

DEUTSCH - ENGLISCH
GERMAN - ENGLISH

A

A, a [a:] *nt* A, a.

Aal [a:l] *m* -(e)s, -e eel.

Aas [a:s] *nt* -es, -e *or* **Äser** carrion; ~**geier** *m* vulture.

ab [ap] *prep +dat* from; *ad* off; **links** ~ to the left; ~ **und zu** *or* **an** now and then *or* again; **von da** ~ from then on; **der Knopf ist** ~ the button has come off.

Abänderung ['ap'ɛndərʊŋ] *f* alteration.

abarbeiten ['ap'arbaɪtən] *vr* wear o.s. out, slave away.

Abart ['ap'a:rt] *f* (*Biol*) variety; **a~ig** *a* abnormal.

Abbau ['apbau] *m* -(e)s dismantling; (*Verminderung*) reduction (*gen* in); (*Verfall*) decline (*gen* in); (*Min*) mining; quarrying; (*Chem*) decomposition; **a~en** *vt* dismantle; (*Min*) mine; quarry; (*verringern*) reduce; (*Chem*) break down.

abbeißen ['apbaɪsən] *vt irreg* bite off.

abberufen ['apbəru:fən] *vt irreg* recall.

Abberufung *f* recall.

abbestellen ['apbəʃtɛlən] *vt* cancel.

abbezahlen ['apbətsa:lən] *vt* pay off.

abbiegen ['apbi:gən] *irreg vi* turn off; (*Straße*) bend; *vt* bend; (*verhindern*) ward off.

Abbild ['apbɪlt] *nt* portrayal; (*einer Person*) image, likeness; **a~en** ['apbɪldən] *vt* portray; ~**ung** *f* illustration.

Abbitte ['apbɪtə] *f*: ~ **leisten** *or* **tun** make one's apologies (*bei* to).

abblasen ['apbla:zən] *vt irreg* blow off; (*fig*) call off.

abblenden ['apblɛndən] *vti* (*Aut*) dip, dim (*US*).

Abblendlicht *nt* dipped *or* dimmed (*US*) headlights *pl*.

abbrechen ['apbrɛçən] *vti irreg* break off; *Gebäude* pull down; *Zelt* take down; (*aufhören*) stop.

abbrennen ['apbrɛnən] *irreg vt* burn off; *Feuerwerk* let off; *vi* (*aux sein*) burn down; **abgebrannt sein** (*col*) be broke.

abbringen ['apbrɪŋən] *vt irreg*: **jdn von etw** ~ dissuade sb from sth; **jdn vom Weg** ~ divert sb; **ich bringe den Verschluß nicht ab** (*col*) I can't get the top off.

abbröckeln ['apbrœkəln] *vti* crumble off *or* away.

Abbruch ['apbrux] *m* (*von Verhandlungen etc*) breaking off; (*von Haus*) demolition; **jdm/etw** ~ **tun** harm sb/sth; **a~reif** *a* only fit for demolition.

abbrühen ['apbry:ən] *vt* scald; **abgebrüht** (*col*) hard-boiled.

abbuchen ['apbu:xən] *vt* debit.

abbürsten ['apbyrstən] *vt* brush off.

abdanken ['apdaŋkən] *vi* resign; (*König*) abdicate.

Abdankung *f* resignation; abdication.

abdecken ['apdɛkən] *vt* uncover; *Tisch* clear; *Loch* cover.

abdichten ['apdɪçtən] *vt* seal; (*Naut*) caulk.

abdrängen ['apdrɛŋən] *vt* push off.

abdrehen ['apdre:ən] *vt Gas* turn off; *Licht* switch off; *Film* shoot; **jdm den Hals** ~ wring sb's neck; *vi* (*Schiff*) change course.

abdrosseln ['apdrɔsəln] *vt* throttle; (*Aut*) stall; *Produktion* cut back.

Abdruck ['apdrʊk] *m* (*Nachdrucken*) reprinting; (*Gedrucktes*) reprint; (*Gips—, Wachs—*) impression; (*Finger—*) print; **a~en** *vt* print, publish.

abdrücken ['apdrʏkən] *vt* make an impression of; *Waffe* fire; *Person* hug, squeeze; **jdm die Luft** ~ squeeze all the breath out of sb; *vr* leave imprints; (*abstoßen*) push o.s. away.

abebben ['ap'ɛbən] *vi* ebb away.

Abend ['a:bənt] *m* -s, -e evening; **zu** ~ **essen** have dinner *or* supper; **a~ ad** evening; ~**brot** *nt*, ~**essen** *nt* supper; **a~füllend** taking up the whole evening; ~**kurs** *m* evening classes *pl*; ~**land** *nt* West; **a~lich** *a* evening; ~**mahl** *nt* Holy Communion; ~**rot** *nt* sunset; **a~s** *ad* in the evening.

Abenteuer ['a:bəntɔyər] *nt* -s, - adventure; **a~lich** *a* adventurous.

Abenteurer *m* -s, - adventurer; ~**in** *f* adventuress.

aber ['a:bər] *cj* but; (*jedoch*) however; **das ist** ~ **schön** that's really nice; **nun ist** ~ **Schluß!** now that's enough!; *ad* **tausend und** ~ **tausend** thousands upon thousands; **A~** *nt* but; **A~glaube** *m* superstition; ~**gläubisch** *a* superstitious.

aberkennen ['ap'ɛrkɛnən] *vt irreg*: **jdm etw** ~ deprive sb of sth, take sth (*away*) from sb.

Aberkennung *f* taking away.

aber- *cpd*: ~**malig** *a* repeated; ~**mals** *ad* once again.

abfahren ['ap-fa:rən] *irreg vi* leave, depart; *vt* take *or* cart away; *Strecke* drive; *Reifen* wear; *Fahrkarte* use.

Abfahrt ['ap-fa:rt] *f* departure; (*Ski*) descent; (*Piste*) run; ~**slauf** *m* (*Ski*) descent, run down; ~**(s)-tag** *m* day of departure; ~**szeit** *f* departure time.

Abfall ['ap-fal] *m* waste; (*von Speisen etc*) rubbish, garbage (*US*); (*Neigung*) slope; (*Verschlechterung*) decline; ~**eimer** *m* rubbish bin, garbage can (*US*); **a~en** *vi irreg* (*lit, fig*) fall *or* drop off; (*Pol, vom*

Glauben) break away; (*sich neigen*) fall *or* drop away.

abfällig ['ap-fɛlɪç] *a* disparaging, deprecatory.

abfangen ['ap-faŋən] *vt irreg* intercept; *Person* catch; (*unter Kontrolle bringen*) check.

abfärben ['ap-fɛrbən] *vi* (*lit*) lose its colour; (*Wäsche*) run; (*fig*) rub off.

abfassen ['ap-fasən] *vt* write, draft.

abfertigen ['ap-fɛrtɪgən] *vt* prepare for dispatch, process; (*an der Grenze*) clear; *Kundschaft* attend to; **jdn kurz ~** give sb short shrift.

Abfertigung *f* preparing for dispatch, processing; clearance.

abfeuern ['ap-fɔʏərn] *vt* fire.

abfinden ['ap-fɪndən] *irreg vt* pay off; *vr* come to terms; **sich mit jdm ~/nicht ~** put up with/not get on with sb.

Abfindung *f* (*von Gläubigern*) payment; (*Geld*) sum in settlement.

abflauen ['ap-flauən] *vi* (*Wind, Erregung*) die away, subside; (*Nachfrage, Geschäft*) fall *or* drop off.

abfliegen ['ap-fli:gən] *irreg vi* (*Flugzeug*) take off; (*Passagier auch*) fly; *vt Gebiet* fly over.

abfließen ['ap-fli:sən] *vi irreg* drain away.

Abflug ['ap-flu:k] *m* departure; (*Start*) take-off; **~zeit** *f* departure time.

Abfluß ['ap-flus] *m* draining away; (*Öffnung*) outlet.

abfragen ['ap-fra:gən] *vt* test; **jdn** *or* **jdm etw ~** question sb on sth.

Abfuhr ['ap-fu:r] *f* **-, -en** removal; (*fig*) snub, rebuff.

Abführ- ['ap-fy:r] *cpd:* **a~en** *vt* lead away; *Gelder, Steuern* pay; *vi* (*Med*) have a laxative effect; **~mittel** *nt* laxative, purgative.

abfüllen ['ap-fʏlən] *vt* draw off; (*in Flaschen*) bottle.

Abgabe ['apga:bə] *f* handing in; (*von Ball*) pass; (*Steuer*) tax; (*eines Amtes*) giving up; (*einer Erklärung*) giving; **a~nfrei** *a* tax-free; **a~npflichtig** *a* liable to tax.

Abgang ['apgaŋ] *m* (*von Schule*) leaving; (*Theat*) exit; (*Med: Ausscheiden*) passing; (*Fehlgeburt*) miscarriage; (*Abfahrt*) departure; (*der Post, von Waren*) dispatch.

Abgas ['apga:s] *nt* waste gas; (*Aut*) exhaust.

abgeben ['apge:bən] *irreg vt Gegenstand* hand *or* give in; *Ball* pass; *Wärme* give off; *Amt* hand over; *Schuß* fire; *Erklärung, Urteil* give; (*darstellen, sein*) make; **jdm etw ~** (*überlassen*) let sb have sth; *vr:* **sich mit jdm/etw ~** associate with sb/bother with sth.

abgedroschen ['apgədrɔʃən] *a* hackneyed; *Witz* corny.

abgefeimt ['apgəfaɪmt] *a* cunning.

abgegriffen ['apgəgrɪfən] *a Buch* well-thumbed; *Redensart* hackneyed.

abgehen ['apge:ən] *irreg vi* go away, leave; (*Theat*) exit; (*Post*) go; (*Med*) be passed; (*Baby*) die; (*Knopf etc*) come off; (*abgezogen werden*) be taken off; (*Straße*) branch off; **etw geht jdm ab** (*fehlt*) sb

lacks sth; *vt Strecke* go *or* walk along.

abgelegen ['apgəle:gən] *a* remote.

abgemacht ['apgəmaxt] *a* fixed; **~!** done.

abgeneigt ['apgənaɪkt] *a* averse to, disinclined.

Abgeordnete(r) ['apgə'ɔrdnətə(r)] *mf* member of parliament; elected representative.

Abgesandte(r) ['apgəzantə(r)] *mf* delegate; (*Pol*) envoy.

abgeschmackt ['apgəʃmakt] *a* tasteless; **A~heit** *f* lack of taste; (*Bemerkung*) tasteless remark.

abgesehen ['apgəze:ən] *a:* **es auf jdn/etw ~ haben** be after sb/sth; **~ von. . .** apart from. . .

abgespannt ['apgəʃpant] *a* tired out.

abgestanden ['apgəʃtandən] *a* stale; *Bier auch* flat.

abgestorben ['apgəʃtɔrbən] *a* numb; (*Biol, Med*) dead.

abgetakelt ['apgəta:kəlt] *a* (*col*) decrepit, past it.

abgetragen ['apgətra:gən] *a* shabby, worn out.

abgewinnen ['apgəvɪnən] *vt irreg:* **jdm Geld ~** win money from sb; **einer Sache etw/Geschmack ~** get sth/pleasure from sth.

abgewöhnen ['apgəvø:nən] *vt:* **jdm/sich etw ~** cure sb of sth/give sth up.

abgleiten ['apglaɪtən] *vi irreg* slip, slide.

Abgott ['apgɔt] *m* idol.

abgöttisch ['apgœtɪʃ] *a:* **~ lieben** idolize.

abgrenzen ['apgrɛntsən] *vt* (*lit, fig*) mark off; fence off.

Abgrund ['apgrunt] *m* (*lit, fig*) abyss.

abgründig ['apgrʏndɪç] *a* unfathomable; *Lächeln* cryptic.

abhacken ['aphakən] *vt* chop off.

abhaken ['apha:kən] *vt* tick off.

abhalten ['aphaltən] *vt irreg Versammlung* hold; **jdn von etw ~** (*fernhalten*) keep sb away from sth; (*hindern*) keep sb from sth.

abhandeln ['aphandəln] *vt Thema* deal with; **jdm die Waren/8 Mark ~** do a deal with sb for the goods/beat sb down 8 marks.

abhanden [ap'handən] *a:* **~ kommen** get lost.

Abhandlung ['aphandluŋ] *f* treatise, discourse.

Abhang ['aphaŋ] *m* slope.

abhängen ['aphɛŋən] *irreg vt Bild* take down; *Anhänger* uncouple; *Verfolger* shake off; *vi* (*Fleisch*) hang; **von jdm/etw ~** depend on sb/sth.

abhängig ['aphɛŋɪç] *a* dependent (*von* on); **A~keit** *f* dependence (*von* on).

abhärten ['aphɛrtən] *vtr* toughen (o.s.) up; **sich gegen etw ~** inure o.s. to sth.

abhauen ['aphauən] *irreg vt* cut off; *Baum* cut down; *vi* (*col*) clear off *or* out.

abheben ['aphe:bən] *irreg vt* lift (up); *Karten* cut; *Masche* slip; *Geld* withdraw, take out; *vi* (*Flugzeug*) take off; (*Rakete*) lift off; (*Cards*) cut; *vr* stand out (*von* from), contrast (*von* with).

abhelfen ['aphɛlfən] vi irreg (+dat) remedy.

abhetzen ['aphɛtsən] vr wear or tire o.s. out.

Abhilfe ['aphılfə] f remedy; ~ **schaffen** put things right.

abholen ['apho:lən] vt Gegenstand fetch, collect; Person call for; (am Bahnhof etc) pick up, meet.

abhorchen ['aphɔrçən] vt (Med) auscultate, sound.

abhören ['aphø:rən] vt Vokabeln test; Telefongespräch tap; Tonband etc listen to.

Abhörgerät nt bug.

Abitur [abi'tu:r] nt **-s, -e** German school leaving examination; ~**i'ent(in f)** m candidate for school leaving certificate.

abkämmen ['apkɛmən] vt Gegend comb, scour.

abkanzeln ['apkantsəln] vt (col) bawl out.

abkapseln ['apkapsəln] vr shut or cut o.s. off.

abkaufen ['apkaufən] vt: **jdm etw** ~ buy sth from sb.

abkehren ['apke:rən] vt Blick avert, turn away; vr turn away.

Abklatsch ['apklatʃ] m **-es, -e** (fig) (poor) copy.

abklingen ['apklıŋən] vi irreg die away; (Radio) fade out.

abknöpfen ['apknœpfən] vt unbutton; **jdm etw** ~ (col) get sth off sb.

abkochen ['apkɔxən] vt boil.

abkommen ['apkɔmən] vi irreg get away; **von der Straße/von einem Plan** ~ leave the road/give up a plan; **A**~ nt **-s, -** agreement.

abkömmlich ['apkœmlıç] a available, free.

abkratzen ['apkratsən] vt scrape off; vi (col) kick the bucket.

abkühlen ['apky:lən] vt cool down; vr (Mensch) cool down or off; (Wetter) get cool; (Zuneigung) cool.

Abkunft ['apkunft] f- origin, birth.

abkürzen ['apkyrtsən] vt shorten; Wort auch abbreviate; **den Weg** ~ take a short cut.

Abkürzung f (Wort) abbreviation; (Weg) short cut.

abladen ['apla:dən] vt irreg unload.

Ablage ['apla:gə] f **-, -n** (für Akten) tray; (für Kleider) cloakroom; **a**~**rn** vt deposit; vr be deposited; vi mature.

ablassen ['aplasən] irreg vt Wasser, Dampf let off; (vom Preis) knock off; vi: **von etw** ~ give sth up, abandon sth.

Ablauf ['aplauf] m (Abfluß) drain; (von Ereignissen) course; (einer Frist, Zeit) expiry; **a**~**en** irreg vi (abfließen) drain away; (Ereignisse) happen; (Frist, Zeit, Paß) expire; vt Sohlen wear (down or out); **jdm den Rang a**~**en** steal a march on sb.

ablegen ['aple:gən] vt put or lay down; Kleider take off; Gewohnheit get rid of; Prüfung take, sit; Zeugnis give.

Ableger m **-s, -** layer; (fig) branch, offshoot.

ablehnen ['aple:nən] vt reject; Einladung decline, refuse; vi decline, refuse.

Ablehnung f rejection; refusal.

ableiten ['aplaıtən] vt Wasser divert; (deduzieren) deduce; Wort derive.

Ableitung f diversion; deduction; derivation; (Wort) derivative.

ablenken ['aplɛŋkən] vt turn away, deflect; (zerstreuen) distract; vi change the subject.

Ablenkung f distraction.

ablesen ['aple:zən] vt irreg read out; Meßgeräte read.

ableugnen ['aplɔygnən] vt deny.

ablichten ['aplıçtən] vt photocopy; photograph.

abliefern ['apli:fərn] vt deliver; **etw bei jdm/einer Dienststelle** ~ hand sth over to sb/in at an office.

Ablieferung f delivery; ~**sschein** m delivery note.

abliegen ['apli:gən] vi irreg be some distance away; (fig) be far removed.

ablisten ['aplıstən] vt: **jdm etw** ~ trick or con sb out of sth.

ablösen ['aplø:zən] vt (abtrennen) take off, remove; (in Amt) take over from; Wache relieve.

Ablösung f removal; relieving.

abmachen ['apmaxən] vt take off; (vereinbaren) agree.

Abmachung f agreement.

abmagern ['apma:gərn] vi get thinner.

Abmagerungskur f diet; **eine** ~ **machen** go on a diet.

Abmarsch ['apmarʃ] m departure; **a**~**bereit** a ready to start; **a**~**ieren** vi march off.

abmelden ['apmɛldən] vt Zeitungen cancel; Auto take off the road; **jdn bei der Polizei** ~ register sb's departure with the police; vr give notice of one's departure; (im Hotel) check out.

abmessen ['apmɛsən] vt irreg measure.

Abmessung f measurement.

abmontieren ['apmɔnti:rən] vt take off.

abmühen ['apmy:ən] vr wear o.s. out.

Abnäher ['apnɛ:ər] m **-s, -** dart.

Abnahme ['apna:mə] f **-, -n** removal; (Comm) buying; (Verringerung) decrease (gen in).

abnehmen ['apne:mən] irreg vt take off, remove; Führerschein take away; Geld get (jdm out of sb); (kaufen, col: glauben) buy (jdm from sb); Prüfung hold; Maschen decrease; **jdm Arbeit** ~ take work off sb's shoulders; vi decrease; (schlanker werden) lose weight.

Abnehmer m **-s, -** purchaser, customer.

Abneigung ['apnaıguŋ] f aversion, dislike.

abnorm [ap'nɔrm] a abnormal.

abnötigen ['apnø:tıgən] vt: **jdm etw/Respekt** ~ force sth from sb/gain sb's respect.

abnutzen ['apnutsən] vt wear out.

Abnutzung f wear (and tear).

Abonnement [abɔn(e)'mã:] nt **-s, -s** subscription.

Abonnent(in f) [abɔ'nɛnt(ɪn)] m subscriber.

abonnieren [abɔ'niːrən] vt subscribe to.

abordnen ['apˈɔrdnən] vt delegate.

Abordnung f delegation.

Abort [a'bɔrt] m -(e)s lavatory.

abpacken ['appakən] vt pack.

abpassen ['appasən] vt Person, Gelegenheit wait for; (in Größe) Stoff etc adjust.

abpfeifen ['appfaifən] vti irreg (Sport) **(das Spiel)** ~ blow the whistle (for the end of the game).

Abpfiff ['appfɪf] m final whistle.

abplagen ['applaːgən] vr wear o.s. out.

Abprall ['appral] m rebound; (von Kugel) ricochet; a~en vi bounce off; ricochet.

abputzen ['apputsən] vt clean.

abquälen ['ap-kvɛːlən] vr drive o.s. frantic; **sich mit etw** ~ struggle with sth.

abraten ['apraːtən] vi irreg advise, warn (jdm von etw sb against sth).

abräumen ['aprɔymən] vt clear up or away.

abreagieren ['apreagiːrən] vt Zorn work off (an + dat on); vr calm down.

abrechnen ['aprɛçnən] vt deduct, take off; vi (lit) settle up; (fig) get even.

Abrechnung f settlement; (Rechnung) bill.

Abrede ['apreːdə] f: **etw in** ~ **stellen** deny or dispute sth.

abregen ['apreːgən] vr (col) calm or cool down.

abreiben ['apraibən] vtr irreg rub off; (säubern) wipe; **jdn mit einem Handtuch** ~ towel sb down.

Abreise ['apraizə] f departure; a~n vi leave, set off.

abreißen ['apraisən] vt irreg Haus tear down; Blatt tear off.

abrichten ['apriçtən] vt train.

abriegeln ['apriːgəln] vt Tür bolt; Straße, Gebiet seal off.

Abriß ['aprɪs] m -sses, -sse (Übersicht) outline.

Abruf ['apruːf] m: **auf** ~ on call; a~en vt irreg Mensch call away; (Comm) Ware request delivery of.

abrunden ['aprundən] vt round off.

abrüsten ['apryˈstən] vi disarm.

Abrüstung f disarmament.

abrutschen ['aprutʃən] vi slip; (Aviat) sideslip.

Absage ['apzaːgə] f -, -n refusal; a~n vt cancel, call off; Einladung turn down; vi cry off; (ablehnen) decline.

absägen ['apzɛːgən] vt saw off.

absahnen ['apzaːnən] vt (lit) skim; **das beste für sich** ~ take the cream.

Absatz ['apzats] m (Comm) sales pl; (Bodensatz) deposit; (neuer Abschnitt) paragraph; (Treppen—) landing; (Schuh—) heel; ~**flaute** f slump in the market; ~**gebiet** nt (Comm) market.

abschaben ['ap-ʃaːbən] vt scrape off; Möhren scrape.

abschaffen ['apʃafən] vt abolish, do away with.

Abschaffung f abolition.

abschalten ['ap-ʃaltən] vti (lit, col) switch off.

abschattieren ['ap-ʃatiːrən] vt shade.

abschätzen ['ap-ʃɛtsən] vt estimate; Lage assess; Person size up.

abschätzig ['ap-ʃɛtsɪç] a disparaging, derogatory.

Abschaum ['ap-ʃaum] m -(e)s scum.

Abscheu ['ap-ʃɔy] m -(e)s loathing, repugnance; a~**erregend** a repulsive, loathsome; a~**lich** [apˈʃɔylɪç] a abominable.

abschicken ['ap-ʃɪkən] vt send off.

abschieben ['ap-ʃiːbən] vt irreg push away; Person pack off.

Abschied ['ap-ʃiːt] m -(e)s, -e parting; (von Armee) discharge; ~ **nehmen** say good-bye (von jdm to sb), take one's leave (von jdm of sb); **seinen** ~ **nehmen** (Mil) apply for discharge; **zum** ~ on parting; ~**sbrief** m farewell letter; ~**sfeier** f farewell party.

abschießen ['ap-ʃiːsən] vt irreg Flugzeug shoot down; Geschoß fire; (col) Minister get rid of.

abschirmen ['ap-ʃɪrmən] vt screen.

abschlagen ['ap-ʃlaːgən] vt irreg (abhacken, Comm) knock off; (ablehnen) refuse; (Mil) repel.

abschlägig ['ap-ʃlɛːgɪç] a negative.

Abschlagszahlung f interim payment.

abschleifen ['ap-ʃlaifən] irreg vt grind down; Rost polish off; vr wear off.

Abschlepp- ['ap-ʃlɛp] cpd: ~**dienst** m (Aut) breakdown service; a~**en** vt take in tow; ~**seil** nt towrope.

abschließen ['ap-ʃliːsən] irreg vt Tür lock; (beenden) conclude, finish; Vertrag, Handel conclude; vr (sich isolieren) cut o.s. off.

Abschluß ['ap-ʃlus] m (Beendigung) close, conclusion; (Comm: Bilanz) balancing; (von Vertrag, Handel) conclusion; **zum** ~ in conclusion; ~**feier** f end-of-term party; ~**rechnung** f final account.

abschmieren ['ap-ʃmiːrən] vt (Aut) grease, lubricate.

abschneiden ['ap-ʃnaidən] irreg vt cut off; vi do, come off.

Abschnitt ['ap-ʃnɪt] m section; (Mil) sector; (Kontroll—) counterfoil; (Math) segment; (Zeit—) period.

abschnüren ['ap-ʃnyːrən] vt constrict.

abschöpfen ['ap-ʃœpfən] vt skim off.

abschrauben ['ap-ʃraubən] vt unscrew.

abschrecken ['ap-ʃrɛkən] vt deter, put off; (mit kaltem Wasser) plunge in cold water; ~d a deterrent; ~**des Beispiel** warning.

abschreiben ['ap-ʃraibən] vt irreg copy; (verlorengehen) write off; (Comm) deduct.

Abschreibung f (Comm) deduction; (Wertverminderung) depreciation.

Abschrift ['ap-ʃrɪft] f copy.

abschürfen ['ap-ʃyrfən] vt graze.

Abschuß ['ap-ʃus] m (eines Geschützes) firing; (Herunterschießen) shooting down; (Tötung) shooting.

abschüssig ['ap-ʃysɪç] a steep.

abschütteln ['ap-ʃytəln] vt shake off.

abschwächen ['ap-ʃvɛçən] vt lessen;

Behauptung, Kritik tone down; *vr* lessen.
abschweifen ['ap-ʃvaifən] *vi* wander.
Abschweifung *f* digression.
abschwellen ['ap-ʃvɛlən] *vi irreg* (*Geschwulst*) go down; (*Lärm*) die down.
abschwenken ['ap-ʃvɛŋkən] *vi* turn away.
abschwören ['ap-ʃvøːrən] *vi irreg* (+*dat*) renounce.

abseh- ['apze:] *cpd*: **~bar** a foreseeable; **in ~barer Zeit** in the foreseeable future; **das Ende ist ~bar** the end is in sight; **~en** *irreg vt* Ende, Folgen foresee; **jdm etw ~en** (*erlernen*) copy sth from sb; *vi*: **von etw ~en** refrain from sth; (*nicht berücksichtigen*) leave sth out of consideration.

abseits ['apzaits] *ad* out of the way; *prep* +*gen* away from; **A~** *nt* (*Sport*) offside; **im A~ stehen** be offside.

Absend- ['apzɛnd] *cpd*: **a~en** *vt irreg* send off, dispatch; **~er** *m* **-s**, - sender; **~ung** *f* dispatch.

absetz- ['apzɛts] *cpd*: **~bar** a *Beamter* dismissible; *Waren* saleable; (*von Steuer*) deductible; **~en** *vt* (*niederstellen, aussteigen lassen*) put down; (*abnehmen*) take off; (*Comm: verkaufen*) sell; (*Fin: abziehen*) deduct; (*entlassen*) dismiss; *König* depose; (*streichen*) drop; (*hervorheben*) pick out; *vr* (*sich entfernen*) clear off; (*sich ablagern*) be deposited; **A~ung** *f* (*Fin: Abzug*) deduction; (*Entlassung*) dismissal; (*von König*) deposing; (*Streichung*) dropping.

absichern ['apzɪçərn] *vtr* make safe; (*schützen*) safeguard.

Absicht ['apzɪçt] *f* intention; **mit ~ on** purpose; **a~lich** a intentional, deliberate; **a~slos** a unintentional.

absinken ['apzɪŋkən] *vi irreg* sink; (*Temperatur, Geschwindigkeit*) decrease.

absitzen ['apzɪtsən] *irreg vi* dismount; *vt Strafe* serve.

absolut [apzo'lu:t] a absolute; **A~ismus** [-'tɪsmʊs] *m* absolutism.

absolvieren [apzɔl'viːrən] *vt* (*Sch*) complete.

absonder- ['apzɔndər] *cpd*: **~lich** [ap'zɔndərlɪç] a odd, strange; **~n** *vt* separate; (*ausscheiden*) give off, secrete; *vr* cut o.s. off; **A~ung** *f* separation; (*Med*) secretion.

abspalten ['ap-ʃpaltən] *vt* split off.
Abspannung ['ap-ʃpanʊŋ] *f* (*Ermüdung*) exhaustion.
absparen ['ap-ʃpa:rən] *vt*: **sich** (*dat*) **etw ~** scrimp and save for sth.
abspeisen ['ap-ʃpaizən] *vt* (*fig*) fob off.
abspenstig ['ap-ʃpɛnstɪç] a: **~ machen** lure away (*jdm* from sb).
absperren ['ap-ʃpɛrən] *vt* block or close off; *Tür* lock.
Absperrung *f* (*Vorgang*) blocking or closing off; (*Sperre*) barricade.
abspielen ['ap-ʃpiːlən] *vt* Platte, Tonband play; (*Sport*) Ball pass; **vom Blatt ~** (*Mus*) sight-read; *vr* happen.
absplittern ['ap-ʃplɪtərn] *vti* chip off.
Absprache ['ap-ʃpra:xə] *f* arrangement.
absprechen ['ap-ʃprɛçən] *vt irreg* (*vereinbaren*) arrange; **jdm etw ~** deny sb sth.

abspringen ['ap-ʃprɪŋən] *vi irreg* jump down/off; (*Farbe, Lack*) flake off; (*Aviat*) bale out; (*sich distanzieren*) back out.
Absprung ['ap-ʃprʊŋ] *m* jump.
abspülen ['ap-ʃpyːlən] *vt* rinse; *Geschirr* wash up.
abstammen ['ap-ʃtamən] *vi* be descended; (*Wort*) be derived.
Abstammung *f* descent; derivation.
Abstand ['ap-ʃtant] *m* distance; (*zeitlich*) interval; **davon ~ nehmen, etw zu tun** refrain from doing sth; **~ halten** (*Aut*) keep one's distance; **mit ~ der beste** by far the best; **~ssumme** *f* compensation.
abstatten ['ap-ʃtatən] *vt* Dank give; Besuch pay.
abstauben ['ap-ʃtaubən] *vti* dust; (*col: stehlen*) pinch; **(den Ball) ~** (*Sport*) tuck the ball away.
abstechen ['ap-ʃtɛçən] *irreg vt* cut; *Tier* cut the throat of; *vi* contrast (*gegen, von* with).
Abstecher *m* **-s**, - detour.
abstecken ['ap-ʃtɛkən] *vt* (*losmachen*) unpin; *Fläche* mark out.
abstehen ['ap-ʃteːən] *vi irreg* (*Ohren, Haare*) stick out; (*entfernt sein*) stand away.
absteigen ['ap-ʃtaigən] *vi irreg* (*vom Rad etc*) get off, dismount; (*in Gasthof*) put up (*in* +*dat* at); (*Sport*) be relegated (*in* +*acc* to).
abstellen ['ap-ʃtɛlən] *vt* (*niederstellen*) put down; (*entfernt stellen*) pull out; (*hinstellen*) Auto park; (*ausschalten*) turn or switch off; Mißstand, Unsitte stop; (*ausrichten*) gear (*auf* +*acc* to).
Abstellgleis *nt* siding.
abstempeln ['ap-ʃtɛmpəln] *vt* stamp.
absterben ['ap-ʃtɛrbən] *vi irreg* die; (*Körperteil*) go numb.
Abstieg ['ap-ʃtiːk] *m* **-(e)s, -e** descent; (*Sport*) relegation; (*fig*) decline.
abstimmen ['ap-ʃtɪmən] *vi* vote; *vt Instrument* tune (*auf* +*acc* to); *Interessen* match (*auf* +*acc* with); *Termine, Ziele* fit in (*auf* +*acc* with); *vr* agree.
Abstimmung *f* vote.
abstinent [apsti'nɛnt] a abstemious; (*von Alkohol*) teetotal.
Abstinenz [apsti'nɛnts] *f* abstinence; teetotalism; **~ler** *m* **-s**, - teetotaller.
abstoßen ['ap-ʃto:sən] *vt irreg* push off or away; (*verkaufen*) unload; (*anekeln*) repel, repulse; **~d** a repulsive.
abstrahieren [apstra'hi:rən] *vti* abstract.
abstrakt [ap'strakt] a abstract; *ad* abstractly, in the abstract; **A~ion** [apstraktsi'o:n] *f* abstraction; **A~um** *nt* **-s**, **-kta** abstract concept/noun.
abstreiten ['ap-ʃtraitən] *vt irreg* deny.
Abstrich ['ap-ʃtrɪç] *m* (*Abzug*) cut; (*Med*) smear; **~e machen** lower one's sights.
abstufen ['ap-ʃtu:fən] *vt* Hang terrace; Farben shade; Gehälter grade.
abstumpfen ['ap-ʃtʊmpfən] *vt* (*lit, fig*) dull, blunt; *vi* (*lit, fig*) become dulled.
Absturz ['ap-ʃtʊrts] *m* fall; (*Aviat*) crash.
abstürzen ['ap-ʃtyrtsən] *vi* fall; (*Aviat*) crash.

absuchen ['apzuːxən] vt scour, search.

absurd [ap'zʊrt] a absurd.

Abszeß [aps'tsɛs] m -sses, -sse abscess.

Abt [apt] m -(e)s, ⁼e abbot.

abtasten ['aptastən] vt feel, probe.

abtauen ['aptaʊən] vti thaw.

Abtei [ap'taɪ] f -, -en abbey.

Abteil [ap'taɪl] nt -(e)s, -e compartment; 'a~en vt divide up; (abtrennen) divide off; ~ung f (in Firma, Kaufhaus) department; (Mil) unit; ~ungsleiter m head of department.

abtönen ['aptøːnən] vt (Phot) tone down.

abtragen ['aptraːgən] vt irreg Hügel, Erde level down; Essen clear away; Kleider wear out; Schulden pay off.

abträglich ['aptrɛːklɪç] a harmful (dat to).

abtransportieren ['aptransportiːrən] vt take away, remove.

abtreiben ['aptraɪbən] irreg vt Boot, Flugzeug drive off course; Kind abort; vi be driven off course; abort.

Abtreibung f abortion; ~sversuch m attempted abortion.

abtrennen ['aptrɛnən] vt (lostrennen) detach; (entfernen) take off; (abteilen) separate off.

abtreten ['aptreːtən] irreg vt wear out; (überlassen) hand over, cede (jdm to sb); vi go off; (zurücktreten) step down.

Abtritt ['aptrɪt] m resignation.

abtrocknen ['aptrɔknən] vti dry.

abtrünnig ['aptrʏnɪç] a renegade.

abtun ['aptuːn] vt irreg take off; (fig) dismiss.

aburteilen ['apʔʊrtaɪlən] vt condemn.

abverlangen ['apfɛrlaŋən] vt: jdm etw ~ demand sth from sb.

abwägen ['apvɛːgən] vt irreg weigh up.

abwählen ['apvɛːlən] vt vote out (of office).

abwandeln ['apvandəln] vt adapt.

abwandern ['apvandərn] vi move away.

abwarten ['apvartən] vt wait for; vi wait.

abwärts ['apvɛrts] ad down.

Abwasch ['apvaʃ] m -(e)s washing-up; a~en vt irreg Schmutz wash off; Geschirr wash (up).

Abwasser ['apvasər] nt -s, -wässer sewage.

abwechseln ['apvɛksəln] vir alternate; (Personen) take turns; ~d a alternate.

Abweg ['apveːk] m: auf ~e geraten/führen go/lead astray; a~ig ['apveːgɪç] a wrong.

Abwehr ['apveːr] f - defence; (Schutz) protection; (—dienst) counter-intelligence (service); a~en vt ward off; Ball stop; a~ende Geste dismissive gesture.

abweichen ['apvaɪçən] vi irreg deviate; (Meinung) differ; ~d a deviant; differing.

abweisen ['apvaɪzən] vt irreg turn away; Antrag turn down; ~d a Haltung cold.

abwenden ['apvɛndən] irreg vt avert; vr turn away.

abwerben ['apvɛrbən] vt irreg woo away (jdm from sb).

abwerfen ['apvɛrfən] vt irreg throw off;

Profit yield; (aus Flugzeug) drop; Spielkarte discard.

abwerten ['apvɛrtən] vt (Fin) devalue.

abwesend ['apveːzənt] a absent.

Abwesenheit ['apveːzənhaɪt] f absence.

abwickeln ['apvɪkəln] vt unwind; Geschäft wind up.

abwiegen ['apviːgən] vt irreg weigh out.

abwimmeln ['apvɪməln] vt (col) Person get rid of; Auftrag get out of.

abwinken ['apvɪŋkən] vi wave it/him etc aside.

abwirtschaften ['apvɪrtʃaftən] vi go downhill.

abwischen ['apvɪʃən] vt wipe off or away; (putzen) wipe.

abwracken ['apvrakən] vt Schiff break (up); abgewrackter Mensch wreck of a person.

Abwurf ['apvʊrf] m throwing off; (von Bomben etc) dropping; (von Reiter, Sport) throw.

abwürgen ['apvʏrgən] vt (col) scotch; Motor stall.

abzahlen ['aptsaːlən] vt pay off.

abzählen ['aptsɛːlən] vt count (up).

Abzahlung f repayment; auf ~ kaufen buy on hire purchase.

abzapfen ['aptsapfən] vt draw off; jdm Blut/Geld ~ take blood from sb/bleed sb.

abzäunen ['aptsɔynən] vt fence off.

Abzeichen ['aptsaɪçən] nt badge; (Orden) decoration.

abzeichnen ['aptsaɪçnən] vt draw, copy; Dokument initial; vr stand out; (fig: bevorstehen) loom.

Abziehbild nt transfer.

abziehen ['aptsiːən] irreg vt take off; Tier skin; Bett strip; Truppen withdraw; (subtrahieren) take away, subtract; (kopieren) run off; vi go away; (Truppen) withdraw.

abzielen ['aptsiːlən] vi be aimed (auf +acc at).

Abzug ['aptsuːk] m departure; (von Truppen) withdrawal; (Kopie) copy; (Subtraktion) subtraction; (Betrag) deduction; (Rauch—) flue; (von Waffen) trigger.

abzüglich ['aptsyːklɪç] prep +gen less.

abzweigen ['aptsvaɪgən] vi branch off; vt set aside.

Abzweigung f junction.

Accessoires [akseso'aːrs] pl accessories pl.

ach [ax] interj oh; mit A~ und Krach by the skin of one's teeth.

Achse ['aksə] f -, -n axis; (Aut) axle; auf ~ sein be on the move.

Achsel ['aksəl] f -, -n shoulder; ~höhle f armpit; ~zucken nt shrug of (one's shoulders).

Achsenbruch m (Aut) broken axle.

Acht [axt] f - attention; (Hist) proscription; sich in ~ nehmen be careful (vor +dat of), watch out (vor +dat for); etw außer a~ lassen disregard sth; ~ f -, -en, a~ num eight; a~ Tage a week; a~bar a worthy; a~e(r,s) a eighth; ~el num eighth; a~en vt respect; vi pay attention (*auf +acc* to); **darauf a~en, daß** ... be careful that ...

ächten ['ɛçtən] *vt* outlaw, ban.

Achter- *cpd:* **~bahn** *f* big dipper, roller coaster; **~deck** *nt* (*Naut*) afterdeck.

acht- *cpd:* **~fach** *a* eightfold; **~geben** *vi irreg* take care (*auf +acc* of); **~los** *a* careless; **~mal** *ad* eight times; **~sam** *a* attentive.

Achtung ['axtʊŋ] *f* attention; (*Ehrfurcht*) respect; *interj* look out!; (*Mil*) attention!; **~ Lebensgefahr/Stufe!** danger/mind the step!

acht- *cpd:* **~zehn** *num* eighteen; **~zig** *num* eighty; **A~ziger(in** *f*) *m* **-s, -** octogenarian; **A~zigerjahre** *pl* eighties *pl*.

ächzen ['ɛçtsən] *vi* groan (*vor +dat* with).

Acker ['akər] *m* **-s, ¨** field; **~bau** *m* agriculture; **a~n** *vti* plough; (*col*) slog away.

addieren [a'di:rən] *vt* add (up).

Addition [aditsi'o:n] *f* addition.

Ade [a'de:] *nt* **-s, -s, a~** *interj* farewell, adieu.

Adel ['a:dəl] *m* **-s** nobility; **a~ig, adlig** *a* noble.

Ader ['a:dər] *f* **-, -n** vein.

Adjektiv ['atjɛkti:f] *nt* **-s, -e** adjective.

Adler ['a:dlər] *m* **-s, -** eagle.

Admiral [atmi'ra:l] *m* **-s, -e** admiral; **~i·tät** *f* admiralty.

adopt- *cpd:* **~ieren** [adɔp'ti:rən] *vt* adopt; **A~ion** [adɔptsi'o:n] *f* adoption; **A~iveltern** [adɔp'ti:f-] *pl* adoptive parents *pl*; **A~ivkind** *nt* adopted child.

Adress- *cpd:* **~ant** [adrɛ'sant] *m* sender; **~at** [adrɛ'sa:t] *m* **-en, -en** addressee; **~e** [a'drɛsə] *f* **-, -n** address; **a~ieren** [adrɛ'si:rən] *vt* address (*an +acc* to).

Advent [at'vɛnt] *m* **-(e)s, -e** Advent; **~skranz** *m* Advent wreath.

Adverb [at'vɛrp] *nt* adverb; **a~ial** [atvɛrbi'a:l] *a* adverbial.

aero- [aero] *pref* aero-.

Affäre [a'fɛ:rə] *f* **-, -n** affair.

Affe ['afə] *m* **-n, -n** monkey.

affektiert [afɛk'ti:rt] *a* affected.

Affen- *cpd:* **a~artig** *a* like a monkey; **mit a~artiger Geschwindigkeit** like a flash; **~hitze** *f* (*col*) incredible heat; **~schande** *f* (*col*) crying shame.

affig ['afiç] *a* affected.

After ['aftər] *m* **-s, -** anus.

Agent [a'gɛnt] *m* agent; **~ur** [-'tu:r] *f* agency.

Aggregat [agre'ga:t] *nt* **-(e)s, -e** aggregate; (*Tech*) · unit; **~zustand** *m* (*Phys*) state.

Aggress- *cpd:* **~ion** [agrɛsi'o:n] *f* aggression; **a~iv** [agrɛ'si:f] *a* aggressive; **~ivität** [agrɛsivi'tɛ:t] *f* aggressiveness.

Agitation [agitatsi'o:n] *f* agitation.

Agrar- [a'gra:r] *cpd:* **~politik** *f* agricultural policy; **~staat** *m* agrarian state.

aha [a'ha:] *interj* aha.

Ahn [a:n] *m* **-en, -en** forebear.

ähneln ['ɛ:nəln] *vi* (*+dat*) be like, resemble; *vr* be alike *or* similar.

ahnen ['a:nən] *vt* suspect; *Tod, Gefahr* have a presentiment of; **du ahnst es nicht** you have no idea.

ähnlich ['ɛ:nliç] *a* similar (*dat* to); **Ä~keit** *f* similarity.

Ahnung ['a:nʊŋ] *f* idea, suspicion; presentiment; **a~slos** *a* unsuspecting.

Ahorn ['a:hɔrn] *m* **-s, -e** maple.

Ähre ['ɛ:rə] *f* **-, -n** ear.

Akademie [akade'mi:] *f* academy.

Akademiker(in *f*) [aka'de:mikər(in)] *m* **-s, -** university graduate.

akademisch *a* academic.

akklimatisieren [aklimati'zi:rən] *vr* become acclimatized.

Akkord [a'kɔrt] *m* **-(e)s, -e** (*Mus*) chord; **im ~ arbeiten** do piecework; **~arbeit** *f* piecework; **~eon** [a'kɔrdeɔn] *nt* **-s, -s** accordion.

Akkusativ ['akuzati:f] *m* **-s, -e** accusative (case).

Akrobat(in *f*) [akro'ba:t(in)] *m* **-en, -en** acrobat.

Akt [akt] *m* **-(e)s, -e** act; (*Art*) nude.

Akte ['aktə] *f* **-, -n** file; **etw zu den ~n legen** (*lit, fig*) file sth away; **a~nkundig** *a* on the files; **~nschrank** *m* filing cabinet; **~ntasche** *f* briefcase.

Aktie ['aktsiə] *f* **-, -n** share; **~ngesellschaft** *f* joint-stock company; **~nkurs** *m* share price.

Aktion [aktsi'o:n] *f* campaign; (*Polizei~, Such~*) action; **~är** ['nɛ:r] *m* **-s, -e** shareholder.

aktiv [ak'ti:f] *a* active; (*Mil*) regular; **A~ nt -s** (*Gram*) active (voice); **A~a** [ak'ti:va] *pl* assets *pl*; **~ieren** [-'vi:rən] *vt* activate; **A~i'tät** *f* activity; **A~saldo** *m* (*Comm*) credit balance.

Aktualität [aktuali'tɛ:t] *f* topicality; (*einer Mode*) up-to-dateness.

aktuell [aktu'el] *a* topical; up-to-date.

Akustik [a'kʊstik] *f* acoustics *pl*.

akut [a'ku:t] *a* acute.

Akzent [ak'tsɛnt] *m* accent; (*Betonung*) stress.

akzeptieren [aktsep'ti:rən] *vt* accept.

Alarm [a'larm] *m* **-(e)s, -e** alarm; **a~bereit** *a* standing by; **~bereitschaft** *f* stand-by; **a~ieren** [-'mi:rən] *vt* alarm.

albern ['albərn] *a* silly.

Album ['albʊm] *nt* **-s, Alben** album.

Algebra ['algebra] *f* - algebra.

alias ['a:lias] *ad* alias.

Alibi ['a:libi] *nt* **-s, -s** alibi.

Alimente [ali'mɛntə] *pl* alimony.

Alkohol ['alkohɔl] *m* **-s, -e** alcohol; **a~frei** *a* non-alcoholic; **~iker(in** *f*) [alko'ho:likər(in)] *m* **-s, -** alcoholic; **a~isch** *a* alcoholic; **~verbot** *nt* ban on alcohol.

All [al] *nt* **-s** universe; **a~'abendlich** *a* every evening; **a~bekannt** *a* universally known; **a~e(r,s)** *a* all; **wir a~e** all of us; **a~e** both of us/you *etc*; **a~e vier Jahre** every four years; *ad* (*col: zu Ende*) finished; **etw a~e machen** finish sth up.

Allee [a'le:] *f* **-, -n** avenue.

allein [a'lain] *ad* alone; (*ohne Hilfe*) on

one's own, by oneself; **nicht** ~ (*nicht nur*) not only; *cj* but, only; **A~gang** *m*: **im A~gang** on one's own; **A~herrscher** *m* autocrat; **A~hersteller** *m* sole manufacturer; ~**stehend** *a* single.

alle- *cpd*: ~**mal** *ad* (*jedesmal*) always; (*ohne weiteres*) with no bother; **ein für ~mal** once and for all; ~**nfalls** *ad* at all events; (*höchstens*) at most; ~**rbeste(r,s)** *a* very best; ~**rdings** *ad* (*zwar*) admittedly; (*gewiß*) certainly.

allerg- *cpd*: ~**isch** [a'lɛrgiʃ] *a* allergic; **A~ie** [-'gi:] *f* allergy.

aller- ['alər] *cpd*: ~**hand** *a inv* (*col*) all sorts of; **das ist doch ~hand!** that's a bit thick; ~**hand!** (*lobend*) good show!; **A~'heiligen** *nt* All Saints' Day; ~**höchste(r,s)** *a* very highest; ~**höchstens** *ad* at the very most; ~**lei** *a inv* all sorts of; ~**letzte(r,s)** *a* very last; ~**seits** *ad* on all sides; **prost ~seits!** cheers everyone!; ~**wenigste(r,s)** *a* very least.

alles *pron* everything; ~ **in allem** all in all.

allgemein ['algə'maɪn] *a* general; ~**gültig** *a* generally accepted; **A~heit** *f* (*Menschen*) general public; (*pl: Redensarten*) general remarks *pl*.

Alliierte(r) [ali'i:rtə(r)] *m* ally.

all- *cpd*: ~**jährlich** *a* annual; ~**mählich** *a* gradual; **A~tag** *m* everyday life; ~**täglich** *a,ad* daily; (*gewöhnlich*) commonplace; ~**tags** *ad* on weekdays; ~**'wissend** *a* omniscient; ~**zu** *ad* all too; ~**zuoft** *ad* all too often; ~**zuviel** *ad* too much.

Almosen ['almo:zən] *nt* **-s, -** alms *pl*.

Alpen ['alpən] *pl* Alps *pl*; ~**blume** *f* alpine flower.

Alphabet [alfa'be:t] *nt* **-(e)s, -e** alphabet; **a~isch** *a* alphabetical.

Alptraum ['alptraum] *m* nightmare.

als [als] *cj* (*zeitlich*) when; (*comp*) than; (*Gleichheit*) as; **nichts** ~ nothing but; ~ **ob** as if.

also ['alzo:] *cj* so; (*folglich*) therefore; **ich komme** ~ **morgen** so I'll come tomorrow; ~ **gut** *or* **schön!** okay then; ~**, so was!** well really!; **na** ~! there you are then!

alt [alt] *a* old; **ich bin nicht mehr der** ~**e** I am not the man I was; **alles beim** ~**en lassen** leave everything as it was; **A~** ~ *m* **-s, -e** (*Mus*) alto; **A~ar** [al'ta:r] *m* **-(e)s, -äre** altar; ~**bekannt** *a* long-known; **A~'eisen** *nt* scrap iron.

Alter ['altər] *nt* **-s, -** age; (*hohes*) old age; **im** ~ **von** at the age of; **a~n** *vi* grow old, age; ~**na'tive** *f* alternative; ~**sgrenze** *f* age limit; ~**sheim** *nt* old people's home; ~**sversorgung** *f* old age pension; ~**tum** *nt* antiquity.

alt- *cpd*: ~**'hergebracht** *a* traditional; ~**klug** *a* precocious; ~**modisch** *a* old-fashioned; **A~papier** *nt* waste paper; **A~stadt** *f* old town; **A~stimme** *f* alto; **A~'weibersommer** *m* Indian summer.

Aluminium [alu'mi:nium] *nt* **-s**

aluminium, aluminum (*US*); ~**folie** *f* tinfoil.

am [am] = **an dem**; ~ **Sterben** on the point of dying; ~ **15. März** on March 15th; ~ **besten/schönsten** best/most beautiful.

Amalgam [amal'ga:m] *nt* **-s, -e** amalgam.

Amateur [ama'tø:r] *m* amateur.

Amboß ['ambɔs] *m* **-sses, -sse** anvil.

ambulant [ambu'lant] *a* outpatient.

Ameise ['a:maɪzə] *f* **-, -n** ant.

Ampel ['ampəl] *f* **-, -n** traffic lights *pl*.

amphibisch [am'fi:biʃ] *a* amphibious.

amputieren [ampu'ti:rən] *vt* amputate.

Amsel ['amzəl] *f* **-, -n** blackbird.

Amt [amt] *nt* **-(e)s, ̈er** office; (*Pflicht*) duty; (*Tel*) exchange; **a~ieren** [am'ti:rən] *vi* hold office; **a~lich** *a* official; ~**sperson** *f* official; ~**srichter** *m* district judge; ~**sstunden** *pl* office hours *pl*; ~**szeit** *f* period of office.

amüsant [amy'zant] *a* amusing.

Amüsement [amyzə'mãː] *nt* amusement.

amüsieren [amy'zi:rən] *vt* amuse; *vr* enjoy o.s.

an [an] *prep* +*dat* (*räumlich*) at; (*auf, bei*) on; (*nahe bei*) near; (*zeitlich*) on; +*acc* (*räumlich*) (on)to; ~ **Ostern** at Easter; ~ **diesem Ort/Tag** at this place/on this day; ~ **und für sich** actually; *ad*: **von . . .** ~ **from . . . on;** ~ **die 5 DM** around 5 marks; **das Licht ist** ~ the light is on.

analog [ana'lo:k] *a* analogous; **A~ie** [-'gi:] *f* analogy.

Analyse [ana'ly:zə] *f* **-, -n** analysis.

analysieren [analy'zi:rən] *vt* analyse.

Ananas ['ananas] *f* **-, -** *or* **-se** pineapple.

Anarchie [anar'çi:] *f* anarchy.

Anatomie [anato'mi:] *f* anatomy.

anbahnen ['anba:nən] *vtr* open up.

anbändeln ['anbɛndəln] *vi* (*col*) flirt.

Anbau ['anbau] *m* (*Agr*) cultivation; (*Gebäude*) extension; **a~en** *vt* (*Agr*) cultivate; *Gebäudeteil* build on.

anbehalten ['anbəhaltən] *vt irreg* keep on.

anbei [an'baɪ] *ad* enclosed.

anbeißen ['anbaɪsən] *irreg vt* bite into; *vi* (*lit*) bite; (*fig*) swallow the bait; **zum A~** (*col*) good enough to eat.

anbelangen ['anbəlaŋən] *vt* concern; **was mich anbelangt** as far as I am concerned.

anberaumen ['anbəraumən] *vt* fix.

anbeten ['anbe:tən] *vt* worship.

Anbetracht ['anbətraxt] *m*: **in** ~ (+*gen*) in view of.

Anbetung *f* worship.

anbiedern ['anbi:dərn] *vr* make up (*bei* to).

anbieten ['anbi:tən] *irreg vt* offer; *vr* volunteer.

anbinden ['anbindən] *irreg vt* tie up; *vi*: **mit jdm** ~ start something with sb; **kurz angebunden** (*fig*) curt.

Anblick ['anblik] *m* sight; **a~en** *vt* look at.

anbrechen ['anbrɛçən] *irreg vt* start; *Vorräte* break into; *vi* start; (*Tag*) break; (*Nacht*) fall.

anbrennen ['anbrɛnən] *vi irreg* catch fire; (*Cook*) burn.

anbringen ['anbrɪŋən] *vt irreg* bring; *Ware* sell; (*festmachen*) fasten.

Anbruch ['anbrux] *m* beginning; ~ **des Tages/der Nacht** dawn/nightfall.

anbrüllen ['anbrʏlən] *vt* roar at.

Andacht ['andaxt] *f* -, **-en** devotion; (*Gottesdienst*) prayers *pl*.

andächtig ['andɛçtɪç] *a* devout.

andauern ['andauərn] *vi* last, go on; ~**d** *a* continual.

Andenken ['andɛŋkən] *nt* **-s,** - memory; souvenir.

andere(r,s) ['andərə(r,z)] *a* other; (*verschieden*) different; **am** ~ **n Tage** the next day; **ein** ~**s Mal** another time; **kein** ~**r** nobody else; **von etw** ~**m sprechen** talk about sth else; ~**nteils,** ~**rseits** *ad* on the other hand.

ändern ['ɛndərn] *vt* alter, change; *vr* change.

ander- *cpd*: ~**nfalls** *ad* otherwise; ~**s** *ad* differently (*als* from); **wer** ~**s?** who else?; **jd/irgendwo** ~**s** sb/somewhere else; ~**s aussehen/klingen** look/sound different; ~**sartig** a different; ~**seits** *ad* on the other hand; ~**sfarbig** *a* of a different colour; ~**sgläubig** *a* of a different faith; ~**sherum** *ad* the other way round; ~**swo** *ad* elsewhere; ~**swoher** *ad* from elsewhere; ~**swohin** *ad* elsewhere.

anderthalb ['andərt'halp] *a* one and a half.

Änderung ['ɛndərʊŋ] *f* alteration, change.

anderweitig ['andər'vaitɪç] *a* other; *ad* otherwise; (*anderswo*) elsewhere.

andeuten ['andɔytən] *vt* indicate; (*Wink geben*) hint at.

Andeutung *f* indication; hint.

Andrang ['andraŋ] *m* crush.

andrehen ['andreːən] *vt* turn *or* switch on; (*col*) **jdm etw** ~ unload sth onto sb.

androhen ['androːən] *vt*: **jdm etw** ~ threaten sb with sth.

aneignen ['an'aignən] *vt*: **sich** (*dat*) **etw** ~ acquire sth; (*widerrechtlich*) appropriate sth.

aneinander [an'ai'nandər] *ad* at/on/to *etc* one another *or* each other; ~**fügen** *vt* put together; ~**geraten** *vi irreg* clash; ~**legen** *vt* put together.

anekeln ['an'e:kəln] *vt* disgust.

Anemone [ane'mo:nə] *f* -, **-n** anemone.

anerkannt ['an'ɛrkant] *a* recognized, acknowledged.

anerkennen ['an'ɛrkɛnən] *vt irreg* recognize, acknowledge; (*würdigen*) appreciate; ~**d** *a* appreciative; ~**swert** *a* praiseworthy.

Anerkennung *f* recognition, acknowledgement; appreciation.

anfachen ['anfaxən] *vt* (*lit*) fan into flame; (*fig*) kindle.

anfahren ['anfa:rən] *irreg vt* deliver; (*fahren gegen*) hit; *Hafen* put into; (*fig*) bawl out; *vi* drive up; (*losfahren*) drive off.

Anfall ['anfal] *m* (*Med*) attack; **a**~**en** *irreg vt* attack; (*fig*) overcome; *vi* (*Arbeit*) come up; (*Produkt*) be obtained.

anfällig ['anfɛlɪç] *a* delicate; ~ **für etw** prone to sth.

Anfang ['anfaŋ] *m* **-(e)s, -fänge** beginning, start; **von** ~ **an** right from the beginning; **zu** ~ at the beginning; ~ **Mai** at the beginning of May; **a**~**en** *vti irreg* begin, start; (*machen*) do.

Anfänger(in *f*) ['anfɛŋər(ɪn)] *m* **-s,** - beginner.

anfänglich ['anfɛŋlɪç] *a* initial.

anfangs *ad* at first; **A**~**buchstabe** *m* initial *or* first letter; **A**~**stadium** *nt* initial stages *pl*.

anfassen ['anfasən] *vt* handle; (*berühren*) touch; *vi* lend a hand; *vr* feel.

anfechten ['anfɛçtən] *vt irreg* dispute; (*beunruhigen*) trouble.

anfertigen ['anfɛrtɪgən] *vt* make.

anfeuern ['anfɔyərn] *vt* (*fig*) spur on.

anflehen ['anfle:ən] *vt* implore.

anfliegen ['anfli:gən] *irreg vt* fly to; *vi* fly up.

Anflug ['anflu:k] *m* (*Aviat*) approach; (*Spur*) trace.

anfordern ['anfordərn] *vt* demand.

Anforderung *f* demand (*gen* for).

Anfrage ['anfra:gə] *f* inquiry; **a**~**n** *vi* inquire.

anfreunden ['anfrɔyndən] *vr* make friends.

anfügen ['anfy:gən] *vt* add; (*beifügen*) enclose.

anfühlen ['anfy:lən] *vtr* feel.

anführen ['anfy:rən] *vt* lead; (*zitieren*) quote; (*col: betrügen*) lead up the garden path.

Anführer *m* leader.

Anführung *f* leadership; (*Zitat*) quotation; ~**sstriche,** ~**szeichen** *pl* quotation marks *pl*, inverted commas *pl*.

Angabe ['anga:bə] *f* statement; (*Tech*) specification; (*col: Prahlerei*) boasting; (*Sport*) service; ~**n** *pl* (*Auskunft*) particulars *pl*.

angeben ['ange:bən] *irreg vt* give; (*anzeigen*) inform on; (*bestimmen*) set; *vi* (*col*) boast; (*Sport*) serve.

Angeber *m* **-s,** - (*col*) show-off; ~**ei** [-'rai] *f* (*col*) showing off.

angeblich ['ange:plɪç] *a* alleged.

angeboren ['angəbo:rən] *a* inborn, innate (*jdm* in sb).

Angebot ['angəbo:t] *nt* offer; (*Comm*) supply (*an* +*dat* of).

angebracht ['angəbraxt] *a* appropriate, in order.

angegriffen ['angəgrɪfən] *a* exhausted.

angeheitert ['angəhaitərt] *a* tipsy.

angehen ['ange:ən] *irreg vt* concern; (*angreifen*) attack; (*bitten*) approach (*um* for); *vi* (*Feuer*) light; (*col: beginnen*) begin; ~**d** *a* prospective; **er ist ein** ~**der Vierziger** he is approaching forty.

angehören ['angəhø:rən] *vi* belong (*dat* to).

Angehörige(r) *mf* relative.

Angeklagte(r) ['angəkla:ktə(r)] *mf* accused.

Angel ['aŋəl] f -, -n fishing rod; (Tür—) hinge.

Angelegenheit ['aŋəle·gənhaɪt] f affair, matter.

Angel- cpd: ~**haken** m fish hook; **a~n** vt catch; vi fish; ~**n** nt -s angling, fishing; ~**rute** f fishing rod.

angemessen ['aŋgəmɛsən] a appropriate, suitable.

angenehm ['aŋgəne:m] a pleasant; ~! (bei Vorstellung) pleased to meet you; **jdm** ~ **sein** be welcome.

angenommen ['aŋgənɔmən] a assumed; ~, **wir** ... assuming we....

angesehen ['aŋgəze:ən] a respected.

angesichts ['aŋgəzɪçts] prep +gen in view of, considering.

angespannt ['aŋgəʃpant] a Aufmerksamkeit close; Arbeit hard.

Angestellte(r) ['aŋgəʃtɛltə(r)] mf employee.

angetan ['aŋgəta:n] a: **von jdm/etw** ~ **sein** be impressed by sb/sth; **es jdm** ~ **haben** appeal to sb.

angewiesen ['aŋgəvi:zən] a: **auf jdn/etw** ~ **sein** be dependent on sb/sth.

angewöhnen ['aŋgəvø:nən] vt: **jdm/sich etw** ~ get sb/become accustomed to sth.

Angewohnheit ['aŋgəvo:nhaɪt] f habit.

angleichen ['aŋglaɪçən] vtr irreg adjust (dat to).

Angler ['aŋlər] m -s, - angler.

angreifen ['aŋgraɪfən] vt irreg attack; (anfassen) touch; Arbeit tackle; (beschädigen) damage.

Angreifer m -s, - attacker.

Angriff ['aŋgrɪf] m attack; **etw in** ~ **nehmen** make a start on sth.

Angst [aŋst] f -, ⁼e fear; ~ **haben** be afraid or scared (vor +dat of); ~ **haben um jdn/etw** be worried about sb/sth; **nur keine** ~! don't be scared; **a~** a: **jdm ist a~** sb is afraid or scared; **jdm a~ machen** scare sb; ~**hase** m (col) chicken, scaredy-cat.

ängst- [ɛŋst] cpd: ~**igen** vt frighten; vr worry (o.s.) (vor +dat, um about); ~**lich** a nervous; (besorgt) worried; **A~lichkeit** f nervousness.

anhaben ['anha:bən] vt irreg have on; **er kann mir nichts** ~ he can't hurt me.

anhalt- ['anhalt] cpd: ~**en** irreg vt stop; (gegen etw halten) hold up (jdm against sb); **jdn zur Arbeit/Höflichkeit** ~**en** make sb work/be polite; vi stop; (andauern) persist; ~**end** a persistent; **A~er** m -s, - hitch-hiker; **A~er fahren** hitch-hike; **A~spunkt** m clue.

anhand [an'hant] prep +gen with.

Anhang ['anhaŋ] m appendix; (Leute) family; supporters pl.

anhäng- ['anhɛŋ] cpd: ~**en** vt irreg hang up; Wagen couple up; Zusatz add (on); **sich an jdn** ~**en** attach to s.to sb; **A~er** m -s, - supporter; (Aut) trailer; (am Koffer) tag; (Schmuck) pendant; **A~erschaft** f supporters pl; **A~eschloß** nt padlock; ~**ig** a (Jur) sub judice; ~**ig machen** Prozeß bring; ~**lich** a devoted; **A~lichkeit** f devotion; **A~sel** nt -s, - appendage.

Anhäufung ['anhɔyfuŋ] f accumulation.

anheben ['anhe:bən] vt irreg lift up; Preise raise.

anheimelnd ['anhaɪməlnt] a comfortable, cosy.

anheimstellen [an'haɪmʃtɛlən] vt: **jdm etw** ~ leave sth up to sb.

Anhieb ['anhi:b] m: **auf** ~ at the very first go; (kurz entschlossen) on the spur of the moment.

Anhöhe ['anhø:ə] f hill.

anhören ['anhø:rən] vt listen to; (anmerken) hear; vr sound.

animieren [ani'mi:rən] vt encourage, urge on.

Anis [a'ni:s] m -es, -e aniseed.

ankaufen ['ankaʊfən] vt purchase, buy.

Anker ['aŋkər] m -s, - anchor; **vor** ~ **gehen** drop anchor; **a~n** vti anchor; ~**platz** m anchorage.

Anklage ['ankla:gə] f accusation; (Jur) charge; ~**bank** f dock; **a~n** vt accuse; (Jur) charge (gen with).

Ankläger ['ankle:gər] m accuser.

Anklang ['anklaŋ] m: **bei jdm** ~ **finden** meet with sb's approval.

Ankleide- ['anklaɪdə] cpd: ~**kabine** f changing cubicle; **a~n** vtr dress.

anklopfen ['anklɔpfən] vi knock.

anknüpfen ['anknʏpfən] vt fasten or tie on; (fig) start; vi (anschließen) refer (an +acc to).

ankommen ['ankɔmən] vi irreg arrive; (näherkommen) approach; (Anklang finden) go down (bei with); **es kommt darauf an** it depends; (wichtig sein) that (is what) matters; **es kommt auf ihn an** it depends on him; **es darauf** ~ **lassen** let things take their course; **gegen jdn/etw** ~ cope with sth/sb.

ankündigen ['ankʏndɪgən] vt announce.

Ankündigung f announcement.

Ankunft ['ankʊnft] f -, -künfte arrival; ~**szeit** f time of arrival.

ankurbeln ['ankʊrbəln] vt (Aut) crank; (fig) boost.

Anlage ['anla:gə] f disposition; (Begabung) talent; (Park) gardens pl; (Beilage) enclosure; (Tech) plant; (Fin) investment; (Entwurf) layout.

anlangen ['anlaŋən] vi arrive.

Anlaß ['anlas] m -sses, -lässe cause (zu for); (Ereignis) occasion; **aus** ~ (+gen) on the occasion of; ~ **zu etw geben** give rise to sth; **etw zum** ~ **nehmen** take the opportunity of sth.

anlassen irreg vt leave on; Motor start; vr (col) start off.

Anlasser m -s, - (Aut) starter.

anläßlich ['anlɛslɪç] prep +gen on the occasion of.

Anlauf ['anlaʊf] m run-up; **a~en** irreg vi begin; (Film) show; (Sport) run up; (Fenster) mist up; (Metall) tarnish; **rot a~en** colour; **gegen etw a~en** run into or up against sth; **angelaufen kommen** come running up; vt call at.

anläuten ['anlɔytən] vi ring.

anlegen ['anle:gən] vt put (an +acc

against/on); (anziehen) put on; (gestalten)
lay out; Geld invest; Gewehr aim (auf +acc
at); **es auf etw** (acc) ~ **be out for sth/to
do sth; sich mit jdm** ~ (col) quarrel with
sb; vi dock.

Anlegestelle f, **Anlegeplatz** m landing
place.

anlehnen ['anle:nən] vt lean (an +acc
against); Tür leave ajar; vr lean (an +acc
on).

anleiten ['anlaitən] vt instruct.

Anleitung f instructions pl.

anlernen ['anlɛrnən] vt teach, instruct.

anliegen ['anli:gən] vi irreg (Kleidung)
cling; **A**~ nt **-s,** - matter; (Wunsch) wish;
~**d** a adjacent; (beigefügt) enclosed.

Anlieger m **-s,** - resident.

anlügen ['anly:gən] vt irreg lie to.

anmachen ['anmaxən] vt attach;
Elektrisches put on; Salat dress.

anmaßen ['anma:sən] vt: **sich** (dat) **etw**
~ lay claim to sth; ~**d** a arrogant.

Anmaßung f presumption.

Anmeld- ['anmeld] cpd: ~**eformular** nt
registration form; **a**~**en** vt announce; vr
(sich ankündigen) make an appointment;
(polizeilich, für Kurs etc) register; ~**ung** f
announcement; appointment; registration.

anmerken ['anmɛrkən] vt observe;
(anstreichen) mark; **jdm etw** ~ notice
sb's sth; **sich** (dat) **nichts** ~ **lassen** not
give anything away.

Anmerkung f note.

Anmut ['anmu:t] f - grace; **a**~**en** vt give a
feeling; **a**~**ig** a charming.

annähen ['annɛ:ən] vt sew on.

annähern ['annɛ:ərn] vr get closer; ~**d** a
approximate.

Annäherung f approach; ~**sversuch** m
advances pl.

Annahme ['anna:mə] f -, **-n** acceptance;
(Vermutung) assumption.

annehm- ['anne:m] cpd: ~**bar** a
acceptable; ~**en** irreg vt accept; Namen
take; Kind adopt; (vermuten) suppose,
assume; **angenommen, das ist so**
assuming that is so; vr take care (gen of);
A~**lichkeit** f comfort.

annektieren [anɛk'ti:rən] vt annex.

Annonce [a'nõ:sə] f -, **-n** advertisement.

annoncieren [anõ'si:rən] vti advertise.

annullieren [anu'li:rən] vt annul.

Anode [a'no:də] f -, **-n** anode.

anöden ['an'ø:dən] vt (col) bore stiff.

anonym [ano'ny:m] a anonymous.

Anorak ['anorak] m **-s,** **-s** anorak.

anordnen ['an'ɔrdnən] vt arrange;
(befehlen) order.

Anordnung f arrangement; order.

anorganisch ['an'ɔrga:nɪʃ] a inorganic.

anpacken ['anpakən] vt grasp; (fig)
tackle; **mit** ~ lend a hand.

anpassen ['anpasən] vt fit (jdm on sb);
(fig) adapt (dat to); vr adapt.

Anpassung f fitting; adaptation;
a~**fähig** a adaptable.

Anpfiff ['anpfɪf] m (Sport) (starting)
whistle; kick-off; (col) rocket.

anpöbeln ['anpø:bəln] vt abuse.

Anprall ['anpral] m collision (gegen, an
+acc with).

anprangern ['anpraŋərn] vt denounce.

anpreisen ['anpraizən] vt irreg extol.

Anprobe ['anpro:bə] f trying on.

anprobieren ['anpro:bi:rən] vt try on.

anrechnen ['anrɛçnən] vt charge; (fig)
count; **jdm etw hoch** ~ value sb's sth
greatly.

Anrecht ['anrɛçt] nt right (auf +acc to).

Anrede ['anre:də] f form of address; **a**~**n**
vt address; (belästigen) accost.

anregen ['anre:gən] vt stimulate;
angeregte Unterhaltung lively discussion; ~**d** a stimulating.

Anregung f stimulation; (Vorschlag)
suggestion.

anreichern ['anraiçərn] vt enrich.

Anreise ['anraizə] f journey; **a**~**n** vi
arrive.

Anreiz ['anraits] m incentive.

Anrichte ['anrɪçtə] f -, **-n** sideboard; **a**~**n**
vt serve up; Unheil **a**~**n** make mischief.

anrüchig ['anryçiç] a dubious.

anrücken ['anrykən] vi approach; (Mil)
advance.

Anruf ['anru:f] m call; **a**~**en** vt irreg call
out to; (bitten) call on; (Tel) ring up,
phone, call.

anrühren ['anry:rən] vt touch; (mischen)
mix.

ans [ans] = **an das.**

Ansage ['anza:gə] f -, **-n** announcement;
a~**n** vt announce; vr say one will come;
~**r(in** f) m **-s,** - announcer.

ansammeln ['anzaməln] vtr collect.

Ansammlung f collection; (Leute) crowd.

ansässig ['anzɛsɪç] a resident.

Ansatz ['anzats] m start; (Haar—) hairline;
(Hals—) base; (Verlängerungsstück) extension; (Veranschlagung) estimate; **die
ersten Ansätze zu etw** the beginnings of
sth; ~**punkt** m starting point.

anschaffen ['anʃafən] vt buy, purchase.

Anschaffung f purchase.

anschalten ['anʃaltən] vt switch on.

anschau- ['anʃau] cpd: ~**en** vt look at;
~**lich** a illustrative; **A**~**ung** f (Meinung)
view; **aus eigener A**~**ung** from one's
own experience; **A**~**ungsmaterial** nt
illustrative material.

Anschein ['anʃain] m appearance; **allem**
~ **nach** to all appearances; **den** ~
haben seem, appear; **a**~**end** a apparent.

Anschlag ['anʃla:k] m notice; (Attentat)
attack; (Comm) estimate; (auf Klavier)
touch; (Schreibmaschine) character; **a**~**en**
['anʃla:gən] irreg vt put up; (beschädigen)
chip; Akkord strike; Kosten estimate; vi hit
(an +acc against); (wirken) have an effect;
(Glocke) ring; (Hund) bark; ~**zettel** m
notice.

anschließen ['anʃli:sən] irreg vt connect
up; Sender link up; vir: (**sich**) **an etw** (acc)
~ adjoin sth; (zeitlich) follow sth; vr join
(jdm/etw sb/sth); (beipflichten) agree
(jdm/etw with sb/sth); ~**d** a adjacent;
(zeitlich) subsequent; ad afterwards; ~**d**
an (+acc) following.

Anschluß ['anʃlus] m (Elec, Rail) connection; (von Wasser etc) supply; **im ~ an** (+acc) following; **~ finden** make friends.

anschmiegsam ['anʃmi:kza:m] a affectionate.

anschmieren ['anʃmi:rən] vt smear; (col) take in.

anschnallen ['anʃnalən] vt buckle on; vr fasten one's seat belt.

anschneiden ['anʃnaɪdən] vt irreg cut into; Thema broach.

Anschnitt ['anʃnɪt] m first slice.

anschreiben ['anʃraɪbən] vt irreg write (up); (Comm) charge up; (benachrichtigen) write to; **bei jdm gut/schlecht angeschrieben sein** be well/badly thought of by sb, be in sb's good/bad books.

anschreien ['anʃraɪən] vt irreg shout at.

Anschrift ['anʃrɪft] f address.

Anschuldigung ['anʃuldɪguŋ] f accusation.

anschwellen ['anʃvɛlən] vi irreg swell (up).

anschwemmen ['anʃvɛmən] vt wash ashore.

anschwindeln ['anʃvɪndəln] vt lie to.

ansehen ['anze:ən] vt irreg look at; **jdm etw ~** see sth (from sb's face); **jdn/etw als etw ~** look on sb/sth as sth; **~ für** consider; **A~** nt -s respect; (Ruf) reputation.

ansehnlich ['anze:nlɪç] a fine-looking; (beträchtlich) considerable.

ansein ['anzaɪn] vi irreg (col) be on.

ansetzen ['anzɛtsən] vt (anfügen) fix on (an +acc to); (anlegen, an Mund etc) put (an +acc to); (festlegen) fix; (entwickeln) develop; Fett put on; Blätter grow; (zubereiten) prepare; **jdn/etw auf jdn/etw ~** set sb/sth on sb/sth; vi (anfangen) start, begin; (Entwicklung) set in; (dick werden) put on weight; **zu etw ~** prepare to do sth; vr (Rost etc) start to develop.

Ansicht ['anzɪçt] f (Anblick) sight; (Meinung) view, opinion; **zur ~** on approval; **meiner ~ nach** in my opinion; **~skarte** f picture postcard; **~ssache** f matter of opinion.

anspannen ['anʃpanən] vt harness; Muskel strain.

Anspannung f strain.

Anspiel ['anʃpi:l] nt (Sport) start; **a~en** vi (Sport) start play; **auf etw** (acc) **a~en** refer or allude to sth; **~ung** f reference, allusion (auf +acc to).

Ansporn ['anʃpɔrn] m -(e)s incentive.

Ansprache ['anʃpra:xə] f address.

ansprechen ['anʃprɛçən] irreg vt speak to; (bitten, gefallen) appeal to; **jdn auf etw** (acc) **(hin) ~** ask sb about sth; **jdn als etw ~** regard sb as sth; vi react (auf +acc to); **~d** a attractive.

anspringen ['anʃprɪŋən] vi irreg (Aut) start.

Anspruch ['anʃprux] m (Recht) claim (auf +acc to); **hohe Ansprüche stellen/haben** demand/ expect a lot; **jdn/etw in ~ nehmen** occupy sb/take

up sth; **a~slos** a undemanding; **a~svoll** a demanding.

anspucken ['anʃpukən] vt spit at.

anstacheln ['anʃtaxəln] vt spur on.

Anstalt ['anʃtalt] f -, -en institution; **~en machen, etw zu tun** prepare to do sth.

Anstand ['anʃtant] m decency.

anständig ['anʃtɛndɪç] a decent; (col) proper; (groß) considerable; **A~keit** f propriety, decency.

anstandslos ad without any ado.

anstarren ['anʃtarən] vt stare at.

anstatt [an'ʃtat] prep +gen instead of; cj: **~ etw zu tun** instead of doing sth.

anstechen ['anʃtɛçən] vt irreg prick; Faß tap.

Ansteck- ['anʃtɛk] cpd: **a~en** vt pin on; (Med) infect; Pfeife light; Haus set fire to; vr: **ich habe mich bei ihm angesteckt** I caught it from him; vi (fig) be infectious; **a~end** a infectious; **~ung** f infection.

anstehen ['anʃte:ən] vi irreg queue (up), line up (US).

anstelle [an'ʃtɛlə] prep +gen in place of; **~n** ['an-] vt (einschalten) turn on; (Arbeit geben) employ; (machen), do; vr queue (up), line up (US); (col) act.

Anstellung f employment; (Posten) post, position.

Anstieg ['anʃti:k] m -(e)s, -e climb; (fig: von Preisen etc) increase (gen in).

anstift- ['anʃtɪft] cpd: **~en** vt Unglück cause; **jdn zu etw ~en** put sb up to sth; **A~er** m -s, instigator.

anstimmen ['anʃtɪmən] vt Lied strike up with; Geschrei set up; vi strike up.

Anstoß ['anʃto:s] m impetus; (Ärgernis) offence; (Sport) kick-off; **der erste ~** the initiative; **~ nehmen an** (+dat) take offence at; **a~en** irreg vt push; (mit Fuß) kick; vi knock, bump; (mit der Zunge) lisp; (mit Gläsern) drink (a toast) (auf +acc to); **an etw** (acc) **a~en** (angrenzen) adjoin sth.

anstößig ['anʃtø:sɪç] a offensive, indecent; **A~keit** f indecency, offensiveness.

anstreben ['anʃtre:bən] vt strive for.

anstreichen ['anʃtraɪçən] vt irreg paint.

Anstreicher m -s, - painter.

anstrengen ['anʃtrɛŋən] vt strain; (Jur) bring; vr make an effort; **angestrengt** ad as hard as one can; **~d** a tiring.

Anstrengung f effort.

Anstrich ['anʃtrɪç] m coat of paint.

Ansturm ['anʃturm] m rush; (Mil) attack.

ansuchen ['anzu:xən] vi: **um etw ~** apply for sth; **A~** nt -s, - request.

Antagonismus [antago'nɪsmus] m antagonism.

antasten ['antastən] vt touch; Recht infringe upon; Ehre question.

Anteil ['antaɪl] m -s, -e share (an +dat in); (Mitgefühl) sympathy; **~ nehmen an** (+dat) share in; (sich interessieren) take an interest in; **~nahme** f sympathy.

Antenne [an'tɛnə] f -, -n aerial; (Zool) antenna.

Anthrazit [antra'tsi:t] m -s, -e anthracite.

Anti- ['anti] in cpds anti; **~alko'holiker** m

teetotaller; **a~autori'tär** *a* anti-authoritarian; **~biotikum** [antibi'o:tikum] *nt* **-s, -ka** antibiotic.

antik [an'ti:k] *a* antique; **A~e** *f* **-, -n** (*Zeitalter*) ancient world; (*Kunstgegenstand*) antique.

Antikörper *m* antibody.

Antilope [anti'lo:pə] *f* **-, -n** antelope.

Antipathie [antipa'ti:] *f* antipathy.

Antiquariat [antikvari'a:t] *nt* **-(e)s, -e** secondhand bookshop.

Antiquitäten [antikvi'tɛ:tən] *pl* antiques *pl*; **~handel** *m* antique business; **~händler** *m* antique dealer.

Antrag ['antra:k] *m* **-(e)s, -träge** proposal; (*Parl*) motion; (*Gesuch*) application.

antreffen ['antrɛfən] *vt irreg* meet.

antreiben ['antraibən] *irreg vt* drive on; *Motor* drive; (*anschwemmen*) wash up; *vi* be washed up.

antreten ['antre:tən] *irreg vt Amt* take up; *Erbschaft* come into; *Beweis* offer; *Reise* start, begin; *vi* (*Mil*) fall in; (*Sport*) line up; **gegen jdn ~** play/fight against sb.

Antrieb ['antri:p] *m* (*lit, fig*) drive; **aus eigenem ~** of one's own accord.

antrinken ['antrɪŋkən] *vt irreg Flasche, Glas* start to drink from; **sich** (*dat*) **Mut/einen Rausch ~** give oneself Dutch courage/get drunk; **angetrunken sein** be tipsy.

Antritt ['antrɪt] *m* beginning, commencement; (*eines Amts*) taking up.

antun ['antu:n] *vt irreg*: **jdm etw ~** do sth to sb; **sich** (*dat*) **Zwang ~** force o.s.

Antwort ['antvɔrt] *f* **-, -en** answer, reply; **um ~ wird gebeten** RSVP; **a~en** *vi* answer, reply.

anvertrauen ['anfertrauən] *vt*: **jdm etw ~** entrust sb with sth; **sich jdm ~** confide in sb.

anwachsen ['anvaksən] *vi irreg* grow; (*Pflanze*) take root.

Anwalt ['anvalt] *m* **-(e)s, -wälte**, **Anwältin** ['anvɛltɪn] *f* solicitor; lawyer; (*fig*) champion.

Anwandlung ['anvandluŋ] *f* caprice; **eine ~ von etw** a fit of sth.

Anwärter ['anvɛrtər] *m* candidate.

anweisen ['anvaizən] *vt irreg* instruct; (*zuteilen*) assign (*jdm etw* sth to sb).

Anweisung *f* instruction; (*Comm*) remittance; (*Post~, Zahlungs~*) money order.

anwend- ['anvɛnd] *cpd*: **~bar** ['anvɛnt-] *a* practicable, applicable; **~en** *vt irreg* use, employ; *Gesetz, Regel* apply; **A~ung** *f* use; application.

Anwesen- ['anve:zən] *cpd*: **a~d** present; **die ~den** those present; **~heit** *f* presence; **~heitsliste** *f* attendance register.

anwidern ['anvi:dərn] *vt* disgust.

Anwuchs ['anvu:ks] *m* growth.

Anzahl ['antsa:l] *f* number (*an* +*dat* of); **a~en** *vt* pay on account; **~ung** *f* deposit, payment on account.

anzapfen ['antsapfən] *vt* tap; *Person* (*um Geld*) touch.

Anzeichen ['antsaiçən] *nt* sign, indication.

Anzeige ['antsaigə] *f* **-, -n** (*Zeitungs~*) announcement; (*Werbung*) advertisement; (*bei Polizei*) report; **~ erstatten gegen jdn** report sb (to the police); **a~n** *vt* (*zu erkennen geben*) show; (*bekanntgeben*) announce; (*bei Polizei*) report; **~nteil** *m* advertisements *pl*; **~r** *m* indicator.

anzetteln ['antsɛtəln] *vt* (*col*) instigate.

anziehen ['antsi:ən] *irreg vt* attract; *Kleidung* put on; *Mensch* dress; *Schraube, Seil* pull tight; *Knie* draw up; *Feuchtigkeit* absorb; *vr* get dressed; **~d** *a* attractive.

Anziehung *f* (*Reiz*) attraction; **~skraft** *f* power of attraction; (*Phys*) force of gravitation.

Anzug ['antsu:k] *m* suit; **im ~ sein** be approaching.

anzüglich ['antsy:klɪç] *a* personal; (*anstößig*) offensive; **A~keit** *f* offensiveness; (*Bemerkung*) personal remark.

anzünden ['antsʏndən] *vt* light.

Anzünder *m* lighter.

anzweifeln ['antsvaifəln] *vt* doubt.

apart [a'part] *a* distinctive.

Apathie [apa'ti:] *f* apathy.

apathisch [a'pa:tɪʃ] *a* apathetic.

Apfel ['apfəl] *m* **-s, ⁻** apple; **~saft** *m* apple juice; **~sine** [apfəl'zi:nə] *f* **-, -n** orange; **~wein** *m* cider.

Apostel [a'pɔstəl] *m* **-s, ⁻** apostle.

Apostroph [apo'stro:f] *m* **-s, -s** apostrophe.

Apotheke [apo'te:kə] *f* **-, -n** chemist's (shop), drugstore (*US*); **~r(in** *f*) *m* **-s,-** chemist, druggist (*US*).

Apparat [apa'ra:t] *m* **-(e)s, -e** piece of apparatus; camera; telephone; (*Rad, TV*) set; **am ~ bleiben** hold the line; **~ur** [-'tu:r] *f* apparatus.

Appartement [apart(ə)'mã:] *nt* **-s, -s** flat.

Appell [a'pɛl] *m* **-s, -e** (*Mil*) muster, parade; (*fig*) appeal; **a~ieren** [apɛ'li:rən] *vi* appeal (*an* +*acc* to).

Appetit [ape'ti:t] *m* **-(e)s, -e** appetite; **guten ~** enjoy your meal; **a~lich** *a* appetizing; **~losigkeit** *f* lack of appetite.

Applaus [a'plaus] *m* **-es, -e** applause.

Appretur [apre'tu:r] *f* finish.

Aprikose [apri'ko:zə] *f* **-, -n** apricot.

April [a'prɪl] *m* **-(s), -e** April; **~wetter** *nt* April showers *pl*.

Aquaplaning [akva'pla:nɪŋ] *nt* **-(s)** aquaplaning.

Aquarell [akva'rɛl] *nt* **-s, -e** watercolour.

Aquarium [a'kva:rium] *nt* aquarium.

Äquator [ɛ'kva:tɔr] *m* **-s** equator.

Arbeit ['arbait] *f* **-, -en** work (*no art*); (*Stelle*) job; (*Erzeugnis*) piece of work; (*wissenschaftliche*) dissertation; (*Klassen~*) test; **das war eine ~** that was a hard job; **a~en** *vi* work; *vt* work, make; **~er(in** *f*) *m* **-s, -** worker; (*ungelernt*) labourer; **~erschaft** *f* workers *pl*, labour force; **~geber** *m* **-s, -** employer; **~nehmer** *m* **-s, -** employee; **a~sam** *a* industrious.

Arbeits- *in cpds* labour; **~amt** *nt* employment exchange; **a~fähig** *a* fit for work, able-bodied; ~**gang** *m* operation; ~**gemeinschaft** *f* study group; ~**kräfte** *pl* workers *pl*, labour; **a**~**los** *a* unemployed, out-of-work; ~**losigkeit** *f* unemployment; ~**platz** *m* job; place of work; **a**~**scheu** *a* work-shy; ~**tag** *m* work(ing) day; ~**teilung** *f* division of labour; **a**~**unfähig** *a* unfit for work; ~**zeit** *f* working hours *pl*.

Archäologe [arçεo'lo:gə] *m* -**n**, -**n** archaeologist.

Architekt(in *f*) [arçi'tεkt(in)] *m* -**en**, -**en** architect; ~**ur** [-'tu:r] *f* architecture.

Archiv [ar'çi:f] *nt* -**s**, -**e** archive.

arg [ark] *a* bad, awful; *ad* awfully, very.

Ärger ['εrgər] *m* -**s** (*Wut*) anger; (*Unannehmlichkeit*) trouble; **ä**~**lich** *a* (*zornig*) angry; (*lästig*) annoying, aggravating; **ä**~**n** *vt* annoy; *vr* get annoyed; ~**nis** *nt* -**ses**, -**se** annoyance; **öffentliches** ~**nis erregen** be a public nuisance.

arg- *cpd*: ~**listig** *a* cunning, insidious; ~**los** *a* guileless, innocent; **A**~**losigkeit** *f* guilelessness, innocence; **A**~**ument** [argu'mεnt] *nt* argument; **A**~**wohn** *m* suspicion; ~**wöhnisch** *a* suspicious.

Arie ['a:riə] *f* -, -**n** aria.

Aristokrat [aristo'kra:t] *m* -**en**,-**en** aristocrat; ~**ie** [-'ti:] *f* aristocracy; **a**~**isch** *a* aristocratic.

arithmetisch [arit'me:tiʃ] *a* arithmetical.

arm [arm] *a* poor; **A**~ *m* -**(e)s**, -**e** arm; (*Fluß*—) branch; **A**~**a'tur** *f* (*Elec*) armature; **A**~**a'turenbrett** *nt* instrument panel; (*Aut*) dashboard; **A**~**band** *nt* bracelet; **A**~**banduhr** *f* (wrist) watch; **A**~**e(r)** *mf* poor man/woman; **die A**~**en** the poor; **A**~**ee** [ar'me:] *f* -, -**n** army; **A**~**eekorps** *nt* army corps.

Ärmel ['εrməl] *m* -**s**, - sleeve; **etw aus dem** ~ **schütteln** (*fig*) produce sth just like that.

ärmlich ['εrmliç] *a* poor.

armselig *a* wretched, miserable.

Armut [ar'mu:t] *f* - poverty.

Aroma [a'ro:ma] *nt* -**s**, **Aromen** aroma; **a**~**tisch** [aro'ma:tiʃ] *a* aromatic.

arrangieren [arã'ʒi:rən] *vt* arrange; *vr* come to an arrangement.

Arrest [a'rεst] *m* -**(e)s**, -**e** detention.

arrogant [aro'gant] *a* arrogant.

Arroganz *f* arrogance.

Arsch [arʃ] *m* -**es**, -**e** (*col*) arse, bum.

Art [a:rt] *f* -, -**en** (*Weise*) way; (*Sorte*) kind, sort; (*Biol*) species; **eine** ~ (**von**) **Frucht** a kind of fruit; **Häuser aller** ~ houses of all kinds; **es ist nicht seine** ~, **das zu tun** it's not like him to do that; **ich mache das auf meine** ~ I do that my (own) way; **nach** ~ **des Hauses** à la maison; **a**~**en** *vi*: **nach jdm a**~**en** take after sb; **der Mensch ist so geartet, daß** . . . human nature is such that . . .

Arterie [ar'te:riə] *f* -, -**n** artery; ~**nverkalkung** *f* arteriosclerosis.

artig ['a:rtiç] *a* good, well-behaved.

Artikel [ar'ti:kəl] *m* -**s**, - article.

Artillerie [artilə'ri:] *f* artillery.

Arznei [a:rts'nai] *f* medicine; ~**mittel** *nt* medicine, medicament.

Arzt [a:rtst] *m* -**es**, -**e**, **Ärztin** ['ε:rtstin] *f* doctor.

ärztlich ['ε:rtstliç] *a* medical.

As [as] *nt* -**ses**, -**se** ace.

Asbest [as'bεst] *m* -**(e)s**, -**e** asbestos.

Asche ['aʃə] *f* -, -**n** ash, cinder; ~**nbahn** *f* cinder track; ~**nbecher** *m* ashtray; ~**nbrödel** *nt* Cinderella; ~**rmittwoch** *m* Ash Wednesday.

asozial ['azotsia:l] *a* antisocial; *Familien* asocial.

Aspekt [as'pεkt] *m* -**(e)s**, -**e** aspect.

Asphalt [as'falt] *m* -**(e)s**, -**e** asphalt; **a**~**ieren** [-'ti:rən] *vt* asphalt; ~**straße** *f* asphalt road.

Assistent(in *f*) [asis'tεnt(in)] *m* assistant.

Assoziation [asotsiatsi'o:n] *f* association.

Ast [ast] *m* -**(e)s**, -**e** bough, branch; ~**er** *f* -, -**n** aster.

ästhetisch [εs'te:tiʃ] *a* aesthetic.

Asthma ['astma] *nt* -**s** asthma; ~**tiker(in** *f*) [ast'ma:tikər(in)] *m* -**s**, - asthmatic.

Astro- [astro] *cpd*: ~**loge** *m* -**n**, -**n** astrologer; ~**lo'gie** *f* astrology; ~**naut** *m* -**en**, -**en** astronaut; ~**nautik** *f* astronautics; ~**nom** *m* -**en**, -**en** astronomer; ~**no'mie** *f* astronomy.

Asyl [a'zy:l] *nt* -**s**, -**e** asylum; (*Heim*) home; (*Obdachlosen*—) shelter.

Atelier [atəli'e:] *nt* -**s**, -**s** studio.

Atem ['a:təm] *m* -**s** breath; **den** ~ **anhalten** hold one's breath; **außer** ~ out of breath; ~**beraubend** a breath-taking; **a**~**los** *a* breathless; ~**pause** *f* breather; ~**zug** *m* breath.

Atheismus [ate'ismus] *m* atheism.

Atheist *m* atheist; **a**~**isch** *a* atheistic.

Äther ['ε:tər] *m* -**s**, - ether.

Athlet [at'le:t] *m* -**en**, -**en** athlete; ~**ik** *f* athletics.

Atlas ['atlas] *m* - *or* -**ses**, -**se** *or* **Atlanten** atlas.

atmen ['a:tmən] *vti* breathe.

Atmosphäre [atmo'sfε:rə] *f* -, -**n** atmosphere.

atmosphärisch *a* atmospheric.

Atmung ['a:tmuŋ] *f* respiration.

Atom [a'to:m] *nt* -**s**, -**e** atom; **a**~**ar** [ato'ma:r] *a* atomic; ~**bombe** *f* atom bomb; ~**energie** *f* atomic or nuclear energy; ~**kern** *m* atomic nucleus; ~**kernforschung** *f* nuclear research; ~**kraftwerk** *nt* nuclear power station; ~**krieg** *m* nuclear or atomic war; ~**macht** *f* nuclear or atomic power; ~**müll** *m* atomic waste; ~**sperrvertrag** *m* (*Pol*) nuclear non-proliferation treaty; ~**versuch** *m* atomic test; ~**waffen** *pl* atomic weapons *pl*; ~**zeitalter** *nt* atomic age.

Attentat [atεn'ta:t] *nt* -**(e)s**, -**e** (attempted) assassination (*auf* +*acc* of).

Attentäter [atεn'tε:tər] *m* (would-be) assassin.

Attest [a'tεst] *nt* -**(e)s**, -**e** certificate.

attraktiv [atrak'ti:f] *a* attractive.

Attrappe [a'trapə] *f* -, -**n** dummy.

Attribut [atri'bu:t] *nt* -(e)s, -e (*Gram*) attribute.

ätzen ['ɛtsən] *vi* be caustic.

auch [aux] *cj* also, too, as well; (*selbst, sogar*) even; (*wirklich*) really; **oder** ~ or; ~ **das ist schön** that's nice too or as well; **das habe ich** ~ **nicht gemacht** I didn't do it either; **ich** ~ **nicht** nor I, me neither; ~ **wenn das Wetter schlecht ist** even if the weather is bad; **wer/was** ~ whoever/whatever; **so sieht es** ~ **aus** it looks like it too; ~ **das noch!** not that as well!

auf [auf] *prep* +acc or dat (*räumlich*) on; (*hinauf:* +acc) up; (*in Richtung:* +acc) to; (*nach*) after; ~ **der Reise** on the way; ~ **der Post/dem Fest** at the post office/party; ~ **das Land** into the country; ~ **der Straße** on the road; ~ **dem Land/den ganzen Welt** in the country/the whole world; ~ **deutsch** in German; ~ **Lebenszeit** for sb's lifetime; **bis** ~ **ihn** except for him; ~ **einmal** at once; *ad:* ~ **und ab** up and down; ~ **und davon** up and away; ~! (*los*) come on!; ~ **sein** (*col*) (*Person*) be up; (*Tür*) be open; **von Kindheit** ~ from childhood onwards; ~ **daß** so that.

aufatmen ['aufʔa:tmən] *vi* heave a sigh of relief.

aufbahren ['aufba:rən] *vt* lay out.

Aufbau ['aufbau] *m* (*Bauen*) building, construction; (*Struktur*) structure; (*aufgebautes Teil*) superstructure; **a** ~ **en** *vt* erect, build (up); *Existenz* make; (*gestalten*) construct; (*gründen*) found, base (*auf* +dat on).

aufbäumen ['aufbɔymən] *vr* rear; (*fig*) revolt, rebel.

aufbauschen ['aufbauʃən] *vt* puff out; (*fig*) exaggerate.

aufbehalten ['aufbəhaltən] *vt irreg* keep on.

aufbekommen ['aufbəkɔmən] *vt irreg* (*öffnen*) get open; *Hausaufgaben* be given.

aufbessern ['aufbɛsərn] *vt Gehalt* increase.

aufbewahren ['aufbəva:rən] *vt* keep; *Gepäck* put in the left-luggage office.

Aufbewahrung *f* (*safe*)keeping; (*Gepäck*—) left-luggage office; **jdm etw zur** ~ **geben** give sb sth for safekeeping; ~ **sort** *m* storage place.

aufbieten ['aufbi:tən] *vt irreg Kraft* summon (up), exert; *Armee, Polizei* mobilize; *Brautpaar* publish the banns of.

aufblasen ['aufbla:zən] *irreg vt* blow up, inflate; *vr* (*col*) become big-headed.

aufbleiben ['aufblaibən] *vi irreg* (*Laden*) remain open; (*Person*) stay up.

aufblenden ['aufblɛndən] *vt Scheinwerfer* turn on full beam.

aufblicken ['aufblɪkən] *vi* (*lit, fig*) look up (*zu* (*lit*) at, (*fig*) to).

aufblühen ['aufbly:ən] *vi* blossom, flourish.

aufbrauchen ['aufbrauxən] *vt* use up.

aufbrausen ['aufbrauzən] *vi* (*fig*) flare up; ~ **d** a hot-tempered.

aufbrechen ['aufbrɛçən] *irreg vt* break or prize open; *vi* burst open; (*gehen*) start, set off.

aufbringen ['aufbrɪŋən] *vt irreg* (*öffnen*) open; (*in Mode*) bring into fashion; (*beschaffen*) procure; (*Fin*) raise; (*ärgern*) irritate; **Verständnis für etw** ~ be able to understand sth.

Aufbruch ['aufbrux] *m* departure.

aufbrühen ['aufbry:ən] *vt Tee* make.

aufbürden ['aufbyrdən] *vt* burden (*jdm etw* sb with sth).

aufdecken ['aufdɛkən] *vt* uncover.

aufdrängen ['aufdrɛŋən] *vt* force (*jdm* on sb); *vr* intrude (*jdm* on sb).

aufdringlich ['aufdrɪŋlɪç] a pushy.

aufeinander [aufʔaɪ'nandər] *ad* **achten** after each other; **schießen** at each other; **vertrauen** each other; **A** ~ **folge** *f* succession, series; ~ **folgen** *vi* follow one another; ~ **folgend** a consecutive; ~ **legen** *vt* lay on top of one another; ~ **prallen** *vi* hit one another.

Aufenthalt ['aufʔɛnthalt] *m* stay; (*Verzögerung*) delay; (*Rail: Halten*) stop; (*Ort*) haunt; ~ **sgenehmigung** *f* residence permit.

auferlegen ['aufʔɛrle:gən] *vt* impose (*jdm etw* sth upon sb).

Auferstehung ['aufʔɛrʃte:uŋ] *f* resurrection.

aufessen ['aufʔɛsən] *vt irreg* eat up.

auffahr- ['auffa:r] *cpd:* ~ **en** *irreg vi* (*Auto*) run, crash (*auf* +acc into); (*herankommen*) draw up; (*hochfahren*) jump up; (*wütend werden*) flare up; (*in den Himmel*) ascend; *vt Kanonen, Geschütz* bring up; ~ **end** a hot-tempered; **A** ~ **t** *f* (*Haus*—) drive; (*Autobahn*—) slip road; **A** ~ **unfall** *m* pile-up.

auffallen ['auffalən] *vi irreg* be noticeable; **jdm** ~ strike sb; ~ **d** a striking.

auffällig ['auffɛlɪç] a conspicuous, striking.

auffang- ['auffaŋ] *cpd:* ~ **en** *vt irreg* catch; *Funkspruch* intercept; *Preise* peg; **A** ~ **lager** *nt* refugee camp.

auffassen ['auffasən] *vt* understand, comprehend; (*auslegen*) see, view.

Auffassung *f* (*Meinung*) opinion; (*Auslegung*) view, concept; (*also* ~ **sgabe**) grasp.

auffindbar ['auffintba:r] a to be found.

auffordern ['aufforдərn] *vt* (*befehlen*) call upon, order; (*bitten*) ask.

Aufforderung *f* (*Befehl*) order; (*Einladung*) invitation.

auffrischen ['auffrɪʃən] *vt* freshen up; *Kenntnisse* brush up; *Erinnerungen* reawaken; *vi* (*Wind*) freshen.

aufführen ['auffy:rən] *vt* (*Theat*) perform; (*in einem Verzeichnis*) list, specify; *vr* (*sich benehmen*) behave.

Aufführung *f* (*Theat*) performance; (*Liste*) specification.

Aufgabe ['aufga:bə] *f* -, -n task; (*Sch*) exercise; (*Haus*—) homework; (*Verzicht*) giving up; (*von Gepäck*) registration; (*von Post*) posting; (*von Inserat*) insertion.

Aufgang ['aufgaŋ] *m* ascent; (*Sonnen*—) rise; (*Treppe*) staircase.

aufgeben ['aufge:bən] *irreg vt* (*verzichten*) give up; *Paket* send, post; *Gepäck* register;

Bestellung give; *Inserat* insert; *Rätsel, Problem* set; vi give up.

Aufgebot ['aufgəbo:t] *nt* supply; (*von Kräften*) utilization; (*Ehe—*) banns *pl*.

aufgedreht ['aufgədre:t] a (*col*) excited.

aufgedunsen ['aufgədunzən] a swollen, puffed up.

aufgehen ['aufge:ən] vi irreg (*Sonne, Teig*) rise; (*sich öffnen*) open; (*klarwerden*) become clear (*jdm* to sb); (*Math*) come out exactly; (*sich widmen*) be absorbed (*in* +*dat* in); **in Rauch/Flammen ~** go up in smoke/flames.

aufgeklärt ['aufgəklɛ:rt] a enlightened; (*sexuell*) knowing the facts of life.

aufgelegt ['aufgəle:kt] a: **gut/schlecht ~ sein** be in a good/bad mood; **zu etw ~ sein** be in the mood for sth.

aufgeregt ['aufgəre:kt] a excited.

aufgeschlossen ['aufgəʃlɔsən] a open, open-minded.

aufgeweckt ['aufgəvɛkt] a bright, intelligent.

aufgießen ['aufgi:sən] vt irreg *Wasser* pour over; *Tee* infuse.

aufgreifen ['aufgraifən] vt irreg *Thema* take up; *Verdächtige* pick up, seize.

aufgrund [auf'grunt] *prep* +*gen* on the basis of; (*wegen*) because of.

aufhaben ['aufha:bən] vt irreg have on; *Arbeit* have to do.

aufhalsen ['aufhalzən] vt (*col*) **jdm etw ~** saddle *or* lumber sb with sth.

aufhalten ['aufhaltən] irreg vt *Person* detain; *Entwicklung* check; *Tür, Hand* hold open; *Augen* keep open; vr (*wohnen*) live; (*bleiben*) stay; **sich über etw/jdn ~** go on about sth/sb; **sich mit etw ~** waste time over.

aufhängen ['aufhɛŋən] irreg vt *Wäsche* hang up; *Menschen* hang; vr hang o.s.

Aufhänger m **-s**, - (*am Mantel*) hook; (*fig*) peg.

aufheben ['aufhe:bən] irreg vt (*hochheben*) raise, lift; *Sitzung* wind up; *Urteil* annul; *Gesetz* repeal, abolish; (*aufbewahren*) keep; **bei jdm gut aufgehoben sein** be well looked after at sb's; vr cancel o.s. out; **viel A~(s) machen** make a fuss (*von* about).

aufheitern ['aufhaitərn] vtr (*Himmel, Miene*) brighten; *Mensch* cheer up.

aufhellen ['aufhɛlən] vtr clear up; *Farbe, Haare* lighten.

aufhetzen ['aufhɛtsən] vt stir up (*gegen* against).

aufholen ['aufho:lən] vt make up; vi catch up.

aufhorchen ['aufhɔrçən] vi prick up one's ears.

aufhören ['aufhø:rən] vi stop; **~ etw zu tun** stop doing sth.

aufklappen ['aufklapən] vt open.

aufklären ['aufklɛ:rən] vt *Geheimnis etc* clear up; *Person* enlighten; (*sexuell*) tell the facts of life to; (*Mil*) reconnoitre; vr clear up.

Aufklärung f (*von Geheimnis*) clearing up; (*Unterrichtung, Zeitalter*) enlightenment; (*sexuell*) sex education; (*Mil, Aviat*) reconnaissance.

aufkleben ['aufkle:bən] vt stick on.

Aufkleber m **-s**, - sticker.

aufknöpfen ['aufknœpfən] vt unbutton.

aufkommen ['aufkɔmən] vi irreg (*Wind*) come up; (*Zweifel, Gefühl*) arise; (*Mode*) start; **für jdn/etw ~** be liable *or* responsible for sb/sth.

aufladen ['aufla:dən] vt irreg load.

Auflage ['aufla:gə] f edition; (*Zeitung*) circulation; (*Bedingung*) condition; **jdm etw zur ~ machen** make sth a condition for sb.

auflassen ['auflasən] vt irreg (*offen*) leave open; (*aufgesetzt*) leave on.

auflauern ['auflauərn] vi: **jdm ~** lie in wait for sb.

Auflauf ['auflauf] m (*Cook*) pudding; (*Menschen—*) crowd.

aufleben ['aufle:bən] vi revive.

auflegen ['aufle:gən] vt put on; *Telefon* hang up; (*Print*) print.

auflehnen ['aufle:nən] vt lean on; vr rebel (*gegen* against).

Auflehnung f rebellion.

auflesen ['aufle:zən] vt irreg pick up.

aufleuchten ['aufləyçtən] vi light up.

aufliegen ['aufli:gən] vi irreg lie on; (*Comm*) be available.

auflockern ['auflɔkərn] vt loosen; (*fig*) *Eintönigkeit etc* liven up.

auflösen ['auflø:zən] vtr dissolve; *Haare etc* loosen; *Mißverständnis* sort out; (**in Tränen) aufgelöst sein** be in tears.

Auflösung f dissolving; (*fig*) solution.

aufmachen ['aufmaxən] vt open; *Kleidung* undo; (*zurechtmachen*) do up; vr set out.

Aufmachung f (*Kleidung*) outfit, get-up; (*Gestaltung*) format.

aufmerksam ['aufmɛrkza:m] a attentive; **jdn auf etw** (*acc*) **~ machen** point sth out to sb; **A~keit** f attention, attentiveness.

aufmuntern ['aufmuntərn] vt (*ermutigen*) encourage; (*erheitern*) cheer up.

Aufnahme ['aufna:mə] f **-**, **-n** reception; (*Beginn*) beginning; (*in Verein etc*) admission; (*in Liste etc*) inclusion; (*Notieren*) taking down; (*Phot*) shot; (*auf Tonband etc*) recording; **a~fähig** a receptive; **~prüfung** f entrance test.

aufnehmen ['aufne:mən] vt irreg receive; (*hochheben*) pick up; (*beginnen*) take up; (*in Verein etc*) admit; (*in Liste etc*) include; (*fassen*) hold; (*notieren*) take down; (*photographieren*) photograph; (*auf Tonband, Platte*) record; (*Fin: leihen*) take out; **es mit jdm ~ können** be able to compete with sb.

aufopfern ['auf'ɔpfərn] vtr sacrifice; **~d** a selfless.

aufpassen ['aufpasən] vi (*aufmerksam sein*) pay attention; **auf jdn/etw ~** look after *or* watch sb/sth; **aufgepaßt!** look out!

Aufprall ['aufpral] m **-s**, **-e** impact; **a~en** vi hit, strike.

Aufpreis ['aufprais] m extra charge.

aufpumpen ['aufpumpən] vt pump up.

aufputschen ['aufputʃən] vt (*aufhetzen*)

inflame; (*erregen*) stimulate.
aufraffen ['aʊfrafən] *vr* rouse o.s.
aufräumen ['aʊfrɔʏmən] *vti* Dinge clear
away; Zimmer tidy up.
aufrecht ['aʊfrɛçt] *a* (*lit, fig*) upright;
~**erhalten** *vt irreg* maintain.
aufreg- ['aʊfreːg] *cpd*: ~**en** *vt* excite; *vr*
get excited; ~**end** *a* exciting; **A~ung** *f*
excitement.
aufreiben ['aʊfraɪbən] *vt irreg* Haut rub
open; (*erschöpfen*) exhaust; ~**d** *a*
strenuous.
aufreißen ['aʊfraɪsən] *vt irreg* Umschlag
tear open; Augen open wide; Tür throw
open; Straße take up.
aufreizen ['aʊfraɪtsən] *vt* incite, stir up;
~**d** *a* exciting, stimulating.
aufrichten ['aʊfrɪçtən] *vt* put up, erect;
(*moralisch*) console; *vr* rise; (*moralisch*)
take heart (*an +dat* from).
aufrichtig ['aʊfrɪçtɪç] *a* sincere, honest;
A~keit *f* sincerity.
aufrücken ['aʊfrʏkən] *vi* move up;
(*beruflich*) be promoted.
Aufruf ['aʊfruːf] *m* summons; (*zur Hilfe*)
call; (*des Namens*) calling out; **a~en** *vt*
irreg (*auffordern*) call upon (*zu* for); Namen
call out.
Aufruhr ['aʊfruːr] *m* -(e)s, -e uprising,
revolt; **in** ~ **sein** be in uproar.
aufrührerisch ['aʊfryːrərɪʃ] *a* rebellious.
aufrunden ['aʊfrʊndən] *vt* Summe round
up.
Aufrüstung ['aʊfrʏstʊŋ] *f* rearmament.
aufrütteln ['aʊfrʏtəln] *vt* (*lit, fig*) shake
up.
aufs [aʊfs] = **auf das**.
aufsagen ['aʊfzaːgən] *vt* Gedicht recite;
Freundschaft put an end to.
aufsammeln ['aʊfzaməln] *vt* gather up.
aufsässig ['aʊfzɛsɪç] *a* rebellious.
Aufsatz ['aʊfzats] *m* (*Geschriebenes*)
essay; (*auf Schrank etc*) top.
aufsaugen ['aʊfzaʊgən] *vt irreg* soak up.
aufschauen ['aʊfʃaʊən] *vi* look up.
aufscheuchen ['aʊfʃɔʏçən] *vt* scare or
frighten away.
aufschieben ['aʊfʃiːbən] *vt irreg* push
open; (*verzögern*) put off, postpone.
Aufschlag ['aʊfʃlaːk] *m* (*Armel—*) cuff;
(*Jacken—*) lapel; (*Hosen—*) turn-up; (*Aufprall*) impact; (*Preis—*) surcharge;
(*Tennis*) service; **a~en** *vt irreg* *vt* (*öffnen*)
open; (*verwunden*) cut; (*hochschlagen*) türn
up; (*aufbauen*) Zelt, Lager pitch, erect;
Wohnsitz take up; *vi* (*aufprallen*) hit; (*teurer
werden*) go up; (*Tennis*) serve.
aufschließen ['aʊfʃliːsən] *irreg* *vt* open up,
unlock; *vi* (*aufrücken*) close up.
Aufschluß ['aʊfʃlʊs] *m* information;
a~reich *a* informative, illuminating.
aufschnappen ['aʊfʃnapən] *vt* (*col*) pick
up; *vi* fly open.
aufschneiden ['aʊfʃnaɪdən] *irreg* *vt*
Geschwür cut open; Brot cut up; (*Med*)
lance; *vi* brag.
Aufschneider *m* -s, - boaster, braggart.
Aufschnitt ['aʊfʃnɪt] *m* (slices of) cold
meat.

aufschnüren ['aʊfʃnyːrən] *vt* unlace; Paket
untie.
aufschrauben ['aʊfʃraʊbən] *vt* (*fest—*)
screw on; (*lösen*) unscrew.
aufschrecken ['aʊfʃrɛkən] *vt* startle; *vi*
irreg start up.
Aufschrei ['aʊfʃraɪ] *m* cry; **a~en** *vi irreg*
cry out.
aufschreiben ['aʊfʃraɪbən] *vt irreg* write
down.
Aufschrift ['aʊfʃrɪft] *f* (*Inschrift*)
inscription; (*auf Etikett*) label.
Aufschub ['aʊfʃuːp] *m* -(e)s, -schübe
delay, postponement.
aufschwatzen ['aʊfʃvatsən] *vt*: **jdm etw**
~ talk sb into (getting/having *etc*) sth.
Aufschwung ['aʊfʃvʊŋ] *n* (*Elan*) boost;
(*wirtschaftlich*) upturn, boom; (*Sport*)
circle.
aufsehen ['aʊfzeːən] *vi irreg* (*lit, fig*) look
up (*zu* (*lit*) at, (*fig*) to); **A~** *nt* -**s** sensation,
stir; ~**erregend** *a* sensational.
Aufseher(in *f*) *m* -**s**, - guard; (*im Betrieb*)
supervisor; (*Museums—*) attendant;
(*Park—*) keeper.
aufsein ['aʊfzaɪn] *vi irreg* (*col*) be open;
(*Person*) be up.
aufsetzen ['aʊfzɛtsən] *vt* put on; Flugzeug
put down; Dokument draw up; *vr* sit
upright; *vi* (*Flugzeug*) touch down.
Aufsicht ['aʊfzɪçt] *f* supervision; **die** ~
haben be in charge.
aufsitzen ['aʊfzɪtsən] *vi irreg* (*aufrecht
hinsitzen*) sit up; (*aufs Pferd, Motorrad*)
mount, get on; (*Schiff*) run aground; **jdn** ~
lassen (*col*) stand sb up; **jdm** ~ (*col*) be
taken in by sb.
aufspalten ['aʊfʃpaltən] *vt* split.
aufsparen ['aʊfʃpaːrən] *vt* save (up).
aufsperren ['aʊfʃpɛrən] *vt* unlock; Mund
open wide.
aufspielen ['aʊfʃpiːlən] *vr* show off; **sich
als etw** ~ try to come on as sth.
aufspießen ['aʊfʃpiːsən] *vt* spear.
aufspringen ['aʊfʃprɪŋən] *vi irreg* jump
(*auf +acc* onto); (*hochspringen*) jump up;
(*sich öffnen*) spring open; (*Hände, Lippen*)
become chapped.
aufspüren ['aʊfʃpyːrən] *vt* track down,
trace.
aufstacheln ['aʊfʃtaxəln] *vt* incite.
Aufstand ['aʊfʃtant] *m* insurrection,
rebellion.
aufständisch ['aʊfʃtɛndɪʃ] *a* rebellious,
mutinous.
aufstechen ['aʊfʃtɛçən] *vt irreg* prick
open, puncture.
aufstecken ['aʊfʃtɛkən] *vt* stick on, pin up;
(*col*) give up.
aufstehen ['aʊfʃteːən] *vi irreg* get up; (*Tür*)
be open.
aufsteigen ['aʊfʃtaɪgən] *vi irreg* (*auf etw*)
get onto; (*hochsteigen*) climb; (*Rauch*) rise.
aufstellen ['aʊfʃtɛlən] *vt* (*aufrecht stellen*)
put up; (*aufreihen*) line up; (*nominieren*)
put up; (*formulieren*) Programm *etc* draw
up; (*leisten*) Rekord set up.
Aufstellung *f* (*Sport*) line-up; (*Liste*) list.
Aufstieg ['aʊfʃtiːk] *m* -(e)s, -e (*auf Berg*)

ascent; *(Fortschritt)* rise; *(beruflich, Sport)* promotion.

aufstoßen ['aʊfʃtoːsən] *irreg vt* push open; *vi* belch.

aufstrebend ['aʊfʃtreːbənd] *a* ambitious; *Land* up-and-coming.

Aufstrich ['aʊfʃtrɪç] *m* spread.

aufstülpen ['aʊfʃtʏlpən] *vt Ärmel* turn up; *Hut* put on.

aufstützen ['aʊfʃtʏtsən] *vr* lean (*auf* +*acc* on); *vt Körperteil* prop, lean; *Person* prop up.

aufsuchen ['aʊfzuːxən] *vt (besuchen)* visit; *(konsultieren)* consult.

auftakeln ['aʊftaːkəln] *vt (Naut)* rig (out); *vr (col)* deck o.s. out.

Auftakt ['aʊftakt] *m (Mus)* upbeat; *(fig)* prelude.

auftanken ['aʊftaŋkən] *vi* get petrol; *vt* refuel.

auftauchen ['aʊftaʊxən] *vi* appear; *(aus Wasser etc)* emerge; *(U-Boot)* surface; *(Zweifel)* arise.

auftauen ['aʊftaʊən] *vti* thaw; *(fig)* relax.

aufteilen ['aʊftaɪlən] *vt* divide up; *Raum* partition.

Aufteilung *f* division; partition.

auftischen ['aʊftɪʃən] *vt* serve (up); *(fig)* tell.

Auftrag ['aʊftraːk] *m* **-(e)s, -träge** order; *(Anweisung)* commission; *(Aufgabe)* mission; **im ~ von** on behalf of; **a~en** [-gən] *irreg vt Essen* serve; *Farbe* put on; *Kleidung* wear out; **jdm etw a~en** tell sb sth; *vi (dick machen)* make you/me *etc* look fat; **dick a~en** *(fig)* exaggerate; **~geber** *m* **-s, -** *(Comm)* purchaser, customer.

auftreiben ['aʊftraɪbən] *vt irreg (col: beschaffen)* raise.

auftreten ['aʊftreːtən] *irreg vt* kick open; *vi* appear; *(mit Füßen)* tread; *(sich verhalten)* behave; **A~** *nt* **-s** *(Vorkommen)* appearance; *(Benehmen)* behaviour.

Auftrieb ['aʊftriːp] *m (Phys)* buoyancy, lift; *(fig)* impetus.

Auftritt ['aʊftrɪt] *m (des Schauspielers)* entrance; *(lit, fig: Szene)* scene.

auftun ['aʊftuːn] *irreg vt* open; *vr* open up.

aufwachen ['aʊfvaxən] *vi* wake up.

aufwachsen ['aʊfvaksən] *vi irreg* grow up.

Aufwand ['aʊfvant] *m* **-(e)s** expenditure; *(Kosten auch)* expense; *(Luxus)* show; **bitte, keinen ~!** please don't go out of your way.

aufwärmen ['aʊfvɛrmən] *vt* warm up; *alte Geschichten* rake up.

aufwärts ['aʊfvɛrts] *ad* upwards; **A~entwicklung** *f* upward trend; **~gehen** *vi irreg* look up.

aufwecken ['aʊfvɛkən] *vt* wake(n) up.

aufweichen ['aʊfvaɪçən] *vt* soften, soak.

aufweisen ['aʊfvaɪzən] *vt irreg* show.

aufwenden ['aʊfvɛndən] *vt irreg* expend; *Geld* spend; *Sorgfalt* devote.

aufwendig *a* costly.

aufwerfen ['aʊfvɛrfən] *irreg vt Fenster etc* throw open; *Probleme* throw up, raise; *vr:* **sich zu etw ~** make o.s. out to be sth.

aufwerten ['aʊfvɛrtən] *vt (Fin)* revalue; *(fig)* raise in value.

aufwiegeln ['aʊfviːgəln] *vt* stir up, incite.

aufwiegen ['aʊfviːgən] *vt irreg* make up for.

Aufwind ['aʊfvɪnt] *m* up-current.

aufwirbeln ['aʊfvɪrbəln] *vt* whirl up; *Staub ~ (fig)* create a stir.

aufwischen ['aʊfvɪʃən] *vt* wipe up.

aufzählen ['aʊftsɛːlən] *vt* count out.

aufzeichnen ['aʊftsaɪçnən] *vt* sketch; *(schriftlich)* jot down; *(auf Band)* record.

Aufzeichnung *f (schriftlich)* note; *(Tonband—)* recording; *(Film—)* record.

aufzeigen ['aʊftsaɪgən] *vt* show, demonstrate.

aufziehen ['aʊftsiːən] *vt irreg (hochziehen)* raise, draw up; *(öffnen)* pull open; *Uhr* wind; *(col: necken)* tease; *(großziehen) Kinder* raise, bring up; *Tiere* rear.

Aufzug ['aʊftsuːk] *m (Fahrstuhl)* lift, elevator; *(Aufmarsch)* procession, parade; *(Kleidung)* get-up; *(Theat)* act.

aufzwingen ['aʊftsvɪŋən] *vt irreg:* **jdm etw ~** force sth upon sb.

Aug- ['aʊg] *cpd:* **~apfel** *m* eyeball; *(fig)* apple of one's eye; **~e** *nt* **-s, -n** eye; *(Fett—)* globule of fat; **unter vier ~en** in private; **~enblick** *m* moment; **im ~enblick** at the moment; **a~enblicklich** *a (sofort)* instantaneous; *(gegenwärtig)* present; **~enbraue** *f* eyebrow; **a~enscheinlich** *a* obvious; **~enweide** *f* sight for sore eyes; **~enzeuge** *m* eye witness.

August [aʊˈgʊst] *m* **-(e)s** *or* **-, -e** August.

Auktion [aʊktsiˈoːn] *f* auction; **~ator** [-ˈnaːtɔr] *m* auctioneer.

Aula ['aʊla] *f-*, **Aulen** *or* **-s** assembly hall.

aus [aʊs] *prep* +*dat* out of; *(von . . . her)* from; *(Material)* made of; **~ ihr wird nie etwas** she'll never get anywhere; *ad* out; *(beendet)* finished, over; *(ausgezogen)* off; **~ und ein gehen** come and go; *(bei jdm)* visit frequently; **weder ~ noch ein wissen** be at sixes and sevens; **auf etw** *(acc)* **~ sein** be after sth; **von Fenster ~** out of the window; **von Rom ~** from Rome; **von sich ~** of one's own accord; **A~** *nt* - outfield; **ins A~ gehen** go out.

ausarbeiten ['aʊsˌarbaɪtən] *vt* work out.

ausarten ['aʊsˌartən] *vi* degenerate; *(Kind)* become overexcited.

ausatmen ['aʊsˌaːtmən] *vi* breathe out.

ausbaden ['aʊsbaːdən] *vt:* **etw ~ müssen** *(col)* carry the can for sth.

Ausbau ['aʊsbaʊ] *m* extension, expansion; removal; **a~en** *vt* extend, expand; *(herausnehmen)* take out, remove; **a~fähig** *a (fig)* worth developing.

ausbedingen ['aʊsbədɪŋən] *vt irreg:* **sich** *(dat)* **etw ~** insist on sth.

ausbessern ['aʊsbɛsərn] *vt* mend, repair.

ausbeulen ['aʊsbɔɪlən] *vt* beat out.

Ausbeute ['aʊsbɔɪtə] *f* yield; *(Fische)* catch; **a~n** *vt* exploit; *(Min)* work.

ausbild- ['aʊsbɪld] *cpd:* **~en** *vt* educate; *Lehrling, Soldat* instruct, train; *Fähigkeiten* develop; *Geschmack* cultivate; **A~er** *m* **-s, -** instructor; **A~ung** *f* education; training, instruction; development, cultivation.

ausbitten ['ausbɪtən] vt irreg: **sich** (dat) **etw ~** (erbitten) ask for sth; (verlangen) insist on sth.

ausbleiben ['ausblaɪbən] vi irreg (Personen) stay away, not come; (Ereignisse) fail to happen, not happen.

Ausblick ['ausblɪk] m (lit, fig) prospect, outlook, view.

ausbomben ['ausbɔmbən] vt bomb out.

ausbrechen ['ausbrɛçən] irreg vi break out; **in Tränen/Gelächter ~** burst into tears/out laughing; vt break off.

ausbreiten ['ausbraɪtən] vt spread (out); Arme stretch out; vr spread; (über Thema) expand, enlarge (über +acc on).

ausbrennen ['ausbrɛnən] irreg vt scorch; Wunde cauterize; vi burn out.

ausbringen ['ausbrɪŋən] vt irreg ein Hoch propose.

Ausbruch ['ausbrux] m outbreak; (von Vulkan) eruption; (Gefühls—) outburst; (von Gefangenen) escape.

ausbrüten ['ausbry:tən] vt (lit, fig) hatch.

Ausbuchtung ['ausbuxtʊŋ] f bulge; (Küste) projection, protuberance.

ausbuhen ['ausbu:ən] vt boo.

ausbürsten ['ausbʏrstən] vt brush out.

Ausdauer ['ausdauər] f perseverance, stamina; **a ~ nd** a persevering.

ausdehnen ['ausde:nən] vtr (räumlich) expand; Gummi stretch; (Nebel) extend; (zeitlich) stretch; (fig) Macht extend.

ausdenken ['ausdɛŋkən] vt irreg (zu Ende denken) think through; **sich** (dat) **etw ~** think sth up.

ausdiskutieren ['ausdɪskuti:rən] vt talk out.

ausdrehen ['ausdre:ən] vt turn or switch off; Licht auch turn out.

Ausdruck ['ausdruk] m expression, phrase; (Kundgabe, Gesichts—) expression.

ausdrücken ['ausdrykən] vt (also vr: formulieren, zeigen) express; Zigarette put out; Zitrone squeeze.

ausdrücklich a express, explicit.

ausdrucks- cpd: **~los** a expressionless, blank; **~voll** a expressive; **A ~ weise** f mode of expression.

auseinander [aus'aɪnandər] ad (getrennt) apart; **~ schreiben** write as separate words; **~ bringen** vt irreg separate; **~ fallen** vi irreg fall apart; **~ gehen** vi irreg (Menschen) separate; (Meinungen) differ; (Gegenstand) fall apart; (col: dick werden) put on weight; **~ halten** vt irreg tell apart; **~ nehmen** vt irreg take to pieces, dismantle; **~ setzen** vt (erklären) set forth, explain; vr (sich verständigen) come to terms, settle; (sich befassen) concern o.s.; **A ~ setzung** f argument.

auserlesen ['aus'ɛrle:zən] a select, choice.

ausfahren ['ausfa:rən] irreg vi drive out; (Naut) put out (to sea); vt take out; (Tech) Fahrwerk drive out; **ausgefahrene Wege** rutted roads.

Ausfahrt f (des Zuges etc) leaving, departure; (Autobahn—, Garagen—) exit, way out; (Spazierfahrt) drive, excursion.

Ausfall ['ausfal] m loss; (Nichtstattfinden

cancellation; (Mil) sortie; (Fechten) lunge; (radioaktiv) fall-out; **a ~ en** vi irreg (Zähne, Haare) fall or come out; (nicht stattfinden) be cancelled; (wegbleiben) be omitted; (Person) drop out; (Lohn) be stopped; (nicht funktionieren) break down; (Resultat haben) turn out; **wie ist das Spiel ausgefallen?** what was the result of the game?; **a ~ end** a impertinent; **~ straße** f arterial road.

ausfegen ['ausfe:gən] vt sweep out.

ausfeilen ['ausfaɪlən] vt file out; Stil polish up.

ausfertigen ['ausfɛrtɪgən] vt draw up; Rechnung make out; **doppelt ~** duplicate.

Ausfertigung f drawing up; making out; (Exemplar) copy.

ausfindig machen ['ausfɪndɪç maxən] vt discover.

ausfliegen ['ausfli:gən] vti irreg fly away; **sie sind ausgeflogen** (col) they're out.

ausflippen ['ausflɪpən] vi (col) freak out.

Ausflucht ['ausfluxt] f-, **-flüchte** excuse.

Ausflug ['ausflu:k] m excursion, outing.

Ausflügler ['ausfly:klər] m **-s,** - tripper.

Ausfluß ['ausflus] m outlet; (Med) discharge.

ausfragen ['ausfra:gən] vt interrogate, question.

ausfransen ['ausfranzən] vi fray.

ausfressen ['ausfrɛsən] vt irreg eat up; (aushöhlen) corrode; (col: anstellen) be up to.

Ausfuhr ['ausfu:r] f-, **-en** export, exportation; in cpds export.

ausführ- ['ausfy:r] cpd: **~ bar** a feasible; (Comm) exportable; **~ en** vt (verwirklichen) carry out; Person take out; Hund take for a walk; (Comm) export; (erklären) give details of; **~ lich** a detailed; ad in detail; **A ~ lichkeit** f detail; **A ~ ung** f execution, performance; (Durchführung) completion; (Herstellungsart) version; (Erklärung) explanation.

ausfüllen ['ausfʏlən] vt fill up; Fragebogen etc fill in; (Beruf) be fulfilling for.

Ausgabe ['ausga:bə] f (Geld) expenditure, outlay; (Aushändigung) giving out; (Gepäck—) left-luggage office; (Buch) edition; (Nummer) issue.

Ausgang ['ausgaŋ] m way out, exit; (Ende) end; (Ausgangspunkt) starting point; (Ergebnis) result; (Ausgehtag) free time, time off; **kein ~** no exit; **~ sbasis** f, **~ spunkt** m starting point; **~ ssperre** f curfew.

ausgeben ['ausge:bən] irreg vt Geld spend; (austeilen) issue, distribute; vr: **sich für etw/jdn ~** pass o.s. off as sth/sb.

ausgebucht ['ausgəbu:xt] a fully booked.

ausgedient ['ausgədi:nt] a Soldat discharged; (verbraucht) no longer in use; **~ haben** have done good service.

ausgefallen ['ausgəfalən] a (ungewöhnlich) exceptional.

ausgeglichen ['ausgəglɪçən] a (well-balanced; **A ~ heit** f balance; (von Mensch) even-temperedness.

Ausgeh- ['ausge:] cpd: **~ anzug** m good suit; **a ~ en** vi irreg go out; (zu Ende gehen) come to an end; (*Benzin*) run out; (*Haare, Zähne*) fall *or* come out; (*Feuer, Ofen, Licht*) go out; (*Strom*) go off; (*Resultat haben*) turn out; **mir ging das Benzin aus** I ran out of petrol; **auf etw** (*acc*) **a~en** aim at sth; **von etw a~en** (*wegführen*) lead away from sth; (*herrühren*) come from sth; (*zugrunde legen*) proceed from sth; **wir können davon a~en, daß ...** we can proceed from the assumption that ..., we can take as our starting point that ...; **leer a~en** get nothing; **schlecht a~en** turn out badly; **~verbot** *nt* curfew.

ausgelassen ['ausgəlasən] *a* boisterous, high-spirited; **A~heit** *f* boisterousness, high spirits *pl*, exuberance.

ausgelastet ['ausgəlastət] *a* fully occupied.

ausgelernt ['ausgəlɛrnt] *a* trained, qualified.

ausgemacht ['ausgəmaxt] *a* (*col*) settled; *Dummkopf etc* out-and-out, downright; **es gilt als ~, daß ...** it is settled that ...; **es war eine ~e Sache, daß ...** it was a foregone conclusion that ...

ausgenommen ['ausgənɔmən] *prep +gen or dat, cj* except; **Anwesende sind ~** present company excepted.

ausgeprägt ['ausgəprɛːkt] *a* prominent.

ausgerechnet ['ausgərɛçnət] *ad* just, precisely; **~ du/heute** you of all people/today of all days.

ausgeschlossen ['ausgəʃlɔsən] *a* (*unmöglich*) impossible, out of the question; **es ist nicht ~, daß ...** it cannot be ruled out that ...

ausgeschnitten ['ausgəʃnitən] *a Kleid* low-necked.

ausgesprochen ['ausgəʃprɔxən] *a Faulheit, Lüge etc* out-and-out; (*unverkennbar*) marked; *ad* decidedly.

ausgezeichnet ['ausgətsaiçnət] *a* excellent.

ausgiebig ['ausgiːbiç] *a Gebrauch* thorough, good; *Essen* generous, lavish; **~ schlafen** have a good sleep.

Ausgleich ['ausglaiç] *m* **-(e)s, -e** balance; (*Vermittlung*) reconciliation; (*Sport*) equalization; **zum ~ (+gen)** in order to offset; **das ist ein guter ~** that's very relaxing; **a~en** *irreg vt* balance (out); reconcile; *Höhe* even up; *vi* (*Sport*) equalize; **~stor** *nt* equalizer.

ausgraben ['ausgraːbən] *vt irreg* dig up; *Leichen* exhume; (*fig*) unearth.

Ausgrabung *f* excavation; (*Ausgraben auch*) digging up.

Ausguß ['ausgus] *m* (*Spüle*) sink; (*Abfluß*) outlet; (*Tülle*) spout.

aushaben ['aushaːbən] *vt irreg* (*col*) *Kleidung* have taken off; *Buch* have finished.

aushalten ['aushaltən] *irreg vt* bear, stand; *Geliebte* keep; *vi* hold out; **das ist nicht zum A~** that is unbearable.

aushandeln ['aushandəln] *vt* negotiate.

aushändigen ['aushɛndiɡən] *vt*: **jdm etw ~** hand sth over to sb.

Aushang ['aushaŋ] *m* notice.

aushängen ['aushɛŋən] *irreg vt Meldung* put up; *Fenster* take off its hinges; *vi* be displayed; *vr* hang out.

Aushängeschild *nt* (shop) sign.

ausharren ['ausharən] *vi* hold out.

ausheben ['ausheːbən] *vt irreg Erde* lift out; *Grube* hollow out; *Tür* take off its hinges; *Diebesnest* clear out; (*Mil*) enlist.

aushecken ['aushɛkən] *vt* (*col*) concoct, think up.

aushelfen ['aushɛlfən] *vi irreg*: **jdm ~** help sb out.

Aushilfe ['aushilfə] *f* help, assistance; (*Person*) (temporary) worker.

Aushilfs- *cpd*: **~kraft** *f* temporary worker; **a~weise** *ad* temporarily, as a stopgap.

ausholen ['aushoːlən] *vi* swing one's arm back; (*zur Ohrfeige*) raise one's hand; (*beim Gehen*) take long strides; **weit ~** (*fig*) be expansive.

aushorchen ['aushɔrçən] *vt* sound out, pump.

aushungern ['aushuŋərn] *vt* starve out.

auskennen ['auskɛnən] *vr irreg* know thoroughly; (*an einem Ort*) know one's way about; (*in Fragen etc*) be knowledgeable.

auskippen ['auskipən] *vt* empty.

ausklammern ['ausklamərn] *vt Thema* exclude, leave out.

Ausklang ['ausklaŋ] *m* end.

auskleiden ['ausklaidən] *vr* undress; *vt Wand* line.

ausklingen ['ausklıŋən] *vi irreg* (*Ton, Lied*) die away; (*Fest*) peter out.

ausklopfen ['ausklɔpfən] *vt Teppich* beat; *Pfeife* knock out.

auskochen ['auskɔxən] *vt* boil; (*Med*) sterilize; **ausgekocht** (*fig*) out-and-out.

auskommen ['auskɔmən] *vi irreg*: **mit jdm ~** get on with sb; **mit etw ~** get by with sth; **A~** *nt* **-s: sein A~ haben** get by.

auskosten ['auskɔstən] *vt* enjoy to the full.

auskugeln ['auskuːɡəln] *vt* (*col*) *Arm* dislocate.

auskundschaften ['auskunt-ʃaftən] *vt* spy out; *Gebiet* reconnoitre.

Auskunft ['auskunft] *f* **-, -künfte** information; (*nähere*) details *pl*, particulars *pl*; (*Stelle*) information office; (*Tel*) inquiries; **jdm ~ erteilen** give sb information.

auskuppeln ['auskupəln] *vi* disengage the clutch.

auslachen ['auslaxən] *vt* laugh at, mock.

ausladen ['auslaːdən] *irreg vt* unload; (*col*) *Gäste* cancel an invitation to; *vi* stick out.

Auslage ['auslaːɡə] *f* shop window (display); **~n** *pl* outlay, expenditure.

Ausland ['auslant] *nt* foreign countries *pl*; **im/ins ~** abroad.

Ausländer(in *f*) ['auslɛndər(ın)] *m* **-s, -** foreigner.

ausländisch *a* foreign.

Auslands- *cpd*: **~gespräch** *nt* international call; **~korrespondent(in** *f*) *m* foreign correspondent; **~reise** *f* trip abroad.

auslassen ['auslasən] *irreg vt* leave out;

Wort etc auch omjt; *Fett* melt; *Kleidungs-stück* let out; *Wut, Ärger* vent (*an* +*dat* on); *vr*: **sich über etw** (*acc*) ~ speak one's mind about sth.

Auslassung *f* omission; ~**szeichen** *nt* apostrophe.

Auslauf ['auslauf] *m* (*für Tiere*) run; (*Ausfluß*) outflow, outlet; **a**~**en** *vi irreg* run out; (*Behälter*) leak; (*Naut*) put out (to sea); (*langsam aufhören*) run down.

Ausläufer ['auslɔyfər] *m* (*von Gebirge*) spur; (*Pflanze*) runner; (*Met*) (*von Hoch*) ridge; (*von Tief*) trough.

ausleeren ['ausleːrən] *vt* empty.

auslegen ['ausleːgən] *vt Waren* lay out; *Köder* put down; *Geld* lend; (*bedecken*) cover; *Text etc* interpret.

Auslegung *f* interpretation.

Ausleihe ['auslaɪə] *f* -, -**n** issuing; (*Stelle*) issue desk; **a**~**n** *vt irreg* (*verleihen*) lend; **sich** (*dat*) **etw a**~**en** borrow sth.

Auslese ['auslɛːzə] *f* -, -**n** selection; (*Elite*) elite; (*Wein*) choice wine; **a**~**n** *vt irreg* select; (*col: zu Ende lesen*) finish.

ausliefern ['ausliːfərn] *vt* deliver (up), hand over; (*Comm*) deliver; **jdm/etw ausgeliefert sein** be at the mercy of sb/sth; *vr*: **sich jdm** ~ give o.s. up to sb.

auslöschen ['auslœʃən] *vt* extinguish; (*fig*) wipe out, obliterate.

auslosen ['ausloːzən] *vt* draw lots for.

auslösen ['auslœːzən] *vt Explosion, Schuß* set off; (*hervorrufen*) cause, produce; *Gefangene* ransom; *Pfand* redeem.

Auslöser *m* -**s**, - (*Phot*) release.

ausmachen ['ausmaxən] *vt Licht, Radio* turn off; *Feuer* put out; (*entdecken*) make out; (*vereinbaren*) agree; (*beilegen*) settle; (*Anteil darstellen, betragen*) represent; (*bedeuten*) matter; **das macht ihm nichts aus** it doesn't matter to him; **macht es Ihnen etwas aus, wenn . . .?** would you mind if . . .?

ausmalen ['ausmaːlən] *vt* paint; (*fig*) describe; **sich** (*dat*) **etw** ~ imagine sth.

Ausmaß ['ausmaːs] *nt* dimension; (*fig auch*) scale.

ausmerzen ['ausmɛrtsən] *vt* eliminate.

ausmessen ['ausmɛsən] *vt irreg* measure.

Ausnahme ['ausnaːmə] *f* -, -**n** exception; **eine** ~ **machen** make an exception; ~**fall** *m* exceptional case; ~**zustand** *m* state of emergency.

ausnahms- *cpd*: ~**los** *ad* without exception; ~**weise** *ad* by way of exception, for once.

ausnehmen ['ausneːmən] *irreg vt* take out, remove; *Tier* gut; *Nest* rob; (*col: Geld abnehmen*) clean out; (*ausschließen*) make an exception of; *vr* look, appear; ~**d** *a* exceptional.

ausnützen ['ausnʏtsən] *vt Zeit, Gelegenheit* use, turn to good account; *Einfluß* use; *Mensch, Gutmütigkeit* exploit.

auspacken ['auspakən] *vt* unpack.

auspfeifen ['auspfaɪfən] *vt irreg* hiss/boo at.

ausplaudern ['ausplaudərn] *vt Geheimnis* blab.

ausprobieren ['ausprobiːrən] *vt* try (out).

Auspuff ['auspuf] *m* -(**e**)**s**, -**e** (*Tech*) exhaust; ~**rohr** *nt* exhaust (pipe); ~**topf** *m* (*Aut*) silencer.

ausradieren ['ausradiːrən] *vt* erase, rub out.

ausrangieren ['ausrãʒiːrən] *vt* (*col*) chuck out.

ausrauben ['ausraubən] *vt* rob.

ausräumen ['ausrɔymən] *vt Dinge* clear away; *Schrank, Zimmer* empty; *Bedenken* put aside.

ausrechnen ['ausrɛçnən] *vt* calculate, reckon.

Ausrechnung *f* calculation, reckoning.

Ausrede ['ausreːdə] *f* excuse; **a**~**n** *vi* have one's say; *vt*: **jdm etw a**~**n** talk sb out of sth.

ausreichen ['ausraɪçən] *vi* suffice, be enough; ~**d** *a* sufficient, adequate; (*Sch*) adequate.

Ausreise ['ausraɪzə] *f* departure; **bei der** ~ when leaving the country; ~**erlaubnis** *f* exit visa; **a**~**n** *vi* leave the country.

ausreißen ['ausraɪsən] *irreg vt* tear or pull out; *vi* (*Riß bekommen*) tear; (*col*) make off, scram.

ausrenken ['ausrɛŋkən] *vt* dislocate.

ausrichten ['ausrɪçtən] *vt Botschaft* deliver; *Gruß* pass on; *Hochzeit etc* arrange; (*erreichen*) get anywhere (*bei* with); (*in gerade Linie bringen*) get in a straight line; (*angleichen*) bring into line; **jdm etw** ~ take a message for sb; **ich werde es ihm** ~ I'll tell him.

ausrotten ['ausrɔtən] *vt* stamp out, exterminate.

ausrücken ['ausrʏkən] *vi* (*Mil*) move off; (*Feuerwehr, Polizei*) be called out; (*col: weglaufen*) run away.

Ausruf ['ausruːf] *m* (*Schrei*) cry, exclamation; (*Verkünden*) proclamation; **a**~**en** *vt irreg* cry out, exclaim; call out; ~**ezeichen** *nt* exclamation mark.

ausruhen ['ausruːən] *vtr* rest.

ausrüsten ['ausrʏstən] *vt* equip, fit out.

Ausrüstung *f* equipment.

ausrutschen ['ausrutʃən] *vi* slip.

Aussage ['auszaːgə] *f* -, -**n** (*Jur*) statement; **a**~**n** *vt* say, state; *vi* (*Jur*) give evidence.

ausschalten ['ausʃaltən] *vt* switch off; (*fig*) eliminate.

Ausschank ['ausʃaŋk] *m* -(**e**)**s**, -**schänke** dispensing, giving out; (*Comm*) selling; (*Theke*) bar.

Ausschau ['ausʃau] *f*: ~ **halten** look out, watch (*nach* for); **a**~**en** *vi* look out (*nach* for), be on the look-out.

ausscheiden ['ausʃaɪdən] *irreg vt* separate; (*Med*) give off, secrete; *vi* leave (*aus etw* sth); (*Sport*) be eliminated or knocked out; **er scheidet für den Posten aus** he can't be considered for the job.

Ausscheidung *f* separation; retiral; elimination.

ausschenken ['ausʃɛŋkən] *vt* pour out; (*Comm*) sell.

ausschimpfen ['aʊʃImpfən] *vt* scold, tell off.

ausschlachten ['aʊʃlaxtən] *vt Auto* cannibalize; (*fig*) make a meal of.

ausschlafen ['aʊʃlaːfən] *irreg vir* have a long lie (in); *vt* sleep off; **ich bin nicht ausgeschlafen** I didn't have or get enough sleep.

Ausschlag ['aʊʃlaːk] *m* (*Med*) rash; (*Pendel—*) swing; (*Nadel*) deflection; **den ~ geben** (*fig*) tip the balance; **a~en** [-gən] *irreg vt* knock out; (*auskleiden*) deck out; (*verweigern*) decline; *vi* (*Pferd*) kick out; (*Bot*) sprout; (*Zeiger*) be deflected; **a~gebend** a decisive.

ausschließen ['aʊʃliːsən] *vt irreg* shut or lock out; (*fig*) exclude; **ich will mich nicht ~** myself not excepted.

ausschließlich a, ad exclusive(ly); *prep +gen* excluding, exclusive of.

Ausschluß ['aʊʃlʊs] *m* exclusion.

ausschmücken ['aʊʃmʏkən] *vt* decorate; (*fig*) embellish.

ausschneiden ['aʊʃnaɪdən] *vt irreg* cut out; *Büsche* trim.

Ausschnitt ['aʊʃnIt] *m* (*Teil*) section; (*von Kleid*) neckline; (*Zeitungs—*) cutting; (*aus Film etc*) excerpt.

ausschreiben ['aʊʃraɪbən] *vt irreg* (*ganz schreiben*) write out (in full); (*ausstellen*) write (out); *Stelle, Wettbewerb etc* announce, advertise.

Ausschreitung ['aʊʃraɪtʊŋ] *f* excess.

Ausschuß ['aʊʃʊs] *m* committee, board; (*Abfall*) waste, scraps *pl*; (*Comm: also ~ware f*) reject.

ausschütten ['aʊʃʏtən] *vt* pour out; *Eimer* empty; *Geld* pay; *vr* shake (with laughter).

ausschweifend ['aʊʃvaɪfənt] a *Leben* dissipated, debauched; *Phantasie* extravagant.

Ausschweifung *f* excess.

ausschweigen ['aʊʃvaɪgən] *vr irreg* keep silent.

ausschwitzen ['aʊʃvItsən] *vt* exude; (*Mensch*) sweat out.

aussehen ['aʊzeːən] *vi irreg* look; **das sieht nach nichts aus** that doesn't look anything special; **es sieht nach Regen aus** it looks like rain; **es sieht schlecht aus** things look bad; **A~** *nt* **-s** appearance.

aussein ['aʊsaɪn] *vi irreg* (*col*) be out; (*zu Ende*) be over.

außen ['aʊsən] *ad* outside; (*nach —*) outwards; **~ ist es rot** it's red (on the outside); **A~antenne** *f* outside aerial; **A~bordmotor** *m* outboard motor.

aussenden ['aʊszɛndən] *vt irreg* send out, emit.

Außen- *cpd*: **~dienst** *m* outside or field service; (*von Diplomat*) foreign service; **~handel** *m* foreign trade; **~minister** *m* foreign minister; **~ministerium** *nt* foreign office; **~politik** *f* foreign policy; **~seite** *f* outside; **~seiter** *m* **-s, -**, **~stehende(r)** *mf* outsider; **~welt** *f* outside world.

außer ['aʊsər] *prep +dat* (*räumlich*) out of; (*abgesehen von*) except; **~ Gefahr sein** be out of danger; **~ Zweifel** beyond any doubt; **~ Betrieb** out of order; **~ sich** (*dat*) **sein/geraten** be beside o.s.; **~ Dienst** retired; **~ Landes** abroad; *cj* (*ausgenommen*) except; **~ wenn** unless; **~ daß** except; **~amtlich** a unofficial, private; **~dem** *cj* besides, in addition; **~dienstlich** a unofficial.

äußere(r,s) ['ɔʏsərə(r,z)] *a* outer, external.

außer- *cpd*: **~ehelich** a extramarital; **~gewöhnlich** a unusual; **~halb** *prep +gen*, *ad* outside; **A~kraftsetzung** *f* putting out of action.

äußer- *cpd*: **~lich** a, *ad* external; **~n** *vt* utter, express; (*zeigen*) show; *vr* give one's opinion; (*sich zeigen*) show itself.

außer- *cpd*: **~ordentlich** a extraordinary; (*außergewöhnlich*) unscheduled; **~'stande** *ad* not in a position, unable.

äußerst ['ɔʏsərst] *ad* extremely, most; **~e(r,s)** a utmost; (*räumlich*) farthest; *Termin* last possible; *Preis* highest; **~enfalls** *ad* if the worst comes to the worst.

aussetzen ['aʊszɛtsən] *vt Kind, Tier* abandon; *Boote* lower; *Belohnung* offer; *Urteil, Verfahren* postpone; **jdn/sich etw** (*dat*) **~** lay sb/o.s. open to sth; **jdm/etw ausgesetzt sein** be exposed to sb/sth; **an jdm/etw etwas ~** find fault with sb/sth; *vi* (*aufhören*) stop; (*Pause machen*) drop out.

Aussicht ['aʊszIçt] *f* view; (*in Zukunft*) prospect; **in ~ sein** be in view; **etw in ~ haben** have sth in view; **a~slos** a hopeless; **~spunkt** *m* viewpoint; **a~sreich** a promising; **~sturm** *m* observation tower.

aussöhnen ['aʊszøːnən] *vt* reconcile; *vr* reconcile o.s., become reconciled.

Aussöhnung *f* reconciliation.

aussondern ['aʊszɔndərn] *vt* separate, select.

aussortieren ['aʊszɔrtiːrən] *vt* sort out.

ausspannen ['aʊʃpanən] *vt* spread or stretch out; *Pferd* unharness; (*col*) *Mädchen* steal (*jdm* from sb); *vi* relax.

aussparen ['aʊʃpaːrən] *vt* leave open.

aussperren ['aʊʃpɛrən] *vt* lock out.

ausspielen ['aʊʃpiːlən] *vt Karte* lead; *Geldprämie* offer as a prize; **jdn gegen jdn ~** play sb off against sb; *vi* (*Cards*) lead; **ausgespielt haben** be finished.

Aussprache ['aʊʃpraːxə] *f* pronunciation; (*Unterredung*) (frank) discussion.

aussprechen ['aʊʃprɛçən] *irreg vt* pronounce; (*zu Ende sprechen*) speak; (*äußern*) say, express; *vr* (*sich äußern*) speak (*über +acc* about); (*sich anvertrauen*) unburden o.s.; (*diskutieren*) discuss; *vi* (*zu Ende sprechen*) finish speaking.

Ausspruch ['aʊʃprʊx] *m Karte* saying, remark.

ausspülen ['aʊʃpyːlən] *vt* wash out; *Mund* rinse.

ausstaffieren ['aʊʃtafiːrən] *vt* equip, kit out; *Zimmer* furnish.

Ausstand ['aʊʃtant] *m* strike; **in den ~ treten** go on strike.

ausstatten ['aʊʃtatən] *vt Zimmer etc*

furnish; **jdn mit etw** ~ equip sb or kit sb out with sth.

Ausstattung f (Ausstatten) provision; (Kleidung) outfit; (Aussteuer) dowry; (Aufmachung) make-up; (Einrichtung) furnishing.

ausstechen ['aʊsʃtɛçən] vt irreg Augen, Rasen, Graben dig out; Kekse cut out; (übertreffen) outshine.

ausstehen ['aʊsʃteːən] irreg vt stand, endure; vi (noch nicht dasein) be outstanding.

aussteigen ['aʊsʃtaɪgən] vi irreg get out, alight.

ausstellen ['aʊsʃtɛlən] vt exhibit, display; (col: ausschalten) switch off; Rechnung etc make out; Paß, Zeugnis issue.

Ausstellung f exhibition; (Fin) drawing up; (einer Rechnung) making out; (eines Passes etc) issuing.

aussterben ['aʊsʃtɛrbən] vi irreg die out.

Aussteuer ['aʊsʃtɔʏər] f dowry.

ausstopfen ['aʊsʃtɔpfən] vt stuff.

ausstoßen ['aʊsʃtoːsən] vt irreg Luft, Rauch give off, emit; (aus Verein etc) expel, exclude; Auge poke out.

ausstrahlen ['aʊsʃtraːlən] vti radiate; (Rad) broadcast.

Ausstrahlung f radiation; (fig) charisma.

ausstrecken ['aʊsʃtrɛkən] vtr stretch out.

ausstreichen ['aʊsʃtraɪçən] vt irreg cross out; (glätten) smooth out.

ausströmen ['aʊsʃtrøːmən] vi (Gas) pour out, escape; vt give off; (fig) radiate.

aussuchen ['aʊszuːxən] vt select, pick out.

Austausch ['aʊstaʊʃ] m exchange; **a~bar** a exchangeable; **a~en** vt exchange, swop; ~**motor** m reconditioned engine.

austeilen ['aʊstaɪlən] vt distribute, give out.

Auster ['aʊstər] f -, -n oyster.

austoben ['aʊstoːbən] vr (Kind) run wild; (Erwachsene) sow one's wild oats.

austragen ['aʊstraːgən] vt irreg Post deliver; Streit etc decide; Wettkämpfe hold.

Austräger ['aʊstrɛːgər] m delivery boy; (Zeitungs—) newspaper boy.

austreiben ['aʊstraɪbən] vt irreg drive out, expel; Geister exorcize.

austreten ['aʊstreːtən] irreg vi (zur Toilette) be excused; **aus etw** ~ leave sth; vt Feuer tread out, trample; Schuhe wear out; Treppe wear down.

austrinken ['aʊstrɪŋkən] irreg vt Glas drain; Getränk drink up; vi finish one's drink, drink up.

Austritt ['aʊstrɪt] m emission; (aus Verein, Partei etc) retirement, withdrawal.

austrocknen ['aʊstrɔknən] vti dry up.

ausüben ['aʊsʔyːbən] vt Beruf practise, carry out; Funktion perform; Einfluß exert; Reiz, Wirkung exercise, have (auf jdn on sb).

Ausübung f practice, exercise.

Ausverkauf ['aʊsfɛrkaʊf] m sale; **a~en** vt sell out; Geschäft sell up; **a~t** a Karten, Artikel sold out; (Theat) Haus full.

Auswahl ['aʊsvaːl] f selection, choice (an +dat of).

auswählen ['aʊsvɛːlən] vt select, choose.

Auswander- ['aʊsvandər] cpd: ~**er** m emigrant; **a~n** vi emigrate; ~**ung** f emigration.

auswärtig ['aʊsvɛrtɪç] a (nicht am/vom Ort) out-of-town; (ausländisch) foreign; **A~e(s) Amt** nt Foreign Office, State Department (US).

auswärts ['aʊsvɛrts] ad outside; (nach außen) outwards; ~ **essen** eat out; **A~spiel** nt away game.

auswechseln ['aʊsvɛksəln] vt change, substitute.

Ausweg ['aʊsveːk] m way out; **a~los** a hopeless.

ausweichen ['aʊsvaɪçən] vi irreg: **jdm/etw** ~ (lit) move aside or make way for sb/sth; (fig) side-step sb/sth; ~**d** a evasive.

ausweinen ['aʊsvaɪnən] vr have a (good) cry.

Ausweis ['aʊsvaɪs] m -es, -e identity card, passport; (Mitglieds—, Bibliotheks—etc) card; **a~en** [-zən] irreg vt expel, banish; vr prove one's identity; ~**karte** f, ~**papiere** pl identity papers pl; ~**ung** f expulsion.

ausweiten ['aʊsvaɪtən] vt stretch.

auswendig ['aʊsvɛndɪç] ad by heart; ~ **lernen** vt learn by heart.

auswert- ['aʊsvert] cpd: ~**en** vt evaluate; **A~ung** f evaluation, analysis; (Nutzung) utilization.

auswirk- ['aʊsvɪrk] cpd: ~**en** vr have an effect; **A~ung** f effect.

auswischen ['aʊsvɪʃən] vt wipe out; **jdm eins** ~ (col) put one over on sb.

Auswuchs ['aʊsvuːks] m (out)growth; (fig) product.

auswuchten ['aʊsvʊxtən] vt (Aut) balance.

auszacken ['aʊstsakən] vt Stoff etc pink.

auszahlen ['aʊstsaːlən] vt Lohn, Summe pay out; Arbeiter pay off; Miterbe buy out; vr (sich lohnen) pay.

auszählen ['aʊstsɛːlən] vt Stimmen count; (Boxen) count out.

auszeichnen ['aʊstsaɪçnən] vt honour; (Mil) decorate; (Comm) price; vr distinguish o.s.

Auszeichnung f distinction; (Comm) pricing; (Ehrung) awarding of decoration; (Ehre) honour; (Orden) decoration; **mit** ~ with distinction.

ausziehen ['aʊstsiːən] irreg vt Kleidung take off; Haare, Zähne, Tisch etc pull out; (nachmalen) trace; vr undress; vi (aufbrechen) leave; (aus Wohnung) move out.

Auszug ['aʊstsuːk] m (aus Wohnung) removal; (aus Buch etc) extract; (Konto—) statement; (Ausmarsch) departure.

Auto ['aʊto] nt -s, -s (motor-)car; ~**fahren** drive; ~**bahn** f motorway; ~**fahrer(in** f) m motorist, driver; ~**fahrt** f drive; **a~gen** [-'geːn] a autogenous; ~**gramm** nt autograph; ~**mat** m -en, -en machine; **a~'matisch** a automatic; **a~'nom** [-'noːm] a autonomous.

Autopsie [aʊtɔ'psiː] f post-mortem, autopsy.

Autor ['autɔr] *m* **-s, -en, Autorin**
['au'to:rɪn] *f* author.
Auto- *cpd*: ~**radio** *nt* car radio; ~**reifen**
m car tyre; ~**rennen** *nt* motor racing.
autoritär [autori'tɛ:r] *a* authoritarian.
Autorität *f* authority.
Auto- *cpd*: ~**unfall** *m* car *or* motor
accident; ~**verleih** *m* car hire.
Axt [akst] *f* -, **-e** axe.

B

B, b [be:] *nt* B, b.
Baby ['be:bi] *nt* **-s, -s** baby;
~**ausstattung** *f* layette; ~**sitter**
['be:bɪzɪtər] *m* -s, - baby-sitter.
Bach [bax] *m* -(e)s, **-e** stream, brook.
Back- [bak] *cpd*: ~**blech** *nt* baking tray;
~**bord** *nt* -(e)s, -e (*Naut*) port; ~**e** *f* -, -n
cheek; **b**~**en** *vti irreg* bake; ~**enbart** *m*
sideboards *pl*; ~**enzahn** *m* molar.
Bäcker ['bɛkər] *m* -s, - baker; ~**ei** [-'raɪ] *f*
bakery; (—*laden*) baker's (shop).
Back- *cpd*: ~**form** *f* baking tin;
~**hähnchen** *nt* roast chicken; ~**obst** *nt*
dried fruit; ~**ofen** *m* oven; ~**pflaume** *f*
prune; ~**pulver** *nt* baking powder;
~**stein** *m* brick.
Bad [ba:t] *nt* -(e)s, **-er** bath; (*Schwimmen*)
bathe; (*Ort*) spa.
Bade- ['ba:də] *cpd*: ~**anstalt** *f* (swimming) baths *pl*; ~**anzug** *m* bathing suit;
~**hose** *f* bathing *or* swimming trunks *pl*;
~**kappe** *f* bathing cap; ~**mantel** *m* bath-
(ing) robe; ~**meister** *m* baths attendant;
b~**n** *vi* bathe, have a bath; *vt* bath; ~**ort**
m spa; ~**tuch** *nt* bath towel; ~**wanne** *f*
bath (tub); ~**zimmer** *nt* bathroom.
baff [baf] *a*: ~ **sein** (*col*) be flabbergasted.
Bagatelle [baga'tɛlə] *f* -, -n trifle.
Bagger ['bagər] *m* -s, - excavator; (*Naut*)
dredger; **b**~**n** *vti* excavate; (*Naut*)
dredge.
Bahn [ba:n] *f* -, -en railway, railroad (*US*);
(*Weg*) road, way; (*Spur*) lane; (*Renn*—)
track; (*Astron*) orbit; (*Stoff*—) length;
b~**brechend** *a* pioneering; ~**damm** *m*
railway embankment; **b**~**en** *vt*:
sich/jdm einen Weg b~**en** clear a
way/a way for sb; ~**fahrt** *f* railway
journey; ~**hof** *m* station; **auf dem** ~**hof**
at the station; ~**hofshalle** *f* station concourse; ~**hofsvorsteher** *m* station-master;
~**hofswirtschaft** *f* station restaurant;
~**linie** *f* (railway) line; ~**steig** *m* platform; ~**steigkarte** *f* platform ticket;
~**strecke** *f* (railway) line; ~**übergang**
m level crossing, grade crossing (*US*);
~**wärter** *m* signalman.
Bahre ['ba:rə] *f* -, -n stretcher.
Bajonett [bajo'nɛt] *nt* -(e)s, -e bayonett.
Bakelit [bake'li:t] *nt* -s Bakelite⸰.
Bakterien [bak'te:riən] *pl* bacteria *pl*.
Balance [ba'lã:sə] *f* -, -n balance, equilibrium.
balan'cieren *vti* balance.
bald [balt] *ad* (*zeitlich*) soon; (*beinahe*)
almost; ~...~... now... now...; ~**ig**

['baldɪç] *a* early, speedy; ~**möglichst** *ad*
as soon as possible.
Baldrian ['baldria:n] *m* -s, -e valerian.
Balken ['balkən] *m* -s, - beam; (*Trag*—)
girder; (*Stütz*—) prop.
Balkon [bal'kõ:] *m* -s, -s *or* -e balcony;
(*Theat*) (dress) circle.
Ball [bal] *m* -(e)s, **-e** ball; (*Tanz*) dance,
ball.
Ballade [ba'la:də] *f* -, -n ballad.
Ballast ['balast] *m* -(e)s, -e ballast; (*fig*)
weight, burden.
Ballen ['balən] *m* -s, - bale; (*Anat*) ball;
b~ *vt* (*formen*) make into a ball; *Faust*
clench; *vr* build up; (*Menschen*) gather.
Ballett [ba'lɛt] *nt* -(e)s, -e ballet;
~**(t)änzer(in** *f*) *m* ballet dancer.
Ball- *cpd*: ~**junge** *m* ball boy; ~**kleid** *nt*
evening dress.
Ballon [ba'lõ:] *m* -s, -s *or* -e balloon.
Ballspiel *nt* ball game.
Ballung ['baluŋ] *f* concentration; (*von
Energie*) build-up; ~**sgebiet** *nt* conur-
bation.
Bambus ['bambus] *m* -ses, -se bamboo;
~**rohr** *nt* bamboo cane.
Bammel ['baməl] *m* -s (*col*) (**einen**) ~
haben vor jdm/etw be scared of sb/sth.
banal [ba'na:l] *a* banal; **B**~**ität**
[banali'tɛ:t] *f* banality.
Banane [ba'na:nə] *f* -, -n banana.
Banause [ba'nauzə] *m* -n, -n philistine.
Band [bant] *m* -(e)s, **-e** (*Buch*—) volume;
nt -(e)s, **-er** (*Stoff*—) ribbon, tape;
(*Fließ*—) production line; (*Faß*—) hoop;
(*Ton*—) tape; (*Anat*) ligament; **etw auf** ~
aufnehmen tape sth; **am laufenden** ~
(*col*) non-stop; *nt* -(e)s, -e (*Freund-
schafts*— *etc*) bond; [bɛnt] *f* -, -s band,
group.
Bandage [ban'da:ʒə] *f* -, -n bandage.
banda'gieren *vt* bandage.
Bande ['bandə] *f* -, -n band; (*Straßen*—)
gang.
bändigen ['bɛndigən] *vt Tier* tame; *Trieb,
Leidenschaft* control, restrain.
Bandit [ban'di:t] *m* -en, -en bandit.
Band- *cpd*: ~**maß** *nt* tape measure;
~**säge** *f* band saw; ~**scheibe** *f* (*Anat*)
disc; ~**wurm** *m* tapeworm.
bange ['baŋə] *a* scared; (*besorgt*) anxious;
jdm wird es ~ sb is becoming scared;
jdm ~ **machen** scare sb; **B**~**macher** *m*
-s, - scaremonger; ~**n** *vi*: **um jdn/etw**
~**n** be anxious *or* worried about sb/sth.
Banjo ['banjo, 'bɛndʒo] *nt* -s, -s banjo.
Bank [baŋk] *f* -, **-e** (*Sitz*—) bench; (*Sand-
etc*) (sand)bank *or* -bar; *f* -, -en (*Geld*—)
bank; ~**anweisung** *f* banker's order;
~**beamte(r)** *m* bank clerk.
Bankett [ban'kɛt] *nt* -(e)s, -e (*Essen*) banquet; (*Straßenrand*) verge.
Bankier [baŋki'e:] *m* -s, -s banker.
Bank- *cpd*: ~**konto** *nt* bank account;
~**note** *f* banknote; ~**raub** *m* bank
robbery.
Bankrott [baŋ'krɔt] *m* -(e)s, -e bankruptcy; ~ **machen** go bankrupt; **b**~ *a*
bankrupt.

Bann [ban] *m* **-(e)s, -e** (*Hist*) ban; (*Kirchen*—) excommunication; (*fig: Zauber*) spell; **b~en** *vt Geister* exorcise; *Gefahr* avert; (*bezaubern*) enchant; (*Hist*) banish; **~er** *nt* **-s, -** banner, flag.

bar [ba:r] *a* (*unbedeckt*) bare; (*frei von*) lacking (*gen* in); (*offenkundig*) utter, sheer; **~e(s) Geld** cash; **etw (in) ~ bezahlen** pay sth (in) cash; **etw für ~ Münze nehmen** (*fig*) take sth at its face value; **B~ f ~, -s** bar.

Bär [bɛ:r] *m* **-en, -en** bear.

Baracke [ba'rakə] *f* **-, -n** hut, barrack.

barbarisch [bar'ba:rɪʃ] *a* barbaric, barbarous.

Bar- *cpd:* **~bestand** *m* money in hand; **b~fuß** *a* barefoot; **~geld** *nt* cash, ready money; **b~geldlos** *a* non-cash; **b~häuptig** *a* bareheaded; **~hocker** *m* bar stool; **~kauf** *m* cash purchase; **~keeper** ['ba:rki:pər] *m* **-s, -**, **~mann** *m* barman, bartender.

barmherzig [barm'hɛrtsɪç] *a* merciful, compassionate; **B~keit** *f* mercy, compassion.

Barometer [baro'me:tər] *nt* **-s, -** barometer.

Baron [ba'ro:n] *m* **-s, -e** baron; **~esse** [baro'nɛsə] *f* **-, -n**, **~in** *f* baroness.

Barren ['barən] *m* **-s, -** parallel bars *pl*; (*Gold*—) ingot.

Barriere [bari'ɛ:rə] *f* **-, -n** barrier.

Barrikade [bari'ka:də] *f* **-, -n** barricade.

Barsch [ba:rʃ] *m* **-(e)s, -e** perch; **b~** [barʃ] *a* brusque, gruff.

Bar- *cpd:* **~schaft** *f* ready money; **~scheck** *m* open *or* uncrossed cheque.

Bart [ba:rt] *m* **-(e)s, -e** beard; (*Schlüssel*—) bit.

bärtig ['bɛ:rtɪç] *a* bearded.

Barzahlung *f* cash payment.

Base ['ba:zə] *f* **-, -n** (*Chem*) base; (*Kusine*) cousin.

basieren [ba'zi:rən] *vt* base; *vi* be based.

Basis ['ba:zɪs] *f* **-, Basen** basis.

basisch ['ba:zɪʃ] *a* (*Chem*) alkaline.

Baß [bas] *m* **Basses, Bässe** bass; **~schlüssel** *m* bass clef; **~stimme** *f* bass voice.

Bassin [ba'sɛ̃] *nt* **-s, -s** pool.

Bassist [ba'sɪst] *m* bass.

Bast [bast] *m* **-(e)s, -e** raffia; **b~eln** *vt* make; *vi* do handicrafts.

Bataillon [batal'jo:n] *nt* **-s, -e** battalion.

Batist [ba'tɪst] *m* **-(e)s, -e** batiste.

Batterie [batə'ri:] *f* battery.

Bau [bau] *m* **-(e)s** (*Bauen*) building, construction; (*Aufbau*) structure; (*Körper*—) frame; (*Baustelle*) building site; *pl* **~e** (*Tier*—) hole, burrow; (*Min*) working(s); *pl* **~ten** (*Gebäude*) building; **sich im ~ befinden** be under construction; **~arbeiter** *m* building worker.

Bauch [baux] *m* **-(e)s, Bäuche** belly; (*Anat auch*) stomach, abdomen; **~fell** *nt* peritoneum; **b~ig** *a* bulging; **~muskel** *m* abdominal muscle; **~redner** *m* ventriloquist; **~tanz** *m* belly dance; belly dancing; **~schmerzen** *pl*, **~weh** *nt* stomach-ache.

bauen ['bauən] *vti* build; (*Tech*) construct; **auf jdn/etw ~** depend *or* count upon sb/sth.

Bauer ['bauər] *m* **-n** *or* **-s, -n** farmer; (*Schach*) pawn; *nt or m* **-s, -** (*Vogel*—) cage.

Bäuerin ['bɔyərɪn] *f* farmer; (*Frau des Bauers*) farmer's wife.

bäuerlich *a* rustic.

Bauern- *cpd:* **~brot** *nt* black bread; **~fänge'rei** *f* deception; **~haus** *nt* farmhouse; **~hof** *m* farm(yard); **~schaft** *f* farming community.

Bau- *cpd:* **b~fällig** *a* dilapidated; **~fälligkeit** *f* dilapidation; **~firma** *f* construction firm; **~führer** *m* site foreman; **~gelände** *nt* building site; **~genehmigung** *f* building permit; **~herr** *m* purchaser; **~kasten** *m* box of bricks; **~kosten** *pl* construction costs *pl*; **~land** *nt* building land; **~leute** *pl* building workers *pl*; **b~lich** *a* structural.

Baum [baum] *m* **-(e)s, Bäume** tree.

baumeln ['bauməln] *vi* dangle.

bäumen ['bɔymən] *vr* rear (up).

Baum- *cpd:* **~schule** *f* nursery; **~stamm** *m* tree trunk; **~stumpf** *m* tree stump; **~wolle** *f* cotton.

Bau- *cpd:* **~plan** *m* architect's plan; **~platz** *m* building site.

Bausch [bauʃ] *m* **-(e)s, Bäusche** (*Watte*—) ball, wad; **in ~ und Bogen** (*fig*) lock, stock and barrel; **b~en** *vtir* puff out; **b~ig** *a* baggy, wide.

Bau- *cpd:* **b~sparen** *vi insep* save with a building society; **~sparkasse** *f* building society; **~stein** *m* building stone, freestone; **~stelle** *f* building site; **~teil** *nt* prefabricated part (of building); **~unternehmer** *m* contractor, builder; **~weise** *f* (method of) construction; **~werk** *nt* building; **~zaun** *m* hoarding.

Bazillus [ba'tsɪlus] *m* **-, Bazillen** bacillus.

beabsichtigen [bə'apzɪçtɪgən] *vt* intend.

beachten [bə'axtən] *vt* take note of; *Vorschrift* obey; *Vorfahrt* observe; **~swert** *a* noteworthy.

beachtlich *a* considerable.

Beachtung *f* notice, attention, observation.

Beamte(r) [bə'amtə(r)] *m* **-n, -n**, **Beamtin** *f* official, civil servant; (*Bank- etc*) employee.

beängstigend [bə'ɛŋstɪgənt] *a* alarming.

beanspruchen [bə'anʃpruxən] *vt* claim; *Zeit, Platz* take up, occupy; *Mensch* take up sb's time.

beanstanden [bə'anʃtandən] *vt* complain about, object to.

Beanstandung *f* complaint.

beantragen [bə'antra:gən] *vt* apply for, ask for.

beantworten [bə'antvɔrtən] *vt* answer.

Beantwortung *f* reply (*gen* to).

bearbeiten [bə'arbaitən] *vt* work; *Material* process; *Thema* deal with; *Land* cultivate; (*Chem*) treat; *Buch* revise; (*col: beeinflussen wollen*) work on.

Bearbeitung *f* processing; treatment; cultivation; revision.

Beatmung [bəˈʔaːtmuŋ] f respiration.
beaufsichtigen [bəˈʔaufzɪçtɪgən] vt supervise.
Beaufsichtigung f supervision.
beauftragen [bəˈʔauftraːgən] vt instruct; **jdn mit etw ~** entrust sb with sth.
bebauen [bəˈbauən] vt build on; (Agr) cultivate.
beben [ˈbeːbən] vi tremble, shake; **B~** nt -s - earthquake.
bebildern [bəˈbɪldərn] vt illustrate.
Becher [ˈbeçər] nt -s, - mug; (ohne Henkel) tumbler.
Becken [ˈbɛkən] nt -s, - basin; (Mus) cymbal; (Anat) pelvis.
bedacht [bəˈdaxt] a thoughtful, careful; **auf etw** (acc) **~ sein** be concerned about sth.
bedächtig [bəˈdɛçtɪç] a (umsichtig) thoughtful, reflective; (langsam) slow, deliberate.
bedanken [bəˈdaŋkən] vr say thank you (bei jdm to sb).
Bedarf [bəˈdarf] m -(e)s need, requirement; (Comm) demand; supply; **je nach ~** according to demand; **bei ~** if necessary; **~ an etw** (dat) **haben** be in need of sth; **~sartikel** m requisite; **~sfall** m case of need; **~shaltestelle** f request stop.
bedauerlich [bəˈdauərlɪç] a regrettable.
bedauern [bəˈdauərn] vt be sorry for; (bemitleiden) pity; **B~** nt -s regret; **~swert** a Zustände regrettable; Mensch pitiable, unfortunate.
bedecken [bəˈdɛkən] vt cover.
bedeckt a covered; Himmel overcast.
bedenken [bəˈdɛŋkən] vt irreg think (over), consider; **B~** nt -s, - (Überlegen) consideration; (Zweifel) doubt; (Skrupel) scruple.
bedenklich a doubtful; (bedrohlich) dangerous, risky.
Bedenkzeit f time for reflection.
bedeuten [bəˈdɔytən] vt mean; signify; (wichtig sein) be of importance; **~d** a important; (beträchtlich) considerable.
Bedeutung f meaning; significance; (Wichtigkeit) importance; **b~slos** a insignificant, unimportant; **b~svoll** a momentous, significant.
bedienen [bəˈdiːnən] vt serve; Maschine work, operate; vr (beim Essen) help o.s.; (gebrauchen) make use (gen of).
Bedienung f service; (Kellnerin) waitress; (Verkäuferin) shop assistant; (Zuschlag) service (charge).
bedingen [bəˈdɪŋən] vt (voraussetzen) demand, involve; (verursachen) cause, occasion.
bedingt a limited, conditional; Reflex conditioned.
Bedingung f condition; (Voraussetzung) stipulation; **~sform** f (Gram) conditional; **b~slos** a unconditional.
bedrängen [bəˈdrɛŋən] vt pester, harass.
Bedrängung f trouble.
bedrohen [bəˈdroːən] vt threaten.
bedrohlich a ominous, threatening.

Bedrohung f threat, menace.
bedrucken [bəˈdrukən] vt print on.
bedrücken [bəˈdrykən] vt oppress, trouble.
bedürf- [bəˈdyrf] cpd: **~en** vi irreg +gen need, require; **B~nis** nt -ses, -se need; **B~nis nach etw haben** need sth; **B~nisanstalt** f public convenience, comfort station (US); **~nislos** a frugal, modest; **~tig** a in need (gen of), poor, needy.
beehren [bəˈʔeːrən] vt honour; **wir ~ uns** we have pleasure in.
beeilen [bəˈʔailən] vt hurry.
beeindrucken [bəˈʔaindrukən] vt impress, make an impression on.
beeinflussen [bəˈʔainflusən] vt influence.
Beeinflussung f influence.
beeinträchtigen [bəˈʔaintrɛçtɪgən] vt affect adversely; Freiheit infringe upon.
beend(ig)en [bəˈʔɛnd(ɪg)ən] vt end, finish, terminate.
Beend(ig)ung f end(ing), finish(ing).
beengen [bəˈʔɛŋən] vt cramp; (fig) hamper, oppress.
beerben [bəˈʔɛrbən] vt inherit from.
beerdigen [bəˈʔeːrdɪgən] vt bury.
Beerdigung f funeral, burial; **~sunternehmer** m undertaker.
Beere [ˈbeːrə] f -, -n berry; (Trauben—) grape.
Beet [beːt] nt -(e)s, -e bed.
befähigen [bəˈfɛːɪgən] vt enable.
befähigt a (begabt) talented; (fähig) capable (für of).
Befähigung f capability; (Begabung) talent, aptitude.
befahrbar [bəˈfaːrbaːr] a passable; (Naut) navigable.
befahren [bəˈfaːrən] vt irreg use, drive over; (Naut) navigate; a used.
befallen [bəˈfalən] vt irreg come over.
befangen [bəˈfaŋən] a (schüchtern) shy, self-conscious; (voreingenommen) biased; **B~heit** f shyness; bias.
befassen [bəˈfasən] vr concern o.s.
Befehl [bəˈfeːl] m -(e)s, -e command, order; **b~en** vt irreg vr order; **jdm etw b~en** order sb to do sth; vi give orders; **b~igen** vt be in command of; **~sempfänger** m subordinate; **~sform** f (Gram) imperative; **~shaber** m -s, - commanding officer; **~sverweigerung** f insubordination.
befestigen [bəˈfɛstɪgən] vt fasten (an +dat to); (stärken) strengthen; (Mil) fortify.
Befestigung f fastening; strengthening; (Mil) fortification.
befeuchten [bəˈfɔyçtən] vt damp(en), moisten.
befinden [bəˈfɪndən] irreg vr be; (sich fühlen) feel; vt: **jdn/etw für** or **als etw ~** deem sb/sth to be sth; vi decide (über +acc on), adjudicate; **B~** nt -s health, condition; (Meinung) view, opinion.
befliegen [bəˈfliːgən] vt irreg fly to.
befolgen [bəˈfolgən] vt comply with, follow.
befördern [bəˈfœrdərn] vt (senden) transport, send; (beruflich) promote.

Beförderung f transport, conveyance; promotion; ~skosten pl transport costs pl.

befragen [bə'fra:gən] vt question.

befreien [bə'fraiən] vt set free; (erlassen) exempt.

Befreier m -s, - liberator.

Befreiung f liberation, release; (Erlassen) exemption.

befremden [bə'frɛmdən] vt surprise, disturb; B~ nt -s surprise, astonishment.

befreunden [bə'frɔyndən] vr make friends; (mit Idee etc) acquaint o.s.

befreundet a friendly.

befriedigen [bə'fri:digən] vt satisfy; ~d a satisfactory.

Befriedigung f satisfaction, gratification.

befristet [bə'fristət] a limited.

befruchten [bə'fruxtən] vt fertilize; (fig) stimulate.

Befugnis [bə'fu:knis] f -, -se authorization, powers pl.

befugt a authorized, entitled.

befühlen [bə'fy:lən] vt feel, touch.

Befund [bə'funt] m -(e)s, -e findings pl; (Med) diagnosis.

befürchten [bə'fyrçtən] vt fear.

Befürchtung f fear, apprehension.

befürwort- [bə'fy:rvɔrt] cpd: ~en vt support, speak in favour of; B~er m -s, - supporter, advocate; B~ung f support(ing), favouring.

begabt [bə'ga:pt] a gifted.

Begabung [bə'ga:bʊŋ] f talent, gift.

begatten [bə'gatən] vr mate; vt mate or pair (with).

begeben [bə'ge:bən] vr irreg (gehen) proceed (zu, nach to); (geschehen) occur; B~heit f occurrence.

begegnen [bə'ge:gnən] vi meet (jdm sb); meet with (etw (dat) sth); (behandeln) treat (jdm sb); Blicke ~ sich eyes meet.

Begegnung f meeting.

begehen [bə'ge:ən] vt irreg Straftat commit; (abschreiten) cover; Straße etc use, negotiate; Feier celebrate.

begehren [bə'ge:rən] vt desire; ~swert a desirable.

begehrt a in demand; Junggeselle eligible.

begeistern [bə'gaistərn] vt fill with enthusiasm, inspire; vr: sich für etw ~ get enthusiastic about sth.

begeistert a enthusiastic.

Begeisterung f enthusiasm.

Begierde [bə'gi:rdə] f -, -n desire, passion.

begierig [bə'gi:riç] a eager, keen.

begießen [bə'gi:sən] vt irreg water; (mit Alkohol) drink to.

Beginn [bə'gin] m -(e)s beginning; zu ~ at the beginning; b~en vti irreg start, begin.

beglaubigen [bə'glaubigən] vt countersign.

Beglaubigung f countersignature; ~sschreiben nt credentials pl.

begleichen [bə'glaiçən] vt irreg settle, pay.

Begleit- [bə'glait] cpd: b~en vt accompany; (Mil) escort; ~er m -s, -

companion; (Freund) escort; (Mus) accompanist; ~erscheinung f concomitant (occurrence); ~paniment; ~schiff nt escort vessel; ~schreiben nt covering letter; ~umstände pl concomitant circumstances pl; ~ung f company; (Mil) escort; (Mus) accompaniment.

beglücken [bə'glʏkən] vt make happy, delight.

beglückwünschen [bə'glʏkvʏnʃən] vt congratulate (zu on).

Beglückwünschung f congratulation, good wishes pl.

begnadigen [bə'gna:digən] vt pardon.

Begnadigung f pardon, amnesty.

begnügen [bə'gny:gən] vr be satisfied, content o.s.

Begonie [bə'go:niə] f begonia.

begraben [bə'gra:bən] vt irreg bury.

Begräbnis [bə'grɛ:pnis] nt -ses, -se burial, funeral.

begradigen [bə'gra:digən] vt straighten (out).

begreifen [bə'graifən] vt irreg understand, comprehend.

begreiflich [bə'graifliç] a understandable.

Begrenztheit [bə'grɛntsthait] f limitation, restriction; (fig) narrowness.

Begriff [bə'grif] m -(e)s, -e concept, idea; im ~ sein, etw zu tun be about to do sth; schwer von ~ (col) slow, dense; ~sbestimmung f definition; b~sstutzig a dense, slow.

begründ- [bə'grʏnd] cpd: ~en vt (Gründe geben) justify; ~et a well-founded, justified; B~ung f justification, reason.

begrüßen [bə'gry:sən] vt greet, welcome; ~swert a welcome.

Begrüßung f greeting, welcome.

begünstigen [bə'gʏnstigən] vt Person favour; Sache further, promote.

begutachten [bə'gu:t'axtən] vt assess.

begütert [bə'gy:tərt] a wealthy, well-to-do.

behaart [bə'ha:rt] a hairy.

behäbig [bə'hɛ:biç] a (dick) portly, stout; (geruhsam) comfortable.

behaftet [bə'haftət] a: mit etw ~ sein be afflicted by sth.

behagen [bə'ha:gən] vi: das behagt ihm nicht he does not like it; B~ nt -s comfort, ease.

behaglich [bə'ha:kliç] a comfortable, cosy; B~keit f comfort, cosiness.

behalten [bə'haltən] vt irreg keep, retain; (im Gedächtnis) remember.

Behälter [bə'hɛltər] m -s, - container, receptacle.

behandeln [bə'handəln] vt treat; Thema deal with; Maschine handle.

Behandlung f treatment; (von Maschine) handling.

beharren [bə'harən] vi: auf etw (dat) ~ stick or keep to sth.

beharrlich [bə'harliç] a (ausdauernd) steadfast, unwavering; (hartnäckig) tenacious, dogged; B~keit f steadfastness; tenacity.

behaupten [bə'hauptən] vt claim, assert,

maintain; *sein Recht* defend; *vr* assert o.s.
Behauptung *f* claim, assertion.
Behausung [bə'hauzuŋ] *f* dwelling, abode; (*armselig*) hovel.
beheimatet [bə'haima:tət] *a* domiciled; *Tier, Pflanze* with its habitat in.
beheizen [bə'haitsən] *vt* heat.
Behelf [bə'hɛlf] *m* **-(e)s, -e** expedient, makeshift; **b~en** *vr irreg*: **sich mit etw b~en** make do with sth; **b~smäßig** *a* improvised, makeshift; (*vorübergehend*) temporary.
behelligen [bə'hɛligən] *vt* trouble, bother.
Behendigkeit [bə'hɛndiçkait] *f* agility, quickness.
beherbergen [bə'hɛrbergən] *vt* put up, house.
beherrschen [bə'hɛrʃən] *vt Volk* rule, govern; *Situation* control; *Sprache, Gefühle* master; *vr* control o.s.
beherrscht *a* controlled; **B~heit** *f* self-control.
Beherrschung *f* rule; control; mastery.
beherzigen [bə'hɛrtsigən] *vt* take to heart.
beherzt *a* spirited, brave.
behilflich [bə'hɪlfliç] *a* helpful; **jdm ~ sein** help sb (*bei* with).
behindern [bə'hindərn] *vt* hinder, impede.
Behinderte(r) *mf* disabled person.
Behinderung *f* hindrance; (*Körper—*) handicap.
Behörde [bə'hø:rdə] *f* -**, -n** authorities *pl*.
behördlich [bə'hø:rtliç] *a* official.
behüten [bə'hy:tən] *vt* guard; **jdn vor etw** (*dat*) — preserve sb from sth.
behutsam [bə'hu:tza:m] *a* cautious, careful; **B~keit** *f* caution, carefulness.
bei [bai] *prep +dat* (*örtlich*) near, by; (*zeitlich*) at, on; (*während*) during; **~m Friseur** at the hairdresser's; **~ uns** at our place; **~ einer Firma arbeiten** work for a firm; **~ Nacht** at night; **~ Nebel** in fog; **~ Regen** if it rains; **etw ~ sich haben** have sth on one; **jdn ~ sich haben** have sb with one; **~ Goethe** in Goethe; **~m Militär** in the army; **~m Fahren** while driving.
beibehalten ['baibəhaltən] *vt irreg* keep, retain.
Beibehaltung *f* keeping, retaining.
Beiblatt ['baiblat] *nt* supplement.
beibringen ['baibriŋən] *vt irreg Beweis, Zeugen* bring forward; *Gründe* adduce; **jdm etw ~** (*zufügen*) inflict sth on sb; (*zu verstehen geben*) make sb understand sth; (*lehren*) teach sb sth.
Beichte ['baiçtə] *f* -**, -n** confession; **b~n** *vt* confess; *vi* go to confession.
Beicht- *cpd*: **~geheimnis** *nt* secret of the confessional; **~stuhl** *m* confessional.
beide(s) ['baidə(z)] *pron, a* both; **meine ~n Brüder** my two brothers, both my brothers; **die ersten ~n** the first two; **wir ~** we two; **diese ~n** one of the two; **alles ~s** both (of them); **~mal** *ad* both times; **~rlei** *a* of both; **~rseitig** *a* mutual, reciprocal; **~rseits** *ad* mutually; *prep +gen* on both sides of.
beidrehen ['baidre:ən] *vi* heave to.

beieinander [bai'ai'nandər] *ad* together.
Beifahrer ['baifa:rər] *m* passenger; **~sitz** *m* passenger seat.
Beifall ['baifal] *m* **-(e)s** applause; (*Zustimmung*) approval.
beifällig ['baifɛliç] *a* approving; *Kommentar* favourable.
Beifilm ['baifilm] *m* supporting film.
beifügen ['baify:gən] *vt* enclose.
beige ['bɛ:ʒə] *a* beige, fawn.
beigeben ['baige:bən] *irreg vt* (*zufügen*) add; (*mitgeben*) give; *vi* (*nachgeben*) give in (*dat* to).
Beigeschmack ['baigəʃmak] *m* aftertaste.
Beihilfe ['baihilfə] *f* aid, assistance; (*Studien—*) grant; (*Jur*) aiding and abetting.
beikommen ['baikɔmən] *vi irreg* (+dat) get at; (*einem Problem*) deal with.
Beil [bail] *nt* **-(e)s, -e** axe, hatchet.
Beilage [baila:gə] *f* (*Buch— etc*) supplement; (*Cook*) vegetables and potatoes *pl*.
beiläufig ['bailɔyfiç] *a* casual, incidental; *ad* casually, by the way.
beilegen ['baile:gən] *vt* (*hinzufügen*) enclose, add; (*beimessen*) attribute, ascribe; *Streit* settle.
beileibe [bai'laibə] : **~ nicht** *ad* by no means.
Beileid ['bailait] *nt* condolence, sympathy; **herzliches ~** deepest sympathy.
beiliegend ['baili:gənt] *a* (*Comm*) enclosed.
beim [baim] = **bei dem**.
beimessen ['baimɛsən] *vt irreg* attribute, ascribe (*dat* to).
Bein [bain] *nt* **-(e)s, -e** leg; **~bruch** *m* fracture of the leg.
beinah(e) ['baina:(ə)] *ad* almost, nearly.
beinhalten [bə'inhaltən] *vt* contain.
beipflichten ['baipfliçtən] *vi*: **jdm/etw ~** agree with sb/sth.
Beirat ['baira:t] *m* legal adviser; (*Körperschaft*) advisory council; (*Eltern—*) parents' council.
beirren [bə'irən] *vt* confuse, muddle; **sich nicht ~ lassen** not let o.s. be confused.
beisammen [bai'zamən] *ad* together; **B~sein** *nt* **-s** get-together.
Beischlaf ['baiʃla:f] *m* sexual intercourse.
Beisein ['baizain] *nt* **-s** presence.
beiseite [bai'zaitə] *ad* to one side, aside; *stehen* on one side, aside; **etw ~ legen** (*sparen*) put sth by; **jdn/etw ~ schaffen** put sb/get sth out of the way.
beisetzen ['baizɛtsən] *vt* bury.
Beisetzung *f* funeral.
Beisitzer ['baizitsər] *m* **-s, -** (*bei Prüfung*) assessor.
Beispiel ['baiʃpi:l] *nt* **-(e)s, -e** example; **sich an jdm ein ~ nehmen** take sb as an example; **zum ~** for example; **b~haft** *a* exemplary; **b~los** *a* unprecedented, unexampled; **b~sweise** *ad* for instance or example.
beispringen ['baiʃpriŋən] *vi irreg*: **jdm ~** come to the aid of sb.
beißen ['baisən] *irreg vti* bite; (*stechen*)

Rauch, Säure) burn; *vr* (*Farben*) clash; ~**d** a biting, caustic; (*fig auch*) sarcastic.

Beißzange ['bais-tsaŋgə] *f* pliers *pl.*

Beistand ['baiʃtant] *m* -(e)s, ⸚e support, help; (*Jur*) adviser.

beistehen ['baiʃte:ən] *vi irreg*: **jdm** ~ stand by sb.

beisteuern ['baiʃtɔyərn] *vt* contribute.

beistimmen ['baiʃtimən] *vi* (+*dat*) agree with.

Beistrich ['baiʃtriç] *m* comma.

Beitrag ['baitra:k] *m* -(e)s, ⸚e contribution; (*Zahlung*) fee, subscription; (*Versicherungs*—) premium; **b**~**en** ['baitra:gən] *vt irreg* contribute (*zu* to); (*mithelfen*) help (*zu* with); ~**szahlende(r)** *mf* fee-paying member.

beitreten ['baitre:tən] *vi irreg* join (*einem Verein* a club).

Beitritt ['baitrit] *m* joining, membership; ~**serklärung** *f* declaration of membership.

Beiwagen ['baiva:gən] *m* (*Motorrad*—) sidecar; (*Straßenbahn*—) extra carriage.

beiwohnen ['baivo:nən] *vi*: **einer Sache** (*dat*) ~ attend or be present at sth.

Beiwort ['baivɔrt] *nt* adjective.

Beize ['baitsə] *f* -, -**n** (*Holz*—) stain; (*Cook*) marinade.

beizeiten [bai'tsaitən] *ad* in time.

bejahen [bə'ja:ən] *vt Frage* say yes to, answer in the affirmative; (*gutheißen*) agree with.

bejahrt [bə'ja:rt] *a* aged, elderly.

bejammern [bə'jamərn] *vt* lament, bewail; ~**swert** a lamentable.

bekämpfen [bə'kɛmpfən] *vt Gegner* fight; *Seuche* combat; *vr* fight.

Bekämpfung *f* fight or struggle against.

bekannt [bə'kant] a (well-)known; (*nicht fremd*) familiar; **mit jdm** ~ **sein** know sb; **jdn mit jdm** ~ **machen** introduce sb to sb; **sich mit etw** ~ **machen** familiarize o.s. with sth; **das ist mir** ~ I know that; **es/sie kommt mir** ~ **vor** it/she seems familiar; **durch etw** ~ **werden** become famous because of sth; **B**~**e(r)** *mf* friend, acquaintance; **B**~**enkreis** *m* circle of friends; **B**~**gabe** *f* announcement; ~**geben** *vt irreg* announce publicly; ~**lich** *ad* as is well known, as you know; ~**machen** *vt* announce; **B**~**machung** *f* publication; announcement; **B**~**schaft** *f* acquaintance.

bekehren [bə'ke:rən] *vt* convert; *vr* become converted.

Bekehrung *f* conversion.

bekennen [bə'kɛnən] *vt irreg* confess; *Glauben* profess; *Farbe* ~ (*col*) show where one stands.

Bekenntnis [bə'kɛntnis] *nt* -**ses**, -**se** admission, confession; (*Religion*) confession, denomination; ~**schule** *f* denominational school.

beklagen [bə'kla:gən] *vt* deplore, lament; *vr* complain; ~**swert** a lamentable, pathetic.

beklatschen [bə'klatʃən] *vt* applaud, clap.

bekleben [bə'kle:bən] *vt*: **etw mit Bildern** ~ stick pictures onto sth.

bekleiden [bə'klaidən] *vt* clothe; *Amt* occupy, fill.

Bekleidung *f* clothing; ~**sindustrie** *f* clothing industry, rag trade.

beklemmen [bə'klɛmən] *vt* oppress.

beklommen [bə'klɔmən] a anxious, uneasy; **B**~**heit** *f* anxiety, uneasiness.

bekommen [bə'kɔmən] *irreg vt* get, receive; *Kind* have; *Zug* catch, get; *vi*: **jdm** ~ agree with sb.

bekömmlich [bə'kœmliç] a wholesome, easily digestible.

bekräftigen [bə'krɛftigən] *vt* confirm, corroborate.

Bekräftigung *f* corroboration.

bekreuzigen [bə'krɔytsigən] *vr* cross o.s.

bekritteln [bə'kritəln] *vt* criticize, pick holes in.

bekümmern [bə'kymərn] *vt* worry, trouble.

bekunden [bə'kundən] *vt* (*sagen*) state; (*zeigen*) show.

belächeln [bə'lɛçəln] *vt* laugh at.

beladen [bə'la:dən] *vt irreg* load.

Belag [bə'la:k] *m* -(e)s, ⸚e covering, coating; (*Brot*—) spread; (*Zahn*—) tartar; (*auf Zunge*) fur; (*Brems*—) lining.

belagern [bə'la:gərn] *vt* besiege.

Belagerung *f* siege; ~**szustand** *m* state of siege.

Belang [bə'laŋ] *m* -(e)s importance; ~**e** *pl* interests *pl*, concerns *pl*; **b**~**en** *vt* (*Jur*) take to court; **b**~**los** a trivial, unimportant; ~**losigkeit** *f* triviality.

belassen [bə'lasən] *vt irreg* (*in Zustand, Glauben*) leave; (*in Stellung*) retain; **es dabei** ~ leave it at that.

belasten [bə'lastən] *vt* (*lit*) burden; (*fig: bedrücken*) trouble, worry; (*Comm*) *Konto* debit; (*Jur*) incriminate; *vr* weigh o.s. down; (*Jur*) incriminate o.s.; ~**d a** (*Jur*) incriminating.

belästigen [bə'lɛstigən] *vt* annoy, pester.

Belästigung *f* annoyance, pestering.

Belastung [bə'lastuŋ] *f* (*lit*) load; (*fig: Sorge etc*) weight; (*Comm*) charge, debit(ing); (*Jur*) incriminatory evidence; ~**sprobe** *f* capacity test; (*fig*) test; ~**szeuge** *m* witness for prosecution.

belaufen [bə'laufən] *vr irreg* amount (*auf* +*acc* to).

belauschen [bə'lauʃən] *vt* eavesdrop on.

belebt [bə'le:pt] a *Straße* crowded.

Beleg [bə'le:k] *m* -(e)s, -**e** (*Comm*) receipt; (*Beweis*) documentary evidence, proof; (*Beispiel*) example; **b**~**en** [bə'le:gən] *vt* cover; *Kuchen, Brot* spread; *Platz* reserve, book; *Kurs, Vorlesung* register for; (*beweisen*) verify, prove; (*Mil: mit Bomben*) bomb; ~**schaft** *f* personnel, staff.

belehren [bə'le:rən] *vt* instruct, teach; **jdn eines Besseren** ~ teach sb better.

Belehrung *f* instruction.

beleibt [bə'laipt] a stout, corpulent.

beleidigen [bə'laidigən] *vt* insult, offend.

Beleidigung *f* insult; (*Jur*) slander, libel.

belesen [bə'le:zən] a a well-read.

beleuchten [bə'lɔʏçtən] vt light, illuminate; (fig) throw light on.

Beleuchtung f lighting, illumination.

belichten [bə'lıçtən] vt expose.

Belichtung f exposure; **~smesser** m exposure meter.

Belieben [bə'li:bən] nt: (ganz) nach ~ (just) as you wish.

beliebig [bə'li:bıç] a any you like, as you like; ~ viel as many as you like; ein ~es Thema any subject you like or want.

beliebt [bə'li:pt] a popular; sich bei jdm ~ machen make o.s. popular with sb; B~heit f popularity.

beliefern [bə'li:fərn] vt supply.

bellen ['bɛlən] vi bark.

belohnen [bə'lo:nən] vt reward.

Belohnung f reward.

belügen [bə'ly:gən] vt irreg lie to, deceive.

belustigen [bə'lʊstıgən] vt amuse.

Belustigung f amusement.

bemächtigen [bə'mɛçtıgən] vr: sich einer Sache (gen) ~ take possession of sth, seize sth.

bemalen [bə'ma:lən] vt paint.

bemängeln [bə'mɛŋəln] vt criticize.

bemannen [bə'manən] vt man.

Bemannung f manning; (Naut, Aviat etc) crew.

bemänteln [bə'mɛntəln] vt cloak, hide.

bemerk- [bə'mɛrk] cpd: ~bar a perceptible, noticeable; sich ~bar machen (Person) make or get o.s. noticed; (Unruhe) become noticeable; ~en vt (wahrnehmen) notice, observe; (sagen) say, mention; ~enswert a remarkable, noteworthy; B~ung f remark; (schriftlich auch) note.

bemitleiden [bə'mıtlaɪdən] vt pity.

bemühen [bə'my:ən] vr take trouble or pains.

Bemühung f trouble, pains pl, effort.

bemuttern [bə'mʊtərn] vt mother.

benachbart [bə'naxba:rt] a neighbouring.

benachrichtigen [bə'na:xrıçtıgən] vt inform.

Benachrichtigung f notification, information.

benachteiligen [bə'na:xtaılıgən] vt (put at a) disadvantage, victimize.

benehmen [bə'ne:mən] vr irreg behave; B~ nt -s behaviour.

beneiden [bə'naɪdən] vt envy; ~swert a enviable.

benennen [bə'nɛnən] vt irreg name.

Bengel ['bɛŋəl] m -s, - (little) rascal or rogue.

benommen [bə'nɔmən] a dazed.

benötigen [bə'nø:tıgən] vt need.

benutzen [bə'nʊtsən], **benützen** [bə'nʏtsən] vt use.

Benutzer m -s, - user.

Benutzung f utilization, use.

Benzin [bɛnt'si:n] nt -s, -e (Aut) petrol, gas(oline) (US); ~kanister m petrol can; ~tank m petrol tank; ~uhr f petrol gauge.

beobacht- [bə'o:baxt] cpd: ~en vt observe; B~er m -s, - observer; (eines

---

Unfalls) witness; (Press, TV) correspondent; B~ung f observation.

bepacken [bə'pakən] vt load, pack.

bepflanzen [bə'pflantsən] vt plant.

bequem [bə'kve:m] a comfortable; (Ausrede) convenient; (Person) lazy, indolent; ~en vr condescend (zu to); B~lichkeit f convenience, comfort; (Faulheit) laziness, indolence.

beraten [bə'ra:tən] irreg vt advise; (besprechen) discuss, debate; vr consult; gut/schlecht ~ sein be well/ill advised; sich ~ lassen get advice.

Berater m -s, - adviser.

beratschlagen [bə'ra:t-ʃla:gən] vti deliberate (on), confer (about).

Beratung f advice, consultation; (Besprechung) consultation; ~sstelle f advice centre.

berauben [bə'raʊbən] vt rob.

berechenbar [bə'rɛçənba:r] a calculable.

berechnen [bə'rɛçnən] vt calculate; (Comm: anrechnen) charge; ~d a Mensch calculating, scheming; B~ung f calculation; (Comm) charge.

berechtig- [bə'rɛçtıg] cpd: ~en vt entitle, authorize; (fig) justify; ~t a (berechtıçt] a justifiable, justified; B~ung f authorization; (fig) justification.

bereden [bə're:dən] vtr (besprechen) discuss; (überreden) persuade.

beredt [bə're:t] a eloquent.

Bereich [bə'raɪç] m -(e)s, -e (Bezirk) area; (Phys) range; (Ressort, Gebiet) sphere.

bereichern [bə'raɪçərn] vt enrich; vr get rich.

Bereifung [bə'raɪfʊŋ] f (set of) tyres pl; (Vorgang) fitting with tyres.

bereinigen [bə'raɪnıgən] vt settle.

bereisen [bə'raɪzən] vt travel through.

bereit [bə'raɪt] a ready, prepared; zu etw ~ sein be ready for sth; sich ~ erklären declare o.s. willing; ~en vt prepare, make ready; Kummer, Freude cause; ~halten vt irreg keep in readiness; ~legen vt lay out; ~machen vtr prepare, get ready; ~s ad already; B~schaft f readiness; (Polizei) alert; in B~schaft sein be on the alert or on stand-by; B~schaftsdienst m emergency service; ~stehen vi irreg (Person) be prepared; (Ding) be ready; ~stellen vt Kisten, Pakete etc put ready; Geld etc make available; Truppen, Maschinen put at the ready; B~ung f preparation; ~willig a willing, ready; B~willigkeit f willingness, readiness.

bereuen [bə'rɔʏən] vt regret.

Berg [bɛrk] m -(e)s, -e mountain, hill; b~ab ad downhill; b~an, b~auf ad uphill; ~arbeiter m miner; ~bahn f mountain railway; ~bau m mining; b~en ['bɛrgən] vt irreg (retten) rescue; Ladung salvage; (enthalten) contain; ~führer m mountain guide; ~gipfel m mountain top, peak, summit; b~ig ['bɛrgıç] a mountainous, hilly; ~kamm m crest, ridge; ~kette f mountain range; ~mann m, pl ~leute miner; ~rutsch *m* landslide; ~**schuh** *m* walking boot; ~**steigen** *nt* mountaineering; ~**steiger(in** *f*) *m* -**s**, - mountaineer, climber; ~**ung** ['ber̩gʊŋ] *f* (*von Menschen*) rescue; (*von Material*) recovery; (*Naut*) salvage; ~**wacht** *f* mountain rescue service; ~**werk** *nt* mine.

Bericht [bə'rɪçt] *m* -**(e)s**, -**e** report, account; **b**~**en** *vti* report; ~**erstatter** *m* -**s**, - reporter, (newspaper) correspondent; ~**erstattung** *f* reporting.

berichtigen [bə'rɪçtɪgən] *vt* correct.

Berichtigung *f* correction.

beritten [bə'rɪtən] *a* mounted.

Bernstein ['bɛrnʃtain] *m* amber.

bersten ['bɛrstən] *vi irreg* burst, split.

berüchtigt [bə'rʏçtɪçt] *a* notorious, infamous.

berücksichtigen [bə'rʏkzɪçtɪgən] *vt* consider, bear in mind.

Berücksichtigung *f* consideration.

Beruf [bə'ru:f] *m* -**(e)s**, -**e** occupation, profession; (*Gewerbe*) trade; **b**~**en** *irreg vt* (*in Amt*) appoint (*in* +*acc* to; *zu* as); *vr*: **sich auf jdn/etw b**~**en** refer *or* appeal to sb/sth; **b**~**en** a competent, qualified; **b**~**lich** a professional; ~**sausbildung** *f* vocational *or* professional training; ~**sberater** *m* careers adviser; ~**sberatung** *f* vocational guidance; ~**sbezeichnung** *f* job description; ~**sgeheimnis** *nt* professional secret; ~**skrankheit** *f* occupational disease; ~**sleben** *nt* professional life; **b**~**smäßig** a professional; ~**srisiko** *nt* occupational hazard; ~**sschule** *f* vocational *or* trade school; ~**ssoldat** *m* professional soldier, regular; ~**ssportler** *m* professional (sportsman); **b**~**stätig** a employed; ~**sverkehr** *m* commuter traffic; ~**swahl** *f* choice of a job; ~**ung** *f* vocation, calling; (*Ernennung*) appointment; (*Jur*) appeal; ~**ung einlegen** appeal.

beruhen [bə'ru:ən] *vi*: **auf etw** (*dat*) ~ be based on sth; **etw auf sich** ~ **lassen** leave sth at that.

beruhigen [bə'ru:ɪgən] *vt* calm, pacify, soothe; *vr* (*Mensch*) calm (o.s.) down; (*Situation*) calm down.

Beruhigung *f* reassurance; (*der Nerven*) calming; **zu jds** ~ to reassure sb; ~**smittel** *nt* sedative; ~**spille** *f* tranquillizer.

berühmt [bə'ry:mt] a famous; **B**~**heit** *f* (*Ruf*) fame; (*Mensch*) celebrity.

berühren [bə'ry:rən] *vt* touch; (*gefühlsmäßig bewegen*) affect; (*flüchtig erwähnen*) mention, touch on; *vr* meet, touch.

Berührung *f* contact; ~**spunkt** *m* point of contact.

besagen [bə'za:gən] *vt* mean.

besagt a *Tag etc* in question.

besänftigen [bə'zɛnftɪgən] *cpd*: ~**en** *vt* soothe, calm; ~**end** a soothing; **B**~**ung** *f* soothing, calming.

Besatz [bə'zats] *m* -**es**, -̈**e** trimming, edging; ~**ung** *f* garrison; (*Naut, Aviat*) crew; ~**ungsmacht** *f* occupying power.

besaufen [bə'zaufən] *vr irreg* (*col*) get drunk *or* stoned.

beschädig- [bə'ʃɛ:dɪg] *cpd*: ~**en** *vt* damage; **B**~**ung** *f* damage; (*Stelle*) damaged spot.

beschaffen [bə'ʃafən] *vt* get, acquire; a constituted; **B**~**heit** *f* constitution, nature.

Beschaffung *f* acquisition.

beschäftigen [bə'ʃɛftɪgən] *vt* occupy; (*beruflich*) employ; *vr* occupy *or* concern o.s.

beschäftigt a busy, occupied.

Beschäftigung *f* (*Beruf*) employment; (*Tätigkeit*) occupation; (*Befassen*) concern.

beschämen [bə'ʃɛ:mən] *vt* put to shame; ~**d** a shameful; *Hilfsbereitschaft* shaming.

beschämt a ashamed.

beschatten [bə'ʃatən] *vt* shade; *Verdächtige* shadow.

beschaulich [bə'ʃaulɪç] a contemplative.

Bescheid [bə'ʃait] *m* -**(e)s**, -**e** information; (*Weisung*) directions *pl*; ~**wissen** be well-informed (*über* +*acc* about); **ich weiß** ~ I know; **jdm** ~ **geben** *or* **sagen** let sb know.

bescheiden [bə'ʃaidən] *vr irreg* content o.s.; a modest; **B**~**heit** *f* modesty.

bescheinen [bə'ʃainən] *vt irreg* shine on.

bescheinigen [bə'ʃainɪgən] *vt* certify; (*bestätigen*) acknowledge.

Bescheinigung *f* certificate; (*Quittung*) receipt.

bescheißen [bə'ʃaisən] *vt irreg* (*col*) cheat.

beschenken [bə'ʃɛŋkən] *vt* give presents to.

bescheren [bə'ʃe:rən] *vt*: **jdm etw** ~ give sb sth as a present; **jdn** ~ give presents to sb.

Bescherung *f* giving of presents; (*col*) mess.

beschildern [bə'ʃɪldərn] *vt* signpost.

beschimpfen [bə'ʃɪmpfən] *vt* abuse.

Beschimpfung *f* abuse, insult.

Beschiß [bə'ʃɪs] *m* -**sses** (*col*) **das ist** ~ that is a swizz *or* a cheat.

Beschlag [bə'ʃla:k] *m* -**(e)s**, -̈**e** (*Metallband*) fitting; (*auf Fenster*) condensation; (*auf Metall*) tarnish; finish; (*Hufeisen*) horseshoe; **jdn/etw in** ~ **nehmen** *or* **mit** -̈ **belegen** monopolize sb/sth; **b**~**en** [bə'ʃla:gən] *irreg vt* cover; *Pferd* shoe; *Fenster, Metall* cover; **b**~**en sein** be well versed (*in or auf* +*dat* in); *vir* (*Fenster etc*) mist over; **b**~**nahmen** *vt* seize, confiscate; requisition; ~**nahmung** *f* confiscation, sequestration.

beschleunigen [bə'ʃlɔynɪgən] *vt* accelerate, speed up; *vi* (*Aut*) accelerate.

Beschleunigung *f* acceleration.

beschließen [bə'ʃli:sən] *vt irreg* decide on; (*beenden*) end, close.

Beschluß [bə'ʃlus] *m* -**sses**, -**schlüsse** decision, conclusion; (*Ende*) close, end.

beschmutzen [bə'ʃmutsən] *vt* dirty, soil.

beschneiden [bə'ʃnaidən] *vt irreg* cut, prune, trim; (*Rel*) circumcise.

beschönigen [bə'ʃø:nɪgən] *vt* gloss over.

beschränken [bə'ʃrɛŋkən] *vt* limit, restrict (*auf* +*acc* to); *vr* restrict o.s.

beschrankt [bə'ʃraŋkt] a *Bahnübergang* with barrier.

beschränk- [bə'ʃrɛŋk] *cpd*: **~t** *a* confined, narrow; *Mensch* limited, narrow-minded; **B~theit** *f* narrowness; **B~ung** *f* limitation.

beschreiben [bə'ʃraɪbən] *vt irreg* describe; *Papier* write on.

Beschreibung *f* description.

beschriften [bə'ʃrɪftən] *vt* mark, label.

Beschriftung *f* lettering.

beschuldigen [bə'ʃʊldɪgən] *vt* accuse.

Beschuldigung *f* accusation.

beschummeln [bə'ʃʊməln] *vti* (*col*) cheat.

beschütz- [bə'ʃyts] *cpd*: **~en** *vt* protect (*vor +dat* from); **B~er** *m* **-s**, **-** protector **B~ung** *f* protection.

Beschwerde [bə'ʃveːrdə] *f* **-**, **-n** complaint; (*Mühe*) hardship; (*pl: Leiden*) pain.

beschweren [bə'ʃveːrən] *vt* weight down; (*fig*) burden; *vr* complain.

beschwerlich *a* tiring, exhausting.

beschwichtigen [bə'ʃvɪçtɪgən] *vt* soothe, pacify.

Beschwichtigung *f* soothing, calming.

beschwindeln [bə'ʃvɪndəln] *vt* (*betrügen*) cheat; (*belügen*) fib to.

beschwingt [bə'ʃvɪŋt] *a* a cheery, in high spirits.

beschwipst [bə'ʃvɪpst] *a* f tipsy.

beschwören [bə'ʃvøːrən] *vt irreg Aussage* swear to; (*anflehen*) implore; *Geister* conjure up.

beseelen [bə'zeːlən] *vt* inspire.

besehen [bə'zeːən] *vt irreg* look at; **genau ~** examine closely.

beseitigen [bə'zaɪtɪgən] *vt* remove.

Beseitigung *f* removal.

Besen ['beːzən] *m* **-s**, **-** broom; **~stiel** *m* broomstick.

besessen [bə'zɛsən] *a* possessed.

besetz- [bə'zɛts] *cpd*: **~en** *vt Haus, Land* occupy; *Platz* take, fill; *Posten* fill; *Rolle* cast; (*mit Edelsteinen*) set; **~t** *a* full; (*Tel*) engaged, busy; *Platz* taken; *WC* engaged; **B~tzeichen** *nt* engaged tone; **B~ung** *f* occupation; filling; (*von Rolle*) casting; (*die Schauspieler*) cast.

besichtigen [bə'zɪçtɪgən] *vt* visit, look at.

Besichtigung *f* visit.

Besied(e)lung [bə'ziːd(ə)lʊŋ] *f* population.

besiegeln [bə'ziːgəln] *vt* seal.

besiegen [bə'ziːgən] *vt* defeat, overcome.

Besiegte(r) [bə'ziːçtə(r)] *m* loser.

besinnen [bə'zɪnən] *vr irreg* (*nachdenken*) think, reflect; (*erinnern*) remember; **sich anders ~** change one's mind.

besinnlich *a* contemplative.

Besinnung *f* consciousness; **zur ~ kommen** recover consciousness; (*fig*) come to one's senses; **b~slos** *a* unconscious.

Besitz [bə'zɪts] *m* **-es** possession; (*Eigentum*) property; **b~anzeigend** *a* (*Gram*) possessive; **b~en** *vt irreg* possess, own; *Eigenschaft* have; **~er(in** *f***)** *m* **-s**, **-** owner, proprietor; **~ergreifung** *f*, **~nahme** *f* occupation, seizure.

besoffen [bə'zɔfən] *a* (*col*) drunk, pissed.

besohlen [bə'zoːlən] *vt* sole.

Besoldung [bə'zɔldʊŋ] *f* salary, pay.

besondere(r,s) [bə'zɔndərə(r,z)] *a* special; (*eigen*) particular; (*gesondert*) separate; (*eigentümlich*) peculiar.

Besonderheit [bə'zɔndərhaɪt] *f* peculiarity.

besonders [bə'zɔndərs] *ad* especially, particularly; (*getrennt*) separately.

besonnen [bə'zɔnən] *a* sensible, level-headed; **B~heit** *f* prudence.

besorg- [bə'zɔrg] *cpd*: **~en** *vt* (*beschaffen*) acquire; (*kaufen auch*) purchase; (*erledigen*) Geschäfte deal with; (*sich kümmern um*) take care of; **es jdm ~en** (*col*) show sb what for; **B~nis** *f* **-**, **-se** anxiety, concern; **~t** [bə'zɔrçt] *a* anxious, worried; **B~theit** *f* anxiety, worry; **B~ung** *f* acquisition; (*Kauf*) purchase.

bespielen [bə'ʃpiːlən] *vt* record.

bespitzeln [bə'ʃpɪtsəln] *vt* spy on.

besprechen [bə'ʃprɛçən] *irreg vt* discuss; *Tonband etc* record, speak onto; *Buch* review; *vr* discuss, consult.

Besprechung *f* meeting, discussion; (*von Buch*) review.

besser ['bɛsər] *a* better; **nur ein ~er . . .** just a glorified . . . ; **~gehen** *vi irreg impers*: **es geht ihm ~** he feels better; **~n** *vt* make better, improve; *vr* improve; *Menschen* reform; **B~ung** *f* improvement; **gute B~ung!** get well soon; **B~wisser** *m* **-s**, **-** know-all.

Bestand [bə'ʃtant] *m* **-(e)s**, **¨e** (*Fortbestehen*) duration, stability; (*Kassen~*) amount, balance; (*Vorrat*) stock; **eiserne(r) ~** iron rations *pl*; **~ haben**, **von ~ sein** last long, endure.

beständig [bə'ʃtɛndɪç] *a* (*ausdauernd*) constant (*auch fig*); *Wetter* settled; *Stoffe* resistant; *Klagen etc* continual.

Bestand- *cpd*: **~saufnahme** *f* stocktaking; **~teil** *m* part, component; (*Zutat*) ingredient.

bestärken [bə'ʃtɛrkən] *vt*: **jdn in etw** (*dat*) **~** strengthen or confirm sb in sth.

bestätigen [bə'ʃtɛːtɪgən] *vt* confirm; (*anerkennen*, *Comm*) acknowledge.

Bestätigung *f* confirmation; acknowledgement.

bestatt- [bə'ʃtat] *cpd*: **~en** *vt* bury; **B~er** *m* **-s**, **-** undertaker; **B~ung** *f* funeral.

bestäuben [bə'ʃtɔybən] *vt* powder, dust; *Pflanze* pollinate.

beste(r,s) ['bɛstə(r,z)] *a* best; **sie singt am ~n** she sings best; **so ist es am ~n** it's best that way; **am ~n gehst du gleich** you'd better go at once; **jdn zum ~n haben** pull sb's leg; **etw zum ~n geben** tell a joke/story *etc*; **aufs ~** in the best possible way; **zu jds B~n** for the benefit of sb.

bestechen [bə'ʃtɛçən] *vt irreg* bribe.

bestechlich *a* corruptible; **B~keit** *f* corruptibility.

Bestechung *f* bribery, corruption.

Besteck [bə'ʃtɛk] *nt* **-(e)s**, **-e** knife, fork and spoon, cutlery; (*Med*) set of instruments.

bestehen [bə'∫te:ən] *irreg vi* be; exist; (*andauern*) last; *vt* Kampf, Probe, Prüfung pass; ~ **auf** (+*dat*) insist on; ~ **aus** consist of.

bestehlen [bə'∫te:lən] *vt irreg* rob.

besteigen [bə'∫taɪgən] *vt irreg* climb, ascend; Pferd mount; Thron ascend.

Bestell- [bə'∫tɛl] *cpd:* ~**buch** *nt* order book; **b~en** *vt* order; (*kommen lassen*) arrange to see; (*nominieren*) name; Acker cultivate; Grüße, Auftrag pass on; ~**schein** *m* order coupon; ~**ung** *f* (Comm) order; (*Bestellen*) ordering.

bestenfalls ['bɛstən'fals] *ad* at best.

bestens ['bɛstəns] *ad* very well.

besteuern [bə'∫tɔʏərn] *vt* tax.

Bestie ['bɛstiə] *f* (lit, fig) beast.

bestimm- [bə'∫tɪm] *cpd:* ~**en** *vt* Regeln lay down; Tag, Ort fix; (*beherrschen*) characterize; (*ausersehen*) mean; (*ernennen*) appoint; (*definieren*) define; (*veranlassen*) induce; ~**t** *a* (*entschlossen*) firm; (*gewiß*) certain, definite; Artikel definite; *ad* (gewiß) definitely, for sure; **B~theit** *f* certainty; **B~ung** *f* (Verordnung) regulation; (Festsetzen) determining; (Verwendungszweck) purpose; (Schicksal) fate; (Definition) definition; **B~ungsort** *m* destination.

Best- *cpd:* ~**leistung** *f* best performance; **b~möglich** *a* best possible.

bestrafen [bə'∫tra:fən] *vt* punish.

Bestrafung *f* punishment.

bestrahlen [bə'∫tra:lən] *vt* shine on; (Med) treat with X-rays.

Bestrahlung *f* (Med) X-ray treatment, radiotherapy.

Bestreben [bə'∫tre:bən] *nt* -s, **Bestrebung** [bə'∫tre:bʊŋ] *f* endeavour, effort.

bestreichen [bə'∫traɪçən] *vt irreg* Brot spread.

bestreiten [bə'∫traɪtən] *vt irreg* (abstreiten) dispute; (finanzieren) pay for, finance.

bestreuen [bə'∫trɔʏən] *vt* sprinkle, dust; Straße (spread with) grit.

bestürmen [bə'∫tʏrmən] *vt* (mit Fragen, Bitten etc) overwhelm, swamp.

bestürzen [bə'∫tʏrtsən] *vt* dismay.

bestürzt *a* dismayed.

Bestürzung *f* consternation.

Besuch [bə'zu:x] *m* **-(e)s, -e** visit; (Person) visitor; **einen** ~ **machen bei jdm** pay sb a visit or call; ~ **haben** have visitors; **bei jdm auf** or **zu** ~ **sein** be visiting sb; **b~en** *vt* visit; (Sch etc) attend; **gut** ~**t** well-attended; ~**er(in** *f*) *m* -s, - visitor, guest; ~**serlaubnis** *f* permission to visit; ~**szeit** *f* visiting hours *pl*.

betagt [bə'ta:kt] *a* aged.

betasten [bə'tastən] *vt* touch, feel.

betätigen [bə'tɛ:tɪgən] *vt* (bedienen) work, operate; *vr* involve o.s.; **sich politisch** ~ be involved in politics; **sich als etw** ~ work as sth.

Betätigung *f* activity; (beruflich) occupation; (Tech) operation.

betäuben [bə'tɔʏbən] *vt* stun; (fig) Gewissen still; (Med) anaesthetize.

Betäubungsmittel *nt* anaesthetic.

Bete ['be:tə] *f* -, **-n: rote** ~ beetroot.

beteiligen [bə'taɪlɪgən] *vr* (an +dat in) take part or participate, share; (an Geschäft: finanziell) have a share; *vt:* **jdn** ~ give sb a share or interest (an +dat in).

Beteiligung *f* participation; (Anteil) share, interest; (Besucherzahl) attendance.

beten ['be:tən] *vti* pray.

beteuern [bə'tɔʏərn] *vt* assert; Unschuld protest; **jdm etw** ~ assure sb of sth.

Beteuerung *f* assertion, protest(ation), assurance.

Beton [be'tõ:] *m* -s, -s concrete.

betonen [bə'to:nən] *vt* stress.

betonieren [beto'ni:rən] *vt* concrete.

Betonung *f* stress, emphasis.

betören [bə'tø:rən] *vt* beguile.

Betracht [bə'traxt] *m:* **in** ~ **kommen** be concerned or relevant; **nicht in** ~ **kommen** be out of the question; **etw in** ~ **ziehen** consider sth; **außer** ~ **bleiben** not be considered; **b~en** *vt* look at; (fig auch) consider; ~**er(in** *f*) *m* -s, - onlooker.

beträchtlich [bə'trɛçtlɪç] *a* considerable.

Betrachtung *f* (Ansehen) examination; (Erwägung) consideration.

Betrag [bə'tra:k] *m* -(e)s, "**e** amount; **b~en** [bə'tra:gən] *irreg vt* amount to; *vr* behave; ~**en** *nt* -s behaviour.

betrauen [bə'trauən] *vt:* **jdn mit etw** ~ entrust sb with sth.

betreffen [bə'trɛfən] *vt irreg* concern, affect; **was mich betrifft** as for me; ~**d** *a* relevant, in question.

betreffs [bə'trɛfs] *prep* +gen concerning, regarding.

betreiben [bə'traɪbən] *vt irreg* (ausüben) practise; Politik follow; Studien pursue; (vorantreiben) push ahead; (Tech: antreiben) drive.

betreten [bə'tre:tən] *vt irreg* enter; Bühne etc step onto; **B~ verboten** keep off/out; *a* embarrassed.

Betrieb [bə'tri:p] *m* -(e)s, -e (Firma) firm, concern; (Anlage) plant; (Tätigkeit) operation; (Treiben) traffic; **außer** ~ **sein** be out of order; **in** ~ **sein** be in operation; ~**sausflug** *m* firm's outing; **b~sfähig** *a* in working order; ~**sferien** *pl* company holidays *pl*; ~**sklima** *nt* (working) atmosphere; ~**skosten** *pl* running costs *pl*; ~**srat** *m* workers' council; **b~ssicher** *a* safe, reliable; ~**sstoff** *m* fuel; ~**sstörung** *f* breakdown; ~**sunfall** *m* industrial accident; ~**swirtschaft** *f* economics.

betrinken [bə'trɪŋkən] *vr irreg* get drunk.

betroffen [bə'trɔfən] *a* (bestürzt) amazed, perplexed; **von etw** ~ **werden** or **sein** be affected by sth.

betrüben [bə'try:bən] *vt* grieve.

betrübt [bə'try:pt] *a* sorrowful, grieved.

Betrug [bə'tru:k] *m* -(e)s deception; (Jur) fraud.

betrügen [bə'try:gən] *irreg vt* cheat; (Jur) defraud; Ehepartner be unfaithful to; *vr* deceive o.s.

Betrüger *m* **-s, -** cheat, deceiver; **b~isch** *a* deceitful; (*Jur*) fraudulent.

betrunken [bə'trʊŋkən] *a* drunk.

Bett [bɛt] *nt* **-(e)s, -en** bed; **ins** *or* **zu ~ gehen** go to bed; **~bezug** *m* duvet cover; **~decke** *f* blanket; (*Daunen~*) quilt; (*Überwurf*) bedspread.

Bettel- ['bɛtəl] *cpd:* **b~arm** *a* very poor, destitute; **~ei** [bɛtə'lai] *f* begging; **b~n** *vi* beg.

Bett- *cpd:* **b~en** *vt* make a bed for; **b~lägerig** *a* bedridden; **~laken** *nt* sheet.

Bettler(in *f*) ['bɛtlər(ɪn)] *m* **-s, -** beggar.

Bett- *cpd:* **~nässer** *m* **-s, -** bedwetter; **~vorleger** *m* bedside rug; **~wäsche** *f*, **~zeug** *nt* bedclothes *pl*, bedding.

beugen ['bɔygən] *vt* bend; (*Gram*) inflect; *vr* (*sich fügen*) bow (*dat* to).

Beule ['bɔylə] *f* **-, -n** bump, swelling.

beunruhigen [bə'ʊnruːɪgən] *vt* disturb, alarm; *vr* become worried.

Beunruhigung *f* worry, alarm.

beurkunden [bə'uːrkʊndən] *vt* attest, verify.

beurlauben [bə'uːrlaubən] *vt* give leave *or* holiday to.

beurteilen [bə'ʊrtailən] *vt* judge; *Buch etc* review.

Beurteilung *f* judgement; review; (*Note*) mark.

Beute ['bɔytə] *f* **-** booty, loot; **~l** *m* **-s, -** bag; (*Geld~*) purse; (*Tabak~*) pouch.

bevölkern [bə'fœlkərn] *vt* populate.

Bevölkerung *f* population.

bevollmächtigen [bə'fɔlmɛçtɪgən] *vt* authorize.

Bevollmächtigte(r) *mf* authorized agent.

Bevollmächtigung *f* authorization.

bevor [bə'foːr] *cj* before; **~munden** *vt* *insep* dominate; **~stehen** *vi irreg* be in store (*dat* for); **~stehend** *a* imminent, approaching; **~zugen** *vt* *insep* prefer; **B~zugung** *f* preference.

bewachen [bə'vaxən] *vt* watch, guard.

Bewachung *f* (*Bewachen*) guarding; (*Leute*) guard, watch.

bewaffnen [bə'vafnən] *vt* arm.

Bewaffnung *f* (*Vorgang*) arming; (*Ausrüstung*) armament, arms *pl*.

bewahren [bə'vaːrən] *vt* keep; **jdn vor jdm/etw ~** save sb from sb/sth.

bewähren [bə'vɛːrən] *vr* prove o.s.; (*Maschine*) prove its worth.

bewahrheiten [bə'vaːrhaitən] *vr* come true.

bewährt *a* reliable.

Bewährung *f* (*Jur*) probation; **~sfrist** *f* (period of) probation.

bewaldet [bə'valdət] *a* wooded.

bewältigen [bə'vɛltɪgən] *vt* overcome; *Arbeit* finish; *Portion* manage.

bewandert [bə'vandərt] *a* expert, knowledgeable.

bewässern [bə'vɛsərn] *vt* irrigate.

Bewässerung *f* irrigation.

Beweg- [bə'veːg] *cpd:* **b~en** *vtr* move; **jdn zu etw b~en** induce sb to (do) sth;

~grund [bə'veːk-] *m* motive; **b~lich** *a* movable, mobile; (*flink*) quick; **b~t** *a* *Leben* eventful; *Meer* rough; (*ergriffen*) touched; **~ung** *f* movement, motion; (*innere*) emotion; (*körperlich*) exercise; **sich** (*dat*) **~ung machen** take exercise; **~ungsfreiheit** *f* freedom of movement or action; **b~ungslos** *a* motionless.

Beweis [bə'vais] *m* **-es, -e** proof; (*Zeichen*) sign; **b~bar** [bə'vaiz-] *a* provable; **b~en** *vt irreg* prove; (*zeigen*) show; **~führung** *f* reasoning; **~kraft** *f* weight, conclusiveness; **b~kräftig** *a* convincing, conclusive; **~mittel** *nt* evidence.

bewenden [bə'vɛndən] *vi:* **etw dabei ~ lassen** leave sth at that.

Bewerb- [bə'vɛrb] *cpd:* **b~en** *vr irreg* apply (*um* for); **~er(in** *f*) *m* **-s, -** applicant; **~ung** *f* application.

bewerkstelligen [bə'vɛrkʃtɛlɪgən] *vt* manage, accomplish.

bewerten [bə'veːrtən] *vt* assess.

bewilligen [bə'vɪlɪgən] *vt* grant, allow.

Bewilligung *f* granting.

bewirken [bə'vɪrkən] *vt* cause, bring about.

bewirten [bə'vɪrtən] *vt* entertain.

bewirtschaften [bə'vɪrt-ʃaftən] *vt* manage.

Bewirtung *f* hospitality.

bewohn- [bə'voːn] *cpd:* **~bar** *a* inhabitable; **~en** *vt* inhabit, live in; **B~er(in** *f*) *m* **-s, -** inhabitant; (*von Haus*) resident.

bewölkt [bə'vœlkt] *a* cloudy, overcast.

Bewölkung *f* clouds *pl*.

Bewunder- [bə'vʊndər] *cpd:* **~er** *m* **-s, -** admirer; **b~n** *vt* admire; **b~nswert** *a* admirable, wonderful; **~ung** *f* admiration.

bewußt [bə'vʊst] *a* conscious; (*absichtlich*) deliberate; **sich** (*dat*) **einer Sache ~ sein** be aware of sth; **~los** *a* unconscious; **B~losigkeit** *f* unconsciousness; **~machen** *vt:* **jdm/sich etw ~machen** make sb/o.s. aware of sth; **B~sein** *nt* consciousness; **bei B~sein** conscious.

bezahlen [bə'tsaːlən] *vt* pay (for); **es macht sich bezahlt** it will pay.

Bezahlung *f* payment.

bezaubern [bə'tsaubərn] *vt* enchant, charm.

bezeichnen [bə'tsaiçnən] *vt* (*kennzeichnen*) mark; (*nennen*) call; (*beschreiben*) describe; (*zeigen*) show, indicate; **~d** *a* characteristic, typical (*für* of).

Bezeichnung *f* (*Zeichen*) mark, sign; (*Beschreibung*) description.

bezeugen [bə'tsɔygən] *vt* testify to.

Bezichtigung [bə'tsɪçtɪgʊŋ] *f* accusation.

beziehen [bə'tsiːən] *irreg vt* (*mit Überzug*) cover; *Bett* make; *Haus, Position* move into; *Standpunkt* take up; (*erhalten*) receive; *Zeitung* subscribe to, take; **etw auf jdn/etw ~** relate sth to sb/sth; *vr* refer (*auf +acc* to); (*Himmel*) cloud over.

Beziehung *f* (*Verbindung*) connection; (*Zusammenhang*) relation; (*Verhältnis*) relationship; (*Hinsicht*) respect; **~en**

haben (*vorteilhaft*) have connections *or* contacts; **b~sweise** *ad* or; (*genauer gesagt auch*) that is, or rather.

Bezirk [bə'tsɪrk] *m* **-(e)s, -e** district.

Bezug [bə'tsu:k] *m* **-(e)s,** ˖e (*Hülle*) covering; (*Comm*) ordering; (*Gehalt*) income, salary; (*Beziehung*) relationship (*zu* to); in **b~ auf** (+*acc*) with reference to; **~ nehmen auf** (+*acc*) refer to.

bezüglich [bə'tsy:klɪç] *prep* +*gen* concerning, referring to; *a* concerning; (*Gram*) relative.

Bezug- *cpd:* **~nahme** *f* reference (*auf* +*acc* to); **~spreis** *m* retail price; **~squelle** *f* source of supply.

bezwecken [bə'tsvɛkən] *vt* aim at.

bezweifeln [bə'tsvaɪfəln] *vt* doubt, query.

Bibel ['bi:bəl] *f* **-, -n** Bible.

Biber ['bi:bər] *m* **-s, -** beaver.

Biblio- *cpd:* **~graphie** [bibliogra'fi:] *f* bibliography; **~thek** [biblio'te:k] *f* **-, -en** library; **~thekar(in** *f*) [bibliote'ka:r(ɪn)] *m* **-s, -e** librarian.

biblisch ['bi:blɪʃ] *a* biblical.

bieder ['bi:dər] *a* upright, worthy; *Kleid etc* plain.

bieg- [bi:g] *cpd:* **~bar** *a* flexible; **~en** *irreg vtr* bend; *vi* turn; **~sam** ['bi:k-] *a* supple; **B~ung** *f* bend, curve.

Biene ['bi:nə] *f* **-, -n** bee; **~nhonig** *m* honey; **~nkorb** *m* beehive; **~nwachs** *nt* beeswax.

Bier [bi:r] *nt* **-(e)s, -e** beer; **~brauer** *m* brewer; **~deckel** *m,* **~filz** *m* beer mat; **~krug** *m,* **~seidel** *nt* beer mug.

bieten ['bi:tən] *irreg vt* offer; (*bei Versteigerung*) bid; *vr* (*Gelegenheit*) be open (*dat* to); **sich** (*dat*) **etw ~ lassen** put up with sth.

Bikini [bi'ki:ni] *m* **-s, -s** bikini.

Bilanz [bi'lants] *f* balance; (*fig*) outcome; **~ ziehen** take stock (*aus* of).

Bild [bɪlt] *nt* **-(e)s, -er** (*lit, fig*) picture; photo; (*Spiegel~*) reflection; **~bericht** *m* pictorial report.

bilden ['bɪldən] *vt* form; (*erziehen*) educate; (*ausmachen*) constitute; *vr* arise; (*erziehen*) educate o.s.

Bilder- ['bɪldər] *cpd:* **~buch** *nt* picture book; **~rahmen** *m* picture frame.

Bild- *cpd:* **~fläche** *f* screen; (*fig*) scene; **~hauer** *m* **-s, -** sculptor; **b~hübsch** *a* lovely, pretty as a picture; **b~lich** *a* figurative; pictorial; **~schirm** *m* television screen; **b~schön** *a* lovely; **~ung** ['bɪldʊŋ] *f* formation; (*Wissen, Benehmen*) education; **~ungslücke** *f* gap in one's education; **~ungspolitik** *f* educational policy; **~weite** *f* (*Phot*) distance.

Billard ['bɪljart] *nt* **-s, -e** billiards; **~ball** *m,* **~kugel** *f* billiard ball.

billig ['bɪlɪç] *a* cheap; (*gerecht*) fair, reasonable; **~en** ['bɪlɪgən] *vt* approve of; **B~ung** *f* approval.

Billion [bɪl'io:n] *f* billion, trillion (*US*).

bimmeln ['bɪməln] *vi* tinkle.

Binde ['bɪndə] *f* **-, -n** bandage; (*Arm—*) band; (*Med*) sanitary towel; **~glied** *nt* connecting link; **b~n** *vt irreg* bind, tie;

~strich *m* hyphen; **~wort** *nt* conjunction.

Bind- *cpd:* **~faden** *m* string; **~ung** *f* bond, tie; (*Ski—*) binding.

binnen ['bɪnən] *prep* +*dat or gen* within; **B~hafen** *m* inland harbour; **B~handel** *m* internal trade.

Binse ['bɪnzə] *f* **-, -n** rush, reed; **~nwahrheit** *f* truism.

Bio- [bio] *cpd* bio-; **~graphie** [-gra'fi:] *f* biography; **~loge** [-'lo:gə] *m* **-n, -n** biologist; **~logie** [-lo'gi:] *f* biology; **b~logisch** [-'lo:gɪʃ] *a* biological.

Birke ['bɪrkə] *f* **-, -n** birch.

Birnbaum *m* pear tree.

Birne ['bɪrnə] *f* **-, -n** pear; (*Elec*) (light) bulb.

bis [bɪs] *ad, prep* +*acc* (*räumlich:* ~ *zu/an* +*acc*) to, as far as; (*zeitlich*) till, until; **Sie haben ~ Dienstag** Zeit you have until *or* till Tuesday; **~ Dienstag muß es fertig sein** it must be ready by Tuesday; **~ hierher** this far; **~ in die Nacht** into the night; **~ auf weiteres** until further notice; **~bald/gleich** see you later/soon; **~ auf etw** (*acc*) (*einschließlich*) including sth; (*ausgeschlossen*) except sth; **~ zu** up to; *cj* (*mit Zahlen*) to; (*zeitlich*) until, till; **von ... ~ ...** from ... to ...

Bischof ['bɪʃɔf] *m* **-s, ˖e** bishop.

bischöflich ['bɪʃøːflɪç] *a* episcopal.

bisher [bɪs'he:r] *ad,* **~ig** *a* till now, hitherto.

Biskuit [bɪs'kvi:t] *m or nt* **-(e)s, -s** *or* **-e** biscuit; **~teig** *m* sponge mixture.

bislang [bɪs'laŋ] *ad* hitherto.

Biß [bɪs] *m* **-sses, -sse** bite.

bißchen ['bɪsçən] *a* a bit.

Bissen ['bɪsən] *m* **-s, -** bite, morsel.

bissig ['bɪsɪç] *a Hund* snappy; *Bemerkung* cutting, biting.

Bistum ['bɪstu:m] *nt* bishopric.

bisweilen [bɪs'vaɪlən] *ad* at times, occasionally.

Bitte ['bɪtə] *f* **-, -n** request; **b~** *interj* please; (*wie b—?*) (I beg your) pardon; (*als Antwort auf Dank*) you're welcome; **b~ schön!** it was a pleasure; **b~n** *vti irreg* ask (*um* for); **b~nd** *a* pleading, imploring.

bitter ['bɪtər] *a* bitter; **~böse** *a* very angry; **B~keit** *f* bitterness; **~lich** *a* bitter.

blähen ['blɛːən] *vtr* swell, blow out.

Blähungen *pl* (*Med*) wind.

blam- *cpd:* **~abel** [bla'ma:bəl] *a* disgraceful; **B~age** [bla'ma:ʒə] *f* **-, -n** disgrace; **~ieren** [bla'mi:rən] *vr* make a fool of o.s., disgrace o.s.; *vt* let down, disgrace.

blank [blaŋk] *a* bright; (*unbedeckt*) bare; (*sauber*) clean, polished; (*col: ohne Geld*) broke; (*offensichtlich*) blatant.

blanko ['blaŋko] *ad* blank; **B~scheck** *m* blank cheque.

Bläschen ['blɛːsçən] *nt* bubble; (*Med*) spot, blister.

Blase ['bla:zə] *f* **-, -n** bubble; (*Med*) blister; (*Anat*) bladder; **~balg** *m* bellows *pl*; **b~n** *vti irreg* blow.

Blas- *cpd:* **~instrument** *nt* brass *or* wind instrument; **~kapelle** *f* brass band.

blaß [blas] a pale.

Blässe ['blɛsə] f - paleness, palour.

Blatt [blat] nt **-(e)s, ̈er** leaf; newspaper; (von Papier) sheet; (Cards) hand; **vom ~ singen/spielen** sight-read.

blättern ['blɛtərn] vi: **in etw** (dat) **~ leaf** through sth.

Blätterteig m flaky or puff pastry.

blau [blau] a blue; (col) drunk, stoned; (Cook) boiled; Auge black; **~er Fleck** bruise; **Fahrt ins B~e** mystery tour; **~äugig** a blue-eyed; **B~licht** nt flashing blue light; **~machen** vi (col) skive off work; **B~strumpf** m (fig) bluestocking.

Blech [blɛç] nt **-(e)s, -e** tin, sheet metal; (Back—) baking tray; **~büchse** f, **~dose** f tin, can; **b~en** vti (col) pay; **~schaden** m (Aut) damage to bodywork.

Blei [blai] nt **-(e)s, -e** lead; **~be** f -, **-n** roof over one's head; **b~ben** vi irreg stay, remain, **b~benlassen** vt irreg leave (alone).

bleich [blaiç] a faded, pale; **~en** vt bleach.

Blei- cpd: **b~ern** a leaden; **~stift** m pencil; **~stiftspitzer** m pencil sharpener.

Blende ['blɛndə] f -, **-n** (Phot) aperture; **b~n** vt blind, dazzle; (fig) hoodwink; **b~nd** a (col) grand; **b~nd aussehen** look smashing.

Blick [blik] m **-(e)s, -e** (kurz) glance, glimpse; (Anschauen) look, gaze; (Aussicht) view; **b~en** vi look; **sich b~en lassen** put in an appearance; **~fang** m eye-catching object; **~feld** nt range of vision (auch fig).

blind [blint] a blind; Glas etc dull; **~er Passagier** stowaway; **B~darm** m appendix; **B~darmentzündung** f appendicitis; **B~enschrift** ['blindən-] f braille; **B~heit** f blindness; **~lings** ad blindly; **B~schleiche** f slow worm; **~schreiben** vi irreg touch-type.

blink- [blink] cpd: **~en** vi twinkle, sparkle; (Licht) flash, signal; (Aut) indicate; vt flash, signal; **B~er** m **-s, -, B~licht** nt (Aut) indicator.

blinzeln ['blintsəln] vi blink, wink.

Blitz [blits] m **-es, -e** (flash of) lightning; **~ableiter** m lightning conductor; **b~en** vi (aufleuchten) glint, shine; **es blitzt** (Met) there's a flash of lightning; **~licht** nt flashlight; **b~schnell** a, ad as quick as a flash.

Block [blɔk] m **-(e)s, ̈e** (lit, fig) block; (von Papier) pad; **~ade** [blɔ'ka:də] f -, **-n** blockade; **~flöte** f recorder; **b~frei** a (Pol) unaligned; **b~ieren** [blɔ'ki:rən] vt block; vi (Räder) jam; **~schrift** f block letters pl.

blöd [blø:t] a silly, stupid; **~eln** ['blø:dəln] vi (col) fool around; **B~heit** f stupidity; **B~sinn** m nonsense; **b~sinnig** a silly, idiotic.

blond [blɔnt] a blond, fair-haired.

bloß [blo:s] a (unbedeckt) bare; (nackt) naked; (nur) mere; ad only, merely; **laß das ~!** just don't do that!

Blöße ['blø:sə] f -, **-n** bareness; nakedness;

(fig) weakness; **sich** (dat) **eine ~ geben** (fig) lay o.s. open to attack.

bloß- cpd: **~legen** vt expose; **~stellen** vt show up.

blühen ['bly:ən] vi (lit) bloom, be in bloom; (fig) flourish.

Blume ['blu:mə] f -, **-n** flower; (von Wein) bouquet; **~nkohl** m cauliflower; **~ntopf** m flowerpot; **~nzwiebel** f bulb.

Bluse ['blu:zə] f -, **-n** blouse.

Blut [blu:t] nt **-(e)s** blood; **b~arm** a anaemic; (fig) penniless; **b~befleckt** a bloodstained; **~buche** f copper beech; **~druck** m blood pressure.

Blüte ['bly:tə] f -, **-n** blossom; (fig) prime; **~zeit** f flowering period; (fig) heyday.

Blut- cpd: **~egel** m leech; **b~en** vi bleed.

Blütenstaub m pollen.

Blut- cpd: **~er** m **-s, -** (Med) haemophiliac; **~erguß** m haemorrhage; (auf Haut) bruise; **~gruppe** f blood group; **b~ig** a bloody; **b~jung** a very young; **~probe** f blood test; **~schande** f incest; **~spender** m blood donor; **~übertragung** f blood transfusion; **~ung** f bleeding, haemorrhage; **~vergiftung** f blood poisoning; **~wurst** f black pudding.

Bö(e) ['bø:(ə)] f -, **-en** squall.

Bock [bɔk] m **-(e)s, ̈e** buck, ram; (Gestell) trestle, support; (Sport) buck.

Boden ['bo:dən] m **-s, ̈** ground; (Fuß—) floor; (Meeres—, Faß—) bottom; (Speicher) attic; **b~los** a bottomless; (col) incredible; **~satz** m dregs pl, sediment; **~schätze** pl mineral wealth; **~turnen** nt floor exercises pl.

Bogen ['bo:gən] m **-s, -** (Biegung) curve; (Archit) arch; (Waffe, Mus) bow; (Papier) sheet; **~gang** m arcade; **~schütze** m archer.

Bohle ['bo:lə] f -, **-n** plank.

Bohne ['bo:nə] f -, **-n** bean; **~nkaffee** m pure coffee; **b~rn** vt wax, polish; **~rwachs** nt floor polish.

Bohr- ['bo:r] cpd: **b~en** vt bore; **~er** m **-s, -** drill; **~insel** f oil rig; **~maschine** f drill; **~turm** m derrick.

Boje ['bo:jə] f -, **-n** buoy.

Bolzen ['bɔltsən] m **-s, -** bolt.

Bomb- cpd: **b~ardieren** [bɔmbar'di:rən] vt bombard; (aus der Luft) bomb; **~e** ['bɔmbə] f -, **-n** bomb; **~enangriff** m bombing raid; **~enerfolg** m (col) huge success.

Bonbon [bõ'bõ:] m or nt **-s, -s** sweet.

Boot [bo:t] nt **-(e)s, -e** boat.

Bord [bɔrt] m **-(e)s, -e** (Aviat, Naut) board; **an ~** on board; nt (Brett) shelf; **~ell** [bɔr'dɛl] nt **-s, -e** brothel; **~funkanlage** f radio; **~stein** m kerb(stone).

borgen ['bɔrgən] vt borrow; **jdm etw ~** lend sb sth.

borniert [bɔr'ni:rt] a narrow-minded.

Börse ['bœrzə] f -, **-n** stock exchange; (Geld—) purse.

Borste ['bɔrstə] f -, **-n** bristle.

Borte ['bɔrtə] f -, **-n** edging; (Band) trimming.

bös [bø:s] a bad, evil; (zornig) angry; **~artig** ['bø:z-] a malicious.

Böschung ['bœʃʊŋ] f slope; (Ufer— etc) embankment.
bos- ['bo:s] cpd: ~**haft** a malicious, spiteful; **B~heit** f malice, spite.
böswillig ['bø:sviliç] a malicious.
Botanik [bo'ta:nik] f botany.
botanisch [bo'ta:nɪʃ] a botanical.
Bot- ['bo:t] cpd: ~**e** m -n, -n messenger; ~**enjunge** m errand boy; ~**schaft** f message, news; (Pol) embassy; ~**schafter** m -s, - ambassador.
Bottich ['bɔtiç] m -(e)s, -e vat, tub.
Bouillon [bu'ljõ:] f -, -s consommé.
Bowle [bo:lə] f -, -n punch.
Box- ['bɔks] cpd: **b~en** vi box; ~**er** m -s, - boxer; ~**handschuh** m boxing glove; ~**kampf** m boxing match.
boykottieren [bɔykɔ'ti:rən] vt boycott.
Branche ['brɑ̃:ʃə] f -, -n line of business; ~**nverzeichnis** nt yellow pages pl.
Brand [brant] m -(e)s, -e fire; (Med) gangrene; **b~en** [brandən] vi surge; (Meer) break; **b~marken** vt brand; (fig) stigmatize; ~**salbe** f ointment for burns; ~**stifter** m arsonist, fire-raiser; ~**stiftung** f arson; ~**ung** f surf; ~**wunde** f burn.
Branntwein ['brantvain] m brandy.
Brat- ['bra:t] cpd: ~**apfel** m baked apple; **b~en** vt irreg roast, fry; ~**en** m -s, - roast, joint; ~**huhn** nt roast chicken; ~**kartoffeln** pl fried or roast potatoes pl; ~**pfanne** f frying pan; ~**rost** m grill.
Bratsche ['bra:tʃə] f -, -n viola.
Brat- cpd: ~**spieß** m spit; ~**wurst** f grilled sausage.
Brauch [braux] m -(e)s, Bräuche custom; **b~bar** a usable, serviceable; Person capable; **b~en** vt (bedürfen) need; (müssen) have to; (verwenden) use.
Braue ['brauə] f -, -n brow; **b~n** vt brew; ~'**rei** f brewery.
braun [braun] a brown; (von Sonne auch) tanned.
Bräune ['brɔynə] f -, -n brownness; (Sonnen—) tan; **b~n** vt make brown; (Sonne) tan.
braungebrannt a tanned.
Brause ['brauzə] f -, -n shower bath; (von Gießkanne) rose; (Getränk) lemonade; **b~n** vi roar; (auch vr: duschen) take a shower; ~**pulver** nt lemonade powder.
Braut [braut] f -, Bräute bride; (Verlobte) fiancée.
Bräutigam ['brɔytigam] m -s, -e bridegroom; fiancé.
Braut- cpd: ~**jungfer** f bridesmaid; ~**paar** nt bride and bridegroom, bridal pair.
brav [bra:f] a (artig) good; (ehrenhaft) worthy, honest.
Brech- ['brɛç] cpd: ~**eisen** nt crowbar; **b~en** vti irreg break; Licht refract; (fig) Mensch crush; (speien) vomit; **die Ehe b~en** commit adultery; ~**reiz** m nausea, retching.
Brei [brai] m -(e)s, -e (Masse) pulp; (Cook) gruel; (Hafer—) porridge.
breit [brait] a wide, broad; **B~e** f -, -n width; breadth; (Geog) latitude; ~**en** vt:

etw über etw (acc) ~**en** spread sth over sth; **B~engrad** m degree of latitude; ~**machen** vr spread o.s. out; ~**schult(e)rig** a broad-shouldered; ~**treten** vt irreg (col) enlarge upon; **B~wandfilm** m wide-screen film.
Brems- ['brɛmz] cpd: ~**belag** m brake lining; ~**e** f -, -n brake; (Zool) horsefly; **b~en** vi brake, apply the brakes; vt Auto brake; (fig) slow down; ~**licht** nt brake light; ~**pedal** nt brake pedal; ~**schuh** m brake shoe; ~**spur** f tyre marks pl; ~**weg** m braking distance.
Brenn- ['brɛn] cpd: **b~bar** a inflammable; **b~en** irreg vi burn, be on fire; (Licht, Kerze etc) burn; vt Holz etc burn; Ziegel, Ton fire; Kaffee roast; **darauf b~en, etw zu tun** be dying to do sth; ~**material** nt fuel; ~**(n)essel** f nettle; ~**spiritus** m methylated spirits; ~**stoff** m liquid fuel.
brenzlig ['brɛntsliç] a smelling of burning, burnt; (fig) precarious.
Brett [brɛt] nt -(e)s, -er board, plank; (Bord) shelf; (Spiel—) board; **Schwarze(s) ~** notice board; ~**er** pl (Ski) skis pl; (Theat) boards pl; ~**erzaun** m wooden fence.
Brezel ['bre:tsəl] f -, -n bretzel, pretzel.
Brief [bri:f] m -(e)s, -e letter; ~**beschwerer** m -s, - paperweight; ~**kasten** m letterbox; **b~lich** a,ad by letter; ~**marke** f postage stamp; ~**öffner** m letter opener; ~**papier** nt notepaper; ~**tasche** f wallet; ~**träger** m postman; ~**umschlag** m envelope; ~**wechsel** m correspondence.
Brikett [bri'kɛt] nt -s, -s briquette.
brillant [bril'jant] a (fig) sparkling, brilliant; **B~** m -en, -en brilliant, diamond.
Brille ['brilə] f -, -n spectacles pl; (Schutz—) goggles pl; (Toiletten—) (toilet) seat.
bringen ['brɪŋən] vt irreg bring; (mitnehmen, begleiten) take; (einbringen) Profit bring in; (veröffentlichen) publish; (Theat, Cine) show; (Rad, TV) broadcast; (in einen Zustand versetzen) get; (col: tun können) manage; **jdn dazu ~, etw zu tun** make sb do sth; **jdn nach Hause ~** take sb home; **jdn um etw ~** make sb lose sth; **jdn auf eine Idee ~** give sb an idea.
Brise ['bri:zə] f -, -n breeze.
bröckelig ['brœkəliç] a crumbly.
Brocken ['brɔkən] m -s, - piece, bit; (Fels—) lump of rock.
brodeln ['bro:dəln] vi bubble.
Brokat [bro'ka:t] m -(e)s, -e brocade.
Brombeere ['brɔmbe:rə] f blackberry, bramble.
bronchial [brɔnçi'a:l] a bronchial.
Bronchien ['brɔnçiən] pl bronchia(l tubes) pl.
Bronze ['brõ:sə] f -, -n bronze.
Brosame ['bro:za:mə] f -, -n crumb.
Brosche ['brɔʃə] f -, -n brooch.
Broschüre [brɔ'ʃy:rə] f -, -n pamphlet.
Brot [bro:t] nt -(e)s, -e bread; (—laib) loaf.

Brötchen ['brø:tçən] *nt* roll.

brotlos ['bro:tlo:s] *a Person* unemployed; *Arbeit etc* unprofitable.

Bruch [brux] *m* -(e)s, ̈e breakage; *(zerbrochene Stelle)* break; *(fig)* split, breach; *(Med: Eingeweide—)* rupture, hernia; *(Bein— etc)* fracture; *(Math)* fraction; ~**bude** *f (col)* shack.

brüchig ['brγçıç] *a* brittle, fragile; *Haus* dilapidated.

Bruch- *cpd:* ~**landung** *f* crash landing; ~**strich** *m (Math)* line; ~**stück** *nt* fragment; ~**teil** *m* fraction.

Brücke ['brγkə] *f* -, -n bridge; *(Teppich)* rug.

Bruder ['bru:dər] *m* -s, ̈ brother.

Brüder- ['bry:dər] *cpd:* **b**~**lich** *a* brotherly; ~**lichkeit** *f* fraternity; ~**schaft** *f* brotherhood, fellowship; ~**schaft trinken** fraternize, address each other as 'du'.

Brühe ['bry:ə] *f* -, -n broth, stock; *(pej)* muck.

brüllen ['brγlən] *vi* bellow, scream.

Brumm- ['brum] *cpd:* ~**bär** *m* grumbler; **b**~**eln** *vti* mumble; **b**~**en** *vi (Bär, Mensch etc)* growl; *(Insekt, Radio)* buzz; *(Motoren)* roar; *(murren)* grumble; *vt* growl; **jdm brummt der Kopf** sb's head is buzzing.

brünett [brγ'nɛt] *a* brunette, dark-haired.

Brunnen ['brunən] *m* -s, - fountain; *(tief)* well; *(natürlich)* spring; ~**kresse** *f* watercress.

brüsk [brγsk] *a* abrupt, brusque.

Brust [brust] *f* -, ̈e breast; *(Männer—)* chest.

brüsten ['brγstən] *vr* boast.

Brust- *cpd:* ~**fellentzündung** *f* pleurisy; ~**kasten** *m* chest; ~**schwimmen** *nt* breast-stroke; ~**warze** *f* nipple.

Brüstung ['brγstuŋ] *f* parapet.

Brut [bru:t] *f* -, -en brood; *(Brüten)* hatching; **b**~**al** [bru'ta:l] *a* brutal; ~**ali-'tät** *f* brutality; ~**apparat** *m*, ~**kasten** *m* incubator.

brüten ['bry:tən] *vi* hatch, brood *(auch fig)*.

brutto ['bruto] *ad* gross; **B**~**einkommen** *nt*, **B**~**gehalt** *nt* gross salary; **B**~**gewicht** *nt* gross weight; **B**~**lohn** *m* gross wages *pl.*

Bub [bu:p] *m* -en, -en boy, lad; ~**e** [bu:bə] *m* -n, -n *(Schurke)* rogue; *(Cards)* jack; ~**ikopf** *m* bobbed hair, shingle.

Buch [bu:x] *nt* -(e)s, ̈er book; *(Comm)* account book; ~**binder** *m* bookbinder; ~**drucker** *m* printer; ~**e** *f* -, -n beech tree; **b**~**en** *vt* book; *Betrag* enter.

Bücher- ['by:çər] *cpd:* ~**brett** *nt* bookshelf; ~**ei** [-'rai] *f* library; ~**regal** *nt* bookshelves *pl*, bookcase; ~**schrank** *m* bookcase.

Buch- *cpd:* ~**fink** *m* chaffinch; ~**führung** *f* book-keeping, accounting; ~**halter(in** *f)* *m* -s, - book-keeper; ~**handel** *m* book trade; ~**händler(in** *f)* *m* bookseller; ~**handlung** *f* bookshop.

Büchse ['byksə] *f* -, -n tin, can; *(Holz—)* box; *(Gewehr)* rifle; ~**nfleisch** *nt* tinned meat; ~**nöffner** *m* tin or can opener.

Buch- *cpd:* ~**stabe** *m* -ns, -n letter (of

the alphabet); **b**~**stabieren** [bu:x-∫ta'bi:rən] *vt* spell; **b**~**stäblich** ['bu:x-∫te:pliç] *a* literal.

Bucht ['buxt] *f* -, -en bay.

Buchung ['bu:xuŋ] *f* booking; *(Comm)* entry.

Buckel ['bukəl] *m* -s, - hump.

bücken ['bykən] *vr* bend.

Bückling ['byklıŋ] *m (Fisch)* kipper; *(Verbeugung)* bow.

Bude ['bu:də] *f* -, -n booth, stall; *(col)* digs *pl.*

Budget [by'dʒe:] *nt* -s, -s budget.

Büffel ['byfəl] *m* -s, - buffalo.

Büf(f)ett [by'fe:] *nt* -s, -s *(Anrichte)* sideboard; *(Geschirrschrank)* dresser; **kaltes** ~ cold buffet.

Bug [bu:k] *m* -(e)s, -e *(Naut)* bow; *(Aviat)* nose.

Bügel ['by:gəl] *m* -s, - *(Kleider—)* hanger; *(Steig—)* stirrup; *(Brillen—)* arm; ~**brett** *nt* ironing board; ~**eisen** *nt* iron; ~**falte** *f* crease; **b**~**n** *vti* iron.

Bühne ['by:nə] *f* -, -n stage; ~**nbild** *nt* set, scenery.

Buhruf [bu:ru:f] *m* boo.

Bulette [bu'lɛtə] *f* meatball.

Bull- ['bul] *cpd:* ~**dogge** *f* bulldog; ~**dozer** ['buldo:zər] *m* -s, - bulldozer; ~**e** *m* -n, -n bull.

Bummel ['buməl] *m* -s, - stroll; *(Schaufenster—)* window-shopping; ~**ant** [-'lant] *m* slowcoach; ~**ei** [-'lai] *f* wandering; dawdling; skiving; **b**~**n** *vi* wander, stroll; *(trödeln)* dawdle; *(faulenzen)* skive, loaf around; ~**streik** *m* go-slow; ~**zug** *m* slow train.

Bummler(in *f)* ['bumlər(ın)] *m* -s, - *(langsamer Mensch)* dawdler; *(Faulenzer)* idler, loafer.

Bund [bunt] *m* -(e)s, ̈e *(Freundschafts- etc)* bond; *(Organisation)* union; *(Pol)* confederacy; *(Hosen—, Rock—)* waistband; *nt* -(e)s, -e bunch; *(Stroh—)* bundle.

Bünd- ['bynd] *cpd:* ~**chen** *nt* ribbing; *(Ärmel—)* cuff; ~**el** *nt* -s, -n bundle, bale; **b**~**eln** *vt* bundle.

Bundes- ['bundəs] *in cpds* Federal *(esp* West German); ~**bahn** *f* Federal Railways *pl*; ~**hauptstadt** *f* Federal capital; ~**kanzler** *m* Federal Chancellor; ~**land** *nt* Land; ~**präsident** *m* Federal President; ~**rat** *m* upper house of West German Parliament; ~**republik** *f* Federal Republic (of West Germany); ~**staat** *m* Federal state; ~**straße** *f* Federal Highway, 'A' road; ~**tag** *m* West German Parliament; ~**verfassungsgericht** *nt* Federal Constitutional Court; ~**wehr** *f* West German Armed Forces *pl.*

Bünd- *cpd:* **b**~**ig** *a (kurz)* concise; ~**nis** *nt* -ses, -se alliance.

Bunker ['buŋkər] *m* -s, - bunker.

bunt [bunt] *a* coloured; *(gemischt)* mixed; **jdm wird es zu** ~ it's getting too much for sb; **B**~**stift** *m* coloured pencil, crayon.

Burg [burk] *f* -, -en castle, fort.

Bürge ['byrgə] *m* -n, -n guarantor; **b**~**n** *vi* vouch; ~**r(in** *f)* *m* -s, - citizen; member

of the middle class; **~rkrieg** m civil war;
b~rlich a *Rechte* civil; *Klasse* middle-
class; (*pej*) bourgeois; **gut b~rliche**
Küche good home cooking; **~rmeister**
m mayor; **~rrecht** nt civil rights pl;
~rschaft f population, citizens pl;
~rsteig m pavement; **~rtum** nt citizens
pl.

Bürg- cpd: **~in** f see **Bürge**; **~schaft** f
surety; **~schaft leisten** give security.

Büro [by'ro:] nt **-s, -s** office;
~angestellte(r) mf office worker;
~klammer f paper clip; **~krat**
[byro'kra:t] m **-en, -en** bureaucrat;
~kra'tie f bureaucracy; **b~'kratisch** a
bureaucratic; **~kra'tismus** m red tape;
~schluß m office closing time.

Bursch(e) [burʃ(ə)] m **-en, -en** lad,
fellow; (*Diener*) servant.

Bürste ['byrstə] f **-, -n** brush; **b~n** vt
brush.

Bus [bus] m **-ses, -se** bus.

Busch [buʃ] m **-(e)s, ⁻e** bush, shrub.

Büschel ['byʃəl] nt **-s, -** tuft.

buschig a bushy.

Busen ['bu:zən] m **-s, -** bosom; (*Meer*)
inlet, bay; **~freund(in** f) m bosom friend.

Buße ['bu:sə] f **-, -n** atonement, penance;
(*Geld*) fine.

büßen ['by:sən] vti do penance (for), atone
(for).

Büste ['bystə] f **-, -n** bust; **~nhalter** m
bra.

Butter ['butər] f **-** butter; **~blume** f
buttercup; **~brot** nt (piece of) bread and
butter; **~brotpapier** nt greaseproof
paper; **~dose** f butter dish; **b~weich** a
soft as butter; (*fig,col*) soft.

Butzen ['butsən] m **-s, -** core.

C

(*see also under K and Z; CH under SCH*)

C, c [tse:] nt C, c.

Café [ka'fe:] nt **-s, -s** café.

Cafeteria [kafete'ri:a] f **-, -s** cafeteria.

Camp- [kɛmp] cpd: **c~en** vi camp;
~er(in f) m **-s, -** camper; **~ing** nt **-s**
camping; **~ingplatz** m (**-ing**) site.

Caravan ['kɛrəvən] m **-s, -s** caravan.

Cellist [tʃe'list] m cellist.

Cello ['tʃɛlo] nt **-s, -s** or **Celli** cello.

Chamäleon [ka'mɛ:leɔn] nt **-s, -s**
chameleon.

Champagner [ʃam'panjər] m **-s, -**
champagne.

Champignon ['ʃampɪnjõ] m **-s, -s** button
mushroom.

Chance ['ʃã:s(ə)] f **-, -n** chance,
opportunity.

Chaos ['ka:ɔs] nt **-s, -** chaos.

chaotisch [ka'o:tɪʃ] a chaotic.

Charakter [ka'raktər] m **-s, -e**
[karak'te:rə] character; **c~fest** a of firm
character; **c~i'sieren** vt characterize;
~istik [karakte'rɪstɪk] f characterization;
c~istisch [karakte'rɪstɪʃ] a characteristic, typical (*für* of); **c~los** a unprincipled; **~losigkeit** f lack of principle;

~schwäche f weakness of character;
~stärke f strength of character; **~zug**
m characteristic, trait.

charmant [ʃar'mant] a charming.

Charme [ʃarm] m **-s** charm.

Chassis [ʃa'si:] nt **-, -** chassis.

Chauffeur [ʃɔ'fø:r] m chauffeur.

Chauvinismus [ʃovi'nɪsmʊs] m
chauvinism, jingoism.

Chauvinist [ʃovi'nɪst] m chauvinist,
jingoist.

Chef [ʃɛf] m **-s, -s** head; (*col*) boss; **~arzt**
m head physician; **~in** f (*col*) boss.

Chemie [çe'mi:] f **-** chemistry; **~faser** f
man-made fibre.

Chemikalie [çemi'ka:liə] f **-, -n** chemical.

Chemiker(in f) ['çe:mikər(ɪn)] m **-s, -**
(industrial) chemist.

chemisch ['çe:mɪʃ] a chemical; **~e**
Reinigung dry cleaning.

Chiffre ['ʃɪfər] f **-, -n** (*Geheimzeichen*)
cipher; (*in Zeitung*) box number.

Chiffriermaschine [ʃifri:rmaʃi:nə] f
cipher machine.

Chips [tʃɪps] pl crisps pl, chips pl (*US*).

Chirurg [çi'rʊrk] m **-en, -en** surgeon;
~ie [-'gi:] f surgery; **c~isch** a surgical.

Chlor [klo:r] nt **-s** chlorine; **~o'form** nt **-s**
chloroform; **c~ofor'mieren** vt
chloroform; **~ophyll** [kloro'fyl] nt **-s**
chlorophyll.

Cholera ['ko:lera] f **-** cholera.

cholerisch [ko'le:rɪʃ] a choleric.

Chor [ko:r] m **-(e), -e** or ⁻e choir; (*Musik-
stück, Theat*) chorus; **~al** [ko'ra:l] m **-s,
-äle** chorale.

Choreograph [koreo'gra:f] m **-en, -en**
choreographer; **~ie** [-'fi:] f choreography.

Chor- cpd: **~gestühl** nt choir stalls pl;
~knabe m choirboy.

Christ ['krɪst] m **-en, -en** Christian;
~baum m Christmas tree; **~enheit** f
Christendom; **~entum** nt Christianity;
~in f Christian; **~kind** nt ≈ Father
Christmas; (*Jesus*) baby Jesus; **c~lich** a
Christian; **~us** m - Christ.

Chrom [kro:m] nt **-s** (*Chem*) chromium;
chrome; **~osom** [kromo'zo:m] nt **-s, -en**
(*Biol*) chromosome.

Chron- ['kro:n] cpd: **~ik** f chronicle;
c~isch a chronic; **~ologie** [-lo'gi:] f
chronology; **c~ologisch** [-'lo:gɪʃ] a
chronological.

Chrysantheme [kryzan'te:mə] f **-, -n**
chrysanthemum.

circa ['tsɪrka] ad about, approximately.

Clown [klaun] m **-s, -s** clown.

Computer [kɔm'pju:tər] m **-s, -** computer.

Conférencier [kõferãsie:] m **-s, -s**
compère.

Coupé [ku'pe:] nt **-s, -s** (*Aut*) coupé, sports
version.

Coupon [ku'põ:] m **-s, -s** coupon; (*Stoff—*)
length of cloth.

Cousin [ku'zɛ̃:] m **-s, -s** cousin; **~e**
[ku'zi:nə] f **-, -n** cousin.

Creme [krɛ:m] f **-, -s** (*lit, fig*) cream;
(*Schuh—*) polish; (*Zahn—*) paste; (*Cook*)
mousse; **c~farben** a cream(-coloured).

Curry(pulver nt) ['kari(pulfər)] m or nt **-s** · curry powder.

Cutter(in f) ['katər(ın)] m **-s,** - (Cine) editor.

D

D, d [de:] nt D, d.

da [da:] ad (dort) there; (hier) here; (dann) then; ~, **wo** where; cj as; ~**behalten** vt irreg keep.

dabei [da'baɪ] ad (räumlich) close to it; (noch dazu) besides; (zusammen mit) with them; (zeitlich) during this; (obwohl doch) but, however; **was ist schon** ~? what of it?; **es ist doch nichts** ~, **wenn . . .** it doesn't matter if . . .; **bleiben wir** ~ let's leave it at that; **es soll nicht** ~ **bleiben** this isn't the end of it; **es bleibt** ~ that's settled; **das Dumme/Schwierige** ~ the stupid/difficult part of it; **er war gerade** ~, **zu gehen** he was just leaving; ~**sein** vi irreg (anwesend) be present; (beteiligt) be involved; ~**stehen** vi irreg stand around.

Dach [dax] nt **-(e)s,** ⁻er roof; ~**boden** m attic, loft; ~**decker** m **-s,** - slater, tiler; ~**fenster** nt, ~**luke** f skylight; ~**pappe** f roofing felt; ~**rinne** f gutter; ~**ziegel** m roof tile.

Dachs [daks] m **-es,** -e badger.

Dackel ['dakəl] m **-s,** - dachshund.

dadurch [da'durç] ad (räumlich) through it; (durch diesen Umstand) thereby, in that way; (deshalb) because of that, for that reason; cj: ~, **daß** because.

dafür [da'fy:r] ad for it; (anstatt) instead; **er kann nichts** ~ he can't help it; **er ist bekannt** ~ he is well-known for that; **was bekomme ich** ~? what will I get for it?; **D**~**halten** nt **-s: nach meinem D**~**halten** in my opinion.

dagegen [da'ge:gən] ad against it; (im Vergleich damit) in comparison with it; (bei Tausch) to it; **ich habe nichts** ~ I don't mind; **ich war** ~ I was against it; ~ **kann man nichts tun** one can't do anything about it; cj however; ~**halten** vt irreg (vergleichen) compare with it; (entgegnen) object to it.

daheim [da'haɪm] ad at home; **D**~ nt **-s** home.

daher [da'he:r] ad (räumlich) from there; (Ursache) from that; ~ **kommt er auch** that's where he comes from too; cj (deshalb) that's why; ~ **die Schwierigkeiten** that's what is causing the difficulties.

dahin [da'hın] ad (räumlich) there; (zeitlich) then; (vergangen) gone; **das tendiert** ~ it is tending towards that; **er bringt es noch** ~, **daß ich . . .** he'll make me . . .; ~**gegen** cj on the other hand; ~**gehend** ad on this matter; ~**stellt** ad: ~**gestellt bleiben** remain to be seen; ~**gestellt sein lassen** leave sth open or undecided.

dahinten [da'hıntən] ad over there.

dahinter [da'hıntər] ad behind it;

~**kommen** vi irreg get to the bottom of sth.

Dahlie ['da:liə] f -, **-n** dahlia.

dalassen ['da:lasən] vt irreg leave (behind).

damalig ['da:ma:lıç] a of that time, then.

damals ['da:ma:ls] ad at that time, then.

Damast [da'mast] m **-(e)s,** -e damask.

Dame ['da:mə] f -, **-n** lady; (Schach, Cards) queen; (Spiel) draughts; **d**~**nhaft** a ladylike; ~**nwahl** f ladies' excuse-me; ~**spiel** nt draughts.

damit [da'mıt] ad with it; (begründend) by that; **was meint er** ~? what does he mean by that?; **genug** ~! that's enough; ~ **basta!** and that's that; ~ **eilt es nicht** there's no hurry; cj in order that or to.

dämlich ['dɛ:mlıç] a (col) silly, stupid.

Damm [dam] m **-(e)s,** ⁻e dyke; (Stau—) dam; (Hafen—) mole; (Bahn—, Straßen—) embankment.

Dämm- ['dɛm] cpd: **d**~**en** vt Wasser dam up; Schmerzen keep back; **d**~**erig** a dim, faint; **d**~**ern** vi (Tag) dawn; (Abend) fall; ~**erung** f twilight; (Morgen—) dawn; (Abend—) dusk.

Dämon ['dɛ:mɔn] m **-s, -en** [dɛ'mo:nən] demon; **d**~**isch** [dɛ'mo:nɪʃ] a demoniacal.

Dampf [dampf] m **-(e)s,** ⁻e steam; (Dunst) vapour; **d**~**en** vi steam.

dämpfen ['dɛmpfən] vt (Cook) steam; (bügeln auch) iron with a damp cloth; (fig) dampen, subdue.

Dampf- cpd: ~**er** m **-s,** - steamer; ~**kochtopf** m pressure cooker; ~**maschine** f steam engine; ~**schiff** nt steamship; ~**walze** f steamroller.

danach [da'na:x] ad after that; (zeitlich auch) afterwards; (gemäß) accordingly; according to which or that; **er sieht** ~ **aus** he looks it.

daneben [da'ne:bən] ad beside it; (im Vergleich) in comparison; ~**benehmen** vr irreg misbehave; ~**gehen** vi irreg miss; (Plan) fail.

Dank [dank] m **-(e)s** thanks pl; **vielen** or **schönen** ~ many thanks; **jdm** ~ **sagen** thank sb; **d**~ prep +dat or gen thanks to; **d**~**bar** a grateful; Aufgabe rewarding; ~**barkeit** f gratitude; **d**~**e** interj thank you, thanks; **d**~**en** vi (+dat) thank; **d**~**enswert** a Arbeit worthwhile; rewarding; Bemühung kind; **d**~**sagen** vi express one's thanks.

dann [dan] ad then; ~ **und wann** now and then.

daran [da'ran] ad on it; stoßen against it; **es liegt** ~, **daß . . .** the cause of it is that . . .; **gut/schlecht** ~ **sein** be well-/badly off; **das Beste/Dümmste** ~ the best/stupidest thing about it; **ich war nahe** ~, **zu . . .** I was on the point of . . .; **er ist** ~ **gestorben** he died from or of it; ~**gehen** vi irreg start; ~**setzen** vt stake; **er hat alles** ~**gesetzt, von Glasgow wegzukommen** he has done his utmost to get away from Glasgow.

darauf [da'raʊf] ad (räumlich) on it; (zielgerichtet) towards it; (danach) afterwards; **es kommt ganz** ~ **an, ob . . .** it depends whether . . .; **die Tage** ~ the days following or thereafter; **am Tag** ~ the next day; ~**folgend** a Tag, Jahr next, following; ~**hin** [-ˈhɪn] ad (im Hinblick darauf) in this respect; (aus diesem Grund) as a result; ~**legen** vt lay or put on top.

daraus [daˈraʊs] ad from it; **was ist** ~ **geworden?** what became of it?; ~ **geht hervor, daß** . . . this means that . . .

Darbietung [ˈdaːrbiːtʊŋ] f performance.

darin [daˈrɪn] ad in (there), in it.

Dar- [ˈdaːr] cpd: **d**~**legen** vt explain, expound, set forth; ~**legung** f explanation; ~**leh(e)n** nt -s, - loan.

Darm [darm] m -(e)s, ~e intestine; (Wurst~) skin; ~**saite** f gut string.

Darstell- [ˈdaːrʃtɛl] cpd: **d**~**en** vt (abbilden, bedeuten) represent; (Theat) act; (beschreiben) describe; vr appear to be; ~**er(in** f) m -s, - actor/actress; ~**ung** f portrayal, depiction.

darüber [daˈryːbər] ad (räumlich) over/above it; (fahren over it; (mehr) more; (währenddessen) meanwhile; sprechen, streiten about it; ~ **geht nichts** there's nothing like it; **seine Gedanken** ~ his thoughts about or on it.

darum [daˈrʊm] ad (räumlich) round it; ~ **herum** round about (it); **er bittet** ~ he is pleading for it; **es geht** ~, **daß** . . . the thing is that . . .; **er würde viel** ~ **geben, wenn** . . . he would give a lot to . . .; cj that's why; **ich tue es** ~, **weil** . . . I am doing it because . . .

darunter [daˈrʊntər] ad (räumlich) under it; (dazwischen) among them; (weniger) less; **ein Stockwerk** ~ one floor below (it); **was verstehen Sie** ~? what do you understand by that?; ~**fallen** vi irreg be included; ~**mischen** vt Mehl mix in; vr mingle.

das [das] def art the; pron that; ~ **heißt** that is.

Dasein [ˈdaːzaɪn] nt -s (Leben) life; (Anwesenheit) presence; (Bestehen) existence; **d**~ vi irreg be there.

daß [das] cj that.

dasselbe [dasˈzɛlbə] art, pron the same.

dastehen [ˈdaːʃteːən] vi irreg stand there.

Datenverarbeitung [ˈdaːtənfɛrˈarbaɪtʊŋ] f data processing.

datieren [daˈtiːrən] vt date.

Dativ [ˈdaːtiːf] m -s, ~e dative.

Dattel [ˈdatəl] f -, ~n date.

Datum [ˈdaːtʊm] nt -s, Daten date; (pl Angaben) data pl; **das heutige** ~ today's date.

Dauer [ˈdaʊər] f -, ~n duration; (gewisse Zeitspanne) length; (Bestand, Fortbestehen) permanence; **es war nur von kurzer** ~ it didn't last long; **auf die** ~ in the long run; (auf längere Zeit) indefinitely; ~**auftrag** m standing order; **d**~**haft** a lasting, durable; ~**haftigkeit** f durability; ~**karte** f season ticket; ~**lauf** m long-distance run; **d**~**n** vi last; **es hat sehr lang gedauert, bis er** . . . it took him a long time to . . .; **d**~**nd** a constant; ~**regen** m continuous rain; ~**welle** f perm(anent wave); ~**wurst** f German

salami; ~**zustand** m permanent condition.

Daumen [ˈdaʊmən] m -s, - thumb; ~**lutscher** m thumb-sucker.

Daune [ˈdaʊnə] f -, ~n down; ~**ndecke** f down duvet or quilt.

davon [daˈfɔn] ad of it; (räumlich) away; (weg von) from it; (Grund) because of it; **das kommt** ~! that's what you get; ~ **abgesehen** apart from that; ~ **sprechen/wissen** talk/know of or about it; **was habe ich** ~? what's the point?; ~**gehen** vi irreg leave, go away; ~**kommen** vi irreg escape; ~**laufen** vi irreg run away; ~**tragen** vt irreg carry off; Verletzung receive.

davor [daˈfoːr] ad (räumlich) in front of it; (zeitlich) before (that); ~ **warnen** warn about it.

dazu [daˈtsuː] ad legen, stellen by it; essen, singen with it; **und** ~ **noch** and in addition; **ein Beispiel/seine Gedanken** ~ one example for/his thoughts on this; **wie komme ich denn** ~? why should I?; ~ **fähig sein** be capable of it; **sich** ~ **äußern** say sth on it; ~**gehören** vi belong to it; ~**gehörig** a appropriate; ~**kommen** vi irreg (Ereignisse) happen too; (an einen Ort) come along; ~**mal** [ˈdaːtsuːmaːl] ad in those days.

dazwischen [daˈtsvɪʃən] ad in between; (räumlich auch) between (them); (zusammen mit) among them; **der Unterschied** ~ the difference between them; ~**kommen** vi irreg (hineingeraten) get caught in it; **es ist etwas** ~**gekommen** something cropped up; ~**reden** vi (unterbrechen) interrupt; (sich einmischen) interfere; ~**treten** vi irreg intervene.

Debatte [deˈbatə] f -, ~n debate.

Deck [dɛk] nt -(e)s, -s or -e deck; **an** ~ **gehen** go on deck; ~e f -, ~n cover; (Bett~) blanket; (Tisch~) tablecloth; (Zimmer~) ceiling; **unter einer** ~e **stecken** be hand in glove; ~**el** m -s, - lid; **d**~**en** vt cover; vr coincide; vi lay the table; ~**mantel** m: **unter dem** ~**mantel von** under the guise of; ~**name** m assumed name; ~**ung** f (Schützen) covering; (Schutz) cover; (Sport) defence; (Übereinstimmen) agreement; **d**~**ungsgleich** a congruent.

Defekt [deˈfɛkt] m -(e)s, -e fault, defect; **d**~ a faulty.

defensiv [defɛnˈsiːf] a defensive.

definieren [defiˈniːrən] vt define.

Definition [definitsiˈoːn] f definition.

definitiv [definiˈtiːf] a definite.

Defizit [ˈdeːfitsɪt] nt -s, -e deficit.

deftig [ˈdɛftɪç] a Essen large; Witz coarse.

Degen [ˈdeːgən] m -s, - sword.

degenerieren [degeneˈriːrən] vi degenerate.

degradieren [degraˈdiːrən] vt degrade.

Dehn- [ˈdeːn] cpd: **d**~**bar** a elastic; (fig) Begriff loose; ~**barkeit** f elasticity; looseness; **d**~**en** vtr stretch; ~**ung** f stretching.

Deich [daɪç] m -(e)s, -e dyke.

Deichsel ['daɪksəl] *f* -, -n shaft; d~n *vt* (*fig, col*) wangle.

dein [daɪn] *pron* (**D~** *in Briefen*) your; ~e(r,s) yours; ~er *pron gen of* du of you; ~erse!ts ad on your part; ~esgleichen *pron* people like you; ~etwegen, ~etwillen ad (*für dich*) for your sake; (*wegen dir*) on your account; ~ige *pron*: der/die/das ~ige yours.

dekadent [deka'dɛnt] *a* decadent.

Dekadenz *f* decadence.

Dekan [de'kaːn] *m* -s, -e dean.

Deklination [deklinatsi'oːn] *f* declension.

deklinieren [dekli'niːrən] *vt* decline.

Dekolleté [dekɔl'teː] *nt* -s, -s low neckline.

Deko- [deko] *cpd*: ~rateur [-ra'töːr] *m* window dresser; ~ration [-ratsi'oːn] *f* decoration; (*in Laden*) window dressing; d~rativ [-ra'tiːf] *a* decorative; d~rieren [-'riːrən] *vt* decorate; *Schaufenster* dress.

Delegation [delegatsi'oːn] *f* delegation.

delikat [deli'kaːt] *a* (*zart, heikel*) delicate; (*köstlich*) delicious.

Delikatesse [delika'tɛsə] *f* -, -n delicacy; (*pl: Feinkost*) delicatessen *pl*; ~n-geschäft *nt* delicatessen (shop).

Delikt [de'lɪkt] *nt* -(e)s, -e (*Jur*) offence.

Delle ['dɛlə] *f*-, -n (*col*) dent.

Delphin [dɛl'fiːn] *m* -s, -e dolphin.

Delta ['dɛltə] *nt* -s, -s delta.

dem [de(ː)m] *art dat of* der.

Demagoge [dema'goːgə] *m* -n, -n demagogue.

Demarkationslinie [demarkatsi'oːnzliːniə] *f* demarcation line.

dementieren [demɛn'tiːrən] *vt* deny.

dem- *cpd*: ~gemäß, ~nach ad accordingly; ~nächst ad shortly.

Demokrat [demo'kraːt] *m* -en, -en democrat; ~ie [-'tiː] *f* democracy; d~isch *a* democratic; d~isieren [-i'siːrən] *vt* democratize.

demolieren [demo'liːrən] *vt* demolish.

Demon- [demɔn] *cpd*: ~strant(in *f*) [-'strant(ɪn)] *m* demonstrator; ~stration [-stratsi'oːn] *f* demonstration; d~strativ [-stra'tiːf] *a* demonstrative; *Protest* pointed; d~strieren [-'striːrən] *vti* demonstrate.

Demoskopie [demosko'piː] *f* public opinion research.

Demut ['deːmuːt] *f*- humility.

demütig ['deːmyːtɪç] *a* humble; ~en ['deːmyːtɪgən] *vt* humiliate; D~ung *f* humiliation.

demzufolge ['deːmtsuːˈfɔlgə] ad accordingly.

den [de(ː)n] *art acc of* der.

denen ['deːnən] *pron dat of* diese.

Denk- [dɛŋk] *cpd*: ~art *f* mentality; d~bar *a* conceivable; d~en *vti irreg* think; ~en *nt* -s thinking; ~er *m* -s, - thinker; ~fähigkeit *f* intelligence; d~faul *a* lazy; ~fehler *m* logical error; ~mal *nt* -s, ̈er monument; d~würdig *a* memorable; ~zettel *m*: jdm einen ~zettel verpassen teach sb a lesson.

denn [dɛn] *cj* for; ad then; (*nach Komparativ*) than.

dennoch ['dɛn'nɔx] *cj* nevertheless.

Denunziant [denʊntsi'ant] *m* informer.

deponieren [depo'niːrən] *vt* (*Comm*) deposit.

Depot [de'poː] *nt* -s, -s warehouse; (*Bus*—, *Rail*) depot; (*Bank*—) strongroom.

Depression [deprɛsi'oːn] *f* depression.

deprimieren [depri'miːrən] *vt* depress.

der [de(ː)r] *def art* the; *rel pron* that, which; (*jemand*) who; *demon pron* this one; ~art ad so; (*solcher Art*) such; ~artig *a* such, this sort of.

derb [dɛrp] *a* sturdy; *Kost* solid; (*grob*) coarse; D~heit *f* sturdiness; solidity; coarseness.

der- *cpd*: '~'gleichen *pron* such; '~jenige *pron* he; she; it; (*rel*) the one (who); that (which); '~'maßen ad to such an extent, so; ~'selbe *art, pron* the same; '~'well(en) ad in the meantime; '~-'zeitig *a* present, current; (*damalig*) then.

des [dɛs] *art gen of* der.

Deserteur [dezɛr'töːr] *m* deserter.

desertieren [dezɛr'tiːrən] *vi* desert.

desgleichen [dɛs'glaɪçən] *pron* the same.

deshalb ['dɛs'halp] ad therefore, that's why.

Desinfektion [dezɪnfɛktsi'oːn] *f* disinfection; ~smittel *nt* disinfectant.

desinfizieren [dezɪnfi'tsiːrən] *vt* disinfect.

dessen ['dɛsən] *pron gen of* der, das; ~ungeachtet ad nevertheless, regardless.

Dessert [dɛ'sɛːr] *nt* -s, -s dessert.

Destillation [dɛstɪlatsi'oːn] *f* distillation.

destillieren [dɛstɪ'liːrən] *vt* distil.

desto ['dɛsto] ad all or so much the; ~ besser all the better.

deswegen ['dɛsˈveːgən] *cj* therefore, hence.

Detail [de'taɪ] *nt* -s, -s detail; d~lieren [deta'jiːrən] *vt* specify, give details of.

Detektiv [detɛk'tiːf] *m* -s, -e detective.

Detektor [de'tɛktɔr] *m* (*Tech*) detector.

deut- ['dɔʏt] *cpd*: ~en *vt* interpret, explain; *vi* point (*auf* +acc to *or* at); ~lich *a* clear; *Unterschied* distinct; D~lichkeit *f* clarity; distinctness; D~ung *f* interpretation.

Devise [de'viːzə] *f* -, -n motto, device; (*pl: Fin*) foreign currency *or* exchange.

Dezember [de'tsɛmbər] *m* -(s), - December.

dezent [de'tsɛnt] *a* discreet.

dezimal [detsi'maːl] *a* decimal; D~bruch *m* decimal (fraction); D~system *nt* decimal system.

Dia ['diːa] *nt* -s, -s *see* **Diapositiv**; ~betes [dia'beːtɛs] *m* -, - (*Med*) diabetes; ~gnose [dia'gnoːzə] *f* -, -n diagnosis; d~gonal [diago'naːl] *a* diagonal; ~gonale *f*-, -n diagonal.

Dialekt [dia'lɛkt] *m* -(e)s, -e dialect; ~ausdruck *m* dialect expression/word; d~frei *a* pure, standard; d~isch *a* dialectal; *Logik* dialectical.

Dialog [dia'loːk] *m* -(e)s, -e dialogue.

Diamant [dia'mant] *m* diamond.

Diapositiv [diapozi'ti:f] *nt* **-s, -e** (*Phot*) slide, transparency.

Diät [di'ɛ:t] *f* - diet; **~en** *pl* (*Pol*) allowance.

dich [dɪç] *pron acc of* **du** you; yourself.

dicht [dɪçt] *a* dense; *Nebel* thick; *Gewebe* close; (*undurchlässig*) (water)tight; (*fig*) concise; *ad:* **~ an/bei** close to; **~bevölkert** *a* densely *or* heavily populated; **D~e** *f* -, **-n** density; thickness; closeness; (water)tightness; (*fig*) conciseness; **~en** *vt* (*dicht machen*) make watertight; seal; (*Naut*) caulk; *vti* (*Liter*) compose, write; **D~er(in** *f)* *m* **-s,** - poet; (*Autor*) writer; **~erisch** *a* poetical; **~halten** *vi irreg* (*col*) keep mum; **D~ung** *f* (*Tech*) washer; (*Aut*) gasket; (*Gedichte*) poetry; (*Prosa*) (piece of) writing.

dick [dɪk] *a* thick; (*fett*) fat; **durch ~ und dünn** through thick and thin; **D~e** *f* -, **-n** thickness; fatness; **~fellig** *a* thickskinned; **~flüssig** *a* viscous; **D~icht** *nt* **-s, -e** thicket; **D~kopf** *m* mule; **D~milch** *f* soured milk.

die [di:] *def art see* **der**.

Dieb(in *f)* [di:p/di:bɪn] *m* **-(e)s, -e** thief; **d~isch** *a* thieving; (*col*) immense; **~stahl** *m* **-(e)s, ⁓e** theft.

Diele ['di:lə] *f* -, **-n** (*Brett*) board; (*Flur*) hall, lobby; (*Eis*—) ice-cream parlour; (*Tanz*—) dance hall.

dienen ['di:nən] *vi* serve (*jdm* sb).

Diener *m* **-s,** - servant; **~in** *f* (maid)-servant; **~schaft** *f* servants *pl*.

Dienst [di:nst] *m* **-(e)s, -e** service; **außer ~** retired; **~ haben** be on duty; **der öffentliche ~** the civil service; **~ag** *m* Tuesday; **d~ags** *ad* on Tuesdays; **d~bote** *m* servant; **d~eifrig** *a* zealous; **d~frei** *a* off duty; **~geheimnis** *nt* professional secret; **~gespräch** *nt* business call; **~grad** *m* rank; **d~habend** *a Arzt* on duty; **d~lich** *a* official; **~mädchen** *nt* domestic servant; **~reise** *f* business trip; **~stelle** *f* office; **d~tuend** *a* on duty; **~vorschrift** *f* service regulations *pl*; **~weg** *m* official channels *pl*; **~zeit** *f* office hours *pl*; (*Mil*) period of service.

dies- [di:s] *cpd:* **~bezüglich** *a Frage* on this matter; **~e(r,s)** [di:zə(r,z)] *pron* this (one); **~elbe** [di:'zɛlbə] *pron, art* the same; **D~elöl** *nt* diesel oil; **~ig** *a* drizzly; **~jährig** *a* this year's; **~mal** *ad* this time; **~seits** *prep +gen* on this side; **D~seits** *nt* - this life.

Dietrich ['di:trɪç] *m* **-s, -e** picklock.

differential [dɪfɛrɛntsi'a:l] *a* differential; **D~getriebe** *nt* differential gear; **D~rechnung** *f* differential calculus.

differenzieren [dɪfɛrɛn'tsi:rən] *vt* make differences in; **differenziert** *a* complex.

Dikt- [dɪkt] *cpd:* **~aphon** [-a'fo:n] *nt* dictaphone; **~at** [-'ta:t] *nt* **-(e)s, -e** dictation; **~ator** [-'ta:tɔr] *m* dictator; **d~atorisch** [-a'to:rɪʃ] *a* dictatorial; **~atur** [-a'tu:r] *f* dictatorship; **d~ieren** [-'ti:rən] *vt* dictate.

Dilemma [di'lɛma] *nt* **-s, -s** *or* **-ta** dilemma.

Dilettant [dilɛ'tant] *m* dilettante, amateur;

d~isch *a* amateurisch, dilettante.

Dimension [dimɛnzi'o:n] *f* dimension.

Ding [dɪŋ] *nt* **-(e)s, -e** thing, object; **d~lich** *a* real, concrete; **~sbums** ['dɪŋksbums] *nt* - (col) thingummybob.

Diözese [diø'tse:zə] *f* -, **-n** diocese.

Diphtherie [dɪfte'ri:] *f* diphtheria.

Diplom [di'plo:m] *nt* **-(e)s, -e** diploma, certificate; **~at** [-'ma:t] *m* **-en, -en** diplomat; **~atie** [-a'ti:] *f* diplomacy; **d~atisch** [-'ma:tɪʃ] *a* diplomatic; **~ingenieur** *m* qualified engineer.

dir [di:r] *pron dat of* **du** (to) you.

direkt [di'rɛkt] *a* direct; **D~or** *m* director; (*Sch*) principal, headmaster; **D~orium** [-'to:rium] *nt* board of directors; **D~übertragung** *f* live broadcast.

Dirigent [diri'gɛnt] *m* conductor.

dirigieren [diri'gi:rən] *vt* direct; (*Mus*) conduct.

Dirne ['dɪrnə] *f* -, **-n** prostitute.

Diskont [dɪs'kɔnt] *m* **-s, -e** discount; **~satz** *m* rate of discount.

Diskothek [dɪsko'te:k] *f* -, **-en** disco-(theque).

Diskrepanz [dɪskre'pants] *f* discrepancy.

diskret [dɪs'kre:t] *a* discreet; **D~ion** [-tsi'o:n] *f* discretion.

Diskussion [dɪskusi'o:n] *f* discussion; debate; **zur ~ stehen** be under discussion.

diskutabel [dɪsku'ta:bəl] *a* debatable.

diskutieren [dɪsku'ti:rən] *vti* discuss; debate.

Dissertation [dɪsɛrtatsi'o:n] *f* dissertation, doctoral thesis.

Distanz [dɪs'tants] *f* distance.

Distel ['dɪstəl] *f* -, **-n** thistle.

Disziplin [dɪstsi'pli:n] *f* discipline.

divers [di'vɛrs] *a* various.

Dividende [divi'dɛndə] *f* -, **-n** dividend.

dividieren [divi'di:rən] *vt* divide (*durch* by).

doch [dɔx] *ad:* **das ist nicht wahr!** ≈ **~!** that's not true! ≈ yes it is!; **nicht ~!** oh no!; **er kam ~ noch** he came after all; *cj* (*aber*) but; (*trotzdem*) all the same.

Docht [dɔxt] *m* **-(e)s, -e** wick.

Dock [dɔk] *nt* **-s, -s** *or* **-e** dock.

Dogge ['dɔgə] *f* -, **-n** bulldog.

Dogma ['dɔgma] *nt* **-s, -men** dogma; **d~tisch** [dɔ'gma:tɪʃ] *a* dogmatic.

Doktor ['dɔktɔr] *m* **-s, -en** [-'to:rən] doctor; **~and** [-'rant] *m* **-en, -en** candidate for a doctorate; **~arbeit** *f* doctoral thesis; **~titel** *m* doctorate.

Dokument [doku'mɛnt] *nt* document; **~arbericht** [-'ta:rbərɪçt] *m* documentary; **~arfilm** *m* documentary (film); **d~arisch** *a* documentary.

Dolch [dɔlç] *m* **-(e)s, -e** dagger.

dolmetschen ['dɔlmɛtʃən] *vti* interpret.

Dolmetscher(in *f)* *m* **-s,** - interpreter.

Dom [do:m] *m* **-(e)s, -e** cathedral.

dominieren [domi'ni:rən] *vt* dominate; *vi* predominate.

Dompfaff ['do:mpfaf] *m* bullfinch.

Dompteur [dɔmp'tø:r] *m*, **Dompteuse** [dɔmp'tø:zə] *f* (*Zirkus*) trainer.

Donner ['dɔnər] *m* **-s**, - thunder; **d~n** *vi impers* thunder; **~stag** *m* Thursday; **~wetter** *nt* thunderstorm; *(fig)* dressing-down; *interj* good heavens!

doof [do:f] *a (col)* daft, stupid.

Doppel ['dɔpəl] *nt* **-s**, - duplicate; *(Sport)* doubles; **~bett** *nt* double bed; **~fenster** *nt* double glazing; **~gänger** *m* **-s**, - double; **~punkt** *m* colon; **d~sinnig** *a* ambiguous; **~stecker** *m* two-way adaptor; **d~t** *a* double; **in d~ter Ausführung** in duplicate; **~verdiener** *pl* two-income family; **~zentner** *m* 100 kilograms; **~zimmer** *nt* double room.

Dorf [dɔrf] *nt* **-(e)s**, **-̈er** village; **~bewohner** *m* villager.

Dorn [dɔrn] *m* **-(e)s**, **-en** *(Bot)* thorn; *pl* **-e** *(Schnallen—)* tongue, pin; **d~ig** *a* thorny; **~röschen** *nt* Sleeping Beauty.

dörren ['dœrən] *vt* dry.

Dörrobst ['dœro:pst] *nt* dried fruit.

Dorsch [dɔrʃ] *m* **-(e)s**, **-e** cod.

dort [dɔrt] *ad* there; **~ drüben** over there; **~her** from there; **~hin** (to) there; **~ig** *a* of that place; in that town.

Dose ['do:zə] *f* **-**, **-n** box; *(Blech—)* tin, can; **~nöffner** *m* tin or can opener.

dösen ['dø:zən] *vi (col)* doze.

Dosis ['do:zɪs] *f* **-**, **Dosen** dose.

Dotter ['dɔtər] *m* **-s**, - egg yolk.

Dozent [do'tsɛnt] *m* university lecturer.

Drache ['draxə] *m* **-n**, **-n** *(Tier)* dragon; **~n** *m* **-**, - kite.

Draht [dra:t] *m* **-(e)s**, **-̈e** wire; **auf ~ sein** be on the ball; **~gitter** *nt* wire grating; **~seil** *nt* cable; **~seilbahn** *f* cable railway, funicular; **~zange** *f* pliers *pl*.

drall [dral] *a* strapping; *Frau* buxom.

Drama ['dra:ma] *nt* **-s**, **Dramen** drama, play; **~tiker** [-'ma:tikər] *m* **-s**, - dramatist; **d~tisch** [-'ma:tiʃ] *a* dramatic.

dran [dran] *ad (col) see* **daran**.

Drang [draŋ] *m* **-(e)s**, **-̈e** *(Trieb)* impulse, urge, desire *(nach* for); *(Druck)* pressure.

drängeln ['drɛŋəln] *vti* push, jostle.

drängen ['drɛŋən] *vt (schieben)* push, press; *(antreiben)* urge; *vi (eilig sein)* be urgent; *(Zeit)* press; **auf etw** *(acc)* **~** press for sth.

drastisch ['drastɪʃ] *a* drastic.

drauf [drauf] *ad (col) see* **darauf**; **D~gänger** *m* **-s**, - daredevil.

draußen ['drausən] *ad* outside, out-of-doors.

Dreck [drɛk] *m* **-(e)s** mud, dirt; **d~ig** *a* dirty, filthy.

Dreh- ['dre:] *cpd:* **~achse** *f* axis of rotation; **~arbeiten** *pl (Cine)* shooting; **~bank** *f* lathe; **d~bar** *a* revolving; **~buch** *nt (Cine)* script; **d~en** *vti* turn, rotate; *Zigaretten* roll; *Film* shoot; *vi* turn; *(handeln von)* be *(um* about); **~orgel** *f* barrel organ; **~tür** *f* revolving door; **~ung** *f (Rotation)* rotation; *(Um—, Wendung)* turn; **~wurm** *m (col)* **den ~wurm haben/bekommen** be/become dizzy; **~zahl** *f* rate of revolutions; **~zahlmesser** *m* rev(olution) counter.

drei [drai] *num* three; **D~eck** *nt* triangle; **~eckig** *a* triangular; **~einhalb** *num* three and a half; **D~einigkeit** [-'ainiçkait] *f*, **D~faltigkeit** [-'faltiçkait] *f* Trinity; **~erlei** *a inv* of three kinds; **~fach** *a,ad* triple, treble; **~hundert** *num* three hundred; **D~königsfest** *nt* Epiphany; **~mal** *ad* three times, thrice; **~malig** *a* three times.

dreinreden ['drainre:dən] *vi:* **jdm ~** *(dazwischenreden)* interrupt sb; *(sich einmischen)* interfere with sb.

dreißig ['draisɪç] *num* thirty.

dreist [draist] *a* bold, audacious; **D~igkeit** *f* boldness, audacity.

drei- *cpd:* **~viertel** *num* three-quarters; **D~viertelstunde** *f* three-quarters of an hour; **~zehn** *num* thirteen.

dreschen ['drɛʃən] *vt irreg* thresh.

dressieren [drɛ'si:rən] *vt* train.

Drill- ['drɪl] *cpd:* **~bohrer** *m* light drill; **d~en** *vt (bohren)* drill, bore; *(Mil)* drill; *(fig)* train; **~ing** *m* triplet.

drin [drɪn] *ad (col) see* **darin**.

dringen ['drɪŋən] *vi irreg (Wasser, Licht, Kälte)* penetrate *(durch* through; *in +acc* into); **auf etw** *(acc)* **~** insist on sth; **in jdn ~** entreat sb.

dringend ['drɪŋənt], **dringlich** ['drɪŋlɪç] *a* urgent.

Dringlichkeit *f* urgency.

drinnen ['drɪnən] *ad* inside, indoors.

dritte(r,s) ['drɪtə(r,z)] *a* third; **D~l** *nt* **-s**, - third; **~ns** *ad* thirdly.

droben ['dro:bən] *ad* above, up there.

Droge ['dro:gə] *f* **-**, **-n** drug; **d~nabhängig** *a* addicted to drugs; **~rie** [-'ri:] *f* chemist's shop.

Drogist [dro'gɪst] *m* pharmacist, chemist.

drohen ['dro:ən] *vi* threaten *(jdm* sb).

dröhnen ['drø:nən] *vi (Motor)* roar; *(Stimme, Musik)* ring, resound.

Drohung ['dro:ʊŋ] *f* threat.

drollig ['drɔlɪç] *a* droll.

Droschke ['drɔʃkə] *f* **-**, **-n** cab; **~nkutscher** *m* cabman.

Drossel ['drɔsəl] *f* **-**, **-n** thrush.

drüben ['dry:bən] *ad* over there, on the other side.

drüber ['dry:bər] *ad (col) see* **darüber**.

Druck [drʊk] *m* **-(e)s**, **-e** *(Phys, Zwang)* pressure; *(Print) (Vorgang)* printing; *(Produkt)* print; *(fig: Belastung)* burden, weight; **~buchstabe** *m* block letter.

Drück- ['drʏk] *cpd:* **~eberger** *m* **-s**, - shirker, dodger; **d~en** *vti* Knopf, Hand press; *(zu eng sein)* pinch; *(fig)* Preise keep down; *(fig: belasten)* oppress, weigh down; **jdm etw in die Hand d~en** press sth into sb's hand; *vr:* **sich vor etw** *(dat)* **d~en** get out of (doing) sth; **d~end** *a* oppressive; **~er** *m* **-s**, - button; *(Tür—)* handle; *(Gewehr—)* trigger.

Druck- *cpd:* **~er** *m* **-s**, - printer; **~e'rei** *f* printing works, press; **~erschwärze** *f* printer's ink; **~fehler** *m* misprint; **~knopf** *m* press stud, snap fastener; **~mittel** *nt* leverage; **~sache** *f* printed matter; **~schrift** *f* block or printed letters *pl*.

drunten ['druntən] *ad* below, down there.

Drüse ['dry:zə] *f* **-**, **-n** gland.

Dschungel ['dʒʊŋəl] *m* **-s,** - jungle.

du [du:] *pron* (**D~** *in Briefen*) you.

ducken ['dʊkən] *vt* Kopf, Person duck; (*fig*) take down a peg or two; *vr* duck.

Duckmäuser ['dʊkmɔʏzər] *m* **-s,** - yesman.

Dudelsack ['du:dəlzak] *m* bagpipes *pl.*

Duell [du'ɛl] *nt* **-s, -e** duel.

Duett [du'ɛt] *nt* **-(e)s, -e** duet.

Duft [dʊft] *m* **-(e)s, ¨e** scent, odour; **d~en** *vi* smell, be fragrant; **d~ig** *a Stoff, Kleid* delicate, diaphanous; *Muster* fine.

duld- ['dʊld] *cpd:* **~en** *vti* suffer; (*zulassen*) tolerate; **~sam** *a* tolerant.

dumm [dʊm] *a* stupid; **das wird mir zu ~** that's just too much; **der D~e sein** be the loser; **~dreist** *a* impudent; **~erweise** *ad* stupidly; **D~heit** *f* stupidity; (*Tat*) blunder, stupid mistake; **D~kopf** *m* blockhead.

dumpf [dʊmpf] *a Ton* hollow, dull; *Luft* close; *Erinnerung, Schmerz* vague; **D~heit** *f* hollowness, dullness; closeness; vagueness; **~ig** *a* musty.

Düne ['dy:nə] *f* **-, -n** dune.

Dung [dʊŋ] *m* **-(e)s** *see* **Dünger.**

düngen ['dyŋən] *vt* manure.

Dünger *m* **-s,** - dung, manure; (*künstlich*) fertilizer.

dunkel ['dʊŋkəl] *a* dark; *Stimme* deep; *Ahnung* vague; (*rätselhaft*) obscure; (*verdächtig*) dubious, shady; **im ~n tappen** (*fig*) grope in the dark.

Dünkel ['dyŋkəl] *m* **-s** self-conceit; **d~haft** *a* conceited.

Dunkel- *cpd:* **~heit** *f* darkness; (*fig*) obscurity; **~kammer** *f* (*Phot*) dark room; **d~n** *vi impers* grow dark; **~ziffer** *f* estimated number of unnotified cases.

dünn [dyn] *a* thin; **~flüssig** *a* watery, thin; **~gesät** *a* scarce; **D~heit** *f* thinness.

Dunst [dʊnst] *m* **-es, ¨e** vapour; (*Wetter*) haze.

dünsten ['dynstən] *vt* steam.

dunstig [dʊnstɪç] *a* vaporous; *Wetter* hazy, misty.

Duplikat [dupli'ka:t] *nt* **-(e)s, -e** duplicate.

Dur [du:r] *nt* **-, -** (*Mus*) major.

durch [dʊrç] *prep* +acc through; (*Mittel, Ursache*) by; (*Zeit*) during; **den Sommer ~** during the summer; **8 Uhr ~** past 8 o'clock; **~ und ~** completely; **~arbeiten** *vti* work through; *vr* work one's way through; **~'aus** *ad* completely; (*unbedingt*) definitely; **~beißen** *irreg vt* bite through; *vr* (*fig*) battle on; **~blättern** *vt* leaf through.

Durchblick ['dʊrçblɪk] *m* view; (*fig*) comprehension; **d~en** *vi* look through; (*col: verstehen*) understand (*bei etw* sth); **etw d~en lassen** (*fig*) hint at sth.

durch'bohren *vt insep* bore through, pierce.

durchbrechen ['dʊrçbrɛçən] *vti irreg* break; [dʊrç'brɛçən] *vt irreg insep* Schranken break through; Schallmauer break; Gewohnheit break free from.

durch- ['dʊrç] *cpd:* **~brennen** *vi irreg* (*Draht, Sicherung*) burn through; (*col*) run

---

away; **~bringen** *irreg vt* get through; *Geld* squander; *vr* make a living.

Durchbruch ['dʊrçbrux] *m* (*Öffnung*) opening; (*Mil*) breach; (*von Gefühlen etc*) eruption; (*der Zähne*) cutting; (*fig*) breakthrough; **zum ~ kommen** break through.

durch- *cpd:* **~dacht** [dʊrç'daxt] *a* well thought-out; **~'denken** *vt irreg insep* think out.

durch- ['dʊrç] *cpd:* **~diskutieren** *vt* talk over, discuss; **~drängen** *vr* force one's way through; **~drehen** *vt Fleisch* mince; *vi* (*col*) crack up.

durchdringen ['dʊrçdrɪŋən] *vi irreg* penetrate, get through; **mit etw ~** get one's way with sth; [dʊrç'drɪŋən] *vt irreg insep* penetrate.

durcheinander [dʊrçʔaɪ'nandər] *ad* in a mess, in confusion; (*col: verwirrt*) confused; **~ trinken** mix one's drinks; **D~** *nt* **-s** (*Verwirrung*) confusion; (*Unordnung*) mess; **~bringen** *vt irreg* mess up; (*verwirren*) confuse; **~reden** *vi* talk at the same time.

durch- *cpd:* **D~'fahrt** *f* transit; (*Verkehr*) thoroughfare; **D~fall** *m* (*Med*) diarrhoea; **~fallen** *vi irreg* fall through; (*in Prüfung*) fail; **~finden** *vr irreg* find one's way through.

durch'forschen *vt insep* explore.

durch- ['dʊrç] *cpd:* **~fressen** *vt irreg* eat through; **~fragen** *vr* find one's way by asking.

durchführ- ['dʊrçfy:r] *cpd:* **~bar** *a* feasible, practicable; **~en** *vt* carry out; **D~ung** *f* execution, performance.

Durchgang ['dʊrçgaŋ] *m* passage(way); (*bei Produktion, Versuch*) run; (*Sport*) round; (*bei Wahl*) ballot; **~ verboten** no thoroughfare; **~shandel** *m* transit trade; **~slager** *nt* transit camp; **~sstadium** *nt* transitory stage; **~sverkehr** *m* through traffic.

durchgefroren ['dʊrçgəfro:rən] *a See* completely frozen; *Mensch* frozen stiff.

durchgehen ['dʊrçge:ən] *irreg vt* (*behandeln*) go over; *vi* go through; (*ausreißen: Pferd*) break loose; (*Mensch*) run away; **mein Temperament ging mit mir durch** my temper got the better of me; **jdm etw ~ lassen** let sb get away with sth; **~d** *a Zug* through; *Öffnungszeiten* continuous.

durch- ['dʊrç] *cpd:* **~greifen** *vi irreg* take strong action; **~halten** *irreg vi* last out; *vt* keep up; **~hecheln** *vt* (*col*) gossip about; **~kommen** *vi irreg* get through; (*überleben*) pull through.

durch'kreuzen *vt insep* thwart, frustrate.

durch- ['dʊrç] *cpd:* **~lassen** *vt irreg Person* let through; *Wasser* let in; **~lässig** *a* leaky; **D~lauf(wasser)erhitzer** *m* **-s,** - (hot water) geyser.

durch- *cpd:* **~'leben** *vt insep* live *or* go through, experience; '**~lesen** *vt irreg* read through; '**~leuchten** *vt insep* X-ray; **~löchern** [-'lœçərn] *vt insep* perforate; (*mit Löchern*) punch holes in; (*mit Kugeln*) riddle; '**~machen** *vt* go through; **die Nacht ~machen** make a night of it.

Durch- ['durç] cpd: ~**marsch** m march through; ~**messer** m -s, - diameter.

durch'nässen vt insep soak (through).

durch- ['durç] cpd: ~**nehmen** vt irreg go over; ~**numerieren** vt number consecutively; ~**pausen** vt trace; ~**peitschen** vt (lit) whip soundly; (fig) Gesetzentwurf, Reform force through.

durchqueren [durç'kve:rən] vt insep cross.

durch- ['durç] cpd: **D~reiche** f -, -n (serving) hatch; **D~reise** f transit; **auf der D~reise** passing through; Güter in transit; ~**ringen** vr irreg reach after a long struggle; ~**rosten** vi rust through.

durchs [durçs] = **durch das**.

Durchsage ['durçza:gə] f -, -n intercom or radio announcement.

durchschauen ['durç'ʃauən] vi (lit) look or see through; [durç'ʃauən] vt insep Person, Lüge see through.

durchscheinen ['durç'ʃainən] vi irreg shine through; ~**d** a translucent.

Durchschlag ['durçʃla:k] m (Doppel) carbon copy; (Sieb) strainer; **d~en** irreg vt (entzweischlagen) split (in two); (sieben) sieve; vi (zum Vorschein kommen) emerge, come out; vr get by; **d~end** a resounding.

durch ['durç] cpd: ~**schlüpfen** vi slip through; ~**schneiden** vt irreg cut through.

Durchschnitt ['durçʃnit] m (Mittelwert) average; **über/unter dem ~** above/below average; **im ~** on average; **d~lich** a average; ad on average; ~**sgeschwindigkeit** f average speed; ~**smensch** m average man, man in the street; ~**swert** m average.

durch- cpd: '**D~schrift** f copy; ~'**schwimmen** vt irreg insep swim across; '~**sehen** vt irreg look through.

durchsetzen ['durçzɛtsən] vt enforce; **seinen Kopf ~** get one's own way; vr (Erfolg haben) succeed; (sich behaupten) get one's way; [durç'zɛtsən] vt insep mix.

Durchsicht ['durçziçt] f looking through, checking; **d~ig** a transparent; ~**igkeit** f transparence.

durch- cpd: '~**sickern** vi seep through; (fig) leak out; '~**sieben** vt sieve; '~**sprechen** vt irreg talk over; '~**stehen** vt irreg live through; ~**stöbern** [-'ʃtø:bərn] vt insep ransack, search through; '~**streichen** vt irreg cross out; '~**suchen** vt insep search; **D~'suchung** f search; ~'**tränken** vt insep soak; ~**trieben** [-'tri:bən] a cunning, wily; ~'**wachsen** a (lit) Speck streaky; (fig: mittelmäßig) so-so.

durch- ['durç] cpd: ~**weg** ad throughout, completely; ~**zählen** vt count; vi count off; ~**ziehen** irreg vt Faden draw through; vi pass through.

durch- cpd: ~'**zucken** vt insep shoot or flash through; '**D~zug** m (Luft) draught; (von Truppen, Vögeln) passage; '~**zwängen** vtr squeeze or force through.

dürfen ['dyrfən] vi irreg be allowed; **darf ich?** may I?; **es darf geraucht werden** you may smoke; **was darf es sein?** what

can I do for you?; **das darf nicht geschehen** that must not happen; **das ~ Sie mir glauben** you can believe me; **es dürfte Ihnen bekannt sein, daß ... as** you will probably know ...

dürftig ['dyrftiç] a (ärmlich) needy, poor; (unzulänglich) inadequate.

dürr [dyr] a dried-up; Land arid; (mager) skinny, gaunt; **D~e** f -, -n aridity; (Zeit) drought; (Magerkeit) skinniness.

Durst [durst] m -(e)s thirst; ~ **haben** be thirsty; **d~ig** a thirsty.

Dusche ['duʃə] f -, -n shower; **d~n** vir have a shower.

Düse ['dy:zə] f -, -n nozzle; (Flugzeug—) jet; ~**nantrieb** m jet propulsion; ~**nflugzeug** nt jet (plane); ~**njäger** m jet fighter.

Dussel ['dusəl] m -s, - (col) twit.

düster ['dy:stər] a dark; Gedanken, Zukunft gloomy; **D~keit** f darkness, gloom; gloominess.

Dutzend ['dutsənt] nt -s, -e dozen; **d~(e)mal** ad a dozen times; ~**mensch** m man in the street; **d~weise** ad by the dozen.

duzen ['du:tsən] vtr use the familiar form of address or 'du' (jdn to or with sb).

Dynamik [dy'na:mik] f (Phys) dynamics; (fig: Schwung) momentum; (von Mensch) dynamism.

dynamisch [dy'na:miʃ] a (lit, fig) dynamic.

Dynamit [dyna'mi:t] nt -s dynamite.

Dynamo [dy'na:mo] m -s, -s dynamo.

D-Zug ['de:tsu:k] m through train.

E

E, e [e:] nt E, e.

Ebbe ['ɛbə] f -, -n low tide.

eben ['e:bən] a level; (glatt) smooth; ad just; (bestätigend) exactly; ~ **deswegen** just because of that; ~**bürtig** a: **jdm ~bürtig sein** be sb's peer; **E~e** f -, -n plain; ~**erdig** a at ground level; ~**falls** ad likewise; **E~heit** f levelness; smoothness; ~**so** ad just as; ~**sogut** ad just as well; ~**sooft** ad just as often; ~**soviel** ad just as much; ~**soweit** ad just as far; ~**sowenig** ad just as little.

Eber ['e:bər] m -s, - boar; ~**esche** f mountain ash, rowan.

ebnen ['e:bnən] vt level.

Echo ['ɛço] nt -s, -s echo.

echt [ɛçt] a genuine; (typisch) typical; **E~heit** f genuineness.

Eck- ['ɛk] cpd: ~**ball** m corner (kick); ~**e** f -, -n corner; (Math) angle; **e~ig** a angular; ~**zahn** m eye tooth.

edel ['e:dəl] a noble; **E~metall** nt rare metal; **E~stein** m precious stone.

Efeu ['e:fɔy] m -s ivy.

Effekt- [ɛ'fɛkt] cpd: ~**en** pl stocks pl; ~**enbörse** f Stock Exchange; ~**hasche'rei** f sensationalism; **e~iv** [-'ti:f] a effective, actual.

egal [e'ga:l] a all the same.

Ego- [ego] cpd: ~**ismus** [-'ismus] m selfishness, egoism; ~**ist** [-'ist] m egoist;

e~istisch *a* selfish, egoistic;
e~zentrisch [-'tsɛntrɪʃ] *a* egocentric, self-centred.

Ehe ['e:ə] *f* -, *in* marriage; **e~** *cj* before;
~brecher *m* -s, - adulterer;
~brecherin *f* adulteress; **~bruch** *m*
adultery; **~frau** *f* married woman; wife;
~leute *pl* married people *pl*; **e~lich** *a*
matrimonial; *Kind* legitimate; **e~malig** *a*
former; **e~mals** *ad* formerly; **~mann** *m*
married man; husband; **~paar** *nt*
married couple.

eher ['e:ər] *ad* (*früher*) sooner; (*lieber*)
rather, sooner; (*mehr*) more.

Ehe- *cpd*: **~ring** *m* wedding ring;
~scheidung *f* divorce; **~schließung** *f*
marriage.

eheste(r,s) ['e:əstə(r,z)] *a* (*früheste*) first,
earliest; **am ~n** (*liebsten*) soonest; (*meist*)
most; (*wahrscheinlichst*) most probably.

Ehr- ['e:r] *cpd*: **e~bar** *a* honourable,
respectable; **~e** *f* -, **-n** honour; **e~en** *vt*
honour; **~engast** *m* guest of honour;
e~enhaft *a* honourable; **~enmann** *m*
man of honour; **~enmitglied** *nt* honorary
member; **~enplatz** *m* place of honour;
~enrechte *pl* civic rights *pl*;
e~enrührig *a* defamatory; **~enrunde** *f*
lap of honour; **~ensache** *f* point of
honour; **e~envoll** *a* honourable;
~enwort *nt* word of honour; **e~erbietig**
a respectful; **~furcht** *f* awe, deep
respect; (*scheu*) **~gefühl** *nt* sense of honour;
~geiz *m* ambition; **e~geizig** *a*
ambitious; **e~lich** *a* honest; **~lichkeit** *f*
honesty; **e~los** *a* dishonourable; **~ung** *f*
honour(ing); **e~würdig** *a* venerable.

Ei [aɪ] *nt* **-(e)s, -er** egg; **e~** *interj* well,
well; (*beschwichtigend*) now, now.

Eich- [aɪç] *cpd*: **~amt** *nt* Office of
Weights and Measures; **~e** *f* -, **-n** oak
(tree); **~el** *f* -, **-n** acorn; (*Cards*) club;
e~en *vt* standardize; **~hörnchen** *nt*
squirrel; **~maß** *nt* standard; **~ung** *f*
standardization.

Eid ['aɪt] *m* **-(e)s, -e** oath; **~echse**
['aɪdɛksə] *f* -, **-n** lizard; **e~esstattliche
Erklärung** affidavit; **~genosse** *m* Swiss;
e~lich *a* (*sworn*) upon oath.

Ei- *cpd*: **~dotter** *nt* egg yolk; **~erbecher**
m eggcup; **~erkuchen** *m* omelette; pancake; **~erschale** *f* eggshell; **~erstock** *m*
ovary; **~eruhr** *f* egg timer.

Eifer ['aɪfər] *m* -s zeal, enthusiasm;
~sucht *f* jealousy; **e~süchtig** *a* jealous
(*auf* +acc of).

eifrig ['aɪfrɪç] *a* zealous, enthusiastic.

Eigelb ['aɪgɛlp] *nt* **-(e)s, -** egg yolk.

eigen ['aɪgən] *a* own; (—*artig*) peculiar;
mit der/dem ihm ~en . . . with that . . .
peculiar to him; **sich** (*dat*) **etw zu ~
machen** make sth one's own; **E~art** *f*
peculiarity; characteristic; **~artig** *a*
peculiar; **E~bedarf** *m* one's own requirements *pl*; **E~gewicht** *nt* dead weight;
~händig *a* with one's own hand;
E~heim *nt* owner-occupied house;
E~heit *f* peculiarity; **E~lob** *nt* self-praise; **~mächtig** *a* high-handed;
E~name *m* proper name; **~s** *ad*

expressly, on purpose; **E~schaft** *f*
quality, property, attribute; **E~schafts-
wort** *nt* adjective; **E~sinn** *m* obstinacy;
~sinnig *a* obstinate; **~tlich** *a* actual,
real; *ad* actually, really; **E~tor** *nt* own
goal; **E~tum** *nt* property; **E~tümer(in**
f) *m* -s, - owner, proprietor; **~tümlich** *a*
peculiar; **E~tümlichkeit** *f* peculiarity;
E~tumswohnung *f* freehold flat.

eignen ['aɪgnən] *vr* be suited.

Eignung *f* suitability.

Eil- ['aɪl] *cpd*: **~bote** *m* courier; **~brief** *m*
express letter; **~e** *f* - haste; **es hat keine
~e** there's no hurry; **e~en** *vi* (*Mensch*)
hurry; (*dringend sein*) be urgent; **e~ends**
ad hastily; **e~fertig** *a* eager, solicitous;
~gut *nt* express goods *pl*, fast freight
(*US*); **e~ig** *a* hasty, hurried; (*dringlich*)
urgent; **es e~ig haben** be in a hurry;
~zug *m* semi-fast train, limited stop
train.

Eimer ['aɪmər] *m* -s, - bucket, pail.

ein(e) [aɪn(ə)] *num* one; *indef art* a, an; *ad*:
nicht ~ noch aus wissen not know
what to do; **~e(r,s)** *pron* one; (*jemand*)
someone.

einander [aɪ'nandər] *pron* one another,
each other.

einarbeiten ['aɪnarbaɪtən] *vr* familiarize
o.s. (*in* +acc with).

einarmig ['aɪn'armɪç] *a* one-armed.

einatmen ['aɪna:tmən] *vti* inhale, breathe
in.

einäugig ['aɪn'ɔygɪç] *a* one-eyed.

Einbahnstraße ['aɪnba:nʃtra:sə] *f* one-way
street.

Einband ['aɪnbant] *m* binding, cover.

einbändig ['aɪnbɛndɪç] *a* one-volume.

einbau- ['aɪnbaʊ] *cpd*: **~en** *vt* build in;
Motor install, fit; **E~möbel** *pl* built-in
furniture.

einbe- ['aɪnbə] *cpd*: **~griffen** *a* included,
inclusive; **~rufen** *vt irreg* convene; (*Mil*)
call up; **E~rufung** *f* convocation; call-up.

einbett- ['aɪnbɛt] *cpd*: **~en** *vt* embed;
E~zimmer *nt* single room.

einbeziehen ['aɪnbətsi:ən] *vt irreg* include.

einbiegen ['aɪnbi:gən] *vi irreg* turn.

einbilden ['aɪnbɪldən] *vt*: **sich** (*dat*) **etw ~**
imagine sth.

Einbildung *f* imagination; (*Dünkel*)
conceit; **~skraft** *f* imagination.

einbinden ['aɪnbɪndən] *vt irreg* bind (up).

einblenden ['aɪnblɛndən] *vt* fade in.

einbleuen ['aɪnblɔyən] *vt* (*col*) **jdm etw
~** hammer sth into sb.

Einblick ['aɪnblɪk] *m* insight.

einbrechen ['aɪnbrɛçən] *vi irreg* (*in Haus*)
break in; (*in Land etc*) invade; (*Nacht*) fall;
(*Winter*) set in; (*durchbrechen*) break.

Einbrecher *m* -s, - burglar.

einbringen ['aɪnbrɪŋən] *vt irreg* bring in;
Geld, Vorteil yield; (*mitbringen*) contribute.

Einbruch ['aɪnbrux] *m* (*Haus—*) break-in,
burglary; (*Eindringen*) invasion; (*des
Winters*) onset; (*Durchbrechen*) break;
(*Met*) approach; (*Mil*) penetration; **~ der
Nacht** nightfall; **e~ssicher** *a* burglar-proof.

einbürgern ['aɪnbyrgərn] *vt* naturalize; *vr*

become adopted; **das hat sich so eingebürgert** that's become a custom.

Einbuße ['aɪnbuːsə] *f* loss, forfeiture.

einbüßen ['aɪnbyːsən] *vt* lose, forfeit.

eindecken ['aɪndɛkən] *vr* lay in stocks (*mit* of).

eindeutig ['aɪndɔʏtɪç] *a* unequivocal.

eindring- ['aɪndrɪŋ] *cpd:* ~**en** *vi irreg* (*in* +*acc*) force one's way in(to); (*in Haus*) break in(to); (*in Land*) invade; (*Gas, Wasser*) penetrate; (*mit Bitten*) pester (*auf jdn* sb); ~**lich** *a* forcible, urgent; **E~ling** *m* intruder.

Eindruck ['aɪndrʊk] *m* impression; **e~sfähig** *a* impressionable; **e~svoll** *a* impressive.

eindrücken ['aɪndrʏkən] *vt* press in.

eineiig ['aɪn|aɪɪç] *a* *Zwillinge* identical.

eineinhalb ['aɪn|aɪn'halp] *num* one and a half.

einengen ['aɪn|ɛŋən] *vt* confine, restrict.

einer- ['aɪnər] *cpd:* **'E~lei** *nt* -**s** sameness; ~**lei** *a* (*gleichartig*) the same kind of; **es ist mir ~lei** it is all the same to me; ~**seits** *ad* on one hand.

einfach ['aɪnfax] *a* simple; (*nicht mehrfach*) single; *ad* simply; **E~heit** *f* simplicity.

einfädeln ['aɪnfɛːdəln] *vt* *Nadel* thread; (*fig*) contrive.

einfahren ['aɪnfaːrən] *irreg vt* bring in; *Barriere* knock down; *Auto* run in; *vi* drive in; (*Zug*) pull in; (*Min*) go down.

Einfahrt *f* (*Vorgang*) driving in; pulling in; (*Min*) descent; (*Ort*) entrance.

Einfall ['aɪnfal] *m* (*Idee*) idea, notion; (*Licht—*) incidence; (*Mil*) raid; **e~en** *vi irreg* (*Licht*) fall; (*Mil*) raid; (*einstimmen*) join in (*in* +*acc* with); (*einstürzen*) fall in, collapse; **etw fällt jdm ein** sth occurs to sb; **das fällt mir gar nicht ein** I wouldn't dream of it; **sich** (*dat*) **etwas e~en lassen** have a good idea.

einfältig ['aɪnfɛltɪç] *a* simple(-minded).

Einfamilienhaus [aɪnfa'miːliənhaus] *nt* detached house.

einfangen ['aɪnfaŋən] *vt irreg* catch.

einfarbig ['aɪnfarbɪç] *a* all one colour; *Stoff etc* self-coloured.

einfass- ['aɪnfas] *cpd:* ~**en** *vt* set; *Beet* enclose; *Stoff* edge, border; *Bier* barrel; **E~ung** *f* setting; enclosure; barrelling.

einfetten ['aɪnfɛtən] *vt* grease.

einfinden ['aɪnfɪndən] *vr irreg* come, turn up.

einfliegen ['aɪnfliːgən] *vt irreg* fly in.

einfließen ['aɪnfliːsən] *vi irreg* flow in.

einflößen ['aɪnfløːsən] *vt:* **jdm etw ~** (*lit*) give sb sth; (*fig*) instil sth in sb.

Einfluß ['aɪnflʊs] *m* influence; ~**bereich** *m* sphere of influence; **e~reich** *a* influential.

einförmig ['aɪnfœrmɪç] *a* uniform; **E~keit** *f* uniformity.

einfrieren ['aɪnfriːrən] *irreg vi* freeze (in); *vt* freeze.

einfügen ['aɪnfyːgən] *vt* fit in; (*zusätzlich*) add.

Einfuhr ['aɪnfuːr] *f* - import; ~**artikel** *m* imported article.

einführ- ['aɪnfyːr] *cpd:* ~**en** *vt* bring in; *Mensch, Sitten* introduce; *Ware* import; **E~ung** *f* introduction; **E~ungspreis** *m* introductory price.

Eingabe ['aɪngaːbə] *f* petition; (*Daten*—) input.

Eingang ['aɪngaŋ] *m* entrance; (*Comm: Ankunft*) arrival; (*Sendung*) post; **e~s** *ad, prep* +*gen* at the outset (of); ~**sbestätigung** *f* acknowledgement of receipt; ~**shalle** *f* entrance hall.

eingeben ['aɪngeːbən] *vt irreg* *Arznei* give; *Daten etc* feed; *Gedanken* inspire.

eingebildet ['aɪngəbɪldət] *a* imaginary; (*eitel*) conceited.

Eingeborene(r) ['aɪngəboːrənə(r)] *mf* native.

Eingebung *f* inspiration.

einge- ['aɪngə] *cpd:* ~**denk** *prep* +*gen* bearing in mind; ~**fallen** *a* *Gesicht* gaunt; ~**fleischt** *a* inveterate; ~**fleischter Junggeselle** confirmed bachelor; ~**froren** *a* frozen.

eingehen ['aɪngeːən] *irreg vi* (*Aufnahme finden*) come in; (*verständlich sein*) be comprehensible (*jdm* to sb); (*Sendung, Geld*) be received; (*Tier, Pflanze*) die; (*Firma*) fold; (*schrumpfen*) shrink; **auf etw** (*acc*) ~ go into sth; **auf jdn ~** respond to sb; *vt* enter into; *Wette* make; ~**d** *a* exhaustive, thorough.

einge- ['aɪngə] *cpd:* **E~machte(s)** *nt* preserves *pl;* ~**meinden** *vt* incorporate; ~**nommen** *a* (*von*) fond (of), partial (to); (*gegen*) prejudiced; ~**schrieben** *a* registered; ~**sessen** *a* old-established; ~**spielt** *a:* **aufeinander ~spielt sein** be in tune with each other; **E~ständnis** *nt* -**ses**, '-**se** admission, confession; ~**stehen** *vt irreg* confess; ~**tragen** *a* (*Comm*) registered; **E~weide** *nt* -**s**, - innards *pl,* intestines *pl;* **E~weihte(r)** *mf* initiate; ~**wöhnen** *vt* accustom.

eingießen ['aɪngiːsən] *vt irreg* pour (out).

eingleisig ['aɪnglaɪzɪç] *a* single-track.

eingraben ['aɪngraːbən] *irreg vt* dig in; *vr* dig o.s. in.

eingreifen ['aɪngraɪfən] *vi irreg* intervene, interfere; (*Zahnrad*) mesh.

Eingriff ['aɪngrɪf] *m* intervention, interference; (*Operation*) operation.

einhaken ['aɪnhaːkən] *vt* hook in; *vr:* **sich bei jdm ~** link arms with sb; *vi* (*sich einmischen*) intervene.

Einhalt ['aɪnhalt] *m:* ~ **gebieten** (+*dat*) put a stop to; **e~en** *irreg vt* *Regel* keep; *vi* stop.

einhändig ['aɪnhɛndɪç] *a* one-handed; ~**en** [-dɪgən] *vt* hand in.

einhängen ['aɪnhɛŋən] *vt* hang; *Telefon* (*auch vi*) hang up; **sich bei jdm ~** link arms with sb.

einheim- ['aɪnhaɪm] *cpd:* ~**isch** *a* native; ~**sen** *vt* (*col*) bring home.

Einheit ['aɪnhaɪt] *f* unity; (*Maß, Mil*) unit; **e~lich** *a* uniform; ~**spreis** *m* uniform price.

einhellig ['aɪnhɛlɪç] *a, ad* unanimous.

einholen ['aɪnhoːlən] vt Tau haul in; Fahne, Segel lower; (Vorsprung aufholen) catch up with; Verspätung make up; Rat, Erlaubnis ask; vi (einkaufen) buy, shop.

Einhorn ['aɪnhɔrn] nt unicorn.

einhüllen ['aɪnhʏlən] vt wrap up.

einig ['aɪnɪç] a (vereint) united; sich (dat) ~ sein in agreement; ~ werden agree; ~e ['aɪnɪgə] pl some; (mehrere) several; ~e(r,s) a some; ~emal ad a few times; ~e vt unite; vr agree (auf +acc on); ~ermaßen ad somewhat; (leidlich) reasonably; ~es pron something; ~gehen vi irreg agree; E~keit f unity; (Übereinstimmung) agreement; E~ung f agreement; (Vereinigung) unification.

einimpfen ['aɪnɪmpfən] vt inoculate (jdm etw sb with sth); (fig) impress (jdm etw sth upon sb).

einjährig ['aɪnjɛːrɪç] a of or for one year; (Alter) one-year-old; Pflanze annual.

einkalkulieren ['aɪnkalkuliːrən] vt take into account, allow for.

Einkauf ['aɪnkaʊf] m purchase; e~en vt buy; vi go shopping; ~sbummel m shopping spree; ~snetz nt string bag; ~spreis m cost price.

einkerben ['aɪnkɛrbən] vt notch.

einklammern ['aɪnklamərn] vt put in brackets, bracket.

Einklang ['aɪnklaŋ] m harmony.

einkleiden ['aɪnklaɪdən] vt clothe; (fig) express.

einklemmen ['aɪnklɛmən] vt jam.

einknicken ['aɪnknɪkən] vt bend in; Papier fold; vi give way.

einkochen ['aɪnkɔxən] vt boil down; Obst preserve, bottle.

Einkommen ['aɪnkɔmən] nt -s, - income; ~(s)steuer f income tax.

einkreisen ['aɪnkraɪzən] vt encircle.

Einkünfte ['aɪnkʏnftə] pl income, revenue.

einlad- ['aɪnlaːd] cpd: ~en vt irreg Person invite; Gegenstände load; jdn ins Kino ~en take sb to the cinema; E~ung f invitation.

Einlage ['aɪnlaːgə] f (Programm—) interlude; (Spar—) deposit; (Schuh—) insole; (Fußstütze) support; (Zahn—) temporary filling; (Cook) noodles pl, vegetables pl etc in soup; e~rn vt store.

Einlaß ['aɪnlas] m -sses, -lässe admission.

einlassen irreg vt let in; (einsetzen) set in; vr: sich mit jdm/auf etw (acc) ~ get involved with sb/sth.

Einlauf ['aɪnlaʊf] m arrival; (von Pferden) finish; (Med) enema; e~en irreg vi arrive, come in; (in Hafen) enter; (Sport) finish; (Wasser) run in; (Stoff) shrink; vt Schuhe break in; jdm das Haus e~en invade sb's house; vr (Sport) warm up; (Motor, Maschine) run in.

einleben ['aɪnleːbən] vr settle down.

Einlege- ['aɪnleːgə] cpd: ~arbeit f inlay; e~n vt (einfügen) Blatt, Sohle insert; (Cook) pickle; (in Holz etc) inlay; Geld deposit; Pause have; Protest make; Veto use; Berufung lodge; ein gutes Wort bei

jdm e~n put in a good word with sb; ~sohle f insole.

einleiten ['aɪnlaɪtən] vt introduce, start; Geburt induce.

Einleitung f introduction; induction.

einleuchten ['aɪnlɔʏçtən] vi be clear or evident (jdm to sb); ~d a clear.

einliefern ['aɪnliːfərn] vt take (in +acc into).

einlösen ['aɪnløːzən] vt Scheck cash; Schuldschein, Pfand redeem; Versprechen keep.

einmachen ['aɪnmaxən] vt preserve.

einmal ['aɪnmaːl] ad once; (erstens) first; (zukünftig) sometime; nehmen wir ~ an just let's suppose; noch ~ once more; nicht ~ not even; auf ~ all at once; es war ~ once upon a time there was/were; E~'eins nt multiplication tables pl; ~ig a unique; (einmal geschehend) single; (prima) fantastic.

Einmann- [aɪn'man] cpd: ~betrieb m one-man business; ~bus m one-man-operated bus.

Einmarsch ['aɪnmarʃ] m entry; (Mil) invasion; e~ieren vi march in.

einmengen ['aɪnmɛŋən], **einmischen** ['aɪnmɪʃən] vr interfere (in +acc with).

einmünden ['aɪnmʏndən] vi run (in +acc into), join.

einmütig ['aɪnmyːtɪç] a unanimous.

Einnahme ['aɪnnaːmə] f -, -n (Geld) takings pl, revenue; (von Medizin) taking; (Mil) capture, taking; ~quelle f source of income.

einnehmen ['aɪnneːmən] vt irreg take; Stellung, Raum take up; ~ für/gegen persuade in favour of/against; ~d a charming.

einnicken ['aɪnnɪkən] vi nod off.

einnisten ['aɪnnɪstən] vr nest; (fig) settle o.s.

Einöde ['aɪnˈøːdə] f -, -n desert, wilderness.

einordnen ['aɪnˈɔrdnən] vt arrange, fit in; vr adapt; (Aut) get into lane.

einpacken ['aɪnpakən] vt pack (up).

einparken ['aɪnparkən] vt park.

einpendeln ['aɪnpɛndəln] vr even out.

einpferchen ['aɪnpfɛrçən] vt pen in, coop up.

einpflanzen ['aɪnpflantsən] vt plant; (Med) implant.

einplanen ['aɪnplaːnən] vt plan for.

einpräg- ['aɪnprɛːg] cpd: ~en vt impress, imprint; (beibringen) impress (jdm on sb); sich (dat) etw ~en memorize sth; ~sam a easy to remember; Melodie catchy.

einrahmen ['aɪnraːmən] vt frame.

einrasten ['aɪnrastən] vi engage.

einräumen ['aɪnrɔʏmən] vt (ordnend) put away; (überlassen) Platz give up; (zugestehen) admit, concede.

einrechnen ['aɪnrɛçnən] vt include; (berücksichtigen) take into account.

einreden ['aɪnreːdən] vt: jdm/sich etw ~ talk sb/o.s. into believing sth.

einreiben ['aɪnraɪbən] vt irreg rub in.

einreichen ['aınraıçən] vt hand in; *Antrag* submit.

Einreise ['aınraızə] f entry; ~**bestimmungen** pl entry regulations pl; ~**erlaubnis** f, ~**genehmigung** f entry permit; **e~n** vi enter (*in ein Land* a country).

einreißen ['aınraısən] vt irreg *Papier* tear; *Gebäude* pull down; vi tear; (*Gewohnheit werden*) catch on.

einrichten ['aınrıçtən] vt *Haus* furnish; (*schaffen*) establish, set up; (*arrangieren*) arrange; (*möglich machen*) manage; vr (*in Haus*) furnish one's house; (*sich vorbereiten*) prepare o.s. (*auf +acc* for); (*sich anpassen*) adapt (*auf +acc* to).

Einrichtung f (*Wohnungs—*) furnishings pl; (*öffentliche Anstalt*) organization; (*Dienste*) service.

einrosten ['aınrɔstən] vi get rusty.

einrücken ['aınrʏkən] vi (*Mil*) (*Soldat*) join up; (*in Land*) move in; vt *Anzeige* insert; *Zeile* indent.

Eins [aıns] f -, -**en** one; **e~** num one; **es ist mir alles e~** it's all one to me.

einsalzen ['aınzaltsən] vt salt.

einsam ['aınza:m] a lonely, solitary; **E~keit** f loneliness, solitude.

einsammeln ['aınzaməln] vt collect.

Einsatz ['aınzats] m (*Teil*) inset; (*an Kleid*) insertion; (*Tisch*) leaf; (*Verwendung*) use, employment; (*Spiel—*) stake; (*Risiko*) risk; (*Mil*) operation; (*Mus*) entry; **im ~** in action; **e~bereit** a ready for action.

einschalten ['aınʃaltən] vt (*einfügen*) insert; *Pause* make; (*Elec*) switch on; (*Aut*) *Gang* engage; *Anwalt* bring in; vr (*dazwischentreten*) intervene.

einschärfen ['aınʃɛrfən] vt impress (*jdm etw* sth on sb).

einschätzen ['aınʃɛtsən] vt estimate, assess; vr rate o.s.

einschenken ['aınʃɛŋkən] vt pour out.

einschicken ['aınʃıkən] vt send in.

einschieben ['aınʃi:bən] vt irreg push in; (*zusätzlich*) insert.

einschiffen ['aınʃıfən] vt take on board; vr embark, go on board.

einschlafen ['aınʃla:fən] vi irreg fall asleep, go to sleep.

einschläfernd ['aınʃlɛ:fərnt] a (*Med*) soporific; (*langweilig*) boring; *Stimme* lulling.

Einschlag ['aınʃla:k] m impact; (*Aut*) lock; (*fig: Beimischung*) touch, hint; **e~en** irreg vt knock in; *Fenster* smash, break; *Zähne, Schädei* smash in; *Steuer* turn; (*kürzer machen*) take up; *Ware* pack, wrap up; *Weg, Richtung* take; vi hit (*in etw* (acc) sth, *auf jdn* sb); (*sich einigen*) agree; (*Anklang finden*) work, succeed.

einschlägig ['aınʃlɛ:gıç] a relevant.

einschleichen ['aınʃlaıçən] vr irreg (*in Haus, Fehler*) creep in, steal in; (*in Vertrauen*) worm one's way in.

einschließen ['aınʃli:sən] vt irreg vt *Kind* lock in; *Häftling* lock up; *Gegenstand* lock away; *Bergleute* cut off; (*umgeben*) surround; (*Mil*) encircle; (*fig*) include, comprise; vr lock o.s. in.

einschließlich ad inclusive; prep +*gen* inclusive of, including.

einschmeicheln ['aınʃmaıçəln] vr ingratiate o.s. (*bei* with).

einschnappen ['aınʃnapən] vi (*Tür*) click to; (*fig*) be touchy; **eingeschnappt sein** be in a huff.

einschneidend ['aınʃnaıdənt] a incisive.

Einschnitt ['aınʃnıt] m cutting; (*Med*) incision; (*Ereignis*) incident.

einschränken ['aınʃrɛŋkən] vt limit, restrict; *Kosten* cut down, reduce; vr cut down (on expenditure); ~**d** a restrictive.

Einschränkung f restriction, limitation; reduction; (*von Behauptung*) qualification.

Einschreib- ['aınʃraıb] cpd: ~**(e)brief** m recorded delivery letter; **e~en** irreg vt write in; *Post* send recorded delivery; vr register; (*Univ*) enrol; ~**en** vt recorded delivery letter; ~**(e)sendung** f recorded delivery packet.

einschreiten ['aınʃraıtən] vi irreg step in, intervene; ~ **gegen** take action against.

Einschub ['aınʃu:p] m -s, -̈e insertion.

einschüchtern ['aınʃʏçtərn] vt intimidate.

einsehen ['aınze:ən] vt irreg (*hineinsehen in*) realize; *Akten* have a look at; (*verstehen*) see; **E~** nt -s understanding; **ein E~ haben** show understanding.

einseifen ['aınzaıfən] vt soap, lather; (*fig*) take in, cheat.

einseitig ['aınzaıtıç] a one-sided; **E~keit** f one-sidedness.

Einsend- ['aınzɛnd] cpd: **e~en** vt irreg send in; ~**er** m -s, - sender, contributor; ~**ung** f sending in.

einsetzen ['aınzɛtsən] vt put (in); (*in Amt*) appoint, install; *Geld* stake; (*verwenden*) use; (*Mil*) employ; vi (*beginnen*) set in; (*Mus*) enter, come in; vr work hard; **sich für jdn/etw ~** support sb/sth.

Einsicht ['aınzıçt] f insight; (*in Akten*) look, inspection; **zu der ~ kommen, daß ...** come to the conclusion that ...; **e~ig** a *Mensch* judicious; ~**nahme** f -, -n examination; **e~slos** a unreasonable; **e~svoll** a understanding.

Einsiedler ['aınzi:dlər] m hermit.

einsilbig ['aınzılbıç] a (*lit,fig*) monosyllabic; **E~keit** f (*fig*) taciturnity.

einsinken ['aınzıŋkən] vi irreg sink in.

Einsitzer ['aınzıtsər] m -s, - single-seater.

einspannen ['aınʃpanən] vt *Werkstück, Papier* put (in), insert; *Pferde* harness; (*col*) *Person* rope in.

einsperren ['aınʃpɛrən] vt lock up.

einspielen ['aınʃpi:lən] vr (*Sport*) warm up; **sich aufeinander ~** become attuned to each other; vt (*Film*) *Geld* bring in; *Instrument* play in; **gut eingespielt** smoothly running.

einspringen ['aınʃprıŋən] vi irreg (*aushelfen*) help out, step into the breach.

einspritzen ['aınʃprıtsən] vt inject.

Einspruch ['aınʃprux] m protest, objection; ~**srecht** nt veto.

einspurig ['aınʃpu:rıç] a single-line.

einst [aınst] ad once; (*zukünftig*) one or some day.

Einstand ['aınʃtant] m (*Tennis*) deuce;

(*Antritt*) entrance (to office).

einstechen ['aɪnʃtɛçən] *vt irreg* stick in.

einstecken ['aɪnʃtɛkən] *vt* stick in, insert; *Brief* post; (*Elec*) *Stecker* plug in; *Geld* pocket; (*mitnehmen*) take; (*überlegen sein*) put in the shade; (*hinnehmen*) swallow.

einstehen ['aɪnʃteːən] *vi irreg* guarantee (*für jdn/etw* sb/sth); (*verantworten*) answer (*für* for).

einsteigen ['aɪnʃtaɪgən] *vi irreg* get in *or* on; (*in Schiff*) go on board; (*sich beteiligen*) come in; (*hineinklettern*) climb in.

einstell- ['aɪnʃtɛl] *cpd*: **~bar** *a* adjustable; **~en** *vti* (*aufhören*) stop; *Geräte* adjust; *Kamera etc* focus; *Sender, Radio* tune in; (*unterstellen*) put; (*in Firma*) employ, take on; *vr* (*anfangen*) set in; (*kommen*) arrive; **sich auf jdn/etw ~en** adapt to sb/prepare o.s. for sth; **E~ung** *f* (*Aufhören*) suspension, cessation; adjustment; focusing; (*von Arbeiter etc*) appointment; (*Haltung*) attitude.

Einstieg ['aɪnʃtiːk] *m* **-(e)s, -e** entry; (*fig*) approach.

einstig ['aɪnstɪç] *a* former.

einstimm- ['aɪnʃtɪm] *cpd*: **~en** *vi* join in; *vt* (*Mus*) tune; (*in Stimmung bringen*) put in the mood; **~ig** *a* unanimous; (*Mus*) for one voice; **E~igkeit** *f* unanimity.

einst- ['aɪnst] *cpd*: **~malig** *a* former; **~mals** *ad* once, formerly.

einstöckig ['aɪnʃtœkɪç] *a* single-storeyed.

einstudieren ['aɪnʃtudiːrən] *vt* study, rehearse.

einstündig ['aɪnʃtyndɪç] *a* one-hour.

einstürmen ['aɪnʃtyrmən] *vi*: **auf jdn ~** rush at sb; (*Eindrücke*) overwhelm sb.

Einsturz ['aɪnʃturts] *m* collapse; **~gefahr** *f* danger of collapse.

einstürzen ['aɪnʃtyrtsən] *vi* fall in, collapse.

einst- ['aɪnst] *cpd*: **~weilen** *ad* meanwhile; (*vorläufig*) temporarily, for the time being; **~weilig** *a* temporary.

eintägig ['aɪntɛːgɪç] *a* one-day.

eintauchen ['aɪntauxən] *vt* immerse, dip in; *vi* dive.

eintauschen ['aɪntauʃən] *vt* exchange.

eintausend ['aɪn'tauzənt] *num* one thousand.

einteil- ['aɪntaɪl] *cpd*: **~en** *vt* (*in Teile*) divide (up); *Menschen* assign; **~ig** *a* one-piece.

eintönig ['aɪntøːnɪç] *a* monotonous; **E~keit** *f* monotony.

Eintopf(gericht *nt*) ['aɪntɔpf(gərɪçt)] *m* stew.

Eintracht ['aɪntraxt] *f* - concord, harmony.

einträchtig ['aɪntrɛçtɪç] *a* harmonious.

Eintrag ['aɪntraːk] *m* **-(e)s, -e** entry; *amtlicher ~* entry in the register; **e~en** *irreg vt* (*in Buch*) enter; *Profit* yield; **jdm etw e~en** bring sb sth; *vr* put one's name down.

einträglich ['aɪntrɛːklɪç] *a* profitable.

eintreffen ['aɪntrɛfən] *vi irreg* happen; (*ankommen*) arrive.

eintreten ['aɪntreːtən] *irreg vi* occur; (*hineingehen*) enter (*in etw* (*acc*) sth); (*sich*

einsetzen) intercede; (*in Club, Partei*) join (*in etw* (*acc*) sth); (*in Stadium etc*) enter; *vt Tür* kick open.

Eintritt ['aɪntrɪt] *m* (*Betreten*) entrance; (*Anfang*) commencement; (*in Club etc*) joining; **~sgeld** *nt*, **~spreis** *m* charge for admission; **~skarte** *f* (admission) ticket.

eintrocknen ['aɪntrɔknən] *vi* dry up.

einüben ['aɪn'yːbən] *vt* practise, drill.

einver- ['aɪnfɛr] *cpd*: **~leiben** *vt* incorporate; *Gebiet* annex; **sich** (*dat*) **etw ~leiben** (*fig*: *geistig*) acquire; **E~nehmen** *nt* **-s, -** agreement, understanding; **~standen** *interj* agreed; *a*: **~standen sein** agree, be agreed; **E~ständnis** *nt* understanding; (*gleiche Meinung*) agreement.

Einwand ['aɪnvant] *m* **-(e)s, -e** objection; **~erer** ['aɪnvandərər] *m* immigrant; **e~ern** *vi* immigrate; **~erung** *f* immigration; **e~frei** *a* perfect; *ad* absolutely.

einwärts ['aɪnvɛrts] *ad* inwards.

einwecken ['aɪnvɛkən] *vt* bottle, preserve.

Einwegflasche ['aɪnveːgflaʃə] *f* no-deposit bottle.

einweichen ['aɪnvaɪçən] *vt* soak.

einweih- ['aɪnvaɪ] *cpd*: **~en** *vt Kirche* consecrate; *Brücke* open; *Gebäude* inaugurate; *Person* initiate (*in* +*acc* in); **E~ung** *f* consecration; opening; inauguration; initiation.

einweis- ['aɪnvaɪs] *cpd*: **~en** *vt irreg* (*in Amt*) install; (*in Arbeit*) introduce; (*in Anstalt*) send; **E~ung** *f* installation; introduction; sending.

einwenden ['aɪnvɛndən] *vt irreg* object, oppose (*gegen* to).

einwerfen ['aɪnvɛrfən] *vt irreg* throw in; *Brief* post; *Geld* put in, insert; *Fenster* smash; (*äußern*) interpose.

einwickeln ['aɪnvɪkəln] *vt* wrap up; (*fig col*) outsmart.

einwillig- ['aɪnvɪlɪç] *cpd*: **~en** *vi* consent, agree (*in* +*acc* to); **E~ung** *f* consent.

einwirk- ['aɪnvɪrk] *cpd*: **~en** *vi*: **auf jdn/etw ~en** influence sb/sth; **E~ung** *f* influence.

Einwohner ['aɪnvoːnər] *m* **-s, -** inhabitant; **~'meldeamt** *nt* registration office; **~schaft** *f* population, inhabitants *pl*.

Einwurf ['aɪnvurf] *m* (*Öffnung*) slot; (*Einwand*) objection; (*Sport*) throw-in.

Einzahl ['aɪntsaːl] *f* singular; **e~en** *vt* pay in; **~ung** *f* paying in.

einzäunen ['aɪntsɔʏnən] *vt* fence in.

einzeichnen ['aɪntsaɪçnən] *vt* draw in.

Einzel ['aɪntsəl] *nt* **-s, -** (*Tennis*) singles; *in cpds* individual; single; **~bett** *nt* single bed; **~fall** *m* single instance, individual case; **~haft** *f* solitary confinement; **~heit** *f* particular, detail; **e~n** *a* single; (*vereinzelt*) the odd; *ad* singly; **e~n angeben** specify; **der/die e~ne** the individual; **das e~ne** the particular; **ins e~ne gehen** go into the particular; **~teil** *nt* component (part); **~zimmer** *nt* single room.

einziehen ['aɪntsiːən] *irreg vt* draw in, take in; *Kopf* duck; *Fühler, Antenne, Fahrgestell* retract; *Steuern, Erkundigungen* collect; (*Mil*) draft, call up; (*aus dem Verkehr ziehen*) withdraw; (*konfiszieren*) confiscate; *vi* move in(to); (*Friede, Ruhe*) come; (*Flüssigkeit*) penetrate.

einzig ['aıntsıç] *a* only; (*ohnegleichen*) unique; **das** ~**e** the only thing; **der/die** ~**e** the only one; ~**artig** *a* unique.

Einzug ['aıntsu:k] *m* entry, moving in.

Eis [aıs] *nt* -**es**, - ice; (*Speise*—) ice cream; ~**bahn** *f* ice *or* skating rink; ~**bär** *m* polar bear; ~**becher** *m* sundae; ~**bein** *nt* pig's trotters *pl*; ~**berg** *m* iceberg; ~**blumen** *pl* ice fern; ~**decke** *f* sheet of ice; ~**diele** *f* ice-cream parlour.

Eisen ['aızən] *nt* -**s**, - iron; ~**bahn** *f* railway, railroad (*US*); ~**bahner** *m* -**s**, - railwayman, railway employee, railroader (*US*); ~**bahnschaffner** *m* railway guard; ~**bahnübergang** *m* level crossing, grade crossing (*US*); ~**bahnwagen** *m* railway carriage; ~**erz** *nt* iron ore; **e**~**haltig** *a* containing iron.

eisern ['aızərn] *a* iron; *Gesundheit* robust; *Energie* unrelenting; *Reserve* emergency.

Eis- *cpd*: **e**~**frei** *a* clear of ice; ~**hockey** *nt* ice hockey; **e**~**ig** ['aızıç] *a* icy; **e**~**kalt** a icy cold; ~**kunstlauf** *m* figure skating; ~**laufen** *nt* ice skating; ~**läufer(in** *f*) *m* ice-skater; ~**pickel** *m* ice-axe; ~**schießen** *nt* = curling; ~**schrank** *m* fridge, ice-box (*US*); ~**zapfen** *m* icicle; ~**zeit** *f* ice age.

eitel ['aıtəl] *a* vain; **E**~**keit** *f* vanity.

Eiter ['aıtər] *m* -**s** pus; **e**~**ig** a suppurating; **e**~**n** *vi* suppurate.

Ei- *cpd*: ~**weiß** *nt* -**es**, -**e** white of an egg; ~**zelle** *f* ovum.

Ekel ['e:kəl] *m* -**s** nausea, disgust; *nt* -**s**, - (*col: Mensch*) nauseating person; **e**~**erregend**, **e**~**haft**, **ek(e)lig** a nauseating, disgusting; **e**~**n** *vt* disgust; **es ekelt jdn** *or* **jdm** sb is disgusted; *vr* loathe, be disgusted (*vor* +*dat* at).

Ekstase [ɛk'sta:zə] *f* -, -**n** ecstasy.

Ekzem [ɛk'tse:m] *nt* -**s**, -**e** (*Med*) eczema.

Elan [e'lã:] *m* -**s** elan.

elastisch [e'lastıʃ] a elastic.

Elastizität [elastitsi'tɛ:t] *f* elasticity.

Elch [ɛlç] *m* -**(e)s**, -**e** elk.

Elefant [ele'fant] *m* elephant.

elegant [ele'gant] a elegant.

Eleganz [ele'gants] *f* elegance.

Elek- ['e:lek] *cpd*: ~**trifizierung** [-trifi'tsi:ruŋ] *f* electrification; ~**triker** [-'trikər] *m* -**s**, - electrician; **e**~**trisch** [-trıʃ] a electric; **e**~**trisieren** [-tri'zi:rən] *vt* (*lit, fig*) electrify; *Mensch* give an electric shock to; *vr* get an electric shock; ~**trizität** [-tritsi'tɛt] *f* electricity; ~**trizitätswerk** *nt* electricity works, power plant.

Elektro- [e'lɛktro] *cpd*: ~**de** [elɛk'tro:də] *f* -, -**n** electrode; ~**herd** *m* electric cooker; ~**lyse** [-'ly:zə] *f*-, -**n** electrolysis; [-ɔn] *nt* -**s**, -**en** electron; **~nen(ge)hirn** [elɛk'tro:nən-] *nt* electronic brain; ~**nenrechner** *m* computer; **e**~**nisch** a electronic; ~**rasierer** *m* -**s**, - electric razor.

Element [ele'mɛnt] *nt* -**s**, -**e** element; (*Elec*) cell, battery; **e**~**ar** [-'ta:r] a elementary; (*naturhaft*) elemental.

Elend ['e:lɛnt] *nt* -(**e**)**s** misery; **e**~ a miserable; **e**~**iglich** ['elɛnd-] *ad* miserably; ~**sviertel** *nt* slum.

elf [ɛlf] *num* eleven; **E**~ *f* -, -**en** (*Sport*) eleven; **E**~**e** *f* -, -**n** elf; **E**~**enbein** *nt* ivory; **E**~**meter** *m* (*Sport*) penalty (kick).

eliminieren [elimi'ni:rən] *vt* eliminate.

Elite [e'li:tə] *f*-, -**n** elite.

Elixier [eli'ksi:r] *nt* -**s**, -**e** elixir.

Ell- *cpd*: ~**e** [e'lə] *f*-, -**n** ell; (*Maß*) yard; ~**(en)bogen** *m* elbow; ~**ipse** [ɛ'lıpsə] *f*-, -**n** ellipse.

Elster ['ɛlstər] *f*-, -**n** magpie.

Elter- ['ɛltər] *cpd*: **e**~**lich** a parental; ~**n** *pl* parents *pl*; ~**nhaus** *nt* home; **e**~**nlos** a parentless.

Email [e'ma:j] *nt* -**s**, -**s** enamel; **e**~**lieren** [ema'ji:rən] *vt* enamel.

Emanzipation [emantsipatsi'o:n] *f* emancipation.

emanzi'pieren *vt* emancipate.

Embryo ['ɛmbryo] *m* -**s**, -**s** *or* -**nen** embryo.

Emi- [emi] *cpd*: ~**grant** [-'grant] *m* emigrant; ~**gration** [-gratsi'o:n] *f* emigration; **e**~**grieren** [-'gri:rən] *vi* emigrate.

Empfang [ɛm'pfaŋ] *m* -**(e)s**, -**e** reception; (*Erhalten*) receipt; **in** ~ **nehmen** receive; **e**~**en** *irreg vt* receive; *vi* (*schwanger werden*) conceive.

Empfäng- [ɛm'pfɛŋ] *cpd*: ~**er** *m* -**s**, - receiver; (*Comm*) addressee, consignee; **e**~**lich** a receptive, susceptible; ~**nis** *f*-, -**se** conception; ~**nisverhütung** *f* contraception.

Empfangs- *cpd*: ~**bestätigung** *f* acknowledgement; ~**dame** *f* receptionist; ~**schein** *m* receipt; ~**zimmer** *nt* reception room.

empfehlen [ɛm'pfe:lən] *irreg vt* recommend; *vr* take one's leave; ~**swert** a recommendable.

Empfehlung *f* recommendation; ~**sschreiben** *nt* letter of recommendation.

empfind- [ɛm'pfınt] *cpd*: ~**en** [ɛm'pfındən] *vt irreg* feel; ~**lich** a sensitive; *Stelle* sore; (*reizbar*) touchy; **E**~**lichkeit** *f* sensitiveness; (*Reizbarkeit*) touchiness; ~**sam** a sentimental; **E**~**ung** *f* feeling, sentiment; ~**ungslos** a unfeeling, insensitive.

empor [ɛm'po:r] *ad* up, upwards.

empören [ɛm'pø:rən] *vt* make indignant; shock; *vr* become indignant; ~**d** a outrageous.

empor- *cpd*: ~**kommen** *vi irreg* rise; succeed; **E**~**kömmling** *m* upstart, parvenu.

Empörung *f* indignation.

emsig ['ɛmzıç] a diligent, busy.

End- ['ɛnt] *in cpds* final; ~**auswertung** *f* final analysis; ~**bahnhof** ['ɛnt-] *m* terminus; **e**~**e** *nt* -**s**, -**n** end; **am** ~**e** at the end; (*schließlich*) in the end; **am** ~**e sein** be at the end of one's tether; ~**e Dezember** at the end of December; **zu**

~**e sein** be finished; **e~en** vi end;
e~gültig a final, definite; **~ivie**
[ɛn'diːviə] f endive; **e~lich** a final; (Math)
finite; ad finally; **e~lich!** at last!; **e~los** a
endless, infinite; **~spiel** nt final(s);
~spurt m (Sport) final spurt; **~station** f
terminus; **~ung** f ending.

Energie [enɛr'giː] f energy; **e~los** a
lacking in energy, weak; **~wirtschaft** f
energy industry.

energisch [e'nɛrgɪʃ] a energetic.

eng [ɛŋ] a narrow; Kleidung tight; (fig)
Horizont auch limited; Freundschaft, Verhältnis close; **~ an etw** (dat) close to sth.

Engagement [ãgaʒ'mãː] nt -s, -s
engagement; (Verpflichtung) commitment.

engagieren [ãga'ʒiːrən] vt engage; **ein
engagierter Schriftsteller** a committed
writer; vr commit o.s.

Enge ['ɛŋə] f -, -n (lit,fig) narrowness;
(Land—) defile; (Meer—) straits pl; **jdn in
die ~ treiben** drive sb into a corner.

Engel ['ɛŋəl] m -s, - angel; **e~haft** a
angelic; **~macher** m -s, - (col) backstreet abortionist.

eng- cpd: **~herzig** a petty; **E~paß** m
defile, pass; (fig, Verkehr) bottleneck.

en gros [ã'groː] ad wholesale.

engstirnig ['ɛŋʃtɪrnɪç] a narrow-minded.

Enkel ['ɛŋkəl] m -s, - grandson; **~in** f
granddaughter; **~kind** nt grandchild.

en masse [ã'mas] ad en masse.

enorm [e'nɔrm] a enormous.

Ensemble [ã'sãbəl] nt -s, -s company,
ensemble.

entarten [ɛnt'ʔaːrten] vi degenerate.

entbehr- [ɛnt'beːr] cpd: **~en** vt do without, dispense with; **~lich** a superfluous;
E~ung f privation.

entbinden [ɛnt'bɪndən] irreg vt release
(gen from); (Med) deliver; vi (Med) give
birth.

Entbindung f release; (Med) confinement; **~sheim** nt maternity hospital.

entblößen [ɛnt'bløːsən] vt denude,
uncover; (berauben) deprive (gen of).

entdeck- [ɛnt'dɛk] cpd: **~en** vt discover;
jdm etw ~en disclose sth to sb; **E~er** m
-s, - discoverer; **E~ung** f discovery.

Ente ['ɛntə] f -, -n duck; (fig) canard, false
report.

entehren [ɛnt'ʔeːrən] vt dishonour,
disgrace.

enteignen [ɛnt'ʔaignən] vt expropriate;
Besitzer dispossess.

enteisen [ɛnt'ʔaizən] vt de-ice, defrost.

enterben [ɛnt'ʔɛrbən] vt disinherit.

entfachen [ɛnt'faxən] vt kindle.

entfallen [ɛnt'falən] vi irreg drop, fall;
(wegfallen) be dropped; **jdm ~**
(vergessen) slip sb's memory; **auf jdn ~**
be allotted to sb.

entfalten [ɛnt'faltən] vt unfold; Talente
develop; vr open; (Mensch) develop one's
potential.

Entfaltung f unfolding; (von Talenten)
development.

entfern- [ɛnt'fɛrn] cpd: **~en** vt remove;
(hinauswerfen) expel; vr go away, retire,
withdraw; **~t** a distant; **weit davon ~t**

sein, etw zu tun be far from doing sth;
E~ung f distance; (Wegschaffen)
removal; **E~ungsmesser** m -s, - (Phot)
rangefinder.

entfesseln [ɛnt'fɛsəln] vt (fig) arouse.

entfetten [ɛnt'fɛtən] vt take the fat from.

entfremd- [ɛnt'frɛmd] cpd: **~en** vt
estrange, alienate; **E~ung** f alienation,
estrangement.

entfrost- [ɛnt'frɔst] cpd: **~en** vt defrost;
E~er m -s, - (Aut) defroster.

entführ- [ɛnt'fyːr] cpd: **~en** vt carry off,
abduct; kidnap; **E~er** m kidnapper;
E~ung f abduction; kidnapping.

entgegen [ɛnt'geːgən] prep +dat contrary
to, against; ad towards; **~bringen** vt irreg
bring; (fig) show (jdm etw sb sth);
~gehen vi irreg (+dat) go to meet, go
towards; **~gesetzt** a opposite; (widersprechend) opposed; **~halten** vt irreg (fig)
object; **~kommen** vi irreg approach;
meet (jdm sb); (fig) accommodate (jdm
sb); **E~kommen** nt obligingness;
~kommend a obliging; **~laufen** vi irreg
(+dat) run towards or to meet; (fig) run
counter to; **~nehmen** vt irreg receive,
accept; **~sehen** vi irreg (+dat) await;
~setzen vt (dat to); **~treten** vi irreg
(+dat) (lit) step up to; (fig) oppose,
counter; **~wirken** vi (+dat) counteract.

entgegnen [ɛnt'geːgnən] vt reply, retort.

Entgegnung f reply, retort.

entgehen [ɛnt'geːən] vi irreg (fig) **jdm ~**
escape sb's notice; **sich** (dat) **etw ~
lassen** miss sth.

entgeistert [ɛnt'gaistərt] a thunderstruck.

Entgelt [ɛnt'gɛlt] nt -(e)s, -e compensation, remuneration; **e~en** vt irreg: **jdm
etw e~en** repay sb for sth.

entgleisen [ɛnt'glaizən] vi (Rail) be
derailed; (fig: Person) misbehave; **~
lassen** derail.

Entgleisung f derailment; (fig) faux pas,
gaffe.

entgleiten [ɛnt'glaitən] vi irreg slip (jdm
from sb's hand).

entgräten [ɛnt'grɛːtən] vt fillet, bone.

Enthaarungsmittel [ɛnt'haːruŋsmɪtəl] nt
depilatory.

enthalten [ɛnt'haltən] irreg vt contain; vr
abstain, refrain (gen from).

enthaltsam [ɛnt'haltzaːm] a abstinent,
abstemious; **E~keit** f abstinence.

enthemmen [ɛnt'hɛmən] vt: **jdn ~** free
sb from his inhibitions.

enthüllen [ɛnt'hylən] vt reveal, unveil.

Enthusiasmus [ɛntuzi'asmʊs] m
enthusiasm.

entkernen [ɛnt'kɛrnən] vt stone; core.

entkommen [ɛnt'kɔmən] vi irreg get
away, escape (dat, aus from).

entkorken [ɛnt'kɔrkən] vt uncork.

entkräften [ɛnt'krɛftən] vt weaken,
exhaust; Argument refute.

entladen [ɛnt'laːdən] irreg vt unload;
(Elec) discharge; vr (Elec, Gewehr) discharge; (Ärger etc) vent itself.

entlang [ɛnt'laŋ] prep +acc or dat, ad
along; **~ dem Fluß, den Fluß ~** along
the river; **~gehen** vi irreg walk along.

entlarven [ɛnt'larfən] vt unmask, expose.

entlassen [ɛnt'lasən] vt irreg discharge; *Arbeiter* dismiss.

Entlassung f discharge; dismissal.

entlasten [ɛnt'lastən] vt relieve; *Achse* relieve the load on; *Angeklagte* exonerate; *Konto* clear.

Entlastung f relief; (*Comm*) crediting; ~szeuge m defence witness.

entledigen [ɛnt'leːdɪgən] vr: sich jds/einer Sache ~ rid o.s. of sb/sth.

entleeren [ɛnt'leːrən] vt empty; evacuate.

entlegen [ɛnt'leːgən] a remote.

entlocken [ɛnt'lɔkən] vt elicit (jdm etw sth from sb).

entlüften [ɛnt'lʏftən] vt ventilate.

entmachten [ɛnt'maxtən] vt deprive of power.

entmenscht [ɛnt'mɛnʃt] a inhuman, bestial.

entmilitarisiert [ɛntmilitariˈziːrt] a demilitarized.

entmündigen [ɛnt'mʏndɪgən] vt certify.

entmutigen [ɛnt'muːtɪgən] vt discourage.

Entnahme [ɛnt'naːmə] f -, -n removal, withdrawal.

entnehmen [ɛnt'neːmən] vt irreg (+dat) take out (of), take (from); (folgern) infer (from).

entpuppen [ɛnt'pʊpən] vr (fig) reveal o.s., turn out (als to be).

entrahmen [ɛnt'raːmən] vt skim.

entreißen [ɛnt'raɪsən] vt irreg snatch (away) (jdm etw sth from sb).

entrichten [ɛnt'rɪçtən] vt pay.

entrosten [ɛnt'rɔstən] vt derust.

entrüst- [ɛnt'rʏst] cpd: ~en vt incense, outrage; vr be filled with indignation; ~et a indignant, outraged; E~ung f indignation.

entsagen [ɛnt'zaːgən] vi renounce (dat sth).

entschädigen [ɛnt'ʃɛːdɪgən] vt compensate.

Entschädigung f compensation.

entschärfen [ɛnt'ʃɛrfən] vt defuse; *Kritik* tone down.

Entscheid [ɛnt'ʃaɪt] m -(e)s, -e decision; e~en vtir irreg decide; e~end a decisive; *Stimme* casting; ~ung f decision; ~ungsspiel nt play-off.

entschieden [ɛnt'ʃiːdən] a decided; (entschlossen) resolute; E~heit f firmness, determination.

entschließen [ɛnt'ʃliːsən] vr irreg decide.

entschlossen [ɛnt'ʃlɔsən] a determined, resolute; E~heit f determination.

Entschluß [ɛnt'ʃlʊs] m decision; e~freudig a decisive; ~kraft f determination, decisiveness.

entschuld- [ɛnt'ʃʊld] cpd: ~bar a excusable; ~igen vt excuse; vr apologize; E~igung f apology; (Grund) excuse; jdn um E~igung bitten apologize to sb; E~igung! excuse me; (Verzeihung) sorry.

entschwinden [ɛnt'ʃvɪndən] vi irreg disappear.

entsetz- [ɛnt'zɛts] cpd: ~en vt horrify; (Mil) relieve; vr be horrified or appalled;

E~en nt -s horror, dismay; ~lich a dreadful, appalling; ~t a horrified.

entsichern [ɛnt'zɪçərn] vt release the safety catch of.

entsinnen [ɛnt'zɪnən] vr irreg remember (gen sth).

entspannen [ɛnt'ʃpanən] vtr *Körper* relax; (Pol) *Lage* ease.

Entspannung f relaxation, rest; (Pol) détente; ~spolitik f policy of détente; ~sübungen pl relaxation exercises pl.

entsprechen [ɛnt'ʃprɛçən] vi irreg (+dat) correspond to; *Anforderungen, Wünschen* meet, comply with; ~d a appropriate; ad accordingly.

entspringen [ɛnt'ʃprɪŋən] vi irreg spring (from).

entstehen [ɛnt'ʃteːən] vi irreg arise, result.

Entstehung f genesis, origin.

entstellen [ɛnt'ʃtɛlən] vt disfigure; *Wahrheit* distort.

entstören [ɛnt'ʃtøːrən] vt (Rad) eliminate interference from; (Aut) suppress.

enttäuschen [ɛnt'tɔʏʃən] vt disappoint.

Enttäuschung f disappointment.

entwaffnen [ɛnt'vafnən] vt (lit,fig) disarm.

Entwarnung [ɛnt'varnʊŋ] f all clear (signal).

entwässer- [ɛnt'vɛsər] cpd: ~n vt drain; E~ung f drainage.

entweder ['ɛntveːdər] cj either.

entweichen [ɛnt'vaɪçən] vi irreg escape.

entweihen [ɛnt'vaɪən] vt irreg desecrate.

entwenden [ɛnt'vɛndən] vt irreg purloin, steal.

entwerfen [ɛnt'vɛrfən] vt irreg *Zeichnung* sketch; *Modell* design; *Vortrag, Gesetz etc* draft.

entwerten [ɛnt'veːrtən] vt devalue; (stempeln) cancel.

entwickeln [ɛnt'vɪkəln] vtr develop (auch Phot); *Mut, Energie* show, display.

Entwickler m -s, - developer.

Entwicklung [ɛnt'vɪklʊŋ] f development; (Phot) developing; ~sabschnitt m stage of development; ~shilfe f aid for developing countries; ~sjahre pl adolescence sing; ~sland nt developing country.

entwirren [ɛnt'vɪrən] vt disentangle.

entwischen [ɛnt'vɪʃən] vi escape.

entwöhnen [ɛnt'vøːnən] vt wean; *Süchtige* cure (dat, von of).

Entwöhnung f weaning; cure, curing.

entwürdigend [ɛnt'vʏrdɪgənt] a degrading.

Entwurf [ɛnt'vʊrf] m outline, design; (Vertrags-, Konzept) draft.

entwurzeln [ɛnt'vʊrtsəln] vt uproot.

entziehen [ɛnt'tsiːən] irreg vt withdraw, take away (dat from); *Flüssigkeit* draw, extract; vr escape (dat from); (jds Kenntnis) be outside; (der Pflicht) shirk.

Entziehung f withdrawal; ~sanstalt f drug addiction/alcoholism treatment centre; ~skur f treatment for drug addiction/alcoholism.

entziffern [ɛnt'tsɪfərn] vt decipher; decode.

entzücken [ɛnt'tsʏkən] vt delight; **E~** nt **-s** delight; **~d** a delightful, charming.

entzünden [ɛnt'tsʏndən] vt light, set light to; (fig, Med) inflame; Streit spark off; vr (lit, fig) catch fire; (Streit) start; (Med) become inflamed.

Entzündung f (Med) inflammation.

entzwei [ɛnt'tsvaɪ] ad broken; in two; **~brechen** vti irreg break in two; **~en** vt set at odds; vr fall out; **~gehen** vi irreg break (in two).

Enzian ['ɛntsia:n] m **-s, -e** gentian.

Enzym [ɛn'tsy:m] nt **-s, -e** enzyme.

Epidemie [epide'mi:] f epidemic.

Epilepsie [epilɛ'psi:] f epilepsy.

episch ['e:pɪʃ] a epic.

Episode [epi'zo:də] f **-, -n** episode.

Epoche [e'pɔxə] f **-, -n** epoch; **e~machend** a epoch-making.

Epos ['e:pɔs] nt **-s, Epen** epic (poem).

er [e:r] pron he; it.

erachten [ɛr''axtən] vt: **~** für or als consider (to be); meines **E~s** in my opinion.

erarbeiten [ɛr'arbaɪtən] vt (auch sich (dat) **~**) work for, acquire; Theorie work out.

erbarmen [ɛr'barmən] vr have pity or mercy (gen on); **E~** nt **-s** pity.

erbärmlich [ɛr'bɛrmlıç] a wretched, pitiful; **E~keit** f wretchedness.

erbarmungs- [ɛr'barmuŋs] cpd: **~los** a pitiless, merciless; **~voll** a compassionate; **~würdig** a pitiable, wretched.

erbau- [ɛr'bau] cpd: **~en** vt build, erect; (fig) edify; **E~er** m **-s, -** builder; **~lich** a edifying; **E~ung** f construction; (fig) edification.

Erbe ['ɛrbə] m **-n, -n** heir; nt **-s** inheritance; (fig) heritage; **e~n** vt inherit.

erbeuten [ɛr'bɔytən] vt carry off; (Mil) capture.

Erb- [ɛrb] cpd: **~faktor** m gene; **~fehler** m hereditary defect; **~folge** f (line of) succession; **~in** f heiress.

erbittern [ɛr'bɪtərn] vt embitter; (erzürnen) incense.

erbittert [ɛr'bɪtərt] a Kampf fierce, bitter.

erblassen [ɛr'blasən] vi, **erbleichen** [ɛr'blaıçən] vi irreg (turn) pale.

erblich ['ɛrplıç] a hereditary.

Erbmasse ['ɛrbmasə] f estate; (Biol) genotype.

erbosen [ɛr'bo:zən] vt anger; vr grow angry.

erbrechen [ɛr'brɛçən] vtr irreg vomit.

Erb- cpd: **~recht** nt right of succession, hereditary right; law of inheritance; **~schaft** f inheritance, legacy.

Erbse ['ɛrpsə] f **-, -n** pea.

Erb- cpd: **~stück** nt heirloom; **~teil** nt inherited trait; (portion of) inheritance.

Erd- [e:rd] cpd: **~achse** f earth's axis; **~atmosphäre** f earth's atmosphere; **~bahn** f orbit of the earth; **~beben** nt earthquake; **~beere** f strawberry;

~boden m ground; **~e** f **-, -n** earth; **zu ebener ~e** at ground level; **e~en** vt (Elec) earth.

erdenkbar [ɛr'dɛŋkba:r], **erdenklich** [-lıç] a conceivable.

Erd- cpd: **~gas** nt natural gas; **~geschoß** nt ground floor; **~kunde** f geography; **~nuß** f peanut; **~oberfläche** f surface of the earth; **~öl** nt (mineral) oil.

erdreisten [ɛr'draɪstən] vr dare, have the audacity (to do sth).

erdrosseln [ɛr'drɔsəln] vt strangle, throttle.

erdrücken [ɛr'drʏkən] vt crush.

Erd- cpd: **~rutsch** m landslide; **~teil** m continent.

erdulden [ɛr'duldən] vt endure, suffer.

ereifern [ɛr''aıfərn] vr get excited.

ereignen [ɛr''aıgnən] vr happen.

Ereignis [ɛr''aıgnıs] nt **-ses, -se** event; **e~reich** a eventful.

erfahren [ɛr'fa:rən] vt irreg learn, find out; (erleben) experience; a experienced.

Erfahrung f experience; **e~sgemäß** ad according to experience.

erfassen [ɛr'fasən] vt seize; (fig) (einbeziehen) include, register; (verstehen) grasp.

erfind- [ɛr'fınd] cpd: **~en** vt irreg invent; **E~er** m **-s, -** inventor; **~erisch** a inventive; **E~ung** f invention; **E~ungsgabe** f inventiveness.

Erfolg [ɛr'fɔlk] m **-(e)s, -e** success; (Folge) result; **e~en** vi follow; (sich ergeben) result; (stattfinden) take place; (Zahlung) be effected; **e~los** a unsuccessful; **~losigkeit** f lack of success; **e~reich** a successful; **e~versprechend** a promising.

erforder- [ɛr'fɔrdər] cpd: **~lich** a requisite, necessary; **~n** vt require, demand; **E~nis** nt **-ses, -se** requirement; prerequisite.

erforsch- [ɛr'fɔrʃ] cpd: **~en** vt Land explore; Problem investigate; Gewissen search; **E~er** m **-s, -** explorer; investigator; **E~ung** f exploration; investigation; searching.

erfragen [ɛr'fra:gən] vt inquire after, ascertain.

erfreuen [ɛr'frɔyən] vr: **sich ~ an** (+dat) enjoy; **sich einer Sache** (gen) **~** enjoy sth; vt delight.

erfreulich [ɛr'frɔylıç] a pleasing, gratifying; **~erweise** ad happily, luckily.

erfrieren [ɛr'fri:rən] vi irreg freeze (to death); (Glieder) get frostbitten; (Pflanzen) be killed by frost.

erfrischen [ɛr'frıʃən] vt refresh.

Erfrischung f refreshment; **~sraum** m snack bar, cafeteria.

erfüllen [ɛr'fʏlən] vt Raum etc fill; (fig) Bitte etc fulfil; vr come true.

ergänzen [ɛr'gɛntsən] vt supplement, complete; vr complement one another.

Ergänzung f completion; (Zusatz) supplement.

ergattern [ɛr'gatərn] vt (col) get hold of, hunt up.

ergaunern [ɛr'gaunərn] *vt (col)* **sich** *(dat)* **etw ~** get hold of sth by underhand methods.

ergeben [ɛr'ge:bən] *irreg vt* yield, produce; *vr* surrender; *(sich hingeben)* give o.s. up, yield *(dat* to); *(folgen)* result; a devoted, humble; *(dem Trunk)* addicted (to); **E~heit** *f* devotion, humility.

Ergebnis [ɛr'ge:pnɪs] *nt* **-ses, -se** result; **e~los** a without result, fruitless.

ergehen [ɛr'ge:ən] *irreg vi* be issued, go out; **etw über sich ~ lassen** put up with sth; *vi impers:* **es ergeht ihm gut/schlecht** he's faring *or* getting on well/badly; *vr:* **sich in etw** *(dat)* **~** indulge in sth.

ergiebig [ɛr'gi:bɪç] a productive.

ergötzen [ɛr'gœtsən] *vt* amuse, delight.

ergreifen [ɛr'graifən] *vt irreg (lit, fig)* seize; *Beruf* take up; *Maßnahmen* resort to; *(rühren)* move; **~d** a moving, affecting.

ergriffen [ɛr'grifən] a deeply moved.

Erguß [ɛr'gus] *m* discharge; *(fig)* out-pouring, effusion.

erhaben [ɛr'ha:bən] a *(lit)* raised, embossed; *(fig)* exalted, lofty; **über etw** *(acc)* **~ sein** be above sth.

erhalten [ɛr'haltən] *vt irreg* receive; *(bewahren)* preserve, maintain; **gut ~** in good condition.

erhältlich [ɛr'hɛltlɪç] a obtainable, available.

Erhaltung *f* maintenance, preservation.

erhängen [ɛr'hɛŋən] *vtr* hang.

erhärten [ɛr'hɛrtən] *vt* harden; *These* substantiate, corroborate.

erhaschen [ɛr'haʃən] *vt* catch.

erheben [ɛr'he:bən] *irreg vt* raise; *Protest, Forderungen* make; *Fakten* ascertain, establish; *vr* rise (up); **sich über etw** *(acc)* **~** rise above sth.

erheblich [ɛr'he:plɪç] a considerable.

erheitern [ɛr'haitərn] *vt* amuse, cheer (up).

Erheiterung *f* exhilaration; **zur allgemeinen ~** to everybody's amusement.

erhellen [ɛr'hɛlən] *vt (lit, fig)* illuminate; *Geheimnis* shed light on; *vr* brighten, light up.

erhitzen [ɛr'hɪtsən] *vt* heat; *vr* heat up; *(fig)* become heated *or* aroused.

erhoffen [ɛr'hɔfən] *vt* hope for.

erhöhen [ɛr'hø:ən] *vt* raise; *(verstärken)* increase.

erhol- [ɛr'ho:l] *cpd:* **~en** *vr* recover; *(entspannen)* have a rest; **~sam** a restful; **E~ung** *f* recovery; relaxation, rest; **~ungsbedürftig** a in need of a rest, run-down; **E~ungsheim** *nt* convalescent/rest home.

erhören [ɛr'hø:rən] *vt Gebet etc* hear; *Bitte etc* yield to.

Erika ['e:rika] ka] *f* -, **Eriken** heather.

erinnern [ɛr'ɪnərn] *vt* remind *(an +acc* of); *vr* remember *(an etw (acc)* sth).

Erinnerung *f* memory; *(Andenken)* reminder; **~stafel** *f* commemorative plaque.

erkalten [ɛr'kaltən] *vi* go cold, cool (down).

erkält- [ɛr'kɛlt] *cpd:* **~en** *vr* catch cold; **~et** a with a cold; **~et sein** have a cold; **E~ung** *f* cold.

erkenn- [ɛr'kɛn] *cpd:* **~bar** a recognizable; **~en** *vt irreg* recognize; *(sehen, verstehen)* see; **~tlich** a: **sich ~tlich zeigen** show one's appreciation; **E~tlichkeit** *f* gratitude; *(Geschenk)* token of one's gratitude; **E~tnis** *f* -, **-se** knowledge; *(das Erkennen)* recognition; *(Einsicht)* insight; **zur E~tnis kommen** realize; **E~ung** *f* recognition; **E~ungsmarke** *f* identity disc.

Erker ['ɛrkər] *m* -s, - bay; **~fenster** *nt* bay window.

erklär- [ɛr'klɛ:r] *cpd:* **~bar** a explicable; **~en** *vt* explain; **~lich** a explicable; *(verständlich)* understandable; **E~ung** *f* explanation; *(Aussage)* declaration.

erklecklich [ɛr'klɛklɪç] a considerable.

erklingen [ɛr'klɪŋən] *vi irreg* resound, ring out.

Erkrankung [ɛr'kraŋkuŋ] *f* illness.

erkund- [ɛr'kund] *cpd:* **~en** *vt* find out, ascertain; *(esp Mil)* reconnitre, scout; **~igen** *vr* inquire *(nach* about); **E~igung** *f* inquiry; **E~ung** *f* reconnaissance, scouting.

erlahmen [ɛr'la:mən] *vi* tire; *(nachlassen)* flag, wane.

erlangen [ɛr'laŋən] *vt* attain, achieve.

Erlaß [ɛr'las] *m* **-sses, -lässe** decree; *(Aufhebung)* remission.

erlassen *vt irreg Verfügung* issue; *Gesetz* enact; *Strafe* remit; **jdm etw ~** release sb from sth.

erlauben [ɛr'laubən] *vt* allow, permit *(jdm etw* sb to do sth); *vr* permit o.s., venture.

Erlaubnis [ɛr'laupnɪs] *f* -, **-se** permission.

erläutern [ɛr'lɔytərn] *vt* explain.

Erläuterung *f* explanation.

Erle ['ɛrlə] *f* -, **-n** alder.

erleben [ɛr'le:bən] *vt* experience; *Zeit* live through; *(mit ~)* witness; *(noch mit ~)* live to see.

Erlebnis [ɛr'le:pnɪs] *nt* **-ses, -se** experience.

erledigen [ɛr'le:dɪgən] *vt* take care of, deal with; *Antrag etc* process; *(col: erschöpfen)* wear out; *(col: ruinieren)* finish; *(col: umbringen)* do in.

erlegen [ɛr'le:gən] *vt* kill.

erleichter- [ɛr'laiçtər] *cpd:* **~n** *vt* make easier; *(fig)* Last lighten; *(lindern, beruhigen)* relieve; **~t** a relieved; **E~ung** *f* facilitation; lightening; relief.

erleiden [ɛr'laidən] *vt irreg* suffer, endure.

erlernbar a learnable.

erlernen [ɛr'lɛrnən] *vt* learn, acquire.

erlesen [ɛr'le:zən] a select, choice.

erleuchten [ɛr'lɔyçtən] *vt* illuminate; *(fig)* inspire.

Erleuchtung *f (Einfall)* inspiration.

erlogen [ɛr'lo:gən] a untrue, made-up.

Erlös [ɛr'lø:s] *m* **-es, -e** proceeds *pl*.

erlöschen [ɛr'lœʃən] *vi (Feuer)* go out;

(*Interesse*) cease, die; (*Vertrag, Recht*) expire.

erlösen [ɛrˈløːzən] *vt* redeem, save.

Erlösung *f* release; (*Rel*) redemption.

ermächtigen [ɛrˈmɛçtɪgən] *vt* authorize, empower.

Ermächtigung *f* authorization; authority.

ermahnen [ɛrˈmaːnən] *vt* exhort, admonish.

Ermahnung *f* admonition, exhortation.

ermäßigen [ɛrˈmɛsɪgən] *vt* reduce.

Ermäßigung *f* reduction.

ermessen [ɛrˈmɛsən] *vt irreg* estimate, gauge; **E~** *nt* **-s** estimation; discretion; **in jds E~ liegen** lie within sb's discretion.

ermitteln [ɛrˈmɪtəln] *vt* determine; *Täter* trace; *vi*: **gegen jdn ~** investigate sb.

Ermittlung [ɛrˈmɪtluŋ] *f* determination; (*Polizei—*) investigation.

ermöglichen [ɛrˈmøːklɪçən] *vt* make possible (*dat* for).

ermord- [ɛrˈmɔrd] *cpd*: **~en** *vt* murder; **E~ung** *f* murder.

ermüden [ɛrˈmyːdən] *vti* tire; (*Tech*) fatigue; **~d** a tiring; (*fig*) wearisome.

Ermüdung *f* fatigue; **~serscheinung** *f* sign of fatigue.

ermuntern [ɛrˈmʊntərn] *vt* rouse; (*ermutigen*) encourage; (*beleben*) liven up; (*aufmuntern*) cheer up.

ermutigen [ɛrˈmuːtɪgən] *vt* encourage.

ernähr- [ɛrˈnɛːr] *cpd*: **~en** *vt* feed, nourish; *Familie* support; *vr* support o.s., earn a living; **sich ~en von** live on; **E~er** *m* **-s**, - breadwinner; **E~ung** *f* nourishment; nutrition; (*Unterhalt*) maintenance.

ernennen [ɛrˈnɛnən] *vt irreg* appoint.

Ernennung *f* appointment.

erneu- [ɛrˈnɔy] *cpd*: **~ern** *vt* renew; restore; renovate; **E~erung** *f* renewal; restoration; renovation; **~t** a renewed, fresh; *ad* once more.

erniedrigen [ɛrˈniːdrɪgən] *vt* humiliate, degrade.

Ernst [ɛrnst] *m* **-es** seriousness; **das ist mein ~** I'm quite serious; **im ~** in earnest; **~ machen mit etw** put sth into practice; **e~** a serious; **~fall** *m* emergency; **e~gemeint** a meant in earnest, serious; **e~haft** a serious; **~haftigkeit** *f* seriousness; **e~lich** a serious.

Ernte [ˈɛrntə] *f* -, **-n** harvest; **~dankfest** *nt* harvest festival; **e~n** *vt* harvest; *Lob etc* earn.

ernüchtern [ɛrˈnʏçtərn] *vt* sober up; (*fig*) bring down to earth.

Ernüchterung *f* sobering up; (*fig*) disillusionment.

Erober- [ɛrˈoːbər] *cpd*: **~er** *m* **-s**, - conqueror; **e~n** *vt* conquer; **~ung** *f* conquest.

eröffnen [ɛrˈœfnən] *vt* open; **jdm etw ~** disclose sth to sb; *vr* present itself.

Eröffnung *f* opening; **~sansprache** *f* inaugural *or* opening address.

erogen [ɛroˈgeːn] a erogenous.

erörtern [ɛrˈœrtərn] *vt* discuss.

Erörterung *f* discussion.

Erotik [eˈroːtɪk] *f* eroticism.

erotisch a erotic.

erpicht [ɛrˈpɪçt] a eager, keen (*auf* +acc on).

erpress- [ɛrˈprɛs] *cpd*: **~en** *vt* Geld etc extort; *Mensch* blackmail; **E~er** *m* **-s**, - blackmailer; **E~ung** *f* blackmail; extortion.

erproben [ɛrˈproːbən] *vt* test.

erraten [ɛrˈraːtən] *vt irreg* guess.

erreg- [ɛrˈreːk] *cpd*: **~bar** a excitable; (*reizbar*) irritable; **E~barkeit** *f* excitability; irritability; **~en** *vt* excite; (*ärgern*) infuriate; (*hervorrufen*) arouse, provoke; *vr* get excited *or* worked up; **E~er** *m* **-s**, - causative agent; **E~theit** *f* excitement; (*Beunruhigung*) agitation; **E~ung** *f* excitement.

erreichbar a accessible, within reach.

erreichen [ɛrˈraiçən] *vt* reach; *Zweck* achieve; *Zug* catch.

errichten [ɛrˈrɪçtən] *vt* erect, put up; (*gründen*) establish, set up.

erringen [ɛrˈrɪŋən] *vt irreg* gain, win.

erröten [ɛrˈrøːtən] *vi* blush, flush.

Errungenschaft [ɛrˈrʊŋənʃaft] *f* achievement; (*col: Anschaffung*) acquisition.

Ersatz [ɛrˈzats] *m* **-es** substitute; replacement; (*Schaden—*) compensation; (*Mil*) reinforcements *pl*; **~befriedigung** *f* vicarious satisfaction; **~dienst** *m* (*Mil*) alternative service; **~mann** *m* replacement; (*Sport*) substitute; **e~pflichtig** a liable to pay compensation; **~reifen** *m* (*Aut*) spare tyre; **~teil** *nt* spare (part).

ersaufen [ɛrˈzaufən] *vi irreg* (*col*) drown.

ersäufen [ɛrˈzɔyfən] *vt* drown.

erschaffen [ɛrˈʃafən] *vt irreg* create.

erscheinen [ɛrˈʃainən] *vi irreg* appear.

Erscheinung *f* appearance; (*Geist*) apparition; (*Gegebenheit*) phenomenon; (*Gestalt*) figure.

erschießen [ɛrˈʃiːsən] *vt irreg* shoot (dead).

erschlaffen [ɛrˈʃlafən] *vi* go limp; (*Mensch*) become exhausted.

erschlagen [ɛrˈʃlaːgən] *vt irreg* strike dead.

erschleichen [ɛrˈʃlaiçən] *vt irreg* obtain by stealth *or* dubious methods.

erschöpf- [ɛrˈʃœpf] *cpd*: **~en** *vt* exhaust; **~end** a exhaustive, thorough; **~t** a exhausted; **E~ung** *f* exhaustion.

erschrecken [ɛrˈʃrɛkən] *vt* startle, frighten; *vi irreg* be frightened *or* startled; **~d** a alarming, frightening.

erschrocken [ɛrˈʃrɔkən] a frightened, startled.

erschüttern [ɛrˈʃʏtərn] *vt* shake; (*ergreifen*) move deeply.

Erschütterung *f* shaking; shock.

erschweren [ɛrˈʃveːrən] *vt* complicate.

erschwingen [ɛrˈʃvɪŋən] *vt irreg* afford.

erschwinglich a within one's means.

ersehen [ɛrˈzeːən] *vt irreg*: **aus etw ~, daß** gather from sth that.

ersetz- [ɛrˈzɛts] *cpd*: **~bar** a replaceable; **~en** *vt* replace; **jdm Unkosten** *etc* **~en** pay sb's expenses *etc*.

ersichtlich [ɛrˈzɪçtlɪç] a evident, obvious.
erspar- [ɛrˈʃpaːr] cpd: ~**en** vt Ärger etc spare; Geld save; **E~nis** f-, -**se** saving.
ersprießlich [ɛrˈʃpriːslɪç] a profitable, useful; (angenehm) pleasant.
erst [eːrst] ad (at) first; (nicht früher, nur) only; (nicht bis) not till; ~ **einmal** first.
erstarren [ɛrˈʃtarən] vi stiffen; (vor Furcht) grow rigid; (Materie) solidify.
erstatten [ɛrˈʃtatən] vt Kosten (re)pay; **Anzeige** etc ~ report sb; **Bericht** ~ make a report.
Erstaufführung [ˈeːrstauffyːruŋ] f first performance.
erstaunen [ɛrˈʃtaunən] vt astonish; vi be astonished; **E~** nt -s astonishment.
erstaunlich a astonishing.
erst- [ˈeːrst] cpd: **E-ausgabe** f first edition; ~**beste(r,s)** a first that comes along; ~**e(r,s)** a first.
erstechen [ɛrˈʃtɛçən] vt irreg stab (to death).
erstehen [ɛrˈʃteːən] vt irreg buy; vi (a)rise.
ersteigen [ɛrˈʃtaɪgən] vt irreg climb, ascend.
erstellen [ɛrˈʃtɛlən] vt erect, build.
erst- cpd: ~**emal** ad (the) first time; ~**ens** ad firstly, in the first place; ~**ere(r,s)** pron (the) former.
ersticken [ɛrˈʃtɪkən] vt (lit, fig) stifle; Mensch suffocate; Flammen smother; vi (Mensch) suffocate; (Feuer) be smothered; **in Arbeit** ~ be snowed under with work.
Erstickung f suffocation.
erst- cpd: ~**klassig** a first-class; **E~kommunion** f first communion; ~**malig** a first; ~**mals** ad for the first time.
erstrebenswert [ɛrˈʃtreːbənsveːrt] a desirable, worthwhile.
erstrecken [ɛrˈʃtrɛkən] vr extend, stretch.
Ersttags- [ˈeːrst-taːgz] cpd: ~**brief** m first-day cover; ~**stempel** m first-day (date) stamp.
ersuchen [ɛrˈzuːxən] vt request.
ertappen [ɛrˈtapən] vt catch, detect.
erteilen [ɛrˈtaɪlən] vt give.
ertönen [ɛrˈtøːnən] vi sound, ring out.
Ertrag [ɛrˈtraːk] m -(e)s, ·e yield; (Gewinn) proceeds pl; **e~en** vt irreg bear, stand.
erträglich [ɛrˈtrɛːklɪç] a tolerable, bearable.
ertränken [ɛrˈtrɛŋkən] vt drown.
erträumen [ɛrˈtrɔʏmən] vt: **sich** (dat) etw ~ dream of sth, imagine sth.
ertrinken [ɛrˈtrɪŋkən] vi irreg drown; **E~** nt -s drowning.
erübrigen [ɛrˈyːbrɪgən] vt spare; vr be unnecessary.
erwachen [ɛrˈvaxən] vi awake.
erwachsen [ɛrˈvaksən] a grown-up; **E~e(r)** mf adult; **E~enbildung** f adult education.
erwägen [ɛrˈvɛːgən] vt irreg consider.
Erwägung f consideration.
erwähn- [ɛrˈvɛːn] cpd: ~**en** vt mention; ~**enswert** a worth mentioning; **E~ung** f mention.

erwärmen [ɛrˈvɛrmən] vt warm, heat; vr get warm, warm up; **sich** ~ **für** warm to.
erwarten [ɛrˈvartən] vt expect; (warten auf) wait for; **etw kaum** ~ **können** hardly be able to wait for sth.
Erwartung f expectation; **e~sgemäß** ad as expected; **e~svoll** a expectant.
erwecken [ɛrˈvɛkən] vt rouse, awake; **den Anschein** ~ give the impression.
erwehren [ɛrˈveːrən] vr fend, ward (gen off); (des Lachens etc) refrain (gen from).
erweichen [ɛrˈvaɪçən] vti soften.
Erweis [ɛrˈvaɪs] m -es, -e proof; **e~en** irreg vt prove; Ehre, Dienst do (jdm sb); vr prove (als to be).
Erwerb [ɛrˈvɛrp] m -(e)s, -e acquisition; (Beruf) trade; **e~en** vt irreg acquire; **e~slos** a unemployed; ~**squelle** f source of income; **e~stätig** a (gainfully) employed; **e~sunfähig** a unemployable.
erwidern [ɛrˈviːdərn] vt reply; (vergelten) return.
erwiesen [ɛrˈviːzən] a proven.
erwischen [ɛrˈvɪʃən] vt (col) catch, get.
erwünscht [ɛrˈvʏnʃt] a desired.
erwürgen [ɛrˈvʏrgən] vt strangle.
Erz [eːrts] nt -es, -e ore.
erzähl- [ɛrˈtsɛːl] cpd: ~**en** vt tell; **E~er** m -s, - narrator; **E~ung** f story, tale.
Erz- cpd: ~**bischof** m archbishop; ~**engel** m archangel.
erzeug- [ɛrˈtsɔʏg] cpd: ~**en** vt produce; Strom generate; **E~erpreis** m producer's price; **E~nis** nt -ses, -se product, produce; **E~ung** f production; generation.
erziehen [ɛrˈtsiːən] vt irreg bring up; (bilden) educate, train.
Erziehung f bringing up; (Bildung) education; ~**sbeihilfe** f educational grant; ~**sberechtigte(r)** mf parent; guardian; ~**sheim** nt approved school.
erzielen [ɛrˈtsiːlən] vt achieve, obtain; Tor score.
erzwingen [ɛrˈtsvɪŋən] vt irreg force, obtain by force.
es [ɛs] pron nom, acc it.
Esche [ˈɛʃə] f-, -n ash.
Esel [ˈeːzəl] m -s, - donkey, ass; ~**sohr** nt dog-ear.
Eskalation [ɛskalatsiˈoːn] f escalation.
eßbar [ˈɛsbaːr] a eatable, edible.
essen [ˈɛsən] vti irreg eat; **E~** nt -s, - meal; food; **E~szeit** f mealtime; dinner time.
Essig [ˈɛsɪç] m -s, -e vinegar; ~**gurke** f gherkin.
Eß- [ˈɛs] cpd: ~**kastanie** f sweet chestnut; ~**löffel** m tablespoon; ~**tisch** m dining table; ~**waren** pl victuals pl, food provisions pl; ~**zimmer** nt dining room.
etablieren [etaˈbliːrən] vr become established; set up business.
Etage [eˈtaːʒə] f-, -n floor, storey; ~**nbetten** pl bunk beds pl; ~**nwohnung** f flat.
Etappe [eˈtapə] f-, -n stage.
Etat [eˈtaː] m -s, -s budget; ~**jahr** nt financial year; ~**posten** m budget item.

etepetete [e:tə'pe:tə] a *(col)* fussy.
Ethik ['e:tık] *f* ethics *sing.*
ethisch ['e:tıʃ] a ethical.
Etikett [eti'kɛt] *nt* **-(e)s, -e** label; tag; ~e *f* etiquette, manners *pl*; **e~ieren** [-'ti:rən] *vt* label; tag.
etliche ['ɛtlıçə] *pron pl* some, quite a few; ~s a thing or two.
Etui [ɛt'vi:] *nt* **-s, -s** case.
etwa ['ɛtva] *ad* *(ungefähr)* about; *(vielleicht)* perhaps; *(beispielsweise)* for instance; **nicht** ~ by no means; ~ig ['ɛtva-ıç] a possible; ~s *pron* something; anything; *(ein wenig)* a little; *ad* a little.
Etymologie [etymolo'gi:] *f* etymology.
euch [ɔʏç] *pron acc of* **ihr** you; yourselves; *dat of* **ihr** (to) you.
euer ['ɔʏər] *pron gen of* **ihr** of you; *pron your;* ~**e(r,s)** yours.
Eule ['ɔʏlə] *f* **-, -n** owl.
eure(r,s) ['ɔʏrə(r,z)] *pron* your; yours; **-rseits** *ad* on your part; ~**twegen**, ~**twillen** *ad (für euch)* for your sakes; *(wegen euch)* on your account.
eurige *pron:* **der/die/das** ~ yours.
Euro- [ɔʏro] *cpd:* ~**krat** [-'kra:t] *m* **-en, -en** eurocrat; ~**pameister** [ɔʏ'ro:pa-] *m* European champion.
Euter ['ɔʏtər] *nt* **-s, -** udder.
evakuieren [evaku'i:rən] *vt* evacuate.
evangelisch [evaŋ'ge:lıʃ] a Protestant.
Evangelium [evaŋ'ge:lıum] *nt* gospel.
Eva(s)kostüm ['e:fa(s)kɔsty:m] *nt:* **im** ~ in one's birthday suit.
eventuell [evɛntu'ɛl] a possible; *ad* possibly, perhaps.
EWG [e:ve:'ge:] *f* - EEC, Common Market.
ewig ['e:vıç] a eternal; **E~keit** *f* eternity.
exakt [ɛ'ksakt] a exact.
Examen [ɛ'ksa:mən] *nt* **-s, -** *or* **Examina** examination.
Exempel [ɛ'ksɛmpəl] *nt* **-s, -** example.
Exemplar [ɛksɛm'pla:r] *nt* **-s, -e** specimen; *(Buch—)* copy; **e~isch** a exemplary.
exerzieren [ɛksɛr'tsi:rən] *vi* drill.
Exil [ɛ'ksi:l] *nt* **-s, -e** exile.
Existenz [ɛksıs'tɛnts] *f* existence; *(Unterhalt)* livelihood, living; *(pej: Mensch)* character; ~**kampf** *m* struggle for existence; ~**minimum** *nt* **-s** subsistence level.
existieren [ɛksıs'ti:rən] *vi* exist.
exklusiv [ɛksklu'zi:f] a exclusive; ~**e** [-'zi:və] *ad, prep* +*gen* exclusive of, not including.
exorzieren [ɛksɔr'tsi:rən] *vt* exorcize.
exotisch [ɛ'kso:tıʃ] a exotic.
Expansion [ɛkspanzi'o:n] *f* expansion.
Expedition [ɛkspeditsi'o:n] *f* expedition; *(Comm)* forwarding department.
Experiment [ɛksperi'mɛnt] *nt* experiment; **e~ell** [-'tɛl] a experimental; **e~ieren** [-'ti:rən] *vi* experiment.
Experte [ɛks'pɛrtə] *m* **-n, -n** expert, specialist.
explo- [ɛksplo] *cpd:* ~**dieren** [-'di:rən] *vi* explode; **E~sion** [ɛksplozi'o:n] *f*

explosion; ~**siv** [-'zi:f] a explosive.
Exponent [ɛkspo'nɛnt] *m* exponent.
Export [ɛks'pɔrt] *m* **-(e)s, -e** export; ~**eur** [-'tø:r] *m* exporter; ~**handel** *m* export trade; **e~ieren** [-'ti:rən] *vt* export; ~**land** *nt* exporting country.
Expreß- [ɛks'prɛs] *cpd:* ~**gut** *nt* express goods *pl or* freight; ~**zug** *m* express (train).
extra ['ɛkstra] a *inv (col: gesondert)* separate; *(besondere)* extra; *ad (gesondert)* separately; *(speziell)* specially; *(absichtlich)* on purpose; *(vor Adjektiven, zusätzlich)* extra; **E~** *nt* **-s, -s** extra; **E~ausgabe** *f*, **E~blatt** *nt* special edition.
Extrakt [ɛks'trakt] *m* **-(e)s, -e** extract.
extrem [ɛks'tre:m] a extreme; ~**istisch** [-'mıstıç] a *(Pol)* extremist; **E~itäten** [-'tɛ:tən] *pl* extremities *pl.*
Exzellenz [ɛkstsɛ'lɛnts] *f* excellency.
exzentrisch [ɛks'tsɛntrıʃ] a eccentric.
Exzeß [ɛks'tsɛs] *m* **-sses, -sse** excess.

F

F, f [ɛf] *nt* F, f.
Fabel ['fa:bəl] *f* **-, -n** fable; **f~haft** a fabulous, marvellous.
Fabrik [fa'bri:k] *f* factory; ~**ant** [-'kant] *m* *(Hersteller)* manufacturer; *(Besitzer)* industrialist; ~**arbeiter** *m* factory worker; ~**at** [-'ka:t] *nt* **-(e)s, -e** manufacture, product; ~**ation** [-atsi'o:n] *f* manufacture, production; ~**besitzer** *m* factory owner; ~**gelände** *nt* factory premises *pl.*
Fach [fax] *nt* **-(e)s, ⁻er** compartment; *(Sachgebiet)* subject; **ein Mann vom** ~ an expert; ~**arbeiter** *m* skilled worker; ~**arzt** *m* *(medical)* specialist; ~**ausdruck** *m* technical term.
Fächer ['fɛçər] *m* **-s, -** fan.
Fach- *cpd:* **f~kundig** a expert, specialist; **f~lich** a professional; expert; ~**mann** *m, pl* **-leute** specialist; ~**schule** *f* technical college; **f~simpeln** *vi* talk shop; ~**werk** *nt* timber frame.
Fackel ['fakəl] *f* **-, -n** torch; **f~n** *vi (col)* dither.
fad(e) ['fa:t, fa:də] a insipid; *(langweilig)* dull.
Faden ['fa:dən] *m* **-s, ⁻** thread; ~**nudeln** *pl* vermicelli *pl*; **f~scheinig** a *(lit, fig)* threadbare.
fähig ['fɛ:ıç] a capable *(zu, gen of)*; able; **F~keit** *f* ability.
Fähnchen ['fɛ:nçən] *nt* pennon, streamer.
fahnden ['fa:ndən] *vi:* ~ **nach** search for.
Fahndung *f* search; ~**sliste** *f* list of wanted criminals, wanted list.
Fahne ['fa:nə] *f* **-, -n** flag, standard; **eine** ~ **haben** *(col)* smell of drink; ~**nflucht** *f* desertion.
Fahrbahn *f* carriageway *(Brit)*, roadway.
Fähre ['fɛ:rə] *f* **-, -n** ferry.
fahren ['fa:rən] *irreg vt* drive; *Rad* ride; *(befördern)* drive, take; *Rennen* drive in; *vi (sich bewegen)* go; *(Schiff)* sail; *(abfahren)* leave; **mit dem Auto/Zug** ~ go *or* travel by car/train; **mit der Hand** ~ **über**

(+*acc*) pass one's hand over.

Fahr- ['fa:r] *cpd:* ~**er** *m* -**s**, - driver; ~**erflucht** *f* hit-and-run; ~**gast** *m* passenger; ~**geld** *nt* fare; ~**gestell** *nt* chassis; (*Aviat*) undercarriage; ~**karte** *f* ticket; ~**kartenausgabe** *f*, ~**kartenschalter** *m* ticket office; **f**~**lässig** *a* negligent; **f**~**lässige Tötung** manslaughter; ~**lässigkeit** *f* negligence; ~**lehrer** *m* driving instructor; ~**plan** *m* timetable; **f**~**planmäßig** *a* (*Rail*) scheduled; ~**preis** *m* fare; ~**prüfung** *f* driving test; ~**rad** *nt* bicycle; ~**schein** *m* ticket; ~**schule** *f* driving school; ~**schüler(in** *f*) *m* learner (driver); ~**stuhl** *m* lift, elevator (*US*).

Fahrt [fa:rt] *f* -, -**en** journey; (*kurz*) trip; (*Aut*) drive; (*Geschwindigkeit*) speed.

Fährte ['fε:rtə] *f*-, -**n** track, trail.

Fahrt- *cpd:* ~**kosten** *pl* travelling expenses *pl*; ~**richtung** *f* course, direction.

Fahr- *cpd:* ~**zeug** *nt* vehicle; ~**zeughalter** *m* -**s**, - owner of a vehicle.

Fak- [fak] *cpd:* **f**~**tisch** *a* actual; ~**tor** *m* factor; ~**tum** *nt* -**s**, -**ten** fact; ~**ul'tät** *f* faculty.

Falke ['falkə] *m* -**n**, -**n** falcon.

Fall [fal] *m* -**(e)s**, ⁒**e** (*Sturz*) fall; (*Sachverhalt, Jur, Gram*) case; **auf jeden** ~, **auf alle** ⁒**e** in any case; (*bestimmt*) definitely; ~**e** *f* -, -**n** trap; **f**~**en** *vi irreg* fall; **etw f**~**en lassen** drop sth.

fällen ['fεlən] *vt Baum* fell; *Urteil* pass.

fallenlassen *vt irreg Bemerkung* make; *Plan* abandon, drop.

fällig ['fεlıç] *a* due ; **F**~**keit** *f* (*Comm*) maturity.

Fall- *cpd:* ~**obst** *nt* fallen fruit, windfall; **f**~**s** *ad* in case, if; ~**schirm** *m* parachute; ~**schirmjäger** *pl*, ~**schirmtruppe** *f* paratroops *pl*; ~**schirmspringer** *m* parachutist; ~**tür** *f* trap door.

falsch [falʃ] *a* false; (*unrichtig*) wrong.

fälschen ['fεlʃən] *vt* forge.

Fälscher *m* -**s**, - forger.

Falsch- *cpd:* ~**geld** *nt* counterfeit money; ~**heit** *f* falsity, falseness; (*Unrichtigkeit*) wrongness.

fälsch- *cpd:* ~**lich** *a* false; ~**licherweise** *ad* mistakenly; **F**~**ung** *f* forgery.

Fältchen ['fεltçən] *nt* crease, wrinkle.

Falte ['faltə] *f* -, -**n** (*Knick*) fold, crease; (*Haut*—) wrinkle; (*Rock*—) pleat; **f**~**n** *vt* fold; *Stirn* wrinkle; **f**~**nlos** *a* without folds; without wrinkles.

familiär [famili'ε:r] *a* familiar.

Familie [fa'mi:liə] *f* family; ~**nähnlichkeit** *f* family resemblance; ~**nkreis** *m* family circle; ~**nname** *m* surname; ~**nstand** *m* marital status; ~**nvater** *m* head of the family.

Fanatiker [fa'na:tikər] *m* -**s**, - fanatic.

fanatisch *a* fanatical.

Fanatismus [fana'tısmʊs] *m* fanaticism.

Fang [faŋ] *m* -**(e)s**, ⁒**e** catch; (*Jagen*) hunting; (*Kralle*) talon, claw; **f**~**en** *irreg vt* catch; *vr* get caught; (*Flugzeug*) level

out; (*Mensch: nicht fallen*) steady o.s.; (*fig*) compose o.s.; (*in Leistung*) get back on form.

Farb- ['farb] *cpd:* ~**abzug** *m* coloured print; ~**aufnahme** *f* colour photograph; ~**band** *m* typewriter ribbon; ~**e** *f* -, -**n** colour; (*zum Malen etc*) paint; (*Stoff*—) dye; **f**~**echt** *a* colourfast.

färben ['fεrbən] *vt* colour; *Stoff, Haar* dye.

farben- ['farbən] *cpd:* ~**blind** *a* colourblind; ~**froh**, ~**prächtig** *a* colourful, gay.

Farb- *cpd:* ~**fernsehen** *nt* colour television; ~**film** *m* colour film; **f**~**ig** *a* coloured; ~**ige(r)** *mf* coloured; ~**kasten** *m* paint-box; **f**~**los** *a* colourless; ~**photographie** *f* colour photography; ~**stift** *m* coloured pencil; ~**stoff** *m* dye; ~**ton** *m* hue, tone.

Färbung ['fεrbʊŋ] *f* colouring; (*Tendenz*) bias.

Farn [farn] *m* -**(e)s**, -**e**, ~**kraut** *nt* fern; bracken.

Fasan [fa'za:n] *m* -**(e)s**, -**e(n)** pheasant.

Fasching ['faʃıŋ] *m* -**s**, -**e** *or* -**s** carnival.

Faschismus [fa'ʃısmus] *m* fascism.

Faschist *m* fascist.

faseln ['fa:zəln] *vi* talk nonsense, drivel.

Faser ['fa:zər] *f* -, -**n** fibre; **f**~**n** *vi* fray.

Faß [fas] *nt* -**sses, Fässer** vat, barrel; (*Öl*) drum; **Bier vom** ~ draught beer; **f**~**bar** *a* comprehensible; ~**bier** *nt* draught beer.

fassen ['fasən] *vt* (*ergreifen*) grasp, take; (*inhaltlich*) hold; *Entschluß etc* take; (*verstehen*) understand; *Ring etc* set; (*formulieren*) formulate, phrase; **nicht zu** ~ unbelievable; *vr* calm down.

faßlich ['faslıç] *a* intelligible.

Fassung ['fasʊŋ] *f* (*Umrahmung*) mounting; (*Lampen*—) socket; (*Wortlaut*) version; (*Beherrschung*) composure; **jdn aus der** ~ **bringen** upset sb; **f**~**slos** *a* speechless; ~**svermögen** *nt* capacity; (*Verständnis*) comprehension.

fast [fast] *ad* almost, nearly.

fasten ['fastən] *vi* fast; **F**~ *nt* -**s** fasting; **F**~**zeit** *f* Lent.

Fastnacht *f* Shrove Tuesday; carnival.

fatal [fa'ta:l] *a* fatal; (*peinlich*) embarrassing.

faul [faʊl] *a* rotten; *Person* lazy; *Ausreden* lame; **daran ist etwas** ~ there's sth fishy about it; ~**en** *vi* rot; ~**enzen** *vi* idle; **F**~**enzer** *m* -**s**, - idler, loafer; **F**~**heit** *f* laziness; ~**ig** *a* putrid.

Fäulnis ['fɔʏlnıs] *f*- decay, putrefaction.

Faust ['faʊst] *f* -, **Fäuste** fist; ~**handschuh** *m* mitten.

Favorit [favo'ri:t] *m* -**en**, -**en** favourite.

Februar ['fe:brua:r] *m* -**(s)**, -**e** February.

fechten ['fεçtən] *vi irreg* fence.

Feder ['fe:dər] *f* -, -**n** feather; (*Schreib*—) pen nib; (*Tech*) spring; ~**ball** *m* shuttlecock; ~**ballspiel** *nt* badminton; ~**bett** *nt* continental quilt; ~**halter** *m* penholder, pen; **f**~**leicht** *a* light as a feather; **f**~**n** *vi* (*nachgeben*) be springy; (*sich bewegen*) bounce; *vt* spring; ~**ung** *f* suspension; ~**vieh** *nt* poultry.

Fee [fe:] f -, -n fairy; f~nhaft ['fe:ən-] a fairylike.

Fege- ['fe:gə] cpd: ~feuer nt purgatory; f~n vt sweep.

fehl [fe:l] a: ~ am Platz or Ort out of place; ~en vi be wanting or missing; (abwesend sein) be absent; etw fehlt jdm sb lacks sth; du fehlst mir I miss you; was fehlt ihm? what's wrong with him?; F~er m -s, - mistake, error; (Mangel, Schwäche) fault; ~erfrei a faultless; without any mistakes; ~erhaft a incorrect; faulty; F~geburt f miscarriage; ~gehen vi irreg go astray; F~griff m blunder; F~konstruktion f badly designed thing; F~schlag m failure; ~schlagen vi irreg fail; F~schluß m wrong conclusion; F~start m (Sport) false start; F~tritt m false move; (fig) blunder, slip; F~zündung f (Aut) misfire, backfire.

Feier ['faɪər] f -, -n celebration; ~abend m time to stop work; ~abend machen stop, knock off; was machst du am ~abend? what are you doing after work?; jetzt ist ~abend! that's enough!; f~lich a solemn; ~lichkeit f solemnity; pl festivities pl; f~n vti celebrate; ~tag m holiday.

feig(e) ['faɪg(ə)] a cowardly; F~e f ~, n fig; F~heit f cowardice; F~ling m coward.

Feil- [faɪl] cpd: ~e f -, -n file; f~en vti file; f~schen vi haggle.

fein [faɪn] a fine; (vornehm) refined; Gehör etc keen; ~! great!

Feind [faɪnt] m -(e)s, -e enemy; f~lich a hostile; ~schaft f enmity; f~selig a hostile; ~seligkeit f hostility.

Fein- cpd: f~fühlend, f~fühlig a sensitive; ~gefühl nt delicacy, tact; ~heit f fineness; refinement; keenness; ~kostgeschäft nt delicatessen (shop); ~schmecker m -s, - gourmet.

feist [faɪst] a fat.

Feld [fɛlt] nt -(e)s, -er field; (Schach) square; (Sport) pitch; ~blume f wild flower; ~herr m commander; ~webel m -s, - sergeant; ~weg m path; ~zug m (lit, fig) campaign.

Felge ['fɛlgə] f -, -n (wheel) rim; ~nbremse f caliper brake.

Fell [fɛl] nt -(e)s, -e fur; coat; (von Schaf) fleece; (von toten Tieren) skin.

Fels [fɛls] m -en, -en, **Felsen** ['fɛlzən] m -s, - rock; (von Dover etc) cliff; f~enfest a firm; ~envorsprung m ledge; f~ig a rocky; ~spalte f crevice.

feminin [femi'ni:n] a feminine; (pej) effeminate.

Fenster ['fɛnstər] nt -s, - window; ~brett nt windowsill; ~laden m shutter; ~putzer m -s, - window cleaner; ~scheibe f windowpane; ~sims m windowsill.

Ferien ['fe:riən] pl holidays pl, vacation (US); ~ haben be on holiday; ~kurs m holiday course; ~reise f holiday; ~zeit f holiday period.

Ferkel ['fɛrkəl] nt -s, - piglet.

fern [fɛːn] a,ad far-off, distant; ~ von hier a long way (away) from here; F~amt nt (Tel) exchange; F~bedienung f remote control; F~e f -, -n distance; ~er a,ad further; (weiterhin) in future; F~flug m long-distance flight; F~gespräch nt trunk call; F~glas nt binoculars pl; ~halten vtr irreg keep away; F~lenkung f remote control; ~liegen vi irreg; jdm ~liegen be far from sb's mind; F~rohr nt telescope; F~schreiber m teleprinter; ~schriftlich a by telex; F~sehapparat m television set; ~sehen vi irreg watch television; F~sehen nt -s television; im F~sehen on television; F~seher m television; F~sprecher m telephone; F~sprechzelle f telephone box or booth (US).

Ferse ['fɛrzə] f -, -n heel.

fertig ['fɛrtɪç] a (bereit) ready; (beendet) finished; (gebrauchs~) ready-made; F~bau m prefab(ricated house); ~bringen vt irreg (fähig sein) manage, be capable of; (beenden) finish; F~keit f skill; ~machen vt (beenden) finish; (col) Person finish; (körperlich) exhaust; (moralisch) get down; vr get ready; ~stellen vt complete; F~ware f finished product.

Fessel ['fɛsəl] f -, -n fetter; f~n vt bind; (mit Fesseln) fetter; (fig) spellbind; f~nd a fascinating, captivating.

fest [fɛst] a firm; Nahrung solid; Gehalt regular; ad schlafen soundly; F~ nt -(e)s, -e party; festival; ~angestellt a permanently employed; F~beleuchtung f illumination; ~binden vt irreg tie, fasten; ~bleiben vi irreg stand firm; F~essen nt banquet; ~fahren vr irreg get stuck; ~halten irreg vt seize, hold fast; Ereignis record; vr hold on (an +dat to); ~igen vt strengthen; F~igkeit f strength; ~klammern vr cling on (an +dat to); F~land nt mainland; ~legen vt fix; vr commit o.s.; ~lich a festive; ~machen vt fasten; Termin etc fix; F~nahme f -, -n capture; ~nehmen vt irreg capture, arrest; F~rede f address; ~schnallen vt strap down; vr fasten one's seat belt; ~setzen vt fix, settle; F~spiel nt festival; ~stehen vi irreg be certain; ~stellen vt establish; (sagen) remark; F~ung f fortress.

Fett [fɛt] nt -(e)s, -e fat, grease; f~ a fat; Essen etc greasy; f~arm a low fat; f~en vt grease; ~fleck m grease spot or stain; f~gedruckt a bold-type; ~gehalt m fat content; f~ig a greasy, fatty; ~näpfchen nt: ins ~näpfchen treten put one's foot in it.

Fetzen ['fɛtsən] m -s, - scrap.

feucht [fɔʏçt] a damp; Luft humid; F~igkeit f dampness; humidity.

Feuer ['fɔʏər] nt -s, - fire; (zum Rauchen) a light; (fig: Schwung) spirit; ~alarm m fire alarm; ~eifer m zeal; f~fest a fireproof; ~gefahr f danger of fire; f~gefährlich a inflammable; ~leiter f fire escape ladder; ~löscher m -s, - fire extinguisher; **~melder** m -s, - fire alarm; **f~n** vti (lit, fig) fire; **f~sicher** a fireproof; **~stein** m flint; **~wehr** f -, -en fire brigade; **~werk** nt fireworks pl; **~zeug** nt (cigarette) lighter.

Fichte ['fɪçtə] f -, -n spruce, pine.

fidel [fi'de:l] a jolly.

Fieber ['fi:bər] nt -s, - fever, temperature; **f~haft** a feverish; **~messer** m, **~thermometer** nt thermometer.

fies [fi:s] a (col) nasty.

Figur [fi'gu:r] f -, -en figure; (Schach—) chessman, chess piece.

Filiale [fili'a:lə] f -, -n (Comm) branch.

Film [fɪlm] m -(e)s, -e film; **~aufnahme** f shooting; **f~en** vti film; **~kamera** f cine-camera; **~vorführgerät** nt cineprojector.

Filter ['fɪltər] m -s, - filter; **f~n** vt filter; **~mundstück** nt filter tip; **~papier** nt filter paper; **~zigarette** f tipped cigarette.

Filz [fɪlts] m -es, -e felt; **f~en** vt (col) frisk; vi (Wolle) mat.

Finale [fi'na:lə] nt -s, -(s) finale; (Sport) final(s).

Finanz [fi'nants] f finance; **~amt** nt Inland Revenue Office; **~beamte(r)** m revenue officer; **f~iell** [-tsi'el] a financial; **f~ieren** [-'tsi:rən] vt finance; **~minister** m Chancellor of the Exchequer (Brit), Minister of Finance.

Find- ['fɪnd] cpd: **f~en** irreg vt find; (meinen) think; vr be (found); (sich fassen) compose o.s.; **ich finde nichts dabei, wenn . . .** I don't see what's wrong if . . .; **das wird sich f~en** things will work out; **~er** m -s, - finder; **~erlohn** m reward; **f~ig** a resourceful.

Finger ['fɪŋər] m -s, - finger.; **~abdruck** m fingerprint; **~handschuh** m glove; **~hut** m thimble; (Bot) foxglove; **~ring** m ring; **~spitze** f fingertip; **~zeig** m -(e)s, -e hint, pointer.

fingieren [fɪŋ'gi:rən] vt feign.

fingiert a made-up, fictitious.

Fink ['fɪŋk] m -en, -en finch.

finster ['fɪnstər] a dark, gloomy; (verdächtig) dubious; (verdrossen) grim; Gedanke dark; **F~nis** f - darkness, gloom.

Finte ['fɪntə] f -, -n feint, trick.

firm [fɪrm] a well-up; **F~a** f -, -men firm; **F~eninhaber** m owner of firm; **F~enschild** nt (shop) sign; **F~enzeichen** nt registered trademark.

Firnis ['fɪrnɪs] m -ses, -se varnish.

Fisch [fɪʃ] m -(e)s, -e fish; pl (Astrol) Pisces; **f~en** vti fish; **~er** m -s, - fisherman; **~e'rei** f fishing, fishery; **~fang** m fishing; **~geschäft** nt fishmonger's (shop); **~gräte** f fishbone; **~zug** m catch or draught of fish.

fix [fɪks] a fixed; Person alert, smart; **~ und fertig** finished; (erschöpft) done in; **~ieren** [fɪ'ksi:rən] vt fix; (anstarren) stare at.

flach [flax] a flat; Gefäß shallow.

Fläche ['flɛçə] f -, -n area; (Ober—) surface; **~ninhalt** m surface area.

Flach- cpd: **~heit** f flatness; shallowness; **~land** nt lowland.

flackern ['flakərn] vi flare, flicker.

Flagge ['flagə] f -, -n flag.

flagrant [fla'grant] a flagrant; **in ~i** redhanded.

Flamme ['flamə] f -, -n flame.

Flanell [fla'nɛl] m -s, -e flannel.

Flanke ['flaŋkə] f -, -n flank; (Sport: Seite) wing.

Flasche ['flaʃə] f -, -n bottle (col: Versager) wash-out; **~nbier** nt bottled beer; **~nöffner** m bottle opener; **~nzug** m pulley.

flatterhaft a flighty, fickle.

flattern ['flatərn] vi flutter.

flau [flau] a weak, listless; Nachfrage slack; **jdm ist ~** sb feels queasy.

Flaum [flaum] m -(e)s (Feder) down; (Haare) fluff.

flauschig ['flauʃɪç] a fluffy.

Flausen ['flauzən] pl silly ideas pl; (Ausflüchte) weak excuses pl.

Flaute ['flautə] f -, -n calm; (Comm) recession.

Flechte ['flɛçtə] f -, -n plait; (Med) dry scab; (Bot) lichen; **f~n** vt irreg plait; Kranz twine.

Fleck [flɛk] m -(e)s, -e, Flecken m -s, - spot; (Schmutz—) stain; (Stoff—) patch; (Makel) blemish; **nicht vom ~ kommen** (lit, fig) not get any further; **vom ~ weg** straight away; **f~enlos** a spotless; **~enmittel** nt, **~enwasser** nt stain remover; **f~ig** a spotted; stained.

Fledermaus ['fle:dərmaus] f bat.

Flegel ['fle:gəl] m -s, - flail; (Person) lout; **f~haft** a loutish, unmannerly; **~jahre** pl adolescence; **f~n** vr lounge about.

flehen ['fle:ən] vi implore; **~tlich** a imploring.

Fleisch [flaɪʃ] nt -(e)s flesh; (Essen) meat; **~brühe** f beef tea, stock; **~er** m -s, - butcher; **~e'rei** f butcher's (shop); **f~ig** a fleshy; **f~lich** a carnal; **~pastete** f meat pie; **~wolf** m mincer; **~wunde** f flesh wound.

Fleiß [flaɪs] m -es diligence, industry; **f~ig** a diligent, industrious.

flektieren [flɛk'ti:rən] vt inflect.

flennen ['flɛnən] vi (col) cry, blubber.

fletschen ['flɛtʃən] vt Zähne show.

flexibel [flɛ'ksi:bəl] a flexible.

Flicken ['flɪkən] m -s, - patch; **f~** vt mend.

Flieder ['fli:dər] m -s, - lilac.

Fliege ['fli:gə] f -, -n fly; (Kleidung) bow tie; **f~n** vti irreg fly; **auf jdn/etw f~en** (col) be mad about sb/sth; **~npilz** m toadstool; **~r** m -s, - flier, airman; **~ralarm** m air-raid warning.

fliehen ['fli:ən] vi irreg flee.

Fliese ['fli:zə] f -, -n tile.

Fließ- ['fli:s] cpd: **~arbeit** f production-line work; **~band** nt production or assembly line; **f~en** vi irreg flow; **f~end** a flowing; Rede, Deutsch fluent; Übergänge smooth; **-heck** nt fastback; **~papier** nt blotting paper.

flimmern ['flɪmərn] vi glimmer.

flink [flɪŋk] a nimble, lively; F~**heit** f nimbleness, liveliness.

Flinte ['flɪntə] f -, -n rifle; shotgun.

Flitter ['flɪtər] m -s, - spangle; tinsel; ~**wochen** pl honeymoon.

flitzen ['flɪtsən] vi flit.

Flocke ['flɔkə] f -, -n flake.

flockig a flaky.

Floh ['floː] m -(e)s, ⁼e flea.

florieren [flo'riːrən] vi flourish.

Floskel ['flɔskəl] f -, -n empty phrase.

Floß [floːs] nt -es, ⁼e raft, float.

Flosse ['flɔsə] f -, -n fin.

Flöte ['fløːtə] f -, -n flute; (Block—) recorder.

Flötist(in f) [flø'tɪst(ɪn)] m flautist.

flott [flɔt] a lively; (elegant) smart; (Naut) afloat; F~**e** f -, -n fleet, navy.

Flöz [fløːts] nt -es, -e layer, seam.

Fluch [fluːx] m -(e)s, ⁼e curse; **f~en** vi curse, swear.

Flucht [fluxt] f -, -en flight; (Fenster—) row; (Reihe) range; (Zimmer—) suite; **f~artig** a hasty.

flücht- ['flʏçt] cpd: ~**en** vir flee, escape; ~**ig** a fugitive; (Chem) volatile; (vergänglich) transitory; (oberflächlich) superficial; (eilig) fleeting; F~**igkeit** f transitoriness; volatility; superficiality; F~**igkeitsfehler** m careless slip; F~**ling** m fugitive, refugee.

Flug [fluːk] m -(e)s, ⁼e flight; **im** ~ airborne, in flight; ~**abwehr** ['fluːg-] f anti-aircraft defence; ~**blatt** nt pamphlet.

Flügel ['flyːgəl] m -s, - wing; (Mus) grand piano.

Fluggast m airline passenger.

flügge ['flʏgə] a (fully-)fledged.

Flug- cpd: ~**geschwindigkeit** f flying or air speed; ~**gesellschaft** f airline (company); ~**hafen** m airport; ~**höhe** f altitude (of flight); ~**plan** m flight schedule; ~**platz** m airport; (klein) airfield; ~**post** f airmail; **f~s** [fluks] ad speedily; ~**schrift** f pamphlet; ~**strecke** f air route; ~**verkehr** m air traffic; ~**wesen** nt aviation; ~**zeug** nt (aero)plane, airplane (US); ~**zeugentführung** f hijacking of a plane; ~**zeughalle** f hangar; ~**zeugträger** m aircraft carrier.

Flunder ['flʊndər] f -, -n flounder.

flunkern ['flʊŋkərn] vi fib, tell stories.

Fluor ['fluːɔr] nt -s fluorine.

Flur [fluːr] m -(e)s, -e hall; (Treppen—) staircase.

Fluß [flʊs] m -sses, ⁼sse river; (Fließen) flow; **im** ~ **sein** (fig) be in a state of flux.

flüssig ['flʏsɪç] a liquid; ~ **machen** vt Geld make available; F~**keit** f liquid; (Zustand) liquidity.

flüster- ['flʏstər] cpd: ~**n** vti whisper; F~**propaganda** f whispering campaign.

Flut [fluːt] f -, -en (lit, fig) flood; (Gezeiten) high tide; **f~en** vi flood; ~**licht** nt flood-light.

Fohlen ['foːlən] nt -s, - foal.

Föhn [føːn] m -(e)s, -e foehn, warm south wind.

Föhre ['føːrə] f -, -n Scots pine.

Folge ['fɔlgə] f -, -n series, sequence; (Fortsetzung) instalment; (Auswirkung) result; **in rascher** ~ in quick succession; **etw zur** ~ **haben** result in sth; ~**n haben** have consequences; **einer Sache** ~ **leisten** comply with sth; **f~n** vi follow (jdm sb); (gehorchen) obey (jdm sb); **jdm f~n können** (fig) follow or understand sb; **f~nd** a following; **f~ndermaßen** ad as follows, in the following way; **f~nreich, f~nschwer** a momentous; **f~richtig** a logical; **f~rn** vt conclude (aus +dat from); ~**rung** f conclusion; **f~widrig** a illogical.

folg- cpd: ~**lich** ad consequently; ~**sam** a obedient.

Folie ['foːliə] f -, -n foil.

Folter ['fɔltər] f -, -n torture; (Gerät) rack; **f~n** vt torture.

Fön ® [føːn] m -(e)s, -e hair-dryer; **f~en** vt (blow) dry.

Fontäne [fɔn'tɛːnə] f -, -n fountain.

foppen ['fɔpən] vt tease.

Förder- ['fœrdər] cpd: ~**band** nt conveyor belt; ~**korb** m pit cage; **f~lich** a beneficial.

fordern ['fɔrdərn] vt demand.

Förder- cpd: **f~n** vt promote; (unterstützen) help; Kohle extract; ~**ung** f promotion; help; extraction.

Forderung ['fɔrdərʊŋ] f demand.

Forelle [fo'rɛlə] f trout.

Form [fɔrm] f -, -en shape; (Gestaltung) form; (Guß—) mould; (Back—) baking tin; **in** ~ **sein** be in good form or shape; **in** ~ **von** in the shape of; **f~ali'sieren** vt formalize; ~**ali'tät** f formality; ~**at** [-'maːt] nt -(e)s, -e format; (fig) distinction; ~**ati'on** f formation; **f~bar** a malleable; ~**el** f -, -n formula; **f~ell** [-'mɛl] a formal; **f~en** vt form, shape; ~**fehler** m faux-pas, gaffe; (Jur) irregularity; **f~ieren** [-'miːrən] vt form; vr form up.

förmlich ['fœrmlɪç] a formal; (col) real; F~**keit** f formality.

Form- cpd: **f~los** a shapeless; Benehmen etc informal; ~**u'lar** nt -s, -e form; **f~u'lieren** vt formulate.

forsch [fɔrʃ] a energetic, vigorous; ~**en** vt search (nach for); vi (wissenschaftlich) (do) research; ~**end** a searching; F~**er** m -s, - research scientist; (Natur—) explorer.

Forschung ['fɔrʃʊŋ] f research; ~**sreise** f scientific expedition.

Forst [fɔrst] m -(e)s, -e forest; ~**arbeiter** m forestry worker; ~**wesen** nt, ~**wirtschaft** f forestry.

Förster ['fœrstər] m -s, - forester; (für Wild) gamekeeper.

fort [fɔrt] ad away; (verschwunden) gone; (vorwärts) on; **und so** ~ and so on; **in einem** ~ on and on; ~**bestehen** vi irreg survive; ~**bewegen** vtr move away; ~**bilden** vr continue one's education; ~**bleiben** vi irreg stay away; ~**bringen** vt irreg take away; F~**dauer** f continuance; ~**fahren** vi irreg depart; (fort-

setzen) go on, continue; ~**führen** vt continue, carry on; ~**gehen** vi irreg go away; ~**geschritten** a advance; ~**kommen** vi irreg get on; (*wegkommen*) get away; ~**können** vi irreg be able to get away; ~**müssen** vi irreg have to go; ~**pflanzen** vr reproduce; F~**pflanzung** f reproduction; ~**schaffen** vt remove; ~**schreiten** vi irreg advance.

Fortschritt ['fɔrt-ʃrɪt] m advance; ~**e machen** make progress; f~**lich** ad progressive.

fort- cpd: ~**setzen** vt continue; F~**setzung** f continuation; (*folgender Teil*) instalment; F~**setzung folgt** to be continued; ~**während** a incessant, continual; ~**ziehen** irreg vt pull away; vi move on; (*umziehen*) move away.

Foto ['fo:to] nt -s, -s photo(graph); m -s, -s (—*apparat*) camera; ~'**graf** m photographer; ~**gra'phie** f photography; (*Bild*) photograph; f~**gra'phieren** vt photograph; vi take photographs.

Foul nt -s, -s foul.

Fracht [fraxt] f -, -en freight; (*Naut*) cargo; (*Preis*) carriage; ~**er** m -s, - freighter, cargo boat; ~**gut** nt freight.

Frack [frak] m -(e)s, ːe tails pl.

Frage ['fra:gə] f -, -n question; etw in ~ **stellen** question sth; **jdm eine** ~ **stellen** ask sb a question, put a question to sb; **nicht in** ~ **kommen** be out of the question; ~**bogen** m questionnaire; f~**n** vti ask; ~**zeichen** nt question mark.

frag- cpd: ~**lich** a questionable, doubtful; ~**los** ad unquestionably.

Fragment [fra'gmɛnt] nt fragment; f~**arisch** [-'taːrɪʃ] a fragmentary.

fragwürdig ['fra:kvʏrdɪç] a questionable, dubious.

Fraktion [fraktsi'o:n] f parliamentary party.

frank [fraŋk] a frank, candid; ~**ieren** [-' kiːrən] vt stamp, frank; ~**o** ad post-paid; carriage paid.

Franse ['franzə] f -, -n fringe; f~**n** vi fray.

Fratze ['fratsə] f -, -n grimace.

Frau [frau] f -, -en woman; (*Ehe*—) wife; (*Anrede*) Mrs; ~ **Doktor** Doctor; ~**enarzt** m gynaecologist; ~**enbewegung** f feminist movement; ~**enzimmer** nt female, broad (US).

Fräulein ['frɔylaɪn] nt young lady; (*Anrede*) Miss.

fraulich ['fraulɪç] a womanly.

frech [frɛç] a cheeky, impudent; F~**dachs** m cheeky monkey; F~**heit** f cheek, impudence.

Fregatte [fre'gatə] f frigate.

frei [fraɪ] a free; *Stelle, Sitzplatz auch* vacant; *Mitarbeiter* freelance; *Geld* available; (*unbekleidet*) bare; **sich** (dat) **einen Tag** ~ **nehmen** take a day off; **von etw** ~ **sein** be free of sth; **im F**~**en** in the open air; ~ **sprechen** talk without notes; F~**bad** nt open-air swimming pool; ~**bekommen** vt irreg: **jdn/einen Tag** ~ **bekommen** get sb freed/get a day off; F~**er** m -s, - suitor; ~**gebig** a generous; F~**gebigkeit** f generosity; ~**halten** vt

irreg keep free; ~**händig** ad *fahren* with no hands; F~**heit** f freedom; ~**heitlich** a liberal; F~**heitsstrafe** f prison sentence; ~**heraus** ad frankly; F~**karte** f free ticket; ~**kommen** vi irreg get free; ~**lassen** vt irreg (set) free; F~**lauf** m freewheeling; ~**legen** vt expose; ~**lich** ad certainly, admittedly; **ja** ~**lich** yes of course; F~**lichtbühne** f open-air theatre; ~**machen** vt Post frank; **Tage** ~ **machen** take days off; vr arrange to be free; ~**sinnig** a liberal; ~**sprechen** vt irreg acquit (*von* of); F~**spruch** m acquittal; ~**stellen** vt: **jdm etw** ~**stellen** leave sth (up) to sb; F~**stoß** m free kick; F~**tag** m Friday; ~**tags** ad on Fridays; F~**übungen** pl (physical) exercises pl; ~**willig** a voluntary; F~**willige(r)** mf volunteer; F~**zeit** f spare or free time; ~**zügig** a liberal, broad-minded; (*mit Geld*) generous.

fremd [frɛmt] a (*unvertraut*) strange; (*ausländisch*) foreign; (*nicht eigen*) someone else's; **etw ist jdm** ~ sth is foreign to sb; ~**artig** a strange; F~**e(r)** ['frɛmdə(r)] mf stranger; (*Ausländer*) foreigner; F~**enführer** m (*tourist*) guide; F~**enlegion** f foreign legion; F~**enverkehr** m tourism; F~**enzimmer** nt guest room; F~**körper** m foreign body; ~**ländisch** a foreign; F~**ling** m stranger; F~**sprache** f foreign language; ~**sprachig** a foreign-language; F~**wort** nt foreign word.

Frequenz [fre'kvɛnts] f (*Rad*) frequency.

fressen ['frɛsən] vti irreg eat.

Freude ['frɔydə] f -, -n joy, delight.

freudig a joyful, happy.

freudlos a joyless.

freuen ['frɔyən] vt impers make happy or pleased; vr be glad or happy; **sich auf etw** (acc) ~ look forward to sth; **sich über etw** (acc) ~ be pleased about sth.

Freund [frɔynt] m -(e)s, -e friend; boyfriend; ~**in** [-dɪn] f friend; girlfriend; f~**lich** a kind, friendly; f~**licherweise** ad kindly; ~**lichkeit** f friendliness, kindness; ~**schaft** f friendship; f~**schaftlich** a friendly.

Frevel ['fre:fəl] m -s, - crime, offence (an +dat against); f~**haft** a wicked.

Frieden ['fri:dən] m -s, - peace; **im** ~ in peacetime; ~**sschluß** m peace agreement; ~**sverhandlungen** pl peace negotiations pl; ~**svertrag** m peace treaty; ~**szeit** f peacetime.

fried- ['fri:t] cpd: ~**fertig** a peaceable; F~**hof** m cemetery; ~**lich** a peaceful.

frieren ['fri:rən] vti irreg freeze; **ich friere, es friert mich I** am freezing, I'm cold.

Fries [fri:s] m -es, -e (*Archit*) frieze.

frigid(e) [fri'gi:t, fri'gi:də] a frigid.

Frikadelle [frika'dɛlə] f meatball.

frisch [frɪʃ] a fresh; (*lebhaft*) lively; ~ **gestrichen!** wet paint!; **sich** ~ **machen** freshen (o.s.) up; F~**e** f - freshness; liveliness.

Friseur [fri'zø:r] m, **Friseuse** [fri'zø:zə] f hairdresser.

Frisier- [fri'ziːr] *cpd:* **f~en** *vtr* do (one's hair); *(fig) Abrechnung* fiddle, doctor; **~salon** *m* hairdressing salon; **~tisch** *m* dressing table.

Frisör [fri'zøːr] *m* **-s, e** hairdresser.

Frist [frɪst] *f* **-, -en** period; *(Termin)* deadline; **f~en** *vt Dasein* lead; *(kümmerlich)* eke out; **f~los** *a Entlassung* instant.

Frisur [fri'zuːr] *f* hairdo, hairstyle.

fritieren [fri'tiːrən] *vt* deep fry.

frivol [fri'voːl] *a* frivolous.

froh [froː] *a* happy, cheerful; **ich bin ~, daß ...** I'm glad that ...

fröhlich [frøːlɪç] *a* merry, happy; **F~keit** *f* merriness, gaiet,.

froh- *cpd:* **~'locken** *vi* exult; *(pej)* gloat; **F~sinn** *m* cheerfulness.

fromm [frɔm] *a* pious, good; *Wunsch* idle.

Frömm- ['frœm] *cpd:* **~e'lei** *f* false piety; **~igkeit** *f* piety.

frönen ['frøːnən] *vi* indulge *(etw (dat)* in sth).

Fronleichnam [froːn'laiçnaːm] *m* **-(e)s** Corpus Christi.

Front [frɔnt] *f* **-, -en** front; **f~al** [frɔn'taːl] *a* frontal.

Frosch [frɔʃ] *m* **-(e)s, ˝e** frog; *(Feuerwerk)* squib; **~mann** *m* frogman; **~schenkel** *m* frog's leg.

Frost [frɔst] *m* **-(e)s, ˝e** frost; **~beule** *f* chilblain.

frösteln ['frœstəln] *vi* shiver.

Frost- *cpd:* **f~ig** *a* frosty; **~schutzmittel** *nt* anti-freeze.

Frottee [frɔ'teː] *nt or m* **-(s), -s** towelling.

frottieren [frɔ'tiːrən] *vt* rub, towel.

Frottier(hand)tuch *nt* towel.

Frucht [fruxt] *f* **-, ˝e** *(lit, fig)* fruit; *(Getreide)* corn; **f~bar** *a* fruitful, fertile; **~barkeit** *f* fertility; **f~en** *vi* be of use; **f~los** *a* fruitless; **~saft** *m* fruit juice.

früh [fryː] *a,ad* early; **heute ~** this morning; **F~aufsteher** *m* **-s, -** early riser; **F~e** *f* - early morning; **~er** *a* earlier; *(ehemalig)* former; *ad* formerly; **~er war das anders** that used to be different; **~estens** *ad* at the earliest; **F~geburt** *f* premature birth/baby; **F~jahr** *nt,* **F~ling** *m* spring; **~reif** *a* precocious; **F~stück** *nt* breakfast; **~stücken** *vi* (have) breakfast; **~zeitig** *a* early; *(pej)* untimely.

frustrieren [frus'triːrən] *vt* frustrate.

Fuchs [fuks] *m* **-es, ˝e** fox; **f~en** *(col) vt* rile, annoy; *vr* be annoyed; **f~teufelswild** *a* hopping mad.

Füchsin ['fyksɪn] *f* vixen.

fuchteln ['fuxtəln] *vi* gesticulate wildly.

Fuge ['fuːgə] *f* **-, -n** joint; *(Mus)* fugue.

fügen ['fyːgən] *vt* place, join; *vr* be obedient *(in +acc* to); *(anpassen)* adapt oneself *(in +acc* to); *impers* happen.

fügsam ['fyːkzaːm] *a* obedient.

fühl- ['fyːl] *cpd:* **~bar** *a* perceptible, noticeable; **~en** *vtir* feel; **F~er** *m* **-s, -** feeler.

führen ['fyːrən] *vt* lead; *Geschäft* run; *Name* bear; *Buch* keep; *vi* lead; *vr* behave.

Führer ['fyːrər] *m* **-s,** - leader; *(Fremden—)* guide; **~schein** *m* driving licence.

Fuhrmann ['fuːrman] *m, pl* **-leute** carter.

Führung ['fyːruŋ] *f* leadership; *(eines Unternehmens)* management; *(Mil)* command; *(Benehmen)* conduct; *(Museums—)* conducted tour; **~szeugnis** *nt* certificate of good conduct.

Fuhrwerk ['fuːrvɛrk] *nt* cart.

Fülle ['fylə] *f* - wealth, abundance; **f~n** *vtr* fill; *(Cook)* stuff; **~n** *nt* **-s, -** foal; **~r** *m* **-s, -, Füllfederhalter** *m* fountain pen.

Füllung ['fyluŋ] *f* filling; *(Holz—)* panel.

fummeln ['fuməln] *vi (col)* fumble.

Fund [funt] *m* **-(e)s, -e** find; **~ament** [-da'mɛnt] *nt* foundation; **f~amen'tal** *a* fundamental; **~büro** *nt* lost property office, lost and found; **~grube** *f (fig)* treasure trove; **f~ieren** [-'diːrən] *vt* back up; **f~iert** *a* sound.

fünf [fynf] *num* five; **~hundert** *num* five hundred; **~te** *num* fifth; **F~tel** *nt* **-s, -** fifth; **~zehn** *num* fifteen; **~zig** *num* fifty.

fungieren [fuŋ'giːrən] *vi* function; *(Person)* act.

Funk [funk] *m* **-s** radio, wireless; **~e(n)** *m* **-ns, -n** *(lit, fig)* spark; **f~eln** *vi* sparkle; **f~en** *vt* radio; **~er** *m* **-s, -** radio operator; **~gerät** *nt* radio set; **~haus** *nt* broadcasting centre; **~spruch** *m* radio signal; **~station** *f* radio station.

Funktion [funktsi'oːn] *f* function; **f~ieren** [-'niːrən] *vi* work, function.

für [fyːr] *prep +acc* for; **was ~** what kind or sort of; **das F~ und Wider** the pros and cons *pl;* **Schritt ~ Schritt** step by step; **F~bitte** *f* intercession.

Furche ['furçə] *f* **-, -n** furrow; **f~n** *vt* furrow.

Furcht [furçt] *f* - fear; **f~bar** *a* terrible, frightful.

fürcht- ['fyrçt] *cpd:* **~en** *vt* be afraid of, fear; *vr* be afraid *(vor +dat* of); **~erlich** *a* awful.

furcht- *cpd:* **~los** *a* fearless; **~sam** *a* timid.

füreinander [fyːr'ai'nandər] *ad* for each other.

Furnier [fur'niːr] *nt* **-s, -e** veneer.

fürs [fyːrs] = **für das**.

Fürsorge ['fyːrzɔrgə] *f* care; *(Sozial—)* welfare; **~amt** *nt* welfare office; **~r(in** *f)* *m* **-s, -** welfare worker; **~unterstützung** *f* social security, welfare benefit *(US).*

Für- *cpd:* **~sprache** *f* recommendation; *(um Gnade)* intercession; **~sprecher** *m* advocate.

Fürst [fyrst] *m* **-en, -en** prince; **~in** *f* princess; **~entum** *nt* principality; **f~lich** *a* princely.

Furt [furt] *f* **-, -en** ford.

Fürwort ['fyːrvɔrt] *nt* pronoun.

Fuß [fuːs] *m* **-es, ˝e** foot; *(von Glas, Säule etc)* base; *(von Möbel)* leg; **zu ~** on foot; **~ball** *m* football; **~ballspiel** *nt* football match; **~ballspieler** *m* footballer; **~boden** *m* floor; **~bremse** *f (Aut)* footbrake; **f~en** *vi* rest, be based *(auf +dat* on); **~ende** *nt* foot; **~gänger(in** *f)* *m* **-s,** -

pedestrian; ~**gängerzone** f pedestrian precinct; ~**note** f footnote; ~**pfleger(in** f) m chiropodist; ~**spur** f footprint; ~**tritt** m kick; (Spur) footstep; ~**weg** m footpath.

Futter ['futər] nt **-s,** - fodder, feed; (Stoff) lining; ~**al** [-'ra:l] nt **-s, -e** case.

füttern ['fγtərn] vt feed; Kleidung line.

Futur [fu'tu:r] nt **-s, -e** future.

G

G, g [ge:] nt G, g.

Gabe ['ga:bə] f **-, -n** gift.

Gabel ['ga:bəl] f **-, -n** fork; ~**frühstück** nt mid-morning snack; ~**ung** f fork.

gackern ['gakərn] vi cackle.

gaffen ['gafən] vi gape.

Gage ['ga:ʒə] f **-, -n** fee; salary.

gähnen ['gε:nən] vi yawn.

Gala ['gala] f - formal dress; ~**vorstellung** f (Theat) gala performance.

galant [ga'lant] a gallant, courteous.

Galerie [galə'ri:] f gallery.

Galgen ['galgən] m **-s,** - gallows pl; ~**frist** f respite; ~**humor** m macabre humour.

Galle ['galə] f **-, -n** gall; (Organ) gallbladder.

Galopp [ga'lɔp] m **-s, -s** or **-e** gallop; **g~ieren** [-'pi:rən] vi gallop.

galvanisieren [galvani'zi:rən] vt galvanize.

Gamasche [ga'maʃə] f **-, -n** gaiter; (kurz) spat.

Gammler ['gamlər] m **-s,** - loafer, layabout.

Gang [gaŋ] m **-(e)s,** ⁻e walk; (Boten—) errand; (—art) gait; (Abschnitt eines Vorgangs) operation; (Essens—, Ablauf) course; (Flur etc) corridor; (Durch—) passage; (Tech) gear; **in** ~ **bringen** start up; (fig) get off the ground; **in** ~ **sein** in operation; (fig) be underway; **g~** f **-, -s** gang; **g~** a: **g~ und gäbe** usual, normal; **g~bar** a passable; Methode practicable.

Gängel- ['gεŋəl] cpd: ~**band** nt: **jdn am** ~**band halten** (fig) spoonfeed sb; **g~n** vt spoonfeed.

gängig ['gεŋɪç] a common, current; Ware in demand, selling well.

Ganove [ga'no:və] m **-n, -n** (col) crook.

Gans [gans] f ⁻e goose.

Gänse- ['gεnzə] cpd: ~**blümchen** nt daisy; ~**braten** m roast goose; ~**füßchen** pl (col) inverted commas pl (Brit), quotes pl; ~**haut** f goose pimples pl; ~**marsch** m: **im** ~**marsch** in single file; ~**rich** m **-s, -e** gander.

ganz [gants] a whole; (vollständig) complete; ~ **Europa** all Europe; **sein** ~**es Geld** all his money; ad quite; (völlig) completely; ~ **und gar nicht** not at all; **es sieht** ~ **so aus** it really looks like it; **aufs G**~**e gehen** go for the lot.

gänzlich ['gεntslɪç] a,ad complete(ly), entire(ly).

gar [ga:r] a cooked, done; ad quite; ~ **nicht/nichts/keiner** not/nothing/nobody at all; ~ **nicht schlecht** not bad at all.

Garage [ga'ra:ʒə] f **-, -n** garage.

Garantie [garan'ti:] f guarantee; **g~ren** vt guarantee.

Garbe ['garbə] f **-, -n** sheaf; (Mil) burst of fire.

Garde ['gardə] f **-, -n** guard(s); **die alte** ~ the old guard; ~'**robe** f **-, -n** wardrobe; (Abgabe) cloakroom; ~'**robenfrau** f cloakroom attendant; ~'**robenständer** m hallstand.

Gardine [gar'di:nə] f curtain.

gären ['gε:rən] vi irreg ferment.

Garn [garn] nt **-(e)s, -e** thread; yarn (auch fig).

Garnele [gar'ne:lə] f **-, -n** shrimp, prawn.

garnieren [gar'ni:rən] vt decorate; Speisen garnish.

Garnison [garni'zo:n] f **-, -en** garrison.

Garnitur [garni'tu:r] f (Satz) set; (Unterwäsche) set of (matching) underwear; (fig) **erste** ~ top rank; **zweite** ~ second rate.

garstig ['garstɪç] a nasty, horrid.

Garten ['gartən] m **-s,** ⁻ garden; ~**arbeit** f gardening; ~**bau** m horticulture; ~**fest** nt garden party; ~**gerät** nt gardening tool; ~**haus** nt summerhouse; ~**kresse** f cress; ~**lokal** nt beer garden; ~**schere** f pruning shears pl; ~**tür** f garden gate.

Gärtner(in f) ['gεrtnər(ɪn)] m **-s,** - gardener; ~**ei** [-'raɪ] f nursery; (Gemüse-) market garden (Brit), truck farm (US); **g~n** vi garden.

Gärung ['gε:rʊŋ] f fermentation.

Gas [ga:s] nt **-es, -e** gas; ~ **geben** (Aut) accelerate, step on the gas; **g~förmig** a gaseous; ~**herd** m, ~**kocher** m gas cooker; ~**leitung** f gas pipeline; ~**maske** f gasmask; ~**pedal** nt accelerator, gas pedal.

Gasse ['gasə] f **-, -n** lane, alley; ~**njunge** m street urchin.

Gast [gast] m **-es,** ⁻e guest; ~**arbeiter(in** f) m foreign worker.

Gästebuch ['gεstəbu:x] nt visitors' book, guest book.

Gast- cpd: **g~freundlich** a hospitable; ~**geber** m **-s,** - host; ~**geberin** f hostess; ~**haus** nt, ~**hof** m hotel, inn; **g~ieren** [-'ti:rən] vi (Theat) (appear as a) guest; **g~lich** a hospitable; ~**lichkeit** f hospitality; ~**rolle** f guest role.

gastronomisch [gastro'no:mɪʃ] a gastronomic(al).

Gast- cpd: ~**spiel** nt (Sport) away game; ~**stätte** f restaurant; pub; ~**wirt** m innkeeper; ~**wirtschaft** f hotel, inn; ~**zimmer** nt (guest) room.

Gas- cpd: ~**vergiftung** f gas poisoning; ~**werk** nt gasworks sing or pl; ~**zähler** m gas meter.

Gatte ['gatə] m **-n, -n** husband, spouse; **die** ~**n** husband and wife.

Gatter ['gatər] nt **-s,** - railing, grating; (Eingang) gate.

Gattin f wife, spouse.

Gattung ['gatʊŋ] f genus; kind.
Gaukler ['gaʊklər] m -s, - juggler, conjurer.
Gaul [gaʊl] m -(e)s, **Gäule** horse; nag.
Gaumen ['gaʊmən] m -s, - palate.
Gauner ['gaʊnər] m -s, - rogue; ~**ei** [-'raı] f swindle.
Gaze ['ga:zə] f -, -n gauze.
Gebäck [gə'bɛk] nt -(e)s, -e pastry.
Gebälk [gə'bɛlk] nt -(e)s timberwork.
Gebärde [gə'bɛːrdə] f -, -n gesture; g~n vr behave.
gebären [gə'bɛːrən] vt irreg give birth to, bear.
Gebärmutter f uterus, womb.
Gebäude [gə'bɔydə] nt -s, - building; ~**komplex** m (building) complex.
Gebein [gə'baɪn] nt -(e)s, -e bones pl.
Gebell [gə'bɛl] nt -(e)s barking.
geben ['ge:bən] irreg vti (jdm etw) give (sb sth or sth to sb); **Karten** deal; **ein Wort gab das andere** one angry word led to another; v impers **es gibt** there is/are; there will be; **gegeben** given; **zu gegebener Zeit** in good time; vr (sich verhalten) behave, act; (aufhören) abate; **sich geschlagen** ~ admit defeat; **das wird sich schon** ~ that'll soon sort itself out.
Gebet [gə'be:t] nt -(e)s, -e prayer.
Gebiet [gə'bi:t] nt -(e)s, -e area; (Hoheits~) territory; (fig) field; g~en vt irreg command, demand; ~**er** m -s, - master; (Herrscher) ruler; g~**erisch** a imperious.
Gebilde [gə'bɪldə] nt -s, - object, structure; g~t a cultured, educated.
Gebimmel [gə'bɪməl] nt -s (continual) ringing.
Gebirge [gə'bɪrgə] nt -s, - mountain chain.
gebirgig a mountainous.
Gebirgszug [gə'bɪrkstsu:k] m mountain range.
Gebiß [gə'bɪs] nt -sses, -sse teeth pl; (künstlich) dentures pl.
geblümt [gə'bly:mt] a flowery.
Geblüt [gə'bly:t] nt -(e)s blood, race.
geboren [gə'bo:rən] a born; **Frau** née.
geborgen [gə'bɔrgən] a secure, safe.
Gebot [gə'bo:t] nt -(e)s, -e command(ment Bibl); (bei Auktion) bid.
Gebräu [gə'brɔy] nt -(e)s, -e brew, concoction.
Gebrauch [gə'braʊx] m -(e)s, **Gebräuche** use; (Sitte) custom; g~en vt use.
gebräuchlich [gə'brɔyçlıç] a usual, customary.
Gebrauchs- cpd: ~**anweisung** f directions pl for use; ~**artikel** m article of everyday use; g~**fertig** a ready for use; ~**gegenstand** m commodity.
gebraucht [gə'braʊxt] a used; **G~wagen** m secondhand or used car.
gebrechlich [gə'brɛçlıç] a frail; **G~keit** f frailty.
Gebrüder [gə'bry:dər] pl brothers pl.
Gebrüll [gə'brYl] nt -(e)s roaring.
Gebühr [gə'by:r] f -, -en charge, fee; **nach** ~ fittingly; **über** ~ unduly; g~en vi:

jdm g~**en** be sb's due or due to sb; vr be fitting; g~**end** a,ad fitting(ly), appropriate(ly); ~**enerlaß** m remission of fees; ~**enermäßigung** f reduction of fees; g~**enfrei** a free of charge; g~**enpflichtig** a subject to charges.
Geburt [gə'bu:rt] f -, -en birth; ~**enbeschränkung** f, ~**enkontrolle** f, ~**enregelung** f birth control; ~**enziffer** f birth-rate.
gebürtig [gə'bYrtıç] a born in, native of; ~**e Schweizerin** native of Switzerland, Swiss-born.
Geburts- cpd: ~**anzeige** f birth notice; ~**datum** nt date of birth; ~**jahr** nt year of birth; ~**ort** m birthplace; ~**tag** m birthday; ~**urkunde** f birth certificate.
Gebüsch [gə'bYʃ] nt -(e)s, -e bushes pl.
Gedächtnis [gə'dɛçtnıs] nt -ses, -se memory; ~**feier** f commemoration; ~**schwund** m loss of memory, failing memory; ~**verlust** m amnesia.
Gedanke [gə'daŋkə] m -ns, -n thought; **sich über etw** (acc) ~**n machen** think about sth; ~**naustausch** m exchange of ideas; g~**nlos** a thoughtless; ~**nlosigkeit** f thoughtlessness; ~**nstrich** m dash; ~**nübertragung** f thought transference, telepathy; g~**nverloren** a lost in thought; g~**nvoll** a thoughtful.
Gedärm [gə'dɛrm] nt -(e)s, -e intestines pl, bowels pl.
Gedeck [gə'dɛk] nt -(e)s, -e cover(ing); (Speisenfolge) menu; **ein** ~ **auflegen** lay a place.
gedeihen [gə'daɪən] vi irreg thrive, prosper.
gedenken [gə'dɛŋkən] vi irreg (sich erinnern) (+gen) remember; (beabsichtigen) intend.
Gedenk- cpd: ~**feier** f commemoration; ~**minute** f minute's silence; ~**tag** m remembrance day.
Gedicht [gə'dıçt] nt -(e)s, -e poem.
gediegen [gə'di:gən] a (good) quality; **Mensch** reliable, honest; **G~heit** f quality; reliability, honesty.
Gedränge [gə'drɛŋə] nt -s crush, crowd; **ins** ~ **kommen** (fig) get into difficulties.
gedrängt a compressed; ~ **voll** packed.
gedrungen [gə'drʊŋən] a thickset, stocky.
Geduld [gə'dʊlt] f - patience; g~en [gə'dʊldən] vr be patient; g~**ig** a patient, forbearing; ~**sprobe** f trial of (one's) patience.
gedunsen [gə'dʊnzən] a bloated.
geeignet [gə'aɪgnət] a suitable.
Gefahr [gə'fa:r] f -, -en danger; ~ **laufen, etw zu tun** run the risk of doing sth; **auf eigene** ~ at one's own risk.
gefährden [gə'fɛːrdən] vt endanger.
Gefahren- cpd: ~**quelle** f source of danger; ~**zulage** f danger money.
gefährlich [gə'fɛːrlıç] a dangerous.
Gefährte [gə'fɛːrtə] m -n, -n, **Gefährtin** f companion.
Gefälle [gə'fɛlə] nt -s, - gradient, incline.
Gefallen [gə'falən] m -s, - favour; nt -s pleasure; **an etw** (dat) ~ **finden** derive

pleasure from sth; **jdm etw zu ~ tun** do sth to please sb; **g~** *vi irreg*: **jdm g~** please sb; **er/es gefällt mir** I like him/it; **das gefällt mir an ihm** that's one thing I like about him; **sich** (*dat*) **etw g~ lassen** put up with sth; *ptp of* **fallen**.

gefällig [gəˈfɛliç] *a* (*hilfsbereit*) obliging; (*erfreulich*) pleasant; **G~keit** *f* favour; helpfulness; **etw aus G~keit tun** do sth as a favour.

gefälligst *ad* kindly.

gefallsüchtig *a* eager to please.

gefangen [gəˈfaŋən] *a* captured; (*fig*) captivated; **G~e(r)** *m* prisoner, captive; **G~enlager** *nt* prisoner-of-war camp; **~halten** *vt irreg* keep prisoner; **G~nahme** *f* -, -n capture; **G~schaft** *f* captivity.

Gefängnis [gəˈfɛŋnis] *nt* -ses, -se prison; **~strafe** *f* prison sentence; **~wärter** *m* prison warder.

Gefasel [gəˈfaːzəl] *nt* -s twaddle, drivel.

Gefäß [gəˈfɛːs] *nt* -es, -e vessel (*auch Anat*), container.

gefaßt [gəˈfast] *a* composed, calm; **auf etw** (*acc*) **~ sein** be prepared *or* ready for sth.

Gefecht [gəˈfɛçt] *nt* -(e)s, -e fight; (*Mil*) engagement.

gefeit [gəˈfait] *a*: **gegen etw ~ sein** be immune to sth.

Gefieder [gəˈfiːdər] *nt* -s, - plumage, feathers *pl*; **g~t** *a* feathered.

gefleckt [gəˈflɛkt] *a* spotted, mottled.

geflissentlich [gəˈflisəntliç] *a,ad* intentional(ly).

Geflügel [gəˈflyːgəl] *nt* -s poultry.

Gefolge [gəˈfɔlgə] *nt* -s, - retinue.

Gefolg- *cpd*: **~schaft** *f* following; (*Arbeiter*) personnel; **~smann** *m* follower.

gefragt [geˈfraːkt] *a* in demand.

gefräßig [gəˈfrɛːsiç] *a* voracious.

Gefreite(r) [gəˈfraitə(r)] *m* -n, -n lance corporal; (*Naut*) able seaman; (*Aviat*) aircraftman.

gefrieren [gəˈfriːrən] *vi irreg* freeze.

Gefrier- *cpd*: **~fach** *nt* icebox; **~fleisch** *nt* frozen meat; **g~getrocknet** *a* freeze-dried; **~punkt** *m* freezing point; **~schutzmittel** *nt* antifreeze; **~truhe** *f* deep-freeze.

Gefüge [gəˈfyːgə] *nt* -s, - structure.

gefügig *a* pliant; *Mensch* obedient.

Gefühl [gəˈfyːl] *nt* -(e)s, -e feeling; **etw im ~ haben** have a feel for sth; **g~los** *a* unfeeling; **g~sbetont** *a* emotional; **~sduselei** [-zduːzəˈlai] *f* emotionalism; **g~smäßig** *a* instinctive.

gegebenenfalls [gəˈgeːbənənfals] *ad* if need be.

gegen [ˈgeːgən] *prep* +*acc* against; (*in Richtung auf*) [in betreffend, kurz vor] towards; (*im Austausch für*) (in return) for; (*ungefähr*) round about; **G~angriff** *m* counter-attack; **G~beweis** *m* counter-evidence.

Gegend [ˈgeːgənt] *f* -, -en area, district.

Gegen- *cpd*: **g~ei'nander** *ad* against one another; **~fahrbahn** *f* oncoming

carriageway; **~frage** *f* counter-question; **~gewicht** *nt* counterbalance; **~gift** *nt* antidote; **~leistung** *f* service in return; **~lichtaufnahme** *f* contre-jour photograph; **~maßnahme** *f* counter-measure; **~probe** *f* cross-check; **~satz** *m* contrast; **~sätze überbrücken** overcome differences; **g~sätzlich** *a* contrary, opposite; (*widersprüchlich*) contradictory; **~schlag** *m* counter attack; **~seite** *f* opposite side; (*Rückseite*) reverse; **g~seitig** *a* mutual, reciprocal; **sich g~seitig helfen** help each other; **~seitigkeit** *f* reciprocity; **~spieler** *m* opponent; **~stand** *m* object; **g~ständlich** *a* objective, concrete; **~stimme** *f* vote against; **~stoß** *m* counterblow; **~stück** *nt* counterpart; **~teil** *nt* opposite; **im ~teil** on the contrary; **ins ~teil umschlagen** swing to the other extreme; **g~teilig** *a* opposite, contrary.

gegenüber [geːgənˈʔyːbər] *prep* +*dat* opposite; (*zu*) to(wards); (*angesichts*) in the face of; *ad* opposite; **G~** *nt* -s, - person opposite; **~liegen** *vr irreg* face each other; **~stehen** *vr irreg* be opposed (to each other); **~stellen** *vt* confront; (*fig*) contrast; **G~stellung** *f* confrontation; (*fig*) contrast; **~treten** *vi irreg* (+*dat*) face.

Gegen- *cpd*: **~verkehr** *m* oncoming traffic; **~vorschlag** *m* counterproposal; **~wart** *f* present; **g~wärtig** *a* present; **das ist mir nicht mehr g~wärtig** that has slipped my mind; *ad* at present; **~wert** *m* equivalent; **~wind** *m* headwind; **~wirkung** *f* reaction; **g~zeichnen** *vti* countersign; **~zug** *m* counter-move; (*Rail*) corresponding train in the other direction.

Gegner [ˈgeːgnər] *m* -s, - opponent; **g~isch** *a* opposing; **~schaft** *f* opposition.

Gehackte(s) [gəˈhaktə(z)] *nt* mince(d meat).

Gehalt [gəˈhalt] *m* -(e)s, -e content; *nt* -(e)s, **̈-er** salary; **~sempfänger** *m* salary earner; **~serhöhung** *f* salary increase; **~szulage** *f* salary increment.

geharnischt [gəˈharniʃt] *a* (*fig*) forceful, angry.

gehässig [gəˈhɛsiç] *a* spiteful, nasty; **G~keit** *f* spite(fulness).

Gehäuse [gəˈhɔʏzə] *nt* -s, - case; casing; (*von Apfel etc*) core.

Gehege [gəˈheːgə] *nt* -s, - enclosure, preserve; **jdm ins ~ kommen** (*fig*) poach on sb's preserve.

geheim [gəˈhaim] *a* secret; **G~dienst** *m* secret service, intelligence service; **~halten** *vt irreg* keep secret; **G~nis** *nt* -ses, -se secret; mystery; **G~niskrämer** *m* secretive type; **~nisvoll** *a* mysterious; **G~polizei** *f* secret police; **G~schrift** *f* code, secret writing.

Geheiß [gəˈhais] *nt* -es command; **auf jds ~** at sb's behest.

gehen [ˈgeːən] *irreg vti* go; (*zu Fuß —*) walk; **~ nach** (*Fenster*) face; *v impers*: **wie**

geht es (dir)? how are you *or* things?; **mir/ihm geht es gut** I'm/he's (doing) fine; **geht das?** is that possible?; **geht's noch?** can you manage?; **es geht** not too bad, O.K.; **das geht nicht** that's not on; **es geht um etw** sth is concerned, it's about sth.

geheuer [gə'hɔɪər] *a*: **nicht ~** eery; (*fragwürdig*) dubious.

Geheul [gə'hɔɪl] *nt* **-(e)s** howling.

Gehilfe [gə'hɪlfə] *m* **-n, -n, Gehilfin** *f* assistant.

Gehirn [gə'hɪrn] *nt* **-(e)s, -e** brain; **~erschütterung** *f* concussion; **~wäsche** *f* brainwashing.

Gehör [gə'hø:r] *nt* **-(e)s** hearing; **musikalisches ~** ear; **~ finden** gain a hearing; **jdm ~ schenken** give sb a hearing.

gehorchen [gə'hɔrçən] *vi* obey (*jdm* sb).

gehören [gə'hø:rən] *vi* belong; *vr impers* be right *or* proper.

gehörig *a* proper; **~ zu** *or* +*dat* belonging to; part of.

gehorsam [gə'ho:rza:m] *a* obedient; **G~** *m* **-s** obedience.

Gehsteig *m*, **Gehweg** *m* ['ge:-] pavement, sidewalk (*US*).

Geier ['gaɪər] *m* **-s, -** vulture.

geifern ['gaɪfərn] *vi* salivate; (*fig*) bitch.

Geige ['gaɪgə] *f* **-, -n** violin; **~r** *m* **-s, -** violinist; **~rzähler** *m* geiger counter.

geil [gaɪl] *a* randy, horny (*US*).

Geisel ['gaɪzəl] *f* **-, -n** hostage.

Geißel ['gaɪsəl] *f* **-, -n** scourge, whip; **g~n** *vt* scourge.

Geist [gaɪst] *m* **-(e)s, -er** spirit; (*Gespenst*) ghost; (*Verstand*) mind; **g~erhaft** *a* ghostly; **g~esabwesend** *a* absent-minded; **~esblitz** *m* brainwave; **~esgegenwart** *f* presence of mind; **~eshaltung** *f* mental attitude; **g~eskrank** *a* mentally ill; **~eskranke(r)** *mf* mentally ill person; **~eskrankheit** *f* mental illness; **~esstörung** *f* mental disturbance; **~eswissenschaften** *pl* arts (subjects) *pl*; **~eszustand** *m* state of mind; **g~ig** *a* intellectual; mental; *Getränke* alcoholic; **g~ig behindert** mentally handicapped; **g~lich** *a* spiritual, religious; clerical; **~liche(r)** *m* clergyman; **~lichkeit** *f* clergy; **g~los** *a* uninspired, dull; **g~reich** *a* clever; witty; **g~tötend** *a* soul-destroying; **g~voll** *a* intellectual; (*weise*) wise.

Geiz [gaɪts] *m* **-es** miserliness, meanness; **g~en** *vi* be miserly; **~ hals** *m*, **~kragen** *m* miser; **g~ig** *a* miserly, mean.

Geklapper [gə'klapər] *nt* **-s** rattling.

geknickt [gə'knɪkt] *a* (*fig*) dejected.

gekonnt [gə'kɔnt] *a* skilful.

Gekritzel [gə'krɪtsəl] *nt* **-s** scrawl, scribble.

gekünstelt [gə'kʏnstəlt] *a* artificial, affected.

Gelächter [gə'lɛçtər] *nt* **-s, -** laughter.

geladen [gə'la:dən] *a* loaded; (*Elec*) live; (*fig*) furious.

Gelage [gə'la:gə] *nt* **-s, -** feast, banquet.

gelähmt [gə'lɛ:mt] *a* paralysed.

Gelände [gə'lɛndə] *nt* **-s, -** land, terrain; (*von Fabrik, Sport—*) grounds *pl*; (*Bau—*) site; **g~gängig** *a* able to go cross-country; **~lauf** *m* cross-country race.

Geländer [gə'lɛndər] *nt* **-s, -** railing; (*Treppen—*) banister(s).

gelangen [gə'laŋən] *vi* (*an* +*acc or zu*) reach; (*erwerben*) attain; **in jds Besitz ~** to come into sb's possession.

gelassen [gə'lasən] *a* calm, composed; **G~heit** *f* calmness, composure.

Gelatine [ʒela'ti:nə] *f* gelatine.

geläufig [gə'lɔʏfɪç] *a* (*üblich*) common; **das ist mir nicht ~** I'm not familiar with that; **G~keit** *f* commonness; familiarity.

gelaunt [gə'laʊnt] *a*: **schlecht/gut ~** in a bad/good mood; **wie ist er ~?** what sort of mood is he in?

Geläut(e) [gə'lɔʏt(ə)] *nt* **-(e)s, -(e)** ringing; (*Läutwerk*) chime.

gelb [gɛlp] *a* yellow; (*Ampellicht*) amber; **~lich** *a* yellowish; **G~sucht** *f* jaundice.

Geld [gɛlt] *nt* **-(e)s, -er** money; **etw zu ~ machen** sell sth off; **~anlage** *f* investment; **~beutel** *m*, **~börse** *f* purse; **~einwurf** *m* slot; **~geber** *m* **-s, -** financial backer; **g~gierig** *a* avaricious; **~mittel** *pl* capital, means *pl*; **~schein** *m* banknote; **~schrank** *m* safe, strongbox; **~strafe** *f* fine; **~stück** *nt* coin; **~verlegenheit** *f*: **in ~verlegenheit sein/kommen** to be/run short of money; **~verleiher** *m* **-s, -** moneylender; **~wechsel** *m* exchange (of money).

Gelee [ʒe'le:] *nt or m* **-s, -s** jelly.

gelegen [gə'le:gən] *a* situated; (*passend*) convenient, opportune; **etw kommt jdm ~** sth is convenient for sb.

Gelegenheit [gə'le:gənhaɪt] *f* opportunity; (*Anlaß*) occasion; **bei jeder ~** at every opportunity; **~sarbeit** *f* casual work; **~sarbeiter** *m* casual worker; **~skauf** *m* bargain.

gelegentlich [gə'le:gəntlɪç] *a* occasional; *ad* occasionally; (*bei Gelegenheit*) some time (or other); *prep* +*gen* on the occasion of.

gelehrig [gə'le:rɪç] *a* quick to learn, intelligent.

gelehrt *a* learned; **G~e(r)** *mf* scholar; **G~heit** *f* scholarliness.

Geleise [gə'laɪzə] *nt* **-s, -** track; *see* **Gleis**.

Geleit [gə'laɪt] *nt* **-(e)s, -e** escort; **g~en** *vt* escort; **~schutz** *m* escort.

Gelenk [gə'lɛŋk] *nt* **-(e)s, -e** joint; **g~ig** *a* supple.

gelernt [gə'lɛrnt] *a* skilled.

Geliebte(r) [gə'li:ptə(r)] *mf* sweetheart, beloved.

gelind(e) [gə'lɪnt, gə'lɪndə] *a* mild, light; (*fig*) *Wut* fierce; **~e gesagt** to put it mildly.

gelingen [gə'lɪŋən] *vi irreg* succeed; **die Arbeit gelingt mir nicht** I'm not being very successful with this piece of work; **es ist mir gelungen, etw zu tun** I succeeded in doing sth.

gellen ['gɛlən] *vi* shrill.

geloben [gə'lo:bən] *vti* vow, swear.
gelten ['gɛltən] *irreg vt* (*wert sein*) be worth; **etw gilt bei jdm viel/wenig** sb values sth highly/sb doesn't value sth very highly; **jdm viel/wenig** ~ mean a lot/not mean much to sb; **was gilt die Wette?** do you want to bet?; *vi* (*gültig sein*) be valid; (*erlaubt sein*) be allowed; **jdm** ~ (*gemünzt sein auf*) be meant for *or* aimed at sb; **etw** ~ **lassen** accept sth; **als** *or* **für etw** ~ be considered to be sth; **jdm** *or* **für jdn** ~ (*betreffen*) apply to *or* for sb; *v impers* **es gilt, etw zu tun** it is necessary to do sth; ~**d** a prevailing; **etw** ~**d machen** to assert sth; **sich** ~**d machen** make itself/o.s. felt.
Geltung ['gɛltʊŋ] *f:* ~ **haben** have validity; **sich/etw** (*dat*) **verschaffen** establish oneself/sth; **etw zur** ~ **bringen** show sth to its best advantage; **zur** ~ **kommen** be seen/heard *etc* to its best advantage; ~**sbedürfnis** *nt* desire for admiration.
Gelübde [gə'lʏpdə] *nt* -s, - vow.
gelungen [gə'lʊŋən] a successful.
gemächlich [gə'mɛ:çlıç] a leisurely.
Gemahl [gə'ma:l] *m* -(e)s, -e husband; ~**in** *f* wife.
Gemälde [gə'mɛ:ldə] *nt* -s, - picture, painting.
gemäß [gə'mɛ:s] *prep* +*dat* in accordance with; *a* appropriate (*dat* to); ~**igt** a moderate; *Klima* temperate.
gemein [gə'maın] a common; (*niederträchtig*) mean; **etw** ~ **haben** (**mit**) have sth in common (with).
Gemeinde [gə'maındə] *f* -, -n district, community; (*Pfarr*—) parish; (*Kirchen*—) congregation; ~**steuer** *f* local rates *pl*; ~**verwaltung** *f* local administration; ~**vorstand** *m* local council; ~**wahl** *f* local election.
Gemein- *cpd*: **g**~**gefährlich** a dangerous to the public; ~**gut** *nt* public property; ~**heit** *f* commonness; mean thing to do/to say; **g**~**hin** *ad* generally; ~**nutz** *m* public good; ~**platz** *m* commonplace, platitude; **g**~**sam** a joint, common (*auch Math*); **g**~**same Sache mit jdm machen** be in cahoots with sb; *ad* together, jointly; **etw g**~**sam haben** have sth in common; ~**samkeit** *f* community, having in common; ~**schaft** *f* community; **in** ~**schaft mit** jointly *or* together with; **g**~**schaftlich** *a see* **g**~**sam**; ~**schaftsarbeit** *f* teamwork; team effort; ~**schaftserziehung** *f* coeducation; ~**sinn** *m* public spirit; **g**~**verständlich** a generally comprehensible; ~**wohl** *nt* common good.
Gemenge [gə'mɛŋə] *nt* -s, - mixture; (*Hand*—) scuffle.
gemessen [gə'mɛsən] a measured.
Gemetzel [gə'mɛtsəl] *nt* -s, - slaughter, carnage, butchery.
Gemisch [gə'mıʃ] *nt* -es, -e mixture; **g**~**t** a mixed.
Gemse ['gɛmzə] *f* -, -n chamois.
Gemunkel [gə'mʊŋkəl] *nt* -s gossip.

Gemurmel [gə'mʊrməl] *nt* -s murmur(ing).
Gemüse [gə'my:zə] *nt* -s, - vegetables *pl*; ~**garten** *m* vegetable garden; ~**händler** *m* greengrocer.
Gemüt [gə'my:t] *nt* -(e)s, -er disposition, nature; person; **sich** (*dat*) **etw zu** ~**e führen** (*col*) indulge in sth; **die** ~**er erregen** arouse strong feelings; **g**~**lich** a comfortable, cosy; *Person* good-natured; ~**lichkeit** *f* comfortableness, cosiness; amiability; ~**sbewegung** *f* emotion; ~**smensch** *m* sentimental person; ~**sruhe** *f* composure; ~**szustand** *m* state of mind; **g**~**voll** a warm, tender.
genau [gə'nau] a,ad exact(ly), precise(ly); **etw** ~ **nehmen** take sth seriously; ~**genommen** ad strictly speaking; **G**~**igkeit** *f* exactness, accuracy.
genehm [gə'ne:m] a agreeable, acceptable; ~**igen** *vt* approve, authorize; **sich** (*dat*) **etw** ~**igen** indulge in sth; **G**~**igung** *f* approval, authorization.
geneigt [gə'naıkt] a well-disposed, willing; ~ **sein, etw zu tun** be inclined to do sth.
General [gene'ra:l] *m* -s, -e *or* ⁼e general; ~**direktor** *m* director general; ~**konsulat** *nt* consulate general; ~**probe** *f* dress rehearsal; ~**stabskarte** *f* ordnance survey map; ~**streik** *m* general strike; **g**~**überholen** *vt* thoroughly overhaul.
Generation [generatsi'o:n] *f* generation; ~**skonflikt** *m* generation gap.
Generator [gene'ra:tɔr] *m* generator, dynamo.
genesen [ge'ne:zən] *vi irreg* convalesce, recover, get well; **G**~**de(r)** *mf* convalescent.
Genesung *f* recovery, convalescence.
genetisch [ge'ne:tıʃ] a genetic.
genial [geni'a:l] a brilliant; **G**~**i'tät** *f* brilliance, genius.
Genick [gə'nık] *nt* -(e)s, -e (back of the) neck; ~**starre** *f* stiff neck.
Genie [ʒe'ni:] *nt* -s, -s genius.
genieren [ʒe'ni:rən] *vt* bother; **geniert es Sie, wenn . . .?** do you mind if . . .?; *vr* feel awkward *or* self-conscious.
genießbar a edible; drinkable.
genießen [gə'ni:sən] *vt irreg* enjoy; eat; drink.
Genießer *m* -s, - epicure; pleasure lover; **g**~**isch** a appreciative; *ad* with relish.
Genosse [gə'nɔsə] *m* -n, -n, **Genossin** *f* comrade (*esp Pol*), companion; ~**nschaft** *f* cooperative (association).
genug [gə'nu:k] *ad* enough.
Genüge [gə'ny:gə] *f* -: **jdm/etw** ~ **tun** *or* **leisten** satisfy sb/sth; **g**~**n** *vi* be enough, suffice; (+*dat*) satisfy; **g**~**nd** a sufficient.
genügsam [gə'ny:kza:m] a modest, easily satisfied; **G**~**keit** *f* moderation.
Genugtuung [gə'nu:ktu:ʊŋ] *f* satisfaction.
Genuß [gə'nus] *m* -sses, ⁼sse pleasure; (*Zusichnehmen*) consumption; **in den** ~ **von etw kommen** receive the benefit of sth; ~**mittel** *pl* (semi-)luxury items *pl*.
genüßlich [gə'nʏslıç] *ad* with relish.

Geograph [geo'graːf] *m* **-en, -en**
geographer; **~ie** [-'fiː] *f* geography;
g~isch *a* geographical.

Geologe [geo'loːgə] *m* **-n, -n** geologist;
~gie [-'giː] *f* geology.

Geometrie [geome'triː] *f* geometry.

Gepäck [gə'pɛk] *nt* **-(e)s** luggage,
baggage; **~abfertigung** *f*, **~annahme** *f*,
~ausgabe *f* luggage desk/office; **~auf-
bewahrung** *f* left-luggage office, check-
room (*US*); **~netz** *nt* luggage-rack;
~träger *m* porter; (*Fahrrad*) carrier;
~wagen *m* luggage van, baggage car
(*US*).

gepflegt [gə'pfleːkt] *a* well-groomed; *Park
etc* well looked after.

Gepflogenheit [gə'pfloːgənhaɪt] *f* custom.

Geplapper [gə'plapər] *nt* **-s** chatter.

Geplauder [gə'plaʊdər] *nt* **-s** chat(ting).

Gepolter [gə'pɔltər] *nt* **-s** din.

gerade [gə'raːdə] *a* straight; *Zahl* even; *ad*
(*genau*) exactly; (*örtlich*) straight; (*eben*)
just; **warum ~ ich?** why me?; **~ weil**
just or precisely because; **nicht ~ schön**
not exactly nice; **das ist es ja ~** that's
just it; **jetzt ~ nicht!** not now!; **~ noch**
just; **~ neben** right next to; **G~ f-n, -n**
straight line; **~aus** *ad* straight ahead;
~heraus *ad* straight out, bluntly; **~so** *ad*
just so; **~so dumm** *etc* just as stupid *etc*;
~so wie just as; **~zu** *ad* (*beinahe*)
virtually, almost.

geradlinig *a* rectilinear.

Gerät [gə'rɛːt] *nt* **-(e)s, -e** device;
(*Werkzeug*) tool; (*Sport*) apparatus;
(*Zubehör*) equipment *no pl*.

geraten [gə'raːtən] *vi irreg* (*gelingen*) turn
out well (*jdm* for sb); (*gedeihen*) thrive;
gut/schlecht ~ turn out well/badly; **an
jdn ~** come across sb; **in etw** (*acc*) **~**
get into sth; **in Angst ~** get frightened;
nach jdm ~ take after sb.

Geratewohl [gəraːtə'voːl] *nt*: **aufs ~** on
the off chance; (*bei Wahl*) at random.

geraum [gə'raʊm] *a*: **seit ~er Zeit** for
some considerable time.

geräumig [gə'rɔymɪç] *a* roomy.

Geräusch [gə'rɔyʃ] *nt* **-(e)s, -e** sound,
noise; **g~los** *a* silent; **g~voll** *a* noisy.

gerben ['gɛrbən] *vt* tan.

Gerber *m* **-s, -** tanner; **~ei** [-'raɪ] *f*
tannery.

gerecht [gə'rɛçt] *a* just, fair; **jdm/etw ~
werden** do justice to sb/sth; **G~igkeit** *f*
justice, fairness.

Gerede [gə'reːdə] *nt* **-s** talk, gossip.

gereizt [gə'raɪtst] *a* irritable; **G~heit** *f*
irritation.

Gericht [gə'rɪçt] *nt* **-(e)s, -e** court; (*Essen*)
dish; **mit jdm ins ~ gehen** (*fig*) judge sb
harshly; **über jdn zu ~ sitzen** sit in
judgement on sb; **das Letzte ~** the Last
Judgement; **g~lich** *a,ad* judicial(ly),
legal(ly); **~sbarkeit** *f* jurisdiction;
~shof *m* court (of law); **~skosten** *pl*
(legal) costs *pl*; **~ssaal** *m* courtroom;
~sverfahren *nt* legal proceedings *pl*;
~sverhandlung *f* court proceedings *pl*;
~svollzieher *m* bailiff.

gerieben [gə'riːbən] *a* grated; (*col: schlau*)
smart, wily.

gering [gə'rɪŋ] *a* slight, small; (*niedrig*)
low; *Zeit* short; **~achten** *vt* think little of;
~fügig *a* slight, trivial; **~schätzig** *a*
disparaging; **G~schätzung** *f* disdain;
~ste(r,s) *a* slightest, least; **~stenfalls**
ad at the very least.

gerinnen [gə'rɪnən] *vi irreg* congeal; (*Blut*)
clot; (*Milch*) curdle.

Gerinnsel [gə'rɪnzəl] *nt* **-s, -** clot.

Gerippe [gə'rɪpə] *nt* **-s, -** skeleton.

gerissen [gə'rɪsən] *a* wily, smart.

gern(e) ['gɛrn(ə)] *ad* willingly, gladly; **~
haben, ~ mögen** like; **etwas ~ tun** like
doing something; **G~egroß** *m* **-, -e** show-
off.

Geröll [gə'rœl] *nt* **-(e)s, -e** scree.

Gerste ['gɛrstə] *f* **-, -n** barley; **~nkorn** *nt*
(*im Auge*) stye.

Gerte ['gɛrtə] *f* **-, -n** switch, rod;
g~nschlank *a* willowy.

Geruch [gə'rʊx] *m* **-(e)s, ̈e** smell, odour;
g~los *a* odourless; **g~tilgend** *a*
deodorant.

Gerücht [gə'rʏçt] *nt* **-(e)s, -e** rumour.

geruhen [gə'ruːən] *vi* deign.

Gerümpel [gə'rʏmpəl] *nt* **-s** junk.

Gerüst [gə'rʏst] *nt* **-(e)s, -e** (*Bau—*)
scaffold(ing); frame.

gesamt [gə'zamt] *a* whole, entire; *Kosten*
total; *Werke* complete; **im ~en** all in all;
G~ausgabe *f* complete edition;
~deutsch *a* all-German; **G~eindruck**
m general impression; **G~heit** *f* totality,
whole.

Gesandte(r) [gə'zantə(r)] *m* envoy.

Gesandtschaft [gə'zant-ʃaft] *f* legation.

Gesang [gə'zaŋ] *m* **-(e)s, ̈e** song; (*Singen*)
singing; **~buch** *nt* (*Rel*) hymn book;
~verein *m* choral society.

Gesäß [gə'zɛːs] *nt* **-es, -e** seat, bottom.

Geschäft [gə'ʃɛft] *nt* **-(e)s, -e** business;
(*Laden*) shop; (*—sabschluß*) deal;
~emacher *m* **-s, -** profiteer; **g~ig** *a*
active, busy; (*pej*) officious; **g~lich** *a*
commercial; *ad* on business; **~sbericht**
m financial report; **~sführer** *m* manager;
(*Klub*) secretary; **~sjahr** *nt* financial
year; **~slage** *f* business conditions *pl*;
~smann *m* businessman; **g~smäßig** *a*
businesslike; **~sreise** *f* business trip;
~sschluß *m* closing time; **~ssinn** *m*
business sense; **~sstelle** *f* office, place of
business; **g~stüchtig** *a* efficient;
~sviertel *nt* business quarter; shopping
centre; **~swagen** *m* company car;
~szweig *m* branch (of a business).

geschehen [gə'ʃeːən] *vi irreg* happen; **es
war um ihn ~** that was the end of him.

gescheit [gə'ʃaɪt] *a* clever.

Geschenk [gə'ʃɛŋk] *nt* **-(e)s, -e** present,
gift; **~packung** *f* gift pack.

Geschicht- [gə'ʃɪçt] *cpd*: **~e** *f* **-, -n** story;
(*Sache*) affair; (*Historie*) history;
~enerzähler *m* storyteller; **g~lich** *a*
historical; **~sschreiber** *m* historian.

Geschick [gə'ʃɪk] *nt* **-(e)s, -e** aptitude;
(*Schicksal*) fate; **~lichkeit** *f* skill,
dexterity; **g~t** *a* skilful.

geschieden [gə'ʃiːdən] a divorced.

Geschirr [gə'ʃɪr] nt -(e)s, -e crockery; pots and pans pl; (Pferd) harness; ~**spülmaschine** f dishwashing machine; ~**tuch** nt dish cloth.

Geschlecht [gə'ʃlɛçt] nt -(e)s, -er sex; (Gram) gender; (Art) species; family; **g~lich** a sexual; ~**skrankheit** f venereal disease; ~**steil** nt or m genitals pl; ~**sverkehr** m sexual intercourse; ~**swort** nt (Gram) article.

Geschmack [gə'ʃmak] m -(e)s, -̈e taste; **nach jds ~** to sb's taste; ~ **finden an** etw (dat) (come to) like sth; **g~los** a tasteless; (fig) in bad taste; ~**(s)sache** f matter of taste; ~**sinn** m sense of taste; **g~voll** a tasteful.

Geschmeide [gə'ʃmaidə] nt -s, - jewellery.

geschmeidig a supple; (formbar) malleable.

Geschmeiß [gə'ʃmais] nt vermin pl.

Geschmiere [gə'ʃmiːrə] nt -s scrawl; (Bild) daub.

Geschöpf [gə'ʃœpf] nt -(e)s, -e creature.

Geschoß [gə'ʃɔs] nt -sses, -sse (Mil) projectile, missile; (Stockwerk) floor.

geschraubt [gə'ʃraupt] a stilted, artificial.

Geschrei [gə'ʃrai] nt -s cries pl, shouting; (fig: Aufhebens) noise, fuss.

Geschütz [gə'ʃʏts] nt -es, -e gun, cannon; **ein schweres ~ auffahren** (fig) bring out the big guns; ~**feuer** nt artillery fire, gunfire; **g~t** a protected.

Geschwader [gə'ʃvaːdər] nt -s, - (Naut) squadron; (Aviat) group.

Geschwafel [gə'ʃvaːfəl] nt -s silly talk.

Geschwätz [gə'ʃvɛts] nt -es chatter, gossip; **g~ig** a talkative; ~**igkeit** f talkativeness.

geschweige [gə'ʃvaigə] ad: ~ **(denn)** let alone, not to mention.

geschwind [gə'ʃvint] a quick, swift; **G~igkeit** [-dıçkait] f speed, velocity; **G~igkeitsbegrenzung** f speed limit; **G~igkeitsmesser** m (Aut) speedometer; **G~igkeitsüberschreitung** f exceeding the speed limit.

Geschwister [gə'ʃvistər] pl brothers and sisters pl.

geschwollen [gə'ʃvɔlən] a pompous.

Geschworene(r) [gə'ʃvoːrənə(r)] mf juror; pl jury.

Geschwulst [gə'ʃvulst] f -, -̈e swelling; growth, tumour.

Geschwür [gə'ʃvyːr] nt -(e)s, -e ulcer.

Gesell- [gə'zɛl] cpd: ~e m -n, -n fellow; (Handwerk-) journeyman; **g~ig** a sociable; ~**igkeit** f sociability; ~**schaft** f society; (Begleitung, Comm) company; (Abend—schaft etc) party; **g~schaftlich** a social; ~**schaftsanzug** m evening dress; **g~schaftsfähig** a socially acceptable; ~**schaftsordnung** f social structure; ~**schaftsreise** f group tour; ~**schaftsschicht** f social stratum.

Gesetz [gə'zɛts] nt -es, -e law; ~**buch** nt statute book; ~**entwurf** m, ~**esvorlage** f bill; **g~gebend** a legislative; ~**geber** m -s, - legislator; ~**gebung** f legislation;

g~lich a legal, lawful; ~**lichkeit** f legality, lawfulness; **g~los** a lawless; **g~mäßig** a lawful; **g~t** a Mensch sedate; **g~tenfalls** ad supposing (that); **g~widrig** a illegal, unlawful.

Gesicht [gə'zıçt] nt -(e)s, -er face; **das zweite ~** second sight; **das ist mir nie zu ~ gekommen** I've never laid eyes on that; ~**sausdruck** m (facial) expression; ~**sfarbe** f complexion; ~**spunkt** m point of view; ~**szüge** pl features pl.

Gesindel [gə'zındəl] nt -s rabble.

gesinnt [gə'zınt] a disposed, minded.

Gesinnung [gə'zınuŋ] f disposition; (Ansicht) views pl; ~**sgenosse** m like-minded person; ~**slosigkeit** f lack of conviction; ~**swandel** m change of opinion, volte-face.

gesittet [gə'zıtət] a well-mannered.

Gespann [gə'ʃpan] nt -(e)s, -e team; (col) couple; **g~t** a tense, strained; (begierig) eager; **ich bin g~t, ob** I wonder if or whether; **auf etw/jdn g~t sein** look forward to sth/meeting sb.

Gespenst [gə'ʃpɛnst] nt -(e)s, -er ghost, spectre; **g~erhaft** a ghostly.

Gespiele [gə'ʃpiːlə] m -n, -n, **Gespielin** f playmate.

Gespött [gə'ʃpœt] nt -(e)s mockery; **zum ~ werden** become a laughing stock.

Gespräch [gə'ʃprɛːç] nt -(e)s, -e conversation; discussion(s); (Anruf) call; **zum ~ werden** become a topic of conversation; **g~ig** a talkative; ~**igkeit** f talkativeness; ~**sthema** nt subject or topic of (conversation).

Gespür [gə'ʃpyːr] nt -s feeling.

Gestalt [gə'ʃtalt] f -, -en form, shape; (Person) figure; **in ~ von** in the form of; ~ **annehmen** take shape; **g~en** vt (formen) shape, form; (organisieren) arrange, organize; vr turn out (zu to be); ~**ung** f formation; organization.

geständig [gə'ʃtɛndıç] a: ~ **sein** have confessed.

Geständnis [gə'ʃtɛntnıs] nt -ses, -se confession.

Gestank [gə'ʃtaŋk] m -(e)s stench.

gestatten [gə'ʃtatən] vt permit, allow; ~ **Sie?** may I?; **sich** (dat) ~, **etw zu tun** take the liberty of doing sth.

Geste ['gɛstə] f -, -n gesture.

gestehen [gə'ʃteːən] vt irreg confess.

Gestein [gə'ʃtain] nt -(e)s, -e rock.

Gestell [gə'ʃtɛl] nt -(e)s, -e frame; (Regal) rack, stand.

gestern ['gɛstərn] ad yesterday; ~ **abend/morgen** yesterday evening/morning.

gestikulieren [gɛstiku'liːrən] vi gesticulate.

Gestirn [gə'ʃtırn] nt -(e)s, -e star; (Stern-bild) constellation.

Gestöber [gə'ʃtøːbər] nt -s, - flurry, blizzard.

Gesträuch [gə'ʃtrɔyç] nt -(e)s, -e shrubbery, bushes pl.

gestreift [gə'ʃtraift] a striped.

gestrig ['gɛstrıç] a yesterday's.

Gestrüpp [gəˈʃtrʏp] *nt* -(e)s, -e under-growth.

Gestüt [gəˈʃtyːt] *nt* -(e)s, -e stud farm.

Gesuch [gəˈzuːx] *nt* -(e)s, -e petition; (*Antrag*) application; **g~t** *a* (*Comm*) in demand; wanted; (*fig*) contrived.

gesund [gəˈzʊnt] *a* healthy; **wieder ~ werden** get better; **G~heit** *f* health(iness); **G~heit!** bless you!; **~heitlich** *a,ad* health *attr*, physical; **wie geht es Ihnen ~heitlich?** how's your health?; **~heitsschädlich** *a* unhealthy; **G~heitswesen** *nt* health service; **G~heitszustand** *m* state of health.

Getöse [gəˈtøːzə] *nt* -s din, racket.

Getränk [gəˈtrɛŋk] *nt* -(e)s, -e drink.

getrauen [gəˈtraʊən] *vr* dare, venture.

Getreide [gəˈtraɪdə] *nt* -s, - cereals *pl*, grain; **~speicher** *m* granary.

getrennt [gəˈtrɛnt] *a* separate.

getreu [gəˈtrɔʏ] *a* faithful.

Getriebe [gəˈtriːbə] *nt* -s, - (*Leute*) bustle; (*Aut*) gearbox; **~öl** *nt* transmission oil.

getrost [gəˈtroːst] *ad* without any bother; **~ sterben** die in peace.

Getue [gəˈtuːə] *nt* -s fuss.

geübt [gəˈyːpt] *a* experienced.

Gewächs [gəˈvɛks] *nt* -es, -e growth; (*Pflanze*) plant.

gewachsen [gəˈvaksən] *a*: **jdm/etw ~ sein** be sb's equal/equal to sth.

Gewächshaus *nt* greenhouse.

gewagt [gəˈvaːkt] *a* daring, risky.

gewählt [gəˈvɛːlt] *a* *Sprache* refined, elegant.

Gewähr [gəˈvɛːr] *f* - guarantee; **keine ~ übernehmen für** accept no responsibility for; **g~en** *vt* grant; (*geben*) provide; **g~leisten** *vt* guarantee.

Gewahrsam [gəˈvaːrzaːm] *m* -s, -e safe-keeping; (*Polizei*—) custody.

Gewähr- *cpd*: **~smann** *m* informant, source; **~ung** *f* granting.

Gewalt [gəˈvalt] *f* -, -en power; (*große Kraft*) force; (—*taten*) violence; **mit aller ~** with all one's might; **~anwendung** *f* use of force; **~herrschaft** *f* tyranny; **g~ig** *a* tremendous; *Irrtum* huge; **~marsch** *m* forced march; **g~sam** *a* forcible; **g~tätig** *a* violent.

Gewand [gəˈvant] *nt* -(e)s, ˝er garment.

gewandt [gəˈvant] *a* deft, skilful; (*erfahren*) experienced; **G~heit** *f* dexterity, skill.

Gewässer [gəˈvɛsər] *nt* -s, - waters *pl*.

Gewebe [gəˈveːbə] *nt* -s, - (*Stoff*) fabric; (*Biol*) tissue.

Gewehr [gəˈveːr] *nt* -(e)s, -e gun; rifle; **~lauf** *m* rifle barrel.

Geweih [gəˈvaɪ] *nt* -(e)s, -e antlers *pl*.

Gewerb- [gəˈvɛrb] *cpd*: **~e** *nt* -s, - trade, occupation; **Handel und ~e** trade and industry; **~eschule** *f* technical school; **g~etreibend** *a* carrying on a trade; industrial; **g~lich** *a* industrial; trade *attr*; **g~smäßig** *a* professional; **~szweig** *m* line of trade.

Gewerkschaft [gəˈvɛrkʃaft] *f* trade union;

~ler *m* -s, - trade unionist; **~sbund** *m* trade unions federation.

Gewicht [gəˈvɪçt] *nt* -(e)s, -e weight; (*fig*) importance; **g~ig** *a* weighty.

gewieft [gəˈviːft] *a*, **gewiegt** [gəˈviːkt] *a* shrewd, cunning.

gewillt [gəˈvɪlt] *a* willing, prepared.

Gewimmel [gəˈvɪməl] *nt* -s swarm.

Gewinde [gəˈvɪndə] *nt* -s, - (*Kranz*) wreath; (*von Schraube*) thread.

Gewinn [gəˈvɪn] *m* -(e)s, -e profit; (*bei Spiel*) winnings *pl*; **etw mit ~ verkaufen** sell sth at a profit; **~beteiligung** *f* profit-sharing; **g~bringend** *a* profitable; **g~en** *vt irreg* win; (*erwerben*) gain; *Kohle, Öl* extract; *vi* win; (*profitieren*) gain; **an etw** (*dat*) **g~en** gain in sth; **g~end** *a* winning, attractive; **~er(in** *f)* *m* -s, - winner; **~spanne** *f* profit margin; **~sucht** *f* love of gain; **~(n)ummer** *f* winning number; **~ung** *f* winning; gaining; (*von Kohle etc*) extraction.

Gewirr [gəˈvɪr] *nt* -(e)s, -e tangle; (*von Straßen*) maze.

gewiß [gəˈvɪs] *a,ad* certain(ly).

Gewissen [gəˈvɪsən] *nt* -s, - conscience; **g~haft** *a* conscientious; **~haftigkeit** *f* conscientiousness; **g~los** *a* unscrupulous; **~sbisse** *pl* pangs of conscience *pl*, qualms *pl*; **~sfrage** *f* matter of conscience; **~sfreiheit** *f* freedom of conscience; **~skonflikt** *m* moral conflict.

gewissermaßen [gəvɪsərˈmaːsən] *ad* more or less, in a way.

Gewiß- *cpd*: **~heit** *f* certainty; **g~lich** *ad* surely.

Gewitter [gəˈvɪtər] *nt* -s, - thunderstorm; **g~n** *vi impers*: **es gewittert** there's a thunderstorm; **g~schwül** *a* sultry and thundery.

gewitzigt [gəˈvɪtsɪçt] *a*: **~ sein** have learned by experience.

gewitzt [gəˈvɪtst] *a* shrewd, cunning.

gewogen [gəˈvoːgən] *a* well-disposed (+*dat* towards).

gewöhnen [gəˈvøːnən] *vt*: **jdn an etw** (*acc*) **~** accustom sb to sth; (*erziehen zu*) teach sb sth; *vr*: **sich an etw** (*acc*) **~** get used *or* accustomed to sth.

Gewohnheit [gəˈvoːnhaɪt] *f* habit; (*Brauch*) custom; **aus ~** from habit; **zur ~ werden** become a habit; **~s-** *in cpds* habitual; **~smensch** *m* creature of habit; **~srecht** *nt* common law; **~stier** *nt* (*col*) creature of habit.

gewöhnlich [gəˈvøːnlɪç] *a* usual; ordinary; (*pej*) common; **wie ~** as usual.

gewohnt [gəˈvoːnt] *a* usual; **etw ~ sein** be used to sth.

Gewöhnung *f* getting accustomed (*an* +*acc* to).

Gewölbe [gəˈvœlbə] *nt* -s, - vault.

Gewühl [gəˈvyːl] *nt* -(e)s throng.

Gewürz [gəˈvʏrts] *nt* -es, -e spice, seasoning; **~nelke** *f* clove.

gezähnt [gəˈtsɛːnt] *a* serrated, toothed.

Gezeiten [gəˈtsaɪtən] *pl* tides *pl*.

Gezeter [gəˈtseːtər] *nt* -s clamour, yelling.

gezielt [gəˈtsiːlt] *a* with a particular aim in mind, purposeful; *Kritik* pointed.

geziemen [gə'tsi:mən] vr impers be fitting; ~d a proper.

geziert [gə'tsi:rt] a affected; G~heit f affectation.

Gezwitscher [gə'tsvɪtʃər] nt -s twitter(ing), chirping.

gezwungen [gə'tsvʊŋən] a forced; ~ermaßen ad of necessity.

Gicht ['gɪçt] f- gout; **g~isch** a gouty.

Giebel ['gi:bəl] m -s, - gable; ~**dach** nt gable(d) roof; ~**fenster** nt gable window.

Gier [gi:r] f- greed; **g~ig** a greedy.

Gieß- ['gi:s] cpd: ~**bach** m torrent; **g~en** vt irreg pour; Blumen water; Metall cast; Wachs mould; ~**e'rei** f foundry; ~**kanne** f watering can.

Gift [gɪft] nt -(e)s, -e poison; **g~ig** a poisonous; (fig: boshaft) venomous; ~**zahn** m fang.

Gilde ['gɪldə] f-, -n guild.

Ginster ['gɪnstər] m -s, - broom.

Gipfel ['gɪpfəl] m -s, - summit, peak; (fig) height; **g~n** vi culminate; ~**treffen** nt summit (meeting).

Gips [gɪps] m -es, -e plaster (of Paris); (Med) plaster (of Paris); ~**abdruck** m plaster cast; **g~en** vt plaster; ~**figur** f plaster figure; ~**verband** m plaster (cast).

Giraffe [gi'rafə] f-, -n giraffe.

Girlande [gɪr'landə] f-, -n garland.

Giro ['ʒi:ro] nt -s, -s giro; ~**konto** nt current account.

girren ['gɪrən] vi coo.

Gischt [gɪʃt] m -(e)s, -e spray, foam.

Gitarre [gi'tarə] f-, -n guitar.

Gitter ['gɪtər] nt -s, - grating, bars pl; (für Pflanzen) trellis; (Zaun) railing(s); ~**bett** nt cot; ~**fenster** nt barred window; ~**zaun** m railing(s).

Glacéhandschuh [gla'se:hant∫u:] m kid glove.

Gladiole [gladi'o:lə] f-, -n gladiolus.

Glanz [glants] m -es shine, lustre; (fig) splendour.

glänzen ['glɛntsən] vi shine (also fig), gleam; vt polish; ~**d** a shining; (fig) brilliant.

Glanz~ cpd: ~**leistung** f brilliant achievement; **g~los** a dull; ~**zeit** f heyday.

Glas [gla:s] nt -es, "er glass; ~**bläser** m -s, - glass blower; ~**er** m -s, - glazier; **g~ieren** [gla'zi:rən] vt glaze; **g~ig** a glassy; ~**scheibe** f pane; ~**ur** [gla'zu:r] f glaze; (Cook) icing.

glatt [glat] a smooth; (rutschig) slippery; Absage flat; Lüge downright; G~**eis** nt (black) ice; jdn aufs G~eis führen (fig) take sb for a ride.

Glätte ['glɛtə] f-, -n smoothness; slipperiness; **g~n** vt smooth out.

Glatze ['glatsə] f-, -n bald head; eine ~ bekommen go bald.

glatzköpfig a bald.

Glaube ['glaubə] m -ns, -n faith (an +acc in); belief (an +acc in); **g~n** vti believe (an +acc in, jdm sb); think; ~**nsbekenntnis** nt creed.

glaubhaft ['glaubhaft] a credible; G~**igkeit** f credibility.

gläubig ['glɔybɪç] a (Rel) devout; (vertrauensvoll) trustful; G~**e(r)** mf believer; **die G~en** the faithful; G~**er** m -s, - creditor.

glaubwürdig ['glaubvʏrdɪç] a credible; Mensch trustworthy; G~**keit** f credibility; trustworthiness.

gleich [glaɪç] a equal; (identisch) (the) same, identical; **es ist mir ~** it's all the same to me; **2 mal 2 ~ 4** 2 times 2 is or equals 4; ad equally; (sofort) straight away; (bald) in a minute; ~ **groß** the same size; ~ **nach/an** right after/at; ~**altrig** a of the same age; ~**artig** a similar; ~**bedeutend** a synonymous; ~**berechtigt** a having equal rights; G~**berechtigung** f equal rights pl; ~**bleibend** a constant; ~**en** vi irreg: jdm/etw ~**en** be like sb/sth; vr be alike; ~**ermaßen** ad equally; ~**falls** ad likewise; **danke ~falls!** the same to you; G~**förmigkeit** f uniformity; ~**gesinnt** a like-minded; G~**gewicht** nt equilibrium, balance; ~**gültig** a indifferent; (unbedeutend) unimportant; G~**gültigkeit** f indifference; G~**heit** f equality; ~**kommen** vi irreg +dat be equal to; G~**mache'rei** f egalitarianism; ~**mäßig** a even, equal; G~**mut** m equanimity; G~**nis** nt -ses, -se parable; ~**sam** ad as it were; ~**sehen** vi irreg (jdm) be or look like (sb); G~**strom** m (Elec) direct current; ~**tun** vi irreg: es jdm ~**tun** match sb; G~**ung** f equation; ~**viel** ad no matter; ~**wohl** ad nevertheless; ~**zeitig** a simultaneous.

Gleis [glaɪs] nt -es, -e track, rails pl; (Bahnsteig) platform.

Gleit- ['glaɪt] cpd: gliding; sliding; **g~en** vi irreg glide; (rutschen) slide; ~**flug** m glide; gliding.

Gletscher ['glɛtʃər] m -s, - glacier; ~**spalte** f crevasse.

Glied [gli:t] nt -(e)s, -er member; (Arm, Bein) limb; (von Kette) link; (Mil) rank(s); **g~ern** vt organize, structure; ~**erung** f structure, organization; ~**maßen** pl limbs pl.

Glimm- ['glɪm] cpd: **g~en** vi irreg glow, gleam; ~**er** m -s, - glow, gleam; (Mineral) mica; ~**stengel** m (col) fag.

glimpflich ['glɪmpflɪç] a mild, lenient; ~ **davonkommen** get off lightly.

glitzern ['glɪtsərn] vi glitter, twinkle.

Globus ['glo:bus] m - or -ses, **Globen** or -se globe.

Glöckchen ['glœkçən] nt (little) bell.

Glocke ['glɔkə] f-, -n bell; etw an die große ~ **hängen** (fig) shout sth from the rooftops; ~**ngeläut** nt peal of bells; ~**nspiel** nt chimes(s); (Mus) glockenspiel.

Glorie ['glo:riə] f-, -n glory; (von Heiligen) halo.

Glosse ['glɔsə] f-, -n comment.

glotzen ['glɔtsən] vi (col) stare.

Glück [glʏk] nt -(e)s luck, fortune; (Freude) happiness; ~ **haben** be lucky; **viel ~** good luck; **zum ~** fortunately;

g~en vi succeed; **es glückte ihm, es zu bekommen** he succeeded in getting it.

gluckern ['glʊkərn] vi glug.

Glück- cpd: **g~lich** a fortunate; (froh) happy; **g~licherweise** ad fortunately; **~bringer** m -s, - lucky charm; **g~-'selig** a blissful; **~sfall** m stroke of luck; **~skind** nt lucky person; **~ssache** f matter of luck; **~sspiel** nt game of chance; **~sstern** m lucky star; **g~strahlend** a radiant (with happiness); **~wunsch** m congratulations pl, best wishes pl.

Glüh- ['gly:] cpd: **~birne** f light bulb; **g~en** vi glow; **~wein** m mulled wine; **~würmchen** nt glow-worm.

Glut [glu:t] f -, -en (Röte) glow; (Feuers—) fire; (Hitze) heat; (fig) ardour.

Gnade ['gna:də] f -, -n (Gunst) favour; (Erbarmen) mercy; (Milde) clemency; **~nfrist** f reprieve, respite; **~ngesuch** nt petition for clemency; **~nstoß** m coup de grâce.

gnädig ['gnɛ:dɪç] a gracious; (voll Erbarmen) merciful.

Gold [gɔlt] nt -(e)s gold; **g~en** a golden; **~fisch** m goldfish; **~grube** f goldmine; **~regen** m laburnum; **~schnitt** m gilt edging; **~währung** f gold standard.

Golf [gɔlf] m -(e)s, -e gulf; nt -s golf; **~platz** m golf course; **~schläger** m golf club; **~spieler** m golfer; **~strom** m Gulf Stream.

Gondel ['gɔndəl] f -, -n gondola; (Seilbahn) cable-car.

gönnen ['gœnən] vt: **jdm etw ~** not begrudge sb sth; **sich** (dat) **etw ~** allow oneself sth.

Gönner m -s, - patron; **g~haft** a patronizing; **~miene** f patronizing air.

Gosse ['gɔsə] f -, -n gutter.

Gott [gɔt] m -es, ̈er god; **um ~es Willen!** for heaven's sake!; **~ sei Dank!** thank God!; **~esdienst** m service; **~eshaus** nt place of worship; **~heit** f deity.

Gött- [gœt] cpd: **~in** f goddess; **g~lich** a divine.

Gott- cpd: **g~los** a godless; **~vertrauen** nt trust in God.

Götze ['gœtsə] m -n, -n idol.

Grab [gra:p] nt -(e)s, ̈er grave; **g~en** ['gra:bən] vt irreg dig; **~en** m -s, ̈ ditch; (Mil) trench; **~rede** f funeral oration; **~stein** m gravestone.

Grad [gra:t] m -(e)s, -e degree; **~einteilung** f graduation; **g~weise** ad gradually.

Graf [gra:f] m -en, -en count, earl; **~schaft** f county.

Gräfin ['grɛ:fɪn] f countess.

Gram [gra:m] m -(e)s grief, sorrow.

grämen ['grɛ:mən] vr grieve.

Gramm [gram] nt -s, -e gram(me); **~atik** [-'matɪk] f grammar; **g~atisch** a grammatical; **~o'phon** nt -s, -e gramophone.

Granat [gra'na:t] m -(e)s, -e (Stein) garnet; **~apfel** m pomegranate; **~e** f -, -n (Mil) shell; (Hand—) grenade.

Granit [gra'ni:t] m -s, -e granite.

graphisch ['gra:fɪʃ] a graphic; **~e Darstellung** graph.

Gras [gra:s] nt -es, ̈er grass; **g~en** vi graze; **~halm** m blade of grass; **g~ig** a grassy; **~narbe** f turf.

grassieren [gra'si:rən] vi be rampant, rage.

gräßlich ['grɛslɪç] a horrible.

Grat [gra:t] m -(e)s, -e ridge.

Gräte ['grɛ:tə] f -, -n fishbone.

gratis ['gra:tɪs] a,ad free (of charge); **G~probe** f free sample.

Gratulation [gratulatsi'o:n] f congratulation(s).

gratulieren [gratu'li:rən] vi: **jdm ~** (zu etw) congratulate sb (on sth); **(ich) gratuliere!** congratulations!

grau [grau] a grey; **~en** vi (Tag) dawn; vi impers: **es graut jdm vor etw** sb dreads sth, sb is afraid of sth; vr: **sich ~en** vor dread, have a horror of; **G~en** nt -s horror; **~enhaft** a horrible; **~haarig** a grey-haired; **~meliert** a grey-flecked.

grausam ['grauza:m] a cruel; **G~keit** f cruelty.

Grausen ['grauzən] nt -s horror; **g~** vi impers, vr see grauen.

gravieren [gra'vi:rən] vt engrave; **~d** a grave.

Grazie ['gra:tsiə] f -, -n grace.

graziös [gratsi'ø:s] a graceful.

greif- [graif] cpd: **~bar** a tangible, concrete; **in ~barer Nähe** within reach; **~en** vt irreg seize; grip; nach etw **~en** reach for sth; **um sich ~en** (fig) spread; **zu etw ~en** (fig) turn to sth.

Greis [grais] m -es, -e old man; **~enalter** nt old age; **g~enhaft** a senile.

grell [grɛl] a harsh.

Grenz- ['grɛnts] cpd: **~beamte(r)** m frontier official; **~e** f -, -n boundary; (Staats—) frontier; (Schranke) limit; **g~en** vi border (an +acc on); **g~enlos** a boundless; **~fall** m borderline case; **~linie** f boundary; **~übergang** m frontier crossing.

Greuel ['grɔyəl] m -s, - horror, revulsion; **etw ist jdm ein ~** sb loathes sth; **~tat** f atrocity.

greulich ['grɔylɪç] a horrible.

griesgrämig ['gri:sgrɛ:mɪç] a grumpy.

Grieß [gri:s] m -es, -e (Cook) semolina.

Griff [grɪf] m -(e)s, -e grip; (Vorrichtung) handle; **g~bereit** a handy.

Griffel ['grɪfəl] m -s, - slate pencil; (Bot) style.

Grille ['grɪlə] f -, -n cricket; (fig) whim; **g~n** vt grill.

Grimasse [gri'masə] f -, -n grimace.

Grimm [grɪm] m -(e)s fury; **g~ig** a furious; (heftig) fierce, severe.

grinsen ['grɪnzən] vi grin.

Grippe ['grɪpə] f -, -n influenza, flu.

grob [gro:p] a coarse, gross; Fehler, Verstoß gross; **G~heit** f coarseness; coarse expression; **g~ia'n** [gro'bia:n] m -s, -e ruffian; **~knochig** a large-boned.

Groll [grɔl] m -(e)s resentment; **g~en** vi

bear ill will (+*dat* or *mit* towards); (*Donner*) rumble.

groß [gro:s] *a* big, large; (*hoch*) tall; (*fig*) great; **im ~en und ganzen** on the whole; *ad* greatly; **~artig** *a* great, splendid; **G~aufnahme** *f* (*Cine*) close-up.

Größe ['grø:sə] *f* -, -n size; (*fig*) greatness; (*Länge*) height.

Groß- *cpd*: **~einkauf** *m* bulk purchase; **~eltern** *pl* grandparents *pl*; **g~enteils** *ad* mostly.

Größen- *cpd*: **~unterschied** *m* difference in size; **~wahn** *m* megalomania.

Groß- *cpd*: **~format** *nt* large size; **~handel** *m* wholesale trade; **~händler** *m* wholesaler; **g~herzig** *a* generous; **~macht** *f* great power; **~maul** *m* braggart; **~mut** *f* - magnanimity; **g~mütig** *a* magnanimous; **~mutter** *f* grandmother; **g~spurig** *a* pompous; **~stadt** *f* city, large town.

größte(r,s) ['grø:stə(r,z)] *a superl* of **groß**; **~nteils** *ad* for the most part.

Groß- *cpd*: **~tuer** *m* -s, - boaster; **g~tun** *vi irreg* boast; **~vater** *m* grandfather; **g~ziehen** *vt irreg* raise; **g~zügig** *a* generous; *Planung* on a large scale.

grotesk [gro'tɛsk] *a* grotesque.

Grotte ['grɔtə] *f* -, -n grotto.

Grübchen ['gry:pçən] *nt* dimple.

Grube ['gru:bə] *f* -, -n pit; mine; **~narbeiter** *m* miner; **~ngas** *nt* firedamp.

grübeln ['gry:bəln] *vi* brood.

Grübler ['gry:blər] *m* -s, - brooder; **g~isch** *a* brooding, pensive.

Gruft [gruft] *f* -, -̈e tomb, vault.

grün [gry:n] *a* green; **G~anlage** *f* park.

Grund [grunt] *m* ground; (*von See, Gefäß*) bottom; (*fig*) reason; **im ~e genommen** basically; **~ausbildung** *f* basic training; **~bedeutung** *f* basic meaning; **~bedingung** *f* fundamental condition; **~besitz** *m* land(ed property), real estate; **~buch** *nt* land register; **g~ehrlich** *a* thoroughly honest.

gründ- [grynd] *cpd*: **~en** *vt* found; **~en auf** (+*acc*) base on; *vr* be based (*auf* +*dat* on); **G~er** *m* -s, - founder; **~lich** *a* thorough; **G~ung** *f* foundation.

Grund- *cpd*: **g~falsch** *a* utterly wrong; **~gebühr** *f* basic charge; **~gedanke** *m* basic idea; **~gesetz** *nt* constitution; **~lage** *f* foundation; **g~legend** *a* fundamental; **g~los** *a* groundless; **~mauer** *f* foundation wall; **~regel** *f* basic rule; **~riß** *m* plan; (*fig*) outline; **~satz** *m* principle; **g~sätzlich** *a,ad* fundamental(ly); *Frage* of principle; (*prinzipiell*) on principle; **~schule** *f* elementary school; **~stein** *m* foundation stone; **~steuer** *f* rates *pl*; **~stück** *nt* estate; plot; **g~verschieden** *a* utterly different; **~zug** *m* characteristic.

Grün- *cpd*: **~e** *nt* -n: **im ~en** in the open air; **~kohl** *m* kale; **~schnabel** *m* greenhorn; **~span** *m* verdigris; **~streifen** *m* central reservation.

grunzen ['gruntsən] *vi* grunt.

Gruppe ['grupə] *f* -, -n group; **g~nweise** *ad* in groups.

gruppieren [gru'pi:rən] *vtr* group.

gruselig *a* creepy.

gruseln ['gru:zəln] *vi impers*: **es gruselt jdm vor etw** sth gives sb the creeps; *vr* have the creeps.

Gruß [gru:s] *m* -es, -̈e greeting; (*Mil*) salute; **viele e best wishes**; **e an** (+*acc*) regards to.

grüßen ['gry:sən] *vt* greet; (*Mil*) salute; **jdn von jdm ~** give sb sb's regards; **jdn ~ lassen** send sb one's regards.

gucken ['gukən] *vi* look.

Gulasch ['gu:laʃ] *nt* -(e)s, -e goulash.

gültig ['gyltıç] *a* valid; **G~keit** *f* validity; **G~keitsdauer** *f* period of validity.

Gummi ['gumi] *nt or m* -s, -s rubber; (*~harze*) gum; (*~band nt*) rubber *or* elastic band; (*Hosen~*) elastic; **g~eren** [gu'mi:rən] *vt* gum; **~knüppel** *m* rubber truncheon; **~strumpf** *m* elastic stocking.

Gunst [gunst] *f* favour.

günstig ['gynstıç] *a* favourable.

Gurgel ['gurgəl] *f* -, -n throat; **g~n** *vi* gurgle; (*im Mund*) gargle.

Gurke ['gurkə] *f* -, -n cucumber; **saure ~** pickled cucumber, gherkin.

Gurt [gurt] *m* -(e)s, -e, **Gurte** *f* -n -n belt.

Gürtel ['gyrtəl] *m* -s, - belt; (*Geog*) zone; **~reifen** *m* radial tyre.

Guß [gus] *m* -sses, **Güsse** casting; (*Regen~*) downpour; (*Cook*) glazing; **~eisen** *nt* cast iron.

Gut [gu:t] *nt* -(e)s, -̈er (*Besitz*) possession; (*pl: Waren*) goods *pl*; **g~** *a* good; *ad* well; **laß es g~ sein** that'll do; **~achten** *nt* -s, - (*expert*) opinion; **~achter** *m* -s, - expert; **g~artig** *a* good-natured; (*Med*) benign; **g~bürgerlich** *a* *Küche* (good) plain; **~dünken** *nt*: **nach ~dünken** at one's discretion.

Güte ['gy:tə] *f* - goodness, kindness; (*Qualität*) quality.

Güter- *cpd*: **~abfertigung** *f* (*Rail*) goods office; **~bahnhof** *m* goods station; **~wagen** *m* goods waggon, freight car (*US*); **~ zug** *m* goods train, freight train (*US*).

Gut- *cpd*: **g~gehen** *v impers irreg* work, come off; **es geht jdm g~** sb's doing fine; **g~gelaunt** *a* good-humoured, in a good mood; **g~gemeint** *a* well meant; **g~gläubig** *a* trusting; **~haben** *nt* -s credit; **g~heißen** *vt irreg* approve (of); **g~herzig** *a* kind(-hearted).

gütig ['gy:tıç] *a* kind.

gütlich ['gy:tlıç] *a* amicable.

Gut- *cpd*: **g~mütig** *a* good-natured; **~mütigkeit** *f* good nature; **~sbesitzer** *m* landowner; **~schein** *m* voucher; **g~schreiben** *vt irreg* credit; **~schrift** *f* credit; **~sherr** *m* squire; **g~tun** *vi irreg*: **jdm g~tun** do sb good; **g~willig** *a* willing.

Gymnasium [gym'na:zium] *nt* grammar school (*Brit*), high school (*US*).

Gymnastik [gym'nastık] *f* exercises *pl*, keep fit.

H

H, h [ha:] *nt* H, h.
Haar [ha:r] *nt* **-(e)s, -e** hair; **um ein ~**
nearly; **~bürste** *f* hairbrush; **h~en** *vir*
lose hair; **~esbreite** *f*: **um ~esbreite**
by a hair's-breadth; **h~genau** *ad*
precisely; **h~ig** *a* hairy; (*fig*) nasty;
~klemme *f* hair grip; **h~los** *a* hairless;
~nadel *f* hairpin; **h~scharf** *ad* beobachten very sharply; *daneben* by a hair's
breadth; **~schnitt** *m* haircut; **~schopf**
m head of hair; **~spalte'rei** *f* hair-
splitting; **~spange** *f* hair slide;
h~sträubend a hair-raising; **~teil** *nt*
hairpiece; **~waschmittel** *nt* shampoo.
Habe ['ha:bə] *f*- property.
haben ['ha:bən] *vt, v* aux *irreg* have;
Hunger/Angst ~ be hungry/afraid;
woher hast du das? where did you get
that from?; **was hast du denn?** what's
the matter (with you)?; **H~** *nt* **-s, -** credit.
Habgier *f* avarice; **h~ig** *a* avaricious.
Habicht ['ha:bɪçt] *m* **-(e)s, -e** hawk.
Habseligkeiten *pl* belongings *pl*.
Hachse ['haksə] *f* **-, -n** (*Cook*) knuckle.
Hacke ['hakə] *f* **-, -n** hoe; (*Ferse*) heel;
h~n *vt* hack, chop; *Erde* hoe.
Hackfleisch *nt* mince, minced meat.
Häcksel ['hɛksəl] *m or nt* **-s** chopped
straw, chaff.
hadern ['ha:dərn] *vi* quarrel.
Hafen ['ha:fən] *m* **-s, ⁼** harbour, port;
~arbeiter *m* docker; **~damm** *m* jetty,
mole; **~stadt** *f* port.
Hafer ['ha:fər] *m* **-s, -** oats *pl*; **~brei** *m*
porridge; **~flocken** *pl* porridge oats *pl*;
~schleim *m* gruel.
Haft [haft] *f* - custody; **h~bar** *a* liable,
responsible; **~befehl** *m* warrant (of
arrest); **h~en** *vi* stick, cling; **h~en für**
be liable or responsible for; **h~enbleiben**
vi irreg stick (an +*dat* to); **~pflicht** *f*
liability; **~pflichtversicherung** *f* third
party insurance; **~schalen** *pl* contact
lenses *pl*; **~ung** *f* liability.
Hage- ['ha:gə] *cpd*: **~butte** *f*-, -n rose hip;
~dorn *m* hawthorn.
Hagel ['ha:gəl] *m* **-s** hail; **h~n** *vi impers*
hail.
hager ['ha:gər] *a* gaunt.
Häher ['hɛ:ər] *m* **-s, -** jay.
Hahn [ha:n] *m* **-(e)s, ⁼e** cock; (*Wasser—*)
tap, faucet (*US*).
Hähnchen ['hɛ:nçən] *nt* cockerel; (*Cook*)
chicken.
Hai(fisch) ['hai(fɪʃ)] *m* **-(e)s, -e** shark.
Häkchen ['hɛ:kçən] *nt* small hook.
Häkel- ['hɛ:kəl] *cpd*: **~arbeit** *f* crochet
work; **h~n** *vt* crochet; **~nadel** *f* crochet
hook.
Haken ['ha:kən] *m* **-s, -** hook; (*fig*) catch;
~kreuz *nt* swastika; **~nase** *f* hooked
nose.
halb [halp] *a* half; **~ eins** half past twelve;
ein ~es Dutzend half a dozen;
H~dunkel *nt* semi-darkness.
halber ['halbər] *prep* +*gen* (*wegen*) on
account of; (*für*) for the sake of.

Halb- *cpd*: **~heit** *f* half-measure;
h~ieren *vt* halve; **~insel** *f* peninsula;
h~jährlich *a* half-yearly; **~kreis** *m*
semicircle; **~kugel** *f* hemisphere;
h~laut *a* in an undertone; **~links** *m* -, -
(*Sport*) inside-left; **~mond** *m* half-moon;
(*fig*) crescent; **h~offen** *a* half-open;
~rechts *m* -, - (*Sport*) inside-right;
~schuh *m* shoe; **~tagsarbeit** *f* part-
time work; **h~wegs** *ad* half-way;
h~wegs besser more or less better;
~wüchsige(r) *mf* adolescent; **~zeit** *f*
(*Sport*) half; (*Pause*) half-time.
Halde ['haldə] *f* -, -n tip; (*Schlacken—*) slag
heap.
Hälfte ['hɛlftə] -, -n *f* half.
Halfter ['halftər] *f* -, -n, *or nt* -s, - halter;
(*Pistolen—*) holster.
Hall [hal] *m* **-(e)s, -e** sound.
Halle ['halə] *f* -, -n hall; (*Aviat*) hangar;
h~n *vi* echo, resound; **~nbad** *nt* indoor
swimming pool.
hallo [ha'lo:] *interj* hallo.
Halluzination [halutsinatsi'o:n] *f*
hallucination.
Halm ['halm] *m* **-(e)s, -e** blade, stalk.
Hals [hals] *m* **-es, ⁼e** neck; (*Kehle*) throat;
~ über Kopf in a rush; **~kette** *f* necklace; **~krause** *f* ruff; **~-Nasen-Ohren-
Arzt** *m* ear nose and throat specialist;
~schlagader *f* carotid artery;
~schmerzen *pl* sore throat; **h~starrig**
a stubborn, obstinate; **~tuch** *nt* scarf;
~weh *nt* sore throat; **~wirbel** *m*
cervical vertebra.
Halt [halt] *m* **-(e)s, -e** stop; (*fester —*)
hold; (*innerer —*) stability; **h~!** stop!, halt!;
h~bar *a* durable; *Lebensmittel* non-perish-
able; (*Mil, fig*) tenable; **~barkeit** *f*
durability; (non-)perishability; tenability.
halten ['haltən] *irreg vt* keep; (*fest—*) hold;
~ für regard as; **~ von** think of; *vi* hold;
(*frisch bleiben*) keep; (*stoppen*) stop; **an
sich ~** restrain oneself; *vr* (*frisch bleiben*)
keep; (*sich behaupten*) hold out; **sich
rechts/links ~** keep to the right/left.
Halt- *cpd*: **~estelle** *f* stop; **h~los** *a*
unstable; **~losigkeit** *f* instability;
h~machen *vi* stop; **~ung** *f* posture; (*fig*)
attitude; (*Selbstbeherrschung*) composure;
~verbot *nt* ban on stopping.
Halunke [ha'lυŋkə] *m* **-n, -n** rascal.
hämisch ['hɛ:mɪʃ] *a* malicious.
Hammel ['haməl] *m* **-s, ⁼ or -** wether;
~fleisch *nt* mutton; **~keule** *f* leg of
mutton.
Hammer ['hamər] *m* **-s, ⁼** hammer.
hämmern ['hɛmərn] *vti* hammer.
Hampelmann ['hampəlman] *m* (*lit, fig*)
puppet.
Hamster ['hamstər] *m* **-s, -** hamster; **~ei**
[-'rai] *f* hoarding; **~er** *m* **-s, -** hoarder;
h~n *vi* hoard.
Hand [hant] *f* -, ⁼e hand; **~arbeit** *f*
manual work; (*Nadelarbeit*) needlework;
~arbeiter *m* manual worker; **~besen** *m*
brush; **~bremse** *f* handbrake; **~buch** *nt*
handbook, manual.
Hände- ['hɛndə] *cpd*: **~druck** *m* handshake; **~klatschen** *nt* clapping, applause.

Handel ['handəl] *m* **-s** trade; (*Geschäft*) transaction; **haben** quarrel.

handeln ['handəln] *vi* trade; act; ~ **von** be about; *vr impers:* **sich** ~ **um** be a question of, be about; **H**~ *nt* **-s** action.

Handels- *cpd:* ~**bilanz** *f* balance of trade; **h**~**einig** *a:* **mit jdm h**~**einig werden** conclude a deal with sb; ~**kammer** *f* chamber of commerce; ~**marine** *f* merchant navy; ~**recht** *nt* commercial law; ~**reisende(r)** *m* commercial traveller; ~**schule** *f* business school; ~**vertreter** *m* sales representative.

Hand- *cpd:* ~**feger** *m* **-s**, - brush; **h**~**fest** *a* hefty; **h**~**gearbeitet** *a* handmade; ~**gelenk** *nt* wrist; ~**gemenge** *nt* scuffle; ~**gepäck** *nt* hand-luggage; **h**~**geschrieben** *a* handwritten; **h**~**greiflich** *a* palpable; **h**~**greiflich werden** become violent; ~**griff** *m* flick of the wrist; **h**~**haben** *vt irreg insep* handle; ~**karren** *m* handcart; ~**kuß** *m* kiss on the hand.

Händler ['hɛndlər] *m* **-s**, - trader, dealer.

handlich ['hantlɪç] *a* handy.

Handlung ['handluŋ] *f* -, **-en** act(ion); (*in Buch*) plot; (*Geschäft*) shop; ~**sbevollmächtigte(r)** *mf* authorized agent; ~**sweise** *f* manner of dealing.

Hand- *cpd:* ~**pflege** *f* manicure; ~**schelle** *f* handcuff; ~**schlag** *m* handshake; ~**schrift** *f* handwriting; (*Text*) manuscript; ~**schuh** *m* glove; ~**tasche** *f* handbag; ~**tuch** *nt* towel; ~**werk** *nt* trade, craft; ~**werker** *m* **-s** - craftsman, artisan; ~**werkzeug** *nt* tools *pl*.

Hanf [hanf] *m* **-(e)s** hemp.

Hang [haŋ] *m* **-(e)s**, **-e** inclination; (*Ab*—) slope.

Hänge- ['hɛŋə] *in cpds* hanging; ~**brücke** *f* suspension bridge; ~**matte** *f* hammock.

hängen ['hɛŋən] *irreg vi* hang; ~ **an** (*fig*) be attached to; *vt* hang (*an* +*acc* on(to)); **sich** ~ **an** (+*acc*) hang on to, cling to; ~**bleiben** *vi irreg* be caught (*an* +*dat* on); (*fig*) remain, stick.

Hängeschloß *nt* padlock.

hänseln ['hɛnzəln] *vt* tease.

hantieren [han'ti:rən] *vi* work, be busy; **mit etw** ~ handle sth.

hapern ['ha:pərn] *vi impers:* **es hapert an etw** (*dat*) sth leaves something to be desired.

Happen ['hapən] *m* **-s**, - mouthful.

Harfe ['harfə] *f* -, **-n** harp.

Harke ['harkə] *f* -, **-n** rake; **h**~**n** *vti* rake.

harmlos ['harmlo:s] *a* harmless; **H**~**igkeit** *f* harmlessness.

Harmonie [harmo'ni:] *f* harmony; **h**~**ren** *vi* harmonize.

Harmonika [har'mo:nika] *f* -, **-s** (*Zieh*—) concertina.

harmonisch [har'mo:nɪʃ] *a* harmonious.

Harmonium [har'mo:niʊm] *nt* **-s**, **-nien** *or* **-s** harmonium.

Harn ['harn] *m* **-(e)s**, **-e** urine; ~**blase** *f* bladder.

Harnisch ['harnɪʃ] *m* **-(e)s**, **-e** armour; **jdn in** ~ **bringen** infuriate sb; **in** ~ **geraten** become angry.

Harpune [har'pu:nə] *f* -, **-n** harpoon.

harren ['harən] *vi* wait (*auf* +*acc* for).

hart [hart] *a* hard; (*fig*) harsh.

Härte ['hɛrtə] *f* -, **-n** hardness; (*fig*) harshness; **h**~**n** *vtr* harden.

hart- *cpd:* ~**gekocht** *a* hard-boiled; ~**gesotten** *a* tough, hard-boiled; ~**herzig** *a* hard-hearted; ~**näckig** *a* stubborn; **H**~**näckigkeit** *f* stubbornness.

Harz [ha:rts] *nt* **-es**, **-e** resin.

Haschee [ha'ʃe:] *nt* **-s**, **-s** hash.

haschen ['haʃən] *vt* catch, snatch; *vi* (*col*) smoke hash.

Haschisch ['haʃɪʃ] *nt* - hashish.

Hase ['ha:zə] *m* **-n**, **-n** hare.

Haselnuß ['ha:zəlnʊs] *f* hazelnut.

Hasen- *cpd:* ~**fuß** *m* coward; ~**scharte** *f* harelip.

Haspe ['haspə] *f* -, **-n** hinge; ~**l** *f* -, **-n** reel, bobbin; (*Winde*) winch.

Haß [has] *m* **-sses** hate, hatred.

hassen ['hasən] *vt* hate; ~**enswert** *a* hateful.

häßlich ['hɛslɪç] *a* ugly; (*gemein*) nasty; **H**~**keit** *f* ugliness; nastiness.

Hast [hast] *f* - haste; **h**~**en** *vir* rush; **h**~**ig** *a* hasty.

hätscheln ['hɛtʃəln] *vt* pamper; (*zärtlich*) cuddle.

Haube ['haubə] *f* -, **-n** hood; (*Mütze*) cap; (*Aut*) bonnet, hood (*US*).

Hauch [haux] *m* **-(e)s**, **-e** breath; (*Luft*—) breeze; (*fig*) trace; **h**~**en** *vi* breathe; **h**~**fein** *a* very fine.

Haue ['hauə] *f* -, **-n** hoe, pick; (*col*) hiding; **h**~**n** *vt irreg* hew, cut; (*col*) thrash.

Haufen ['haufən] *m* **-s**, - heap; (*Leute*) crowd; **ein** ~ (*x*) (*col*) loads *or* a lot (of x); **auf einem** ~ in one heap; **h**~**weise** *ad* in heaps; in droves; **etw h**~**weise haben** have piles of sth.

häufen ['hɔyfən] *vt* pile up; *vr* accumulate.

häufig ['hɔyfɪç] *a,ad* frequent(ly); **H**~**keit** *f* frequency.

Haupt [haupt] *nt* **-(e)s**, **Häupter** head; (*Ober*—) chief; *in cpds* main; ~**bahnhof** *m* central station; **h**~**beruflich** *ad* as one's main occupation; ~**buch** *nt.* (*Comm*) ledger; ~**darsteller(in** *f*) *m* leading actor/actress; ~**eingang** *m* main entrance; ~**fach** *nt* main subject; ~**film** *m* main film.

Häuptling ['hɔyptlɪŋ] *m* chief(tain).

Haupt- *cpd:* ~**mann** *m*, *pl* **-leute** (*Mil*) captain; ~**postamt** *nt* main post office; ~**quartier** *nt* headquarters *pl*; ~**rolle** *f* leading part; ~**sache** *f* main thing; **h**~**sächlich** *a,ad* chief(ly); ~**satz** *m* main clause; ~**schlagader** *f* aorta; ~**stadt** *f* capital; ~**straße** *f* main street; ~**wort** *nt* noun.

Haus [haus] *nt* **-es**, **Häuser** house; **nach** ~**e** home; **zu** ~**e** at home; ~**angestellte** *f* domestic servant; ~**arbeit** *f* housework; (*Sch*) homework; ~**arzt** *m* family doctor; ~**aufgabe** *f* (*Sch*) homework; ~**besitzer(in** *f*) *m*, ~**eigentümer(in** *f*) *m* house-owner.

hausen ['hauzən] *vi* live (in poverty); (*pej*) wreak havoc.

Häuser- ['hɔʏzər] cpd: ~block m block (of houses); ~makler m estate agent.

Haus- cpd: ~frau f housewife; ~freund m family friend; (col) lover; h~gemacht a home-made; ~halt m household; (Pol) budget; h~halten vi irreg keep house; (sparen) economize; ~hälterin f housekeeper; ~haltsgeld nt housekeeping (money); ~haltsgerät nt domestic appliance; ~haltsplan m budget; ~haltung f housekeeping; ~herr m host; (Vermieter) landlord; h~hoch ad: h~hoch verlieren lose by a mile.

hausieren [hau'ziːrən] vi hawk, peddle.

Hausierer m -s, - hawker, peddlar.

häuslich ['hɔʏslɪç] a domestic; H~keit f domesticity.

Haus- cpd: ~meister m caretaker, janitor; ~ordnung f house rules pl; ~putz m house cleaning; ~schlüssel m front-door key; ~schuh m slipper; ~suchung f police raid; ~tier nt domestic animal; ~verwalter m caretaker; ~wirt m landlord; ~wirtschaft f domestic science.

Haut [haut] f-, Häute skin; (Tier—) hide.

häuten ['hɔʏtən] vt skin; vr slough one's skin.

Haut- cpd: h~eng a skin-tight; ~farbe f complexion.

Haxe ['haksə] f-, -n see Hachse.

Hebamme ['he:p'amə] f-, -n midwife.

Hebel ['he:bəl] m -s, - lever.

heben ['he:bən] vt irreg raise, lift.

hecheln ['hɛçəln] vi (Hund) pant.

Hecht [hɛçt] m -(e)s, -e pike.

Heck [hɛk] nt -(e)s, -e stern; (von Auto) rear.

Hecke ['hɛkə] f-, -n hedge; ~nrose f dog rose; ~schütze m sniper.

Heer [he:r] nt -(e)s, -e army.

Hefe ['he:fə] f-, -n yeast.

Heft [hɛft] nt -(e)s, -e exercise book; (Zeitschrift) number; (von Messer) haft; h~en vt fasten (an +acc to); (nähen) tack; ~er m -s, - folder.

heftig a fierce, violent; H~keit f fierceness, violence.

Heft- cpd: ~klammer f paper clip; ~maschine f stapling machine; ~pflaster nt sticking plaster; ~zwecke f drawing pin.

hegen ['he:gən] vt nurse; (fig) harbour, foster.

Hehl [he:l] m or nt: kein(en) ~ aus etw (dat) machen make no secret of sth; ~er m -s, - receiver (of stolen goods), fence.

Heide ['haidə] f-, -n heath, moor; (—kraut) heather; m -n, -n heathen, pagan; ~kraut nt heather; ~lbeere f bilberry; h~nmäßig a (col) terrific; ~ntum nt paganism.

heidnisch ['haidnɪʃ] a heathen, pagan.

heikel ['haikəl] a awkward, thorny; (wählerisch) fussy.

Heil [hail] nt -(e)s well-being; (Seelen—) salvation; h~ a in one piece, intact; h~ interj hail; ~and m -(e)s, -e saviour; h~bar a curable; h~en vt cure; vi heal;

h~froh a very relieved; ~gymnastin f physiotherapist.

heilig ['hailɪç] a holy; H~abend m Christmas Eve; H~e(r) mf saint; ~en vt sanctify, hallow; H~enschein m halo; H~keit f holiness; ~sprechen vt irreg canonize; H~tum nt shrine; (Gegenstand) relic.

Heil- cpd: h~los a unholy; ~mittel nt remedy; h~sam a (fig) salutary; ~sarmee f Salvation Army; ~ung f cure.

Heim [haim] nt -(e), -e home; h~ ad home.

Heimat ['haima:t] f-, -en home (town/country etc); ~land nt homeland; h~lich a native, home attr; (Gefühle) nostalgic; h~los a homeless; ~ort m home town/area; ~vertriebene(r) mf displaced person.

Heim- cpd: h~begleiten vt accompany home; h~elig a homely; h~fahren vi irreg drive/go home; ~fahrt f journey home; ~gang m return home; (Tod) decease; h~gehen vi irreg go home; (sterben) pass away; h~isch a (gebürtig) native; sich h~isch fühlen feel at home; ~kehr f-, -en homecoming; h~kehren vi return home; h~lich a secret; ~lichkeit f secrecy; ~reise f journey home; h~suchen vt afflict; (Geist) haunt; h~tückisch a malicious; h~wärts ad homewards; ~weg m way home; ~weh nt homesickness; ~weh haben be homesick; h~zahlen vt: jdm etw h~zahlen pay back sb for sth.

Heirat ['haira:t] f-, -en marriage; h~en vti marry; ~santrag m proposal.

heiser ['haizər] a hoarse; H~keit f hoarseness.

heiß [hais] a hot; ~e(r) Draht hot line; ~blütig a hot-blooded.

heißen ['haisən] irreg vi be called; (bedeuten) mean; vt command; (nennen) name; v impers it says; it is said.

Heiß- cpd: h~ersehnt a longed for; ~hunger m ravenous hunger; h~laufen vir irreg overheat.

heiter ['haitər] a cheerful; Wetter bright; H~keit f cheerfulness; (Belustigung) amusement.

Heiz- ['haits] cpd: h~bar a heated; Raum with heating; leicht h~bar easily heated; ~decke f electric blanket; h~en vt heat; ~er m -s, - stoker; ~körper m radiator; ~öl nt fuel oil; ~sonne f electric fire; ~ung f heating; ~ungsanlage f heating system.

hektisch ['hɛktɪʃ] a hectic.

Held [hɛlt] m -en, -en hero; ~in f heroine.

helfen ['hɛlfən] irreg vi help (jdm sb, bei with); (nützen) be of use; sich (dat) zu ~ wissen be resourceful; v impers: es hilft nichts, du mußt . . . it's no use, you have to . . .

Helfer m -s, - helper, assistant; ~shelfer m accomplice.

hell [hɛl] a clear, bright; Farbe light; ~blau a light blue; ~blond a ash-blond;

H~e f - clearness, brightness; **H~er** m
-s, - farthing; **~hörig** a keen of hearing;
Wand poorly soundproofed; **H~igkeit** f
clearness, brightness; lightness;
H~seher m clairvoyant; **~wach** a wide-
awake.

Helm ['hɛlm] m **-(e)s, -e** (*auf Kopf*)
helmet.

Hemd [hɛmt] nt **-(e)s, -en** shirt; (*Unter—*)
vest; **~bluse** f blouse; **~enknopf** m shirt
button.

hemmen ['hɛmən] vt check, hold up;
gehemmt sein be inhibited.

Hemmung f check; (*Psych*) inhibition;
h~slos a unrestrained, without restraint.

Hengst [hɛŋst] m **-es, -e** stallion.

Henkel ['hɛŋkəl] m **-s,** - handle; **~krug** m
jug.

henken ['hɛŋkən] vt hang.

Henker m **-s,** - hangman.

Henne ['hɛnə] f **-, -n** hen.

her [he:r] ad here; (*Zeit*) ago; **~ damit!**
hand it over!

herab [hɛ'rap] ad down(ward(s));
~hängen vi irreg hang down; **~lassen**
irreg vt let down; vr condescend;
H~lassung f condescension; **~sehen** vi
irreg look down (*auf +acc on*); **~setzen** vt
lower, reduce; (*fig*) belittle, disparage;
H~setzung f reduction; (*fig*) disparagement;
~würdigen vt belittle, disparage.

heran [hɛ'ran] ad: **näher ~!** come up
closer!; **~ zu mir!** come up to me!;
~bilden vt train; **~bringen** vt irreg
bring up (*an +acc to*); **~fahren** vi irreg
drive up (*an +acc to*); **~kommen** vi irreg
(*an +acc*) approach, come near;
~machen vr: **sich an jdn ~machen**
make up to sb; **~wachsen** vi irreg grow
up; **~ziehen** vt irreg pull nearer;
(*aufziehen*) raise; (*ausbilden*) train; **jdn zu
etw ~ziehen** call upon sb to help in sth.

herauf [hɛ'raʊf] ad up(ward(s)), up here;
~beschwören vt irreg conjure up, evoke;
~bringen vt irreg bring up; **~ziehen**
irreg vt draw or pull up; vi approach;
(*Sturm*) gather.

heraus [hɛ'raʊs] ad out; outside; from;
~arbeiten vt work out; **~bekommen** vt
irreg get out; (*fig*) find or figure out;
~bringen vt irreg bring out; *Geheimnis*
elicit; **~finden** vt irreg find out;
~fordern vt challenge; **H~forderung** f
challenge; provocation; **~geben** vt irreg
give up, surrender; *Geld* give back; *Buch*
edit; (*veröffentlichen*) publish; **~geber** m
-s, - editor; (*Verleger*) publisher; **~gehen**
vi irreg: **aus sich** (*dat*) **~gehen** come out
of one's shell; **~halten** vr irreg: **sich aus
etw ~halten** keep out of sth; **~hängen**
vti irreg hang out; **~holen** vt get out (*aus
of*); **~kommen** vi irreg come out; **dabei
kommt nichts ~** nothing will come of it;
~nehmen vt irreg take out; **sich** (*dat*)
Freiheiten **~nehmen** take liberties;
~reißen vt irreg tear out; pull out;
~rücken vt *Geld* fork out, hand over; **mit
etw ~rücken** (*fig*) come out with sth;
~rutschen vi slip out; **~schlagen** vt
irreg knock out; (*fig*) obtain; **~stellen** vr

turn out (*als* to be); **~wachsen** vi irreg
grow out (*aus* of); **~ziehen** vt irreg pull
out, extract.

herb [hɛrp] a (slightly) bitter, acid; *Wein*
dry; (*fig*) (*schmerzlich*) bitter; (*streng*)
stern, austere.

herbei [hɛr'baɪ] ad (over) here; **~führen**
vt bring about; **~lassen** vr irreg: **sich
~lassen zu** condescend or deign to;
~schaffen vt procure.

herbemühen ['hɛrbəmy:ən] vr take the
trouble to come.

Herberge ['hɛrbɛrgə] f **-, -n** shelter;
hostel, inn.

Herbergsmutter f, **Herbergsvater** m
warden.

her- ['hɛr] cpd: **~bitten** vt irreg ask to
come (here); **~bringen** vt irreg bring
here.

Herbst [hɛrpst] m **-(e)s, -e** autumn, fall
(*US*); **h~lich** a autumnal.

Herd [he:rt] m **-(e)s, -e** cooker; (*fig, Med*)
focus, centre.

Herde ['he:rdə] f **-, -n** herd; (*Schaf—*)
flock.

herein [hɛ'raɪn] ad in (here), here; **~!**
come in!; **~bitten** vt irreg ask in;
~brechen vi irreg set in; **~bringen** vt
irreg bring in; **~dürfen** vi irreg have permission to enter; **H~fall** m letdown;
~fallen vi irreg be caught, taken in;
~fallen auf (*+acc*) fall for; **~kommen**
vi irreg come in; **~lassen** vt irreg admit;
~legen vt: **jdn ~legen** take sb in;
~platzen vi burst in.

Her- ['hɛr] cpd: **~fahrt** f journey here;
h~fallen vi irreg: **h~fallen über** fall
upon; **~gang** m course of events, circumstances pl; **h~geben** vt irreg give, hand
(over); **sich zu etw h~geben** lend one's
name to sth; **h~gehen** vi irreg: **hinter
jdm h~gehen** follow sb; **es geht hoch
h~** there are a lot of goings-on;
h~halten vt irreg hold out; **h~halten
müssen** (*col*) have to suffer; **h~hören** vi
listen; **hör mal h~!** listen here!

Hering ['he:rɪŋ] m **-s, -e** herring.

her- ['hɛr] cpd: **~kommen** vi irreg come;
komm mal ~! come here!; **~kömmlich**
a traditional; **H~kunft** f **-, -künfte** origin;
~laufen vi irreg; **~laufen hinter**
(*+dat*) run after; **~leiten** vr derive;
~machen vr: **sich ~machen über**
(*+acc*) set about or upon.

Hermelin [hɛrmə'li:n] m or nt **-s, -e**
ermine.

hermetisch [hɛr'me:tɪʃ] a,ad her-
metic(ally).

her- cpd: **~'nach** ad afterwards; **~-
'nieder** ad down.

heroisch [he'ro:ɪʃ] a heroic.

Herold ['he:rɔlt] m **-(e)s, -e** herald.

Herr [hɛr] m **-(e)n, -en** master; (*Mann*)
gentleman; (*adliger, Rel*) Lord; (*vor
Namen*) Mr.; **mein ~!** sir!; **meine ~en!**
gentlemen!; **~enbekanntschaft** f gentleman friend; **~endoppel** nt men's doubles;
~eneinzel nt men's singles; **~enhaus** nt
mansion; **h~enlos** a ownerless.

herrichten ['hɛrɪçtən] vt prepare.

Herr- cpd: ~**in** f mistress; **h~isch** a domineering; **h~lich** a marvellous, splendid; ~**lichkeit** f splendour, magnificence; ~**schaft** f power, rule; (Herr und Herrin) master and mistress; **meine ~schaften!** ladies and gentlemen!

herrschen ['hɛrʃən] vt rule; (bestehen) prevail, be.

Herrscher(in f) m **-s,** - ruler.

Herrschsucht f domineering behaviour.

her- ['hɛr] cpd: ~**rühren** vi arise, originate; ~**sagen** vt recite; ~**stammen** vi descend, come from; ~**stellen** vt make, manufacture; **H~steller** m **-s,** - manufacturer; **H~stellung** f manufacture; **H~stellungskosten** pl manufacturing costs pl.

herüber [hɛ'ry:bər] ad over (here), across.

herum [hɛ'rum] ad about, (a)round; **um etw ~** around sth; ~**ärgern** vr get annoyed (mit with); ~**führen** vt show around; ~**gehen** vi irreg walk or go round (um etw sth); walk about; ~**irren** vi wander about; ~**kriegen** vt bring or talk around; ~**lungern** vi lounge about; ~**sprechen** vr irreg get around, be spread; ~**treiben** vir irreg drift about; ~**ziehen** vir irreg wander about.

herunter [hɛ'runtər] ad downward(s), down (there); ~**gekommen** a run-down; ~**hängen** vi irreg hang down; ~**holen** vt bring down; ~**kommen** vi irreg come down; (fig) come down in the world; ~**machen** vt take down; (schimpfen) abuse, criticise severely.

hervor [hɛr'fo:r] ad out, forth; ~**brechen** vi irreg burst forth, break out; ~**bringen** vt irreg produce; Wort utter; ~**gehen** vi irreg emerge, result; ~**heben** vt irreg stress; (als Kontrast) set off; ~**ragend** a excellent; (lit) projecting; ~**rufen** vt irreg cause, give rise to; ~**treten** vi irreg come out.

Herz [hɛrts] nt **-ens, -en** heart; ~**anfall** m heart attack; **h~en** vt caress, embrace; ~**enslust** f: **nach ~enslust** to one's heart's content; ~**fehler** m heart defect; **h~haft** a hearty; ~**infarkt** m heart attack; ~**klopfen** nt palpitation; **h~lich** a cordial; **h~lichen Glückwunsch** congratulations pl; **h~liche Grüße** best wishes; ~**lichkeit** f cordiality; **h~los** a heartless; ~**losigkeit** f heartlessness.

Herzog ['hɛrtso:k] m **-(e)s,** ⸚e duke; ~**in** f duchess; **h~lich** a ducal; ~**tum** nt duchy.

Herz- cpd: ~**schlag** m heartbeat; (Med) heart attack; **h~zerreißend** a heart-rending.

heterogen [hetero'ge:n] a heterogeneous.

Hetze ['hɛtsə] f **-, -n** (Eile) rush; **h~n** vt hunt; (verfolgen) chase; **jdn/etw auf jdn/etw ~** set sb/sth on sb/sth; vi (eilen) rush; **h~n gegen** stir up feeling against; **h~n zu** agitate for; ~'**rei** f agitation; (Eile) rush.

Heu [hɔy] nt **-(e)s** hay; ~**boden** m hayloft.

Heuchelei [hɔyçə'lai] f hypocrisy.

heucheln ['hɔyçəln] vt pretend, feign; vi be hypocritical.

Heuchler(in f) [hɔyçlər(in)] m **-s,** - hypocrite; **h~isch** a hypocritical.

Heuer ['hɔyər] f **-, -n** (Naut) pay; **h~** ad this year.

Heugabel f pitchfork.

heulen ['hɔylən] vi howl; cry; **das ~de Elend bekommen** get the blues.

heurig ['hɔyriç] a this year's.

Heu- cpd: ~**schnupfen** m hay fever; ~**schrecke** f grasshopper, locust.

heute ['hɔytə] ad today; ~**abend/früh** this evening/morning; **das H~** today.

heutig ['hɔytiç] a today's.

heutzutage ['hɔyttsuta:gə] ad nowadays.

Hexe ['hɛksə] f **-, -n** witch; **h~n** vi practise witchcraft; **ich kann doch nicht h~n** I can't work miracles; ~**nkessel** m (lit, fig) cauldron; ~**nmeister** m wizard; ~**nschuß** m lumbago; ~'**rei** f witchcraft.

Hieb [hi:p] m **-(e)s, -e** blow; (Wunde) cut, gash; (Stichelei) cutting remark; ~**e bekommen** get a thrashing.

hier [hi:r] ad here; ~**auf** ad thereupon; (danach) after that; ~**behalten** vt irreg keep here; ~**bei** ad herewith, enclosed; ~**bleiben** vi irreg stay here; ~**durch** ad by this means; (örtlich) through here; ~**her** ad this way, here; ~**lassen** vt irreg leave here; ~**mit** ad hereby; ~**nach** ad hereafter; ~**von** ad about this, hereof; ~**zulande** ad in this country.

hiesig ['hi:ziç] a of this place, local.

Hilfe ['hilfə] f **-, -n** help; aid; **Erste ~** first aid; ~**!** help!

Hilf- cpd: **h~los** a helpless; ~**losigkeit** f helplessness; **h~reich** a helpful; ~**saktion** f relief measures pl; ~**sarbeiter** m labourer; **h~sbedürftig** a needy; **h~sbereit** a ready to help; ~**skraft** f assistant, helper; ~**sschule** f school for backward children; ~**szeitwort** nt auxiliary verb.

Himbeere ['himbe:rə] f **-, -n** raspberry.

Himmel ['himəl] m **-s, -** sky; (Rel, liter) heaven; **h~angst** a: **es ist mir h~angst** I'm scared to death; **h~blau** a sky-blue; ~**fahrt** f Ascension; **h~schreiend** a outrageous; ~**srichtung** f direction.

himmlisch ['himliʃ] a heavenly.

hin [hin] ad there; ~ **und her** to and fro; **bis zur Mauer ~** up to the wall; **Geld ~, Geld her** money or no money; **mein Glück ist ~** my happiness has gone.

hinab [hi'nap] ad down; ~**gehen** vi irreg go down; ~**sehen** vi irreg look down.

hinauf [hi'nauf] ad up; ~**arbeiten** vr work one's way up; ~**steigen** vi irreg climb.

hinaus [hi'naus] ad out; ~**befördern** vt kick/throw out; ~**gehen** vi irreg go out; ~**gehen über** (+acc) exceed; ~**laufen** vi irreg run out; ~**laufen auf** (+acc) come to, amount to; ~**schieben** vt irreg put off, postpone; ~**werfen** vt irreg throw out; ~**wollen** vi want to go out; ~**wollen auf** (+acc) drive at, get at; ~**ziehen** irreg vt draw out; vr be protracted.

Hinblick ['hinblik] m: **in** or **im ~ auf** (+acc) in view of.

hinder- ['hindər] cpd: ~**lich** a awkward;

~n vt hinder, hamper; **jdn an etw** (dat)
~n prevent sb from doing sth; **H~nis** nt
-ses, -se obstacle.

hindeuten ['hɪndɔytən] vi point (auf +acc
to).

hindurch [hɪn'durç] ad through; across;
(zeitlich) over.

hinein [hɪ'naɪn] ad in; ~**fallen** vi irreg fall
in; ~**fallen in** (+acc) fall into; ~**gehen**
vi irreg go in; ~**gehen in** (+acc) go into,
enter; ~**geraten** vi irreg: ~**geraten in**
(+acc) get into; ~**passen** vi fit in;
~**passen in** (+acc) fit into; ~**reden** vi:
jdm ~**reden** interfere in sb's affairs;
~**steigern** vr get worked up;
~**versetzen** vr: **sich** ~**versetzen in**
(+acc) put oneself in the position of.

hin- ['hɪn] cpd: ~**fahren** vi irreg go; drive;
vt take; drive; **H~fahrt** f journey there;
~**fallen** vi irreg fall down; ~**fällig** a
frail, decrepit; Regel etc unnecessary,
otiose; **H~gabe** f devotion; ~**geben** vr
irreg +dat give oneself up to, devote
oneself to; ~**gehen** vi irreg go; (Zeit) pass;
~**halten** vt irreg hold out; (warten lassen)
put off, stall.

hinken ['hɪŋkən] vi limp; (Vergleich) be
unconvincing.

hin- ['hɪn] cpd: ~**legen** vt put down; vr lie
down; ~**nehmen** vt irreg (fig) put up
with, take; ~**reichen** vi be adequate; vt:
jdm etw ~**reichen** hand sb sth;
H~reise f journey out; ~**reißen** vt irreg
carry away, enrapture; **sich** ~**reißen
lassen, etw zu tun** get carried away and
do sth; ~**richten** vt execute;
H~richtung f execution; ~**sichtlich**
prep +gen with regard to; **H~spiel** nt
(Sport) first leg; ~**stellen** vt put (down);
vr place o.s.

hintanstellen [hɪnt'anʃtɛlən] vt (fig)
ignore.

hinten ['hɪntən] ad at the back; behind;
~**herum** ad round the back; (fig)
secretly.

hinter ['hɪntər] prep +dat or acc behind;
(nach) after; ~ **jdm hersein** be after sb;
H~achse f rear axle; **H~bein** nt hind
leg; **sich auf die H~beine stellen** get
tough; **H~bliebene(r)** mf surviving
relative; ~**drein** ad afterwards; ~**e(r,s)**
a rear, back; ~**einander** ad one after the
other; **H~gedanke** m ulterior motive;
~**gehen** vt irreg deceive; **H~grund** m
background; **H~halt** m ambush;
~**hältig** a underhand, sneaky; ~**her** ad
afterwards, after; **H~hof** m backyard;
H~kopf m back of one's head; ~**lassen**
vt irreg leave; **H~'lassenschaft** f
(testator's) estate; ~**'legen** vt deposit;
H~list f cunning, trickery; (Handlung)
trick, dodge; ~**listig** a cunning, crafty;
H~mann m, pl ~**männer** person
behind; **H~rad** nt back wheel;
H~radantrieb m (Aut) rear wheel drive;
~**rücks** ad from behind; **H~teil** nt
behind; **H~treffen** nt: **ins H~treffen
kommen** lose ground; ~**treiben** vt irreg
prevent, frustrate; **H~tür** f back door;
(fig: Ausweg) escape, loophole; ~**'ziehen**

vt irreg Steuern evade (paying).

hinüber [hɪ'ny:bər] ad across, over;
~**gehen** vi irreg go over or across.

hinunter [hɪ'nʊntər] ad down; ~**bringen**
vt irreg take down; ~**schlucken** vt (lit,
fig) swallow; ~**steigen** vi irreg descend.

hin- ['hɪn] cpd: **H~weg** m journey out;
~'**weghelfen** vi irreg: **jdm über etw**
(acc) ~'**weghelfen** help sb to get over
sth; ~'**wegsetzen** vr: **sich** ~**wegsetzen
über** (+acc) disregard; **H~weis** m **-es,
-e** (Andeutung) hint; (Anweisung)
instruction; (Verweis) reference;
~**weisen** vi irreg (auf +acc) (anzeigen)
point to; (sagen) point out, refer to;
~**werfen** vt irreg throw down; ~**ziehen**
vr irreg (fig) drag on; ~**zielen** vi aim (auf
+acc at).

hinzu [hɪn'tsu:] ad in addition; ~**fügen** vt
add.

Hirn [hɪrn] nt **-(e)s, -e** brain(s);
~**gespinst** nt **-(e)s, -e** fantasy;
h~verbrannt a half-baked, crazy.

Hirsch [hɪrʃ] m **-(e)s, -e** stag.

Hirse ['hɪrzə] f -, -n millet.

Hirt ['hɪrt] m **-en, -en** herdsman; (Schaf-,
fig) shepherd.

hissen ['hɪsən] vt hoist.

Historiker [hɪs'to:rikər] m **-s, -** historian.

historisch [hɪs'to:rɪʃ] a historical.

Hitze ['hɪtsə] f - heat; **h~beständig** a
heat-resistant; ~**welle** f heatwave.

hitzig a hot-tempered; Debatte heated.

Hitz- cpd: ~**kopf** m hothead; **h~köpfig** a
fiery, hotheaded; ~**schlag** m heatstroke.

Hobel ['ho:bəl] m **-s, -** plane; ~**bank** f carpenter's bench; **h~n** vti plane; ~**späne**
pl wood shavings pl.

hoch [ho:x] a high; **H~** nt **-s, -s** (Ruf)
cheer; (Met) anticyclone; ~**achten** vt
respect; **H~achtung** f respect, esteem;
~**achtungsvoll** ad yours faithfully;
H~amt nt high mass; ~**arbeiten** vr
work one's way up; ~**begabt** a extremely
gifted; ~**betagt** a very old, aged;
H~betrieb m intense activity; (Comm)
peak time; ~**bringen** vt irreg bring up;
H~burg f stronghold; **H~deutsch** nt
High German; ~**dotiert** a highly paid;
H~druck m high pressure; ~**ebene** f
plateau; ~**erfreut** a highly delighted;
~**fliegend** a (fig) high-flown; **H~form** f
top form; ~**gradig** a intense, extreme;
~**halten** vt irreg hold up; (fig) uphold,
cherish; **H~haus** nt multi-storey building;
~**heben** vt irreg lift (up);
H~konjunktur f boom; **H~land** nt high-
lands pl; ~**leben** vi: **jdn** ~**leben lassen**
give sb three cheers; **H~mut** m pride;
~**mütig** a proud, haughty; ~**näsig** a
stuck-up, snooty; **H~ofen** m blast
furnace; ~**prozentig** a Alkohol strong;
H~rechnung f projected result;
H~saison f high season; **H~schätzung**
f high esteem; **H~schule** f college; university; **H~sommer** m middle of summer; **H~spannung** f high tension;
H~sprache f standard language;
~**springen** vi irreg jump up, **H~sprung**
m high jump.

höchst [høːçst] ad highly, extremely; **~e(r,s)** a highest; (äußerste) extreme.
Hochstapler ['hoːxstaplər] m **-s, -** swindler.
Höchst- cpd: **h~ens** ad at the most; **~geschwindigkeit** f maximum speed; **h~persönlich** ad in person; **~preis** m maximum price; **h~wahrscheinlich** ad most probably.
Hoch- cpd **h~trabend** a pompous; **~verrat** m high treason; **~wasser** nt high water; (Überschwemmung) floods pl; **h~wertig** a high-class, first-rate; **~würden** m Reverend; **~zahl** f (Math) exponent.
Hochzeit ['hoxtsait] f **-, -en** wedding; **~sreise** f honeymoon.
hocken ['hɔkən] vir squat, crouch.
Hocker m **-s, -** stool.
Höcker ['hœkər] m **-s, -** hump.
Hode ['hoːdə] m **-n, -n** testicle.
Hof [hoːf] m **-(e)s, ⸚e** (Hinter~) yard; (Bauern~) farm; (Königs~) court.
hoffen ['hɔfən] vi hope (auf +acc for); **~tlich** ad I hope, hopefully.
Hoffnung ['hɔfnuŋ] f hope; **h~slos** a hopeless; **~slosigkeit** f hopelessness; **~sschimmer** m glimmer of hope; **h~svoll** a hopeful.
höflich ['høːflıç] a polite, courteous; **H~keit** f courtesy, politeness.
hohe(r,s) ['hoːə(r,z)] a see **hoch**.
Höhe ['høːə] f **-, -n** height; (An~) hill.
Hoheit ['hoːhait] f (Pol) sovereignty; (Titel) Highness; **~sgebiet** nt sovereign territory; **~sgewässer** nt territorial waters pl; **~szeichen** nt national emblem.
Höhen- ['høːən] cpd: **~angabe** f altitude reading; (auf Karte) height marking; **~messer** m **-s, -** altimeter; **~sonne** f sun lamp; **~unterschied** m difference in altitude; **~zug** m mountain chain.
Höhepunkt m climax.
höher a,ad higher.
hohl [hoːl] a hollow.
Höhle ['høːlə] f **-, -n** cave, hole; (Mund~) cavity; (fig, Zool) den.
Hohl- cpd: **~heit** f hollowness; **~maß** nt measure of volume; **~saum** m hemstitch.
Hohn [hoːn] m **-(e)s** scorn.
höhnen ['høːnən] vt taunt, scoff at.
höhnisch ['høːnıʃ] a scornful, taunting.
hold [hɔlt] a charming, sweet.
holen ['hoːlən] vt get, fetch; Atem take; **jdn/etw ~ lassen** send for sb/sth.
Hölle ['hœlə] f **-, -n** hell; **~nangst** f: **eine ~nangst haben** be scared to death.
höllisch ['hœlıʃ] a hellish, infernal.
holperig ['hɔlpərıç] a rough, bumpy.
holpern ['hɔlpərn] vi jolt.
Holunder [ho'lundər] m **-s, -** elder.
Holz [hɔlts] nt **-es, ⸚er** wood.
hölzern ['hœltsərn] a (lit, fig) wooden.
Holz- cpd: **~fäller** m **-s, -** lumberjack, woodcutter; **h~ig** a woody; **~klotz** m wooden block; **~kohle** f charcoal; **~scheit** nt log; **~schuh** m clog; **~weg** m (fig) wrong track; **~wolle** f fine wood

shavings pl; **~wurm** m woodworm.
homosexuell [homozɛksu'ɛl] a homosexual.
Honig ['hoːnıç] m **-s, -e** honey; **~wabe** f honeycomb.
Honorar [hono'raːr] nt **-s, -e** fee.
honorieren [hono'riːrən] vt remunerate; Scheck honour.
Hopfen ['hɔpfən] m **-s, -** hops pl.
hopsen ['hɔpsən] vi hop.
Hör- cpd: **~apparat** m hearing aid; **h~bar** a audible.
horch [hɔrç] interj listen; **~en** vi listen; (pej) eavesdrop; **H~er** m **-s, -** listener; eavesdropper.
Horde ['hɔrdə] f **-, -n** horde.
hören ['høːrən] vti hear; **H~sagen** nt: **vom H~sagen** from hearsay.
Hörer m **-s, -** hearer; (Rad) listener; (Univ) student; (Telefon~) receiver.
Horizont [hori'tsɔnt] m **-(e)s, -e** horizon; **h~al** ['taːl] a horizontal.
Hormon [hɔr'moːn] nt **-s, -e** hormone.
Hörmuschel f (Tel) earpiece.
Horn [hɔrn] nt **-(e)s, ⸚er** horn; **~haut** f horny skin.
Hornisse [hɔr'nısə] f **-, -n** hornet.
Horoskop [horo'skoːp] nt **-s, -e** horoscope.
Hör- cpd: **~rohr** nt ear trumpet; (Med) stethoscope; **~saal** m lecture room; **~spiel** nt radio play.
Hort [hɔrt] m **-(e)s, -e** hoard; (Sch) nursery school; **h~en** vt hoard.
Hose ['hoːzə] f **-, -n** trousers pl, pants (US) pl; **~nanzug** m trouser suit; **~nrock** m culottes pl; **~ntasche** f (trouser) pocket; **~nträger** m braces pl, suspenders (US) pl.
Hostie ['hɔstiə] f (Rel) host.
Hotel [ho'tɛl] nt **-s, -s** hotel; **~ier** [hoteli'eː] m **-s, -s** hotelkeeper, hotelier.
Hub [huːp] m **-(e)s, ⸚e** lift; (Tech) stroke.
hüben ['hyːbən] ad on this side, over here.
Hubraum m (Aut) cubic capacity.
hübsch [hypʃ] a pretty, nice.
Hubschrauber m **-s, -** helicopter.
hudeln ['huːdəln] vi be sloppy.
Huf ['huːf] m **-(e)s, -e** hoof; **~eisen** nt horseshoe; **~nagel** m horseshoe nail.
Hüft- ['hyft] cpd: **~e** f **-, -n** hip; **~gürtel** m, **~halter** m **-s, -** girdle.
Hügel ['hyːgəl] m **-s, -** hill; **h~ig** a hilly.
Huhn [huːn] nt **-(e)s, ⸚er** hen; (Cook) chicken.
Hühner- ['hyːnər] cpd: **~auge** nt corn; **~brühe** f chicken broth.
Huld [hult] f **-** favour; **h~igen** ['huldigən] vi pay homage (jdm to sb); **~igung** f homage.
Hülle ['hylə] f **-, -n** cover(ing); wrapping; **in ~ und Fülle** galore; **h~n** vt cover, wrap (in +acc with).
Hülse ['hylzə] f **-, -n** husk, shell; **~nfrucht** f legume.
human [hu'maːn] a humane; **~itär** a humanitarian; **H~ität** f humanity.
Hummel ['huməl] f **-, -n** bumblebee.
Hummer ['humər] m **-s, -** lobster.
Humor [hu'moːr] m **-s, -e** humour; **~**

haben have a sense of humour; ~**ist** [-'rɪst] m humorist; **h**~**istisch** a, **h**~**voll** a humorous.

humpeln ['hʊmpəln] vi hobble.

Humpen ['hʊmpən] m **-s,** - tankard.

Hund [hʊnt] m -(e)s, -e dog; ~**ehütte** f (dog) kennel; ~**ekuchen** m dog biscuit; **h**~**emüde** a (col) dog-tired.

hundert ['hʊndərt] num hundred; **H**~-'**jahrfeier** f centenary; ~**prozentig** a,ad one hundred per cent.

Hündin ['hʏndɪn] f bitch.

Hunger ['hʊŋər] m -s hunger; ~ **haben** be hungry; ~**lohn** m starvation wages pl; **h**~**n** vi starve; ~**snot** f famine; ~**streik** m hunger strike.

hungrig ['hʊŋrɪç] a hungry.

Hupe ['hu:pə] f -, -n horn, hooter; **h**~**n** vi hoot, sound one's horn.

hüpfen ['hʏpfən] vi hop, jump.

Hürde ['hʏrdə] f -, -n hurdle; (für Schafe) pen; ~**nlauf** m hurdling.

Hure ['hu:rə] f -, -n whore.

hurtig ['hʊrtɪç] a,ad brisk(ly), quick(ly).

huschen ['hʊʃən] vi flit, scurry.

Husten ['hu:stən] m -s cough; **h**~ vi cough; ~**anfall** m coughing fit; ~**bonbon** m or nt cough drop; ~**saft** m cough mixture.

Hut [hu:t] m -(e)s, ᵉe hat; f - care; **auf der** ~ **sein** be on one's guard.

hüten ['hy:tən] vt guard; **h** watch out; **sich** ~, **zu** take care not to; **sich** ~ **vor** beware of.

Hütte ['hʏtə] f -, -n hut, cottage; (Eisen—) forge; ~**nwerk** nt foundry.

hutzelig ['hʊtsəlɪç] a shrivelled.

Hyäne ['hyːnə] f -, -n hyena.

Hyazinthe [hya'tsɪntə] f -, -n hyacinth.

Hydr- cpd: ~**ant** [hy'drant] m hydrant; **h**~**aulisch** [hy'draʊlɪʃ] a hydraulic; ~**ierung** [hy'dri:rʊŋ] f hydrogenation.

Hygiene [hygi'eːnə] f - hygiene.

hygienisch [hygi'eːnɪʃ] a hygienic.

Hymne ['hʏmnə] f -, -n hymn, anthem.

hyper- ['hyper] pref hyper-.

Hypno- [hʏp'no] cpd: ~**se** f -, -n hypnosis; **h**~**tisch** a hypnotic; ~**tiseur** [-ti'zøːr] m hypnotist; **h**~**ti'sieren** vt hypnotize.

Hypothek [hypo'teːk] f -, -en mortgage.

Hypothese [hypo'teːzə] f -, -n hypothesis.

hypothetisch [hypo'teːtɪʃ] a hypothetical.

Hysterie [hʏste'riː] f hysteria.

hysterisch [hʏs'teːrɪʃ] a hysterical.

I

I, i [iː] nt I, i.

ich [ɪç] pron I; ~ **bin's!** it's me!; **I**~ nt -(s), -(s) self; (Psych) ego.

Ideal [ide'aːl] nt -s, -e ideal; **i**~ a ideal; ~**ist** [-'lɪst] m idealist; **i**~**istisch** [-'lɪstɪʃ] a idealistic.

Idee [i'deː] f -, -n [i'deːən] idea; **i**~**ll** [ide'ɛl] a ideal.

identi- [i'dɛnti] cpd: ~**fizieren** [-fi'tsiːrən] vt identify; ~**sch** a identical; **I**~**tät** [-'tɛːt] f identity.

Ideo- [ideo] cpd: ~**loge** [-'loːgə] m -n, -n

ideologist; ~**logie** [-lo'giː] f ideology; **i**~**logisch** [-'loːgɪʃ] a ideological.

idiomatisch [idio'maːtɪʃ] a idiomatic.

Idiot [idi'oːt] m -en, -en idiot; **i**~**isch** a idiotic.

idyllisch [i'dʏlɪʃ] a idyllic.

Igel ['iːgəl] m -s, - hedgehog.

ignorieren [ɪgno'riːrən] vt ignore.

ihm [iːm] pron dat of **er, es** (to) him, (to) it.

ihn [iːn] pron acc of **er** him; it; ~**en** pron dat of **sie** pl (to) them; **I**~**en** pron dat of **Sie** (to) you.

ihr [iːr] pron nom pl you; dat of **sie** sing (to) her; ~(**e**) poss pron sing her; its; pl their; **I**~(**e**) poss pron your; ~**e**(**r,s**) poss pron sing hers; its; pl theirs; **I**~**e**(**r,s**) poss pron yours; ~**er** pron gen of **sie** sing/pl of her/them; **I**~**er** pron gen of **Sie** of you; ~**erseits** ad for her/their part; ~**esgleichen** pron people like her/them; (von Dingen) others like it; ~**etwegen,** ~**etwillen** ad (für sie) for her/its/their sake; (wegen ihr) on her/its/their account; ~**ige** pron: **der/die/das** ~**ige** hers; its; theirs.

Ikone [i'koːnə] f -, -n icon.

illegal ['ɪlegaːl] a illegal.

Illusion [ɪluzi'oːn] f illusion.

illusorisch [ɪlu'zoːrɪʃ] a illusory.

illustrieren [ɪlus'triːrən] vt illustrate.

Illustrierte f -n, -n picture magazine.

Iltis ['ɪltɪs] m -ses, -se polecat.

im [ɪm] = **in dem**.

imaginär [imagi'nɛːr] a imaginary.

Imbiß ['ɪmbɪs] m -sses, -sse snack; ~**halle** f, ~**stube** f snack bar.

imitieren [imi'tiːrən] vt imitate.

Imker ['ɪmkər] m -s, - beekeeper.

Immatrikulation [ɪmatrikulatsi'oːn] f (Univ) registration.

immatrikulieren [ɪmatriku'liːrən] vir register.

immer ['ɪmər] ad always; ~ **wieder** again and again; ~ **noch** still; ~ **noch nicht** still not; **für** ~ forever; ~ **wenn ich . . .** everytime I . . .; ~ **schöner/trauriger** more and more beautiful/sadder and sadder; **was/wer (auch)** ~ whatever/whoever; ~**hin** ad all the same; ~**zu** ad all the time.

Immobilien [ɪmo'biːliən] pl real estate.

immun [ɪ'muːn] a immune; **I**~**ität** [-i'tɛːt] f immunity.

Imperativ ['ɪmperatiːf] m -s, -e imperative.

Imperfekt ['ɪmpɛrfɛkt] nt -s, -e imperfect (tense).

Imperialist [ɪmperia'lɪst] m imperialist; **i**~**isch** a imperialistic.

Impf- [ɪmpf] cpd: ~**en** vt vaccinate; ~**stoff** m vaccine; ~**ung** f vaccination; ~**zwang** m compulsory vaccination.

implizieren [ɪmpli'tsiːrən] vt imply (mit by).

imponieren [ɪmpo'niːrən] vi impress (jdm sb).

Import [ɪm'pɔrt] m -(e)s, -e import; **i**~**ieren** [-'tiːrən] vt import.

imposant [ɪmpo'zant] a imposing.

impotent ['ɪmpotɛnt] a impotent.
imprägnieren [ɪmprɛ'gni:rən] vt (water)proof.
Improvisation [ɪmprovizatsi'o:n] f improvization.
improvisieren [ɪmprovi'zi:rən] vti improvize.
Impuls [ɪm'pʊls] m -es, -e impulse; i~iv [-'zi:f] a impulsive.
imstande [ɪm'ʃtandə] a: ~ sein be in a position; (fähig) be able.
in [ɪn] prep +acc in(to); to; +dat in; ~ der/die Stadt in/into town; ~ der/die Schule at/to school.
Inanspruchnahme [ɪn''anʃpruxna:mə] f -, -n demands pl (gen on).
Inbegriff ['ɪnbəgrɪf] m embodiment, personification; i~en ad included.
inbrünstig ['ɪnbrʏnstɪç] a ardent.
indem [ɪn'de:m] cj while; ~ man etw macht (dadurch) by doing sth.
indes(sen) [ɪn'dɛs(ən)] ad meanwhile; cj while.
Indianer(in f) [ɪndi'a:nər(ɪn)] m -s, - Red Indian.
indianisch a Red Indian.
indigniert [ɪndɪ'gni:rt] a indignant.
Indikativ ['ɪndikati:f] m -s, -e indicative.
indirekt ['ɪndirɛkt] a indirect.
indiskret ['ɪndiskre:t] a indiscreet; I~ion [ɪndɪskretsi'o:n] f indiscretion.
indiskutabel ['ɪndɪskuta:bəl] a out of the question.
Individu- [ɪndividu] cpd: ~alist [-a'lɪst] m individualist; ~alität [-ali'tɛt] f individuality; i~ell [-'ɛl] a individual; ~um [ɪndi'vi:duum] nt -s, -en individual.
Indiz [ɪn'di:ts] nt -es, -ien sign (für of); (Jur) clue; ~ienbeweis m circumstantial evidence.
indoktrinieren [ɪndɔktri'ni:rən] vt indoctrinate.
industrialisieren [ɪndʊstriali'zi:rən] vt industrialize.
Industrie [ɪndʊs'tri:] f industry; in cpds industrial; ~gebiet nt industrial area; i~ll [ɪndʊstri'ɛl] a industrial; ~zweig m branch of industry.
ineinander [ɪn'aɪ'nandər] ad in(to) one another or each other.
Infanterie [ɪnfantə'ri:] f infantry.
Infarkt [ɪn'farkt] m -(e)s, -e coronary (thrombosis).
Infektion [ɪnfɛktsi'o:n] f infection; ~skrankheit f infectious disease.
Infinitiv ['ɪnfiniti:f] m -s, -e infinitive.
infizieren [ɪnfi'tsi:rən] vt infect; vr be infected (bei by).
Inflation [ɪnflatsi'o:n] f inflation.
inflatorisch [ɪnfla'to:rɪʃ] a inflationary.
infolge [ɪn'fɔlgə] prep +gen as a result of, owing to; ~dessen [-'dɛsən] ad consequently.
Informatik [ɪnfɔr'ma:tɪk] f information studies pl.
Information [ɪnfɔrmatsi'o:n] f information no pl.
informieren [ɪnfɔr'mi:rən] vt inform; vr find out (über +acc about).

Infusion [ɪnfuzi'o:n] f infusion.
Ingenieur [ɪnʒeni'ø:r] m engineer; ~schule f school of engineering.
Ingwer ['ɪŋvər] m -s ginger.
Inhaber(in f) ['ɪnha:bər(ɪn)] m -s, - owner; (Haus—) occupier; (Lizenz—) licensee, holder; (Fin) bearer.
inhaftieren [ɪnhaf'ti:rən] vt take into custody.
inhalieren [ɪnha'li:rən] vti inhale.
Inhalt ['ɪnhalt] m -(e)s, -e contents pl; (eines Buchs etc) content; (Math) area; volume; i~lich a as regards content; ~sangabe f summary; i~slos a empty; i~(s)reich a full; ~sverzeichnis nt table of contents.
inhuman ['ɪnhuma:n] a inhuman.
Initiative [initsia'ti:və] f initiative.
Injektion [ɪnjɛktsi'o:n] f injection.
inklusive [ɪnklu'zi:və] prep, ad inclusive (gen of).
inkognito [ɪn'kɔgnito] ad incognito.
inkonsequent ['ɪnkɔnzekvɛnt] a inconsistent.
inkorrekt ['ɪnkɔrɛkt] a incorrect.
Inkrafttreten [ɪn'krafttre:tən] nt -s coming into force.
Inland ['ɪnlant] nt -(e)s (Geog) inland; (Pol, Comm) home (country); ~sporto nt inland postage.
inmitten [ɪn'mɪtən] prep +gen in the middle of; ~ von amongst.
innehaben ['ɪnəha:bən] vt irreg hold.
innen ['ɪnən] ad inside; I~aufnahme f indoor photograph; I~einrichtung f (interior) furnishings pl; I~minister m minister of the interior, Home Secretary (Brit); I~politik f domestic policy; I~stadt f town/city centre.
inner- ['ɪnər] cpd: ~e(r,s) a inner; (im Körper, inländisch) internal; I~e(s) nt inside; (Mitte) centre; (fig) heart; I~eien [-'raɪən] pl innards pl; ~halb ad, prep +gen within; (räumlich) inside; ~lich a internal; (geistig) inward; I~ste(s) nt heart; ~ste(r,s) a innermost.
innig ['ɪnɪç] a profound; Freundschaft intimate.
inoffiziell ['ɪn'ɔfitsiɛl] a unofficial.
ins [ɪns] = in das.
Insasse ['ɪnzasə] m -n, -n (Anstalt) inmate; (Aut) passenger.
insbesondere [ɪnsbə'zɔndərə] ad (e)specially.
Inschrift ['ɪnʃrɪft] f inscription.
Insekt [ɪn'zɛkt] nt -(e)s, -en insect.
Insel ['ɪnzəl] f -, -n island.
Inser- cpd: ~at [ɪnze'ra:t] nt -(e)s, -e advertisement; ~ent [ɪnze'rɛnt] m advertiser; i~ieren [ɪnze'ri:rən] vti advertise.
insgeheim [ɪnsgə'haɪm] ad secretly.
insgesamt [ɪnsgə'zamt] ad altogether, all in all.
insofern ['ɪnzo'fɛrn], **insoweit** ['ɪnzo'vaɪt] ad in this respect; ~ als in so far as; cj if; (deshalb) and) so.
Installateur [ɪnstala'tø:r] m electrician; plumber.
Instand- [ɪn'ʃtant] cpd: ~haltung f main-

tenance; ~**setzung** f overhaul; (*eines Gebäudes*) restoration.

Instanz [ɪn'stants] f authority; (*Jur*) court; ~**enweg** m official channels pl.

Instinkt [ɪn'stɪŋkt] m -(e)s, -e instinct; i~**iv** [-'tiːf] a instinctive.

Institut [ɪnsti'tuːt] nt -(e)s, -e institute.

Instrument [ɪnstru'mɛnt] nt instrument.

inszenieren [ɪnstse'niːrən] vt direct; (*fig*) stage-manage.

Intell- [ɪntɛl] cpd: **i~ektuell** [-ɛktu'ɛl] a intellectual; **i~igent** [-i'gɛnt] a intelligent; ~**igenz** [-i'gɛnts] f intelligence; (*Leute*) intelligentsia pl.

Intendant [ɪntɛn'dant] m director.

intensiv [ɪntɛn'ziːf] a intensive.

Interess- cpd: **i~ant** [ɪntɛrɛ'sant] a interesting; **i~anterweise** ad interestingly enough; ~**e** [ɪntɛ'rɛsə] nt -s, -n interest; ~**e haben** be interested (an +dat in); ~**ent** [ɪntɛrɛ'sɛnt] m interested party; **i~ieren** [ɪntɛrɛ'siːrən] vt interest; vr be interested (für in).

Inter- [ɪntɛr] cpd: ~**nat** [-'naːt] nt -(e)s, -e boarding school; **i~national** [-natsio'naːl] a international; **i~nieren** [-'niːrən] vt intern; **i~pretieren** [-pre'tiːrən] vt interpret; ~**punktion** [-puŋktsi'oːn] f punctuation; ~**vall** [-'val] nt -s, -e interval; ~**view** [-'vjuː] nt -s, -s interview; **i~viewen** [-'vjuːən] vt interview.

intim [ɪn'tiːm] a intimate; **I~ität** [ɪntimi'tɛːt] f intimacy.

intolerant ['ɪntolerant] a intolerant.

intransitiv ['ɪntranzitiːf] a (*Gram*) intransitive.

Intrige [ɪn'triːgə] f -, -n intrigue, plot.

Invasion [ɪnvazi'oːn] f invasion.

Inventar [ɪnvɛn'taːr] nt -s, -e inventory.

Inventur [ɪnvɛn'tuːr] f stocktaking; ~**machen** stocktake.

investieren [ɪnvɛs'tiːrən] vt invest.

inwiefern [ɪnvi'fɛrn], **inwieweit** [ɪnvi'vaɪt] ad how far, to what extent.

inzwischen [ɪn'tsvɪʃən] ad meanwhile.

irdisch ['ɪrdɪʃ] a earthly.

irgend ['ɪrgənt] ad at all; **wann/was/wer** ~ whenever/whatever/whoever; **jemand/etwas** somebody/something, anybody/anything; ~**ein(e,s)** a some, any; ~**einmal** ad sometime or other; (*fragend*) ever; ~**wann** ad sometime; ~**wie** ad somehow; ~**wo** ad somewhere, anywhere.

Ironie [iro'niː] f irony.

ironisch [i'roːnɪʃ] a ironic(al).

irre ['ɪrə] a crazy, mad; **I~(r)** mf lunatic; ~**führen** vt mislead; ~**machen** vt confuse; ~**n** vir be mistaken; (*umher—*) wander, stray; **I~nanstalt** f lunatic asylum.

irrig ['ɪrɪç] a incorrect, wrong.

Irr- cpd: **i~sinnig** a mad, crazy; (*col*) terrific; ~**tum** m -s, -tümer mistake, error; **i~tümlich** a mistaken.

Isolation [izolatsi'oːn] f isolation; (*Elec*) insulation.

Isolator [izo'laːtɔr] m insulator.

Isolier- [izo'liːr] cpd: ~**band** nt insulating tape; **i~en** vt isolate; (*Elec*) insulate;

~**station** f (*Med*) isolation ward; ~**ung** f isolation; (*Elec*) insulation.

J

J, j [jɔt] nt J, j.

ja [jaː] ad yes; **tu das ~ nicht!** don't do that!

Jacht [jaxt] f -, -en yacht.

Jacke ['jakə] f -, -n jacket; (*Woll—*) cardigan.

Jackett [ʒa'kɛt] nt -s, -s or -e jacket.

Jagd [jaːkt] f -, -en hunt; (*Jagen*) hunting; ~**beute** f kill; ~**flugzeug** nt fighter; ~**gewehr** nt sporting gun.

jagen ['jaːgən] vi hunt; (*eilen*) race; vt hunt; (*weg—*) drive (off); (*verfolgen*) chase.

Jäger ['jɛːgər] m -s, - hunter.

jäh [jɛː] a sudden, abrupt; (*steil*) steep, precipitous; ~**lings** ad abruptly.

Jahr [jaːr] nt -(e)s, -e year; **j~elang** ad for years; ~**esabonnement** nt annual subscription; ~**esabschluß** m end of the year; (*Comm*) annual statement of account; ~**esbericht** m annual report; ~**eswechsel** m turn of the year; ~**eszahl** f date, year; ~**eszeit** f season; ~**gang** m age group; (*von Wein*) vintage; ~**hundert** nt -s, -e century; ~**'hundertfeier** f centenary.

jährlich ['jɛːrlɪç] a, ad yearly.

Jahr- cpd: ~**markt** m fair; ~'**zehnt** nt decade.

Jähzorn ['jɛːtsɔrn] m sudden anger; hot temper; **j~ig** a hot-tempered.

Jalousie [ʒalu'ziː] f venetian blind.

Jammer ['jamər] m -s misery; **es ist ein ~, daß ...** it is a crying shame that ...

jämmerlich ['jɛmərlɪç] a wretched, pathetic; **J~keit** f wretchedness.

jammer- cpd: ~**n** vi wail; vt impers: **es jammert jdn** it makes sb feel sorry; ~**schade** a: **es ist ~schade** it is a crying shame.

Januar ['januaːr] m -s, -e January.

Jargon [ʒar'gõː] m -s, -s jargon.

jäten ['jɛːtən] vt: **Unkraut ~** weed.

jauchzen ['jauxtsən] vi rejoice, shout (with joy).

Jauchzer m -s, - shout of joy.

jaulen ['jaulən] vi howl.

ja- cpd: ~'**wohl** ad yes (of course); **J~wort** nt consent.

Jazz [dʒɛs] m - Jazz.

je [jeː] ad ever; (*jeweils*) each; ~ **nach** depending on; ~ **nachdem** it depends; ~ ... **desto** or ~ ... **je** ...

jede(r,s) ['jeːdə(r,z)] a every, each; pron everybody; (~ *einzelne*) each; **ohne ~ x** without any x; ~**nfalls** ad in any case; ~**rmann** pron everone; ~**rzeit** ad at any time; ~**smal** ad every time, each time.

jedoch [je'dɔx] ad however.

jeher ['jeːheːr] ad: **von ~** all along.

jemals ['jeːmaːls] ad ever.

jemand ['jeːmant] pron somebody, anybody.

jene(r,s) ['jeːnə(r,z)] a that; pron that one.

jenseits ['jeːnzaɪts] ad on the other side;

prep +*gen* on the other side of, beyond; **das J**~ the hereafter, the beyond.
jetzig ['jɛtsɪç] *a* present.
jetzt [jɛtst] *ad* now.
je~ *cpd:* ~**weilig** *a* respective; ~**weils** *ad* ~**weils zwei zusammen** two at a time; **zu** ~**weils 5 DM** at 5 marks each; ~**weils das erste** the first each time.
Joch [jɔx] *nt* -**(e)s, -e** yoke.
Jockei ['dʒɔke] *m* -**s, -s** jockey.
Jod [jo:t] *nt* -**(e)s** iodine.
jodeln ['jo:dəln] *vi* yodel.
Joghurt ['jo:gurt] *m or nt* -**s, -s** yogurt.
Johannisbeere [jo'hanɪsbe:rə] *f* red-currant; **schwarze** ~ blackcurrant.
johlen ['jo:lən] *vi* yell.
Jolle ['jɔlə] *f* -, -**n** dinghy.
jonglieren [ʒõ'gli:rən] *vi* juggle.
Joppe ['jɔpə] *f* -, -**n** jacket.
Journal [ʒur'na:l] *cpd:* ~**ismus** [-'lɪsmʊs] *m* journalism; ~**ist(in** *f*) [-'lɪst] *m* journalist; **j**~**istisch** *a* journalistic.
Jubel ['ju:bəl] *m* -**s** rejoicing; **j**~**n** *vi* rejoice.
Jubiläum [jubi'lɛʊm] *nt* -**s, Jubiläen** anniversary, jubilee.
jucken ['jʊkən] *vi* itch; *vt* **es juckt mich am Arm** my arm is itching; **das juckt mich** that's itchy.
Juckreiz ['jʊkraɪts] *m* itch.
Jude ['ju:də] *m* -**n, -n** Jew; ~**ntum** *nt* - Judaism; Jewry; ~**nverfolgung** *f* persecution of the Jews.
Jüd- [jy:d] *cpd:* ~**in** *f* Jewess; **j**~**isch** *a* Jewish.
Judo ['ju:do] *nt* -**(s)** judo.
Jugend ['ju:gənt] *f* - youth; ~**herberge** *f* youth hostel; ~**kriminalität** *f* juvenile crime; **j**~**lich** *a* youthful; ~**liche(r)** *mf* teenager, young person; ~**richter** *m* juvenile court judge.
Juli ['ju:li] *m* -**(s), -s** July.
jung [jʊŋ] *a* young; **J**~**e** *m* -**n, -n** boy, lad; **J**~**e(s)** *nt* young animal; (*pl*) young *pl*.
Jünger ['jyŋər] *m* -**s,** - disciple; **j**~ *a* younger.
Jung- *cpd:* ~**fer** *f* -, -**n**: **alte** ~**fer** old maid; ~**fernfahrt** *f* maiden voyage; ~**frau** *f* virgin; (*Astrol*) Virgo; ~**geselle** *m* bachelor.
Jüngling ['jyŋlɪŋ] *m* youth.
jüngst ['jyŋst] *ad* lately, recently; ~**e(r,s)** *a* youngest; (*neueste*) latest.
Juni ['ju:ni] *m* -**(s), -s** June.
Junior ['ju:nior] *m* -**s, -en** [-'o:rən] junior.
Jurist [ju'rɪst] *m* jurist, lawyer; **j**~**isch** *a* legal.
Justiz [jus'ti:ts] *f* - justice; ~**beamte(r)** *m* judicial officer; ~**irrtum** *m* miscarriage of justice.
Juwel [ju've:l] *nt or m* -**s, -en** jewel; ~**ier** *m* [-'li:r] *m* -**s, -e** jeweller; ~**iergeschäft** *nt* jeweller's (shop).
Jux [jʊks] *m* -**es, -e** joke, lark.

K

K, k [ka:] *nt* K, k.
Kabarett [kaba'rɛt] *nt* -**s, -e** *or* -**s** cabaret; ~**ist** [-'tɪst] *m* cabaret artiste.
Kabel ['ka:bəl] *nt* -**s,** - (*Elec*) wire; (*stark*) cable; ~**jau** [-jaʊ] *m* -**s, -e** *or* -**s** cod; **k**~**n** *vti* cable.
Kabine [ka'bi:nə] *f* cabin; (*Zelle*) cubicle.
Kabinett [kabi'nɛt] *nt* -**s, -e** (*Pol*) cabinet; small room.
Kachel ['kaxəl] *f* -, -**n** tile; **k**~**n** *vt* tile; ~**ofen** *m* tiled stove.
Kadaver [ka'da:vər] *m* -**s,** - carcass.
Kadett [ka'dɛt] *m* -**en, -en** cadet.
Käfer ['kɛ:fər] *m* -**s,** - beetle.
Kaffee ['kafe] *m* -**s, -s** coffee; ~**kanne** *f* coffeepot; ~**klatsch** *m,* ~**kränzchen** *nt* hen party; coffee morning; ~**löffel** *m* coffee spoon; ~**mühle** *f* coffee grinder; ~**satz** *m* coffee grounds *pl*.
Käfig ['kɛ:fɪç] *m* -**s, -e** cage.
kahl [ka:l] *a* bald; ~**fressen** *vt irreg* strip bare; ~**geschoren** *a* shaven, shorn; **K**~**heit** *f* baldness; ~**köpfig** *a* bald-headed.
Kahn [ka:n] *m* -**(e)s, ˝e** boat, barge.
Kai [kaɪ] *m* -**s, -e** *or* -**s** quay.
Kaiser ['kaɪzər] *m* -**s,** - emperor; ~**in** *f* empress; **k**~**lich** *a* imperial; ~**reich** *nt* empire; ~**schnitt** *m* (*Med*) Caesarian (section).
Kajüte [ka'jy:tə] *f* -, -**n** cabin.
Kakao [ka'ka:o] *m* -**s, -s** cocoa.
Kaktee [kak'te:(ə)] *f* -, -**n, Kaktus** ['kaktus] *m* -, -**se** cactus.
Kalb [kalp] *nt* -**(e)s, ˝er** calf; **k**~**en** ['kalbən] *vi* calve; ~**fleisch** *nt* veal; ~**sleder** *nt* calf(skin).
Kalender [ka'lɛndər] *m* -**s,** - calendar; (*Taschen*—) diary.
Kali ['ka:li] *nt* -**s, -s** potash.
Kaliber [ka'li:bər] *nt* -**s,** - (*lit, fig*) calibre.
Kalk [kalk] *m* -**(e)s, -e** lime; (*Biol*) calcium; ~**stein** *m* limestone.
Kalkulation [kalkulatsi'o:n] *f* calculation.
kalkulieren [kalku'li:rən] *vt* calculate.
Kalorie [kalo'ri:] *f* calorie.
kalt [kalt] *a* cold; **mir ist (es)** ~ I am cold; ~**bleiben** *vi irreg* be unmoved; ~**blütig** *a* cold-blooded; (*ruhig*) cool; **K**~**blütigkeit** *f* cold-bloodedness; coolness.
Kälte ['kɛltə] *f* - cold; coldness; ~**grad** *m* degree of frost *or* below zero; ~**welle** *f* cold spell.
kalt- *cpd:* ~**herzig** *a* cold-hearted; ~**schnäuzig** *a* cold, unfeeling; ~**stellen** *vt* chill; (*fig*) leave out in the cold.
Kamel [ka'me:l] *nt* -**(e)s, -e** camel.
Kamera ['kamera] *f* -, -**s** camera.
Kamerad [kamə'ra:t] *m* -**en, -en** comrade, friend; ~**schaft** *f* comradeship; **k**~**schaftlich** *a* comradely.
Kamera- *cpd:* ~**führung** *f* camera work; ~**mann** *m* cameraman.
Kamille [ka'mɪlə] *f* -, -**n** camomile; ~**ntee** *m* camomile tea.

Kamin [ka'mi:n] *m* **-s, -e** (*außen*) chimney; (*innen*) fireside, fireplace; ~**feger**, ~**kehrer** *m* **-s, -** chimney sweep.

Kamm [kam] *m* **-(e)s, ¨e** comb; (*Berg—*) ridge; (*Hahnen—*) crest.

kämmen ['kɛmən] *vt* comb.

Kammer ['kamər] *f* **-, -n** chamber; small bedroom; ~**diener** *m* valet.

Kampf [kampf] *m* **-(e)s, ¨e** fight, battle; (*Wettbewerb*) contest; (*fig: Anstrengung*) struggle; k~**bereit** a ready for action.

kämpfen ['kɛmpfən] *vi* fight.

Kämpfer *m* **-s, -** fighter, combatant.

Kampfer ['kampfər] *m* **-s** camphor.

Kampf- *cpd:* ~**handlung** *f* action; k~**los** a without a fight; k~**lustig** a pugnacious; ~**richter** *m* (*Sport*) referee; (*Tennis*) umpire.

Kanal [ka'na:l] *m* **-s, Kanäle** (*Fluß*) canal; (*Rinne, Ärmel—*) channel; (*für Abfluß*) drain; ~**isation** [-izatsi'o:n] *f* sewage system; k~**isieren** [-i'zi:rən] *vt* provide with a sewage system.

Kanarienvogel [ka'na:riənfo:gəl] *m* canary.

Kandi- [kandi] *cpd:* ~**dat** [-'da:t] *m* **-en, -en** candidate; ~**datur** [-da'tu:r] *f* candidature, candidacy; k~**dieren** [-'di:rən] *vi* stand, run.

Kandis(zucker) ['kandɪs] *m* **-** candy.

Känguruh ['kɛŋguru] *nt* **-s, -s** kangaroo.

Kaninchen [ka'ni:nçən] *nt* rabbit.

Kanister [ka'nɪstər] *m* **-s, -** can, canister.

Kanne ['kanə] *f* **-, -n** (*Krug*) jug; (*Kaffee—*) pot; (*Milch—*) churn; (*Gieß—*) can.

Kanon ['ka:nɔn] *m* **-s, -s** canon.

Kanone [ka'no:nə] *f* **-, -n** gun; (*Hist*) cannon; (*fig: Mensch*) ace.

Kantate [kan'ta:tə] *f* **-, -n** cantata.

Kante ['kantə] *f* **-, -n** edge.

Kantine [kan'ti:nə] *f* canteen.

Kantor ['kantɔr] *m* choirmaster.

Kanu ['ka:nu] *nt* **-s, -s** canoe.

Kanzel ['kantsəl] *f* **-, -n** pulpit.

Kanzlei [kants'lai] *f* chancery; (*Büro*) chambers *pl*.

Kanzler ['kantslər] *m* **-s, -** chancellor.

Kap [kap] *nt* **-s, -e** cape.

Kapazität [kapatsi'tɛ:t] *f* capacity; (*Fachmann*) authority.

Kapelle [ka'pɛlə] *f* (*Gebäude*) chapel; (*Mus*) band.

Kaper ['ka:pər] *f* **-, -n** caper; k~**n** *vt* capture.

kapieren [ka'pi:rən] *vti* (*col*) understand.

Kapital [kapi'ta:l] *nt* **-s, -e** *or* **-ien** capital; ~**anlage** *f* investment; ~**ismus** [-'lɪsmus] *m* capitalism; ~**ist** [-'lɪst] *m* capitalist; k~**kräftig** a wealthy; ~**markt** *m* money market.

Kapitän [kapi'tɛ:n] *m* **-s, -e** captain.

Kapitel [ka'pɪtəl] *nt* **-s, -** chapter.

Kapitulation [kapitulatsi'o:n] *f* capitulation.

kapitulieren [kapitu'li:rən] *vi* capitulate.

Kaplan [ka'pla:n] *m* **-s, Kapläne** chaplain.

Kappe ['kapə] *f* **-, -n** cap; (*Kapuze*) hood; k~**n** *vt* cut.

Kapsel ['kapsəl] *f* **-, -n** capsule.

kaputt [ka'put] a (*col*) smashed, broken; *Person* exhausted, finished; ~**gehen** *vi irreg* break; (*Schuhe*) fall apart; (*Firma*) go bust; (*Stoff*) wear out; (*sterben*) cop it; ~**lachen** *vr* laugh o.s. silly; ~**machen** *vt* break; *Mensch* exhaust, wear out.

Kapuze [ka'pu:tsə] *f* **-, -n** hood.

Karaffe [ka'rafə] *f* **-, -n** caraffe; (*geschliffen*) decanter.

Karambolage [karambo'la:ʒə] *f* **-, -n** (*Zusammenstoß*) crash.

Karamel [kara'mɛl] *m* **-s** caramel; ~**bonbon** *m or nt* toffee.

Karat [ka'ra:t] *nt* **-(e)s, -e** carat; ~**e** *nt* **-s** karate.

Karawane [kara'va:nə] *f* **-, -n** caravan.

Kardinal [kardi'na:l] *m* **-s, Kardinäle** cardinal; ~**zahl** *f* cardinal number.

Karfreitag [ka:r'fraita:k] *m* Good Friday.

karg [kark] a scanty, poor; *Mahlzeit auch* meagre; ~ **mit Worten sein** use few words; **K~heit** *f* poverty, scantiness; meagreness.

kärglich ['kɛrklıç] a poor, scanty.

kariert [ka'ri:rt] a *Stoff* checked; *Papier* squared.

Karies ['ka:ries] *f* **-** caries.

Karikatur [karika'tu:r] *f* caricature; ~**ist** [-'rɪst] *m* cartoonist.

karikieren [kari'ki:rən] *vt* caricature.

Karneval ['karnəval] *m* **-s, -e** *or* **-s** carnival.

Karo ['ka:ro] *nt* **-s, -s** square; (*Cards*) diamonds; ~**As** *nt* ace of diamonds.

Karosse [ka'rɔsə] *f* **-, -n** coach, carriage; ~**rie** [-'ri:] *f* (*Aut*) body(work).

Karotte [ka'rɔtə] *f* **-, -n** carrot.

Karpfen ['karpfən] *m* **-s, -** carp.

Karre ['karə] *f* **-, -n,** ~ *m* **-s, -** cart, barrow; k~**n** *vt* cart, transport.

Karriere [kari'ɛ:rə] *f* **-, -n** career; ~**machen** get on, get to the top; ~**macher** *m* **-s, -** careerist.

Karte ['kartə] *f* **-, -n** card; (*Land—*) map; (*Speise—*) menu; (*Eintritts—, Fahr—*) ticket; **alles auf eine ~ setzen** put all one's eggs in one basket.

Kartei [kar'tai] *f* card index; ~**karte** *f* index card.

Kartell [kar'tɛl] *nt* **-s, -e** cartel.

Karten- *cpd:* ~**haus** *nt* (*lit, fig*) house of cards; ~**spiel** *nt* card game; pack of cards.

Kartoffel [kar'tɔfəl] *f* **-, -n** potato; ~**brei** *m*, ~**püree** *nt* mashed potatoes *pl*; ~**salat** *m* potato salad.

Karton [kar'tɔ̃] *m* **-s, -s** cardboard; (*Schachtel*) cardboard box; k~**iert** [karto'ni:rt] a hardback.

Karussell [karu'sɛl] *nt* **-s, -s** roundabout (*Brit*), merry-go-round.

Karwoche [ka:r'vɔxə] *f* Holy Week.

Kaschemme [ka'ʃɛmə] *f* **-, -n** dive.

Käse ['kɛ:zə] *m* **-s, -** cheese; ~**blatt** *nt* (*col*) (local) rag; ~**kuchen** *m* cheesecake.

Kaserne [ka'zɛrnə] *f* -, -n barracks *pl*; ~nhof *m* parade ground.

Kasino [ka'zi:no] *nt* -s, -s club; (*Mil*) officers' mess; (*Spiel*—) casino.

Kasper ['kaspər] *m* -s, - Punch; (*fig*) clown.

Kasse ['kasə] *f* -, -n (*Geldkasten*) cashbox; (*in Geschäft*) till, cash register; (*Kino*—, *Theater*— *etc*) box office; ticket office; (*Kranken*—) health insurance; (*Spar*—) savings bank; ~ **machen** count the money; **getrennte ~ führen** pay separately; **an der ~** (*in Geschäft*) at the desk; **gut bei ~ sein** be in the money; ~**narzt** *m* panel doctor (*Brit*); ~**nbestand** *m* cash balance; ~**npatient** *m* panel patient (*Brit*); ~**nprüfung** *f* audit; ~**nsturz** *m*: ~**nsturz machen** check one's money; ~**nzettel** *m* receipt.

Kasserolle [kasə'rɔlə] *f* -, -n casserole.

Kassette [ka'sɛtə] *f* small box; (*Tonband, Phot*) cassette; (*Bücher*—) case; ~**nrecorder** *m* -s, - cassette recorder.

kassieren [ka'si:rən] *vt* take; *vi*: **darf ich ~?** would you like to pay now?

Kassierer [ka'si:rər] *m* -s, - cashier; (*von Klub*) treasurer.

Kastanie [kas'ta:niə] *f* chestnut; ~**nbaum** *m* chestnut tree.

Kästchen ['kɛstçən] *nt* small box, casket.

Kaste ['kastə] *f* -, -n caste.

Kasten ['kastən] *m* -s, ⁻ box (*Sport auch*), case; (*Truhe*) chest; ~**wagen** *m* van.

kastrieren [kas'tri:rən] *vt* castrate.

Katalog [kata'lo:k] *m* -(e)s, -e catalogue; **k**~**isieren** [katalogi'zi:rən] *vt* catalogue.

Katapult [kata'pult] *m or nt* -(e)s, -e catapult.

Katarrh [ka'tar] *m* -s, -e catarrh.

katastrophal [katastro'fa:l] *a* catastrophic.

Katastrophe [kata'stro:fə] *f* -, -n catastrophe, disaster.

Kategorie [katego'ri:] *f* category.

kategorisch [kate'go:rɪʃ] *a* categorical.

kategorisieren [kategori'zi:rən] *vt* categorize.

Kater ['ka:tər] *m* -s, - tomcat; (*col*) hangover.

Katheder [ka'te:dər] *nt* -s, - lecture desk.

Kathedrale [kate'dra:lə] *f* -, -n cathedral.

Kathode [ka'to:də] *f* -, -n cathode.

Katholik [kato'li:k] *m* -en, -en Catholic.

katholisch [ka'to:lɪʃ] *a* Catholic.

Katholizismus [katoli'tsɪsmus] *m* Catholicism.

Kätzchen ['kɛtsçən] *nt* kitten.

Katze ['katsə] *f* -, -n cat; **für die Katz** (*col*) in vain, for nothing; ~**nauge** *nt* cat's eye; (*Fahrrad*) rear light; ~**njammer** *m* (*col*) hangover; ~**nsprung** *m* (*col*) stone's throw; short journey; ~**nwäsche** *f* lick and a promise.

Kauderwelsch ['kaudərvɛlʃ] *nt* -(s) jargon; (*col*) double Dutch.

kauen ['kauən] *vti* chew.

kauern ['kauərn] *vi* crouch.

Kauf [kauf] *m* -(e)s, **Käufe** purchase, buy; (*Kaufen*) buying; **ein guter ~** a bargain; **etw in ~ nehmen** put up with sth; **k**~**en** *vt* buy.

Käufer(in *f*) ['kɔyfər(ɪn)] *m* -s, - buyer.

Kauf- *cpd*: ~**haus** *nt* department store; ~**kraft** *f* purchasing power; ~**laden** *m* shop, store.

käuflich ['kɔyflɪç] *a,ad* purchasable, for sale; (*pej*) venal; ~ **erwerben** purchase.

Kauf- *cpd*: ~**lustig** *a* interested in buying; ~**mann** *m, pl* -**leute** businessman; shopkeeper; **k**~**männisch** *a* commercial; ~**männischer Angestellter** clerk.

Kaugummi ['kaugumi] *m* chewing gum.

Kaulquappe ['kaulkvapə] *f* -, -n tadpole.

kaum [kaum] *ad* hardly, scarcely.

Kaution [kautsi'o:n] *f* deposit; (*Jur*) bail.

Kautschuk ['kautʃuk] *m* -s, -e india-rubber.

Kauz [kauts] *m* -es, **Käuze** owl; (*fig*) queer fellow.

Kavalier [kava'li:r] *m* -s, -e gentleman, cavalier; ~**sdelikt** *nt* peccadillo.

Kavallerie [kavalə'ri:] *f* cavalry.

Kavallerist [kavalə'rɪst] *m* trooper, cavalryman.

Kaviar ['ka:viar] *m* caviar.

keck [kɛk] *a* daring, bold; **K**~**heit** *f* daring, boldness.

Kegel ['ke:gəl] *m* -s, - skittle; (*Math*) cone; ~**bahn** *f* skittle alley; bowling alley; **k**~**förmig** *a* conical; **k**~**n** *vi* play skittles.

Kehle ['ke:lə] *f* -, -n throat.

Kehl- *cpd*: ~**kopf** *m* larynx; ~**laut** *m* guttural.

Kehre ['ke:rə] *f* -, -n turn(ing), bend; **k**~**n** *vti* (*wenden*) turn; (*mit Besen*) sweep; **sich an etw** (*dat*) **nicht k**~**n** not heed sth.

Kehr- *cpd*: ~**icht** *m* -s sweepings *pl*; ~**maschine** *f* sweeper; ~**reim** *m* refrain; ~**seite** *f* reverse, other side; wrong side; bad side; **k**~**tmachen** *vi* turn about, about-turn.

keifen ['kaifən] *vi* scold, nag.

Keil [kail] *m* -(e)s, -e wedge; (*Mil*) arrowhead; **k**~**en** *vt* wedge; *vr* fight; ~**e'rei** *f* (*col*) punch-up; ~**riemen** *m* (*Aut*) fan belt.

Keim [kaim] *m* -(e)s, -e bud; (*Med, fig*) germ; **etw im ~ ersticken** nip sth in the bud; **k**~**en** *vi* germinate; **k**~**frei** *a* sterile; **k**~**tötend** *a* antiseptic, germicidal; ~**zelle** *f* (*fig*) nucleus.

kein [kain] *a* no, not any; ~**e(r,s)** *pron* no one, nobody; none; ~**esfalls** *ad* on no account; ~**eswegs** *ad* by no means; ~**mal** *ad* not once.

Keks [ke:ks] *m or nt* -es, -e biscuit.

Kelch [kɛlç] *m* -(e)s, -e cup, goblet, chalice.

Kelle ['kɛlə] *f* -, -n ladle; (*Maurer*—) trowel.

Keller ['kɛlər] *m* -s, - cellar; ~**assel** *f* -, -n woodlouse; ~**wohnung** *f* basement flat.

Kellner ['kɛlnər] *m* -s, - waiter; ~**in** *f* waitress.

keltern ['kɛltərn] *vt* press.

kennen ['kɛnən] vt irreg know; ~**lernen** vt get to know; **sich** ~**lernen** get to know each other; (zum erstenmal) meet.

Kenn- cpd: ~**er** m -s, - connoisseur; ~**karte** f identity card; **k~tlich** a distinguishable, discernible; **etw k~tlich machen** mark sth; ~**tnis** f -, -se knowledge no pl; **etw zur ~tnis nehmen** note sth; **von etw ~tnis nehmen** take notice of sth; **jdn in ~tnis setzen** inform sb; ~**zeichen** nt mark, characteristic; **k~zeichnen** vt insep characterize; **k~zeichnenderweise** ad characteristically; ~**ziffer** f reference number.

kentern ['kɛntərn] vi capsize.

Keramik [ke'ra:mık] f -, -en ceramics pl, pottery.

Kerb- [kɛrb] cpd: ~**e** f -, -n notch, groove; ~**el** m -s, - chervil; **k~en** vt notch; ~**holz** nt: **etw auf dem ~holz haben** have done sth wrong.

Kerker ['kɛrkər] m -s, - prison.

Kerl [kɛrl] m -s, -e chap, bloke (Brit), guy.

Kern [kɛrn] m -(e)s, -e (Obst—) pip, stone; (Nuß—) kernel; (Atom—) nucleus; (fig) heart, core; ~**energie** f nuclear energy; ~**forschung** f nuclear research; ~**frage** f central issue; ~**gehäuse** nt core; **k~gesund** a thoroughly healthy, fit as a fiddle; **k~ig** a robust; Ausspruch pithy; ~**kraftwerk** nt nuclear power station; **k~los** a seedless, pipless; ~**physik** f nuclear physics; ~**reaktion** f nuclear reaction; ~**spaltung** f nuclear fission; ~**waffen** pl nuclear weapons pl.

Kerze ['kɛrtsə] f -, -n candle; (Zünd—) plug; **k~ngerade** a straight as a die; ~**nständer** m candle holder.

keß [kɛs] a saucy.

Kessel ['kɛsəl] m -s, - kettle; (von Lokomotive etc) boiler; (Geog) depression; (Mil) encirclement; ~**treiben** nt -s, - (fig) witch hunt.

Kette ['kɛtə] f -, -n chain; **k~n** vt chain; ~**nhund** m watchdog; ~**nladen** m chain store; ~**nrauchen** nt chain smoking; ~**nreaktion** f chain reaction.

Ketzer ['kɛtsər] m -s, - heretic; **k~isch** a heretical.

keuchen ['kɔʏçən] vi pant, gasp.

Keuchhusten m whooping cough.

Keule ['kɔʏlə] f -, -n club; (Cook) leg.

keusch [kɔʏʃ] a chaste; **K~heit** f chastity.

Kfz [ka:ɛftsɛt] abbr of **Kraftfahrzeug**.

kichern ['kıçərn] vi giggle.

kidnappen ['kıdnæpən] vt kidnap.

Kiebitz ['ki:bıts] m -es, -e peewit.

Kiefer ['ki:fər] m -s, - jaw; f -, -n pine; ~**nzapfen** m pine cone.

Kiel [ki:l] m -(e)s, -e (Feder—) quill; (Naut) keel; **k~holen** vt Person keelhaul; Schiff career; ~**wasser** nt wake.

Kieme ['ki:mə] f -, -n gill.

Kies [ki:s] m -es, -e gravel; ~**el** [ki:zəl] m -s, - pebble; ~**elstein** m pebble; ~**grube** f gravel pit; ~**weg** m gravel path.

Kilo ['ki:lo] kilo; ~**gramm** [kilo'gram] nt -s, -e kilogram; ~**meter** [kilo'me:tər] m -s, - kilometre; ~**meterzähler** m ≈ milometer.

Kimme ['kımə] f -, -n notch; (Gewehr) backsight.

Kind [kınt] nt -(e)s, -er child; **von ~ auf** from childhood; **sich bei jdm lieb ~ machen** ingratiate o.s. with sb; ~**erbett** ['kındərbɛt] nt cot; ~**erei** [kındə'raı] f childishness; ~**ergarten** m nursery school, playgroup; ~**ergeld** nt family allowance; ~**erlähmung** f poliomyelitis; **k~erleicht** a childishly easy; **k~erlos** a childless; ~**ermädchen** nt nursemaid; **k~erreich** a with a lot of children; ~**erspiel** nt child's play; ~**erstube** f: **eine gute ~erstube haben** be well-mannered; ~**erwagen** m pram, baby carriage (US); ~**esalter** nt infancy; **k~esbeine** pl: **von ~esbeinen an** from early childhood; ~**heit** f childhood; **k~isch** a childish; **k~lich** a childlike; **k~sköpfig** a childish.

Kinn [kın] nt -(e)s, -e chin; ~**haken** m (Boxen) uppercut; ~**lade** f jaw.

Kino ['ki:no] nt -s, -s cinema; ~**besucher** m cinema-goer; ~**programm** nt film programme.

Kiosk [ki'ɔsk] m -(e)s, -e kiosk.

Kipp- ['kıp] cpd: ~**e** f -, -n cigarette end; (col) fag; **auf der ~e stehen** (fig) be touch and go; **k~en** vi topple over, overturn; vt tilt.

Kirch- ['kırç] cpd: ~**e** f -, -n church; ~**endiener** m churchwarden; ~**enfest** nt church festival; ~**enlied** nt hymn; ~**gänger** m -s, - churchgoer; ~**hof** m churchyard; **k~lich** a ecclesiastical; ~**turm** m church tower, steeple.

Kirsche ['kırʃə] f -, -n cherry.

Kissen ['kısən] nt -s, - cushion; (Kopf—) pillow; ~**bezug** m pillowslip.

Kiste ['kıstə] f -, -n box; chest.

Kitsch [kıtʃ] m -(e)s trash; **k~ig** a trashy.

Kitt [kıt] m -(e)s, -e putty; ~**chen** nt (col) clink; ~**el** m -s, - overall, smock; **k~en** vt putty; (fig) Ehe etc cement.

Kitz [kıts] nt -es, -e kid; (Reh—) fawn.

kitzel- ['kıtsəl] cpd: ~**ig** a (lit, fig) ticklish; ~**n** vi tickle.

klaffen ['klafən] vi gape.

kläffen ['klɛfən] vi yelp.

Klage ['kla:gə] f -, -n complaint; (Jur) action; **k~n** vi (weh—) lament, wail; (sich beschweren) complain; (Jur) take legal action.

Kläger(in f) ['klɛ:gər(ın)] m -s, - plaintiff.

kläglich ['klɛ:klıç] a wretched.

Klamm [klam] f -, -en ravine; **k~ a** Finger numb; (feucht) damp.

Klammer ['klamər] f -, -n clamp; (in Text) bracket; (Büro—) clip; (Wäsche—) peg; (Zahn—) brace; **k~n** vr cling (an +acc to).

Klang [klaŋ] m -(e)s, -e sound; **k~voll** a sonorous.

Klappe ['klapə] f -, -n valve; (Ofen—) damper; (col: Mund) trap; (Geräusch) click; vti Sitz etc tip; v impers work.

Klapper ['klapər] f -, -n rattle; **k~ig** a run-down, worn-out; **k~n** vi clatter, rattle;

~schlange f rattlesnake; ~storch m stork.

Klapp- cpd: ~messer nt jack-knife; ~rad nt collapsible bicycle; ~stuhl m folding chair.

Klaps [klaps] m -es, -e slap; k~en vi slap.

klar [klɑːr] a clear; (Naut) ready for sea; (Mil) ready for action; sich (dat) im K~en sein über (+acc) be clear about; ins K~e kommen get clear.

Klär- ['klɛːr] cpd: ~anlage f purification plant; k~en vt Flüßigkeit purify; Probleme clarify; vr clear (itself) up.

Klar- cpd: ~heit f clarity; ~inette [klari'nɛtə] f clarinet; k~legen vt clear up, explain; k~machen vt Schiff get ready for sea; jdm etw k~machen make sth clear to sb; k~sehen vi irreg see clearly; ~sichtfolie f transparent film; k~stellen vt clarify.

Klärung ['klɛːruŋ] f purification; clarification.

Klasse ['klasə] f -, -n class; (Sch auch) form; k~ a (col) smashing; ~narbeit f test; ~nbewußtsein nt class consciousness; ~ngesellschaft f class society; ~nkampf m class conflict; ~nlehrer m form master; ~nlos a classless; ~nsprecher(in f) m form prefect; ~nzimmer nt classroom.

klassifizieren [klasifi'tsiːrən] vt classify.

Klassifizierung f classification.

Klassik ['klasɪk] f (Zeit) classical period; (Stil) classicism; ~er m -s, - classic.

klassisch a (lit, fig) classical.

Klatsch [klatʃ] m -(e)s, -e smack, crack; (Gerede) gossip; ~base f gossip, scandalmonger; ~e f -, -n (col) crib; k~en vi (Geräusch) clash; (reden) gossip; (Beifall) applaud, clap; ~mohn m (corn) poppy; k~naß a soaking wet; ~spalte f gossip column.

klauben ['klaubən] vt pick.

Klaue ['klauə] f -, -n claw; (col: Schrift) scrawl; k~n vt claw; (col) pinch.

Klause ['klauzə] f -, -n cell; hermitage.

Klausel ['klauzəl] f -, -n clause.

Klausur [klau'zuːr] f seclusion; ~arbeit f examination paper.

Klaviatur [klavia'tuːr] f keyboard.

Klavier [kla'viːr] nt -s, -e piano.

Kleb- ['kleːb] cpd: ~emittel nt glue; k~en vt stick (an +acc to); k~rig a sticky; ~stoff m glue; ~streifen m adhesive tape.

kleckern ['klɛkərn] vi slobber.

Klecks [klɛks] m -es, -e blot, stain; k~en vi blot; (pej) daub.

Klee [kleː] m -s clover; ~blatt nt cloverleaf; (fig) trio.

Kleid [klaɪt] nt -(e)s, -er garment; (Frauen~) dress; pl clothes pl; k~en ['klaɪdən] vt clothe, dress; (auch vi) suit; vr dress; ~erbügel m coat hanger; ~erbürste f clothes brush; ~erschrank m wardrobe; k~sam a becoming; ~ung f clothing; ~ungsstück nt garment.

Kleie ['klaɪə] f -, -n bran.

klein [klaɪn] a little, small;

K~bürgertum nt petite bourgeoisie; **K~e(r,s)** little one; **K~format** nt small size; im **K~format** small-scale; **K~geld** nt small change; ~gläubig a of little faith; ~hacken vt chop up, mince; **K~holz** nt firewood; **K~holz aus jdm machen** make mincemeat of sb; **K~igkeit** f trifle; **K~kind** nt infant; **K~kram** m details pl; ~laut a dejected, quiet; ~lich a petty, paltry; **K~lichkeit** f pettiness, paltriness; ~mütig a fainthearted; **K~od** ['klaɪnoːt] nt -s, -odien gem, jewel; treasure; ~schneiden vt irreg chop up; ~städtisch a provincial; ~stmöglich a smallest possible.

Kleister ['klaɪstər] m -s, - paste; k~n vt paste.

Klemme ['klɛmə] f -, -n clip; (Med) clamp; (fig) jam; k~n vt (festhalten) jam; (quetschen) pinch, nip; vr catch o.s.; (sich hineinzwängen) squeeze o.s.; sich hinter jdn/etw k~n get on to sb/get down to sth; vi (Tür) stick, jam.

Klempner ['klɛmpnər] m -s, - plumber.

Kleptomanie [klɛptoma'niː] f kleptomania.

Kleriker ['kleːrikər] m -s, - cleric.

Klerus ['kleːrus] m - clergy.

Klette ['klɛtə] f -, -n burr.

Kletter- ['klɛtər] cpd: ~er m -s, - climber; k~n vi climb; ~pflanze f creeper; ~seil nt climbing rope.

klicken ['klɪkən] vi click.

Klient(in f) [kli'ɛnt(ɪn)] m client.

Klima ['kliːma] nt -s, -s or -te [kli'maːtə] climate; ~anlage f air conditioning; k~tisieren [-i'ziːrən] vt air-condition; ~wechsel m change of air.

klimpern ['klɪmpərn] vi tinkle; (mit Gitarre) strum.

Klinge ['klɪŋə] f -, -n blade, sword.

Klingel ['klɪŋəl] f -, -n bell; ~beutel m collection bag; k~n vi ring.

klingen ['klɪŋən] vi irreg sound; (Gläser) clink.

Klinik ['kliːnɪk] f hospital, clinic.

klinisch ['kliːnɪʃ] a clinical.

Klinke ['klɪŋkə] f -, -n handle.

Klinker ['klɪŋkər] m -s, - clinker.

Klippe ['klɪpə] f -, -n cliff; (im Meer) reef; (fig) hurdle; k~nreich a rocky.

klipp und klar ['klɪp'untklaːr] a clear and concise.

Klips [klɪps] m -es, -e clip; (Ohr~) earring.

klirren ['klɪrən] vi clank, jangle; (Gläser) clink; ~de Kälte biting cold.

Klischee [kli'ʃeː] nt -s, -s (Druckplatte) plate, block; (fig) cliché; ~vorstellung f stereotyped idea.

Klo [kloː] nt -s, -s (col) loo.

Kloake [klo'aːkə] f -, -n sewer.

klobig ['kloːbɪç] a clumsy.

klopfen ['klɔpfən] vti knock; (Herz) thump; es klopft sb's knocking; jdm auf die Schulter ~ tap sb on the shoulder; vt beat.

Klopfer m -s, - (Teppich~) beater; (Tür~) knocker.

Klöppel ['klœpəl] *m* -s, - (*von Glocke*) clapper; **k~n** *vi* make lace.

Klops [klɔps] *m* -es, -e meatball.

Klosett [klo'zɛt] *nt* -s, -e *or* -s lavatory, toilet; **~papier** *nt* toilet paper.

Kloß [klo:s] *m* -es, ˙e (*Erd—*) clod; (*im Hals*) lump; (*Cook*) dumpling.

Kloster ['klo:stər] *nt* -s, ˙ (*Männer—*) monastery; (*Frauen—*) convent.

klösterlich ['klø:stərlıç] *a* monastic; convent.

Klotz [klɔts] *m* -es, ˙e log; (*Hack—*) block; **ein ~ am Bein** (*fig*) drag, millstone round (sb's) neck.

Klub [klup] *m* -s, -s club; **~sessel** *m* easy chair.

Kluft [kluft] *f* -, ˙e cleft, gap; (*Geol*) gorge, chasm.

klug [klu:k] *a* clever, intelligent; **K~heit** *f* cleverness, intelligence.

Klümpchen ['klʏmpçən] *nt* clot, blob.

Klumpen ['klumpən] *m* -s, - (*Erd—*) clod; (*Blut—*) lump, clot; (*Gold—*) nugget; (*Cook*) lump; **k~** *vi* go lumpy, clot.

Klumpfuß ['klump-fu:s] *m* club-foot.

knabbern ['knabərn] *vti* nibble.

Knabe ['kna:bə] *m* -n, -n boy; **k~nhaft** *a* boyish.

Knäckebrot ['knɛkəbro:t] *nt* crispbread.

knacken ['knakən] *vti* (*lit, fig*) crack.

Knall [knal] *m* -(e)s, -e bang; (*Peitschen—*) crack; **~ und Fall** (*col*) unexpectedly; **~bonbon** *m* cracker; **~effekt** *m* surprise effect, spectacular effect; **k~en** *vi* bang; crack; **k~rot** *a* bright red.

knapp [knap] *a* tight; *Geld* scarce; *Sprache* concise; **K~ e** *m* -n, -n (*Edelmann*) young knight; **~halten** *vt irreg* stint; **K~heit** *f* tightness; scarcity; conciseness.

knarren ['knarən] *vi* creak.

knattern ['knatərn] *vi* rattle; (*MG*) chatter.

Knäuel ['knɔyəl] *m or nt* -s, - (*Woll—*) ball; (*Menschen—*) knot.

Knauf [knauf] *m* -(e)s, **Knäufe** knob; (*Schwert—*) pommel.

Knauser ['knauzər] *m* -s, - miser; **k~ig** *a* miserly; **k~n** *vi* be mean.

knautschen ['knautʃən] *vti* crumple.

Knebel ['kne:bəl] *m* -s, - gag; **k~n** *vt* gag; (*Naut*) fasten.

Knecht [knɛçt] *m* -(e)s, -e farm labourer; servant; **k~en** *vt* enslave; **~schaft** *f* servitude.

kneifen ['knaifən] *vti irreg* pinch; (*sich drücken*) back out; **vor etw ~** dodge sth.

Kneipe ['knaipə] *f* -, -n (*col*) pub.

Knet- [kne:t] *cpd*: **k~en** *vt* knead; *Wachs* mould; **~masse** *f* Plasticine ®.

Knick [knık] *m* -(e)s, -e (*Sprung*) crack; (*Kurve*) bend; (*Falte*) fold; **k~en** *vti* (*springen*) crack; (*brechen*) break; *Papier* fold; **geknickt sein** *vi* be downcast.

Knicks [knıks] *m* -es, -e curtsey; **k~en** *vi* curtsey.

Knie [kni:] *nt* -s, - knee; **~beuge** *f* -, -n knee bend; **k~n** *vi* kneel; **~fall** *m* genuflection; **~gelenk** *nt* knee joint; **~kehle** *f*

back of the knee; **~scheibe** *f* kneecap; **~strumpf** *m* knee-length sock.

Kniff [knıf] *m* -(e)s, -e (*Zwicken*) pinch; (*Falte*) fold; (*fig*) trick, knack; **k~elig** *a* tricky.

knipsen ['knıpsən] *vti Fahrkarte* punch; (*Phot*) take a snap (of), snap.

Knirps [knırps] *m* -es, -e little chap; ' (*Schirm*) telescopic umbrella.

knirschen ['knırʃən] *vi* crunch; **mit den Zähnen ~** grind one's teeth.

knistern ['knıstərn] *vi* crackle.

Knitter- ['knitər] *cpd*: **~falte** *f* crease; **k~frei** *a* non-crease; **k~n** *vi* crease.

Knoblauch ['kno:plaux] *m* -(e)s garlic.

Knöchel ['knœçəl] *m* -s, - knuckle; (*Fuß—*) ankle.

Knochen ['knɔxən] *m* -s, - bone; **~bau** *m* bone structure; **~bruch** *m* fracture; **~gerüst** *nt* skeleton.

knöchern ['knœçərn] *a* bone.

knochig ['knɔxıç] *a* bony.

Knödel ['knø:dəl] *m* -s, - dumpling.

Knolle ['knɔlə] *f* -, -n bulb.

Knopf [knɔpf] *m* -(e)s, ˙e button; (*Kragen—*) stud; **~loch** *nt* buttonhole.

knöpfen ['knœpfən] *vt* button.

Knorpel ['knɔrpəl] *m* -s, - cartilage, gristle; **k~ig** *a* gristly.

knorrig ['knɔrıç] *a* gnarled, knotted.

Knospe ['knɔspə] *f* -, -n bud; **k~n** *vi* bud.

Knoten ['kno:tən] *m* -s, - knot; (*Bot*) node; (*Med*) lump; **k~** *vt* knot; **~punkt** *m* junction.

knuffen ['knufən] *vt* (*col*) cuff.

Knüller ['knʏlər] *m* -s, - (*col*) hit; (*Reportage*) scoop.

knüpfen ['knʏpfən] *vt* tie; *Teppich* knot; *Freundschaft* form.

Knüppel ['knʏpəl] *m* -s, - cudgel; (*Polizei—*) baton, truncheon; (*Aviat*) (joy)stick; **~schaltung** *f* (*Aut*) floor-mounted gear change.

knurren ['knurən] *vi* (*Hund*) snarl, growl; (*Magen*) rumble; (*Mensch*) mutter.

knusperig ['knuspərıç] *a* crisp; *Keks* crunchy.

Koalition [koalitsi'o:n] *f* coalition.

Kobalt ['ko:balt] *nt* -s cobalt.

Kobold ['ko:bolt] *m* -(e)s, -e goblin, imp.

Kobra ['ko:bra] *f* -, -s cobra.

Koch [kɔx] *m* -(e)s, ˙e cook; **~buch** *nt* cookery book; **k~en** *vti* cook; *Wasser* boil; **~er** *m* -s, - stove, cooker.

Köcher ['kœçər] *m* -s, - quiver.

Kochgelegenheit ['kɔxgəle:gənhait] *f* cooking facilities *pl*.

Köchin ['kœçın] *f* cook.

Koch- *cpd*: **~löffel** *m* kitchen spoon; **~nische** *f* kitchenette; **~platte** *f* boiling ring, hotplate; **~salz** *nt* cooking salt; **~topf** *m* saucepan, pot.

Köder ['kø:dər] *m* -s, - bait, lure; **k~n** *vt* lure, entice.

Koexistenz [koɛksıs'tɛnts] *f* coexistence.

Koffein [kɔfe'i:n] *nt* -s caffeine; **k~frei** *a* decaffeinated.

Koffer ['kɔfər] *m* -s, - suitcase; (*Schrank—*) trunk; **~radio** *nt* portable

radio; ~**raum** m (Aut) boot, trunk (US).
Kognak ['kɔnjak] m **-s**, **-s** brandy, cognac.
Kohl [ko:l] m **-(e)s**, **-e** cabbage.
Kohle ['ko:lə] f **-**, **-n** coal; (Holz—) charcoal; (Chem) carbon; ~**hydrat** nt **-(e)s**, **-e** carbohydrate; ~**ndioxyd** nt **-(e)s**, **-e** carbon dioxide; ~**ngrube** f coal pit, mine; ~**nhändler** m coal merchant, coalman; ~**nsäure** f carbon dioxide; ~**nstoff** m carbon; ~**papier** nt carbon paper; ~**stift** m charcoal pencil.
Köhler ['kø:lər] m **-s**, **-** charcoal burner.
Kohl- cpd: ~**rübe** f turnip; **k**~**schwarz** a coal-black.
Koje ['ko:jə] f **-**, **-n** cabin; (Bett) bunk.
Kokain [koka'i:n] nt **-s** cocaine.
kokett [ko'kɛt] a coquettish, flirtatious; ~**ieren** [-'ti:rən] vi flirt.
Kokosnuß ['ko:kɔsnʊs] f coconut.
Koks [ko:ks] m **-es**, **-e** coke.
Kolben ['kɔlbən] m **-s**, **-** (Gewehr—) rifle butt; (Keule) club; (Chem) flask; (Tech) piston; (Mais—) cob.
Kolchose [kɔl'çoːzə] f **-**, **-n** collective farm.
Kolik ['ko:lɪk] f colic, gripe.
Kollaps [kɔ'laps] m **-es**, **-e** collapse.
Kolleg [kɔl'e:k] nt **-s**, **-s** or **-ien** lecture course; ~**e** [kɔ'le:gə] m **-n**, **-n**, ~**in** f colleague; ~**ium** nt board; (Sch) staff.
Kollekte [kɔ'lɛktə] f **-**, **-n** (Rel) collection.
kollektiv [kɔlɛk'ti:f] a collective.
kollidieren [kɔli'di:rən] vi collide; (zeitlich) clash.
Kollision [kɔlizi'o:n] f collision; (zeitlich) clash.
kolonial [koloni'a:l] a colonial; **K**~**warenhändler** m grocer.
Kolonie [kolo'ni:] f colony.
kolonisieren [koloni'zi:rən] vt colonize.
Kolonist [kolo'nɪst] m colonist.
Kolonne [ko'lɔnə] f **-**, **-n** column; (von Fahrzeugen) convoy.
Koloß [ko'lɔs] m **-sses**, **-sse** colossus.
kolossal [kolɔ'sa:l] a colossal.
Kombi- ['kɔmbi] cpd: ~**nation** [-natsi'o:n] f combination; (Vermutung) conjecture; (Hemdhose) combinations pl; (Aviat) flying suit; **k**~**nieren** [-'ni:rən] vt combine; vi deduce, work out; (vermuten) guess; ~**wagen** m station wagon; ~**zange** f (pair of) pliers.
Komet [ko'me:t] m **-en**, **-en** comet.
Komfort [kɔm'fo:r] m **-s** luxury.
Komik ['ko:mɪk] f humour, comedy; ~**er** m **-s**, **-** comedian.
komisch ['ko:mɪʃ] a funny.
Komitee [komi'te:] nt **-s**, **-s** committee.
Komma ['kɔma] nt **-s**, **-s** or **-ta** comma.
Kommand- [kɔ'mand] cpd: ~**ant** [-'dant] m commander, commanding officer; ~**eur** [-'dø:r] m commanding officer; **k**~**ieren** [-'di:rən] vti command; ~**o** nt **-s**, **-s** command, order; (Truppe) detachment, squad; **auf** ~**o** to order.
kommen [kɔmən] vi irreg come; (näher —) approach; (passieren) happen; (gelangen, geraten) get; (Blumen, Zähne, Tränen etc) appear; (in die Schule, das

Zuchthaus etc) go; ~ **lassen** send for; **das kommt in den Schrank** that goes in the cupboard; **zu sich** ~ come round or to; **zu etw** ~ acquire sth; **um etw** ~ lose sth; **nichts auf jdn/etw** ~ **lassen** have nothing said against sb/sth; **jdm frech** ~ get cheeky with sb; **auf jeden vierten kommt ein Platz** there's one place to every fourth person; **wer kommt zuerst?** who's first?; **unter ein Auto** ~ be run over by a car; **wie hoch kommt das?** what does that cost?; ~ **s** coming.
Kommentar [kɔmɛn'ta:r] m commentary; **kein** ~ no comment; **k**~**los** a without comment.
Kommentator [kɔmɛn'ta:tor] m (TV) commentator.
kommentieren [kɔmɛn'ti:rən] vt comment on.
kommerziell [kɔmɛrtsi'ɛl] a commercial.
Kommilitone [kɔmili'to:nə] m **-n**, **-n** fellow student.
Kommiß [kɔ'mɪs] m **-sses** (life in the) army; ~**brot** nt army bread.
Kommissar [kɔmɪ'sa:r] m police inspector.
Kommission [kɔmɪsɪ'o:n] f (Comm) commission; (Ausschuß) committee.
Kommode [kɔ'mo:də] f **-**, **-n** (chest of) drawers.
Kommune [kɔ'mu:nə] f **-**, **-n** commune.
Kommunikation [kɔmunɪkatsɪ'o:n] f communication.
Kommunion [kɔmuni'o:n] f communion.
Kommuniqué [kɔmyni'ke:] nt **-s**, **-s** communiqué.
Kommunismus [kɔmu'nɪsmʊs] m communism.
Kommunist [kɔmu'nɪst] m communist; **k**~**isch** a communist.
kommunizieren [kɔmuni'tsi:rən] vi communicate; (Eccl) receive communion.
Komödiant [komødi'ant] m comedian; ~**in** f comedienne.
Komödie [ko'mø:diə] f comedy.
Kompagnon [kɔmpan'jõ:] m **-s**, **-s** (Comm) partner.
kompakt [kɔm'pakt] a compact.
Kompanie [kɔmpa'ni:] f company.
Komparativ ['kɔmparati:f] m **-s**, **-e** comparative.
Kompaß ['kɔmpas] m **-sses**, **-sse** compass.
kompetent [kɔmpe'tɛnt] a competent.
Kompetenz f competence, authority.
komplett [kɔm'plɛt] a complete.
Komplikation [kɔmplikatsɪ'o:n] f complication.
Kompliment [kɔmpli'mɛnt] nt compliment.
Komplize [kɔm'pli:tsə] m **-n**, **-n** accomplice.
komplizieren [kɔmpli'tsi:rən] vt complicate.
Komplott [kɔm'plɔt] nt **-(e)s**, **-e** plot.
komponieren [kɔmpo'ni:rən] vt compose.
Komponist [kɔmpo'nɪst] m composer.
Komposition [kɔmpozitsɪ'o:n] f composition.

Kompost [kɔm'pɔst] *m* **-(e)s, -e** compost; **~haufen** *m* compost heap.

Kompott [kɔm'pɔt] *nt* **-(e)s, -e** stewed fruit.

Kompresse [kɔm'prɛsə] *f* **-, -n** compress.

Kompressor [kɔm'prɛsɔr] *m* compressor.

Kompromiß [kɔmprɔ'mɪs] *m* **-sses, -sse** compromise; **k~bereit** a willing to compromise; **~lösung** *f* compromise solution.

kompromittieren [kɔmprɔmɪ'tiːrən] *vt* compromise.

Kondens- [kɔn'dɛns] *cpd*: **~ation** [kɔndɛnzatsi'oːn] *f* condensation; **~ator** [kɔndɛn'zaːtɔr] *m* condenser; **k~ieren** [kɔndɛn'ziːrən] *vt* condense; **~milch** *f* condensed milk; **~streifen** *m* vapour trail.

Kondition [kɔnditsi'oːn] *cpd*: **~alsatz** [kɔnditsio'naːlzats] *m* conditional clause; **~straining** *nt* fitness training.

Konditor [kɔn'diːtɔr] *m* pastrycook; **~ei** [kɔndito'raɪ] *f* café; cake shop.

kondolieren [kɔndo'liːrən] *vi* condole (*jdm* with sb).

Kondom [kɔn'doːm] *nt* **-s, -e** condom.

Konfektion [kɔnfɛktsi'oːn] *f* production of ready-made clothing; **~skleidung** *f* ready-made clothing.

Konferenz [kɔnfe'rɛnts] *f* conference, meeting.

konferieren [kɔnfe'riːrən] *vi* confer, have a meeting.

Konfession [kɔnfɛsi'oːn] *f* religion; (*christlich*) denomination; **k~ell** [-'nɛl] a denominational; **k~slos** a non-denominational; **~sschule** *f* denominational school.

Konfetti [kɔn'fɛti] *nt* **-(s)** confetti.

Konfirmand [kɔnfɪr'mant] *m* candidate for confirmation.

Konfirmation [kɔnfɪrmatsi'oːn] *f* (*Eccl*) confirmation.

konfirmieren [kɔnfɪr'miːrən] *vt* confirm.

konfiszieren [kɔnfɪs'tsiːrən] *vt* confiscate.

Konfitüre [kɔnfi'tyːrə] *f* **-, -n** jam.

Konflikt [kɔn'flɪkt] *m* **-(e)s, -e** conflict.

konform [kɔn'fɔrm] a concurring; **~ gehen** be in agreement.

konfrontieren [kɔnfrɔn'tiːrən] *vt* confront.

konfus [kɔn'fuːs] a confused.

Kongreß [kɔn'grɛs] *m* **-sses, -sse** congress.

Kongruenz [kɔngru'ɛnts] *f* agreement, congruence.

König ['køːnɪç] *m* **-(e)s, -e** king; **~in** ['køːnɪgɪn] *f* queen; **k~lich** a royal; **~reich** *nt* kingdom; **~tum** *nt* **-(e)s, -er** kingship.

konisch ['koːnɪʃ] a conical.

Konjugation [kɔnjugatsi'oːn] *f* conjugation.

konjugieren [kɔnju'giːrən] *vt* conjugate.

Konjunktion [kɔnjuŋktsi'oːn] *f* conjunction.

Konjunktiv ['kɔnjuŋktiːf] *m* **-s, -e** subjunctive.

Konjunktur [kɔnjuŋk'tuːr] *f* economic situation; (*Hoch—*) boom.

konkav [kɔn'kaːf] a concave.

konkret [kɔn'kreːt] a concrete.

Konkurrent(in *f*) [kɔnku'rɛnt(ɪn)] *m* competitor.

Konkurrenz [kɔnku'rɛnts] *f* competition; **k~fähig** a competitive; **~kampf** *m* competition; (*col*) rat race.

konkurrieren [kɔnku'riːrən] *vi* compete.

Konkurs [kɔn'kurs] *m* **-es, -e** bankruptcy.

können ['kœnən] *vti irreg* be able to, can; (*wissen*) know; **~ Sie Deutsch?** can you speak German?; **ich kann nicht . . .** I can't *or* cannot . . .; **kann ich gehen?** can I go?; **das kann sein** that's possible; **ich kann nicht mehr** I can't go on; **K~** *nt* **-s** ability.

konsequent [kɔnze'kvɛnt] a consistent.

Konsequenz [kɔnze'kvɛnts] *f* consistency; (*Folgerung*) conclusion.

Konserv- [kɔn'zɛrv] *cpd*: **k~ativ** [-a'tiːf] a conservative; **~atorium** [-a'toːrium] *nt* academy of music, conservatory; **~e** *f* **-, -n** tinned food; **~enbüchse** *f* tin, can; **k~ieren** [-'viːrən] *vt* preserve; **~ierung** *f* preservation; **~ierungsmittel** *nt* preservative.

Konsonant [kɔnzo'nant] *m* consonant.

konstant [kɔn'stant] a constant.

Konstitution [kɔnstitutsi'oːn] *f* constitution; **k~ell** [-'nɛl] a constitutional.

konstruieren [kɔnstru'iːrən] *vt* construct.

Konstrukteur [kɔnstruk'tøːr] *m* engineer, designer.

Konstruktion [kɔnstruktsi'oːn] *f* construction.

konstruktiv [kɔnstruk'tiːf] a constructive.

Konsul ['kɔnzul] *m* **-s, -n** consul; **~at** [-'laːt] *nt* consulate.

konsultieren [kɔnzul'tiːrən] *vt* consult.

Konsum [kɔn'zuːm] *m* **-s** consumption; **~artikel** *m* consumer article; **~ent** [-'mɛnt] *m* consumer; **k~ieren** [-'miːrən] *vt* consume.

Kontakt [kɔn'takt] *m* **-(e)s, -e** contact; **k~arm** a unsociable; **k~freudig** a sociable; **~linsen** *pl* contact lenses *pl*.

Konterfei ['kɔntərfaɪ] *nt* **-s, -s** picture.

kontern ['kɔntərn] *vti* counter.

Konterrevolution [kɔntərrevolutsio:n] *f* counter-revolution.

Kontinent ['kɔntinɛnt] *m* continent.

Kontingent [kɔntiŋ'gɛnt] *nt* **-(e)s, -e** quota; (*Truppen—*) contingent.

kontinuierlich [kɔntinu'iːrlɪç] a continuous.

Kontinuität [kɔntinui'tɛːt] *f* continuity.

Konto ['kɔnto] *nt* **-s, Konten** account; **~auszug** *m* statement (of account); **~inhaber(in** *f*) *m* account holder; **~r** [kɔn'toːr] *nt* **-s, -e** office; **~rist** [-'rɪst] *m* clerk, office worker; **~stand** *m* state of account.

Kontra ['kɔntra] *nt* **-s, -s** (*Cards*) double; **jdm ~ geben** (*fig*) contradict sb; **~baß** *m* double bass; **~hent** [-'hɛnt] *m* contracting party; **~punkt** *m* counterpoint.

Kontrast [kɔn'trast] *m* **-(e)s, -e** contrast.

Kontroll- [kɔn'trɔl] *cpd*: **~e** *f* **-, -n** control, supervision; (*Paß—*) passport control; **~eur** [-'løːr] *m* inspector; **k~ieren**

[-'li:rən] vt control, supervise; (nachprüfen) check.

Kontur [kɔn'tu:r] f contour.

Konvention [kɔnvɛntsi'o:n] f convention; k~ell [-'nɛl] a conventional.

Konversation [kɔnvɛrzatsi'o:n] f conversation; ~slexikon nt encyclopaedia.

konvex [kɔn'vɛks] a convex.

Konvoi [ˈkɔnvɔy] m -s, -s convoy.

Konzentration [kɔntsɛntratsi'o:n] f concentration; ~slager nt concentration camp.

konzentrieren [kɔntsɛn'tri:rən] vtr concentrate.

konzentriert a concentrated; ad zuhören, arbeiten intently.

Konzept [kɔn'tsɛpt] nt -(e)s, -e rough draft; jdn aus dem ~ bringen confuse sb.

Konzern [kɔn'tsɛrn] m -s, -e combine.

Konzert [kɔn'tsɛrt] nt -(e)s, -e concert; (Stück) concerto; ~saal m concert hall.

Konzession [kɔntsesi'o:n] f licence; (Zugeständnis) concession; k~ieren [-'ni:rən] vt license.

Konzil [kɔn'tsi:l] nt -s, -e or -ien council.

konzipieren [kɔntsi'pi:rən] vt conceive.

Kopf [kɔpf] m -(e)s, ⁻e head; ~ bedeckung f headgear.

köpfen ['kœpfən] vt behead; Baum lop; Ei take the top off; Ball head.

Kopf- cpd: ~haut f scalp; ~hörer m headphone; ~kissen nt pillow; k~los a panic-stricken; ~losigkeit f panic; k~rechnen vi do mental arithmetic; ~salat m lettuce; ~schmerzen pl headache; ~sprung m header, dive; ~stand m headstand; ~tuch nt headscarf; k~über ad head over heels; ~weh nt headache; ~zerbrechen nt: jdm ~zerbrechen machen give sb a lot of headaches.

Kopie [ko'pi:] f copy; k~ren vt copy.

Koppel ['kɔpəl] f -, -n (Weide) enclosure; nt -s, - (Gürtel) belt; k~n vt couple; ~ung f coupling; ~ungsmanöver nt docking manoeuvre.

Koralle [ko'ralə] f -, -n coral; ~nkette f coral necklace; ~nriff nt coral reef.

Korb [kɔrp] m -(e)s, ⁻e basket; jdm einen ~ geben (fig) turn sb down; ~ball m basketball; ~stuhl m wicker chair.

Kord [kɔrt] m -(e)s, -e corduroy.

Kordel ['kɔrdəl] f -, -n cord, string.

Kork [kɔrk] m -(e)s, -e cork; ~en m -s, - stopper, cork; ~enzieher m -s, - corkscrew.

Korn [kɔrn] nt -(e)s, ⁻er corn, grain; (Gewehr) sight; ~blume f cornflower; ~kammer f granary.

Körnchen ['kœrnçən] nt grain, granule.

Körper ['kœrpər] m -s, - body; ~bau m build; k~behindert a disabled; ~gewicht nt weight; ~größe f height; ~haltung f carriage, deportment; k~lich a physical; ~pflege f personal hygiene; ~schaft f corporation; ~teil m part of the body.

Korps [ko:r] nt -, - (Mil) corps; students' club.

korpulent [kɔrpu'lɛnt] a corpulent.

korrekt [kɔ'rɛkt] a correct; K~heit f correctness; K~or m proofreader; K~ur [-'tu:r] f (eines Textes) proofreading; (Text) proof; (Sch) marking, correction.

Korrespond- [kɔrespɔnd] cpd: ~ent(in f) [-'dɛnt(ɪn)] m correspondent; ~enz [-'dɛnts] f correspondence; k~ieren [-'di:rən] vi correspond.

Korridor ['korido:r] m -s, -e corridor.

korrigieren [kɔri'gi:rən] vt correct.

korrumpieren [kɔrum'pi:rən] vt corrupt.

Korruption [kɔruptsi'o:n] f corruption.

Korsett [kɔr'zɛt] nt -(e)s, -e corset.

Kose- ['ko:zə] cpd: ~form f pet form; k~n vt caress; vi bill and coo; ~name m pet name; ~wort nt term of endearment.

Kosmetik [kɔs'me:tɪk] f cosmetics pl; ~erin f beautician.

kosmetisch a cosmetic; Chirurgie plastic.

kosmisch ['kɔsmɪʃ] a cosmic.

Kosmo- [kɔsmo] cpd: ~naut [-'naut] m -en, -en cosmonaut; ~polit [-po'li:t] m -en, -en cosmopolitan; k~politisch [-po'li:tɪʃ] a cosmopolitan; ~s m - cosmos.

Kost [kɔst] f - (Nahrung) food; (Verpflegung) board; k~bar a precious; (teuer) costly, expensive; ~barkeit f preciousness; costliness, expensiveness; (Wertstück) valuable; ~en pl cost(s); (Ausgaben) expenses pl; auf ~ von at the expense of; k~en vt cost; vti (versuchen) taste; ~enanschlag m estimate; k~enlos a free (of charge); ~geld nt board.

köstlich ['kœstlɪç] a precious; Einfall delightful; Essen delicious; sich ~ amüsieren have a marvellous time.

Kost- cpd: ~probe f taste; (fig) sample; k~spielig a expensive.

Kostüm [kɔs'ty:m] nt -s, -e costume; (Damen—) suit; ~fest nt fancy-dress party; k~ieren [kɔsty'mi:rən] vtr dress up; ~verleih m costume agency.

Kot [ko:t] m -(e)s excrement.

Kotelett [kotə'lɛt] nt -(e)s, -e or -s cutlet, chop; ~en pl sideboards pl.

Köter ['kø:tər] m -s, - cur.

Kotflügel m (Aut) wing.

Krabbe ['krabə] f -, -n shrimp; k~ln vi crawl.

Krach [krax] m -(e)s, -s or -e crash; (andauernd) noise; (col: Streit) quarrel, row; k~en vi crash; (beim Brechen) crack; vr (col) row, quarrel.

krächzen ['krɛçtsən] vi croak.

Kraft [kraft] f -, ⁻e strength, power, force; (Arbeits—) worker; in ~ treten come into effect; k~ prep +gen by virtue of; ~ausdruck m swearword; ~fahrer m motor driver; ~fahrzeug nt motor vehicle; ~fahrzeugbrief m logbook; ~fahrzeugsteuer f ≈ road tax.

kräftig ['krɛftɪç] a strong; ~en [krɛftɪgən] vt strengthen.

Kraft- cpd: k~los a weak; powerless; (Jur) invalid; ~probe f trial of strength; ~rad nt motorcycle; k~voll a vigorous;

~wagen m motor vehicle; **~werk** nt power station.

Kragen ['kra:gən] m **-s, -** collar; **~weite** f collar size.

Krähe ['krɛ:ə] f **-, -n** crow; **k~n** vi crow.

krakeelen [kra'ke:lən] vi (col) make a din.

Kralle ['kralə] f **-, -n** claw; (Vogel—) talon; **k~n** vt clutch; (krampfhaft) claw.

Kram [kra:m] m **-(e)s** stuff, rubbish; **k~en** vi rummage; **~laden** m (pej) small shop.

Krampf [krampf] m **-(e)s, ¨e** cramp; (zuckend) spasm; **~ader** f varicose vein; **k~haft** a convulsive; (fig) Versuche desperate.

Kran [kra:n] m **-(e)s, ¨e** crane; (Wasser—) tap.

Kranich ['kra:nɪç] m **-s, -e** (Zool) crane.

krank [kraŋk] a ill, sick; **K~e(r)** mf sick person; invalid, patient.

kränkeln ['krɛŋkəln] vi be in bad health.

kranken ['kraŋkən] vi: **an etw** (dat) **~** (fig) suffer from sth.

kränken ['krɛŋkən] vt hurt.

Kranken- cpd: **~bericht** m medical report; **~geld** nt sick pay; **~haus** nt hospital; **~kasse** f health insurance; **~pfleger** m nursing orderly; **~schwester** f nurse; **~versicherung** f health insurance; **~wagen** m ambulance.

Krank- cpd: **k~haft** a diseased; Angst etc morbid; **~heit** f illness, disease; **~heitserreger** m disease-carrying agent.

kränk- ['krɛŋk] cpd: **~lich** a sickly; **K~ung** f insult, offence.

Kranz [krants] m **-es, ¨e** wreath, garland.

Kränzchen ['krɛntsçən] nt small wreath; ladies' party.

Krapfen ['krapfən] m **-s, -** fritter; (Berliner) doughnut.

kraß [kras] a crass.

Krater ['kra:tər] m **-s, -** crater.

Kratz- ['krats] cpd: **~bürste** f (fig) crosspatch; **k~en** vti scratch; **~er** m **-s, -** scratch; (Werkzeug) scraper.

Kraul(schwimmen) ['kraul(ʃvimən)] nt **-s** crawl; **k~en** vi (schwimmen) do the crawl; vt (streicheln) tickle.

kraus [kraus] a crinkly; Haar frizzy; Stirn wrinkled; **K~e** ['krauzə] f **-, -n** frill, ruffle.

kräuseln ['krɔyzəln] vt Haar make frizzy; Stoff gather; Stirn wrinkle; vr (Haar) go frizzy; (Stirn) wrinkle; (Wasser) ripple.

Kraut [kraut] nt **-(e)s, Kräuter** plant; (Gewürz) herb; (Gemüse) cabbage.

Krawall [kra'val] m **-s, -e** row, uproar.

Krawatte [kra'vatə] f **-, -n** tie.

kreativ [krea'ti:f] a creative.

Kreatur [krea'tu:r] f creature.

Krebs [kre:ps] m **-es, -e** crab; (Med, Astrol) cancer.

Kredit [kre'di:t] m **-(e)s, -e** credit.

Kreide ['kraidə] f **-, -n** chalk; **k~bleich** a as white as a sheet.

Kreis [krais] m **-es, -e** circle; (Stadt— etc) district; **im ~ gehen** (lit, fig) go round in circles.

kreischen ['kraiʃən] vi shriek, screech.

Kreis- cpd: **~el** ['kraizəl] m **-s, -** top; (Verkehrs—) roundabout; **k~en** ['kraizən] vi spin; **k~förmig** a circular; **~lauf** m (Physiol) circulation; (fig: der Natur etc) cycle; **~säge** f circular saw; **~stadt** f county town; **~verkehr** m roundabout traffic.

Kreißsaal ['krais-za:l] m delivery room.

Krem [kre:m] f **-, -s** cream, mousse.

Krematorium [krema'to:riʊm] nt crematorium.

Krempe ['krɛmpə] f **-, -n** brim; **~l** m **-s** (col) rubbish.

krepieren [kre'pi:rən] vi (col: sterben) die, kick the bucket.

Krepp [krɛp] m **-s, -s** or **-e** crepe; **~papier** nt crepe paper; **~sohle** f crepe sole.

Kresse ['krɛsə] f **-, -n** cress.

Kreuz [krɔyts] nt **-es, -e** cross; (Anat) small of the back; (Cards) clubs; **k~en** vtr cross; vi (Naut) cruise; **~er** m **-s, -** (Schiff) cruiser; **~fahrt** f cruise; **~feuer** nt (fig) **im ~feuer stehen** be caught in the crossfire; **~gang** m cloisters pl; **k~igen** vt crucify; **~igung** f crucifixion; **~otter** f adder; **~ung** f (Verkehrs—) crossing, junction; (Züchten) cross; **~verhör** nt cross-examination; **~weg** m crossroads; (Rel) Way of the Cross; **~worträtsel** nt crossword puzzle; **~zeichen** nt sign of the cross; **~zug** m crusade.

Kriech- ['kri:ç] cpd: **k~en** vi irreg crawl, creep; (pej) grovel, crawl; **~er** m **-s, -** crawler; **~spur** f crawler lane; **~tier** nt reptile.

Krieg [kri:k] m **-(e)s, -e** war; **k~en** ['kri:gən] vt (col) get; **~er** m **-s, -** warrior; **k~erisch** a warlike; **~führung** f warfare; **~sbemalung** f war paint; **~serklärung** f declaration of war; **~sfuß** m: **mit jdm/etw auf ~sfuß stehen** be at loggerheads with sb/not get on with sth; **~sgefangene(r)** m prisoner of war; **~sgefangenschaft** f captivity; **~sgericht** nt court-martial; **~sschiff** nt warship; **~sschuld** f war guilt; **~sverbrecher** m war criminal; **~sversehrte(r)** m person disabled in the war; **~szustand** m state of war.

Krimi ['kri:mi] m **-s, -s** (col) thriller; **k~nal** ['-na:l] a criminal; **~'nalbeamte(r)** m detective; **~nali'tät** f criminality; **~'nalpolizei** f detective force, CID (Brit); **~'nalroman** m detective story; **k~nell** [-'nɛl] a criminal; **~'nelle(r)** m criminal.

Krippe ['krɪpə] f **-, -n** manger, crib; (Kinder—) crèche.

Krise ['kri:zə] f **-, -n** crisis; **k~ln** vi: **es kriselt** there's a crisis; **~nherd** m trouble spot.

Kristall [krɪs'tal] m **-s, -e** crystal; nt **-s** (Glas) crystal.

Kriterium [kri'te:riʊm] nt criterion.

Kritik [kri'ti:k] f criticism; (Zeitungs—) review, write-up; **~er** ['kri:tikər] m **-s, -** critic; **k~los** a uncritical.

kritisch ['kri:tiʃ] a critical.

kritisieren [kriti'zi:rən] vti criticize.

kritteln ['krɪtəln] *vi* find fault, carp.
kritzeln ['krɪtsəln] *vti* scribble, scrawl.
Krokodil [kroko'diːl] *nt* -**s**, -**e** crocodile.
Krokus ['kroːkus] *m* -, - *or* -**se** crocus.
Krone ['kroːnə] *f* -, -**n** crown; (*Baum*—) top.
krönen ['kröːnən] *vt* crown.
Kron- *cpd:* ~**korken** *m* bottle top; ~**leuchter** *m* chandelier; ~**prinz** *m* crown prince.
Krönung ['kröːnʊŋ] *f* coronation.
Kropf [krɔpf] *m* -(**e**)**s**, ⁻**e** (*Med*) goitre; (*im Vogel*) crop.
Kröte ['kröːtə] *f* -, -**n** toad.
Krücke ['krʏkə] *f* -, -**n** crutch.
Krug [kruːk] *m* -(**e**)**s**, ⁻**e** jug; (*Bier*—) mug.
Krümel ['kryːməl] *m* -**s**, - crumb; **k**~**n** *vti* crumble.
krumm [krʊm] *a* (*lit, fig*) crooked; (*kurvig*) curved; ~**beinig** *a* bandy-legged.
krümm- ['krʏm] *cpd:* ~**en** *vtr* curve, bend; **K**~**ung** *f* bend, curve.
krumm- *cpd:* ~**lachen** *vr* (*col*) laugh o.s. silly; ~**nehmen** *vt irreg* (*col*) **jdm etw** ~ **nehmen** take sth amiss.
Krüppel ['krʏpəl] *m* -**s**, - cripple.
Kruste ['krustə] *f* -, -**n** crust.
Kruzifix [krutsi'fɪks] *nt* -**es**, -**e** crucifix.
Kübel ['kyːbəl] *m* -**s**, - tub; (*Eimer*) pail.
Küche ['kʏçə] *f* -, -**n** kitchen; (*Kochen*) cooking, cuisine.
Kuchen ['kuːxən] *m* -**s**, - cake; ~**blech** *nt* baking tray; ~**form** *f* baking tin; ~**gabel** *f* pastry fork; ~ **teig** *m* cake mixture.
Küchen- *cpd:* ~**herd** *m* range; (*Gas, Elec*) cooker, stove; ~**schabe** *f* cockroach; ~**nschrank** *m* kitchen cabinet.
Kuckuck ['kukuk] *m* -**s**, -**e** cuckoo.
Kufe ['kuːfə] *f* -, -**n** (*Faß*) vat; (*Schlitten*—) runner; (*Aviat*) skid.
Kugel ['kuːgəl] *f* -, -**n** ball; (*Math*) sphere; (*Mil*) bullet; (*Erd*—) globe; (*Sport*) shot; **k**~**förmig** *a* spherical; ~**lager** *nt* ball bearing; **k**~**n** *vt* roll; (*Sport*) bowl; *vr* (*vor Lachen*) double up; **k**~**rund** *a* (*Gegenstand*) round; (*col*) *Person* tubby; ~**schreiber** *m* ball-point (pen), biro ®; **k**~**sicher** *a* bulletproof; ~**stoßen** *nt* -**s** shot-put.
Kuh [kuː] *f* -, ⁻**e** cow.
kühl [kyːl] *a* (*lit, fig*) cool; **K**~**anlage** *f* refrigerating plant; **K**~**e** *f* - coolness; ~**en** *vt* cool; **K**~**er** *m* -**s**, - (*Aut*) radiator; **K**~**erhaube** (*Aut*) bonnet, hood (*US*); **K**~**raum** *m* cold-storage chamber; **K**~**schrank** *m* refrigerator; **K**~**truhe** *f* freezer; **K**~**ung** *f* cooling; **K**~**wagen** *m* (*Rail*) refrigerator van; **K**~**wasser** *nt* cooling water.
kühn [kyːn] *a* bold, daring; **K**~**heit** *f* boldness.
Küken ['kyːkən] *nt* -**s**, - chicken.
kulant [ku'lant] *a* obliging.
Kuli [ku'liː] *m* -**s**, -**s** coolie; (*col: Kugelschreiber*) biro ®.
Kulisse [ku'lɪsə] *f* -, -**n** scene.
kullern ['kulərn] *vi* roll.
Kult [kult] *m* -(**e**)**s**, -**e** worship, cult; **mit etw** ~ **treiben** make a cult out of sth; **k**~**ivieren** [-i'viːrən] *vt* cultivate;

k~**iviert** *a* cultivated, refined; ~**ur** [kul'tuːr] *f* culture; civilization; (*das Boden*) cultivation; **k**~**urell** [-u'rɛl] *a* cultural; ~**urfilm** *m* documentary film.
Kümmel ['kyməl] *m* -**s**, - caraway seed; (*Branntwein*) kümmel.
Kummer ['kumər] *m* -**s** grief, sorrow.
kümmer- ['kymər] *cpd:* ~**lich** *a* miserable, wretched; ~**n** *vr:* **sich um jdn** ~ **n** look after sb; *jdn um etw* ~ **n** see to sth; *vt* concern; **das kümmert mich nicht** that doesn't worry me.
Kumpan [kum'paːn] *m* -**s**, -**e** mate; (*pej*) accomplice.
Kumpel ['kumpəl] *m* -**s**, - (*col*) mate.
kündbar ['kʏntbaːr] *a* redeemable, recallable; *Vertrag* terminable.
Kunde ['kundə] *m* -**n**, -**n**, **Kundin** *f* customer; *f* -, -**n** (*Botschaft*) news; ~**ndienst** *m* after-sales service.
Kund- *cpd:* ~**gabe** *f* announcement; **k**~**geben** *vt irreg* announce; ~**gebung** *f* announcement; (*Versammlung*) rally; **k**~**ig** *a* expert, experienced.
Künd- ['kʏnd] *cpd:* **k**~**igen** *vi* give in one's notice; **jdm k**~**igen** give sb his notice; *vt* cancel; (**jdm**) **die Stellung/Wohnung** ~ give (sb) notice; ~**igung** *f* notice; ~**igungsfrist** *f* period of notice.
Kundschaft *f* customers *pl*, clientele.
künftig ['kʏnftɪç] *a* future; *ad* in future.
Kunst [kunst] *f* -, ⁻**e** art; (*Können*) skill; **das ist doch keine** ~ it's easy; ~**akademie** *f* academy of art; ~**dünger** *m* artificial manure; ~**faser** *f* synthetic fibre; ~**fertigkeit** *f* skilfulness; ~**geschichte** *f* history of art; ~**gewerbe** *nt* arts and crafts *pl*; ~**griff** *m* trick, knack; ~**händler** *m* art dealer; ~**harz** *nt* artificial resin.
Künstler(in *f*) ['kʏnstlər(ɪn)] *m* -**s**, - artist; **k**~**isch** *a* artistic; ~**name** *m* stagename; pseudonym.
künstlich ['kʏnstlɪç] *a* artificial.
Kunst- *cpd:* ~**sammler** *m* -**s**, - art collector; ~**seide** *f* artificial silk; ~**stoff** *m* synthetic material; ~**stopfen** *nt* -**s** invisible mending; ~**stück** *nt* trick; ~**turnen** *nt* gymnastics; **k**~**voll** *a* ingenious, artistic; ~**werk** *nt* work of art.
kunterbunt ['kuntərbunt] *a* higgledy-piggledy.
Kupfer ['kupfər] *nt* -**s**, - copper; ~**geld** *nt* coppers *pl*; **k**~**n** *a* copper; ~**stich** *m* copperplate engraving.
Kuppe ['kupə] *f* -, -**n** (*Berg*—) top; (*Finger*—) tip; ~**l** *f* -, -**n** cupola, dome; ~**'lei** *f* (*Jur*) procuring; **k**~**ln** *vi* (*Jur*) procure; (*Aut*) declutch; *vt* join.
Kupp- ['kup] *cpd:* ~**ler** *m* -**s**, - pimp; ~**lerin** *f* matchmaker; ~**lung** *f* coupling; (*Aut*) clutch.
Kur [kuːr] *f* -, -**en** cure, treatment.
Kür [kyːr] *f* -, -**en** (*Sport*) free skating/exercises *pl*.
Kurbel ['kurbəl] *f* -, -**n** crank, winch; (*Aut*) starting handle; ~**welle** *f* crankshaft.
Kürbis ['kʏrbɪs] *m* -**ses**, -**se** pumpkin; (*exotisch*) gourd.
Kur- ['kuːr] *cpd:* ~**gast** *m* visitor (to a

health resort); **k~ieren** [kuˈriːrən] vt cure; **k~ios** [kuriˈoːs] a curious, odd; **~iosiˈtät** f curiosity; **~ort** m health resort; **~pfuscher** m quack.

Kurs [kʊrs] m -es, -e course; (Fin) rate; **hoch im ~ stehen** (fig) be highly thought of; **~buch** nt timetable; **k~ieren** [kʊrˈziːrən] vi circulate; **k~iv** ad in italics; **~ive** [kʊrˈziːvə] f -, -n italics pl; **~us** [ˈkʊrzʊs] m -, **Kurse** course; **~wagen** m (Rail) through carriage.

Kurve [ˈkʊrvə] f -, -n curve; (Straßen— auch) bend; **k~nreich, kurvig** a Straße bendy.

kurz [kʊrts] a short; **zu ~ kommen** come off badly; **den eren ziehen** get the worst of it; **K~arbeit** f short-time work; **~ärm(e)lig** a short-sleeved.

Kürze [ˈkʏrtsə] f -, -n shortness, brevity; **k~n** vt cut short; (in der Länge) shorten; Gehalt reduce.

kurz- cpd: **~erhand** ad on the spot; **K~fassung** f shortened version; **~fristig** a short-term; **~gefaßt** a concise; **K~geschichte** f short story; **~halten** vt irreg keep short; **~lebig** a shortlived.

kürzlich [ˈkʏrtslɪç] ad lately, recently.

Kurz- cpd: **~schluß** m (Elec) short circuit; **~schrift** f shorthand; **k~sichtig** a short-sighted; **~welle** f shortwave.

kuscheln [ˈkʊʃəln] vr snuggle up.

Kusine [kuˈziːnə] f cousin.

Kuß [kʊs] m -sses, ˙sse kiss.

küssen [ˈkʏsən] vtr kiss.

Küste [ˈkʏstə] f -, -n coast, shore; **~nwache** f coastguard (station).

Küster [ˈkʏstər] m -s, - sexton, verger.

Kutsche [ˈkʊtʃə] f -, -n coach, carriage; **~r** m -s, - coachman.

Kutte [ˈkʊtə] f -, -n cowl.

Kuvert [kuˈvert] nt -s, -e or -s envelope; cover.

Kybernetik [kybɛrˈneːtɪk] f cybernetics.

kybernetisch [kybɛrˈneːtɪʃ] a cybernetic.

L

L, l [ɛl] nt L, l.

laben [ˈlaːbən] vtr refresh (o.s.); (fig) relish (an etw dat) sth).

Labor [laˈboːr] nt -s, -e or -s lab; **~ant(in** f) [laboˈrant(ɪn)] m lab(oratory) assistant; **~atorium** [laboraˈtoːriʊm] nt laboratory.

Labyrinth [labyˈrɪnt] nt -s, -e labyrinth.

Lache [ˈlaxə] f -, -n (Wasser) pool, puddle; (col: Gelächter) laugh.

lächeln [ˈlɛçəln] vi smile; **L~** nt -s smile.

lachen [ˈlaxən] vi laugh.

lächerlich [ˈlɛçərlɪç] a ridiculous; **L~keit** f absurdity.

Lach- cpd: **~gas** nt laughing gas; **l~haft** a laughable.

Lachs [laks] m -es, -e salmon.

Lack [lak] m -(e)s, -e lacquer, varnish; (von Auto) paint; **l~ieren** [laˈkiːrən] vt varnish; Auto spray; **~ierer** [laˈkiːrər] m -s, - varnisher; **~leder** nt patent leather.

Lackmus [ˈlakmʊs] m or nt - litmus.

Lade [ˈlaːdə] f -, -n box, chest; **~baum** m derrick; **~fähigkeit** f load capacity.

laden [ˈlaːdən] vt irreg Lasten load; (Jur) summon; (einladen) invite.

Laden [ˈlaːdən] m -s, ˙ shop; (Fenster—) shutter; **~besitzer** m shopkeeper; **~dieb** m shoplifter; **~diebstahl** m shoplifting; **~hüter** m -s, - unsaleable item; **~preis** m retail price; **~schluß** m closing time; **~tisch** m counter.

Laderaum m (Naut) hold.

Ladung [ˈlaːdʊŋ] f (Last) cargo, load; (Beladen) loading; (Jur) summons; (Einladung) invitation; (Spreng—) charge.

Lage [ˈlaːgə] f -, -n position, situation; (Schicht) layer; **in der ~ sein** be in a position; **l~nweise** ad in layers.

Lager [ˈlaːgər] nt -s, - camp; (Comm) warehouse; (Schlaf—) bed; (von Tier) lair; (Tech) bearing; **~arbeiter(in** f) m storehand; **~bestand** m stocks pl; **~geld** nt storage (charges pl); **~haus** nt warehouse, store.

lagern [ˈlaːgərn] vi (Dinge) be stored; (Menschen) camp; (auch vr: rasten) lie down; vt store; (betten) lay down; Maschine bed.

Lager- cpd: **~schuppen** m store shed; **~stätte** f resting place; **~ung** f storage.

Lagune [laˈguːnə] f -, -n lagoon.

lahm [laːm] a lame; **~en** vi be lame, limp.

lähmen [ˈlɛːmən] vt paralyse.

lahmlegen vt paralyse.

Lähmung f paralysis.

Laib [laɪp] m -s, -e loaf.

Laich [laɪç] m -(e)s, -e spawn; **l~en** vi spawn.

Laie [ˈlaɪə] m -n, -n layman; **l~nhaft** a amateurish.

Lakai [laˈkaɪ] m -en, -en lackey.

Laken [ˈlaːkən] nt -s, - sheet.

Lakritze [laˈkrɪtsə] f -, -n liquorice.

lallen [ˈlalən] vti slur; (Baby) babble.

Lamelle [laˈmɛlə] f lamella; (Elec) lamina; (Tech) plate.

lamentieren [lamɛnˈtiːrən] vi lament.

Lametta [laˈmɛta] nt -s tinsel.

Lamm [lam] nt -(e)s, ˙er lamb; **~fell** nt lambskin; **l~fromm** a like a lamb; **~wolle** f lambswool.

Lampe [ˈlampə] f -, -n lamp; **~nfieber** nt stage fright; **~nschirm** m lampshade.

Lampion [lãpiˈõ] m -s, -s Chinese lantern.

Land [lant] nt -(e)s, ˙er land; (Nation, nicht Stadt) country; (Bundes—) state; **auf dem ~(e)** in the country; **~arbeiter** m farm or agricultural worker; **~besitz** m landed property; **~besitzer** m landowner; **~ebahn** f runway; **l~einwärts** ad inland; **l~en** [ˈlandən] vti land.

Ländereien [lɛndəˈraɪən] pl estates pl.

Landes- [ˈlandəs] cpd: **~farben** pl national colours pl; **~innere(s)** nt inland region; **~tracht** f national costume; **l~üblich** a customary; **~verrat** m high treason; **~verweisung** f banishment; **~währung** f national currency.

Land- cpd: **~gut** nt estate; **~haus** nt

country house; ~**karte** f map; ~**kreis** m
administrative region; **l~läufig** a
customary.

ländlich ['lentlıç] a rural.

Land- cpd: ~**schaft** f countryside; (Art)
landscape; **l~schaftlich** a scenic;
regional; ~**smann** m, ~**smännin** f, pl
-**sleute** compatriot, fellow countryman or
countrywoman; ~**straße** f country road;
~**streicher** m -**s**, - tramp; ~**strich** m
region; ~**tag** m (Pol) regional parliament.

Landung ['landʊŋ] f landing; ~**sboot** nt
landing craft; ~**sbrücke** f jetty, pier;
~**sstelle** f landing place.

Land- cpd: ~**vermesser** m surveyor;
~**wirt** m farmer; ~**wirtschaft** f agriculture; ~**zunge** f spit.

lang [laŋ] a long; Mensch tall; ~**atmig** a
long-winded; ~**e** ad for a long time;
dauern, brauchen a long time.

Länge ['leŋə] f -, -**n** length; (Geog) longitude; ~**ngrad** m longitude; ~**nmaß** nt
linear measure.

langen ['laŋən] vi (ausreichen) do, suffice;
(fassen) reach (nach for); **es langt mir**
I've had enough.

lang- cpd: **L~eweile** f boredom; ~**lebig** a
a long-lived.

länglich a longish.

lang- cpd: **L~mut** f forbearance,
patience; ~**mütig** a forbearing.

längs [leŋs] prep +gen or dat along; ad
lengthwise.

lang- cpd: ~**sam** a slow; **L~samkeit** f
slowness; **L~schläfer(in** f) m late riser;
L~spielplatte f long-playing record.

längst ['leŋst] ad **das ist ~ fertig** that
was finished a long time ago, that has
been finished for a long time; ~**e(r,s)** a
longest.

lang- cpd: ~**weilig** a boring, tedious;
L~welle f long wave; ~**wierig** a
lengthy, long-drawn-out.

Lanze ['lantsə] f -, -**n** lance.

Lanzette [lan'tsetə] f lancet.

lapidar [lapi'daːr] a terse, pithy.

Lappalie [la'paːliə] f trifle.

Lappen ['lapən] m -**s**, - cloth, rag; (Anat)
lobe.

läppisch ['lepıʃ] a foolish.

Lapsus ['lapsʊs] m -, - slip.

Lärche ['lerçə] f -, -**n** larch.

Lärm [lerm] m -(e)s noise; **l~en** vi be
noisy, make a noise.

Larve ['larfə] f -, -**n** mask; (Biol) larva.

lasch [laʃ] a slack; Geschmack tasteless.

Lasche ['laʃə] f -, -**n** (Schuh-) tongue; (Rail)
fishplate.

Laser ['leızə] m -**s**, - laser.

lassen ['lasən] vti irreg leave; (erlauben)
let; (aufhören mit) stop; (veranlassen)
make; **etw machen** ~ to have sth done;
es läßt sich machen it can be done; **es
läßt sich öffnen** it can be opened, it
opens.

lässig ['lesıç] a casual; **L~keit** f
casualness.

läßlich ['lesliç] a pardonable, venial.

Last [last] f -, -**en** load, burden; (Naut,
Aviat) cargo; (usu pl: Gebühr) charge; **jdm
zur ~ fallen** be a burden to sb; ~**auto** nt
lorry, truck; **l~en** vi (auf +dat) weigh on.

Laster ['lastər] nt -**s**, - vice.

Lästerer ['lestərər] m -**s**, - mocker;
(Gottes—) blasphemer.

lasterhaft a immoral.

lästerlich a scandalous.

lästern ['lestərn] vti Gott blaspheme;
(schlecht sprechen) mock.

Lästerung f jibe; (Gottes—) blasphemy.

lästig ['lestıç] a troublesome, tiresome.

Last- cpd: ~**kahn** m barge; ~**kraft-
wagen** m heavy goods vehicle; ~**schrift**
f debiting; debit item; ~**tier** nt beast of
burden; ~**träger** m porter; ~**wagen** m
lorry, truck.

latent [la'tent] a latent.

Laterne [la'ternə] f -, -**n** lantern;
(Straßen—) lamp, light; ~**npfahl** m lamp-
post.

Latrine [la'triːnə] f latrine.

Latsche ['latʃə] f -, -**n** dwarf pine; **l~n**
['laːtʃən] vi (col) (gehen) wander, go;
(lässig) slouch.

Latte ['latə] f -, -**n** lath; (Sport) goalpost;
(quer) crossbar; ~**nzaun** m lattice fence.

Latz [lats] m -**es**, -ˀe bib; (Hosen—) flies pl.

Lätzchen ['letsçən] nt bib.

Latzhose f dungarees pl.

lau [lau] a Nacht balmy; Wasser lukewarm.

Laub [laup] nt -(e)s foliage; ~**baum** m
deciduous tree; ~**e** f ['laubə] f -, -**n** arbour;
~**frosch** m tree frog; ~**säge** f fretsaw.

Lauch [laux] m -(e)s, -**e** leek.

Lauer ['lauər] f: **auf der ~ sein** or
liegen, l~n vi lie in wait; (Gefahr) lurk.

Lauf [lauf] m -(e)s, **Läufe** run; (Wett—)
race; (Entwicklung, Astron) course;
(Gewehr) barrel; **einer Sache ihren ~
lassen** let sth take its course; ~**bahn** f
career; ~**bursche** m errand boy.

laufen ['laufən] vti irreg run; (col: gehen)
walk; ~**d** a running; Monat, Ausgaben
current; **auf dem ~den sein/halten**
be/keep up to date; **am ~den Band** (fig)
continuously; ~ **lassen** vt irreg leave
running; ~**lassen** vt irreg Person let go.

Läufer ['lɔyfər] m -**s**, - (Teppich, Sport)
runner; (Fußball) half-back; (Schach)
bishop.

Lauf- cpd: ~**kundschaft** f passing trade;
~**masche** f run, ladder (Brit); **im
~schritt** at a run; ~**stall** m playpen;
~**steg** m dais; ~**zettel** m circular.

Lauge ['laugə] f -, -**n** soapy water; (Chem)
alkaline solution.

Laune ['launə] f -, -**n** mood, humour;
(Einfall) caprice; (schlechte) temper;
l~nhaft a capricious, changeable.

launisch a moody; bad-tempered.

Laus [laus] f, **Läuse** louse; ~**bub** m
rascal, imp.

lauschen ['lauʃən] vi eavesdrop, listen in.

lauschig ['lauʃıç] a snug.

lausen ['lauzən] vt delouse.

laut [laut] a loud; ad loudly; lesen aloud;

prep +*gen or dat* according to; **L~** *m*
-**(e)s**, -**e** sound.

Laute ['lautə] *f -*, -**n** lute.

lauten ['lautən] *vi* say; (*Urteil*) be.

läuten ['lɔytən] *vti* ring, sound.

lauter ['lautər] *a Wasser* clear, pure;
Wahrheit, Charakter honest; *inv Freude,
Dummheit etc* sheer; (*mit pl*) nothing but,
only; **L~keit** *f* purity; honesty, integrity.

läutern ['lɔytərn] *vt* purify.

Läuterung *f* purification.

laut- *cpd:* ~**hals** *ad* at the top of one's
voice; ~**los** *a* noiseless, silent; ~**malend**
a onomatopoeic; **L~schrift** *f* phonetics
pl; **L~sprecher** *m* loudspeaker;
L~sprecherwagen *m* loudspeaker van;
~**stark** *a* vociferous; **L~stärke** *f* (*Rad*)
volume.

lauwarm ['lauvarm] *a* (*lit, fig*) lukewarm.

Lava ['la:va] *f-*, **Laven** lava.

Lavendel [la'vɛndəl] *m* -**s**, - lavender.

Lawine [la'vi:nə] *f* avalanche; ~**ngefahr** *f*
danger of avalanches.

lax [laks] *a* lax.

Lazarett [latsa'rɛt] *nt* -**(e)s**, -**e** (*Mil*)
hospital, infirmary.

Lebe- *cpd:* ~**hoch** *nt* three cheers *pl*;
~**mann** *m*, *pl* -**männer** man about
town.

leben ['le:bən] *vti* live; **L~** *nt* -**s**, - life; ~**d**
a living; ~**dig** [le'bɛndɪç] *a* living, alive;
(*lebhaft*) lively; **L~digkeit** *f* liveliness.

Lebens- *cpd:* ~**alter** *nt* age; ~**art** *f* way
of life; ~**erwartung** *f* life expectancy;
l~fähig *a* able to live; **l~froh** *a* full of
the joys of life; ~**gefahr** *f:* ~**gefahr!**
danger!; **in** ~**gefahr** dangerously ill;
l~gefährlich *a* dangerous; *Verletzung*
critical; ~**haltungskosten** *pl* cost of
living *sing*; ~**jahr** *nt* year of life; ~**lage** *f*
situation in life; ~**lauf** *m* curriculum
vitae; **l~lustig** *a* cheerful, lively;
~**mittel** *pl* food *sing*; ~**mittelgeschäft**
nt grocer's; **l~müde** *a* tired of life;
~**retter** *m* lifesaver; ~**standard** *m*
standard of living; ~**stellung** *f*
permanent post; ~**unterhalt** *m* livelihood; ~**versicherung** *f* life insurance;
~**wandel** *m* way of life; ~**weise** *f* way of
life, habits *pl*; ~**zeichen** *nt* sign of life;
~**zeit** *f* lifetime.

Leber ['le:bər] *f -*, -**n** liver; ~**fleck** *m*
mole; ~**tran** *m* cod-liver oil; ~**wurst** *f*
liver sausage.

Lebe- *cpd:* ~**wesen** *nt* creature; ~**wohl**
nt farewell, goodbye.

leb- ['le:p] *cpd:* ~**haft** *a* lively, vivacious;
L~haftigkeit *f* liveliness, vivacity;
L~kuchen *m* gingerbread; ~**los** *a* life-
less.

lechzen ['lɛçtsən] *vi:* **nach etw** ~ long for
sth.

leck [lɛk] *a* leaky, leaking; **L~** *nt* -**(e)s**, -**e**
leak; ~**en** *vi* (*Loch haben*) leak; *vti*
(*schlecken*) lick.

lecker ['lɛkər] *a* delicious, tasty;
L~bissen *m* dainty morsel; **L~maul** *nt:*
ein L~maul sein enjoy one's food.

Leder ['le:dər] *nt* -**s**, - leather; **l~n** *a*
leather; ~**waren** *pl* leather goods *pl*.

ledig ['le:dɪç] *a* single; **einer Sache** ~
sein be free of sth; ~**lich** *ad* merely,
solely.

leer [le:r] *a* empty; vacant; **L~e** *f* - empti-
ness; ~**en** *vt* empty; *vr* become empty;
L~gewicht *nt* weight when empty;
L~lauf *m* neutral; ~**stehend** *a* empty;
L~ung *f* emptying; (*Post*) collection.

legal [le'ga:l] *a* legal, lawful; ~**i'sieren** *vt*
legalize; **L~i'tät** *f* legality.

legen ['le:gən] *vt* lay, put, place; *Ei* lay; *vr*
lie down; (*fig*) subside.

Legende [le'gɛndə] *f-*, -**n** legend.

leger [le'ʒɛ:r] *a* casual.

legieren [le'gi:rən] *vt* alloy.

Legierung *f* alloy.

Legislative [legisla'ti:və] *f* legislature.

legitim [legi'ti:m] *a* legitimate; **L~ation**
[-atsi'o:n] *f* legitimation; ~**ieren** [-'mi:rən]
vt legitimate; *vr* prove one's identity;
L~i'tät *f* legitimacy.

Lehm [le:m] *m* -**(e)s**, -**e** loam; **l~ig** *a*
loamy.

Lehne ['le:nə] *f -*, -**n** arm; back; **l~n** *vtr*
lean.

Lehnstuhl *m* armchair.

Lehr- *cpd:* ~**amt** *nt* teaching profession;
~**brief** *m* indentures *pl*; ~**buch** *nt* text-
book.

Lehre ['le:rə] *f -*, -**n** teaching, doctrine;
(*beruflich*) apprenticeship; (*moralisch*)
lesson; (*Tech*) gauge; **l~n** *vt* teach; ~**r(in**
f) *m* -**s**, - teacher.

Lehr- *cpd:* ~**gang** *m* course; ~**jahre** *pl*
apprenticeship; ~**kraft** *f* teacher; ~**ling**
m apprentice; ~**plan** *m* syllabus;
l~reich *a* instructive; ~**satz** *m* proposition; ~**stelle** *f* apprenticeship; ~**stuhl**
m chair; ~**zeit** *f* apprenticeship.

Leib [laip] *m* -**(e)s**, -**er** body; **halt ihn
mir vom** ~! keep him away from me;
~**eserziehung** ['laibəs-] *f* physical
education; ~**esübung** *f* physical exercise;
l~haftig *a* personified; *Teufel* incarnate;
l~lich *a* bodily; *Vater etc* own; ~**wache** *f*
bodyguard.

Leiche ['laiçə] *f -*, -**n** corpse;
~**nbeschauer** *m* -**s**, - doctor who makes
out death certificate; ~**nhemd** *nt* shroud;
~**nträger** *m* bearer; ~**nwagen** *m*
hearse.

Leichnam ['laiçna:m] *m* -**(e)s**, -**e** corpse.

leicht [laiçt] *a* light; (*einfach*) easy;
L~athletik *f* athletics *sing*; ~**fallen** *vi
irreg:* **jdm** ~**fallen** be easy for sb;
~**fertig** *a* frivolous; ~**gläubig** *a* gullible,
credulous; **L~gläubigkeit** *f* gullibility,
credulity; ~**hin** *ad* lightly; **L~igkeit** *f*
easiness; **mit L~igkeit** with ease;
~**lebig** *a* easy-going; ~**machen** *vt:* **es
sich** (*dat*) ~**machen** make things easy
for oneself; ~**nehmen** *vt irreg* take
lightly; **L~sinn** *m* carelessness; ~**sinnig**
a careless.

Leid [lait] *nt* -**(e)s** grief, sorrow; **l~** *a:*
etw l~ haben *or* **sein** be tired of sth; **es
tut mir/ihm l~** I am/he is sorry; **er/das
tut mir l~** I am sorry for him/it; **l~en**
['laidən] *irreg vt* suffer; (*erlauben*) permit;
jdn/etw nicht l~en können not be able

to stand sb/sth; *vi* suffer; ~**en** *nt* -s, -
suffering; (*Krankheit*) complaint; ~**en-
schaft** *f* passion; **l**~**enschaftlich** *a*
passionate.
leider ['laɪdər] *ad* unfortunately; **ja,** ~ yes,
I'm afraid so; ~ **nicht** I'm afraid not.
leidig ['laɪdɪç] *a* miserable, tiresome.
leidlich *a* tolerable; *ad* tolerably.
Leid- *cpd:* ~**tragende(r)** *mf* bereaved;
(*Benachteiligter*) one who suffers;
~**wesen** *nt:* **zu jds** ~**wesen** to sb's
dismay.
Leier ['laɪər] *f* -, -**n** lyre; (*fig*) old story;
~**kasten** *m* barrel organ; **l**~**n** *vti* **Kurbel**
turn; (*col*) *Gedicht* rattle off.
Leihbibliothek *f* lending library.
leihen ['laɪən] *vt irreg* lend; **sich** (*dat*) **etw**
~ borrow sth.
Leih- *cpd:* ~**gebühr** *f* hire charge;
~**haus** *nt* pawnshop; ~**schein** *m* pawn
ticket; (*Buch*— *etc*) borrowing slip;
~**wagen** *m* hired car.
Leim [laɪm] *m* -(**e)s,** -**e** glue; **l**~**en** *vt*
glue.
Leine ['laɪnə] *f* -, -**n** line, cord; (*Hunde*—)
leash, lead; ~**n** *nt* -**s,** - linen; **l**~**n** *a* linen.
Lein- *cpd:* ~**tuch** *nt* (*Bett*—) sheet; linen
cloth; ~**wand** *f* (*Art*) canvas; (*Cine*)
screen.
leise ['laɪzə] *a* quiet; (*sanft*) soft, gentle.
Leiste ['laɪstə] *f* -, -**n** ledge; (*Zier*—) strip;
(*Anat*) groin.
leisten ['laɪstən] *vt Arbeit* do; *Gesellschaft*
keep; *Ersatz* supply; (*vollbringen*) achieve;
sich (*dat*) **etw** ~ **können** be able to
afford sth.
Leistung *f* performance; (*gute*) achievement; ~**sdruck** *m* pressure; **l**~**sfähig** *a*
efficient; ~**sfähigkeit** *f* efficiency;
~**szulage** *f* productivity bonus.
Leit- *cpd:* ~**artikel** *m* leading article;
~**bild** *nt* model.
leiten ['laɪtən] *vt* lead; *Firma* manage; (*in
eine Richtung*) direct; (*Elec*) conduct.
Leiter ['laɪtər] *m* -s, - leader, head; (*Elec*)
conductor; *f* -, -**n** ladder.
Leit- *cpd:* ~**faden** *m* guide; ~**fähigkeit** *f*
conductivity; ~**motiv** *nt* leitmotiv;
~**planke** *f* -, -**n** crash barrier.
Leitung *f* (*Führung*) direction; (*Cine, Theat
etc*) production; (*von Firma*) management;
directors *pl*; (*Wasser*—) pipe; (*Kabel*)
cable; **eine lange** ~ **haben** be slow on
the uptake; ~**sdraht** *m* wire; ~**smast** *m*
telegraph pole; ~**srohr** *nt* pipe;
~**swasser** *nt* tap water.
Lektion [lɛktsi'oːn] *f* lesson.
Lektor(in *f*) *m* ['lɛktɔr(ɪn)] (*Univ*) lector;
(*Verlag*) editor.
Lektüre [lɛk'tyːrə] *f* -, -**n** (*Lesen*) reading;
(*Lesestoff*) reading matter.
Lende ['lɛndə] *f* -, -**n** loin; ~**nbraten** *m*
roast sirloin; ~**nstück** *nt* fillet.
lenk- ['lɛŋk] *cpd:* ~**bar** *a Fahrzeug* steer-
able; *Kind* manageable; ~**en** *vt* steer; *Kind*
guide; *Blick, Aufmerksamkeit* direct (*auf
+acc* at); **L**~**rad** *nt* steering wheel;
L~**stange** *f* handlebars *pl*.
Lenz [lɛnts] *m* -**es,** -**e** (*liter*) spring.
Leopard [leo'part] *m* -**en,** -**en** leopard.

Lepra ['leːpra] *f*- leprosy.
Lerche ['lɛrçə] *f* -, -**n** lark.
lern- [lɛrn] *cpd:* ~**begierig** *a* eager to
learn; ~**en** *vt* learn.
lesbar ['leːsbaːr] *a* legible.
Lesbierin ['lɛsbiərɪn] *f* lesbian.
lesbisch ['lɛsbɪʃ] *a* lesbian.
Lese ['leːzə] *f* -, -**n** gleaning; (*Wein*)
harvest; ~**buch** *nt* reading book, reader;
l~**n** *vti irreg* read; (*ernten*) gather, pick;
~**r(in** *f*) *m* -**s,** - reader; ~**rbrief** *m*
reader's letter; ~**rlich** *a* legible; ~**saal**
m reading room; ~**zeichen** *nt* bookmark.
Lesung ['leːzʊŋ] *f* (*Parl*) reading; (*Eccl*)
lesson.
letzte(r, s) ['lɛtstə(r,z)] *a* last; (*neueste*)
latest; **zum** ~**nmal** *ad* for the last time;
~**ns** *ad* lately; ~**re(r,s)** *a* latter.
Leuchte ['lɔʏçtə] *f* -, -**n** lamp, light; **l**~**n**
vi shine, gleam; ~**r** *m* -**s,** - candlestick.
Leucht- *cpd:* ~**farbe** *f* fluorescent colour;
~**feuer** *nt* beacon; ~**käfer** *m* glow-
worm; ~**kugel** *f*, ~**rakete** *f* flare;
~**reklame** *f* neon sign; ~**röhre** *f* strip
light; ~**turm** *m* lighthouse; ~**zifferblatt**
nt luminous dial.
leugnen ['lɔʏgnən] *vti* deny.
Leugnung *f* denial.
Leukämie [lɔʏkɛ'miː] *f* leukaemia.
Leukoplast[Ⓡ] [lɔʏko'plast] *nt* -(**e)s,** -**e**
elastoplast Ⓡ.
Leumund ['lɔʏmʊnt] *m* -(**e)s,** -**e**
reputation; ~**szeugnis** *nt* character
reference.
Leute ['lɔʏtə] *pl* people *pl*.
Leutnant ['lɔʏtnant] *m* -**s,** -**s** *or* -**e**
lieutenant.
leutselig ['lɔʏtzeːlɪç] *a* affable; **L**~**keit** *f*
affability.
Lexikon ['lɛksikɔn] *nt* -**s,** **Lexiken** *or*
Lexika dictionary.
Libelle [li'bɛlə] *f* -, -**n** dragonfly; (*Tech*)
spirit level.
liberal [libe'raːl] *a* liberal; **L**~**ismus**
[libera'lɪsmʊs] *m* liberalism.
Libero ['liːbero] *m* -**s,** -**s** (*Fußball*)
sweeper.
Licht [lɪçt] *nt* -(**e)s,** -**er** light; **l**~ *a* light,
bright; ~**bild** *nt* photograph; (*Dia*) slide;
~**blick** *m* cheering prospect; **l**~
empfindlich *a* sensitive to light; **l**~**en**
vt clear; *Anker* weigh; *vr* clear up; (*Haar*)
thin; **l**~**erloh** *ad:* **l**~**erloh brennen**
blaze; ~**hupe** *f* flashing of headlights;
~**jahr** *nt* light year; ~**maschine** *f*
dynamo; ~**meß** *f* - Candlemas;
~**schalter** *m* light switch.
Lichtung *f* clearing, glade.
Lid [liːt] *nt* -(**e)s,** -**er** eyelid; ~**schatten**
m eyeshadow.
lieb [liːp] *a* dear; ~**äugeln** *vi insep* ogle
(*mit jdm/etw* sb/sth).
Liebe ['liːbə] *f* -, -**n** love; **l**~**bedürftig** *a:*
l~**bedürftig sein** need love; ~**lei** *f*
flirtation; **l**~**n** *vt* love; like; **l**~**nswert** *a*
loveable; **l**~**nswürdig** *a* kind;
l~**nswürdigerweise** *ad* kindly;
~**nswürdigkeit** *f* kindness.
lieber ['liːbər] *ad* rather, preferably; **ich**

gehe ~ **nicht** I'd rather not go; *see* **gern, lieb.**

Liebes- *cpd:* ~**brief** *m* love letter; ~**dienst** *m* good turn; ~**kummer** *m:* ~**kummer haben be** lovesick; ~**paar** *nt* courting couple, lovers *pl.*

liebevoll a loving.

lieb- ['li:p] *cpd:* ~**gewinnen** *vt irreg* get fond of; ~**haben** *vt irreg* be fond of; **L**~**haber** *m -s,* - lover; **L**~**habe'rei** *f* hobby; ~**kosen** [li:p'ko:zən] *vt insep* caress; ~**lich** a lovely, charming; **L**~**ling** *m* darling; **L**~**lings-** *in cpds* favourite; ~**los** a unloving; **L**~**schaft** *f* love affair.

Lied [li:t] *nt* **-(e)s, -er** song; *(Eccl)* hymn; ~**erbuch** *nt* songbook; hymn book.

liederlich ['li:dərlɪç] a slovenly; *Lebenswandel* loose, immoral; **L**~**keit** *f* slovenliness; immorality.

Lieferant [li:fə'rant] *m* supplier.

liefern ['li:fərn] *vt* deliver; *(versorgen mit)* supply; *Beweis* produce.

Liefer- *cpd:* ~**schein** *m* delivery note; ~**termin** *m* delivery date; ~**ung** *f* delivery; supply; ~**wagen** *m* van.

Liege ['li:gə] *f* **-, -n** bed.

liegen ['li:gən] *vi irreg* lie; *(sich befinden)* be; **mir liegt nichts/viel daran** it doesn't matter to me/it matters a lot to me; **es liegt bei Ihnen, ob . . .** it rests with you whether . . .; **Sprachen** ~ **mir nicht** languages are not my line; **woran liegt es?** what's the cause?; ~**bleiben** *vi irreg (Person)* stay in bed; stay lying down; *(Ding)* be left (behind); ~**lassen** *vt irreg (vergessen)* leave behind; **L**~**schaft** *f* real estate.

Liege- *cpd:* ~**sitz** *m (Aut)* reclining seat; ~**stuhl** *m* deck chair; ~**wagen** *m (Rail)* couchette.

Lift [lɪft] *m* **-(e)s, -e** or **-s** lift.

Likör [li'kø:r] *m* **-s, -e** liqueur.

lila ['li:la] a purple, lilac; **L**~ *nt* **-s, -s** *(Farbe)* purple, lilac.

Lilie ['li:liə] *f* lily.

Limonade [limo'na:də] *f* lemonade.

lind [lɪnt] a gentle, mild; **L**~**e** ['lɪndə] *f* **-, -n** lime tree, linden; ~**ern** *vt* alleviate, soothe; **L**~**erung** *f* alleviation; ~**grün** a lime green.

Lineal [line'a:l] *nt* **-s, -e** ruler.

Linie ['li:niə] *f* line; ~**nblatt** *nt* ruled sheet; ~**nflug** *m* scheduled flight; ~**nrichter** *m* linesman.

linieren [lini'i:rən] *vt* line.

Linke ['lɪŋkə] *f* **-, -n** left side; left hand; *(Pol)* left; **l**~**(r,s)** a left; **l**~ **Masche** purl.

linkisch a awkward, gauche.

links [lɪŋks] ad left; to *or* on the left; ~ **von mir** on *or* to my left; **L**~**außen** [lɪŋks'ausən] *m -s,* - *(Sport)* outside left; **L**~**händer(in** *f)* *m* **-s,** - left-handed person; **L**~**kurve** *f* left-hand bend; **L**~**verkehr** *m* traffic on the left.

Linoleum [li'no:leum] *nt* **-s** lino(leum).

Linse ['lɪnzə] *f* **-, -n** lentil; *(optisch)* lens.

Lippe ['lɪpə] *f* **-, -n** lip; ~**nstift** *m* lipstick.

liquidieren [likvi'di:rən] *vt* liquidate.

lispeln ['lɪspəln] *vi* lisp.

List [lɪst] *f* **-, -en** cunning; trick, ruse.

Liste ['lɪstə] *f* **-, -n** list.

listig ['lɪstɪç] a cunning, sly.

Litanei [lita'nai] *f* litany.

Liter ['li:tər] *m or nt* **-s,** - litre.

literarisch [lite'ra:rɪʃ] a literary.

Literatur [litera'tu:r] *f* literature; ~**preis** *m* award for literature.

Litfaßsäule ['lɪtfaszɔylə] *f* advertising pillar.

Lithographie [litogra'fi:] *f* lithography.

Liturgie [litur'gi:] *f* liturgy.

liturgisch [li'turgɪʃ] a liturgical.

Litze ['lɪtsə] *f* **-, -n** braid; *(Elec)* flex.

live [laif] ad *(Rad, TV)* live.

Livree [li'vre:] *f* **-, -n** livery.

Lizenz [li'tsɛnts] *f* licence.

Lkw [ɛlka:'ve:] *m* **Lastkraftwagen**

Lob [lo:p] *nt* **-(e)s** praise; **l**~**en** ['lo:bən] *vt* praise; **l**~**enswert** a praiseworthy.

löblich ['lø:plɪç] a praiseworthy, laudable.

Lobrede *f* eulogy.

Loch [lɔx] *nt* **-(e)s,** ⁻**er** hole; **l**~**en** *vt* punch holes in; ~**er** *m -s,* - punch.

löcherig ['lœçərɪç] a full of holes.

Loch- *cpd:* ~**karte** *f* punch card; ~**streifen** *m* punch tape.

Locke ['lɔkə] *f* **-, -n** lock, curl; **l**~**n** *vt* entice; *Haare* curl; ~**nwickler** *m -s,* - curler.

locker ['lɔkər] a loose; ~**lassen** *vi irreg:* **nicht** ~**lassen** not let up; ~**n** *vt* loosen.

lockig ['lɔkɪç] a curly.

Lock- *cpd:* ~**ruf** *m* call; ~**ung** *f* enticement; ~**vogel** *m* decoy, bait.

Lodenmantel ['lo:dənmantəl] *m* thick woollen coat.

lodern ['lo:dərn] *vi* blaze.

Löffel ['lœfəl] *m -s,* - spoon; **l**~**n** *vt* (eat with a) spoon; **l**~**weise** ad by spoonfuls.

Logarithmentafel [loga'rɪtmənta:fəl] *f* log(arithm) tables *pl.*

Logarithmus [loga'rɪtmus] *m* logarithm.

Loge ['lo:ʒə] *f* **-, -n** *(Theat)* box; *(Freimaurer)* *(masonic)* lodge; *(Pförtner—)* office.

logieren [lo'ʒi:rən] *vi* lodge, stay.

Logik ['lo:gɪk] *f* logic.

logisch ['lo:gɪʃ] a logical.

Lohn [lo:n] *m* **-(e)s,** ⁻**e** reward; *(Arbeits—)* pay, wages *pl;* ~**büro** *nt* wages office; ~**empfänger** *m* wage earner.

lohnen ['lo:nən] *vt (liter)* reward *(jdm etw sb for sth); vr impers* be worth it; ~**d** a worthwhile.

Lohn- *cpd:* ~**steuer** *f* income tax; ~**streifen** *m* pay slip; ~**tüte** *f* pay packet.

lokal [lo'ka:l] a local; **L**~ *nt* **-(e)s, -e** pub(lic house); **l**~**isieren** *vt* localize; **L**~**i'sierung** *f* localization.

Lokomotive [lokomo'ti:və] *f* **-, -n** locomotive.

Lokomotivführer *m* engine driver.

Lorbeer ['lɔrbe:r] *m* **-s, -en** *(lit, fig)* laurel; ~**blatt** *nt (Cook)* bay leaf.

Lore ['lo:rə] *f* **-, -n** *(Min)* truck.

Los [lo:s] *nt* **-es, -e** *(Schicksal)* lot, fate; lottery ticket.

los [lo:s] a loose; ~**!** go on!; **etw** ~ **sein** be rid of sth; **was ist** ~**?** what's the matter?; **dort ist nichts/viel** ~ there's nothing/a lot going on there; **etw** ~ **haben** (col) be clever; ~ **binden** vt irreg untie.

löschen ['lœʃən] vt Feuer, Licht put out, extinguish; Durst quench; (Comm) cancel; Tonband erase; Fracht unload; vi (Feuerwehr) put out a fire; (Papier) blot.

Lösch- cpd: ~**fahrzeug** nt fire engine; fire boat; ~**gerät** nt fire extinguisher; ~**papier** nt blotting paper; ~**ung** f extinguishing; (Comm) cancellation; (Fracht) unloading.

lose ['lo:zə] a loose.

Lösegeld nt ransom.

losen ['lo:zən] vi draw lots.

lösen ['lø:zən] vt loosen; Rätsel etc solve; Verlobung call off; (Chem) dissolve; Partnerschaft break up; Fahrkarte buy; vr (aufgehen) come loose; (Zucker etc) dissolve; (Problem, Schwierigkeit) (re)solve itself.

los- cpd: ~**fahren** vi irreg leave; ~**gehen** vi irreg set out; (anfangen) start; (Bombe) go off; **auf jdn** ~ **gehen** go for sb; ~**kaufen** vt Gefangene, Geißeln pay ransom for; ~**kommen** vi irreg: **von etw** ~ **kommen** get away from sth; ~**lassen** vt irreg Seil let go of; Schimpfe let loose; ~**laufen** vi irreg run off.

löslich ['lø:slɪç] a soluble; **L**~**keit** f solubility.

los- cpd: ~**lösen** vtr free; ~**machen** vt loosen; Boot unmoor; vr get free; ~**sagen** vr renounce (von jdm/etw sb/sth); ~**schrauben** vt unscrew; ~**sprechen** vt irreg absolve.

Losung ['lo:zʊŋ] f watchword, slogan.

Lösung ['lø:zʊŋ] f (Lockermachen) loosening; (eines Rätsels, Chem) solution; ~**smittel** nt solvent.

los- cpd: ~**werden** vt irreg get rid of; ~**ziehen** vi irreg (sich aufmachen) set out; **gegen jdn** ~ **ziehen** run sb down.

Lot [lo:t] nt **-(e)s, -e** plummet; **im** ~ vertical; (fig) on an even keel; **l**~**en** vti plumb, sound.

löten ['lø:tən] vt solder.

Lötkolben m soldering iron.

Lotse ['lo:tsə] m **-n, -n** pilot; (Aviat) air traffic controller; see **Schüler**~; **l**~**n** vt pilot; (col) lure.

Lotterie [lɔtə'ri:] f lottery.

Löwe ['lø:və] m **-n, -n** lion; (Astrol) Leo; ~**nanteil** m lion's share; ~**nmaul** nt snapdragon; ~**nzahn** m dandelion.

Löwin ['lø:vɪn] f lioness.

loyal [loa'ja:l] a loyal; **L**~**i'tät** f loyalty.

Luchs ['lʊks] m **-es, -e** lynx.

Lücke ['lʏkə] f **-, -n** gap; ~**nbüßer** m **-s, -** stopgap; **l**~**nhaft** a defective, full of gaps; **l**~**nlos** a complete.

Luder ['lu:dər] nt **-s, -** (pej: Frau) hussy; (bedauernswert) poor wretch.

Luft [lʊft] f **-, ⸚e** air; (Atem) breath; **in der** ~ **liegen** be in the air; **jdn wie** ~ **behandeln** ignore sb; ~**angriff** m air raid; ~**ballon** m balloon; ~**blase** f air

bubble; **l**~**dicht** a airtight; ~**druck** m atmospheric pressure.

lüften ['lʏftən] vti air; Hut lift, raise.

Luft- cpd: ~**fahrt** f aviation; **l**~**gekühlt** a air-cooled; **l**~**ig** a Ort breezy; Raum airy; Kleider summery; ~**kissenfahrzeug** nt hovercraft; ~**krieg** m war in the air; aerial warfare; ~**kurort** m health resort; **l**~**leer** a: ~**leerer Raum** vacuum; ~**linie** f: **in der** ~**linie** as the crow flies; ~**loch** nt air-hole; (Aviat) air-pocket; ~**matratze** f lilo ®, air mattress; ~**pirat** m hijacker; ~**post** f airmail; ~**röhre** f (Anat) wind pipe; ~**schlange** f streamer; ~**schutz** m anti-aircraft defence; ~**schutzkeller** m air-raid shelter; ~**sprung** m: (fig) **einen** ~**sprung machen** jump for joy.

Lüftung ['lʏftʊŋ] f ventilation.

Luft- cpd: ~**verkehr** m air traffic; ~**waffe** f air force; ~**zug** m draught.

Lüge ['ly:gə] f **-, -n** lie; **jdn/etw** ~**n strafen** give the lie to sb/sth; **l**~**n** vi irreg lie.

Lügner(in f) m **-s, -** liar.

Luke ['lu:kə] f **-, -n** dormer window, hatch.

Lümmel ['lʏməl] m **-s, -** lout; **l**~**n** vr lounge (about).

Lump [lʊmp] m **-en, -en** scamp, rascal.

Lumpen ['lʊmpən] m **-s, -** rag; **sich nicht l**~ **lassen** not be mean.

lumpig ['lʊmpɪç] a shabby.

Lunge ['lʊŋə] f **-, -n** lung; ~**nentzündung** f pneumonia; **l**~**nkrank** a consumptive.

lungern ['lʊŋərn] vi hang about.

Lunte ['lʊntə] f **-, -n** fuse; ~ **riechen** smell a rat.

Lupe ['lu:pə] f **-, -n** magnifying glass; **unter die** ~ **nehmen** (fig) scrutinize.

Lupine [lu'pi:nə] f lupin.

Lust [lʊst] f **-, ⸚e** joy, delight; (Neigung) desire; ~ **haben zu** or **auf etw** (acc)/**etw zu tun** feel like sth/doing sth.

lüstern ['lʏstərn] a lustful, lecherous.

Lustgefühl nt pleasurable feeling.

lustig ['lʊstɪç] a (komisch) amusing, funny; (fröhlich) cheerful.

Lüstling m lecher.

Lust- cpd: **l**~**los** a unenthusiastic; ~**mord** m sex(ual) murder; ~**spiel** nt comedy; **l**~**wandeln** vi stroll about.

lutschen ['lʊtʃən] vti suck; **am Daumen** ~ suck one's thumb.

Lutscher m **-s, -** lollipop.

luxuriös [lʊksuri'ø:s] a luxurious.

Luxus ['lʊksʊs] m **-** luxury; ~**artikel** pl luxury goods pl; ~**hotel** nt luxury hotel; ~**steuer** f tax on luxuries.

Lymphe ['lʏmfə] f **-, -n** lymph.

lynchen ['lʏnçən] vt lynch.

Lyrik ['ly:rɪk] f lyric poetry; ~**er** m **-s, -** lyric poet.

lyrisch ['ly:rɪʃ] a lyrical.

M

M, m [ɛm] nt M, m.

Mach- [max] cpd: ~**art** f make; **m**~**bar** a feasible; ~**e** f **-** (col) show, sham;

m~en *vt* make; (*tun*) do; (*col: reparieren*) fix; (*betragen*) be; **das macht nichts** that doesn't matter; **mach's gut!** good luck!; *vr* m~en set about sth; *vi:* **in etw** (*dat*) m~en (*Comm*) be *or* deal in sth.

Macht [maxt] *f* -s, ·e power; ~haber *m* -s, - ruler.

mächtig ['mɛçtıç] *a* powerful, mighty; (*col: ungeheuer*) enormous.

Macht- *cpd:* m~los *a* powerless; ~probe *f* trial of strength; ~stellung *f* position of power; ~wort *nt:* **ein** ~wort **sprechen** lay down the law.

Machwerk *nt* work; (*schlechte Arbeit*) botched-up job.

Mädchen ['mɛ:tçən] *nt* girl; m~haft *a* girlish; ~name *m* maiden name.

Made ['ma:də] *f* -, -n maggot.

madig ['ma:dıç] *a* maggoty; **jdm etw** ~ **machen** spoil sth for sb.

Magazin [maga'tsi:n] *nt* -s, -e magazine.

Magd [ma:kt] *f* -, ·e maid(servant).

Magen ['ma:gən] *m* -s, - *or* · stomach; ~schmerzen *pl* stomachache.

mager ['ma:gər] *a* lean; (*dünn*) thin; M~keit *f* leanness; thinness.

Magie [ma'gi:] *f* magic; ~r ['ma:giər] *m* -s, - magician.

magisch ['ma:gıʃ] *a* magical.

Magnet [ma'gne:t] *m* -s *or* -en, -en magnet; m~isch *a* magnetic; m~i-'sieren *vt* magnetize; ~nadel *f* magnetic needle.

Mahagoni [maha'go:ni] *nt* -s mahogany.

mähen ['mɛ:ən] *vti* mow.

Mahl [ma:l] *nt* -(e)s, -e meal; m~en *vt* irreg. grind; ~stein *m* grindstone; ~zeit *f* meal; *interj* enjoy your meal.

Mahnbrief *m* reminder.

Mähne ['mɛ:nə] *f* -, -n mane.

Mahn- [ma:n] *cpd:* m~en *vt* remind; (*warnend*) warn; (*wegen Schuld*) demand payment from; ~ung *f* reminder; admonition, warning.

Mähre ['mɛ:rə] *f* -, -n mare.

Mai [maı] *m* -(e)s, -e May; ~glöckchen *nt* lily of the valley; ~käfer *m* cockchafer.

Mais [maıs] *m* -es, -e maize, corn (*US*); ~kolben *m* corncob.

Majestät [majɛs'tɛ:t] *f* majesty; m~isch *a* majestic.

Major [ma'jo:r] *m* -s, -e (*Mil*) major; (*Aviat*) squadron leader.

Majoran [majo'ra:n] *m* -s, -e marjoram.

makaber [ma'ka:bər] *a* macabre.

Makel ['ma:kəl] *m* -s, - blemish; (*moralisch*) stain; m~los *a* immaculate, spotless.

mäkeln ['mɛ:kəln] *vi* find fault.

Makkaroni [maka'ro:ni] *pl* macaroni *sing.*

Makler ['ma:klər] *m* -s, - broker.

Makrele [ma'kre:lə] *f* -, -n mackerel.

Makrone [ma'kro:nə] *f* -, -n macaroon.

Mal [ma:l] *nt* -(e)s, -e mark, sign; (*Zeitpunkt*) time; m~ *ad* times, (*col*) see **einmal**; **-m~** *suff* -times; m~en *vti* paint; ~er *m* -s, - painter; ~e'rei *f*

painting; m~erisch *a* picturesque; ~kasten *m* paintbox; m~nehmen *vti* multiply.

Malz [malts] *nt* -es malt; ~bonbon *nt* cough drop; ~kaffee *m* malt coffee.

Mama ['mama:] *f* -, -s, **Mami** ['mami] *f* -, -s (*col*) mum(my).

Mammut ['mamut] *nt* -s, -e *or* -s irreg mammoth.

man [man] *pron* one, people *pl*, you.

manche(r,s) ['mançə(r,z)] *a* many a; (*pl*) a number of; *pron* some; ~rlei *a inv* various; *pron* a variety of things.

manchmal *ad* sometimes.

Mandant(in *f*) [man'dant(ın)] *m* (*Jur*) client.

Mandarine [manda'ri:nə] *f* mandarin, tangerine.

Mandat [man'da:t] *nt* -(e)s, -e mandate.

Mandel ['mandəl] *f* -, -n almond; (*Anat*) tonsil.

Manege [ma'ne:ʒə] *f* -, -n ring, arena.

Mangel ['maŋəl] *f* -, -n mangle; *m* -s, · lack; (*Knappheit*) shortage (*an* +*dat* of); (*Fehler*) defect, fault; ~erscheinung *f* deficiency symptom; m~haft *a* poor; (*fehlerhaft*) defective, faulty; m~n *vi impers:* **es mangelt jdm an etw** (*dat*) sb lacks sth; *vt Wäsche* mangle; m~s *prep* +*gen* for lack of.

Manie [ma'ni:] *f* mania.

Manier [ma'ni:r] *f* - manner; style; (*pej*) mannerism; ~en *pl* manners *pl*; m~iert [mani'ri:rt] *a* mannered, affected; m~lich *a* well-mannered.

Manifest [mani'fɛst] *nt* -es, -e manifesto.

Maniküre [mani'ky:rə] *f* -, -n manicure; m~n *vt* manicure.

manipulieren [manipu'li:rən] *vt* manipulate.

Manko ['maŋko] *nt* -s, -s deficiency; (*Comm*) deficit.

Mann [man] *m* -(e)s, ·er man; (*Ehe—*) husband; (*Naut*) hand; **seinen** ~ **stehen** hold one's own.

Männchen ['mɛnçən] *nt* little man; (*Tier*) male.

Mannequin [manə'kɛ̃:] *nt* -s, -s fashion model.

mannigfaltig ['manıçfaltıç] *a* various, varied; M~keit *f* variety.

männlich ['mɛnlıç] *a* (*Biol*) male; (*fig, Gram*) masculine.

Mann- *cpd:* ~schaft *f* (*Sport, fig*) team; (*Naut, Aviat*) crew; (*Mil*) other ranks *pl*; ~sleute *pl* (*col*) menfolk *pl*; ~weib *nt* (*pej*) mannish woman.

Manöver [ma'nø:vər] *nt* -s, - manoeuvre.

manövrieren [manø'vri:rən] *vti* manoeuvre.

Mansarde [man'zardə] *f* -, -n attic.

Manschette [man'ʃɛtə] *f* cuff; (*Papier—*) paper frill; (*Tech*) collar; sleeve; ~knopf *m* cufflink.

Mantel ['mantəl] *m* -s, · coat; (*Tech*) casing, jacket.

Manuskript [manu'skrıpt] *nt* -(e)s, -e manuscript.

Mappe ['mapə] f -, -n briefcase; (Akten—) folder.

Märchen ['mɛːrçən] nt fairy tale; m~haft a fabulous; ~prinz m prince charming.

Marder ['mardər] m -s, - marten.

Margarine [marga'riːnə] f margarine.

Marienkäfer [ma'riːənkɛːfər] m ladybird.

Marine [ma'riːnə] f navy; m~blau a navy-blue.

marinieren [mari'niːrən] vt marinate.

Marionette [mario'nɛtə] f puppet.

Mark [mark] f -, - (Münze) mark; nt -(e)s (Knochen—) marrow; durch ~ und Bein gehen go right through sb; m~ant [mar'kant] a striking.

Marke ['markə] f -, -n mark; (Warensorte) brand; (Fabrikat) make; (Rabatt—, Brief—) stamp; (Essens—) ticket; (aus Metall etc) token, disc.

Mark- cpd: ~ieren [mar'kiːrən] vt mark; vti (col) act; ~ierung f marking; m~ig ['makiç] a (fig) pithy; ~ise [mar'kiːzə] f -, -n awning; ~stück nt one-mark piece.

Markt [markt] m -(e)s, ¨e market; ~forschung f market research; ~platz m market place; ~wirtschaft f market economy.

Marmelade [marmə'laːdə] f -, -n jam.

Marmor ['marmɔr] m -s, -e marble; m~ieren [-'riːrən] vt marble; m~n a marble.

Marone [ma'roːnə] f -, -n or **Maroni** chestnut.

Marotte [ma'rɔtə] f -, -n fad, quirk.

Marsch [marʃ] m -(e)s, ¨e march; m~ interj march; f -, -en marsh; ~befehl m marching orders pl; m~bereit a ready to move; m~ieren [mar'ʃiːrən] vi march.

Marter ['martər] f -, -n torment; m~n vt torture.

Märtyrer(in f) ['mɛrtyrər(ın)] m -s, - martyr.

März [mɛrts] m -(es), -e March.

Marzipan [martsi'paːn] nt -s, -e marzipan.

Masche ['maʃə] f -, -n mesh; (Strick—) stitch; das ist die neueste ~ that's the latest dodge; ~ndraht m wire mesh; m~nfest a runproof.

Maschine [ma'ʃiːnə] f machine; (Motor) engine; m~ll [maʃi'nɛl] a machine(-); mechanical; ~nbauer m mechanical engineer; ~ngewehr nt machine gun; ~npistole f submachine gun; ~nschaden m mechanical fault; ~nschlosser m fitter; ~nschrift f typescript; m~schreiben vi irreg type.

Maschinist [maʃi'nıst] m engineer.

Maser ['maːzər] f -, -n grain; speckle; ~n pl (Med) measles sing; ~ung f grain(ing).

Maske ['maskə] f -, -n mask; ~nball m fancy-dress ball; ~rade [-'raːdə] f masquerade.

maskieren [mas'kiːrən] vt mask; (verkleiden) dress up; vr disguise o.s., dress up.

Maß [maːs] nt -es, -e measure; (Mäßigung) moderation; (Grad) degree, extent; f -, -(e) litre of beer.

Massage [ma'saːʒə] f -, -n massage.

Maß- cpd: ~anzug m made-to-measure suit; ~arbeit f (fig) neat piece of work.

Masse ['masə] f -, -n mass; ~nartikel m mass-produced article; ~ngrab nt mass grave; m~nhaft a loads of; ~nmedien pl mass media pl.

Mass- cpd: ~eur [ma'søːr] m masseur; ~euse [ma'søːzə] f masseuse.

maß- cpd: ~gebend a authoritative; ~halten vi irreg exercise moderation.

massieren [ma'siːrən] vt massage; (Mil) mass.

massig ['masıç] a massive; (col) massive amount of.

mäßig ['mɛːsıç] a moderate; ~en ['mɛːsıgən] vt restrain, moderate; M~keit f moderation.

massiv [ma'siːf] a solid; (fig) heavy, rough; M~ nt -s, -e massif.

Maß- cpd: ~krug m tankard; m~los a extreme; ~nahme f -, -n measure, step; m~regeln vt insep reprimand; ~stab m rule, measure; (fig) standard; (Geog) scale; m~voll a moderate.

Mast ['mast] m -(e)s, -e(n) mast; (Elec) pylon.

mästen ['mɛstən] vt fatten.

Material [materi'aːl] nt -s, -ien material(s); ~fehler m material defect; ~ismus [-'lismus] m materialism; ~ist [-'lıst] m materialist; m~istisch [-'lıstıʃ] a materialistic.

Materie [ma'teːriə] f matter, substance; m~ll [materi'ɛl] a material.

Mathematik [matema'tiːk] f mathematics sing; ~er(in f) [mate'maːtikər(ın)] m -s, - mathematician.

mathematisch [mate'maːtıʃ] a mathematical.

Matratze [ma'tratsə] f -, -n mattress.

Matrize [ma'triːtsə] f -, -n matrix; (zum Abziehen) stencil.

Matrose [ma'troːzə] m -n, -n sailor.

Matsch [matʃ] m -(e)s mud; (Schnee—) slush; m~ig a muddy; slushy.

matt [mat] a weak; (glanzlos) dull; (Phot) matt; (Schach) mate.

Matte ['matə] f -, -n mat.

Matt- cpd: ~igkeit f weakness; dullness; ~scheibe f (TV) screen; ~scheibe haben (col) be not quite with it.

Mauer ['mauər] f -, -n wall; m~n vti build; lay bricks; ~werk nt brickwork; (Stein) masonry.

Maul [maul] nt -(e)s, Mäuler mouth; m~en vi (col) grumble; ~esel m mule; ~korb m muzzle; ~sperre f lockjaw; ~tier nt mule; ~wurf m mole; ~wurfshaufen m molehill.

Maurer ['maurər] m -s, - bricklayer.

Maus [maus] f -, Mäuse mouse.

mäuschenstill ['mɔysçən'ʃtıl] a very quiet.

Maus- cpd: ~efalle f mousetrap; m~en vt (col) flinch; vi catch mice; m~ern vr moult; m~(e)tot a stone dead.

maximal [maksi'maːl] a maximum.

Maxime [ma'ksi:mə] f -, -n maxim.

Mayonnaise [majɔ'nɛːzə] f -, -n mayonnaise.

Mechan- [me'ça:n] cpd: ~**ik** f mechanics sing; (Getriebe) mechanics pl; ~**iker** m -s, - mechanic, engineer; **m~isch** a mechanical; **m~i'sieren** vt mechanize; ~**i'sierung** f mechanization; ~**ismus** [meça'nısmʊs] m mechanism.

meckern ['mɛkərn] vi bleat; (col) moan.

Medaille [me'daljə] f -, -n medal.

Medaillon [medal'jõ:] nt -s, -s (Schmuck) locket.

Medikament [medika'mɛnt] nt medicine.

meditieren [medi'ti:rən] vi meditate.

Medizin [medi'tsi:n] f -, -en medicine; **m~isch** a medical.

Meer [me:r] nt -(e)s, -e sea; ~**busen** m bay, gulf; ~**enge** f straits pl; ~**esspiegel** m sea level; ~**rettich** m horseradish; ~**schweinchen** nt guinea-pig.

Megaphon [mega'fo:n] nt -s, -e megaphone.

Mehl ['me:l] nt -(e)s, -e flour; **m~ig** a floury.

mehr [me:r] a,ad more; **M~aufwand** m additional expenditure; ~**deutig** a ambiguous; ~**ere** a several; ~**eres** pron several things; ~**fach** a multiple; (wiederholt) repeated; **M~heit** f majority; ~**malig** a repeated; ~**mals** ad repeatedly; ~**stimmig** a for several voices; ~**stimmig singen** harmonize; **M~wertsteuer** f value added tax, VAT; **M~zahl** f majority; (Gram) plural.

meiden ['maidən] vt irreg avoid.

Meile ['mailə] f -, -n mile; ~**nstein** m milestone; **m~nweit** a for miles.

mein [main] pron my; ~**e(r,s)** mine.

Meineid ['main'ait] m perjury.

meinen ['mainən] vti think; (sagen) say; (sagen wollen) mean; **das will ich** ~ I should think so.

mein- cpd: ~**er** pron gen of ich of me; ~**erseits** ad for my part; ~**esgleichen** pron people like me; ~**etwegen**, ~**etwillen** ad (für mich) for my sake; (wegen mir) on my account; (von mir aus) as far as I'm concerned; I don't care or mind; ~**ige** pron: **der/die/das ~ige** mine.

Meinung ['mainʊŋ] f opinion; **jdm die ~ sagen** give sb a piece of one's mind; ~**saustausch** m exchange of views; ~**sumfrage** f opinion poll; ~**sverschiedenheit** f difference of opinion.

Meise ['maizə] f -, -n tit(mouse).

Meißel ['maisəl] m -s, - chisel; **m~n** vt chisel.

meist ['maist] a,ad most(ly); ~**ens** ad generally, usually.

Meister ['maistər] m -s, - master; (Sport) champion; **m~haft** a masterly; **m~n** vt master; ~**schaft** f mastery; (Sport) championship; ~**stück** nt, ~**werk** nt masterpiece.

Melancholie [melaŋko'li:] f melancholy.

melancholisch [melaŋ'ko:lɪʃ] a melancholy.

Melde- ['mɛldə] cpd: ~**frist** f registration period; **m~n** vt report; vr report (bei to); (Sch) put one's hand up; (freiwillig) volunteer; (auf etw, am Telefon) answer; **sich zu Wort m~n** ask to speak; ~**pflicht** f obligation to register with the police; ~**stelle** f registration office.

Meldung ['mɛldʊŋ] f announcement; (Bericht) report.

meliert [me'li:rt] a mottled, speckled.

melken ['mɛlkən] vt irreg milk.

Melodie [melo'di:] f melody, tune.

melodisch [me'lo:dɪʃ] a melodious, tuneful.

Melone [me'lo:nə] f -, -n melon; (Hut) bowler (hat).

Membran(e) [mɛm'bra:n(ə)] f -, -en (Tech) diaphragm.

Memoiren [memo'a:rən] pl memoirs pl.

Menge ['mɛŋə] f -, -n quantity; (Menschen—) crowd; (große Anzahl) lot (of); **m~n** vt mix; vr: **sich m~n in** (+acc) meddle with; ~**nlehre** f (Math) set theory; ~**nrabatt** m bulk discount.

Mensch [mɛnʃ] m -en, -en human being, man; person; **kein ~** nobody; nt -(e)s, -er hussy; ~**enalter** nt generation; ~**enfeind** m misanthrope; **m~enfreundlich** a philanthropical; ~**enkenner** m -s, - judge of human nature; ~**enliebe** f philanthropy; **m~enmöglich** a humanly possible; ~**enrecht** nt human rights pl; **m~enscheu** a shy; **m~enunwürdig** a degrading; ~**enverstand** m: **gesunder ~enverstand** common sense; ~**heit** f humanity, mankind; **m~lich** a human; (human) humane; ~**lichkeit** f humanity.

Menstruation [mɛnstruatsi'o:n] f menstruation.

Mentalität [mɛntali'tɛ:t] f mentality.

Menü [me'ny:] nt -s, -s menu.

Merk- [mɛrk] cpd: ~**blatt** nt instruction sheet or leaflet; **m~en** vt notice; **sich** (dat) **etw m~en** remember sth; **m~lich** a noticeable; ~**mal** nt sign, characteristic; **m~würdig** a odd.

Meß- [mɛs] cpd: **m~bar** a measurable; ~**becher** m measuring cup; ~**buch** nt missal.

Messe ['mɛsə] f -, -n fair; (Eccl) mass; (Mil) mess; **m~n** irreg vt measure; vr compete; ~**r** nt -s, - knife; ~**rspitze** f knife point; (in Rezept) pinch; ~**stand** m exhibition stand.

Meß- cpd: ~**gerät** nt measuring device, gauge; ~**gewand** nt chasuble.

Messing ['mɛsɪŋ] nt -s brass.

Metall [me'tal] nt -s, -e metal; **m~en**, **m~isch** a metallic.

Metaphysik [metafy'zi:k] f metaphysics sing.

Metastase [meta'sta:zə] f -, -n (Med) secondary growth.

Meteor [mete'o:r] nt -s, -e meteor.

Meter ['me:tər] nt or m -s, - metre; ~**maß** nt tape measure.

Methode [me'to:də] f -, -n method.

methodisch [me'to:dɪʃ] a methodical.

Metropole [metro'po:lə] f -, -n
metropolis.

Metzger ['mɛtsgər] m -s, - butcher; ~ei
[-'raɪ] f butcher's (shop).

Meuchelmord ['mɔʏçəlmɔrt] m
assassination.

Meute ['mɔʏtə] f -, -n pack; ~'rei f
mutiny; ~rer m -s, - mutineer; m~rn vi
mutiny.

miauen [mi'auən] vi miaow.

mich [mɪç] pron acc of **ich** me; myself.

Miene ['mi:nə] f -, -n look, expression.

mies [mi:s] a (col) lousy.

Miet- ['mi:t] cpd: ~**auto** nt hired car; ~e
f -, -n rent; **zur ~e wohnen** live in
rented accommodation; m~en vt rent;
Auto hire; ~er(in f) m -s, - tenant;
~shaus nt tenement, block of flats;
~vertrag m tenancy agreement.

Migräne [mi'grɛ:nə] f -, -n migraine.

Mikro- cpd: ~**be** [mi'kro:bə] f -, -n
microbe; ~**fon**, ~**phon** [mikro'fo:n] nt -s,
-e microphone; ~**skop** [mikro'sko:p] nt -s,
-e microscope; m~**skopisch** a microscopic.

Milch [mɪlç] f - milk; (Fisch~) milt, roe;
~**glas** nt frosted glass; m~**ig** a milky;
~**kaffee** m white coffee; ~**pulver** nt
powdered milk; ~**straße** f Milky Way;
~**zahn** m milk tooth.

mild [mɪlt] a mild; Richter lenient;
(freundlich) kind, charitable; M~e
['mɪldə] f -, -n mildness; leniency; ~ern vt
mitigate, soften; Schmerz alleviate;
~ernde Umstände extenuating circumstances.

Milieu [mili'ø] nt -s, -s background,
environment; m~**geschädigt** a
maladjusted.

Mili- [mili] cpd: m~**tant** [-'tant] a militant;
~**tär** [-'tɛ:r] nt -s military, army; ~-
'**tärgericht** nt military court; m~-
'**tärisch** a military; ~**tarismus**
[-ta'rɪsmus] m militarism; m~ta'**ristisch**
a militaristic; ~**tärpflicht** f
(compulsory) military service.

Milli- ['mɪli] cpd: ~**ardär** [-ar'dɛ:r] m
multimillionaire; ~**arde** [-'ardə] f -, -n
milliard; billion (esp US); ~**meter** m millimetre; ~**on** [-'o:n] f -, -en million; ~**onär**
[-o'nɛ:r] m millionaire.

Milz ['mɪlts] f -, -en spleen.

Mimik ['mi:mɪk] f mime.

Mimose [mi'mo:zə] f -, -n mimosa; (fig)
sensitive person.

minder ['mɪndər] a inferior; ad less;
M~**heit** f minority; ~**jährig** a minor;
M~**jährigkeit** f minority; ~n vtr
decrease, diminish; M~**ung** f decrease;
~**wertig** a inferior; M~**wertigkeits-
gefühl** nt, M~**wertigkeitskomplex** m
inferiority complex.

Mindest- ['mɪndəst] cpd: ~**alter** nt
minimum age; ~**betrag** m minimum
amount; m~e a least; m~**ens, zum**
m~en ad at least; ~**lohn** m minimum
wage; ~**maß** nt minimum.

Mine ['mi:nə] f -, -n mine; (Bleistift~)
lead; (Kugelschreiber~) refill; ~**nfeld** nt
minefield.

Mineral [mine'ra:l] nt -s, -e or -ien
mineral; m~**isch** a mineral; ~**wasser** nt
mineral water.

Miniatur [minia'tu:r] f miniature.

minimal [mini'ma:l] a minimal.

Minister [mi'nɪstər] m -s, - minister;
m~**iell** [minɪsteri'ɛl] a ministerial; ~**ium**
[minɪs'te:riom] nt ministry; ~**präsident**
m prime minister.

minus ['mi:nus] ad minus; M~ nt -, -
deficit; M~**pol** m negative pole;
M~**zeichen** nt minus sign.

Minute [mi'nu:tə] f -, -n minute;
~**nzeiger** m minute hand.

mir [mi:r] pron dat of **ich** (to) me; ~
nichts, dir nichts just like that.

Misch- ['mɪʃ] cpd: ~**ehe** f mixed
marriage; m~**en** vt mix; ~**ling** m half-
caste; ~**ung** f mixture.

Miß- ['mɪs] cpd: m~'**achten** vt insep
disregard; ~'**achtung** f disregard;
~**behagen** nt discomfort, uneasiness;
~**bildung** f deformity; m~'**billigen** vt
insep disapprove of; ~'**billigung** f disapproval; ~**brauch** m abuse; (falscher
Gebrauch) misuse; m~'**brauchen** vt insep
abuse; misuse (zu for); m~'**deuten** vt
insep misinterpret; ~**erfolg** m failure.

Misse- ['mɪsə] cpd: ~**tat** f misdeed;
~**täter(in** f) m criminal; (col) scoundrel.

Miß- cpd: m~'**fallen** vi irreg insep
displease (jdm sb); ~**fallen** nt -s displeasure; ~**geburt** f freak; (fig) abortion;
~**geschick** nt misfortune; m~**glücken**
[mɪs'glʏkən] vi insep fail; jdm m~**glückt
etw** sb does not succeed with sth; ~**griff**
m mistake; ~**gunst** f envy; m~**günstig** a
envious; m~'**handeln** vt insep ill-treat;
~'**handlung** f ill-treatment; ~**helligkeit**
f: ~**helligkeiten haben be** at variance.

Mission [mɪsi'o:n] f mission; ~**ar**
[mɪsio'na:r] m missionary.

Miß- cpd: ~**klang** m discord; ~**kredit** m
discredit; m~**lingen** [mɪs'lɪŋən] vi irreg
insep fail; ~'**lingen** nt -s failure; ~**mut**
nt bad temper; m~**mutig** a cross; m~-
'**raten** vi irreg insep turn out badly; a ill-
bred; ~**stand** m state of affairs; abuse;
~**stimmung** f ill-humour, discord; m~-
'**trauen** vi insep mistrust; ~**trauen** nt -s
distrust, suspicion (of); ~**trauensantrag**
m (Pol) motion of no confidence;
~**trauensvotum** nt -s, -voten (Pol) vote
of no confidence; m~**trauisch** a distrust-
ful, suspicious; ~**verhältnis** nt dis-
proportion; ~**verständnis** nt misunder-
standing; m~**verstehen** vt irreg insep
misunderstand.

Mist [mɪst] m -(e)s dung; dirt; (col)
rubbish; ~**el** f -, -n mistletoe; ~**haufen**
m dungheap.

mit [mɪt] prep +dat with; (mittels) by; ~
der Bahn by train; ~ **10 Jahren** at the
age of 10; ad along, too; **wollen Sie ~?** do
you want to come along?

Mitarbeit ['mɪt'arbaɪt] f cooperation;
m~**en** vi cooperate, collaborate; ~**er(in**
f) m collaborator; co-worker; pl staff.

Mit- cpd: ~**bestimmung** f participation
in decision-making; (Pol) determination;

m~bringen vt irreg bring along; **~bürger(in** f) m fellow citizen; **m~denken** vi irreg follow; **du hast ja m~gedacht!** good thinking!

miteinander [mɪt'aɪ'nandər] ad together, with one another.

Mit- cpd: **m~erleben** vt see, witness; **~esser** ['mɪt'ɛsər] m -s, - blackhead; **m~geben** vt irreg give; **~gefühl** nt sympathy; **m~gehen** vi irreg go/come along; **m~genommen** a done in, in a bad way; **~gift** f dowry.

Mitglied ['mɪtgliːt] nt member; **~sbeitrag** m membership fee; **~schaft** f membership.

Mit- cpd: **m~halten** vi irreg keep up; **~hilfe** f help, assistance; **m~hören** vt listen in to; **m~kommen** vi irreg come along; (verstehen) keep up, follow; **~läufer** m hanger-on; (Pol) fellow-traveller.

Mitleid nt sympathy; (Erbarmen) compassion; **~enschaft** f: **in ~enschaft ziehen** affect; **m~ig** a sympathetic; **m~slos** a pitiless, merciless.

Mit- cpd: **m~machen** vt join in, take part in; **~mensch** m fellow man; **m~nehmen** vt irreg take along/away; (anstrengen) wear out, exhaust.

mitsamt [mɪt'zamt] prep +dat together with.

Mitschuld f complicity; **m~ig** a also guilty (an +dat of); **~ige(r)** mf accomplice.

Mit- cpd: **~schüler(in** f) m schoolmate; **m~spielen** vi join in, take part; **~spieler(in** f) m partner; **~spracherecht** ['mɪtʃpraːxərɛçt] nt voice, say.

Mittag ['mɪtaːk] m -(e)s, -e midday, lunchtime; **(zu) ~ essen** have lunch; **m~** ad at lunchtime or noon; **~essen** nt lunch, dinner; **m~s** ad at lunchtime or noon; **~spause** f lunch break; **~sschlaf** m early afternoon nap, siesta.

Mittäter(in f) [mɪttɛ:tər(ɪn)] m accomplice.

Mitte ['mɪtə] f -, -n middle; **aus unserer ~** from our midst.

mitteil- ['mɪttaɪl] cpd: **~en** vt: **jdm etw ~en** inform sb of sth, communicate sth to sb; **~sam** a communicative; **M~ung** f communication.

Mittel ['mɪtəl] nt -s - means; method; (Math) average; (Med) medicine; **ein ~ zum Zweck** a means to an end; **~alter** nt Middle Ages pl; **m~alterlich** a mediaeval; **m~bar** a indirect; **~ding** nt cross; **m~los** a without means; **m~mäßig** a mediocre, middling; **~mäßigkeit** f mediocrity; **~punkt** m centre; **m~s** prep +gen by means of; **~stand** m middle class; **~streifen** m central reservation; **~stürmer** m centre-forward; **~weg** m middle course; **~welle** f (Rad) medium wave; **~wert** m average value, mean.

mitten ['mɪtən] ad in the middle; **~ auf der Straße/in der Nacht** in the middle of the street/night; **~hindurch** ad

[-hɪn'dʊrç] through the middle.

Mitternacht ['mɪtərnaxt] f midnight; **m~s** ad at midnight.

mittlere(r,s) ['mɪtlərə(r,z)] a middle; (durchschnittlich) medium, average.

mittlerweile ['mɪtlər'vaɪlə] ad meanwhile.

Mittwoch [mɪtvɔx] m -(e)s, -e Wednesday; **m~s** ad on Wednesdays.

mitunter [mɪt'ʊntər] ad occasionally, sometimes.

Mit- cpd: **m~verantwortlich** a also responsible; **~verschulden** ['mɪtfɛr-ʃʊldən] nt contributory negligence; **m~wirken** vi contribute (bei to); (Theat) take part (bei in); **~wirkung** f contribution; participation; **~wisser** ['mɪtvɪsər] m -s, - sb in the know.

Möbel ['mø:bəl] nt -s, - (piece of) furniture; **~wagen** m furniture or removal van.

mobil [mo'bi:l] a mobile; (Mil) mobilized; **M~iar** [mobili'a:r] nt -s, -e movable assets pl; **M~machung** f mobilization.

möblieren [mø'bli:rən] vt furnish; **möbliert wohnen** live in furnished accommodation.

Mode ['mo:də] f -, -n fashion.

Modell [mo'dɛl] nt -s, -e model; **m~ieren** [-'li:rən] vt model.

Mode- cpd: **~(n)schau** f fashion show; **m~rn** [mo'dɛrn] a modern; (modisch) fashionable; **m~rni'sieren** vt modernize; **~schmuck** m fashion jewellery; **~wort** nt fashionable word.

modisch ['mo:dɪʃ] a fashionable.

mogeln [mo:gəln] vi (col) cheat.

mögen ['mø:gən] vti irreg like; **ich möchte ... I** would like ...; **das mag wohl sein** that may well be so.

möglich ['mø:klɪç] a possible; **~erweise** ad possibly; **M~keit** f possibility; **nach M~keit** if possible; **~st** ad as ... as possible.

Mohn [mo:n] m -(e)s, -e (—blume) poppy; (—samen) poppy seed.

Möhre ['mø:rə] f -, -n, **Mohrrübe** f carrot.

mokieren [mo'ki:rən] vr make fun (über +acc of).

Mole ['mo:lə] f -, -n (harbour) mole; **~kül** [mole'ky:l] nt -s, -e molecule.

Molkerei [mɔlkə'raɪ] f dairy.

Moll [mɔl] nt -, - (Mus) minor (key); **m~ig** a cosy; (dicklich) plump.

Moment [mo'mɛnt] m -(e)s, -e moment; **im ~** at the moment; nt factor, element; **m~an** [-'ta:n] a momentary; ad at the moment.

Monarch [mo'narç] m -en, -en monarch; **~ie** [monar'çi:] f monarchy.

Monat [mo:nat] m -(e)s, -e month; **m~elang** ad for months; **m~lich** a monthly; **~skarte** f monthly ticket.

Mönch ['mœnç] m -(e)s, -e monk.

Mond [mo:nt] m -(e)s, -e moon; **~fähre** f lunar (excursion) module; **~finsternis** f eclipse of the moon; **m~hell** a moonlit; **~landung** f moon landing; **~schein** m moonlight; **~sonde** f moon probe.

Mono- [mono] *in cpds* mono; **~log** [-'lo:k] *m* **-s, -e** monologue; **~pol** [-'po:l] *nt* **-s, -e** monopoly; **m~polisieren** [-poli'tsi:rən] *vt* monopolize; **m~ ton** [-'to:n] *a* monotonous; **~ tonie** [-to'ni:] *f* monotony.

Monsun [mɔn'zu:n] *m* **-s, -e** monsoon.

Montag ['mo:nta:k] *m* **-(e)s, -e** Monday; **m~s** *ad* on Mondays.

Montage ['mɔn'ta:ʒə] *f* **-, -n** (*Phot etc*) montage; (*Tech*) assembly; (*Einbauen*) fitting.

Monteur [mɔn'tø:r] *m* fitter, assembly man.

montieren [mɔn'ti:rən] *vt* assemble, set up.

Monument [monu'mɛnt] *nt* monument; **m~al** [-'ta:l] *a* monumental.

Moor [mo:r] *nt* **-(e)s, -e** moor.

Moos [mo:s] *nt* **-es, -e** moss.

Moped ['mo:pɛt] *nt* **-s, -s** moped.

Mops [mɔps] *m* **-es, -e** pug.

Moral [mo'ra:l] *f* **-, -en** morality; (*einer Geschichte*) moral; **m~isch** *a* moral.

Moräne [mo're:nə] *f* **-, -n** moraine.

Morast [mo'rast] *m* **-(e)s, -e** morass, mire; **m~ig** *a* boggy.

Mord [mɔrt] *m* **-(e)s, -e** murder; **~anschlag** *m* murder attempt.

Mörder ['mœrdər] *m* **-s, -** murderer; **~in** *f* murderess.

Mord- *cpd*: **~kommission** *f* murder squad; **~sglück** *nt* (*col*) amazing luck; **m~smäßig** *a* (*col*) terrific, enormous; **~sschreck** *m* (*col*) terrible fright; **~verdacht** *m* suspicion of murder; **~waffe** *f* murder weapon.

morgen ['mɔrgən] *ad*, **M~** *nt* tomorrow; **~ früh** tomorrow morning; **M~** *m* **-s, -** morning; **M~mantel** *m*, **M~rock** *m* dressing gown; **M~röte** *f* dawn; **~s** *ad* in the morning.

morgig ['mɔrgiç] *a* tomorrow's; **der ~e Tag** tomorrow.

Morphium ['mɔrfium] *nt* morphine.

morsch [mɔrʃ] *a* rotten.

Morse- ['mɔrzə] *cpd*: **~alphabet** *nt* Morse code; **m~n** *vi* send a message by morse code.

Mörtel ['mœrtəl] *m* **-s, -** mortar.

Mosaik [moza'i:k] *nt* **-s, -en** *or* **-e** mosaic.

Moschee [mɔ'ʃe:] *f* **-, -n** [mɔ'ʃe:ən] mosque.

Moskito [mɔs'ki:to] *m* **-s, -s** mosquito.

Most [mɔst] *m* **-(e)s, -e** (*unfermented*) fruit juice; (*Apfelwein*) cider.

Motel [mo'tel] *nt* **-s, -s** motel.

Motiv [mo'ti:f] *nt* **-s, -e** motive; (*Mus*) theme; **m~ieren** [moti'vi:rən] *vt* motivate; **~ierung** *f* motivation.

Motor ['mo:tɔr] *m* **-s, -en** [mo'to:rən] engine; (*esp Elec*) motor; **~boot** *nt* motorboat; **~enöl** *nt* motor oil; **m~isieren** [motori'zi:rən] *vt* motorize; **~rad** *nt* motorcycle; **~roller** *m* motor scooter; **~schaden** *m* engine trouble *or* failure.

Motte ['mɔtə] *f* **-, -n** moth; **~nkugel** *f*, **~npulver** *nt* mothball(s).

Motto ['mɔto] *nt* **-s, -s** motto.

Möwe ['mø:və] *f* **-, -n** seagull.

Mucke ['mʊkə] *f* **-, -n** (*usu pl*) caprice; (*von*

Ding) snag, bug; **seine ~n haben** be temperamental.

Mücke ['mʏkə] *f* **-, -n** midge, gnat; **~nstich** *m* midge *or* gnat bite.

mucksen ['mʊksən] *vr* (*col*) budge; (*Laut geben*) open one's mouth.

müde ['my:də] *a* tired.

Müdigkeit ['my:dɪçkaɪt] *f* tiredness.

Muff [mʊf] *m* **-(e)s, -e** (*Handwärmer*) muff; **~el** *m* **-s, -** (*col*) killjoy, sourpuss; **m~ig** *a* (*Luft*) musty.

Mühe ['my:ə] *f* **-, -n** trouble, pains *pl*; **mit Müh und Not** with great difficulty; **sich** (*dat*) **~ geben** go to a lot of trouble; **m~los** *a* without trouble, easy.

muhen ['mu:ən] *vi* low, moo.

mühevoll *a* laborious, arduous.

Mühle ['my:lə] *f* **-, -n** mill; (*Kaffee—*) grinder.

Müh- *cpd*: **~sal** *f* **-, -e** hardship, tribulation; **m~sam** *a* arduous, troublesome; **m~selig** *a* arduous, laborious.

Mulatte [mu'latə] *m* **-, -n**, **Mulattin** *f* mulatto.

Mulde ['mʊldə] *f* **-, -n** hollow, depression.

Mull [mʊl] *m* **-(e)s, -e** thin muslin; **~binde** *f* gauze bandage.

Müll [mʏl] *m* **-(e)s, -e** refuse; **~abfuhr** *f* rubbish disposal; (*Leute*) dustmen *pl*; **~abladeplatz** *m* rubbish dump; **~eimer** *m* dustbin, garbage can (*US*); **~er** *m* **-s, -** miller; **~haufen** *m* rubbish heap; **~schlucker** *m* **-s, -** garbage disposal unit; **~wagen** *m* dustcart, garbage truck (*US*).

mulmig ['mʊlmiç] *a* rotten; (*col*) dodgy; **jdm ist ~** sb feels funny.

multiplizieren [multipli'tsi:rən] *vt* multiply.

Mumie ['mu:miə] *f* mummy.

Mumm [mʊm] *m* **-s** (*col*) gumption, nerve.

Mund [mʊnt] *m* **-(e)s, ¨er** ['mʏndər] mouth; **~art** *f* dialect.

Mündel ['mʏndəl] *nt* **-s, -** ward.

münden ['mʏndən] *vi* flow (*in +acc* into).

Mund- *cpd*: **m~faul** *a* taciturn; **~fäule** *f* - (*Med*) ulcerative stomatitis; **~geruch** *m* bad breath; **~harmonika** *f* mouth organ.

mündig ['mʏndiç] *a* of age; **M~keit** *f* majority.

mündlich ['mʏntliç] *a* oral.

Mund- *cpd*: **~stück** *nt* mouthpiece; (*Zigaretten—*) tip; **m~tot** *a*: **jdn m~tot machen** muzzle sb.

Mündung ['mʏnduŋ] *f* mouth; (*Gewehr*) muzzle.

Mund- *cpd*: **~wasser** *nt* mouthwash; **~werk** *nt*: **ein großes ~werk haben** have a big mouth; **~winkel** *m* corner of the mouth.

Munition [munitsi'o:n] *f* ammunition; **~slager** *nt* ammunition dump.

munkeln ['mʊŋkəln] *vi* whisper, mutter.

Münster ['mʏnstər] *nt* **-s, -** minster.

munter ['mʊntər] *a* lively; **M~keit** *f* liveliness.

Münze ['mʏntsə] *f* **-, -n** coin; **m~n** *vt* coin, mint; **auf jdn gemünzt sein** be aimed at sb.

Münzfernsprecher ['mʏntsfɛrnʃpreçər] *m* callbox, pay phone (*US*).

mürb(e) ['mʏrb(ə)] *a Gestein* crumbly; *Holz* rotten; *Gebäck* crisp; **jdn ~ machen** wear sb down; **M~(e)teig** *m* shortcrust pastry.

murmeln ['murməln] *vti* murmer, mutter.

Murmeltier ['murməltiːr] *nt* marmot.

murren ['murən] *vi* grumble, grouse.

mürrisch ['mʏrɪʃ] *a* sullen.

Mus [muːs] *nt* **-es, -e** puree.

Muschel ['muʃəl] *f* **-, -n** mussel; (*—schale*) shell; (*Telefon—*) receiver.

Muse ['muːzə] *f* **-, -n** muse.

Museum [mu'zeːʊm] *nt* **-s, Museen** museum.

Musik [mu'ziːk] *f* music; (*Kapelle*) band; **m~alisch** [-'kaːlɪʃ] *a* musical; **~box** *f* jukebox; **~er** ['muːzikər] *m* **-s, -** musician; **~hochschule** *f* music school; **~instrument** *nt* musical instrument; **~truhe** *f* radiogram.

musizieren [muziˈtsiːrən] *vi* make music.

Muskat [musˈkaːt] *m* **-(e)s, -e** nutmeg.

Muskel ['muskəl] *m* **-s, -n** muscle; **~kater** *m*: **einen ~kater haben** be stiff.

Muskulatur [muskulaˈtuːr] *f* muscular system.

muskulös [muskuˈløːs] *a* muscular.

Muß [mus] *nt* - necessity, must.

Muße ['muːsə] *f* - leisure.

müssen ['mʏsən] *vi irreg* must, have to; **er hat gehen ~** he (has) had to go.

müßig ['myːsɪç] *a* idle; **M~gang** *m* idleness.

Muster ['mustər] *nt* **-s, -** model; (*Dessin*) pattern; (*Probe*) sample; **~ ohne Wert** free sample; **m~gültig** *a* exemplary; **m~n** *vt Tapete* pattern; (*fig, Mil*) examine; *Truppen* inspect; **~schüler** *m* model pupil; **~ung** *f* (*von Stoff*) pattern; (*Mil*) inspection.

Mut [muːt] *m* courage; **nur ~!** cheer up!; **jdm ~ machen** encourage sb; **m~ig** *a* courageous; **m~los** *a* discouraged, despondent.

mutmaßlich ['muːtmaːslɪç] *a* presumed; *ad* probably.

Mutter ['mutər] *f* **-, ⁻** mother; *pl* **~n** (*Schrauben—*) nut; **~land** *nt* mother country.

mütterlich ['mʏtərlɪç] *a* motherly; **~erseits** *ad* on the mother's side.

Mutter- *cpd*: **~liebe** *f* motherly love; **~mal** *nt* birthmark, mole; **~schaft** *f* motherhood, maternity; **~schutz** *m* maternity regulations; **'m~'seelen-a'llein** *a* all alone; **~sprache** *f* native language; **~tag** *m* Mother's Day.

mutwillig ['muːtvɪlɪç] *a* malicious, deliberate.

Mütze ['mʏtsə] *f* **-, -n** cap.

mysteriös [mʏsteriˈøːs] *a* mysterious.

Mystik ['mʏstɪk] *f* mysticism; **~er** *m* **-s, -** mystic.

Mythos ['myːtɔs] *m* **-, Mythen** myth.

N

N, n [ɛn] *nt* N, n.

na [na] *interj* well.

Nabel ['naːbəl] *m* **-s, -** navel; **~schnur** *f* umbilical cord.

nach [naːx] *prep +dat* after; (*in Richtung*) to; (*gemäß*) according to; **~ oben/hinten** up/back; **ihm ~!** after him!; **~ wie vor** still; **~ und ~** gradually; **dem Namen ~** judging by his name; **~ahmen** *vt* ape; **~ahmen** *vt* imitate; **N~ahmung** *f* imitation.

Nachbar(in *f*) ['naxbaːr(ɪn)] *m* **-s, -n** neighbour; **~haus** *nt*: **im ~haus** next door; **n~lich** *a* neighbourly; **~schaft** *f* neighbourhood; **~staat** *m* neighbouring state.

nach- *cpd*: **~bestellen** *vt* order again; **N~bestellung** *f* (*Comm*) repeat order; **~bilden** *vt* copy; **N~bildung** imitation, copy; **~blicken** *vi* look *or* gaze after; **~datieren** *vt* postdate.

nachdem [naːxˈdeːm] *cj* after; (*weil*) since; **je ~ (ob)** it depends (whether).

nach- *cpd*: **~denken** *vi irreg* think (*über +acc* about); **N~denken** *nt* **-s** reflection, meditation; **~denklich** *a* thoughtful, pensive.

Nachdruck ['naːxdrʊk] *m* emphasis; (*Print*) reprint, reproduction.

nachdrücklich ['naːxdrʏklɪç] *a* emphatic.

nacheifern ['naːxaifərn] *vi* emulate (*jdm* sb).

nacheinander [naːxʔaiˈnandər] *ad* one after the other.

nachempfinden ['naːxɛmpfɪndən] *vt irreg*: **jdm etw ~** feel sth with sb.

Nacherzählung ['naːxɛrtsɛːluŋ] *f* reproduction (of a story).

Nachfahr ['naːxfaːr] *m* **-s, -en** descendant.

Nachfolge ['naːxfɔlgə] *f* succession; **n~n** *vi* (*lit*) follow (*jdm/etw* sb/sth); **~r(in** *f*) *m* **-s, -** successor.

nach- *cpd*: **~forschen** *vti* investigate; **N~forschung** *f* investigation.

Nachfrage ['naːxfraːgə] *f* inquiry; (*Comm*) demand; **n~n** *vi* inquire.

nach- *cpd*: **~fühlen** *vt* see **~empfinden**; **~füllen** *vt* refill; **~geben** *vi irreg* give way, yield.

Nach- *cpd*: **~gebühr** *f* surcharge; (*Post*) excess postage; **~geburt** *f* afterbirth.

nachgehen ['naːxgeːən] *vi irreg* follow (*jdm* sb); (*erforschen*) inquire (*einer Sache* into sth); (*Uhr*) be slow.

Nachgeschmack ['naːxgəʃmak] *m* aftertaste.

nachgiebig ['naːxgiːbɪç] *a* soft, accommodating; **N~keit** *f* softness.

Nachhall ['naːxhal] *m* resonance; **n~en** *vi* resound.

nachhaltig ['naːxhaltɪç] *a* lasting; *Widerstand* persistent.

nachhelfen ['naːxhɛlfən] *vi irreg* assist, help (*jdm* sb).

nachher [naːxˈheːr] *ad* afterwards.

Nachhilfeunterricht ['naːxhɪlfə-ʊntɛrrɪçt] *m* extra tuition.
nachholen ['naːxhoːlən] *vt* catch up with; *Versäumtes* make up for.
Nachkomme ['naːxkɔmə] *m* -, -n descendant; **n~n** *vi irreg* follow; *einer Verpflichtung* fulfil; **~nschaft** *f* descendants *pl*.
Nachkriegs- ['naːxkriːks] *in cpds* postwar; **~zeit** *f* postwar period.
Nach- *cpd*: **~laß** *m* **-lasses, -lässe** (*Comm*) discount, rebate; (*Erbe*) estate; **n~lassen** *irreg vt Strafe* remit; *Summe* take off; *Schulden* cancel; *vi* decrease, ease off; (*Sturm auch*) die down; (*schlechter werden*) deteriorate; **er hat n~gelassen** he has got worse; **n~lässig** *a* negligent, careless; **~lässigkeit** *f* negligence, carelessness.
nachlaufen ['naːxlaufən] *vi irreg* run after, chase (*jdm* sb).
nachmachen ['naːxmaxən] *vt* imitate, copy (*jdm etw* sth from sb); (*fälschen*) counterfeit.
Nachmittag ['naːxmɪtaːk] *m* afternoon; **am ~, n~s** *ad* in the afternoon.
Nach- *cpd*: **~nahme** *f* -, -n cash on delivery; **per ~nahme** C.O.D.; **~name** *m* surname; **~porto** *nt* excess postage.
nachprüfen ['naːxpryːfən] *vt* check, verify.
nachrechnen ['naːxrɛçnən] *vt* check.
Nachrede ['naːxreːdə] *f*: **üble ~** libel; slander.
Nachricht ['naːxrɪçt] *f* -, -en (piece of) news; (*Mitteilung*) message; **~en** *pl* news; **~enagentur** *f* news agency; **~endienst** *m* (*Mil*) intelligence service; **~ensprecher(in** *f*) *m* newsreader; **~entechnik** *f* telecommunications *sing*.
nachrücken ['naːxrʏkən] *vi* move up.
Nachruf ['naːxruːf] *m* obituary (notice).
nachsagen ['naːxzaːgən] *vt* repeat; **jdm etw ~** say sth of sb.
nachschicken ['naːxʃɪkən] *vt* forward.
Nachschlag- ['naːxʃlaːg] *cpd*: **n~en** *vt irreg* look up; *vi*: **jdm n~en** take after sb; **~ewerk** *nt* reference boook.
Nach- *cpd*: **~schlüssel** *m* master key; **~schub** *m* supplies *pl*; (*Truppen*) reinforcements *pl*.
nachsehen ['naːxzeːən] *irreg vt* (*prüfen*) check; **jdm etw ~** forgive sb sth; *vi* look after (*jdm* sb); (*erforschen*) look and see; **das N~ haben** come off worst.
nachsenden ['naːxzɛndən] *vt irreg* send on, forward.
Nachsicht ['naːxzɪçt] *f* - indulgence, leniency; **n~ig** *a* indulgent, lenient.
nachsitzen ['naːxzɪtsən] *vi irreg* (*Sch*) be kept in.
Nachspeise ['naːxʃpaizə] *f* dessert, sweet, pudding.
Nachspiel ['naːxʃpiːl] *nt* epilogue; (*fig*) sequel.
nachsprechen ['naːxʃprɛçən] *vt irreg* repeat (*jdm* after sb).
nächst [nɛːçst] *prep* +*dat* (*räumlich*) next to; (*außer*) apart from; **~beste(r,s)** *a* first that comes along; (*zweitbeste*) next best;

N~e(r) *mf* neighbour; **~e(r,s)** next; (*nächstgelegen*) nearest; **N~enliebe** *f* love for one's fellow men; **~ens** *ad* shortly, soon; **~liegend** *a* (*lit*) nearest; (*fig*) obvious; **~möglich** *a* next possible.
nachsuchen ['naːxzuːxən] *vi*: **um etw ~** ask *or* apply for sth.
Nacht [naxt] *f* -, -̈e night.
Nachteil ['naːxtail] *m* disadvantage; **n~ig** *a* disadvantageous.
Nachthemd *nt* nightshirt; nightdress.
Nachtigall ['naxtɪgal] *f* -, -en nightingale.
Nachtisch ['naːxtɪʃ] *m see* **Nachspeise**.
nächtlich ['nɛçtlɪç] *a* nightly.
Nach- *cpd*: **~trag** *m* -(e)s, -träge supplement; **n~tragen** *vt irreg* carry (*jdm* after sb); (*zufügen*) add; **jdm etw n~tragen** hold sth against sb; **n~tragend** *a* resentful; **n~träglich** *a,ad* later, subsequent(ly); additional(ly); **n~trauern** *vi*: **jdm/etw n~trauern** mourn the loss of sb/sth.
Nacht- *cpd*: **~ruhe** *f* sleep; **n~s** *ad* by night; **~schicht** *f* nightshift; **n~süber** *ad* during the night; **~tarif** *m* off-peak tariff; **~tisch** *m* bedside table; **~topf** *m* chamberpot; **~wächter** *m* night watchman.
Nach- *cpd*: **~untersuchung** *f* checkup; **n~wachsen** *vi irreg* grow again; **~wehen** *pl* afterpains *pl*; (*fig*) aftereffects *pl*.
Nachweis ['naːxvais] *m* -es, -e proof; **n~bar** *a* provable, demonstrable; **n~en** ['naːxvaizən] *vt irreg* prove; **jdm etw n~en** point sth out to sb; **n~lich** *a* evident, demonstrable.
nach- *cpd*: **~winken** *vi* wave (*jdm* after sb); **~wirken** *vi* have after-effects; **N~wirkung** *f* after-effect; **N~wort** *nt* appendix; **N~wuchs** *m* offspring; (*beruflich etc*) new recruits *pl*; **~zahlen** *vti* pay extra; **N~zahlung** *f* additional payment; (*zurückdatiert*) back pay; **~zählen** *vt* count again; **N~zügler** *m* -s, - straggler.
Nacken ['nakən] *m* -s, - nape of the neck.
nackt [nakt] *a* naked; *Tatsachen* plain, bare; **N~heit** *f* nakedness; **N~kultur** *f* nudism.
Nadel ['naːdəl] *f* -, -n needle; (*Steck—*) pin; **~kissen** *nt* pincushion; **~öhr** *nt* eye of a needle; **~wald** *m* coniferous forest.
Nagel ['naːgəl] *m* -s, -̈ nail; **~feile** *f* nail-file; **~haut** *f* cuticle; **~lack** *m* nail varnish; **n~n** *vti* nail; **n~neu** *a* brand-new; **~schere** *f* nail scissors *pl*.
nagen ['naːgən] *vti* gnaw.
Nagetier ['naːgətiːr] *nt* rodent.
nah(e) ['naː(ə)] *a,ad* (*räumlich*) near(by); *Verwandte* near; *Freunde* close; (*zeitlich*) near, close; *prep* +*dat* near (to), close to; **N~aufnahme** *f* close-up.
Nähe ['nɛːə] *f* - nearness, proximity; (*Umgebung*) vicinity; **in der ~** close by; at hand; **aus der ~** from close to.
nahe- *cpd*: **~bei** *ad* nearby; **~gehen** *vi irreg* grieve (*jdm* sb); **~kommen** *vi irreg* get close (*jdm* to sb); **~legen** *vt*: **jdm etw ~legen** suggest sth to sb; **~liegen** *vi*

irreg be obvious; **~liegend** *a* obvious; **~n** *vir* approach, draw near.

Näh- ['nɛː] *cpd*: **n~en** *vti* sew; **n~er** *a,ad* nearer; *Erklärung, Erkundigung* more detailed; **~ere(s)** *nt* details *pl*, particulars *pl*; **~erei** *f* sewing, needlework; **~erin** *f* seamstress; **n~erkommen** *vir irreg* get closer; **n~ern** *vr* approach; **~erungswert** *m* approximate value.

nahe- *cpd*: **~stehen** *vi irreg* be close (*jdm* to sb); **einer Sache ~stehen** sympathize with sth; **~stehend** *a* close; **~treten** *vi irreg*: **jdm (zu) ~treten** offend sb; **~zu** *ad* nearly.

Näh- *cpd*: **~garn** *nt* thread; **~kasten** *m* workbox; **~maschine** *f* sewing machine; **~nadel** *f* needle.

nähren ['nɛːrən] *vtr* feed.

nahrhaft ['naːrhaft] *a* nourishing, nutritious.

Nähr- ['nɛːr] *cpd*: **~gehalt** *m* nutritional value; **~stoffe** *pl* nutrients *pl*.

Nahrung [naːrʊŋ] *f* food; (*fig auch*) sustenance; **~smittel** *nt* foodstuffs *pl*; **~smittelindustrie** *f* food industry; **~ssuche** *f* search for food.

Nährwert *m* nutritional value.

Naht [naːt] *f* -, **⁻e** seam; (*Med*) suture; (*Tech*) join; **n~los** *a* seamless; **n~los ineinander übergehen** follow without a gap.

Nah- *cpd*: **~verkehr** *m* local traffic; **~verkehrszug** *m* local train; **~ziel** *nt* immediate objective.

naiv [naˈiːf] *a* naive; **N~ität** [naiviˈtɛːt] *f* naivety.

Name ['naːmə] *m* -ns, -n name; **im ~n von** on behalf of; **n~ns** *ad* by the name of; **n~ntlich** *a* by name; *ad* particularly, especially.

namhaft ['naːmhaft] *a* (*berühmt*) famed, renowned; (*beträchtlich*) considerable; **~machen** name.

nämlich ['nɛːmlıç] *ad* that is to say, namely; (*denn*) since; **der/die/das ~e** the same.

Napf [napf] *m* -(e)s, **⁻e** bowl, dish.

Narbe ['narbə] *f* -, -n scar.

narbig ['narbıç] *a* scarred.

Narkose [narˈkoːzə] *f* -, -n anaesthetic.

Narr [nar] *m* -en, -en fool; **n~en** *vt* fool; **~heit** *f* foolishness.

Närr- ['nɛr] *cpd*: **~in** *f* fool; **n~isch** *a* foolish, crazy.

Narzisse [narˈtsɪsə] *f* -, -n narcissus; daffodil.

nasch- ['naʃ] *cpd*: **~en** *vti* nibble; eat secretly; **~haft** *a* sweet-toothed.

Nase ['naːzə] *f* -, -n nose; **~nbluten** *nt* -s nosebleed; **~nloch** *nt* nostril; **~nrücken** *m* bridge of the nose; **~ntropfen** *pl* nose drops *pl*; **n~weis** *a* pert, cheeky; (*neugierig*) nosey.

Nashorn ['naːshɔrn] *nt* rhinoceros.

naß [nas] *a* wet.

Nässe ['nɛsə] *f* - wetness; **n~n** *vt* wet.

Naß- *cpd*: **n~kalt** *a* wet and cold; **~rasur** *f* wet shave.

Nation [natsiˈoːn] *f* nation.

national [natsioˈnaːl] *a* national;

N~hymne *f* national anthem; **~isieren** [-iˈziːrən] *vt* nationalize; **N~i'sierung** *f* nationalization; **N~ismus** [-ˈlɪsmus] *m* nationalism; **~istisch** [-ˈlɪstıʃ] *a* nationalistic; **N~i'tät** *f* nationality; **N~mannschaft** *f* national team; **N~sozialismus** *m* national socialism.

Natron ['naːtrɔn] *nt* -s soda.

Natter ['natər] *f* -, -n adder.

Natur [naˈtuːr] *f* nature; (*körperlich*) constitution; **~alien** [natuˈraːliən] *pl* natural produce; **in ~alien** in kind; **~a'lismus** *m* naturalism; **~erscheinung** *f* natural phenomenon *or* event; **n~farben** *a* natural coloured; **n~gemäß** *a* natural; **~geschichte** *f* natural history; **~gesetz** *nt* law of nature; **~katastrophe** *f* natural disaster.

natürlich [naˈtyːrlıç] *a* natural; *ad* naturally; **~erweise** *ad* naturally, of course; **N~keit** *f* naturalness.

Natur- *cpd*: **~produkt** *nt* natural product; **n~rein** *a* natural, pure; **~schutzgebiet** *nt* nature reserve; **~wissenschaft** *f* natural science; **~wissenschaftler(in** *f*) *m* scientist; **~zustand** *m* natural state.

nautisch ['nautıʃ] *a* nautical.

Navelorange ['naːvəlorˈãːʒə] *f* navel orange.

Navigation [navigatsiˈoːn] *f* navigation; **~sfehler** *m* navigationai error; **~sinstrumente** *pl* navigation instruments *pl*.

Nazi ['naːtsi] *m* -s, -s Nazi.

Nebel ['neːbəl] *m* -s, - fog, mist; **n~ig** *a* foggy, misty; **~scheinwerfer** *m* foglamp.

neben ['neːbən] *prep* +*acc or dat* next to; (*außer*) apart from, besides; **~an** [neːbənˈan] *ad* next door; **N~anschluß** *m* (*Tel*) extension; **~bei** [neːbənˈbai] *ad* at the same time; (*außerdem*) additionally; (*beiläufig*) incidentally; **N~beschäftigung** *f* sideline; **N~buhler(in** *f*) *m* -s, - rival; **~einander** [neːbənˈaiˈnandər] *ad* side by side; **~einanderlegen** *vt* put next to each other; **N~eingang** *m* side entrance; **N~erscheinung** *f* side effect; **N~fach** *nt* subsidiary subject; **N~fluß** *m* tributary; **N~geräusch** *nt* (*Rad*) atmospherics *pl*, interference; **~her** [neːbənˈheːr] *ad* (*auch zusätzlich*) besides; (*gleichzeitig*) at the same time; (*daneben*) alongside; **~herfahren** *vi irreg* drive alongside; **N~kosten** *pl* extra charges *pl*, extras *pl*; **N~produkt** *nt* by-product; **N~rolle** *f* minor part; **N~sache** *f* trifle, side issue; **~sächlich** *a* minor, peripheral; **N~straße** *f* side street; **N~zimmer** *nt* adjoining room.

Necessaire [nesɛˈsɛːr] *nt* -s, -s (*Näh-*) needlework box; (*Nagel-*) manicure case.

neck- ['nɛk] *cpd*: **~en** *vt* tease; **N~e'rei** *f* teasing; **~isch** *a* coy; *Einfall, Lied* amusing.

Neffe ['nɛfə] *m* -n, -n nephew.

negativ [negaˈtiːf] *a* negative; **N~** *nt* -s, -e (*Phot*) negative.

Neger ['neːgər] *m* -s, - negro; **~in** *f* negress.

negieren [ne'gi:rən] *vt* (*bestreiten*) deny; (*verneinen*) negate.

nehmen ['ne:mən] *vt irreg* take; **jdn zu sich** ~ take sb in; **sich ernst** ~ take o.s. seriously; **nimm dir noch einmal** help yourself.

Neid [nait] *m* ~**(e)s** envy; ~**er** *m* ~**s**, - envier; **n**~**isch** *a* envious, jealous.

neigen ['naigən] *vt* incline, lean; *Kopf* bow; *vi:* **zu etw** ~ tend to sth.

Neigung *f* (*des Geländes*) slope; (*Tendenz*) tendency, inclination; (*Vorliebe*) liking; (*Zuneigung*) affection; ~**swinkel** *m* angle of inclination.

nein [nain] *ad* no.

Nelke ['nɛlkə] *f* -, -**n** carnation, pink; (*Gewürz*) clove.

Nenn- ['nɛn] *cpd:* **n**~**en** *vt irreg* name; (*mit Namen*) call; **n**~**enswert** *a* worth mentioning; ~**er** *m* -**s**, - denominator; ~**ung** *f* naming; ~**wert** *m* nominal value; (*Comm*) par.

Neon ['ne:ɔn] *nt* -**s** neon; ~**licht** *nt* neon light; ~**röhre** *f* neon tube.

Nerv [nɛrf] *m* -**s**, -**en** nerve; **jdm auf die** ~**en** **gehen** get on sb's nerves; **n**~**enaufreibend** *a* nerve-racking; ~**enbündel** *nt* bundle of nerves; ~**enheilanstalt** *f* mental home; **n**~**enkrank** *a* mentally ill; ~**enschwäche** *f* neurasthenia; ~**ensystem** *nt* nervous system; ~**enzusammenbruch** *m* nervous breakdown; **n**~**ös** [nɛr'vø:s] *a* nervous; ~**osi'tät** *f* nervousness; **n**~**tötend** *a* nerve-racking; *Arbeit* soul-destroying.

Nerz [nɛrts] *m* -**es**, -**e** mink.

Nessel ['nɛsəl] *f* -, -**n** nettle.

Nest [nɛst] *nt* -(**e**)**s**, -**er** nest; (*col: Ort*) dump; **n**~**eln** *vi* fumble *or* fiddle about (*an* +*dat* with).

nett [nɛt] *a* nice; (*freundlich auch*) kind; ~**erweise** *ad* kindly; ~**o** *ad* net.

Netz [nɛts] *nt* -**es**, -**e** net; (*Gepäck*~) rack; (*Einkaufs*~) string bag; (*Spinnen*~) web; (*System*) network; **jdm ins** ~ **gehen** (*fig*) fall into sb's trap; ~**anschluß** *m* mains connection; ~**haut** *f* retina.

neu [nɔy] *a* new; *Sprache, Geschichte* modern; **seit** ~ **estem** (*since*) recently; ~ **schreiben** rewrite, write again; **N**~**anschaffung** *f* new purchase *or* acquisition; ~**artig** *a* a new kind of; **N**~**auflage** *f*, **N**~**ausgabe** *f* new edition; **N**~**bau** *m* -**s**, -**ten** new building; ~**erdings** *ad* (*kürzlich*) (since) recently; (*von neuem*) again; **N**~**erung** *f* innovation, new departure; **N**~**gier** *f* curiosity; ~**gierig** *a* curious; **N**~**heit** *f* newness; novelty; **N**~**igkeit** *f* news; **N**~**jahr** *nt* New Year; ~**lich** *ad* recently, the other day; **N**~**ling** *m* novice; **N**~**mond** *m* new moon.

neun [nɔyn] *num* nine; ~**zehn** *num* nineteen; ~**zig** *num* ninety.

neureich *a* nouveau riche; **N**~**e(r)** *mf* nouveau riche.

Neur- *cpd:* ~**ose** [nɔy'ro:zə] *f* -, -**n** neurosis; ~**otiker** [nɔy'ro:tikər] *m* -**s**, - neurotic; ~**otisch** *a* neurotic.

Neutr- *cpd:* **n**~**al** [nɔy'tra:l] *a* neutral; ~**ali'tät** *f* neutrality; **n**~**ali'sieren** *vt* neutralize; ~**on** ['nɔytrɔn] *nt* -**s**, -**en** neutron; ~**um** ['nɔytrʊm] *nt* -**s**, -**a** *or* -**en** neuter.

Neu- *cpd:* ~**wert** *m* purchase price; ~**zeit** *f* modern age; **n**~**zeitlich** *a* modern, recent.

nicht [nɪçt] *ad* not; *pref* non-; ~ **wahr?** isn't it/he?, don't you *etc*; ~ **doch!** don't!; ~ **berühren!** do not touch! **was du** ~ **sagst!** the things you say!; **N**~**achtung** *f* disregard; **N**~**angriffspakt** *m* non-aggression pact.

Nichte ['nɪçtə] *f* -, -**n** niece.

nichtig ['nɪçtɪç] *a* (*ungültig*) null, void; (*wertlos*) futile; **N**~**keit** *f* nullity, invalidity; (*Sinnlosigkeit*) futility.

Nicht- *cpd:* ~**raucher**(**in** *f*) *m* non-smoker; **n**~**rostend** *a* stainless.

nichts [nɪçts] *pron* nothing; **für** ~ **und wieder** ~ for nothing at all; **N**~ *nt* -**s** nothingness; (*pej: Person*) nonentity; ~**desto'weniger** *ad* nevertheless; **N**~**nutz** *m* -**es**, -**e** good-for-nothing; ~**nutzig** *a* worthless, useless; ~**sagend** *a* meaningless; **N**~**tun** *nt* -**s** idleness.

Nickel ['nɪkəl] *nt* -**s** nickel.

nicken ['nɪkən] *vi* nod.

Nickerchen ['nɪkərçən] *nt* nap.

nie [ni:] *ad* never; ~ **wieder** *or* **mehr** never again; ~ **und nimmer** never ever.

nieder ['ni:dər] *a* low; (*gering*) inferior; *ad* down; **N**~**gang** *m* decline; ~**gehen** *vi irreg* descend; (*Aviat*) come down; (*Regen*) fall; (*Boxer*) go down; ~**geschlagen** *a* depressed, dejected; **N**~**geschlagenheit** *f* depression, dejection; **N**~**lage** *f* defeat; (*Lager*) depot; (*Filiale*) branch; ~**lassen** *vr irreg* (*sich setzen*) sit down; (*an Ort*) settle (down); (*Arzt, Rechtsanwalt*) set up a practice; **N**~**lassung** *f* settlement; (*Comm*) branch; ~**legen** *vt* lay down; *Arbeit* stop; *Amt* resign; ~**machen** *vt* mow down; **N**~**schlag** *m* (*Chem*) precipitate, sediment; (*Met*) precipitation; rainfall; (*Boxen*) knockdown; ~**schlagen** *irreg vt Gegner* beat down; *Gegenstand* knock down; *Augen* lower; (*Jur*) *Prozeß* dismiss; *Aufstand* put down; *vr* (*Chem*) precipitate; **N**~**schrift** *f* transcription; ~**trächtig** *a* base, mean; **N**~**trächtigkeit** *f* meanness, baseness; outrage; **N**~**ung** *f* (*Geog*) depression; flats *pl*.

niedlich ['ni:tlɪç] *a* sweet, nice, cute.

niedrig ['ni:drɪç] *a* low; *Stand* lowly, humble; *Gesinnung* mean.

niemals ['ni:ma:ls] *ad* never.

niemand ['ni:mant] *pron* nobody, no one; **N**~**sland** *nt* no-man's land.

Niere ['ni:rə] *f* -, -**n** kidney; ~**nentzündung** *f* kidney infection.

nieseln ['ni:zəln] *vi* drizzle.

niesen ['ni:zən] *vi* sneeze.

Niet ['ni:t] *m* -(**e**)**s**, -**e**, ~**e** *f* -, -**n** (*Tech*) rivet; (*Los*) blank; (*Reinfall*) flop; (*Mensch*) failure; **n**~**en** *vt* rivet.

Nihil- *cpd:* ~**ismus** [nihi'lɪsmʊs] *m*

nihilism; ~ist [nihi'lɪst] m nihilist; n~istisch a nihilistic.

Nikotin [niko'tiːn] nt -s nicotine.

Nilpferd ['niːlpfeːrt] nt hippopotamus.

nimmersatt ['nɪmərzat] a insatiable; N~ m -(e)s, -e glutton.

nippen ['nɪpən] vti sip.

Nippsachen ['nɪpzaxən] pl knick-knacks pl.

nirgends ['nɪrgənts], nirgendwo ['nɪrgəntvoː] ad nowhere.

Nische ['niːʃə] f-, -n niche.

nisten ['nɪstən] vi nest.

Nitrat [ni'traːt] nt -(e)s, -e nitrate.

Niveau [ni'voː] nt -s, -s level.

Nixe ['nɪksə] f-, -n water nymph.

noch [nɔx] ad still; (in Zukunft) still, yet; one day; (außerdem) else; cj nor; ~ nie never (yet); ~ nicht not yet; immer ~ still; ~ heute today; ~ vor einer Woche only a week ago; und wenn es ~ so schwer ist however hard it is; ~ einmal again; ~ dreimal three more times; ~ und ~ heaps of; (mit Verb) again and again; ~mal(s) ad again, once more; ~malig a repeated.

Nockenwelle ['nɔkənvɛlə] f camshaft.

Nominativ ['noːminatiːf] m -s, -e nominative.

nominell [nomi'nɛl] a nominal.

Nonne ['nɔnə] f-, -n nun; ~nkloster nt convent.

Nord(en) ['nɔrd(ən)] m -s north; n~isch a northern; n~ische Kombination (Ski) nordic combination.

nördlich ['nœrtlɪç] a northerly, northern; ~ von, ~ prep +gen (to the) north of.

Nord- cpd: ~pol m North Pole; n~wärts ad northwards.

Nörg- ['nœrg] cpd: ~e'lei f grumbling; n~eln vi grumble; ~ler m -s, - grumbler.

Norm [nɔrm] f -, -en norm; (Größenvorschrift) standard; n~al [nɔr'maːl] a normal; n~alerweise ad normally; n~ali'sieren vt normalize; vr return to normal; n~en vt standardize.

Not [noːt] f -, ̈-e need; (Mangel) want; (Mühe) trouble; (Zwang) necessity; zur ~ if necessary; (gerade noch) just about; ~ar [no'taːr] m -s, -e notary; n~ari'ell a notarial; ~ausgang m emergency exit; ~behelf m -s, -e makeshift; ~bremse f emergency brake; n~dürftig a scanty; (behelfsmäßig) makeshift; sich n~dürftig verständigen just about understand each other.

Note ['noːtə] f -, -n note; (Sch) mark; ~nblatt nt sheet of music; ~nschlüssel m clef; ~nständer m music stand.

Not- cpd: ~fall m (case of) emergency; n~falls ad if need be; n~gedrungen a necessary, unavoidable; etw n~gedrungen machen be forced to do sth.

notieren [no'tiːrən] vt note; (Comm) quote.

Notierung f (Comm) quotation.

nötig ['nøːtɪç] a necessary; etw ~ haben need sth; ~en vt compel, force; ~enfalls ad if necessary.

Notiz [no'tiːts] f -, -en note; (Zeitungs—)

item; ~ nehmen take notice; ~buch nt notebook; ~zettel m piece of paper.

Not- cpd: ~lage f crisis, emergency; n~landen vi make a forced or emergency landing; n~leidend a needy; ~lösung f temporary solution; ~lüge f white lie.

notorisch [no'toːrɪʃ] a notorious.

Not- cpd: ~ruf m emergency call; ~stand m state of emergency; ~standsgesetz nt emergency law; ~unterkunft f emergency accommodation; ~verband m emergency dressing; ~wehr f - self-defence; n~wendig a necessary; ~wendigkeit f necessity; ~zucht f rape.

Novelle [no'vɛlə] f -, -n short story; (Jur) amendment.

November [no'vɛmbər] m -(s), - November.

Nu [nuː] m: im ~ in an instant.

Nuance [nyˈãːsə] f-, -n nuance.

nüchtern ['nʏçtərn] a sober; Magen empty; Urteil prudent; N~heit f sobriety.

Nudel ['nuːdəl] f-, -n noodle.

Null [nʊl] f -, -en nought, zero; (pej: Mensch) washout; n~ num zero; Fehler no; n~ Uhr midnight; n~ und nichtig null and void; ~punkt m zero; auf dem ~punkt at zero.

numerieren [nume'riːrən] vt number.

numerisch [nu'meːrɪʃ] a numerical.

Nummer ['nʊmər] f -, -n number; ~nscheibe f telephone dial; ~nschild nt (Aut) number or license (US) plate.

nun [nuːn] ad now; interj well.

nur [nuːr] ad just, only.

Nuß [nʊs] f -, Nüsse nut; ~baum m walnut tree; hazelnut tree; ~knacker m -s, - nutcracker.

Nüster ['nyːstər] f-, -n nostril.

Nutte ['nʊtə] f-, -n tart.

nutz [nʊts], nütze ['nʏtsə] a: zu nichts ~ sein be useless; ~bar a: ~bar machen utilize; N~barmachung f utilization; ~bringend a profitable; ~en, nützen vt use (zu etw for sth); vi be of use; was nützt es? what's the use?, what use is it?; N~en m -s usefulness; profit; von N~en useful.

nützlich ['nʏtslɪç] a useful; N~keit f usefulness.

Nutz- cpd: n~los a useless; ~losigkeit f uselessness; ~nießer m -s, - beneficiary.

Nymphe ['nʏmfə] f-, -n nymph.

O

O, o [oː] nt O, o.

Oase [o'aːzə] f-, -n oasis.

ob [ɔp] cj if, whether; ~ das wohl wahr ist? can that be true?; und ~! you bet!

Obacht ['oːbaxt] f: ~ geben pay attention.

Obdach ['ɔpdax] nt -(e)s shelter, lodging; o~los a homeless; ~lose(r) mf homeless person.

Obduktion [ɔpdʊktsi'oːn] f post-mortem.

obduzieren [ɔpdu'tsiːrən] *vt* do a post mortem on.

O-Beine ['oːbaɪnə] *pl* bow *or* bandy legs *pl.*

oben ['oːbən] *ad* above; (*in Haus*) upstairs; **nach ~** up; **von ~** down; **~ ohne** topless; **jdn von ~ bis unten ansehen** look sb up and down; **Befehl von ~** orders from above; **~an** *ad* at the top; **~auf** *ad* up above, on the top; *a* (*munter*) in form; **~drein** *ad* into the bargain; **~erwähnt**, **~genannt** *a* above-mentioned; **~hin** *ad* cursorily, superficially.

Ober ['oːbər] *m* **-s**, **-** waiter; **~arm** *m* upper arm; **~arzt** *m* senior physician; **~aufsicht** *f* supervision; **~befehl** *m* supreme command; **~befehlshaber** *m* commander-in-chief; **~begriff** *m* generic term; **~bekleidung** *f* outer clothing; **~-'bürgermeister** *m* lord mayor; **~deck** *nt* upper *or* top deck; **o~e(r,s)** *a* upper; **die ~en** the bosses; (*Eccl*) the superiors; **~fläche** *f* surface; **o~flächlich** *a* superficial; **~geschoß** *nt* upper storey; **o~halb** *ad*, *prep* +*gen* above; **~haupt** *nt* head, chief; **~haus** *nt* upper house; House of Lords; **~hemd** *nt* shirt; **~herrschaft** *f* supremacy, sovereignty; **~in** *f* matron; (*Eccl*) Mother Superior; **o~irdisch** *a* above ground; *Leitung* overhead; **~kellner** *m* head waiter; **~kiefer** *m* upper jaw; **~kommando** *nt* supreme command; **~körper** *m* trunk, upper part of body; **~leitung** *f* direction; (*Elec*) overhead cable; **~licht** *nt* skylight; **~lippe** *f* upper lip; **~prima** *f* **-**, **-primen** final year of secondary school; **~schenkel** *m* thigh; **~schicht** *f* upper classes *pl*; **~schule** *f* grammar school (*Brit*), high school (*US*); **~schwester** *f* (*Med*) matron; **~sekunda** *f* **-**, **-sekunden** seventh year of secondary school.

Oberst ['oːbərst] *m* **-en** *or* **-s**, **-en** *or* **-e** colonel; **o~e(r,s)** *a* very top, topmost.

Ober- *cpd*: **~stufe** *f* upper school; **~teil** *nt* upper part; **~tertia** [-tɛrtsia] *f* **-**, **-tertien** fifth year of secondary school; **~wasser** *nt*: **~wasser haben/bekommen** be/get on top (of things); **~weite** *f* bust/chest measurement.

obgleich [ɔp'glaɪç] *cj* although.

Obhut ['ɔphuːt] *f* **-** care, protection; **in jds ~ sein** be in sb's care.

obig ['oːbɪç] *a* above.

Objekt [ɔp'jɛkt] *nt* **-(e)s**, **-e** object; **~iv** [-'tiːf] *nt* **-s**, **-e** lens; **o~iv** *a* objective; **~ivi'tät** *f* objectivity.

Oblate [o'blaːtə] *f* **-**, **-n** (*Gebäck*) wafer; (*Eccl*) host.

obligatorisch [ɔbliga'toːrɪʃ] *a* compulsory, obligatory.

Oboe [o'boːə] *f* **-**, **-n** oboe.

Obrigkeit ['oːbrɪçkaɪt] *f* (*Behörden*) authorities *pl*, administration; (*Regierung*) government.

obschon [ɔp'ʃoːn] *cj* although.

Observatorium [ɔpzɛrva'toːriʊm] *nt* observatory.

obskur [ɔps'kuːr] *a* obscure; (*verdächtig*) dubious.

Obst [oːpst] *nt* **-(e)s** fruit; **~bau** *m* fruit-

growing; **~baum** *m* fruit tree; **~garten** *m* orchard; **~händler** *m* fruiterer, fruit merchant; **~kuchen** *m* fruit tart.

obszön [ɔps'tsøːn] *a* obscene; **O~i'tät** *f* obscenity.

obwohl [ɔp'voːl] *cj* although.

Ochse ['ɔksə] *m* **-n**, **-n** ox; **o~n** *vti* (*col*) cram, swot; **~nschwanzsuppe** *f* oxtail soup; **~nzunge** *f* oxtongue.

öd(e) ['øːd(ə)] *a Land* waste, barren; (*fig*) dull; **Ö~e** *f* **-**, **-n** desert, waste(land); (*fig*) tedium.

oder ['oːdər] *cj* or.

Ofen ['oːfən] *m* **-s**, **-** oven; (*Heiz—*) fire, heater; (*Kohle—*) stove; (*Hoch—*) furnace; (*Herd*) cooker, stove; **~rohr** *nt* stovepipe.

offen ['ɔfən] *a* open; (*aufrichtig*) frank; *Stelle* vacant; **~ gesagt** to be honest; **~bar** *a* obvious; **~baren** [ɔfən'baːrən] *vt* reveal, manifest; **O~barung** *f* (*Rel*) revelation; **~bleiben** *vi irreg* (*Fenster*) stay open; (*Frage*, *Entscheidung*) remain open; **~halten** *vt irreg* keep open; **O~heit** *f* candour, frankness; **~herzig** *a* candid, frank; *Kleid* revealing; **O~herzigkeit** *f* frankness; **~kundig** *a* well-known; (*klar*) evident; **~lassen** *vt irreg* leave open; **~sichtlich** *a* evident, obvious; **~siv** [ɔfɛn'ziːf] *a* offensive; **O~-'sive** *f* **-**, **-n** offensive; **~stehen** *vi irreg* be open; (*Rechnung*) be unpaid; **es steht Ihnen ~**, **es zu tun** you are at liberty to do it.

öffentlich ['œfəntlɪç] *a* public; **Ö~keit** *f* (*Leute*) public; (*einer Versammlung etc*) public nature; **in aller Ö~keit** in public; **an die Ö~keit dringen** reach the public ear.

offerieren [ɔfe'riːrən] *vt* offer.

Offerte [ɔ'fɛrtə] *f* **-**, **-n** offer.

offiziell [ɔfitsi'ɛl] *a* official.

Offizier [ɔfi'tsiːr] *m* **-s**, **-e** officer; **~skasino** *nt* officers' mess.

öffnen ['œfnən] *vtr* open; **jdm die Tür ~** open the door for sb.

Öffner ['œfnər] *m* **-s**, **-** opener.

Öffnung ['œfnʊŋ] *f* opening; **~szeiten** *pl* opening times *pl.*

oft [ɔft] *ad* often.

öfter ['œftər] *ad* more often *or* frequently; **~s** *ad* often, frequently.

oftmals *ad* often, frequently.

ohne ['oːnə] *prep* +*acc*, *cj* without; **das ist nicht ~** (*col*) it's not bad; **~ weiteres** without a second thought; (*sofort*) immediately; **~dies** [oːnə'diːs] *ad* anyway; **~einander** [oːnə'aɪˈnandər] *ad* without each other; **~gleichen** [oːnə'glaɪçən] *a* unsurpassed, without equal; **~hin** [oːnə'hɪn] *ad* anyway, in any case.

Ohnmacht ['oːnmaxt] *f* faint; (*fig*) impotence; **in ~ fallen** faint.

ohnmächtig ['oːnmɛçtɪç] *a* in a faint, unconscious; (*fig*) weak, impotent; **sie ist ~** she has fainted.

Ohr [oːr] *nt* **-(e)s**, **-en** ear; (*Gehör*) hearing.

Öhr [øːr] *nt* **-(e)s**, **-e** eye.

Ohr- *cpd*: **~enarzt** *m* ear specialist; **o~enbetäubend** *a* deafening; **~en-**

schmalz nt earwax; ~**enschmerzen** pl earache; ~**enschützer** m -s, - earmuff; ~**feige** f slap on the face; box on the ears; **o**~**feigen** vt slap sb's face; box sb's ears; ~**läppchen** nt ear lobe; ~**ringe** pl earrings pl; ~**wurm** m earwig; (Mus) catchy tune.

okkupieren [ɔku'piːrən] vt occupy.

ökonomisch [øko'noːmɪʃ] a economical.

Oktanzahl [ɔk'taːntsaːl] f (bei Benzin) octane.

Oktave [ɔk'taːfə] f -, -n octave.

Oktober [ɔk'toːbər] m -(s), - October.

ökumenisch [øku'meːnɪʃ] a ecumenical.

Öl [øːl] nt -(e)s, -e oil; ~**baum** m olive tree; **ö**~**en** vt oil; (Tech) lubricate; ~**farbe** f oil paint; ~**feld** nt oilfield; ~**film** m film of oil; ~**heizung** f oil-fired central heating; **ö**~**ig** a oily.

oliv [o'liːf] a olive-green; **O**~**e** [o'liːvə] f -, -n olive.

Öl- cpd: ~**meßstab** m dipstick; ~**pest** f oil pollution; ~**sardine** f sardine; ~**scheich** m oil sheik; ~**standanzeiger** m (Aut) oil gauge; ~**ung** f lubrication; oiling; (Eccl) anointment; **die Letzte** ~**ung** Extreme Unction; ~**wechsel** m oil change; ~**zeug** nt oilskins pl.

Olymp- [o'lvmp] cpd: ~**iade** [-i'aːdə] f Olympic Games pl; ~**iasieger(in** f) [-iazi:gər(ɪn)] m Olympic champion; ~**iateilnehmer(in** [-io'niːkə] m, ~**io'nikin** f Olympic competitor; **o**~**isch** a Olympic.

Oma ['oːma] f -, -s (col) granny.

Omelett [ɔm(ə)'lɛt] nt -(e)s, -s, **Omelette** f omlet(te).

Omen ['oːmɛn] nt -s, - or **Omina** omen.

Omnibus ['ɔmnibʊs] m (omni)bus.

Onanie [ona'niː] f masturbation; **o**~**ren** vi masturbate.

Onkel ['ɔŋkəl] m -s, - uncle.

Opa ['oːpa] m -s, -s (col) grandpa.

Opal [o'paːl] m -s, -e opal.

Oper ['oːpər] f -, -n opera; opera house; ~**ation** [operatsi'oːn] f operation; ~**ationssaal** m operating theatre; ~**ette** [ope'rɛtə] f operetta; **o**~**ieren** [ope'riːrən] vti operate; ~**nglas** nt opera glasses pl; ~**nhaus** nt opera house; ~**nsänger(in** f) m operatic singer.

Opfer ['ɔpfər] nt -s, - sacrifice; (Mensch) victim; **o**~**n** vt sacrifice; ~**stock** m (Eccl) offertory box; ~**ung** f sacrifice.

Opium ['oːpiʊm] nt -s opium.

opponieren [ɔpo'niːrən] vi oppose (gegen jdn/etw sb/sth).

opportun [ɔpɔr'tuːn] a opportune; **O**~**ismus** [-'nɪsmʊs] m opportunism; **O**~**ist** [-'nɪst] m opportunist.

Opposition [ɔpozitsi'oːn] f opposition; **o**~**ell** [-'nɛl] a opposing.

Optik ['ɔptɪk] f optics sing; ~**er** m -s, - optician.

optimal [ɔpti'maːl] a optimal, optimum.

Optimismus [ɔpti'mɪsmʊs] m optimism.

Optimist [ɔpti'mɪst] m optimist; **o**~**isch** a optimistic.

optisch ['ɔptɪʃ] a optical.

Orakel [o'raːkəl] nt -s, - oracle.

Orange [o'rãːʒə] f -, -n orange; **o**~ a orange; ~**ade** [orãːʒa'də] f orangeade; ~**at** [orãːʒaːt] nt -s, -e candied peel; ~**nmarmelade** f marmelade; ~**nschale** f orange peel.

Orchester [ɔr'kɛstər] nt -s, - orchestra.

Orchidee [ɔrçi'deːə] f -, -n orchid.

Orden ['ɔrdən] m -s, - (Eccl) order; (Mil) decoration; ~**sschwester** f nun.

ordentlich ['ɔrdəntlɪç] a (anständig) decent, respectable; (geordnet) tidy, neat; (col: annehmbar) not bad; (col: tüchtig) real, proper; ~**er Professor** (full) professor; ad properly; **O**~**keit** f respectability; tidiness, neatness.

Ordinalzahl [ɔrdi'naːltsaːl] f ordinal number.

ordinär [ɔrdi'nɛːr] a common, vulgar.

ordnen ['ɔrdnən] vt order, put in order.

Ordner m -s, - steward; (Comm) file.

Ordnung f order; (Ordnen) ordering; (Geordnetsein) tidiness; **o**~**sgemäß** a proper, according to the rules; **o**~**shalber** ad as a matter of form; ~**sliebe** f tidiness, orderliness; ~**sstrafe** f fine; **o**~**swidrig** a contrary to the rules, irregular; ~**szahl** f ordinal number.

Organ [ɔr'gaːn] nt -s, -e organ; (Stimme) voice; ~**isation** [-izatsi'oːn] f organisation; ~**isationstalent** nt organizing ability; (Person) good organizer; ~**isator** [-i'zaːtɔr] m organizer; **o**~**isch** a organic; **o**~**isieren** [-i'ziːrən] vt organize, arrange; (col: beschaffen) acquire; vr organize; ~**ismus** [-'nɪsmʊs] m organism; ~**ist** [-'nɪst] m organist; ~**verpflanzung** f transplantation (of organs).

Orgasmus [ɔr'gasmʊs] m orgasm.

Orgel ['ɔrgəl] f -, -n organ; ~**pfeife** f organ pipe; **wie die** ~**pfeifen stehen** stand in order of height.

Orgie ['ɔrgiə] f orgy.

Orient ['oːrient] m -s Orient, east; ~**ale** [-'taːlə] m -n, -n Oriental; **o**~**alisch** [-'taːlɪʃ] a oriental; **o**~**ieren** [-'tiːrən] vt (örtlich) locate; (fig) inform; vr find one's way or bearings; inform oneself; ~**ierung** [-'tiːrʊŋ] f orientation; (fig) information; ~**ierungssinn** m sense of direction.

original [origi'naːl] a original; **O**~ nt -s, -e original; **O**~**fassung** f original version; **O**~**i'tät** f originality.

originell [origi'nɛl] a original.

Orkan [ɔr'kaːn] m -(e)s, -e hurricane.

Ornament [ɔrna'mɛnt] nt decoration, ornament; **o**~**al** [-'taːl] a decorative, ornamental.

Ort [ɔrt] m -(e)s, -e or -er place; **an** ~ **und Stelle** on the spot; **o**~**en** vt locate.

ortho- [ɔrto] cpd: ~**dox** [-'dɔks] a orthodox; **O**~**graphie** [-gra'fiː] f spelling, orthography; ~**'graphisch** a orthographic; **O**~**päde** [-'pɛːdə] m -n, -n orthopaedic specialist, orthopaedist; **O**~**pädie** [-pɛ'diː] f orthopaedics sing; ~**'pädisch** a orthopaedic.

örtlich ['œrtlɪç] a local; **O**~**keit** f locality.

Ort- cpd: ~**sangabe** f (name of the) town; **o**~**sansässig** a local; ~**schaft** f village, small town; **o**~**sfremd** a non-local;

~**sfrende(r)** *mf* stranger; ~**sgespräch**
nt local (phone)call; ~**sname** *m* place-
name; ~**snetz** *nt* (*Tel*) local telephone
exchange area; ~**ssinn** *m* sense of
direction; ~**szeit** *f* local time; ~**ung** *f*
locating.

Öse ['ø:zə] *f* -, -n loop, eye.

Ost- [ɔst] *cpd:* ~**block** *m* (*Pol*) Eastern
bloc; ~**en** *m* -s east; **o**~**entativ**
[ɔstɛnta'ti:f] *a* pointed, ostentatious.

Oster- ['o:stər] *cpd:* ~**ei** *nt* Easter egg;
~**fest** *nt* Easter; ~**glocke** *f* daffodil;
~**hase** *m* Easter bunny; ~**montag** *m*
Easter Monday; ~**n** *nt* -s, - Easter;
~**sonntag** *m* Easter Day *or* Sunday.

östlich ['œstlɪç] *a* eastern, easterly.

Ost- *cpd:* ~**see** *f* Baltic Sea; **o**~**wärts** *ad*
eastwards; ~**wind** *m* east wind.

oszillieren [ɔstsi'li:rən] *vi* oscillate.

Otter ['ɔtər] *m* -s, - otter; *f* -, -n (*Schlange*)
adder.

Ouvertüre [uver'ty:rə] *f* -, -n overture.

oval [o'va:l] *a* oval.

Ovation [ovatsi'o:n] *f* ovation.

Ovulation [ovulatsi'o:n] *f* ovulation.

Oxyd [ɔ'ksy:t] *nt* -(e)s, -e oxide; **o**~**ieren**
[ɔksy'di:rən] *vti* oxidize; ~**ierung** *f*
oxidization.

Ozean ['o:tsea:n] *m* -s, -e ocean;
~**dampfer** *m* (ocean-going) liner;
o~**isch** [otse'a:nɪʃ] *a* oceanic.

Ozon [o'tso:n] *nt* -s ozone.

P

P, p [pe:] *nt* P, p.

Paar [pa:r] *nt* -(e)s, -e pair; (*Ehe*—)
couple; **ein p**~ a few; **p**~**en** *vtr* couple;
Tiere mate; ~**lauf** *m* pair skating;
p~**mal** *ad:* **ein p**~**mal** a few times;
~**ung** *f* combination; mating; **p**~**weise**
ad in pairs; in couples.

Pacht [paxt] *f* -, -en lease; **p**~**en** *vt* lease.

Pächter ['pɛçtər] *m* -s, - leaseholder,
tenant.

Pack [pak] *m* -(e)s *or* ≟e bundle, pack;
nt -(e)s (*pej*) mob, rabble.

Päckchen ['pɛkçən] *nt* small package;
(*Zigaretten*) packet; (*Post*—) small parcel.

Pack- *cpd:* **p**~**en** *vt* pack; (*fassen*) grasp,
seize; (*col: schaffen*) manage; (*fig: fesseln*)
grip; ~**en** *m* -s, - bundle; (*fig: Menge*)
heaps of; ~**esel** *m* (*lit, fig*) packhorse;
~**papier** *nt* brown paper, wrapping
paper; ~**ung** *f* packet; (*Pralinen*—) box;
(*Med*) compress.

Pädagoge [pɛda'go:gə] *cpd:* ~**e** *m* -n, -n
teacher; ~**ik** *f* education; **p**~**isch** *a*
educational, pedagogical.

Paddel ['padəl] *nt* -s, - paddle; ~**boot** *nt*
canoe; **p**~**n** *vi* paddle.

paffen ['pafən] *vti* puff.

Page ['pa:ʒə] *m* -n, -n page; ~**nkopf** *m*
pageboy.

Paillette [paɪ'jɛtə] *f* sequin.

Paket [pa'ke:t] *nt* -(e)s, -e packet;
(*Post*—) parcel; ~**karte** *f* dispatch note;
~**post** *f* parcel post; ~**schalter** *m*
parcels counter.

Pakt [pakt] *m* -(e)s, -e pact.

Palast [pa'last] *m* -es, **Paläste** palace.

Palette [pa'letə] *f* palette; (*Lade*—) pallet.

Palme ['palmə] *f* -, -n palm (tree).

Palmsonntag *m* Palm Sunday.

Pampelmuse ['pampəlmu:zə] *f* -, -n
grapefruit.

pampig ['pampɪç] *a* (*col: frech*) fresh.

panieren [pa'ni:rən] *vt* (*Cook*) coat with
egg and breadcrumbs.

Paniermehl [pa'ni:rme:l] *nt* breadcrumbs
pl.

Panik ['pa:nɪk] *f* panic.

panisch ['pa:nɪʃ] *a* panic-stricken.

Panne ['panə] *f* -, -n (*Aut etc*) breakdown;
(*Mißgeschick*) slip.

panschen ['panʃən] *vi* splash about; *vt*
water down.

Panther ['pantər] *m* -s, - panther.

Pantoffel [pan'tɔfəl] *m* -s, -n slipper;
~**held** *m* (*col*) henpecked husband.

Pantomime [panto'mi:mə] *f* -, -n mime.

Panzer ['pantsər] *m* -s, - armour; (*Platte*)
armour plate; (*Fahrzeug*) tank; ~**glas** *nt*
bulletproof glass; **p**~**n** *vtr* armour; (*fig*)
arm *o.s.*; ~**schrank** *m* strongbox.

Papa [pa'pa:] *m* -s, -s (*col*) dad, daddy;
~**gei** [-'gai] *m* -s, -en parrot.

Papier [pa'pi:r] *nt* -s, -e paper; (*Wert*—)
share; ~**fabrik** *f* paper mill; ~**geld** *nt*
paper money; ~**korb** *m* wastepaper
basket; ~**krieg** *m* red tape; angry correspondence; ~**tüte** *f* paper bag.

Papp- [pap] *cpd:* ~**deckel** *m,* ~**e** *f* -, -n
cardboard; ~**einband** *m* pasteboard;
~**el** *f* -, -n poplar; **p**~**en** *vti* (*col*) stick;
~**enstiel** *m* (*col*): **keinen** ~**enstiel**
wert sein not be worth a thing; **für einen**
~**enstiel bekommen** get for a song;
p~**erlapapp** *interj* rubbish; **p**~**ig** *a*
sticky; ~**maché** [-ma'ʃe] *nt* -s, -s papier-
mâché.

Paprika [paprika] *m* -s, -s (*Gewürz*)
paprika; (*—schote*) pepper.

Papst [pa:pst] *m* -(e)s, ≟e pope.

päpstlich ['pe:pstlɪç] *a* papal.

Parabel [pa'ra:bəl] *f* -, -n parable; (*Math*)
parabola.

Parade [pa'ra:də] *f* (*Mil*) parade, review;
(*Sport*) parry; ~**marsch** *m* march-past;
~**schritt** *m* goose-step.

Paradies [para'di:s] *nt* -es, -e paradise;
p~**isch** *a* heavenly.

paradox [para'dɔks] *a* paradoxical; **P**~ *nt*
-es, -e paradox.

Paragraph [para'gra:f] *m* -en, -en paragraph; (*Jur*) section.

parallel [para'le:l] *a* parallel; **P**~**e** *f*
parallel.

paramilitärisch [paramili'tɛ:rɪʃ] *a* para-
military.

Paranuß ['pa:ranus] *f* Brazil nut.

paraphieren [para'fi:rən] *vt Vertrag*
initial.

Parasit [para'zi:t] *m* -en, -en (*lit, fig*)
parasite.

parat [pa'ra:t] *a* ready.

Pärchen ['pe:rçən] *nt* couple.

Parfüm [par'fy:m] *nt* -s, -s *or* -e perfume;

~erie [-ə'ri:] f perfumery; ~flasche f scent bottle; p~ieren [-'mi:rən] vt scent, perfume.

parieren [pa'ri:rən] vt parry; vi (col) obey.

Parität [pari'tɛ:t] f parity.

Park [park] m -s, -s park; ~anlage f park; (um Gebäude) grounds pl; p~en vti park; ~ett [par'kɛt] nt -(e)s, -e parquet (floor); (Theat) stalls pl; ~haus nt multistorey car park; ~lücke f parking space; ~platz m parking place; car park, parking lot (US); ~scheibe f parking disc; ~uhr f parking meter; ~verbot nt no parking.

Parlament [parla'mɛnt] nt parliament; ~arier [-'ta:riər] m -s, - parliamentarian; p~arisch [-'ta:rɪʃ] a parliamentary; ~sbeschluß nt vote of parliament; ~smitglied nt member of parliament; ~ssitzung f sitting (of parliament).

Parodie [paro'di:] f parody; p~ren vt parody.

Parole [pa'ro:lə] f -, -n password; (Wahlspruch) motto.

Partei [par'tai] f party; ~ ergreifen für jdn take sb's side; ~führung f party leadership; ~genosse m party member; p~isch a partial, biased; p~los a neutral; ~nahme f -, -n support, taking the part of; ~tag m party conference.

Parterre [par'tɛr] nt -s, -s ground floor; (Theat) stalls pl.

Partie [par'ti:] f part; (Spiel) game; (Ausflug) outing; (Mann, Frau) catch; (Comm) lot; mit von der ~ sein join in.

Partikel [par'ti:kəl] f -n particle.

Partisan [parti'za:n] m -s or -en, -en partisan.

Partitur [parti'tu:r] f (Mus) score.

Partizip [parti'tsi:p] nt -s, -ien participle.

Partner(in f) ['partnər] m -s, - partner; p~schaftlich a as partners.

Party ['pa:rti] f -, -s or Parties party.

Parzelle [par'tsɛlə] f plot, allotment.

Paß [pas] m -sses, ̈sse pass; (Ausweis) passport.

Pass- cpd: p~abel [pa'sa:bəl] a passable, reasonable; ~age [pa'sa:ʒə] f -, -n passage; ~agier [pa'si:r] m -s, -e passenger; ~agierdampfer m passenger steamer; ~agierflugzeug nt airliner; ~ant [pa'sant] m passer-by.

Paß- cpd: ~amt nt passport office; ~bild nt passport photograph.

passen [pasən] vi fit; (Farbe) go (zu with); (auf Frage, Cards, Sport) pass; das paßt mir nicht that doesn't suit me; er paßt nicht zu dir he's not right for you; ~d a suitable; (zusammen-) matching; (angebracht) fitting; Zeit convenient.

passier- [pa'si:r] cpd: ~bar a passable; ~en vt (pass); (durch Sieb) strain; vi happen; P~schein m pass, permit.

Passion [pasi'o:n] f passion; p~iert [-'ni:rt] a enthusiastic, passionate; ~sspiel nt Passion Play.

passiv ['pasi:f] a passive; P~ nt -s, -e passive; P~a pl (Comm) liabilities pl; P~i'tät f passiveness.

Paß- cpd: ~kontrolle f passport control;

~stelle f passport office; ~straße f (mountain) pass; ~zwang m requirement to carry a passport.

Paste ['pastə] f -, -n paste.

Pastell [pas'tɛl] nt -(e)s, -e pastel.

Pastete [pas'te:tə] f -, -n pie.

pasteurisieren [pastöri'zi:rən] vt pasteurize.

Pastor ['pastər] m vicar; pastor, minister.

Pate ['pa:tə] m -n, -n godfather; ~nkind nt godchild.

Patent [pa'tɛnt] nt -(e)s, -e patent; (Mil) commission; p~ a clever; ~amt nt patent office; p~ieren [-'ti:rən] vt patent; ~inhaber m patentee; ~schutz m patent right.

Pater ['pa:tər] m -s, - or Patres (Eccl) Father.

pathetisch [pa'te:tɪʃ] a emotional; bombastic.

Pathologe [pato'lo:gə] m -n, -n pathologist.

pathologisch a pathological.

Pathos ['pa:tɔs] nt - emotiveness, emotionalism.

Patient(in f) [patsi'ɛnt(ɪn)] m patient.

Patin ['pa:tɪn] f godmother; ~a [pa'ti:na] f - patina.

Patriarch [patri'arç] m -en, -en patriarch; p~alisch [-'ça:lɪʃ] a patriarchal.

Patriot [patri'o:t] m -en, -en patriot; p~isch a patriotic; ~ismus [-'tɪsmʊs] m patriotism.

Patron [pa'tro:n] m -s, -e patron; (pej) beggar; ~e f -, -n cartridge; ~enhülse f cartridge case; ~in f patroness.

Patrouille [pa'trʊljə] f -, -n patrol.

patrouillieren [patrʊl'ji:rən] vi patrol.

patsch [patʃ] interj splash; P~e f -, -n (col: Händchen) paw; (Fliegen—) swat; (Feuer—) beater; (Bedrängnis) mess, jam; ~en vti smack, slap; (im Wasser) splash; ~naß a soaking wet.

patzig ['patsɪç] a (col) cheeky, saucy.

Pauke ['paukə] f -, -n kettledrum; auf die ~ hauen live it up; p~n vti (Sch) swot, cram; ~r m -s, - (col) teacher.

pausbäckig ['pausbɛkɪç] a chubby-cheeked.

pauschal [pau'ʃa:l] a Kosten inclusive; Urteil sweeping; P~e f -, -n, P~gebühr f flat rate; P~preis m all-in price; P~reise f package tour; P~summe f lump sum.

Pause ['pauzə] f -, -n break; (Theat) interval; (Innehalten) pause; (Kopie) tracing; p~n vt trace; p~nlos a nonstop; ~nzeichen nt call sign; (Mus) rest.

pausieren [pau'zi:rən] vi make a break.

Pauspapier ['pauspapi:r] nt tracing paper.

Pavian ['pa:via:n] m -s, -e baboon.

Pazifist [patsi'fɪst] m pacifist; p~isch a pacifist.

Pech ['pɛç] nt -s, -e pitch; (fig) bad luck; ~ haben be unlucky; p~schwarz a pitch-black; ~strähne m (col) unlucky patch; ~vogel m (col) unlucky person.

Pedal [pe'daːl] *nt* **-s, -e** pedal.
Pedant [pe'dant] *m* pedant; ~**e'rie** *f* pedantry; **p**~**isch** *a* pedantic.
Peddigrohr ['pɛdɪçroːr] *nt* cane.
Pegel ['peːgəl] *m* **-s, -** water gauge; ~**stand** *m* water level.
peilen ['paɪlən] *vt* get a fix on.
Pein [paɪn] *f* - agony, pain; **p**~**igen** *vt* torture; (*plagen*) torment; **p**~**lich** *a* (*unangenehm*) embarrassing, awkward, painful; (*genau*) painstaking; **P**~**lichkeit** *f* painfulness, awkwardness; scrupulousness.
Peitsche ['paɪtʃə] *f* -, **-n** whip; **p**~**n** *vt* whip; (*Regen*) lash.
Pelikan ['peːlikaːn] *m* **-s, -e** pelican.
Pelle ['pɛlə] *f* -, **-n** skin; **p**~**n** *vt* skin, peel.
Pellkartoffeln *pl* jacket potatoes *pl*.
Pelz [pɛlts] *m* **-es, -e** fur.
Pendel ['pɛndəl] *nt* **-s, -** pendulum; ~**verkehr** *m* shuttle traffic; (*für Pendler*) commuter traffic.
Pendler ['pɛndlər] *m* **-s, -** commuter.
penetrant [pene'trant] *a* sharp; *Person* pushing.
Penis ['peːnɪs] *m* -, **-se** penis.
Pension [pɛnzi'oːn] *f* (*Geld*) pension; (*Ruhestand*) retirement; (*für Gäste*) boarding *or* guest-house; **halbe/volle** ~ half/full board; ~**är(in** *f*) ['nɛr(ɪn)] *m* **-s, -e** pensioner; ~**at** [-'naːt] *nt* **-(e)s, -e** boarding school; **p**~**ieren** [-'niːrən] *vt* pension (off); **p**~**iert** *a* retired; ~**ierung** *f* retirement; ~**sgast** *m* boarder, paying guest.
Pensum ['pɛnzʊm] *nt* **-s, Pensen** quota; (*Sch*) curriculum.
per [pɛr] *prep* +*acc* by, per; (*pro*) per; (*bis*) by.
Perfekt ['pɛrfɛkt] *nt* **-(e)s, -e** perfect; **p**~ [pɛr'fɛkt] *a* perfect; ~**ionismus** [pɛrfɛktsio'nɪsmus] *m* perfectionism.
perforieren [pɛrfo'riːrən] *vt* perforate.
Pergament [pɛrga'mɛnt] *nt* parchment; ~**papier** *nt* greaseproof paper.
Periode [peri'oːdə] *f* -, **-n** period.
periodisch [peri'oːdɪʃ] *a* periodic; (*dezimal*) recurring.
Peripherie [perife'riː] *f* periphery; (*um Stadt*) outskirts *pl*; (*Math*) circumference.
Perle ['pɛrlə] *f* -, **-n** (*lit, fig*) pearl; **p**~**n** *vi* sparkle; (*Tropfen*) trickle.
Perlmutt ['pɛrlmʊt] *nt* **-s** mother-of-pearl.
perplex [pɛr'plɛks] *a* dumbfounded.
Persianer [pɛrzi'aːnər] *m* **-s, -** Persian lamb.
Person [pɛr'zoːn] *f* -, **-en** person; **ich für meine** ~ personally I; **klein von** ~ of small build; ~**al** [-'naːl] *nt* **-s** personnel; (*Bedienung*) servants *pl*; ~**alausweis** *m* identity card; ~**alien** [-'naːliən] *pl* particulars *pl*; ~**ali'tät** *f* personality; ~**alpronomen** *nt* personal pronoun; ~**enaufzug** *m* lift, elevator (*US*); ~**enkraftwagen** *m* private motorcar; ~**enkreis** *m* group of people; ~**enschaden** *m* injury to persons; ~**enwaage** *f* scales *pl*; ~**enzug** *m* stopping train; passenger train; **p**~**ifizieren** [-ifi'tsiːrən] *vt* personify.

persönlich [pɛr'zøːnlɪç] *a* personal; *ad* in person; personally; **P**~**keit** *f* personality.
Perspektive [pɛrspɛk'tiːvə] *f* perspective.
Perücke [pe'rʏkə] *f* -, **-n** wig.
pervers [pɛr'vɛrs] *a* perverse; **P**~**i'tät** *f* perversity.
Pessimismus [pɛsi'mɪsmus] *m* pessimism.
Pessimist [pɛsi'mɪst] *m* pessimist; **p**~**isch** *a* pessimistic.
Pest [pɛst] *f* - plague.
Petersilie [petər'ziːliə] *f* parsley.
Petroleum [pe'troːleum] *nt* **-s** paraffin, kerosene (*US*).
petzen ['pɛtsən] *vi* (*col*) tell tales.
Pfad [pfaːt] *m* **-(e)s, -e** path; ~**finder** *m* **-s, -** boy scout; ~**finderin** *f* girl guide.
Pfahl [pfaːl] *m* **-(e)s, -e** post, stake; ~**bau** *m* pile dwelling.
Pfand [pfant] *nt* **-(e)s, -er** pledge, security; (*Flaschen*—) deposit; (*im Spiel*) forfeit; (*fig: der Liebe etc*) pledge; ~**brief** *m* bond.
pfänden ['pfɛndən] *vt* seize, distrain.
Pfänderspiel *nt* game of forfeits.
Pfand- *cpd*: ~**haus** *nt* pawnshop; ~**leiher** *m* **-s, -** pawnbroker; ~**schein** *m* pawn ticket.
Pfändung ['pfɛndʊŋ] *f* seizure, distraint.
Pfanne ['pfanə] *f* -, **-n** (frying) pan.
Pfannkuchen *m* pancake; (*Berliner*) doughnut.
Pfarr- ['pfar] *cpd*: ~**ei** [-'raɪ] *f* parish; ~**er** *m* **-s, -** priest; (*evangelisch*) vicar; minister; ~**haus** *nt* vicarage; manse.
Pfau [pfau] *m* **-(e)s, -en** peacock; ~**enauge** *nt* peacock butterfly.
Pfeffer ['pfɛfər] *m* **-s, -** pepper; ~**korn** *nt* peppercorn; ~**kuchen** *m* gingerbread; ~**minz** *nt* **-es, -e** peppermint; ~**mühle** *f* pepper-mill; **p**~**n** *vt* pepper; (*col: werfen*) fling; **gepfefferte Preise/Witze** steep prices/spicy jokes.
Pfeife ['pfaɪfə] *f* -, **-n** whistle; (*Tabak*—, *Orgel*—) pipe; **p**~**n** *vti irreg* whistle; ~**r** *m* **-s, -** piper.
Pfeil [pfaɪl] *m* **-(e)s, -e** arrow.
Pfeiler ['pfaɪlər] *m* **-s, -** pillar, prop; (*Brücken*—) pier.
Pfennig ['pfɛnɪç] *m* **-(e)s, -e** pfennig (*hundredth part of a mark*).
Pferd [pfeːrt] *nt* **-(e)s, -e** horse; ~**erennen** *nt* horse-race; horse-racing; ~**eschwanz** *m* (*Frisur*) ponytail; ~**estall** *m* stable.
Pfiff [pfɪf] *m* **-(e)s, -e** whistle; (*Kniff*) trick; ~**erling** ['pfɪfərlɪŋ] *m* yellow chanterelle; **keinen** ~**erling wert** not worth a thing; **p**~**ig** *a* sly, sharp.
Pfingsten ['pfɪŋstən] *nt* -, -Whitsun.
Pfingstrose ['pfɪŋstroːzə] *f* peony.
Pfirsich ['pfɪrzɪç] *m* **-s, -e** peach.
Pflanz- ['pflants] *cpd*: ~**e** *f* -, **-n** plant; **p**~**en** *vt* plant; ~**enfett** *nt* vegetable fat; ~**er** *m* **-s, -** planter; ~**ung** *f* plantation.
Pflaster ['pflastər] *nt* **-s, -** plaster; (*Straße*) pavement; **p**~**müde** *a* dead on one's feet; **p**~**n** *vt* pave; ~**stein** *m* paving stone.

Pflaume ['pflaʊmə] *f* -, **-n** plum.
Pflege ['pfle:gə] *f* -, **-n** care; (*von Idee*) cultivation; (*Kranken—*) nursing; **in ~ sein** (*Kind*) be fostered out; **p~bedürftig** a needing care; **~eltern** *pl* foster parents *pl*; **~kind** *nt* foster child; **p~leicht** a easy-care; **~mutter** *f* foster mother; **p~n** *vt* look after; *Kranke* nurse; *Beziehungen* foster; **~r** *m* -s, - orderly; male nurse; **~rin** *f* nurse, attendant; **~vater** *m* foster father.
Pflicht [pflɪçt] *f* -, **-en** duty; (*Sport*) compulsory section; **p~bewußt** a conscientious; **~fach** *nt* (*Sch*) compulsory subject; **~gefühl** *nt* sense of duty; **p~gemäß** a dutiful; *ad* as in duty bound; **p~vergessen** a irresponsible; **~versicherung** *f* compulsory insurance.
Pflock [pflɔk] *m* -(e)s, **⸚e** peg; (*für Tiere*) stake.
pflücken ['pflʏkən] *vt* pick; *Blumen auch* pluck.
Pflug [pflu:k] *m* -(e)s, **⸚e** plough.
pflügen ['pfly:gən] *vt* plough.
Pforte ['pfɔrtə] *f* -, **-n** gate; door.
Pförtner ['pfœrtnər] *m* -s, - porter, doorkeeper, doorman.
Pfosten ['pfɔstən] *m* -s, - post.
Pfote ['pfo:tə] *f* -, **-n** paw; (*col: Schrift*) scrawl.
Pfropf [pfrɔpf] *m* -(e)s, **-e** (*Flaschen—*) stopper; (*Blut—*) clot; **p~en** *vt* (*stopfen*) cram; *Baum* graft; **P~en** *m* -s, **-e** *see* **Pfropf**.
pfui [pfʊi] *interj* ugh; (*na na*) tut tut.
Pfund [pfʊnt] *nt* -(e)s, **-e** pound; **p~ig** a (*col*) great; **p~weise** *ad* by the pound.
pfuschen ['pfʊʃən] *vi* (*col*) be sloppy; **jdm in etw** (*acc*) **~** interfere in sth.
Pfuscher ['pfʊʃər] *m* -s, - (*col*) sloppy worker; (*Kur—*) quack; **~ei** [-'raɪ] *f* (*col*) sloppy work; (*Kur—*) quackery.
Pfütze ['pfʏtsə] *f* -, **-n** puddle.
Phänomen [fɛnoˈmeːn] *nt* -s, **-e** phenomenon; **p~al** [-'naːl] a phenomenal.
Phantasie [fanta'ziː] *f* imagination; **p~los** a unimaginative; **p~ren** *vi* fantasize; **p~voll** a imaginative.
phantastisch [fan'tastɪʃ] a fantastic.
Pharisäer [fariˈzɛːər] *m* -s, - (*lit, fig*) pharisee.
Pharmazeut(in *f*) [farmaˈtsɔʏt(ɪn)] *m* **-en, -en** pharmacist.
Phase ['faːzə] *f* -, **-n** phase.
Philanthrop [filanˈtroːp] *m* **-en, -en** philanthropist; **p~isch** a philanthropic.
Philologe [filoˈloːgə] *m* **-n, -n** philologist.
Philologie [filoloˈgiː] *f* philology.
Philosoph [filoˈzoːf] *m* **-en, -en** philosopher; **~ie** [-'fiː] *f* philosophy; **p~isch** a philosophical.
Phlegma ['flɛgma] *nt* -s lethargy; **p~tisch** [flɛˈgmaːtɪʃ] a lethargic.
Phonet- [foˈneːt] *cpd:* **~ik** *f* phonetics *sing;* **p~isch** a phonetic.
Phosphor ['fɔsfɔr] *m* -s phosphorus; **p~eszieren** [fɔsfɔresˈtsiːrən] *vt* phosphoresce.
Photo ['foːto] *nt* -s, -s *etc see* **Foto**.

Phrase ['fraːzə] *f* -, **-n** phrase; (*pej*) hollow phrase.
Physik [fyˈziːk] *f* physics *sing;* **p~alisch** [-ˈkaːlɪʃ] a of physics; **~er(in** *f*) ['fyːzikər(ɪn)] *m* -s, - physicist.
Physiologe [fyzioˈloːgə] *m* **-n, -n** physiologist.
Physiologie [fyzioloˈgiː] *f* physiology.
physisch ['fyːzɪʃ] a physical.
Pianist(in *f*) [piaˈnɪst(ɪn)] *m* pianist.
picheln ['pɪçəln] *vi* (*col*) booze.
Pickel ['pɪkəl] *m* -s, - pimple; (*Werkzeug*) pickaxe; (*Berg—*) ice-axe; **p~ig** a pimply.
picken ['pɪkən] *vi* pick, peck.
Picknick ['pɪknɪk] *nt* -s, **-e** *or* -s picnic; **~ machen** have a picnic.
piepen ['piːpən], **piepsen** ['piːpsən] *vi* chirp.
piesacken ['piːzakən] *vt* (*col*) torment.
Pietät [pieˈtɛːt] *f* piety, reverence; **p~los** a impious, irreverent.
Pigment [pɪgˈmɛnt] *nt* pigment.
Pik [piːk] *nt* -s, -s (*Cards*) spades; **einen ~ auf jdn haben** (*col*) have it in for sb; **p~ant** [piˈkant] a spicy, piquant; (*anzüglich*) suggestive; **p~iert** [piˈkiːrt] a offended.
Pilger ['pɪlgər] *m* -s, - pilgrim; **~fahrt** *f* pilgrimage.
Pille ['pɪlə] *f* -, **-n** pill.
Pilot [piˈloːt] *m* **-en, -en** pilot.
Pilz [pɪlts] *m* **-es, -e** (*eßbar*) mushroom; (*giftig*) toadstool; **~krankheit** *f* fungal disease.
pingelig ['pɪŋəlɪç] a (*col*) fussy.
Pinguin ['pɪŋguiːn] *m* -s, **-e** penguin.
Pinie ['piːniə] *f* pine.
pinkeln ['pɪŋkəln] *vi* (*col*) pee.
Pinsel ['pɪnzəl] *m* -s, - paintbrush.
Pinzette [pɪnˈtsɛtə] *f* tweezers *pl.*
Pionier [pioˈniːr] *m* -s, **-e** pioneer; (*Mil*) sapper, engineer.
Pirat [piˈraːt] *m* **-en, -en** pirate; **~ensender** *m* pirate radio station.
Pirsch [pɪrʃ] *f* - stalking.
Piste ['pɪstə] *f* -, **-n** (*Ski*) run, piste; (*Aviat*) runway.
Pistole [pɪsˈtoːlə] *f* -, **-n** pistol.
Pizza ['pɪtsa] *f* -, -s pizza.
Pkw [pekaˈveː] *m* **-(s), -(s)** *see* **Personenkraftwagen.**
Plackerei [plakəˈraɪ] *f* drudgery.
plädieren [plɛˈdiːrən] *vi* plead.
Plädoyer [plɛdoaˈjeː] *nt* -s, **-s** speech for the defence; (*fig*) plea.
Plage ['plaːgə] *f* -, **-n** plague; (*Mühe*) nuisance; **~geist** *m* pest, nuisance; **p~n** *vt* torment; *vr* toil, slave.
Plakat [plaˈkaːt] *nt* -(e)s, **-e** placard; poster.
Plan [plaːn] *m* -(e)s, **⸚e** plan; (*Karte*) map; **~e** *f* -, **-n** tarpaulin; **p~en** *vt* plan; *Mord etc* plot; **~er** *m* -s, - planner; **~et** [plaˈneːt] *m* **-en -en** planet; **~etenbahn** *f* orbit (of a planet); **p~gemäß** according to schedule *or* plan; (*Rail*) on time; **p~ieren** [plaˈniːrən] *vt* plane, level; **~ierraupe** *f* bulldozer.
Planke ['plaŋkə] *f* -, **-n** plank.

Plänkelei [plɛŋkə'laɪ] f skirmish(ing).
plänkeln ['plɛŋkəln] vi skirmish.
Plankton ['plaŋktɔn] nt -s plankton.
Plan- cpd: p~los a Vorgehen unsystematic; Umherlaufen aimless;
p~mäßig a according to plan;
systematic; (Rail) scheduled.
Plansch- [planʃ] cpd: ~becken nt
paddling pool; p~en vi splash.
Plan- cpd: ~soll nt -s output target;
~stelle f post.
Plantage [plan'ta:ʒə] f -, -n plantation.
Plan- cpd: ~ung f planning; ~wagen m
covered wagon; ~wirtschaft f planned
economy.
plappern ['plapərn] vi chatter.
plärren ['plɛrən] vi (Mensch) cry, whine;
(Radio) blare.
Plasma ['plasma] nt -s, Plasmen
plasma.
Plastik ['plastɪk] f sculpture; nt -s
(Kunststoff) plastic; ~folie f plastic film.
Plastilin [plasti'li:n] nt -s plasticine.
plastisch ['plastɪʃ] a plastic; stell dir das
~ vor! just picture it!
Platane [pla'ta:nə] f -, -n plane (tree).
Platin [pla'ti:n] nt -s platinum.
Platitüde [plati'ty:də] f -, -n platitude.
platonisch [pla'to:nɪʃ] a platonic.
platsch [platʃ] interj splash; ~en vi splash;
~naß a drenched.
plätschern ['plɛtʃərn] vi babble.
platt [plat] a flat; (col: überrascht) flabber-
gasted; (fig: geistlos) flat, boring;
~deutsch a low German; P~e f -, -n
(Speisen—, Phot, Tech) plate; (Stein—) flag;
(Kachel) tile; (Schall—) record.
Plätt- ['plɛt] cpd: ~eisen nt iron; p~en
vti iron.
Platt- cpd: ~enspieler m record player;
~enteller m turntable; ~fuß m flat foot;
(Reifen) flat tyre.
Platz [plats] m -es, ⁼e place; (Sitz—) seat;
(Raum) space, room; (in Stadt) square;
(Sport—) playing field; jdm ~ machen
make room for sb; ~angst f (Med) agora-
phobia; (col) claustrophobia; ~anwei-
ser(in f) m -s, - usher(ette).
Plätzchen ['plɛtsçən] nt spot; (Gebäck)
biscuit.
Platz- cpd: p~en vi burst; (Bombe)
explode; vor Wut p~en (col) be bursting
with anger; ~karte f seat reservation;
~mangel m lack of space; ~patrone f
blank cartridge; ~regen m downpour;
~wunde f cut.
Plauderei [plaudə'raɪ] f chat, conversation; (Rad) talk.
plaudern ['plaudərn] vi chat, talk.
plausibel [plau'zi:bəl] a plausible.
plazieren [pla'tsi:rən] vt place; vr (Sport)
be placed; (Tennis) be seeded.
Plebejer [ple'be:jər] m -s, - plebeian.
plebejisch [ple'be:jɪʃ] a plebeian.
pleite ['plaɪtə] a (col) broke; P~ f -, -n
bankruptcy; (col: Reinfall) flop; P~
machen go bust.
Plenum ['ple:num] nt -s plenum.

Pleuelstange ['plɔyəlʃtaŋə] f connecting
rod.
Plissee [plɪ'se:] nt -s, -s pleat.
Plombe ['plɔmbə] f -, -n lead seal;
(Zahn—) filling.
plombieren [plɔm'bi:rən] vt seal; Zahn fill.
plötzlich ['plœtslɪç] a sudden; ad suddenly.
plump [plump] a clumsy; Hände coarse;
Körper shapeless; ~sen vi (col) plump
down, fall.
Plunder ['plundər] m -s rubbish.
plündern ['plyndərn] vti plunder; Stadt
sack.
Plünderung ['plyndəruŋ] f plundering,
sack, pillage.
Plural ['plu:ra:l] m -s, -e plural;
p~istisch [plura'lɪstɪʃ] a pluralistic.
Plus [plus] nt -, - plus; (Fin) profit;
(Vorteil) advantage; p~ ad plus.
Plüsch [ply:ʃ] m -(e)s, -e plush.
Plus- cpd: ~pol m (Elec) positive pole;
~punkt m point; (fig) point in sb's favour;
~quamperfekt nt -s, -e pluperfect.
Po [po:] m -s, -s (col) bottom, bum.
Pöbel ['pø:bəl] m -s mob, rabble; ~ei
[-'laɪ] f vulgarity; p~haft a low, vulgar.
pochen ['pɔxən] vi knock; (Herz) pound;
auf etw (acc) ~ (fig) insist on sth.
Pocken ['pɔkən] pl smallpox.
Podium ['po:diʊm] nt podium;
~sdiskussion f panel discussion.
Poesie [poe'zi:] f poetry.
Poet [po'e:t] m -en, -en poet; p~isch a
poetic.
Pointe [po'ɛ̃:tə] f -, -n point.
Pokal [po'ka:l] m -s, -e goblet; (Sport) cup;
~spiel nt cup-tie.
Pökel- ['pø:kal] cpd: ~fleisch nt salt
meat; p~n vt pickle, salt.
Pol [po:l] m -s, -e pole; p~ar [po'la:r] a
polar; ~arkreis m arctic circle.
Polemik [po'le:mɪk] f polemics.
polemisch a polemical.
polemisieren [polemi'zi:rən] vi
polemicize.
Police [po'li:s(ə)] f -, -n insurance policy.
Polier [po'li:r] m -s, -e foreman; p~en vt
polish.
Poliklinik [poli'kli:nɪk] f outpatients.
Politik [poli'ti:k] f politics sing; (eine
bestimmte) policy; ~er(in f)
[po'li:tikər(ɪn)] m -s, - politician.
politisch [po'li:tɪʃ] a political.
politisieren [politi'zi:rən] vi talk politics;
vt politicize.
Politur [poli'tu:r] f polish.
Polizei [poli'tsaɪ] f police; ~beamte(r) m
police officer; p~lich a police; sich
p~lich melden register with the police;
~revier nt police station; ~spitzel m
police spy, informer; ~staat m police
state; ~streife f police patrol; ~stunde
f closing time; p~widrig a illegal.
Polizist [poli'tsɪst] m -en, -en policeman;
~in f policewoman.
Pollen ['pɔlən] m -s, - pollen.
Polster ['pɔlstər] nt -s, - cushion;
(Polsterung) upholstery; (in Kleidung)
padding; (fig: Geld) reserves pl; ~er m -s,

- upholsterer; **~möbel** pl upholstered furniture; **p~n** vt upholster; pad; **~ung** f upholstery.
Polter- ['pɔltər] cpd: **~abend** m party on eve of wedding; **p~n** vi (Krach machen) crash; (schimpfen) rant.
Polygamie [polyga'mi:] f polygamy.
Polyp [po'ly:p] m **-en -en** polyp; (pl: Med) adenoids pl; (col) cop.
Pomade [po'ma:də] f pomade.
Pommes frites [pɔm'frit] pl chips pl, French fried potatoes pl.
Pomp [pɔmp] m **-(e)s** pomp.
Pony ['pɔni] m **-s, -s** (Frisur) fringe; nt **-s, -s** (Pferd) pony.
Popo [po'po:] m **-s, -s** bottom, bum.
populär [popu'lɛ:r] a popular.
Popularität [populari'tɛ:t] f popularity.
Pore ['po:rə] f **-, -n** pore.
Pornographie [pɔrnogra'fi:] f pornography.
porös [po'rø:s] a porous.
Porree ['pɔre] m **-s, -s** leek.
Portal [pɔr'ta:l] nt **-s, -e** portal.
Portemonnaie [pɔrtmɔ'ne:] nt **-s, -s** purse.
Portier [pɔrti'e:] m **-s, -s** porter; see **Pförtner**.
Portion [pɔrtsi'o:n] f portion, helping; (col: Anteil) amount.
Porto ['pɔrto] nt **-s, -s** postage; **p~frei** a post-free, (postage) prepaid.
Porträt [pɔr'trɛ:] nt **-s, -s** portrait; **p~ieren** [pɔrtrɛ'ti:rən] vt paint, portray.
Porzellan [pɔrtsɛ'la:n] nt **-s, -e** china, porcelain; (Geschirr) china.
Posaune [po'zaunə] f **-, -n** trombone.
Pose ['po:zə] f **-, -n** pose.
posieren [po'zi:rən] vi pose.
Position [pozitsi'o:n] f position; **~slichter** pl (Aviat) position lights pl.
positiv ['po:ziti:f] a positive; **P~** nt **-s, -e** (Phot) positive.
Positur [pozi'tu:r] f posture, attitude.
possessiv ['pɔsɛsi:f] a possessive; **P~(pronomen)** nt **-s, -e** possessive pronoun.
possierlich [po'si:rlɪç] a funny.
Post [pɔst] f **-, -en** post (office); (Briefe) mail; **~amt** nt post office; **~anweisung** f postal order, money order; **~bote** m postman; **~en** m **-s, -** post, position; (Comm) item; (auf Liste) entry; (Mil) sentry; (Streik—) picket; **~fach** nt post-office box; **~karte** f postcard; **p~lagernd** ad poste restante; **~leitzahl** f postal code; **~scheckkonto** nt postal giro account; **~sparkasse** f post office savings bank; **~stempel** m postmark; **p~wendend** ad by return of (post).
potent [po'tɛnt] a potent; (fig) high-powered.
Potential [potɛntsi'a:l] nt **-s, -e** potential.
potentiell [potɛntsi'ɛl] a potential.
Potenz [po'tɛnts] f power; (eines Mannes) potency.
Pracht [praxt] f **-** splendour, magnificence.
prächtig ['prɛçtɪç] a splendid.

Pracht- cpd: **~stück** nt showpiece; **p~voll** a splendid, magnificent.
Prädikat [prɛdi'ka:t] nt **-(e)s, -e** title; (Gram) predicate; (Zensur) distinction.
prägen ['prɛ:gən] vt stamp; Münze mint; Ausdruck coin; Charakter form.
prägnant [prɛ'gnant] a precise, terse.
Prägnanz [prɛ'gnants] f conciseness, terseness.
Prägung ['prɛ:guŋ] f minting; forming; (Eigenart) character, stamp.
prahlen ['pra:lən] vi boast, brag.
Prahlerei [pra:lə'rai] f boasting.
prahlerisch a boastful.
Praktik ['praktɪk] f practice; **p~abel** [-'ka:bəl] a practicable; **~ant(in** f) [-'kant(ɪn)] m trainee; **~um** nt **-s, Praktika** or **Praktiken** practical training.
praktisch ['praktɪʃ] a practical, handy; **~er Arzt** general practitioner.
praktizieren [prakti'tsi:rən] vti practise.
Praline [pra'li:nə] f chocolate.
prall [pral] a firmly rounded; Segel taut; Arme plump; Sonne blazing; **~en** vi bounce, rebound; (Sonne) blaze.
Prämie ['prɛ:miə] f premium; (Belohnung) award, prize; **p~ren** [prɛ'mi:rən] vt give an award to.
Pranger ['praŋər] m **-s, -** (Hist) pillory; **jdn an den ~ stellen** (fig) pillory sb.
Präparat [prɛpa'ra:t] nt **-(e)s, -e** (Biol) preparation; (Med) medicine.
Präposition [prɛpozitsi'o:n] f preposition.
Prärie [prɛ'ri:] f prairie.
Präsens ['prɛ:zɛns] nt **-** present tense.
präsentieren [prɛzɛn'ti:rən] vt present.
Präservativ [prɛzɛrva'ti:f] nt **-s, -e** contraceptive.
Präsident(in f) [prɛzi'dɛnt(ɪn)] m president; **~schaft** f presidency; **~schaftskandidat** m presidential candidate.
Präsidium [prɛ'zi:diʊm] nt presidency, chair(manship); (Polizei—) police headquarters pl.
prasseln ['prasəln] vi (Feuer) crackle; (Hagel) drum; (Wörter) rain down.
prassen ['prasən] vi live it up.
Präteritum [prɛ'te:ritʊm] nt **-s, Präterita** preterite.
Pratze ['pratsə] f **-, -n** paw.
Präventiv- [prɛvɛn'ti:f] in cpds preventive.
Praxis ['praksɪs] f **-, Praxen** practice; (Behandlungsraum) surgery; (von Anwalt) office.
Präzedenzfall [prɛtse'dɛntsfal] m precedent.
präzis [prɛ'tsi:s] a precise; **P~ion** [prɛtsizi'o:n] f precision.
predigen ['pre:dɪgən] vti preach.
Prediger m **-s, -** preacher.
Predigt ['pre:dɪçt] f **-, -en** sermon.
Preis [prais] m **-es, -e** price; (Sieges-) prize; **um keinen ~** not at any price; **~elbeere** f cranberry; **p~en** [praizən] vi irreg praise; **p~geben** vt irreg abandon; (opfern) sacrifice; (zeigen) expose;

p~gekrönt a prize-winning; ~gericht nt jury; p~günstig a inexpensive; ~lage f price range; p~lich a price, in price; ~sturz m slump; ~träger(in f) m prizewinner; p~wert a inexpensive.

prekär [preˈkɛːr] a precarious.

Prell- [prɛl] cpd: ~bock m buffers pl; p~en vt bump; (fig) cheat, swindle; ~ung f bruise.

Premiere [prəmiˈɛːrə] f-, -n premiere.

Premierminister [prəmiˈeːministər] m prime minister, premier.

Presse [ˈprɛsə] f-, -n press; ~freiheit f freedom of the press; ~meldung f press report; p~n vt press.

pressieren [prɛˈsiːrən] vi (be in a) hurry.

Preß- [ˈprɛs] cpd: ~luft f compressed air; ~luftbohrer m pneumatic drill.

Prestige [prɛsˈtiːʒə] nt -s prestige.

prickeln [ˈprɪkəln] vti tingle, tickle.

Priester [ˈpriːstər] m -s, - priest.

prima [ˈpriːma] a first-class, excellent; P~ f-, Primen sixth form, top class.

primär [priˈmɛːr] a primary.

Primel [ˈpriːməl] f-, -n primrose.

primitiv [primiˈtiːf] a primitive.

Prinz [prɪnts] m -en, -en prince; ~essin [prɪnˈtsɛsɪn] f princess.

Prinzip [prɪnˈtsiːp] nt -s, -ien principle; p~iell [-iˈɛl] a,ad on principle; p~ienlos a unprincipled.

Priorität [prioriˈtɛːt] f priority.

Prise [ˈpriːzə] f-, -n pinch.

Prisma [ˈprɪsma] nt -s, Prismen prism.

privat [priˈvaːt] a privat; P~ in cpds private.

pro [proː] prep +acc per; P~ nt - pro.

Probe [ˈproːbə] f -, -n test; (Teststück) sample; (Theat) rehearsal; jdn auf die ~ stellen put sb to the test; ~exemplar nt specimen copy; ~fahrt f test drive; p~n vt try; (Theat) rehearse; p~weise ad on approval; ~zeit f probation period.

probieren [proˈbiːrən] vti try; Wein, Speise taste, sample.

Problem [proˈbleːm] nt -s, -e problem; ~atik [-ˈmaːtɪk] f problem; p~atisch [-ˈmaːtɪʃ] a problematic; p~los a problemfree.

Produkt [proˈdʊkt] nt -(e)s, -e product; (Agr) produce no pl; ~ion [prodʊktsiˈoːn] f production; output; p~iv [-ˈtiːf] a productive; ~ivität f productivity.

Produzent [produˈtsɛnt] m manufacturer; (Film) producer.

produzieren [produˈtsiːrən] vt produce.

Professor [proˈfɛsɔr] m professor.

Professur [profɛˈsuːr] f chair.

Profil [proˈfiːl] nt -s, -e profile; (fig) image; p~ieren [profiˈliːrən] vr create an image for o.s.

Profit [proˈfiːt] m -(e)s, -e profit; p~ieren [profiˈtiːrən] vi profit (von from).

Prognose [proˈgnoːzə] f -, -n prediction, prognosis.

Programm [proˈgram] nt -s, -e programme; p~(m)äßig a according to plan; p~ieren [-ˈmiːrən] vt programme; ~ierer(in f) m -s, - programmer.

progressiv [progrɛˈsiːf] a progressive.

Projekt [proˈjɛkt] nt -(e)s, -e project; ~or [proˈjɛktɔr] m projector.

projizieren [projiˈtsiːrən] vt project.

proklamieren [proklaˈmiːrən] vt proclaim.

Prolet [proˈleːt] m -en, -en prole, pleb; ~ariat [-ariˈaːt] nt -(e)s, -e proletariat; ~arier [-ˈtaːriər] m -s, - proletarian.

Prolog [proˈloːk] m -(e)s, -e prologue.

Promenade [proməˈnaːdə] f promenade.

Promille [proˈmɪlə] nt -(s), - alcohol level.

prominent [promiˈnɛnt] a prominent.

Prominenz [promiˈnɛnts] f VIPs pl.

Promotion [promotsiˈoːn] f doctorate, Ph.D.

promovieren [promoˈviːrən] vi do a doctorate or Ph.D.

prompt [prɔmpt] a prompt.

Pronomen [proˈnoːmən] nt -s, - pronoun.

Propaganda [propaˈganda] f - propaganda.

Propeller [proˈpɛlər] m -s, - propeller.

Prophet [proˈfeːt] m -en, -en prophet; ~in f prophetess.

prophezeien [profeˈtsaɪən] vt prophesy.

Prophezeiung f prophecy.

Proportion [proˈpɔrtsiˈoːn] f proportion; p~al [-ˈnaːl] a proportional.

Prosa [ˈproːza] f - prose; p~isch [proˈzaːɪʃ] a prosaic.

prosit [ˈproːzɪt] interj cheers.

Prospekt [proˈspɛkt] m -(e)s, -e leaflet, brochure.

prost [proːst] interj cheers.

Prostituierte [prostituˈiːrtə] f -n, -n prostitute.

Prostitution [prostitutsiˈoːn] f prostitution.

Protest [proˈtɛst] m -(e)s, -e protest; ~ant(in f) [protɛsˈtant] m Protestant; p~antisch [protɛsˈtantɪʃ] a Protestant; p~ieren [protɛsˈtiːrən] vi protest; ~kundgebung f (protest) rally.

Prothese [proˈteːzə] f -, -n artificial limb; (Zahn~) dentures pl.

Protokoll [protoˈkɔl] nt -s, -e register; (von Sitzung) minutes pl; (diplomatisch) protocol; (Polizei~) statement; p~ieren [-ˈliːrən] vt take down in the minutes.

Proton [ˈproːtɔn] nt -s, -en proton.

Protz [prɔts] m -en, -e(n) swank; p~en vi show off; p~ig a ostentatious.

Proviant [proviˈant] m -s, -e provisions pl, supplies pl.

Provinz [proˈvɪnts] f -, -en province; p~iell a provincial.

Provision [provɪziˈoːn] f (Comm) commission.

provisorisch [proviˈzoːrɪʃ] a provisional.

Provokation [provokatsiˈoːn] f provocation.

provozieren [provoˈtsiːrən] vt provoke.

Prozedur [protseˈduːr] f procedure; (pej) carry-on.

Prozent [proˈtsɛnt] nt -(e)s, -e per cent, percentage; ~rechnung f percentage calculation; ~satz m percentage; p~ual

[-u'a:l] a percentage; as a percentage.

Prozeß [pro'tsɛs] m **-sses, -sse** trial, case; ~**kosten** pl (legal) costs pl.

prozessieren [protsɛ'si:rən] vi bring an action, go to law (mit against).

Prozession [protsɛsi'o:n] f procession.

prüde ['pry:də] a prudish; **P~rie** [-'ri:] f prudery.

Prüf- ['pry:f] cpd: **p~en** vt examine, test; (nach—) check; ~**er** m -s, - examiner; ~**ling** m examinee; ~**stein** m touchstone; ~**ung** f examination; checking; ~**ungsausschuß** m, ~**ungskommission** f examining board.

Prügel ['pry:gəl] m -s, - cudgel; pl beating; ~**ei** [-'laɪ] f fight; ~**knabe** m scapegoat; **p~n** vt beat; vr fight; ~**strafe** f corporal punishment.

Prunk [prʊŋk] m **-(e)s** pomp, show; **p~voll** a splendid, magnificent.

Psalm [psalm] m -s, -en psalm.

pseudo- [psɔʏdo] in cpds pseudo-.

Psych- ['psyç] cpd: ~**iater** [-i'a:tər] m -s, - psychiatrist; **p~isch** a psychological; ~**oanalyse** [-o'analy:zə] f psychoanalysis; ~**ologe** [-o'lo:gə] m -n, -n psychologist; ~**ologie** f psychology; **p~ologisch** a psychological.

Pubertät [pubɛr'tɛ:t] f puberty.

Publikum ['pu:blikʊm] nt -s audience; (Sport) crowd.

publizieren [publi'tsi:rən] vt publish, publicize.

Pudding ['pʊdɪŋ] m -s, -e or -s blancmange.

Pudel ['pu:dəl] m -s poodle.

Puder ['pu:dər] m -s, - powder; ~**dose** f powder compact; **p~n** vt powder; ~**zucker** m icing sugar.

Puff [pʊf] m -s, -e (Wäsche-) linen basket; (Sitz—) pouf; pl -e (col: Stoß) push; pl -s (col: Bordell) brothel; ~**er** m -s, - buffer; ~**erstaat** m buffer state.

Pulli ['pʊli] m -s, -s (col), **Pullover** [pʊ'lo:vər] m -s, - pullover, jumper.

Puls [pʊls] m **-es, -e** pulse; ~**ader** f artery; **p~ieren** [pʊl'zi:rən] vi throb, pulsate.

Pult [pʊlt] nt **-(e)s, -e** desk.

Pulver ['pʊlfər] nt -s, - powder; **p~ig** a powdery; **p~isieren** [pʊlveri'zi:rən] vt pulverize; ~**schnee** m powdery snow.

pummelig ['pʊməlɪç] a chubby.

Pumpe ['pʊmpə] f -, -n pump; **p~n** vt pump; (col) lend; borrow.

Punkt [pʊŋkt] m **-(e)s, -e** point; (bei Muster) dot; (Satzzeichen) full stop; **p~ieren** [-'ti:rən] vt dot; (Med) aspirate.

pünktlich ['pʏŋktlɪç] a punctual; **P~keit** f punctuality.

Punkt- cpd: ~**sieg** m victory on points; ~**zahl** f score.

Punsch [pʊnʃ] m **-(e)s, -e** punch.

Pupille [pu'pɪlə] f -, -n pupil.

Puppe ['pʊpə] f -, -n doll; (Marionette) puppet; (Insekten—) pupa, chrysalis; ~**nspieler** m puppeteer; ~**nstube** f doll's house.

pur [pu:r] a pure; (völlig) sheer; Whisky neat.

Püree [py're:] nt -s, -s mashed potatoes pl.

Purzel- ['pʊrtsəl] cpd: ~**baum** m somersault; **p~n** vi tumble.

Puste ['pu:stə] f - (col) puff; (fig) steam; ~**l** ['pʊstəl] f -, -n pustule; **p~n** vi puff, blow.

Pute ['pu:tə] f -, -n turkey-hen; ~**r** m -s, - turkey-cock.

Putsch [pʊtʃ] m **-(e)s, -e** revolt, putsch; **p~en** vi revolt; ~**ist** m rebel.

Putz [pʊts] m **-es** (Mörtel) plaster, roughcast; **p~en** vt clean; Nase wipe, blow; vr clean oneself; dress oneself up; ~**frau** f charwoman; **p~ig** a quaint, funny; ~**lappen** m cloth; ~**tag** m cleaning day; ~**zeug** nt cleaning things pl.

Puzzle ['pasəl] nt -s, -s jigsaw.

Pyjama [pi'dʒa:ma] m -s, -s pyjamas pl.

Pyramide [pyra'mi:də] f -, -n pyramid.

Q

Q, q [ku:] nt Q, q.

quabb(e)lig ['kvab(ə)lɪç] a wobbly; Frosch slimy.

Quacksalber ['kvakzalbər] m -s, - quack (doctor).

Quader ['kva:dər] m -s, - square stone; (Math) cuboid.

Quadrat [kva'dra:t] nt **-(e)s, -e** square; **q~isch** a square; ~**meter** m square metre.

quadrieren [kva'dri:rən] vt square.

quaken ['kva:kən] vi croak; (Ente) quack.

quäken ['kvɛ:kən] vi screech; ~**d** a screeching.

Qual [kva:l] f -, -en pain, agony; (seelisch) anguish.

Qual- [kvɛ:l] cpd: **q~en** vt torment; vr struggle; (geistig) torment oneself; ~**erei** [-ə'raɪ] f torture, torment; ~**geist** m pest.

qualifizieren [kvalifi'tsi:rən] vtr qualify; (einstufen) label.

Qualität [kvali'tɛ:t] f quality; ~**sware** f article of high quality.

Qualle ['kvalə] f -, -n jellyfish.

Qualm [kvalm] m **-(e)s** thick smoke; **q~en** vti smoke.

qualvoll ['kva:lfɔl] a excruciating, painful, agonizing.

Quant- ['kvant] cpd: ~**entheorie** f quantum theory; ~**ität** [-i'tɛ:t] f quantity; **q~itativ** [-ita'ti:f] a quantitative; ~**um** nt -s, Quanten quantity, amount.

Quarantäne [karan'tɛ:nə] f -, -n quarantine.

Quark [kvark] m -s curd cheese; (col) rubbish.

Quarta ['kvarta] f -, **Quarten** third year of secondary school; ~**l** [kvar'ta:l] nt -s, -e quarter (year).

Quartier [kvar'ti:r] nt -s, -e accommodation; (Mil) quarters pl; (Stadt—) district.

Quarz [kva:rts] m **-es, -e** quartz.

quasseln ['kvasəln] vi (col) natter.

Quatsch [kvatʃ] m **-es** rubbish; **q~en** vi chat, natter.

Quecksilber ['kvɛkzɪlbər] nt mercury.

Quelle ['kvɛlə] f -, -n spring; (eines Flusses)

source; **q~n** *vi (hervor—)* pour *or* gush forth; *(schwellen)* swell.

quengel- ['kveŋəl] *cpd:* **Q~ei** [-'laɪ] *f (col)* whining; **~ig** *a (col)* whining; **~n** *vi (col)* whine.

quer [kveːr] *ad* crossways, diagonally; *(rechtwinklig)* at right angles; **~ auf dem Bett** across the bed; **Q~balken** *m* crossbeam; **~feldein** *ad* across country; **Q~flöte** *f* flute; **Q~kopf** *m* awkward customer; **Q~schiff** *nt* transept; **Q~schnitt** *m* cross-section; **~schnittsgelähmt** *a* paralysed below the waist; **Q~straße** *f* intersecting road; **Q~treiber** *m* **-s, -** obstructionist; **Q~verbindung** *f* connection, link.

quetschen ['kvɛtʃən] *vt* squash, crush; *(Med)* bruise.

Quetschung *f* bruise, contusion.

quieken ['kviːkən] *vi* squeak.

quietschen ['kviːtʃən] *vi* squeak.

Quint- ['kvɪnt] *cpd:* **~a** *f* **-, -en** second form in secondary school; **~essenz** [-'ɛsɛnts] *f* quintessence; **~ett** [-'tɛt] *nt* **-(e)s, -e** quintet.

Quirl [kvɪrl] *m* **-(e)s, -e** whisk.

quitt [kvɪt] *a* quits, even; **Q~e** *f* **-, -n** quince; **~engelb** *a* sickly yellow; **~ieren** [-'tiːrən] *vt* give a receipt for; *Dienst* leave; **Q~ung** *f* receipt.

Quiz [kvɪs] *nt* **-, -** quiz.

Quote ['kvoːtə] *f* **-, -n** number, rate.

R

R, r [ɛr] *nt* R, r.

Rabatt [ra'bat] *m* **-(e)s, -e** discount; **~e** *f* **-, -n** flowerbed, border; **~marke** *f* trading stamp.

Rabe ['raːbə] *m* **-n, -n** raven; **~nmutter** *f* bad mother.

rabiat [rabi'aːt] *a* furious.

Rache ['raxə] *f* **-** revenge, vengeance; **~n** *m* **-s, -** throat.

rächen ['rɛçən] *vt* avenge, revenge; *vr* take (one's) revenge; **das wird sich ~** you'll pay for that.

Rach- ['rax] *cpd:* **~itis** [ra'xiːtɪs] *f* **-** rickets *sing;* **~sucht** *f* vindictiveness; **r~süchtig** *a* vindictive.

Racker ['rakər] *m* **-s, -** rascal, scamp.

Rad [raːt] *nt* **-(e)s, -̈er** wheel; *(Fahr—)* bike; **~ar** [ra'daːr] *m or nt* **-s** radar; **~arkontrolle** *f* radar-controlled speed trap; **~au** [ra'dau] *m* **-s** *(col)* row; **~dampfer** *m* paddle steamer; **r~ebrechen** *vi insep:* **deutsch** *etc* **r~ebrechen** speak broken German *etc*; **r~eln** *vi,* **r~fahren** *vi irreg* cycle; **~fahrer(in** *f) m* cyclist; **~fahrweg** *m* cycle track *or* path.

Radier- [ra'diːr] *cpd:* **r~en** *vt* rub out, erase; *(Art)* etch; **~gummi** *m* rubber, eraser; **~ung** *f* etching.

Radieschen [ra'diːsçən] *nt* radish.

radikal [radi'kaːl] *a,* **R~e(r)** *mf* radical.

Radio ['raːdio] *nt* **-s, -s** radio, wireless; **r~ak'tiv** *a* radioactive; **~aktivi'tät** *f* radioactivity; **~apparat** *m* radio, wireless set.

Radium ['raːdium] *nt* **-s** radium.

Radius ['raːdius] *m* **-, Radien** radius.

Rad- *cpd:* **~kappe** *f (Aut)* hub cap; **~ler(in** *f) m* **-s, -** cyclist; **~rennbahn** *f* cycling (race)track; **~rennen** *nt* cycle race; cycle racing; **~sport** *m* cycling.

raff- [raf] *cpd:* **~en** *vt* snatch, pick up; *Stoff* gather (up); *Geld* pile up, rake in; **R~inade** [-i'naːdə] *f* refined sugar; **~inieren** [-i'niːrən] *vt* refine; **~i'niert** *a* crafty, cunning; *Zucker* refined.

ragen ['raːgən] *vi* tower, rise.

Rahm [raːm] *m* **-s** cream; **~en** *m* **-s, -** frame(work); **im ~en des Möglichen** within the bounds of possibility; **r~en** *vt* frame; **r~ig** *a* creamy.

Rakete [ra'keːtə] *f* **-, -n** rocket; **ferngelenkte ~** guided missile.

rammen ['ramən] *vt* ram.

Rampe ['rampə] *f* **-, -n** ramp; **~nlicht** *vt (Theat)* footlights *pl.*

ramponieren [rampo'niːrən] *vt (col)* damage.

Ramsch [ramʃ] *m* **-(e)s, -e** junk.

ran [ran] *ad (col) =* **heran.**

Rand [rant] *m* **-(e)s, -̈er** edge; *(von Brille, Tasse etc)* rim; *(Hut—)* brim; *(auf Papier)* margin; *(Schmutz—, unter Augen)* ring; *(fig)* verge, brink; **außer ~ und Band** wild; **am ~e bemerkt** mentioned in passing; **r~alieren** [randa'liːrən] *vi* (go on the) rampage; **~bemerkung** *f* marginal note; *(fig)* odd comment; **~erscheinung** *f* unimportant side effect, marginal phenomenon.

Rang [raŋ] *m* **-(e)s, -̈e** rank; *(Stand)* standing; *(Wert)* quality; *(Theat)* circle; **~abzeichen** *nt* badge of rank; **~älteste(r)** *m* senior officer.

Rangier- [rãˈʒiːr] *cpd:* **~bahnhof** *m* marshalling yard; **r~en** *vt (Rail)* shunt, switch *(US); vi* rank, be classed; **~gleis** *nt* siding.

Rang- *cpd:* **~ordnung** *f* hierarchy; *(Mil)* rank; **~unterschied** *m* social distinction; *(Mil)* difference in rank.

Ranke ['raŋkə] *f* **-, -n** tendril, shoot.

Ränke ['rɛŋkə] *pl* intrigues *pl;* **~schmied** *m* intriguer; **r~voll** *a* scheming.

Ranzen ['rantsən] *m* **-s, -** satchel; *(col: Bauch)* gut, belly.

ranzig ['rantsɪç] *a* rancid.

Rappe ['rapə] *m* **-n, -n** black horse.

Raps [raps] *m* **-es, -e** *(Bot)* rape.

rar [raːr] *a* rare; **sich ~ machen** *(col)* keep oneself to oneself; **R~i'tät** *f* rarity; *(Sammelobjekt)* curio.

rasant [ra'zant] *a* quick, rapid.

rasch [raʃ] *a* quick; **~eln** *vi* rustle.

Rasen ['raːzən] *m* **-s, -** lawn; grass; **r~** *vi* rave; *(schnell)* race; **r~d** *a* furious; **r~de Kopfschmerzen** a splitting head-ache; **~mäher** *m* **-s, -, ~mähmaschine** *f* lawnmower; **~platz** *m* lawn.

Raserei [raːzə'raɪ] *f* raving, ranting; *(Schnelle)* reckless speeding.

Rasier- [ra'ziːr] *cpd:* **~apparat** *m* shaver; **~creme** *f* shaving cream; **r~en** *vtr* shave; **~klinge** *f* razor blade; **~messer** *nt* razor; **~pinsel** *m* shaving brush;

~**seife** f shaving soap or stick; ~**wasser** nt shaving lotion.

Rasse [ˈrasə] f -, -n race; (Tier—) breed; ~**hund** m thoroughbred dog; ~**l** f -, -n rattle; **r**~**ln** vi rattle, clatter; ~**nhaß** m race or racial hatred; ~**ntrennung** f racial segregation.

Rast [rast] f -, -en rest; **r**~**en** vi rest; ~**haus** nt (Aut) service station; **r**~**los** a tireless; (unruhig) restless; ~**platz** m (Aut) layby.

Rasur [raˈzuːr] f shaving; (Radieren) erasure.

Rat [raːt] m -(e)s, ~**schläge** (piece of) advice; **jdn zu** ~**e ziehen** consult sb; **keinen** ~ **wissen** not know what to do; ~**e** f -, -**n** instalment; **r**~**en** vti irreg guess; (empfehlen) advise (jdm sb); **r**~**enweise** ad by instalments; ~**enzahlung** f hire purchase; ~**geber** m -s, - adviser; ~**haus** nt town hall.

ratifizier- [ratifiˈtsiːr] cpd: ~**en** vt ratify; **R**~**ung** f ratification.

Ration [ratsiˈoːn] f ration; **r**~**al** [-ˈnaːl] a rational; **r**~**ali'sieren** vt rationalize; **r**~**ell** [-ˈnɛl] a efficient; **r**~**ieren** [-ˈniːrən] vt ration.

Rat- cpd: **r**~**los** a at a loss, helpless; ~**losigkeit** f helplessness; **r**~**sam** a advisable; ~**schlag** m (piece of) advice.

Rätsel [ˈrɛːtsəl] nt -s, - puzzle; (Wort—) riddle; **r**~**haft** a mysterious; **es ist mir r**~**haft** it's a mystery to me.

Rats- cpd: ~**herr** m councillor; ~**keller** m town-hall restaurant.

Ratte [ˈratə] f -, -n rat; ~**nfänger** m -s, - ratcatcher.

rattern [ˈratərn] vi rattle, clatter.

Raub [raup] m -(e)s robbery; (Beute) loot, booty; ~**bau** m ruthless exploitation; **r**~**en** [ˈraubən] vt rob; Mensch kidnap, abduct.

Räuber [ˈrɔybər] m -s, - robber; **r**~**isch** a thieving.

Raub- cpd: **r**~**gierig** a rapacious; ~**mord** m robbery with murder; ~**tier** nt predator; ~**überfall** m robbery with violence; ~**vogel** m bird of prey.

Rauch [ˈraux] m -(e)s smoke; **r**~**en** vti smoke; ~**er** m -s, - smoker; ~**erabteil** nt (Rail) smoker.

räuchern [ˈrɔyçərn] vt smoke, cure.

Rauch- cpd: ~**fahne** f smoke trail; ~**fleisch** nt smoked meat; **r**~**ig** a smoky.

räudig [ˈrɔydiç] a mangy.

rauf [rauf] ad (col) = **herauf**; **R**~**bold** m -(e)s, -e rowdy, hooligan; ~**en** vt Haare pull out; vir fight; **R**~**e'rei** f brawl, fight; ~**lustig** a spoiling for a fight, rowdy.

rauh [rau] a rough, coarse; Wetter harsh; ~**haarig** a wire-haired; **R**~**reif** m hoarfrost.

Raum [raum] m -(e)s, **Räume** space; (Zimmer, Platz) room; (Gebiet) area; ~**bild** nt 3D picture.

räumen [ˈrɔymən] vt clear; Wohnung, Platz vacate; (wegbringen) shift, move; (in Schrank etc) put away.

Raum- cpd: ~**fahrt** f space travel;

~**inhalt** m cubic capacity, volume.

räumlich [ˈrɔymliç] a spatial; **R**~**keiten** pl premises pl.

Raum- cpd: ~**mangel** m lack of space; ~**meter** m cubic metre; ~**pflegerin** f cleaner; ~**schiff** nt spaceship; ~**schiffahrt** f space travel; **r**~**sparend** a space-saving.

Räumung [ˈrɔymuŋ] f vacating, evacuation; clearing (away); ~**sverkauf** m clearance sale.

raunen [ˈraunən] vti whisper mysteriously.

Raupe [ˈraupə] f -, -n caterpillar; (—nkette) (caterpillar) track; ~**n-schlepper** m caterpillar tractor.

raus [raus] ad (col) = **heraus, hinaus.**

Rausch [rauʃ] m -(e)s, **Räusche** intoxication; **r**~**en** vi (Wasser) rush; (Baum) rustle; (Radio etc) hiss; (Mensch) sweep, sail; **r**~**end** a Beifall thunderous; Fest sumptuous; ~**gift** nt drug; ~**giftsüchtige(r)** mf drug addict.

räuspern [ˈrɔyspərn] vr clear one's throat.

Raute [ˈrautə] f -, -n diamond; (Math) rhombus; **r**~**nförmig** a rhombic.

Razzia [ˈratsia] f -, **Razzien** raid.

Reagenzglas [reaˈgɛntsglaːs] nt test tube.

reagieren [reaˈgiːrən] vi react (auf +acc to).

Reakt- cpd: ~**ion** [reaktsiˈoːn] f reaction; **r**~**io'när** a reactionary; ~**ionsgeschwindigkeit** f speed of reaction; ~**or** [reˈaktɔr] m reactor.

real [reˈaːl] a real, material; **R**~**ismus** [-ˈlismus] m realism; **R**~**ist** [-ˈlist] m realist; ~**istisch** a realistic.

Rebe [ˈreːbə] f -, -n vine.

Rebell [reˈbɛl] m -en, -en rebel; ~**ion** f rebellion; **r**~**isch** a rebellious.

Reb- cpd: ~**ensaft** m grape juice; ~**huhn** [ˈrɛphuːn] nt partridge; ~**stock** m vine.

Rechen [ˈrɛçən] m -s, - rake; **r**~ vti rake; ~**aufgabe** f sum, mathematical problem; ~**fehler** m miscalculation; ~**maschine** f calculating machine; ~**schaft** f account; ~**schaftsbericht** m report; ~**schieber** m slide rule.

Rech- [ˈrɛç] cpd: **r**~**nen** vti calculate; **jdn/etw r**~**nen zu** or **unter** (+acc) count sb/sth among; **r**~**nen mit** reckon with; **r**~**nen auf** (+acc) count on; ~**ner** m -s, calculator; ~**nung** f calculation(s); (Comm) bill, check (US); **jdm/etw** ~**nung tragen** take sb/sth into account; ~**nungsbuch** nt account book; ~**nungsjahr** nt financial year; ~**nungsprüfer** m auditor; ~**nungsprüfung** f audit(ing).

recht [rɛçt] a, ad right; (vor Adjektiv) really, quite; **das ist mir** ~ that suits me; **jetzt erst** ~ now more than ever; ~ **haben** be right; **jdm** ~ **geben** agree with sb; **r**~**en** nt -(e)s, -e right; (Jur) law; **R**~ **sprechen** administer justice; **mit R**~ rightly, justly; **von R**~**s wegen** by rights; **R**~**e** f -n, -**n** right (hand); (Pol) Right; ~**e(r,s)** a right; (Pol) right-wing; **R**~**e(r)** mf right person; **R**~**e(s)** nt right thing; **etwas/nichts R**~**es** something/nothing proper; **R~eck** nt -s, -e rectangle; **~eckig** a rectangular; **~fertigen** vtr insep justify (o.s.); **R~fertigung** f justification; **~haberisch** a dogmatic; **~lich** a, **~mäßig** a legal, lawful.

rechts [rɛçts] ad on/to the right; **R~anwalt** m, **R~anwältin** f lawyer, barrister; **R~'außen** m -, - (Sport) outside right; **R~beistand** m legal adviser.

Recht- cpd: **r~schaffen** a upright; **~schreibung** f spelling.

Rechts- cpd: **~drehung** f clockwise rotation; **~fall** m (law) case; **~frage** f legal question; **~händer** m -s, - right-handed person; **r~kräftig** a valid, legal; **~kurve** f right-hand bend; **~pflege** f administration of justice; **r~radikal** a (Pol) extreme right-wing; **~spruch** m verdict; **~verkehr** m driving on the right; **r~widrig** a illegal; **~wissenschaft** f jurisprudence.

recht- cpd: **~winklig** a right-angled; **~zeitig** a timely; ad in time.

Reck [rɛk] nt -(e)s, -e horizontal bar; **r~en** vtr stretch.

Redak- cpd: **~teur** [redak'tøːr] m editor; **~tion** [redaktsi'oːn] f editing; (Leute) editorial staff; (Büro) editorial office(s).

Rede ['reːdə] f -, -n speech; (Gespräch) talk; **jdn zur ~ stellen** take sb to task; **~freiheit** f freedom of speech; **r~gewandt** a eloquent; **r~n** vi talk, speak; vt say; Unsinn etc talk; **~n** nt -s talking, speech; **~nsart** f set phrase; **~wendung** f expression, idiom.

red- cpd: **~lich** ['reːtlɪç] a honest; **R~lichkeit** f honesty; **R~ner** m -s, - speaker, orator; **~selig** ['reːtzeːlɪç] a talkative, loquacious; **R~seligkeit** f talkativeness.

reduzieren [redu'tsiːrən] vt reduce.

Reede ['reːdə] f -, -n protected anchorage; **~r** m -s, - shipowner; **~rei** f shipping line or firm.

reell [re'ɛl] a fair, honest; (Math) real.

Refer- cpd: **~at** [refe'raːt] nt -(e)s, -e report; (Vortrag) paper; (Gebiet) section; **~ent** [refe'rɛnt] m speaker; (Berichterstatter) reporter; (Sachbearbeiter) expert; **~enz** [refe'rɛnts] f reference; **r~ieren** [refe'riːrən] vi: **r~ieren über** (+acc) speak or talk on.

reflektieren [reflɛk'tiːrən] vti reflect; **~auf** (+acc) be interested in.

Reflex [re'flɛks] m -es, -e reflex; **~bewegung** f reflex action; **r~iv** [-'ksiːf] a (Gram) reflexive.

Reform [re'fɔrm] f -, -en reform; **~ati'on** f reformation; **~ator** [-'maːtɔr] m reformer; **r~atorisch** a reformatory, reforming; **~haus** nt health food shop; **r~ieren** [-'miːrən] vt reform.

Refrain [rə'frɛː] m -s, -s refrain, chorus.

Regal [re'gaːl] nt -s, -e (book)shelves pl, bookcase; stand, rack.

rege ['reːgə] a lively, active; Geschäft brisk.

Regel ['reːgəl] f -, -n rule; (Med) period; **r~los** a irregular, unsystematic; **r~mäßig** a regular; **~mäßigkeit** f

regularity; **r~n** vt regulate, control; Angelegenheit settle; vr: **sich von selbst r~n** take care of itself; **r~recht** a regular, proper, thorough; **~ung** f regulation; settlement; **r~widrig** a irregular, against the rules.

regen ['reːgən] vtr move, stir; **R~** m -s, - rain; **R~bogen** m rainbow; **R~bogenhaut** f (Anat) iris; **R~guß** m downpour; **R~mantel** m raincoat, mac(kintosh); **R~menge** f rainfall; **R~schauer** m shower (of rain); **R~schirm** m umbrella.

Regent [re'gɛnt] m regent; **~schaft** f regency.

Regen- cpd: **~tag** m rainy day; **~wurm** m earthworm; **~zeit** f rainy season, rains pl.

Regie [re'ʒiː] f (Film etc) direction; (Theat) production; **r~ren** [re'giːrən] vti govern, rule; **~rung** f government; (Monarchie) reign; **~rungswechsel** m change of government; **~rungszeit** f period in government; (von König) reign.

Regiment [regi'mɛnt] nt -s, -er regiment.

Region [regi'oːn] f region.

Regisseur [reʒi'søːr] m director; (Theat) (stage) producer.

Register [re'gɪstər] nt -s, - register; (in Buch) table of contents, index.

Registratur [regɪs'traːtuːr] f registry, record office.

registrieren [regɪs'triːrən] vt register.

reg- ['reːg] cpd: **R~ler** m -s, - regulator, governor; **~los** ['reːkloːs] a motionless; **~nen** vi impers rain; **~nerisch** a rainy; **~sam** ['reːkzaːm] a active.

regulär [regu'lɛːr] a regular.

regulieren [regu'liːrən] vt regulate; (Comm) settle.

Regung ['reːgʊŋ] f motion; (Gefühl) feeling, impulse; **r~slos** a motionless.

Reh [reː] nt -(e)s, -e deer, roe; **~bock** m roebuck; **~kalb** nt, **~kitz** nt fawn.

Reib- ['raɪb] cpd: **~e** f -, -n, **~eisen** nt grater; **r~en** vt irreg rub; (Cook) grate; **~erei** f friction no pl; **~fläche** f rough surface; **~ung** f friction; **r~ungslos** a smooth.

reich [raɪç] a rich; **R~** nt -(e)s, -e empire, kingdom; (fig) realm; **das Dritte R~** the Third Reich; **~en** vi reach; (genügen) be enough or sufficient (jdm for sb); vt hold out; (geben) pass, hand; (anbieten) offer; **~haltig** a ample, rich; **~lich** a ample, plenty of; **R~tum** m -s, -tümer wealth; **R~weite** f range.

reif [raɪf] a ripe; Mensch, Urteil mature; **R~** m -(e)s hoarfrost; -(e)s, -e (Ring) ring, hoop; **R~e** f - ripeness; maturity; **~en** vi mature; ripen; **R~en** m -s, - ring, hoop; (Fahrzeug-) tyre; **R~enschaden** m puncture; **R~eprüfung** f school leaving exam; **R~ezeugnis** nt school leaving certificate.

Reihe ['raɪə] f -, -n row; (von Tagen etc, col: Anzahl) series sing; **der ~ nach** in turn; **er ist an der ~** it's his turn; **an die ~ kommen** have one's turn; **r~n** vt set in a row; arrange in series; Perlen string;

~nfolge f sequence; **alphabetische ~nfolge** alphabetical order; **~nhaus** nt terraced house; **~r** m **-s, -** heron.

Reim [raim] m **-(e)s, -e** rhyme; **r~en** vt rhyme.

rein [rain] ad (col) = **herein, hinein**; a, ad pure(ly); (sauber) clean; **etw ins ~e schreiben** make a fair copy of sth; **etw ins ~e bringen** clear up sth; **R~** in cpds (Comm) net(t); **R~(e)machefrau** f charwoman; **R~fall** m (col) let-down; **R~gewinn** m net profit; **R~heit** f purity; cleanliness; **~igen** vt clean; Wasser purify; **R~igung** f cleaning; purification; (Geschäft) cleaners; **chemische R~igung** dry cleaning; dry cleaners; **~lich** a clean; **R~lichkeit** f cleanliness; **~rassig** a pedigree; **R~schrift** f fair copy; **~waschen** vr irreg clear oneself.

Reis [rais] m **-es, -e** rice; nt **-es, -er** twig, sprig.

Reise ['raizə] f **-, -n** journey; (Schiff~) voyage; **~n** pl travels pl; (Schiff~) voyage; **~andenken** nt souvenir; **~büro** nt travel agency; **r~fertig** a ready to start; **~führer** m guide(book); (Mensch) travel guide; **~gepäck** nt luggage; **~gesellschaft** f party of travellers; **~kosten** pl travelling expenses pl; **~leiter** m courier; **~lektüre** f reading matter for the journey; **r~n** vi travel; go (nach to); **~nde(r)** mf traveller; **~paß** m passport; **~pläne** pl plans pl for a journey; **~proviant** m provisions pl for the journey; **~scheck** m traveller's cheque; **~tasche** f travelling bag or case; **~verkehr** m tourist/holiday traffic; **~wetter** nt holiday weather; **~ziel** nt destination.

Reisig ['raiziç] nt **-s** brushwood.

Reiß- [rais'] cpd: **~aus nehmen** run away, flee; **~brett** nt drawing board; **r~en** vti irreg tear; (ziehen) pull, drag; Witz crack; **etw an sich r~en** snatch sth up; (fig) take over sth; **sich um etw r~en** scramble for sth; **r~end** a Fluß torrential; (Comm) rapid; **~er** m **-s, -** (col) thriller; **r~erisch** a sensationalistic; **~leine** f (Aviat) ripcord; **~nagel** m drawing pin, thumbtack (US); **~schiene** f drawing rule, square; **~verschluß** m zip(per), zip fastener; **~zeug** nt geometry set; **~zwecke** f = **~nagel.**

Reit- ['rait] cpd: **r~en** vti irreg ride; **~er(in** f) m **-s, -** rider; (Mil) cavalryman, trooper; **~e'rei** f cavalry; **~hose** f riding breeches pl; **~pferd** nt saddle horse; **~stiefel** m riding boot; **~zeug** nt riding outfit.

Reiz [raits] m **-es, -e** stimulus; (angenehm) charm; (Verlockung) attraction; **~bar** a irritable; **~barkeit** f irritability; **r~en** vt stimulate; (unangenehm) irritate; (verlocken) appeal to, attract; **r~end** a charming; **~los** a unattractive; **r~voll** a attractive; **~wäsche** f sexy underwear.

rekeln ['re:kəln] vr stretch out; (lümmeln) lounge or loll about.

Reklam- cpd: **~ation** [reklamatsi'o:n] f

complaint; **~e** [re'kla:mə] f **-, -n** advertising; advertisement; **~e machen für etw** advertise sth; **r~ieren** [rekla'mi:rən] vti complain (about); (zurückfordern) reclaim.

rekon- cpd: **~struieren** [stru'i:rən] vt reconstruct; **R~valeszenz** [-valεs'tsεnts] f convalescence.

Rekord [re'kort] m **-(e)s, -e** record; **~leistung** f record performance.

Rekrut [re'kru:t] m **-en, -en** recruit; **r~ieren** [-'ti:rən] vt recruit; vr be recruited.

Rektor ['rεktɔr] m (Univ) rector, vice-chancellor; (Sch) headmaster; **~at** [-'ra:t] nt **-(e)s, -e** rectorate, vice-chancellorship; headship; (Zimmer) rector's etc office.

Relais [rə'lε:] nt **-, -** relay.

relativ [rela'ti:f] a relative; **R~ität** [relativi'tε:t] f relativity.

relevant [rele'vant] a relevant.

Relief [reli'εf] nt **-s, -s** relief.

Religion [religi'o:n] f religion; **~slehre** f, **~sunterricht** m religious instruction.

religiös [religi'ø:s] a religious.

Relikt [re'likt] nt **-(e)s, -e** relic.

Reling ['re:liŋ] f **-, -s** (Naut) rail.

Reliquie [re'li:kviə] f relic.

Reminiszenz [reminis'tsεnts] f reminiscence, recollection.

Remoulade [remu'la:də] f remoulade.

Ren [rεn] nt **-s, -s or -e** reindeer.

Rendezvous [rãde'vu:] nt **-, -** rendezvous.

Renn- ['rεn] cpd: **~bahn** f racecourse; (Aut) circuit, race track; **r~en** vti irreg run, race; **R~en** nt **-s, -** running; (Wettbewerb) race; **~fahrer** m racing driver; **~pferd** nt racehorse; **~platz** m racecourse; **~wagen** m racing car.

renovier- [reno'vi:r] cpd: **~en** vt renovate; **R~ung** f renovation.

rentabel [rεn'ta:bəl] a profitable, lucrative.

Rentabilität [rεntabili'tε:t] f profitability.

Rente ['rεntə] f **-, -n** pension; **~nempfänger** m pensioner.

Rentier ['rεnti:r] nt reindeer.

rentieren [rεn'ti:rən] vr pay, be profitable.

Rentner(in f) ['rεntnər(in)] m **-s, -** pensioner.

Repar- [repa] cpd: **~ation** [-atsi'o:n] f reparation; **~atur** [-ra'tu:r] f repairing; repair; **r~a'turbedürftig** a in need of repair; **~a'turwerkstatt** f repair shop; (Aut) garage; **r~ieren** [-'ri:rən] vt repair.

Repertoire [reperto'a:r] nt **-s, -s** repertoire.

Report- cpd: **~age** [repor'ta:ʒə] f **-, -n** (on-the-spot) report; (TV, Rad) live commentary or coverage; **~er** [re'portər] m **-s, -** reporter, commentator.

Repräsent- cpd: **~ant** [reprεzεn'tant] m representative; **r~a'tiv** a representative; Geschenk etc prestigious; **r~ieren** [reprεzεn'ti:rən] vt represent.

Repressalien [reprε'sa:liən] pl reprisals pl.

Reproduktion [reproduktsi'o:n] f reproduction.

reproduzieren [reprodu'tsi:rən] *vt* reproduce.
Reptil [rɛp'ti:l] *nt* **-s, -ien** reptile.
Republik [repu'bli:k] *f* republic; **~aner** [-'ka:nər] *m* **-s,** - republican; **~anisch** [-'ka:nɪʃ] *a* republican.
Reserv- *cpd:* **~at** [rɛzɛr'va:t] *nt* **-(e)s, -e** reservation; **~e** [re'zɛrvə] *f* **-, -n** reserve; **~erad** *nt* (*Aut*) spare wheel; **~espieler** *m* reserve; **~etank** *m* reserve tank; **r~ieren** [rɛzɛr'vi:rən] *vt* reserve; **~ist** [rɛzɛr'vɪst] *m* reservist; **~oir** [rɛzɛrvo'a:r] *nt* **-s, -e** reservoir.
Residenz [rɛzi'dɛnts] *f* residence, seat.
Resignation [rɛziɡnatsi'o:n] *f* resignation.
resignieren [rɛzi'ɡni:rən] *vi* resign.
resolut [rɛzo'lu:t] *a* resolute; **R~ion** [rɛzolutsi'o:n] *f* resolution.
Resonanz [rɛzo'nants] *f* (*lit*, *fig*) resonance; **~boden** *m* sounding board; **~kasten** *m* resonance box.
Resopal ' [rɛzo'pa:l] *nt* **-s** formica '.
Resozialisierung [rɛzotsiali'zi:ruŋ] *f* rehabilitation.
Respekt [rɛ'spɛkt] *m* **-(e)s** respect; **r~abel** [-'ta:bəl] *a* respectable; **r~ieren** [-'ti:rən] *vt* respect; **r~los** *a* disrespectful; **~sperson** *f* person commanding respect; **r~voll** *a* respectful.
Ressort [rɛ'so:r] *nt* **-s, -s** department.
Rest [rɛst] *m* **-(e)s, -e** remainder, rest; (*Über—*) remains *pl*; **~er** *pl* (*Comm*) remnants *pl*.
Restaur- *cpd:* **~ant** [rɛsto'rã:] *nt* **-s, -s** restaurant; **~ation** [rɛstauratsi'o:n] *f* restoration; **r~ieren** [rɛstau'ri:rən] *vt* restore.
Rest- *cpd:* **~betrag** *m* remainder, outstanding sum; **r~lich** *a* remaining; **r~los** *a* complete.
Resultat [rɛzul'ta:t] *nt* **-(e)s, -e** result.
Retorte [re'tortə] *f* **-, -n** retort.
retten [rɛtən] *vt* save, rescue.
Retter *m* **-s,** - rescuer, saviour.
Rettich [rɛtɪç] *m* **-s, -e** radish.
Rettung *f* rescue; (*Hilfe*) help; **seine letzte ~** his last hope; **~sboot** *nt* lifeboat; **~sgürtel** *m*, **~sring** *m* lifebelt, life preserver (*US*); **r~slos** *a* hopeless.
retuschieren [retu'ʃi:rən] *vt* (*Phot*) retouch.
Reue ['rɔyə] *f* - remorse; (*Bedauern*) regret; **r~n** *vt*: **es reut ihn** he regrets (it) *or* is sorry (about it).
reuig ['rɔyɪç] *a* penitent.
Revanche [re'vã:ʃə] *f* -, -n revenge; (*Sport*) return match.
revanchieren [revã'ʃi:rən] *vr* (*sich rächen*) get one's own back, have one's revenge; (*erwidern*) reciprocate, return the compliment.
Revers [re've:r] *m or nt* **-,** - lapel.
revidieren [revi'di:rən] *vt* revise.
Revier [re'vi:r] *nt* **-s, -e** district; (*Jagd—*) preserve; police station/beat; (*Mil*) sickbay.
Revision [revizi'o:n] *f* revision; (*Comm*) auditing; (*Jur*) appeal.
Revolte [re'voltə] *f* -, -n revolt.

Revolution [revolutsi'o:n] *f* revolution; **~är** [-'nɛ:r] *m* **-s, -e** revolutionary; **r~ieren** [-'ni:rən] *vt* revolutionize.
Revolver [re'volvər] *m* **-s,** - revolver.
Rezen- [retsɛn] *cpd:* **~sent** [-'zɛnt] *m* reviewer, critic; **r~sieren** [-'zi:rən] *vt* review; **~sion** [-zi'o:n] *f* review, criticism.
Rezept [re'tsɛpt] *nt* **-(e)s, -e** recipe; (*Med*) prescription; **r~pflichtig** *a* available only on prescription.
rezitieren [retsi'ti:rən] *vt* recite.
Rhabarber [ra'barbər] *m* **-s** rhubarb.
Rhesusfaktor ['re:zusfaktor] *m* rhesus factor.
Rhetorik [re'to:rɪk] *f* rhetoric.
rhetorisch [re'to:rɪʃ] *a* rhetorical.
Rheuma ['rɔyma] *nt* **-s, Rheumatismus** [rɔyma'tɪsmus] *m* rheumatism.
Rhinozeros [ri'no:tserɔs] *nt* - *or* **-ses, -se** rhinoceros.
rhyth- ['rʏt] *cpd:* **~misch** *a* rythmical; **R~mus** *m* rhythm.
Richt- ['rɪçt] *cpd:* **r~en** *vt* direct (*an* +*acc* at; (*fig*) to); *Waffe* aim (*auf* +*acc* at); (*einstellen*) adjust; (*instand setzen*) repair; (*zurechtmachen*) prepare; (*bestrafen*) pass judgement on; *vr:* **sich r~en nach** go by; **~er(in** *f*) *m* **-s,** - judge; **r~erlich** *a* judicial; **r~ig** *a* right, correct; (*echt*) proper; *ad* (*col: sehr*) really; **der/die ~ige** the right one/person; **das ~ige** the right thing; **~igkeit** *f* correctness; **~igstellung** *f* correction, rectification; **~preis** *m* recommended price; **~ung** *f* direction; tendency, orientation.
riechen ['ri:çən] *vti* *irreg* smell (*an etw* (*dat*) sth; *nach* of); **ich kann das/ihn nicht ~** (*col*) I can't stand it/him.
Ried [ri:t] *nt* **-(e)s, -e** reed; marsh.
Riege ['ri:ɡə] *f* -, -n team, squad.
Riegel ['ri:ɡəl] *m* **-s,** - bolt, bar.
Riemen ['ri:mən] *m* **-s,** - strap; (*Gürtel, Tech*) belt; (*Naut*) oar.
Riese ['ri:zə] *m* **-n, -n** giant; **r~ln** *vi* trickle; (*Schnee*) fall gently; **~nerfolg** *m* enormous success; **r~ngroß** *a*, **r~nhaft** *a* colossal, gigantic, huge.
ries- ['ri:z] *cpd:* **~ig** *a* enormous, huge, vast; **R~in** *f* giantess.
Riff [rɪf] *nt* **-(e)s, -e** reef.
Rille ['rɪlə] *f* -, -n groove.
Rind [rɪnt] *nt* **-(e)s, -er** ox; cow; cattle *pl*; (*Cook*) beef; **~e** *f* ['rɪndə] -, -n rind; (*Baum—*) bark; (*Brot—*) crust; **~fleisch** *nt* beef; **~sbraten** *m* roast beef; **~vieh** *nt* cattle *pl*; (*col*) blockhead, stupid oaf.
Ring [rɪŋ] *m* **-(e)s, -e** ring; **~buch** *nt* loose-leaf book; **~elnatter** *f* grass snake; **r~en** *vi* *irreg* wrestle; **~en** *nt* **-s** wrestling; **~finger** *m* ring finger; **r~förmig** *a* ring-shaped; **~kampf** *m* wrestling bout; **~richter** *m* referee; **r~s um** *ad* round; **r~sherum** *ad* round about; **~straße** *f* ring road; **r~sum(her)** *ad* (*rundherum*) round about; (*überall*) all round.
Rinn- ['rɪn] *cpd:* **~e** *f* -, -n gutter, drain; **r~en** *vi* *irreg* run, trickle; **~sal** *nt* **-s, -e** trickle of water; **~stein** *m* gutter.
Rippchen ['rɪpçən] *nt* small rib; cutlet.

Rippe ['rɪpə] f -, -n rib; ~nfell-
entzündung f pleurisy.
Risiko ['ri:ziko] nt -s, -s or **Risiken** risk.
riskant [rɪs'kant] a risky, hazardous.
riskieren [rɪs'ki:rən] vt risk.
Riß [rɪs] m -sses, -sse tear; (in Mauer,
Tasse etc) crack; (in Haut) scratch; (Tech)
design.
rissig ['rɪsɪç] a torn; cracked; scratched.
Ritt [rɪt] m -(e)s, -e ride; ~er m -s, -
knight; r~erlich a chivalrous;
~erschlag m knighting; ~ertum nt -s
chivalry; ~erzeit f age of chivalry;
r~lings ad astride.
Ritus ['ri:tus] m -, **Riten** rite.
Ritze ['rɪtsə] f -, -n crack, chink; r~n vt
scratch.
Rivale [ri'va:lə] m -n, -n rival.
Rivalität [rivali'tɛ:t] f rivalry.
Rizinusöl ['ri:tsinusø:l] nt castor oil.
Robbe ['rɔbə] f -, -n seal.
Robe ['ro:bə] f -, -n robe.
Roboter ['rɔbɔtər] m -s, - robot.
röcheln ['rœçəln] vi wheeze.
Rock [rɔk] m -(e)s, ⁓e skirt; (Jackett)
jacket; (Uniform~) tunic.
Rodel ['ro:dəl] m -s, - toboggan; ~bahn f
toboggan run; r~n vi toboggan.
roden ['ro:dən] vti clear.
Rogen ['ro:gən] m -s, - roe, spawn.
Roggen ['rɔgən] m -s, - rye; ~brot nt rye
bread, black bread.
roh [ro:] a raw; Mensch coarse, crude;
R~bau m shell of a building; R~eisen
nt pig iron; R~ling m ruffian;
R~material nt raw material; R~öl nt
crude oil.
Rohr ['ro:r] nt -(e)s, -e pipe, tube; (Bot)
cane; (Schilf) reed; (Gewehr~) barrel;
~bruch m burst pipe.
Röhre ['rø:rə] f -, -n tube, pipe; (Rad etc)
valve; (Back~) oven.
Rohr- cpd: ~geflecht nt wickerwork;
~leger m -s, - plumber; ~leitung f pipeline; ~post f pneumatic post; ~stock m
cane; ~stuhl m basket chair; ~zucker
m cane sugar.
Roh- cpd: ~seide f raw silk; ~stoff m
raw material.
Rokoko ['rɔkoko] nt -s rococo.
Roll- ['rɔl] cpd: ~(l)aden m shutter;
~bahn f, ~feld nt (Aviat) runway.
Rolle ['rɔlə] f -, -n roll; (Theat, soziologisch)
role; (Garn~ etc) reel, spool; (Walze)
roller; (Wäsche~) mangle; **keine ~
spielen** not matter; r~n vti roll; (Aviat)
taxi; Wäsche mangle; ~nbesetzung f
(Theat) cast; ~r m -s, - scooter; (Welle)
roller.
Roll- cpd: ~mops m pickled herring;
~schuh m roller skate; ~stuhl m
wheelchair; ~treppe f escalator.
Roman [ro'ma:n] m -s, -e novel;
~schreiber m, ~schriftsteller m
novelist; ~tik [ro'mantɪk] f romanticism;
~tiker m -s, - romanticist;
r~tisch [ro'mantɪʃ] a romantic; ~ze
[ro'mantsə] f -, -n romance.

Römer ['rø:mər] m -s, - wineglass;
(Mensch) Roman.
röntgen ['rœntgən] vt X-ray;
R~aufnahme f, R~bild nt X-ray;
R~strahlen pl X-rays pl.
rosa ['ro:za] a pink, rose-(coloured).
Rose ['ro:zə] f -, -n rose; ~nkohl m
Brussels sprouts pl; ~nkranz m rosary;
~nmontag m Shrove Monday.
Rosette [ro'zɛtə] f rosette; rose window.
rosig ['ro:zɪç] a rosy.
Rosine [ro'zi:nə] f raisin, currant.
Roß [rɔs] nt -sses, -sse horse, steed;
~kastanie f horse chestnut.
Rost [rɔst] m -(e)s, -e rust; (Gitter) grill,
gridiron; (Bett~) springs pl; ~braten m
roast(ed) meat, joint; r~en vi rust.
rösten ['rø:stən] vt roast; toast; grill.
Rost- cpd: r~frei a rust-free; rustproof;
stainless; r~ig a rusty; ~schutz m rust-
proofing.
rot [ro:t] a red; R~ation [rotatsi'o:n] f
rotation; ~bäckig a red-cheeked;
~blond a strawberry blond.
Röte ['rø:tə] f - redness; ~ln pl German
measles sing; r~n vtr redden.
rot- cpd: ~haarig a red-haired; ~ieren
[ro'ti:rən] vi rotate; R~käppchen nt
Little Red Riding Hood; R~kehlchen nt
robin; R~stift m red pencil; R~wein m
red wine.
Rotz [rɔts] m -es, -e (col) snot.
Roulade [ru'la:də] f (Cook) beef olive.
Route ['ru:tə] f -, -n route.
Routine [ru'ti:nə] f experience; routine.
Rübe ['ry:bə] f -, -n turnip; **gelbe ~**
carrot; **rote ~** beetroot; ~nzucker m
beet sugar.
Rubin [ru'bi:n] m -s, -e ruby.
Rubrik [ru'bri:k] f heading; (Spalte)
column.
Ruck [ruk] m -(e)s, -e jerk, jolt.
Rück- ['rYk] cpd: ~antwort f reply,
answer; r~bezüglich a reflexive;
r~blenden vi flash back; r~blickend a
retrospective; r~en vti move; ~en m -s,
- back; (Berg~) ridge; ~endeckung f
backing; ~enlehne f back (of chair);
~enmark nt spinal cord;
~enschwimmen nt backstroke;
~enwind m following wind;
~erstattung f return, restitution;
~fahrt f return journey; ~fall m
relapse; r~fällig a relapsing; r~fällig
werden relapse; ~flug m return flight;
~frage f question; ~gabe f return;
~gang m decline, fall; r~gängig a: etw
r~gängig machen cancel sth; ~grat nt
-(e)s, -e spine, backbone; ~griff m
recourse; ~halt m backing; reserve;
r~haltlos a unreserved; ~kehr f -, -en
return; ~koppelung f feedback; ~lage f
reserve, savings pl; r~läufig a declining,
falling; ~licht nt back light; ~lings ad
from behind; backwards; ~nahme f -, -n
taking back; ~porto nt return postage;
~reise f return journey; (Naut) home
voyage; ~ruf m recall.
Rucksack ['rukzak] m rucksack.
Rück- cpd: ~schau f reflection;

r~schauend a, ad retrospective, in retrospect; **~schluß** m conclusion; **~schritt** m retrogression; **r~schrittlich** a reactionary; retrograde; **~seite** f back; (von Münze etc) reverse; **~sicht** f consideration; **~sicht nehmen auf** (+acc) show consideration for; **r~sichtslos** a inconsiderate; Fahren reckless; (unbarmherzig) ruthless; **r~sichtsvoll** a considerate; **~sitz** m back seat; **~spiegel** m (Aut) rear-view mirror; **~spiel** nt return match; **~sprache** f further discussion or talk; **~stand** m arrears pl; **r~ständig** a backward, out-of-date; Zahlungen in arrears; **~stoß** m recoil; **~strahler** m -s, - rear reflector; **~tritt** m resignation; **~trittbremse** f pedal brake; **~vergütung** f repayment; (Comm) refund; **~versicherung** f reinsurance; **r~wärtig** a rear; **r~wärts** ad backward(s), back; **~wärtsgang** m (Aut) reverse gear; **~weg** m return journey, way back; **r~wirkend** a retroactive; **~wirkung** f reaction; retrospective effect; **~zahlung** f repayment; **~zug** m retreat.

Rüde ['ry:də] m -n, -n male dog/fox/wolf; **r~** a blunt, gruff.

Rudel ['ru:dəl] nt -s, - pack; herd.

Ruder ['ru:dər] nt -s, - oar; (Steuer) rudder; **~boot** nt rowing boat; **~er** m -s, - rower; **r~n** vti row.

Ruf [ru:f] m -(e)s, -e call, cry; (Ansehen) reputation; **r~en** vti irreg call; cry; **~name** m usual (first) name; **~nummer** f (tele)phone number; **~zeichen** nt (Rad) call sign; (Tel) ringing tone.

Rüge ['ry:gə] f -, -n reprimand, rebuke; **r~n** vt reprimand.

Ruhe ['ru:ə] f - rest; (Ungestörtheit) peace, quiet; (Gelassenheit, Stille) calm; (Schweigen) silence; **sich zur ~ setzen** retire; **~! be quiet!,** silence!; **r~los** a restless; **r~n** vi rest; **~pause** f break; **~platz** m resting place; **~stand** m retirement; **letzte ~stätte** f final resting place; **~störung** f breach of the peace; **~tag** m closing day.

ruhig ['ru:ɪç] a quiet; (bewegungslos) still; Hand steady; (gelassen, friedlich) calm; Gewissen clear; **tu das ~** feel free to do that.

Ruhm [ru:m] m -(e)s fame, glory.

rühm- ['ry:m] cpd: **~en** vt praise; vr boast; **~lich** a laudable.

ruhm- cpd: **~los** a inglorious; **~reich** a glorious.

Ruhr ['ru:r] f - dysentery.

Rühr- ['ry:r] cpd: **~ei** nt scrambled egg; **r~en** vtr (lit, fig) move, stir (auch Cook); vi: **r~en von** come or stem from; **r~en an** (+acc) touch; (fig) touch on; **r~end** a touching, moving; **r~ig** a active, lively; **r~selig** a sentimental, emotional; **~ung** f emotion.

Ruin [ru'i:n] m -s, -e, f -, -n ruin; **r~ieren** [rui'ni:rən] vt ruin.

rülpsen ['rʏlpsən] vi burp, belch.

Rum [rʊm] m -s, -s rum.

Rummel ['rʊməl] m -s (col) hubbub; (Jahrmarkt) fair; **~platz** m fairground, fair.

rumoren [ru'mo:rən] vi be noisy, make a noise.

Rumpel- ['rʊmpəl] cpd: **~kammer** f junk room; **r~n** vi rumble; (holpern) jolt.

Rumpf [rʊmpf] m -(e)s, -̈e trunk, torso; (Aviat) fuselage; (Naut) hull.

rümpfen ['rʏmpfən] vt Nase turn up.

rund [rʊnt] a round; ad (etwa) around; **~ um etw** round sth; **R~bogen** m Norman or Romanesque arch; **R~brief** m circular; **R~e** ['rʊndə] f -, -n round; (in Rennen) lap; (Gesellschaft) circle; **~en** vt make round; vr (fig) take shape; **~erneuert** a Reifen remoulded; **R~fahrt** f (round) trip.

Rundfunk ['rʊntfʊŋk] m -(e)s broadcasting; (~anstalt) broadcasting service; **im ~ on** the radio; **~empfang** m reception; **~gebühr** f licence; **~gerät** nt wireless set; **~sendung** f broadcast, radio programme.

Rund- cpd: **r~heraus** ad straight out, bluntly; **r~herum** ad round about; all round; **r~lich** a plump, rounded; **~reise** f round trip; **~schreiben** nt (Comm) circular; **~ung** f curve, roundness.

runter ['rʊntər] ad (col) **= herunter, hinunter.**

Runzel ['rʊntsəl] f -, -n wrinkle; **r~ig** a wrinkled; **r~n** vt wrinkle; **die Stirn r~n** frown.

Rüpel ['ry:pəl] m -s, - lout; **r~haft** a loutish.

rupfen ['rʊpfən] vt pluck; **R~** m -s, - sackcloth.

ruppig ['rʊpɪç] a rough, gruff.

Rüsche ['ry:ʃə] f -, -n frill.

Ruß [ru:s] m -es soot; **r~en** vi smoke; (Ofen) be sooty; **r~ig** a sooty.

Rüssel ['rʏsəl] m -s, - snout; (Elefanten—) trunk.

rüsten ['rʏstən] vtri prepare; (Mil) arm.

rüstig ['rʏstɪç] a sprightly, vigorous; **R~keit** f sprightliness, vigour.

Rüstung ['rʏstʊŋ] f preparation; arming; (Ritter—) armour; (Waffen etc) armaments pl; **~skontrolle** f armaments control.

Rüstzeug nt tools pl; (fig) capacity.

Rute ['ru:tə] f -, -n rod, switch.

Rutsch [rʊtʃ] m -(e)s, -e slide; (Erd—) landslide; **~bahn** f slide; **r~en** vi slide; (ausr—en) slip; **r~ig** a slippery.

rütteln ['rʏtəln] vti shake, jolt.

S

S,s [ɛs] nt S,s.

Saal [za:l] m -(e)s, Säle hall; room.

Saat [za:t] f -, -en seed; (Pflanzen) crop; (Säen) sowing.

sabbern ['zabərn] vi (col) dribble.

Säbel ['zɛ:bəl] m -s, - sabre, sword.

Sabotage [zabo'ta:ʒə] f -, -n sabotage.

sabotieren [zabo'ti:rən] vt sabotage.

Sach- [zax] *cpd*: **~bearbeiter** *m* specialist; **s~dienlich** *a* relevant, helpful; **~e** *f* -, **-n** thing; *(Angelegenheit)* affair, business; *(Frage)* matter; *(Pflicht)* task; **zur ~e** to the point; **s~gemäß** *a* appropriate, suitable; **s~kundig** *a* expert; **~lage** *f* situation, state of affairs; **s~lich** *a* matter-of-fact, objective; *Irrtum, Angabe* factual.

sächlich ['zɛxlıç] *a* neuter.

Sach- *cpd*: **~schaden** *m* material damage; **s~t(e)** *ad* softly, gently; **~verständige(r)** *mf* expert.

Sack [zak] *m* **-(e)s,** ⁛e sack; **s~en** *vi* sag, sink; **~gasse** *f* cul-de-sac, dead-end street *(US)*.

Sadismus [za'dısmʊs] *m* sadism.

Sadist [za'dıst] *m* sadist; **s~isch** *a* sadistic.

säen ['zɛːn] *vti* sow.

Saft [zaft] *m* **-(e)s,** ⁛e juice; *(Bot)* sap; **s~ig** *a* juicy; **s~los** *a* dry.

Sage ['zaːgə] *f* -, **-n** saga.

Säge ['zɛːgə] *f* -, **-n** saw; **~mehl** *nt* sawdust; **s~n** *vti* saw.

sagen ['zaːgən] *vti* say *(jdm* to sb), tell *(jdm* sb); **~haft** *a* legendary; *(col)* great, smashing.

Sägewerk *nt* sawmill.

Sahne ['zaːnə] *f* - cream.

Saison [zɛ'zõ] *f* -, **-s** season; **~arbeiter** *m* seasonal worker.

Saite ['zaɪtə] *f* -, **-n** string; **~ninstrument** *nt* string instrument.

Sakko ['zako] *m or nt* **-s, -s** jacket.

Sakrament [zakramɛnt] *nt* sacrament.

Sakristei [zakrıs'taı] *f* sacristy.

Salat [za'laːt] *m* **-(e)s, -e** salad; *(Kopfsalat)* lettuce; **~soße** *f* salad dressing.

Salb- ['zalb] *cpd*: **~e** *f* -, **-n** ointment; **~en** *vt* *[zal'baı]* *m or f* **-s** *or* **-** sage; **s~en** *vt* anoint; **~ung** *f* anointing; **s~ungsvoll** *a* unctuous.

Saldo ['zaldo] *m* **-s, Salden** balance.

Salmiak [zalmi'ak] *m* **-s** sal ammoniac; **~geist** *m* liquid ammonia.

Salon [za'lõ] *m* **-s, -s** salon.

salopp [za'lɔp] *a* casual.

Salpeter [zal'peːtər] *m* **-s** saltpetre; **~säure** *f* nitric acid.

Salut [za'luːt] *m* **-(e)s, -e** salute; **s~ieren** [-'tiːrən] *vi* salute.

Salve ['zalvə] *f* -, **-n** salvo.

Salz [zalts] *nt* **-es, -e** salt; **s~en** *vt irreg* salt; **s~ig** *a* salty; **~kartoffeln** *pl* boiled potatoes *pl*; **~säure** *f* hydrochloric acid.

Samen ['zaːmən] *m* **-s, -** seed; *(Anat)* sperm.

Sammel- ['zaməl] *cpd*: **~band** *m* anthology; **~becken** *nt* reservoir; **~bestellung** *f* collective order; **s~n** *vt* collect; *vr* assemble, gather; *(konzentrieren)* concentrate; **~name** *m* collective term; **~surium** [-'zuːrium] *nt* hotchpotch.

Sammlung ['zamlʊŋ] *f* collection; assembly, gathering; concentration.

Samstag ['zamstaːk] *m* Saturday; **s~s** *ad* (on) Saturdays.

Samt [zamt] *m* **-(e)s, -e** velvet; **s~** *prep*

+dat (along) with, together with; **s~ und sonders** each and every one (of them).

sämtlich ['zɛmtlıç] *a* all (the), entire.

Sand [zant] *m* **-(e)s, -e** sand; **~ale** [zan'daːlə] *f* -, **-n** sandal; **~bank** *f* sandbank; **s~ig** [zandıç] *a* sandy; **~kasten** *m* sandpit; **~kuchen** *m* Madeira cake; **~papier** *nt* sandpaper; **~stein** *m* sandstone; **~uhr** *f* hourglass.

sanft [zanft] *a* soft, gentle; **~mütig** *a* gentle, meek.

Sänger(in *f)* ['zɛŋər(ın)] *m* **-s, -** singer.

Sani- *cpd*: **s~eren** [za'niːrən] *vt* redevelop; *Betrieb* make financially sound; *vr* line one's pocket; become financially sound; **~erung** *f* redevelopment; making viable; **s~tär** [zani'tɛːr] *a* sanitary; **s~täre Anlagen** sanitation; **~täter** [zani'tɛːtər] *m* **-s, -** first-aid attendant; *(Mil)* (medical) orderly.

sanktionieren [zaŋktsio'niːrən] *vt* sanction.

Saphir ['zaːfiːr] *m* **-s, -e** sapphire.

Sardelle [zar'dɛlə] *f* anchovy.

Sardine [zar'diːnə] *f* sardine.

Sarg [zark] *m* **-(e)s, -e** coffin.

Sarkasmus [zar'kasmʊs] *m* sarcasm.

sarkastisch [zar'kastıʃ] *a* sarcastic.

Satan ['zaːtan] *m* **-s, -e** Satan; devil.

Satellit [zatɛ'liːt] *m* **-en, -en** satellite.

Satire [za'tiːrə] *f* -, **-n** satire.

satirisch [za'tiːrıʃ] *a* satirical.

satt [zat] *a* full; *Farbe* rich, deep; **jdn/etw ~ sein** *or* **haben** be fed up with sb/sth; **sich ~ hören/sehen an** *(+dat)* see/hear enough of; **sich ~ essen** eat one's fill; **~ machen** be filling.

Sattel ['zatəl] *m* **-s,** ⁛ saddle; *(Berg)* ridge; **s~fest** *a (fig)* proficient; **s~n** *vt* saddle.

sättigen ['zɛtıgən] *vt* satisfy; *(Chem)* saturate.

Satz [zats] *m* **-es,** ⁛e *(Gram)* sentence; *(Neben-, Adverbial—)* clause; *(Theorem)* theorem; *(Mus)* movement; *(Tennis, Briefmarken etc)* set; *(Kaffee)* grounds *pl*; *(Comm)* rate; *(Sprung)* jump; **~gegenstand** *m (Gram)* subject; **~lehre** *f* syntax; **~teil** *m* constituent (of a sentence); **~ung** *f* statute, rule; **s~ungsgemäß** *a* statutory; **~zeichen** *nt* punctuation mark.

Sau [zau] *f* -, **Säue** sow; *(col)* dirty pig.

sauber ['zaubər] *a* clean; *(ironisch)* fine; **~halten** *vt irreg* keep clean; **S~keit** *f* cleanness; *(einer Person)* cleanliness.

säuber- ['zɔybər] *cpd*: **~lich** *ad* neatly; **~n** *vt* clean; *(Pol etc)* purge; **S~ung** *f* cleaning; purge.

Sauce ['zoːsə] *f* -, **-n** sauce, gravy.

sauer ['zauər] *a* sour; *(Chem)* acid; *(col)* cross.

Sauerei [zauə'raı] *f (col)* rotten state of affairs, scandal; *(Schmutz etc)* mess; *(Unanständigkeit)* obscenity.

säuerlich ['zɔyərlıç] *a* sourish, tart.

Sauer- *cpd*: **~milch** *f* sour milk; **~stoff** *m* oxygen; **~stoffgerät** *nt* breathing apparatus; **~teig** *m* leaven.

saufen ['zaufən] *vti irreg (col)* drink, booze.

Säufer ['zɔyfər] *m* **-s, -** *(col)* boozer.

Sauferei [zaufə'raı] f drinking, boozing; booze-up.
saugen ['zaʊgən] vti irreg suck.
säugen ['zɔygən] vt suckle.
Sauger ['zaʊgər] m -s, - dummy, comforter (US); (auf Flasche) teat; (Staub-) vacuum cleaner, hoover ®.
Säug- ['zɔyg] cpd: ~etier nt mammal; ~ling m infant, baby.
Säule ['zɔylə] f -, -n column, pillar; ~ngang m arcade.
Saum [zaʊm] m -(e)s, Säume hem; (Naht) seam.
säumen ['zɔymən] vt hem; seam; vi delay, hesitate.
Sauna ['zaʊna] f -, -s sauna.
Säure ['zɔyrə] f -, -n acid; (Geschmack) sourness, acidity; s~beständig a acidproof; s~haltig a acidic.
säuseln ['zɔyzəln] vti murmur, rustle.
sausen ['zaʊzən] vi blow; (col: eilen) rush; (Ohren) buzz; etw ~ lassen (col) give sth a miss.
Saustall ['zaʊʃtal] m (col) pigsty.
Saxophon [zakso'fo:n] nt -s, -e saxophone.
Schabe ['ʃa:bə] f -, -n cockroach; s~n vt scrape; ~rnack ['ʃa:bərnak] m -(e)s, -e trick, prank.
schäbig ['ʃe:bıç] a shabby; S~keit f shabbiness.
Schablone [ʃa'blo:nə] f -, -n stencil; (Muster) pattern; (fig) convention; s~nhaft a stereotyped, conventional.
Schach [ʃax] nt -s, -s chess; (Stellung) check; ~brett nt chessboard; ~figur f chessman; 's~'matt a checkmate; ~partie f, ~spiel nt game of chess.
Schacht [ʃaxt] m -(e)s, -e shaft; ~el f -, -n box; (pej: Frau) bag, cow.
schade ['ʃa:də] a a pity or shame; sich (dat) zu ~ sein für etw consider oneself too good for sth; interj (what a) pity or shame.
Schädel ['ʃe:dəl] m -s, - skull; ~bruch m fractured skull.
Schaden ['ʃa:dən] m -s, ⸚ damage; (Verletzung) injury; (Nachteil) disadvantage; s~ vi (+dat) hurt; einer Sache s~ damage sth; ~ersatz m compensation, damages pl; s~ersatzpflichtig a liable for damages; ~freude f malicious delight; s~froh a gloating, with malicious delight.
schadhaft ['ʃa:thaft] a faulty, damaged.
schäd- ['ʃe:t] cpd: ~igen vt damage; Person do harm to, harm; S~igung f damage; harm; ~lich a harmful (für to); S~lichkeit f harmfulness; S~ling m pest; S~lingsbekämpfungsmittel nt pesticide.
schadlos ['ʃa:tlo:s] a: sich ~ halten an (+dat) take advantage of.
Schaf [ʃa:f] nt -(e)s, -e sheep; ~bock m ram.
Schäfchen ['ʃe:fçən] nt lamb; ~wolken pl cirrus clouds pl.
Schäfer ['ʃe:fər] m -s, -e shepherd; ~hund m Alsatian; ~in f shepherdess.
schaffen ['ʃafən] vt irreg create; Platz make; sich (dat) etw ~ get o.s. sth; vt (erreichen) manage, do; (erledigen) finish;

Prüfung pass; (transportieren) take; vi (col: arbeiten) work; sich an etw (dat) zu ~ machen busy oneself with sth; S~ nt -s (creative) activity; S~sdrang m creative urge; energy; S~skraft f creativity.
Schaffner(in f) ['ʃafnər(ın)] m -s, - (Bus) conductor/conductress; (Rail) guard.
Schaft [ʃaft] m -(e)s, -e shaft; (von Gewehr) stock; (von Stiefel) leg; (Bot) stalk; tree trunk; ~stiefel m high boot.
Schakal [ʃa'ka:l] m -s, -e jackal.
Schäker ['ʃe:kər] m -s, - flirt; joker; s~n vi flirt; joke.
schal [ʃa:l] a flat; (fig) insipid; S~ m -s, -e or -s scarf.
Schälchen ['ʃe:lçən] nt cup, bowl.
Schale ['ʃa:lə] f -, -n skin; (abgeschält) peel; (Nuß-, Muschel-, Ei-) shell; (Geschirr) dish, bowl.
schälen ['ʃe:lən] vt peel; shell; vr peel.
Schall [ʃal] m -(e)s, -e sound; ~dämpfer m -s, - (Aut) silencer; s~dicht a soundproof; s~en vi (re)sound; s~end a resounding, loud; ~mauer f sound barrier; ~platte f (gramophone) record.
Schalt- ['ʃalt] cpd: ~bild nt circuit diagram; ~brett nt switchboard; s~en vt switch, turn; vi (Aut) change (gear); (col: begreifen) catch on; s~en und walten do as one pleases; ~er m -s, - counter; (an Gerät) switch; ~erbeamte(r) m counter clerk; ~hebel m switch; (Aut) gear-lever; ~jahr nt leap year; ~ung f switching; (Elec) circuit; (Aut) gear change.
Scham [ʃa:m] f - shame; (-gefühl) modesty; (Organe) private parts pl.
schämen ['ʃe:mən] vr be ashamed.
Scham- cpd: ~haare pl pubic hair; s~haft a modest, bashful; s~los a shameless.
Schande ['ʃandə] f - disgrace.
schändlich ['ʃentlıç] a disgraceful, shameful; S~keit f disgracefulness.
Schandtat ['ʃantta:t] f (col) escapade, shenanigan.
Schändung ['ʃendʊŋ] f violation, defilement.
Schank- ['ʃaŋk] cpd: ~erlaubnis f, ~konzession f (publican's) licence; ~tisch m bar.
Schanze ['ʃantsə] f -, -n (Mil) fieldwork, earthworks pl; (Sprung-) skijump.
Schar [ʃa:r] f -, -en band, company; (Vögel) flock; (Menge) crowd; in ~en in droves; ~ade [ʃa'ra:də] f charade; s~en vr assemble, rally; s~enweise ad in droves.
scharf [ʃarf] a sharp; Essen hot; Munition live; ~ nachdenken think hard; auf etw (acc) ~ sein (col) be keen on sth; S~blick m (fig) penetration.
Schärf- ['ʃerf] cpd: ~e f -, -n sharpness; (Strenge) rigour; s~en vt sharpen.
Scharf- cpd: s~machen vt (col) stir up; ~richter m executioner; ~schießen nt firing live ammunition; ~schütze m marksman, sharpshooter; ~sinn m penetration, astuteness; s~sinnig a astute, shrewd.

Scharmützel [ʃarˈmʏtsəl] *nt* -s, - skirmish.

Scharnier [ʃarˈniːr] *nt* -s, -e hinge.

Schärpe [ˈʃɛrpə] *f* -, -n sash.

scharren [ˈʃarən] *vti* scrape, scratch.

Scharte [ˈʃartə] *f* -, -n notch, nick; *(Berg)* wind gap.

schartig [ˈʃartiç] *a* jagged.

Schaschlik [ˈʃaʃlɪk] *m or nt* -s, -s (shish) kebab.

Schatten [ˈʃatən] *m* -s, - shadow; **~bild** *nt*, **~riß** *m* silhouette; **~seite** *f* shady side, dark side.

schattieren [ʃaˈtiːrən] *vti* shade.

Schattierung *f* shading.

schattig [ˈʃatiç] *a* shady.

Schatulle [ʃaˈtʊlə] *f* -, -n casket; *(Geld—)* coffer.

Schatz [ʃats] *m* -es, -̈e treasure; *(Person)* darling; **~amt** *nt* treasury.

schätz- [ˈʃets] *cpd:* **~bar** *a* assessable; **S~chen** *nt* darling, love; **~en** *vt (abschätzen)* estimate; *Gegenstand* value; *(würdigen)* value, esteem; *(vermuten)* reckon; **~enlernen** *vt* learn to appreciate; **S~ung** *f* estimate; estimation; valuation; **nach meiner S~ung ...** I reckon that . . .; **~ungsweise** *ad* approximately; **it is thought; **S~wert** *m* estimated value.

Schau [ʃaʊ] *f* - show; *(Ausstellung)* display, exhibition; **etw zur ~ stellen** make a show of sth, show sth off; **~bild** *nt* diagram.

Schauder [ˈʃaʊdər] *m* -s, -s shudder; *(wegen Kälte)* shiver; **s~haft** *a* horrible; **s~n** *vi* shudder; shiver.

schauen [ˈʃaʊən] *vi* look.

Schauer [ˈʃaʊər] *m* -s, - *(Regen—)* shower; *(Schreck)* shudder; **~geschichte** *f* horror story; **s~lich** *a* horrific, spine-chilling.

Schaufel [ˈʃaʊfəl] *f* -, -n shovel; *(Naut)* paddle; *(Tech)* scoop; **s~n** *vt* shovel, scoop.

Schau- *cpd:* **~fenster** *nt* shop window; **~fensterauslage** *f* window display; **~fensterbummel** *m* window shopping (expedition); **~fensterdekorateur** *m* window dresser; **~geschäft** *nt* show business; **~kasten** *m* showcase.

Schaukel [ˈʃaʊkəl] *f* -, -n swing; **s~n** *vi* swing, rock; **~pferd** *nt* rocking horse; **~stuhl** *m* rocking chair.

Schaulustige(r) [ˈʃaʊlʊstɪgə(r)] *mf* onlooker.

Schaum [ʃaʊm] *m* -(e)s, **Schäume** foam; *(Seifen—)* lather.

schäumen [ˈʃɔʏmən] *vi* foam.

Schaum- *cpd:* **~gummi** *m* foam (rubber); **s~ig** *a* frothy, foamy; **~krone** *f* white crest; **~schläger** *m* *(fig)* windbag; **~wein** *m* sparkling wine.

Schau- *cpd:* **~platz** *m* scene; **s~rig** *a* horrific, dreadful; **~spiel** *nt* spectacle; *(Theat)* play; **~spieler** *m* actor; **~spielerin** *f* actress; **s~spielern** *vi insep* act.

Scheck [ʃek] *m* -s, -s cheque; **~buch** *nt* cheque book; **s~ig** *a* dappled, piebald.

scheel [ʃeːl] *a (col)* dirty; **jdn ~ ansehen** give sb a dirty look.

scheffeln [ˈʃefəln] *vt* amass.

Scheibe [ˈʃaɪbə] *f* -, -n disc; *(Brot etc)* slice; *(Glas—)* pane *(Mil)* target; **~nbremse** *f (Aut)* disc brake; **~nwaschanlage** *f (Aut)* windscreen washers *pl*; **~nwischer** *m (Aut)* windscreen wiper.

Scheich [ʃaɪç] *m* -s, -e *or* -s sheik(h).

Scheide [ˈʃaɪdə] *f* -, -n sheath; *(Grenze)* boundary; *(Anat)* vagina; **~n** *irreg vt* separate; *Ehe* dissolve; **sich s~n lassen** get a divorce; *vi (de)*part.

Scheidung *f (Ehe—)* divorce; **~sgrund** *m* grounds *pl* for divorce; **~sklage** *f* divorce suit.

Schein [ʃaɪn] *m* -(e)s, -e light; *(An—)* appearance; *(Geld)* (bank)note; *(Bescheinigung)* certificate; **zum ~** in pretence; **s~bar** *a* apparent; **s~en** *vi irreg* shine; *(Anschein haben)* seem; **s~heilig** *a* hypocritical; **~tod** *m* apparent death; **~werfer** *m* -s, - floodlight; spotlight; *(Such—)* searchlight; *(Aut)* headlamp.

Scheiß- [ˈʃaɪs] *in cpds (col)* bloody; **~e** *f - (col)* shit.

Scheit [ʃaɪt] *nt* -(e)s, -e *or* -er log, billet.

Scheitel [ˈʃaɪtəl] *m* -s, - top; *(Haar)* parting; **s~n** *vt* part; **~punkt** *m* zenith, apex.

scheitern [ˈʃaɪtərn] *vi* fail.

Schelle [ˈʃɛlə] *f* -, -n small bell; **s~n** *vi* ring.

Schellfisch [ˈʃɛlfɪʃ] *m* haddock.

Schelm [ʃɛlm] *m* -(e)s, -e rogue; **s~isch** *a* mischievous, roguish.

Schelte [ˈʃɛltə] *f* -, -n scolding; **s~n** *vt irreg* scold.

Schema [ˈʃeːma] *nt* -s, -s *or* -ta scheme, plan; *(Darstellung)* schema; **nach ~** quite mechanically; **s~tisch** [ʃeˈmaːtɪʃ] *a* schematic; *(pej)* mechanical.

Schemel [ˈʃeːməl] *m* -s, - (foot)stool.

Schenkel [ˈʃɛŋkəl] *m* -s, - thigh.

schenken [ˈʃɛŋkən] *vt (lit, fig)* give; *Getränk* pour; **sich** *(dat)* **etw ~** *(col)* skip sth; **das ist geschenkt!** *(billig)* that's a giveaway!; *(nichts wert)* that's worthless!

Schenkung [ˈʃɛŋkʊŋ] *f* gift; **~surkunde** *f* deed of gift.

Scherbe [ˈʃɛrbə] *f* -, -n broken piece, fragment; *(archäologisch)* potsherd.

Schere [ˈʃeːrə] *f* -, -n scissors *pl*; *(groß)* shears *pl*; **s~n** *vt irreg* cut; *Schaf* shear; *(sich kümmern)* bother; *vr* care; **scher dich (zum Teufel)!** get lost!; **~n-schleifer** *m* -s, - knife-grinder; **~'rei** *f (col)* bother, trouble.

Scherflein [ˈʃɛrflaɪn] *nt* mite, bit.

Scherz [ʃɛrts] *m* -es, -e joke; fun; **~frage** *f* conundrum; **s~haft** *a* joking, jocular.

scheu [ʃɔʏ] *a* shy; **S~** *f* - shyness; *(Angst)* fear *(vor +dat of)*; *(Ehrfurcht)* awe; **S~che** *f* -, -n scarecrow; **~chen** *vt* scare (off); **~en** *vr:* **sich ~en vor** *(+dat)* be afraid of, shrink from; *vt* shun; *vi (Pferd)* shy.

Scheuer- [ˈʃɔʏər] *cpd:* **~bürste** *f* scrubbing brush; **~lappen** *m* floorcloth;

~**leiste** f skirting board; **s~n** vt scour, scrub.

Scheuklappe f blinker.

Scheune ['ʃɔʏnə] f -, -n barn.

Scheusal ['ʃɔʏzaːl] nt -s, -e monster.

scheußlich ['ʃɔʏslɪç] a dreadful, frightful; **S~keit** f dreadfulness.

Schi [ʃiː] m see **Ski**.

Schicht [ʃɪçt] f -, -en layer; (Klasse) class, level; (in Fabrik etc) shift; ~**arbeit** f shift work; **s~en** vt layer, stack.

schick [ʃɪk] a stylish, chic; ~**en** vt send; vr resign oneself (in +acc to); v impers (anständig sein) be fitting; ~**lich** a proper, fitting; **S~sal** nt -s, -e fate; ~**salsschlag** m great misfortune, blow.

Schieb- ['ʃiːb] cpd: ~**edach** nt (Aut) sunshine roof; **s~en** vti irreg push; Schuld put (auf jdn on sb); ~**er** m -s, - slide; (Besteckteil) pusher; (Person) profiteer; ~**etür** f sliding door; ~**lehre** f (Math) calliper rule; ~**ung** f fiddle.

Schieds- ['ʃiːts] cpd: ~**gericht** nt court of arbitration; ~**richter** m referee, umpire; (Schlichter) arbitrator; **s~richtern** vti insep referee, umpire; arbitrate; ~**spruch** m (arbitration) award.

schief [ʃiːf] a crooked; Ebene sloping; Turm leaning; Winkel oblique; Blick funny; Vergleich distorted; ad crooked(ly); ansehen askance; etw ~ **stellen** slope sth.

Schiefer ['ʃiːfər] m -s, - slate; ~**dach** nt slate roof; ~**tafel** f (child's) slate.

schief- cpd: ~**gehen** vi irreg (col) go wrong; ~**lachen** vr (col) double up with laughter; ~**liegen** vi irreg (col) be wrong.

schielen ['ʃiːlən] vi squint; **nach etw ~** (fig) eye sth.

Schienbein nt shinbone.

Schiene ['ʃiːnə] f -, -n rail; (Med) splint; **s~n** vt put in splints; ~**nstrang** m (Rail etc) (section of) track.

schier [ʃiːr] a pure; Fleisch lean and boneless; (fig) sheer; ad nearly, almost.

Schieß- ['ʃiːs] cpd: ~**bude** f shooting gallery; ~**budenfigur** f (col) clown, ludicrous figure; **s~en** vti irreg shoot (auf +acc at); (Salat etc) run to seed; Ball kick; Geschoß fire; ~**e'rei** f shooting incident, shoot-up; ~**platz** m firing range; ~**pulver** nt gunpowder; ~**scharte** f embrasure; ~**stand** m rifle or shooting range.

Schiff [ʃɪf] nt -(e)s, -e ship, vessel; (Kirchen—) nave; **s~bar** a navigable; ~**bau** m shipbuilding; ~**bruch** m shipwreck; **s~brüchig** a shipwrecked; ~**chen** nt small boat; (Weben) shuttle; (Mütze) forage cap; ~**er** m -s, - bargeman, boatman; ~**(f)ahrt** f shipping; (Reise) voyage; ~**(f)ahrtslinie** f shipping route; ~**sjunge** m cabin boy; ~**sladung** f cargo, shipload; ~**splanke** f gangplank.

Schikane [ʃi'kaːnə] f -, -n harassment; dirty trick; **mit allen ~n** with all the trimmings.

schikanieren [ʃikaˈniːrən] vt harass, torment.

Schild [ʃɪlt] m -(e)s, -e shield; (Mützen—)

peak, visor; **etw im ~ führen** be up to sth; nt -(e)s, -er sign; nameplate; (Etikett) label; ~**bürger** m duffer, blockhead; ~**drüse** f thyroid gland; **s~ern** ['ʃɪldərn] vt depict, portray; ~**erung** f description, portrayal; ~**kröte** f tortoise; (Wasser—) turtle.

Schilf [ʃɪlf] nt -(e)s, -e, ~**rohr** nt (Pflanze) reed; (Material) reeds pl, rushes pl.

schillern ['ʃɪlərn] vi shimmer; ~**d** a iridescent.

Schimmel ['ʃɪməl] m -s, - mould; (Pferd) white horse; **s~ig** a mouldy; **s~n** vi get mouldy.

Schimmer ['ʃɪmər] m -s glimmer; **s~n** vi glimmer, shimmer.

Schimpanse [ʃɪm'panzə] m -n, -n chimpanzee.

Schimpf [ʃɪmpf] m -(e)s, -e disgrace; **s~en** vti scold; vi curse, complain; ~**wort** nt term of abuse.

Schind- ['ʃɪnd] cpd: ~**el** f -, -n shingle; **s~en** irreg vt maltreat, drive too hard; (col) Eindruck **s~en** create an impression; vr sweat and strain, toil away (mit at); ~**er** m -s, - knacker; (fig) slave driver; ~**e'rei** f grind, drudgery; ~**luder** nt: ~**luder treiben mit** muck or mess about; Vorrecht abuse.

Schinken ['ʃɪŋkən] m -s, - ham.

Schippe ['ʃɪpə] f -, -n shovel; **s~n** vt shovel.

Schirm [ʃɪrm] m -(e)s, -e (Regen—) umbrella; (Sonnen—) parasol, sunshade; (Wand—, Bild—) screen; (Lampen—) (lamp)shade; (Mützen—) peak; (Pilz—) cap; ~**bildaufnahme** f X-ray; ~**herr** m patron, protector; ~**mütze** f peaked cap; ~**ständer** m umbrella stand.

schizophren [ʃitso'freːn] a schizophrenic.

Schlacht [ʃlaxt] f -, -en battle; **s~en** vt slaughter, kill; ~**enbummler** m football supporter; ~**er** m -s, - butcher; ~**feld** nt battlefield; ~**haus** nt, ~**hof** m slaughterhouse, abattoir; ~**plan** m (lit, fig) battle plan; ~**ruf** m battle cry, war cry; ~**schiff** nt battle ship; ~**vieh** nt animals kept for meat; beef cattle.

Schlacke ['ʃlakə] f -, -n slag.

Schlaf [ʃlaːf] m -(e)s sleep; ~**anzug** m pyjamas pl.

Schläf- ['ʃlɛːf] cpd: ~**chen** nt nap; ~**e** f -, -n temple.

schlafen ['ʃlaːfən] vi irreg sleep; **S~gehen** nt -s going to bed; **S~szeit** f bedtime.

Schläfer(in f) ['ʃlɛːfər(ɪn)] m -s, - sleeper.

schlaff [ʃlaf] a slack; (energielos) limp; (erschöpft) exhausted; **S~heit** f slackness; limpness; exhaustion.

Schlaf- cpd: ~**gelegenheit** f sleeping accommodation; ~**lied** nt lullaby; **s~los** a sleepless; ~**losigkeit** f sleeplessness, insomnia; ~**mittel** nt soporific, sleeping pill.

schläfrig ['ʃlɛːfrɪç] a sleepy.

Schlaf- cpd: ~**saal** m dormitory; ~**sack** m sleeping bag; ~**tablette** f sleeping pill; **s~trunken** a drowsy, half-asleep; ~**wagen** m sleeping car, sleeper;

s~**wandeln** vi insep sleepwalk;
~**zimmer** nt bedroom.

Schlag [ʃlaːk] m -(e)s, ˵e (lit, fig) blow;
stroke (auch Med); (Puls-, Herz-) beat;
(pl: Tracht Prügel) beating; (Elec) shock;
(Blitz-) bolt, stroke; (Autotür) car door;
(col: Portion) helping; (Art) kind, type; mit
einem ~ all at once; ~ **auf** ~ in rapid
succession; ~**ader** f artery; ~**anfall** m
stroke; s~**artig** a sudden, without
warning; ~**baum** m barrier; s~en
[ˈʃlaːgən] irreg vti strike, hit; (wiederholt ~,
besiegen) beat; (Glocke) ring; Stunde strike;
Sahne whip; Schlacht fight; (einwickeln)
wrap; **nach jdm** s~**en** (fig) take after sb;
vr fight; **sich gut** s~**en** (fig) do well;
s~**end** a Beweis convincing; s~**ende**
Wetter (Min) firedamp; ~**er** [ˈʃlaːgər] m
-s, - (lit, fig) hit; ~**ersänger(in** f) m pop
singer.

Schläg- [ˈʃlɛːg] cpd: ~**er** m -s, - brawler;
(Sport) bat; (Tennis etc) racket; (golf) club;
hockey stick; (Waffe) rapier; ~**e'rei** f
fight, punch-up.

Schlag- cpd: s~**fertig** a quick-witted;
~**fertigkeit** f ready wit, quickness of
repartee; ~**instrument** nt percussion
instrument; ~**loch** nt pothole; ~**rahm** m,
~**sahne** f (whipped) cream; ~**seite** f
(Naut) list; ~**wort** nt slogan, catch phrase;
~**zeile** f headline; ~**zeug** nt percussion;
drums pl; ~**zeuger** m -s, - drummer.

Schlamassel [ʃlaˈmasəl] m -s, - (col)
mess.

Schlamm [ʃlam] m -(e)s, -e mud; s~**ig** a
muddy.

Schlamp- [ˈʃlamp] cpd: ~**e** f -, -n (col)
slattern, slut; s~**en** vi (col) be sloppy;
~**e'rei** f (col) disorder, untidiness; sloppy
work; s~**ig** a (col) slovenly, sloppy.

Schlange [ˈʃlaŋə] f -, -n snake;
(Menschen-) queue (Brit), line-up (US); ~
stehen (form a) queue, line up.

schlängeln [ˈʃlɛŋəln] vr twist, wind; (Fluß)
meander.

Schlangen- cpd: ~**biß** m snake bite;
~**ngift** nt snake venom; ~**linie** f wavy
line.

schlank [ʃlaŋk] a slim, slender; S~**heit** f
slimness, slenderness; S~**heitskur** f diet.

schlapp [ʃlap] a limp; (locker) slack; S~**e** f
-, -n (col) setback; S~**heit** f limpness,
slackness; S~**hut** m slouch hat;
~**machen** vi (col) wilt, droop.

Schlaraffenland [ʃlaˈrafənlant] nt land of
milk and honey.

schlau [ʃlau] a crafty, cunning.

Schlauch [ʃlaux] m -(e)s, Schläuche
hose; (in Reifen) inner tube; (col:
Anstrengung) grind; ~**boot** nt rubber
dinghy; s~**en** vt (col) tell on, exhaust;
s~**los** a Reifen tubeless.

Schlau- cpd: ~**heit** f, Schläue [ˈʃlɔyə] f -
cunning; ~**kopf** m clever dick.

schlecht [ʃlɛçt] a bad; ~ **und recht** after
a fashion; **jdm ist** ~ sb feels sick or bad;
~**erdings** ad simply; ~**gehen** vi impers
irreg: **jdm geht es** ~ sb is in a bad way;
S~**heit** f badness; '~**hin** ad simply; **der**
Dramatiker ~**hin** THE playwright;

S~**igkeit** f badness; bad deed;
~**machen** vt run down; etw ~ **machen**
do sth badly; ~**weg** ad simply.

schlecken [ˈʃlɛkən] vti lick.

Schlegel [ˈʃleːgal] m -s, - (drum)stick;
(Hammer) mallet, hammer; (Cook) leg.

Schleie [ˈʃlaiə] f -, -n tench.

schleichen [ˈʃlaiçən] vi irreg creep, crawl;
~**d** a gradual; creeping.

Schleier [ˈʃlaiər] m -s, - veil; s~**haft** a
(col) **jdm** s~**haft sein** to be a mystery to sb.

Schleif- [ʃlaif] cpd: ~**e** f -, -n loop; (Band)
bow; s~**en** vt drag; (Mil) Festung raze; vi
drag; vt irreg grind; Edelstein cut; (Mil)
Soldaten drill; ~**stein** m grindstone.

Schleim [ʃlaim] m -(e)s, -e slime; (Med)
mucus; (Cook) gruel; s~**ig** a slimy.

Schlemm- [ˈʃlɛm] cpd: s~**en** vi feast;
~**er** m -s, - gourmet; ~**e'rei** f gluttony,
feasting.

schlendern [ˈʃlɛndərn] vi stroll.

Schlendrian [ˈʃlɛndriaːn] m -(e)s sloppy
way of working.

schlenkern [ˈʃlɛŋkərn] vti swing, dangle.

Schlepp- [ˈʃlɛp] cpd: ~**e** f -, -n train;
s~**en** vt drag; Auto, Schiff tow; (tragen)
lug; s~**end** a dragging, slow; ~**er** m -s, -
tractor; (Schiff) tug; ~**tau** nt towrope; **jdn**
ins ~**tau nehmen** (fig) take sb in tow.

Schleuder [ˈʃlɔydər] f -, -n catapult;
(Wäsche-) spin-drier; (Butter-) etc)
centrifuge; s~**n** vt hurl; Wäsche spin-dry;
vi (Aut) skid; ~**preis** m give-away price;
~**sitz** m (Aviat) ejector seat; (fig) hot
seat; ~**ware** f cheap or cut-price goods pl.

schleunig [ˈʃlɔyniç] a quick, prompt; ~**st**
ad straight away.

Schleuse [ˈʃlɔyzə] f -, -n lock; (~ntor)
sluice.

Schlich [ʃliç] m -(e)s, -e dodge, trick.

schlicht [ʃliçt] a simple, plain; ~**en** vt
smooth, dress; Streit settle; S~**er** m -s, -
mediator, arbitrator; S~**ung** f settlement;
arbitration.

Schlick [ʃlik] m -(e)s, -e mud; (Öl-) a) slick.

Schließ- [ˈʃliːs] cpd: ~**e** f -, -n fastener;
s~**en** irreg vtir close, shut; (beenden)
close; Freundschaft, Bündnis, Ehe enter into;
(folgern) infer (aus +dat from); **etw in**
sich s~**en** include sth; ~**fach** nt locker;
s~**lich** ad finally; (~ doch) after all.

Schliff [ʃlif] m -(e)s, -e cut(ting); (fig)
polish.

schlimm [ʃlim] a bad; ~**er** a worse;
~**ste(r,s)** a worst; ~**stenfalls** ad at (the)
worst.

Schling- [ˈʃliŋ] cpd: ~**e** f -, -n loop; (esp
Henkers-) noose; (Falle) snare; (Med)
sling; ~**el** m -s, - rascal; s~**en** irreg vt
wind; vti (essen) bolt (one's food), gobble;
s~**ern** vi roll.

Schlips [ʃlips] m -es, -e tie.

Schlitten [ˈʃlitən] m -s, - sledge, sleigh;
~**bahn** f toboggan run; ~**fahren** nt -s
tobogganing.

schlittern [ˈʃlitərn] vi slide.

Schlittschuh [ˈʃlitʃuː] m skate; ~ **laufen**
skate; ~**bahn** f skating rink; ~**läufer(in**
f) m skater.

Schlitz [ʃlits] m -es, -e slit; (für Münze)

slot; *(Hosen—)* flies *pl*; **s~äugig** *a* slant-eyed; **s~en** *vt* slit.

schlohweiß ['ʃloː'vaɪs] *a* snow-white.

Schloß [ʃlɔs] *nt* **-sses, ˙sser** lock; *(an Schmuck etc)* clasp; *(Bau)* castle; chateau.

Schlosser ['ʃlɔsər] *m* **-s, -** *(Auto—)* fitter; *(für Schlüssel etc)* locksmith; **~ei** [-'raɪ] *f* metal (working) shop.

Schlot [ʃloːt] *m* **-(e)s, -e** chimney; *(Naut)* funnel.

schlottern ['ʃlɔtərn] *vi* shake, tremble; *(Kleidung)* be baggy.

Schlucht [ʃluxt] *f -, -en* gorge, ravine.

schluchzen ['ʃluxtsən] *vi* sob.

Schluck [ʃlʊk] *m* **-(e)s, -e** swallow; *(Menge)* drop; **~auf** *m* **-s, ~en** *m* **-s, -** hiccups *pl*; **s~en** *vti* swallow.

schludern ['ʃluːdərn] *vi* skimp, do sloppy work.

Schlummer ['ʃlʊmər] *m* **-s** slumber; **s~n** *vi* slumber.

Schlund [ʃlʊnt] *m* **-(e)s, ˙e** gullet; *(fig)* jaw.

schlüpfen ['ʃlʏpfən] *vi* slip; *(Vogel etc)* hatch (out).

Schlüpfer ['ʃlʏpfər] *m* **-s, -** panties *pl*, knickers *pl*.

Schlupfloch ['ʃlʊpflɔx] *nt* hole; hide-out; *(fig)* loophole.

schlüpfrig ['ʃlʏpfrɪç] *a* slippery; *(fig)* lewd; **S~keit** *f* slipperiness; *(fig)* lewdness.

schlurfen ['ʃlʊrfən] *vi* shuffle.

schlürfen ['ʃlʏrfən] *vti* slurp.

Schluß [ʃlʊs] *m* **-sses, ˙sse** end; *(—folgerung)* conclusion; **am ~** at the end; **~ machen mit** finish with.

Schlüssel ['ʃlʏsəl] *m* **-s, -** *(lit, fig)* key; *(Schraub—)* spanner, wrench; *(Mus)* clef; **~bein** *nt* collarbone; **~blume** *f* cowslip, primrose; **~bund** *m* bunch of keys; **~kind** *nt* latchkey child; **~loch** *nt* keyhole; **~position** *f* key position; **~wort** *f* combination.

schlüssig ['ʃlʏsɪç] *a* conclusive.

Schluß- *cpd*: **~licht** *nt* taillight; *(fig)* tailender; **~strich** *m (fig)* final stroke; **~verkauf** *m* clearance sale; **~wort** *nt* concluding words *pl*.

Schmach [ʃmaːx] *f -* disgrace, ignominy.

schmachten ['ʃmaxtən] *vi* languish; long *(nach* for).

schmächtig ['ʃmɛçtɪç] *a* slight.

schmachvoll *a* ignominious, humiliating.

schmackhaft ['ʃmakhaft] *a* tasty.

schmäh- ['ʃmɛː] *cpd*: **~en** *vt* abuse, revile; **~lich** *a* ignominious, shameful; **S~ung** *f* abuse.

schmal [ʃmaːl] *a* narrow; *Person, Buch etc* slender, slim; *(karg)* meagre.

schmälern ['ʃmɛːlərn] *vt* diminish; *(fig)* belittle.

Schmal- *cpd*: **~film** *m* cine film; **~spur** *f* narrow gauge.

Schmalz [ʃmalts] *nt* **-es, -e** dripping, lard; *(fig)* sentiment, schmaltz; **s~ig** *a (fig)* schmaltzy, slushy.

schmarotzen [ʃma'rɔtsən] *vi* sponge; *(Bot)* be parasitic.

Schmarotzer *m* **-s, -** parasite; sponger.

Schmarren ['ʃmarən] *m* **-s, -** *(Aus)* small

piece of pancake; *(fig)* rubbish, tripe.

schmatzen [ʃmatsən] *vi* smack one's lips; eat noisily.

Schmaus [ʃmaʊs] *m* **-es, Schmäuse** feast; **s~en** *vi* feast.

schmecken ['ʃmɛkən] *vti* taste; **es schmeckt ihm** he likes it.

Schmeichel- ['ʃmaɪçəl] *cpd*: **~ei** [-'laɪ] *f* flattery; **s~haft** *a* flattering; **s~n** *vi* flatter.

schmeißen ['ʃmaɪsən] *vt irreg (col)* throw, chuck.

Schmeißfliege *f* bluebottle.

Schmelz [ʃmɛlts] *m* **-es, -e** enamel; *(Glasur)* glaze; *(von Stimme)* melodiousness; **s~bar** *a* fusible; **s~en** *vti irreg* melt; *Erz* smelt; **~hütte** *f* smelting works *pl*; **~punkt** *m* melting point; **~wasser** *nt* melted snow.

Schmerz [ʃmerts] *m* **-es, -en** pain; *(Trauer)* grief; **s~empfindlich** *a* sensitive to pain; **s~en** *vti* hurt; **~ensgeld** *nt* compensation; **s~haft, s~lich** *a* painful; **s~los** *a* painless; **s~stillend** *a* soothing.

Schmetterling ['ʃmɛtərlɪŋ] *m* butterfly.

schmettern ['ʃmɛtərn] *vti* smash; *Melodie* sing loudly, bellow out; *(Trompete)* blare.

Schmied [ʃmiːt] *m* **-(e)s, -e** blacksmith; **~e** ['ʃmiːdə] *f -, -n* smithy, forge; **~eeisen** *nt* wrought iron; **s~en** *vt* forge; *Pläne* devise, concoct.

schmiegen ['ʃmiːgən] *vt* press, nestle; *vr* cling, nestle (up) (*an +acc* to).

schmiegsam ['ʃmiːkzaːm] *a* flexible, pliable.

Schmier- ['ʃmiːr] *cpd*: **~e** *f -, -n* grease; *(Theat)* greasepaint, make-up; **s~en** *vt* smear; *(ölen)* lubricate, grease; *(bestechen)* bribe; *vti (schreiben)* scrawl; **~fett** *nt* grease; **~fink** *m* messy person; **~geld** *nt* bribe; **s~ig** *a* greasy; **~mittel** *nt* lubricant; **~seife** *f* soft soap.

Schminke ['ʃmɪŋkə] *f -, -n* make-up; **s~n** *vtr* make up.

schmirgel- ['ʃmɪrgəl] *cpd*: **~n** *vt* sand (down); **S~papier** *nt* emery paper.

Schmöker ['ʃmøːkər] *m* **-s, -** *(col)* (trashy) old book; **s~n** *vi (col)* browse.

schmollen ['ʃmɔlən] *vi* sulk, pout; **~d** *a* sulky.

Schmor- ['ʃmoːr] *cpd*: **~braten** *m* stewed *or* braised meat; **s~en** *vt* stew, braise.

Schmuck [ʃmʊk] *m* **-(e)s, -e** jewellery; *(Verzierung)* decoration.

schmücken ['ʃmʏkən] *vt* decorate.

Schmuck- *cpd*: **s~los** *a* unadorned, plain; **~losigkeit** *f* simplicity; **~sachen** *pl* jewels *pl*, jewellery.

Schmuggel ['ʃmʊgəl] *m* **-s** smuggling; **s~n** *vti* smuggle.

Schmuggler *m* **-s, -** smuggler.

schmunzeln ['ʃmʊntsəln] *vi* smile benignly.

Schmutz [ʃmʊts] *m* **-es** dirt, filth; **s~en** *vi* get dirty; **~fink** *m* filthy creature; **~fleck** *m* stain; **s~ig** *a* dirty.

Schnabel ['ʃnaːbəl] *m* **-s, ˙** beak, bill; *(Ausguß)* spout.

Schnake ['ʃnaːkə] *f -, -n* cranefly; *(Stechmücke)* gnat.

Schnalle ['ʃnalə] f -, -n buckle, clasp; s~n vt buckle.

schnalzen ['ʃnaltsən] vi snap; (mit Zunge) click.

Schnapp- ['ʃnap] cpd: s~en vt grab, catch; vi snap; ~schloß nt spring lock; ~schuß m (Phot) snapshot.

Schnaps [ʃnaps] m -es, ⁻e spirits pl; schnapps.

schnarchen ['ʃnarçən] vi snore.

schnattern ['ʃnatərn] vi chatter; (zittern) shiver.

schnauben ['ʃnaubən] vi snort; vr blow one's nose.

schnaufen ['ʃnaufən] vi puff, pant.

Schnauz- ['ʃnauts] cpd: ~bart m moustache; ~e f -, -n snout, muzzle; (Ausguß) spout; (col) gob.

Schnecke ['ʃnɛkə] f -, -n snail; ~nhaus nt snail's shell.

Schnee [ʃne:] m -s snow; (Ei—) beaten egg white; ~ball m snowball; ~flocke f snowflake; ~gestöber nt snowstorm; ~glöckchen nt snowdrop; ~kette f (Aut) (snow) chain; ~pflug m snowplough; ~schmelze f -, -n thaw; ~wehe f snowdrift; ~wittchen nt Snow White.

Schneid [ʃnaɪt] m -(e)s (col) pluck; ~e f ['ʃnaɪdə] f -, -n edge; (Klinge) blade; s~en vtr irreg cut (o.s.); (kreuzen) cross, intersect; s~end a cutting; ~er m -s, - tailor; ~erin f dressmaker; s~ern vt make; vi be a tailor; ~ezahn m incisor; s~ig a dashing; (mutig) plucky.

schneien ['ʃnaɪən] vi snow.

Schneise ['ʃnaɪzə] f -, -n clearing.

schnell [ʃnɛl] a,ad quick(ly), fast; ~en vi shoot, fly; S~hefter m -s, - loose-leaf binder; S~igkeit f speed; ~stens ad as quickly as possible; S~straße f expressway; S~zug m fast or express train.

schneuzen ['ʃnɔytsən] vr blow one's nose.

schnippisch ['ʃnɪpɪʃ] a sharp-tongued.

Schnitt [ʃnɪt] m -(e)s, -e cut(ting); (—punkt) intersection; (Quer—) (cross) section; (Durch—) average; (—muster) pattern; (Ernte) crop; (an Buch) edge; (col: Gewinn) profit; ~blumen pl cut flowers pl; ~e f -, -n slice; (belegt) sandwich; ~fläche f section; ~lauch m chive; ~muster nt pattern; ~punkt m (point of) intersection; ~wunde f cut.

Schnitz- ['ʃnɪts] cpd: ~arbeit f wood carving; ~el nt -s, - chip; (Cook) escalope; s~en vt carve; ~er m -s, - carver; (col) blunder; ~e'rei f carving, carved woodwork.

schnodderig ['ʃnɔdərɪç] a (col) snotty.

schnöde ['ʃnø:də] a base, mean.

Schnorchel ['ʃnɔrçəl] m -s, - snorkel.

Schnörkel ['ʃnœrkəl] m -s, - flourish; (Archit) scroll.

schnorren ['ʃnɔrən] vti cadge.

schnüffeln ['ʃnyfəln] vi sniff.

Schnüffler m -s, - snooper.

Schnuller ['ʃnulər] m -s, - dummy, comforter (US).

Schnupfen ['ʃnupfən] m -s, - cold.

schnuppern ['ʃnupərn] vi sniff.

Schnur [ʃnu:r] f -, ⁻e string, cord; (Elec)

flex; s~gerade a straight (as a die or arrow).

schnüren ['ʃny:rən] vt tie.

Schnurr- ['ʃnur] cpd: ~bart m moustache; s~en vi purr; (Kreisel) hum.

Schnür- ['ʃny:r] cpd: ~schuh m lace-up (shoe); ~senkel m shoelace.

schnurstracks ad straight (away).

Schock [ʃɔk] m -(e)s, -e shock; s~ieren [ʃɔ'ki:rən] vt shock, outrage.

Schöffe ['ʃœfə] m -n, -n lay magistrate; ~ngericht nt magistrates' court.

Schöffin f lay magistrate.

Schokolade [ʃoko'la:də] f -, -n chocolate.

Scholle ['ʃɔlə] f -, -n clod; (Eis—) ice floe; (Fisch) plaice.

schon [ʃo:n] ad already; (zwar) certainly; warst du ~ einmal da? have you ever been there?; ich war ~ einmal da I've been there before; das ist ~ immer so that has always been the case; das wird ~ (noch) gut that'll be OK; wenn ich das ~ höre . . . I only have to hear that . . .; ~ der Gedanke the very thought.

schön [ʃø:n] a beautiful; (nett) nice; ~e Grüße best wishes; ~en Dank (many) thanks.

schonen ['ʃo:nən] vt look after; vr take it easy; ~d a careful, gentle.

Schön- cpd: ~geist m cultured person, aesthete; ~heit f beauty; ~heitsfehler m blemish, flaw; ~heitsoperation f cosmetic plastic surgery; s~machen vr make oneself look nice.

Schon- cpd: ~ung f good care; (Nachsicht) consideration; (Forst) plantation of young trees; s~ungslos a unsparing, harsh; ~zeit f close season.

Schöpf- ['ʃœpf] cpd: s~en vt scoop, ladle; Mut summon up; Luft breath in; ~er m -s, - creator; s~erisch a creative; ~kelle f ladle; ~löffel m skimmer, scoop; ~ung f creation.

Schorf ['ʃɔrf] m -(e)s, -e scab.

Schornstein ['ʃɔrnʃtaɪn] m chimney; (Naut) funnel; ~feger m -s, - chimney sweep.

Schoß [ʃo:s] m -es, ⁻e lap; (Rock—) coat tail; ~hund m pet dog, lapdog.

Schote ['ʃo:tə] f -, -n pod.

Schotter ['ʃɔtər] m -s broken stone, road metal; (Rail) ballast.

schraffieren [ʃra'fi:rən] vt hatch.

schräg [ʃrɛ:k] a slanting, not straight; etw ~ stellen put sth at an angle; ~ gegenüber diagonally opposite; S~e f -, -n slant; S~schrift f italics pl; S~streifen m bias binding; S~strich m oblique stroke.

Schramme ['ʃramə] f -, -n scratch; s~n vt scratch.

Schrank [ʃraŋk] m -(e)s, ⁻e cupboard; (Kleider—) wardrobe; ~e f -, -n barrier; s~enlos a boundless; (zügellos) unrestrained; ~enwärter m (Rail) level crossing attendant; ~koffer m trunk.

Schraube ['ʃraubə] f -, -n screw; s~n vt screw; ~nschlüssel m spanner; ~nzieher m -s, - screwdriver.

Schraubstock ['fraubftɔk] m (Tech) vice.
Schrebergarten ['freːbərgartən] m allotment.
Schreck [frɛk] m -(e)s, -e, ~en m -s, - terror; fright; s~en vt frighten, scare; ~gespenst nt spectre, nightmare; s~haft a jumpy, easily frightened; s~lich a terrible, dreadful; ~schuß m shot fired in the air.
Schrei [fraɪ] m -(e)s, -e scream; (Ruf) shout.
Schreib- ['fraɪb] cpd: ~block m writing pad; s~en vti irreg write; (buchstabieren) spell; ~en nt -s, - letter, communication; ~er m -s, - writer; (Büro~) clerk; s~faul a bad about writing letters; ~fehler m spelling mistake; ~maschine f typewriter; ~papier nt notepaper; ~tisch m desk; ~ung f spelling; ~waren pl stationery; ~weise f spelling; way of writing; ~zeug nt writing materials pl.
schreien ['fraɪən] vti irreg scream; (rufen) shout; ~d a (fig) glaring; Farbe loud.
Schreiner ['fraɪnər] m -s, - joiner; (Zimmermann) carpenter; (Möbel~) cabinetmaker; ~ei [-'raɪ] f joiner's workshop.
schreiten ['fraɪtən] vi irreg stride.
Schrift [frɪft] f -, -en writing; handwriting; (~art) script; (Gedrucktes) pamphlet, work; ~deutsch nt written German; ~führer m secretary; s~lich a written; ad in writing; ~setzer m compositor; ~sprache f written language; ~steller(in f) m -s, - writer; ~stück nt document.
schrill [frɪl] a shrill; ~en vi sound or ring shrilly.
Schritt [frɪt] m -(e)s, -e step; (Gangart) walk; (Tempo) pace; (von Hose) crutch; ~macher m -s, pacemaker; ~tempo nt: im ~(t)empo at a walking pace.
schroff [frɔf] a steep; (zackig) jagged; (fig) brusque; (ungeduldig) abrupt.
schröpfen ['frœpfən] vt (fig) fleece.
Schrot [froːt] m or nt -(e)s, -e (Blei) (small) shot; (Getreide) coarsely ground grain, groats pl; ~flinte f shotgun.
Schrott [frɔt] m -(e)s, -e scrap metal; ~haufen m scrap heap; s~reif a ready for the scrap heap.
schrubben ['frubən] vt scrub.
Schrubber m -s, - scrubbing brush.
Schrulle ['frulə] f -, -n eccentricity, queer idea/habit.
schrumpfen ['frumpfən] vi shrink; (Apfel) shrivel.
Schub- ['fuːb] cpd: ~fach nt drawer; ~karren m wheelbarrow; ~lade f drawer.
schüchtern ['fʏçtərn] a shy; S~heit f shyness.
Schuft [fuft] m -(e)s, -e scoundrel; s~en vi (col) graft, slave away.
Schuh [fuː] m -(e)s, -e shoe; ~band nt shoelace; ~creme f shoe polish; ~löffel m shoehorn; ~macher m -s, - shoemaker.
Schul- ['fuːl] cpd: ~aufgaben pl

homework; ~besuch m school attendance.
Schuld [fult] f -, -en guilt; (Fin) debt; (Verschulden) fault; s~ a: s~ sein or haben be to blame (an +dat for); er ist or hat s~ it's his fault; jdm s~ geben blame sb; s~en ['fuldən] vt owe; s~enfrei a free from debt; ~gefühl nt feeling of guilt; s~ig a guilty (an +dat of); (gebührend) due; jdm etw s~ig sein owe sb sth; jdm etw s~ig bleiben not provide sb with sth; s~los a innocent, without guilt; ~ner m -s, - debtor; ~schein m promissory note, IOU; ~spruch m verdict of guilty.
Schule ['fuːlə] f -, -n school; s~n vt train, school.
Schüler(in f) ['fyːlər(ɪn)] m -s, - pupil.
Schul- ['fuːl] cpd: ~ferien pl school holidays pl; s~frei a: s~freier Tag holiday; s~frei sein be a holiday; ~funk m schools' broadcasts pl; ~geld nt school fees pl; ~hof m playground; ~jahr nt school year; ~junge m schoolboy; ~mädchen nt schoolgirl; s~pflichtig a of school age; ~schiff nt (Naut) training ship; ~stunde f period, lesson; ~tasche f satchel.
Schulter ['fultər] f -, -n shoulder; ~blatt nt shoulder blade; s~n vt shoulder.
Schul- cpd: ~ung f education, schooling; ~wesen nt educational system; ~zeugnis nt school report.
Schund [funt] m -(e)s trash, garbage; ~roman m trashy novel.
Schuppe ['fupə] f -, -n scale; pl (Haar~) dandruff; s~n vt scale; vr peel; ~n m -s, - shed.
schuppig ['fupɪç] a scaly.
Schur [fuːr] f -, -en shearing.
Schür- ['fyːr] cpd: ~eisen nt poker; s~en vt rake; (fig) stir up; s~fen ['fʏrfən] vti scrape, scratch; (Min) prospect; dig; ~fung f abrasion; (Min) prospecting; ~haken m poker.
Schurke ['furkə] m -n, -n rogue.
Schurz [furts] m -es, -e, **Schürze** ['fʏrtsə] f -, -n apron.
Schuß [fus] m -sses, -sse shot; (Weben) woof; ~bereich m effective range.
Schüssel ['fʏsəl] f -, -n bowl.
Schuß- cpd: ~linie f line of fire; ~verletzung f bullet wound; ~waffe f firearm; ~weite f range (of fire).
Schuster ['fuːstər] m -s, - cobbler, shoemaker.
Schutt [fut] m -(e)s rubbish; (Bau~) rubble; ~abladeplatz m refuse dump.
Schütt- ['fʏt] cpd: ~elfrost m shivering; s~eln vtr shake; s~en vt pour; (Zucker, Kies etc) tip; (ver~) spill; vi impers pour (down); s~er a Haare sparse, thin.
Schutt- cpd: ~halde f dump; ~haufen m heap of rubble.
Schutz [futs] m -es protection; (Unterschlupf) shelter; jdn in ~ nehmen stand up for sb; ~anzug m overalls pl; ~befohlene(r) mf charge; ~blech nt mudguard; ~brille f goggles pl.
Schütze ['fʏtsə] m -n, -n gunman;

(Gewehr—) rifleman; *(Scharf-, Sport—)* marksman; *(Astrol)* Sagittarius.

Schutz- cpd: **~engel** m guardian angel; **~gebiet** nt protectorate; *(Natur—)* reserve; **~haft** f protective custody; **~impfung** f immunisation; **s~los** a defenceless; **~mann** m, pl **-leute** or **-männer** policeman; **~maßnahme** f precaution; **~patron** m patron saint; **~umschlag** m (book) jacket; **~vorrichtung** f safety device.

schwach [ʃvax] a weak, feeble.

Schwäche ['ʃvɛçə] f -, **-n** weakness; **s~n** vt weaken.

Schwach- cpd: **~heit** f weakness; **s~köpfig** a silly, lame-brained.

Schwäch- cpd: **s~lich** a weakly, delicate; **~ling** m weakling.

Schwach- cpd: **~sinn** m imbecility; **s~sinnig** a mentally deficient; *Idee* idiotic; **~strom** m weak current.

Schwächung ['ʃvɛçʊŋ] f weakening.

Schwaden ['ʃvaːdən] m -s, - cloud.

schwafeln ['ʃvaːfəln] vti blather, drivel.

Schwager ['ʃvaːgər] m -s, - brother-in-law.

Schwägerin ['ʃvɛːgərɪn] f sister-law.

Schwalbe ['ʃvalbə] f -, **-n** swallow.

Schwall [ʃval] m -(e)s, **-e** surge; *(Worte)* flood, torrent.

Schwamm [ʃvam] m -(e)s, **-e** sponge; *(Pilz)* fungus; **s~ig** a spongy; *Gesicht* puffy.

Schwan [ʃvaːn] m -(e)s, **-e** swan; **s~en** vi impers: **jdm schwant etw** sb has a foreboding of sth.

schwanger ['ʃvaŋɡər] a pregnant.

schwängern ['ʃvɛŋərn] vt make pregnant.

Schwangerschaft f pregnancy.

Schwank [ʃvaŋk] m -(e)s, **-e** funny story; **s~en** vi sway; *(taumeln)* stagger, reel; *(Preise, Zahlen)* fluctuate; *(zögern)* hesitate, vacillate; **~ung** f fluctuation.

Schwanz [ʃvants] m -es, **-e** tail.

schwänzen ['ʃvɛntsən] *(col)* vt skip, cut; vi play truant.

Schwänzer ['ʃvɛntsər] m -s, - *(col)* truant.

Schwarm [ʃvarm] m -(e)s, **-e** swarm; *(col)* heart-throb, idol.

schwärm- ['ʃvɛrm] cpd: **~en** vi swarm; **~en für** be mad or wild about; **S~erei** f [-ə'raɪ] f enthusiasm; **~erisch** a impassioned, effusive.

Schwarte ['ʃvaːrtə] f -, **-n** hard skin; *(Speck—)* rind.

schwarz [ʃvarts] a black; **ins S~e treffen** *(lit, fig)* hit the bull's eye; **S~arbeit** f illicit work, moonlighting; **S~brot** nt black bread.

Schwärze ['ʃvɛrtsə] f -, **-n** blackness; *(Farbe)* blacking; *(Drucker—)* printer's ink; **s~n** vt blacken.

Schwarz- cpd: **s~fahren** vi irreg travel without paying; drive without a licence; **~handel** m black-market *(trade)*; **s~hören** vi listen to the radio without a licence.

schwärzlich ['ʃvɛrtslɪç] a blackish, darkish.

Schwarz- cpd: **~markt** m black market; **s~sehen** vi irreg *(col)* see the gloomy side

of things; *(TV)* watch TV without a licence; **~seher** m pessimist; *(TV)* viewer without a licence; **s~weiß** a black and white.

schwatzen ['ʃvatsən], **schwätzen** ['ʃvɛtsən] vi chatter.

Schwätzer ['ʃvɛtsər] m -s, - gasbag; **~in** f chatterbox, gossip.

schwatzhaft a talkative, gossipy.

Schwebe ['ʃveːbə] f: **in der ~** *(fig)* in abeyance; **~bahn** f overhead railway; **~balken** m *(Sport)* beam; **s~n** vi drift, float; *(hoch)* soar; *(unentschieden sein)* be in the balance.

Schwefel ['ʃveːfəl] m -s sulphur; **s~ig** a sulphurous; **~säure** f sulphuric acid.

Schweif [ʃvaɪf] m -(e)s, **-e** tail; **s~en** vi wander, roam.

Schweig- ['ʃvaɪɡ] cpd: **~egeld** nt hush money; **s~en** vi irreg be silent; stop talking; **~en** nt -s silence; **s~sam** ['ʃvaɪkzaːm] a silent, taciturn; **~samkeit** f taciturnity, quietness.

Schwein [ʃvaɪn] nt -(e)s, **-e** pig; *(fig)* (good) luck; **~efleisch** nt pork; **~ehund** m *(col)* stinker, swine; **~erei** [-ə'raɪ] f mess; *(Gemeinheit)* dirty trick; **~estall** m pigsty; **s~isch** a filthy; **~sleder** nt pigskin.

Schweiß [ʃvaɪs] m -es sweat, perspiration; **s~en** vti weld; **~er** m -s, - welder; **~füße** pl sweaty feet pl; **~naht** f weld.

schwelen ['ʃveːlən] vi smoulder.

schwelgen ['ʃvɛlɡən] vi indulge.

Schwelle ['ʃvɛlə] f -, **-n** threshold *(auch fig)*; doorstep; *(Rail)* sleeper; **s~n** vi irreg swell.

Schwellung f swelling.

Schwengel ['ʃvɛŋəl] m -s, - pump handle; *(Glocken-)* clapper.

Schwenk- ['ʃvɛŋk] cpd: **s~bar** a swivel-mounted; **s~en** vt swing; *Fahne* wave; *(abspülen)* rinse; vi turn, swivel; *(Mil)* wheel; **~ung** f turn; wheel.

schwer [ʃveːr] a heavy; *(schwierig)* difficult, hard; *(schlimm)* serious, bad; ad *(sehr)* very (much); *verletzt etc* seriously, badly; **S~arbeiter** m manual worker, labourer; **S~e** f -, in weight, heaviness; *(Phys)* gravity; **~elos** a weightless; *Kammer* zero-G; **S~enöter** m -s, - casanova, ladies' man; **~erziehbar** a difficult (to bring up); **~fallen** vi irreg: **jdm ~fallen** be difficult for sb; **~fällig** a ponderous; **S~gewicht** nt heavyweight; *(fig)* emphasis; **~hörig** a hard of hearing; **S~industrie** f heavy industry; **S~kraft** f gravity; **S~kranke(r)** mf person who is seriously ill; **~lich** ad hardly; **~machen** vt: **jdm/sich etw ~machen** make sth difficult for sb/o.s.; **S~metall** nt heavy metal; **~mütig** a melancholy; **~nehmen** vt irreg take to heart; **S~punkt** m centre of gravity; *(fig)* emphasis, crucial point.

Schwert [ʃveːrt] nt -(e)s, **-er** sword; **~lilie** f iris.

schwer- cpd: **~tun** vi irreg: **sich** *(dat or acc)* **~tun** have difficulties; **S~verbrecher(in** f) m criminal, serious offender; **~verdaulich** a indigestible, heavy; ~**verletzt** a badly injured; ~**verwundet** a seriously wounded; ~**wiegend** a weighty, important.

Schwester ['ʃvɛstər] f -, -n sister; (Med) nurse; s~**lich** a sisterly.

Schwieger- ['ʃviːgər] cpd: ~**eltern** pl parents-in-law pl; ~**mutter** f mother-in-law; ~**sohn** m son-in-law; ~**tochter** f daughter-in-law; ~**vater** m father-in-law.

Schwiele ['ʃviːlə] f -, -n callus.

schwierig ['ʃviːrɪç] a difficult, hard; S~**keit** f difficulty.

Schwimm- ['ʃvɪm] cpd: ~**bad** nt swimming baths pl; ~**becken** nt swimming pool; s~**en** vi irreg swim; (treiben, nicht sinken) float; (fig: unsicher sein) be all at sea; ~**er** m -s, - swimmer; (Angeln) float; ~**lehrer** m swimming instructor; ~**sport** m swimming; ~**weste** f life jacket.

Schwindel ['ʃvɪndəl] m -s giddiness; dizzy spell; (Betrug) swindle, fraud; (Zeug) stuff; s~**frei** a free from giddiness; s~**n** vi (col: lügen) fib; **jdm schwindelt es** sb feels giddy.

schwinden ['ʃvɪndən] vi irreg disappear; (sich verringern) decrease; (Kräfte) decline.

Schwindler ['ʃvɪndlər] m -s, - swindler; (Lügner) liar; s~**lig** a giddy; **mir ist** s~**lig** I feel giddy.

Schwing- ['ʃvɪŋ] cpd: s~**en** vti irreg swing; Waffe etc brandish; (vibrieren) vibrate; (klingen) sound; ~**er** m -s, - (Boxen) swing; ~**tür** f swing door(s); ~**ung** f vibration; (Phys) oscillation.

Schwips [ʃvɪps] m -es, -e **einen** ~ **haben** to be tipsy.

schwirren ['ʃvɪrən] vi buzz.

schwitzen ['ʃvɪtsən] vi sweat, perspire.

schwören ['ʃvøːrən] vti irreg swear.

schwul [ʃvuːl] a (col) gay, queer.

schwül [ʃvyːl] a sultry, close; S~**e** f - - sultriness, closeness.

Schwulst [ʃvʊlst] f -(e)s, ¨e bombast.

schwülstig ['ʃvʏlstɪç] a pompous.

Schwund [ʃvʊnt] m -(e)s loss; (Schrumpfen) shrinkage.

Schwung [ʃvʊŋ] m -(e)s, ¨e swing; (Triebkraft) momentum; (fig: Energie) verve, energy; (col: Menge) batch; s~**haft** a brisk, lively; ~**rad** nt flywheel; s~**voll** a vigorous.

Schwur [ʃvuːr] m -(e)s, ¨e oath; ~**gericht** nt court with a jury.

sechs [zɛks] num six; ~**hundert** num six hundred; ~**te(r,s)** a sixth; S~**tel** nt -s - sixth.

sechzehn ['zɛçtseːn] num sixteen.

sechzig ['zɛçtsɪç] num sixty.

See [zeː] f -, -n sea; m -s, -n lake; ~**bad** nt seaside resort; ~**fahrt** f seafaring; (Reise) voyage; ~**gang** m (motion of the) sea; ~**gras** nt seaweed; ~**hund** m seal; ~**igel** ['zeːʔiːgəl] m sea urchin; s~**krank** a seasick; ~**krankheit** f seasickness; ~**lachs** m rock salmon.

Seel- ['zeːl] cpd: ~**e** f -, -n soul; ~**enfriede(n)** m peace of mind; s~**enruhig** ad calmly.

Seeleute ['zeːlɔytə] pl seamen pl.

Seel- cpd: s~**isch** a mental; ~**sorge** f pastoral duties pl; ~**sorger** m -s, - clergyman.

See- cpd: ~**macht** f naval power; ~**mann** m, pl -**leute** seaman, sailor; ~**meile** f nautical mile; ~**not** f distress; ~**pferd(chen)** nt sea horse; ~**räuber** m pirate; ~**rose** f water lily; ~**stern** m starfish; s~**tüchtig** a seaworthy; ~**weg** m sea route; **auf dem** ~**weg** by sea; ~**zunge** f sole.

Segel ['zeːgəl] nt -s, - sail; ~**boot** nt yacht; ~**fliegen** nt -s gliding; ~**flieger** m glider pilot; ~**flugzeug** nt glider; s~**n** vti sail; ~**schiff** nt sailing vessel; ~**sport** m sailing; ~**tuch** nt canvas.

Segen ['zeːgən] m -s, - blessing; s~**sreich** a beneficial.

Segler ['zeːglər] m -s, - sailor, yachtsman; (Boot) sailing boat.

segnen ['zeːgnən] vt bless.

Seh- [zeː] cpd: s~**en** vti irreg see; (in bestimmte Richtung) look; s~**enswert** a worth seeing; ~**enswürdigkeiten** pl sights pl (of a town); ~**er** m -s, - seer; ~**fehler** m sight defect.

Sehn- ['zeːn] cpd: ~**e** f -, -n sinew; (an Bogen) string; s~**en** vr long, yearn (nach for); s~**ig** a sinewy; s~**lich** a ardent; ~**sucht** f longing; s~**süchtig** a longing.

sehr [zeːr] ad (vor a,ad) very; (mit Verben) a lot, (very) much; **zu** ~ too much.

seicht [zaɪçt] a (lit, fig) shallow.

Seide ['zaɪdə] f -, -n silk; ~**l** nt -s, - tankard, beer mug; s~**n** a silk; ~**npapier** nt tissue paper.

seidig ['zaɪdɪç] a silky.

Seife ['zaɪfə] f -, -n soap; ~**nlauge** f soapsuds pl; ~**nschale** f soap dish; ~**nschaum** m lather.

seifig ['zaɪfɪç] a soapy.

seihen ['zaɪən] vt strain, filter.

Seil [zaɪl] nt -(e)s, -e rope; cable; ~**bahn** f cable railway; ~**hüpfen** nt -s, ~**springen** nt -s skipping; ~**tänzer(in** f) m tightrope walker; ~**zug** m tackle.

sein [zaɪn] vi irreg be; **laß das** ~! leave that!; stop that!; **es ist an dir, zu . . .** it's up to you to . . .

sein [zaɪn] pron sein; its; ~**e(r,s)** his; its; ~**er** pron gen of er of him; ~**erseits** ad for his part; ~**erzeit** ad in those days, formerly; ~**esgleichen** pron people like him; ~**etwegen**, ~**etwillen** ad (für ihn) for his sake; (wegen ihm) on his account; (von ihm aus) as far as he is concerned; ~**ige** pron: **der/die/das** ~ his.

Seismograph [zaɪsmoˈgraːf] m -en, -en seismograph.

seit [zaɪt] prep, cj since; **er ist** ~ **einer Woche hier** he has been here for a week; ~ **langem** for a long time; ~**dem** [zaɪtˈdeːm] ad,cj since.

Seite ['zaɪtə] f -, -n side; (Buch-) page; (Mil) flank; ~**nansicht** f side view; ~**nhieb** m (fig) passing shot, dig; ~**nruder** nt (Aviat) rudder; s~**ns** prep +gen on the part of; ~**nschiff** nt aisle; ~**nsprung** m extramarital escapade; ~**nstechen** nt (a) stitch; ~**nstraße** f side road; ~**nwagen** m sidecar; ~**nzahl** f page number; number of pages.

seit- cpd: ~**her** [zaɪt'heːr] ad,cj since (then); ~**lich** a on one or the side; side; ~**wärts** ad sidewards.

Sekretär [zekre'tɛːr] m secretary; (Möbel) bureau; ~**in** f secretary.

Sekretariat [zekretari'aːt] nt -(e)s, -e secretary's office, secretariat.

Sekt [zɛkt] m -(e)s, -e champagne; ~**e** f -, -n sect.

sekundär [zekun'dɛːr] a secondary.

Sekunde [ze'kundə] f -, -n second.

selber ['zɛlbər] = **selbst.**

selbst [zɛlpst] pron myself; itself; themselves etc; von ~ by itself etc; ad even; S~ nt - self; S~**achtung** f self-respect; ~**ändig** ['zɛlpʃtɛndɪç] a independent; S~**ändigkeit** f independence; S~**auslöser** m (Phot) delayed-action shutter release; S~**bedienung** f self-service; S~**befriedigung** f masturbation; S~**beherrschung** f self-control; ~**bewußt** a (self-)confident; S~**bewußtsein** nt self-confidence; S~**erhaltung** f self-preservation; S~**erkenntnis** f self-knowledge; ~**gefällig** a smug, self-satisfied; ~**gemacht** a home-made; S~**gespräch** nt conversation with oneself; S~**kostenpreis** m cost price; ~**los** a unselfish, selfless; S~**mord** m suicide; S~**mörder(in** f) m suicide; ~**mörderisch** a suicidal; ~**sicher** a self-assured; ~**süchtig** a selfish; ~**tätig** a auto-matic; ~**verständlich** a obvious; ad naturally; **ich halte das für** ~**verständlich** I take that for granted; S~**vertrauen** nt self-confidence; S~**verwaltung** f autonomy, self-government; S~**zweck** m end in itself.

selig ['zeːlɪç] a happy, blissful; (Rel) blessed; (tot) late; S~**keit** f bliss.

Sellerie ['zɛləri:] m -s, -(s) or f -, -n celery.

selten ['zɛltən] a rare; ad seldom, rarely; S~**heit** f rarity.

Selterswasser ['zɛltərsvasər] nt soda water.

seltsam ['zɛltzaːm] a strange, curious; ~**erweise** ad curiously, strangely; S~**keit** f strangeness.

Semester [ze'mɛstər] nt -s, - semester.

Semi- [zemi] in cpds semi-; ~**kolon** [-'koːlon] nt -s, -s semicolon; ~**nar** [-'naːr] nt -s, -e seminary; (Kurs) seminar; (Univ: Ort) department building.

Semmel ['zɛməl] f -, -n roll.

Senat [ze'naːt] m -(e)s, -e senate, council.

Sende- ['zɛndə] cpd: ~**bereich** m range of transmission; ~**folge** f (Serie) series; s~n vt irreg send; vti (Rad, TV) transmit, broadcast; ~**r** m -s, - station; (Anlage) transmitter; ~**reihe** f series (of broadcasts); ~**station** f, ~**stelle** f transmitting station.

Sendung ['zɛnduŋ] f consignment; (Aufgabe) mission; (Rad, TV) transmission; (Programm) programme.

Senf [zɛnf] m -(e)s, -e mustard.

sengen ['zɛŋən] vt singe; vi scorch.

Senk- ['zɛŋk] cpd: ~**blei** nt plumb; ~**e** f -, -n depression; ~**el** m -s, - (shoe)lace; s~**en** vt lower; vr sink, drop gradually; ~**fuß** m flat foot; s~**recht** a vertical, perpendicular; ~**rechte** f -n, -n perpendicular; ~**rechtstarter** m (Aviat) vertical take-off plane; (fig) high-flier.

Sensation [zenzatsi'oːn] f sensation; s~**ell** [-'nɛl] a sensational; ~**ssucht** f sensationalism.

Sense ['zɛnzə] f -, -n scythe.

sensibel [zɛn'ziːbəl] a sensitive.

Sensibilität [zɛnzibili'tɛːt] f sensitivity.

sentimental [zentimɛn'taːl] a sentimental; S~**i'tät** f sentimentality.

separat [zepa'raːt] a separate.

September [zɛp'ɛmbər] m -(s), - September.

septisch ['zɛptɪʃ] a septic.

Serie ['zeːriə] f series; ~**nherstellung** f mass production; s~**nweise** ad in series.

seriös [zeri'øːs] a serious, bona fide.

Serpentine [zɛrpɛn'tiːn(ə)] f hairpin (bend).

Serum ['zeːrum] nt -s, **Seren** serum.

Service [zɛr'viːs] nt -(s), - set, service; ['zøːrvɪs] m -, - service.

servieren [zɛr'viːrən] vti serve.

Serviette [zɛrvi'ɛtə] f napkin, serviette.

Sessel ['zɛsəl] m -s, - armchair; ~**lift** m chairlift.

seßhaft ['zɛshaft] a settled; (ansässig) resident.

Sets [zɛts] pl tablemats pl.

setzen ['zɛtsən] vt put, set; Baum etc plant; Segel, (Print) set; vr settle; (person) sit down; vi leap.

Setz- [zɛts] cpd: ~**er** m -s, - (Print) compositor; ~**e'rei** f caseroom; ~**ling** m young plant; ~**maschine** f (Print) typesetting machine.

Seuche ['zɔʏçə] f -, -n epidemic; ~**ngebiet** nt infected area.

seufzen ['zɔʏftsən] vti sigh.

Seufzer ['zɔʏftsər] m -s, - sigh.

Sex [zɛks] m -(es) sex; ~**ualität** [-uali'tɛt] f sex, sexuality; s~**uell** [-u'ɛl] a sexual.

Sexta ['zɛksta] f -, **Sexten** first year of secondary school.

sezieren [ze'tsiːrən] vt dissect.

sich [zɪç] pron himself; herself; itself; oneself; yourself; yourselves; themselves; each other.

Sichel ['zɪçəl] f -, -n sickle; (Mond~) crescent.

sicher ['zɪçər] a safe (vor +dat from); (gewiß) certain (+gen of); (zuverlässig) secure, reliable, (selbst~) confident; ~**gehen** vi irreg make sure.

Sicherheit ['zɪçərhaɪt] f safety; security (auch Fin); (Gewißheit) certainty; (Selbst~) confidence; ~**sabstand** m safe distance; ~**sglas** nt safety glass; s~**shalber** ad for safety; to be on the safe side; ~**snadel** f safety pin; ~**sschloß** nt safety lock; ~**sverschluß** m safety clasp; ~**svorkehrung** f safety precaution.

sicher- *cpd*: **~lich** *ad* certainly, surely; **~n** *vt* secure; *(schützen)* protect; *Waffe* put the safety catch on; **jdm/sich etw ~n** secure sth for sb/(for o.s.); **~stellen** *vt* impound; **S~ung** *f (Sichern)* securing; *(Vorrichtung)* safety device; *(an Waffen)* safety catch; *(Elec)* fuse.

Sicht [zɪçt] *f* ~ sight; *(Aus—)* view; **auf** *or* **nach ~** *(Fin)* at sight; **auf lange ~** on a long-term basis; **s~bar** *a* visible; **~barkeit** *f* visibility; **s~en** *vt* sight; *(auswählen)* sort out; **s~lich** *a* evident, obvious; **~verhältnisse** *pl* visibility; **~vermerk** *m* visa; **~weite** *f* visibility.

sickern [ˈzɪkərn] *vi* trickle, seep.

Sie [zi:] *pron sing, pl, nom, acc* you.

sie [zi:] *pron sing nom* she; *acc* her; *pl nom* they; *acc* them.

Sieb [zi:p] *nt* **-(e)s, -e** sieve; *(Cook)* strainer; **s~en** [ˈzi:bən] *vt* sift; *Flüssigkeit* strain.

sieben [ˈzi:bən] *num* seven; **~hundert** *num* seven hundred; **S~sachen** *pl* belongings *pl*.

siebte(r,s) [ˈzi:ptə(r,z)] *a* seventh; **S~l** *nt* **-s, -** seventh.

siebzehn [ˈzi:ptse:n] *num* seventeen.

siebzig [ˈzi:ptsɪç] *num* seventy.

sied- [zi:d] *cpd*: **~eln** *vi* settle; **~en** *vti* boil, simmer; **S~epunkt** *m* boiling point; **S~ler** *m* **-s, -** settler; **S~lung** *f* settlement; *(Häuser—)* housing estate.

Sieg [zi:k] *m* **-(e)s, -e** victory; **~el** [ˈzi:gəl] *nt* **-s, -** seal; **~ellack** *m* sealing wax; **~elring** *m* signet ring; **s~en** *vi* be victorious; *(Sport)* win; **~er** *m* **-s, -** victor; *(Sport etc)* winner; **s~essicher** *a* sure of victory; **~eszug** *m* triumphal procession; **s~reich** *a* victorious.

siehe [zi:ə] *(Imperativ)* see; *(— da)* behold.

siezen [ˈzi:tsən] *vt* address as 'Sie'.

Signal [zɪˈgna:l] *nt* **-s, -e** signal.

Signatur [zɪgnaˈtu:r] *f* signature.

Silbe [ˈzɪlbə] *f* **-, -n** syllable.

Silber [ˈzɪlbər] *nt* **-s** silver; **~bergwerk** *nt* silver mine; **~blick** *m*: **einen ~blick haben** have a slight squint; **s~n** *a* silver; **~papier** *nt* silver paper.

Silhouette [zɪluˈɛtə] *f* silhouette.

Silo [ˈzi:lo] *nt or m* **-s, -s** silo.

Silvester(abend *m)* [zɪlˈvɛstər(a:bənt)] *nt* **-s, -** New Year's Eve, Hogmanay *(Scot)*.

simpel [ˈzɪmpəl] *a* simple; **S~** *m* **-s, -** *(col)* simpleton.

Sims [zɪms] *nt or m* **-es, -e** *(Kamin—)* mantlepiece; *(Fenster—)* (window)sill.

simulieren [zimuˈli:rən] *vti* simulate; *(vortäuschen)* feign.

simultan [zimulˈta:n] *a* simultaneous.

Sinfonie [zɪnfoˈni:] *f* symphony.

singen [ˈzɪŋən] *vti irreg* sing.

Singular [ˈzɪŋgula:r] *m* singular.

Singvogel [ˈzɪŋfo:gəl] *m* songbird.

sinken [ˈzɪŋkən] *vi irreg* sink; *(Preise etc)* fall, go down.

Sinn [zɪn] *m* **-(e)s, -e** mind; *(Wahrnehmungs—)* sense; *(Bedeutung)* sense, meaning; **~ für etw** sense of sth; **von ~en sein** be out of one's mind;

~bild *nt* symbol; **s~bildlich** *a* symbolic; **s~en** *vi irreg* ponder; **auf etw** *(acc)* **s~en** contemplate sth; **~enmensch** *m* sensualist; **~estäuschung** *f* illusion; **s~gemäß** *a* faithful; *Wiedergabe* in one's own words; **s~ig** *a* clever; **s~lich** *a* sensual, sensuous; *Wahrnehmung* sensory; **~lichkeit** *f* sensuality; **s~los** *a* senseless; meaningless; **~losigkeit** *f* senselessness; meaninglessness; **s~voll** *a* meaningful; *(vernünftig)* sensible.

Sintflut [ˈzɪntflu:t] *f* Flood.

Sinus [ˈzi:nus] *m* **-, -** *or* **-se** *(Anat)* sinus; *(Math)* sine.

Siphon [ziˈfõ:] *m* **-s, -s** siphon.

Sippe [ˈzɪpə] *f* **-, -n** clan, kin.

Sippschaft [ˈzɪpʃaft] *f (pej)* relations *pl*, tribe; *(Bande)* gang.

Sirene [ziˈre:nə] *f* **-, -n** siren.

Sirup [ˈzi:rup] *m* **-s, -e** syrup.

Sitt- [zɪt] *cpd*: **~e** *f* **-, -n** custom; *pl* morals *pl*; **~enpolizei** *f* vice squad; **s~lich** *a* moral; **~lichkeit** *f* morality; **~lichkeitsverbrechen** *nt* sex offence; **s~sam** *a* modest, demure.

Situation [zituatsiˈo:n] *f* situation.

Sitz [zɪts] *m* **-es, -e** seat; **der Anzug hat einen guten ~** the suit is a good fit; **s~en** *vi irreg* sit; *(Bemerkung, Schlag)* strike home, tell; *(Gelerntes)* have sunk in; **s~en bleiben** remain seated; **s~enbleiben** *vi irreg (Sch)* have to repeat a year; **auf etw** *(dat)* **s~enbleiben** be lumbered with sth; **s~end** *a Tätigkeit* sedentary; **s~enlassen** *vt irreg (Sch)* make (sb) repeat a year; *Mädchen* jilt; *Wartenden* stand up; **etw auf sich** *(dat)* **s~enlassen** take sth lying down; **~gelegenheit** *f* place to sit down; **~platz** *m* seat; **~streik** *m* sit-down strike; **~ung** *f* meeting.

Skala [ˈska:la] *f* **-, Skalen** scale.

Skalpell [skalˈpɛl] *nt* **-s, -e** scalpel.

Skandal [skanˈda:l] *m* **-s, -e** scandal; **s~ös** [skandaˈlø:s] *a* scandalous.

Skelett [skeˈlɛt] *nt* **-(e)s, -e** skeleton.

Skepsis [ˈskɛpsɪs] *f* **-** scepticism.

skeptisch [ˈskɛptɪʃ] *a* sceptical.

Ski, Schi [ʃi:] *m* **-s, -er** ski; **~ laufen** *or* **fahren** ski; **~fahrer** *m*, **~läufer** *m* skier; **~lehrer** *m* ski instructor; **~lift** *m* ski-lift; **~springen** *nt* ski-jumping.

Skizze [ˈskɪtsə] *f* **-, -n** sketch.

skizzieren [skɪˈtsi:rən] *vti* sketch.

Sklave [ˈskla:və] *m* **-n, -n**, **Sklavin** *f* slave; **~rei** *f* slavery.

Skonto [ˈskɔnto] *m or nt* **-s, -s** discount.

Skorpion [skɔrpiˈo:n] *m* **-s, -e** scorpion; *(Astrol)* Scorpio.

Skrupel [ˈskru:pəl] *m* **-s, -** scruple; **s~los** *a* unscrupulous.

Slalom [ˈsla:lɔm] *m* **-s, -s** slalom.

Smaragd [smaˈrakt] *m* **-(e)s, -e** emerald.

Smoking [ˈsmo:kɪŋ] *m* **-s, -s** dinner jacket.

so [zo:] *ad* so; *(auf diese Weise)* like this; *(etwa)* roughly; **~ ein** such a; **~, das ist fertig** well, that's finished; **~ etwas!** well, well!; **~ . . . wie . . .** as . . . as . . .; **~ daß** so that, with the result that; *cj so; (vor a)* as.

Socke ['zɔkə] *f* -, -n sock.

Sockel ['zɔkəl] *m* -s, - pedestal, base.

Sodawasser ['zo:davasər] *nt* soda water.

Sodbrennen ['zo:tbrɛnən] *nt* -s, - heartburn.

soeben [zo'e:bən] *ad* just (now).

Sofa ['zo:fa] *nt* -s, -s sofa.

sofern [zo'fɛrn] *cj* if, provided (that).

sofort [zo'fɔrt] *ad* immediately, at once; ~ig *a* immediate.

Sog [zo:k] *m* -(e)s, -e suction.

so- *cpd:* ~**gar** [zo'ga:r] *ad* even; ~**genannt** ['zo:gənant] *a* so-called; ~**gleich** [zo'glaiç] *ad* straight away, at once.

Sohle ['zo:lə] *f* -, -n sole; (*Tal*— *etc*) bottom; (*Min*) level.

Sohn [zo:n] *m* -(e)s, -e son.

solang(e) [zo'laŋ(ə)] *cj* as *or* so long as.

Solbad ['zo:lba:t] *nt* saltwater bath.

solch [zɔlç] *pron* such; **ein** ~**e(r,s)** . . . such a . . .

Sold [zɔlt] *m* -(e)s, -e pay; ~**at** [zɔl'da:t] *m* -en, -en soldier; **s**~**atisch** a soldierly.

Söldner ['zœldnər] *m* -s, - mercenary.

solid(e) [zo'li:d(ə)] *a* solid; *Leben, Person* staid, respectable; ~**arisch** [zoli'da:rɪʃ] *a* in/with solidarity; **sich** ~**arisch erklären** declare one's solidarity.

Solist(in *f*) [zo'lɪst(ɪn)] *m* soloist.

Soll [zɔl] *nt* -(s), -(s) (*Fin*) debit (side); (*Arbeitsmenge*) quota, target.

sollen ['zɔlən] *vi* be supposed to; (*Verpflichtung*) shall, ought to; **du hättest nicht gehen** ~ you shouldn't have gone; **soll ich?** shall I?; **was soll das?** what's that supposed to mean?

Solo ['zo:lo] *nt* -s, -s *or* **Soli** solo.

somit [zo'mɪt] *cj* and so, therefore.

Sommer ['zɔmər] *m* -s, - summer; **s**~**lich** *a* summery; summer; ~**sprossen** *pl* freckles *pl*.

Sonate [zo'na:tə] *f* -, -n sonata.

Sonde ['zɔndə] *f* -, -n probe.

Sonder- ['zɔndər] *in cpds* special; ~**angebot** *nt* special offer; **s**~**bar** *a* strange, odd; ~**fahrt** *f* special trip; ~**fall** *m* special case; **s**~**gleichen** *a inv* without parallel, unparalleled; **s**~**lich** *a* particular; (*außergewöhnlich*) remarkable; (*eigenartig*) peculiar; ~**ling** *m* eccentric; **s**~**n** *cj* but; **nicht nur . . .,** **s**~**n auch** not only . . ., but also; *vt* separate; ~**zug** *m* special train.

sondieren [zɔn'di:rən] *vt* suss out; *Gelände* scout out.

Sonett [zo'nɛt] *nt* -(e)s, -e sonnet.

Sonnabend ['zɔn'a:bənt] *m* Saturday.

Sonne ['zɔnə] *f* -, -n sun; **s**~**n** *vt* put out in the sun; *vr* sun oneself; ~**naufgang** *m* sunrise; **s**~**nbaden** *vi* sunbathe; ~**nbrand** *m* sunburn; ~**nbrille** *f* sunglasses *pl*; ~**nfinsternis** *f* solar eclipse; ~**nschein** *m* sunshine; ~**nschirm** *m* parasol, sunshade; ~**nstich** *m* sunstroke; ~**nuhr** *f* sundial; ~**nuntergang** *m* sunset; ~**nwende** *f* solstice.

sonnig ['zɔnıç] *a* sunny.

Sonntag ['zɔnta:k] *m* Sunday; **s**~**s** *ad* (on) Sundays.

sonst [zɔnst] *ad* otherwise (*auch cj*); (*mit pron, in Fragen*) else; (*zu anderer Zeit*) at other times, normally; ~ **noch etwas?** anything else?; ~ **nichts** nothing else; ~**ig** *a* other; ~**jemand** *pron* anybody (at all); ~**wo(hin)** *ad* somewhere else; ~**woher** *ad* from somewhere else.

sooft [zo'ɔft] *cj* whenever.

Sopran [zo'pra:n] *m* -s, -e soprano; ~**istin** [zopra'nıstın] *f* soprano.

Sorge ['zɔrgə] *f* -, -n care, worry; **s**~**n** *vi*: **für jdn s**~**n** look after sb; **für etw s**~**n** take care of *or* see to sth; *vr* worry (*um* about); **s**~**nfrei** *a* carefree; ~**nkind** *nt* problem child; **s**~**nvoll** *a* troubled, worried; ~**recht** *nt* custody (of a child).

Sorg- *cpd:* ~**falt** *f* - care(fulness); **s**~**fältig** *a* careful; **s**~**los** *a* careless; (*ohne Sorgen*) carefree; **s**~**sam** *a* careful.

Sorte ['zɔrtə] *f* -, -n sort; (*Waren*—) brand; ~**n** *pl* (*Fin*) foreign currency.

sortieren [zɔr'ti:rən] *vt* sort (out).

Sortiment [zɔrti'mɛnt] *nt* assortment.

sosehr [zo'ze:r] *cj* as much as.

Soße ['zo:sə] *f* -, -n sauce; (*Braten*—) gravy.

Souffleur [zu'flø:r] *m*, **Souffleuse** [zu'flø:zə] *f* prompter.

soufflieren [zu'fli:rən] *vti* prompt.

souverän [zuvə'rɛ:n] *a* sovereign; (*überlegen*) superior.

so- *cpd:* ~**viel** [zo'fi:l] *cj* as far as; *pron* as much (*wie* as); **rede nicht** ~**viel** don't talk so much; ~**weit** [zo'vait] *cj* as far as; *a:* ~**weit sein** be ready; ~**weit wie** *or* **als möglich** as far as possible; **ich bin** ~**weit zufrieden** by and large I'm quite satisfied; ~**wenig** [zo've:nıç] *cj* little as; *pron* as little (*wie* as); ~**wie** [zo'vi:] *cj* (*sobald*) as soon as; (*ebenso*) as well as; ~**wieso** [zovi'zo:] *ad* anyway; ~**wohl** [zo'vo:l] *cj*: ~**wohl . . . als** *or* **wie auch** both . . . and.

sozial [zotsi'a:l] *a* social; **S**~**abgaben** *pl* national insurance contributions *pl*; **S**~**demokrat** *m* social democrat; ~**i- 'sieren** *vt* socialize; **S**~**ismus** [-'lısmus] *m* socialism; **S**~**ist** [-'lıst] *m* socialist; ~**istisch** *a* socialist; **S**~**politik** *f* social welfare policy; **S**~**produkt** *nt* (gross/net) national product; **S**~**staat** *m* welfare state.

Sozio- [zotsio] *cpd:* ~**loge** [-'lo:gə] *m* -n, -n sociologist; ~**logie** [-'lo:gi:] *f* sociology; **s**~**logisch** [-'lo:gıʃ] *a* sociological.

Sozius ['zo:tsius] *m* -, -se (*Comm*) partner; (*Motorrad*) pillion rider; ~**sitz** *m* pillion (seat).

sozusagen [zotsu'za:gən] *ad* so to speak.

Spachtel ['ʃpaxtəl] *m* -s, - spatula.

spähen ['ʃpɛ:ən] *vi* peep, peek.

Spalier [ʃpa'li:r] *nt* -s, -e (*Gerüst*) trellis; (*Leute*) guard of honour.

Spalt [ʃpalt] *m* -(e)s, -e crack; (*Tür*—) chink; (*fig: Kluft*) split; ~**e** *f* -, -n crack, fissure; (*Gletscher*—) crevasse; (*in Text*) column; **s**~**en** *vtr* (*lit, fig*) split; ~**ung** *f* splitting.

Span [ʃpaːn] **-(e)s,** ⁻e shaving; ~**ferkel** nt sucking-pig.

Spange ['ʃpaŋə] f -, -n clasp; (Haar—) hair slide; (Schnalle) buckle; (Armreif) bangle.

Spann ['ʃpan] cpd: ~**beton** m pre-stressed concrete; ~**e** f -, -n (Zeit—) space; (Differenz) gap; s~**en** vt (straffen) tighten, tauten; (befestigen) brace; vi be tight; s~**end** a exciting, gripping; ~**kraft** f elasticity; (fig) energy; ~**ung** f tension; (Elec) voltage; (fig) suspense; (unangenehm) tension.

Spar- ['ʃpaːr] cpd: ~**buch** nt savings book; ~**büchse** f moneybox; s~**en** vti save; **sich** (dat) **etw** s~**en** save oneself sth; Bemerkung keep sth to oneself; **mit etw** (dat) s~**en** be sparing with sth; **an etw** (dat) s~**en** economize on sth; ~**er** m -s, - saver.

Spargel ['ʃpargəl] m -s, - asparagus.

Spar- cpd: ~**kasse** f savings bank; ~**konto** nt savings account.

spärlich ['ʃpɛːrlɪç] a meagre; Bekleidung scanty.

Spar- cpd: ~**maßnahme** f economy measure, cut; s~**sam** a economical, thrifty; ~**samkeit** f thrift, economizing; ~**schwein** nt piggy bank.

Sparte ['ʃpartə] f -, -n field; line of business; (Press) column.

Spaß [ʃpaːs] m -es, ⁻e joke; (Freude) fun; **jdm** ~ **machen** be fun (for sb); s~**en** vi joke; **mit ihm ist nicht zu** s~**en** you can't take liberties with him; s~**eshalber** ad for the fun of it; s~**haft,** s~**ig** a funny, droll; ~**macher** m -s, - joker, funny man; ~**verderber** m -s, - spoilsport.

spät [ʃpɛːt] a, ad late; ~**er** a, ad later; ~**estens** ad at the latest.

Spaten ['ʃpaːtən] m -s, - spade.

Spatz [ʃpats] m -en, -en sparrow.

spazier- [ʃpaˈtsiːr] cpd: ~**en** vi stroll, walk; ~**enfahren** vi irreg go for a drive; ~**engehen** vi irreg go for a walk; S~**gang** m walk; S~**stock** m walking stick; S~**weg** m path, walk.

Specht [ʃpɛçt] m -(e)s, -e woodpecker.

Speck [ʃpɛk] m -(e)s, -e bacon.

Spediteur [ʃpediˈtøːr] m carrier; (Möbel—) furniture remover.

Spedition [ʃpediˈtsiˈoːn] f carriage; (—sfirma) road haulage contractor; removal firm.

Speer [ʃpeːr] m -(e)s, -e spear; (Sport) javelin.

Speiche ['ʃpaɪçə] f -, -n spoke.

Speichel ['ʃpaɪçəl] m -s saliva, spit(tle).

Speicher ['ʃpaɪçər] m -s, - storehouse; (Dach—) attic, loft; (Korn—) granary; (Wasser—) tank; (Tech) store; s~**n** vt store.

speien ['ʃpaɪən] vti irreg spit; (erbrechen) vomit; (Vulkan) spew.

Speise ['ʃpaɪzə] f -, -n food; ~**eis** [-'aɪs] nt ice-cream; ~**kammer** f larder, pantry; ~**karte** f menu; s~**n** vt feed; eat; vi dine; ~**röhre** f gullet, oesophagus; ~**saal** m dining room; ~**wagen** m dining car; ~**zettel** m menu.

Spektakel [ʃpɛkˈtaːkəl] m -s, - (col) row; nt -s, - spectacle.

Speku- [ʃpeku] cpd: ~**lant** [-'lant] m speculator; ~**lation** [-'latsiˈoːn] f speculation; s~**lieren** [-'liːrən] vi (fig) speculate; **auf etw** (acc) s~**lieren** have hopes of sth.

Spelunke [ʃpeˈluŋkə] f -, -n dive.

Spende ['ʃpɛndə] f -, -n donation; s~**n** vt donate, give; ~**r** m -s, - donor, donator.

spendieren [ʃpɛnˈdiːrən] vt pay for, buy; **jdm etw** ~ treat sb to sth, stand sb sth.

Sperling ['ʃpɛrlɪŋ] m sparrow.

Sperma ['ʃpɛrma] nt -s, **Spermen** sperm.

Sperr- ['ʃpɛr] cpd: s~**angelweit** ['-'aŋəl'vaɪt] a wide open; ~**e** f -, -n barrier; (Verbot) ban; s~**en** vt block; (Sport) suspend, bar; (vom Ball) obstruct; (einschließen) lock; (verbieten) ban; vr baulk, jib(e); ~**gebiet** nt prohibited area; ~**holz** nt plywood; s~**ig** a bulky; ~**müll** m bulky refuse; ~**sitz** m (Theat) stalls pl; ~**stunde** f, ~**zeit** f closing time.

Spesen ['ʃpeːzən] pl expenses pl.

Spezial- [ʃpetsiˈaːl] in cpds special; s~**i-'sieren** vr specialize; ~**i'sierung** f specialization; ~**ist** [-'lɪst] m specialist; ~**i'tät** f speciality.

speziell [ʃpetsiˈɛl] a special.

spezifisch [ʃpeˈtsiːfɪʃ] a specific.

Sphäre ['sfɛːrə] f -, -n sphere.

spicken ['ʃpɪkən] vt lard; vi (Sch) copy, crib.

Spiegel ['ʃpiːgəl] m -s, - mirror; (Wasser—) level; (Mil) tab; ~**bild** nt reflection; s~**bildlich** a reversed; ~**ei** [-'aɪ] nt fried egg; ~**fechterei** [-fɛçtəˈraɪ] f shadow-boxing, bluff; s~**n** vt mirror, reflect; vr be reflected; vi gleam; (wider—) be reflective; ~**schrift** f mirror-writing; ~**ung** f reflection.

Spiel [ʃpiːl] nt -(e)s, -e game; (Schau—) play; (Tätigkeit) playing; (Cards) deck; (Tech) (free) play; s~**en** vti play; (um Geld) gamble; (Theat) perform, act; s~**end** ad easily; ~**er** m -s, - player; (um Geld) gambler; ~**e'rei** f trifling pastime; s~**erisch** a playful; Leichtigkeit effortless; s~**erisches Können** skill as a player; acting ability; ~**feld** nt pitch, field; ~**film** m feature film; ~**plan** m (Theat) programme; ~**platz** m playground; ~**raum** m room to manoeuvre, scope; ~**sachen** pl toys pl; ~**verderber** m -s, - spoilsport; ~**waren** pl, ~**zeug** nt toys pl.

Spieß [ʃpiːs] m -es, -e spear; (Brat—) spit; ~**bürger** m, ~**er** m -s, - bourgeois; ~**rutenlaufen** nt running the gauntlet.

Spikes [ʃpaɪks] pl spikes pl; (Aut) studs pl.

Spinat [ʃpiˈnaːt] m -(e)s, -e spinach.

Spind [ʃpɪnt] m or nt -(e)s, -e locker.

Spinn- ['ʃpɪn] cpd: ~**e** f -, -n spider; s~**en** vti irreg spin; (col) talk rubbish; (verrückt) be crazy or mad; ~**e'rei** f spinning mill; ~**(en)gewebe** nt cobweb; ~**rad** nt spinning-wheel; ~**webe** f cobweb.

Spion [ʃpiˈoːn] m -s, -e spy; (in Tür) spyhole; ~**age** [ʃpioˈnaːʒə] f -, -n espionage; s~**ieren** [ʃpioˈniːrən] vi spy.

Spirale [ʃpiˈraːlə] f -, -n spiral.

Spirituosen [ʃpiritu'oːzən] *pl* spirits *pl*.

Spiritus ['spiːritus] *m* -, -se (methylated) spirit.

Spital [ʃpi'taːl] *nt* -s, ⁻er hospital.

spitz [ʃpits] *a* pointed; *Winkel* acute; *(fig) ·Zunge* sharp; *Bemerkung* caustic; **S~** *m* -es, -e spitz; **S~bogen** *m* pointed arch; **S~bube** *m* rogue; **S~e** *f* -, -n point, tip; *(Berg—)* peak; *(Bemerkung)* taunt, dig; *(erster Platz)* lead, top; *(usu pl: Gewebe)* lace; **S~el** *m* -s, - police informer; **~en** *vt* sharpen; **S~en-** *in cpds* top; **S~enleistung** *f* top performance; **S~enlohn** *m* top wages *pl*; **S~ensportler** *m* topclass sportsman; **S~findig** *a* (over)subtle; **~ig** *a see* **spitz**; **S~name** *m* nickname.

Splitter ['ʃplitər] *m* -s, - splinter; **s~nackt** *a* stark naked.

spontan [ʃpɔn'taːn] *a* spontaneous.

Sport [ʃpɔrt] *m* -(e)s, -e sport; *(fig)* hobby; **~lehrer(in** *f)* *m* games *or* P.E. teacher; **~ler(in** *f)* *m* -s, - sportsman/woman; **s~lich** *a* sporting; *Mensch* sporty; **~platz** *m* playing *or* sports field; **~verein** *m* sports club; **~wagen** *m* sports car; **~zeug** *nt* sports gear.

Spott [ʃpɔt] *m* -(e)s mockery, ridicule; **s~billig** *a* dirt-cheap; **s~en** *vi* mock *(über +acc* at), ridicule.

spöttisch ['ʃpœtiʃ] *a* mocking.

Sprach- ['ʃpraːx] *cpd:* **s~begabt** *a* good at languages; **~e** *f* -, -n language; **~fehler** *m* speech defect; **~fertigkeit** *f* fluency; **~führer** *m* phrasebook; **~gebrauch** *m* (linguistic) usage; **~gefühl** *nt* feeling for language; **s~lich** *a* linguistic; **s~los** *a* speechless; **~rohr** *nt* megaphone; *(fig)* mouthpiece.

Spray [spreː] *m or nt* -s, -s spray.

Sprech- ['ʃprɛç] *cpd:* **~anlage** *f* intercom; **s~en** *irreg* *vi* speak, talk *(mit* to); **das spricht für ihn** that's a point in his favour; *vt* say; *Sprache* speak; *Person* speak to; **~er(in** *f)* *m* -s, - speaker; *(für Gruppe)* spokesman; *(Rad, TV)* announcer; **~stunde** *f* consultation (hour); (doctor's) surgery; **~stundenhilfe** *f* (doctor's) receptionist; **~zimmer** *nt* consulting room, surgery.

spreizen ['ʃpraitsən] *vt* spread; *vr* put on airs.

Spreng- ['ʃprɛŋ] *cpd:* **~arbeiten** *pl* blasting operations *pl*; **s~en** *vt* sprinkle; *(mit Sprengstoff)* blow up; *Gestein* blast; *Versammlung* break up; **~ladung** *f* explosive charge; **~stoff** *m* explosive(s).

Spreu [ʃprɔy] *f* - chaff.

Sprich- ['ʃpriç] *cpd:* **~wort** *nt* proverb; **s~wörtlich** *a* proverbial.

Spring- ['ʃpriŋ] *cpd:* **~brunnen** *m* fountain; **s~en** *vi irreg* jump; *(Glas)* crack; *(mit Kopfsprung)* dive; **~er** *m* -s, - jumper; *(Schach)* knight.

Sprit [ʃprit] *m* -(e)s, -e *(col)* petrol, fuel.

Spritz- ['ʃprits] *cpd:* **~e** *f* -, -n syringe; injection; *(an Schlauch)* nozzle; **s~en** *vt* spray; *(Med)* inject; *vi* splash; *(heraus—)* spurt; *(Med)* give injections; **~pistole** *f* spray gun.

spröde ['ʃprøːdə] *a* brittle; *Person* reserved, coy.

Sproß [ʃprɔs] *m* -sses, -sse shoot; *(Kind)* scion.

Sprosse ['ʃprɔsə] *f* -, -n rung.

Sprößling ['ʃprœslɪŋ] *m* offspring *no pl*.

Spruch [ʃprux] *m* -(e)s, ⁻e saying, maxim; *(Jur)* judgement.

Sprudel ['ʃpruːdəl] *m* -s, - mineral water; lemonade; **s~n** *vi* bubble.

Sprüh- ['ʃpryː] *cpd:* **~dose** *f* aerosol (can); **s~en** *vti* spray; *(fig)* sparkle; **~regen** *m* drizzle.

Sprung [ʃpruŋ] *m* -(e)s, ⁻e jump; *(Riß)* crack; **~brett** *nt* springboard; **s~haft** *a* erratic; *Aufstieg* rapid; **~schanze** *f* skijump.

Spucke ['ʃpukə] *f* - spit; **s~en** *vti* spit.

Spuk [ʃpuːk] *m* -(e)s, -e haunting; *(fig)* nightmare; **s~en** *vi* *(Geist)* walk; **hier spukt es** this place is haunted.

Spule ['ʃpuːlə] *f* -, -n spool; *(Elec)* coil.

Spül- ['ʃpyːl] *cpd:* **~e** *f* -, -n (kitchen) sink; **s~en** *vti* rinse; *Geschirr* wash up; *Toilette* flush; **~maschine** *f* dishwasher; **~stein** *m* sink; **~ung** *f* rinsing; flush; *(Med)* irrigation.

Spur [ʃpuːr] *f* -, -en trace; *(Fuß—, Rad—, Tonband—)* track; *(Fährte)* trail; *(Fahr—)* lane; **s~los** *ad* without (a) trace.

spür- ['ʃpyːr] *cpd:* **~bar** *a* noticeable, perceptible; **~en** *vt* feel; **S~hund** *m* tracker dog; *(fig)* sleuth.

Spurt [ʃpurt] *m* -(e)s, -s *or* -e spurt.

sputen ['ʃpuːtən] *vr* make haste.

Staat [ʃtaːt] *m* -(e)s, -en state; *(Prunk)* show; *(Kleidung)* finery; **mit etw ~machen** show off *or* parade sth; **s~enlos** *a* stateless; **s~lich** *a* state(-); state-run; **~sangehörigkeit** *f* nationality; **~sanwalt** *m* public prosecutor; **~sbürger** *m* citizen; **~sdienst** *m* civil service; **s~seigen** *a* state-owned; **~sexamen** *nt (Univ)* degree; **~sfeindlich** *a* subversive; **~smann** *m, pl* **-männer** statesman; **~ssekretär** *m* secretary of state.

Stab [ʃtaːp] *m* -(e)s, ⁻e rod; *(Gitter—)* bar; *(Menschen)* staff; **~hochsprung** *m* pole vault; **s~il** [ʃta'biːl] *a* stable; *Möbel* sturdy; **s~ili'sieren** *vt* stabilize; **~reim** *m* alliteration.

Stachel ['ʃtaxəl] *m* -s, -n spike; *(von Tier)* spine; *(von Insekten)* sting; **~beere** *f* gooseberry; **~draht** *m* barbed wire; **s~ig** *a* prickly; **~schwein** *nt* porcupine.

Stadion ['ʃtaːdiɔn] *nt* -s, **Stadien** stadium.

Stadium ['ʃtaːdiʊm] *nt* stage, phase.

Stadt [ʃtat] *f* -, ⁻e town.

Städt- ['ʃtɛːt] *cpd:* **~chen** *nt* small town; **~ebau** *m* town planning; **~er(in** *f)* *m* -s, - town dweller; **s~isch** *a* municipal; *(nicht ländlich)* urban.

Stadt- *cpd:* **~mauer** *f* city wall(s); **~plan** *m* street map; **~rand** *m* outskirts *pl*; **~teil** *m* district, part of town.

Staffel ['ʃtafəl] *f* -, -n rung; *(Sport)* relay (team); *(Aviat)* squadron; **~ei** [-'lai] *f* easel; **s~n** *vt* graduate; **~ung** *f* graduation.

Stahl [ʃtaːl] m -(e)s, ⁼e steel; ~helm m steel helmet.

Stall [ʃtal] m -(e)s, ⁼e stable; (Kaninchen—) hutch; (Schweine—) sty; (Hühner—) henhouse.

Stamm [ʃtam] m -(e)s, ⁼e (Baum—) trunk; (Menschen—) tribe; (Gram) stem; ~baum m family tree; (von Tier) pedigree; s~eln vti stammer; s~en vi: s~en von or aus come from; ~gast m regular (customer); ~halter m -s, - son and heir.

stämmig [ʃtɛmɪç] a sturdy; Mensch stocky; S~keit f sturdiness; stockiness.

stampfen [ʃtampfən] vti stamp; (stapfen) tramp; (mit Werkzeug) pound.

Stand [ʃtant] m -(e)s, ⁼e position; (Wasser—, Benzin— etc) level; (Stehen) standing position; (Zustand) state; (Spiel—) score; (Messe— etc) stand; (Klasse) class; (Beruf) profession.

Standard [ʃtandart] m -s, -s standard.

Ständ- [ʃtɛnd] cpd: ~chen nt serenade; ~er m -s, - stand.

Stand- [ʃtant] cpd: ~esamt nt registry office; ~esbeamte(r) m registrar; ~esbewußtsein nt status consciousness; s~esgemäß a,ad according to one's social position; ~esunterschied m social difference; s~haft a steadfast; ~haftigkeit f steadfastness; s~halten vi irreg stand firm (jdm/etw against sb/sth), resist (jdm/etw sb/sth).

ständig [ʃtɛndɪç] a permanent; (ununterbrochen) constant, continual.

Stand- cpd: ~licht nt sidelights pl, parking lights pl (US); ~ort m location; (Mil) garrison; ~punkt m standpoint.

Stange [ʃtaŋə] f -, -n stick; (Stab) pole, bar; rod; (Zigaretten) carton; von der ~ (Comm) off the peg; eine ~ Geld quite a packet.

Stanniol [ʃtaniˈoːl] nt -s, -e tinfoil.

Stanze [ʃtantsə] f -, -n stanza; (Tech) stamp; s~n vt stamp.

Stapel [ˈʃtaːpəl] m -s, - pile; (Naut) stocks pl; ~lauf m launch; s~n vt pile (up).

Star [ʃtaːr] m -(e)s, -e starling; (Med) cataract; m -s, -s (Film etc) star.

stark [ʃtark] a strong; (heftig, groß) heavy; (Maßangabe) thick.

Stärke [ˈʃtɛrkə] f -, -n strength; heaviness; thickness; (Cook, Wäsche—) starch; s~n vt strengthen; Wäsche starch.

Starkstrom m heavy current.

Stärkung [ˈʃtɛrkʊŋ] f strengthening; (Essen) refreshment.

starr [ʃtar] a stiff; (unnachgiebig) rigid; Blick staring; ~en vi stare; ~en vor or von be covered in; Waffen be bristling with; S~heit f rigidity; ~köpfig a stubborn; S~sinn m obstinacy.

Start [ʃtart] m -(e)s, -e start; (Aviat) takeoff; ~automatik f (Aut) automatic choke; ~bahn f runway; s~en vti start; take off; ~er m -s, - starter; ~erlaubnis f takeoff clearance; ~zeichen nt start signal.

Station [ʃtatsiˈoːn] f station; hospital ward; s~ieren [-ˈniːrən] vt station.

Statist [ʃtaˈtɪst] m extra, supernumerary;

~ik f statistics; ~iker m -s, - statistician; s~isch a statistical.

Stativ [ʃtaˈtiːf] nt -s, -e tripod.

statt [ʃtat] cj, prep +gen or dat instead of; S~ f - place.

Stätte [ˈʃtɛtə] f -, -n place.

statt- cpd: ~finden vi irreg take place; ~haft a admissible; ~lich a imposing, handsome.

Statue [ˈʃtaːtuə] f -, -n statue.

Statur [ʃtaˈtuːr] f stature.

Status [ˈʃtaːtʊs] m -, - status.

Stau [ʃtaʊ] m -(e)s, -e blockage; (Verkehrs—) (traffic) jam.

Staub [ʃtaʊp] m -(e)s dust; s~en [ˈʃtaʊbən] vi be dusty; ~faden m stamen; s~ig a dusty; ~sauger m vacuum cleaner; ~tuch nt duster.

Staudamm m dam.

Staude [ˈʃtaʊdə] f -, -n shrub.

stauen [ˈʃtaʊən] vt Wasser dam up; Blut stop the flow of; vr (Wasser) become dammed up; (Med, Verkehr) become congested; (Menschen) collect together; (Gefühle) build up.

staunen [ˈʃtaʊnən] vi be astonished; S~ nt -s amazement.

Stauung [ˈʃtaʊʊŋ] f (von Wasser) damming-up; (von Blut, Verkehr) congestion.

Stech- [ˈʃtɛç] cpd: ~becken nt bedpan; s~en vt irreg (mit Nadel etc) prick; (mit Messer) stab; (mit Finger) poke; (Biene etc) sting; (Mücke) bite; (Sonne) burn; (Cards) take; (Art) engrave; Torf, Spargel cut; in See s~en put to sea; ~en nt -s, - (Sport) play-off; jump-off; s~end a piercing, stabbing; Geruch pungent; ~ginster m gorse; ~palme f holly; ~uhr f time clock.

Steck- [ˈʃtɛk] cpd: ~brief m 'wanted' poster; ~dose f (wall) socket; s~en vt put, insert; Nadel stick; Pflanzen plant; (beim Nähen) pin; vi irreg be; (festsitzen) be stuck; (Nadeln) stick; s~enbleiben vi irreg get stuck; s~enlassen vt irreg leave in; ~enpferd nt hobby-horse; ~er m -s, - plug; ~nadel f pin; ~rübe f swede, turnip; ~zwiebel f bulb.

Steg [ʃteːk] m -(e)s, -e small bridge; (Anlege—) landing stage; ~reif m: aus dem ~reif just like that.

stehen [ˈʃteːən] irreg vi stand (zu by); (sich befinden) be; (in Zeitung) say; (still—) have stopped; jdm ~ suit sb; vi impers: es steht schlecht um things are bad for; wie steht's? how are things?; (Sport) what's the score?; ~ bleiben remain standing; ~bleiben vi irreg (Uhr) stop; (Fehler) stay as it is; ~lassen vt irreg leave; Bart grow.

stehlen [ˈʃteːlən] vt irreg steal.

steif [ʃtaif] a stiff; S~heit f stiffness.

Steig- [ʃtaik] cpd: ~bügel m stirrup; ~e [ˈʃtaigə] f -, -n (in Straße) steep road; (Kiste) crate; ~eisen nt crampon; s~en vi irreg rise; (klettern) climb; s~en in (+acc)/auf (+acc) get in/on; s~ern vt raise; (Gram) compare; vi (Auktion) bid; vr increase; ~erung f raising; (Gram) comparison; ~ung f incline, gradient, rise.

steil [ʃtaɪl] a steep.
Stein [ʃtaɪn] m -(e)s, -e stone; *(in Uhr)* jewel; s~**alt** a ancient; ~**bock** m *(Astrol)* Capricorn; ~**bruch** m quarry; ~**butt** m -s, -e turbot; s~**ern** a (made of) stone; *(fig)* stony; ~**gut** nt stoneware; s~**hart** a hard as stone; s~**ig** a stony; s~**igen** vt stone; ~**kohle** f mineral coal; ~**metz** m -es, -e stonemason.
Steiß [ʃtaɪs] m -es, -e rump.
Stell- ['ʃtɛl] cpd: ~**dichein** nt -(s), -(s) rendezvous; ~**e** f -, -n place; *(Arbeit)* post, job; *(Amt)* office; s~**en** vt put; *Uhr etc* set; *(zur Verfügung —)* supply; *(fassen)* *Dieb* apprehend; vr *(sich aufstellen)* stand; *(sich einfinden)* present oneself; *(bei Polizei)* give oneself up; *(vorgeben)* pretend (to be); **sich zu etw** s~**en** have an opinion of sth; ~**enangebot** nt offer of a post; *(Zeitung)* vacancies; ~**engesuch** nt application for a post; ~**ennachweis** m, ~**envermittlung** f employment agency; ~**ung** f position; *(Mil)* line; ~**ung nehmen zu** comment on; ~**ungnahme** f -, -n comment; s~**vertretend** a deputy, acting; ~**vertreter** m deputy; ~**werk** nt *(Rail)* signal box.
Stelze ['ʃtɛltsə] f -, -n stilt.
Stemm- ['ʃtɛm] cpd: ~**bogen** m *(Ski)* stem turn; s~**en** vt lift (up); *(drücken)* press; **sich** s~**en gegen** *(fig)* resist, oppose.
Stempel ['ʃtɛmpəl] m -s, - stamp; *(Bot)* pistil; ~**kissen** nt inkpad; s~**n** vt stamp; *Briefmarke* cancel; s~**n gehen** *(col)* be/go on the dole.
Stengel ['ʃtɛŋəl] m -s, - stalk.
Steno- [ʃteno] cpd: ~**gramm** [-'gram] nt shorthand report; ~**graphie** [-gra'fi:] f shorthand; s~**graphieren** [-gra'fi:rən] vti write (in) shorthand; ~**typist(in** f) [-ty'pɪst(ɪn)] m shorthand typist.
Stepp- ['ʃtɛp] cpd: ~**decke** f quilt; ~**e** f -, -n prairie; steppe; s~**en** vt stitch; vi tapdance.
Sterb- ['ʃtɛrb] cpd: ~**ebett** nt deathbed; ~**efall** m death; s~**en** vi irreg die; ~**eurkunde** f death certificate; s~**lich** ['ʃtɛrplɪç] a mortal; ~**lichkeit** f mortality; ~**lichkeitsziffer** f death rate.
stereo- [ʃteːreo] in cpds stereo(-); ~**typ** [stereo'ty:p] a stereotype.
steril [ʃteˈriːl] a sterile; ~**i'sieren** vt sterilize; S~**i'sierung** f sterilization.
Stern [ʃtɛrn] m -(e)s, -e star; ~**bild** nt constellation; ~**chen** nt asterisk; ~**schnuppe** f -, -n meteor, falling star; ~**stunde** f historic moment.
stet [ʃteːt] a steady, ~**ig** a constant, continual; ~**s** ad continually, always.
Steuer ['ʃtɔʏər] nt -s, - *(Naut)* helm; *(—ruder)* rudder; *(Aut)* steering wheel; f -, -n tax; ~**bord** nt starboard; ~**erklärung** f tax return; ~**klasse** f tax group; ~**knüppel** m control column; *(Aviat)* joystick; ~**mann** m, pl -**männer** or -**leute** helmsman; s~**n** vti steer; *Flugzeug* pilot; *Entwicklung, Tonstärke* control; s~**pflichtig** a taxable; *Person* liable to pay tax; ~**rad** nt steering wheel; ~**ung** f steering *(auch Aut)*; piloting; control;

(Vorrichtung) controls pl; ~**zahler** m -s, - taxpayer; ~**zuschlag** m additional tax.
Steward ['stjuːərt] m -s, -s steward; ~**eß** ['stjuːərdɛs] f -, -**essen** stewardess; air hostess.
stibitzen [ʃtiˈbɪtsən] vt *(col)* pilfer, steal.
Stich [ʃtɪç] m -(e)s, -e *(Insekten—)* sting; *(Messer—)* stab; *(beim Nähen)* stitch; *(Färbung)* tinge; *(Cards)* trick; *(Art)* engraving; **jdn im** ~ **lassen** leave sb in the lurch; ~**el** m -s, - engraving tool, style; ~**e'lei** f jibe, taunt; s~**eln** vi *(fig)* jibe; s~**haltig** a sound, tenable; ~**probe** f spot check; ~**wahl** f final ballot; ~**wort** nt cue; *(in Wörterbuch)* headword; *(für Vortrag)* note; ~**wortverzeichnis** nt index.
Stick- [ʃtɪk] cpd: s~**en** vti embroider; ~**e'rei** f embroidery; s~**ig** a stuffy, close; ~**stoff** m nitrogen.
Stiefel ['ʃtiːfəl] m -s, - boot.
Stief- ['ʃtiːf] in cpds step; ~**kind** nt stepchild; *(fig)* Cinderella; ~**mutter** f stepmother; ~**mütterchen** nt pansy.
Stiege ['ʃtiːgə] f -, -n staircase.
Stiel [ʃtiːl] m -(e)s, -e handle; *(Bot)* stalk.
stier [ʃtiːr] a staring, fixed; S~ m -(e)s, -e bull; *(Astrol)* Taurus; ~**en** vi stare.
Stift [ʃtɪft] m -(e)s, -e peg; *(Nagel)* tack; *(Farb—)* crayon; *(Blei—)* pencil; nt -(e)s, -e *(charitable)* foundation; *(Eccl)* religious institution; s~**en** vt found; *Unruhe* cause; *(spenden)* contribute; ~**er(in** f) m -s, - founder; ~**ung** f donation; *(Organisation)* foundation; ~**zahn** m crown tooth.
Stil [ʃtiːl] m -(e)s, -e style; ~**blüte** f howler.
still [ʃtɪl] a quiet; *(unbewegt)* still; *(heimlich)* secret; S~**e** f -, -n stillness, quietness; **in aller** S~**e** quietly; ~**en** vt stop; *(befriedigen)* satisfy; *Säugling* breast-feed; ~**gestanden** interj attention; ~**halten** vi irreg keep still; ~**(l)egen** vt close down; ~**schweigen** vi irreg be silent; S~**schweigen** nt silence; ~**schweigend** a,ad silent(ly); *Einverständnis* tacit(ly); S~**stand** m standstill; ~**stehen** vi irreg stand still.
Stimm- ['ʃtɪm] cpd: ~**abgabe** f voting; ~**bänder** pl vocal chords pl; s~**berechtigt** a entitled to vote; ~**e** f -, -n voice; *(Wahl—)* vote; s~**en** vt *(Mus)* tune; **das stimmte ihn traurig** that made him feel sad; vi be right; s~**en für/gegen** vote for/against; ~**enmehrheit** f majority (of votes); ~**enthaltung** f abstention; ~**gabel** f tuning fork; s~**haft** a voiced; ~**lage** f register; s~**los** a voiceless; ~**recht** nt right to vote; ~**ung** f mood; atmosphere; s~**ungsvoll** a enjoyable; full of atmosphere; ~**zettel** m ballot paper.
stinken ['ʃtɪŋkən] vi irreg stink.
Stipendium [ʃtiˈpɛndiʊm] nt grant.
Stirn ['ʃtɪrn] f -, -**en** forehead, brow; *(Frechheit)* impudence; ~**höhle** f sinus; ~**runzeln** nt -s frown(ing).
stöbern ['ʃtøːbərn] vi rummage.
stochern ['ʃtɔxərn] vi poke (about).
Stock [ʃtɔk] m -(e)s, ⸚e stick; *(Bot)* stock; pl

-werke storey; **s~**-*in* cpds vor a (col) completely; **s~en** vi stop, pause; **s~end** a halting; **s~finster** a (col) pitch-dark; **s~taub** a stone-deaf; **~ung** f stoppage; **~werk** nt storey, floor.

Stoff [ʃtɔf] m -(e)s, -e (Gewebe) material, cloth; (Materie) matter; (von Buch etc) subject (matter); **s~lich** a material; with regard to subject matter; **~wechsel** m metabolism.

stöhnen [ˈʃtøːnən] vi groan.

stoisch [ˈʃtoːɪʃ] a stoical.

Stollen [ˈʃtɔlən] m -s, - (Min) gallery; (Cook) cake eaten at Christmas; (von Schuhen) stud.

stolpern [ˈʃtɔlpərn] vi stumble, trip.

Stolz [ʃtɔlts] m -es pride; **s~** a proud; **s~ieren** [ʃtɔlˈtsiːrən] vi strut.

Stopf- [ˈʃtɔpf] cpd: **s~en** vt (hinein—) stuff; (voll—) fill (up); (nähen) darn; vi (Med) cause constipation; **~garn** nt darning thread.

Stoppel [ˈʃtɔpəl] f -, -n stubble.

Stopp- [ˈʃtɔp] cpd: **s~en** vti stop; (mit Uhr) time; **~schild** nt stop sign; **~uhr** f stopwatch.

Stöpsel [ˈʃtœpsəl] m -s, - plug; (für Flaschen) stopper.

Stör [ʃtøːr] m -(e)s, -e sturgeon.

Storch m -(e)s, **-e** stork.

Stör- [ʃtøːr] cpd: **s~en** vt disturb; (behindern, Rad) interfere with; vr **sich an etw** (dat) **s~en** let sth bother one; **s~end** a disturbing, annoying; **~enfried** m -(e)s, -e troublemaker.

störrig [ˈʃtœrɪç], **störrisch** [ˈʃtœrɪʃ] a stubborn, perverse.

Stör- cpd: **~sender** m jammer; **~ung** f disturbance; interference.

Stoß [ʃtoːs] m -es, **-e** (Schub) push; (Schlag) blow; knock; (mit Schwert) thrust; (mit Fuß) kick; (Erd—) shock; (Haufen) pile; **~dämpfer** m -s, - shock absorber; **s~en** irreg vt (mit Druck) shove, push; (mit Schlag) knock, bump; (mit Fuß) kick; Schwert etc thrust; (an—) Kopf etc bump; (zerkleinern) pulverize; vr get a knock; **sich s~en** an (+dat) (fig) take exception to; vi: **s~en an** or **auf** (+acc) bump into; (finden) come across; (angrenzen) be next to; **~stange** f (Aut) bumper.

Stotterer [ˈʃtɔtərər] m -s, - stutterer.

stottern [ˈʃtɔtərn] vti stutter.

stracks [ʃtraks] ad straight.

Straf- [ˈʃtraːf] cpd: **~anstalt** f penal institution; **~arbeit** f (Sch) punishment; lines pl; **s~bar** a punishable; **~barkeit** f criminal nature; **~e** f -, -n punishment; (Jur) penalty; (Gefängnis—) sentence; (Geld—) fine; **s~en** vt punish.

straff [ʃtraf] a tight; (streng) strict; Stil etc concise; Haltung erect; **s~en** vt tighten, tauten.

Straf- cpd: **~gefangene(r)** mf prisoner, convict; **~gesetzbuch** nt penal code; **~kolonie** f penal colony.

Sträf- [ˈʃtrɛːf] cpd: **s~lich** a criminal; **~ling** m convict.

Straf- cpd: **~porto** nt excess postage (charge); **~predigt** f severe lecture;

~raum m (Sport) penalty area; **~recht** nt criminal law; **~stoß** m (Sport) penalty (kick); **~tat** f punishable act; **~zettel** m ticket.

Strahl [ʃtraːl] m -s, -en ray, beam; (Wasser—) jet; **s~en** vi radiate; (fig) beam; **~enbehandlung**, **~entherapie** f radiotherapy; **~ung** f radiation.

Strähne [ˈʃtrɛːnə] f -, -n strand.

stramm [ʃtram] a tight; Haltung erect; Mensch robust; **~stehen** vi irreg (Mil) stand to attention.

strampeln [ˈʃtrampəln] vi kick (about), fidget.

Strand [ʃtrant] m -(e)s, **-e** shore; (mit Sand) beach; **~bad** nt open-air swimming pool, lido; **s~en** [ˈʃtrandən] vi run aground; (fig: Mensch) fail; **~gut** nt flotsam; **~korb** m beach chair.

Strang [ʃtraŋ] m -(e)s, **-e** cord, rope; (Bündel) skein; (Schienen—) track; **über die e schlagen** (col) kick over the traces.

Strapaz- cpd: **~e** [ʃtraˈpaːtsə] f - -n strain, exertion; **s~ieren** [ʃtrapaˈtsiːrən] vt Material treat roughly, punish; Mensch, Kräfte wear out, exhaust; **s~ierfähig** a hard-wearing; **s~iös** [ʃtrapatsiˈøːs] a exhausting, tough.

Straße [ˈʃtraːsə] f -, -n street, road; **~nbahn** f tram, streetcar (US); **~nbeleuchtung** f street lighting; **~nfeger**, **~nkehrer** m -s, - roadsweeper; **~nsperre** f roadblock; **~nverkehrsordnung** f highway code.

Strateg- [ʃtraˈteːg] cpd: **~e** m -n, -n strategist; **~ie** [ʃtrateˈgiː] f strategy; **s~isch** a strategic.

Stratosphäre [ʃtratoˈsfɛːrə] f - stratosphere.

sträuben [ˈʃtrɔybən] vt ruffle; vr bristle; (Mensch) resist (gegen etw sth).

Strauch [ʃtraux] m -(e)s, **Sträucher** bush, shrub; **s~eln** vi stumble, stagger.

Strauß [ʃtraus] m -es, **Sträuße** bunch; bouquet; pl -e ostrich.

Streb- [ˈʃtreːb] cpd: **~e** f -, -n strut; **~ebalken** m buttress; **s~en** vi strive (nach for), endeavour; **s~en zu** or **nach** (sich bewegen) make for; **~er** m -s, - (pej) pusher, climber; (Sch) swot; **s~sam** a industrious; **~samkeit** f industry.

Strecke [ˈʃtrɛkə] f -, -n stretch; (Entfernung) distance; (Rail) line; (Math) line; **s~n** vt stretch; Waffen lay down; (Cook) eke out; vr stretch (oneself); vi (Sch) put one's hand up.

Streich [ʃtraɪç] m -(e)s, -e trick, prank; (Hieb) blow; **s~eln** vt stroke; **s~en** irreg vt (berühren) stroke; (auftragen) spread; (anmalen) paint; (durch—) delete; (nicht genehmigen) cancel; vi (berühren) brush; (schleichen) prowl; **~holz** nt match; **~instrument** nt string instrument.

Streif- [ˈʃtraɪf] cpd: **~band** nt wrapper; **~e** f -, -n patrol; **s~en** vt (leicht berühren) brush against, graze; (Blick) skim over; Thema, Problem touch on; (ab—) take off; vi (gehen) roam; **~en** m -s, - (Linie) stripe; (Stück) strip; (Film) film; **~endienst** m patrol duty; **~enwagen** m patrol car; ~**schuß** m graze, grazing shot; ~**zug** m scouting trip.

Streik [ʃtraık] m -(e)s, -s strike; ~**brecher** m -s, - blackleg, strikebreaker; **s~en** vi strike; ~**kasse** f strike fund; ~**posten** m (strike) picket.

Streit [ʃtraıt] m -(e)s, -e argument; dispute; **s~en** vir irreg argue; dispute; ~**frage** f point at issue; **s~ig** a: **jdm etw s~ig machen** dispute sb's right to sth; ~**igkeiten** pl quarrel, dispute; ~**kräfte** pl (Mil) armed forces pl; **s~lustig** a quarrelsome; ~**sucht** f quarrelsomeness.

streng [ʃtrɛŋ] a severe; Lehrer, Maßnahme strict; Geruch etc sharp; **S~e** f - severity; strictness; sharpness; ~**genommen** ad strictly speaking; ~**gläubig** a orthodox, strict.

Streu [ʃtrɔy] f -, -en litter, bed of straw; **s~en** vt strew, scatter, spread; ~**ung** f dispersion.

Strich [ʃtrıç] m -(e)s, -e (Linie) line; (Feder–, Pinsel–) stroke; (von Geweben) nap; (von Fell) pile; **auf den ~ gehen** (col) walk the streets; **jdm gegen den ~ gehen** rub sb up the wrong way; **einen ~ machen durch** (lit) cross out; (fig) foil; ~**einteilung** f calibration; (fig) ~**mädchen** nt streetwalker; ~**punkt** m semicolon; **s~weise** ad here and there.

Strick [ʃtrık] m -(e)s, -e rope; (col: Kind) rascal; **s~en** vti knit; ~**jacke** f cardigan; ~**leiter** f rope ladder; ~**nadel** f knitting needle; ~**waren** pl knitwear.

Strieme [ʃtriːmə] f -, -n, **Striemen** [ʃtriːmən] m -s, - weal.

strikt [ʃtrıkt] a strict.

strittig [ʃtrıtıç] a disputed, in dispute.

Stroh [ʃtroː] nt -(e)s straw; ~**blume** f everlasting flower; ~**dach** nt thatched roof; ~**halm** m (drinking) straw; ~**mann** m, pl ~**männer** dummy, straw man; ~**witwe** f grass widow.

Strolch [ʃtrɔlç] m -(e)s, -e layabout, bum.

Strom [ʃtroːm] m -(e)s, -e river; (fig) stream; (Elec) current; **s~abwärts** [-ˈapvɛrts] ad downstream; **s~aufwärts** [-ˈaufvɛrts] ad upstream.

strömen [ˈʃtrøːmən] vi stream, pour.

Strom- cpd: ~**kreis** m circuit; **s~linienförmig** a streamlined; ~**rechnung** f electricity bill; ~**sperre** f power cut; ~**stärke** f amperage.

Strömung [ˈʃtrøːmʊŋ] f current.

Strophe [ʃtroːfə] f -, -n verse.

strotzen [ˈʃtrɔtsən] vi: ~**vor** or **von** abound in, be full of.

Strudel [ˈʃtruːdəl] m -s, - whirlpool, vortex; (Cook) strudel; **s~n** vi swirl, eddy.

Struktur [ʃtrʊkˈtuːr] f structure; **s~ell** [-ˈrɛl] a structural.

Strumpf [ʃtrʊmpf] m -(e)s, -e stocking; ~**band** nt garter; ~**hose** f (pair of) tights.

Strunk [ʃtrʊŋk] m -(e)s, -e stump.

struppig [ˈʃtrʊpıç] a shaggy, unkempt.

Stube [ˈʃtuːbə] f -, -n room; ~**narrest** m confinement to one's room; (Mil) confinement to quarters; ~**nhocker** m

(col) stay-at-home; **s~nrein** a housetrained.

Stuck [ʃtʊk] m -(e)s stucco.

Stück [ʃtyk] nt -(e)s, -e piece; (etwas) bit; (Theat) play; ~**arbeit** f piecework; ~**chen** nt little piece; ~**lohn** m piecework wages pl; **s~weise** ad bit by bit, piecemeal; (Comm) individually; ~**werk** nt bits and pieces pl.

Student(in f) [ʃtuˈdɛnt(ın)] m student; **s~isch** a student, academic.

Studie [ˈʃtuːdiə] f study.

studieren [ʃtuˈdiːrən] vti study.

Studio [ˈʃtuːdio] nt -s, -s studio.

Studium [ˈʃtuːdiʊm] nt studies pl.

Stufe [ˈʃtuːfə] f -, -n step; (Entwicklungs–) stage; ~**nleiter** f (fig) ladder; **s~nweise** ad gradually.

Stuhl [ʃtuːl] m -(e)s, -e chair; ~**gang** m bowel movement.

stülpen [ˈʃtylpən] vt (umdrehen) turn upside down; (bedecken) put.

stumm [ʃtʊm] a silent; (Med) dumb; **S~el** m -s, - stump; (Zigaretten–) stub; **S~film** m silent film; **S~heit** f silence; dumbness.

Stümper [ˈʃtympər] m -s, - incompetent, duffer; **s~haft** a bungling, incompetent; **s~n** vi (col) bungle.

stumpf [ʃtʊmpf] a blunt; (teilnahmslos, glanzlos) dull; Winkel obtuse; **S~** m -(e)s, -e stump; **S~heit** f bluntness; dullness; **S~sinn** m tediousness; ~**sinnig** a dull.

Stunde [ˈʃtʊndə] f -, -n hour; **s~n** vt: **jdm etw s~en** give sb time to pay sth; ~**ngeschwindigkeit** f average speed per hour; ~**nkilometer** pl kilometres per hour; **s~nlang** a for hours; ~**nlohn** m hourly wage; ~**nplan** m timetable; **s~nweise** a by the hour; every hour.

stündlich [ˈʃtyntlıç] a hourly, hour.

Stups [ʃtʊps] m -es, -e (col) push; ~**nase** f snub nose.

stur [ʃtuːr] a obstinate, pigheaded.

Sturm [ʃtʊrm] m -(e)s, -e storm, gale; (Mil etc) attack, assault.

stürm- [ˈʃtyrm] cpd: ~**en** vi (Wind) blow hard, rage; (rennen) storm; vt (Mil, fig) storm; v impers **es ~t** there's a gale blowing; **S~er** m -s, - (Sport) forward, striker; ~**isch** a stormy.

Sturm- cpd: ~**warnung** f gale warning; ~**wind** m storm, gale.

Sturz [ʃtʊrts] m -es, -e fall; (Pol) overthrow.

stürzen [ˈʃtyrtsən] vt (werfen) hurl; (Pol) overthrow; (umkehren) overturn; vr rush; (hinein–) plunge; vi fall; (Aviat) dive; (rennen) dash.

Sturz- cpd: ~**flug** m nose-dive; ~**helm** m crash helmet.

Stute [ˈʃtuːtə] f -, -n mare.

Stütz- [ˈʃtyts] cpd: ~**balken** m brace, joist; ~**e** f -, -n support; help; **s~en** vt (lit, fig) support; Ellbogen etc prop up.

stutz- [ˈʃtʊts] cpd: ~**en** vt trim; Ohr, Schwanz dock; Flügel clip; vi hesitate; become suspicious; ~**ig** a perplexed, puzzled; (mißtrauisch) suspicious.

Stütz- cpd: ~**mauer** f supporting wall;

~**punkt** m point of support; (von Hebel) fulcrum; (Mil, fig) base.

Styropor ® [ʃtyro'po:r] nt -s polystyrene.

Subjekt [zup'jɛkt] nt -(e)s, -e subject; s~**iv** [-'ti:f] a subjective; ~**ivi'tät** f subjectivity.

Substantiv [zupstan'ti:f] nt -s, -e noun.

Substanz [zup'stants] f substance.

subtil [zup'ti:l] a subtle.

subtrahieren [zuptra'hi:rən] vt subtract.

Subvention [zupvɛntsi'o:n] f subsidy; s~**ieren** [-'ni:rən] vt subsidize.

subversiv [zupvɛr'zi:f] a subversive.

Such- ['zu:x] cpd: ~**aktion** f search; ~**e** f -, -n search; s~**en** vti look (for), seek; (ver—) try; ~**er** m -s, - seeker, searcher; (Phot) viewfinder.

Sucht [zuxt] f -, -̈e mania; (Med) addiction, craving.

süchtig ['zyçtıç] a addicted; S~**e(r)** mf addict.

Süd- [zy:t] cpd: ~**en** ['zy:dən] m -s south; ~**früchte** pl Mediterranean fruit; s~**lich** a southern; s~**lich von** (to the) south of; s~**wärts** ad southwards.

süff- cpd: ~**ig** ['zyfıç] a Wein pleasant to the taste; ~**isant** [zyfi'zant] a smug.

suggerieren [zuge'ri:rən] vt suggest (jdm etw sth to sb).

Sühne ['zy:nə] f -, -n atonement, expiation; s~**n** vt atone for, expiate.

Sulfonamid [zulfona'mi:t] nt -(e)s, -e (Med) sulphonamide.

Sultan ['zʊltan] m -s, -e sultan; ~**ine** [zulta'ni:nə] f sultana.

Sülze ['zyltsə] f -, -n brawn.

Summ- [zum] cpd: s~**arisch** [zʊ'ma:rıʃ] a summary; ~**e** f -, -n sum, total; s~**en** vti buzz; Lied hum; s~**ieren** [zʊ'mi:rən] vtr add up (to).

Sumpf [zʊmpf] m -(e)s, -̈e swamp, marsh; s~**ig** a marshy.

Sünde ['zyndə] f -, -n sin; ~**nbock** m (col) scapegoat; ~**nfall** m Fall (of man); ~**r(in** f) m -s, - sinner.

Super ['zu:pər] nt -s (Benzin) four star (petrol); ~**lativ** [-lati:f] m -s, -e superlative; ~**markt** m supermarket.

Suppe ['zʊpə] f -, -n soup.

surren ['zʊrən] vi buzz, hum.

Surrogat [zʊro'ga:t] nt -(e)s, -e substitute, surrogate.

suspekt [zʊs'pɛkt] a suspect.

süß [zy:s] a sweet; S~**e** f - sweetness; ~**en** vt sweeten; S~**igkeit** f sweetness; (Bonbon etc) sweet, candy (US); ~**lich** a sweetish; (fig) sugary; S~**speise** f pudding, sweet; S~**stoff** m sweetening agent; S~**wasser** nt fresh water.

Sylvester [zyl'vəstər] nt -s, - see **Silvester.**

Symbol [zym'bo:l] nt -s, -e symbol; s~**isch** a symbolic(al).

Symmetrie [zyme'tri:] f symmetry; ~**achse** f symmetric axis.

symmetrisch [zy'me:trıʃ] a symmetrical.

Sympath- cpd: ~**ie** [zympa'ti:] f liking, sympathy; s~**isch** [zym'pa:tıʃ] a likeable,

congenial; **er ist mir s~isch** I like him; s~**i'sieren** vi sympathize.

Symptom [zymp'to:m] nt -s, -e symptom; s~**atisch** [zympto'ma:tıʃ] a symptomatic.

Synagoge [zyna'go:gə] f -, -n synagogue.

synchron [zyn'kro:n] a synchronous; S~**getriebe** nt synchromesh (gears pl); ~**i'sieren** vt synchronize; Film dub.

Syndikat [zyndi'ka:t] nt -(e)s, -e combine, syndicate.

Synonym [zyno'ny:m] nt -s, -e synonym; s~ a synonymous.

Syntax ['zyntaks] f -, -en syntax.

Synthese [zyn'te:zə] f -, -n synthesis.

synthetisch [zyn'te:tıʃ] a synthetic.

Syphilis ['zyfilıs] f - syphilis.

System [zys'te:m] nt -s, -e system; s~**atisch** [zyste'ma:tıʃ] a systematic; s~**ati'sieren** vt systematize.

Szene ['stse:nə] f -, -n scene; ~**rie** [stsenə'ri:] f scenery.

Szepter ['stsɛptər] nt -s, - sceptre.

T

T, t [te:] T, t.

Tabak ['ta:bak] m -s, -e tobacco.

Tabell- [ta'bɛl] cpd: t~**arisch** [tabe'la:rıʃ] a tabular; ~**e** f table; ~**enführer** m top of the table, league leader.

Tabernakel [tabɛr'na:kəl] m -s, - tabernacle.

Tablette [ta'blɛtə] f tablet, pill.

Tachometer [taxo'me:tər] m -s, - (Aut) speedometer.

Tadel ['ta:dəl] m -s, - censure, scolding; (Fehler) blemish, fault; t~**los** a faultless, irreproachable; t~**n** vt scold; t~**nswert** a blameworthy.

Tafel ['ta:fəl] f -, -n table (auch Math); (Anschlag—) board; (Wand—) blackboard; (Schiefer—) slate; (Gedenk—) plaque; (Illustration) plate; (Schalt—) panel; (Schokolade etc) bar.

Täfel- ['tɛ:fəl] cpd: t~**n** vt panel; ~**ung** f panelling.

Taft [taft] m -(e)s, -e taffeta.

Tag [ta:k] m -(e)s, -e day; daylight; **unter/über** ~ (Min) underground/on the surface; **an den** ~ **kommen** come to light; **guten** ~! good morning/afternoon!; t~**aus**, t~**ein** ad day in, day out; ~**dienst** m day duty; ~**ebuch** ['ta:gəbu:x] nt diary, journal; ~**edieb** m idler; ~**egeld** nt daily allowance; t~**elang** ad for days; t~**en** vi sit, meet; v impers: **es tagt** dawn is breaking; ~**esablauf** m course of the day; ~**esanbruch** m dawn; ~**eslicht** nt daylight; ~**esordnung** f agenda; ~**essatz** m daily rate; ~**eszeit** f time of day; ~**eszeitung** f daily (paper).

täglich ['tɛ:klıç] a,ad daily.

Tag- cpd: t~**süber** ad during the day; ~**ung** f conference.

Taille ['taljə] f -, -n waist.

Takel ['ta:kəl] nt -s, - tackle; t~**n** vt rig.

Takt [takt] m -(e)s, -e tact; (Mus) time; ~**gefühl** nt tact; ~**ik** f tactics pl; t~**isch** a tactical; t~**los** a tactless; ~**losigkeit** f tactlessness; ~**stock** m (conductor's) baton; t~**voll** a tactful.

Tal [taːl] nt -(e)s, ᵉer valley.

Talar [taˈlaːr] m -s, -e (Jur) robe; (Univ) gown.

Talent [taˈlɛnt] nt -(e)s, -e talent; t~**iert** [talɛnˈtiːrt], t~**voll** a talented, gifted.

Taler [ˈtaːlər] m -s, - taler, florin.

Talg [talk] m -(e)s, -e tallow; ~**drüse** f sebaceous gland.

Talisman [ˈtaːlisman] m -s, -e talisman.

Tal- cpd: ~**sohle** f bottom of a valley; ~**sperre** f dam.

Tamburin [tambuˈriːn] nt -s, -e tambourine.

Tampon [ˈtampɔn] m -s, -s tampon.

Tang [taŋ] m -(e)s, -e seaweed; ~**ente** [taŋˈgɛntə] f -, -n tangent; t~**ieren** [taŋgiˈrən] vt (lit) be tangent to; (fig) affect.

Tank [taŋk] m -s, -s tank; t~**en** vi fill up with petrol or gas (US); (Aviat) (re)fuel; ~**er** m -s, -, ~**schiff** nt tanker; ~**stelle** f petrol or gas (US) station; ~**wart** m petrol pump or gas station (US) attendant.

Tanne [ˈtanə] f -, -n fir; ~**nbaum** m fir tree; ~**nzapfen** m fir cone.

Tante [ˈtantə] f -, -n aunt.

Tanz [tants] m -es, ᵉe dance.

Tänz- [ˈtɛnts] cpd: t~**eln** vi dance along; ~**er(in** f) m -s, - dancer.

Tanz- cpd: t~**en** vti dance; ~**fläche** f (dance) floor; ~**schule** f dancing school.

Tape- cpd: ~**te** [taˈpeːtə] f -, -n wallpaper; ~**tenwechsel** m (fig) change of scenery; t~**zieren** [tapeˈtsiːrən] vt (wall)paper; ~**zierer** [tapeˈtsiːrər] m -s, - (interior) decorator.

tapfer [ˈtapfər] a brave; T~**keit** f courage, bravery.

tappen [ˈtapən] vi walk uncertainly or clumsily.

täppisch [ˈtɛpiʃ] a clumsy.

Tarif [taˈriːf] m -s, -e tariff, (scale of) fares/charges; ~**lohn** m standard wage rate.

Tarn- [ˈtarn] cpd: t~**en** vt camouflage; Person, Absicht disguise; ~**farbe** f camouflage paint; ~**ung** f camouflaging, disguising.

Tasche [ˈtaʃə] f -, -n pocket; handbag; ~**n** in cpds pocket; ~**nbuch** nt paperback; ~**ndieb** m pickpocket; ~**ngeld** nt pocket money; ~**nlampe** f (electric) torch, flashlight (US); ~**nmesser** nt penknife; ~**nspieler** m conjurer; ~**ntuch** nt handkerchief.

Tasse [ˈtasə] f -, -n cup.

Tast- [ˈtast] cpd: ~**atur** [-aˈtuːr] f keyboard; ~**e** f -, -n push-button control; (an Schreibmaschine) key; t~**en** vt feel, touch; vi feel, grope; vr feel one's way; ~**sinn** m sense of touch.

Tat [taːt] f -, -en act, deed, action; **in der** ~ indeed, as a matter of fact; ~**bestand** m facts pl of the case; t~**enlos** a inactive.

Tät- [ˈtɛːt] cpd: ~**er(in** f) m -s, - perpetrator, culprit; ~**erschaft** f guilt; t~**ig** a active; **in einer Firma** t~**ig sein** work for a firm; T~**igkeit** f activity;

(Beruf) occupation; t~**lich** a violent; ~**lichkeit** f violence; pl blows pl.

tätowieren [tɛtoˈviːrən] vt tattoo.

Tat- cpd: ~**sache** f fact; t~**sächlich** a actual; ad really.

Tatze [ˈtatsə] f -, -n paw.

Tau [tau] nt -(e)s, -e rope; m -(e)s dew.

taub [taup] a deaf; Nuß hollow; T~**heit** f deafness; ~**stumm** a deaf-and-dumb.

Taube [ˈtaubə] f -, -n dove; pigeon; ~**nschlag** m dovecote.

Tauch- [ˈtaux] cpd: t~**en** vt dip; vi dive; (Naut) submerge; ~**er** m -s, - diver; ~**eranzug** m diving suit; ~**sieder** m -s, - portable immersion heater.

tauen [ˈtauən] vti, v impers thaw.

Tauf- [ˈtauf] cpd: ~**becken** nt font; ~**e** f -, -n baptism; t~**en** vt christen, baptize; ~**name** m Christian name; ~**pate** m godfather; ~**patin** f godmother; ~**schein** m certificate of baptism.

Taug- [ˈtaug] cpd: t~**en** vi be of use; t~**en für** do or be good for; **nicht** t~**en** be no good or useless; ~**enichts** m -es, -e good-for-nothing; t~**lich** [ˈtauklɪç] a suitable; (Mil) fit (for service); ~**lichkeit** f suitability.

Taumel [ˈtauməl] m -s dizziness; (fig) frenzy; t~**ig** a giddy, reeling; t~**n** vi reel, stagger.

Tausch [tauʃ] m -(e)s, -e exchange; t~**en** vt exchange, swap; ~**handel** m barter.

täuschen [ˈtɔyʃən] vt deceive; vi be deceptive; vr be wrong; ~**d** a deceptive.

Täuschung f deception; (optisch) illusion.

tausend [ˈtauzənt] num (a) thousand; T~**füßler** m -s, - centipede; millipede.

Tau- cpd: ~**tropfen** m dew drop; ~**wetter** nt thaw; ~**ziehen** nt -s, - tug-of-war.

Taxi [ˈtaksi] nt -(s), -(s) taxi; ~**fahrer** m taxi driver.

Tech- [ˈtɛç] cpd: ~**nik** f technology; (Methode, Kunstfertigkeit) technique; ~**niker** m -s, technician; t~**nisch** a technical; ~**nolo'gie** f technology; t~**nologisch** a technological.

Tee [teː] m -s, -s tea; ~**kanne** f teapot; ~**löffel** m teaspoon.

Teer [teːr] m -(e)s, -e tar; t~**en** vt tar.

Tee- cpd: ~**sieb** nt tea strainer; ~**wagen** m tea trolley.

Teich [taiç] m -(e)s, -e pond.

Teig [taik] m -(e)s, -e dough; t~**ig** a doughy; ~**waren** pl pasta sing.

Teil [tail] m or nt -(e)s, -e part; (An—) share; (Bestand—) component; **zum** ~ partly; t~**bar** a divisible; ~**betrag** m instalment; ~**chen** nt (atomic) particle; t~**en** vtr divide; (mit jdm) share; t~**haben** vi irreg share (an +dat in); ~**haber** m -s, - partner; ~**kaskoversicherung** f third party, fire and theft insurance; ~**nahme** f -, -n participation; (Mitleid) sympathy; t~**nahmslos** a disinterested, apathetic; t~**nehmen** vi irreg take part (an +dat in); ~**nehmer** m -s, - participant; t~**s** ad partly; ~**ung** f division; t~**weise** ad partially, in part;

~zahlung f payment by instalments.
Teint [tɛ̃:] m **-s, -s** complexion.
Telefon [tele'fo:n] nt **-s, -e** telephone; **~amt** nt telephone exchange; **~anruf** m, **~at** [telefo'na:t] nt **-(e)s, -e** (tele)phone call; **~buch** nt telephone directory; **t~ieren** [telefo'ni:rən] vi telephone; **t~isch** [-ɪʃ] a telephone; Benachrichtigung by telephone; **~ist(in** f) [telefo'nɪst(ɪn)] m telephonist; **~nummer** f (tele)phone number; **~verbindung** f telephone connection; **~zelle** f telephone kiosk, callbox; **~zentrale** f telephone exchange.
Telegraf [tele'gra:f] m **-en, -en** telegraph; **~enleitung** f telegraph line; **~enmast** m telegraph pole; **~ie** [-'fi:] f telegraphy; **t~ieren** [-'fi:rən] vti telegraph, wire; **t~isch** a telegraphic.
Telegramm [tele'gram] nt **-s, -e** telegram, cable; **~adresse** f telegraphic address; **~formular** nt telegram form.
Tele- cpd: **~graph** = **~graf**; **~kolleg** ['teleko:lek] nt university of the air; **~objektiv** [te:le'ɔpjekti:f] nt telephoto lens; **~pathie** [telepa'ti:] f telepathy; **t~pathisch** [tele'pa:tɪʃ] a telepathic; **~phon** = **~fon**; **~skop** [tele'sko:p] nt **-s, -e** telescope.
Teller ['tɛlər] m **-s, -** plate.
Tempel ['tɛmpəl] m **-s, -** temple.
Temperafarbe ['tɛmpərafarbə] f distemper.
Temperament [tɛmpəra'mɛnt] nt temperament; (Schwung) vivacity, liveliness; **t~los** a spiritless; **t~voll** a high-spirited, lively.
Temperatur [tɛmpəra'tu:r] f temperature.
Tempo ['tɛmpo] nt **-s, -s** speed, pace; pl **Tempi** (Mus) tempo; **~!** get a move on!; **t~rär** [-'rɛ:r] a temporary; **~taschentuch** nt paper handkerchief.
Tendenz [tɛn'dɛnts] f tendency; (Absicht) intention; **t~iös** [-i'ø:s] a biased, tendentious.
tendieren [tɛn'di:rən] vi show a tendency, incline (zu to(wards)).
Tenne ['tɛnə] f **-, -n** threshing floor.
Tennis ['tɛnɪs] nt **-** tennis; **~platz** m tennis court; **~schläger** m tennis racket; **~spieler(in** f) m tennis player.
Tenor [te'no:r] m **-s, ̈e** tenor.
Teppich ['tɛpɪç] m **-s, -e** carpet; **~boden** m wall-to-wall carpeting; **~kehrmaschine** f carpet sweeper; **~klopfer** m carpet beater.
Termin [tɛr'mi:n] m **-s, -e** (Zeitpunkt) date; (Frist) time limit, deadline; (Arzt-etc) appointment; **~kalender** m diary, appointments book; **~ologie** [-olo'gi:] f terminology.
Termite [tɛr'mi:tə] f **-, -n** termite.
Terpentin [tɛrpɛn'ti:n] nt **-s, -e** turpentine, turps sing.
Terrasse [tɛ'rasə] f **-, -n** terrace.
Terrine [tɛ'ri:nə] f tureen.
territorial [tɛritori'a:l] a territorial.
Territorium [tɛri'to:rium] nt territory.
Terror [tɛ'ro:r] m **-s** terror; reign of terror; **t~isieren** [tɛrori'zi:rən] vt terrorize;

~ismus [-'rɪsmus] m terrorism; **~ist** [-'rɪst] m terrorist.
Terz [tɛrts] f **-, -en** (Mus) third; **~ett** [tɛr'tsɛt] nt trio.
Tesafilm ® ['te:zafɪlm] m sellotape ®.
Testament [tɛsta'mɛnt] nt will, testament; (Rel) Testament; **t~arisch** [-'ta:rɪʃ] a testamentary; **~svollstrecker** m executor (of a will).
Test- [tɛst] cpd: **~at** [tɛs'ta:t] nt **-(e)s, -e** certificate; **~ator** [tɛs'ta:tor] m testator; **~bild** nt (TV) test card; **t~en** vt test.
Tetanus ['te:tanus] m **-** tetanus; **~impfung** f (anti-)tetanus injection.
teuer ['tɔyər] a dear, expensive; **T~ung** f increase in prices; **T~ungszulage** f cost of living bonus.
Teufel ['tɔyfəl] m **-s, -** devil; **~ei** [-'lai] f devilry; **~saustreibung** f exorcism.
teuflisch ['tɔyflɪʃ] a fiendish, diabolical.
Text [tɛkst] m **-(e)s, -e** text; (Lieder—) words pl; **t~en** vi write the words.
textil [tɛks'ti:l] a textile; **T~ien** pl textiles pl; **T~industrie** f textile industry; **~waren** pl textiles pl.
Theater [te'a:tər] nt **-s, -** theatre; (col) fuss; **~ spielen** (lit, fig) playact; **~besucher** m playgoer; **~kasse** f box office; **~stück** nt (stage-)play.
theatralisch [tea'tra:lɪʃ] a theatrical.
Theke ['te:kə] f **-, -n** (Schanktisch) bar; (Ladentisch) counter.
Thema ['te:ma] nt **-s, Themen** or **-ta** theme, topic, subject.
Theo- [teo] cpd: **~loge** [-'lo:gə] m **-n, -n** theologian; **~logie** [-lo'gi:] f theology; **t~logisch** [-'lo:gɪʃ] a theological; **~retiker** [-'re:tikər] m **-s, -** theorist; **t~retisch** [-'re:tɪʃ] a theoretical; **~rie** [-'ri:] f theory.
Thera- [tera] cpd: **~peut** [-'pɔyt] m **-en, -en** therapist; **t~peutisch** [-'pɔytɪʃ] a therapeutic; **~pie** [-'pi:] f therapy.
Therm- cpd: **~albad** [tɛrm'a:lba:t] nt thermal bath; thermal spa; **~ometer** [tɛrmo'me:tər] nt **-s,** thermometer; **~osflasche** ['tɛrmɔsflaʃə] f Thermos flask; **~ostat** [tɛrmo'sta:t] m **-(e)s** or **-en, -e(n)** thermostat.
These ['te:zə] f **-, -n** thesis.
Thrombose [trɔm'bo:zə] f **-, -n** thrombosis.
Thron [tro:n] m **-(e)s, -e** throne; **~besteigung** f accession (to the throne); **~erbe** m heir to the throne; **~folge** f succession (to the throne).
Thunfisch ['tu:nfɪʃ] m tuna.
Thymian ['ty:mia:n] m **-s, -e** thyme.
Tick [tɪk] m **-(e)s, -e** tic; (Eigenart) quirk; (Fimmel) craze; **t~en** vi tick.
tief [ti:f] a deep; (tiefsinnig) profound; Ausschnitt, Ton low; **T~** nt **-s, -s** (Met) depression; **T~druck** m low pressure; **T~e** f **-, -n** depth; **T~ebene** f plain; **T~enpsychologie** f depth psychology; **T~enschärfe** f (Phot) depth of focus; **~ernst** a very grave or solemn; **T~gang** m (Naut) draught; (geistig) depth; **~gekühlt** a frozen; **~greifend** a far-reaching; **T~kühlfach** nt deep-freeze

compartment; **T~kühltruhe** f deep-freeze, freezer; **T~land** nt lowlands pl; **T~punkt** m low point; (fig) low ebb; **T~schlag** m (Boxen, fig) blow below the belt; **~schürfend** a profound; **T~see** f deep sea; **T~sinn** m profundity; **~sinnig** a profound; melancholy; **T~stand** m low level; **~stapeln** vi be overmodest; **T~start** m (Sport) crouch start; **T~stwert** m minimum or lowest value.

Tiegel ['tiːgəl] m -s, - saucepan; (Chem) crucible.

Tier [tiːr] nt -(e)s, -e animal; **~arzt** m vet(erinary surgeon); **~garten** m zoo(logical gardens pl); **t~isch** a animal; (lit, fig) brutish; (fig) Ernst etc deadly; **~kreis** m zodiac; **~kunde** f zoology; **t~liebend** a fond of animals; **~quälerei** [-kvɛːləˈraɪ] f cruelty to animals; **~schutzverein** m society for the prevention of cruelty to animals.

Tiger ['tiːgər] m -s, - tiger; **~in** f tigress.

tilgen ['tɪlgən] vt erase, expunge; Sünden expiate; Schulden pay off.

Tilgung f erasing, blotting out; expiation; repayment.

Tinktur [tɪŋkˈtuːr] f tincture.

Tinte ['tɪntə] f -, -n ink; **~nfaß** nt inkwell; **~nfisch** m cuttlefish; **~nfleck** m ink stain, blot; **~nstift** m copying or indelible pencil.

tippen ['tɪpən] vti tap, touch; (col: schreiben) type; (col: raten) tip (auf jdn sb); (im Lotto etc) bet (on).

Tipp- [ʊp] cpd: **~fehler** m (col) typing error; **~se** f -, -n (col) typist; **t~topp** a (col) tip-top; **~zettel** m (pools) coupon.

Tisch [tɪʃ] m -(e)s, -e table; **bei ~** at table; **vor/nach ~** before/ after eating; **unter den ~ fallen** (fig) be dropped; **~decke** f tablecloth; **~ler** m -s, - carpenter, joiner; **~le'rei** f joiner's workshop; (Arbeit) carpentry, joinery; **t~lern** vi do carpentry etc; **~rede** f after-dinner speech; **~tennis** nt table tennis.

Titel ['tiːtəl] m -s, - title; **~anwärter** m (Sport) challenger; **~bild** nt cover (picture); (von Buch) frontispiece; **~rolle** f title role; **~seite** f cover; (Buch—) title page; **~verteidiger** m defending champion, title holder.

titulieren [tituˈliːrən] vt entitle; (anreden) address.

Toast [toːst] m -(e)s, -s or -e toast; **~er** m -s, - toaster.

tob- ['toːb] cpd: **~en** vi rage; (Kinder) romp about; **T~sucht** f raving madness; **~süchtig** a maniacal; **~suchtsanfall** m maniacal fit.

Tochter ['tɔxtər] f -, ˸ daughter.

Tod [toːt] m -(e)s, -e death; **t~ernst** a (col) deadly serious; **ad** in dead earnest; **~esangst** [toːdəsaŋst] f mortal fear; **~esanzeige** f obituary (notice); **~esfall** m death; **~eskampf** m throes pl of death; **~esstoß** m death-blow; **~esstrafe** f death penalty; **~estag** m anniversary of death; **~esursache** f cause of death; **~esurteil** nt death sentence;

~esverachtung f utter disgust; **t~krank** a dangerously ill.

tödlich ['tøːtlɪç] a deadly, fatal.

tod- cpd: **~müde** a dead tired; **~schick** a (col) smart, classy; **~sicher** a (col) absolutely or dead certain; **T~sünde** f deadly sin.

Toilette [toaˈlɛtə] f toilet, lavatory; (Frisiertisch) dressing table; (Kleidung) outfit; **~nartikel** pl toiletries pl, toilet articles pl; **~npapier** nt toilet paper; **~ntisch** m dressing table.

toi, toi, toi ['tɔy, 'tɔy, 'tɔy] interj touch wood.

tolerant [toleˈrant] a tolerant.

Toleranz [toleˈrants] f tolerance.

tolerieren [toleˈriːrən] vt tolerate.

toll [tɔl] a mad; Treiben wild; (col) terrific; **~en** vi romp; **T~heit** f madness, wildness; **T~kirsche** f deadly nightshade; **~kühn** a daring; **T~wut** f rabies.

Tölpel ['tœlpəl] m -s, - oaf, clod.

Tomate [toˈmaːtə] f -, -n tomato; **~nmark** nt tomato puree.

Ton [toːn] m -(e)s, -e (Erde) clay; pl ˸e (Laut) sound; (Mus) note; (Redeweise) tone; (Farb—, Nuance) shade; (Betonung) stress; **~abnehmer** m pick-up; **t~angebend** a leading; **~art** f (musical) key; **~band** nt tape; **~bandgerät** nt tape recorder.

tönen ['tøːnən] vi sound; vt shade; Haare tint.

tönern ['tøːnərn] a clay.

Ton- cpd: **~fall** m intonation; **~film** m sound film; **t~haltig** a clayey; **~höhe** f pitch; **~ika** f -, -iken (Mus), **~ikum** nt -s, -ika (Med) tonic; **~künstler** m musician; **~leiter** f (Mus) scale; **t~los** a soundless.

Tonne f (Naut) f -, -n barrel; (Maß) ton.

Ton- cpd: **~spur** f soundtrack; **~taube** f clay pigeon; **~waren** pl pottery, earthenware.

Topf [tɔpf] m -(e)s, ˸e pot; **~blume** f pot plant.

Töpfer ['tœpfər] m -s, - potter; **~ei** [-'raɪ] f piece of pottery; potter's workshop; **~scheibe** f potter's wheel.

topographisch [topoˈɡraːfɪʃ] a topographic.

topp [tɔp] interj O.K.

Tor [toːr] m -en, -en fool; nt -(e)s, -e gate; (Sport) goal; **~bogen** m archway.

Torf [tɔrf] m -(e)s peat; **~stechen** nt peat-cutting.

Tor- cpd: **~heit** f foolishness; foolish deed; **~hüter** m -s, - goalkeeper.

töricht ['tøːrɪçt] a foolish.

torkeln ['tɔrkəln] vi stagger, reel.

torpedieren [tɔrpeˈdiːrən] vt (lit, fig) torpedo.

Torpedo [tɔrˈpeːdo] m -s, -s torpedo.

Torte ['tɔrtə] f -, -n cake; (Obst—) flan, tart.

Tortur [tɔrˈtuːr] f ordeal.

Tor- cpd: **~verhältnis** nt goal average; **~wart** m -(e)s, -e goalkeeper.

tosen ['toːzən] vi roar.

tot [toːt] a dead; **einen ~en Punkt haben** be at one's lowest.

total [to'ta:l] a total; **~itär** [totali'tɛ:r] a totalitarian; **T~schaden** m (Aut) complete write-off.

tot- cpd: **~arbeiten** vr work oneself to death; **~ärgern** vr (col) get really annoyed.

töten ['tø:tən] vti kill.

Tot- cpd: **~enbett** nt death bed; **t~enblaß** a deathly pale, white as a sheet; **~engräber** m -s, - gravedigger; **~enhemd** nt shroud; **~enkopf** m skull; **~enschein** m death certificate; **~enstille** f deathly silence; **~entanz** m danse macabre; **~e(r)** mf dead person; **t~fahren** vt irreg run over; **t~geboren** a stillborn; **t~lachen** vr (col) laugh one's head off.

Toto ['to:to] m or nt -s, -s pools pl; **~schein** m pools coupon.

tot- cpd: **~sagen** vt: **jdn ~sagen** say that sb is dead; **~schlagen** vt irreg (lit, fig) kill; **T~schläger** m killer; (Waffe) cosh; **~schweigen** vt irreg hush up; **~stellen** vr pretend to be dead; **~treten** vt irreg trample to death.

Tötung ['tø:tuŋ] f killing.

Toupet [tu'pe:] nt -s, -s toupee.

toupieren [tu'pi:rən] vt back-comb.

Tour [tu:r] f -, -en tour, trip; (Umdrehung) revolution; (Verhaltensart) way; **in einer ~** incessantly; **~enzahl** f number of revolutions; **~enzähler** m rev counter; **~ismus** [tu'rismʊs] m tourism; **~ist** [tu'rist] m tourist; **~istenklasse** f tourist class; **~nee** [tur'ne:] f -, -n (Theat etc) tour; **auf ~nee gehen** go on tour.

Trab [tra:p] m -(e)s trot; **~ant** [tra'bant] m satellite; **~antenstadt** f satellite town; **t~en** vi trot.

Tracht [traxt] f -, -en (Kleidung) costume, dress; **eine ~ Prügel** a sound thrashing; **t~en** vi strive (nach for), endeavour; **jdm nach dem Leben t~en** seek to kill sb.

trächtig ['trɛçtɪç] a Tier pregnant; (fig) rich, fertile.

Tradition [traditsi'o:n] f tradition; **t~ell** [-'nɛl] a traditional.

Trag- [tra:g] cpd: **~bahre** f stretcher; **t~bar** a Gerät portable; Kleidung wearable; (erträglich) bearable.

träge ['trɛ:gə] a sluggish, slow; (Phys) inert.

tragen ['tra:gən] irreg vt carry; Kleidung, Brille wear; Namen, Früchte bear; (erdulden) endure; **sich mit einem Gedanken ~** have an idea in mind; vi (schwanger sein) be pregnant; (Eis) hold; **zum T~ kommen** have an effect.

Träger ['trɛ:gər] m -s, - carrier; wearer; bearer; (Ordens-) holder; (an Kleidung) (shoulder) strap; (Körperschaft etc) sponsor; **~rakete** f launch vehicle; **~rock** m skirt with shoulder straps.

Trag- ['tra:k] cpd: **~fähigkeit** f load-carrying capacity; **~fläche** f (Aviat) wing; **~flügelboot** nt hydrofoil.

Trägheit ['trɛ:khait] f laziness; (Phys) inertia.

Tragi- ['tra:gi] cpd: **~k** f tragedy; **t~komisch** a tragi-comic; **~sch** a tragic.

Tragödie [tra'gø:diə] f tragedy.

Trag- ['tra:k] cpd: **~weite** f range; (fig) scope; **~werk** nt wing assembly.

Train- [trɛ:n] cpd: **~er** m -s, - (Sport) trainer, coach; (Fußball) manager; **t~ieren** [trɛ'ni:rən] vti train; Mensch auch coach; Übung practise; **Fußball t~ieren** do football practice; **~ing** nt -s, -s training; **~ingsanzug** m track suit.

Traktor ['traktor] m tractor.

trällern ['trɛlərn] vti trill, sing.

trampeln ['trampəln] vti trample, stamp.

trampen ['trampən] vi hitch-hike.

Tran [tra:n] m -(e)s, -e train oil, blubber.

tranchieren [trã'ʃi:rən] vt carve.

Tranchierbesteck [trã'ʃi:rbəʃtɛk] nt (pair of) carvers.

Träne ['trɛ:nə] f -, -n tear; **t~n** vi water; **~ngas** nt teargas.

Tränke ['trɛŋkə] f -, -n watering place; **t~n** vt (naß machen) soak; Tiere water.

Trans- cpd: **~formator** [transfor'ma:tor] m transformer; **~istor** [tran'zistor] m transistor; **t~itiv** ['tranziti:f] a transitive; **t~parent** [transpa'rɛnt] a transparent; **~parent** nt -(e)s, -e (Bild) transparency; (Spruchband) banner; **t~pirieren** [transpi'ri:rən] vi perspire; **~plantation** [transplantatsi'o:n] f transplantation; (Haut-) graft(ing); **~port** [trans'port] m -(e)s, -e transport; **t~portieren** [transpor'ti:rən] vt transport; **~portkosten** pl transport charges pl, carriage; **~portmittel** nt means of transportation; **~portunternehmen** nt carrier.

Trapez [tra'pe:ts] nt -es, -e trapeze; (Math) trapezium.

Traube ['traubə] f -, -n grape; bunch (of grapes); **~nlese** f vintage; **~nzucker** m glucose.

trauen ['trauən] vi: **jdm/etw ~** trust sb/sth; vr dare; vt marry.

Trauer ['trauər] f - sorrow; (für Verstorbenen) mourning; **~fall** m death, bereavement; **~marsch** m funeral march; **t~n** vi mourn (um for); **~rand** m black border; **~spiel** nt tragedy.

Traufe ['traufə] f -, -n eaves pl.

träufeln ['trɔyfəln] vti drip.

traulich ['trauliç] a cosy, intimate.

Traum [traum] m -(e)s, **Träume** dream; **~a** nt -s, -men trauma; **~bild** nt vision.

träum- ['trɔym] cpd: **t~en** vti dream; **T~er** m -s, - dreamer; **T~e'rei** f dreaming; **~erisch** a dreamy.

traumhaft a dreamlike; (fig) wonderful.

traurig ['trauriç] a sad; **T~keit** f sadness.

Trau- ['trau] cpd: **~ring** m wedding ring; **~schein** m marriage certificate; **~ung** f wedding ceremony; **~zeuge** m witness (to a marriage).

treffen ['trɛfən] irreg vti strike, hit; (Bemerkung) hurt; (begegnen) meet; Entscheidung etc make; Maßnahmen take; **er hat es gut getroffen** he did well; **~ auf** (+ acc) come across, meet with; vr meet: **es traf sich, daß...** it so happened that...; **es trifft sich gut** it's convenient; **wie es so trifft** as these things happen;

T~ nt **-s,** - meeting; **~d** a pertinent, apposite.
Treff- cpd: **~er** m **-s,** - hit; (Tor) goal; (Los) winner; **t~lich** a excellent; **~punkt** m meeting place.
Treib- ['traib] cpd: **~eis** nt drift ice; **t~en** irreg vt drive; Studien etc pursue; Sport do, go in for; **Unsinn t~en** fool around; vi (Schiff etc) drift; (Pflanzen) sprout; (Cook: aufgehen) rise; (Tee, Kaffee) be diuretic; **~en** nt **-s** activity; **~haus** nt hothouse; **~stoff** m fuel.
trenn- ['trɛn] cpd: **~bar** a separable; **~en** vt separate; (teilen) divide; vr separate; **sich ~en von** part with; **T~schärfe** f (Rad) selectivity; **T~ung** f separation; **T~wand** f partition (wall).
Trepp- [trɛp] cpd: **t~ab** ad downstairs; **t~auf** ad upstairs; **~e** f-, **-n** stair(case); **~engeländer** nt banister; **~enhaus** nt staircase.
Tresor [tre'zo:r] m **-s, -e** safe.
treten ['tre:tən] irreg vi step; (Tränen, Schweiß) appear; **~ nach** kick at; **~ in** (+acc) step in(to); **in Verbindung ~** get in contact; **in Erscheinung ~** appear; vt (mit Fußtritt) kick; (nieder—) tread, trample.
treu [trɔy] a faithful, true; **T~e** f - loyalty, faithfulness; **T~händer** m **-s,** - trustee; **T~handgesellschaft** f trust company; **~herzig** a innocent; **~lich** ad faithfully; **~los** a faithless.
Tribüne [tri'by:nə] f -, **-n** grandstand; (Redner—) platform.
Tribut [tri'bu:t] nt **-(e)s, -e** tribute.
Trichter ['trɪçtər] m **-s,** - funnel; (in Boden) crater.
Trick [trɪk] m **-s, -e** or **-s** trick; **~film** m cartoon.
Trieb [tri:p] m **-(e)s, -e** urge, drive; (Neigung) inclination; (an Baum etc) shoot; **~feder** f (fig) motivating force; **t~haft** a impulsive; **~kraft** f (fig) drive; **~täter** m sex offender; **~wagen** m (Rail) diesel railcar; **~werk** nt engine.
triefen ['tri:fən] vi drip.
triftig ['trɪftɪç] a good, convincing.
Trigonometrie [trigonome'tri:] f trigonometry.
Trikot [tri'ko:] nt **-s, -s** vest; (Sport) shirt; m **-s, -s** (Gewebe) tricot.
Triller ['trɪlər] m **-s,** - (Mus) trill; **t~n** vi trill, warble; **~pfeife** f whistle.
Trimester [tri'mɛstər] nt **-s,** - term.
trink- ['trɪŋk] cpd: **~bar** a drinkable; **~en** vti irreg drink; **T~er** m **-s,** - drinker; **T~geld** nt tip; **T~halm** m (drinking) straw; **T~spruch** m toast; **T~wasser** nt drinking water.
trippeln ['trɪpəln] vi toddle.
Tripper ['trɪpər] m **-s,** - gonorrhoea.
Tritt [trɪt] m **-(e)s, -e** step; (Fuß—) kick; **~brett** nt (Rail) step; (Aut) running-board.
Triumph [tri'umf] m **-(e)s, -e** triumph; **~bogen** m triumphal arch; **t~ieren** [-'fi:rən] vi triumph; (jubeln) exult.
trivial [trivi'a:l] a trivial.
trocken ['trɔkən] a dry; **T~dock** nt dry dock; **T~element** nt dry cell; **T~haube**

f hair-dryer; **T~heit** f dryness; **~legen** vt Sumpf drain; Kind put a clean nappy on; **T~milch** f dried milk.
trocknen ['trɔknən] vti dry.
Troddel ['trɔdəl] f-, **-n** tassel.
Trödel ['trø:dəl] m **-s** (col) junk; **t~n** vi (col) dawdle.
Trödler ['trø:dlər] m **-s,** - secondhand dealer.
Trog [tro:k] **-(e)s,** ˙e trough.
Trommel ['trɔməl] f-, **-n** drum; **~fell** nt eardrum; **t~n** vti drum; **~revolver** m revolver; **~waschmaschine** f tumble-action washing machine.
Trommler ['trɔmlər] m **-s,** - drummer.
Trompete [trɔm'pe:tə] f-, **-n** trumpet; **~r** m **-s,** - trumpeter.
Tropen ['tro:pən] pl tropics pl; **t~beständig** a suitable for the tropics; **~helm** m topee, sun helmet.
Tropf [trɔpf] m **-(e)s,** ˙e (col) rogue; **armer ~** poor devil.
tröpfeln ['trœpfəln] vi drop, trickle.
Tropfen ['trɔpfən] m **-s,** - drop; **t~** vti drip; v impers: **es tropft** a few raindrops are falling; **~weise** ad in drops.
Tropfsteinhöhle f stalactite cave.
tropisch ['tro:pɪʃ] a tropical.
Trost [tro:st] m **-es** consolation, comfort; **t~bedürftig** a in need of consolation.
tröst- ['trø:st] cpd: **~en** vt console, comfort; **T~er(in** f) m **-s,** - comfort(er); **~lich** a comforting.
trost- cpd: **~los** a bleak; Verhältnisse wretched; **T~preis** m consolation prize; **~reich** a comforting.
Tröstung ['trø:stʊŋ] f comfort; consolation.
Trott [trɔt] m **-(e)s, -e** trot; (Routine) routine; **~el** m **-s,** - (col) fool, dope; **t~en** vi trot; **~oir** [trɔto'a:r] nt **-s, -s** or **-e** pavement, sidewalk (US).
Trotz [trɔts] m **-es** pigheadedness; **etw aus ~ tun** do sth just to show them; **jdm zum ~** in defiance of sb; **t~** prep +gen or dat in spite of; **~alter** nt obstinate phase; **t~dem** ad nevertheless; cj although; **t~ig** a defiant, pig-headed; **~kopf** m obstinate child; **~reaktion** f fit of pique.
trüb [try:p] a dull; Flüssigkeit, Glas cloudy; (fig) gloomy; **~en** ['try:bən] vt cloud; vr become clouded; **T~heit** f dullness; cloudiness; gloom; **T~sal** f-, **-e** distress; **~selig** a sad, melancholy; **T~sinn** m depression; **~sinnig** a depressed, gloomy.
trudeln ['tru:dəln] vi (Aviat) (go into a) spin.
Trüffel ['tryfəl] f-, **-n** truffle.
trüg- ['try:g] cpd: **~en** vt irreg deceive; vi be deceptive; **~erisch** a deceptive.
Trugschluß ['tru:gʃlʊs] m false conclusion.
Truhe ['tru:ə] f-, **-n** chest.
Trümmer ['trymər] pl wreckage; (Bau—) ruins pl; **~haufen** m heap of rubble.
Trumpf [trumpf] m **-(e)s,** ˙e (lit, fig) trump; **t~en** vti trump.
Trunk [truŋk] m **-(e)s,** ˙e drink; **t~en** a intoxicated; **~enbold** m **-(e)s, -e** drunkard; **~enheit** f intoxication;

~enheit am Steuer drunken driving;
~sucht f alcoholism.

Trupp [trʊp] m -s, -s troop; ~e f -, -n
troop; (Waffengattung) force; (Schauspiel—)
troupe; ~en pl troops pl; ~enführer m
(military) commander; ~enteil m unit;
~enübungsplatz m training area.

Truthahn ['tru:tha:n] m turkey.

Tube ['tu:bə] f -, -n tube.

Tuberkulose [tubɛrku'lo:zə] f -, -n
tuberculosis.

Tuch [tu:x] nt -(e)s, "er cloth; (Hals—)
scarf; (Kopf—) headscarf; (Hand—) towel.

tüchtig ['tʏçtɪç] a efficient, (cap)able; (col:
kräftig) good, sound; T~keit f efficiency,
ability.

Tücke ['tʏkə] f -, -n (Arglist) malice;
(Trick) trick; (Schwierigkeit) difficulty,
problem; seine ~n haben be temperamental.

tückisch ['tʏkɪʃ] a treacherous; (böswillig)
malicious.

Tugend ['tu:gənt] f -, -en virtue; t~haft a
virtuous.

Tüll [tʏl] m -s, -e tulle; ~e f -, -n spout.

Tulpe ['tʊlpə] f -, -n tulip.

tummeln ['tʊməln] vr romp, gambol; (sich
beeilen) hurry.

Tumor ['tu:mɔr] m -s, -e tumour.

Tümpel ['tʏmpəl] m -s, - pool, pond.

Tumult [tu'mʊlt] m -(e)s, -e tumult.

tun [tu:n] irreg vt (machen) do; (legen) put;
jdm etw ~ (antun) do sth to sb; etw tut
es auch sth will do; das tut nichts that
doesn't matter; das tut nichts zur Sache
that's neither here nor there; vi act; so ~,
als ob act as if; vr: es tut sich
etwas/viel something/a lot is happening.

Tünche ['tʏnçə] f -, -n whitewash; t~n vt
whitewash.

Tunke ['tʊŋkə] f -, -n sauce; t~n vt dip,
dunk.

tunlichst ['tu:nlɪçst] ad if at all possible; ~
bald as soon as possible.

Tunnel ['tʊnəl] m -s, -s or - tunnel.

Tüpfel ['tʏpfəl] m -s, - dot, spot; ~chen nt
(small) dot; t~n vt dot, spot.

tupfen ['tʊpfən] vti dab; (mit Farbe) dot;
T~ m -s, - dot, spot.

Tür [ty:r] f -, -en door.

Turbine [tʊr'bi:nə] f turbine.

Türkis [tʏr'ki:s] m -es, -e turquoise; t~ a
turquoise.

Turm [tʊrm] m -(e)s, "e tower; (Kirch—)
steeple; (Sprung—) diving platform;
(Schach) castle, rook.

Türm- ['tʏrm] cpd: ~chen nt turret;
t~en vr tower up; vt heap up; vi (col)
scarper, bolt.

Turn- ['tʊrn] cpd: t~en vi do gymnastic
exercises; vt perform; ~en nt -s gymnastics; (Sch) physical education, P.E.;
~er(in f) m -s, - gymnast; ~halle f
gym(nasium); ~hose f gym shorts pl.

Turnier [tʊr'ni:r] nt -s, -e tournament.

Turnus ['tʊrnʊs] m -, -se rota; im ~ in
rotation.

Turn- cpd: ~verein m gymnastics club;
~zeug nt gym things pl.

Tusche ['tʊʃə] f -, -n Indian ink.

tuscheln ['tʊʃəln] vti whisper.

Tuschkasten m paintbox.

Tüte ['ty:tə] f -, -n bag.

tuten ['tu:tən] vi (Aut) hoot.

TÜV [tʏf] m MOT.

Typ [ty:p] m -s, -en type; ~e f -, -n
(Print) type.

Typhus ['ty:fʊs] m - typhoid (fever).

typisch ['ty:pɪʃ] a typical (für of).

Tyrann [ty'ran] m -en, -en tyrant; ~ei
[-'nai] f tyranny; t~isch a tyrannical;
t~i'sieren vt tyrannize.

U

U, u [u:] nt U, u.

U-Bahn ['u:ba:n] f underground, tube.

übel ['y:bəl] a bad; (moralisch auch) wicked;
jdm ist ~ sb feels sick; U~ nt -s, - evil;
(Krankheit) disease; ~gelaunt a bad-
tempered, ill-humoured; U~keit f
nausea; ~nehmen vt irreg: jdm eine
Bemerkung etc ~nehmen be offended
at sb's remark etc; U~stand m bad state
of affairs, abuse; ~wollend a malevolent.

üben ['y:bən] vti exercise, practise.

über ['y:bər] prep +dat or acc over; (hoch —
auch) above; (quer — auch) across; (Route)
via; (betreffend) about; ad over; den
ganzen Tag ~ all day long; jdm in etw
(dat) ~ sein (col) be superior to sb in sth;
~ und ~ all over; ~all [y:bər'al] ad
everywhere.

überanstrengen [y:bər'anʃtrɛŋən] vtr
insep overexert (o.s.).

überantworten [y:bər'antvɔrtən] vt insep
hand over, deliver (up).

überarbeiten [y:bər'arbaitən] vt insep
revise, rework; vr overwork (o.s.).

überaus ['y:bər'aus] ad exceedingly.

überbelichten ['y:bərbəliçtən] vt (Phot)
overexpose.

über'bieten vt irreg insep outbid;
(übertreffen) surpass; Rekord break.

Überbleibsel ['y:bərblaipsəl] nt -s, -
residue, remainder.

Überblick ['y:bərblɪk] m view; (fig)
(Darstellung) survey, overview; (Fähigkeit)
overall view, grasp (über +acc of); ü~en
[-'blɪkən] vt insep survey.

überbring- [y:bər'brɪŋ] cpd: ~en vt irreg
insep deliver, hand over; U~er m -s, -
bearer; U~ung f delivery.

überbrücken [y:bər'brʏkən] vt insep
bridge (over).

über'dauern vt insep outlast.

über'denken vt irreg insep think over.

überdies [y:bər'di:s] ad besides.

überdimensional ['y:bərdimenziona:l] a
oversize.

Überdruß ['y:bərdrʊs] m -sses weariness;
bis zum ~ ad nauseam.

überdrüssig ['y:bərdrʏsɪç] a tired, sick
(gen of).

übereifrig ['y:bəraifrɪç] a overkeen,
overzealous.

übereilen [y:bər'ailən] vt insep hurry.

übereilt a (over)hasty, premature.

überein- [y:bər''aɪn] cpd: ~ander
[y:bər'aɪ'nandər] ad one upon the other;
sprechen about each other;
~anderschlagen vt irreg fold, cross;
~kommen vi irreg agree; Ü~kunft f -,
-künfte agreement; ~stimmen vi agree;
Ü~stimmung f agreement.

überempfindlich ['y:bərεmpfɪntlɪç] a
hypersensitive.

überfahren ['y:bərfa:rən] irreg vt take
across; vi (go a)cross; [-'fa:rən] vt insep
(Aut) run over; (fig) walk all over.

Überfahrt ['y:bərfa:rt] f crossing.

Überfall ['y:bərfal] m (Bank—, Mil) raid;
(auf jdn) assault; ü~en [-'falən] vt irreg
insep attack; Bank raid; (besuchen)
surprise.

überfällig ['y:bərfεlɪç] a overdue.

über'fliegen vt irreg insep fly over,
overfly; Buch skim through.

Überfluß ['y:bərflʊs] m (super)abundance,
excess (an +dat of).

überflüssig ['y:bərflʏsɪç] a superfluous.

über'fordern vt insep demand too much
of; Kräfte etc overtax.

über'führen vt insep Leiche etc transport;
Täter have convicted (gen of).

Über'führung f transport; conviction;
(Brücke) bridge, overpass.

Übergabe ['y:bərga:bə] f handing over;
(Mil) surrender.

Übergang ['y:bərgaŋ] m crossing; (Wandel,
Überleitung) transition; ~serscheinung f
transitory phenomenon; ~slösung f
provisional solution, stopgap; ~sstadium
nt state of transition; ~szeit f transitional
period.

über'geben irreg insep vt hand over; (Mil)
surrender; dem Verkehr ~ open to
traffic; vr be sick.

übergehen ['y:bərge:ən] irreg vi (Besitz)
pass; (zum Feind etc) go over, defect;
(Überleiten) go on (zu to); (sich verwandeln)
turn (in +acc into); [-'ge:ən] vt insep pass
over, omit.

Übergewicht ['y:bərgəvɪçt] nt excess
weight; (fig) preponderance.

überglücklich ['y:bərglʏklɪç] a overjoyed.

übergroß ['y:bərgro:s] a outsize, huge.

überhaben ['y:bərha:bən] vt irreg (col) be
fed up with.

überhandnehmen [y:bər'hantne:mən] vi
irreg gain the ascendancy.

überhängen ['y:bərhεŋən] vi irreg
overhang.

überhaupt [y:bər'haupt] ad at all; (im
allgemeinen) in general; (besonders)
especially; ~ nicht not at all.

überheblich [y:bər'he:plɪç] a arrogant;
Ü~keit f arrogance.

über'holen vt insep overtake; (Tech)
overhaul.

überholt a out-of-date, obsolete.

über'hören vt insep not hear; (absichtlich)
ignore.

überirdisch ['y:bər'ɪrdɪʃ] a supernatural,
unearthly.

überkompensieren ['y:bərkɔmpεnzi:rən]
vt insep overcompensate for.

über'laden vt irreg insep overload; a (fig)
cluttered.

über'lassen irreg insep vt: jdm etw ~
leave sth to sb; vr: sich etw (dat) ~ give
o.s. over to sth.

über'lasten vt insep overload; Mensch
overtax.

überlaufen ['y:bərlaufən] irreg vi
(Flüssigkeit) flow over; (zum Feind etc) go
over, defect; [-'laufən] insep vt (Schauer etc)
come over; ~ sein be inundated or
besieged.

Überläufer ['y:bərlɔyfər] m -s, - deserter.

über'leben vt insep survive; Ü~de(r) mf
survivor.

über'legen vt insep consider; a superior;
Ü~heit f superiority.

Überlegung f consideration, deliberation.

über'liefern vt insep hand down,
transmit.

Überlieferung f tradition.

überlisten [y:bər'lɪstən] vt insep outwit.

überm ['y:bərm] = über dem.

Übermacht ['y:bərmaxt] f superior force,
superiority.

übermächtig ['y:bərmεçtɪç] a superior (in
strength); Gefühl etc overwhelming.

übermannen [y:bər'manən] vt insep
overcome.

Übermaß ['y:bərma:s] nt excess (an +dat
of).

übermäßig ['y:bərmε:sɪç] a excessive.

Übermensch ['y:bərmεnʃ] m superman;
ü~lich a superhuman.

übermitteln [y:bər'mɪtəln] vt insep
convey.

übermorgen ['y:bərmɔrgən] ad the day
after tomorrow.

Übermüdung [y:bər'my:dʊŋ] f fatigue,
overtiredness.

Übermut ['y:bərmu:t] m exuberance.

übermütig ['y:bərmy:tɪç] a exuberant,
high-spirited; ~ werden get
overconfident.

übernachten [y:bər'naxtən] vi insep spend
the night (bei jdm at sb's place).

übernächtigt [y:bər'nεçtɪçt] a tired,
sleepy.

Übernahme ['y:bərna:mə] f -, -n taking
over or on, acceptance.

über'nehmen irreg insep vt take on,
accept; Amt, Geschäft take over; vr take on
too much.

über'prüfen vt insep examine, check.

Überprüfung f examination.

überqueren [y:bər'kve:rən] vt insep cross.

überragen [y:bər'ra:gən] vt insep tower
above; (fig) surpass; ['y:bərra:gən] vi
project, stick out.

überraschen [y:bər'raʃən] vt insep
surprise.

Überraschung f surprise.

überreden [y:bər're:dən] vt insep
persuade.

überreich ['y:bərraɪç] a very/too rich;
~en [-'raɪçən] vt insep present, hand over;
~lich a, ad (more than) ample.

überreizt [y:bər'raɪtst] a overwrought.

Überreste ['y:bərrɛstə] pl remains pl, remnants pl.

überrumpeln [y:bər'rumpəln] vt insep take by surprise.

überrunden [y:bər'rundən] vt insep lap.

übers ['y:bərs] = **über das.**

übersättigen [y:bər'zɛtɪgən] vt insep satiate.

Überschall- ['y:bərʃal] cpd: **~flugzeug** nt supersonic jet; **~geschwindigkeit** f supersonic speed.

über'schätzen vt insep overestimate.

überschäumen ['y:bərʃɔymən] vi froth over; (fig) bubble over.

Überschlag ['y:bərʃla:k] m (Fin) estimate; (Sport) somersault; **ü~en** [-'ʃla:gən] irreg insep vt (berechnen) estimate; (auslassen) Seite omit; vr somersault; (Stimme) crack; (Aviat) loop the loop; a lukewarm, tepid; ['y:bərʃla:gən] irreg vt Beine cross; vi (Wellen) break over; (Funken) flash over.

überschnappen ['y:bərʃnapən] vi (Stimme) crack; (col: Mensch) flip one's lid.

über'schneiden vr irreg insep (lit, fig) overlap; (Linien) intersect.

über'schreiben vt irreg insep provide with a heading; jdm etw ~ transfer or make over sth to sb.

über'schreiten vt irreg insep cross over; (fig) exceed; (verletzen) transgress.

Überschrift ['y:bərʃrɪft] f heading, title.

Überschuß ['y:bərʃus] m surplus (an +dat of).

überschüssig ['y:bərʃʏsɪç] a surplus, excess.

über'schütten vt insep jdn/etw mit etw ~ (lit) pour sth over sb/sth; jdn mit etw ~ (fig) shower sb with sth.

Überschwang ['y:bərʃvaŋ] m exuberance, excess.

überschwemmen [y:bər'ʃvɛmən] vt insep flood.

Überschwemmung f flood.

überschwenglich ['y:bərʃvɛŋlɪç] a effusive; **Ü~keit** f effusion.

Übersee ['y:bərze:] f nach/in ~ overseas; **ü~isch** a overseas.

über'sehen vt irreg insep look (out) over; (fig) Folgen see, get an overall view of; (nicht beachten) overlook.

über'senden vt irreg insep send, forward.

übersetz- cpd **~en** [y:bər'zɛtsən] vt insep translate; ['y:bərzɛtsən] vi cross; **Ü~er(in** f) [-'zɛtsər(ɪn)] m -s, - translator; **Ü~ung** [-zɛtsuŋ] f translation; (Tech) gear ratio.

Übersicht ['y:bərzɪçt] f overall view; (Darstellung) survey; **ü~lich** a clear; Gelände open; **~lichkeit** f clarity, lucidity.

übersiedeln ['y:bərzi:dəln] or [y:bər'zi:dəln] vi sep or insep move.

über'spannen vt irreg insep (zu sehr spannen) overstretch; (überdecken) cover.

überspannt a eccentric; Idee wild, crazy; **Ü~keit** f eccentricity.

überspitzt [y:bər'ʃpɪtst] a exaggerated.

über'springen vt irreg insep jump over; (fig) skip.

übersprudeln ['y:bərʃpru:dəln] vi bubble over.

überstehen [y:bər'ʃte:ən] irreg vt insep overcome, get over; Winter etc survive, get through; ['y:bərʃte:ən] vi project.

über'steigen vt irreg insep climb over; (fig) exceed.

über'stimmen vt insep outvote.

Überstunden ['y:bərʃtundən] pl overtime.

über'stürzen vt rush; vr follow (one another) in rapid succession.

überstürzt a (over)hasty.

über'tölpeln [y:bər'tœlpən] vt insep dupe.

über'tönen vt insep drown (out).

Übertrag ['y:bərtra:k] m -(e)s, -träge (Comm) amount brought forward; **ü~bar** [-'tra:kba:r] a transferable; (Med) infectious; **ü~en** [-'tra:gən] irreg insep vt transfer (auf +acc to); (Rad) broadcast; (übersetzen) render; Krankheit transmit; jdm etw **ü~en** assign sth to sb; vr spread (auf +acc to); a figurative; **~ung** [-'tra:guŋ] f transfer(ence); (Rad) broadcast; rendering; transmission.

über'treffen vt irreg insep surpass.

über'treiben vt irreg insep exaggerate.

Übertreibung f exaggeration.

übertreten [y:bər'tre:tən] irreg vt insep cross; Gebot etc break; ['y:bərtre:tən] vi (über Linie, Gebiet) step (over); (Sport) overstep; (in andere Partei) go over (in +acc to); (zu anderem Glauben) be converted.

Über'tretung f violation, transgression.

übertrieben [y:bər'tri:bən] a exaggerated, excessive.

übertrumpfen [y:bər'trumpfən] vt insep outdo; (Cards) overtrump.

übervölkert [y:bər'fœlkərt] a overpopulated.

übervoll ['y:bərfɔl] a overfull.

übervorteilen [y:bər'fɔrtaɪlən] vt insep dupe, cheat.

über'wachen vt insep supervise; Verdächtigen keep under surveillance.

Überwachung f supervision; surveillance.

überwältigen [y:bər'vɛltɪgən] vt insep overpower; **~d** a overwhelming.

überweisen [y:bər'vaɪzən] vt irreg insep transfer.

Überweisung f transfer.

über'wiegen vi irreg insep predominate; **~d** a predominant.

über'winden irreg insep vt overcome; vr make an effort, bring oneself (to do sth).

Überwindung f effort, strength of mind.

Überwurf ['y:bərvurf] m wrap, shawl.

Überzahl ['y:bərtsa:l] f superiority, superior numbers pl; in der ~ sein outnumber sb, be numerically superior.

überzählig ['y:bərtsɛ:lɪç] a surplus.

über'zeugen vt insep convince; **~d** a convincing.

Überzeugung f conviction; **~skraft** f power of persuasion.

überziehen ['y:bərtsi:ən] irreg vt put on [-'tsi:ən]; Konto overdraw.

Überzug ['y:bərtsu:k] m cover; (Belag) coating.

üblich ['y:plɪç] a usual.

U-Boot ['u:bo:t] *nt* submarine.
übrig ['y:brɪç] *a* remaining; **für jdn etwas ~ haben** *(col)* be fond of sb; **die ~en** ['y:brɪgən] the others; **das ~e** the rest; **im ~en** besides; **~bleiben** *vi irreg* remain, be left (over); **~ens** *ad* besides; *(nebenbei bemerkt)* by the way; **~lassen** *vt irreg* leave (over).
Übung ['y:bʊŋ] *f* practice; *(Turn-, Aufgabe etc)* exercise; **~ macht den Meister** practice makes perfect.
Ufer ['u:fər] *nt* **-s, -** bank; *(Meeres-)* shore; **~befestigung** *f* embankment.
Uhr [u:r] *f* **-, -en** clock; *(Armband-)* watch; **wieviel ~ ist es?** what time is it?; **1 ~** 1 o'clock; **20 ~** 8 o'clock, 20.00 (twenty hundred) hours; **~band** *nt* watch strap; **~(en)gehäuse** *nt* clock/ watch case; **~kette** *f* watch chain; **~macher** *m* **-s, -** watchmaker; **~werk** *nt* clockwork; works of a watch; **~zeiger** *m* hand; **~zeigersinn** *m*: **im ~zeigersinn** clockwise; **entgegen dem ~zeigersinn** anticlockwise; **~zeit** *f* time (of day).
Uhu ['u:hu] *m* **-s, -s** eagle owl.
UKW [u:ka:'ve:] *abbr* VHF.
Ulk [ʊlk] *m* **-s, -e** lark; **u~ig** *a* funny.
Ulme ['ʊlmə] *f* **-, -n** elm.
Ultimatum [ʊlti'ma:tʊm] *nt* **-s, Ultimaten** ultimatum.
Ultra- *cpd*: **~kurzwellen** [ʊltra-'kʊrtsvɛlən] *pl* very high frequency; **u~violett** [ʊltra-] *a* ultraviolet.
um [ʊm] *prep* +*acc* (a)round; *(zeitlich)* at; *(mit Größenangabe)* by; *(für)* for; **er schlug ~ sich** he hit about him; **Stunde ~ Stunde** hour after hour; **Auge ~ Auge** an eye for an eye; **~ vieles (besser)** (better) by far; **~ nichts besser** not in the least better; **~ so besser** so much the better; **~ ... willen** for the sake of; *cj (damit)* (in order) to; **zu klug, ~ zu ...** clever to ...; *ad (ungefähr)* about.
umadressieren ['ʊmadrɛsi:rən] *vt* readdress.
umänder- ['ʊm'ɛndər] *cpd*: **~n** *vt* alter; **U~ung** *f* alteration.
umarbeiten ['ʊm'arbaɪtən] *vt* remodel; *Buch etc* revise, rework.
umarmen ['ʊm'armən] *vt insep* embrace.
Umbau ['ʊmbau] *m* **-(e)s, -e** *or* **-ten** reconstruction, alteration(s); **u~en** *vt* rebuild, reconstruct.
umbenennen ['ʊmbənɛnən] *vt irreg* rename.
umbiegen ['ʊmbi:gən] *vt irreg* bend (over).
umbilden ['ʊmbɪldən] *vt* reorganize; *(Pol)* Kabinett reshuffle.
umbinden ['ʊmbɪndən] *vt irreg* Krawatte etc put on; [-'bɪndən] *vt irreg insep* tie (sth) round.
umblättern ['ʊmblɛtərn] *vt* turn over.
umblicken ['ʊmblɪkən] *vr* look around.
umbringen ['ʊmbrɪŋən] *vt irreg* kill.
Umbruch ['ʊmbrʊx] *m* radical change; *(Print)* make-up.
umbuchen ['ʊmbu:xən] *vti* change one's reservation/flight *etc*.
umdenken ['ʊmdɛŋkən] *vi irreg* adjust one's views.

um'drängen *vt insep* crowd round.
umdrehen ['ʊmdre:ən] *vtr* turn (round); Hals wring.
Um'drehung *f* revolution; rotation.
umeinander [ʊm'aɪnandər] *ad* round one another; *(für einander)* for one another.
umfahren ['ʊmfa:rən] *vt irreg* run over; [-'fa:rən] *insep* drive/sail round.
umfallen ['ʊmfalən] *vi irreg* fall down *or* over.
Umfang ['ʊmfaŋ] *m* extent; *(von Buch)* size; *(Reichweite)* range; *(Fläche)* area; *(Math)* circumference; **u~reich** *a* extensive; *Buch etc* voluminous.
um'fassen *vt insep* embrace; *(umgeben)* surround; *(enthalten)* include; **~d** *a* comprehensive, extensive.
umform- ['ʊmfɔrm] *cpd*: **~en** *vt* transform; **U~er** *m* **-s, -** *(Elec)* transformer, converter.
Umfrage ['ʊmfra:gə] *f* poll.
umfüllen ['ʊmfʏlən] *vt* transfer; Wein decant.
umfunktionieren ['ʊmfʊŋktsioni:rən] *vt* convert, transform.
Umgang ['ʊmgaŋ] *m* company; *(mit jdm)* dealings *pl*; *(Behandlung)* way of behaving.
umgänglich ['ʊmgɛŋlɪç] *a* sociable.
Umgangs- *cpd*: **~formen** *pl* manners *pl*; **~sprache** *f* colloquial language.
umgeb- [ʊm'ge:b] *cpd*: **~en** *vt irreg insep* surround; **U~ung** *f* surroundings *pl*; *(Milieu)* environment; *(Personen)* people in one's circle.
umgehen ['ʊmge:ən] *irreg vi* go (a)round; **im Schlosse ~** haunt the castle; **mit jdm grob** *etc* **~** treat sb roughly *etc*; **mit Geld sparsam ~** be careful with one's money; [-'ge:ən] *vt insep* bypass; *(Mil)* outflank; Gesetz etc circumvent; *(vermeiden)* avoid; **'~d** *a* immediate.
Um'gehung *f* bypassing; outflanking; circumvention; avoidance; **~sstraße** *f* bypass.
umgekehrt ['ʊmgəke:rt] *a* reverse(d); *(gegenteilig)* opposite; *ad* the other way around; **und ~** and vice versa.
umgraben ['ʊmgra:bən] *vt irreg* dig up.
umgruppieren ['ʊmgrupi:rən] *vt* regroup.
Umhang ['ʊmhaŋ] *m* wrap, cape.
umhängen ['ʊmhɛŋən] *vt* Bild hang somewhere else; **jdm etw ~** put sth on sb.
umhauen ['ʊmhauən] *vt* fell; *(fig)* bowl over.
umher [ʊm'he:r] *ad* about, around; **~gehen** *vi irreg* walk about; **~reisen** *vi* travel about; **~schweifen** *vi* roam about; **~ziehen** *vi irreg* wander from place to place.
umhinkönnen [ʊm'hɪnkœnən] *vi irreg* **ich kann nicht umhin, das zu tun** I can't help doing it.
umhören ['ʊmhø:rən] *vr* ask around.
Umkehr ['ʊmke:r] *f* **-** turning back; *(Änderung)* change; **u~en** *vi* turn back; *vt* turn round, reverse; Tasche etc turn inside out; Gefäß etc turn upside down.
umkippen ['ʊmkɪpən] *vt* tip over; *vi* overturn; *(fig: Meinung ändern)* change one's mind; *(col: Mensch)* keel over.

Umkleideraum ['ʊmklaɪdəraʊm] *m* changing *or* dressing room.

umkommen ['ʊmkɔmən] *vi irreg* die, perish; *(Lebensmittel)* go bad.

Umkreis ['ʊmkraɪs] *m* neighbourhood; *(Math)* circumcircle; **im ~ von** within a radius of; **u~en** [ʊm'kraɪzən] *vt insep* circle (round); *(Satellit)* orbit.

umladen ['ʊmlaːdən] *vt irreg* transfer, reload.

Umlage ['ʊmlaːgə] *f* share of the costs.

Umlauf ['ʊmlaʊf] *m (Geld—)* circulation; *(von Gestirn)* revolution; *(Schreiben)* circular; **~bahn** *f* orbit.

Umlaut ['ʊmlaʊt] *m* umlaut.

umlegen ['ʊmleːgən] *vt* put on; *(verlegen)* move, shift; *Kosten* share out; *(umkippen)* tip over; *(col: töten)* bump off.

umleiten ['ʊmlaɪtən] *vt* divert.

Umleitung *f* diversion.

umlernen ['ʊmlɛrnən] *vi* learn something new; adjust one's views.

umliegend ['ʊmliːgənt] *a* surrounding.

Umnachtung [ʊm'naxtʊŋ] *f* (mental) derangement.

um'rahmen *vt insep* frame.

um'randen *vt insep* border, edge.

umrechnen ['ʊmrɛçnən] *vt* convert.

Umrechnung *f* conversion; **~skurs** *m* rate of exchange.

um'reißen *vt irreg insep* outline, sketch.

um'ringen *vt insep* surround.

Umriß ['ʊmrɪs] *m* outline.

umrühren ['ʊmryːrən] *vti* stir.

ums [ʊms] = **um das.**

umsatteln ['ʊmzatəln] *vi (col)* change one's occupation; switch.

Umsatz ['ʊmzats] *m* turnover.

umschalten ['ʊmʃaltən] *vt* switch.

Umschau ['ʊmʃaʊ] *f* look(ing) round; **~ halten nach** look around for; **u~en** *vr* look round.

Umschlag ['ʊmʃlaːk] *m* cover; *(Buch- auch)* jacket; *(Med)* compress; *(Brief—)* envelope; *(Wechsel)* change; *(von Hose)* turn-up; **u~en** ['ʊmʃlaːgən] *irreg vi* change; *(Naut)* capsize; *vt* knock over; *Armel* turn up; *Seite* turn over; *Waren* transfer; **~platz** *m (Comm)* distribution centre.

umschreiben *vt irreg* ['ʊmʃraɪbən] *(neu—)* rewrite; *(übertragen)* transfer *(auf +acc* to); [-'ʃraɪbən] *insep* paraphrase; *(abgrenzen)* circumscribe, define.

umschulen ['ʊmʃuːlən] *vt* retrain; *Kind* send to another school.

umschwärmen [ʊm'ʃvɛrmən] *vt insep* swarm round; *(fig)* surround, idolize.

Umschweife ['ʊmʃvaɪfə] *pl:* **ohne ~** without beating about the bush, straight out.

Umschwung ['ʊmʃvʊŋ] *m* change (around), revolution.

umsehen ['ʊmzeːən] *vr irreg* look around or about; *(suchen)* look out *(nach* for).

umseitig ['ʊmzaɪtɪç] *ad* overleaf.

Umsicht ['ʊmzɪçt] *f* prudence, caution; **u~ig** *a* cautious, prudent.

umsonst [ʊm'zɔnst] *ad* in vain; *(gratis)* for nothing.

umspringen ['ʊmʃprɪŋən] *vi irreg* change; *(Wind auch)* veer; **mit jdm ~** treat sb badly.

Umstand ['ʊmʃtant] *m* circumstance; **Umstände** *pl (fig: Schwierigkeiten)* fuss; **in anderen Umständen sein** be pregnant; **Umstände machen** go to a lot of trouble; **unter Umständen** possibly; **mildernde Umstände** *(Jur)* extenuating circumstances.

umständlich ['ʊmʃtɛntlɪç] *a,ad* Methode cumbersome, complicated; *Ausdrucksweise, Erklärung auch* long-winded; *Mensch* ponderous.

Umstands- *cpd:* **~kleid** *nt* maternity dress; **~wort** *nt* adverb.

Umstehende(n) ['ʊmʃteːəndə(n)] *pl* bystanders *pl.*

Umsteig- ['ʊmʃtaɪg] *cpd:* **~ekarte** *f* transfer ticket; **u~en** *vi irreg (Rail)* change.

umstellen ['ʊmʃtɛlən] *vt (an anderen Ort)* change round, rearrange; *(Tech)* convert; *vr* adapt o.s. *(auf +acc* to); [ʊm'ʃtɛlən] *vt insep* surround.

Umstellung ['ʊmʃtɛlʊŋ] *f* change; *(Umgewöhnung)* adjustment; *(Tech)* conversion.

umstimmen ['ʊmʃtɪmən] *vt (Mus)* retune; **jdn ~** make sb change his mind.

umstoßen ['ʊmʃtoːsən] *vt irreg (lit)* overturn; *Plan etc* change, upset.

umstritten [ʊm'ʃtrɪtən] *a* disputed.

Umsturz ['ʊmʃtʊrts] *m* overthrow.

umstürzen ['ʊmʃtʏrtsən] *vt (umwerfen)* overturn; *vi* collapse, fall down; *Wagen* overturn.

umstürzlerisch *a* revolutionary.

Umtausch ['ʊmtaʊʃ] *m* exchange; **u~en** *vt* exchange.

Umtriebe ['ʊmtriːbə] *pl* machinations *pl,* intrigues *pl.*

umtun ['ʊmtuːn] *vr irreg* see; **sich nach etw ~** look for sth.

umwandeln ['ʊmvandəln] *vt* change, convert; *(Elec)* transform.

umwechseln ['ʊmvɛksəln] *vt* change.

Umweg ['ʊmveːk] *m* detour, roundabout way.

Umwelt ['ʊmvɛlt] *f* environment; **~verschmutzung** *f* environmental pollution.

umwenden ['ʊmvɛndən] *vtr irreg* turn (round).

um'werben *vt irreg insep* court, woo.

umwerfen ['ʊmvɛrfən] *vt irreg (lit)* upset, overturn; *Mantel* throw on; *(fig: erschüttern)* upset, throw.

umziehen ['ʊmtsiːən] *irreg vtr* change; *vi* move.

umzingeln [ʊm'tsɪŋəln] *vt insep* surround, encircle.

Umzug ['ʊmtsuːk] *m* procession; *(Wohnungs—)* move, removal.

unab- ['ʊn'ap] *cpd:* **~'änderlich** *a* irreversible, unalterable; **~hängig** *a* independent; **U~hängigkeit** *f* independence; **~hängig** *a* indispensable; **zur Zeit ~kömmlich** not free 'at the moment; **~lässig** *a* incessant, constant; **~sehbar** *a* immeasurable; *Folgen* unforeseeable; *Kosten* incalculable; ~**sichtlich** a unintentional; ~'**wendbar** a inevitable.

unachtsam ['ʊn'axtza:m] a careless; U~**keit** f carelessness.

unan- ['ʊn'an] cpd: ~'**fechtbar** a indisputable; ~**gebracht** a uncalled-for; ~**gemessen** a inadequate; ~**genehm** a unpleasant; U~**nehmlichkeit** f inconvenience; pl trouble; ~**sehnlich** a unsightly; ~**ständig** a indecent, improper; U~**ständigkeit** f indecency, impropriety.

unappetitlich ['ʊn'apeti:tlɪç] a unsavoury.

Unart ['ʊn'a:rt] f bad manners pl; *(Angewohnheit)* bad habit; **u~ig** a naughty, badly behaved.

unauf- ['ʊn'aʊf] cpd: ~**fällig** a unobtrusive; *Kleidung* inconspicuous; ~'**findbar** a undiscoverable, not to be found; ~**gefordert** a unasked; ad spontaneously; ~**haltsam** a irresistible; ~'**hörlich** a incessant, continuous; ~**merksam** a inattentive; ~**richtig** a insincere.

unaus- ['ʊn'aʊs] cpd: ~'**bleiblich** a inevitable, unavoidable; ~**geglichen** a volatile; ~'**sprechlich** a inexpressible; ~'**stehlich** a intolerable; ~'**weichlich** a inescapable, ineluctable.

unbändig ['ʊnbɛndɪç] a extreme, excessive.

unbarmherzig ['ʊnbarmhɛrtsɪç] a pitiless, merciless.

unbeabsichtigt ['ʊnbə'apzɪçtɪçt] a unintentional.

unbeachtet ['ʊnbə'axtət] a unnoticed, ignored.

unbedenklich ['ʊnbədɛŋklɪç] a unhesitating; *Plan* unobjectionable; ad without hesitation.

unbedeutend ['ʊnbədɔytənt] a insignificant, unimportant; *Fehler* slight.

unbedingt ['ʊnbədɪŋt] a unconditional; ad absolutely; **mußt du** ~ **gehen?** do you really have to go?

unbefangen ['ʊnbəfaŋən] a impartial, unprejudiced; *(ohne Hemmungen)* uninhibited; U~**heit** f impartiality; uninhibitedness.

unbefriedig- ['ʊnbəfri:dɪg] cpd: ~**end** a unsatisfactory; ~**t** [-dɪçt] a unsatisfied, dissatisfied.

unbefugt ['ʊnbəfu:kt] a unauthorized.

unbegabt ['ʊnbəga:pt] a untalented.

unbegreiflich ['ʊnbə'graɪflɪç] a inconceivable.

unbegrenzt ['ʊnbəgrɛntst] a unlimited.

unbegründet ['ʊnbəgryndət] a unfounded.

Unbehag- ['ʊnbəha:g] cpd: ~**en** nt discomfort; **u~lich** [-klɪç] a uncomfortable; *Gefühl* uneasy.

unbeholfen ['ʊnbəhɔlfən] a awkward, clumsy; U~**heit** f awkwardness, clumsiness.

unbeirrt ['ʊnbə'ɪrt] a imperturbable.

unbekannt ['ʊnbəkant] a unknown.

unbekümmert ['ʊnbəkʏmərt] a unconcerned.

unbeliebt ['ʊnbəli:pt] a unpopular; U~**heit** f unpopularity.

unbequem ['ʊnbəkve:m] a *Stuhl*

uncomfortable; *Mensch* bothersome; *Regelung* inconvenient.

unberech- ['ʊnbə'rɛç] cpd: ~**enbar** [ʊnbə'reçənba:r] a incalculable; *Mensch, Verhalten* unpredictable; ~**tigt** ['ʊnbəreçtɪçt] a unjustified; *(nicht erlaubt)* unauthorized.

unberufen ['ʊnbə'ru:fən] interj touch wood.

unberührt ['ʊnbəry:rt] a untouched, intact; **sie ist noch** ~ she is still a virgin.

unbescheiden ['ʊnbəʃaɪdən] a presumptuous.

unbeschreiblich [ʊnbə'ʃraɪplɪç] a indescribable.

unbesonnen ['ʊnbəzɔnən] a unwise, rash, imprudent.

unbeständig ['ʊnbəʃtɛndɪç] a *Mensch* inconstant; *Wetter* unsettled; *Lage* unstable.

unbestechlich [ʊnbə'ʃtɛçlɪç] a incorruptible.

unbestimmt ['ʊnbəʃtɪmt] a indefinite; *Zukunft auch* uncertain; U~**heit** f vagueness.

unbeteiligt [ʊnbə'taɪlɪçt] a unconcerned, indifferent.

unbeugsam ['ʊnbɔ*ykza:m] a inflexible, stubborn; *Wille auch* unbending.

unbewacht ['ʊnbəvaxt] a unguarded, unwatched.

unbeweglich ['ʊnbəve:klɪç] a immovable.

unbewußt ['ʊnbəvʊst] a unconscious.

unbrauchbar ['ʊnbrauxba:r] a *Arbeit* useless; *Gerät auch* unusable; U~**keit** f uselessness.

und [ʊnt] cj and; ~ **so weiter** and so on.

Undank ['ʊdaŋk] m ingratitude; **u~bar** a ungrateful; ~**barkeit** f ingratitude.

undefinierbar [ʊndefi'ni:rba:r] a indefinable.

undenkbar [ʊn'dɛŋkba:r] a inconceivable.

undeutlich ['ʊndɔytlɪç] a indistinct.

undicht ['ʊndɪçt] a leaky.

Unding ['ʊndɪŋ] nt absurdity.

unduldsam ['ʊnduldsa:m] a intolerant.

undurch- ['ʊndʊrç] cpd: ~**führbar** [-'fy:rba:r] a impracticable; ~**lässig** [-lɛsɪç] a waterproof, impermeable; ~**sichtig** [-zɪçtɪç] a opaque; *(fig)* obscure.

uneben ['ʊn'e:bən] a uneven.

unehelich ['ʊn'e:əlɪç] a illegitimate.

uneigennützig ['ʊn'aɪgənnʏtsɪç] a unselfish.

uneinig ['ʊn'aɪnɪç] a divided; ~ **sein** disagree; U~**keit** f discord, dissension.

uneins ['ʊn'aɪns] a at variance, at odds.

unempfindlich ['ʊn'ɛmpfɪntlɪç] a insensitive; U~**keit** f insensitivity.

unendlich [ʊn"ɛntlɪç] a infinite; U~**keit** f infinity.

unent- ['ʊn'ɛnt] cpd: ~**behrlich** [-'be:rlɪç] a indispensable; ~**geltlich** [-gɛltlɪç] a free (of charge); ~**schieden** [-'ʃi:dən] a undecided; ~**schieden enden** *(Sport)* end in a draw; ~**schlossen** [-'ʃlɔsən] a undecided; irresolute; ~**wegt** [-'ve:kt] a unswerving; *(unaufhörlich)* incessant.

uner- [ʊn'ɛr] cpd: ~**bittlich** [-bɪtlɪç] a unyielding, inexorable; ~**fahren** [-fa:rən] a inexperienced; ~**freulich** [-frɔ*ylɪç] unpleasant; ~**gründlich** [-'gryntlıç] a unfathomable; ~**heblich** [-he:plıç] a unimportant; ~**hört** [-hø:rt] a unheard-of; *Bitte* outrageous; ~**läßlich** [-'lɛslıç] a indispensable; ~**laubt** [-laupt] a unauthorized; ~**meßlich** [-'mɛslıç] a immeasurable, immense; ~**müdlich** [-'my:tlıç] a indefatigable; ~**sättlich** [-'zɛtlıç] a insatiable; ~**schöpflich** [-'ʃœpflıç] a inexhaustible; ~**schütterlich** [-'ʃytərlıç] a unshakeable; ~**schwinglich** [-'ʃvıŋlıç] a *Preis* exorbitant; too expensive; ~**träglich** [-'trɛ:klıç] a unbearable; *Frechheit* insufferable; ~**wartet** [-vartət] a unexpected; ~**wünscht** [-vynʃt] a undesirable, unwelcome; ~**zogen** [-tso:gən] a ill-bred, rude.

unfähig ['unfɛ:ıç] a incapable (*zu* of); incompetent; **U~keit** f incapacity; incompetence.

unfair ['unfɛ:r] a unfair.

Unfall ['unfal] m accident; ~**flucht** f hit-and-run (driving); ~**stelle** f scene of the accident; ~**versicherung** f accident insurance.

unfaßbar [ʊn'fasba:r] a inconceivable.

unfehlbar [ʊn'fe:lba:r] a infallible; *ad* inevitably; **U~keit** f infallibility.

unflätig ['unflɛ:tıç] a rude.

unfolgsam ['unfɔlkza:m] a disobedient.

unfrankiert ['unfraŋki:rt] a unfranked.

unfrei ['unfraɪ] a not free, unfree; ~**willig** a involuntary, against one's will.

unfreundlich ['unfrɔyntlıç] a unfriendly; **U~keit** f unfriendliness.

Unfriede(n) ['unfri:də(n)] m dissension, strife.

unfruchtbar ['unfrʊxtba:r] a infertile; *Gespräche* unfruitful; **U~keit** f infertility; unfruitfulness.

Unfug ['unfu:k] m -s (*Benehmen*) mischief; (*Unsinn*) nonsense; **grober** ~ (*Jur*) gross misconduct; malicious damage.

ungeachtet ['ungə'axtət] prep +gen notwithstanding.

ungeahnt ['ungə'a:nt] a unsuspected, undreamt-of.

ungebeten ['ungəbe:tən] a uninvited.

ungebildet ['ungəbıldət] a uneducated; uncultured.

ungebräuchlich ['ungəbrɔyçlıç] a unusual, uncommon.

ungedeckt ['ungədɛkt] a *Scheck* uncovered.

Ungeduld ['ungədult] f impatience; **u~ig** [-dıç] a impatient.

ungeeignet ['ungə'aıgnət] a unsuitable.

ungefähr ['ungəfɛ:r] a rough, approximate; **das kommt nicht von** ~ that's hardly surprising; ~**lich** a not dangerous, harmless.

ungehalten ['ungəhaltən] a indignant.

ungeheuer ['ungəhɔyər] a huge; *ad* (*col*) enormously; **U~** *nt* -s, - monster; ~**lich** [-'hɔyərlıç] a monstrous.

ungehobelt ['ungəho:bəlt] a (*fig*) uncouth.

ungehörig ['ungəhø:rıç] a impertinent, improper; **U~keit** f impertinence.

ungehorsam ['ungəho:rza:m] a disobedient; **U~** m disobedience.

ungeklärt ['ungəklɛ:rt] a not cleared up; *Rätsel* unsolved; *Abwasser* untreated.

ungeladen ['ungəla:dən] a not loaded; (*Elec*) uncharged; *Gast* uninvited.

ungelegen ['ungəle:gən] a inconvenient.

ungelernt ['ungəlɛrnt] a unskilled.

ungelogen ['ungəlo:gən] *ad* really, honestly.

ungemein ['ungəmaın] a uncommon.

ungemütlich ['ungəmy:tlıç] a uncomfortable; *Person* disagreeable.

ungenau ['ungənau] a inaccurate; **U~igkeit** f inaccuracy.

ungeniert ['unʒeni:rt] a free and easy, unceremonious; *ad* without embarrassment, freely.

ungenießbar ['ungəni:sba:r] a inedible; undrinkable; (*col*) unbearable.

ungenügend ['ungəny:gənt] a insufficient, inadequate.

ungepflegt ['ungəpfle:kt] a *Garten etc* untended; *Person* unkempt; *Hände* neglected.

ungerade ['ungəra:də] a uneven, odd.

ungerecht ['ungərɛçt] a unjust; ~**fertigt** a unjustified; **U~igkeit** f injustice, unfairness.

ungern ['ungɛrn] *ad* unwillingly, reluctantly.

ungeschehen ['ungəʃe:ən] a: ~ **machen** undo.

Ungeschick- ['ungəʃık] cpd: ~**lichkeit** f clumsiness; **u~t** a awkward, clumsy.

ungeschminkt ['ungəʃmıŋkt] a without make-up; (*fig*) unvarnished.

ungesetzlich ['ungəzɛtslıç] a illegal.

ungestempelt ['ungəʃtɛmpəlt] a *Briefmarke* unfranked, uncancelled.

ungestört ['ungəʃtø:rt] a undisturbed.

ungestraft ['ungəʃtra:ft] ad with impunity.

ungestüm ['ungəʃty:m] a impetuous; tempestuous; **U~** *nt* -(e)s impetuosity; passion.

ungesund ['ungəzʊnt] a unhealthy.

ungetrübt ['ungətry:pt] a clear; (*fig*) untroubled; *Freude* unalloyed.

Ungetüm ['ungəty:m] *nt* -(e)s, -e monster.

ungewiß ['ungəvıs] a uncertain; **U~heit** f uncertainty.

ungewöhnlich ['ungəvø:nlıç] a unusual.

ungewohnt ['ungəvo:nt] a unaccustomed.

Ungeziefer ['ungətsi:fər] *nt* -s vermin.

ungezogen ['ungətso:gən] a rude, impertinent; **U~heit** f rudeness, impertinence.

ungezwungen ['ungətsvʊŋən] a natural, unconstrained.

ungläubig ['unglɔybıç] a unbelieving; **ein ~er Thomas** a doubting Thomas; **die U~en** the infidel(s).

unglaub- cpd: ~**lich** [ʊn'glauplıç] a incredible; ~**würdig** ['unglaupvyrdıç] a untrustworthy, unreliable; *Geschichte* improbable.

ungleich ['unglaıç] a dissimilar; unequal; *ad* incomparably; ~**artig** a different; **U~heit** f dissimilarity; inequality.

Unglück ['ungyk] *nt* -(e)s, -e misfortune; (*Pech*) bad luck; (~*sfall*) calamity, disaster; *(Verkehrs—)* accident; **u~lich** *a* unhappy; *(erfolglos)* unlucky; *(unerfreulich)* unfortunate; **u~licherweise** [-'waɪɪzə] *ad* unfortunately; **u~selig** *a* calamitous; *Person* unfortunate; **~sfall** *m* accident, calamity.

ungültig ['ʊngʏltɪç] *a* invalid; **U~keit** *f* invalidity.

ungünstig ['ʊngʏnstɪç] *a* unfavourable.

ungut ['ʊngu:t] *a Gefühl* uneasy; **nichts für ~** no offence.

unhaltbar ['ʊnhaltba:r] *a* untenable.

Unheil ['ʊnhaɪl] *nt* evil; *(Unglück)* misfortune; **~ anrichten** cause mischief; **u~bar** *a* incurable; **u~bringend** *a* fatal, fateful; **u~voll** *a* disastrous.

unheimlich ['ʊnhaɪmlɪç] *a* weird, uncanny; *ad (col)* tremendously.

unhöflich ['ʊnhö:flɪç] *a* impolite; **U~keit** *f* impoliteness.

unhygienisch ['ʊnhygie'e:nɪʃ] *a* unhygienic.

Uni ['ʊni] *f-, -s* university; **u~** [y'ni:] *a* self-coloured.

Uniform [uni'fɔrm] *f* uniform; **u~iert** [-'mi:rt] *a* uniformed.

uninteressant ['ʊn'ɪnterɛsant] *a* uninteresting.

Universität [univerzi'tɛ:t] *f* university.

unkenntlich ['ʊnkɛntlɪç] *a* unrecognizable.

Unkenntnis ['ʊnkɛntnɪs] *f* ignorance.

unklar ['ʊnkla:r] *a* unclear; **im ~en sein über** *(+acc)* be in the dark about; **U~heit** *f* unclarity; *(Unentschiedenheit)* uncertainty.

unklug ['ʊnklu:k] *a* unwise.

Unkosten ['ʊnkɔstən] *pl* expense(s).

Unkraut ['ʊnkraut] *nt* weed; weeds *pl*.

unlängst ['ʊnlɛŋst] *ad* not long ago.

unlauter ['ʊnlautər] *a* unfair.

unleserlich ['ʊnle:zərlɪç] *a* illegible.

unlogisch ['ʊnlo:gɪʃ] *a* illogical.

unlösbar ['ʊn'lö:sbar], **unlöslich** ['ʊn'lö:slɪç] *a* insoluble.

Unlust ['ʊnlʊst] *f* lack of enthusiasm; **u~ig** *a* unenthusiastic.

unmäßig ['ʊnmɛ:sɪç] *a* immoderate.

Unmenge ['ʊnmɛŋə] *f* tremendous number, hundreds *pl*.

Unmensch ['ʊnmɛnʃ] *m* ogre, brute; **u~lich** *a* inhuman, brutal; *(ungeheuer)* awful.

unmerklich [ʊn'mɛrklɪç] *a* imperceptible.

unmißverständlich ['ʊnmɪsfɛrʃtɛntlɪç] *a* unmistakable.

unmittelbar ['ʊnmɪtəlba:r] *a* immediate.

unmöbliert ['ʊnmöbli:rt] *a* unfurnished.

unmöglich ['ʊnmö:klɪç] *a* impossible; **U~keit** *f* impossibility.

unmoralisch ['ʊnmora:lɪʃ] *a* immoral.

Unmut ['ʊnmu:t] *m* ill humour.

unnachgiebig ['ʊnna:xgi:bɪç] *a* unyielding.

unnahbar [ʊn'na:ba:r] *a* unapproachable.

unnötig ['ʊnnö:tɪç] *a* unnecessary; **~erweise** *ad* unnecessarily.

unnütz ['ʊnnʏts] *a* useless.

unordentlich ['ʊn'ɔrdəntlɪç] *a* untidy.

Unordnung ['ʊn'ɔrdnʊŋ] *f* disorder.

unparteiisch ['ʊnpartaɪʃ] *a* impartial; **U~e(r)** *m* umpire; *(Fußball)* referee.

unpassend ['ʊnpasənt] *a* inappropriate; *Zeit* inopportune.

unpäßlich ['ʊnpɛslɪç] *a* unwell.

unpersönlich ['ʊnpɛrzö:nlɪç] *a* impersonal.

unpolitisch ['ʊnpoli:tɪʃ] *a* apolitical.

unpraktisch ['ʊnpraktɪʃ] *a* unpractical.

unproduktiv ['ʊnprodukti:f] *a* unproductive.

unproportioniert ['ʊnproportsioni:rt] *a* out of proportion.

unpünktlich ['ʊnpʏnktlɪç] *a* unpunctual.

unrationell ['ʊnratsionɛl] *a* inefficient.

unrecht ['ʊnrɛçt] *a* wrong; **U~ ~** *nt* wrong; **zu U~** wrongly; **U~ haben, im U~ sein** be wrong; **~mäßig** *a* unlawful, illegal.

unregelmäßig ['ʊnre:gəlmɛsɪç] *a* irregular; **U~keit** *f* irregularity.

unreif ['ʊnraɪf] *a Obst* unripe; *(fig)* immature.

unrentabel ['ʊnrɛnta:bəl] *a* unprofitable.

unrichtig ['ʊnrɪçtɪç] *a* incorrect, wrong.

Unruhe ['ʊnru:ə] *f-, -en (von Uhr)* balance; **~e** *f-, -n* unrest; **~estifter** *m* troublemaker; **u~ig** *a* restless.

uns [ʊns] *pron acc, dat* of **wir** us; ourselves.

unsachlich ['ʊnzaxlɪç] *a* not to the point, irrelevant; *(persönlich)* personal.

unsagbar [ʊn'za:kba:r], **unsäglich** [ʊn'zɛ:klɪç] *a* indescribable.

unsanft ['ʊnzanft] *a* rough.

unsauber ['ʊnzaubər] *a* unclean, dirty; *(fig)* crooked; *(Mus)* fuzzy.

unschädlich ['ʊnʃɛ:tlɪç] *a* harmless; **jdn/etw ~ machen** render sb/sth harmless.

unscharf ['ʊnʃarf] *a* indistinct; *Bild etc* out of focus, blurred.

unscheinbar ['ʊnʃaɪnba:r] *a* insignificant; *Aussehen, Haus etc.* unprepossessing.

unschlagbar [ʊn'ʃla:kba:r] *a* invincible.

unschlüssig ['ʊnʃlʏsɪç] *a* undecided.

Unschuld ['ʊnʃʊlt] *f* innocence; **u~ig** [-dɪç] *a* innocent.

unselbständig ['ʊnzɛlpʃtɛndɪç] *a* dependent, over-reliant on others.

unser ['ʊnzər] *pron acc, gen* of **wir** of us; **~e(r,s)** ours; **~einer, ~eins, ~esgleichen** *pron* people like us; **~erseits** *ad* on our part; **~twegen, ~twillen** *ad (für uns)* for our sake; *(wegen uns)* on our account; **~ige** *pron:* **der/die/das ~ige** ours.

unsicher ['ʊnzɪçər] *a* uncertain; *Mensch* insecure; **U~heit** *f* uncertainty; insecurity.

unsichtbar ['ʊnzɪçtba:r] *a* invisible; **U~keit** *f* invisibility.

Unsinn ['ʊnzɪn] *m* nonsense; **u~ig** *a* non-sensical.

Unsitte ['ʊnzɪtə] *f* deplorable habit.

unsittlich ['ʊnzɪtlɪç] *a* indecent; **U~keit** *f* indecency.

unsportlich ['ʊnʃpɔrtlɪç] *a* not sporty; unfit; *Verhalten* unsporting.

unsre ['ʊnzrə] = unsere.
unsrige ['ʊnzrɪgə] = unserige.
unsterblich ['ʊnʃtɛrplɪç] a immortal;
U~keit f immortality.
Unstimmigkeit ['ʊnʃtɪmɪçkaɪt] f inconsistency; (Streit) disagreement.
unsympathisch ['ʊnzympa:tɪʃ] a
unpleasant; er ist mir ~ I don't like him.
untätig ['ʊntɛ:tɪç] a idle.
untauglich ['ʊntaʊklɪç] a unsuitable; (Mil)
unfit; U~keit f unsuitability; unfitness.
unteilbar [ʊn'taɪlba:r] a indivisible.
unten ['ʊntən] ad below; (im Haus) downstairs; (an der Treppe etc) at the bottom;
nach ~ down; ~ am Berg etc at the
bottom of the mountain etc; ich bin bei
ihm ~ durch (col) he's through with me.
unter ['ʊntər] prep +acc or dat under,
below; (bei Menschen) among; (während)
during; ad under.
Unter- ['ʊntər] cpd: ~abteilung f subdivision; ~arm m forearm.
unterbe- ['ʊntərbə] cpd: ~lichten vt
(Phot) underexpose; U~wußtsein nt subconscious; ~zahlt a underpaid.
unterbieten [ʊntər'bi:tən] vt irreg insep
(Comm) undercut; Rekord lower, reduce.
unterbinden [ʊntər'bɪndən] vt irreg insep
stop, call a halt to.
Unterbodenschutz [ʊntər'bo:dənʃʊts] m
(Aut) underseal.
unterbrech- [ʊntər'brɛç] cpd: ~en vt
irreg insep interrupt; U~ung f
interruption.
unterbringen ['ʊntərbrɪŋən] vt irreg (in
Koffer) stow; (in Zeitung) place; Person (in
Hotel etc) accommodate, put up; (beruflich)
fix up (auf, in with).
unterdessen [ʊntər'dɛsən] ad meanwhile.
Unterdruck ['ʊntərdrʊk] m low pressure.
unterdrücken [ʊntər'drykən] vt insep
suppress; Leute oppress.
untere(r,s) ['ʊntərə(r,z)] a lower.
untereinander [ʊntəraɪ'nandər] ad with
each other; among themselves etc.
unterentwickelt ['ʊntərɛntvɪkəlt] a
underdeveloped.
unterernährt ['ʊntərɛrnɛːrt] a under-
nourished, underfed.
Unterernährung f malnutrition.
Unter'führung f subway, underpass.
Untergang ['ʊntərgaŋ] m (down-)fall,
decline; (Naut) sinking; (von Gestirn)
setting.
unter'geben a subordinate.
untergehen ['ʊntərgeːən] vi irreg go down;
(Sonne auch) set; (Staat) fall; (Volk) perish;
(Welt) come to an end; (im Lärm) be
drowned.
Untergeschoß ['ʊntərgəʃɔs] nt basement.
unter'gliedern vt insep subdivide.
Untergrund ['ʊntərgrʊnt] m foundation;
(Pol) underground; ~bahn f underground, tube, subway (US); ~bewegung f
underground (movement).
unterhalb ['ʊntərhalp] prep +gen, ad
below; ~ von below.
Unterhalt ['ʊntərhalt] m maintenance;
u~en [ʊntər'haltən] irreg insep vt main-

tain; (belustigen) entertain; vr talk; (sich
belustigen) enjoy o.s.; u~end
[ʊntər'haltənt] a entertaining; ~ung f
maintenance; (Belustigung) entertainment,
amusement; (Gespräch) talk.
Unterhändler ['ʊntərhɛntlər] m
negotiator.
Unterhemd ['ʊntərhɛmt] nt vest, undershirt (US).
Unterhose ['ʊntərhoːzə] f underpants pl.
unterirdisch ['ʊntər'ɪrdɪʃ] a underground.
Unterkiefer ['ʊntərkiːfər] m lower jaw.
unterkommen ['ʊntərkɔmən] vi irreg find
shelter; find work; das ist mir noch nie
untergekommen I've never met with
that.
Unterkunft ['ʊntərkʊnft] f -, -künfte
accommodation.
Unterlage ['ʊntərlaːgə] f foundation;
(Beleg) document; (Schreib– etc) pad.
unter'lassen vt irreg insep (versäumen)
fail (to do); (sich enthalten) refrain from.
unterlaufen [ʊntər'laʊfən] vi irreg insep
happen, a: mit Blut ~ suffused with
blood; (Augen) bloodshot.
unterlegen ['ʊntərleːgən] vt lay or put
under; [ʊntər'leːgən] a inferior (dat to);
(besiegt) defeated.
Unterleib ['ʊntərlaɪp] m abdomen.
unter'liegen vi irreg insep be defeated or
overcome (jdm by sb); (unterworfen sein)
be subject to.
Untermiete ['ʊntərmiːtə] f: zur ~
wohnen be a subtenant or lodger; ~r(in
f) m subtenant, lodger.
unter'nehmen vt irreg insep undertake;
U~ nt -s, - undertaking, enterprise (auch
Comm); ~d a enterprising, daring.
Unternehmer [ʊntər'neːmər] m -s, -
entrepreneur, businessman.
Unterprima ['ʊntərpriːma] f -, -primen
eighth year of secondary school.
Unterredung [ʊntər'reːdʊŋ] f discussion,
talk.
Unterricht ['ʊntərrɪçt] m -(e)s, -e
instruction, lessons pl; u~en [ʊntər-
'rɪçtən] insep vt instruct; (Sch) teach; vr
inform o.s. (über +acc about).
Unterrock [ʊntər'rɔk] m petticoat, slip.
unter'sagen vt insep forbid (jdm etw sb to
do sth).
unter'schätzen vt insep underestimate.
unter'scheiden irreg insep vt distinguish;
vr differ.
Unter'scheidung f (Unterschied)
distinction; (Unterscheiden) differentiation.
Unterschied ['ʊntərʃiːt] m -(e)s, -e
difference, distinction; im ~ zu as
distinct from; u~lich a varying, differing;
(diskriminierend) discriminatory; u~slos
ad indiscriminately.
unter'schlagen vt irreg insep embezzle;
(verheimlichen) suppress.
Unter'schlagung f embezzlement.
Unterschlupf ['ʊntərʃlʊpf] m -(e)s,
-schlüpfe refuge.
unter'schreiben vt irreg insep sign.
Unterschrift ['ʊntərʃrɪft] f signature.

Unterseeboot ['ʊntərzeːboːt] *nt* submarine.

Untersekunda ['ʊntərzekʊnda] *f* -, -sekunden sixth year of secondary school.

Untersetzer ['ʊntərzɛtsər] *m* tablemat; *(für Gläser)* coaster.

untersetzt [ʊntər'zɛtst] a stocky.

unterste(r,s) ['ʊntərstə(r,z)] a lowest, bottom.

unterstehen [ʊntər'ʃteːən] *irreg vi insep* be under *(jdm* sb); *vr* dare; ['ʊntərʃteːən] *vi* shelter.

unterstellen [ʊntər'ʃtɛlən] *vt insep* subordinate *(dat* to); *(fig)* impute *(jdm etw* sth to sb); ['ʊntərʃtɛlən] *vt Auto* garage, park; *vr* take shelter.

unter'streichen *vt irreg insep (lit, fig)* underline.

Unterstufe ['ʊntərʃtuːfə] *f* lower grade.

unter'stützen *vt insep* support.

Unter'stützung *f* support, assistance.

unter'suchen *vt insep (Med)* examine; *(Polizei)* investigate.

Unter'suchung *f* examination; investigation, inquiry; **~sausschuß** *m* committee of inquiry; **~shaft** *f* imprisonment on remand.

Untertan ['ʊntərtaːn] *m* -s, -en subject.

untertänig ['ʊntərtɛːnɪç] a submissive, humble.

Untertasse ['ʊntərtasə] *f* saucer.

untertauchen ['ʊntərtauxən] *vi* dive; *(fig)* disappear, go underground.

Unterteil ['ʊntərtail] *nt or m* lower part, bottom; **u~en** [ʊntər'tailən] *vt insep* divide up.

Untertertia ['ʊntərtɛrtsia] *f* -, -tertien fourth year of secondary school.

Unterwäsche ['ʊntərvɛʃə] *f* underwear.

unterwegs [ʊntər'veːks] *ad* on the way.

unter'weisen *vt irreg insep* instruct.

unter'werfen *irreg insep vt* subject; *Volk* subjugate; *vr* submit *(dat* to).

unterwürfig [ʊntər'vʏrfɪç] a obsequious, servile.

unter'zeichnen *vt insep* sign.

unter'ziehen *irreg insep vt* subject *(dat* to); *vr* undergo *(etw (dat)* sth); *(einer Prüfung)* take.

untreu ['ʊntrɔy] a unfaithful; **U~e** *f* unfaithfulness.

untröstlich [ʊn'trøːstlɪç] a inconsolable.

Untugend ['ʊntuːgənt] *f* vice, failing.

unüber- ['ʊn'yːbər] *cpd:* **~legt** [-leːkt] a ill-considered; *ad* without thinking; **~sehbar** [-'zeːbaːr] a incalculable.

unum- [ʊn'ʊm] *cpd:* **~gänglich** ['-gɛŋlɪç] a indispensable, vital; absolutely necessary; **~wunden** ['-vʊndən] a candid; *ad* straight out.

ununterbrochen ['ʊn'ʊntərbrɔxən] a uninterrupted.

unver- [ʊnfɛr] *cpd* **~änderlich** ['-'ɛndərlɪç] a unchangeable; **~antwortlich** ['-'antvɔrtlɪç] a irresponsible; *(unentschuldbar)* inexcusable; **~äußerlich** ['-ɔysərlɪç] a inalienable; **~besserlich** [-'bɛsərlɪç] a incorrigible; **~bindlich**

['-bɪntlɪç] a not binding; *Antwort* curt; *ad (Comm)* without obligation; **~blümt** [-'blyːmt] a,ad plain(ly), blunt(ly); **~daulich** ['-daulɪç] a indigestible; **~dorben** ['-dɔrbən] a unspoilt; **~einbar** [-'ainbaːr] a incompatible; **~fänglich** [-fɛŋlɪç] a harmless; **~froren** [-'froːrən] a impudent; **~hofft** ['-hɔft] a unexpected; **~kennbar** [-'kɛnbaːr] a unmistakable; **~meidlich** [-'maitlɪç] a unavoidable; **~mutet** ['-muːtət] a unexpected; **~nünftig** [-nynftɪç] a foolish; **~schämt** ['-ʃɛːmt] a impudent; **U~schämtheit** *f* impudence, insolence; **~sehens** ['-zeːəns] *ad* all of a sudden; **~sehrt** ['-zeːrt] a uninjured; **~söhnlich** ['-zøːnlɪç] a irreconcilable; **~ständlich** [-ʃtɛntlɪç] a unintelligible; **~träglich** [-'trɛːklɪç] a quarrelsome; *Meinungen, (Med)* incompatible; **~wüstlich** [-'vyːstlɪç] a indestructible; *Mensch* irrepressible; **~zeihlich** [-'tsailɪç] a unpardonable; **~züglich** [-'tsyːklɪç] a immediate.

unvoll- ['ʊnfɔl] *cpd:* **~kommen** a imperfect; **~ständig** a incomplete.

unvor- ['ʊnfoːr] *cpd:* **~bereitet** a unprepared; **~eingenommen** a unbiased; **~hergesehen** [-heːrgəzeːən] a unforeseen; **~sichtig** [-zɪçtɪç] a careless, imprudent; **~stellbar** [-'ʃtɛlbaːr] a inconceivable; **~teilhaft** [-tailhaft] a disadvantageous.

unwahr ['ʊnvaːr] a untrue; **~haftig** a untruthful; **~scheinlich** a improbable, unlikely; *ad (col)* incredibly; **U~scheinlichkeit** *f* improbability, unlikelihood.

unweigerlich [ʊn'vaigərlɪç] a unquestioning; *ad* without fail.

Unwesen ['ʊnveːzən] *nt* nuisance; *(Unfug)* mischief; **sein ~ treiben** wreak havoc; **u~tlich** a inessential, unimportant; **u~tlich besser** marginally better.

Unwetter ['ʊnvɛtər] *nt* thunderstorm.

unwichtig ['ʊnvɪçtɪç] a unimportant.

unwider- [ʊnviːdər] *cpd:* **~legbar** [-'leːkbaːr] a irrefutable; **~ruflich** [-'ruːflɪç] a irrevocable; **~stehlich** [-ʃteːlɪç] a irresistible.

unwill- ['ʊnvɪl] *cpd:* **U~e(n)** *m* indignation; **~ig** a indignant; *(widerwillig)* reluctant; **~kürlich** [-kyːrlɪç] a involuntary; *ad* instinctively; *lachen* involuntarily.

unwirklich ['ʊnvɪrklɪç] a unreal.

unwirsch ['ʊnvɪrʃ] a cross, surly.

unwirtlich ['ʊnvɪrtlɪç] a inhospitable.

unwirtschaftlich ['ʊnvɪrt-ʃaftlɪç] a uneconomical.

unwissen- ['ʊnvɪsən] *cpd:* **~d** a ignorant; **U~heit** *f* ignorance; **~schaftlich** a unscientific.

unwohl ['ʊnvoːl] a unwell, ill; **U~sein** *nt* -s indisposition.

unwürdig ['ʊnvʏrdɪç] a unworthy *(jds* of sb).

unzählig [ʊn'tsɛːlɪç] a innumerable, countless.

unzer- [ʊntsɛr] *cpd:* **~brechlich** [-'brɛçlɪç] a unbreakable; **~reißbar**

[-'raisba:r] *a* untearable; **~störbar** [-'ʃtø:rba:r] *a* indestructible; **~trennlich** [-'trɛnlɪç] *a* inseparable.

Unzucht ['ʊntsʊxt] *f* sexual offence.

unzüchtig ['ʊntsʏçtɪç] *a* immoral; lewd.

unzu- ['ʊntsu] *cpd:* **~frieden** *a* dissatisfied; **U~friedenheit** *f* discontent; **~länglich** ['ʊntsu:lɛŋlɪç] *a* inadequate; **~lässig** ['ʊntsu:lɛsɪç] *a* inadmissible; **~rechnungsfähig** ['ʊntsu:rɛçnʊŋsfɛ:ɪç] *a* irresponsible; **~sammenhängend** *a* disconnected; *Außerung* incoherent; **~treffend** ['ʊntsu:-] *a* incorrect; **~verlässig** ['ʊntsu:-] *a* unreliable.

unzweideutig ['ʊntsvaidɔytɪç] *adj* unambiguous.

üppig ['ʏpɪç] *adj Frau* curvaceous; *Busen* full, ample; *Essen* sumptuous, lavish; *Vegetation* luxuriant, lush.

uralt ['u:r'alt] *a* ancient, very old.

Uran [u'ra:n] *nt* **-s** uranium.

Ur- ['u:r] *in cpds* original; **~aufführung** *f* first performance; **~einwohner** *m* original inhabitant; **~eltern** *pl* ancestors *pl*; **~enkel(in** *f)* *m* great-grandchild; **~großmutter** *f* great-grandmother; **~großvater** *m* great-grandfather; **~heber** *m* **-s**, **-** originator; *(Autor)* author.

Urin [u'ri:n] *m* **-s**, **-e** urine.

ur- *cpd:* **~komisch** *a* incredibly funny; **U~kunde** *f* **-**, **-n** document, deed; **~kundlich** ['u:rkʊntlɪç] *a* documentary; **~laub** *m* **-(e)s**, **-e** holiday(s *pl*), vacation *(US)*; *(Mil etc)* leave; **~lauber** *m* **-s**, **-** holiday-maker, vacationist *(US)*; **~mensch** *m* primitive man.

Urne ['ʊrnə] *f* **-**, **-n** urn.

Ursache ['u:rzaxə] *f* cause.

Ursprung ['u:rʃprʊŋ] *m* origin, source; *(von Fluß)* source.

ursprünglich [u:rʃprʏŋlɪç] *a, ad* original(ly).

Urteil ['ʊrtail] *nt* **-s**, **-e** opinion; *(Jur)* sentence, judgement; **u~en** *vi* judge; **~sspruch** *m* sentence, verdict.

Ur- *cpd:* **~wald** *m* jungle; **~zeit** *f* prehistoric times *pl*.

usw [u:sve:] *abbr of* **und so weiter** etc.

Utensilien [uten'zi:liən] *pl* utensils *pl*.

Utopie [uto'pi:] *f* pipedream.

utopisch [u'to:pɪʃ] *a* utopian.

V

V, v [fau] *nt* V, v.

vag(e) [va:k, va:gə] *a* vague.

Vagina [va'gi:na] *f* **-**, **Vaginen** vagina.

Vakuum ['va:kuʊm] *nt* **-s**, **Vakua** *or* **Vakuen** vacuum.

Vanille [va'nɪljə] *f* **-** vanilla.

Variation [variatsi'o:n] *f* variation.

variieren [vari'i:rən] *vti* vary.

Vase ['va:zə] *f* **-**, **-n** vase.

Vater ['fa:tər] *m* **-s**, **:** father; **~land** *nt* native country; Fatherland; **~landsliebe** *f* patriotism.

väterlich ['fɛ:tərlɪç] *a* fatherly; **~erseits** *ad* on the father's side.

Vater- *cpd:* **~schaft** *f* paternity; **~unser** *nt* **-s**, **-** Lord's prayer.

Vegetarier(in *f)* [vege'ta:riər(in)] *m* **-s**, **-** vegetarian.

Veilchen ['failçən] *nt* violet.

Vene ['ve:nə] *f* **-**, **-n** vein.

Ventil [vɛn'ti:l] *nt* **-s**, **-e** valve; **~ator** [vɛnti'la:tor] *m* ventilator.

verab- [fɛr'ap] *cpd:* **~reden** *vt* agree, arrange; *vr* arrange to meet *(mit jdm sb)*; **V~redung** *f* arrangement; *(Treffen)* appointment; **~scheuen** *vt* detest, abhor; **~schieden** *vt Gäste* say goodbye to; *(entlassen)* discharge; *Gesetz* pass; *vr* take one's leave *(von* of); **V~schiedung** *f* leave-taking; discharge; passing.

ver- [fɛr] *cpd:* **~achten** [-'axtən] *vt* despise; **~ächtlich** [-'ɛçtlɪç] *a* contemptuous; *(verachtenswert)* contemptible; **jdn ~ächtlich machen** run sb down; **V~achtung** *f* contempt.

verallgemein- [fɛr'algə'main] *cpd:* **~ern** *vt* generalize; **V~erung** *f* generalization.

veralten [fɛr'altən] *vi* become obsolete *or* out-of-date.

Veranda [ve'randa] *f* **-**, **Veranden** veranda.

veränder- [fɛr'ɛndər] *cpd:* **~lich** *a* changeable; **V~lichkeit** *f* variability, instability; **~n** *vtr* change, alter; **V~ung** *f* change, alteration.

veran- [fɛr'an] *cpd:* **~lagt** *a* with a ... nature; **V~lagung** *f* disposition, aptitude; **~lassen** *vt* cause; **Maßnahmen ~lassen** take measures; **sich ~laßt sehen** feel prompted; **V~lassung** *f* cause; motive; **auf jds ~lassung (hin)** at the instance of sb; **~schaulichen** *vt* illustrate; **~schlagen** *vt* estimate; **~stalten** *vt* organize, arrange; **V~stalter** *m* **-s**, **-** organizer; **V~staltung** *f (Veranstalten)* organizing; *(Veranstaltetes)* event, function.

verantwort- [fɛr'antvort] *cpd:* **~en** *vt* answer for; *vr* justify o.s.; **~lich** *a* responsible; **V~ung** *f* responsibility; **~ungsbewußt** *a* responsible; **~ungslos** *a* irresponsible.

verarbeiten [fɛr'arbaitən] *vt* process; *(geistig)* assimilate; **etw zu etw ~** make sth into sth.

Verarbeitung *f* processing; assimilation.

verärgern [fɛr'ɛrgərn] *vt* annoy.

verausgaben [fɛr'ausga:bən] *vr* run out of money; *(fig)* exhaust o.s.

veräußern [fɛr'ɔysərn] *vt* dispose of, sell.

Verb [vɛrp] *nt* **-s**, **-en** verb.

Verband [fɛr'bant] *m* **-(e)s**, **:e** *(Med)* bandage, dressing; *(Bund)* association, society; *(Mil)* unit; **~(s)kasten** *m* medicine chest, first-aid box; **~stoff** *m*, **~zeug** *nt* bandage, dressing material.

verbannen [fɛr'banən] *vt* banish.

Verbannung *f* exile.

verbergen [fɛr'bɛrgən] *vtr irreg* hide *(vor +dat* from).

verbessern [fɛr'bɛsərn] *vtr* improve; *(berichtigen)* correct (o.s.).

Verbesserung *f* improvement; correction.

ver'beugen [fɛr'bɔʏgən] vr bow.
Verbeugung f bow.
ver'biegen vi irreg bend.
ver'bieten vt irreg forbid (jdm etw sb to do sth).
ver'binden irreg vt connect; (kombinieren) combine; (Med) bandage; **jdm die Augen** ~ blindfold sb; vr combine (auch Chem), join.
verbindlich [fɛr'bɪntlɪç] a binding; (freundlich) friendly: **V~keit** f obligation; (Höflichkeit) civility.
Ver'bindung f connection; (Zusammensetzung) combination; (Chem) compound; (Univ) club.
verbissen [fɛr'bɪsən] a grim, dogged; **V~heit** f grimness, doggedness.
ver'bitten vt irreg: **sich** (dat) etw ~ not tolerate sth, not stand for sth.
verbittern [fɛr'bɪtərn] vt embitter; vi get bitter.
verblassen [fɛr'blasən] vi fade.
Verbleib [fɛ'blaɪp] m -(e)s whereabouts; **v~en** [fɛr'blaɪbən] vi irreg remain.
Verblendung [fɛr'blɛndʊŋ] f (fig) delusion.
verblöden [fɛr'blø:dən] vi get stupid.
verblüffen [fɛr'blʏfən] vt stagger, amaze. **Verblüffung** f stupefaction.
ver'blühen vi wither, fade.
ver'bluten vi bleed to death.
verborgen [fɛr'bɔrgən] a hidden.
Verbot [fɛr'bo:t] nt -(e)s, -e prohibition, ban; **v~en** a forbidden; **Rauchen v~en!** no smoking; **v~enerweise** ad though it is forbidden; **~sschild** nt prohibitory sign.
Verbrauch [fɛr'braux] m -(e)s consumption; **v~en** vt use up; **~er** m -s, - consumer; **v~t** a used up, finished; Luft stale; Mensch worn-out.
Verbrechen [fɛr'brɛçən] nt -s, - crime; **v~** vt irreg perpetrate.
Verbrecher [fɛr'brɛçər] m -s, - criminal; **v~isch** a criminal; **~tum** nt -s criminality.
ver'breiten vtr spread; **sich über etw** (acc) ~ expound on sth.
verbreitern [fɛr'braɪtərn] vt broaden.
Verbreitung f spread(ing), propagation.
verbrenn- [fɛr'brɛn] cpd: **~bar** a combustible; **~en** irreg burn; Leiche cremate; **V~ung** f burning; (in Motor) combustion; (von Leiche) cremation; **V~ungsmotor** m internal combustion engine.
ver'bringen vt irreg spend.
Verbrüderung [fɛr'bry:dərʊŋ] f fraternization.
verbrühen [fɛr'bry:ən] vt scald.
verbuchen [fɛr'bu:xən] vt (Fin) register; Erfolg enjoy; Mißerfolg suffer.
verbunden [fɛr'bʊndən] a connected; **jdm** ~ **sein** be obliged or indebted to sb; **falsch** ~ (Tel) wrong number; **V~heit** f bond, relationship.
verbünden [fɛr'byndən] vr ally o.s.
Verbündete(r) [fɛr'byndətə(r)] mf ally.
ver'bürgen vr: **sich** ~ **für** vouch for.
ver'büßen vt: **eine Strafe** ~ serve a sentence.

verchromt [fɛr'kro:mt] a chromium-plated.
Verdacht [fɛr'daxt] m -(e)s suspicion.
verdächtig [fɛr'dɛçtɪç] a suspicious, suspect; **~en** [fɛr'dɛçtɪgən] vt suspect.
verdammen [fɛr'damən] vt damn, condemn.
Verdammnis [fɛr'damnɪs] f -, -se perdition, damnation.
ver'dampfen vi vaporize, evaporate.
ver'danken vt: **jdm etw** ~ owe sb sth.
verdauen [fɛr'dauən] vt (lit, fig) digest.
verdaulich [fɛr'daulɪç] a digestible; **das ist schwer** ~ that is hard to digest.
Verdauung f digestion.
Verdeck [fɛr'dɛk] nt -(e)s, -e (Aut) hood; (Naut) deck; **v~en** vt cover (up); (verbergen) hide.
ver'denken vt irreg: **jdm etw** ~ blame sb for sth, hold sth against sb.
Verderb- [fɛr'dɛrp] cpd: **~en** [fɛr'dɛrbən] nt -s ruin; **v~en** irreg vt spoil; (schädigen) ruin; (moralisch) corrupt; **es mit jdm v~en** get into sb's bad books; vi (Essen) spoil, rot; (Mensch) go to the bad; **v~lich** a Einfluß pernicious; Lebensmittel perishable; **v~t** a depraved; **~theit** f depravity.
verdeutlichen [fɛr'dɔʏtlɪçən] vt make clear.
ver'dichten vtr condense.
ver'dienen vt earn; (moralisch) deserve.
Ver'dienst m -(e)s, -e earnings pl; nt -(e)s, -e merit; (Leistung) service (um to).
verdient [fɛr'di:nt] a well-earned; Person deserving of esteem; **sich um etw** ~ **machen** do a lot for sth.
verdoppeln [fɛr'dɔpəln] vt double.
Verdopp(e)lung f doubling.
verdorben [fɛr'dɔrbən] a spoilt; (geschädigt) ruined; (moralisch) corrupt.
verdrängen [fɛr'drɛŋən] vt oust, displace (auch Phys); (Psych) repress.
Verdrängung f displacement; (Psych) repression.
ver'drehen vt (lit, fig) twist; Augen roll; **jdm den Kopf** ~ (fig) turn sb's head.
verdreifachen [fɛr'draɪfaxən] vt treble.
verdrießlich [fɛr'dri:slɪç] a peevish, annoyed.
verdrossen [fɛr'drɔsən] a cross, sulky.
ver'drücken vt (col) put away, eat; vr (col) disappear.
Verdruß [fɛr'drʊs] m -sses, -sse annoyance, worry.
ver'duften vi evaporate; vir (col) disappear.
verdummen [fɛr'dumən] vt make stupid; vi grow stupid.
verdunkeln [fɛr'dʊŋkəln] vtr darken; (fig) obscure.
Verdunk(e)lung f blackout; (fig) obscuring.
verdünnen [fɛr'dynən] vt dilute.
verdunsten [fɛr'dʊnstən] vi evaporate.
verdursten [fɛr'dʊrstən] vi die of thirst.
verdutzt [fɛr'dʊtst] a nonplussed, taken aback.
verehr- [fɛr''e:r] cpd: **~en** vt venerate,

worship *(auch Rel)*; **jdm etw ~ en** present sb with sth; **V~er(in** *f)* *m* **-s, -** admirer, worshipper *(auch Rel)*; **~t** *a* esteemed; **V~ung** *f* respect; *(Rel)* worship.

vereidigen [fɛr'aɪdɪgən] *vt* put on oath.

Vereidigung *f* swearing in.

Verein [fɛr'aɪn] *m* **-(e)s, -e** club, association; **v~bar** *a* compatible; **v~baren** [-ba:rən] *vt* agree upon; **~barung** *f* agreement; **v~fachen** [-faxən] *vt* simplify; **v~heitlichen** *vt* standardize; **v~igen** [-ɪgən] *vtr* unite; **~igung** *f* union; *(Verein)* association; **v~samen** [-za:mən] *vi* become lonely; **v~t** *a* united; **~zelt** *a* isolated.

vereisen [fɛr'aɪzən] *vi* freeze, ice over; *vt (Med)* freeze.

vereiteln [fɛr'aɪtəln] *vt* frustrate.

ver'eitern *vi* suppurate, fester.

verengen [fɛr'ɛŋən] *vr* narrow.

vererb- [fɛr'ɛrb] *cpd*: **~en** *vt* bequeath; *(Biol)* transmit; *vr* be hereditary; **~lich** [fɛr'ɛrplɪç] *a* hereditary; **V~ung** *f* bequeathing; *(Biol)* transmission; *(Lehre)* heredity.

verewigen [fɛr'e:vɪgən] *vt* immortalize; *vr (col)* leave one's name.

ver'fahren *irreg vi* act; **~ mit** deal with; *vr* get lost; *a* tangled; **V~** *nt* **-s, -** procedure; *(Tech)* process; *(Jur)* proceedings *pl.*

Verfall [fɛr'fal] *m* **-(e)s** decline; *(von Haus)* dilapidation; *(Fin)* expiry; **v~en** *vi irreg* decline; *(Haus)* be falling down; *(Fin)* lapse; **v~en in** *(+acc)* lapse. into; **v~en auf** *(+acc)* hit upon; **einem Laster v~en sein** be addicted to a vice.

verfänglich [fɛr'fɛŋlɪç] *a* awkward, tricky.

ver'färben *vr* change colour.

Verfasser(in *f)* [fɛr'fasər(ɪn)] *m* **-s, -** author, writer.

Verfassung *f* constitution *(auch Pol)*; **~sgericht** *nt* constitutional court; **v~smäßig** *a* constitutional; **v~swidrig** *a* unconstitutional.

ver'faulen *vi* rot.

ver'fechten *vt irreg* advocate; defend.

Verfechter [fɛr'fɛçtər] *m* **-s, -** champion; defender.

ver'fehlen *vt* miss; **etw für verfehlt halten** regard sth as mistaken.

verfeinern [fɛr'faɪnərn] *vt* refine.

ver'fliegen *vi irreg* evaporate; *(Zeit)* pass, fly.

verflossen [fɛr'flɔsən] *a* past, former.

ver'fluchen *vt* curse.

verflüchtigen [fɛr'flʏçtɪgən] *vr* vaporize, evaporate; *(Geruch)* fade.

verflüssigen [fɛr'flʏsɪgən] *vr* become liquid.

verfolg- [fɛr'fɔlg] *cpd*: **~en** *vt* pursue; *(gerichtlich)* prosecute; *(grausam, esp Pol)* persecute; **V~er** *m* **-s, -** pursuer; **V~ung** *f* pursuit; persecution; **V~ungswahn** *m* persecution mania.

verfremden [fɛr'frɛmdən] *vt* alienate, distance.

verfrüht [fɛr'fry:t] *a* premature.

verfüg- [fɛr'fy:g] *cpd*: **~bar** *a* available; **~en** *vt* direct, order; *vr* proceed; *vi*: **~en über** *(+acc)* have at one's disposal; **V~ung** *f* direction, order; **zur V~ung** at one's disposal; **jdm zur V~ung stehen** be available to sb.

verführ- [fɛr'fy:r] *cpd*: **~en** *vt* tempt; *(sexuell)* seduce; **V~er** *m* tempter; seducer; **~erisch** *a* seductive; **V~ung** *f* seduction; *(Versuchung)* temptation.

ver'gammeln *vi (col)* go to seed; *(Nahrung)* go off.

vergangen [fɛr'gaŋən] *a* past; **V~heit** *f* past.

vergänglich [fɛr'gɛŋlɪç] *a* transitory; **V~keit** *f* transitoriness, impermanence.

vergasen [fɛr'ga:zən] *vt* gasify; *(töten)* gas.

Vergaser *m* **-s, -** *(Aut)* carburettor.

vergeb- [fɛr'ge:b] *cpd*: **~en** *vt irreg* forgive *(jdm etw* sb for sth); *(weggeben)* give away; **~en sein** be occupied; *(col: Mädchen)* be spoken for; **~ens** *ad* in vain; **~lich** [fɛr'ge:plɪç] *ad* in vain; *a* vain, futile; **V~ung** *f* forgiveness.

vergegenwärtigen [fɛr'ge:gənvɛrtɪgən] *vr*: **sich** *(dat)* **etw ~** recall or visualize sth.

ver'gehen *vi irreg* pass by or away; **jdm vergeht etw** sb loses sth; *vr* commit an offence *(gegen etw* against sth); **sich an jdm ~** *(sexually)* assault sb; **V~** *nt* **-s, -** offence.

ver'gelten *vt irreg* pay back *(jdm etw* sb for sth), repay.

Ver'geltung *f* retaliation, reprisal; **~sschlag** *m (Mil)* reprisal.

vergessen [fɛr'gɛsən] *vt irreg* forget; **V~heit** *f* oblivion.

vergeßlich [fɛr'gɛslɪç] *a* forgetful; **V~heit** *f* forgetfulness.

vergeuden [fɛr'gɔydən] *vt* squander, waste.

vergewaltigen [fɛrgə'valtɪgən] *vt* rape; *(fig)* violate.

Vergewaltigung *f* rape.

vergewissern [fɛrgə'vɪsərn] *vr* make sure.

ver'gießen *vt irreg* shed.

vergiften [fɛr'gɪftən] *vt* poison.

Vergiftung *f* poisoning.

Vergißmeinnicht [fɛr'gɪsmaɪnnɪçt] *nt* **-(e)s, -e** forget-me-not.

verglasen [fɛr'gla:zən] *vt* glaze.

Vergleich [fɛr'glaɪç] *m* **-(e)s, -e** comparison; *(Jur)* settlement; **im ~ mit** or **zu** compared with or to; **v~bar** *a* comparable; **v~en** *irreg vt* compare; *vr* reach a settlement.

vergnügen [fɛr'gny:gən] *vr* enjoy or amuse o.s.; **V~** *nt* **-s, -** pleasure; **viel V~!** enjoy yourself!

vergnügt [fɛr'gny:kt] *a* cheerful.

Vergnügung *f* pleasure, amusement; **~spark** *m* amusement park; **v~ssüchtig** *a* pleasure-loving.

vergolden [fɛr'gɔldən] *vt* gild.

ver'gönnen *vt* grant.

vergöttern [fɛr'gœtərn] *vt* idolize.

ver'graben *vt* bury.

ver'greifen vr irreg: **sich an jdm ~** lay hands on sb; **sich an etw ~** misappropriate sth; **sich im Ton ~** say the wrong thing.

vergrifien [fɛr'grifən] a Buch out of print; Ware out of stock.

vergrößern [fɛr'grø:sərn] vt enlarge; (mengenmäßig) increase; (Lupe) magnify.

Vergrößerung f enlargement; increase; magnification; **~sglas** nt magnifying glass.

Vergünstigung [fɛr'gʏnstɪgʊŋ] f concession, privilege.

vergüten [fɛr'gy:tən] vt: **jdm etw ~** compensate sb for sth.

Vergütung f compensation.

verhaften [fɛr'haftən] vt arrest.

Verhaftete(r) mf prisoner.

Verhaftung f arrest; **~sbefehl** m warrant (for arrest).

ver'hallen vi die away.

ver'halten irreg vr be, stand; (sich benehmen) behave; (Math) be in proportion to; vt hold or keep back; Schritt check; **V~** nt **-s** behaviour; **V~sforschung** f behavioural science; **V~smaßregel** f rule of conduct.

Verhältnis [fɛr'hɛltnɪs] nt **-ses, -se** relationship; (Math) proportion, ratio; pl (Umstände) conditions pl; **über seine ~se leben** live beyond one's means; **v~mäßig** a,ad relative(ly), comparative(ly).

verhandeln [fɛr'handəln] vi negotiate (über etw (acc) sth); (Jur) hold proceedings; vt discuss; (Jur) hear.

Verhandlung f negotiation; (Jur) proceedings pl.

ver'hängen vt (fig) impose, inflict.

Verhängnis [fɛr'hɛŋnɪs] nt **-ses, -se** fate, doom; **jdm zum ~ werden** be sb's undoing; **v~voll** a fatal, disastrous.

verharmlosen [fɛr'harmlo:zən] vt make light of, play down.

verharren [fɛr'harən] vi remain; (hartnäckig) persist.

verhärten [fɛr'hɛrtən] vr harden.

verhaßt [fɛr'hast] a odious, hateful.

verheerend [fɛr'he:rənt] a disastrous, devastating.

verhehlen [fɛr'he:lən] vt conceal.

ver'heilen vi heal.

verheimlichen [fɛr'haɪmlɪçən] vt keep secret (jdm from sb).

verheiratet [fɛr'haɪra:tət] a married.

ver'heißen vt irreg: **jdm etw ~** promise sb sth.

ver'helfen vi irreg: **jdm ~ zu** help sb to get.

verherrlichen [fɛr'hɛrlɪçən] vt glorify.

ver'hexen vt bewitch; **es ist wie verhext** it's jinxed.

ver'hindern vt prevent; **verhindert sein** be unable to make it.

Ver'hinderung f prevention.

verhöhnen [fɛr'hø:nən] vt mock, sneer at.

Verhör [fɛr'hø:r] nt **-(e)s, -e** interrogation; (gerichtlich) (cross-)examination;

v~en vt interrogate; (cross-)examine; vr misunderstand, mishear.

ver'hungern vi starve, die of hunger.

ver'hüten vt prevent, avert.

Ver'hütung f prevention; **~smittel** nt contraceptive.

verirren [fɛr'ɪrən] vr go astray.

ver'jagen vt drive away or out.

verjüngen [fɛr'jʏŋən] vt rejuvenate; vr taper.

verkalken [fɛr'kalkən] vi calcify; (col) become senile.

verkalkulieren [fɛrkalku'li:rən] vr miscalculate.

verkannt [fɛr'kant] a unappreciated.

Verkauf [fɛr'kaʊf] m sale; **v~en** vt sell.

Verkäufer(in f) [fɛr'kɔʏfər(ɪn)] m **-s, -** seller; salesman; (in Laden) shop assistant.

verkäuflich [fɛr'kɔʏflɪç] a saleable.

Verkehr [fɛr'ke:r] m **-s, -e** traffic; (Umgang, esp sexuell) intercourse; (Umlauf) circulation; **v~en** vi (Fahrzeug) ply, run; (besuchen) visit regularly (bei jdm sb); **v~en mit** associate with; vtr turn, transform; **~sampel** f traffic lights pl; **~sdelikt** nt traffic offence; **~sinsel** f traffic island; **~sstockung** f traffic jam, stoppage; **~sunfall** m traffic accident; **v~swidrig** a contrary to traffic regulations; **~szeichen** nt traffic sign; **v~t** a wrong; (umgekehrt) the wrong way round.

ver'kennen vt irreg misjudge, not appreciate.

ver'klagen vt take to court.

verklären [fɛr'klɛ:rən] vt transfigure; **verklärt lächeln** smile radiantly.

ver'kleben vt glue up, stick; vi stick together.

verkleiden [fɛr'klaɪdən] vtr disguise (o.s.), dress up.

Verkleidung f disguise; (Archit) wainscoting.

verkleinern [fɛr'klaɪnərn] vt make smaller, reduce in size.

verklemmt [fɛr'klɛmt] a (fig) inhibited.

ver'klingen vi irreg die away.

ver'kneifen vt (col): **sich (dat) etw ~** Lachen stifle; Schmerz hide; (sich versagen) do without.

verknüpfen [fɛr'knʏpfən] vt tie (up), knot; (fig) connect.

Verknüpfung f connection.

verkohlen [fɛr'ko:lən] vti carbonize; vt (col) fool.

ver'kommen vi irreg deteriorate, decay; (Mensch) go downhill, come down in the world; a (moralisch) dissolute, depraved; **V~heit** f depravity.

verkörpern [fɛr'kœrpərn] vt embody, personify.

verköstigen [fɛr'kœstɪgən] vt feed.

verkraften [fɛr'kraftən] vt cope with.

ver'kriechen vr irreg creep away, creep into a corner.

verkrümmt [fɛr'krʏmt] a crooked.

Verkrümmung f bend, warp; (Anat) curvature.

verkrüppelt [fɛr'krʏpəlt] a crippled.

verkrustet [fɛr'krʊstət] a encrusted.

ver'kühlen *vr* get a chill.
ver'kümmern *vi* waste away.
verkünden [fɛr'kʏndən] *vt* proclaim; *Urteil* pronounce.
verkürzen [fɛr'kʏrtsən] *vt* shorten; *Wort* abbreviate; **sich** *(dat)* **die Zeit** ~ while away the time.
Verkürzung *f* shortening; abbreviation.
ver'laden *vt irreg* load.
Verlag [fɛr'la:k] *m* **-(e)s, -e** publishing firm.
verlangen [fɛr'laŋən] *vt* demand; desire; ~ **Sie Herrn X** ask for Mr X; *vi* ~ **nach** ask for, desire; **V**~ *nt* **-s, -** desire *(nach* for*);* **auf jds V**~ **(hin)** at sb's request.
verlängern [fɛr'lɛŋərn] *vt* extend; *(länger machen)* lengthen.
Verlängerung *f* extension; *(Sport)* extra time; ~**schnur** *f* extension cable.
verlangsamen [fɛr'laŋza:mən] *vtr* decelerate, slow down.
Verlaß [fɛr'las] *m:* **auf ihn/das ist kein** ~ he/it cannot be relied upon.
ver'lassen *irreg vt* leave; *vr* depend *(auf +acc* on*);* a desolate; *Mensch* abandoned; **V**~**heit** *f* loneliness.
verläßlich [fɛr'lɛslɪç] a reliable.
Verlauf [fɛr'lauf] *m* course; **v**~**en** *irreg vi* *(zeitlich)* pass; *(Farben)* run; *vr* get lost; *(Menschenmenge)* disperse.
ver'lauten *vi:* **etw** ~ **lassen** disclose sth; **wie verlautet** as reported.
ver'leben *vt* spend.
verlebt [fɛr'le:pt] a dissipated, worn out.
ver'legen *vt* move; *(verlieren)* mislay; *(abspielen lassen)* Handlung set *(nach* in*);* *Buch* publish; *vr:* **sich auf etw** *(acc)* ~ take up or to sth; a embarrassed; **nicht** ~ **um** never at a loss for; **V**~**heit** *f* embarrassment; *(Situation)* difficulty, scrape.
Verleger [fɛr'le:gər] *m* **-s, -** publisher.
Verleih [fɛr'lai] *m* **-(e)s, -e** hire service; **v**~**en** *vt irreg* lend; *Kraft, Anschein* confer, bestow; *Preis, Medaille* award; ~**ung** *f* lending; bestowal; award.
ver'leiten *vt* lead astray; ~ **zu** talk into, tempt into.
ver'lernen *vt* forget, unlearn.
ver'lesen *irreg vt* read out; *(aussondern)* sort out; *vr* make a mistake in reading.
verletz- [fɛr'lɛts] *cpd:* ~**bar** a vulnerable; ~**en** *vt (lit, fig)* injure, hurt; *Gesetz etc* violate; ~**end** a *(fig)* Worte hurtful; ~**lich** a vulnerable, sensitive; **V**~**te(r)** *mf* injured person; **V**~**ung** *f* injury; *(Verstoß)* violation, infringement.
verleugnen [fɛr'lɔygnən] *vt* deny; *Menschen* disown.
Verleugnung *f* denial.
verleumd- [fɛr'lɔymd] *cpd:* ~**en** *vt* slander; ~**erisch** a slanderous; **V**~**ung** *f* slander, libel.
ver'lieben *vr* fall in love *(in jdn* with sb*).*
verliebt [fɛr'li:pt] a in love; **V**~**heit** *f* being in love.
verlieren [fɛr'li:rən] *irreg vt* lose; *vr* get lost; *(verschwinden)* disappear.
verlob- [fɛr'lo:b] *cpd:* ~**en** *vr* get engaged

(mit to*);* **V**~**te(r)** [fɛr'lo:ptə(r)] *mf* fiancé(e); **V**~**ung** *f* engagement.
ver'locken *vt* entice, lure.
Ver'lockung *f* temptation, attraction.
verlogen [fɛr'lo:gən] a untruthful; **V**~**heit** *f* untruthfulness.
verloren [fɛr'lo:rən] a lost; *Eier* poached; **der** ~**e Sohn** the prodigal son; **etw** ~ **geben** give sth up for lost; ~**gehen** *vi irreg* get lost.
ver'losen [fɛr'lo:zən] *vt* raffle, draw lots for.
Verlosung *f* raffle, lottery.
verlottern [fɛr'lɔtərn], **verludern** [fɛr'lu:dərn] *vi (col)* go to the dogs.
Verlust [fɛr'lʊst] *m* **-(e)s, -e** loss; *(Mil)* casualty.
ver'machen *vt* bequeath, leave.
Vermächtnis [fɛr'mɛçtnɪs] *nt* **-ses, -se** legacy.
vermählen [fɛr'mɛ:lən] *vr* marry.
Vermählung *f* wedding, marriage.
vermehren [fɛr'me:rən] *vtr* multiply; *(Menge)* increase.
Vermehrung *f* multiplying; increase.
ver'meiden *vt irreg* avoid.
vermeintlich [fɛr'maintlɪç] a supposed.
vermengen [fɛr'mɛŋən] *vtr* mix; *(fig)* mix up, confuse.
Vermerk [fɛr'mɛrk] *m* **-(e)s, -e** note; *(in Ausweis)* endorsement; **v**~**en** *vt* note.
ver'messen *irreg vt* survey; *vr (falsch messen)* measure incorrectly; a presumptuous, bold; **V**~**heit** *f* presumptuousness; recklessness.
Ver'messung *f* survey(ing).
ver'mieten *vt* let, rent (out); *Auto* hire out, rent.
Ver'mieter(in *f)* *m* **-s, -** landlord/ landlady.
Ver'mietung *f* letting, renting (out); *(von Autos)* hiring (out).
vermindern [fɛr'mɪndərn] *vtr* lessen, decrease; *Preise* reduce.
Verminderung *f* reduction.
ver'mischen *vtr* mix, blend.
vermissen [fɛr'mɪsən] *vt* miss.
vermißt [fɛr'mɪst] a missing.
vermitteln [fɛr'mɪtəln] *vi* mediate; *vt Gespräch* connect; **jdm etw** ~ help sb to obtain sth.
Vermittler [fɛr'mɪtlər] *m* **-s, -** *(Schlichter)* agent, mediator.
Vermittlung *f* procurement; *(Stellen—)* agency; *(Tel)* exchange; *(Schlichtung)* mediation.
ver'mögen *vt irreg* be capable of; ~ **zu** be able to; **V**~ *nt* **-s, -** wealth; *(Fähigkeit)* ability; **ein V**~ **kosten** cost a fortune; ~**d** a wealthy.
vermuten [fɛr'mu:tən] *vt* suppose, guess; *(argwöhnen)* suspect.
vermutlich a supposed, presumed; *ad* probably.
Vermutung *f* supposition; suspicion.
vernachlässigen [fɛr'na:xlɛsɪgən] *vt* neglect.
vernarben [fɛr'narbən] *vi* heal up.
ver'nehmen *vt irreg* perceive, hear;

(erfahren) learn; *(Jur)* (cross-)examine; **dem V~** nach from what I/we *etc* hear.

vernehmlich [fɛr'neːmlɪç] *a* audible.

Vernehmung *f* (cross-)examination; **v~sfähig** *a* in a condition to be (cross-) examined.

verneigen [fɛr'naɪgən] *vr* bow.

verneinen [fɛr'naɪnən] *vt Frage* answer in the negative; *(ablehnen)* deny; *(Gram)* negate; **~d** *a* negative.

Verneinung *f* negation.

vernichten [fɛr'nɪçtən] *vt* annihilate, destroy; **~d** *a (fig)* crushing; *Blick* withering; *Kritik* scathing.

Vernichtung *f* destruction, annihilation.

verniedlichen [fɛr'niːtlɪçən] *vt* play down.

Vernunft [fɛr'nʊnft] *f* - reason, understanding.

vernünftig [fɛr'nʏnftɪç] *a* sensible, reasonable.

veröden [fɛr'øːdən] *vi* become desolate; *vt (Med)* remove.

veröffentlichen [fɛr'œfəntlɪçən] *vt* publish.

Veröffentlichung *f* publication.

verordnen [fɛr'ɔrdnən] *vt (Med)* prescribe.

Verordnung *f* order, decree; *(Med)* prescription.

ver'pachten *vt* lease (out).

ver'packen *vt* pack.

Ver'packung *f*, **~smaterial** *nt* packing, wrapping.

ver'passen *vt* miss; **jdm eine Ohrfeige ~** *(col)* give sb a clip round the ear.

verpesten [fɛr'pɛstən] *vt* pollute.

ver'pflanzen *vt* transplant.

Ver'pflanzung *f* transplant(ing).

ver'pflegen *vt* feed, cater for.

Ver'pflegung *f* feeding, catering; *(Kost)* food; *(in Hotel)* board.

verpflichten [fɛr'pflɪçtən] *vt* oblige, bind; *(anstellen)* engage; *vr* undertake; *(Mil)* sign on; *vi* carry obligations; **jdm zu Dank verpflichtet sein** be obliged to sb.

Verpflichtung *f* obligation, duty.

ver'pfuschen *vt (col)* bungle, make a mess of.

verplempern [fɛr'plɛmpərn] *vt (col)* waste.

verpönt [fɛr'pøːnt] *a* disapproved (of), taboo.

verprassen [fɛr'prasən] *vt* squander.

ver'prügeln *vt (col)* beat up, do over.

Verputz [fɛr'pʊts] *m* plaster, roughcast; **v~en** *vt* plaster; *(col) Essen* put away.

verquollen [fɛr'kvɔlən] *a* swollen; *Holz* warped.

verrammeln [fɛr'raməln] *vt* barricade.

Verrat [fɛr'raːt] *m* **-(e)s** treachery; *(Pol)* treason; **v~en** *irreg vt* betray; *Geheimnis* divulge; *vr* give o.s. away.

Verräter [fɛr'rɛːtər] *m* **-s, -** traitor; **~in** *f* traitress; **v~isch** *a* treacherous.

ver'rechnen *vt:* **~ mit** set off against; *vr* miscalculate.

Verrechnungsscheck [fɛr'rɛçnʊŋsʃɛk] *m* crossed cheque.

verregnet [fɛr'reːgnət] *a* spoilt by rain, rainy.

ver'reisen *vi* go away (on a journey).

ver'reißen *vt irreg* pull to pieces.

verrenken [fɛr'rɛŋkən] *vt* contort; *(Med)* dislocate; **sich** *(dat)* **den Knöchel ~** sprain one's ankle.

Verrenkung *f* contortion; *(Med)* dislocation, sprain.

ver'richten *vt* do, perform.

verriegeln [fɛr'riːgəln] *vt* bolt up, lock.

verringern [fɛr'rɪŋərn] *vt* reduce; *vr* diminish.

Verringerung *f* reduction; lessening.

ver'rinnen *vi irreg* run out *or* away; *(Zeit)* elapse.

ver'rosten *vi* rust.

verrotten [fɛr'rɔtən] *vi* rot.

ver'rücken *vt* move, shift.

verrückt [fɛr'rʏkt] *a* crazy, mad; **V~e(r)** *mf* lunatic; **V~heit** *f* madness, lunacy.

Verruf [fɛr'ruːf] *m:* **in ~ geraten/bringen** fall/bring into disrepute; **v~en** *a* notorious, disreputable.

Vers [fɛrs] *m* **-es, -e** verse.

ver'sagen *vt:* **jdm/sich** *(dat)* **etw ~** deny sb/o.s. sth; *vi* fail; **V~** *nt* **-s** failure.

Versager [fɛr'zaːgər] *m* **-s, -** failure.

ver'salzen *vt irreg* put too much salt in; *(fig)* spoil.

ver'sammeln *vtr* assemble, gather.

Ver'sammlung *f* meeting, gathering.

Versand [fɛr'zant] *m* **-(e)s** forwarding; dispatch; *(—abteilung)* dispatch department; **~haus** *nt* mail-order firm.

versäumen [fɛr'zɔymən] *vt* miss; *(unterlassen)* neglect, fail.

Versäumnis *f* **-, -se** neglect; omission.

ver'schaffen *vt:* **jdm/sich etw ~** get *or* procure sth for sb/o.s. **verschämt** [fɛr'ʃɛːmt] *a* bashful.

verschandeln [fɛr'ʃandəln] *vt (col)* spoil.

verschanzen [fɛr'ʃantsən] *vr:* **sich hinter etw** *(dat)* **~** dig in behind sth; *(fig)* take refuge behind.

verschärfen [fɛr'ʃɛrfən] *vtr* intensify; *Lage* aggravate.

ver'schätzen *vr* be out in one's reckoning.

ver'schenken *vt* give away.

verscherzen [fɛr'ʃɛrtsən] *vt:* **sich** *(dat)* **etw ~** lose sth, throw away sth.

verscheuchen [fɛr'ʃɔyçən] *vt* frighten away.

ver'schicken *vt* send off; *Sträfling* transport, deport.

ver'schieben *vt irreg* shift; *(Rail)* shunt; *Termin* postpone; *(Comm)* push.

Ver'schiebung *f* shift, displacement; shunting; postponement.

verschieden [fɛr'ʃiːdən] *a* different; *(pl: mehrere)* various; **sie sind ~ groß** they are of different sizes; **~e** *pl* various people/things *pl;* **~es** *pron* various things *pl;* **etwas V~es** something different; **~artig** *a* various, of different kinds; **zwei so ~artige ...** two such differing ...; **V~heit** *f* difference; **~tlich** *ad* several times.

verschlafen [fɛr'ʃlaːfən] *irreg vt* sleep through; *(fig: versäumen)* miss; *vir* oversleep; *a* sleepy.

Verschlag [fɛr'ʃlaːk] *m* shed; **v~en** [fɛr'ʃlaːɡən] *vt irreg* board up; *(Tennis)* hit out of play; *Buchseite* lose; **jdm den Atem v~en** take sb's breath away; **an einen Ort v~en werden** wind up in a place; *a* cunning.

verschlampen [fɛr'ʃlampən] *vi* fall into neglect; *vt* lose, mislay.

verschlechtern [fɛr'ʃlɛçtərn] *vt* make worse; *vr* deteriorate, get worse.

Verschlechterung *f* deterioration.

Verschleierung [fɛr'ʃlaɪərʊŋ] *f* veiling; *(fig)* concealment; *(Mil)* screening; **~staktik** *f* smoke-screen tactics *pl*.

Verschleiß [fɛr'ʃlaɪs] *m* **-es, -e** wear and tear; *(Aus)* retail trade; **v~en** *irreg vt* wear out; retail; *vir* wear out.

ver'schleppen *vt* carry off, abduct; *(zeitlich)* drag out, delay.

ver'schleudern *vt* squander; *(Comm)* sell dirt-cheap.

verschließ- [fɛr'ʃliːs] *cpd:* **~bar** *a* lockable; **~en** *irreg vt* close; lock; *vr* **sich einer Sache ~en** close one's mind to sth.

verschlimmern [fɛr'ʃlɪmərn] *vt* make worse, aggravate; *vr* get worse, deteriorate.

Verschlimmerung *f* deterioration.

verschlingen [fɛr'ʃlɪŋən] *vt irreg* devour, swallow up; *Fäden* twist.

verschlossen [fɛr'ʃlɔsən] *a* locked; *(fig)* reserved; **V~heit** *f* reserve.

ver'schlucken *vt* swallow; *vr* choke.

Verschluß [fɛr'ʃlʊs] *m* lock; *(von Kleid etc)* fastener; *(Phot)* shutter; *(Stöpsel)* plug; **unter ~ halten** keep under lock and key.

verschlüsseln [fɛr'ʃlʏsəln] *vt* encode.

verschmähen [fɛr'ʃmɛːən] *vt* disdain, scorn.

ver'schmelzen *vti irreg* merge, blend.

verschmerzen [fɛr'ʃmɛrtsən] *vt* get over.

verschmutzen [fɛr'ʃmʊtsən] *vt* soil; *Umwelt* pollute.

verschneit [fɛr'ʃnaɪt] *a* snowed up, covered in snow.

verschnüren [fɛr'ʃnyːrən] *vt* tie up.

verschollen [fɛr'ʃɔlən] *a* lost, missing.

ver'schonen *vt* spare *(jdn mit etw sb sth)*.

verschönern [fɛr'ʃøːnərn] *vt* decorate; *(verbessern)* improve.

verschränken [fɛr'ʃrɛŋkən] *vt* cross, fold.

ver'schreiben *irreg vt Papier* use up; *(Med)* prescribe; *vr* make a mistake (in writing); **sich einer Sache ~** devote oneself to sth.

verschrien [fɛr'ʃriːən] *a* notorious.

verschroben [fɛr'ʃroːbən] *a* eccentric, odd.

verschrotten [fɛr'ʃrɔtən] *vt* scrap.

verschüchtert [fɛr'ʃʏçtərt] *a* subdued, intimidated.

verschuld- [fɛr'ʃʊld] *cpd:* **~en** *vt* be guilty of; **V~en** *nt* **-s** fault, guilt; **~et** *a* in debt; **V~ung** *f* fault; *(Geld)* debts *pl*.

ver'schütten *vt* spill; *(zuschütten)* fill; *(unter Trümmern)* bury.

ver'schweigen *vt irreg* keep secret; **jdm etw ~** keep sth from sb.

verschwend- [fɛr'ʃvɛnd] *cpd:* **~en** *vt* squander; **V~er** *m* **-s, -** spendthrift; **~erisch** *a* wasteful, extravagant; **V~ung** *f* waste; extravagance.

verschwiegen [fɛr'ʃviːɡən] *a* discreet; *Ort* secluded; **V~heit** *f* discretion; seclusion.

ver'schwimmen *vi irreg* grow hazy, become blurred.

ver'schwinden *vi irreg* disappear, vanish; **V~** *nt* **-s** disappearance.

ver'schwitzen *vt* stain with sweat; *(col)* forget.

verschwommen [fɛr'ʃvɔmən] *a* hazy, vague.

verschwör- [fɛr'ʃvøːr] *cpd:* **~en** *vr irreg* plot, conspire; **V~er** *m* **-s, -** conspirator; **V~ung** *f* conspiracy, plot.

ver'sehen *irreg vt* supply, provide; *Pflicht* carry out; *Amt* fill; *Haushalt* keep; *vr (fig)* make a mistake; **ehe er (es) sich ~ hatte ...** before he knew it ... ; **V~** *nt* **-s, -** oversight; **aus V~** by mistake; **~tlich** *ad* by mistake.

Versehrte(r) [fɛr'zeːrtə(r)] *mf* disabled person.

ver'senden *vt irreg* forward, dispatch.

ver'senken *vt* sink; *vr* become engrossed *(in +acc* in).

versessen [fɛr'zɛsən] *a:* **~ auf** *(+acc)* mad about.

ver'setzen *vt* transfer; *(verpfänden)* pawn; *(col)* stand up; **jdm einen Tritt/Schlag ~** kick/hit sb; **etw mit etw ~** mix sth with sth; **jdn in gute Laune ~** put sb in a good mood; *vr:* **sich in jdn** *or* **in jds Lage ~** put o.s. in sb's place.

Ver'setzung *f* transfer.

verseuchen [fɛr'zɔʏçən] *vt* contaminate.

ver'sichern *vt* assure; *(mit Geld)* insure; *vr* **sich ~** *(+gen)* make sure of.

Versicherung *f* assurance; insurance; **~spolice** *f* insurance policy.

versiegeln [fɛr'ziːɡəln] *vt* seal (up).

ver'siegen *vi* dry up.

ver'sinken *vi irreg* sink.

versöhnen [fɛr'zøːnən] *vt* reconcile; *vr* become reconciled.

Versöhnung *f* reconciliation.

ver'sorgen *vt* provide, supply *(mit* with); *Familie etc* look after; *vr* look after o.s.

Ver'sorgung *f* provision; *(Unterhalt)* maintenance; *(Alters— etc)* benefit, assistance.

verspäten [fɛr'ʃpɛːtən] *vr* be late.

Verspätung *f* delay; **~ haben** be late.

ver'sperren *vt* bar, obstruct.

Ver'sperrung *f* barrier.

ver'spielen *vti* lose.

verspielt [fɛr'ʃpiːlt] *a* playful; **bei jdm ~ haben** be in sb's bad books.

ver'spotten *vt* ridicule, scoff at.

ver'sprechen *irreg vt* promise; **sich** *(dat)* **etw von etw ~** expect sth from sth; **V~** *nt* **-s, -** promise.

verstaatlichen [fɛr'ʃtaːtlɪçən] vt nationalize.

Verstand [fɛr'ʃtant] m intelligence; mind; **den ~ verlieren** go out of one's mind; **über jds ~ gehen** go beyond sb; **v~esmäßig** a rational; intellectual.

verständig [fɛr'ʃtɛndɪç] a sensible; **~en** [fɛr'ʃtɛndɪgən] vt inform; vr communicate; (sich einigen) come to an understanding; **V~keit** f good sense; **V~ung** f communication; (Benachrichtigung) informing; (Einigung) agreement.

verständ- [fɛr'ʃtɛnt] cpd: **~lich** a understandable, comprehensible; **V~lichkeit** f clarity, intelligibility; **V~nis** nt **-ses, -se** understanding; **~nislos** a uncomprehending; **~nisvoll** a understanding, sympathetic.

verstärk- [fɛr'ʃtɛrk] cpd: **~en** vt strengthen; Ton amplify; (erhöhen) intensify; vr intensify; **V~er** m **-s, -** amplifier; **V~ung** f strengthening; (Hilfe) reinforcements pl; (von Ton) amplification.

verstauchen [fɛr'ʃtauxən] vt sprain.

verstauen [fɛr'ʃtauən] vt stow away.

Versteck [fɛr'ʃtɛk] nt **-(e)s, -e** hiding (place); **v~en** vtr hide; **~spiel** nt hide-and-seek; **v~t** a hidden.

ver'stehen irreg vt understand; vr get on.

versteifen [fɛr'ʃtaifən] vt stiffen, brace; vr (fig) insist (auf +acc on).

versteigern [fɛr'ʃtaigərn] vt auction.

Versteigerung f auction.

verstell- [fɛr'ʃtɛl] cpd: **~bar** a adjustable, variable; **~en** vt move, shift; Uhr adjust; (versperren) block; (fig) disguise; vr pretend, put on an act; **V~ung** f pretence.

verstiegen [fɛr'ʃtiːgən] a exaggerated.

verstimmt [fɛr'ʃtɪmt] a out of tune; (fig) cross, put out.

verstockt [fɛr'ʃtɔkt] a stubborn; **V~heit** f stubbornness.

verstohlen [fɛr'ʃtoːlən] a stealthy.

ver'stopfen vt block, stop up; (Med) constipate.

Ver'stopfung f obstruction; (Med) constipation.

verstorben [fɛr'ʃtɔrbən] a deceased, late.

verstört [fɛr'ʃtøːrt] a Mensch distraught.

Verstoß [fɛr'ʃtoːs] m infringement, violation (gegen of); **v~en** irreg vt disown, reject; vi: **v~en gegen** offend against.

ver'streichen irreg vt spread; vi elapse.

ver'streuen vt scatter (about).

ver'stricken vt (fig) entangle, ensnare; vr get entangled (in +acc in).

verstümmeln [fɛr'ʃtʏməln] vt maim, mutilate (auch fig).

verstummen [fɛr'ʃtumən] vi go silent; (Lärm) die away.

Versuch [fɛr'zuːx] m **-(e)s, -e** attempt; (Sci) experiment; **v~en** vt try; (verlocken) tempt; vr: **sich an etw** (dat) **v~en** try one's hand at sth; **~skaninchen** nt guinea-pig; **v~sweise** ad tentatively; **~ung** f temptation.

versunken [fɛr'zuŋkən] a sunken; **~ sein in** (+acc) be absorbed or engrossed in.

versüßen [fɛr'zyːsən] vt: **jdm etw ~** (fig) make sth more pleasant for sb.

vertagen [fɛr'taːgən] vti adjourn.

Vertagung f adjournment.

ver'tauschen vt exchange; (versehentlich) mix up.

verteidig- [fɛr'taidɪg] cpd: **~en** vt defend; **V~er** m **-s, -** defender; (Jur) defence counsel; **V~ung** f defence.

ver'teilen vt distribute; Rollen assign; Salbe spread.

Verteilung f distribution, allotment.

verteufelt [fɛr'tɔyfəlt] a,ad (col) awful(ly), devilish(ly).

vertiefen [fɛr'tiːfən] vt deepen; vr: **sich in etw** (acc) **~** become engrossed or absorbed in sth.

Vertiefung f depression.

vertikal [vɛrti'kaːl] a vertical.

vertilgen [fɛr'tɪlgən] vt exterminate; (col) eat up, consume.

vertippen [fɛr'tɪpən] vr make a typing mistake.

vertonen [fɛr'toːnən] vt set to music.

Vertrag [fɛr'traːk] m **-(e)s, ²e** contract, agreement; (Pol) treaty; **v~en** [fɛr'traːgən] irreg vt tolerate, stand; vr get along; (sich aussöhnen) become reconciled; **v~lich** a contractual.

verträglich [fɛr'trɛːklɪç] a good-natured, sociable; Speisen easily digested; (Med) easily tolerated; **V~keit** f sociability; good nature; digestibility.

Vertrags- cpd: **~bruch** m breach of contract; **v~brüchig** a in breach of contract; **v~mäßig** a,ad stipulated, according to contract; **~partner** m party to a contract; **~spieler** m (Sport) contract professional; **v~widrig** a contrary to contract.

vertrauen [fɛr'trauən] vi trust (jdm sb); **~ auf** (+acc) rely on; **V~** nt **-s** confidence; **~erweckend** a inspiring trust; **~sselig** a too trustful; **~svoll** a trustful; **~swürdig** a trustworthy.

vertraulich [fɛr'traulɪç] a familiar; (geheim) confidential; **V~keit** f familiarity; confidentiality.

vertraut [fɛr'traut] a familiar; **V~e(r)** mf confidant, close friend; **V~heit** f familiarity.

ver'treiben vt irreg drive away; (aus Land) expel; (Comm) sell; Zeit pass.

Ver'treibung f expulsion.

vertret- [fɛr'treːt] cpd: **~en** vt irreg represent; Ansicht hold, advocate; **sich** (dat) **die Beine ~en** stretch one's legs; **V~er** m **-s, -** representative; (Verfechter) advocate; **V~ung** f representation; advocacy.

Vertrieb [fɛr'triːp] m **-(e)s, -e** marketing.

ver'trocknen vi dry up.

ver'trödeln vt (col) fritter away.

ver'trösten vt put off.

vertun [fɛr'tuːn] irreg vt (col) waste; vr make a mistake.

vertuschen [fɛr'tuʃən] vt hush or cover up.

verübeln [fɛr'yːbəln] vt: **jdm etw ~** be cross or offended with sb on account of sth.

verüben [fɛr'yːbən] vt commit.

verun- [fɛr'un] cpd: **~glimpfen**

[-glimpfən] vt disparage; ~glücken [-glykən] vi have an accident; tödlich ~glücken be killed in an accident; ~reinigen vt soil; Umwelt pollute; ~sichern vt rattle; ~stalten [-ʃtaltən] vt disfigure; Gebäude etc deface; ~treuen vt embezzle.

verur- [fer'u:r] cpd: ~sachen [-zaxən] vt cause; ~teilen [-tailən] vt condemn; V~teilung f condemnation; (Jur) sentence.

verviel- [fer'fi:l] cpd: ~fachen [-faxən] vt multiply; ~fältigen [—fɛltıgən] vt duplicate, copy; V~fältigung f duplication, copying.

vervolli- [fer'fɔl] cpd: ~kommnen [-kɔmnən] vt perfect; ~ständigen [-ʃtɛndıgən] vt complete.

ver'wackeln vt Photo blur.

ver'wählen vr (Tel) dial the wrong number.

verwahr- [fer'va:r] ~en vt keep, lock away; vr protest; ~losen [-lo:zən] vi become neglected; (moralisch) go to the bad; ~lost [-lo:st] a neglected; wayward.

verwaist [fer'vaist] a orphaned.

verwalt- [fer'valt] cpd: ~en vt manage; administer; V~er m -s, - manager; (Vermögens—) trustee; V~ung f administration; management; V~ungsbezirk m administrative district.

ver'wandeln vtr change, transform.

Ver'wandlung f change, transformation.

verwandt [fer'vant] a related (mit to); V~e(r) mf relative, relation; V~schaft f relationship; (Menschen) relations pl.

ver'warnen vt caution.

Ver'warnung f caution.

ver'waschen a faded; (fig) vague.

verwässern [fer'vɛsərn] vt dilute, water down.

ver'wechseln vt confuse (mit with); mistake (mit for); zum V~ ähnlich as like as two peas.

Ver'wechslung f confusion, mixing up.

verwegen [fer've:gən] a daring, bold; V~heit f daring, audacity, boldness.

Verwehung [fer've:uŋ] f snow-/ sanddrift.

verweichlich- [fer'vaiçlıç] cpd: ~en vt mollycoddle; ~t a effeminate, soft.

ver'weigern vt refuse (jdm etw sb sth); den Gehorsam/die Aussage ~ refuse to obey/testify.

Ver'weigerung f refusal.

verweilen [fer'vailən] vi stay; (fig) dwell (bei on).

Verweis [fer'vais] m -es, -e reprimand, rebuke; (Hinweis) reference; v~en [fer'vaizən] vt irreg refer; jdm etw v~en (tadeln) scold sb for sth; jdn von der Schule v~en expel sb (from school); jdn des Landes v~en deport or expel sb; ~ung f reference; (Tadel) reprimand; (Landes—) deportation.

ver'welken vi fade.

ver'wenden irreg vt use; Mühe, Zeit, Arbeit spend; vr intercede.

Ver'wendung f use.

ver'werfen vt irreg reject.

verwerflich [fer'verflıç] a reprehensible.

ver'werten vt utilize.

Ver'wertung f utilization.

verwesen [fer've:zən] vi decay.

Verwesung f decomposition.

ver'wickeln vt tangle (up); (fig) involve (in +acc in); vr get tangled (up); sich ~ in (+acc) (fig) get involved in.

Verwicklung f complication, entanglement.

verwildern [fer'vıldərn] vi run wild.

ver'winden vt irreg get over.

verwirklichen [fer'vırklıçən] vt realize, put into effect.

Verwirklichung f realization.

verwirren [fer'vırən] vt tangle (up); (fig) confuse.

Verwirrung f confusion.

verwittern [fer'vıtərn] vi weather.

verwitwet [fer'vıtvət] a widowed.

verwöhnen [fer'vø:nən] vt spoil.

Verwöhnung f spoiling, pampering.

verworfen [fer'vɔrfən] a depraved; V~heit f depravity.

verworren [fer'vɔrən] a confused.

verwund- cpd: ~bar [fer'vʊntba:r] a vulnerable; ~en [fer'vʊndən] vt wound; ~erlich [fer'vʊndərlıç] a surprising; V~erung [fer'vʊndəruŋ] f astonishment; V~ete(r) mf injured (person); V~ung f wound, injury.

ver'wünschen vt curse.

verwüsten [fer'vy:stən] vt devastate.

Verwüstung f devastation.

verzagen [fer'tsa:gən] vi despair.

ver'zählen vr miscount.

verzehren [fer'tse:rən] vt consume.

ver'zeichnen vt list; Niederlage, Verlust register.

Verzeichnis [fer'tsaıçnıs] nt -ses, -se list, catalogue; (in Buch) index.

verzeih- [fer'tsai] cpd: ~en vti irreg forgive (jdm etw sb for sth); ~lich a pardonable; V~ung f forgiveness, pardon; V~ung! sorry!, excuse me!

ver'zerren vt distort.

Verzicht [fer'tsıçt] m -(e)s, -e renunciation (auf +acc of); v~en vi forgo, give up (auf etw (acc) sth).

ver'ziehen irreg vi move; vt put out of shape; Kind spoil; Pflanzen thin out; das Gesicht ~ pull a face; vr go out of shape; (Gesicht) contort; (verschwinden) disappear.

verzieren [fer'tsi:rən] vt decorate, ornament.

verzinsen [fer'tsınzən] vt pay interest on.

ver'zögern vt delay.

Ver'zögerung f delay, time-lag; ~staktik f delaying tactics pl.

verzollen [fer'tsɔlən] vt declare, pay duty on.

verzück- [fer'tsʏk] cpd: ~en vt send into ecstasies, enrapture; ~t a enraptured; V~ung f ecstasy.

verzweif- [fer'tsvaif] cpd: ~eln vi despair; ~elt a desperate; V~lung f despair.

verzweigen [fer'tsvaigən] vr branch out.

verzwickt [fɛr'tsvɪkt] *a (col)* awkward, complicated.
Veto ['ve:to] *nt* **-s, -s** veto.
Vetter ['fɛtər] *m* **-s, -n** cousin; ~**nwirtschaft** *f* nepotism.
vibrieren [vi'bri:rən] *vi* vibrate.
Vieh [fi:] *nt* **-(e)s** cattle *pl*; **v**~**isch** *a* bestial.
viel [fi:l] *a* lot of, much; ~**e** *pl* a lot of, many; *ad* a lot, much; ~ **zuwenig** much too little; ~**erlei** *a* a great variety of; ~**es** a a lot; ~**fach** *a,ad* many times; **auf** ~**fachen Wunsch** at the request of many people; **V**~**falt** *f* - variety; ~**fältig** a varied, many-sided.
vielleicht [fi'laɪçt] *ad* perhaps.
viel- *cpd*: ~**mal(s)** *ad* many times; **danke** ~**mals** many thanks; ~**mehr** *ad* rather, on the contrary; ~**sagend** a significant; ~**seitig** a many-sided; ~**versprechend** a promising.
vier [fi:r] *num* four; **V**~**eck** *nt* **-(e)s, -e** four-sided figure; *(gleichseitig)* square; ~**eckig** a four-sided; square; ~**taktmotor** *m* four-stroke engine; ~**te(r,s)** ['fi:rtə(r,z)] a fourth; ~**teilen** *vt* quarter; **V**~**tel** ['fɪrtəl] *nt* **-s, -** quarter; ~**teljährlich** a quarterly; ~**tel** f crotchet; **V**~**elstunde** [fɪrtəl'ʃtundə] f quarter of an hour; ~**zehn** ['fɪrtse:n] *num* fourteen; **in** ~**zehn Tagen** in a fortnight; ~**zehntägig** a fortnightly; ~**zig** ['fɪrtsɪç] *num* forty.
Vikar [vi'ka:r] *m* **-s, -e** curate.
Villa ['vɪla] f-, **Villen** villa.
Villenviertel ['vɪlənfɪrtəl] *nt* (prosperous) residential area.
violett [vio'lɛt] a violet.
Violin- [vio'li:n] *cpd*: ~**bogen** *m* violin bow; ~**e** f-, **-n** violin; ~**konzert** *nt* violin concerto; ~**schlüssel** *m* treble clef.
Virus ['vi:rus] *m or nt* -, **Viren** virus.
Visier [vi'zi:r] *nt* **-s, -e** gunsight; *(am Helm)* visor.
Visite [vi'zi:tə] f-, **-n** *(Med)* visit; ~**nkarte** f visiting card.
visuell [vizu'ɛl] a visual.
Visum ['vi:zum] *nt* **-s, Visa** *or* **Visen** visa.
vital [vi'ta:l] a lively, full of life, vital.
Vitamin [vita'mi:n] *nt* **-s, -e** vitamin.
Vogel ['fo:gəl] *m* **-s, ∸** bird; **einen** ~ **haben** *(col)* have bats in the belfry; **jdm den** ~ **zeigen** *(col)* tap one's forehead *(to indicate that one thinks sb stupid)*; ~**bauer** *nt* birdcage; ~**beerbaum** *m* rowan tree; ~**schau** f bird's-eye view; ~**scheuche** f -, **-n** scarecrow.
Vokab- *cpd*: ~**el** [vo'ka:bəl] f -, **-n** word; ~**ular** [vokabu'la:r] *nt* **-s, -e** vocabulary.
Vokal [vo'ka:l] *m* **-s, -e** vowel.
Volk [fɔlk] *nt* **-(e)s, ∸er** people; nation.
Völker- ['fœlkər] *cpd*: ~**bund** *m* League of Nations; ~**recht** *nt* international law; **v**~**rechtlich** a according to international law; ~**verständigung** f international understanding; ~**wanderung** f migration.
Volks- *cpd*: ~**abstimmung** f referendum; ~**hochschule** f adult education classes *pl*; ~**lied** *nt* folksong; ~**republik** f

people's republic; ~**schule** f elementary school; ~**tanz** *m* folk dance; **v**~**wirtschaft** f economics.
voll [fɔl] a full; ~ **und ganz** completely; **jdn für** ~ **nehmen** *(col)* take sb seriously; ~**auf** [fɔl'auf] *ad* amply; ~**blütig** a full-blooded; ~'**bringen** *vt irreg insep* accomplish; ~**enden** *vt insep* finish, complete; ~**ends** ['fɔlɛnts] *ad* completely; **V**~'**endung** f completion; ~**er** a fuller; *(+gen)* full of; **V**~**eyball** ['vɔliba:l] *m* volleyball; **V**~**gas** *nt*: **mit** **V**~**gas** at full throttle; **V**~**gas geben** step on it.
völlig ['fœlɪç] a,*ad* complete(ly).
voll- *cpd*: ~**jährig** a of age; **V**~**kaskoversicherung** f fully comprehensive insurance; ~'**kommen** a perfect; **V**~'**kommenheit** f perfection; **V**~**kornbrot** *nt* wholemeal bread; ~**machen** *vt* fill (up); **V**~**macht** f -, **-en** authority, full powers *pl*; **V**~**mond** *m* full moon; **V**~**pension** f full board; ~**ständig** a complete; ~'**strecken** *vt insep* execute; ~**tanken** *vti* fill up; ~**zählig** a complete; in full number; ~'**ziehen** *vt irreg insep* carry out; *vr* happen; **V**~'**zug** *m* execution.
Volt [vɔlt] *nt* - *or* **-(e)s, -** volt.
Volumen [vo'lu:mən] *nt* **-s, -** *or* **Volumina** volume.
vom [fɔm] = **von dem**.
von [fɔn] *prep +dat* from; *(statt Genitiv, bestehend aus)* of; *(im Passiv)* by; **ein Freund** ~ **mir** a friend of mine; ~ **mir aus** *(col)* OK by me; ~ **wegen** no way!; ~**ei'nander** *ad* from each other; ~**statten** [fɔn'ʃtatən] *ad*: ~**statten gehen** proceed, go.
vor [fo:r] *prep +dat or acc* before; *(räumlich)* in front of; ~ **Wut/Liebe** with rage/love; ~ **2 Tagen** 2 days ago; ~ **allem/allen** above all; **V**~**abend** *m* evening before, eve.
voran [fo'ran] *ad* before, ahead; ~**gehen** *vi irreg* go ahead; **einer Sache** *(dat)* ~**gehen** precede sth; ~**gehend** a previous; ~**kommen** *vi irreg* come along, make progress.
Vor- ['fo:r] *cpd*: ~**anschlag** *m* estimate; ~**arbeiter** *m* foreman.
voraus [fo'raus] *ad* ahead; *(zeitlich)* in advance; **jdm** ~ **sein** be ahead of sb; **im** ~ in advance; ~**bezahlen** *vt* pay in advance; ~**gehen** *vi irreg* go (on) ahead; *(fig)* precede; ~**haben** *vt irreg*: **jdm etw** ~**haben** have the edge on sb in sth; **V**~**sage** f -, **-n** prediction; ~**sagen** *vt* predict; ~**sehen** *vt irreg* foresee; ~**setzen** *vt* assume; ~**gesetzt, daß** . . . provided that . . . ; **V**~**setzung** f requirement, prerequisite; **V**~**sicht** f foresight; **aller** **V**~**sicht nach** in all probability; **in der V**~**sicht, daß** . . . anticipating that . . . ; ~**sichtlich** *ad* probably.
vorbauen ['fo:rbauən] *vt* build up in front; *vi* take precautions *(dat* against).
Vorbehalt ['fo:rbəhalt] *m* **-(e)s, -e** reservation, proviso; **v**~**en** *vt irreg*:

sich/jdm etw **v~en** reserve sth (to o.s.)/to sb; **v~los** a,ad unconditional(ly).

vorbei [fɔr'baɪ] ad by, past; **~gehen** vi irreg pass by, go past.

vorbe- cpd: **~lastet** ['fo:rbəlastət] a (fig) handicapped; **~reiten** ['fo:rbəraɪtən] vt prepare; **V~reitung** f preparation; **~straft** ['fo:rbəʃtraft] a previously convicted, with a record.

vorbeugen ['fo:rbɔʏgən] vtr lean forward; vi prevent (einer Sache (dat) sth); **~d** a preventive.

Vorbeugung f prevention; **zur ~ gegen** for the prevention of.

Vorbild ['fo:rbɪlt] nt model; **sich** (dat) **jdn zum ~ nehmen** model o.s. on sb; **v~lich** a model, ideal.

vorbringen ['fo:rbrɪŋən] vt irreg advance, state; (col: nach vorne) bring to the front.

Vorder- ['fɔrdər] cpd: **~achse** f front axle; **~ansicht** f front view; **v~e(r,s)** a front; **~grund** m foreground; **v~hand** ad for the present; **~mann** m, pl **-männer** man in front; **jdn auf ~mann bringen** (col) tell sb to pull his socks up; **~seite** f front (side); **v~ste(r,s)** a front.

vordrängen ['fo:rdrɛŋən] vt push to the front.

vorehelich ['fo:r'e:əlɪç] a premarital.

voreilig ['fo:r'aɪlɪç] a hasty, rash.

voreingenommen ['fo:r'aɪngənɔmən] a biased; **V~heit** f bias.

vorenthalten ['fo:r'ɛnthaltən] vt irreg: **jdm etw ~** withhold sth from sb.

vorerst ['fo:r'e:rst] ad for the moment or present.

Vorfahr ['fo:rfa:r] m **-en**, **-en** ancestor; **v~en** vi irreg drive (on) ahead; (vors Haus etc) drive up; **~t** f (Aut) right of way; **~t achten!** give way!; **~tsregel** f right of way; **~tsschild** nt give way sign.

Vorfall ['fo:rfal] m incident; **v~en** vi irreg occur.

vorfinden ['fo:rfɪndən] vt irreg find.

vorführen ['fo:rfy:rən] vt show, display; **dem Gericht ~** bring before the court.

Vorgabe ['fo:rga:bə] f (Sport) start, handicap.

Vorgang ['fo:rgaŋ] m course of events; (esp Sci) process; **der ~ von etw** how sth happens.

Vorgänger(in f) ['fo:rgɛŋər(ɪn)] m **-s, -** predecessor.

vorgeben ['fo:rge:bən] vt irreg pretend, use as a pretext; (Sport) give an advantage or a start of.

vorge- ['fo:rgə] cpd: **~faßt** [-fast] a preconceived; **~fertigt** [-fɛrtɪçt] a prefabricated; **V~fühl** [-fy:l] nt presentiment, anticipation.

vorgehen ['fo:rge:ən] vi irreg (voraus) go (on) ahead; (nach vorn) go up front; (handeln) act, proceed; (Uhr) be fast; (Vorrang haben) take precedence; (passieren) go on; **V~** nt -s action.

Vorgeschmack ['fo:rgəʃmak] m foretaste.

Vorgesetzte(r) ['fo:rgəzɛtstə(r)] mf superior.

vorgestern ['fo:rgɛstərn] ad the day before yesterday.

vorgreifen ['fo:rgraɪfən] vi irreg anticipate, forestall.

vorhaben ['fo:rha:bən] vt irreg intend; **hast du schon was vor?** have you got anything on?; **V~** nt -s, - intention.

vorhalten ['fo:rhaltən] irreg vt hold or put up; (fig) reproach (jdm etw sb for sth); vi last.

Vorhaltung f reproach.

vorhanden [fo:r'handən] a existing, extant; (erhältlich) available; **V~sein** nt -s existence, presence.

Vorhang ['fo:rhaŋ] m curtain.

Vorhängeschloß ['fo:rhɛŋəʃlɔs] nt padlock.

Vorhaut ['fo:rhaʊt] f (Med) foreskin.

vorher [fo:r'he:r] ad before(hand); **~bestimmen** vt Schicksal preordain; **~gehen** vi irreg precede; **~ig** [fo:r'he:rɪç] a previous.

Vorherrschaft ['fo:rhɛrʃaft] f predominance, supremacy.

vorherrschen ['fo:rhɛrʃən] vi predominate.

vorher- [fo:r'he:r] cpd: **V~sage** f -, -n forecast; **~sagen** vt forecast, predict; **~sehbar** a predictable; **~sehen** vt irreg foresee.

vorhin [fo:r'hɪn] ad not long ago, just now; **~ein** ['fo:rhɪnaɪn] ad: **im ~ein** beforehand.

vorig ['fo:rɪç] a previous, last.

vorjährig ['fo:rjɛ:rɪç] a of the previous year; last year's.

Vorkehrung ['fo:rke:ruŋ] f precaution.

vorkommen ['fo:rkɔmən] vi irreg come forward; (geschehen, sich finden) occur; (scheinen) seem (to be); **sich** (dat) **dumm etc ~** feel stupid etc; **V~** nt -s, - occurrence.

Vorkommnis ['fo:rkɔmnɪs] nt **-ses, -se** occurrence.

Vorkriegs- ['fo:rkri:ks] in cpds prewar.

Vorladung ['fo:rla:duŋ] f summons.

Vorlage ['fo:rla:gə] f model, pattern; (Gesetzes~) bill; (Sport) pass.

vorlassen ['fo:rlasən] vt irreg admit; (vorgehen lassen) allow to go in front.

vorläufig ['fo:rlɔʏfɪç] a temporary, provisional.

vorlaut ['fo:rlaʊt] a impertinent, cheeky.

Vorleg- ['fo:rle:g] cpd: **v~en** vt put in front; (fig) produce, submit; **jdm etw v~en** put sth before sb; **~er** m -s, - mat.

vorlesen ['fo:rle:zən] vt irreg read (out).

Vorlesung f (Univ) lecture.

vorletzte(r, s) ['fo:rlɛtstə(r,s)] a last but one.

Vorliebe ['fo:rli:bə] f preference, partiality.

vorliebnehmen [fo:r'li:pne:mən] vi irreg: **~ mit** make do with.

vorliegen ['fo:rli:gən] vi irreg be (here); **etw liegt jdm vor** sb has sth; **~d** a present, at issue.

vormachen ['fo:rmaxən] vt: **jdm etw ~** show sb how to do sth; (fig) fool sb; have sb on.

Vormachtstellung ['foːrmaxtʃtɛlʊŋ] f supremacy, hegemony.

Vormarsch ['foːrmarʃ] m advance.

vormerken ['foːrmɛrkən] vt book.

Vormittag ['foːrmɪtaːk] m morning; **v~s** ad in the morning, before noon.

Vormund ['foːrmʊnt] m **-(e)s, -e** or **-münder** guardian.

vorn(e) ['fɔrn(ə)] ad in front; **von ~ anfangen** start at the beginning; **nach ~** to the front.

Vorname ['foːrnaːmə] m first or Christian name.

vornan [fɔrn''an] ad at the front.

vornehm ['foːrneːm] a distinguished; refined; elegant; **~en** vt irreg (fig) carry out; **sich** (dat) etw **~en** start on sth; (beschließen) decide to do sth; **sich** (dat) **jdn ~en** tell sb off; **~lich** ad chiefly, specially.

vornherein ['fɔrnhɛraɪn] ad: **von ~** from the start.

Vorort ['foːr'ɔrt] m suburb; **~zug** m commuter train.

Vorrang ['foːrraŋ] m precedence, priority; **v~ig** a of prime importance, primary.

Vorrat ['foːrraːt] m stock, supply; **~skammer** f pantry.

vorrätig ['foːrrɛːtɪç] a in stock.

Vorrecht ['foːrrɛçt] nt privilege.

Vorrichtung ['foːrrɪçtʊŋ] f device, contrivance.

vorrücken ['foːrrʏkən] vi advance; vt move forward.

vorsagen ['foːrzaːgən] vt recite, say out loud; (Sch: zuflüstern) tell secretly, prompt.

Vorsatz ['foːrzats] m intention; (Jur) intent; **einen ~ fassen** make a resolution.

vorsätzlich ['foːrzɛtslɪç] a,ad intentional(ly); (Jur) premeditated.

Vorschau ['foːrʃau] f (Rad, TV) (programme) preview; (Film) trailer.

vorschieben ['foːrʃiːbən] vt irreg push forward; (vor etw) push across; (fig) put forward as an excuse; **jdn ~** use sb as a front.

Vorschlag ['foːrʃlaːk] m suggestion, proposal; **v~en** vt irreg suggest, propose.

vorschnell ['foːrʃnɛl] ad hastily, too quickly.

vorschreiben ['foːrʃraɪbən] vt irreg prescribe, specify.

Vorschrift ['foːrʃrɪft] f regulation(s); rule(s); (Anweisungen) instruction(s); **Dienst nach ~** work-to-rule; **v~smäßig** a as per regulations/instructions.

Vorschuß ['foːrʃʊs] m advance.

vorschweben ['foːrʃveːbən] vi: **jdm schwebt etw vor** sb has sth in mind.

vorsehen ['foːrzeːən] irreg vt provide for, plan; vr take care, be careful; vi be visible.

Vorsehung f providence.

vorsetzen ['foːrzɛtsən] vt move forward; (vor etw) put in front; (anbieten) offer.

Vorsicht ['foːrzɪçt] f caution, care; **~!** look out!, take care!; (auf Schildern) caution!, danger!; **~, Stufe!** mind the step!; **v~ig** a cautious, careful; **v~shalber** ad just in case.

Vorsilbe ['foːrzɪlbə] f prefix.

Vorsitz ['foːrzɪts] m chair(manship); **~ende(r)** mf chairman/-woman.

Vorsorge ['foːrzɔrgə] f precaution(s), provision(s); **v~n** vi: **v~en für** make provision(s) for.

vorsorglich ['foːrzɔrklɪç] ad as a precaution.

Vorspeise ['foːrʃpaɪzə] f hors d'oeuvre, appetizer.

Vorspiel ['foːrʃpiːl] nt prelude.

vorsprechen ['foːrʃprɛçən] irreg vt say out loud, recite; vi: **bei jdm ~** call on sb.

Vorsprung ['foːrʃprʊŋ] m projection, ledge; (fig) advantage, start.

Vorstadt ['foːrʃtat] f suburbs pl.

Vorstand ['foːrʃtant] m executive committee; (Comm) board (of directors); (Person) director, head.

vorstehen ['foːrʃteːən] vi irreg project; **etw** (dat) **~** (fig) be the head of sth.

vorstell- ['foːrʃtɛl] cpd: **~bar** a conceivable; **~en** vt put forward; (vor etw) put in front; (bekannt machen) introduce; (darstellen) represent; **sich** (dat) etw **~en** imagine sth; **V~ung** f (Bekanntmachen) introduction; (Theat etc) performance; (Gedanke) idea, thought.

Vorstoß ['foːrʃtoːs] m advance; **v~en** vti irreg push forward.

Vorstrafe ['foːrʃtraːfə] f previous conviction.

vorstrecken [foːrʃtrɛkən] vt stretch out; Geld advance.

Vorstufe ['foːrʃtuːfə] f first step(s).

Vortag ['foːrtak] m day before (einer Sache sth).

vortäuschen ['foːrtɔʏʃən] vt feign, pretend.

Vorteil ['fɔrtaɪl] m **-s, -e** advantage (gegenüber over); **im ~ sein** have the advantage; **v~haft** a advantageous.

Vortrag ['foːrtraːk] m **-(e)s, Vorträge** talk, lecture; (—sart) delivery, rendering; (Comm) balance carried forward; **v~en** vt irreg carry forward (auch Comm); (fig) recite; Rede deliver; Lied perform; Meinung etc express.

vortrefflich [foːrtrɛflɪç] a excellent.

vortreten ['foːrtreːtən] vi irreg step forward; (Augen etc) protrude.

vorüber [fo'ryːbər] ad past, over; **~gehen** vi irreg pass (by); **~gehen an** (+dat) (fig) pass over; **~gehend** a temporary, passing.

Vorurteil ['foːr'urtaɪl] nt prejudice; **v~sfrei, v~slos** a unprejudiced, open-minded.

Vorverkauf ['foːrfɛrkauf] m advance booking.

Vorwahl ['foːrvaːl] f preliminary election; (Tel) dialling code.

Vorwand ['foːrvant] m **-(e)s, Vorwände** pretext.

vorwärts ['foːrvɛrts] ad forward; **V~gang** m (Aut etc) forward gear; **~gehen** vi irreg progress; **~kommen** vi irreg get on, make progress.

vorweg [foːr'vɛk] ad in advance; **V~nahme** f **-, -n** anticipation;

~nehmen vt irreg anticipate.

vorweisen ['foːrvaɪzən] vt irreg show, produce.

vorwerfen ['foːrvɛrfən] vt irreg: **jdm etw ~** reproach sb for sth, accuse sb of sth; **sich** (dat) **nichts vorzuwerfen haben** have nothing to reproach o.s. with.

vorwiegend ['foːrviːgənt] a,ad predominant(ly).

Vorwitz ['foːrvɪts] m cheek; **v~ig** a saucy, cheeky.

Vorwort ['foːrvɔrt] nt -(e)s, -e preface.

Vorwurf ['foːrvʊrf] m reproach; **jdm/sich Vorwürfe machen** reproach sb/o.s.; **v~svoll** a reproachful.

vorzeigen ['foːrtsaɪgən] vt show, produce.

vorzeitig ['foːrtsaɪtɪç] a premature.

vorziehen ['foːrtsiːən] vt irreg pull forward; Gardinen draw; (lieber haben) prefer.

Vorzug ['foːrtsuːk] m preference; (gute Eigenschaft) merit, good quality; (Vorteil) advantage; (Rail) relief train.

vorzüglich [foːr'tsyːklɪç] a excellent, first-rate.

vulgär [vʊl'gɛːr] a vulgar.

Vulkan [vʊl'kaːn] m -s, -e volcano; **v~i-'sieren** vt vulcanize.

W

W, w [veː] nt W, w.

Waage ['vaːgə] f -, -n scales pl; (Astrol) Libra; **w~recht** a horizontal.

wabb(e)lig ['vab(ə)lɪç] a wobbly.

Wabe ['vaːbə] f -, -n honeycomb.

wach [vax] a awake; (fig) alert; **W~e** f -, -n guard, watch; **W~e halten** keep watch; **W~e stehen** stand guard; **~en** vi be awake; (W—e halten) guard.

Wacholder [va'xɔldər] m -s, - juniper.

Wachs [vaks] nt -es, -e wax.

wachsam ['vaxzaːm] a watchful, vigilant, alert; **W~keit** f vigilance.

Wachs- cpd: **w~en** vi irreg grow; vt Skier wax; **~tuch** nt oilcloth; **~tum** nt -s growth.

Wächter ['vɛçtər] m -s, - guard, warder, keeper; (Parkplatz—) attendant.

Wacht- [vaxt] cpd: **~meister** m officer; **~posten** m guard, sentry.

wackel- ['vakəl] cpd: **~ig** a shaky, wobbly; **W~kontakt** m loose connection; **~n** vi shake; (fig: Position) be shaky.

wacker ['vakər] a valiant, stout; ad well, bravely.

Wade ['vaːdə] f -, -n (Anat) calf.

Waffe ['vafə] f -, -n weapon; **~l** f -, -n waffle; wafer; **~nschein** m gun licence; **~nstillstand** m armistice, truce.

Wagemut ['vaːgəmuːt] m daring.

wagen ['vaːgən] vt venture, dare.

Wagen ['vaːgən] m -s, - vehicle; (Auto) car; (Rail) carriage; (Pferde—) cart; **~führer** m driver; **~heber** m -s, - jack.

Waggon [va'gõ] m -s, -s carriage; (Güter—) goods van, freight truck (US).

waghalsig ['vaːkhalzɪç] a foolhardy.

Wagnis ['vaːknɪs] nt -ses, -se risk.

Wahl ['vaːl] f -, -en choice; (Pol) election;

zweite **~** seconds pl; **w~berechtigt** a entitled to vote.

wähl- ['vɛːl] cpd: **~bar** a eligible; **~en** vti choose; (Pol) elect, vote (for); (Tel) dial; **W~er(in** f) m -s, voter; **~erisch** a fastidious, particular; **W~erschaft** f electorate.

Wahl- cpd: **~fach** nt optional subject; **~gang** m ballot; **~kabine** f polling booth; **~kampf** m election campaign; **~kreis** m constituency; **~liste** f electoral register; **~lokal** nt polling station; **w~los** ad at random; **~recht** nt franchise; **~spruch** m motto; **~urne** f ballot box.

Wahn [vaːn] m -(e)s delusion; folly; **~sinn** m madness; **w~sinnig** a insane, mad; ad (col) incredibly.

wahr [vaːr] a true; **~en** vt maintain, keep.

während ['vɛːrən] vi last; **~d** prep +gen during; cj while; **~ddessen** [vɛːrənt'dɛsən] ad meanwhile.

wahr- cpd: **~haben** vt irreg: **etw nicht ~haben wollen** refuse to admit sth; **~haft** ad (tatsächlich) truly; **~haftig** [vaːr'haftɪç] a true, real; ad really; **W~heit** f truth; **~nehmen** vt irreg perceive, observe; **W~nehmung** f perception; **~sagen** vi prophesy, tell fortunes; **W~sager(in** f) m -s, - fortune teller; **~scheinlich** [vaːr'ʃaɪnlɪç] a probable; ad probably; **W~'scheinlichkeit** f probability; **aller W~scheinlichkeit nach** in all probability; **W~zeichen** nt emblem.

Währung ['vɛːrʊŋ] f currency.

Waise ['vaɪzə] f -, -n orphan; **~nhaus** nt orphanage; **~nkind** nt orphan.

Wald [valt] m -(e)s, -er wood(s); (groß) forest; **w~ig** ['valdɪç] a wooded.

Wäldchen ['vɛltçən] nt copse, grove.

Wal(fisch) ['vaːl(fɪʃ)] m -(e)s, -e whale.

Wall [val] m -(e)s, -e embankment; (Bollwerk) rampart; **w~fahren** vi irreg insep go on a pilgrimage; **~fahrer(in** f) m pilgrim; **~fahrt** f pilgrimage.

Wal- ['val] cpd: **~nuß** f walnut; **~roß** nt walrus.

Walze ['valtsə] f -, -n (Gerät) cylinder; (Fahrzeug) roller; **w~n** vt roll (out).

wälzen ['vɛltsən] vt roll (over); Bücher hunt through; Probleme deliberate on; vr wallow; (vor Schmerzen) roll about; (im Bett) toss and turn.

Walzer ['valtsər] m -s, - waltz.

Wälzer ['vɛltsər] m -s, - (col) tome.

Wand [vant] f -, -e wall; (Trenn—) partition; (Berg—) precipice.

Wandel ['vandəl] m -s change; **w~bar** a changeable, variable; **w~n** vtr change; vi (gehen) walk.

Wander- ['vandər] cpd: **~bühne** f travelling theatre; **~er** m -s, - hiker, rambler; **w~n** vi hike; (Blick) wander; (Gedanken) stray; **~preis** m challenge trophy; **~schaft** f travelling; **~ung** f walking tour, hike.

Wand- cpd: **~lung** f change, transformation; (Rel) transubstantiation; **~schirm** m (folding) screen; **~schrank**

m cupboard; ~**teppich** *m* tapestry; ~**verkleidung** *f* wainscoting.

Wange ['vaŋə] *f* -, -n cheek.

wankelmütig [vaŋkəlmy:tiç] *a* vacillating, inconstant.

wanken ['vaŋkən] *vi* stagger; (*fig*) waver.

wann [van] *ad* when.

Wanne ['vanə] *f* -, -n tub.

Wanze ['vantsə] *f* -, -n bug.

Wappen ['vapən] *nt* -s, - coat of arms, crest; ~**kunde** *f* heraldry.

Ware ['va:rə] *f* -, -n ware; ~**nhaus** *nt* department store; ~**nlager** *nt* stock, store; ~**nprobe** *f* sample; ~**nzeichen** *nt* trademark.

warm [varm] *a* warm; *Essen* hot.

Wärm- ['verm] *cpd:* ~**e** *f* -, -n warmth; **w~en** *vtr* warm, heat; ~**flasche** *f* hot-water bottle.

warm- *cpd:* ~**herzig** *a* warm-hearted; ~**laufen** *vi irreg* (*Aut*) warm up; **W~ 'wassertank** *m* hot-water tank.

warnen ['varnən] *vt* warn.

Warnung *f* warning.

warten ['vartən] *vi* wait (*auf +acc* for); **auf sich ~ lassen** take a long time.

Wärter(in *f*) ['vertər(in)] *m* -s, - attendant.

Warte- ['vartə] *cpd:* ~**saal** *m* (*Rail*), ~**zimmer** *nt* waiting room.

Wartung *f* servicing; service.

warum [va'rʊm] *ad* why.

Warze ['vartsə] *f* -, -n wart.

was [vas] *pron* what; (*col:* etwas) something.

Wasch- ['vaʃ] *cpd:* **w~bar** *a* washable; ~**becken** *nt* washbasin; **w~echt** *a* colourfast; (*fig*) genuine.

Wäsche ['vɛʃə] *f* -, -n wash(ing); (*Bett—*) linen; (*Unter—*) underclothing; ~**klammer** *f* clothes peg, clothespin (*US*); ~**leine** *f* washing line.

waschen ['vaʃən] *irreg vti* wash; *vr* (have a) wash; **sich** (*dat*) **die Hände ~** wash one's hands; **~ und legen** *Haare* shampoo and set.

Wäsche- *cpd:* ~**'rei** *f* laundry; ~**schleuder** *f* spin-drier.

Wasch- *cpd:* ~**küche** *f* laundry room; ~**lappen** *m* face flannel, washcloth (*US*); (*col*) sissy; ~**maschine** *f* washing machine; ~**mittel** *nt*, ~**pulver** *nt* detergent, washing powder; ~**tisch** *m* washhand basin.

Wasser ['vasər] *nt* -s, - water; **w~dicht** *a* watertight, waterproof; ~**fall** *m* waterfall; ~**farbe** *f* watercolour; **w~gekühlt** *a* (*Aut*) water-cooled; ~**hahn** *m* tap, faucet (*US*).

wässerig ['vɛsəriç] *a* watery.

Wasser- *cpd:* ~**kraftwerk** *nt* hydroelectric power station; ~**leitung** *f* water pipe; ~**mann** *m* (*Astrol*) Aquarius; **w~n** *vi* land on the water.

wässern ['vɛsərn] *vti* water.

Wasser- *cpd:* **w~scheu** *a* afraid of the water; ~**schi** *nt* water-skiing; ~**stand** *m* water level; ~**stoff** *m* hydrogen; ~**stoffbombe** *f* hydrogen bomb; ~**waage** *f*

spirit level; ~**welle** *f* shampoo and set; ~**zeichen** *nt* watermark.

waten ['va:tən] *vi* wade.

watscheln ['va:tʃəln] *vi* waddle.

Watt [vat] *nt* -(e)s, -en mud flats *pl*; *nt* -s, - (*Elec*) watt; ~**e** *f* -, -n cotton wool, absorbent cotton (*US*); **w~ieren** [va'ti:rən] *vt* pad.

Web- ['ve:b] *cpd:* **w~en** *vt irreg* weave; ~**er** *m* -s, - weaver; ~**e'rei** *f* (*Betrieb*) weaving mill; ~**stuhl** *m* loom.

Wechsel ['vɛksəl] *m* -s, - change; (*Comm*) bill of exchange; ~**beziehung** *f* correlation; ~**geld** *nt* change; **w~haft** *a Wetter* variable; ~**jahre** *pl* change of life; ~**kurs** *m* rate of exchange; **w~n** *vt* change; *Blicke* exchange; *vi* change; vary; (*Geld* —) have change; ~**strom** *m* alternating current; ~**wirkung** *f* interaction.

wecken ['vɛkən] *vt* wake (up); call.

Wecker ['vɛkər] *m* -s, - alarm clock.

wedeln ['ve:dəln] *vi* (*mit Schwanz*) wag; (*mit Fächer*) fan; (*Ski*) wedeln.

weder ['ve:dər] *cj* neither; ~ ... **noch** ... neither ... nor ...

weg [vɛk] *ad* away, off; **über etw** (*acc*) ~ **sein** be over sth; **er war schon ~** he had already left; **Finger ~!** hands off!; **W~** ['ve:k] *m* -(e)s, -e way; (*Pfad*) path; (*Route*) route; **sich auf den W~ machen** be on one's way; **jdm aus dem W~ gehen** keep out of sb's way; **W~bereiter** *m* -s, - pioneer; ~**blasen** *vt irreg* blow away; ~**bleiben** *vi irreg* stay away.

wegen ['ve:gən] *prep +gen or* (*col*) *dat* because of.

weg- ['vɛk] *cpd:* ~**fahren** *vi irreg* drive away; leave; ~**fallen** *vi irreg* be left out; (*Ferien, Bezahlung*) be cancelled; (*aufhören*) cease; ~**gehen** *vi irreg* go away; leave; ~**jagen** *vt* chase away; ~**lassen** *vt irreg* leave out; ~**laufen** *vi irreg* run away or off; ~**legen** *vt* put aside; ~**machen** *vt* (*col*) get rid of; ~**müssen** *vi irreg* (*col*) have to go; ~**nehmen** *vt irreg* take away; ~**räumen** *vt* clear away; ~**schaffen** *vt* clear away; ~**schnappen** *vt* snatch away (*jdm etw* sth from sb); ~**tun** *vt irreg* put away; **W~weiser** ['ve:gvaizər] *m* -s, - road sign, signpost; ~**werfen** *vt irreg* throw away; ~**werfend** *a* disparaging; ~**ziehen** *vi irreg* move away.

weh [ve:] *a* sore; ~ **tun** hurt, be sore; **jdm/sich ~ tun** hurt sb/o.s.; ~**(e)** *interj:* ~(e), **wenn du** ... woe betide you if ... ; **o ~!** oh dear!; **W~e** *f* -, -n drift; ~**en** *vti* blow; (*Fahnen*) flutter; **W~en** *pl* (*Med*) labour pains *pl*; ~**klagen** *vi insep* wail; ~**leidig** *a* whiny, whining; **W~mut** *f* melancholy; ~**mütig** *a* melancholy.

Wehr [ve:r] *nt* -(e)s, -e weir; *f:* **sich zur ~ setzen** defend o.s.; ~**dienst** *m* military service; **w~en** *vr* defend o.s.; **w~los** *a* defenceless; ~**macht** *f* armed forces *pl*; ~**pflicht** *f* compulsory military service; **w~pflichtig** *a* liable for military service.

Weib [vaip] *nt* -(e)s, -er woman, female; wife; ~**chen** *nt* female; **w~isch** ['vaibiʃ] *a* sissyish; **w~lich** *a* feminine.

weich [vaiç] *a* soft; **W~e** *f* -, **-n** (Rail) points *pl*; **~en** *vi irreg* yield, give away; **W~ensteller** *m* -s, - pointsman; **W~heit** *f* softness; **~lich** *a* soft, namby-pamby; **W~ling** *m* weakling.

Weide [vaidə] *f* -, **-n** (Baum) willow; (Gras) pasture; **w~n** *vi* graze; *vr*: **sich an etw** (dat) **w~n** delight in sth.

weidlich [vaitliç] *ad* thoroughly.

weigern [vaigərn] *vr* refuse.

Weigerung [vaigəruŋ] *f* refusal.

Weih- [vai] *cpd*: **~e** *f* -, **-n** consecration; (Priester—) ordination; **w~en** *vt* consecrate; ordain; **~er** *m* -s, - pond; **~nacht** *f* -, **~nachten** *nt* - Christmas; **w~nachtlich** *a* Christmas; **~nachts-abend** *m* Christmas Eve; **~nachtslied** *nt* Christmas carol; **~nachtsmann** *m* Father Christmas, Santa Claus; **zweiter ~nachtstag** *m* Boxing Day; **~rauch** *m* incense; **~wasser** *nt* holy water.

weil [vail] *cj* because.

Weile [vailə] *f* - while, short time.

Wein [vain] *m* **-(e)s, -e** wine; (Pflanze) vine; **~bau** *m* cultivation of vines; **~beere** *f* grape; **~berg** *m* vineyard; **~bergschnecke** *f* snail; **~brand** *m* brandy; **w~en** *vti* cry; **das ist zum ~en** it's enough to make you cry *or* weep; **w~erlich** *a* tearful; **~geist** *m* spirits of wine; **~lese** *f* vintage; **~rebe** *f* vine; **~stein** *m* tartar; **~stock** *m* vine; **~traube** *f* grape.

weise [vaizə] *a* wise; **W~(r)** *mf* wise old man/woman, sage.

Weise [vaizə] *f* -, **-n** manner, way; (Lied) tune; **auf diese ~** in this way; **w~n** *vt irreg* show.

Weisheit [vaishait] *f* wisdom; **~szahn** *m* wisdom tooth.

weiß [vais] *a* white; **W~brot** *nt* white bread; **~en** *vt* whitewash; **W~glut** *f* (Tech) incandescence; **jdn bis zur W~glut bringen** (fig) make sb see red; **W~kohl** *m* (white) cabbage; **W~wein** *m* white wine.

Weisung [vaizuŋ] *f* instruction.

weit [vait] *a* wide; (Begriff) broad; Reise, Wurf long; **wie ~ ist es . . .?** how far is it . . .?; **in ~er Ferne** in the far distance; **das geht zu ~** that's going too far; *ad* far; **~aus** *ad* by far; **~blickend** *a* far-seeing; **W~e** *f* -, **-n** width; (Raum) space; (von Entfernung) distance; **~en** *vtr* widen.

weiter [vaitər] *a* wider; broader; farther (away); (zusätzlich) further; **ohne ~es** without further ado; just like that; *ad* further; **~ nichts/niemand** nothing/nobody else; **~arbeiten** *vi* go on working; **~bilden** *vr* continue one's studies; **~empfehlen** *vt irreg* recommend (to others); **W~fahrt** *f* continuation of the journey; **~gehen** *vi irreg* go on; **~hin** *ad*: **etw ~hin tun** go on doing sth; **~leiten** *vt* pass on; **~machen** *vti* continue; **~reisen** *vi* continue one's journey.

weit- *cpd*: **~gehend** *a* considerable; *ad* largely; **~läufig** *a* Gebäude spacious; Erklärung lengthy; Verwandter distant;

~schweifig *a* long-winded; **~sichtig** *a* (lit) long-sighted; (fig) far-sighted; **W~sprung** *m* long jump; **~verbreitet** *a* widespread; **W~winkelobjektiv** *nt* (Phot) wide-angle lens.

Weizen [vaitsən] *m* -s, - wheat.

welch [vɛlç] *pron*: **~ ein(e) . . .** what a . . .; **~e** *indef pron* (col: einige) some; **~e(r,s)** *rel pron* (für Personen) who; (für Sachen) which; *interrog pron* (adjektivisch) which; (substantivisch) which one.

welk [vɛlk] *a* withered; **~en** *vi* wither.

Well- [vɛl] *cpd*: **~blech** *nt* corrugated iron; **~e** *f* -, **-n** wave; (Tech) shaft; **~enbereich** *m* waveband; **~enbrecher** *m* -s, - breakwater; **~enlänge** *f* (lit, fig) wavelength; **~enlinie** *f* wavy line; **~ensittich** *m* budgerigar; **~pappe** *f* corrugated cardboard.

Welt [vɛlt] *f* -, **-en** world; **~all** *nt* universe; **~anschauung** *f* philosophy of life; **w~berühmt** *a* world-famous; **w~fremd** *a* unworldly; **~krieg** *m* world war; **w~lich** *a* worldly; (nicht kirchlich) secular; **~macht** *f* world power; **w~männisch** *a* sophisticated; **~meister** *m* world champion; **~raum** *m* space; **~reise** *f* trip round the world; **~stadt** *f* metropolis; **w~weit** *a* world-wide; **~wunder** *nt* wonder of the world.

wem [ve:m] *pron* (dat) to whom.

wen [ve:n] *pron* (acc) whom.

Wende [vɛndə] *f* -, **-n** turn; (Veränderung) change; **~kreis** *m* (Geog) tropic; (Aut) turning circle; **~ltreppe** *f* spiral staircase; **w~n** *vtir irreg* turn; **sich an jdn w~n** go/come to sb; **~punkt** *m* turning point.

Wendung *f* turn; (Rede—) idiom.

wenig [ve:niç] *a,ad* little; **~e** [ve:nigə] *pl* few *pl*; **W~keit** *f* trifle; **meine W~keit** yours truly, little me; **~ste(r,s)** *a* least; **~stens** *ad* at least.

wenn [vɛn] *cj* if; (zeitlich) when; **~ auch . . .** even if . . .; **~ ich doch . . .** if only I . . .; **~schon** *ad*: **na ~schon** so what?; **~schon, dennschon** if a thing's worth doing, it's worth doing properly.

wer [ve:r] *pron* who.

Werbe- [vɛrbə] *cpd*: **~fernsehen** *nt* commercial television; **~kampagne** *f* advertising campaign; **w~n** *irreg vt* win; Mitglied recruit; *vi* advertise; **um jdn/etw w~n** try to win sb/sth; **für jdn/etw w~n** promote sb/sth.

Werbung *f* advertising; (von Mitgliedern) recruitment; (um jdn/etw) promotion (um of).

Werdegang [ve:rdəgaŋ] *m* development; (beruflich) career.

werden [ve:rdən] *vi irreg* become; *v aux* (Futur) shall, will; (Passiv) be; **was ist aus ihm/aus der Sache geworden?** what became of him/it?; **es ist nichts/gut geworden** it came to nothing/turned out well; **mir wird kalt** I'm getting cold; **das muß anders ~** that will have to change; **zu Eis ~** turn to ice.

werfen [vɛrfən] *vt irreg* throw.

Werft [vɛrft] *f* -, **-en** shipyard, dockyard.

Werk [vɛrk] nt -(e)s, -e work; (Tätigkeit) job; (Fabrik, Mechanismus) works pl; ans ~ gehen set to work; ~statt f -, -stätten workshop; (Aut) garage; ~student m self-supporting student; ~tag m working day; w~tags ad on working days; w~tägig a working; ~zeug nt tool; ~zeugschrank m tool chest.

Wermut ['veːrmuːt] m -(e)s wormwood; (Wein) vermouth.

Wert [veːrt] m -(e)s, -e worth; (Fin) value; ~ legen auf (+acc) attach importance to; es hat doch keinen ~ it's useless; w~ a worth; (geschätzt) dear; worthy; das ist nichts/viel w~ it's not worth anything/it's worth a lot; das ist es/er mir w~ it's/he's worth that to me; ~angabe f declaration of value; w~en vt rate; ~gegenstand m article of value; w~los a worthless; ~losigkeit f worthlessness; ~papier nt security; w~voll a valuable; ~zuwachs m appreciation.

Wesen ['veːzən] nt -s, - (Geschöpf) being; (Natur, Character) nature; w~tlich a significant; (beträchtlich) considerable.

weshalb [vɛsˈhalp] ad why.

Wespe ['vɛspə] f -, -n wasp.

wessen ['vɛsən] pron (gen) whose.

West- [vɛst] cpd: ~e f -, -n waistcoat, vest (US); (Woll—) cardigan; ~en m -s west; w~lich a western; ad to the west; w~wärts ad westwards.

weswegen [vɛsˈveːɡən] ad why.

wett [vɛt] a even; W~bewerb m competition; W~e f -, -n bet, wager; W~eifer m rivalry; ~en vti bet.

Wetter ['vɛtɐr] nt -s, - weather; ~bericht m weather report; ~dienst m meteorological service; ~lage f (weather) situation; ~vorhersage f weather forecast; ~warte f -, -n weather station; w~wendisch a capricious.

Wett- cpd: ~kampf m contest; ~lauf m race; w~laufen vi irreg race; w~machen vt make good; ~spiel nt match; ~streit m contest.

wetzen ['vɛtsən] vt sharpen.

Wicht [vɪçt] m -(e)s, -e titch; (pej) worthless creature; w~ig a important; ~igkeit f importance.

wickeln ['vɪkəln] vt wind; Haare set; Kind change; jdn/etw in etw (acc) ~ wrap sb/sth in sth.

Widder ['vɪdɐr] m -s, - ram; (Astrol) Aries.

wider ['vɪːdɐr] prep +acc against; ~-'fahren vi irreg happen (jdm to sb); ~'legen vt refute.

widerlich ['vɪːdɐrlɪç] a disgusting, repulsive; W~keit f repulsiveness.

wider- ['vɪːdɐr] cpd: ~rechtlich a unlawful; W~rede f contradiction.

Widerruf ['vɪːdɐruːf] m retraction; countermanding; w~en vt irreg insep retract; Anordnung revoke; Befehl countermand.

wider'setzen vr insep oppose (jdm/etw sb/sth).

widerspenstig ['vɪːdɐrʃpɛnstɪç] a wilful; W~keit f wilfulness.

widerspiegeln ['vɪːdɐrʃpiːɡəln] vt reflect.

wider'sprechen vi irreg insep contradict (jdm sb); ~d a contradictory.

Widerspruch ['vɪːdɐrʃprʊx] m contradiction; w~slos ad without arguing.

Widerstand ['vɪːdɐrʃtant] m resistance; ~sbewegung f resistance (movement); w~sfähig a resistant, tough; w~slos a unresisting.

wider'stehen vi irreg insep withstand (jdm/etw sb/sth).

widmen ['vɪtmən] vt dedicate; vtr devote (o.s.).

Widmung f dedication.

widrig ['vɪːdrɪç] a Umstände adverse; Mensch repulsive.

wie [viː] ad how; cj ~ ich schon sagte as I said; (so) schön ~ ... as beautiful as ...; ~ du like you; singen ~ ein ... sing like a ...

wieder ['viːdɐr] ad again; ~ da sein be back (again); gehst du schon ~? are you off again?; ~ ein(e) ... another ... .; W~aufbau [-ˈʔaʊfbaʊ] m rebuilding; W~aufnahme [-ˈʔaʊfnaːmə] f resumption; ~aufnehmen vt irreg resume; ~bekommen vt irreg get back; ~bringen vt irreg bring back; ~erkennen vt irreg recognize; W~erstattung f reimbursement; ~gabe f reproduction; ~geben vt irreg (zurückgeben) return; Erzählung etc repeat; Gefühle etc convey; ~gutmachen [-ˈguːtmaxən] vt make up for; Fehler put right; W~'gutmachung f reparation; ~'herstellen vt restore; ~'holen vt insep repeat; W~'holung f repetition; W~hören nt: auf W~hören (Tel) goodbye; W~kehr f - return; (von Vorfall) repetition, recurrence; W~kunft f -, -e return; ~sehen vt irreg see again; auf W~sehen goodbye; ~um ad again; (andererseits) on the other hand; ~vereinigen vt reunite; W~wahl f re-election.

Wiege ['viːɡə] f -, -n cradle; w~n vt (schaukeln) rock; vti irreg (Gewicht) weigh; ~nfest nt birthday.

wiehern ['viːɐrn] vi neigh, whinny.

Wiese ['viːzə] f -, -n meadow; ~l nt -s, - weasel.

wieso [viːˈzoː] ad why.

wieviel [viːˈfiːl] a how much; ~ Menschen how many people; ~mal ad how often; ~te(r,s) a: zum ~ten Mal? how many times?; den W~ten haben wir? what's the date?; an ~ter Stelle? in what place?; der ~te Besucher war er? how many visitors were there before him?

wieweit [viːvaɪt] ad to what extent.

wild [vɪlt] a wild; W~ nt -(e)s game; ~ern ['vɪldɐrn] vi poach; ~fremd a (col) quite strange or unknown; W~heit f wildness; W~leder nt suede; W~nis f -, -se wilderness; W~schwein nt (wild) boar.

Wille ['vɪlə] m **-ns, -n** will; **w~n** prep +gen: **um . . . w~n** for the sake of . . .; **w~nlos** a weak-willed; **w~nsstark** a strong-willed.

will- cpd: **~ig** a willing; **~kommen** [vɪl'kɔmən] a welcome; **jdn ~kommen heißen** welcome sb; **W~kommen** nt **-s, -** welcome; **~kürlich** a arbitrary; Bewegung voluntary.

wimmeln ['vɪməln] vi swarm (von with).

wimmern ['vɪmərn] vi whimper.

Wimper ['vɪmpər] f **-, -n** eyelash.

Wind [vɪnt] m **-(e)s, -e** wind; **~beutel** m cream puff; (fig) windbag; **~e** ['vɪndə] f **-, -n** (Tech) winch, windlass; (Bot) bindweed; **~el** ['vɪndəl] f **-, -n** nappy, diaper (US); **w~en** ['vɪndən] vi impers be windy; irreg vt wind; Kranz weave; (ent—) twist; vr wind; (Person) writhe; **~hose** f whirlwind; **~hund** m greyhound; (Mensch) fly-by-night; **w~ig** ['vɪndɪç] a windy; (fig) dubious; **~mühle** f windmill; **~pocken** pl chickenpox; **~schutzscheibe** f (Aut) windscreen, windshield (US); **~stärke** f wind force; **~stille** f calm; **~stoß** m gust of wind.

Wink [vɪŋk] m **-(e)s, -e** hint; (mit Kopf) nod; (mit Hand) wave.

Winkel ['vɪŋkəl] m **-s, -** (Math) angle; (Gerät) set square; (in Raum) corner.

winken ['vɪŋkən] vti wave.

winseln ['vɪnzəln] vi whine.

Winter ['vɪntər] m **-s, -** winter; **w~lich** a wintry; **~sport** m winter sports pl.

Winzer ['vɪntsər] m **-s, -** vine grower.

winzig ['vɪntsɪç] a tiny.

Wipfel ['vɪpfəl] m **-s, -** treetop.

wir [viːr] pron we; **~ alle** all of us, we all.

Wirbel ['vɪrbəl] m **-s, -** whirl, swirl; (Trubel) hurly-burly; (Aufsehen) fuss; (Anat) vertebra; **w~n** vi whirl, swirl; **~säule** f spine; **~tier** nt vertebrate; **~wind** m whirlwind.

wirken ['vɪrkən] vi have an effect; (erfolgreich sein) work; (scheinen) seem; vt Wunder work.

wirklich ['vɪrklɪç] a real; **W~keit** f reality.

wirksam ['vɪrkzaːm] a effective; **W~keit** f effectiveness, efficacy.

Wirkung ['vɪrkuŋ] f effect; **w~slos** a ineffective; **w~slos bleiben** have no effect; **w~svoll** a effective.

wirr [vɪr] a confused, wild; **W~warr** [-var] m **-s** disorder, chaos.

Wirsing(kohl) ['vɪrzɪŋ(koːl)] m **-s** savoy cabbage.

Wirt [vɪrt] m **-(e)s, -e** landlord; **~in** f landlady; **~schaft** f (Gaststätte) pub; (Haushalt) housekeeping; (eines Landes) economy; (col: Durcheinander) mess; **w~schaftlich** a economical; (Pol) economic; **~schaftskrise** f economic crisis; **~schaftsprüfer** m chartered accountant; **~schaftswunder** nt economic miracle; **~shaus** nt inn.

Wisch [vɪʃ] m **-(e)s, -e** scrap of paper; **w~en** vt wipe; **~er** m **-s, -** (Aut) wiper.

wispern ['vɪspərn] vti whisper.

Wißbegier(de) ['vɪsbəgiːr(də)] f thirst for knowledge; **w~ig** a inquisitive, eager for knowledge.

wissen ['vɪsən] vt irreg know; **W~** nt **-s** knowledge; **W~schaft** f science; **W~schaftler(in** f) m **-s,** scientist; **~schaftlich** a scientific; **~swert** a worth knowing; **~tlich** a knowing.

wittern ['vɪtərn] vt scent; (fig) suspect.

Witterung f weather; (Geruch) scent.

Witwe ['vɪtvə] f **-, -n** widow; **~r** m **-s, -** widower.

Witz [vɪts] m **-es, -e** joke; **~blatt** nt comic (paper); **~bold** m **-(e)s, -e** joker, wit; **w~eln** vi joke; **w~ig** a funny.

wo [voː] ad where; (col: irgendwo) somewhere; **im Augenblick, ~ . . .** the moment (that) . . .; **die Zeit, ~ . . .** the time when . . .; cj (wenn) if; **~anders** [voː'andərs] ad elsewhere; **~bei** [voː'baɪ] ad (rel) by/with which; (interrog) what . . . in/by/with.

Woche ['vɔxə] f **-, -n** week; **~nende** nt weekend; **w~nlang** a,ad for weeks; **~nschau** f newsreel.

wöchentlich ['væçəntlɪç] a,ad weekly.

wo- cpd: **~durch** [voː'durç] ad (rel) through which; (interrog) what . . . through; **~für** [voː'fyːr] ad (rel) for which; (interrog) what . . . for.

Woge ['voːgə] f **-, -n** wave; **w~n** vi heave, surge.

wo- cpd: **~gegen** [voː'geːgən] ad (rel) against which; (interrog) what . . . against; **~her** [voː'heːr] ad where . . . from; **~hin** [voː'hɪn] ad where . . . to.

wohl [voːl] ad well; (behaglich) at ease, comfortable; (vermutlich) I suppose, probably; (gewiß) certainly; **er weiß das ~** he knows that perfectly well; **W~** nt **-(e)s** welfare; **zum W~!** cheers!; **~auf** [voːl'aʊf] ad well; **W~behagen** nt comfort; **~behalten** ad safe and sound; **W~fahrt** f welfare; **~habend** a wealthy; **~ig** a contented, comfortable; **W~klang** m melodious sound; **~schmeckend** a delicious; **W~stand** m prosperity; **W~standsgesellschaft** f affluent society; **W~tat** f relief; act of charity; **W~täter(in** f) m benefactor; **~tätig** a charitable; **~tun** vi irreg do good (jdm sb); **~verdient** a well-earned, well-deserved; **~weislich** ad prudently; **W~wollen** nt **-s** good will; **~wollend** a benevolent.

wohn- cpd: **~en** vi live; **~haft** a resident; **~lich** a comfortable; **W~ort** m domicile; **W~sitz** place of residence; **W~ung** f house; (Etagen—) flat, apartment (US); **W~ungsnot** f housing shortage; **W~wagen** m caravan; **W~zimmer** nt living room.

wölben ['vœlbən] vtr curve.

Wölbung f curve.

Wolf [vɔlf] m **-(e)s, ̈-e** wolf.

Wölfin ['vœlfɪn] f she-wolf.

Wolke ['vɔlkə] f **-, -n** cloud; **~nkratzer** m skyscraper.

wolkig ['vɔlkɪç] a cloudy.

Wolle ['vɔlə] f **-, -n** wool; **w~n** a woollen.

wollen ['vɔlən] vti want.

wollüstig ['vɔlʏstɪç] a lusty, sensual.
wo- cpd: ~**mit** [vo:'mɪt] ad (rel) with which; (interrog) what . . . with; ~**möglich** [vo:'mø:klɪç] ad probably, I suppose; ~**nach** [vo:'na:x] ad (rel) after/for which; (interrog) what . . . for/after.
Wonne ['vɔnə] f -, -n joy, bliss.
wo- cpd: ~**ran** [vo:'ran] ad (rel) on/at which; (interrog) what . . . on/at; ~**rauf** [vo:'rauf] ad (rel) on which; (interrog) what . . . on; ~**raus** [vo:'raus] ad (rel) from/out of which; (interrog) what . . . from/out of; ~**rin** [vo:'rɪn] ad (rel) in which; (interrog) what . . . in.
Wort [vɔrt] nt -(e)s, ⁻er, -e word; **jdn beim** ~ **nehmen** take sb at his word; **w~brüchig** a not true to one's word.
Wörterbuch ['vœrtərbuːx] nt dictionary.
Wort- cpd: ~**führer** m spokesman; **w~getreu** a true to one's word; Übersetzung literal; **w~karg** a taciturn; ~**laut** m wording.
wörtlich ['vœrtlɪç] a literal.
Wort- cpd: **w~los** a mute; **w~reich** a wordy, verbose; ~**schatz** m vocabulary; ~**spiel** nt play on words, pun; ~**wechsel** m dispute.
wo- cpd: ~**rüber** [vo:'ry:bər] ad (rel) over/about which; (interrog) what . . . over/about; ~**rum** [vo:'rum] ad (rel) about/round which; (interrog) what . . . about/round; ~**runter** [vo:'runtər] ad (rel) under which; (interrog) what . . . under; ~**von** [vo:'fɔn] ad (rel) from which; (interrog) what . . . from; ~**vor** [vo:'fɔːr] ad (rel) in front of/before which; (interrog) in front of/before what; of what; ~**zu** [vo:'tsu:] ad (rel) to/for which; (interrog) what . . . for/to; (warum) why.
Wrack [vrak] nt -(e)s, -s wreck.
wringen ['vrɪŋən] vt irreg wring.
Wucher ['vu:xər] m -s profiteering; ~**er** m -s, - profiteer; **w~isch** a profiteering; **w~n** vi (Pflanzen) grow wild; ~**ung** f (Med) growth, tumour.
Wuchs [vu:ks] m -es (Wachstum) growth; (Statur) build.
Wucht [vuxt] f - force; **w~ig** a solid, massive.
wühlen ['vy:lən] vi scrabble; (Tier) root; (Maulwurf) burrow; (col: arbeiten) slave away; vt dig.
Wulst [vulst] -es, ⁻e bulge; (an Wunde) swelling.
wund [vunt] a sore, raw; **W~e** ['vundə] f -, -n wound.
Wunder ['vundər] nt -s, - miracle; **es ist kein** ~ it's no wonder; **w~bar** a wonderful, marvellous; **w~kind** nt infant prodigy; **w~lich** a odd, peculiar; **w~n** vr be surprised (über +acc at); vt surprise; **w~schön** a beautiful; **w~voll** a wonderful.
Wundstarrkrampf ['vuntʃtarkrampf] m tetanus, lockjaw.
Wunsch [vunʃ] m -(e)s, ⁻e wish.
wünschen ['vʏnʃən] vt wish; **sich** (dat) **etw** ~ want sth, wish for sth; ~**swert** a desirable.

Würde ['vʏrdə] f -, -n dignity; (Stellung) honour; ~**nträger** m dignitary; **w~voll** a dignified.
würdig ['vʏrdɪç] a worthy; (würdevoll) dignified; ~**en** ['vʏrdɪgən] vt appreciate; **jdn keines Blickes** ~**en** not so much as look at sb.
Wurf [vurf] m -s, ⁻e throw; (Junge) litter.
Würfel ['vʏrfəl] m -s, - dice; (Math) cube; ~**becher** m (dice) cup; **w~n** vi play dice; vt dice; ~**spiel** nt game of dice; ~**zucker** m lump sugar.
würgen ['vʏrgən] vti choke.
Wurm [vurm] m -(e)s, ⁻er worm; **w~en** vt (col) rile, nettle; ~**fortsatz** m (Med) appendix; **w~ig** a worm-eaten; ~**stichig** a worm-ridden.
Wurst [vurst] f -, ⁻e sausage; **das ist mir** ~ (col) I don't care, I don't give a damn.
Würze ['vʏrtsə] f -, -n seasoning, spice.
Wurzel ['vurtsəl] f -, -n root.
würz- ['vʏrts] cpd: ~**en** vt season, spice; ~**ig** a spicy.
wüst [vy:st] a untidy, messy; (ausschweifend) wild; (öde) waste; (col: heftig) terrible; **W~e** f -, -n desert; **W~ling** m rake.
Wut [vu:t] f - rage, fury; ~**anfall** m fit of rage.
wüten ['vy:tən] vi rage; ~**d** a furious, mad.

X

X,x [ɪks] nt X,x.
X-Beine ['ɪksbaɪnə] pl knock-knees pl.
x-beliebig [ɪksbə'li:bɪç] a any (whatever).
xerokopieren [kseroko'pi:rən] vt xerox, photocopy.
x-mal ['ɪksma:l] ad any number of times, n times.
Xylophon [ksylo'fo:n] nt -s, -e xylophone.

Y

Y,y ['ʏpsilɔn] nt Y,y.
Ypsilon nt -(s), -s the letter Y.

Z

Z,z [tsɛt] nt Z,z.
Zacke ['tsakə] f -, -n point; (Berg—) jagged peak; (Gabel—) prong; (Kamm—) tooth.
zackig ['tsakɪç] a jagged; (col) smart; Tempo brisk.
zaghaft ['tsa:khaft] a timid; **Z~igkeit** f timidity.
zäh [tsɛ:] a tough; Mensch tenacious; Flüssigkeit thick; (schleppend) sluggish; **Z~igkeit** f toughness; tenacity.
Zahl [tsa:l] f -, -en number; **z~bar** a payable; **z~en** vti pay; **z~en bitte!** the bill please!
zählen ['tsɛ:lən] vti count (auf +acc on); ~**zu** be numbered among.
Zahl- cpd: **z~enmäßig** a numerical; ~**er** m -s, - payer.
Zähler ['tsɛ:lər] m -s, - (Tech) meter; (Math) numerator.
Zahl- cpd: **z~los** a countless; **z~reich** a

numerous; ~**tag** m payday; ~**ung** f payment; z~**ungsfähig** a solvent; ~**wort** nt numeral.

zahm [tsa:m] a tame.

zähmen ['tsɛ:mən] vt tame; (fig) curb.

Zahn [tsa:n] m -(e)s, ⸚e tooth; ~**arzt** m dentist; ~**bürste** f toothbrush; z~**en** vi cut teeth; ~**fäule** f · tooth decay, caries; ~**fleisch** nt gums pl; ~**pasta**, ~**paste** f toothpaste; ~**rad** nt cog(wheel); ~**radbahn** f rack railway; ~**schmelz** m (tooth) enamel; ~**schmerzen** pl toothache; ~**stein** m tartar; ~**stocher** m -s, · toothpick.

Zange ['tsaŋə] f -, -n pliers pl; (Zucker— etc) tongs pl; (Beiß—, Zool) pincers pl; (Med) forceps pl; ~**ngeburt** f forceps delivery.

Zank- [tsaŋk] cpd: ~**apfel** m bone of contention; z~**en** vir quarrel.

zänkisch ['tsɛŋkɪʃ] a quarrelsome.

Zäpfchen ['tsɛpfçən] nt (Anat) uvula; (Med) suppository.

Zapfen ['tsapfən] m -s, · plug; (Bot) cone; (Eis—) icicle; z~ vt tap; ~**streich** m (Mil) tattoo.

zappelig ['tsapəlɪç] a wriggly; (unruhig) fidgety.

zappeln ['tsapəln] vi wriggle; fidget.

zart [tsart] a (weich, leise) soft; (Braten etc) tender; (fein, schwächlich) delicate; Z~**gefühl** nt tact; Z~**heit** f softness; tenderness; delicacy.

zärtlich ['tsɛ:rtlɪç] a tender, affectionate; Z~**keit** f tenderness; pl caresses pl.

Zauber ['tsaubər] m -s, · magic; (—bann) spell; ~**ei** [-'raɪ] f magic; ~**er** m -s, · magician; conjuror; z~**haft** a magical, enchanting; ~**künstler** m conjuror; z~**n** vi conjure, practise magic; ~**spruch** m (magic) spell.

zaudern ['tsaudərn] vi hesitate.

Zaum [tsaum] m -(e)s, **Zäume** bridle; etw im ~ **halten** keep sth in check.

Zaun [tsaun] m -(e)s, **Zäune** fence; vom ~(e) **brechen** (fig) start; ~**könig** m wren; ~**pfahl** m: ein Wink mit dem ~ **pfahl** a broad hint.

Zeche ['tsɛçə] f -, -n bill; (Bergbau) mine.

Zecke ['tsɛkə] f -, -n tick.

Zehe ['tse:ə] f -, -n toe; (Knoblauch—) clove.

zehn [tse:n] num ten; ~**te(r,s)** a tenth; Z~**tel** nt -s, · tenth (part).

Zeich- ['tsaɪç] cpd: ~**en** nt -s, · sign; z~**nen** vti draw; (kenn—) mark; (unter—) sign; ~**ner** m -s, · artist; technischer ~**ner** draughtsman; ~**nung** f drawing; (Markierung) markings pl.

Zeig- ['tsaɪg] cpd: ~**efinger** m index finger; z~**en** vt show; vi point (auf +acc to, at); vr show o.s.; **es wird sich** z~**en** time will tell; **es zeigte sich, daß** . . . it turned out that . . .; ~**er** m -s, · pointer; (Uhr—) hand.

Zeile ['tsaɪlə] f -, -n line; (Häuser—) row; ~**nabstand** m line spacing.

Zeit [tsaɪt] f -, -en time; (Gram) tense; **zur** ~ **at the** moment; **sich** (dat) ~ **lassen** take one's time; **von** ~ **zu** ~ from time to time; ~**alter** nt age; z~**gemäß** a in

keeping with the times; ~**genosse** m contemporary; z~**ig** a early; z~'**lebens** ad all one's life; z~**lich** a temporal; ~**lupe** f slow motion; ~**raffer** m -s time-lapse photography; z~**raubend** a time-consuming; ~**raum** m period; ~**rechnung** f time, era; **nach/vor unserer** ~**rechnung** A.D./B.C.; ~**schrift** f periodical; ~**ung** f newspaper; ~**verschwendung** f waste of time; ~**vertreib** m pastime, diversion; z~**weilig** a temporary; z~**weise** ad for a time; ~**wort** nt verb; ~**zeichen** nt (Rad) time signal; ~**zünder** m time fuse.

Zell- ['tsɛl] cpd: ~**e** f -, -n cell; (Telefon—) callbox; ~**kern** m cell, nucleus; ~**stoff** m cellulose; ~**teilung** f cell division.

Zelt [tsɛlt] nt -(e)s, -e tent; ~**bahn** f tarpaulin, groundsheet; z~**en** vi camp.

Zement [tse'mɛnt] m -(e)s, -e cement; z~**ieren** [-'ti:rən] vt cement.

zensieren [tsɛn'zi:rən] vt censor; (Sch) mark.

Zensur [tsɛn'zu:r] f censorship; (Sch) mark.

Zent- cpd: ~**imeter** [tsɛnti'me:tər] m or nt centimetre; ~**ner** ['tsɛntnər] m -s, · hundredweight.

zentral [tsɛn'tra:l] a central; Z~**e** f -, -n central office; (Tel) exchange; Z~**heizung** f central heating; ~**isieren** [tsɛntrali'zi:rən] vt centralize.

Zentri- [tsɛntri] cpd: ~**fugalkraft** [-fu'ga:lkraft] f centrifugal force; ~**fuge** [-'fu:gə] f -, -n centrifuge; (für Wäsche) spindryer.

Zentrum ['tsɛntrum] nt -s, **Zentren** centre.

Zepter ['tsɛptər] nt -s, · sceptre.

zerbrech- [tsɛr'brɛç] cpd: ~**en** vti irreg break; ~**lich** a fragile.

zerbröckeln [tsɛr'brœkəln] vti crumble. (to pieces).

zer'drücken vt squash, crush; Kartoffeln mash.

Zeremonie [tseremo'ni:] f ceremony.

zer'fahren a scatterbrained, distracted.

Zerfall [tsɛr'fal] m decay; z~**en** vi irreg disintegrate, decay; (sich gliedern) fall (in +acc into).

zerfetzen [tsɛr'fɛtsən] vt tear to pieces.

zer'fließen vi irreg dissolve, melt away.

zer'gehen vi irreg melt, dissolve.

zerkleinern [tsɛr'klaɪnərn] vt reduce to small pieces.

zerleg- [tsɛr'le:g] cpd: ~**bar** a able to be dismantled; ~**en** vt take to pieces; Fleisch carve; Satz analyse.

zerlumpt [tsɛr'lumpt] a ragged.

zermalmen [tsɛr'malmən] vt crush.

zermürben [tsɛr'myrbən] vt wear down.

zer'platzen vi burst.

zerquetschen [tsɛr'kvɛtʃən] vt squash.

Zerrbild ['tsɛrbɪlt] nt caricature, distorted picture.

zer'reden vt Problem flog to death.

zer'reiben vt irreg grind down.

zer'reißen irreg vt tear to pieces; vi tear, rip.

zerren ['tsɛrən] vt drag; vi tug (an +dat at).

zer'rinnen vi irreg melt away.

zerrissen [tsɛr'rɪsən] a torn, tattered; **Z~heit** f tattered state; (Pol) disunion, discord; (innere —) disintegration.

zerrütten [tsɛr'rʏtən] vt wreck, destroy.

zerrüttet a wrecked, shattered.

zer'schießen vt irreg shoot to pieces.

zer'schlagen irreg vt shatter, smash; vr fall through.

zerschleißen [tsɛr'ʃlaɪsən] vti irreg wear out.

zer'schneiden vt irreg cut up.

zer'setzen vtr decompose, dissolve.

zersplittern [tsɛr'ʃplɪtərn] vti split (into pieces); (Glas) shatter.

zer'springen vi irreg shatter, burst.

zerstäub- [tsɛr'ʃtɔʏb] cpd: **~en** vt spray; **Z~er** m **-s, -** atomizer.

zerstör- [tsɛr'ʃtøːr] cpd: **~en** vt destroy; **Z~ung** f destruction.

zer'stoßen vt irreg pound, pulverize.

zer'streiten vr irreg fall out, break up.

zerstreu- [tsɛr'ʃtrɔʏ] cpd: **~en** vtr disperse, scatter; (unterhalten) divert; Zweifel etc dispel; **~t** a scattered; Mensch absent-minded; **Z~theit** f absent-mindedness; **Z~ung** f dispersion; (Ablenkung) diversion.

zerstückeln [tsɛr'ʃtʏkəln] vt cut into pieces.

zer'teilen vt divide into parts.

zer'treten vt irreg crush underfoot.

zertrümmern [tsɛr'trʏmərn] vt shatter; Gebäude etc demolish.

Zerwürfnis [tsɛr'vʏrfnɪs] nt **-ses, -se** dissension, quarrel.

zerzausen [tsɛr'tsaʊzən] vt Haare ruffle up, tousle.

zetern ['tseːtərn] vi shout, shriek.

Zettel ['tsɛtəl] m **-s, -** piece of paper, slip; (Notiz—) note; (Formular) form; **~kasten** m card index (box).

Zeug [tsɔʏk] nt **-(e)s, -e** (col) stuff; (Ausrüstung) gear; **dummes ~** (stupid) nonsense; **das ~ haben zu** have the makings of; **sich ins ~ legen** put one's shoulder to the wheel.

Zeuge ['tsɔʏgə] m **-n, -n, Zeugin** ['tsɔʏgɪn] f witness; **z~n** vi bear witness, testify; **es zeugt von . . .** it testifies to . . .; vt Kind father; **~naussage** f evidence; **~nstand** m witness box.

Zeugnis ['tsɔʏgnɪs] nt **-ses, -se** certificate; (Sch) report; (Referenz) reference; (Aussage) evidence, testimony; **~ geben von** be evidence of, testify to.

Zeugung ['tsɔʏgʊŋ] f procreation; **z~sunfähig** a sterile.

Zickzack ['tsɪktsak] m **-(e)s, -e** zigzag.

Ziege ['tsiːgə] f **-, -n** goat; **~nieder** nt kid.

Ziegel ['tsiːgəl] m **-s, -** brick; (Dach—) tile; **~ei** [-'laɪ] f brickworks.

ziehen ['tsiːən] irreg vt draw; (zerren) pull; (Schach etc) move; (züchten) rear; **etw nach sich ~** lead to sth, entail sth; vi draw; (um—, wandern) move; (Rauch, Wolke etc) drift; (reißen) pull; v impers: **es zieht** there is a draught, it's draughty; vr (Gummi) stretch; (Grenze etc) run; (Gespräche) be drawn out.

Ziehharmonika ['tsiː'harmoːnika] f concertina; accordion.

Ziehung ['tsiːʊŋ] f (Los—) drawing.

Ziel [tsiːl] nt **-(e)s, -e** (einer Reise) destination; (Sport) finish; (Mil) target; (Absicht) goal, aim; **z~en** vi aim (auf +acc at); **~fernrohr** nt telescopic sight; **z~los** a aimless; **~scheibe** f target; **z~strebig** a purposeful.

ziemlich ['tsiːmlɪç] a quite a; fair; ad rather; quite a bit.

zieren ['tsiːrən] vr act coy.

Zier- [tsiːr] cpd: **z~lich** a dainty; **~lichkeit** f daintiness; **~strauch** m flowering shrub.

Ziffer ['tsɪfər] f **-, -n** figure, digit; **~blatt** nt dial, clock-face.

zig [tsɪk] a (col) umpteen.

Zigarette [tsiga'rɛtə] f cigarette; **~nautomat** m cigarette machine; **~nschachtel** f cigarette packet; **~nspitze** f cigarette holder.

Zigarillo [tsiga'rɪlo] nt or m **-s, -s** cigarillo.

Zigarre [tsi'garə] f **-, -n** cigar.

Zigeuner(in f) [tsi'gɔʏnər(ɪn)] m **-s, -** gipsy.

Zimmer ['tsɪmər] nt **-s, -** room; **~antenne** f indoor aerial; **~decke** f ceiling; **~herr** m lodger; **~lautstärke** f reasonable volume; **~mädchen** nt chambermaid; **~mann** m carpenter; **z~n** vt make, carpenter; **~pflanze** f indoor plant.

zimperlich ['tsɪmpərlɪç] a squeamish; (pingelig) fussy, finicky.

Zimt [tsɪmt] m **-(e)s, -e** cinnamon; **~stange** f cinnamon stick.

Zink [tsɪŋk] nt **-(e)s** zinc; **~e** f **-, -n** (Gabel—) prong; (Kamm—) tooth; **z~en** vt Karten mark; **~salbe** f zinc ointment.

Zinn [tsɪn] nt **-(e)s** (Element) tin; (in —waren) pewter; **z~oberrot** [tsiˈnoːbərrot] a vermilion; **~soldat** m tin soldier; **~waren** pl pewter.

Zins [tsɪns] m **-es, -en** interest; **~eszins** m compound interest; **~fuß** m, **~satz** m rate of interest; **z~los** a interest-free.

Zipfel ['tsɪpfəl] m **-s, -** corner; (spitz) tip; (Hemd—) tail; (Wurst—) end; **~mütze** f stocking cap; nightcap.

zirka ['tsɪrka] ad (round) about.

Zirkel ['tsɪrkəl] m **-s, -** circle; (Math) pair of compasses; **~kasten** m geometry set.

Zirkus ['tsɪrkʊs] m **-, -se** circus.

Zirrhose [tsiˈroːzə] f **-, -n** cirrhosis.

zischeln ['tsɪʃəln] vti whisper.

zischen ['tsɪʃən] vi hiss.

Zitat [tsi'taːt] nt **-(e)s, -e** quotation, quote.

zitieren [tsi'tiːrən] vt quote.

Zitronat [tsitro'naːt] nt **-(e)s, -e** candied lemon peel.

Zitrone [tsi'troːnə] f **-, -n** lemon; **~nlimonade** f lemonade; **~nsaft** m lemon juice; **~nscheibe** f lemon slice.

zittern ['tsɪtərn] vi tremble.

Zitze ['tsɪtsə] f **-, -n** teat, dug.

zivil [tsi'viːl] a civil; *Preis* moderate; **Z~** *nt* **-s** plain clothes *pl; (Mil)* civilian clothing; **Z~bevölkerung** *f* civilian population; **Z~courage** *f* courage of one's convictions; **Z~isation** [tsivilizatsi'oːn] *f* civilization; **Z~isationserscheinung** *f* phenomenon of civilization; **Z~isationskrankheit** *f* disease peculiar to civilization; **~i'sieren** *vt* civilize; **Z~ist** [tsivi'list] *m* civilian; **Z~recht** *nt* civil law.

Zölibat [tsøli'baːt] *nt or m* **-(e)s** celibacy.

Zoll [tsɔl] *m* **-(e)s**, **ˑe** customs *pl: (Abgabe)* duty; **~abfertigung** *f* customs clearance; **~amt** *nt* customs office; **~beamte(r)** *m* customs official; **~erklärung** *f* customs declaration; **z~frei** a duty-free; **z~pflichtig** a liable to duty, dutiable.

Zone ['tsoːnə] *f* **-**, **-n** zone.

Zoo [tsoː] *m* **-s**, **-s** zoo; **~loge** [tsoo'loːgə] *m* **-n**, **-n** zoologist; **~lo'gie** *f* zoology; **z~'logisch** a zoological.

Zopf [tsɔpf] *m* **-(e)s**, **ˑe** plait; pigtail; *alter* **~** antiquated custom.

Zorn [tsɔrn] *m* **-(e)s** anger; **z~ig** a angry.

Zote [tsoːtə] *f* **-**, **-n** smutty joke/remark.

zottig ['tsɔtɪç] a shaggy.

zu [tsuː] *(mit Infinitiv)* to; *prep +dat (bei Richtung, Vorgang)* to; *(bei Orts-, Zeit-, Preisangabe)* at; *(Zweck)* for; **~m Fenster herein** through the window; **~ meiner Zeit** in my time; ad too; *(in Richtung)* towards (sb/sth); a *(col)* shut.

zualler- [tsu'alər] *cpd:* **~erst** ad first of all; **~letzt** ad last of all.

Zubehör ['tsuːbəhøːr] *nt* **-(e)s**, **-e** accessories *pl.*

Zuber ['tsuːbər] *m* **-s**, **-** tub.

zubereiten ['tsuːbəraɪtən] *vt* prepare.

zubilligen ['tsuːbɪlɪgən] *vt* grant.

zubinden ['tsuːbɪndən] *vt irreg* tie up.

zubleiben ['tsuːblaɪbən] *vi irreg (col)* stay shut.

zubringen ['tsuːbrɪŋən] *vt irreg* spend; *(col) Tür* get shut.

Zubringer *m* **-s**, **-** *(Tech)* feeder, conveyor; **~straße** *f* approach or slip road.

Zucht [tsʊxt] *f* **-**, **-en** *(von Tieren)* breed(ing); *(von Pflanzen)* cultivation; *(Rasse)* breed; *(Erziehung)* raising; *(Disziplin)* discipline.

züchten ['tsʏçtən] *vt Tiere* breed; *Pflanzen* cultivate, grow.

Züchter *m* **-s**, **-** breeder; grower.

Zucht- *cpd:* **~haus** *nt* prison, penitentiary *(US);* **~hengst** *m* stallion, stud.

züchtig ['tsʏçtɪç] a modest, demure; **~en** ['tsʏçtɪgən] *vt* chastise; **Z~ung** *f* chastisement.

zucken ['tsʊkən] *vi* jerk, twitch; *(Strahl etc)* flicker; *vt* shrug.

zücken ['tsʏkən] *vt Schwert* draw; *Geldbeutel* pull out.

Zucker ['tsʊkər] *m* **-s**, **-** sugar; *(Med)* diabetes; **~dose** *f* sugar bowl; **~guß** *m* icing; **z~krank** a diabetic; **z~n** *vt* sugar; **~rohr** *nt* sugar cane; **~rübe** *f* sugar beet.

Zuckung ['tsʊkʊŋ] *f* convulsion, spasm; *(leicht)* twitch.

zudecken ['tsuːdɛkən] *vt* cover (up).

zudem [tsuː'deːm] ad in addition (to this).

zudrehen ['tsuːdreːən] *vt* turn off.

zudringlich ['tsuːdrɪŋlɪç] a forward, pushing, obtrusive; **Z~keit** *f* forwardness, obtrusiveness.

zudrücken ['tsuːdrʏkən] *vt* close; **ein Auge ~** turn a blind eye.

zueinander [tsuːaɪ'nandər] ad to one other; *(in Verbverbindung)* together.

zuerkennen ['tsuːˈɛrkɛnən] *vt irreg* award *(jdm etw* sth to sb, sb sth).

zuerst [tsuː'eːrst] ad first; *(zu Anfang)* at first; **~ einmal** first of all.

Zufahrt ['tsuːfaːrt] *f* approach; **~sstraße** *f* approach road; *(von Autobahn etc)* slip road.

Zufall ['tsuːfal] *m* chance; *(Ereignis)* coincidence; **durch ~** by accident; **so ein ~** what a coincidence; **z~en** *vi irreg* close, shut itself; *(Anteil, Aufgabe)* fall *(jdm* to sb).

zufällig ['tsuːfɛlɪç] a chance; ad by chance; *(in Frage)* by any chance.

Zuflucht ['tsuːflʊxt] *f* recourse; *(Ort)* refuge.

Zufluß ['tsuːflʊs] *m* *(Zufließen)* inflow, influx; *(Geog)* tributary; *(Comm)* supply.

zufolge [tsu'fɔlgə] *prep +dat or gen* judging by; *(laut)* according to.

zufrieden [tsuː'friːdən] a content(ed), satisfied; **Z~heit** *f* satisfaction, contentedness; **~stellen** *vt* satisfy.

zufrieren ['tsuː'friːrən] *vi irreg* freeze up or over.

zufügen ['tsuːfyːgən] *vt* add *(dat* to); *Leid etc* cause *(jdm etw* sth to sb).

Zufuhr ['tsuːfuːr] *f* **-**, **-en** *(Herbeibringen)* supplying; *(Met)* influx; *(Mil)* supplies *pl.*

zuführen ['tsuːfyːrən] *vt (leiten)* bring, conduct; *(transportieren)* convey to; *(versorgen)* supply; *vi:* **auf etw** *(acc)* **~** lead to sth.

Zug [tsuːk] *m* **-(e)s**, **ˑe** *(Eisenbahn)* train; *(Luft~)* draught; *(Ziehen)* pull(ing); *(Gesichts~)* feature; *(Schach etc)* move; *(Klingel~)* pull; *(Schrift~)* stroke; *(Atem~)* breath; *(Charakter~)* trait; *(an Zigarette)* puff, pull, drag; *(Schluck)* gulp; *(Menschengruppe)* procession; *(von Vögeln)* flight; *(Mil)* platoon; **etw in vollen en genießen** enjoy sth to the full.

Zu- ['tsuː] *cpd:* **~gabe** *f* extra; *(in Konzert etc)* encore; **~gang** *m* access, approach; **z~gänglich** a accessible; *Mensch* approachable.

Zug- *cpd:* **~abteil** *nt* train compartment; **~brücke** *f* drawbridge.

zugeben ['tsuːgeːbən] *vt irreg (beifügen)* add, throw in; *(zugestehen)* admit; *(erlauben)* permit.

zugehen ['tsuːgeːən] *vi irreg (schließen)* shut; *v impers (sich ereignen)* go on, proceed; **auf jdn/etw ~** walk towards sb/sth; **dem Ende ~** be finishing.

Zugehörigkeit ['tsuːgəhøːrɪçkaɪt] *f* membership *(zu* of), belonging *(zu* to); **~sgefühl** *nt* feeling of belonging.

zugeknöpft ['tsuːgəknœpft] a *(col)* reserved, stand-offish.

Zügel ['tsyːgəl] *m* **-s**, **-** rein(s); *(fig auch)* curb; z~los a unrestrained, licentious; ~losigkeit f lack of restraint, licentiousness; z~n vt curb; Pferd auch rein in.

zuge- ['tsu:gə] cpd: ~sellen vr join (jdm up with); Z~ständnis nt -ses, -se concession; ~stehen vt irreg admit; Rechte concede (jdm to sb).

Zug- cpd: ~führer m (Rail) inspector; (Mil) platoon commander; z~ig a draughty.

zügig ['tsy:gɪç] a speedy, swift.

Zug- cpd: ~luft f draught; ~maschine f traction engine, tractor.

zugreifen ['tsu:graifən] vi irreg seize or grab it; (helfen) help; (beim Essen) help o.s.

zugrunde [tsu'grundə] ad: ~ gehen collapse; (Mensch) perish; einer Sache etw ~ legen base sth on sth; einer Sache ~ liegen be based on sth; ~ richten ruin, destroy.

zugunsten [tsu'gunstən] prep +gen or dat in favour of.

zugute [tsu'gu:tə] ad: jdm etw ~ halten concede sth; jdm ~ kommen be of assistance to sb.

Zug- cpd: ~verbindung f train connection; ~vogel m migratory bird.

zuhalten ['tsu:haltən] irreg vt hold shut; vi: auf jdn/etw ~ make for sb/sth.

Zuhälter ['tsu:hɛltər] m -s, - pimp.

Zuhause [tsu'hausə] nt - home.

Zuhilfenahme [tsu'hɪlfəna:mə] f: unter ~ von with the help of.

zuhören ['tsu:høːrən] vi listen (dat to).

Zuhörer m -s, - listener; ~schaft f audience.

zujubeln ['tsu:ju:bəln] vi cheer (jdm sb).

zukleben ['tsu:kle:bən] vt paste up.

zuknöpfen ['tsu:knœpfən] vt button up, fasten.

zukommen ['tsu:kɔmən] vi irreg come up (auf +acc to); (sich gehören) be fitting (jdm for sb); (Recht haben auf) be entitled to; jdm etw ~ lassen give sb sth; etw auf sich ~ lassen wait and see.

Zukunft ['tsu:kunft] f -, Zükunfte future.

zukünftig ['tsu:kynftɪç] a future; mein ~er Mann my husband to be; ad in future.

Zukunfts- cpd: ~aussichten pl future prospects pl; ~musik f (col) wishful thinking; crystal ball gazing; ~roman m science-fiction novel.

Zulage ['tsu:la:gə] f bonus, allowance.

zulassen ['tsu:lasən] vt irreg (hereinlassen) admit; (erlauben) permit; Auto license; (col: nicht öffnen) (keep) shut.

zulässig ['tsu:lɛsɪç] a permissible, permitted.

zulaufen ['tsu:laufən] vi irreg run (auf +acc towards); (Tier) adopt (jdm sb); spitz ~ come to a point.

zulegen ['tsu:le:gən] vt add; Geld put in; Tempo accelerate, quicken; (schließen) cover over; sich (dat) etw ~ (col) get hold of sth.

zuleide [tsu'laidə] a: jdm etw ~ tun hurt or harm sb.

zuleiten ['tsu:laitən] vt direct (dat to); (schicken) send.

zuletzt [tsu'lɛtst] ad finally, at last.

zuliebe [tsu'li:bə] ad: jdm ~ to please sb.

zum [tsum] = zu dem; ~ dritten Mal for the third time; ~ Scherz as a joke; ~ Trinken for drinking.

zumachen ['tsu:maxən] vt shut; Kleidung do up, fasten; vi shut; (col) hurry up.

zumal [tsu'ma:l] cj especially (as).

zumeist [tsu'maist] ad mostly.

zumindest [tsu'mɪndəst] ad at least.

zumut- cpd: ~bar ['tsu:mu:tba:r] a reasonable; ~e wie ist ihm ~e? how does he feel?; ~en ['tsu:mu:tən] vt expect, ask (jdm of sb); Z~ung ['tsu:mu:tuŋ] f unreasonable expectation or demand, impertinence.

zunächst [tsu'nɛ:çst] ad first of all; ~ einmal to start with.

zunähen ['tsu:nɛ:ən] vt sew up.

Zunahme ['tsu:na:mə] f -, -n increase.

Zuname ['tsu:na:mə] m surname.

Zünd- [tsynd] cpd: z~en vi (Feuer) light, ignite; (Motor) fire; (begeistern) fire (with enthusiasm) (bei jdm sb); z~end a fiery; ~er m -s, - fuse; (Mil) detonator; ~holz ['tsynt-] nt match; ~kerze f (Aut) spark(ing) plug; ~schlüssel m ignition key; ~schnur f fuse wire; ~stoff m fuel; (fig) dynamite; ~ung f ignition.

zunehmen ['tsu:ne:mən] vi irreg increase, grow; (Mensch) put on weight.

zuneigen ['tsu:naigən] vi incline, lean; sich dem Ende ~ draw to a close; einer Auffassung ~ incline towards a view; jdm zugeneigt sein be attracted to sb.

Zuneigung f affection.

Zunft [tsunft] f -, ²e guild.

zünftig ['tsynftɪç] a proper, real; Handwerk decent.

Zunge ['tsuŋə] f -, -n tongue; (Fisch) sole; z~nfertig a glib.

zunichte [tsu'nɪçtə] ad: ~ machen ruin, destroy; ~ werden come to nothing.

zunutze [tsu'nutsə] ad: sich (dat) etw ~ machen make use of sth.

zuoberst [tsu'o:bərst] ad at the top.

zupfen ['tsupfən] vt pull, pick, pluck; Gitarre pluck.

zur [tsu:r] = zu der.

zurech- ['tsu:rɛç] cpd: ~nungsfähig a responsible, accountable; Z~nungsfähigkeit f responsibility, accountability.

zurecht- [tsu'rɛçt] cpd: ~finden vr irreg find one's way (about); ~kommen vi irreg (be able to) deal (mit with); manage; ~legen vt get ready; Ausrede etc have ready; ~machen vt prepare; vr get ready; ~weisen vt irreg reprimand; Z~weisung f reprimand, rebuff.

zureden ['tsu:re:dən] vi persuade, urge (jdm sb).

zurichten ['tsu:rɪçtən] vt Essen prepare; (beschädigen) batter, bash up.

zürnen ['tsyrnən] vi be angry (jdm with sb).

zurück [tsu'ryk] ad back; ~behalten vt irreg keep back; ~bekommen vt irreg get back; ~bezahlen vt repay, pay back; ~bleiben vi irreg (Mensch) remain behind; (nicht nachkommen) fall behind, lag; *(Schaden)* remain; **~bringen** *vt irreg* bring back; **~drängen** *vt Gefühle* repress; *Feind* push back; **~drehen** *vt* turn back; **~erobern** *vt* reconquer; **~fahren** *irreg vi* travel back; *(vor Schreck)* recoil, start; *vt* drive back; **~fallen** *vi irreg* fall back; *(in Laster)* relapse; **~finden** *vi irreg* find one's way back; **~fordern** *vt* demand back; **~führen** *vt* lead back; *etw* **auf etw** *(acc)* **~führen** trace sth back to sth; **~geben** *vt irreg* give back; *(antworten)* retort with; **~geblieben** *a* retarded; **~gehen** *vi irreg* go back; *(zeitlich)* date back *(auf +acc* to); *(fallen)* go down, fall; **~gezogen** *a* retired, withdrawn; **~halten** *irreg vt* hold back; *Mensch* restrain; *(hindern)* prevent; *vr (reserviert sein)* be reserved; *(im Essen)* hold back; **~haltend** *a* reserved; **Z~haltung** *f* reserve; **~kehren** *vi* return; **~kommen** *vi irreg* come back; **auf etw** *(acc)* **~kommen** return to sth; **~lassen** *vt irreg* leave behind; **~legen** *vt* put back; *Geld* put by; *(reservieren)* keep back; *Strecke* cover; **~nehmen** *vt irreg* take back; **~rufen** *vti irreg* call back; **etw ins Gedächtnis ~rufen** recall sth; **~schrecken** *vi* shrink *(vor +dat* from); **~setzen** *vt* put back; *(im Preis)* reduce; *(benachteiligen)* put at a disadvantage; **~stecken** *vt* put back; *vi (fig)* moderate (one's wishes); **~stellen** *vt* put back, replace; *(aufschieben)* put off, postpone; *(Mil)* turn down; *Interessen* defer; *Ware* keep; **~stoßen** *vt irreg* repulse; **~treten** *vi irreg* step back; *(vom Amt)* retire; **gegenüber** *or* **hinter etw ~treten** diminish in importance in view of sth; **~weisen** *vt irreg* turn down; *Mensch* reject; **Z~zahlung** *f* repayment; **~ziehen** *irreg vt* pull back; *Angebot* withdraw; *vr* retire.

Zuruf ['tsuːruːf] *m* shout, cry.

Zusage ['tsuːzaːɡə] *f* -, **-n** promise; *(Annahme)* consent; **z~n** *vt* promise; *vi* accept; **jdm z~n** *(gefallen)* agree with *or* please sb.

zusammen [tsuˈzamən] *ad* together; **Z~arbeit** *f* cooperation; **~arbeiten** *vi* cooperate; **~beißen** *vt irreg Zähne* clench; **~bleiben** *vi irreg* stay together; **~brechen** *vi irreg* collapse; *(Mensch auch)* break down; **~bringen** *vt irreg* bring *or* get together; *Geld* get; *Sätze* put together; **Z~bruch** *m* collapse; **~fahren** *vi irreg* collide; *(erschrecken)* start; **~fassen** *vt* summarize; *(vereinigen)* unite; **~fassend** *a* summarizing; *ad* to summarize; **Z~fassung** *f* summary, résumé; **~finden** *vir irreg* meet (together); **~fließen** *vi irreg* flow together, meet; **Z~fluß** *m* confluence; **~fügen** *vt* join (together), unite; **~gehören** *vi* belong together; *(Paar)* match; **~gesetzt** *a* compound, composite; **~halten** *vt irreg* stick together; **Z~hang** *m* connection; **im/aus dem Z~hang** in/out of context; **~hängen** *vi irreg* be connected *or* linked; **~hang(s)los** *a* incoherent, disconnected; **~klappbar** *a* folding, collapsible;

~kommen *vi irreg* meet, assemble; *(sich ereignen)* occur at once *or* together; **Z~kunft** *f* meeting; **~laufen** *vi irreg* run *or* come together; *(Straßen, Flüsse etc)* converge, meet; *(Farben)* run into one another; **~legen** *vt* put together; *(stapeln)* pile up; *(falten)* fold; *(verbinden)* combine, unite; *Termine, Fest* amalgamate; *Geld* collect; **~nehmen** *irreg vt* summon up; **alles ~genommen** all in all; *vr* pull o.s. together; **~passen** *vi* go well together, match; **~prallen** *vi* collide; **~schlagen** *vt irreg Mensch* beat up; *Dinge* smash up; *(falten)* fold; *Hände* clap; *Hacken* click; **~schließen** *vtr irreg* join (together); **Z~schluß** *m* amalgamation; **~schreiben** *vt irreg* write together; *Bericht* put together; **~schrumpfen** *vi* shrink, shrivel up; **Z~sein** *nt* -s get-together; **~setzen** *vt* put together; *vr* be composed of; **Z~setzung** *f* composition; **~stellen** *vt* put together; compile; **Z~stellung** *f* list; *(Vorgang)* compilation; **Z~stoß** *m* collision; **~stoßen** *vi irreg* collide; **~treffen** *vi irreg* coincide; *Menschen* meet; **Z~treffen** *nt* meeting; coincidence; **~wachsen** *vi irreg* grow together; **~zählen** *vt* add up; **~ziehen** *irreg vt (verengern)* draw together; *(vereinigen)* bring together; *(addieren)* add up; *vr* shrink; *(Gewitter)* form, develop.

Zusatz ['tsuːzats] *m* addition; **~antrag** *m (Pol)* amendment.

zusätzlich ['tsuːzɛtslɪç] *a* additional.

zuschauen ['tsuːʃaʊən] *vi* watch, look on.

Zuschauer *m* **-s, -** spectator; *pl (Theat)* audience.

zuschicken ['tsuːʃɪkən] *vt* send, forward *(jdm etw* sth to sb).

zuschießen ['tsuːʃiːsən] *irreg vt* fire *(auf* at); *Geld* put in; *vi:* **~ auf** *(+acc)* rush towards.

Zuschlag ['tsuːʃlaːk] *m* extra charge, surcharge; **z~en** ['tsuːʃlaːɡən] *irreg vt Tür* slam; *Ball* hit *(jdm* to sb); *(bei Auktion)* knock down; *Steine etc* knock into shape; *vi (Fenster, Tür)* shut; *(Mensch)* hit, punch; **~skarte** *f (Rail)* surcharge ticket; **z~spflichtig** *a* subject to surcharge.

zuschließen ['tsuːʃliːsən] *vt irreg* lock (up).

zuschmeißen ['tsuːʃmaɪsən] *vt irreg (col)* slam, bang shut.

zuschneiden ['tsuːʃnaɪdən] *vt irreg* cut out *or* to size.

zuschnüren ['tsuːʃnyːrən] *vt* tie up.

zuschrauben ['tsuːʃraʊbən] *vt* screw down *or* up.

zuschreiben ['tsuːʃraɪbən] *vt irreg (fig)* ascribe, attribute; *(Comm)* credit.

Zuschrift ['tsuːʃrɪft] *f* letter, reply.

zuschulden [tsuːˈʃʊldən] *ad:* **sich** *(dat)* **etw ~ kommen lassen** make o.s. guilty of sth.

Zuschuß ['tsuːʃʊs] *m* subsidy, allowance.

zuschütten ['tsuːʃʏtən] *vt* fill up.

zusehen ['tsuːzeːən] *vi irreg* watch *(jdm/etw* sb/sth); *(dafür sorgen)* take care; **~ds** *ad* visibly.

zusenden ['tsuːzɛndən] *vt irreg* forward, send on *(jdm etw* sth to sb).

zusetzen ['tsu:zɛtsən] vt (beifügen) add; Geld lose; vi: **jdm ~** harass sb; (Krankheit) take a lot out of sb.

zusichern ['tsu:zɪçərn] vt assure (jdm etw sb of sth).

zusperren ['tsu:ʃpɛrən] vt bar.

zuspielen ['tsu:ʃpiːlən] vti pass (jdm to sb).

zuspitzen ['tsu:ʃpɪtsən] vt sharpen; vr (Lage) become critical.

zusprechen ['tsu:ʃprɛçən] irreg vt (zuerkennen) award (jdm etw sb sth, sth to sb); **jdm Trost ~** comfort sb; vi speak (jdm to sb); **dem Essen/Alkohol ~** eat/drink a lot.

Zuspruch ['tsu:ʃprʊx] m encouragement; (Anklang) appreciation, popularity.

Zustand ['tsu:ʃtant] m state, condition; **z~e** [tsu:ʃtɛndə] ad: **z~e bringen** vt irreg bring about; **z~e kommen** vi irreg come about.

zuständig ['tsu:ʃtɛndɪç] a competent, responsible; **Z~keit** f competence, responsibility.

zustehen ['tsu:ʃteːən] vi irreg: **jdm ~** be sb's right.

zustellen ['tsu:ʃtɛlən] vt (verstellen) block; Post etc send.

zustimmen ['tsu:ʃtɪmən] vi agree (dat to).

Zustimmung f agreement, consent.

zustoßen ['tsu:ʃtoːsən] vi irreg (fig) happen (jdm to sb).

zutage [tsu:'taːgə] ad: **~ bringen** bring to light; **~ treten** come to light.

Zutaten ['tsu:taːtən] pl ingredients pl.

zuteilen ['tsu:taɪlən] vt allocate, assign.

zutiefst [tsu'tiːfst] ad deeply.

zutragen ['tsu:traːgən] irreg vt bring (jdm etw sth to sb); Klatsch tell; vr happen.

zuträglich ['tsu:trɛːklɪç] a beneficial.

zutrau- ['tsu:trau] cpd: **~en** vt credit (jdm etw sb with sth); **Z~en** nt -s trust (zu in); **~lich** a trusting, friendly; **Z~lichkeit** f trust.

zutreffen ['tsu:trɛfən] vi irreg be correct; apply; **Z~des bitte unterstreichen** please underline where applicable.

zutrinken ['tsu:trɪŋkən] vi irreg drink to (jdm sb).

Zutritt ['tsu:trɪt] m access, admittance.

Zutun ['tsu:tuːn] nt -s assistance; vt irreg add; (schließen) shut.

zuverlässig ['tsu:fɛrlɛsɪç] a reliable; **Z~keit** f reliability.

Zuversicht ['tsu:fɛrzɪçt] f · confidence; **z~lich** a confident; **~lichkeit** f confidence, hopefulness.

zuviel [tsu:'fiːl] ad too much.

zuvor [tsu'foːr] ad before, previously; **~kommen** vi irreg anticipate (jdm sb), beat (sb) to it; **~kommend** a obliging, courteous.

Zuwachs ['tsu:vaks] m -es increase, growth; (col) addition; **z~en** vi irreg become overgrown; (Wunde) heal (up).

zuwandern ['tsu:vandərn] vi immigrate.

zuwege [tsu:'veːgə] ad: **etw ~ bringen** accomplish sth; **mit etw ~ kommen** manage sth; **gut ~ sein** be (doing) well.

zuweilen [tsu'vaɪlən] ad at times, now and then.

zuweisen ['tsu:vaɪzən] vt irreg assign, allocate (jdm to sb).

zuwenden ['tsu:vɛndən] irreg vt turn (dat towards); **jdm seine Aufmerksamkeit ~** give sb one's attention; vr devote o.s., turn (dat to).

zuwenig [tsu:'veːnɪç] ad too little.

zuwerfen ['tsu:vɛrfən] vt irreg throw (jdm to sb).

zuwider [tsu:'viːdər] ad: **etw ist jdm ~** sb loathes sth, sb finds sth repugnant; prep +dat contrary to; **~handeln** vi act contrary (dat to); **einem Gesetz ~handeln** contravene a law; **Z~handlung** f contravention; **~laufen** vi irreg run counter (dat to).

zuziehen ['tsu:tsiːən] irreg vt (schließen) Vorhang draw, close; (herbeirufen) Experten call in; **sich** (dat) **etw ~** Krankheit catch; Zorn incur; vi move in, come.

zuzüglich ['tsu:tsyːklɪç] prep +gen plus, with the addition of.

Zwang [tsvaŋ] m -(e)s, ⁻e compulsion, coercion.

zwängen ['tsvɛŋən] vtr squeeze.

Zwang- cpd: **z~los** a informal; **~losigkeit** f informality; **~sarbeit** f forced labour; (Strafe) hard labour; **~sjacke** f straightjacket; **~slage** f predicament, tight corner; **z~släufig** a necessary, inevitable; **~smaßnahme** f sanction, coercive measure; **z~sweise** ad compulsorily.

zwanzig ['tsvantsɪç] num twenty.

zwar [tsvaːr] ad to be sure, indeed; **das ist ~ . . ., aber . . .** that may be . . . but . . .; **und ~ am Sonntag** on Sunday to be precise; **und ~ so schnell, daß . . .** in fact so quickly that . . .

Zweck ['tsvɛk] m -(e)s, -e purpose, aim; **z~dienlich** a practical; expedient; **~e** f -, -n hobnail; (Heft-) drawing pin, thumbtack (US); **~entfremdung** f misuse; **z~los** a pointless; **z~mäßig** a suitable, appropriate; **~mäßigkeit** f suitability; **z~widrig** a unsuitable.

zwei [tsvaɪ] num two; **~deutig** a ambiguous; (unanständig) suggestive; **~erlei** a: **~erlei Stoff** two different kinds of material; **~erlei Meinung** of differing opinions; **~erlei zu tun haben** have two different things to do; **~fach** a double.

Zweifel ['tsvaɪfəl] m -s, · doubt; **z~haft** a doubtful, dubious; **z~los** a doubtless; **z~n** vi doubt (an etw (dat) sth); **~sfall** m: **im ~sfall** in case of doubt.

Zweig [tsvaɪk] m -(e)s, -e branch; **~geschäft** nt (Comm) branch; **~stelle** f branch (office).

zwei- cpd: **Z~heit** f duality; **~hundert** num two hundred; **Z~kampf** m duel; **~mal** ad twice; **~motorig** a twin-engined; **~reihig** a (Anzug) double-breasted; **~schneidig** a (fig) two-edged; **Z~sitzer** m -s, · two-seater; **~sprachig** a bilingual; **~spurig** a (Aut) two-lane; **~stimmig** a for two voices;

Z~taktmotor *m* two-stroke engine.

zweit- [tsvaɪt] *cpd:* **~ens** *ad* secondly; **~größte(r,s)** *a* second largest; **~klassig** *a* second-class; **~letzte(r,s)** *a* last but one, penultimate; **~rangig** *a* second-rate; **Z~wagen** *m* second car.

Zwerchfell ['tsvɛrçfɛl] *nt* diaphragm.

Zwerg [tsvɛrk] *m* **-(e)s, -e** dwarf.

Zwetsche ['tsvɛtʃə] *f* **-, -n** plum.

Zwickel ['tsvɪkəl] *m* **-s, -** gusset.

zwicken ['tsvɪkən] *vt* pinch, nip.

Zwieback ['tsviːbak] *m* **-(e)s, -e** rusk.

Zwiebel ['tsviːbəl] *f* **-, -n** onion; *(Blumen—)* bulb; **z~artig** *a* bulbous.

Zwie- ['tsviː] *cpd:* **~gespräch** *vt* dialogue; **~licht** *nt* twilight; **z~lichtig** *a* shady, dubious; **~spalt** *m* conflict, split; **z~spältig** *a Gefühle* conflicting; *Charakter* contradictory; **~tracht** *f* discord, dissension.

Zwilling ['tsvɪlɪŋ] *m* **-s, -e** twin; *pl (Astrol)* Gemini.

zwingen ['tsvɪŋən] *vt irreg* force; **~nd** *a Grund etc* compelling.

zwinkern ['tsvɪŋkərn] *vi* blink; *(absichtlich)* wink.

Zwirn [tsvɪrn] *m* **-(e)s, -e** thread.

zwischen ['tsvɪʃən] *prep +acc or dat* between; **Z~bemerkung** *f* (incidental) remark; **~blenden** *vt (TV)* insert; **Z~ding** *nt* cross; **~durch** [-'dʊrç] *ad* in between; *(räumlich)* here and there; **Z~ergebnis** *nt* intermediate result; **Z~fall** *m* incident; **Z~frage** *f* question; **Z~gas** *nt:* **Z~gas geben** double-declutch; **Z~handel** *m* middlemen *pl;* middleman's trade; **Z~händler** *m* middleman, agent; **Z~landung** *f* stop, intermediate landing; **~menschlich** *a* interpersonal; **Z~raum** *m* space; **Z~ruf** *m* interjection, interruption; **Z~spiel** *nt* interlude; **~staatlich** *f* interstate; international; **Z~station** *f* intermediate station; **Z~stecker** *m (Elec)* adaptor; **Z~wand** *f* partition; **Z~zeit** *f* interval; **in der Z~zeit** in the interim, meanwhile.

Zwist [tsvɪst] *m* **-es, -e** dispute, feud.

zwitschern ['tsvɪtʃərn] *vti* twitter, chirp.

Zwitter ['tsvɪtər] *m* **-s, -** hermaphrodite.

zwölf [tsvœlf] *num* twelve.

Zyklus ['tsyːklʊs] *m* **-, Zyklen** cycle.

Zylinder [tsiˈlɪndər] *m* **-s, -** cylinder; *(Hut)* top hat; **z~förmig** *a* cylindrical.

Zyniker ['tsyːnikər] *m* **-s, -** cynic.

zynisch ['tsyːnɪʃ] *a* cynical.

Zynismus [tsyˈnɪsmʊs] *m* cynicism.

Zyste ['tsʏstə] *f* **-, -n** cyst.

ENGLISH - GERMAN
ENGLISCH - DEUTSCH

A

A, a [eɪ] n A nt, a nt.

a, an [eɪ, ə; æn, ən] indef art ein/eine/ein. **£1 a metre** 1£ pro or das Meter.

aback [ə'bæk] ad: **to be taken** ~ verblüfft sein.

abandon [ə'bændən] vt (give up) aufgeben; (desert) verlassen; n Hingabe f.

abashed [ə'bæʃt] a verlegen.

abate [ə'beɪt] vi nachlassen, sich legen.

abattoir ['æbətwɑː*] n Schlachthaus nt.

abbey ['æbɪ] n Abtei f.

abbot ['æbət] n Abt m.

abbreviate [ə'briːvɪeɪt] vt abkürzen.

abbreviation [əbriːvɪ'eɪʃən] n Abkürzung f.

ABC ['eɪbiː'siː] n (lit, fig) Abc nt.

abdicate ['æbdɪkeɪt] vt aufgeben; vi abdanken.

abdication [æbdɪ'keɪʃən] n Abdankung f; (Amts)niederlegung f.

abdomen ['æbdəmən] n Unterleib m.

abdominal [æb'dɒmɪnl] a Unterleibs-.

abduct [æb'dʌkt] vt entführen; ~**ion** [æb'dʌkʃən] Entführung f.

aberration [æbə'reɪʃən] n (geistige) Verwirrung f.

abet [ə'bet] vt see **aid** vt.

abeyance [ə'beɪəns] n: **in** ~ in der Schwebe; (disuse) außer Kraft.

abhor [əb'hɔː*] vt verabscheuen.

abhorrent [əb'hɒrənt] a verabscheuungswürdig.

abide [ə'baɪd] vt vertragen; leiden; ~ **by** vt sich halten an (+acc).

ability [ə'bɪlɪtɪ] n (power) Fähigkeit f; (skill) Geschicklichkeit f.

abject ['æbdʒekt] a: a liar übel; poverty größte(r, s); apology zerknirscht.

ablaze [ə'bleɪz] a in Flammen; ~ **with lights** hell erleuchtet.

able ['eɪbl] a geschickt, fähig; **to be** ~ **to do sth** etw tun können; ~-**bodied** a kräftig; seaman Voll-; (Mil) wehrfähig.

ably ['eɪblɪ] ad geschickt.

abnormal [æb'nɔːml] a regelwidrig, abnorm; ~**ity** [æbnɔː'mælɪtɪ] Regelwidrigkeit f; (Med) krankhafte Erscheinung f.

aboard [ə'bɔːd] ad, prep an Bord (+gen).

abode [ə'bəʊd] n: **of no fixed** ~ ohne festen Wohnsitz.

abolish [ə'bɒlɪʃ] vt abschaffen.

abolition [æbə'lɪʃən] n Abschaffung f.

abominable a, **abominably** ad [ə'bɒmɪnəbl, -blɪ] scheußlich.

aborigine [æbə'rɪdʒɪniː] n Ureinwohner m.

abort [ə'bɔːt] vt abtreiben; fehlgebären; ~**ion** [ə'bɔːʃən] Abtreibung f; (miscarriage) Fehlgeburt f; ~**ive** a mißlungen.

abound [ə'baʊnd] vi im Überfluß vor-

handen sein; **to** ~ **in** Überfluß haben an (+dat).

about [ə'baʊt] ad (nearby) in der Nähe; (roughly) ungefähr; (around) umher, herum; prep (topic) über (+acc); (place) um, um ... herum; **to be** ~ **to** im Begriff sein zu; **I was** ~ **to go out** ich wollte gerade weggehen.

above [ə'bʌv] ad oben; prep über; a obig; ~ **all** vor allem; ~**board** a offen, ehrlich.

abrasion [ə'breɪʒən] n Abschürfung f.

abrasive [ə'breɪzɪv] n Schleifmittel nt; a Abschleif-; personality zermürbend, aufreibend.

abreast [ə'brest] ad nebeneinander; **to keep** ~ **of** Schritt halten mit.

abridge [ə'brɪdʒ] vt (ab)kürzen.

abroad [ə'brɔːd] ad be im Ausland; go ins Ausland.

abrupt [ə'brʌpt] a (sudden) abrupt, jäh; (curt) schroff.

abscess ['æbsɪs] n Geschwür nt.

abscond [əb'skɒnd] vi flüchten, sich davonmachen.

absence ['æbsəns] n Abwesenheit f.

absent ['æbsənt] a abwesend, nicht da; (lost in thought) geistesabwesend; ~**ee** [æbsən'tiː] Abwesende(r) m; ~**eeism** [æbsən'tiːɪzəm] Fehlen nt (am Arbeitsplatz/in der Schule); ~-**minded** a zerstreut.

absolute ['æbsəluːt] a absolut; power unumschränkt; rubbish vollkommen, rein; ~**ly** ['æbsəluːtlɪ] ad absolut, vollkommen, ~! ganz bestimmt!

absolve [əb'zɒlv] vt entbinden; freisprechen.

absorb [əb'zɔːb] vt aufsaugen, absorbieren; (fig) ganz in Anspruch nehmen, fesseln; ~**ent** a absorbierend; ~**ent cotton** (US) Verbandwatte f; ~**ing** a aufsaugend; (fig) packend.

abstain [əb'steɪn] vi (in vote) sich enthalten; **to** ~ **from** (keep from) sich enthalten (+gen).

abstemious [əb'stiːmɪəs] a mäßig, enthaltsam.

abstention [əb'stenʃən] n (in vote) (Stimm)enthaltung f.

abstinence ['æbstɪnəns] n Enthaltsamkeit f.

abstract ['æbstrækt] a abstrakt; n Abriß m; [æb'strækt] vt abstrahieren, aussondern.

abstruse [æb'struːs] a verworren, abstrus.

absurd [əb'sɜːd] a absurd; ~**ity** Unsinnigkeit f, Absurdität f.

abundance [ə'bʌndəns] n Überfluß m (of an +dat).

abundant [ə'bʌndənt] a reichlich.

abuse [ə'bju:s] n (rude language) Beschimpfung f; (ill usage) Mißbrauch m; (bad practice) (Amts)mißbrauch m; [ə'bju:z] vt
(misuse) mißbrauchen.
abusive [ə'bju:sɪv] a beleidigend, Schimpf-.
abysmal [ə'bɪzməl] a scheußlich; ignorance
bodenlos.
abyss [ə'bɪs] n Abgrund m.
academic [ækə'demɪk] a akademisch;
(theoretical) theoretisch.
academy [ə'kædəmɪ] n (school) Hochschule f; (society) Akademie f.
accede [æk'si:d] vi: ~ to office antreten;
throne besteigen; request zustimmen
(+dat).
accelerate [æk'seləreɪt] vi schneller werden; (Aut) Gas geben; vt beschleunigen.
acceleration [ækselə'reɪʃən] n Beschleunigung f.
accelerator [ək'seləreɪtə*] n Gas(pedal)
nt.
accent ['æksent] n Akzent m, Tonfall m;
(mark) Akzent m; (stress)' Betonung f;
~uate [æk'sentjueɪt] vt betonen.
accept [ək'sept] vt (take) annehmen;
(agree to) akzeptieren; ~able a
annehmbar; ~ance Annahme f.
access ['ækses] n Zugang m; ~ible
[æk'sesibl] a (easy to approach) zugänglich;
(within reach) (leicht) erreichbar; ~ion
[æk'seʃən] (to throne) Besteigung f; (to
office) Antritt m.
accessory [æk'sesərɪ] n Zubehörteil nt;
accessories pl Zubehör nt; **toilet accessories** pl Toilettenartikel pl.
accident ['æksɪdənt] n Unfall m;
(coincidence) Zufall m; **by** ~ zufällig; ~**al**
[æksɪ'dentl] a unbeabsichtigt; ~**ally**
[æksɪ'dentəlɪ] ad zufällig; **to be** ~**-prone**
zu Unfällen neigen.
acclaim [ə'kleɪm] vt zujubeln (+dat); n
Beifall m.
acclimatize [ə'klaɪmətaɪz] vt: **to become**
~**d** sich gewöhnen (to an +acc), sich akklimatisieren.
accolade ['ækəleɪd] n Auszeichnung f.
accommodate [ə'kɔmədeɪt] vt unterbringen; (hold) Platz haben für; (oblige)
(aus)helfen (+dat).
accommodating [ə'kɔmədeɪtɪŋ] a
entgegenkommend.
accommodation [ə'kɔmə'deɪʃən] n Unterkunft f.
accompaniment [ə'kʌmpənɪmənt] n
Begleitung f.
accompanist [ə'kʌmpənɪst] n Begleiter m.
accompany [ə'kʌmpənɪ] vt begleiten.
accomplice [ə'kʌmplɪs] n Helfershelfer m,
Komplize m.
accomplish [ə'kʌmplɪʃ] vt (fulfil) durch-
führen; (finish) vollenden; aim erreichen;
~**ed** a vollendet, ausgezeichnet; ~**ment**
(skill) Fähigkeit f; (completion) Vollen-
dung f; (feat) Leistung f.
accord [ə'kɔ:d] n Übereinstimmung f; **of
one's own** ~ freiwillig; vt gewähren;
~**ance: in** ~**ance with** in Übereinstimmung mit; ~**ing to** nach, laut (+gen);
~**ingly** ad danach, dementsprechend.
accordion [ə'kɔ:dɪən] n Ziehharmonika f,

Akkordeon nt; ~**ist** Akkordeonspieler m.
accost [ə'kɔst] vt ansprechen.
account [ə'kaunt] n (bill) Rechnung f;
(narrative) Bericht m; (report)
Rechenschaftsbericht m; (in bank) Konto
nt; (importance) Geltung f; **on** ~ auf
Rechnung; **of·no** ~ ohne Bedeutung; **on
no** ~ keinesfalls; **on** ~ **of** wegen; **to
take into** ~ berücksichtigen; ~ **for** vt
expenditure Rechenschaft ablegen für;
how do you ~ **for that?** wie erklären Sie
(sich) das?; ~**able** a verantwortlich;
~**ancy** Buchhaltung f; ~**ant** Wirtschafts-
prüfer(in f) m.
accoutrements [ə'ku:trəmənts] npl Ausrüstung f.
accredited [ə'kredɪtɪd] a beglaubigt, ak-
kreditiert.
accretion [ə'kri:ʃən] n Zunahme f.
accrue [ə'kru:] vi erwachsen, sich ansammeln.
accumulate [ə'kju:mjuleɪt] vt ansammeln;
vi sich ansammeln.
accumulation [əkju:mju'leɪʃən] n (act)
Aufhäufung f; (result) Ansammlung f.
accuracy ['ækjurəsɪ] n Genauigkeit f.
accurate ['ækjurɪt] a genau; ~**ly** ad
genau, richtig.
accursed, accurst [ə'kɜ:st] a verflucht.
accusation [ækju:'zeɪʃən] n Anklage f,
Beschuldigung f.
accusative [ə'kju:zətɪv] n Akkusativ m,
vierte(r) Fall m.
accuse [ə'kju:z] vt anklagen, beschuldigen;
~**d** Angeklagte(r) mf.
accustom [ə'kʌstəm] vt gewöhnen (to an
+acc); ~**ed** a gewohnt.
ace [eɪs] n As nt; (col) As nt, Kanone f.
ache [eɪk] n Schmerz m; vi (be sore)
schmerzen, weh tun; **I** ~ **all over** mir tut
es überall weh.
achieve [ə'tʃi:v] vt zustande bringen; aim
erreichen; ~**ment** Leistung f; (act)
Erreichen nt.
acid ['æsɪd] n Säure f; a sauer, scharf; ~**ity**
[ə'sɪdɪtɪ] Säuregehalt m; ~ **test** (fig)
Nagelprobe f.
acknowledge [ək'nɔlɪdʒ] vt receipt bestätigen; (admit) zugeben; ~**ment** Anerkennung f; (letter) Empfangsbestätigung f.
acne ['æknɪ] n Akne f.
acorn ['eɪkɔ:n] n Eichel f.
acoustic [ə'ku:stɪk] a akustisch; ~**s** pl
Akustik f.
acquaint [ə'kweɪnt] vt vertraut machen;
~**ance** (person) Bekannte(r) m; (knowledge) Kenntnis f.
acquiesce [ækwɪ'es] vi sich abfinden (in
mit).
acquire [ə'kwaɪə*] vt erwerben.
acquisition [ækwɪ'zɪʃən] n Errungenschaft
f; (act) Erwerb m.
acquisitive [ə'kwɪzɪtɪv] a gewinnsüchtig.
acquit [ə'kwɪt] vt (free) freisprechen; **to**
~ **o.s.** sich bewähren; ~**tal** Freispruch
m.
acre ['eɪkə*] n Morgen m; ~**age** Fläche f.
acrimonious [ækrɪ'məunɪəs] a bitter.
acrobat ['ækrəbæt] n Akrobat m.

acrobatics [ækrə'bætıks] npl akrobatische Kunststücke pl.

across [ə'krɒs] prep über (+acc); **he lives ~ the river** er wohnt auf der anderen Seite des Flusses; ad hinüber, herüber; **ten metres ~** zehn Meter breit; **he lives ~ from us** er wohnt uns gegenüber; **~-the-board** a pauschal.

act [ækt] n (deed) Tat f; (Jur) Gesetz nt; (Theat) Akt m; (Theat: turn) Nummer f; vi (take action) handeln; (behave) sich verhalten; (pretend) vorgeben; (Theat) spielen; vt (in play) spielen; **~ing** a stellvertretend; n Schauspielkunst f; (performance) Aufführung f.

action ['ækʃən] n (deed) Tat f; Handlung f; (motion) Bewegung f; (way of working) Funktionieren nt; (battle) Einsatz m, Gefecht nt; (lawsuit) Klage f, Prozeß m; **to take ~** etwas unternehmen.

activate ['æktıveıt] vt in Betrieb setzen, aktivieren.

active ['æktıv] a (brisk) rege, tatkräftig; (working) aktiv; (Gram) aktiv, Tätigkeits-; **~ly** ad aktiv, tätig.

activist ['æktıvıst] n Aktivist m.

activity [æk'tıvıtı] n Aktivität f; (doings) Unternehmungen pl; (occupation) Tätigkeit f.

actor ['æktə*] n Schauspieler m.

actress ['æktrıs] n Schauspielerin f.

actual ['æktjʊəl] a wirklich; **~ly** ad tatsächlich; **~ly no** eigentlich nicht.

acumen ['ækjumen] n Scharfsinn m.

acupuncture ['ækjʊpʌŋktʃə*] n Akupunktur f.

acute [ə'kju:t] a (severe) heftig, akut; (keen) scharfsinnig; **~ly** ad akut, scharf.

ad [æd] n abbr of **advertisement**.

adage ['ædıdʒ] n Sprichwort nt.

Adam ['ædəm] n Adam m; **~'s apple** Adamsapfel m.

adamant ['ædəmənt] a eisern; hartnäckig.

adapt [ə'dæpt] vt anpassen; vi sich anpassen (to an +acc); **~able** a anpassungsfähig; **~ation** [ædæp'teıʃən] (Theat etc) Bearbeitung f; (adjustment) Anpassung f; **~er** (Elec) Zwischenstecker m.

add [æd] vt (join) hinzufügen; numbers addieren; **~ up** vi (make sense) stimmen; **~ up to** vt ausmachen.

addendum [ə'dendəm] n Zusatz m.

adder ['ædə*] n Kreuzotter f, Natter f.

addict ['ædıkt] n Süchtige(r) mf; **~ed** a [ə'dıktıd] **~ed to** -süchtig; **~ion** [ə'dıkʃən] Sucht f.

adding machine ['ædıŋməʃi:n] n Addiermaschine f.

addition [ə'dıʃən] n Anhang m, Addition f; (Math) Addition f, Zusammenzählen nt; **in ~** zusätzlich, außerdem; **~al** a zusätzlich, weiter.

additive ['ædıtıv] n Zusatz m.

addled ['ædld] a faul, schlecht; (fig) verwirrt.

address [ə'dres] n Adresse f; (speech) Ansprache f; **form of ~** Anredeform f; vt letter adressieren; (speak to) ansprechen; (make speech to) eine Ansprache halten

an (+acc); **~ee** [ædre'si:] Empfänger(in f) m, Adressat m.

adenoids ['ædənɔıdz] npl Polypen pl.

adept ['ædept] a geschickt; **to be ~ at** gut sein in (+dat).

adequacy ['ædıkwəsı] n Angemessenheit f.

adequate ['ædıkwıt] a angemessen; **~ly** ad hinreichend.

adhere [əd'hıə*] vi: **~ to** (lit) haften an (+dat); (fig) festhalten an (+dat).

adhesion [əd'hi:ʒən] n Festhaften nt; (Phys) Adhäsion f.

adhesive [əd'hi:zıv] a klebend; Kleb(e)-; n Klebstoff m.

adieu [ə'dju:] n Adieu nt, Lebewohl nt.

adjacent [ə'dʒeısənt] a benachbart.

adjective ['ædʒəktıv] n Adjektiv nt, Eigenschaftswort nt.

adjoining [ə'dʒɔınıŋ] a benachbart, Neben-.

adjourn [ə'dʒɜ:n] vt vertagen; vi abbrechen.

adjudicate [ə'dʒu:dıkeıt] vti entscheiden, ein Urteil fällen.

adjudication [ədʒu:dı'keıʃən] n Entscheidung f.

adjudicator [ə'dʒu:dıkeıtə*] n Schiedsrichter m, Preisrichter m.

adjust [ə'dʒʌst] vt (alter) anpassen; (put right) regulieren, richtig stellen; **~able** a verstellbar; **~ment** (rearrangement) Anpassung f; (settlement) Schlichtung f.

adjutant ['ædʒətənt] n Adjutant m.

ad-lib [æd'lıb] vi improvisieren; n Improvisation f; a, ad improvisiert.

administer [æd'mınıstə*] vt (manage) verwalten; (dispense) ausüben; justice sprechen; medicine geben.

administration [ædmınıs'treıʃən] n Verwaltung f; (Pol) Regierung f.

administrative [əd'mınıstrətıv] a Verwaltungs-.

administrator [əd'mınıstreıtə*] n Verwaltungsbeamte(r) m.

admirable ['ædmərəbl] a bewundernswert.

admiral ['ædmərəl] n Admiral m; **A~ty** Admiralität f.

admiration [ædmı'reıʃən] n Bewunderung f.

admire [əd'maıə*] vt (respect) bewundern; (love) verehren; **~r** Bewunderer m.

admission [əd'mıʃən] n (entrance) Einlaß m; (fee) Eintritt(spreis) m; (confession) Geständnis nt.

admit [əd'mıt] vt (let in) einlassen; (confess) gestehen; (accept) anerkennen; **~tance** Zulassung f; **~tedly** ad zugegebenermaßen.

ado [ə'du:] n: **without more ~** ohne weitere Umstände.

adolescence [ædə'lesns] n Jugendalter nt.

adolescent [ædə'lesnt] a heranwachsend, jugendlich; n Jugendliche(r) mf.

adopt [ə'dɒpt] vt child adoptieren; idea übernehmen; **~ion** [ə'dɒpʃən] (of child) Adoption f; (of idea) Übernahme f.

adorable [ə'dɔ:rəbl] a anbetungswürdig; (likeable) entzückend.

adoration [ædɔ'reɪʃən] n Anbetung f; Verehrung f.

adore [ə'dɔː*] vt anbeten; verehren.

adoring [ə'dɔːrɪŋ] a verehrend.

adorn [ə'dɔːn] vt schmücken.

adornment [ə'dɔːnmənt] n Schmuck m, Verzierung f.

adrenalin [ə'drenəlɪn] n Adrenalin nt.

adrift [ə'drɪft] ad Wind und Wellen preisgegeben.

adroit [ə'drɔɪt] a gewandt.

adulation [ædju'leɪʃən] n Lobhudelei f.

adult ['ædʌlt] a erwachsen; n Erwachsene(r) mf.

adulterate [ə'dʌltəreɪt] vt verfälschen, mischen.

adultery [ə'dʌltərɪ] n Ehebruch m.

advance [əd'vɑːns] n (progress) Vorrücken nt; (money) Vorschuß m; vt (move forward) vorrücken; money vorschießen; argument vorbringen; vi vorwärtsgehen; **in** ~ im voraus; **in** ~ **of** vor (+dat); ~ **booking** Vorbestellung f, Vorverkauf m; ~**d** a (ahead) vorgerückt; (modern) fortgeschritten; study für Fortgeschrittene; ~**ment** Förderung f; (promotion) Beförderung f.

advantage [əd'vɑːntɪdʒ] n Vorteil m; ~**ous** [ædvən'teɪdʒəs] a vorteilhaft; **to have an** ~ **over sb** jdm gegenüber im Vorteil sein; **to be of** ~ von Nutzen sein; **to take** ~ **of** (misuse) ausnutzen; (profit from) Nutzen ziehen aus.

advent ['ædvent] n Ankunft f; A~ Advent m.

adventure [əd'ventʃə*] n Abenteuer nt.

adventurous [əd'ventʃərəs] a abenteuerlich, waghalsig.

adverb ['ædvɜːb] n Adverb nt, Umstandswort nt.

adversary ['ædvəsərɪ] n Gegner m.

adverse ['ædvɜːs] a widrig.

adversity [əd'vɜːsɪtɪ] n Widrigkeit f, Mißgeschick nt.

advert ['ædvɜːt] n Anzeige f; ~**ise** vt anzeigen; vi annoncieren; ~**isement** [əd'vɜːtɪsmənt] Anzeige f, Annonce f, Inserat nt; ~**ising** Werbung f; ~**ising campaign** Werbekampagne f.

advice [əd'vaɪs] n Rat(schlag) m.

advisable [əd'vaɪzəbl] a ratsam.

advise [əd'vaɪz] vt raten (+dat); ~**r** Berater m.

advisory [əd'vaɪzərɪ] a beratend, Beratungs-.

advocate ['ædvəkeɪt] vt vertreten.

aegis ['iːdʒɪs] n: **under the** ~ **of** unter der Schirmherrschaft von.

aerial ['ɛərɪəl] n Antenne f; a Luft-.

aero- ['ɛərəu] pref Luft-.

aeroplane ['ɛərəpleɪn] n Flugzeug nt.

aerosol ['ɛərəsɒl] n Aerosol nt; Sprühdose f.

aesthetic [ɪs'θetɪk] a ästhetisch; ~**s** Ästhetik f.

afar [ə'fɑː*] ad: **from** ~ aus der Ferne.

affable ['æfəbl] a umgänglich.

affair [ə'fɛə*] n (concern) Angelegenheit f;

(event) Ereignis nt; (love ~) (Liebes)verhältnis nt.

affect [ə'fekt] vt (influence) (ein)wirken auf (+acc); (move deeply) bewegen; **this change doesn't** ~ **us** diese Änderung betrifft uns nicht; ~**ation** [æfek'teɪʃən] Affektiertheit f, Verstellung f; ~**ed** a affektiert, gekünstelt; ~**ion** [ə'fekʃən] Zuneigung f; ~**ionate** [ə'fekʃənɪt] a liebevoll, lieb; ~**ionately** [ə'fekʃənɪtlɪ] ad liebevoll; ~**ionately yours** herzlichst Dein.

affiliated [ə'fɪlieɪtɪd] a angeschlossen (to dat).

affinity [ə'fɪnɪtɪ] n (attraction) gegenseitige Anziehung f; (relationship) Verwandtschaft f.

affirmation [æfə'meɪʃən] n Behauptung f.

affirmative [ə'fɜːmətɪv] a bestätigend; n: **in the** ~ (Gram) nicht verneint; **to answer in the** ~ mit Ja antworten.

affix [ə'fɪks] vt aufkleben, anheften.

afflict [ə'flɪkt] vt quälen, heimsuchen; ~**ion** [ə'flɪkʃən] Kummer m; (illness) Leiden nt.

affluence ['æfluəns] n (wealth) Wohlstand m.

affluent ['æfluənt] a wohlhabend, Wohlstands-.

afford [ə'fɔːd] vt (sich) leisten, erschwingen; (yield) bieten, einbringen.

affront [ə'frʌnt] n Beleidigung f; ~**ed** a beleidigt.

afield [ə'fiːld] ad: **far** ~ weit fort.

afloat [ə'fləut] a: **to be** ~ schwimmen.

afoot [ə'fut] ad im Gang.

aforesaid [ə'fɔːsed] a obengenannt.

afraid [ə'freɪd] a ängstlich; **to be** ~ **of** Angst haben vor (+dat); **to be** ~ **to** sich scheuen; **I am** ~ **I have...** ich habe leider...; **I'm** ~ **so/not** leider/leider nicht.

afresh [ə'freʃ] ad von neuem.

aft [ɑːft] ad achtern.

after ['ɑːftə*] prep nach; (following, seeking) hinter... (dat)... her; (in imitation) nach, im Stil von; ad: **soon** ~ bald danach; ~ **all** letzten Endes; ~**effects** pl Nachwirkungen pl; ~**life** Leben nt nach dem Tode; ~**math** Auswirkungen pl; ~**noon** Nachmittag m; **good** ~**noon!** guten Tag!; ~**shave** (lotion) Rasierwasser nt; ~**thought** nachträgliche(r) Einfall m; ~**wards** ad danach, nachher.

again [ə'gen] ad wieder, noch einmal; (besides) außerdem, ferner; ~ **and** ~ immer wieder.

against [ə'genst] prep gegen.

age [eɪdʒ] n (of person) Alter nt; (in history) Zeitalter nt; vi altern, alt werden; vt älter machen; **to come of** ~ mündig werden; ~**d** a ... Jahre alt, -jährig; ['eɪdʒɪd] (elderly) betagt; **the** ~**d** die Bejahrten pl; ~ **group** Altersgruppe f, Jahrgang m; ~**less** a zeitlos; ~ **limit** Altersgrenze f.

agency ['eɪdʒənsɪ] n Agentur f; Vermittlung f; (Chem) Wirkung f.

agenda [ə'dʒendə] n Tagesordnung f.

agent ['eɪdʒənt] n (Comm) Vertreter m; (spy) Agent m.

aggravate ['ægrəveɪt] vt (make worse) verschlimmern; (irritate) reizen.

aggravating ['ægrəveɪtɪŋ] a verschlimmernd; ärgerlich.

aggravation [ægrə'veɪʃən] n Verschlimmerung f, Verärgerung f.

aggregate ['ægrɪgɪt] n Summe f.

aggression [ə'greʃən] n Aggression f.

aggressive a, **~ly** ad [ə'gresɪv, -lɪ] aggressiv; **~ness** Aggressivität f.

aggrieved [ə'griːvd] a bedrückt, verletzt.

aghast [ə'gɑːst] a entsetzt.

agile ['ædʒaɪl] a flink; agil; mind rege.

agitate ['ædʒɪteɪt] vt rütteln; vi agitieren; **~d** a aufgeregt.

agitator ['ædʒɪteɪtə*] n Agitator m; (pej) Hetzer m.

agnostic [æg'nɒstɪk] n Agnostiker (in f) m.

ago [ə'gəʊ] ad: two days **~** vor zwei Tagen; **not long ~** vor kurzem; **it's so long ~** ist schon so lange her.

agog [ə'gɒg] a, ad gespannt.

agonized ['ægənaɪzd] a gequält.

agonizing ['ægənaɪzɪŋ] a quälend.

agony ['ægənɪ] n Qual f.

agree [ə'griː] vt date vereinbaren; vi (have same opinion, correspond) übereinstimmen (with mit); (consent) zustimmen; (be in harmony) sich vertragen; **to ~ to do sth** sich bereit erklären, etw zu tun; **garlic doesn't ~ with me** Knoblauch vertrage ich nicht; **I ~** einverstanden, ich stimme zu; **to ~ on sth** sich auf etw (acc) einigen; **~able** a (pleasing) liebenswürdig; (willing to consent) einverstanden; **~ably** ad angenehm; **~d** a vereinbart; **~ment** (agreeing) Übereinstimmung f, (contract) Vereinbarung f, Vertrag m.

agricultural [ægrɪ'kʌltʃərəl] a landwirtschaftlich, Landwirtschafts-.

agriculture ['ægrɪkʌltʃə*] n Landwirtschaft f.

aground [ə'graʊnd] a, ad auf Grund.

ahead [ə'hed] ad vorwärts; **to be ~** voraus sein.

ahoy [ə'hɔɪ] interj ahoi!

aid [eɪd] n (assistance) Hilfe f, Unterstützung f; (person) Hilfe f; (thing) Hilfsmittel nt; vt unterstützen, helfen (+dat); **~ and abet** vti Beihilfe leisten (sb jdm).

aide [eɪd] n (person) Gehilfe m; (Mil) Adjutant m.

ailing ['eɪlɪŋ] a kränkelnd.

ailment ['eɪlmənt] n Leiden nt.

aim [eɪm] vt gun, camera richten auf (+acc); **that was ~ed at you** das war auf dich gemünzt; vi (with gun) zielen; (intend) beabsichtigen; **to ~ at sth** etw anstreben; n (intention) Absicht f, Ziel nt; (pointing) Zielen nt, Richten nt; **to take ~** zielen; **~less** a, **~lessly** ad ziellos.

air [ɛə*] n Luft f, Atmosphäre f; (manner) Miene f, Anschein m; (Mus) Melodie f; vt lüften; (fig) an die Öffentlichkeit bringen; **~bed** Luftmatratze f; **~conditioned** a mit Klimaanlage; **~conditioning** Klimaanlage f; **~craft** Flugzeug nt, Maschine f; **~craft carrier** Flugzeugträger m; **~ force** Luftwaffe f; **~gun** Luftgewehr nt; **~ hostess**

Stewardeß f; **~ily** ad leichtfertig; **~letter** Luftpost(leicht)brief m; **~line** Luftverkehrsgesellschaft f; **~liner** Verkehrsflugzeug nt; **~lock** Luftblase f; by **~mail** mit Luftpost; **~port** Flughafen m, Flugplatz m; **~ raid** Luftangriff m; **~sick** a luftkrank; **~strip** Landestreifen m; **~tight** a luftdicht; **~y** a luftig; manner leichtfertig.

aisle [aɪl] n Gang m.

ajar [ə'dʒɑː*] ad angelehnt; ein Spalt offen.

alabaster ['æləbɑːstə*] n Alabaster m.

à la carte [ælæ'kɑːt] a nach der (Speise)karte, à la carte.

alacrity [ə'lækrɪtɪ] n Bereitwilligkeit f.

alarm [ə'lɑːm] n (warning) Alarm m; (bell etc) Alarmanlage f; vt erschrecken; **~clock** Wecker m; **~ing** a beängstigend; **~ist** Bangemacher m.

alas [ə'læs] interj ach.

album [ælbəm] n Album nt.

alcohol ['ælkəhɒl] n Alkohol m; **~ic** [ælkə'hɒlɪk] a drink alkoholisch; n Alkoholiker(in f) m; **~ism** Alkoholismus m.

alcove ['ælkəʊv] n Alkoven m.

alderman ['ɔːldəmən] n Stadtrat m.

ale [eɪl] n Ale f.

alert [ə'lɜːt] a wachsam; n Alarm m; **~ness** Wachsamkeit f.

algebra ['ældʒɪbrə] n Algebra f.

alias ['eɪlɪəs] ad alias; n Deckname m.

alibi ['ælɪbaɪ] n Alibi nt.

alien ['eɪlɪən] n Ausländer m; (foreign) ausländisch; (strange) fremd; **~ate** vt entfremden; **~ation** [eɪlɪə'neɪʃən] Entfremdung f.

alight [ə'laɪt] a, ad brennend; (of building) in Flammen; vi (descend) aussteigen; (bird) sich setzen.

align [ə'laɪn] vt ausrichten; **~ment** Ausrichtung f; Gruppierung f.

alike [ə'laɪk] a gleich, ähnlich; ad gleich, ebenso.

alimony ['ælɪmənɪ] n Unterhalt m, Alimente pl.

alive [ə'laɪv] a (living) lebend; (lively) lebendig, aufgeweckt; (full of) voll (with von), wimmelnd (with von).

alkali ['ælkəlaɪ] n Alkali nt.

all [ɔːl] a (every one of) alle; n (the whole) alles, das Ganze; **~ of the books** alle Bücher; **~** (completely) vollkommen, ganz; **it's ~ mine** das geht alles mir; **it's ~ over** es ist alles aus or vorbei; **~ around the edge** rund um den Rand; **~ at once** auf einmal; **~ but** alle(s) außer; (almost) fast; **~ in** alles in allem; **~ over town** in der ganzen Stadt; **~ right** okay, in Ordnung; **not at ~** ganz und gar nicht; (don't mention it!) bitte.

allay [ə'leɪ] vt fears beschwichtigen.

allegation [ælɪ'geɪʃən] n Behauptung f.

allege [ə'ledʒ] vt (declare) behaupten; (falsely) vorgeben; **~dly** [ə'ledʒɪdlɪ] ad angeblich.

allegiance [ə'liːdʒəns] n Treue f, Ergebenheit f.

allegory ['ælɪgərɪ] n Allegorie f.

all-embracing ['ɔːlɪm'breɪsɪŋ] a allumfassend.

allergic [ə'lɜːdʒɪk] a allergisch (*to* gegen).

allergy ['ælədʒɪ] n Allergie f.

alleviate [ə'liːvɪeɪt] vt erleichtern, lindern.

alleviation [əliːvɪ'eɪʃən] n Erleichterung f.

alley ['ælɪ] n Gasse f, Durchgang m.

alliance [ə'laɪəns] n Bund m, Allianz f.

allied ['ælaɪd] a vereinigt; *powers* alliiert; verwandt (*to* mit).

alligator ['ælɪgeɪtə*] n Alligator m.

all-important ['ɔːlɪm'pɔːtənt] a äußerst wichtig.

all-in ['ɔːlɪn] a, ad *charge* alles inbegriffen, Gesamt-; (*exhausted*) erledigt, kaputt.

alliteration [əlɪtə'reɪʃən] n Alliteration f, Stabreim m.

all-night ['ɔːlnaɪt] a *café, cinema* die ganze Nacht geöffnet, Nacht-.

allocate ['æləkeɪt] vt zuweisen, zuteilen.

allocation [ælə'keɪʃən] n Zuteilung f.

allot [ə'lɒt] vt zuteilen; ~**ment** (*share*) Anteil m; (*plot*) Schrebergarten m.

all-out ['ɔːl'aut] a, ad total.

allow [ə'lau] vt (*permit*) erlauben, gestatten (*sb* jdm); (*grant*) bewilligen; (*deduct*) abziehen; ~ **for** vt berücksichtigen, einplanen; ~**ance** Beihilfe f; **to make** ~**ances for** berücksichtigen.

alloy ['ælɔɪ] n Metallegierung f.

all-round ['ɔːl'raund] a *sportsman* allseitig, Allround-.

all-rounder ['ɔːl'raundə*] n (*Sport*) vielseitige(r) Sportler; (*general*) Allerweltskerl m.

all-time ['ɔːl'taɪm] a *record, high* ... aller Zeiten, Höchst-.

allude [ə'luːd] vi hinweisen, anspielen (*to* auf +acc).

alluring [ə'ljuərɪŋ] a verlockend.

allusion [ə'luːʒən] n Anspielung f, Andeutung f.

alluvium [ə'luːvɪəm] n Schwemmland nt.

ally ['ælaɪ] n Verbündete(r) mf; (*Pol*) Alliierte(r) m.

almanac ['ɔːlmənæk] n Kalender m.

almighty [ɔːl'maɪtɪ] a allmächtig; **the A**~ der Allmächtige.

almond ['ɑːmənd] n Mandel f.

almost ['ɔːlməust] ad fast, beinahe.

alms [ɑːmz] n Almosen nt.

alone [ə'ləun] a, ad allein.

along [ə'lɒŋ] prep entlang, längs; ad (*onward*) vorwärts, weiter; ~ **with** zusammen mit; ~**side** ad *walk* nebenher; *come* nebendran; *be* daneben; prep (*walk, compared with*) neben (+dat); (*come*) neben (+acc); (*be*) entlang, neben (+dat); (*of ship*) längsseits (+gen); ~ **the river** den Fluß entlang; **I knew all** ~ ich wußte die ganze Zeit.

aloof [ə'luːf] a zurückhaltend; ad fern; ~**ness** Zurückhaltung f, Sich-Fernhalten nt.

aloud [ə'laud] ad laut.

alphabet ['ælfəbet] n Alphabet nt; ~**ical** [ælfə'betɪkl] a alphabetisch.

alpine ['ælpaɪn] a alpin, Alpen-.

already [ɔːl'redɪ] ad schon, bereits.

also ['ɔːlsəu] ad auch, außerdem.

altar ['ɔːltə*] n Altar m.

alter ['ɔːltə*] vti ändern; *dress* umändern; ~**ation** [ɔltə'reɪʃən] Änderung f; Umänderung f; (*to building*) Umbau m.

alternate [ɒl'tɜːnɪt] a abwechselnd; [ɒltə'neɪt] vi abwechseln (*with* mit); ~**ly** ad abwechselnd, wechselweise.

alternative [ɒl'tɜːnətɪv] a andere(r, s); n (*Aus*)wahl f, Alternative f; **what's the** ~? welche Alternative gibt es?; **we have no** ~ uns bleibt keine andere Wahl; ~**ly** ad im anderen Falle.

although [ɔːl'ðəu] cj obwohl, wenn auch.

altitude ['æltɪtjuːd] n Höhe f.

alto ['æltəu] n Alt m.

altogether [ɔːltə'geðə*] ad (*on the whole*) im ganzen genommen; (*entirely*) ganz und gar.

altruistic [æltru'ɪstɪk] a uneigennützig, altruistisch.

aluminium [ælju'mɪnɪəm], (*US*) **aluminum** [ə'luːmɪnəm] n Aluminium nt.

always ['ɔːlweɪz] ad immer; **it was** ~ **that way** es war schon immer so.

amalgam [ə'mælgəm] n Amalgam nt; (*fig*) Mischung f.

amalgamate [ə'mælgəmeɪt] vi (*combine*) sich vereinigen; vt (*mix*) amalgamieren.

amalgamation [əmælgə'meɪʃən] n Verschmelzung f, Zusammenschluß m.

amass [ə'mæs] vt anhäufen.

amateur ['æmətə*] n Amateur m; (*pej*) Amateur m, Bastler m, Stümper m; a Amateur-, Bastler-; ~**ish** a (*pej*) dilettantisch, stümperhaft.

amaze [ə'meɪz] vt erstaunen, in Staunen versetzen; ~**ment** höchste(s) (Er)staunen nt.

amazing [ə'meɪzɪŋ] a höchst erstaunlich.

ambassador [æm'bæsədə*] n Botschafter m.

amber ['æmbə*] n Bernstein m.

ambidextrous [æmbɪ'dekstrəs] a beidhändig.

ambiguity [æmbɪ'gjuɪtɪ] n Zweideutigkeit f, Unklarheit f.

ambiguous [æm'bɪgjuəs] a zweideutig; (*not clear*) unklar.

ambition [æm'bɪʃən] n Ehrgeiz m.

ambitious [æm'bɪʃəs] a ehrgeizig.

ambivalent [æm'bɪvələnt] n *attitude* zwiespältig.

amble ['æmbl] vi schlendern.

ambulance ['æmbjuləns] n Krankenwagen m.

ambush ['æmbuʃ] n Hinterhalt m; vt aus dem Hinterhalt angreifen, überfallen.

ameliorate [ə'miːlɪəreɪt] vt verbessern.

amelioration [əmiːlɪə'reɪʃən] n Verbesserung f.

amen ['ɑː'men] interj amen.

amenable [ə'miːnəbl] a gefügig; (*to reason*) zugänglich (*to* dat); (*to flattery*) empfänglich (*to* für); (*to law*) unterworfen (*to* dat).

amend [ə'mend] vt *law etc* abändern, ergänzen; **to make** ~**s** etw wiedergutmachen; ~**ment** Abänderung f.

amenity [ə'miːnɪtɪ] n (moderne) Einrichtung f.

Americanize [ə'merıkənaız] *vt* amerikanisieren.

amethyst ['æmıθıst] *n* Amethyst *m.*

amiable ['eımıəbl] *a* liebenswürdig, sympathisch.

amicable ['æmıkəbl] *a* freundschaftlich; *settlement* gütlich.

amid(st) [ə'mıd(st)] *prep* mitten in *or* unter (+*dat*).

amiss [ə'mıs] *a* verkehrt, nicht richtig; *ad* **to take sth ~** etw übelnehmen.

ammeter ['æmıtə*] *n* (*Aut*) Amperemeter *m.*

ammunition [æmju'nıʃən] *n* Munition *f.*

amnesia [æm'niːzıə] *n* Gedächtnisverlust *m.*

amnesty ['æmnıstı] *n* Amnestie *f.*

amock [ə'mɒk] *ad see* **amuck.**

amoeba [ə'miːbə] *n* Amöbe *f.*

among(st) [ə'mʌŋ(st)] *prep* unter.

amoral [æ'mɒrəl] *a* unmoralisch.

amorous ['æmərəs] *a* verliebt.

amorphous [ə'mɔːfəs] *a* formlos, gestaltlos.

amount [ə'maunt] *n* (*of money*) Betrag *m*; (*of time, energy*) Aufwand *m* (*of* an +*dat*); (*of water, sand*) Menge *f*; **no ~ of ...** kein(e) ...; *vi*: **~ to** (*total*) sich belaufen auf (+*acc*); **this ~s to treachery** das kommt Verrat gleich; **it ~s to the same** es läuft aufs gleiche hinaus; **he won't ~ to much** aus ihm wird nie was.

amp [æmp] *n*, **ampere** ['æmpɛə*] *n* Ampere *nt.*

amphibious [æm'fıbıəs] *a* amphibisch, Amphibien-.

amphitheatre ['æmfıθıətə*] *n* Amphitheater *nt.*

ample ['æmpl] *a portion* reichlich; *dress* weit, groß; **~ time** genügend Zeit.

amplifier ['æmplıfaıə*] *n* Verstärker *m.*

amply ['æmplı] *ad* reichlich.

amputate ['æmpjuteıt] *vt* amputieren, abnehmen.

amuck [ə'mʌk] *ad*: **to run ~** Amok laufen.

amuse [ə'mjuːz] *vt* (*entertain*) unterhalten; (*make smile*) belustigen; (*occupy*) unterhalten; **I'm not ~d** das find' ich gar nicht lustig; **if that ~s you** wenn es dir Spaß macht; **~ment** (*feeling*) Unterhaltung *f*; (*recreation*) Zeitvertreib *m.*

amusing [ə'mjuːzıŋ] *a* amüsant, unterhaltend.

an [æn, ən] *indef art* ein(e).

anaemia [ə'niːmıə] *n* Anämie *f.*

anaemic [ə'niːmık] *a* blutarm.

anaesthetic [ænıs'θetık] *n* Betäubungsmittel *nt*; **under ~** unter Narkose.

anagram ['ænəgræm] *n* Anagramm *nt.*

analgesic [ænæl'dʒiːsık] *n* schmerzlindernde(s) Mittel *nt.*

analogous [ə'næləgəs] *a* analog.

analogy [ə'nælədʒı] *n* Analogie *f.*

analyse ['ænəlaız] *vt* analysieren.

analysis [ə'nælısıs] *n* Analyse *f.*

analytic [ænə'lıtık] *a* analytisch.

anarchist ['ænəkıst] *n* Anarchist(in *f*) *m.*

anarchy ['ænəkı] *n* Anarchie *f.*

anathema [ə'næθımə] *n* (*fig*) Greuel *nt.*

anatomical [ænə'tɒmıkəl] *a* anatomisch.

anatomy [ə'nætəmı] *n* (*structure*) anatomische(r) Aufbau *m*; (*study*) Anatomie *f.*

ancestor ['ænsestə*] *n* Vorfahr *m.*

ancestral [æn'sestrəl] *n* angestammt, Ahnen-.

ancestry ['ænsıstrı] *n* Abstammung *f*; Vorfahren *pl.*

anchor ['æŋkə*] *n* Anker *m*; *vi* ankern, vor Anker liegen; *vt* verankern; **~age** Ankerplatz *m.*

anchovy ['æntʃəvı] *n* Sardelle *f.*

ancient ['eınʃənt] *a* alt; *car etc* uralt.

and [ænd, ənd, ən] *cj* und.

anecdote ['ænıkdəut] *n* Anekdote *f.*

anemia [ə'niːmıə] *n* (*US*) = **anaemia.**

anemone [ə'nemənı] *n* Anemone *f.*

anesthetic [ænıs'θetık] *n* (*US*) = **anaesthetic.**

anew [ə'njuː] *ad* von neuem.

angel ['eındʒəl] *n* Engel *m*; **~ic** [æn'dʒelık] *a* engelhaft.

anger ['æŋgə*] *n* Zorn *m*; *vt* ärgern.

angina [æn'dʒaınə] *n* Angina *f*, Halsentzündung *f.*

angle ['æŋgl] *n* Winkel *m*; (*point of view*) Standpunkt *m*; **at an ~** nicht gerade; *vt* stellen; **to ~ for** aussein auf (+*acc*); **~r** Angler *m.*

Anglican ['æŋglıkən] *a* anglikanisch; *n* Anglikaner(in *f*) *m.*

anglicize ['æŋglısaız] *vt* anglisieren.

angling ['æŋglıŋ] *n* Angeln *nt.*

Anglo- ['æŋgləu] *pref* Anglo-.

angrily ['æŋgrılı] *ad* ärgerlich, böse.

angry ['æŋgrı] *a* ärgerlich, ungehalten, böse; *wound* entzündet.

anguish ['æŋgwıʃ] *n* Qual *f.*

angular ['æŋgjulə*] *a* eckig, winkelförmig; *face* kantig.

animal ['ænıməl] *n* Tier *nt*; (*living creature*) Lebewesen *nt*; *a* tierisch, animalisch.

animate ['ænımeıt] *vt* beleben; ['ænımət] *a* lebhaft; **~d** *a* lebendig; *film* Zeichentrick-.

animation [ænı'meıʃən] *n* Lebhaftigkeit *f.*

animosity [ænı'mɒsıtı] *n* Feindseligkeit *f*, Abneigung *f.*

aniseed ['ænısiːd] *n* Anis *m.*

ankle ['æŋkl] *n* (Fuß)knöchel *m.*

annex ['æneks] *n* Anbau *m*; [ə'neks] *vt* anfügen; (*Pol*) annektieren, angliedern.

annihilate [ə'naıəleıt] *vt* vernichten.

anniversary [ænı'vɜːsərı] *n* Jahrestag *m.*

annotate ['ænəteıt] *vt* kommentieren.

announce [ə'nauns] *vt* ankündigen, anzeigen; **~ment** Ankündigung *f*; (*official*) Bekanntmachung *f*; **~r** Ansager(in *f*) *m.*

annoy [ə'nɔı] *vt* ärgern; **~ance** Ärgernis *nt*, Störung *f*; **~ing** *a* ärgerlich; *person* lästig.

annual ['ænjuəl] *a* jährlich; *salary* Jahres-; *n* (*plant*) einjährige Pflanze *f*; (*book*) Jahrbuch *nt*; **~ly** *ad* jährlich.

annuity [ə'njuːıtı] *n* Jahresrente *f.*

annul [ə'nʌl] *vt* aufheben, annullieren; **~ment** Aufhebung *f*, Annullierung *f.*

anoint [ə'nɔɪnt] vt salben.
anomalous [ə'nɒmələs] a unregelmäßig, anomal.
anomaly [ə'nɒməlɪ] n Abweichung f von der Regel.
anon [ə'nɒn] a = **anonymous**.
anonymity [ænə'nɪmɪtɪ] n Anonymität f.
anonymous [ə'nɒnɪməs] a anonym.
anorak ['ænəræk] n Anorak m, Windjacke f.
another [ə'nʌðə*] a, pron (different) ein(e) andere(r, s); (additional) noch eine(r, s).
answer ['ɑ:nsə*] n Antwort f; vi antworten; (on phone) sich melden; vt person antworten (+dat); letter, question beantworten; telephone gehen an (+acc), abnehmen; door öffnen; ~able a beantwortbar; (responsible) verantwortlich, haftbar; ~ back vi frech sein; to ~ for sth für etw verantwortlich sein; to ~ to the name of auf den Namen ... hören.
ant [ænt] n Ameise f.
antagonism [æn'tægənɪzəm] n Antagonismus m.
antagonist [æn'tægənɪst] n Gegner m, Antagonist m; ~ic [æntægə'nɪstɪk] a feindselig.
antagonize [æn'tægənaɪz] vt reizen.
anteater ['æntiːtə*] n Ameisenbär m.
antecedent [æntɪ'siːdənt] n Vorhergehende(s) nt; ~s pl Vorleben nt, Vorgeschichte f.
antelope ['æntɪləʊp] n Antilope f.
antenatal [æntɪ'neɪtl] a vor der Geburt.
antenna [æn'tenə] n (Biol) Fühler m; (Rad) Antenne f.
anteroom ['æntɪrʊm] n Vorzimmer nt.
anthem ['ænθəm] n Hymne f.
anthology [æn'θɒlədʒɪ] n Gedichtsammlung f, Anthologie f.
anthropologist [ænθrə'pɒlədʒɪst] n Anthropologe m.
anthropology [ænθrə'pɒlədʒɪ] n Anthropologie f.
anti- ['æntɪ] pref Gegen-, Anti-.
anti-aircraft ['æntɪ'ɛəkrɑːft] a Flugabwehr-.
antibiotic ['æntɪbaɪ'ɒtɪk] n Antibiotikum nt.
anticipate [æn'tɪsɪpeɪt] vt (expect) trouble, question erwarten, rechnen mit; (look forward to) sich freuen auf (+acc); (do first) vorwegnehmen; (foresee) ahnen, vorhersehen.
anticipation [æntɪsɪ'peɪʃən] n Erwartung f; (foreshadowing) Vorwegnahme f; that was good ~ das war gut vorausgesehen.
anticlimax ['æntɪ'klaɪmæks] n Ernüchterung f.
anticlockwise ['æntɪ'klɒkwaɪz] a entgegen dem Uhrzeigersinn.
antics ['æntɪks] npl Possen pl.
anticyclone ['æntɪ'saɪkləʊn] n Hoch nt, Hochdruckgebiet nt.
antidote ['æntɪdəʊt] n Gegenmittel nt.
antifreeze ['æntɪfriːz] n Frostschutzmittel nt.
antipathy [æn'tɪpəθɪ] n Abneigung f, Antipathie f.

antiquarian [æntɪ'kwɛərɪən] a altertümlich; n Antiquitätensammler m.
antiquated ['æntɪkweɪtɪd] a antiquiert.
antique [æn'tiːk] n Antiquität f; a antik; (old-fashioned) altmodisch.
antiquity [æn'tɪkwɪtɪ] n Antike f, Altertum nt.
antiseptic [æntɪ'septɪk] n Antiseptikum nt; a antiseptisch.
antisocial [æntɪ'səʊʃl] a person ungesellig; law unsozial.
antithesis [æn'tɪθɪsɪs] n Gegensatz m, Antithese f.
antlers ['æntləz] npl Geweih nt.
anus ['eɪnəs] n After m.
anvil ['ænvɪl] n Amboß m.
anxiety [æŋ'zaɪətɪ] n Angst f; (worry) Sorge f.
anxious ['æŋkʃəs] a ängstlich; (worried) besorgt; ~ly ad besorgt; to be ~ to do sth etw unbedingt tun wollen.
any ['enɪ] a: take ~ one nimm irgendein(e,n,s)!; do you want ~ apples? willst du ~ Apfel (haben)?; do you want ~? willst du welche?; not ~ keine; ad: ~ faster schneller; ~body pron irgend jemand; (everybody) jedermann; ~how ad sowieso, ohnehin; (carelessly) einfach so; ~one pron = ~body; ~thing pron irgend etwas; ~time ad jederzeit; ~way ad sowieso, ohnehin; ~way, let's stop na ja or sei's drum, hören wir auf; ~where ad irgendwo; (everywhere) überall.
apace [ə'peɪs] ad rasch.
apart [ə'pɑːt] ad (parted) auseinander; (away) beiseite, abseits; ~ from außer.
apartheid [ə'pɑːteɪt] n Apartheid f.
apartment [ə'pɑːtmənt] n (US) Wohnung f; ~s pl (möblierte Miet)wohnung f.
apathetic [æpə'θetɪk] a teilnahmslos, apathisch.
apathy ['æpəθɪ] n Teilnahmslosigkeit f, Apathie f.
ape [eɪp] n (Menschen)affe m; vt nachahmen.
aperitif [ə'perɪtɪv] n Aperitif m.
aperture ['æpətjʊə*] n Öffnung f; (Phot) Blende f.
apex ['eɪpeks] n Spitze f, Scheitelpunkt m.
aphorism ['æfərɪzəm] n Aphorismus m.
aphrodisiac [æfrəʊ'dɪzɪæk] n Aphrodisiakum nt.
apiece [ə'piːs] ad pro Stück; (per person) pro Kopf.
aplomb [ə'plɒm] n selbstbewußte(s) Auftreten nt.
apocryphal [ə'pɒkrɪfəl] a apokryph, unecht.
apologetic [əpɒlə'dʒetɪk] a entschuldigend; to be ~ sich sehr entschuldigen.
apologize [ə'pɒlədʒaɪz] vi sich entschuldigen.
apology [ə'pɒlədʒɪ] n Entschuldigung f.
apoplexy ['æpəpleksɪ] n Schlaganfall m.
apostle [ə'pɒsl] n Apostel m; (pioneer) Vorkämpfer m.
apostrophe [ə'pɒstrəfɪ] n Apostroph m.

appal [ə'pɔːl] vt erschrecken; ~**ling** a schrecklich.

apparatus ['æpəreitəs] n Apparat m, Gerät nt.

apparent [ə'pærənt] a offenbar; ~**ly** ad anscheinend.

apparition [æpə'rɪʃən] n (ghost) Erscheinung f, Geist m; (appearance) Erscheinen nt.

appeal [ə'piːl] vi dringend ersuchen; dringend bitten (for um); sich wenden (to an +acc); (to public) appellieren (to an +acc); (Jur) Berufung einlegen; n Aufruf m; (Jur) Berufung f; ~**ing** a ansprechend.

appear [ə'pɪə*] vi (come into sight) erscheinen; (be seen) auftauchen; (seem) scheinen; ~**ance** (coming into sight) Erscheinen nt; (outward show) Äußere(s) nt; **to put in** or **make an** ~**ance** sich zeigen.

appease [ə'piːz] vt beschwichtigen.

appendage [ə'pendɪdʒ] n Anhang m, Anhängsel nt.

appendicitis [əpendi'saitis] n Blinddarmentzündung f.

appendix [ə'pendiks] n (in book) Anhang m; (Med) Blinddarm m.

appetite ['æpitait] n Appetit m; (fig) Lust f.

appetizing ['æpitaiziŋ] a appetitanregend.

applaud [ə'plɔːd] vti Beifall klatschen (+dat), applaudieren.

applause [ə'plɔːz] n Beifall m, Applaus m.

apple ['æpl] n Apfel m; ~ **tree** Apfelbaum m.

appliance [ə'plaɪəns] n Gerät nt.

applicable [ə'plɪkəbl] a anwendbar; (in forms) zutreffend.

applicant ['æplɪkənt] n Bewerber(in f) m.

application [æplɪ'keiʃən] n (request) Antrag m; (for job) Bewerbung f; (putting into practice) Anwendung f; (hard work) Fleiß m.

applied [ə'plaid] a angewandt.

apply [ə'plai] vi (ask) sich wenden (to an +acc), sich melden; (be suitable) zutreffen; vt (place on) auflegen; cream auftragen; (put into practice) anwenden; (devote o.s.) sich widmen (+dat).

appoint [ə'pɔint] vt (to office) ernennen, berufen; (settle) festsetzen; ~**ment** (meeting) Verabredung f; (at hairdresser etc) Bestellung f; (in business) Termin m; (choice for a position) Ernennung f; (Univ) Berufung f.

apportion [ə'pɔːʃən] vt zuteilen.

appreciable [ə'priːʃəbl] a (perceptible) merklich; (able to be estimated) abschätzbar.

appreciate [ə'priːʃieit] vt (value) zu schätzen wissen; (understand) einsehen; vi (increase in value) im Wert steigen.

appreciation [əpriːʃi'eiʃən] n Wertschätzung f; (Comm) Wertzuwachs m.

appreciative [ə'priːʃiətiv] a (showing thanks) dankbar; (showing liking) anerkennend.

apprehend [æpri'hend] vt (arrest) festnehmen; (understand) erfassen.

apprehension [æpri'henʃən] n Angst f.

apprehensive [æpri'hensiv] a furchtsam.

apprentice [ə'prentis] n Lehrling m; ~**ship** Lehrzeit f.

approach [ə'prəutʃ] vi sich nähern; vt herantreten an (+acc); problem herangehen an (+acc); n Annäherung f; (to problem) Ansatz m; (path) Zugang m, Zufahrt f; ~**able** a zugänglich.

approbation [æprə'beiʃən] n Billigung f.

appropriate [ə'prəuprieit] vt (take for o.s.) sich aneignen; (set apart) bereitstellen; [ə'prəupriət] a angemessen; remark angebracht; ~**ly** [ə'prəupriətli] ad passend.

approval [ə'pruːvəl] n (show of satisfaction) Beifall m; (permission) Billigung f; (Comm) **on** ~ bei Gefallen.

approve [ə'pruːv] vti billigen (of acc); **I don't** ~ **of it/him** ich halte nichts davon/von ihm.

approximate [ə'prɔksimit] a annähernd, ungefähr; [ə'prɔksimeit] vt nahekommen (+dat); ~**ly** ad rund, ungefähr.

approximation [əprɔksi'meiʃən] n Annäherung f.

apricot ['eiprikɔt] n Aprikose f.

April ['eiprəl] n April m.

apron ['eiprən] n Schürze f.

apt [æpt] a (suitable) passend; (able) begabt; (likely) geneigt.

aptitude ['æptitjuːd] n Begabung f.

aqualung ['ækwəlʌŋ] n Unterwasseratmungsgerät nt.

aquarium [ə'kwεəriəm] n Aquarium nt.

Aquarius [ə'kwεəriəs] n Wassermann m.

aquatic [ə'kwætik] a Wasser-.

aqueduct ['ækwidʌkt] n Aquädukt m.

arable ['εrəbl] a bebaubar, Kultur-.

arbiter ['ɑːbitə*] n (Schieds)richter m.

arbitrary ['ɑːbitrəri] a willkürlich.

arbitrate ['ɑːbitreit] vti schlichten.

arbitration [ɑːbi'treiʃən] n Schlichtung f; **to go to** ~ vor ein Schiedsgericht gehen.

arbitrator ['ɑːbitreitə*] n Schiedsrichter m, Schlichter m.

arc [ɑːk] n Bogen m.

arcade [ɑː'keid] n Säulengang m.

arch [ɑːtʃ] n Bogen m; vt überwölben; back krumm machen; vi sich wölben; a durchtrieben; ~ **enemy** Erzfeind m.

archaeologist [ɑːki'ɔlədʒist] n Archäologe m.

archaeology [ɑːki'ɔlədʒi] n Archäologie f.

archaic [ɑː'keiik] a altertümlich.

archbishop [ɑːtʃ'biʃəp] n Erzbischof m.

archer ['ɑːtʃə*] n Bogenschütze m; ~**y** Bogenschießen nt.

archipelago [ɑːki'peligəu] n Archipel m; (sea) Inselmeer nt.

architect ['ɑːkitekt] n Architekt(in f) m; ~**ural** [ɑːki'tektʃərəl] a architektonisch; ~**ure** Architektur f.

archives ['ɑːkaivz] npl Archiv nt.

archivist ['ɑːkivist] n Archivar m.

archway ['ɑːtʃwei] n Bogen m.

ardent ['ɑːdənt] a glühend.

ardour ['ɑːdə*] n Eifer m.

arduous ['ɑːdjuəs] a mühsam.

are [ɑː*] see **be**.

area ['εəriə] n Fläche f; (of land) Gebiet nt;

(part of sth) Teil m, Abschnitt m.
arena [ə'ri:nə] n Arena f.
aren't [ɑ:nt] = **are not.**
arguable ['ɑ:gjuəbl] a (doubtful) diskutabel; (possible) **it's ~ that . . . man könnte argumentieren daß ...**
argue ['ɑ:gju:] vt case vertreten; vi diskutieren; (angrily) streiten; **don't ~!** keine Widerrede!; **to ~ with sb** sich mit jdm streiten.
argument ['ɑ:gjumənt] n (theory) Argument nt; (reasoning) Argumentation f; (row) Auseinandersetzung f, Streit m; **~ative** [ɑ:gju'mentətɪv] a streitlustig; **to have an ~** sich streiten.
aria ['ɑ:rɪə] n Arie f.
arid ['ærɪd] a trocken; **~ity** [ə'rɪdɪtɪ] n Dürre f.
Aries ['eəri:z] n Widder m.
arise [ə'raɪz] vi irreg aufsteigen; (get up) aufstehen; (difficulties etc) entstehen; (case) vorkommen; **to ~ out of sth** herrühren von etw.
aristocracy [ærɪs'tɒkrəsɪ] n Adel m, Aristokratie f.
aristocrat ['ærɪstəkræt] n Adlige(r) mf, Aristokrat(in f) m; **~ic** [ærɪstə'krætɪk] a adlig, aristokratisch.
arithmetic [ə'rɪθmətɪk] n Rechnen nt, Arithmetik f.
ark [ɑ:k] n: **Noah's A~** die Arche Noah.
arm [ɑ:m] n Arm m; (branch of military service) Zweig m; vt bewaffnen; **~s** pl (weapons) Waffen pl; **~chair** Lehnstuhl m; **~ed** a forces Streit-, bewaffnet; robbery bewaffnet; **~ful** Armvoll m.
armistice ['ɑ:mɪstɪs] n Waffenstillstand m.
armour ['ɑ:mə*] n (knight's) Rüstung f; (Mil) Panzerplatte f; **~y** Waffenlager nt; (factory) Waffenfabrik f.
armpit ['ɑ:mpɪt] n Achselhöhle f.
army ['ɑ:mɪ] n Armee f, Heer nt; (host) Heer nt.
aroma [ə'rəumə] n Duft m, Aroma nt; **~tic** [ærə'mætɪk] a aromatisch, würzig.
around [ə'raund] ad ringsherum; (almost) ungefähr; prep um . . . herum; **is he ~?** ist er hier?
arouse [ə'rauz] vt wecken.
arrange [ə'reɪndʒ] vt time, meeting festsetzen; holidays festlegen; flowers, hair, objects anordnen; **I ~d to meet him** ich habe mit ihm ausgemacht, ihn zu treffen; **it's all ~d** es ist alles arrangiert; **~ment** (order) Reihenfolge f; (agreement) Übereinkommen nt; (plan) Vereinbarung f.
array [ə'reɪ] n Aufstellung f.
arrears [ə'rɪəz] npl (of debts) Rückstand m; (of work) Unerledigte(s) nt; **in ~** im Rückstand.
arrest [ə'rest] vt person verhaften; (stop) aufhalten; n Verhaftung f; **under ~** in Haft; **you're under ~** Sie sind verhaftet.
arrival [ə'raɪvəl] n Ankunft f.
arrive [ə'raɪv] vi ankommen (at in +dat, bei); **to ~ at a decision** zu einer Entscheidung kommen.
arrogance ['ærəgəns] n Überheblichkeit f, Arroganz f.

arrogant ['ærəgənt] a anmaßend, arrogant.
arrow ['ærəu] n Pfeil m.
arse [ɑ:s] n (col) Arsch m.
arsenal ['ɑ:sɪnl] n Waffenlager nt, Zeughaus nt.
arsenic ['ɑ:snɪk] n Arsen nt.
arson ['ɑ:sn] n Brandstiftung f.
art [ɑ:t] n Kunst f; **~s** pl Geisteswissenschaften pl; **~ gallery** Kunstgalerie f.
artery ['ɑ:tərɪ] n Schlagader f, Arterie f.
artful ['ɑ:tful] a verschlagen.
arthritis [ɑ:'θraɪtɪs] n Arthritis f.
artichoke ['ɑ:tɪtʃəuk] n Artischocke f.
article ['ɑ:tɪkl] n (Press, Gram) Artikel m; (thing) Gegenstand m, Artikel m; (clause) Abschnitt m, Paragraph m.
articulate [ɑ:'tɪkjulɪt] a (able to express o.s.) redegewandt; (speaking clearly) deutlich, verständlich; **to be ~** sich gut ausdrücken können; [ɑ:'tɪkjuleɪt] vt (connect) zusammenfügen, gliedern; **~d vehicle** Sattelschlepper m.
artifice ['ɑ:tɪfɪs] n (skill) Kunstgriff m; (trick) Kniff m, List f.
artificial [ɑ:tɪ'fɪʃəl] a künstlich, Kunst-; **~ respiration** künstliche Atmung f.
artillery [ɑ:'tɪlərɪ] n Artillerie f.
artisan ['ɑ:tɪzæn] n gelernte(r) Handwerker m.
artist ['ɑ:tɪst] n Künstler(in f) m; **~ic** [ɑ:'tɪstɪk] a künstlerisch; **~ry** künstlerische(s) Können nt.
artless ['ɑ:tlɪs] a ungekünstelt; character arglos.
arty ['ɑ:tɪ] a: **to be ~** auf Kunst machen.
as [æz] ad, cj (since) da, weil; (while) als; (like) wie; (in role of) als; **~ soon ~ he comes** sobald er kommt; **~ big ~** so groß wie; **~ well** auch; **~ well ~** und auch; **~ for him** was ihn anbetrifft; **~ if, ~ though** als ob; **~ it were** sozusagen; **old ~ he was** so alt er auch war.
asbestos [æz'bestəs] n Asbest m.
ascend [ə'send] vi aufsteigen; vt besteigen; **~ancy** Oberhand f.
ascension [ə'senʃən] n (Eccl) Himmelfahrt f.
ascent [ə'sent] n Aufstieg m; Besteigung f.
ascertain [æsə'teɪn] vt feststellen.
ascetic [ə'setɪk] a asketisch.
ascribe [əs'kraɪb] vt zuschreiben (to dat).
ash [æʃ] n (dust) Asche f; (tree) Esche f.
ashamed [ə'feɪmd] a beschämt.
ashen [æʃən] a (pale) aschfahl.
ashore [ə'ʃɔ:*] ad an Land.
ashtray ['æʃtreɪ] n Aschenbecher m.
aside [ə'saɪd] ad beiseite; **~ from** (US) abgesehen von; n beiseite gesprochene Worte pl.
ask [ɑ:sk] vti fragen; permission bitten um; **~ him his name** frage ihn nach seinem Namen; **he ~ed to see you** er wollte dich sehen; **you ~ed for that!** da bist du selbst schuld.
askance [əs'kɑ:ns] ad: **to look ~ at s.o.** jdn schief ansehen.
askew [əs'kju:] ad schief.

asleep [ə'sliːp] *a, ad*: **to be ~** schlafen; **to fall ~** einschlafen.

asp [æsp] *n* Espe *f*.

asparagus [əs'pærəgəs] *n* Spargel *m*.

aspect ['æspekt] *n* (*appearance*) Aussehen *nt*; Aspekt *m*.

asphalt ['æsfælt] *n* Asphalt *m*.

asphyxiate [əs'fɪksɪeɪt] *vt* ersticken.

asphyxiation [əsfɪksɪ'eɪʃən] *n* Erstickung *f*.

aspirate ['æspərɪt] *n* Hauchlaut *m*.

aspiration [æspə'reɪʃən] *n* Trachten *nt*; **to have ~s towards sth** etw anstreben.

aspire [əs'paɪə*] *vi* streben (*to* nach).

aspirin ['æsprɪn] *n* Aspirin *nt*.

ass [æs] *n* (*lit, fig*) Esel *m*.

assailant [ə'seɪlənt] *n* Angreifer *m*.

assassin [ə'sæsɪn] *n* Attentäter(in *f*) *m*; **~ate** *vt* ermorden; **~ation** [əsæsɪ'neɪʃən] Ermordung *f*.

assault [ə'sɔːlt] *n* Angriff *m*; *vt* überfallen; **woman** herfallen über (+*acc*).

assemble [ə'sembl] *vt* versammeln; *parts* zusammensetzen; *vi* sich versammeln.

assembly [ə'semblɪ] *n* (*meeting*) Versammlung *f*; (*construction*) Zusammensetzung *f*, Montage *f*; **~ line** Fließband *nt*.

assent [ə'sent] *n* Zustimmung *f*; *vi* zustimmen (*to* dat).

assert [ə'sɜːt] *vt* erklären; **~ion** [ə'sɜːʃən] Behauptung *f*; **~ive** *a* selbstsicher.

assess [ə'ses] *vt* schätzen; **~ment** Bewertung *f*, Einschätzung *f*; **~or** Steuerberater *m*.

asset ['æset] *n* Vorteil *m*, Wert *m*; **~s** *pl* Vermögen *nt*; (*estate*) Nachlaß *m*.

assiduous [ə'sɪdjuəs] *a* fleißig, aufmerksam.

assign [ə'saɪn] *vt* zuweisen.

assignment [ə'saɪnmənt] *n* Aufgabe *f*, Auftrag *m*.

assimilate [ə'sɪmɪleɪt] *vt* sich aneignen, aufnehmen.

assimilation [əsɪmɪ'leɪʃən] *n* Assimilierung *f*, Aufnahme *f*.

assist [ə'sɪst] *vt* beistehen (+*dat*); **~ance** Unterstützung *f*, Hilfe *f*; **~ant** Assistent(in *f*) *m*, Mitarbeiter(in *f*) *m*; (*in shop*) Verkäufer(in *f*) *m*.

assizes [ə'saɪzɪz] *npl* Landgericht *nt*.

associate [ə'səuʃɪɪt] *n* (*partner*) Kollege *m*, Teilhaber *m*; (*member*) außerordentliche(s) Mitglied *nt*; [ə'səuʃɪeɪt] *vt* verbinden (*with* mit); *vi* (*keep company*) verkehren (*with* mit).

association [əsəusɪ'eɪʃən] *a* Verband *m*, Verein *m*; (*Psych*) Assoziation *f*; (*link*) Verbindung *f*; **~ football** (*Brit*) Fußball *nt*.

assorted [ə'sɔːtɪd] *a* gemischt, verschieden.

assortment [ə'sɔːtmənt] *n* Sammlung *f*; (*Comm*) Sortiment *nt* (*of* von), Auswahl *f* (*of* an +*dat*).

assume [ə'sjuːm] *vt* (*take for granted*) annehmen; (*put on*) annehmen, sich geben; **~d name** Deckname *m*.

assumption [ə'sʌmpʃən] *n* Annahme *f*.

assurance [ə'fuərəns] *n* (*firm statement*) Versicherung *f*; (*confidence*) Selbstsicherheit *f*; (*insurance*) (Lebens)versicherung *f*.

assure [ə'fuə*] *vt* (*make sure*) sicherstellen; (*convince*) versichern (+*dat*); *life* versichern.

assuredly [ə'fuərɪdlɪ] *ad* sicherlich.

asterisk ['æstərɪsk] *n* Sternchen *nt*.

astern [əs'tɜːn] *ad* achtern.

asthma ['æsmə] *n* Asthma *nt*; **~tic** [æs'mætɪk] *a* asthmatisch; *n* Asthmatiker(in *f*) *m*.

astir [ə'stɜː*] *ad* in Bewegung.

astonish [əs'tonɪʃ] *vt* erstaunen; **~ing** *a* erstaunlich; **~ment** Erstaunen *nt*.

astound [əs'taund] *vt* verblüffen; **~ing** *a* verblüffend.

astray [əs'treɪ] *ad* in die Irre; auf Abwege; *a* irregehend.

astride [əs'traɪd] *ad* rittlings; *prep* rittlings auf.

astringent [əs'trɪndʒənt] *a* (*Med*) zusammenziehend; (*severe*) streng.

astrologer [əs'trolədʒə*] *n* Astrologe *m*, Astrologin *f*.

astrology [əs'trolədʒɪ] *n* Astrologie *f*.

astronaut ['æstrənɔːt] *n* Astronaut(in *f*) *m*.

astronomer [əs'tronəmə*] *n* Astronom *m*.

astronomical [æstrə'nomɪkəl] *a* astronomisch; *numbers* astronomisch; *success* riesig.

astronomy [əs'tronəmɪ] *n* Astronomie *f*.

astute [əs'tjuːt] *a* scharfsinnig; schlau, gerissen.

asunder [ə'sʌndə*] *ad* entzwei.

asylum [ə'saɪləm] *n* (*home*) Heim *nt*; (*refuge*) Asyl *nt*.

at [æt] *prep* **~ home** zuhause; **~ John's** bei John; **~ table** bei Tisch; **~ school** in der Schule; **~ Easter** an Ostern; **~ 2 o'clock** um 2 Uhr; **~ (the age of) 16** mit 16; **~ £5** zu 5 Pfund; **~ 20 mph** mit 20 Meilen pro Stunde; **~ that** darauf; (*also*) dazu.

ate [et, eɪt] *pt of* **eat**.

atheism ['eɪθɪɪzəm] *n* Atheismus *m*.

atheist ['eɪθɪɪst] *n* Atheist(in *f*) *m*.

athlete ['æθliːt] *n* Athlet *m*, Sportler *m*.

athletic [æθ'letɪk] *a* sportlich, athletisch; **~s** *pl* Leichtathletik *f*.

atlas ['ætləs] *n* Atlas *m*.

atmosphere ['ætməsfɪə*] *n* Atmosphäre *f*.

atoll ['ætol] *n* Atoll *nt*.

atom ['ætəm] *n* Atom *nt*; (*fig*) bißchen *nt*; **~ic** [ə'tomɪk] *a* atomar, Atom-; **~(ic) bomb** Atombombe *f*; **~ic power** Atomkraft *f*; **~izer** Zerstäuber *m*.

atone [ə'təun] *vi* sühnen (*for* acc).

atrocious [ə'trəuʃəs] *a* gräßlich.

atrocity [ə'trosɪtɪ] *n* Scheußlichkeit *f*; (*deed*) Greueltat *f*.

attach [ə'tætʃ] *vt* (*fasten*) befestigen; *importance etc* legen (*to* auf +*acc*), beimessen (*to* dat); **to be ~ed to sb/sth** an jdm/etw hängen; **~é** [ə'tæʃeɪ] Attaché *m*.

attack [ə'tæk] *vti* angreifen; *n* Angriff *m*; (*Med*) Anfall *m*.

attain [ə'teɪn] *vt* erreichen; **~ment** Erreichung *f*; **~ments** *pl* Kenntnisse *pl*.

attempt [ə'tempt] n Versuch m; vti versuchen.

attend [ə'tend] vt (go to) teilnehmen (an +dat); lectures besuchen; vi (pay attention) aufmerksam sein; **to ~ to** needs nachkommen (+dat); person sich kümmern um; **~ance** (presence) Anwesenheit f; (people present) Besucherzahl f; **good ~ance** gute Teilnahme; **~ant** n (companion) Begleiter(in f) m; Gesellschafter(in f) m; (in car park etc) Wächter(in f) m; (servant) Bediente(r) mf, a begleitend; (fig) verbunden mit.

attention [ə'tenʃən] n Aufmerksamkeit f; (care) Fürsorge f; (for machine etc) Pflege f.

attentive a, **~ly** ad [ə'tentɪv, -lɪ] aufmerksam.

attenuate [ə'tenjʊeɪt] vt verdünnen.

attest [ə'test] vt bestätigen; **to ~ to** sich verbürgen für.

attic ['ætɪk] n Dachstube f, Mansarde f.

attire [ə'taɪə*] n Gewand nt.

attitude ['ætɪtjuːd] n (position) Haltung f; (mental) Einstellung f.

attorney [ə'tɜːnɪ] n (solicitor) Rechtsanwalt m; (representative) Bevollmächtigte(r) mf; **A~ General** Justizminister m.

attract [ə'trækt] vt anziehen; attention erregen; employees anlocken; **~ion** [ə'trækʃən] n Anziehungskraft f; (thing) Attraktion f; **~ive** a attraktiv; **the idea ~s me** ich finde die Idee attraktiv.

attribute ['ætrɪbjuːt] n Eigenschaft f, Attribut nt; [ə'trɪbjuːt] vt zuschreiben (to dat).

attrition [ə'trɪʃən] n Verschleiß m; **war of ~** Zermürbungskrieg m.

aubergine ['əʊbəʒiːn] n Aubergine f.

auburn ['ɔːbən] a kastanienbraun.

auction ['ɔːkʃən] n Versteigerung f, Auktion f; vt versteigern; **~eer** [ɔːkʃə'nɪə*] Versteigerer m.

audacious [ɔː'deɪʃəs] a (daring) verwegen; (shameless) unverfroren.

audacity [ɔː'dæsɪtɪ] n (boldness) Wagemut m; (impudence) Unverfrorenheit f.

audible ['ɔːdɪbl] a hörbar.

audience ['ɔːdɪəns] n Zuhörer pl, Zuschauer pl; (with king etc) Audienz f.

audit ['ɔːdɪt] n Bücherrevision f; vt prüfen.

audition [ɔː'dɪʃən] n Probe f.

auditorium [ɔːdɪ'tɔːrɪəm] n Zuschauerraum m.

augment [ɔːg'ment] vt vermehren; vi zunehmen.

augur ['ɔːgə*] vti bedeuten, voraussagen; **this ~s well** das ist ein gutes Omen; **~y** ['ɔːgjʊrɪ] Vorbedeutung f, Omen nt.

August ['ɔːgəst] n August m.

august [ɔː'gʌst] a erhaben.

aunt [ɑːnt] n Tante f; **~y, ~ie** Tantchen nt.

au pair ['əʊ 'pɛə*] n (also **~ girl**) Au-pair-Mädchen nt.

aura ['ɔːrə] n Nimbus m.

auspices ['ɔːspɪsɪz] npl: **under the ~ of** unter der Schirmherrschaft von.

auspicious [ɔːs'pɪʃəs] a günstig; verheißungsvoll.

austere [ɒs'tɪə*] a streng; room nüchtern.

austerity [ɒs'terɪtɪ] n Strenge f; (Pol) wirtschaftliche Einschränkung f.

authentic [ɔː'θentɪk] a echt, authentisch; **~ate** vt beglaubigen; **~ity** [ɔːθen'tɪsɪtɪ] n Echtheit f.

author ['ɔːθə*] n Autor m, Schriftsteller m; (beginner) Urheber m, Schöpfer m.

authoritarian [ɔːθɒrɪ'tɛərɪən] a autoritär.

authoritative [ɔː'θɒrɪtətɪv] a account maßgeblich; manner herrisch.

authority [ɔː'θɒrɪtɪ] n (power) Autorität f; (expert) Autorität f, Fachmann m; **the authorities** pl die Behörden pl.

authorize ['ɔːθəraɪz] vt bevollmächtigen; (permit) genehmigen.

auto ['ɔːtəʊ] n (US) Auto nt, Wagen m.

autobiographical [ɔːtəbaɪə'græfɪkəl] a autobiographisch.

autobiography [ɔːtəbaɪ'ɒgrəfɪ] n Autobiographie f.

autocracy [ɔː'tɒkrəsɪ] n Autokratie f.

autocratic [ɔːtə'krætɪk] a autokratisch.

autograph ['ɔːtəgrɑːf] n (of celebrity) Autogramm nt; vt mit Autogramm versehen.

automate ['ɔːtəmeɪt] vt automatisieren, auf Automation umstellen.

automatic [ɔːtə'mætɪk] a automatisch; n Selbstladepistole f; (car) Automatik m; **~ally** ad automatisch.

automation [ɔːtə'meɪʃən] n Automation f.

automaton [ɔː'tɒmətən] n Automat m, Roboter m.

automobile ['ɔːtəməbiːl] n (US) Auto(mobil) nt.

autonomous [ɔː'tɒnəməs] a autonom.

autonomy [ɔː'tɒnəmɪ] n Autonomie f, Selbstbestimmung f.

autopsy ['ɔːtɒpsɪ] n Autopsie f.

autumn ['ɔːtəm] n Herbst m.

auxiliary [ɔːg'zɪlɪərɪ] a Hilfs-; n Hilfskraft f; (Gram) Hilfsverb nt.

avail [ə'veɪl] vt: **~ o.s. of sth** sich einer Sache bedienen; n: **to no ~** nutzlos; **~ability** [əveɪlə'bɪlɪtɪ] Erhältlichkeit f, Vorhandensein nt; **~able** erhältlich; zur Verfügung stehend; person erreichbar, abkömmlich.

avalanche ['ævəlɑːnʃ] n Lawine f.

avant-garde ['ævãŋ'gɑːd] a avant-gardistisch; n Avantgarde f.

avarice ['ævərɪs] n Habsucht f, Geiz m.

avaricious [ævə'rɪʃəs] a geizig, habsüchtig.

avenge [ə'vendʒ] vt rächen, sühnen.

avenue ['ævənjuː] n Allee f.

average ['ævərɪdʒ] n Durchschnitt m; a durchschnittlich, Durchschnitts-; vt figures den Durchschnitt nehmen von; (perform) durchschnittlich leisten; (in car etc) im Schnitt fahren; **on ~** durchschnittlich, im Durchschnitt.

averse [ə'vɜːs] a: **to be ~ to** eine Abneigung haben gegen.

aversion [ə'vɜːʃən] n Abneigung f.

avert [ə'vɜːt] vt (turn away) abkehren; (prevent) abwehren.

aviary ['eɪvɪərɪ] n Vogelhaus nt.

aviation [eɪvɪ'eɪʃən] n Luftfahrt f, Flugwesen nt.

aviator ['eɪvɪeɪtə*] n Flieger m.

avid ['ævɪd] a gierig (for auf +acc); ~ly ad gierig.

avocado [ævə'kɑːdəʊ] n (also ~ pear) Avocado(birne) f.

avoid [ə'vɔɪd] vt vermeiden; ~able a vermeidbar; ~ance Vermeidung f.

avowal [ə'vaʊəl] n Erklärung f.

await [ə'weɪt] vt erwarten, entgegensehen (+dat).

awake [ə'weɪk] a wach; irreg vi aufwachen; vt (auf)wecken; ~ning Erwachen nt.

award [ə'wɔːd] n (judgment) Urteil nt; (prize) Preis m; vt zuerkennen.

aware [ə'wɛə*] a bewußt; **to be ~** sich bewußt sein (of gen); ~ness Bewußtsein nt.

awash [ə'wɒʃ] a überflutet.

away [ə'weɪ] ad weg, fort.

awe [ɔː] n Ehrfurcht f; ~-inspiring, ~some a ehrfurchtgebietend; ~-struck a von Ehrfurcht ergriffen.

awful ['ɔːful] a (very bad) furchtbar; ~ly ad furchtbar, sehr.

awhile [ə'waɪl] ad eine kleine Weile, ein bißchen.

awkward ['ɔːkwəd] a (clumsy) ungeschickt, linkisch; (embarrassing) peinlich; ~ness Ungeschicklichkeit f.

awning ['ɔːnɪŋ] n Markise f.

awry [ə'raɪ] ad, a schief; **to go ~** (person) fehlgehen; (plans) schiefgehen.

ax (US), **axe** [æks] n Axt f, Beil nt; vt (to end suddenly) streichen.

axiom ['æksɪəm] n Grundsatz m, Axiom nt; ~atic [æksɪə'mætɪk] a axiomatisch.

axis ['æksɪs] n Achse f.

axle ['æksl] n Achse f.

ay(e) [aɪ] interj (yes) ja; **the ~es** pl die Jastimmen pl.

azure ['eɪʒə*] a himmelblau.

B

B, b [biː] n B nt, b nt.

babble ['bæbl] vi schwätzen; (stream) murmeln; n Geschwätz nt.

babe [beɪb] n Baby nt.

baboon [bə'buːn] n Pavian m.

baby ['beɪbɪ] n Baby nt, Säugling m; ~ **carriage** (US) Kinderwagen m; ~**ish** a kindisch; ~-**sit** vi irreg Kinder hüten, babysitten; ~-**sitter** Babysitter m.

bachelor ['bætʃələ*] n Junggeselle m; **B~ of Arts** Bakkalaureus m der philosophischen Fakultät; **B~ of Science** Bakkalaureus m der Naturwissenschaften.

back [bæk] n (of person, horse) Rücken m; (of house) Rückseite f; (of train) Ende nt; (Ftbl) Verteidiger m; vt (support) unterstützen; (wager) wetten auf (+acc); car rückwärts fahren; vi (go backwards) rückwärts gehen or fahren; a hinter(e, s); ad zurück; (to the rear) nach hinten; ~ **down** vi zurückstecken; ~ **out** vi sich zurückziehen; kneifen (col); ~**biting** Verleumdung f; ~**bone** Rückgrat nt;

(support) Rückhalt m; ~**cloth** Hintergrund m; ~**er** Förderer m; ~**fire** vi (plan) fehlschlagen; (Tech) fehlzünden; ~**ground** Hintergrund m; (information) Hintergrund m, Umstände pl; (person's education) Vorbildung f; ~**hand** (Sport) Rückhand f; a Rückhand-; ~**handed** a shot Rückhand-; compliment zweifelhaft; ~**ing** (support) Unterstützung f; ~**lash** (Tech) tote(r) Gang m; (fig) Gegenschlag m; ~**log** (of work) Rückstand m; ~ **number** (Press) alte Nummer f; ~ **pay** (Gehalts-, Lohn)nachzahlung f; ~**side** (col) Hintern m; ~**stroke** Rückenschwimmen nt; ~**ward** a (less developed) zurückgeblieben; (primitive) rückständig; ~**wardness** (of child) Unterentwicklung f; (of country) Rückständigkeit f; ~**wards** ad (in reverse) rückwärts; (towards the past) zurück, rückwärts; ~**water** (fig) Kaff nt; ~**cultural ~water** tiefste Provinz f; ~**yard** Hinterhof m.

bacon ['beɪkən] n Schinkenspeck m.

bacteria [bæk'tɪərɪə] npl Bakterien pl.

bad [bæd] a schlecht, schlimm.

badge [bædʒ] n Abzeichen nt.

badger ['bædʒə*] n Dachs m; vt plagen.

badly ['bædlɪ] ad schlecht, schlimm; ~ **off:** **he is ~ off** es geht ihm schlecht.

badminton ['bædmɪntən] n Federballspiel nt.

bad-tempered ['bæd'tempəd] a schlecht gelaunt.

baffle ['bæfl] vt (puzzle) verblüffen.

bag [bæg] n (sack) Beutel m; (paper) Tüte f; (hand—) Tasche f; (suitcase) Koffer m; (booty) Jagdbeute f; (col: old woman) alte Schachtel f; vi sich bauschen; vt (put in sack) in einen Sack stecken; (hunting) erlegen; ~**ful** Sackvoll m; ~**gage** ['bægɪdʒ] Gepäck nt; ~**gy** a bauschig, sackartig; ~**pipes** pl Dudelsack m.

bail [beɪl] n (money) Kaution f; vt prisoner gegen Kaution freilassen; (also ~ **out**) boat ausschöpfen; see **bale**.

bailiff ['beɪlɪf] n Gerichtsvollzieher(in f) m.

bait [beɪt] n Köder m; vt mit einem Köder versehen; (fig) ködern.

bake [beɪk] vti backen; ~**r** Bäcker m; ~**ry** Bäckerei f; ~**r's dozen** dreizehn.

baking ['beɪkɪŋ] n Backen nt; ~ **powder** Backpulver nt.

balance ['bæləns] n (scales) Waage f; (equilibrium) Gleichgewicht nt; (Fin: state of account) Saldo m; (difference) Bilanz f; (amount remaining) Restbetrag m; vt (weigh) wägen; (make equal) ausgleichen; ~**d** a ausgeglichen; ~ **sheet** Bilanz f, Rechnungsabschluß m.

balcony ['bælkənɪ] n Balkon m.

bald [bɔːld] a kahl; statement knapp.

bale [beɪl] n Ballen m; **to ~** or **bail out** (from a plane) abspringen.

baleful ['beɪlful] a (sad) unglückselig; (evil) böse.

balk [bɔːk] vt (hinder) vereiteln; vi scheuen (at vor +dat).

ball [bɔːl] n Ball m.

ballad ['bæləd] n Ballade f.

ballast ['bæləst] n Ballast m.

ball bearing ['bɔːl'bɛərɪŋ] n Kugellager nt.

ballerina [bælə'riːnə] n Ballerina f.

ballet ['bæleɪ] n Ballett nt.

ballistics [bə'lɪstɪks] n Ballistik f.

balloon [bə'luːn] n (Luft)ballon m.

ballot ['bælət] n (geheime) Abstimmung f.

ball-point (pen) ['bɔːlpɔɪnt('pen)] n Kugelschreiber m.

ballroom ['bɔːlrʊm] n Tanzsaal m.

balmy ['bɑːmɪ] a lindernd; mild.

balsa ['bɔːlsə] n (also ~ **wood**) Balsaholz nt.

balustrade [bæləs'treɪd] n Brüstung f.

bamboo [bæm'buː] n Bambus m.

bamboozle [bæm'buːzl] vt übers Ohr hauen.

ban [bæn] n Verbot nt; vt verbieten.

banal [bə'nɑːl] a banal.

banana [bə'nɑːnə] n Banane f.

band [bænd] n Band nt; (group) Gruppe f; (of criminals) Bande f; (Mus) Kapelle f, Band f; vi (+together) sich zusammentun; ~**age** Verband m; (elastic) Bandage f.

bandit ['bændɪt] n Bandit m.

bandy ['bændɪ] vt wechseln; ~(**-legged**) a o-beinig.

bang [bæŋ] n (explosion) Knall m; (blow) Hieb m; vti knallen.

bangle ['bæŋgl] n Armspange f.

banish ['bænɪʃ] vt verbannen.

banister(s) ['bænɪstə*(z)] n(pl) (Treppen)geländer nt.

banjo ['bændʒəʊ] n Banjo nt.

bank [bæŋk] n (raised ground) Erdwall m; (of lake etc) Ufer nt; (Fin) Bank f; vt (tilt: Aviat) in die Kurve neigen; (money einzahlen); **to ~ on sth** mit etw rechnen; ~**account** Bankkonto nt; (employee) Bankbeamte(r) m; ~ **holiday** gesetzliche(r) Feiertag m; ~**ing** Bankwesen nt, Bankgeschäft nt; ~**note** Banknote f; ~**rupt** a Zahlungsunfähige(r) mf; vt bankrott machen; **to go ~rupt** Pleite machen; ~**ruptcy** Bankrott m.

banner ['bænə*] n Banner nt.

banns [bænz] npl Aufgebot nt.

banquet ['bæŋkwɪt] n Bankett nt, Festessen nt.

banter ['bæntə*] n Neckerei f.

baptism ['bæptɪzəm] n Taufe f.

baptize [bæp'taɪz] vt taufen.

bar [bɑː*] n (rod) Stange f; (obstacle) Hindernis nt; (of chocolate) Tafel f; (of soap) Stück nt; (for food, drink) Buffet nt, Bar f; (pub) Wirtschaft f; (Mus) Takt-(strich) m; vt (fasten) verriegeln; (hinder) versperren; (exclude) ausschließen; **the B~: to be called to the B~** als Anwalt zugelassen werden; ~ **none** ohne Ausnahme.

barbarian [bɑː'bɛərɪən] n Barbar(in f) m.

barbaric [bɑː'bærɪk] a primitiv, unkultiviert.

barbarity [bɑː'bærɪtɪ] n Grausamkeit f.

barbarous ['bɑːbərəs] a grausam, barbarisch.

barbecue ['bɑːbɪkjuː] n Barbecue nt.

barbed wire ['bɑːbd'waɪə*] n Stacheldraht m.

barber ['bɑːbə*] n Herrenfriseur m.

barbiturate [bɑː'bɪtjʊrɪt] n Barbiturat nt, Schlafmittel nt.

bare [bɛə*] a nackt; trees, country kahl; (mere) bloß; vt entblößen; ~**back** ad ungesattelt; ~**faced** a unverfroren; ~**foot** a barfuß; ~**headed** a mit bloßem Kopf; ~**ly** ad kaum, knapp; ~**ness** Nacktheit f; Kahlheit f.

bargain ['bɑːgɪn] n (sth cheap) günstiger Kauf; (agreement) (written) Kaufvertrag m; (oral) Geschäft nt; **into the ~** obendrein; ~ **for** vt rechnen mit.

barge [bɑːdʒ] n Lastkahn m; ~ **in** vi hereinplatzen.

baritone ['bærɪtəʊn] n Bariton m.

bark [bɑːk] n (of tree) Rinde f; (of dog) Bellen nt; vi (dog) bellen.

barley ['bɑːlɪ] n Gerste f.

barmaid ['bɑːmeɪd] n Bardame f.

barman ['bɑːmən] n Barkellner m.

barn [bɑːn] n Scheune f.

barnacle ['bɑːnəkl] n Entenmuschel f.

barometer [bə'rɒmɪtə*] n Barometer nt.

baron ['bærən] n Baron m; ~**ess** Baronin f; ~**ial** [bə'rəʊnɪəl] a freiherrlich.

baroque [bə'rɒk] a barock.

barracks ['bærəks] npl Kaserne f.

barrage ['bærɑːʒ] n (gunfire) Sperrfeuer nt; (dam) Staudamm m; Talsperre f.

barrel ['bærəl] n Faß nt; (of gun) Lauf m; ~ **organ** Drehorgel f.

barren ['bærən] a unfruchtbar.

barricade [bærɪ'keɪd] n Barrikade f; vt verbarrikadieren.

barrier ['bærɪə*] n (obstruction) Hindernis nt; (fence) Schranke f.

barrister ['bærɪstə*] n (Brit) Rechtsanwalt m.

barrow ['bærəʊ] n (cart) Schubkarren m.

bartender ['bɑːtendə*] n (US) Barmann or -kellner m.

barter ['bɑːtə*] n Tauschhandel m; vi Tauschhandel treiben.

base [beɪs] n (bottom) Boden m, Basis f; (Mil) Stützpunkt m; vt gründen; **to be ~d on** basieren auf (+dat); a (low) gemein; ~**ball** Baseball m; ~**less** a grundlos; ~**ment** Kellergeschoß nt.

bash [bæʃ] vt (col) (heftig) schlagen.

bashful ['bæʃful] a schüchtern.

basic ['beɪsɪk] a grundlegend; ~**ally** ad im Grunde.

basin ['beɪsn] n (dish) Schüssel f; (for washing, also valley) Becken nt; (dock) (Trocken)becken nt.

basis ['beɪsɪs] n Basis f, Grundlage f.

bask [bɑːsk] vi sich sonnen.

basket ['bɑːskɪt] n Korb m; ~**ball** Basketball m.

bass [beɪs] n (Mus, also instrument) Baß m; (voice) Baßstimme f; ~ **clef** Baßschlüssel m.

bassoon [bə'suːn] n Fagott nt.

bastard ['bɑːstəd] n Bastard m; Arschloch nt.

baste [beɪst] vt meat mit Fett begießen.

bastion ['bæstɪən] n (lit, fig) Bollwerk nt.

bat [bæt] n (Sport) Schlagholz nt; Schläger

m; (*Zool*) Fledermaus *f*; *vt*: **he didn't ~ an eyelid** er hat nicht mit der Wimper gezuckt; **off one's own ~** auf eigene Faust.

batch [bætʃ] *n* (*of letters*) Stoß *m*; (*of samples*) Satz *m*.

bated ['beɪtɪd] *a*: **with ~ breath** mit verhaltenem Atem.

bath [bɑːθ] *n* Bad *nt*; (*tub*) Badewanne *f*; *vt* baden; **~s** [bɑːðz] *pl* (Schwimm)bad *nt*; **~chair** Rollstuhl *m*.

bathe [beɪð] *vti* baden; **~r** Badende(r) *mf*.

bathing ['beɪðɪŋ] *n* Baden *nt*; **~ cap** Badekappe *f*; **~ costume** Badeanzug *m*.

bathmat ['bɑːθmæt] *n* Badevorleger *m*.

bathroom ['bɑːθrʊm] *n* Bad(ezimmer) *nt*.

baths [bɑːðz] *npl* see **bath**.

bath towel ['bɑːθtaʊəl] *n* Badetuch *nt*.

batman ['bætmən] *n* (*Offiziers*)bursche *m*.

baton ['bætən] *n* (*of police*) Gummiknüppel *m*; (*Mus*) Taktstock *m*.

battalion [bəˈtælɪən] *n* Bataillon *nt*.

batter ['bætə*] *vt* verprügeln; *n* Schlagteig *m*; (*for cake*) Biskuitteig *m*.

battery ['bætərɪ] *n* (*Elec*) Batterie *f*; (*Mil*) Geschützbatterie *f*.

battle ['bætl] *n* Schlacht *f*; (*small*) Gefecht *nt*; *vi* kämpfen; **~-axe** (*col*) Xanthippe *f*; **~field** Schlachtfeld *nt*; **~ments** *pl* Zinnen *pl*; **~ship** Schlachtschiff *nt*.

batty ['bætɪ] *a* (*col*) plemplem.

bauble ['bɔːbl] *n* Spielzeug *nt*.

bawdy ['bɔːdɪ] *a* unflätig.

bawl [bɔːl] *vi* brüllen; **to ~ sb out** jdn zur Schnecke machen.

bay [beɪ] *n* (*of sea*) Bucht *f*; **at ~** gestellt, in die Enge getrieben; **to keep at ~** unter Kontrolle halten.

bayonet ['beɪənet] *n* Bajonett *nt*.

bay window ['beɪ'wɪndəʊ] *n* Erkerfenster *nt*.

bazaar [bəˈzɑː*] *n* Basar *m*.

bazooka [bəˈzuːkə] *n* Panzerfaust *f*.

be [biː] *vi irreg* sein; (*become, for passive*) werden; (*be situated*) liegen, sein; **the book is 40p** das Buch kostet 40p; **he wants to ~ a teacher** er will Lehrer werden; **how long have you been here?** wie lange sind Sie schon da?; **have you been to Rome?** warst du schon einmal in Rom?, bist du schon einmal in Rom gewesen?; **his name is on the list** sein Name steht auf der Liste; **there is/are** es gibt.

beach [biːtʃ] *n* Strand *m*; *vt* **ship** auf den Strand setzen; **~wear** Strandkleidung *f*.

beacon ['biːkən] *n* (*signal*) Leuchtfeuer *nt*; (*traffic ~*) Bake *f*.

bead [biːd] *n* Perle *f*; (*drop*) Tropfen *m*.

beak [biːk] *n* Schnabel *m*.

beaker ['biːkə*] *n* Becher *m*.

beam [biːm] *n* (*of wood*) Balken *m*; (*of light*) Strahl *m*; (*smile*) strahlende(s) Lächeln *nt*; *vi* strahlen.

bean [biːn] *n* Bohne *f*.

bear [beə*] *vt irreg* **weight, crops** tragen; (*tolerate*) ertragen; **young** gebären; *n* Bär *m*; **~able** *a* erträglich; **to ~ on** relevant sein für.

beard [bɪəd] *n* Bart *m*; **~ed** a bärtig.

bearer ['beərə*] *n* Träger *m*.

bearing ['beərɪŋ] *n* (*posture*) Haltung *f*; (*relevance*) Relevanz *f*; (*relation*) Bedeutung *f*; (*Tech*) Kugellager *nt*; **~s** *pl* (*direction*) Orientierung *f*.

bearskin ['beəskɪn] *n* Bärenfellmütze *f*.

beast [biːst] *n* Tier *nt*, Vieh *nt*; (*person*) Bestie *f*; (*nasty person*) Biest *nt*; **~ly** *ad* viehisch; (*col*) scheußlich; **~ of burden** Lasttier *nt*.

beat [biːt] *n* (*stroke*) Schlag *m*; (*pulsation*) (Herz)schlag *m*; (*police round*) Runde *f*; Revier *nt*; (*Mus*) Takt *m*; Beat *m*; *vt irreg* schlagen; **to ~ about the bush** wie die Katze um den warmen Brei herumgehen; **to ~ time** den Takt schlagen; **~ off** *vt* abschlagen; **~ up** *vt* zusammenschlagen; **~en track** gebahnte(r) Weg *m*; (*fig*) herkömmliche Art und Weise; **off the ~en track** abgelegen; **~er** (*for eggs, cream*) Schneebesen *m*.

beautiful ['bjuːtɪfʊl] *a* schön; **~ly** *ad* ausgezeichnet.

beautify ['bjuːtɪfaɪ] *vt* verschönern.

beauty ['bjuːtɪ] *n* Schönheit *f*.

beaver ['biːvə*] *n* Biber *m*.

becalm [bɪˈkɑːm] *vt*: **to be ~ed** eine Flaute haben.

because [bɪˈkɒz] *ad*, *cj* weil; *prep*: **~ of** wegen (+*gen or col* +*dat*).

beckon ['bekən] *vti* ein Zeichen geben (*sb* jdm).

become [bɪˈkʌm] *vt irreg* werden; (*clothes*) stehen (+*dat*).

becoming [bɪˈkʌmɪŋ] *a* (*suitable*) schicklich; **clothes** kleidsam.

bed [bed] *n* Bett *nt*; (*of river*) Flußbett *nt*; (*foundation*) Schicht *f*; (*in garden*) Beet *nt*; **~ and breakfast** Übernachtung *f* mit Frühstück; **~clothes** *pl* Bettwäsche *f*; **~ding** Bettzeug *nt*.

bedeck [bɪˈdek] *vt* schmücken.

bedlam ['bedləm] *n* (*uproar*) tolle(s) Durcheinander *nt*.

bedraggled [bɪˈdrægld] *a* ramponiert.

bedridden ['bedrɪdn] *a* bettlägerig.

bedroom ['bedrʊm] *n* Schlafzimmer *nt*.

bedside ['bedsaɪd] *n*: **at the ~** am Bett.

bed-sitter ['bed'sɪtə*] *n* Einzimmerwohnung *f*, möblierte(s) Zimmer *nt*.

bedtime ['bedtaɪm] *n* Schlafenszeit *f*.

bee [biː] *n* Biene *f*.

beech [biːtʃ] *n* Buche *f*.

beef [biːf] *n* Rindfleisch *nt*.

beehive ['biːhaɪv] *n* Bienenstock *m*.

beeline ['biːlaɪn] *n*: **to make a ~ for** schnurstracks zugehen auf (+*acc*).

beer [bɪə*] *n* Bier *nt*.

beetle ['biːtl] *n* Käfer *m*.

beetroot ['biːtruːt] *n* rote Bete *f*.

befall [bɪˈfɔːl] *irreg* *vi* sich ereignen; *vt* zustoßen (+*dat*).

befit [bɪˈfɪt] *vt* sich schicken für.

before [bɪˈfɔː*] *prep* vor; *cj* bevor; *ad* (*of time*) zuvor; früher; **I've done it ~** das hab' ich schon mal getan.

befriend [bɪˈfrend] *vt* sich (jds) annehmen.

beg [beg] *vti* (*implore*) dringend bitten;

alms betteln; ~**gar** Bettler(in *f*) *m*.

begin [bɪ'gɪn] *vti irreg* anfangen, beginnen; (*found*) gründen; **to ~ with** zunächst (einmal); ~**ner** Anfänger *m*; ~**ning** Anfang *m*.

begrudge [bɪ'grʌdʒ] *vt* (be)neiden; **to ~ sb sth** jdm etw mißgönnen.

behalf [bɪ'hɑːf] *n*: **on** *or* **in** (*US*) ~ **of** im Namen (+*gen*); **on my** ~ für mich.

behave [bɪ'heɪv] *vi* sich benehmen.

behaviour, (*US*) **behavior** [bɪ'heɪvjə*] *n* Benehmen *nt*.

behead [bɪ'hed] *vt* enthaupten.

behind [bɪ'haɪnd] *prep* hinter; *ad* (*late*) im Rückstand; (*in the rear*) hinten; *n* (*col*) Hinterteil *nt*.

behold [bɪ'həʊld] *vt irreg* (*old*) erblicken.

beige [beɪʒ] *a* beige.

being ['biːɪŋ] *n* (*existence*) (Da)sein *nt*; (*person*) Wesen *nt*.

belch [beltʃ] *n* Rülpsen *nt*; *vi* rülpsen; *vt smoke* ausspeien.

belfry ['belfrɪ] *n* Glockenturm *m*.

belie [bɪ'laɪ] *vt* Lügen strafen (+*acc*).

belief [bɪ'liːf] *n* Glaube *m* (*in an* +*acc*); (*conviction*) Überzeugung *f*.

believable [bɪ'liːvəbl] *a* glaubhaft.

believe [bɪ'liːv] *vt* glauben (+*dat*); (*think*) glauben, meinen, denken; *vi* (*have faith*) glauben; ~**r** Gläubige(r) *mf*.

belittle [bɪ'lɪtl] *vt* herabsetzen.

bell [bel] *n* Glocke *f*.

belligerent [bɪ'lɪdʒərənt] *a* person streitsüchtig; *country* kriegsführend.

bellow ['beləʊ] *vt* brüllen; *n* Gebrüll *nt*.

bellows ['beləʊz] *npl* (*Tech*) Gebläse *nt*; (*for fire*) Blasebalg *m*.

belly ['belɪ] *n* Bauch *m*; *vi* sich ausbauchen.

belong [bɪ'lɒŋ] *vi* gehören (*to sb* jdm); (*to club*) angehören (+*dat*); **it does not ~ here** es gehört nicht hierher; ~**ings** *pl* Habe *f*.

beloved [bɪ'lʌvɪd] *a* innig geliebt; *n* Geliebte(r) *mf*.

below [bɪ'ləʊ] *prep* unter; *ad* unten.

belt [belt] *n* (*band*) Riemen *m*; (*round waist*) Gürtel *m*; *vt* (*fasten*) mit Riemen befestigen; (*col: beat*) schlagen; *vi* (*col: go fast*) rasen.

bench [bentʃ] *n* (*seat*) Bank *f*; (*workshop*) Werkbank *f*; (*judge's seat*) Richterbank *f*; (*judges*) Richterstand *m*.

bend [bend] *vt irreg* (*curve*) biegen; (*stoop*) beugen; *n* Biegung *f*; (*in road*) Kurve *f*.

beneath [bɪ'niːθ] *prep* unter; *ad* darunter.

benefactor ['benɪfæktə*] *n* Wohltäter(in *f*) *m*.

beneficial [benɪ'fɪʃl] *a* vorteilhaft; (*to health*) heilsam.

beneficiary [benɪ'fɪʃərɪ] *n* Nutznießer(in *f*) *m*.

benefit ['benɪfɪt] *n* (*advantage*) Nutzen *m*; *vt* fördern; *vi* Nutzen ziehen (*from* aus).

benevolence [bɪ'nevələns] *n* Wohlwollen *nt*.

benevolent [bɪ'nevələnt] *a* wohlwollend.

benign [bɪ'naɪn] *a* person gütig; *climate* mild.

bent [bent] *n* (*inclination*) Neigung *f*; *a* (*col:*

dishonest) unehrlich; **to be ~ on** versessen sein auf (+*acc*).

bequeath [bɪ'kwiːð] *vt* vermachen.

bequest [bɪ'kwest] *n* Vermächtnis *nt*.

bereaved [bɪ'riːvd] *n* (*person*) Hinterbliebene(r) *mf*.

bereavement [bɪ'riːvmənt] *n* schmerzliche(r) Verlust *m*.

beret ['beɪ] *n* Baskenmütze *f*.

berry ['berɪ] *n* Beere *f*.

berserk [bə'sɜːk] *a*: **to go ~** wild werden.

berth [bɜːθ] *n* (*for ship*) Ankerplatz *m*; (*in ship*) Koje *f*; (*in train*) Bett *nt*; *vt* am Kai festmachen; *vi* anlegen.

beseech [bɪ'siːtʃ] *vt irreg* anflehen.

beset [bɪ'set] *vt irreg* bedrängen.

beside [bɪ'saɪd] *prep* neben, bei; (*except*) außer; **to be ~ o.s.** außer sich sein (*with* vor +*dat*).

besides [bɪ'saɪdz] *prep* außer, neben; *ad* zudem, überdies.

besiege [bɪ'siːdʒ] *vt* (*Mil*) belagern; (*surround*) umlagern, bedrängen.

besmirch [bɪ'smɜːtʃ] *vt* besudeln.

bespectacled [bɪ'spektɪkld] *a* bebrillt.

bespoke **tailor** [bɪ'spəʊk'teɪlə*] *n* Maßschneider *m*.

best [best] *a* beste(r, s); *ad* am besten; **at ~** höchstens; **to make the ~ of it** das Beste daraus machen; **for the ~** zum Besten; ~ **man** Trauzeuge *m*.

bestial ['bestɪəl] *a* bestialisch.

bestow [bɪ'stəʊ] *vt* verleihen.

bestseller ['best'selə*] *n* Bestseller *m*, meistgekaufte(s) Buch *nt*.

bet [bet] *n* Wette *f*; *vti irreg* wetten.

betray [bɪ'treɪ] *vt* verraten; ~**al** Verrat *m*.

better ['betə*] *a, ad* besser; *vt* verbessern; *n*: **to get the ~ of sb** jdn überwinden; **he thought ~ of it** er hat sich eines Besseren besonnen; **you had ~ leave** Sie gehen jetzt wohl besser; ~ **off** *a* (*richer*) wohlhabender.

betting ['betɪŋ] *n* Wetten *nt*; ~ **shop** Wettbüro *nt*.

between [bɪ'twiːn] *prep* zwischen; (*among*) unter; *ad* dazwischen.

bevel ['bevəl] *n* Abschrägung *f*.

beverage ['bevərɪdʒ] *n* Getränk *nt*.

beware [bɪ'weə*] *vt* sich hüten vor (+*dat*); '~ **of the dog**' 'Vorsicht, bissiger Hund!'

bewildered [bɪ'wɪldəd] *a* verwirrt.

bewildering [bɪ'wɪldərɪŋ] *a* verwirrend.

bewitching [bɪ'wɪtʃɪŋ] *a* bestrickend.

beyond [bɪ'jɒnd] *prep* (*place*) jenseits (+*gen*); (*time*) über . . . hinaus; (*out of reach*) außerhalb (+*gen*); **it's ~ me** das geht über meinen Horizont; *ad* darüber hinaus.

bias ['baɪəs] *n* (*slant*) Neigung *f*; (*prejudice*) Vorurteil *nt*; ~**(s)ed** *a* voreingenommen.

bib [bɪb] *n* Latz *m*.

Bible ['baɪbl] *n* Bibel *f*.

biblical ['bɪblɪkəl] *a* biblisch.

bibliography [bɪblɪ'ɒɡrəfɪ] *n* Bibliographie *f*.

bicentenary [baɪsen'tiːnərɪ] *n* Zweihundertjahrfeier *f*.

biceps ['baɪseps] *npl* Bizeps *m*.

bicker ['bɪkə*] vi zanken; ~ing Gezänk nt, Gekeife nt.

bicycle ['baɪsɪkl] n Fahrrad nt.

bid [bɪd] n (offer) Gebot nt; (attempt) Versuch m; vt irreg (offer) bieten; **to ~ farewell** Lebewohl sagen; ~der (person) Steigerer m; ~ding (command) Geheiß nt.

bide [baɪd] vt: ~ one's time abwarten.

big [bɪg] a groß.

bigamy ['bɪgəmɪ] n Bigamie f.

bigheaded ['bɪg'hedɪd] a eingebildet.

bigot ['bɪgət] n Frömmler m; ~ed a bigott; ~ry Bigotterie f.

bigwig ['bɪgwɪg] n (col) hohe(s) Tier nt.

bike [baɪk] n Rad nt.

bikini [bɪ'ki:nɪ] n Bikini m.

bilateral [baɪ'lætərəl] a bilateral.

bile [baɪl] n (Biol) Galle(nflüssigkeit) f.

bilge [bɪldʒ] n (water) Bilgenwasser nt.

bilingual [baɪ'lɪŋgwəl] a zweisprachig.

bilious ['bɪlɪəs] a (sick) gallenkrank; (peevish) verstimmt.

bill [bɪl] n (account) Rechnung f; (Pol) Gesetzentwurf m; (US Fin) Geldschein m; ~ of exchange Wechsel m.

billet ['bɪlɪt] n Quartier nt.

billfold ['bɪlfəʊld] n (US) Geldscheintasche f.

billiards ['bɪlɪədz] n Billard nt.

billion ['bɪlɪən] n Billion f; (US) Milliarde f.

billy goat ['bɪlɪgəʊt] n Ziegenbock m.

bin [bɪn] n Kasten m; (dust~) (Abfall)eimer m.

bind [baɪnd] vt irreg (tie) binden; (tie together) zusammenbinden; (oblige) verpflichten; ~ing (Buch)einband m; a verbindlich.

binge [bɪndʒ] n (col) Sauferei f.

bingo ['bɪŋgəʊ] n Bingo nt.

binoculars [bɪ'nɒkjʊləz] npl Fernglas nt.

biochemistry ['baɪəʊ'kemɪstrɪ] n Biochemie f.

biographer [baɪ'ɒgrəfə*] n Biograph m.

biographic(al) [baɪəʊ'græfɪk(l)] a a biographisch.

biography [baɪ'ɒgrəfɪ] n Biographie f.

biological [baɪə'lɒdʒɪkəl] a biologisch.

biologist [baɪ'ɒlədʒɪst] n Biologe m.

biology [baɪ'ɒlədʒɪ] n Biologie f.

biped ['baɪped] n Zweifüßler m.

birch [bɜ:tʃ] n Birke f.

bird [bɜ:d] n Vogel m; (col: girl) Mädchen nt; ~'s-eye view Vogelschau f.

birth [bɜ:θ] n Geburt f; **of good ~** aus gutem Hause; ~ certificate Geburtsurkunde f; ~ control Geburtenkontrolle f; ~day Geburtstag m; ~place Geburtsort m; ~ rate Geburtenrate f.

biscuit ['bɪskɪt] n Keks m.

bisect [baɪ'sekt] vt halbieren.

bishop ['bɪʃəp] n Bischof m.

bit [bɪt] n bißchen, Stückchen nt; (horse's) Gebiß nt; **a ~ tired** etwas müde.

bitch [bɪtʃ] n (dog) Hündin f; (unpleasant woman) Weibsstück nt.

bite [baɪt] vti irreg beißen; n Biß m; (mouthful) Bissen m; ~ to eat Happen m.

biting ['baɪtɪŋ] a beißend.

bitter ['bɪtə*] a bitter; memory etc schmerzlich; person verbittert; n (beer) dunkles Bier; **to the ~ end** bis zum bitteren Ende; ~ness Bitterkeit f; ~sweet bittersüß.

bivouac ['bɪvʊæk] n Biwak nt.

bizarre [bɪ'zɑ:*] a bizarr.

blab [blæb] vi klatschen; vt ausplaudern.

black [blæk] a schwarz; night finster; vt schwärzen; shoes wichsen; eye blau schlagen; (industry) boykottieren; ~ and blue grün und blau; ~berry Brombeere f; ~bird Amsel f; ~board (Wand)tafel f; ~currant schwarze Johannisbeere f; ~guard ['blægɑ:d] Schuft m; ~leg Streikbrecher(in f) m; ~list schwarze Liste f; ~mail Erpressung f; vt erpressen; ~mailer Erpresser(in f) m; ~market Schwarzmarkt m; ~ness Schwärze f; ~out Verdunklung f; (Med) to have a ~out bewußtlos werden; ~ sheep schwarze(s) Schaf nt; ~smith Schmied m.

bladder ['blædə*] n Blase f.

blade [bleɪd] n (of weapon) Klinge f; (of grass) Halm m; (of oar) Ruderblatt nt.

blame [bleɪm] n Tadel m, Vorwürfe machen (+dat) **he is to ~** er ist daran schuld; ~less a untadelig.

blanch [blɑ:ntʃ] vi bleich werden.

blancmange [blə'mɒnʒ] n Pudding m.

bland [blænd] a mild.

blank [blæŋk] a leer, unbeschrieben; look verdutzt; cheque Blanko-; verse Blank-; n (space) Lücke f; Zwischenraum m; (cartridge) Platzpatrone f.

blanket ['blæŋkɪt] n (Woll)decke f.

blankly ['blæŋklɪ] ad leer; look verdutzt.

blare [blɛə*] vi (radio) plärren; (horn) tuten; (Mus) schmettern; n Geplärr nt; Getute nt; Schmettern nt.

blasé ['blɑ:zeɪ] a blasiert.

blaspheme [blæs'fi:m] vi (Gott) lästern.

blasphemous ['blæsfɪməs] a lästernd, lästerlich.

blasphemy ['blæsfəmɪ] n (Gottes)lästerung f, Blasphemie f.

blast [blɑ:st] n Explosion f; (of wind) Windstoß m; vt (blow up) sprengen; ~! (col) verflixt!; ~ furnace Hochofen m; ~-off (Space) (Raketen)abschuß m.

blatant ['bleɪtənt] a offenkundig.

blaze [bleɪz] n (fire) lodernde(s) Feuer nt; vi lodern; vt: ~ a trail Bahn brechen.

blazer ['bleɪzə*] n Klubjacke f, Blazer m.

bleach [bli:tʃ] n Bleichmittel nt; vt bleichen.

bleak [bli:k] a kahl, rauh; future trostlos.

bleary-eyed ['blɪərɪaɪd] a triefäugig; (on waking up) mit verschlafenen Augen.

bleat [bli:t] n (of sheep) Blöken nt; (of goat) Meckern nt; vi blöken; meckern.

bleed [bli:d] irreg vi bluten; vt (draw blood) Blut abnehmen; **to ~ to death** verbluten.

bleeding ['bli:dɪŋ] a blutend.

blemish ['blemɪʃ] n Makel m; vt verunstalten.

blench [blentʃ] vi zurückschrecken; see **blanch**.

blend [blend] *n* Mischung *f*; *vt* mischen; *vi* sich mischen.

bless [bles] *vt* segnen; *(give thanks)* preisen; *(make happy)* glücklich machen; **~ you!** Gesundheit!; **~ing** Segen *m*; *(at table)* Tischgebet *nt*; *(happiness)* Wohltat *f*; Segen *m*; *(good wish)* Glück *nt*.

blight [blaɪt] *n* *(Bot)* Mehltau *m*; *(fig)* schädliche(r) Einfluß *m*; *vt* zunichte machen.

blimey ['blaɪmɪ] *interj (Brit col)* verflucht.

blind [blaɪnd] *a* blind; *corner* unübersichtlich; *n* *(for window)* Rouleau *nt*; *vt* blenden; **~ alley** Sackgasse *f*; **~fold** Augenbinde *f*; *a* mit verbundenen Augen; *vt* die Augen verbinden *(sb jdm)*; **~ly** *ad* blind; *(fig)* blindlings; **~ness** Blindheit *f*; **~ spot** *(Aut)* toter Winkel *m*; *(fig)* schwache(r) Punkt *m*.

blink [blɪŋk] *vti* blinzeln; **~ers** *pl* Scheuklappen *pl*.

bliss [blɪs] *n* (Glück)seligkeit *f*; **~fully** *ad* glückselig.

blister ['blɪstə*] *n* Blase *f*; *vt* Blasen werfen auf (*+dat*); *vi* Blasen werfen.

blithe [blaɪð] *a* munter; **~ly** *ad* fröhlich.

blitz [blɪts] *n* Luftkrieg *m*; *vt* bombardieren.

blizzard ['blɪzəd] *n* Schneesturm *m*.

bloated ['bləʊtɪd] *a* aufgedunsen; *(col: full)* nudelsatt.

blob [blɒb] *n* Klümpchen *nt*.

bloc [blɒk] *n* *(Pol)* Block *m*.

block [blɒk] *n* *(of wood)* Block *m*, Klotz *m*; *(of houses)* Häuserblock *m*; *vt* hemmen; **~ade** [blɒ'keɪd] Blockade *f*; *vt* blockieren; **~age** Verstopfung *f*.

bloke [bləʊk] *n* *(col)* Kerl *m*, Typ *m*.

blonde [blɒnd] *a* blond; *n* Blondine *f*.

blood [blʌd] *n* Blut *nt*; **~ donor** Blutspender *m*; **~ group** Blutgruppe *f*; **~less** *a* blutleer; **~ poisoning** Blutvergiftung *f*; **~ pressure** Blutdruck *m*; **~shed** Blutvergießen *nt*; **~shot** *a* blutunterlaufen; **~stained** *a* blutbefleckt; **~stream** Blut *n*, Blutkreislauf *m*; **~thirsty** *a* blutrünstig; **~ transfusion** Blutübertragung *f*; **~y** *a* *(col)* verdammt, saumäßig; *(lit)* blutig; **~y-minded** *a* stur.

bloom [blu:m] *n* Blüte *f*; *(freshness)* Glanz *m*; *vi* blühen; **in ~** in Blüte.

blossom ['blɒsəm] *n* Blüte *f*; *vi* blühen.

blot [blɒt] *n* Klecks *m*; *vt* beklecksen; *ink* (ab)löschen; **~ out** *vt* auslöschen.

blotchy ['blɒtʃɪ] *a* fleckig.

blotting paper ['blɒtɪŋpeɪpə*] *n* Löschpapier *nt*.

blouse [blaʊz] *n* Bluse *f*.

blow [bləʊ] *n* Schlag *m*; *irreg vt* blasen; *vi* *(wind)* wehen; **to ~ one's top** *(vor Wut)* explodieren; **~ over** *vi* vorübergehen; **~ up** *vi* explodieren; *vt* sprengen; **~lamp** Lötlampe *f*; **~-out** *(Aut)* geplatzte(r) Reifen *m*; **~-up** *(Phot)* Vergrößerung *f*; **~y** *a* windig.

blubber ['blʌbə*] *n* Walfischspeck *m*.

bludgeon ['blʌdʒən] *vt* *(fig)* zwingen.

blue [blu:] *a* blau; *(col: unhappy)* niedergeschlagen; *(obscene)* pornographisch; *joke* anzüglich; **to have the ~s** traurig

sein; **~bell** Glockenblume *f*; **~-blooded** *a* blaublütig; **~bottle** Schmeißfliege *f*; **~print** *(fig)* Entwurf *m*; **~s** *pl* *(Mus)* Blues *m*.

bluff [blʌf] *vt* bluffen, täuschen; *n* *(deception)* Bluff *m*; *a* gutmütig und derb.

bluish ['blu:ɪʃ] *a* bläulich.

blunder ['blʌndə*] *n* grobe(r) Fehler *m*, Schnitzer *m*; *vi* einen groben Fehler machen.

blunt [blʌnt] *a* *knife* stumpf; *talk* unverblümt; *vt* abstumpfen; **~ly** *ad* frei heraus; **~ness** Stumpfheit *f*; *(fig)* Plumpheit *f*.

blur [blɜ:*] *n* Fleck *m*; *vi* verschwimmen; *vt* verschwommen machen.

blurb [blɜ:b] *n* Waschzettel *m*.

blurt [blɜ:t] *vt*: **~ out** herausplatzen mit.

blush [blʌʃ] *vi* erröten; *n* (Scham)röte *f*; **~ing** *a* errötend.

bluster ['blʌstə*] *n* *(wind)* brausen; *(person)* darauf lospoltern, schwadronieren; **~y** *a* sehr windig.

boa ['bəʊə] *n* Boa *f*.

boar [bɔ:*] *n* Keiler *m*, Eber *m*.

board [bɔ:d] *n* *(of wood)* Brett *nt*; *(of card)* Pappe *f*; *(committee)* Ausschuß *m*; *(of firm)* Aufsichtsrat *m*; *(Sch)* Direktorium *nt*; *vt* *train* einsteigen in (*+acc*); *ship* an Bord gehen (*+gen*); **~ and lodging** Unterkunft *f* und Verpflegung; **to go by the ~** flachfallen, über Bord gehen; **~ up** *vt* mit Brettern vernageln; **~er** Kostgänger *m*; *(Sch)* Internatsschüler(in *f*) *m*; **~ing house** Pension *f*; **~ing school** Internat *nt*; **~ room** Sitzungszimmer *nt*.

boast [bəʊst] *vi* prahlen; *n* Großtuerei *f*, Prahlerei *f*; **~ful** *a* prahlerisch; **~fulness** Überheblichkeit *f*.

boat [bəʊt] *n* Boot *nt*; *(ship)* Schiff *nt*; **~er** *(hat)* Kreissäge *f*; **~ing** Bootfahren *nt*; **~swain** ['bəʊsn] = **bosun**; **~ train** Zug *m* mit Schiffsanschluß.

bob [bɒb] *vi* sich auf und nieder bewegen.

bobbin ['bɒbɪn] *n* Spule *f*.

bobsleigh ['bɒbsleɪ] *n* Bob *m*.

bodice ['bɒdɪs] *n* Mieder *nt*.

-bodied ['bɒdɪd] *a* -gebaut.

bodily ['bɒdɪlɪ] *a*, *ad* körperlich.

body ['bɒdɪ] *n* Körper *m*; *(dead)* Leiche *f*; *(group)* Mannschaft *f*; *(Aut)* Karosserie *f*; *(trunk)* Rumpf *m*; **in a ~** in einer Gruppe; **the main ~ of the work** der Hauptanteil der Arbeit; **~guard** Leibwache *f*; **~work** Karosserie *f*.

bog [bɒg] *n* Sumpf *m*; *vi*: **to get ~ged down** sich festfahren.

bogey ['bəʊgɪ] *n* Schreckgespenst *nt*.

boggle ['bɒgl] *vi* stutzen.

bogus ['bəʊgəs] *a* unecht, Schein-.

boil [bɔɪl] *vti* kochen; *n* *(Med)* Geschwür *nt*; **to come to the ~** zu kochen anfangen; **~er** Boiler *m*; **~ing point** Siedepunkt *m*.

boisterous ['bɔɪstərəs] *a* ungestüm.

bold [bəʊld] *a* *(fearless)* unerschrocken; *handwriting* fest und klar; **~ly** *ad* keck; **~ness** Kühnheit *f*; *(cheekiness)* Dreistigkeit *f*.

bollard ['bɒləd] *n* *(Naut)* Poller *m*; *(on road)* Pfosten *m*.

bolster ['bəʊlstə*] n Polster nt; ~ **up** vt
unterstützen.

bolt [bəʊlt] n Bolzen m; (lock) Riegel m; vt
verriegeln; (swallow) verschlingen; vi
(horse) durchgehen.

bomb [bɒm] n Bombe f; vt bombardieren;
~**ard** [bɒm'bɑːd] vt bombardieren;
~**ardment** [bɒm'bɑːdmənt] Beschießung
f; ~**er** Bomber m; ~**ing** Bombenangriff
m; ~**shell** (fig) Bombe f.

bombastic [bɒm'bæstɪk] a bombastisch.

bona fide ['bəʊnə'faɪdɪ] a echt.

bond [bɒnd] n (link) Band nt; (Fin)
Schuldverschreibung f.

bone [bəʊn] n Knochen m; (of fish) Gräte f;
(piece of ~) Knochensplitter m; ~ **of
contention** Zankapfel m; vt die Knochen
herausnehmen (+dat); fish entgräten;
~**dry** a knochentrocken; ~**r** (US col)
Schnitzer m.

bonfire ['bɒnfaɪə*] n Feuer nt im Freien.

bonnet ['bɒnɪt] n Haube f; (for baby)
Häubchen nt; (Brit Aut) Motorhaube f.

bonny ['bɒnɪ] a (Scot) hübsch.

bonus ['bəʊnəs] n Bonus m; (annual ~)
Prämie f.

bony ['bəʊnɪ] a knochig, knochendürr.

boo [buː] vt auspfeifen.

book [bʊk] n Buch nt; vt ticket etc vor-
bestellen; person verwarnen; ~**able** a im
Vorverkauf   erhältlich;   ~**case**
Bücherregal nt, Bücherschrank m; ~**ing
office** (Rail) Fahrkartenschalter m;
(Theat) Vorverkaufsstelle f; ~**keeping**
Buchhaltung f; ~**let** Broschüre f;
~**maker** Buchmacher m; ~**seller** Buch-
händler m; ~**shop** Buchhandlung f;
~**stall** Bücherstand m; (Rail) Bahnhofs-
buchhandlung f; ~**worm** Bücherwurm m.

boom [buːm] n (noise) Dröhnen nt; (busy
period) Hochkonjunktur f; vi dröhnen.

boomerang ['buːməræŋ] n Bumerang m.

boon [buːn] n Wohltat f, Segen m.

boorish ['bʊərɪʃ] a grob.

boost [buːst] n Auftrieb m; (fig) Reklame f;
vt Auftrieb geben.

boot [buːt] n Stiefel m; (Brit Aut)
Kofferraum m; vt (kick) einen Fußtritt
geben; **to** ~ (in addition) obendrein.

booty ['buːtɪ] n Beute f.

booze [buːz] n (col) Alkohol m, Schnaps m;
vi saufen.

border ['bɔːdə*] n Grenze f; (edge) Kante f;
(in garden) (Blumen)rabatte f; ~ **on** vt
grenzen an (+acc); ~**line** Grenze f.

bore [bɔː*] vt bohren; (weary) langweilen;
n (person) langweilige(r) Mensch m;
(thing) langweilige Sache f; (of gun)
Kaliber nt; ~**dom** Langeweile f.

boring ['bɔːrɪŋ] a langweilig.

born [bɔːn] **to be** ~ geboren werden.

borough ['bʌrə] n Stadt(gemeinde) f, Stadt-
bezirk m.

borrow ['bɒrəʊ] vt borgen; ~**ing** (Fin)
Anleihe f.

bosom ['bʊzəm] n Busen m.

boss [bɒs] n Chef m, Boß m; vt: ~ **around**
herumkommandieren; ~**y** a herrisch.

bosun ['bəʊsn] n Bootsmann m.

botanical [bə'tænɪkəl] a botanisch.

botanist ['bɒtənɪst] n Botaniker(in f) m.

botany ['bɒtənɪ] n Botanik f.

botch [bɒtʃ] vt verpfuschen.

both [bəʊθ] a beide(s); ~ **(of) the books**
beide Bücher; **I like them** ~ ich mag
(sie) beide; pron beide(s); ad: ~ **X and Y**
sowohl X wie or als auch Y.

bother ['bɒðə*] vt (pester) quälen; vi (fuss)
sich aufregen; (take trouble) sich Mühe
machen; n Mühe f, Umstand m.

bottle ['bɒtl] n Flasche f; vt (in Flaschen)
abfüllen; ~**neck** (lit, fig) Engpaß m.

bottom ['bɒtəm] n Boden m; (of person)
Hintern m; (riverbed) Flußbett nt; **at** ~
im Grunde; a unterste(r, s); ~**less** a
bodenlos.

bough [baʊ] n Zweig m, Ast m.

boulder ['bəʊldə*] n Felsbrocken m.

bounce [baʊns] vi (ball) hochspringen;
(person) herumhüpfen; (cheque) platzen;
vt (auf)springen lassen; n (rebound) Aufprall m; ~**r** Rausschmeißer m.

bound [baʊnd] n Grenze f; (leap) Sprung
m; vi (spring, leap) (auf)springen; a
gebunden, verpflichtet; **out of** ~**s** Zutritt
verboten; **to be** ~ **to do sth** verpflichtet
sein, etw zu tun, etw tun müssen; **it's** ~ **to
happen** es muß so kommen; **to be** ~ **for
. . .** nach . . . fahren; ~**ary** Grenze f,
Grenzlinie f; ~**less** a grenzenlos.

bouquet [bʊ'keɪ] n Strauß m; (of wine)
Blume f.

bourgeois ['bʊəʒwɑː] a kleinbürgerlich,
bourgeois.

bout [baʊt] n (of illness) Anfall m; (of
contest) Kampf m.

bow[1] [bəʊ] n (ribbon) Schleife f; (weapon,
Mus) Bogen m.

bow[2] [baʊ] vi sich verbeugen; (submit) sich
beugen (+dat); n Verbeugung f; (of ship)
Bug m.

bowels ['baʊlz] npl Darm m; (centre)
Innere nt.

bowl [bəʊl] n (basin) Schüssel f; (of pipe)
(Pfeifen)kopf m; (wooden ball) (Holz)kugel
f; vti (die Kugel) rollen; ~**s** pl (game)
Bowls-Spiel nt.

bow-legged ['bəʊlegɪd] a o-beinig.

bowler ['bəʊlə*] n Werfer m; (hat) Melone
f.

bowling ['bəʊlɪŋ] n Kegeln nt; ~ **alley**
Kegelbahn f; ~ **green** Rasen m zum
Bowling-Spiel.

bow tie ['bəʊ'taɪ] n Fliege f.

box [bɒks] n Schachtel f; (bigger) Kasten
m; (Theat) Loge f; vt einpacken; **to** ~ **sb's
ears** jdm eine Ohrfeige geben; vi boxen;
~**er** Boxer m; ~ **in** vt einpferchen;
~**ing** (Sport) Boxen nt; **B**~**ing Day**
zweiter Weihnachtsfeiertag; ~**ing ring**
Boxring m; ~ **office** (Theater)kasse f; ~
room Rumpelkammer f.

boy [bɔɪ] n Junge m; ~ **scout** Pfadfinder
m.

boycott ['bɔɪkɒt] n Boykott m; vt boykottieren.

boyfriend ['bɔɪfrend] n Freund m.

boyish ['bɔɪʃ] a jungenhaft.

bra [brɑː] n BH m.

brace [breɪs] n (Tech) Stütze f; (Med) Klammer f; vt stützen; ~s pl Hosenträger pl.

bracelet ['breɪslɪt] n Armband nt.

bracing ['breɪsɪŋ] a kräftigend.

bracken ['brækən] n Farnkraut nt.

bracket ['brækɪt] n Halter m, Klammer f; (in punctuation) Klammer f; (group) Gruppe f; vt einklammern; (fig) in dieselbe Gruppe einordnen.

brag [bræg] vi sich rühmen.

braid [breɪd] n (hair) Flechte f; (trim) Borte f.

Braille [breɪl] n Blindenschrift f.

brain [breɪn] n (Anat) Gehirn nt; (intellect) Intelligenz f, Verstand m; (person) kluge(r) Kopf m; ~s pl Verstand m; ~less a dumm; ~storm verrückte(r) Einfall m; ~wash vt Gehirnwäsche f vornehmen bei; ~wave gute(r) Einfall m, Geistesblitz m; ~y gescheit.

braise [breɪz] vt schmoren.

brake [breɪk] n Bremse f; vti bremsen.

branch [brɑːntʃ] n Ast m; (division) Zweig m; vi (road) sich verzweigen.

brand [brænd] n (Comm) Marke f, Sorte f; (on cattle) Brandmal nt; vt brandmarken; (Comm) eine Schutzmarke geben (+dat).

brandish ['brændɪʃ] vt (drohend) schwingen.

brand-new ['brænd'njuː] a funkelnagelneu.

brandy ['brændɪ] n Weinbrand m, Kognak m.

brash [bræʃ] a unverschämt.

brass [brɑːs] n Messing nt; ~ band Blaskapelle f.

brassière ['bræsɪə*] n Büstenhalter m.

brat [bræt] n ungezogene(s) Kind nt, Gör nt.

bravado [brə'vɑːdəʊ] n Tollkühnheit f.

brave [breɪv] a tapfer; n indianische(r) Krieger m; vt die Stirn bieten (+dat); ~ly ad tapfer; ~ry ['breɪvərɪ] Tapferkeit f.

bravo ['brɑː'vəʊ] interj bravo!

brawl [brɔːl] n Rauferei f; vi Krawall machen.

brawn [brɔːn] n (Anat) Muskeln pl; (strength) Muskelkraft f; ~y a muskulös, stämmig.

bray [breɪ] n Eselsschrei m; vi schreien.

brazen ['breɪzn] a (shameless) unverschämt; vt: ~ it out sich mit Lügen und Betrügen durchsetzen.

brazier ['breɪzɪə*] n (of workmen) offene(r) Kohlenofen m.

breach [briːtʃ] n (gap) Lücke f; (Mil) Durchbruch m; (of discipline) Verstoß m (gegen die Disziplin); (of faith) Vertrauensbruch m; vt durchbrechen; ~ of the peace öffentliche Ruhestörung f.

bread [bred] n Brot nt; ~ and butter Butterbrot nt; ~crumbs pl Brotkrumen pl; (Cook) Paniermehl nt; to be on the ~line sich gerade so durchschlagen; ~winner Ernährer m.

breadth [bretθ] n Breite f.

break [breɪk] irreg vt (destroy) (ab- or zer)brechen; promise brechen, nicht einhalten; vi (fall apart) auseinanderbrechen; (collapse) zusammenbrechen; (of dawn) anbrechen; n (gap) Lücke f; (chance) Chance f, Gelegenheit f; (fracture) Bruch m; (rest) Pause f; ~ down vi (car) eine Panne haben; (person) zusammenbrechen; to ~ free or loose sich losreißen; ~ in vt animal abrichten; horse zureiten; vi (burglar) einbrechen; ~ out vi ausbrechen; ~ up vi (partnership) (fig) sich zerstreuen; (Sch) in die Ferien gehen; vt brechen; ~able a zerbrechlich; ~age Bruch m, Beschädigung f; ~down (Tech) Panne f; (of nerves) Zusammenbruch m; ~er Brecher m; ~fast ['brekfəst] Frühstück nt; ~through Durchbruch m; ~water Wellenbrecher m.

breast [brest] n Brust f; ~ stroke Brustschwimmen nt.

breath [breθ] n Atem m; out of ~ außer Atem; under one's ~ flüsternd.

breathalize ['breθəlaɪz] vt blasen lassen.

breathe [briːð] vti atmen; ~r Verschnaufpause f.

breathless ['breθlɪs] a atemlos.

breath-taking ['breθteɪkɪŋ] a atemberaubend.

breed [briːd] irreg vi sich vermehren; vt züchten; n (race) Rasse f, Zucht f; ~er (person) Züchter m; ~ing Züchtung f; (upbringing) Erziehung f; (education) Bildung f.

breeze [briːz] n Brise f.

breezy ['briːzɪ] a windig; manner munter.

brevity ['brevɪtɪ] n Kürze f.

brew [bruː] vt brauen; plot anzetteln; vi (storm) sich zusammenziehen; ~ery Brauerei f.

bribe ['braɪb] n Bestechungsgeld nt or -geschenk nt; vt bestechen; ~ry ['braɪbərɪ] Bestechung f.

bric-à-brac ['brɪkəbræk] n Nippes pl.

brick [brɪk] n Backstein m; ~layer Maurer m; ~work Mauerwerk nt; ~works Ziegelei f.

bridal ['braɪdl] a Braut-, bräutlich.

bride [braɪd] n Braut f; ~groom Bräutigam m; ~smaid Brautjungfer f.

bridge [brɪdʒ] n Brücke f; (Naut) Kommandobrücke f; (Cards) Bridge nt; (Anat) Nasenrücken m; vt eine Brücke schlagen über (+acc); (fig) überbrücken.

bridle ['braɪdl] n Zaum m; vt (fig) zügeln; horse aufzäumen; ~ path Saumpfad m.

brief [briːf] a kurz; n (Jur) Akten pl; vt instruieren; ~s pl Schlüpfer m, Slip m; ~case Aktentasche f; ~ing (genaue) Anweisung f; ~ly ad kurz; ~ness Kürze f.

brigade [brɪ'geɪd] n Brigade f.

brigadier [brɪgə'dɪə*] n Brigadegeneral m.

bright [braɪt] a hell; (cheerful) heiter; idea klug; ~en up vt aufhellen; person aufheitern; vi sich aufheitern; ~ly ad hell; heiter.

brilliance ['brɪljəns] n Glanz m; (of person) Scharfsinn m.

brilliant a, ~ly ad ['brɪlɪənt, -lɪ] glänzend.

brim [brɪm] n Rand m; vi voll sein; ~ful a übervoll.

brine [braɪn] n Salzwasser nt.

bring [brɪŋ] vt irreg bringen; ~ **about** vt zustande bringen; ~ **off** vt davontragen; success erzielen; ~ **round** or **to** vt wieder zu sich bringen; ~ **up** vt aufziehen; question zur Sprache bringen.

brisk [brɪsk] a lebhaft.

bristle [ˈbrɪsl] n Borste f; vi sich sträuben; bristling with strotzend vor (+dat).

brittle [ˈbrɪtl] a spröde.

broach [brəʊtʃ] vt subject anschneiden.

broad [brɔːd] a breit; hint deutlich; daylight hellicht; (general) allgemein; accent stark; ~ cast n Rundfunkübertragung f; vti irreg übertragen, senden; ~ **casting** Rundfunk m; ~ **en** vt erweitern; vi sich erweitern; ~ly ad allgemein gesagt; ~ **-minded** a tolerant.

brocade [brəˈkeɪd] n Brokat m.

broccoli [ˈbrɒkəlɪ] n Spargelkohl m, Brokkoli pl.

brochure [ˈbrəʊʃʊə*] n Broschüre f.

broiler [ˈbrɔɪlə*] n Bratrost m.

broke [brəʊk] a (col) pleite.

broken-hearted [ˈbrəʊkənˈhɑːtɪd] a untröstlich.

broker [ˈbrəʊkə*] n Makler m.

bronchitis [brɒŋˈkaɪtɪs] n Bronchitis f.

bronze [brɒnz] n Bronze f; ~ **d** a sonnengebräunt.

brooch [brəʊtʃ] n Brosche f.

brood [bruːd] n Brut f; vi brüten; ~y a brütend.

brook [brʊk] n Bach m.

broom [bruːm] n Besen m; ~ **stick** Besenstiel m.

broth [brɒθ] n Suppe f, Fleischbrühe f.

brothel [ˈbrɒθl] n Bordell nt.

brother [ˈbrʌðə*] n Bruder m; ~ **hood** Bruderschaft f; ~ **-in-law** Schwager m; ~ly a brüderlich.

brow [braʊ] n (eyebrow) (Augen)braue f; (forehead) Stirn f; (of hill) Bergkuppe f; ~ **beat** vt irreg einschüchtern.

brown [braʊn] a braun; n Braun nt; vt bräunen; ~ **ie** Wichtel m; ~ **paper** Packpapier nt.

browse [braʊz] vi (in books) blättern; (in shop) schmökern, herumschauen.

bruise [bruːz] n Bluterguß m, blaue(r) Fleck m; vti einen blauen Fleck geben/bekommen.

brunette [bruːˈnet] n Brünette f.

brunt [brʌnt] n volle Wucht f.

brush [brʌʃ] n Bürste f; (for sweeping) Handbesen m; (for painting) Pinsel m; (fight) kurze(r) Kampf m; (Mil) Scharmützel nt; (fig) Auseinandersetzung f; vt (clean) bürsten; (sweep) fegen; (touch) streifen; **give sb the** ~ **-off** (col) jdm eine Abfuhr erteilen; ~ **aside** vt abtun; ~ **wood** Gestrüpp nt.

brusque [bruːsk] a schroff.

Brussels sprout [ˈbrʌslzˈspraʊt] n Rosenkohl m.

brutal [ˈbruːtl] a brutal; ~ity [bruːˈtælɪtɪ] n Brutalität f.

brute [bruːt] n (person) Scheusal nt; ~

force rohe Kraft; (violence) nackte Gewalt f.

brutish [ˈbruːtɪʃ] a tierisch.

bubble [ˈbʌbl] n (Luft)blase f; vi sprudeln; (with joy) übersprudeln.

buck [bʌk] n Bock m; (US col) Dollar m; vi bocken; ~ **up** vi (col) sich zusammenreißen.

bucket [ˈbʌkɪt] n Eimer m.

buckle [ˈbʌkl] n Schnalle f; vt (an- or zusammen)schnallen; vi (bend) sich verziehen.

bud [bʌd] n Knospe f; vi knospen, keimen.

Buddhism [ˈbʊdɪzəm] n Buddhismus m.

Buddhist [ˈbʊdɪst] n Buddhist(in f) m; a buddhistisch.

budding [ˈbʌdɪŋ] a angehend.

buddy [ˈbʌdɪ] n (col) Kumpel m.

budge [bʌdʒ] vti (sich) von der Stelle rühren.

budgerigar [ˈbʌdʒərɪgɑː*] n Wellensittich m.

budget [ˈbʌdʒɪt] n Budget nt; (Pol) Haushalt m; vi haushalten.

budgie [ˈbʌdʒɪ] n = **budgerigar.**

buff [bʌf] n a colour lederfarben; n (enthusiast) Fan m.

buffalo [ˈbʌfələʊ] n Büffel m.

buffer [ˈbʌfə*] n Puffer m.

buffet [ˈbʌfɪt] n (blow) Schlag m; [ˈbʊfeɪ] (bar) Imbißraum m, Erfrischungsraum m; (food) (kaltes) Büffet nt; vt [ˈbʌfɪt] (herum)stoßen.

buffoon [bʌˈfuːn] n Hanswurst m.

bug [bʌg] n (lit, fig) Wanze f; vt verwanzen; ~ **bear** Schreckgespenst nt.

bugle [ˈbjuːgl] n Jagd-, Bügelhorn nt.

build [bɪld] vt irreg bauen; n Körperbau m; ~ **er** n Bauunternehmer m; ~ **ing** Gebäude nt; ~ **ing society** Baugenossenschaft f; ~ **-up** Aufbau m; (publicity) Reklame f.

built [bɪlt]: **well-**~ a person gut gebaut; ~ **-in** a cupboard eingebaut; ~ **-up area** Wohngebiet nt.

bulb [bʌlb] n (Bot) (Blumen)zwiebel f; (Elec) Glühlampe f, Birne f; ~ **ous** a knollig.

bulge [bʌldʒ] n (Aus)bauchung f; vi sich (aus)bauchen.

bulk [bʌlk] n Größe f, Masse f; (greater part) Großteil m; ~ **head** Schott nt; ~y a (sehr) umfangreich; goods sperrig.

bull [bʊl] n (animal) Bulle m; (cattle) Stier m; (papal) Bulle f; ~ **dog** Bulldogge f.

bulldoze [ˈbʊldəʊz] vt planieren; (fig) durchboxen; ~ **r** Planierraupe f, Bulldozer m.

bullet [ˈbʊlɪt] n Kugel f.

bulletin [ˈbʊlɪtɪn] n Bulletin nt, Bekanntmachung f.

bullfight [ˈbʊlfaɪt] n Stierkampf m.

bullion [ˈbʊlɪən] n Barren m.

bullock [ˈbʊlək] n Ochse m.

bull's-eye [ˈbʊlzaɪ] n das Schwarze nt.

bully [ˈbʊlɪ] n Raufbold m; vt einschüchtern.

bum [bʌm] n (col: backside) Hintern m; (tramp) Landstreicher m; (nasty person) fieser Kerl *m*; ~ **around** *vi* herumgammeln.

bumblebee ['bʌmblbi:] *n* Hummel *f*.

bump [bʌmp] *n* (*blow*) Stoß *m*; (*swelling*) Beule *f*; *vti* stoßen, prallen; ~**er** (*Brit Aut*) Stoßstange *f*; *a* edition dick; harvest Rekord-.

bumptious ['bʌmpʃəs] *a* aufgeblasen.

bumpy ['bʌmpɪ] *a* holprig.

bun [bʌn] *n* Korinthenbrötchen *nt*.

bunch [bʌntʃ] *n* (*of flowers*) Strauß *m*; (*of keys*) Bund *m*; (*of people*) Haufen *m*.

bundle ['bʌndl] *n* Bündel *nt*; *vt* bündeln; ~**off** *vt* fortschicken.

bung [bʌŋ] *n* Spund *m*; *vt* (*col: throw*) schleudern.

bungalow ['bʌŋgələʊ] *n* einstöckige(s) Haus *nt*, Bungalow *m*.

bungle ['bʌŋgl] *vt* verpfuschen.

bunion ['bʌnɪən] *n* entzündete(r) Fußballen *m*.

bunk [bʌŋk] *n* Schlafkoje *f*; ~ **bed** Etagenbett *nt*.

bunker ['bʌŋkə*] *n* (*coal store*) Kohlenbunker *m*; (*golf*) Sandloch *nt*.

bunny ['bʌnɪ] *n* Häschen *nt*.

Bunsen burner ['bʌnsn 'bɜːnə*] *n* Bunsenbrenner *m*.

bunting ['bʌntɪŋ] *n* Fahnentuch *nt*.

buoy [bɔɪ] *n* Boje *f*; (*lifebuoy*) Rettungsboje *f*; ~**ancy** Schwimmkraft *f*; ~**ant** *a* (*floating*) schwimmend; (*fig*) heiter; ~ **up** *vt* Auftrieb geben (+*dat*).

burden ['bɜːdn] *n* (*weight*) Ladung *f*, Last *f*; (*fig*) Bürde *f*; *vt* belasten.

bureau ['bjuːrəʊ] *n* (*desk*) Sekretär *m*; (*for information etc*) Büro *nt*.

bureaucracy [bjuː'rɒkrəsɪ] *n* Bürokratie *f*.

bureaucrat ['bjuːrəkræt] *n* Bürokrat(in *f*) *m*; ~**ic** [bjuːrə'krætɪk] *a* bürokratisch.

burglar ['bɜːglə*] *n* Einbrecher *m*; ~ **alarm** Einbruchssicherung *f*; ~**ize** *vt* (*US*) einbrechen in (+*acc*); ~**y** Einbruch *m*.

burgle ['bɜːgl] *vt* einbrechen in (+*acc*).

burial ['berɪəl] *n* Beerdigung *f*; ~ **ground** Friedhof *m*.

burlesque [bɜː'lesk] *n* Burleske *f*.

burly ['bɜːlɪ] *a* stämmig.

burn [bɜːn] *irreg vt* verbrennen; *vi* brennen; *n* Brandwunde *f*; to ~ **one's fingers** sich die Finger verbrennen; ~**ing question** brennende Frage *f*.

burnish ['bɜːnɪʃ] *vt* polieren.

burrow ['bʌrəʊ] *n* (*of fox*) Bau *m*; (*of rabbit*) Höhle *f*; *vi* sich eingraben; *vt* eingraben.

bursar ['bɜːsə*] *n* Kassenverwalter *m*, Quästor *m*.

burst [bɜːst] *irreg vt* zerbrechen; *vi* platzen; (*into tears*) ausbrechen; *n* Explosion *f*; (*outbreak*) Ausbruch *m*; (*in pipe*) Bruch(stelle *f*) *m*.

bury ['berɪ] *vt* vergraben; (*in grave*) beerdigen; to ~ **the hatchet** das Kriegsbeil begraben.

bus [bʌs] *n* (*Auto*)bus *m*, Omnibus *m*.

bush [bʊʃ] *n* Busch *m*.

bushel ['bʊʃl] *n* Scheffel *m*.

bushy ['bʊʃɪ] *a* buschig.

busily ['bɪzɪlɪ] *ad* geschäftig.

business ['bɪznɪs] *n* Geschäft *nt*; (*concern*) Angelegenheit *f*; **it's none of your** ~ es geht dich nichts an; **to mean** ~ es ernst meinen; ~**man** Geschäftsmann *m*.

bus-stop ['bʌsstɒp] *n* Bushaltestelle *f*.

bust [bʌst] *n* Büste *f*; *a* (*broken*) kaputt-(gegangen); business pleite; **to go** ~ pleite machen.

bustle ['bʌsl] *n* Getriebe *nt*; *vi* hasten.

bustling ['bʌslɪŋ] *a* geschäftig.

bust-up ['bʌstʌp] *n* (*col*) Krach *m*.

busy ['bɪzɪ] *a* beschäftigt; road belebt; *vt*: ~ **o.s.** sich beschäftigen; ~**body** Übereifrige(r) *mf*.

but [bʌt, bət] *cj* aber; **not this** ~ **that** nicht dies, sondern das; (*only*) nur; (*except*) außer.

butane ['bjuːteɪn] *n* Butan *nt*.

butcher ['bʊtʃə*] *n* Metzger *m*; (*murderer*) Schlächter *m*; *vt* schlachten; (*kill*) abschlachten.

butler ['bʌtlə*] *n* Butler *m*.

butt [bʌt] *n* (*cask*) große(s) Faß *nt*; (*target*) Zielscheibe *f*; (*thick end*) dicke(s) Ende *nt*; (*of gun*) Kolben *m*; (*of cigarette*) Stummel *m*; *vt* (mit dem Kopf) stoßen.

butter ['bʌtə*] *n* Butter *f*; *vt* buttern; ~**fly** Schmetterling *m*.

buttocks ['bʌtəks] *npl* Gesäß *nt*.

button ['bʌtn] *n* Knopf *m*; *vti* zuknöpfen; ~**hole** Knopfloch *nt*; Blume *f* im Knopfloch; *vt* rankriegen.

buttress ['bʌtrɪs] *n* Strebepfeiler *m*; Stützbogen *m*.

buxom ['bʌksəm] *a* drall.

buy [baɪ] *vt irreg* kaufen; ~ **up** *vt* aufkaufen; ~**er** Käufer(in *f*) *m*.

buzz [bʌz] *n* Summen *nt*; *vi* summen.

buzzard ['bʌzəd] *n* Bussard *m*.

buzzer ['bʌzə*] *n* Summer *m*.

by [baɪ] *prep* (*near*) bei; (*via*) über (+*acc*); (*past*) an (+*dat*) . . . vorbei; (*before*) bis; ~ **day/night** tags/nachts; ~ **train/bus** mit dem Zug/Bus; done ~ **sb/sth** von jdm/durch etw gemacht; ~ **oneself** allein; ~ **and large** im großen und ganzen; ~-**election** Nachwahl *f*; ~**gone** *a* vergangen; *n*: let ~**gones be** ~**gones** laß(t) das Vergangene vergangen sein; ~-**(e)-law** Verordnung *f*; ~**pass** Umgehungsstraße *f*; ~-**product** Nebenprodukt *nt*; ~**stander** Zuschauer *m*; ~**word** Inbegriff *m*.

C

C, c [si:] *n* C *nt*, c *nt*.

cab [kæb] *n* Taxi *nt*; (*of train*) Führerstand *m*; (*of truck*) Führersitz *m*.

cabaret ['kæbəreɪ] *n* Kabarett *nt*.

cabbage ['kæbɪdʒ] *n* Kohl(kopf) *m*.

cabin ['kæbɪn] *n* Hütte *f*; (*Naut*) Kajüte *f*; (*Aviat*) Kabine *f*; ~ **cruiser** Motorjacht *f*.

cabinet ['kæbɪnɪt] *n* Schrank *m*; (*for china*) Vitrine *f*; (*Pol*) Kabinett *nt*; ~**maker** Kunsttischler *m*.

cable ['keɪbl] *n* Drahtseil *nt*, Tau *nt*; (*Tel*)

(Leitungs)kabel *nt*; (*telegram*) Kabel *nt*; *vti* kabeln, telegraphieren; ~-**car** Seilbahn *f*; ~**gram** (Übersee)telegramm *nt*; ~ **railway** (Draht)seilbahn *f*.

cache [kæʃ] *n* Versteck *nt*; (*for ammunition*) geheimes Munitionslager *nt*; (*for food*) geheimes Proviantlager *nt*; (*supplies of ammunition*) Munitionsvorrat *m*; (*supplies of food*) Lebensmittelvorrat *m*.

cackle ['kækl] *n* Gegacker *nt*; *vi* gacken.

cactus ['kæktəs] *n* Kaktus *m*, Kaktee *f*.

caddie ['kædɪ] *n* Golfjunge *m*.

caddy ['kædɪ] *n* Teedose *f*.

cadence ['keɪdəns] *n* Tonfall *m*; (*Mus*) Kadenz *f*.

cadet [kə'det] *n* Kadett *m*.

cadge [kædʒ] *vt* schmarotzen, nassauern.

Caesarean [siː'zɛərɪən] *a*: ~ (**section**) Kaiserschnitt *m*.

café ['kæfɪ] *n* Café *nt*, Restaurant *nt*.

cafeteria [kæfɪ'tɪərɪə] *n* Selbstbedienungsrestaurant *nt*.

caffein(e) ['kæfiːn] *n* Koffein *nt*.

cage [keɪdʒ] *n* Käfig *m*; *vt* einsperren.

cagey ['keɪdʒɪ] *a* geheimnistuerisch, zurückhaltend.

cajole [kə'dʒəʊl] *vt* überreden.

cake [keɪk] *n* Kuchen *m*; (*of soap*) Stück *nt*; ~**d** *a* verkrustet.

calamine ['kæləmaɪn] *n* Galmei *m*.

calamitous [kə'læmɪtəs] *a* katastrophal, unglückselig.

calamity [kə'læmɪtɪ] *n* Unglück *nt*, (Schicksals)schlag *m*.

calcium ['kælsɪəm] *n* Kalzium *nt*.

calculate ['kælkjʊleɪt] *vt* berechnen, kalkulieren.

calculating ['kælkjʊleɪtɪŋ] *a* berechnend.

calculation [kælkjʊ'leɪʃən] *n* Berechnung *f*.

calculator ['kælkjʊleɪtə*] *n* Rechner *m*.

calculus ['kælkjʊləs] *n* Rechenart *f*.

calendar ['kælɪndə*] *n* Kalender *m*.

calf [kɑːf] *n* Kalb *nt*; (*leather*) Kalbsleder *nt*; (*Anat*) Wade *f*.

calibre, (*US*) **caliber** ['kælɪbə*] *n* Kaliber *nt*.

call [kɔːl] *vt* rufen; (*summon*) herbeirufen; (*name*) nennen; (*meeting*) einberufen; (*awaken*) wecken; (*Tel*) anrufen; *vi* (*for help*) rufen, schreien; (*visit*) vorbeikommen; *n* (*shout*) Schrei *m*, Ruf *m*; (*visit*) Besuch *m*; (*Tel*) Anruf *m*; **on** ~ in Bereitschaft; ~**box** Fernsprechzelle *f*; ~**er** Besucher(in *f*) *m*; (*Tel*) Anrufer *m*; ~ **girl** Call-Girl *nt*; ~**ing** (*vocation*) Berufung *f*; **to be** ~**ed** heißen; ~ **for** *vt* rufen (nach); (*fetch*) abholen; (*fig: require*) erfordern, verlangen; ~ **off** *vt meeting* absagen; ~ **on** *vt* besuchen, aufsuchen; (*request*) fragen; ~ **up** *vt* (*Mil*) einziehen, einberufen.

callous *a*, ~**ly** *ad* ['kæləs, -lɪ] herzlos; ~**ness** Herzlosigkeit *f*.

callow ['kæləʊ] *a* unerfahren, noch nicht flügge.

calm [kɑːm] *n* Stille *f*, Ruhe *f*; (*Naut*) Flaute *f*; *vt* beruhigen; *a* still, ruhig; *person* gelassen; ~**ly** *ad* ruhig, still; ~**ness** Stille

f, Ruhe *f*; (*mental*) Gelassenheit *f*; ~ **down** *vi* sich beruhigen; *vt* beruhigen, besänftigen.

calorie ['kælərɪ] *n* Kalorie *f*, Wärmeeinheit *f*.

calve [kɑːv] *vi* kalben.

camber ['kæmbə*] *n* Wölbung *f*.

camel ['kæməl] *n* Kamel *nt*.

cameo ['kæmɪəʊ] *n* Kamee *f*.

camera ['kæmərə] *n* Fotoapparat *m*, Kamera *f*; **in** ~ unter Ausschluß der Öffentlichkeit; ~**man** Kameramann *m*.

camomile ['kæməmaɪl] *n*: ~ **tea** Kamillentee *m*.

camouflage ['kæməflɑːʒ] *n* Tarnung *f*; *vt* tarnen; (*fig*) verschleiern, bemänteln.

camp [kæmp] *n* Lager *nt*, Camp *nt*; (*Mil*) Feldlager *nt*; (*permanent*) Kaserne *f*; (*camping place*) Zeltplatz *m*; *vi* zelten, campen.

campaign [kæm'peɪn] *n* Kampagne *f*; (*Mil*) Feldzug *m*; *vi* (*Mil*) Krieg führen; (*participate*) in den Krieg ziehen; (*fig*) werben, Propaganda machen; (*Pol*) den Wahlkampf führen; **electoral** ~ Wahlkampf *m*.

campbed ['kæmp'bed] *n* Campingbett *nt*.

camper ['kæmpə*] *n* Zeltende(r) *mf*, Camper *m*.

camping ['kæmpɪŋ] *n*: **to go** ~ zelten, Camping machen.

campsite ['kæmpsaɪt] *n* Zeltplatz *m*, Campingplatz *m*.

campus ['kæmpəs] *n* (*Sch*) Schulgelände *nt*; (*Univ*) Universitätsgelände *nt*, Campus *m*.

can [kæn] *v aux irreg* (*be able*) können, fähig sein; (*be allowed*) dürfen, können; *n* Büchse *f*, Dose *f*; (*for water*) Kanne *f*; *vt* konservieren, in Büchsen einmachen.

canal [kə'næl] *n* Kanal *m*.

canary [kə'nɛərɪ] *n* Kanarienvogel *m*; *a* hellgelb.

cancel ['kænsəl] *vt* (*delete*) durchstreichen; (*Math*) kürzen; *arrangement* aufheben; *meeting* absagen; *treaty* annullieren; *stamp* entwerten; ~**lation** [kænsə'leɪʃən] Aufhebung *f*; Absage *f*; Annullierung *f*; Entwertung *f*.

cancer ['kænsə*] *n* (*also Astrol* **C**~) Krebs *m*.

candid ['kændɪd] *a* offen, ehrlich; ~**ly** *ad* ehrlich.

candidate ['kændɪdeɪt] *n* Bewerber(in *f*) *m*; (*Pol*) Kandidat(in *f*) *m*.

candle ['kændl] *n* Kerze *f*; ~**light** Kerzenlicht *nt*; ~**stick** Kerzenleuchter *m*.

candour ['kændə*] *n* Offenheit *f*.

candy ['kændɪ] *n* Kandis(zucker) *m*; (*US*) Bonbons *pl*.

cane [keɪn] *n* (*Bot*) Rohr *nt*; (*for walking*, *Sch*) Stock *m*; *vt* schlagen.

canister ['kænɪstə*] *n* Blechdose *f*.

cannabis ['kænəbɪs] *n* Hanf *m*, Haschisch *nt*.

canned [kænd] *a* Büchsen-, eingemacht.

cannibal ['kænɪbəl] *n* Menschenfresser *m*; ~**ism** Kannibalismus *m*.

cannon ['kænən] *n* Kanone *f*.

cannot ['kænɒt] = can not.
canny ['kænɪ] a (*shrewd*) schlau, erfahren; (*cautious*) umsichtig, vorsichtig.
canoe [kə'nuː] n Paddelboot nt, Kanu nt; ~**ing** Kanufahren nt; ~**ist** Kanufahrer(in f) m.
canon ['kænən] n Domherr m; (*in church law*) Kanon m; (*standard*) Grundsatz m.
canonize ['kænənaɪz] vt heiligsprechen.
can opener ['kænəʊpnə*] n Büchsenöffner m.
canopy ['kænəpɪ] n Baldachin m.
can't [kænt] = can not.
cantankerous [kæn'tæŋkərəs] a zänkisch, mürrisch.
canteen [kæn'tiːn] n (*in factory*) Kantine f; (*case of cutlery*) Besteckkasten m.
canter ['kæntə*] n Kanter m, kurzer leichter Galopp m; vi in kurzem Galopp reiten.
cantilever ['kæntɪliːvə*] n Träger m, Ausleger m.
canvas ['kænvəs] n Segeltuch m, Zeltstoff m; (*sail*) Segel nt; (*for painting*) Leinwand f; (*painting*) Ölgemälde nt; **under** ~ (*people*) in Zelten; (*boat*) unter Segel.
canvass ['kænvəs] vt werben; ~**er** Wahlwerber(in f) m.
canyon ['kænjən] n Felsenschlucht f.
cap [kæp] n Kappe f, Mütze f, (*lid*) (Verschluß)kappe f, Deckel m; vt verschließen; (*surpass*) übertreffen.
capability [keɪpə'bɪlɪtɪ] n Fähigkeit f.
capable ['keɪpəbl] a fähig; **to be** ~ **of sth** zu etw fähig or imstande sein.
capacity [kə'pæsɪtɪ] n Fassungsvermögen nt; (*ability*) Fähigkeit f; (*position*) Eigenschaft f.
cape [keɪp] n (*garment*) Cape nt, Umhang m; (*Geog*) Kap nt.
caper ['keɪpə*] n Kaper f.
capital ['kæpɪtl] n (— *city*) Hauptstadt f; (*Fin*) Kapital nt; (— *letter*) Großbuchstabe m; ~**ism** Kapitalismus m; ~**ist** a kapitalistisch; n Kapitalist(in f) m; ~ **punishment** Todesstrafe f.
capitulate [kə'pɪtjʊleɪt] vi kapitulieren.
capitulation [kəpɪtjʊ'leɪʃən] n Kapitulation f.
capricious [kə'prɪʃəs] a launisch.
Capricorn ['kæprɪkɔːn] n Steinbock m.
capsize [kæp'saɪz] vti kentern.
capstan ['kæpstən] n Ankerwinde f, Poller m.
capsule ['kæpsjuːl] n Kapsel f.
captain ['kæptɪn] n (*Naut*) Führer m; (*Naut*) Kapitän m; (*Mil*) Hauptmann m; (*Sport*) (Mannschafts)kapitän m; vt anführen.
caption ['kæpʃən] n Unterschrift f, Text m.
captivate ['kæptɪveɪt] vt fesseln.
captive ['kæptɪv] n Gefangene(r) mf; a gefangen(gehalten).
captivity [kæp'tɪvɪtɪ] n Gefangenschaft f.
capture ['kæptʃə*] vt fassen, gefangennehmen; n Gefangennahme f.
car [kɑː*] n Auto nt, Wagen m.
carafe [kə'ræf] n Karaffe f.
caramel ['kærəməl] n Karamelle f.
carat ['kærət] n Karat nt.

caravan ['kærəvæn] n Wohnwagen m; (*in desert*) Karawane f.
caraway ['kærəweɪ] n: ~ **seed** Kümmel m.
carbohydrate [kɑːbəʊ'haɪdreɪt] n Kohlenhydrat nt.
carbon ['kɑːbən] n Kohlenstoff m; (— *paper*) Kohlepapier nt; ~ **copy** Durchschlag m.
carburettor ['kɑːbjʊretə*] n Vergaser m.
carcass ['kɑːkəs] n Kadaver m.
card [kɑːd] n Karte f, ~**board** Pappe f; ~**board box** Pappschachtel f; ~ **game** Kartenspiel nt.
cardiac ['kɑːdɪæk] a Herz-.
cardigan ['kɑːdɪgən] n Strickjacke f.
cardinal ['kɑːdɪnl] a: ~ . **number** Kardinalzahl f.
care [keə*] n Sorge f, Mühe f; (*charge*) Obhut f, Fürsorge f; vi: **I don't** ~ es ist mir egal; **to** ~ **about sb/sth** sich kümmern um jdn/etw; **to take** ~ (*watch*) vorsichtig sein; (*take pains*) darauf achten; **take** ~ **of** vt sorgen für; ~ **for** vt (*look after*) sorgen für; (*like*) mögen, gern haben.
career [kə'rɪə*] n Karriere f, Laufbahn f; vi rasen.
carefree ['keəfriː] a sorgenfrei.
careful a, ~**ly** ad ['keəfʊl, -fəlɪ] sorgfältig.
careless a, ~**ly** ad ['keəlɪs, -lɪ] unvorsichtig; ~**ness** Unachtsamkeit f; (*neglect*) Nachlässigkeit f.
caress [kə'res] n Liebkosung f; vt liebkosen.
caretaker ['keəteɪkə*] n Hausmeister m.
car-ferry ['kɑːferɪ] n Autofähre f.
cargo ['kɑːgəʊ] n Kargo m, Schiffsladung f.
caricature ['kærɪkətjʊə*] n Karikatur f; vt karikieren.
carnage ['kɑːnɪdʒ] n Blutbad nt.
carnal ['kɑːnl] a fleischlich, sinnlich.
carnation [kɑː'neɪʃən] n Nelke f.
carnival ['kɑːnɪvəl] n Karneval m, Fastnacht f, Fasching m.
carnivorous [kɑː'nɪvərəs] a fleischfressend.
carol ['kærl] n (Weihnachts)lied nt.
carp [kɑːp] n (*fish*) Karpfen m; ~ **at** vt herumnörgeln an (+dat).
car park ['kɑːpɑːk] n Parkplatz m; Parkhaus nt.
carpenter ['kɑːpɪntə*] n Zimmermann m.
carpentry ['kɑːpɪntrɪ] n Zimmerei f.
carpet ['kɑːpɪt] n Teppich m; vt mit einem Teppich auslegen.
carping ['kɑːpɪŋ] a (*critical*) krittelnd, Mecker-.
carriage ['kærɪdʒ] n Wagen m; (*of goods*) Beförderung f; (*bearing*) Haltung f; ~**way** (*on road*) Fahrbahn f.
carrier ['kærɪə*] n Träger(in f) m; (*Comm*) Spediteur m; ~ **bag** Tragetasche m; ~ **pigeon** Brieftaube f.
carrion ['kærɪən] n Aas nt.
carrot ['kærət] n Möhre f, Mohrrübe f, Karotte f.
carry ['kærɪ] vt tragen; vi weit tragen, reichen; ~**cot** Babytragetasche f; **to be**

carried away (fig) hingerissen sein; ~ **on** vti fortführen, weitermachen; ~ **out** vt orders ausführen.

cart [kɑːt] n Wagen m, Karren m; vt schleppen.

cartilage ['kɑːtilidʒ] n Knorpel m.

cartographer [kɑːˈtɒgrəfə*] n Kartograph(in f) m.

carton ['kɑːtən] n (Papp)karton m; (of cigarettes) Stange f.

cartoon [kɑːˈtuːn] n (Press) Karikatur f; (Cine) (Zeichen)trickfilm m.

cartridge ['kɑːtridʒ] n (for gun) Patrone f; (film) Rollfilm m; (of record player) Tonabnehmer m.

carve [kɑːv] vti wood schnitzen; stone meißeln; meat (vor)schneiden.

carving ['kɑːviŋ] n (in wood etc) Schnitzerei f; ~ **knife** Tranchiermesser nt.

car wash ['kɑːwɒʃ] n Autowäsche f.

cascade [kæsˈkeid] n Wasserfall m; vi kaskadenartig herabfallen.

case [keis] n (box) Kasten m, Kiste f; (suit—) Koffer m; (Jur, matter) Fall m; in ~ falls, im Falle; in any ~ jedenfalls, auf jeden Fall.

cash [kæʃ] n (Bar)geld nt; vt einlösen; ~ **desk** Kasse f; ~**ier** [kæˈʃiə*] Kassier(er)in f) m; ~ **on delivery** per Nachnahme; ~ **register** Registrierkasse f.

cashmere ['kæʃmiə*] n Kaschmirwolle f.

casing ['keisiŋ] n Gehäuse nt.

casino [kəˈsiːnəu] n Kasino nt.

cask [kɑːsk] n Faß nt.

casket ['kɑːskit] n Kästchen nt; (US: coffin) Sarg m.

casserole ['kæsərəul] n Kasserole f; (food) Auflauf m.

cassock ['kæsək] n Soutane f, Talar m.

cast [kɑːst] irreg vt werfen; horns etc verlieren; metal gießen; (Theat) besetzen; roles verteilen; n (Theat) Besetzung f; ~ **off** vi (Naut) losmachen; ~-**off clothing** abgelegte Kleidung.

castanets [kæstəˈnets] npl Kastagnetten pl.

castaway ['kɑːstəwei] n Schiffbrüchige(r) mf.

caste [kɑːst] n Kaste f.

casting ['kɑːstiŋ] a: ~ **vote** entscheidende Stimme f.

castiron ['kɑːstˈaiən] n Gußeisen nt; a gußeisern; alibi todsicher.

castle ['kɑːsl] n Burg f, Schloß nt; (country mansion) Landschloß nt; (chess) Turm m.

castor ['kɑːstə*] n (wheel) Laufrolle f; ~ **oil** Rizinusöl nt; ~ **sugar** Streuzucker m.

castrate [kæsˈtreit] vt kastrieren.

casual ['kæʒjul] a arrangement beiläufig; attitude nachlässig; dress leger; meeting zufällig; ~**ly** ad dress zwanglos, leger; remark beiläufig.

casualty ['kæʒjultı] n Verletzte(r) mf; Tote(r) mf; (department in hospital) Unfallstation f.

cat [kæt] n Katze f.

catalog (US), **catalogue** ['kætəlɒg] n Katalog m; vt katalogisieren.

catalyst ['kætəlist] n (lit, fig) Katalysator m.

catapult ['kætəpʌlt] n Katapult nt; Schleuder f.

cataract ['kætərækt] n Wasserfall m; (Med) graue(r) Star m.

catarrh [kəˈtɑː*] n Katarrh m.

catastrophe [kəˈtæstrəfı] n Katastrophe f.

catastrophic [kætəsˈtrɒfik] a katastrophal.

catch [kætʃ] vt irreg fangen; train etc nehmen; erreichen; (surprise) ertappen; (understand) begreifen; n (of lock) Sperrhaken m; (of fish) Fang m; **to** ~ **a cold** sich erkälten.

catching ['kætʃiŋ] a (Med, fig) ansteckend.

catch phrase ['kætʃfreiz] n Schlagwort nt, Slogan m.

catchy ['kætʃi] a tune eingängig.

catechism ['kætikizəm] n Katechismus m.

categorical a, ~**ly** ad [kætəˈgɒrikl, -klı] kategorisch.

categorize ['kætigəraiz] vt kategorisieren.

category ['kætigərı] n Kategorie f.

cater ['keitə*] vi versorgen; ~**ing** Gastronomie f; Bewirtung f; ~ **for** vt (lit) party ausrichten; (fig) eingestellt sein auf (+acc); berücksichtigen.

caterpillar ['kætəpilə*] n Raupe f; ~ **track** Gleiskette f.

cathedral [kəˈθiːdrəl] n Kathedrale f, Dom m.

Catholic ['kæθəlik] a (Rel) katholisch; n Katholik(in f) m; c~ vielseitig.

cattle ['kætl] npl Vieh nt.

catty ['kætı] a gehässig.

cauliflower ['kɒlifauə*] n Blumenkohl m.

cause [kɒz] n Ursache f; Grund m; (purpose) Sache f; **in a good** ~ zu einem guten Zweck; vt verursachen.

causeway ['kɒzwei] n Damm m.

caustic ['kɒstik] a ätzend; (fig) bissig.

cauterize ['kɒtəraiz] vt ätzen, ausbrennen.

caution ['kɒʃən] n Vorsicht f, (warning) Warnung f; (Jur) Verwarnung f; vt (ver)warnen.

cautious a, ~**ly** ad ['kɒʃəs, -lı] vorsichtig.

cavalcade [kævəlˈkeid] n Kavalkade f.

cavalier [kævəˈliə*] a blasiert.

cavalry ['kævəlrı] npl Kavallerie f.

cave [keiv] n Höhle f; ~**man** Höhlenmensch m; ~ **in** vi einstürzen.

cavern ['kævən] n Höhle f; ~**ous** a cheeks hohl; eyes tiefliegend.

cavil ['kævil] vi kritteln (at an +dat).

cavity ['kævitı] n Höhlung f; (in tooth) Loch nt.

cavort [kəˈvɔːt] vi umherspringen.

cease [siːs] vi aufhören; vt beenden; ~**fire** Feuereinstellung f; ~**less** a unaufhörlich.

cedar ['siːdə*] n Zeder f.

cede [siːd] vt abtreten.

ceiling ['siːliŋ] n Decke f; (fig) Höchstgrenze f.

celebrate ['selibreit] vt feiern; anniversary begehen; vi feiern; ~**d** a gefeiert.

celebration [seliˈbreiʃən] n Feier f.

celebrity [sɪ'lebrɪtɪ] n gefeierte Persönlichkeit f.

celery ['selərɪ] n Sellerie m or f.

celestial [sɪ'lestɪəl] a himmlisch.

celibacy ['selɪbəsɪ] n Zölibat nt or m.

cell [sel] n Zelle f; (Elec) Element nt.

cellar ['selə*] n Keller m.

cellist ['tʃelɪst] n Cellist(in f) m.

cello [tʃeləʊ] n Cello nt.

cellophane · ['seləfeɪn] n Cellophan nt.

cellular ['seljʊlə*] a zellenförmig, zellular.

cellulose ['seljʊləʊs] n Zellulose f.

cement [sɪ'ment] n Zement m; vt (lit) zementieren; (fig) festigen.

cemetery ['semɪtrɪ] n Friedhof m.

cenotaph ['senətɑːf] n Ehrenmal nt, Zenotaph m.

censor ['sensə*] n Zensor m; ~ship Zensur f.

censure ['senʃə*] vt rügen.

census ['sensəs] n Volkszählung f.

centenary [sen'tiːnərɪ] n Jahrhundertfeier f.

center ['sentə*] n (US) = centre.

centigrade ['sentɪgreɪd] a: **10 (degrees)** ~ 10 Grad Celsius.

centilitre, (US) ~**liter** ['sentɪliːtə*] n Zentiliter nt or m.

centimetre, (US) ~**meter** ['sentɪmiːtə*] n Zentimeter nt.

centipede ['sentɪpiːd] n Tausendfüßler m.

central ['sentrəl] a zentral ; ~ **heating** Zentralheizung f; ~**ize** vt zentralisieren.

centre ['sentə*] n Zentrum nt; ~ **of gravity** Schwerpunkt m; **to** ~ **on** (sich) konzentrieren auf (+acc).

century ['sentjʊrɪ] n Jahrhundert nt.

ceramic [sɪ'ræmɪk] a keramisch.

cereal ['sɪərɪəl] n (any grain) Getreide nt; (at breakfast) Getreideflocken pl.

ceremonial [serɪ'məʊnɪəl] a zeremoniell.

ceremony ['serɪmənɪ] n Feierlichkeiten pl, Zeremonie f.

certain ['sɜːtən] a sicher; (particular) gewiß; **for** ~ ganz bestimmt; ~**ly** ad sicher, bestimmt; ~**ty** Gewißheit f.

certificate [sə'tɪfɪkɪt] n Bescheinigung f; (Sch etc) Zeugnis nt.

certify ['sɜːtɪfaɪ] vti bescheinigen.

cessation [se'seɪʃən] n Einstellung f, Ende nt.

chafe [tʃeɪf] vti (wund)reiben, scheuern.

chaffinch ['tʃæfɪntʃ] n Buchfink m.

chain [tʃeɪn] n Kette f; vt (also ~ **up**) anketten; mit Ketten fesseln; ~ **reaction** Kettenreaktion f; ~ **smoker** Kettenraucher(in f) m; ~ **store** Kettenladen m.

chair [tʃeə*] n Stuhl m; (arm—) Sessel m; (Univ) Lehrstuhl m; vt: **to** ~ **a meeting** in einer Versammlung den Vorsitz führen; ~**lift** Sessellift m; ~**man** Vorsitzende(r) m; (of firm) Präsident m.

chalet ['ʃæleɪ] n Chalet nt.

chalice ['tʃælɪs] n (Abendmahls)kelch m.

chalk ['tʃɔːk] n Kreide f.

challenge ['tʃælɪndʒ] n Herausforderung f; vt auffordern; (contest) bestreiten; ~**r** Herausforderer m.

challenging ['tʃælɪndʒɪŋ] a statement herausfordernd; work anspruchsvoll.

chamber ['tʃeɪmbə*] n Kammer f; ~ **of commerce** Handelskammer f; ~**maid** Zimmermädchen nt; ~ **music** Kammermusik f; ~**pot** Nachttopf m.

chameleon [kə'miːlɪən] n Chamäleon nt.

chamois ['ʃæmwɑː] n Gemse f; ~ **leather** ['ʃæmɪˈleðə*] Sämischleder nt.

champagne [ʃæm'peɪn] n Champagner m, Sekt m.

champion ['tʃæmpɪən] n (Sport) Sieger(in f) m, Meister m; (of cause) Verfechter(in f) m; ~**ship** Meisterschaft f.

chance [tʃɑːns] n (luck, fate) Zufall m; (possibility) Möglichkeit f; (opportunity) Gelegenheit f, Chance f; (risk) Risiko nt; a zufällig; vt: **to** ~ **it** es darauf ankommen lassen; **by** ~ zufällig; **to take a** ~ ein Risiko eingehen; **no** ~ keine Chance.

chancel ['tʃɑːnsəl] n Altarraum m, Chor m.

chancellor ['tʃɑːnsələ*] n Kanzler m; **C~ of the Exchequer** Schatzkanzler m.

chancy ['tʃɑːnsɪ] a (col) riskant.

chandelier [ʃændɪ'lɪə*] n Kronleuchter m.

change [tʃeɪndʒ] vt verandern; money wechseln; vi sich verändern; (trains) umsteigen; (colour etc) sich verwandeln; (clothes) sich umziehen; n Veränderung f; (money) Wechselgeld nt; (coins) Kleingeld nt; ~**able** a weather wechselhaft; ~**over** Umstellung f, Wechsel m.

changing ['tʃeɪndʒɪŋ] a veränderlich; ~**room** Umkleideraum m.

channel ['tʃænl] n (stream) Bachbett nt; (Naut) Straße f, Meerenge f; (Rad, TV) Kanal m; (fig) Weg m; vt (hindurch)leiten, lenken; **through official** ~**s** durch die Instanzen; **the (English) C~** der Ärmelkanal; **C~ Islands** Kanalinseln pl.

chant [tʃɑːnt] n liturgische(r) Gesang m; Sprechgesang m, Sprechchor m; vt intonieren.

chaos ['keɪɒs] n Chaos nt, Durcheinander nt.

chaotic [keɪ'ɒtɪk] a chaotisch.

chap [tʃæp] n (col) Bursche m, Kerl m; vt skin rissig machen; vi (hands etc) aufspringen.

chapel ['tʃæpəl] n Kapelle f.

chaperon ['ʃæpərəʊn] n Anstandsdame f; vt begleiten.

chaplain ['tʃæplɪn] n Geistliche(r) m, Pfarrer m, Kaplan m.

chapter ['tʃæptə*] n Kapitel nt.

char [tʃɑː*] vt (burn) verkohlen; vi (cleaner) putzen gehen.

character ['kærɪktə*] n Charakter m, Wesen nt; (Liter) Figur f, Gestalt f; (Theat) Person f, Rolle f; (peculiar person) Original nt; (in writing) Schriftzeichen nt; ~**istic** [kærɪktə'rɪstɪk] a charakteristisch, bezeichnend (of für); n Kennzeichen nt, Eigenschaft f; ~**ize** vt charakterisieren, kennzeichnen.

charade [ʃə'rɑːd] n Scharade f.

charcoal ['tʃɑːkəʊl] n Holzkohle f.

charge [tʃɑːdʒ] n (cost) Preis m; (Jur) Anklage f; (of gun) Ladung f; (attack) Angriff m; vt gun, battery laden; price verlangen; (Mil) angreifen; vi (rush) angreifen, (an)stürmen; **to be in ~ of** verantwortlich sein für; **to take ~** (die Verantwortung) übernehmen.

chariot ['tʃærɪət] n (Streit)wagen m.

charitable ['tʃærɪtəbl] a wohltätig; (lenient) nachsichtig.

charity ['tʃærɪtɪ] n (institution) Wohlfahrtseinrichtung f, Hilfswerk nt; (attitude) Nächstenliebe f, Wohltätigkeit f.

charlady ['tʃɑːleɪdɪ] n Reinemachefrau f, Putzfrau f.

charlatan ['ʃɑːlətən] n Scharlatan m, Schwindler(in f) m.

charm [tʃɑːm] n Charme m, gewinnende(s) Wesen nt; (in superstition) Amulett nt; Talisman m; vt bezaubern; **~ing** a reizend, liebenswürdig, charmant.

chart [tʃɑːt] n Tabelle f; (Naut) Seekarte f.

charter ['tʃɑːtə*] vt (Naut, Aviat) chartern; n Schutzbrief m; (cost) Schiffsmiete f; **~flight** Charterflug m; **~ed accountant** Wirtschaftsprüfer(in f) m.

charwoman ['tʃɑːwumən] n Reinemachefrau f, Putzfrau f.

chary ['tʃɛərɪ] a zurückhaltend (of sth mit etw).

chase [tʃeɪs] vt jagen, verfolgen; n Jagd f.

chasm ['kæzəm] n Kluft f.

chassis ['ʃæsɪ] n Chassis nt, Fahrgestell nt.

chaste [tʃeɪst] a keusch.

chastity ['tʃæstɪtɪ] n Keuschheit f.

chat [tʃæt] vi plaudern, sich (zwanglos) unterhalten; n Plauderei f.

chatter ['tʃætə*] vi schwatzen; (teeth) klappern; n Geschwätz nt; **~box** Quasselstrippe f.

chatty ['tʃætɪ] a geschwätzig.

chauffeur ['ʃoufə*] n Chauffeur m, Fahrer m.

cheap [tʃiːp] a billig; (joke schlecht; (of poor quality) minderwertig; **to ~ en o.s.** sich herablassen; **~ly** ad billig.

cheat [tʃiːt] vti betrügen; (Sch) mogeln; n Betrüger(in f) m; **~ing** Betrug nt.

check [tʃek] vt prüfen; (look up, make sure) nachsehen; (control) kontrollieren; (restrain) zügeln; (stop) anhalten; n (examination, restraint) Kontrolle f; (restaurant bill) Rechnung f; (pattern) Karo(muster) nt; (US) = **cheque**; **~ers** (US) Damespiel nt; **~list** Kontroll-liste f; **~mate** Schachmatt nt; **~point** Kontrollpunkt m; **~up** (Nach)prüfung f; (Med) (ärztliche) Untersuchung f.

cheek [tʃiːk] n Backe f, Wange f; (fig) Frechheit f, Unverschämtheit f; **~bone** Backenknochen m; **~y** a frech, übermütig.

cheep [tʃiːp] n Pieps(er) nt.

cheer [tʃɪə*] n Beifallsruf m, Hochruf m; **~s!** Prost!; vt zujubeln; (encourage) ermuntern, aufmuntern; vi jauchzen, Hochrufe ausbringen; **~ful** a fröhlich; **~fulness** Fröhlichkeit f, Munterkeit f; **~ing** Applaus m; a aufheiternd; **~io** interj tschüs!; **~less** a prospect trostlos; person verdrießlich; **~ up** vt ermuntern; vi: **~ up!** Kopf hoch!

cheese [tʃiːz] n Käse m; **~board**

(gemischte) Käseplatte f; **~cake** Käsekuchen m.

cheetah ['tʃiːtə] n Gepard m.

chef [ʃef] n Küchenchef m.

chemical ['kemɪkəl] a chemisch.

chemist ['kemɪst] n (Med) Apotheker m, Drogist m; (Chem) Chemiker m; **~ry** Chemie f; **~'s (shop)** (Med) Apotheke f, Drogerie f.

cheque [tʃek] n Scheck m; **~book** Scheckbuch nt; **~ card** Scheckkarte f.

chequered ['tʃekəd] a (fig) bewegt.

cherish ['tʃerɪʃ] vt person lieben; hope hegen; memory bewahren.

cheroot [ʃə'ruːt] n Zigarillo nt or m.

cherry ['tʃerɪ] n Kirsche f.

chervil ['tʃɜːvɪl] n Kerbel m.

chess [tʃes] n Schach nt; **~board** Schachbrett nt; **~man** Schachfigur f; **~player** Schachspieler(in f) m.

chest [tʃest] n Brust f, Brustkasten m; (box) Kiste f, Kasten m; **to get sth off one's ~** seinem Herzen Luft machen; **~ of drawers** Kommode f.

chestnut ['tʃesnʌt] n Kastanie f; **~ (tree)** Kastanienbaum m.

chew [tʃuː] vti kauen; **~ing gum** Kaugummi m.

chic [ʃiːk] a schick, elegant.

chicanery [ʃɪ'keɪnərɪ] n Schikane f.

chick [tʃɪk] n Küken nt; **~en** Huhn nt; (food: roast) Hähnchen nt; **~enpox** Windpocken pl; **~pea** Kichererbse f.

chicory ['tʃɪkərɪ] n Zichorie f; (plant) Chicorée f.

chief [tʃiːf] n (Ober)haupt nt; Anführer m; (Comm) Chef m; a höchst, Haupt-; **~ly** ad hauptsächlich.

chieftain ['tʃiːftən] n Häuptling m.

chilblain ['tʃɪlbleɪn] n Frostbeule f.

child [tʃaɪld] n Kind nt; **~birth** Entbindung f; **~hood** Kindheit f; **~ish** a kindisch; **~like** a kindlich; **~ren** ['tʃɪldrən] npl of **child**; **~'s play** (fig) Kinderspiel nt.

chill [tʃɪl] n Kühle f; (Med) Erkältung f; **~y** a kühl, frostig.

chime [tʃaɪm] n Glockenschlag m, Glockenklang m; vi ertönen, (er)klingen.

chimney ['tʃɪmnɪ] n Schornstein m, Kamin m.

chimpanzee [tʃɪmpæn'ziː] n Schimpanse m.

chin [tʃɪn] n Kinn nt.

china ['tʃaɪnə] n Porzellan nt.

chink [tʃɪŋk] n (opening) Ritze f, Spalt m; (noise) Klirren nt.

chintz [tʃɪnts] n Kattun m.

chip [tʃɪp] n (of wood etc) Splitter m; (potato) **~s** pl Pommes frites pl; (US: crisp) Chip m; vt absplittern; **~ in** vi Zwischenbemerkungen machen.

chiropodist [kɪ'rɒpədɪst] n Fußpfleger(in f) m.

chirp [tʃɜːp] n Zwitschern nt; vi zwitschern.

chisel ['tʃɪzl] n Meißel m.

chit [tʃɪt] n Notiz f; **~chat** Plauderei f.

chivalrous ['ʃɪvəlrəs] a ritterlich.

chivalry ['ʃɪvəlrɪ] n Ritterlichkeit f; (honour) Ritterschaft f.

chive [tʃaɪv] n Schnittlauch m.
chloride [ˈklɔːraɪd] n Chlorid nt.
chlorine [ˈklɔːriːn] n Chlor nt.
chock [tʃɔk] n Keil m; ~-a-block a vollgepfropft.
chocolate [ˈtʃɔklɪt] n Schokolade f.
choice [tʃɔɪs] n Wahl f; (of goods) Auswahl f; a auserlesen, Qualitäts-.
choir [ˈkwaɪə*] n Chor m; ~boy Chorknabe m.
choke [tʃəʊk] vi ersticken; vt erdrosseln; (block) (ab)drosseln; n (Aut) Starterklappe f.
cholera [ˈkɔlərə] n Cholera f.
choose [tʃuːz] vt irreg wählen; (decide) beschließen.
chop [tʃɔp] vt (zer)hacken; wood spalten; vi: to ~ and change schwanken; n Hieb m; (meat) Kotelett nt; ~py a bewegt; ~sticks pl (Eß)stäbchen pl.
choral [ˈkɔːrəl] a Chor-.
chord [kɔːd] n Akkord m; (string) Saite f.
chore [tʃɔː*] n Pflicht f; harte Arbeit f.
choreographer [kɔrɪˈɔgrəfə*] n Choreograph(in f) m.
chorister [ˈkɔrɪstə*] n Chorsänger(in f) m.
chortle [ˈtʃɔːtl] vi glucksen, tief lachen.
chorus [ˈkɔːrəs] n Chor m; (in song) Refrain m.
chow [tʃaʊ] n (dog) Chow-Chow m.
Christ [kraɪst] n Christus m.
christen [ˈkrɪsn] vt taufen; ~ing Taufe f.
Christian [ˈkrɪstɪən] a christlich; n Christ(in f) m; ~ name Vorname m; ~ity [krɪstɪˈænɪtɪ] Christentum nt.
Christmas [ˈkrɪsməs] n Weihnachten pl; ~ card Weihnachtskarte f; ~ tree Weihnachtsbaum m.
chrome [krəʊm] n = **chromium plating**.
chromium [ˈkrəʊmɪəm] n Chrom nt; ~ plating Verchromung f.
chronic [ˈkrɔnɪk] a (Med) chronisch; (terrible) scheußlich.
chronicle [ˈkrɔnɪkl] n Chronik f.
chronological [krɔnəˈlɔdʒɪkəl] a chronologisch.
chrysalis [ˈkrɪsəlɪs] n (Insekten)puppe f.
chrysanthemum [krɪsˈænθɪməm] n Chrysantheme f.
chubby [ˈtʃʌbɪ] a child pausbäckig; adult rundlich.
chuck [tʃʌk] vt werfen; n (Tech) Spannvorrichtung f.
chuckle [ˈtʃʌkl] vi in sich hineinlachen.
chum [tʃʌm] n (child) Spielkamerad m; (adult) Kumpel m.
chunk [tʃʌŋk] n Klumpen m; (of food) Brocken m.
church [tʃɜːtʃ] n Kirche f; (clergy) Geistlichkeit f; ~yard Kirchhof m.
churlish [ˈtʃɜːlɪʃ] a grob.
churn [tʃɜːn] n Butterfaß nt; (for transport) (große) Milchkanne f; ~ out vt (col) produzieren.
chute [ʃuːt] n Rutsche f.
cicada [sɪˈkɑːdə] n Zikade f.
cider [ˈsaɪdə*] n Apfelwein m.
cigar [sɪˈgɑː*] n Zigarre f; ~ette [sɪgəˈret]

Zigarette f; ~ette case Zigarettenetui nt; ~ette end Zigarettenstummel m; ~ette holder Zigarettenspitze f.
cinch [sɪntʃ] n (col) klare(r) Fall m; (easy) Kinderspiel nt.
cinder [ˈsɪndə*] n Zinder m.
Cinderella [sɪndəˈrelə] n Aschenbrödel nt.
cine [ˈsɪnɪ] n: ~-camera Filmkamera f; ~ film Schmalfilm m.
cinema [ˈsɪnəmə] n Kino nt.
cine-projector [sɪnɪprəˈdʒektə*] n Filmvorführapparat m.
cinnamon [ˈsɪnəmən] n Zimt m.
cipher [ˈsaɪfə*] n (code) Chiffre f; (numeral) Ziffer f.
circle [ˈsɜːkl] n Kreis m; vi kreisen; vt umkreisen; (attacking) umzingeln.
circuit [ˈsɜːkɪt] n Umlauf m; (Elec) Stromkreis m; ~ous [sɜːˈkjuːɪtəs] a weitschweifig.
circular [ˈsɜːkjulə*] a (kreis)rund, kreisförmig; n Rundschreiben nt.
circularize [ˈsɜːkjuləraɪz] vt (inform) benachrichtigen; letter herumschicken.
circulate [ˈsɜːkjuleɪt] vi zirkulieren; vt in Umlauf setzen.
circulation [sɜːkjuˈleɪʃən] n (of blood) Kreislauf m; (of newspaper) Auflage f; (of money) Umlauf m.
circumcise [ˈsɜːkəmsaɪz] vt beschneiden.
circumference [səˈkʌmfərəns] n (Kreis)umfang m.
circumspect [ˈsɜːkəmspekt] a umsichtig.
circumstances [ˈsɜːkəmstənsəz] npl (facts connected with sth) Umstände pl; (financial condition) Verhältnisse pl.
circumvent [sɜːkəmˈvent] vt umgehen.
circus [ˈsɜːkəs] n Zirkus m.
cissy [ˈsɪsɪ] n Weichling m.
cistern [ˈsɪstən] n Zisterne f; (of W.C.) Spülkasten m.
citation [saɪˈteɪʃən] n Zitat nt.
cite [saɪt] vt zitieren, anführen.
citizen [ˈsɪtɪzn] n Bürger(in f) m; (of nation) Staatsangehörige(r) mf; ~ship Staatsangehörigkeit f.
citrus [ˈsɪtrəs] adj: ~ fruit Zitrusfrucht f.
city [ˈsɪtɪ] n Großstadt f; (centre) Zentrum nt, City f.
civic [ˈsɪvɪk] a städtisch, Bürger-.
civil [ˈsɪvɪl] a (of town) Bürger-; (of state) staatsbürgerlich; (not military) zivil; (polite) höflich; ~ engineer Bauingenieur m; ~ engineering Hoch- und Tiefbau m; ~ian [sɪˈvɪlɪən] n Zivilperson f; a zivil, Zivil-; ~ization [sɪvɪlaɪˈzeɪʃən] n Zivilisation f, Kultur f; ~ized a zivilisiert; Kultur-; ~ law bürgerliche(s) Recht, Zivilrecht nt; ~ rights pl Bürgerrechte pl; ~ servant Staatsbeamte(r) m; ~ service Staatsdienst m; ~ war Bürgerkrieg m.
clad [klæd] a gekleidet; ~ in gehüllt in (+acc).
claim [kleɪm] vt beanspruchen; (have opinion) behaupten; n (demand) Forderung f; (right) Anspruch m; Behauptung f; ~ant Antragsteller(in f) m.

clairvoyant [klɛə'vɔɪənt] n Hellseher(in f) m; a hellseherisch.
clam [klæm] n Venusmuschel f.
clamber ['klæmbə*] vi kraxeln.
clammy ['klæmɪ] a feucht(kalt); klamm.
clamorous ['klæmərəs] a lärmend, laut.
clamp [klæmp] n Schraubzwinge f; vt einspannen.
clan [klæn] n Sippe f, Clan m.
clang [klæŋ] n Klang m; Scheppern nt; vi klingen; scheppern.
clap [klæp] vi klatschen; vt Beifall klatschen (+dat); ~**ping** (Beifall)klatschen nt.
claret ['klærɪt] n rote(r) Bordeaux(wein) m.
clarification [klærɪfɪ'keɪʃən] n Erklärung f.
clarify ['klærɪfaɪ] vt klären, erklären.
clarinet [klærɪ'net] n Klarinette f.
clarity ['klærɪtɪ] n Klarheit f.
clash [klæʃ] n (fig) Konflikt m, Widerstreit m; (sound) Knall m; vi zusammenprallen; (colours) sich beißen; (argue) sich streiten.
clasp [klɑːsp] n Klammer f, Haken m; (on belt) Schnalle f; vt umklammern.
class [klɑːs] n Klasse f; vt einordnen, einstufen; ~**conscious** a klassenbewußt.
classic ['klæsɪk] n Klassiker(in f) m; a (traditional) klassisch; ~**al** a klassisch.
classification [klæsɪfɪ'keɪʃən] n Klassifizierung f; Einteilung f.
classify ['klæsɪfaɪ] vt klassifizieren, einteilen.
classroom ['klɑːsrʊm] n Klassenzimmer nt.
classy ['klɑːsɪ] a (col) todschick.
clatter ['klætə*] n Klappern nt, Rasseln nt; (of feet) Getrappel nt; vi klappern, rasseln; (feet) trappeln.
clause [klɔːz] n (Jur) Klausel f; (Gram) Satz(teil) m, Satzglied nt.
claustrophobia [klɒstrə'fəʊbɪə] n Platzangst f, Klaustrophobie f.
claw [klɔː] n Kralle f; vt (zer)kratzen.
clay [kleɪ] n Lehm m; (for pots) Ton m.
clean [kliːn] a sauber; (fig) schuldlos; shape ebenmäßig; cut glatt; vt saubermachen, reinigen, putzen; ~**er** (person) Putzfrau f; (for grease etc) Scheuerpulver nt; ~**ers** pl Chemische Reinigung f; ~**ing** Reinigen nt, Säubern nt; ~**liness** ['klenlɪnɪs] Sauberkeit f, Reinlichkeit f; ~**ly** ad reinlich; ~**se** [klenz] vt reinigen, säubern; ~**-shaven** a glattrasiert; ~**-up** Reinigung f; ~ **out** vt gründlich putzen; ~ **up** vt aufräumen.
clear [klɪə*] a water klar; glass durchsichtig; sound deutlich, klar, hell; meaning genau, klar; (certain) klar, sicher; road frei; **to stand** ~ **of sth** etw frei halten; vt road etc freimachen; vi (become clear) klarwerden; ~**ance** ['klɪərns] (removal) Räumung f; (free space) Lichtung f; (permission) Freigabe f; ~**-cut** a scharf umrissen; case eindeutig; ~**ing** Lichtung f; ~**ly** ad klar, deutlich, zweifellos; ~**way** (Brit) (Straße f mit) Halteverbot nt; ~ **up** vi (weather) sich aufklären; vt reinigen, säubern; (solve) aufklären.

clef [klef] n Notenschlüssel m.
clench [klentʃ] vt teeth zusammenbeißen; fist ballen.
clergy ['klɜːdʒɪ] n Geistliche(n) pl; ~**man** Geistliche(r) m.
clerical ['klerɪkəl] a (office)Schreib-, Büro-; (Eccl) geistlich, Pfarr(er)-; ~ **error** Schreibfehler m.
clerk [klɑːk, US klɜːk] n (in office) Büroangestellte(r) mf; (US: salesman) Verkäufer(in f) m.
clever a, ~**ly** ad ['klevə*, -əlɪ] klug, geschickt, gescheit.
cliché ['kliːʃeɪ] n Klischee nt.
click [klɪk] vi klicken; n Klicken nt; (of door) Zuklinken nt.
client ['klaɪənt] n Klient(in f) m; ~**ele** [kliːãn'tel] Kundschaft f.
cliff [klɪf] n Klippe f.
climate ['klaɪmɪt] n Klima nt.
climatic [klaɪ'mætɪk] a klimatisch.
climax ['klaɪmæks] n Höhepunkt m.
climb [klaɪm] vt besteigen; vi steigen, klettern; n Aufstieg m; ~**er** Bergsteiger m, Kletterer m; (fig) Streber m; ~**ing** Bergsteigen nt, Klettern nt.
clinch [klɪntʃ] vt (decide) entscheiden; deal festmachen; n (boxing) Clinch m.
cling [klɪŋ] vi irreg anhaften, anhängen.
clinic ['klɪnɪk] n Klinik f; ~**al** a klinisch.
clink [klɪŋk] n (of coins) Klimpern nt; (of glasses) Klirren nt; (col: prison) Knast m; vi klimpern; vt klimpern mit; glasses anstoßen.
clip [klɪp] n Spange f; **paper** ~ (Büro-, Heft)klammer f; vt papers heften; hair, hedge stutzen; ~**pers** pl (instrument) (for hedge) Heckenschere f; (for hair) Haarschneidemaschine f.
clique [kliːk] n Clique f, Gruppe f.
cloak [kləʊk] n lose(r) Mantel m, Umhang m; ~**room** (for coats) Garderobe f; (W.C.) Toilette f.
clobber ['klɒbə*] n (col) Klamotten pl; vt schlagen.
clock [klɒk] n Uhr f; ~**wise** ad im Uhrzeigersinn; ~**work** Uhrwerk nt; like ~**work** wie am Schnürchen.
clog [klɒg] n Holzschuh m; vt verstopfen.
cloister ['klɔɪstə*] n Kreuzgang m.
close [kləʊs] a nahe; march geschlossen; thorough genau, gründlich; weather schwül; ad knapp; ~**ly** ad gedrängt, dicht; ~ **to** prep in der Nähe (+gen); **I had a** ~ **shave** das war knapp; ~**-up** Nahaufnahme f.
close [kləʊz] vt schließen, abschließen; vi sich schließen; n (end) Ende nt, Schluß m; **to** ~ **with sb** jdn angreifen; ~ **down** vt Geschäft aufgeben; vi eingehen; ~**d** a road gesperrt; shop etc geschlossen; ~**d shop** Gewerkschaftszwang m.
closet ['klɒzɪt] n Abstellraum m, Schrank m.
closure ['kləʊʒə*] n Schließung f.
clot [klɒt] n Klumpen m; (of blood) Blutgerinnsel nt; (fool) Blödmann m; vi gerinnen.
cloth [klɒθ] n (material) Stoff m, Tuch nt;

(*for washing etc*) Lappen *m*, Tuch *nt*.

clothe [kləʊð] *vt* kleiden, bekleiden; **~s** *pl* Kleider *pl*, Kleidung *f*; *see* **bedclothes**; **~s brush** Kleiderbürste *f*; **~s line** Wäscheleine *f*; **~s peg** Wäscheklammer *f*.

clothing [ˈkləʊðɪŋ] *n* = **clothes**.

cloud [klaʊd] *n* Wolke *f*; **~burst** Wolkenbruch *m*; **~y** a wolkig, bewölkt.

clout [klaʊt] (*col*) *n* Schlag *m*; *vt* hauen.

clove [kləʊv] *n* Gewürznelke *f*; **~ of garlic** Knoblauchzehe *f*.

clover [ˈkləʊvə*] *n* Klee *m*; **~leaf** Kleeblatt *nt*.

clown [klaʊn] *n* Clown *m*, Hanswurst *m*; *vi* kaspern, sich albern benehmen.

cloy [klɔɪ] *vi*: **it ~s** es übersättigt einen.

club [klʌb] *n* Knüppel *m*; (*society*) Klub *m*; (*golf*) Golfschläger *m*; (*Cards*) Kreuz *nt*; *vt* prügeln; **~ together** *vi* (*with money etc*) zusammenlegen; **~house** Klubhaus *nt*.

cluck [klʌk] *vi* glucken.

clue [kluː] *n* Anhaltspunkt *m*, Fingerzeig *m*, Spur *f*; **he hasn't a ~** er hat keine Ahnung.

clump [klʌmp] *n* Gebüsch *nt*.

clumsy [ˈklʌmzɪ] a *person* ungelenk, unbeholfen; *object, shape* unförmig.

cluster [ˈklʌstə*] *n* Traube *f*; (*of trees etc*) Gruppe *f*; **~ round** *vi* sich scharen um; umschwarmen.

clutch [klʌtʃ] *n* feste(r) Griff *m*; (*Aut*) Kupplung *f*; *vt* sich festklammern an (*+dat*); *book* an sich klammern.

clutter [ˈklʌtə*] *vt* vollpropfen; *desk etc* übersäen; *n* Unordnung *f*.

coach [kəʊtʃ] *n* Omnibus *m*, (Überland)bus *m*; (*old*) Kutsche *f*, (*Rail*) (Personen)-wagen *m*; (*trainer*) Trainer *m*; *vt* (*Sch*) Nachhilfeunterricht geben (*+dat*); (*Sport*) trainieren.

coagulate [kəʊˈægjuleɪt] *vi* gerinnen.

coal [kəʊl] *n* Kohle *f*.

coalesce [kəʊəˈles] *vi* sich verbinden.

coal face [ˈkəʊlfeɪs] *n* (Abbau)sohle *f*, Streb *m*; **at the ~** vor Ort.

coalfield [ˈkəʊlfiːld] *n* Kohlengebiet *nt*.

coalition [kəʊəˈlɪʃən] *n* Zusammenschluß *m*; (*Pol*) Koalition *f*.

coalmine [ˈkəʊlmaɪn] *n* Kohlenbergwerk *nt*; **~r** Bergarbeiter *m*.

coarse [kɔːs] a (*lit*) grob; (*fig*) ordinär.

coast [kəʊst] *n* Küste *f*; **~al** Küsten-; **~er** Küstenfahrer *m*; **~guard** Küstenwache *f*; **~line** Küste(nlinie) *f*.

coat [kəʊt] *n* Mantel *m*; (*on animals*) Fell *nt*, Pelz *m*; (*of paint*) Schicht *f*; *vt* überstreichen; (*cover*) bedecken; **~ of arms** Wappen *nt*; **~hanger** Kleiderbügel *m*; **~ing** Schicht *f*, Überzug *m*; (*of paint*) Schicht *f*.

coax [kəʊks] *vt* beschwatzen.

cobble(stone)s [ˈkɒbl(stəʊn)z] *npl* Pflastersteine *pl*.

cobra [ˈkɒbrə] *n* Kobra *f*.

cobweb [ˈkɒbweb] *n* Spinnennetz *nt*.

cocaine [kəˈkeɪn] *n* Kokain *nt*.

cock [kɒk] *n* Hahn *m*; *vt ears* spitzen; *gun* den Hahn spannen; **~erel** junge(r) Hahn

m; **~-eyed** a (*fig*) verrückt.

cockle [ˈkɒkl] *n* Herzmuschel *f*.

cockney [ˈkɒknɪ] *n* echte(r) Londoner *m*.

cockpit [ˈkɒkpɪt] *n* (*Aviat*) Pilotenkanzel *f*.

cockroach [ˈkɒkrəʊtʃ] *n* Küchenschabe *f*.

cocktail [ˈkɒkteɪl] *n* Cocktail *m*; **~ cabinet** Hausbar *f*; **~ party** Cocktailparty *f*; **~ shaker** Mixbecher *m*.

cocoa [ˈkəʊkəʊ] *n* Kakao *m*.

coconut [ˈkəʊkənʌt] *n* Kokosnuß *f*.

cocoon [kəˈkuːn] *n* Puppe *f*, Kokon *m*.

cod [kɒd] *n* Kabeljau *m*.

code [kəʊd] *n* Kode *m*; (*Jur*) Kodex *m*; **in ~** verschlüsselt, in Kode.

codeine [ˈkəʊdiːn] *n* Kodein *nt*.

codify [ˈkəʊdɪfaɪ] *vt message* verschlüsseln; (*Jur*) kodifizieren.

coeducational [kəʊedjʊˈkeɪʃənl] a koedukativ, gemischt.

coerce [kəʊˈɜːs] *vt* nötigen, zwingen.

coercion [kəʊˈɜːʃən] *n* Zwang *m*, Nötigung *f*.

coexistence [kəʊɪgˈzɪstəns] *n* Koexistenz *f*.

coffee [ˈkɒfɪ] *n* Kaffee *m*; **~ bar** Kaffeeausschank *m*, Café *nt*.

coffin [ˈkɒfɪn] *n* Sarg *m*.

cog [kɒg] *n* (*Rad*)zahn *m*.

cogent [ˈkəʊdʒənt] a triftig, überzeugend, zwingend.

cognac [ˈkɒnjæk] *n* Kognak *m*.

coherent [kəʊˈhɪərənt] a zusammenhängend, einheitlich.

coil [kɔɪl] *n* Rolle *f*; (*Elec*) Spule *f*; *vt* aufrollen, aufwickeln.

coin [kɔɪn] *n* Münze *f*; *vt* prägen; **~age** (*word*) Prägung *f*.

coincide [kəʊɪnˈsaɪd] *vi* (*happen together*) zusammenfallen; (*agree*) übereinstimmen; **~nce** [kəʊˈɪnsɪdəns] Zufall *m*; **by a strange ~nce** merkwürdigerweise; **~ntal** [kəʊɪnsɪˈdentl] a zufällig.

coke [kəʊk] *n* Koks *m*.

colander [ˈkɒləndə*] *n* Durchschlag *m*.

cold [kəʊld] a kalt; **I'm ~** mir ist kalt, ich friere; *n* Kälte *f*; (*illness*) Erkältung *f*; **to have ~ feet** (*fig*) kalte Füße haben, Angst haben; **to give sb the ~ shoulder** jdm die kalte Schulter zeigen; **~ly** ad kalt; (*fig*) gefühllos; **~ sore** Erkältungsbläschen *nt*.

coleslaw [ˈkəʊlslɔː] *n* Krautsalat *m*.

colic [ˈkɒlɪk] *n* Kolik *f*.

collaborate [kəˈlæbəreɪt] *vi* zusammenarbeiten.

collaboration [kəlæbəˈreɪʃən] *n* Zusammenarbeit *f*; (*Pol*) Kollaboration *f*.

collaborator [kəˈlæbəreɪtə*] *n* Mitarbeiter *m*; (*Pol*) Kollaborateur *m*.

collage [kɒˈlɑːʒ] *n* Collage *f*.

collapse [kəˈlæps] *vi* (*people*) zusammenbrechen; (*things*) einstürzen; *n* Zusammenbruch *m*, Einsturz *m*.

collapsible [kəˈlæpsəbl] a zusammenklappbar, Klapp-.

collar [ˈkɒlə*] *n* Kragen *m*; **~bone** Schlüsselbein *nt*.

collate [kɒˈleɪt] *vt* zusammenstellen und vergleichen.

colleague [ˈkɒliːg] *n* Kollege *m*, Kollegin *f*.

collect [kə'lekt] *vt* sammeln; (*fetch*) abholen; *vi* sich sammeln; ~ **call** (*US*) R-Gespräch *nt*; ~**ed** *a* gefaßt; ~**ion** [kə'lekʃən] Sammlung *f*; (*Eccl*) Kollekte *f*; ~**ive** *a* gemeinsam; (*Pol*) kollektiv; ~**or** Sammler *m*; (*tax* ~*or*) (Steuer)einnehmer *m*.

college [kɔlɪdʒ] *n* (*Univ*) College *nt*; (*Tech*) Fach-, Berufsschule *f*.

collide [kə'laɪd] *vi* zusammenstoßen; kollidieren; im Widerspruch stehen (*with* zu).

collie ['kɔlɪ] *n* schottische(r) Schäferhund *m*, Collie *m*.

colliery ['kɔlɪərɪ] *n* (Kohlen)bergwerk *nt*, Zeche *f*.

collision [kə'lɪʒən] *n* Zusammenstoß *m*; (*of opinions*) Konflikt *m*.

colloquial [kə'ləʊkwɪəl] *a* umgangssprachlich.

collusion [kə'lu:ʒən] *n* geheime(s) Einverständnis *nt*, Zusammenspiel *nt*.

colon ['kəʊlən] *n* Doppelpunkt *m*.

colonel ['kɜːnl] *n* Oberst *m*.

colonial [kə'ləʊnɪəl] *a* Kolonial-.

colonize ['kɔlənaɪz] *vt* kolonisieren.

colonnade [kɔlə'neɪd] *n* Säulengang *m*.

colony ['kɔlənɪ] *n* Kolonie *f*.

color ['kʌlə*] (*US*) = colour.

Colorado beetle [kɔlə'rɑːdəʊ 'biːtl] *n* Kartoffelkäfer *m*.

colossal [kə'lɔsl] *a* kolossal, riesig.

colour ['kʌlə*] *n* Farbe *f*; off ~ nicht wohl; *vt* (*lit, fig*) färben; *vi* sich verfärben; ~**s** *pl* Fahne *f*; ~ **bar** Rassenschranke *f*; ~**blind** *a* farbenblind; ~**ed** *a* farbig; ~**ed** (**wo**)**man** Farbige(r) *mf*; ~ **film** Farbfilm *m*; ~**ful** *a* bunt; ~ **scheme** Farbgebung *f*; ~ **television** Farbfernsehen *nt*.

colt [kəʊlt] *n* Fohlen *nt*.

column ['kɔləm] *n* Säule *f*; (*Mil*) Kolonne *f*; (*of print*) Spalte *f*; ~**ist** ['kɔləmnɪst] Kolumnist *m*.

coma ['kəʊmə] *n* Koma *nt*.

comb [kəʊm] *n* Kamm *m*; *vt* kämmen; (*search*) durchkämmen.

combat ['kɔmbæt] *n* Kampf *m*; *vt* bekämpfen.

combination [kɔmbɪ'neɪʃən] *n* Verbindung *f*, Kombination *f*.

combine [kəm'baɪn] *vt* verbinden; *vi* sich vereinigen; ['kɔmbaɪn] *n* (*Comm*) Konzern *m*, Verband *m*; ~ **harvester** Mähdrescher *m*.

combustible [kəm'bʌstɪbl] *a* brennbar, leicht entzündlich.

combustion [kəm'bʌstʃən] *n* Verbrennung *f*.

come [kʌm] *irreg vi* kommen; (*reach*) ankommen, gelangen; ~ **about** *vi* geschehen; ~ **across** *vt* (*find*) stoßen auf (+*acc*); ~ **away** *vi* (*person*) weggehen; (*handle etc*) abgehen; ~ **by** *vi* vorbeikommen; *vt* (*find*) zu etw kommen; ~ **down** *vi* (*price*) fallen; ~ **forward** *vi* (*volunteer*) sich melden; ~ **from** *vi* (*result*) kommen von; **where do you** ~ **from?** wo kommen Sie her?; **I** ~ **from London** ich komme aus London; ~ **in for**

vt abkriegen; ~ **into** *vi* eintreten in (+*acc*); (*inherit*) erben; ~ **of** *vi*: **what came of it?** was ist daraus geworden?; ~ **off** *vi* (*handle*) abgehen; (*happen*) stattfinden; (*succeed*) klappen; ~ **off it!** laß den Quatsch!; ~ **on** *vi* (*progress*) vorankommen; **how's the book coming on?** was macht das Buch?; ~ **on!** komm!; (*hurry*) beeil dich!; (*encouraging*) los!; ~ **out** *vi* herauskommen; ~ **out with** *vt* herausrücken mit; ~ **round** *vi* (*visit*) vorbeikommen; (*Med*) wieder zu sich kommen; ~ **to** *vi* (*Med*) wieder zu sich kommen; (*bill*) sich belaufen auf; ~ **up** *vi* hochkommen; (*problem*) auftauchen; ~ **upon** *vt* stoßen auf (+*acc*); ~ **up to** *vi* (*approach*) zukommen auf (+*acc*); (*water*) reichen bis; (*expectation*) entsprechen (+*dat*); **to** ~ **up with sth** sich etw einfallen lassen; ~**back** Wiederauftreten *nt*, Comeback *nt*.

comedian [kə'miːdɪən] *n* Komiker *m*.

comedown ['kʌmdaʊn] *n* Abstieg *m*.

comedy ['kɔmədɪ] *n* Komödie *f*.

comet ['kɔmɪt] *n* Komet *m*.

comfort ['kʌmfət] *n* Bequemlichkeit *f*; (*of body*) Behaglichkeit *f*; (*of mind*) Trost *m*; *vt* trösten; ~**s** *pl* Annehmlichkeiten *pl*; ~**able** *a* bequem, gemütlich; ~ **station** (*US*) öffentliche Toilette *f*.

comic ['kɔmɪk] *n* Comic(heft) *nt*; (*comedian*) Komiker *m*; *a* (*also* ~**al**) komisch, humoristisch.

coming ['kʌmɪŋ] *n* Kommen *nt*, Ankunft *f*.

comma ['kɔmə] *n* Komma *nt*.

command [kə'mɑːnd] *n* Befehl *m*; (*control*) Führung *f*; (*Mil*) Kommando *nt*, (Ober)befehl *m*; *vt* befehlen (+*dat*); (*Mil*) kommandieren; (*be able to get*) verfügen über (+*acc*); *vi* befehlen; ~**eer** [kɔmən'dɪə*] *vt* (*Mil*) requirieren; ~**er** Befehlshaber *m*, Kommandant *m*; ~**ing officer** Kommandeur *m*; ~**ment** Gebot *nt*; ~**o** (Mitglied einer) Kommandotruppe *f*.

commemorate [kə'meməreɪt] *vt* gedenken (+*gen*).

commemoration [kəmemə'reɪʃən] *n*: **in** ~ **of** zum Gedächtnis *or* Andenken an (+*acc*).

commemorative [kə'memərətɪv] *a* Gedächtnis-; Gedenk-.

commence [kə'mens] *vti* beginnen; ~**ment** Beginn *m*.

commend [kə'mend] *vt* (*recommend*) empfehlen; (*praise*) loben; ~**able** *a* empfehlenswert, lobenswert; ~**ation** [kɔmen'deɪʃən] Empfehlung *f*; (*Sch*) Lob *nt*.

commensurate [kə'mensjurɪt] *a* vergleichbar, entsprechend (*with dat*).

comment ['kɔment] *n* (*remark*) Bemerkung *f*; (*note*) Anmerkung *f*; (*opinion*) Stellungnahme *f*; *vi* etw sagen (*on zu*); sich äußern (*on zu*); ~**ary** ['kɔməntrɪ] Kommentar *m*; Erläuterungen *pl*; ~**ator** ['kɔmənteɪtə*] Kommentator *m*.

commerce ['kɔmɜːs] *n* Handel *m*.

commercial [kə'mɜːʃəl] *a* kommerziell, geschäftlich; *training* kaufmännisch; *n* (*TV*) Fernsehwerbung *f*; ~**ize** *vt* kommerzialisieren;   ~ **television** Werbefernsehen *nt*; ~ **vehicle** Lieferwagen *m*.

commiserate [kə'mɪzəreɪt] *vi* Mitleid haben.

commission [kə'mɪʃən] *n* Auftrag *m*; (*fee*) Provision *f*; (*Mil*) Offizierspatent *nt*; (*of offence*) Begehen *nt*; (*reporting body*) Kommission *f*; *vt* bevollmächtigen, beauftragen; **out of** ~ außer Betrieb; ~**aire** [kəmɪʃə'nɛə*] Portier *m*; ~**er** (Regierungs)bevollmächtigte(r) *m*.

commit [kə'mɪt] *vt crime* begehen; (*undertake*) sich verpflichten; (*entrust*) übergeben, anvertrauen; **I don't want to** ~ **myself** ich will mich nicht festlegen; ~**ment** Verpflichtung *f*.

committee [kə'mɪtɪ] *n* Ausschuß *m*, Komitee *nt*.

commodious [kə'məʊdɪəs] *a* geräumig.

commodity [kə'mɒdɪtɪ] *n* Ware *f*; (Handels-, Gebrauchs)artikel *m*.

commodore ['kɒmədɔ:*] *n* Flotillenadmiral *m*.

common ['kɒmən] *a cause* gemeinsam; (*public*) öffentlich, allgemein; *experience* allgemein, alltäglich; (*pej*) gewöhnlich; (*widespread*) üblich, häufig, gewöhnlich; *n* Gemeindeland *nt*; öffentliche Anlage *f*; ~**ly** *ad* im allgemeinen, gewöhnlich; **C~ Market** Gemeinsame(r) Markt *m*; ~**place** *a* alltäglich; *n* Gemeinplatz *m*; ~**room** Gemeinschaftsraum *m*; ~**sense** gesunde(r) Menschenverstand *m*; **the C~wealth** das Commonwealth.

commotion [kə'məʊʃən] *n* Aufsehen *nt*, Unruhe *f*.

communal ['kɒmjuːnl] *a* Gemeinde-; Gemeinschafts-.

commune ['kɒmjuːn] *n* Kommune *f*; *vi* sich mitteilen (*with dat*), vertraulich verkehren.

communicate [kə'mjuːnɪkeɪt] *vt* (*transmit*) übertragen; *vi* (*be in touch*) in Verbindung stehen; (*make self understood*) sich verständlich machen.

communication [kəmjuːnɪ'keɪʃən] *n* (*message*) Mitteilung *f*; (*Rad, TV etc*) Kommunikationsmittel *nt*; (*making understood*) Kommunikation *f*; ~**s** *pl* (*transport etc*) Verkehrswege *pl*; ~ **cord** Notbremse *f*.

communion [kə'mjuːnɪən] *n* (*group*) Gemeinschaft *f*; (*Rel*) Religionsgemeinschaft *f*; **(Holy) C~** Heilige(s) Abendmahl *nt*, Kommunion *f*.

communiqué [kə'mjuːnɪkeɪ] *n* Kommuniqué *nt*, amtliche Verlautbarung *f*.

communism ['kɒmjunɪzəm] *n* Kommunismus *m*.

communist ['kɒmjunɪst] *n* Kommunist(in *f*) *m*; *a* kommunistisch.

community [kə'mjuːnɪtɪ] *n* Gemeinschaft *f*; (*public*) Gemeinwesen *nt*; ~ **centre** Gemeinschaftszentrum *nt*; ~ **chest** (*US*) Wohltätigkeitsfonds *m*.

commutation ticket [kɒmjuː'teɪʃən'tɪkɪt] *n* (*US*) Zeitkarte *f*.

commute [kə'mjuːt] *vi* pendeln; ~**r** Pendler *m*.

compact [kəm'pækt] *a* kompakt, fest,

dicht; ['kɒmpækt] *n* Pakt *m*, Vertrag *m*; (*for make-up*) Puderdose *f*.

companion [kəm'pænɪən] *n* Begleiter(in *f*) *m*; ~**ship** Gesellschaft *f*.

company ['kʌmpənɪ] *n* Gesellschaft *f*; (*Comm also*) Firma *f*; (*Mil*) Kompanie *f*; **to keep sb** ~ jdm Gesellschaft leisten.

comparable ['kɒmpərəbl] *a* vergleichbar.

comparative [kəm'pærətɪv] *a* (*relative*) verhältnismäßig, relativ; (*Gram*) steigernd; ~**ly** *ad* verhältnismäßig.

compare [kəm'pɛə*] *vt* vergleichen; *vi* sich vergleichen lassen.

comparison [kəm'pærɪsn] *n* Vergleich *m*; (*object*) Vergleichsgegenstand *m*; **in** ~ **(with)** im Vergleich (mit *or* zu).

compartment [kəm'pɑ:tmənt] *n* (*Rail*) Abteil *nt*; (*in drawer etc*) Fach *nt*.

compass ['kʌmpəs] *n* Kompaß *m*; ~**es** *pl* Zirkel *m*.

compassion [kəm'pæʃən] *n* Mitleid *nt*; ~**ate** *a* mitfühlend.

compatible [kəm'pætɪbl] *a* vereinbar, im Einklang; **we're not** ~ wir vertragen uns nicht.

compel [kəm'pel] *vt* zwingen; ~**ling** *a argument* zwingend.

compendium [kəm'pendɪəm] *n* Kompendium *nt*.

compensate ['kɒmpenseɪt] *vt* entschädigen; **to** ~ **for** Ersatz leisten für, kompensieren.

compensation [kɒmpen'seɪʃən] *n* Entschädigung *f*; (*money*) Schadenersatz *m*; Entschädigung *f*; (*Jur*) Abfindung *f*; (*Psych etc*) Kompensation *f*.

compère ['kɒmpɛə*] *n* Conférencier *m*.

compete [kəm'piːt] *vi* sich bewerben; konkurrieren, sich messen mit.

competence ['kɒmpɪtəns] *n* Fähigkeit *f*; (*Jur*) Zuständigkeit *f*.

competent ['kɒmpɪtənt] *a* kompetent, fähig; (*Jur*) zuständig.

competition [kɒmpɪ'tɪʃən] *n* Wettbewerb *m*; (*Comm*) Konkurrenz *f*.

competitive [kəm'petɪtɪv] *a* Konkurrenz-; (*Comm*) konkurrenzfähig.

competitor [kəm'petɪtə*] *n* Mitbewerber(in *f*) *m*; (*Comm*) Konkurrent(in *f*) *m*; (*Sport*) Teilnehmer(in *f*) *m*.

compile [kəm'paɪl] *vt* zusammenstellen.

complacency [kəm'pleɪsnsɪ] *n* Selbstzufriedenheit *f*, Gleichgültigkeit *f*.

complacent [kəm'pleɪsnt] *a* selbstzufrieden, gleichgültig.

complain [kəm'pleɪn] *vi* sich beklagen, sich beschweren (*about* über +*acc*); ~**t** Beschwerde *f*; (*Med*) Leiden *nt*.

complement ['kɒmplɪmənt] *n* Ergänzung *f*; (*ship's crew etc*) Bemannung *f*; ~**ary** [kɒmplɪ'mentərɪ] *a* Komplementär-, (sich) ergänzend.

complete [kəm'pliːt] *a* vollständig, vollkommen, ganz; *vt* vervollständigen; (*finish*) beenden; ~**ly** *ad* vollständig, ganz.

completion [kəm'pliːʃən] *n* Vervollständigung *f*; (*of building*) Fertigstellung *f*.

complex ['kɒmpleks] *a* kompliziert, verwickelt; *n* Komplex *m*.

complexion [kəm'plekʃən] *n* Gesichtsfarbe f, Teint m; (fig) Anstrich m, Aussehen nt.

complexity [kəm'pleksıtı] n Verwicklung f, Kompliziertheit f.

compliance [kəm'plaıəns] n Fügsamkeit f, Einwilligung f.

complicate ['komplıkeıt] vt komplizieren, verwickeln; ~**d** a kompliziert, verwickelt.

complication [komplı'keıʃən] a Komplikation f, Erschwerung f.

compliment ['komplımənt] n Kompliment nt; ['komplıment] vt ein Kompliment machen (sb jdm); ~**s** pl Grüße pl, Empfehlung f; ~**ary** [komplı'mentərı] a schmeichelhaft; (free) Frei-, Gratis-.

comply [kəm'plaı] vi: ~ **with** erfüllen (+acc); entsprechen (+dat).

component [kəm'pəunənt] a Teil-; n Bestandteil m.

compose [kəm'pəuz] vt (arrange) zusammensetzen; music komponieren; poetry schreiben; thoughts sammeln; features beherrschen; ~**d** a ruhig, gefaßt; **to be** ~**d of** bestehen aus; ~**r** Komponist(in f) m.

composite ['kompəzıt] a zusammengesetzt.

composition [kompə'zıʃən] n (Mus) Komposition f; (Sch) Aufsatz m; (composing) Zusammensetzung f, Gestaltung f; (structure) Zusammensetzung f, Aufbau m.

compositor [kəm'pozıtə*] n Schriftsetzer m.

compos mentis ['kompos'mentıs] a klar im Kopf.

compost ['kompost] n Kompost m; ~ **heap** Komposthaufen m.

composure [kəm'pəuʒə*] n Gelassenheit f, Fassung f.

compound ['kompaund] n (Chem) Verbindung f; (mixture) Gemisch nt; (enclosure) eingezäunte(s) Gelände nt; (Ling) Kompositum nt; a zusammengesetzt; ~ **fracture** komplizierte(r) Bruch m; ~ **interest** Zinseszinsen pl.

comprehend [komprı'hend] vt begreifen; (include) umfassen, einschließen.

comprehension [komprı'henʃən] n Fassungskraft f, Verständnis nt.

comprehensive [komprı'hensıv] a umfassend; ~ **school** Gesamtschule f.

compress [kəm'pres] vt zusammendrücken, komprimieren; ['kompres] (Med) Kompresse f, Umschlag m; ~**ion** [kəm'preʃən] Komprimieren nt.

comprise [kəm'praız] vt (also be ~**d of**) umfassen, bestehen aus.

compromise ['komprəmaız] n Kompromiß m, Verständigung f; vt reputation kompromittieren; vi einen Kompromiß schließen.

compulsion [kəm'pʌlʃən] n Zwang m.

compulsive [kəm'pʌlsıv] a Gewohnheits-.

compulsory [kəm'pʌlsərı] a (obligatory) obligatorisch, Pflicht-.

computer [kəm'pjuːtə*] n Computer m, Rechner m.

comrade ['komrıd] n Kamerad m; (Pol) Genosse m; ~**ship** Kameradschaft f.

concave ['kon'keıv] a konkav, hohlgeschliffen.

conceal [kən'siːl] vt secret verschweigen; **to** ~ **o.s.** sich verbergen.

concede [kən'siːd] vt (grant) gewähren; point zugeben; vi (admit) zugeben.

conceit [kən'siːt] n Eitelkeit f, Einbildung f; ~**ed** a eitel, eingebildet.

conceivable [kən'siːvəbl] a vorstellbar.

conceive [kən'siːv] vt idea ausdenken; imagine sich vorstellen; , vti baby empfangen.

concentrate ['konsəntreıt] vi sich konzentrieren (on auf +acc); vt (gather) konzentrieren.

concentration [konsən'treıʃən] n Konzentration f; ~ **camp** Konzentrationslager nt, KZ nt.

concentric [kon'sentrık] a konzentrisch.

concept ['konsept] n Begriff m; ~**ion** [kon'sepʃən] (idea) Vorstellung f; (Physiol) Empfängnis f.

concern [kən'sɜːn] n (affair) Angelegenheit f; (Comm) Unternehmen nt, Konzern m; (worry) Sorge f, Unruhe f; vt (interest) angehen; (be about) handeln von; (have connection with) betreffen; ~**ed** a (anxious) besorgt; ~**ing** prep betreffend, hinsichtlich (+gen).

concert ['konsət] n Konzert nt; **in** ~ (**with**) im Einverständnis (mit); ~**ed** [kən'sɜːtıd] a gemeinsam; (Fin) konzertiert; ~ **hall** Konzerthalle f.

concertina [konsə'tiːnə] n Handharmonika f.

concerto [kən'tʃɑːtəu] n Konzert nt.

concession [kən'seʃən] n (yielding) Zugeständnis nt; (right to do sth) Genehmigung f.

conciliation [kənsılı'eıʃən] n Versöhnung f; (official) Schlichtung f.

conciliatory [kən'sılıətrı] a vermittelnd; versöhnlich.

concise [kən'saıs] a knapp, gedrängt.

conclave ['konkleıv] n Konklave nt.

conclude [kən'kluːd] vt (end) beenden; treaty (ab)schließen; (decide) schließen, folgern; vi (finish) schließen.

conclusion [kən'kluːʒən] n (Ab)schluß m; **in** ~ zum Schluß, schließlich.

conclusive [kən'kluːsıv] a überzeugend, schlüssig; ~**ly** ad endgültig.

concoct [kən'kokt] vt zusammenbrauen.

concord ['konkɔːd] n Eintracht f.

concourse ['konkɔːs] n (Bahnhofs)halle f, Vorplatz m.

concrete ['konkriːt] n Beton m; a konkret.

concur [kən'kɜː*] vi übereinstimmen.

concurrently [kən'kʌrəntlı] ad gleichzeitig.

concussion [kon'kʌʃən] n (Gehirn)erschütterung f.

condemn [kən'dem] vt verdammen; (Jur) verurteilen; building abbruchreif erklären; ~**ation** [kondem'neıʃən] Verurteilung f; (of object) Verwerfung f.

condensation [konden'seıʃən] n Kondensation f.

condense [kən'dens] vi (Chem) kondensieren; *vt* (*fig*) zusammendrängen; ~**d milk** Kondensmilch *f*.

condescend [kɒndɪ'send] *vi* sich herablassen; ~**ing** *a* herablassend.

condition [kən'dɪʃən] *n* (*state*) Zustand *m*, Verfassung *f*; (*presupposition*) Bedingung *f*; *vt* *hair etc* behandeln; (*regulate*) regeln; **on ~ that . . .** unter der Bedingung, daß . . .; ~**ed to** gewöhnt an (+*acc*); ~**ed reflex** bedingter Reflex; ~**s** *pl* (*circumstances*, *weather*) Verhältnisse *f*; ~**al** *a* bedingt; (*Gram*) Bedingungs-.

condolences [kən'dəʊlənsɪz] *npl* Beileid *nt*.

condone [kən'dəʊn] *vt* gutheißen.

conducive [kən'djuːsɪv] *a* dienlich (*to dat*).

conduct ['kɒndʌkt] *n* (*behaviour*) Verhalten *nt*; (*management*) Führung *f*; [kən'dʌkt] *vt* führen, leiten; (*Mus*) dirigieren; ~**ed tour** Führung *f*; ~**or** [kən'dʌktə*] (*of orchestra*) Dirigent *m*; (*in bus*) Schaffner *m*; ~**ress** [kən'dʌktrɪs] (*in bus*) Schaffnerin *f*.

conduit ['kɒndɪt] *n* (*water*) Rohrleitung *f*; (*Elec*) Isolierrohr *nt*.

cone [kəʊn] *n* (*Math*) Kegel *m*; (*for ice cream*) (Waffel)tüte *f*; (*fir*) Tannenzapfen *m*.

confectioner [kən'fekʃənə*] *n* Konditor *m*; ~**'s** (**shop**) Konditorei *f*; ~**y** (*cakes*) Konfekt *nt*, Konditorwaren *pl*; (*sweets*) Süßigkeiten *pl*.

confederation [kənfedə'reɪʃən] *n* Bund *m*.

confer [kən'fɜː*] *vt* *degree* verleihen; *vi* (*discuss*) konferieren, verhandeln; ~**ence** ['kɒnfərəns] Konferenz *f*.

confess [kən'fes] *vti* gestehen; (*Eccl*) beichten; ~**ion** [kən'feʃən] Geständnis *nt*; (*Eccl*) Beichte *f*; ~**ional** [kən'feʃənl] Beichtstuhl *m*; ~**or** (*Eccl*) Beichtvater *m*.

confetti [kən'fetɪ] *n* Konfetti *nt*.

confide [kən'faɪd] *vi*: ~ **in** (sich) anvertrauen (+*dat*); (*trust*) vertrauen (+*dat*); ~**nce** ['kɒnfɪdəns] Vertrauen *nt*; (*assurance*) Selbstvertrauen *nt*; (*secret*) vertrauliche Mitteilung *f*, Geheimnis *nt*; ~**nce trick** ['kɒnfɪdənstrɪk] Schwindel *m*.

confident ['kɒnfɪdənt] *a* (*sure*) überzeugt; sicher; (*self-assured*) selbstsicher; ~**ial** [kɒnfɪ'denʃəl] *a* (*secret*) vertraulich, geheim; (*trusted*) Vertrauens-.

confine [kən'faɪn] *vt* (*limit*) begrenzen, einschränken; (*lock up*) einsperren; ~**s** ['kɒnfaɪnz] *pl* Grenze *f*; ~**d** *a space* eng, begrenzt; ~**ment** (*of room*) Beengtheit *f*; (*in prison*) Haft *f*; (*Med*) Wochenbett *nt*.

confirm [kən'fɜːm] *vt* bestätigen; ~**ation** [kɒnfə'meɪʃən] Bestätigung *f*; (*Rel*) Konfirmation *f*; ~**ed** *a* unverbesserlich, hartnäckig; *bachelor* eingefleischt.

confiscate ['kɒnfɪskeɪt] *vt* beschlagnahmen, konfiszieren.

confiscation [kɒnfɪs'keɪʃən] *n* Beschlagnahme *f*.

conflagration [kɒnflə'greɪʃən] *n* Feuersbrunst *f*.

conflict ['kɒnflɪkt] *n* Kampf *m*; (*of words*, *opinions*) Konflikt *m*, Streit *m*; [kən'flɪkt] *vi* im Widerspruch stehen; ~**ing** [kən'flɪktɪŋ] *a* gegensätzlich; *testimony* sich widersprechend.

conform [kən'fɔːm] *vi* sich anpassen (*to dat*); (*to rules*) sich fügen (*to dat*); (*to general trends*) sich richten (*to* nach); ~**ist** Konformist(in *f*) *m*.

confront [kən'frʌnt] *vt* *enemy* entgegentreten (+*dat*); *sb with sth* konfrontieren; *sb with sb* gegenüberstellen (*with dat*); ~**ation** [kɒnfrən'teɪʃən] Gegenüberstellung *f*; (*quarrel*) Konfrontation *f*.

confuse [kən'fjuːz] *vt* verwirren; (*sth with sth*) verwechseln.

confusing [kən'fjuːzɪŋ] *a* verwirrend.

confusion [kən'fjuːʒən] *n* (*disorder*) Verwirrung *f*; (*tumult*) Aufruhr *m*; (*embarrassment*) Bestürzung *f*.

congeal [kən'dʒiːl] *vi* (*freeze*) gefrieren; (*clot*) gerinnen.

congenial [kən'dʒiːnɪəl] *a* (*agreeable*) angenehm.

congenital [kən'dʒenɪtəl] *a* angeboren.

conger eel ['kɒŋgər'iːl] *n* Meeraal *m*.

congested [kən'dʒestɪd] *a* überfüllt.

congestion [kən'dʒestʃən] *n* Stauung *f*; Stau *m*.

conglomeration [kənglɒmə'reɪʃən] *n* Anhäufung *f*.

congratulate [kən'grætjuleɪt] *vt* beglückwünschen (*on zu*).

congratulations [kən'grætju'leɪʃənz] *npl* Glückwünsche *pl*; ~**!** gratuliere!, herzlichen Glückwunsch!

congregate ['kɒŋgrɪgeɪt] *vi* sich versammeln.

congregation [kɒŋgrɪ'geɪʃən] *n* Gemeinde *f*.

congress ['kɒŋgres] *n* Kongreß *m*; ~**ional** [kən'greʃənl] *a* Kongreß-; ~**man** (*US*) Mitglied *nt* des amerikanischen Repräsentantenhauses.

conical ['kɒnɪkəl] *a* kegelförmig, konisch.

conifer ['kɒnɪfə*] *n* Nadelbaum *m*; ~**ous** [kə'nɪfərəs] *a* zapfentragend.

conjecture [kən'dʒektʃə*] *n* Vermutung *f*; *vti* vermuten.

conjugal ['kɒndʒʊgəl] *a* ehelich.

conjunction [kən'dʒʌŋkʃən] *n* Verbindung *f*; (*Gram*) Konjunktion *f*, Verbindungswort *nt*.

conjunctivitis [kəndʒʌŋktɪ'vaɪtɪs] *n* Bindehautentzündung *f*.

conjure ['kʌndʒə*] *vti* zaubern; ~ **up** *vt* heraufbeschwören; ~**r** Zauberer *m*; (*entertainer*) Zauberkünstler(in *f*) *m*.

conjuring ['kʌndʒərɪŋ] *n*: ~ **trick** Zauberkunststück *nt*.

conk [kɒŋk]: ~ **out** *vi* (*col*) stehenbleiben, streiken.

connect [kə'nekt] *vt* verbinden; *train* koppeln; ~**ion** [kə'nekʃən] Verbindung *f*; (*relation*) Zusammenhang *m*; **in** ~**ion with** in Verbindung mit.

connexion [kə'nekʃən] *n* = **connection**.

connoisseur [kɒnɪ'sɜː*] *n* Kenner *m*.

connotation [kɒnə'teɪʃən] *n* Konnotation *f*.

conquer ['kɒŋkə*] *vt* (*overcome*) überwinden, besiegen; (*Mil*) besiegen; *vi* siegen; ~**or** Eroberer *m*.

conquest ['kɒŋkwest] *n* Eroberung *f*.

conscience ['kɒnʃəns] *n* Gewissen *nt*.

conscientious [kɒnʃɪ'enʃəs] a gewissenhaft; ~ **objector** Wehrdienstverweigerer m (aus Gewissensgründen).

conscious ['kɒnʃəs] a bewußt; (Med) bei Bewußtsein; ~**ness** Bewußtsein nt.

conscript ['kɒnskrɪpt] n Wehrpflichtige(r) m; ~ **ion** [kən'skrɪpʃən] Wehrpflicht f.

consecrate ['kɒnsɪkreɪt] vt weihen.

consecutive [kən'sekjʊtɪv] a aufeinanderfolgend.

consensus [kən'sensəs] n allgemeine Übereinstimmung f.

consent [kən'sent] n Zustimmung f; vi zustimmen (to dat).

consequence ['kɒnsɪkwəns] n (importance) Bedeutung f, Konsequenz f; (result, effect) Wirkung f.

consequently ['kɒnsɪkwəntlɪ] ad folglich.

conservation [kɒnsə'veɪʃən] n Erhaltung f, Schutz m.

conservative [kən'sɜːvətɪv] a konservativ; (cautious) mäßig, vorsichtig; **C**~ a party konservativ; n Konservative(r) mf.

conservatory [kən'sɜːvətrɪ] n (greenhouse) Gewächshaus nt; (room) Wintergarten m.

conserve [kən'sɜːv] vt erhalten.

consider [kən'sɪdə*] vt überlegen; (take into account) in Betracht ziehen; (regard) halten für; ~**able** a beträchtlich; ~**ate** a rücksichtsvoll, aufmerksam; ~**ation** [kənsɪdə'reɪʃən] Rücksicht(nahme) f; (thought) Erwägung f; (reward) Entgelt nt; ~**ing** prep in Anbetracht (+gen); cj da; **on no** ~**ation** unter keinen Umständen.

consign [kən'saɪn] vt übergeben; ~**ment** (of goods) Sendung f, Lieferung f.

consist [kən'sɪst] vi bestehen (of aus).

consistency [kən'sɪstənsɪ] n (of material) Festigkeit f; (of argument) Folgerichtigkeit f; (of person) Konsequenz f.

consistent [kən'sɪstənt] a gleichbleibend, stetig; argument folgerichtig; **she's not** ~ sie ist nicht konsequent.

consolation [kɒnsə'leɪʃən] n Trost m; ~ **prize** Trostpreis m.

console [kən'səʊl] vt trösten.

consolidate [kən'sɒlɪdeɪt] vt festigen.

consommé [kən'sɒmeɪ] n Fleischbrühe f.

consonant ['kɒnsənənt] n Konsonant m, Mitlaut m.

consortium [kən'sɔːtɪəm] n Gruppe f, Konsortium nt.

conspicuous [kən'spɪkjʊəs] a (prominent) auffallend; (visible) deutlich, sichtbar.

conspiracy [kən'spɪrəsɪ] n Verschwörung f, Komplott nt.

conspire [kən'spaɪə*] vi sich verschwören.

constable ['kʌnstəbl] n Polizist(in f) m.

constabulary [kən'stæbjʊlərɪ] n Polizei f.

constancy ['kɒnstənsɪ] n Beständigkeit f, Treue f.

constant ['kɒnstənt] a dauernd; ~**ly** ad (continually) andauernd; (faithfully) treu, unwandelbar.

constellation [kɒnstə'leɪʃən] n (temporary) Konstellation f; (permanent) Sternbild nt.

consternation [kɒnstə'neɪʃən] n (dismay) Bestürzung f.

constipated ['kɒnstɪpeɪtəd] a verstopft.

constipation [kɒnstɪ'peɪʃən] n Verstopfung f.

constituency [kən'stɪtjʊənsɪ] n Wahlkreis m.

constituent [kən'stɪtjʊənt] n (person) Wähler m; (part) Bestandteil m.

constitute ['kɒnstɪtjuːt] vt ausmachen.

constitution [kɒnstɪ'tjuːʃən] n Verfassung f; ~**al** a Verfassungs-; monarchy konstitutionell.

constrain [kən'streɪn] vt zwingen; ~**t** Zwang m; (Psych) Befangenheit f.

constrict [kən'strɪkt] vt zusammenziehen; ~**ion** [kən'strɪkʃən] Zusammenziehung f; (of chest) Zusammenschnürung f, Beklemmung f.

construct [kən'strʌkt] vt bauen; ~**ion** [kən'strʌkʃən] (action) (Er)bauen nt, Konstruktion f; (building) Bau m; **under** ~**ion** im Bau befindlich; ~**ive** a konstruktiv.

construe [kən'struː] vt (interpret) deuten.

consul ['kɒnsl] n Konsul m; ~**ate** ['kɒnsjʊlət] Konsulat nt.

consult [kən'sʌlt] vt um Rat fragen; doctor konsultieren; book nachschlagen in (+dat); ~**ant** (Med) Facharzt m; (other specialist) Gutachter m; ~**ation** [kɒnsəl'teɪʃən] Beratung f; (Med) Konsultation f; ~**ing room** Sprechzimmer nt.

consume [kən'sjuːm] vt verbrauchen; food verzehren, konsumieren; ~**r** Verbraucher m.

consummate ['kɒnsʌmeɪt] vt vollenden; marriage vollziehen.

consumption [kən'sʌmpʃən] n Verbrauch m; (of food) Konsum m.

contact ['kɒntækt] n (touch) Berührung f; (connection) Verbindung f; (person) Kontakt m, Beziehung f; vt sich in Verbindung setzen mit; ~ **lenses** pl Kontaktlinsen pl.

contagious [kən'teɪdʒəs] a ansteckend.

contain [kən'teɪn] vt enthalten; **to** ~ **o.s.** sich zügeln; ~**er** Behälter m; (transport) Container m.

contaminate [kən'tæmɪneɪt] vt verunreinigen; (germs) infizieren.

contamination [kəntæmɪ'neɪʃən] n Verunreinigung f.

contemplate ['kɒntəmpleɪt] vt (nachdenklich) betrachten; (think about) überdenken; (plan) vorhaben.

contemplation [kɒntəm'pleɪʃən] n Betrachtung f; (Rel) Meditation f.

contemporary [kən'tempərərɪ] a zeitgenössisch; n Zeitgenosse m.

contempt [kən'tempt] n Verachtung f; ~**ible** a verächtlich, nichtswürdig; ~**uous** a voller Verachtung (of für).

contend [kən'tend] vt (fight) kämpfen (um); (argue) behaupten; ~**er** (for post) Bewerber(in f) m; (Sport) Wettkämpfer(in f) m.

content [kən'tent] a zufrieden; vt befriedigen; ['kɒntent] n (also ~**s**) Inhalt m; ~**ed** a zufrieden.

contention [kən'tenʃən] n (dispute) Streit

m; (*argument*) Behauptung *f*.

contentment [kən'tentmənt] *n* Zufriedenheit *f*.

contest ['kɒntest] *n* (Wett)kampf *m*; [kən'test] *vt* (*dispute*) bestreiten; (*Pol*) kandidieren (*in dat*); ~**ant** [kən'testənt] Bewerber(in *f*) *m*.

context ['kɒntekst] *n* Zusammenhang *m*.

continent ['kɒntinənt] *n* Kontinent *m*, Festland *nt*; **the C**~ das europäische Festland, der Kontinent; ~**al** [kɒnti'nentl] *a* kontinental; *n* Bewohner(in *f*) *m* des Kontinents.

contingency [kən'tindʒənsi] *n* Möglichkeit *f*.

contingent [kən'tindʒənt] *n* (*Mil*) Kontingent *nt*; *a* abhängig (*upon* von).

continual [kən'tinjuəl] *a* (*endless*) fortwährend; (*repeated*) immer wiederkehrend; ~**ly** *ad* immer wieder.

continuation [kəntinju'eiʃən] *n* Verlängerung *f*; Fortsetzung *f*.

continue [kən'tinju:] *vi* (*go on*) anhalten; (*last*) fortbestehen; **shall we** ~? wollen wir weitermachen?; **if this** ~**s** wenn das so weitergeht; **the rain** ~**d** es regnete weiter; *vt* fortsetzen; **to** ~ **doing sth** fortfahren, etw zu tun.

continuity [kɒnti'njuiti] *n* Kontinuität *nt*; (*wholeness*) Zusammenhang *m*.

continuous [kən'tinjuəs] *a* ununterbrochen.

contort [kən'tɔ:t] *vt* verdrehen; ~**ion** [kən'tɔ:ʃən] Verzerrung *f*; ~**ionist** [kən'tɔ:ʃənist] Schlangenmensch *m*.

contour ['kɒntuə*] *n* Umriß *m*; (*height*) Höhenlinie *f*.

contraband ['kɒntrəbænd] *n* Schmuggelware *f*.

contraception [kɒntrə'sepʃən] *n* Empfängnisverhütung *f*.

contraceptive [kɒntrə'septiv] *n* empfängnisverhütende(s) Mittel *nt*; *a* empfängnisverhütend.

contract ['kɒntrækt] *n* (*agreement*) Vertrag *m*, Kontrakt *m*; [kən'trækt] *vi* (*to do sth*) sich vertraglich verpflichten; (*muscle*) sich zusammenziehen; (*become smaller*) schrumpfen; ~**ion** [kən'trækʃən] (*shortening*) Verkürzung *f*; ~**or** [kən'træktə*] Unternehmer *m*; (*supplier*) Lieferant *m*.

contradict [kɒntrə'dikt] *vt* widersprechen (+*dat*); ~**ion** [kɒntrə'dikʃən] Widerspruch *m*.

contralto [kən'træltəu] *n* (tiefe) Altstimme *f*.

contraption [kən'træpʃən] *n* (*col*) komische Konstruktion *f*, komische(s) Ding *nt*.

contrary ['kɒntrəri] *a* entgegengesetzt; *wind* ungünstig, Gegen-; (*obstinate*) widerspenstig, eigensinnig; *n* Gegenteil *nt*; **on the** ~ im Gegenteil.

contrast ['kɒntrɑ:st] *n* Kontrast *m*; [kən'trɑ:st] *vt* entgegensetzen; ~**ing** [kən'trɑ:stiŋ] *a* Kontrast-.

contravene [kɒntrə'vi:n] *vt* verstoßen gegen.

contribute [kən'tribju:t] *vti* beitragen; *money* spenden.

contribution [kɒntri'bju:ʃən] *n* Beitrag *m*.

contributor [kən'tribjutə*] *n* Beitragende(r) *mf*.

contrite ['kɒntrait] *a* zerknirscht.

contrivance [kən'traivəns] *n* Vorrichtung *f*, Kniff *m*, Erfindung *f*.

contrive [kən'traiv] *vt* zustande bringen; **to** ~ **to do sth** es schaffen, etw zu tun.

control [kən'trəul] *vt* (*direct, test*) kontrollieren; *n* Kontrolle *f*; (*business*) Leitung *f*; ~**s** *pl* (*of vehicle*) Steuerung *f*; (*of engine*) Schalttafel *f*; ~ **point** Kontrollstelle *f*; **out of** ~ außer Kontrolle; **under** ~ unter Kontrolle.

controversial [kɒntrə'vɜ:ʃəl] *a* umstritten, kontrovers.

controversy ['kɒntrəvɜ:si] *n* Meinungsstreit *m*, Kontroverse *f*.

convalesce [kɒnvə'les] *vi* gesund werden; ~**nce** Genesung *f*; ~**nt** *a* auf dem Wege der Besserung; *n* Genesende(r) *mf*.

convector [kən'vektə*] *n* Heizlüfter *m*.

convene [kən'vi:n] *vt* zusammenrufen; *vi* sich versammeln.

convenience [kən'vi:niəns] *n* Annehmlichkeit *f*; (*thing*) bequeme Einrichtung *f*; **public**.

convenient [kən'vi:niənt] *a* günstig.

convent ['kɒnvənt] *n* Kloster *nt*.

convention [kən'venʃən] *n* Versammlung *f*; (*Pol*) Übereinkunft *f*; (*custom*) Konvention *f*; ~**al** *a* herkömmlich, konventionell.

converge [kən'vɜ:dʒ] *vi* zusammenlaufen.

conversant [kən'vɜ:sənt] *a* vertraut; (*in learning*) bewandert (*with* in +*dat*).

conversation [kɒnvə'seiʃən] *n* Unterhaltung *f*; ~**al** *a* Unterhaltungs-.

converse [kən'vɜ:s] *vi* sich unterhalten; ['kɒnvɜ:s] *a* gegenteilig; ~**ly** [kɒn'vɜ:sli] *ad* umgekehrt.

conversion [kən'vɜ:ʃən] *n* Umwandlung *f*; (*esp Rel*) Bekehrung *f*; ~ **table** Umrechnungstabelle *f*.

convert [kən'vɜ:t] *vt* (*change*) umwandeln; (*Rel*) bekehren; ['kɒnvɜ:t] *n* Bekehrte(r) *mf*, Konvertit(in *f*) *m*; ~**ible** (*Aut*) Kabriolett *nt*; *a* umwandelbar; (*Fin*) konvertierbar.

convex ['kɒnveks] *a* konvex.

convey [kən'vei] *vt* (*carry*) befördern; *feelings* vermitteln; ~**or belt** Fließband *nt*.

convict [kən'vikt] *vt* verurteilen; ['kɒnvikt] *n* Häftling *m*; ~**ion** [kən'vikʃən] (*verdict*) Verurteilung *f*; (*belief*) Überzeugung *f*.

convince [kən'vins] *vt* überzeugen.

convincing [kən'vinsiŋ] *a* überzeugend.

convivial [kən'viviəl] *a* festlich, froh.

convoy ['kɒnvɔi] *n* (*of vehicles*) Kolonne *f*; (*protected*) Konvoi *m*.

convulse [kən'vʌls] *vt* zusammenzucken lassen; **to be** ~**d with laughter** sich vor Lachen krümmen.

convulsion [kən'vʌlʃən] *n* (*esp Med*) Zuckung *f*, Krampf *m*.

coo [ku:] *vi* (*dove*) gurren.

cook [kuk] *vti* kochen; *n* Koch *m*, Köchin *f*;

~book Kochbuch nt; ~er Herd m; ~ery Kochkunst f; ~ery book = ~book; ~ie (US) Plätzchen nt; ~ing Kochen nt.

cool [ku:l] a kühl; vti (ab)kühlen; ~ down vti (fig) (sich) beruhigen; ~ing-tower Kühlturm m; ~ness Kühle f; (of temperament) kühle(r) Kopf.

coop [ku:p] n Hühnerstall m; vt: ~ up (fig) einpferchen.

co-op ['kəʊɒp] n = cooperative.

cooperate [kəʊ'ɒpəreit] vi zusammenarbeiten.

cooperation [kəʊɒpə'reiʃən] n Zusammenarbeit f.

cooperative [kəʊ'ɒpərətiv] a hilfsbereit; (Comm) genossenschaftlich; n (of farmers) Genossenschaft f; (— store) Konsumladen m.

coordinate [kəʊ'ɔːdineit] vt koordinieren.

coordination [kəʊɔː'dineiʃən] n Koordination f.

coot [ku:t] n Wasserhuhn nt.

cop [kɒp] n (col) Polyp m, Bulle m.

cope [kəʊp] vi fertig werden, schaffen (with acc).

co-pilot ['kəʊpailɒt] n Kopilot m.

copious ['kəʊpiəs] a reichhaltig.

copper ['kɒpə*] n Kupfer nt; Kupfermünze f; (col: policeman) Polyp m, Bulle m.

coppice ['kɒpis], copse [kɒps] n Unterholz nt.

copulate ['kɒpjʊleit] vi sich paaren.

copy ['kɒpi] n (imitation) Nachahmung f; (of book etc) Exemplar nt; (of newspaper) Nummer f; vt kopieren, abschreiben; ~cat Nachäffer m; ~right Copyright nt; ~right reserved alle Rechte vorbehalten, Nachdruck verboten.

coral ['kɒrəl] n Koralle f; ~ reef Korallenriff nt.

cord [kɔːd] n Schnur f, Kordel f; see vocal.

cordial ['kɔːdiəl] a herzlich; n Fruchtsaft m; ~ly ad herzlich.

cordon ['kɔːdn] n Absperrkette f.

corduroy ['kɔːdərɔi] n Kord(samt) m.

core [kɔː*] n Kern m; vt entkernen.

cork [kɔːk] n (bark) Korkrinde f; (stopper) Korken m; ~age Korkengeld nt; ~screw Korkenzieher m.

corm [kɔːm] n Knolle f.

cormorant ['kɔːmərənt] n Kormoran m.

corn [kɔːn] n Getreide nt, Korn nt; (US: maize) Mais m; (on foot) Hühnerauge nt.

cornea ['kɔːniə] n Hornhaut f.

corned beef ['kɔːnd'biːf] n Corned Beef nt.

corner ['kɔːnə*] n Ecke f; (nook) Winkel m; (on road) Kurve f; vt in die Enge treiben; vi (Aut) in die Kurve gehen; ~ flag Eckfahne f; ~ kick Eckball m; ~stone Eckstein m.

cornet ['kɔːnit] n (Mus) Kornett nt; (for ice cream) Eistüte f.

cornflour ['kɔːnflaʊə*] n Maizena " nt, Maismehl nt.

cornice ['kɔːnis] n Gesims nt.

cornstarch ['kɔːnstɑːtʃ] n (US) = cornflour.

cornucopia [kɔːnjʊ'kəʊpiə] n Füllhorn nt.

corny ['kɔːni] a joke blöd(e).

corollary [kə'rɒləri] n Folgesatz m.

coronary ['kɒrənəri] a (Med) Koronar-; n Herzinfarkt m; ~ thrombosis Koronarthrombose f.

coronation [kɒrə'neiʃən] n Krönung f.

coroner ['kɒrənə*] n Untersuchungsrichter m und Leichenbeschauer m.

coronet ['kɒrənit] n Adelskrone f.

corporal ['kɔːpərəl] n Obergefreite(r) m; a: ~ punishment Prügelstrafe f.

corporate ['kɔːpərit] a gemeinschaftlich, korporativ.

corporation [kɔːpə'reiʃən] n Gemeinde f, Stadt f; (esp business) Körperschaft f, Aktiengesellschaft f.

corps [kɔː*] n (Armee)korps nt.

corpse [kɔːps] n Leiche f.

corpulent ['kɔːpjʊlənt] a korpulent.

Corpus Christi ['kɔːpəs'kristi] n Fronleichnamsfest nt.

corpuscle ['kɔːpʌsl] n Blutkörperchen nt.

corral [kə'rɑːl] n Pferch m, Korral m.

correct [kə'rekt] a (accurate) richtig; (proper) korrekt; vt mistake berichtigen; pupil tadeln; ~ion [kə'rekʃən] Berichtigung f; ~ly ad richtig; korrekt.

correlate ['kɒrileit] vt aufeinander beziehen; vi korrelieren.

correlation [kɒri'leiʃən] n Wechselbeziehung f.

correspond [kɒris'pɒnd] vi übereinstimmen; (exchange letters) korrespondieren; ~ence (similarity) Entsprechung f; Briefwechsel m, Korrespondenz f; ~ence course Fernkurs m; ~ent (Press) Berichterstatter m; ~ing a entsprechend, gemäß (to dat).

corridor ['kɒridɔː*] n Gang m.

corroborate [kə'rɒbəreit] vt bestätigen, erhärten.

corroboration [kərɒbə'reiʃən] n Bekräftigung f.

corrode [kə'rəʊd] vt zerfressen; vi rosten.

corrosion [kə'rəʊʒən] n Rost m, Korrosion f.

corrugated ['kɒrəgeitid] a gewellt; ~ cardboard Wellpappe f; ~ iron Wellblech nt.

corrupt [kə'rʌpt] a korrupt; vt verderben; (bribe) bestechen; ~ion [kə'rʌpʃən] (of society) Verdorbenheit f; (bribery) Bestechung f.

corset ['kɔːsit] n Korsett nt.

cortège [kɔː'teːʒ] n Zug m; (of funeral) Leichenzug m.

cortisone ['kɔːtizəʊn] n Kortison nt.

cosh [kɒʃ] n Totschläger m; vt über den Schädel hauen.

cosignatory [kəʊ'signətəri] n Mitunterzeichner(in f) m.

cosine ['kəʊsain] n Kosinus m.

cosiness ['kəʊzinis] n Gemütlichkeit f.

cosmetic [kɒz'metik] n Schönheitsmittel nt, kosmetische(s) Mittel nt; a kosmetisch.

cosmic ['kɒzmik] a kosmisch.

cosmonaut ['kɒzmənɔːt] n Kosmonaut(in f) m.

cosmopolitan [kɔzmə'pɔlitən] *a* international; *city* Welt-.

cosmos ['kɔzmɒs] *n* Weltall *nt*, Kosmos *m*.

cost [kɔst] *n* Kosten *pl*, Preis *m*; *vt irreg* kosten; **it ~ him his life/job** es kostete ihm sein Leben/seine Stelle; **at all ~s** um jeden Preis; **~ of living** Lebenshaltungskosten *pl*.

co-star ['kəustɑː*] *n* zweite(r) *or* weitere(r) Hauptdarsteller(in *f*) *m*.

costing ['kɔstɪŋ] *n* Kostenberechnung *f*.

costly ['kɔstlɪ] *a* kostspielig.

cost price ['kɔst'praɪs] *n* Selbstkostenpreis *m*.

costume ['kɔstjuːm] *n* Kostüm *nt*; *(fancy dress)* Maskenkostüm *nt*; *(for bathing)* Badeanzug *m*; **~ jewellery** Modeschmuck *m*.

cosy ['kəuzɪ] *a* behaglich, gemütlich.

cot [kɔt] *n* Kinderbett(chen) *nt*.

cottage ['kɔtɪdʒ] *n* kleine(s) Haus *nt* (auf dem Land); **~ cheese** Hüttenkäse *m*.

cotton ['kɔtn] *n* (*material*) Baumwollstoff *m*; *a dress etc* Baumwoll-, Kattun-; **~ wool** Watte *f*.

couch [kautʃ] *n* Couch *f*; *vt* (in Worte) fassen, formulieren.

cougar ['kuːgə*] *n* Puma *m*.

cough [kɔf] *vi* husten; *n* Husten *m*; **~ drop** Hustenbonbon *nt*.

could [kud] *pt of* **can**; **~n't** = **could not**.

council ['kaunsl] *n* (*of town*) Stadtrat *m*; **~ estate/house** Siedlung *f*/Haus *nt* des sozialen Wohnungsbaus; **~lor** ['kaunslə*] Stadtrat *m*.

counsel ['kaunsl] *n* (*barrister*) Anwalt *m*, Rechtsbeistand *m*; (*advice*) Rat(schlag) *m*; **~lor** Berater *m*.

count [kaunt] *vti* zählen; *vi* (*be important*) zählen, gelten; *vi* (*reckoning*) Abrechnung *f*; (*nobleman*) Graf *m*; **~down** Countdown *m*; **~ on** *vt* zählen auf (+*acc*); **~ up** *vt* zusammenzählen.

counter ['kauntə*] *n* (*in shop*) Ladentisch *m*; (*in café*) Tresen *m*, Theke *f*; (*in bank, post office*) Schalter *m*; *vt* entgegnen; *ad* entgegen; **~act** [kauntə'rækt] *vt* entgegenwirken (+*dat*); **~attack** Gegenangriff *m*; **~balance** *vt* aufwiegen; **~clockwise** *ad* entgegen dem Uhrzeigersinn; **~espionage** Spionageabwehr *f*; **~feit** Fälschung *f*; *vt* fälschen; *a* gefälscht, unecht; **~foil** (Control)abschnitt *m*; **~part** (*object*) Gegenstück *nt*; (*person*) Gegenüber *nt*.

countess ['kauntɪs] *n* Gräfin *f*.

countless ['kauntlɪs] *a* zahllos, unzählig.

countrified ['kʌntrɪfaɪd] *a* ländlich.

country ['kʌntrɪ] *n* Land *nt*; **in the ~** auf dem Land(e); **~ dancing** Volkstanztanzen *nt*; **~ house** Landhaus *nt*; **~man** (*national*) Landsmann *m*; (*rural*) Bauer *m*; **~side** Landschaft *f*.

county ['kauntɪ] *n* Landkreis *m*; (*Brit*) Grafschaft *f*; **~ town** Kreisstadt *f*.

coup [kuː] *n* Coup *m*; **~ d'état** Staatsstreich *m*, Putsch *m*.

coupé [kuː'peɪ] *n* (*Aut*) Coupé *nt*.

couple ['kʌpl] *n* Paar *nt*; **a ~ of** ein paar; *vt* koppeln.

couplet ['kʌplɪt] *n* Reimpaar *nt*.

coupling ['kʌplɪŋ] *n* Kupplung *f*.

coupon ['kuːpɔn] *n* Gutschein *m*.

courage ['kʌrɪdʒ] *n* Mut *m*; **~ous** [kə'reɪdʒəs] *a* mutig.

courier ['kurɪə*] *n* (*for holiday*) Reiseleiter *m*; (*messenger*) Kurier *m*, Eilbote *m*.

course [kɔːs] *n* (*race*) Strecke *f*, Bahn *f*; (*of stream*) Lauf *m*; (*of action*) Richtung *f*; (*of lectures*) Vortragsreihe *f*; (*of study*) Studiengang *m*; **summer ~** Sommerkurs *m*; (*Naut*) Kurs *m*; (*in meal*) Gang *m*; **of ~** natürlich; **in the ~ of** im Laufe (+*gen*); **in due ~** zu gegebener Zeit; *see* **golf**.

court [kɔːt] *n* (*royal*) Hof *m*; (*Jur*) Gericht *nt*; *vt* gehen mit; *see* **tennis**.

courteous ['kɜːtɪəs] *a* höflich, zuvorkommend.

courtesan [kɔːtɪ'zæn] *n* Kurtisane *f*.

courtesy ['kɜːtəsɪ] *n* Höflichkeit *f*.

courthouse ['kɔːthaus] *n* (*US*) Gerichtsgebäude *nt*.

courtier ['kɔːtɪə*] *n* Höfling *m*.

court-martial ['kɔːt'mɑːʃəl] *n* Kriegsgericht *nt*; *vt* vor ein Kriegsgericht stellen.

courtroom ['kɔːtrum] *n* Gerichtssaal *m*.

courtyard ['kɔːtjɑːd] *n* Hof *m*.

cousin ['kʌzn] *n* Cousin *m*, Vetter *m*; Kusine *f*.

cove [kəuv] *n* kleine Bucht *f*.

covenant ['kʌvənənt] *n* feierliche(s) Abkommen *nt*.

cover ['kʌvə*] *vt* (*spread over*) bedecken; (*shield*) abschirmen; (*include*) sich erstrecken über (+*acc*); (*protect*) decken; (*lid*) Deckel *m*; (*for bed*) Decke *f*; (*Mil*) Bedeckung *f*; **~age** ['kʌvrɪdʒ] (*Press*) (*reports*) Berichterstattung *f*; (*distribution*) Verbreitung *f*; **~ charge** Bedienungsgeld *nt*; **~ing** Bedeckung *f*; **~ing letter** Begleitbrief *m*.

covet ['kʌvɪt] *vt* begehren.

covetous ['kʌvɪtəs] *a* begehrlich.

cow [kau] *n* Kuh *f*.

coward ['kauəd] *n* Feigling *m*; **~ice** ['kauədɪs] Feigheit *f*; **~ly** *a* feige.

cowboy ['kaubɔɪ] *n* Cowboy *m*.

cower ['kauə*] *vi* kauern; (*movement*) sich kauern.

co-worker ['kəu'wɜːkə*] *n* Mitarbeiter(in *f*) *m*.

cowshed ['kaufed] *n* Kuhstall *m*.

coxswain ['kɔksn] *n* (*abbr* **cox**) Steuermann *m*.

coy [kɔɪ] *a* schüchtern; *girl* spröde.

coyote [kɔɪ'əutɪ] *n* Präriewolf *m*.

crab [kræb] *n* Krebs *m*; **~apple** Holzapfel *m*.

crack [kræk] *n* Riß *m*, Sprung *m*; (*noise*) Knall *m*; *vt* (*break*) springen lassen; (*joke*) reißen; *vi* (*noise*) krachen, knallen; *a* erstklassig; *troops* Elite-; **~er** (*firework*) Knallkörper *m*, Kracher *m*; (*biscuit*) Keks *m*; (*Christmas ~*) Knallbonbon *m*; **~ up** *vi* (*fig*) zusammenbrechen.

crackle ['krækl] *vi* knistern; (*fire*) prasseln.

crackling ['kræklɪŋ] *n* Knistern *n*; (*rind*) Kruste *f* (des Schweinebratens).

cradle ['kreɪdl] n Wiege f.

craft [krɑ:ft] n (skill) (Hand- or Kunst-)fertigkeit f; (trade) Handwerk nt; (cunning) Verschlagenheit f; (Naut) Fahrzeug nt, Schiff nt; ~**sman** gelernte(r) Handwerker m; ~**smanship** (quality) handwerkliche Ausführung f; (ability) handwerkliche(s) Können nt; ~**y** a schlau, gerieben.

crag [kræg] n Klippe f; ~**gy** a schroff, felsig.

cram [kræm] vt vollstopfen; (col) (teach) einpauken; vi (learn) pauken.

cramp [kræmp] n Krampf m; vt (hinder) einengen, hemmen.

crampon ['kræmpɒn] n Steigeisen nt.

cranberry ['krænbərɪ] n Preiselbeere f.

crane [kreɪn] n (machine) Kran m; (bird) Kranich m.

cranium ['kreɪnɪəm] n Schädel m.

crank [kræŋk] n (lever) Kurbel f; (person) Spinner m; vt ankurbeln; ~**shaft** Kurbelwelle f.

cranky ['kræŋkɪ] a verschroben.

cranny ['krænɪ] n Ritze f.

crap [kræp] n (col) Mist m, Scheiße f.

craps [kræps] n (US) Würfelspiel nt.

crash [kræʃ] n (noise) Krachen nt; (with cars) Zusammenstoß m; (with plane) Absturz m; vi stürzen; (cars) zusammenstoßen; (plane) abstürzen; (economy) zusammenbrechen; (noise) knallen; a course Schnell-; ~ **helmet** Sturzhelm m; ~ **landing** Bruchlandung f.

crass [kræs] a kraß.

crate [kreɪt] n (lit, fig) Kiste f.

crater ['kreɪtə*] n Krater m.

cravat(e) [krə'væt] n Krawatte f.

crave [kreɪv] vi verlangen (for nach).

craving ['kreɪvɪŋ] n Verlangen nt.

crawl [krɔ:l] vi kriechen; (baby) krabbeln; n Kriechen nt; (swim) Kraul nt.

crayon ['kreɪən] n Buntstift m.

craze [kreɪz] n Fimmel m.

crazy ['kreɪzɪ] a (foolish) verrückt; (insane) wahnsinnig; (eager for) versessen (auf +acc); ~ **paving** Mosaikpflaster m.

creak [kri:k] n Knarren nt; vi quietschen, knarren.

cream [kri:m] n (from milk) Rahm m, Sahne f; (polish, cosmetic) Creme f; (colour) Cremefarbe f; (fig: people) Elite f; ~ **cake** (small) Sahnetörtchen nt; (big) Sahnekuchen m; ~ **cheese** Rahmquark m; ~**ery** Molkerei f; ~**y** a sahnig.

crease [kri:s] n Falte f; vt falten; (untidy) zerknittern.

create [kri'eɪt] vt erschaffen; (cause) verursachen.

creation [kri'eɪʃən] n Schöpfung f.

creative [kri'eɪtɪv] a schöpferisch, kreativ.

creator [kri'eɪtə*] n Schöpfer m.

creature ['kri:tʃə*] n Geschöpf nt.

credence ['kri:dəns] n Glauben m.

credentials [krɪ'denʃəlz] npl Beglaubigungsschreiben nt.

credibility [kredɪ'bɪlɪtɪ] n Glaubwürdigkeit f.

credible ['kredɪbl] a person glaubwürdig; story glaubhaft.

credit ['kredɪt] n (Comm) Kredit m; Guthaben nt; vt Glauben schenken (+dat); to sb's ~ zu jds Ehre; ~**s** pl (of film) die Mitwirkenden; ~**able** a rühmlich; ~ **card** Kreditkarte m; ~**or** Gläubiger m.

credulity [krɪ'dju:lɪtɪ] n Leichtgläubigkeit f.

creed [kri:d] n Glaubensbekenntnis nt.

creek [kri:k] n (inlet) kleine Bucht f; (US: river) kleine(r) Wasserlauf m.

creep [kri:p] vi irreg kriechen; ~**er** Kletterpflanze f; ~**y** a (frightening) gruselig.

cremate [krɪ'meɪt] vt einäschern.

cremation [krɪ'meɪʃən] n Einäscherung f.

crematorium [kremə'tɔ:rɪəm] n Krematorium nt.

creosote ['krɪəsəʊt] n Kreosot nt.

crepe [kreɪp] n Krepp m; ~ **bandage** Elastikbinde f.

crescent ['kresnt] n (of moon) Halbmond m.

cress [kres] n Kresse f.

crest [krest] n (of cock) Kamm m; (of wave) Wellenkamm m; (coat of arms) Wappen nt; ~**fallen** a niedergeschlagen.

cretin ['kretɪn] n Idiot m.

crevasse [krɪ'væs] n Gletscherspalte f.

crevice ['krevɪs] n Riß m; (in rock) Felsspalte f.

crew [kru:] n Besatzung f, Mannschaft f; ~**-cut** Bürstenschnitt m; ~**-neck** runde(r) Ausschnitt m.

crib [krɪb] n (bed) Krippe f; (translation) wortwörtliche Übersetzung f, Klatsche f.

crick [krɪk] n Muskelkrampf m.

cricket ['krɪkɪt] n (insect) Grille f; (game) Kricket nt; ~**er** Kricketspieler m.

crime [kraɪm] n Verbrechen nt.

criminal ['krɪmɪnl] n Verbrecher m; a kriminell, strafbar.

crimp [krɪmp] vt hair drehen.

crimson ['krɪmzn] n Karmesin nt; a leuchtend rot.

cringe [krɪndʒ] vi sich ducken.

crinkle ['krɪŋkl] vt zerknittern; vi knittern.

crinkly ['krɪŋklɪ] a hair kraus.

cripple ['krɪpl] n Krüppel m; vt lahmlegen; (Med) lähmen, verkrüppeln.

crisis ['kraɪsɪs] n Krise f.

crisp [krɪsp] a knusprig; n Chip m.

criss-cross ['krɪskrɒs] a gekreuzt, Kreuz-.

criterion [kraɪ'tɪərɪən] n Kriterium nt.

critic ['krɪtɪk] n Kritiker(in f) m; ~**al** a kritisch; ~**ally** ad kritisch; ill gefährlich; ~**ism** ['krɪtɪsɪzəm] Kritik f; ~**ize** ['krɪtɪsaɪz] vt kritisieren; (comment) beurteilen.

croak [krəʊk] vi krächzen; (frog) quaken; n Krächzen nt; Quaken nt.

crochet ['krəʊʃeɪ] n Häkelei f.

crockery ['krɒkərɪ] n Geschirr nt.

crocodile ['krɒkədaɪl] n Krokodil nt.

crocus ['krəʊkəs] n Krokus m.

croft [krɒft] n kleine(s) Pachtgut nt; ~**er** Kleinbauer m.

crony ['krəʊnɪ] n (col) Kumpel m.

crook [kruk] n (criminal) Gauner m, Schwindler m; (stick) Hirtenstab m; ~ed ['krukɪd] a krumm.

crop [krɒp] n (harvest) Ernte f; (col: series) Haufen m; ~ up vi auftauchen; (thing) passieren.

croquet ['krəʊkeɪ] n Krocket nt.

croquette [krɔˈket] n Krokette f.

cross [krɒs] n Kreuz nt; (Biol) Kreuzung f; vt road überqueren; legs übereinander legen; (write) einen Querstrich ziehen; (Biol) kreuzen; cheque als Verrechnungsscheck kennzeichnen; a (annoyed) ärgerlich, böse; ~bar Querstange f; ~breed Kreuzung f; ~country (race) Geländelauf m; ~examination Kreuzverhör nt; ~examine vt ins Kreuzverhör nehmen; ~eyed a: to be ~eyed schielen; ~ing (crossroads) (Straßen)kreuzung f; (of ship) Überfahrt f; (for pedestrians) Fußgängerüberweg m; ~ out vt streichen; to be at ~ purposes reden; von verschiedenen Dingen ~reference Querverweis m; ~roads Straßenkreuzung f; (fig) Scheideweg m; ~section Querschnitt m; ~wind Seitenwind m; ~word (puzzle) Kreuzworträtsel nt.

crotch [krɒtʃ] n Zwickel m; (Anat) Unterleib nt.

crotchet ['krɒtʃɪt] n Viertelnote f.

crotchety ['krɒtʃɪtɪ] a person launenhaft.

crouch [krautʃ] vi hocken.

crouton ['kruːtɔ̃n] n geröstete(r) Brotwürfel m.

crow [krəʊ] n Krähen nt; vi krähen.

crowbar ['krəʊbɑː*] n Stemmeisen nt.

crowd [kraud] n Menge f, Gedränge nt; vt (fill) überfüllen; vi drängen; ~ed a überfüllt.

crown [kraun] n Krone f; (of head, hat) Kopf m; vt krönen; ~ jewels pl Kronjuwelen pl; ~ prince Kronprinz m.

crow's-nest ['krəʊznest] n Krähennest f, Ausguck m.

crucial ['kruːʃəl] a entscheidend.

crucifix ['kruːsɪfɪks] n Kruzifix nt; ~ion [kruːsɪˈfɪkʃən] Kreuzigung f.

crucify ['kruːsɪfaɪ] vt kreuzigen.

crude [kruːd] a (raw) roh; humour, behaviour grob, unfein; ~ly ad grob; ~ness Roheit f.

crudity ['kruːdɪtɪ] n = **crudeness**.

cruel ['kruəl] a grausam; (distressing) schwer; (hard-hearted) hart, gefühllos; ~ty Grausamkeit f.

cruet ['kruːɪt] n Gewürzständer m, Menage f.

cruise [kruːz] n Kreuzfahrt f; vi kreuzen; ~r (Mil) Kreuzer m.

cruising-speed ['kruːzɪŋspiːd] n Reisegeschwindigkeit f.

crumb [krʌm] n Krume f; (fig) Bröckchen nt.

crumble ['krʌmbl] vti zerbröckeln.

crumbly ['krʌmblɪ] a krümelig.

crumpet ['krʌmpɪt] n Tee(pfann)kuchen m.

crumple ['krʌmpl] vt zerknittern.

crunch [krʌntʃ] n Knirschen nt; (fig) der entscheidende Punkt; vt knirschen; ~y a knusprig.

crusade [kruːˈseɪd] n Kreuzzug m; ~r Kreuzfahrer m.

crush [krʌʃ] n Gedränge nt; vt zerdrücken; (rebellion) unterdrücken, niederwerfen; vi (material) knittern; ~ing a überwältigend.

crust [krʌst] n (of bread) Rinde f, Kruste f; (Med) Schorf m.

crutch [krʌtʃ] n Krücke f; see also **crotch**.

crux [krʌks] n (crucial point) der springende Punkt, Haken m (col).

cry [kraɪ] vi (call) ausrufen; (shout) schreien; (weep) weinen; n (call) Schrei m; ~ing a (fig) himmelschreiend; ~ off vi (plötzlich) absagen.

crypt [krɪpt] n Krypta f.

cryptic ['krɪptɪk] a (secret) geheim; (mysterious) rätselhaft.

crystal ['krɪstl] n Kristall m; (glass) Kristallglas nt; (mineral) Bergkristall m; ~clear a kristallklar; ~lize vti (lit) kristallisieren; (fig) klären.

cub [kʌb] n Junge(s) nt; (young Boy Scout) Wölfling m.

cubbyhole ['kʌbɪhəʊl] n Eckchen nt.

cube [kjuːb] n Würfel m; (Math) Kubikzahl f.

cubic ['kjuːbɪk] a würfelförmig; centimetre etc Kubik-.

cubicle ['kjuːbɪkl] n Kabine f.

cubism ['kjuːbɪzəm] n Kubismus m.

cuckoo ['kuku:] n Kuckuck m; ~ clock Kuckucksuhr f.

cucumber ['kjuːkʌmbə*] n Gurke f.

cuddle ['kʌdl] vti herzen, drücken (col); n enge Umarmung f.

cuddly ['kʌdlɪ] a anschmiegsam; teddy zum Drücken.

cudgel ['kʌdʒəl] n Knüppel m.

cue [kjuː] n Wink m; (Theat) Stichwort nt; Billardstock m.

cuff [kʌf] n (of shirt, coat etc) Manschette f; Aufschlag m; (US) = **turn-up**; ~link Manschettenknopf m.

cuisine [kwɪˈziːn] n Kochkunst f, Küche f.

cul-de-sac ['kʌldəsæk] n Sackgasse f.

culinary ['kʌlɪnərɪ] a Koch-.

culminate ['kʌlmɪneɪt] vi gipfeln.

culmination [kʌlmɪˈneɪʃən] n Höhepunkt m.

culpable ['kʌlpəbl] a strafbar, schuldhaft.

culprit ['kʌlprɪt] n Täter m.

cult [kʌlt] n Kult m.

cultivate ['kʌltɪveɪt] vt (Agr) bebauen; mind bilden; ~d a (Agr) bebaut; (cultured) kultiviert.

cultivation [kʌltɪˈveɪʃən] n (Agr) Bebauung f; (of person) Bildung f.

cultural ['kʌltʃərəl] a kulturell, Kultur-.

culture ['kʌltʃə*] n (refinement) Kultur f, Bildung f; (of community) Kultur f; ~d a gebildet, kultiviert.

cumbersome ['kʌmbəsəm] a task beschwerlich; object schwer zu handhaben.

cummberbund ['kʌməbʌnd] n Kummerbund m.

cumulative ['kju:mjulɔtɪv] a gehäuft; **to be ~** sich häufen.

cunning ['kʌnɪŋ] n Verschlagenheit f; a schlau.

cup [kʌp] n Tasse f; (prize) Pokal m; **~board** ['kʌbɔd] Schrank m; **~ final** Meisterschaftsspiel m; **~ful** Tasse(voll) f.

cupola ['kju:pɔlɔ] n Kuppel f.

curable ['kjurɔbɔl] a heilbar.

curator [kju'reɪtɔ*] n Kustos m.

curb [kɜ:b] vt zügeln; n Zaum m; (on spending etc) Einschränkung f.

cure [kjuɔ*] n Heilmittel nt; (process) Heilverfahren nt; **there's no ~ for ...** es gibt kein Mittel gegen ...; vt heilen.

curfew ['kɜ:fju:] n Ausgangssperre f; Sperrstunde f.

curiosity [kjuɔrɪ'ɔsɪtɪ] n Neugier f; (for knowledge) Wißbegierde f; (object) Merkwürdigkeit f.

curious ['kjuɔrɪɔs] a neugierig; (strange) seltsam; **~ly** ad besonders.

curl [kɜ:l] n Locke f; vti locken; **~er** Lockenwickler m.

curlew ['kɜ:lju:] n Brachvogel m.

curly ['kɜ:lɪ] a lockig.

currant ['kʌrɔnt] n Korinthe f; Johannisbeere f.

currency ['kʌrɔnsɪ] n Währung f; (of ideas) Geläufigkeit f.

current ['kʌrɔnt] n Strömung f; a expression gängig, üblich; (issue neueste; **~ account** Girokonto nt; **~ affairs** pl Zeitgeschehen nt; **~ly** ad zur Zeit.

curriculum [kɔ'rɪkjuləm] n Lehrplan m; **~ vitae** Lebenslauf m.

curry ['kʌrɪ] n Currygericht nt; **~ powder** Curry(pulver) nt.

curse [kɜ:s] vi (swear) fluchen (at auf +acc); vt (insult) verwünschen; n Fluch m.

cursory ['kɜ:sɔrɪ] a flüchtig.

curt [kɜ:t] a schroff.

curtail [kɜ:'teɪl] vt abkürzen; rights einschränken.

curtain ['kɜ:tn] n Vorhang m, Gardine f; (Theat) Vorhang m.

curtsy ['kɜ:tsɪ] n Knicks m; vi knicksen.

cushion ['kuʃn] n Kissen nt; vt polstern.

custard ['kʌstɔd] n Vanillesoße f.

custodian [kʌs'tɔudɪɔn] n Kustos m, Verwalter(in f) m.

custody ['kʌstɔdɪ] n Aufsicht f; (police) Polizeigewahrsam m.

custom ['kʌstɔm] n (tradition) Brauch m; (business dealing) Kundschaft f; **~s** (taxes) Einfuhrzoll m; **C~s** Zollamt nt; **~ary** a üblich; **~er** Kunde m, Kundin f; **~-made** a speziell angefertigt; **C~s officer** Zollbeamte(r) mf.

cut [kʌt] vt irreg schneiden; wages kürzen; prices heruntersetzen; **I ~ my hand** ich habe mir in die Hand geschnitten; n Schnitt m; (wound) Schnittwunde f; (in book, income etc) Kürzung f; (share) Anteil m.

cute [kju:t] a reizend, niedlich.

cuticle ['kju:tɪkl] n (on nail) Nagelhaut f.

cutlery ['kʌtlɔrɪ] n Besteck nt.

cutlet ['kʌtlɪt] n (pork) Kotelett nt; (veal) Schnitzel nt.

cutout ['kʌtaut] n (Elec) Sicherung f.

cut-price ['kʌtpraɪs] a verbilligt.

cutting ['kʌtɪŋ] a schneidend; n (from paper) Ausschnitt m.

cyanide ['saɪɔnaɪd] n Zyankali nt.

cybernetics [saɪbɔ'netɪks] n Kybernetik f.

cyclamen ['sɪklɔmɔn] n Alpenveilchen nt.

cycle ['saɪkl] n Fahrrad nt; (series) Reihe f; (of songs) Zyklus m; vi radfahren.

cycling ['saɪklɪŋ] n Radfahren nt; (Sport) Radsport m.

cyclist ['saɪklɪst] n Radfahrer(in f) m.

cyclone ['saɪklɔun] n Zyklon m.

cygnet ['sɪgnɪt] n junge(r) Schwan m.

cylinder ['sɪlɪndɔ*] n Zylinder m; (Tech) Walze f; **~ block** Zylinderblock m; **~ capacity** Zylindervolumen nt, Zylinderinhalt m; **~ head** Zylinderkopf m.

cymbals ['sɪmbɔlz] npl Becken nt.

cynic ['sɪnɪk] n Zyniker(in f) m; **~al** a zynisch; **~ism** Zynismus m.

cypress ['saɪprɪs] n Zypresse f.

cyst [sɪst] n Zyste f.

czar [zɑ:*] n Zar m; **~ina** [zɑ'ri:nɔ] Zarin f.

D

D, d [di:] n D nt, d nt.

dab [dæb] vt wound, paint betupfen; n (little bit) bißchen nt; (of paint) Tupfer m; (smear) Klecks m.

dabble ['dæbl] vi (splash) plätschern; (fig) **to ~ in sth** in etw (dat) machen.

dachshund ['dækshund] n Dackel m.

dad(dy) [dæd, -ɪ] n Papa m, Vati m; **daddy-long-legs** Weberknecht m.

daffodil ['dæfɔdɪl] n Osterglocke f.

daft [dɑ:ft] a (col) blöd(e), doof.

dagger ['dægɔ*] n Dolch m.

dahlia ['deɪlɪɔ] n Dahlie f.

daily ['deɪlɪ] a täglich; n (Press) Tageszeitung f; (woman) Haushaltshilfe f.

dainty ['deɪntɪ] a zierlich; (attractive) reizend.

dairy ['dɛɔrɪ] n (shop) Milchgeschäft nt; (on farm) Molkerei f; a Milch-.

daisy ['deɪzɪ] n Gänseblümchen nt.

dally ['dælɪ] vi tändeln.

dam [dæm] n (Stau)damm m; vt stauen.

damage ['dæmɪdʒ] n Schaden m; vt beschädigen; **~s** (Jur) Schaden(s)ersatz m.

dame [deɪm] n Dame f; (col) Weibsbild nt.

damn [dæm] vt verdammen, verwünschen; a (col) verdammt; **~ it!** verflucht!; **~ing** a vernichtend.

damp [dæmp] a feucht; n Feuchtigkeit f; vt (also **~en**) befeuchten; (discourage) dämpfen; **~ness** Feuchtigkeit f.

damson ['dæmzɔn] n Damaszenerpflaume f.

dance [dɑ:ns] n Tanz m; (party) Tanz(abend) m; vi tanzen; **~ hall** Tanzlokal nt; **~r** Tänzer m.

dancing ['dɑ:nsɪŋ] n Tanzen nt.

dandelion ['dændɪlaɪɔn] n Löwenzahn m.

dandruff ['dændrɔf] n (Kopf)schuppen pl.

dandy ['dændɪ] n Dandy m.

danger ['deɪndʒə*] n Gefahr f; ~! (sign) Achtung!; **in** ~ in Gefahr; **on the** ~-**list** in Lebensgefahr; ~**ous** a, ~**ously** ad gefährlich.

dangle ['dæŋgl] vi baumeln; vt herabhängen lassen.

dapper ['dæpə*] a elegant.

dare [dɛə*] vt herausfordern; vi: ~ **(to) do sth** es wagen, etw zu tun; **I** ~ **say** ich würde sagen.

daring ['dɛərɪŋ] a (audacious) verwegen; (bold) wagemutig; dress gewagt; n Mut m.

dark [dɑːk] a dunkel; (fig) düster, trübe; (deep colour) dunkel-; n Dunkelheit f; **after** ~ nach Anbruch der Dunkelheit; **D**~ **Ages** (finsteres) Mittelalter nt; ~**en** vti verdunkeln; ~**ness** Finsternis nt; ~**room** Dunkelkammer f.

darling ['dɑːlɪŋ] n Liebling m; a lieb.

darn [dɑːn] n Gestopfte(s) nt; vt stopfen.

dart [dɑːt] n (leap) Satz m; (weapon) Pfeil m; vi sausen; ~**s** (game) Pfeilwerfen nt; ~**board** Zielscheibe f.

dash [dæʃ] n Sprung m; (mark) (Gedanken)strich m; vt (lit) schleudern; vi stürzen; ~**board** Armaturenbrett nt; ~**ing** a schneidig.

data ['deɪtə] npl Einzelheiten pl, Daten pl; ~ **processing** Datenverarbeitung f.

date [deɪt] n Datum nt; (for meeting etc) Termin m; (with person) Verabredung f; (fruit) Dattel f; vt letter etc datieren; person gehen mit; ~**d** a altmodisch; ~-**line** Datumsgrenze f.

dative ['deɪtɪv] n Dativ m; a Dativ-.

daub [dɔːb] vt beschmieren; paint schmieren.

daughter ['dɔːtə*] n Tochter f; ~-**in-law** Schwiegertochter f.

daunt [dɔːnt] vt entmutigen.

davenport ['dævnpɔːt] n Sekretär m; (US: sofa) Sofa nt.

dawdle ['dɔːdl] vi trödeln.

dawn [dɔːn] n Morgendämmerung f; vi dämmern; (fig) dämmern (on dat).

day [deɪ] n Tag m; (daylight) Tageslicht nt; ~ **by** ~ Tag für Tag, täglich; **one** ~ eines Tages; ~**break** Tagesanbruch m; ~**dream** n Wachtraum m, Träumerei f; vi irreg (mit offenen Augen) träumen; ~**light** Tageslicht nt; ~**time** Tageszeit f.

daze [deɪz] vt betäuben; n Betäubung f; ~**d** a benommen.

dazzle ['dæzl] vt blenden; n Blenden nt.

deacon ['diːkən] n Diakon m; Kirchenvorsteher m.

dead [ded] a tot, gestorben; (without feeling) gefühllos; (without movement) leer, verlassen; ~ **centre** genau in der Mitte; ad völlig; **the** ~ pl die Toten pl; ~**en** vt pain abtöten; sound ersticken; ~ **end** Sackgasse f; ~ **heat** tote(s) Rennen nt; ~**line** Frist(ablauf) m, Stichtag m; ~**lock** Stillstand m; ~**ly** a tödlich; ~**pan** a undurchdringlich.

deaf [def] a taub; ~-**aid** Hörgerät nt; ~**en** vt taub machen; ~**ening** a ohrenbetäubend; ~**ness** Taubheit f; ~-**mute** Taubstumme(r) m.

deal [diːl] n Geschäft nt; vti irreg austeilen; **a great** ~ **of** sehr viel; **to** ~ **with** person behandeln; department sich befassen mit; ~**er** (Comm) Händler m; (Cards) Kartengeber m; ~**ings** pl (Fin) Geschäfte pl; (relations) Beziehungen pl, Geschäftsverkehr m.

dean [diːn] n (Protestant) Superintendent m; (Catholic) Dechant m; (Univ) Dekan m.

dear [dɪə*] a lieb; (expensive) teuer; n Liebling m; ~ **me!** du liebe Zeit!; **D**~ **Sir** Sehr geehrter Herr!; **D**~ **John** Lieber John!; ~**ly** ad love herzlich; pay teuer.

dearth [dɜːθ] n Mangel m (of an +dat).

death [deθ] n Tod m; (end) Ende nt; (statistic) Sterbefall m; ~-**bed** Sterbebett nt; ~ **certificate** Totenschein m; ~ **duties** (Brit) Erbschaftssteuer f; ~**ly** a totenähnlich, Toten-; ~ **penalty** Todesstrafe f; ~ **rate** Sterblichkeitsziffer f.

debar [dɪ'bɑː*] vt ausschließen.

debase [dɪ'beɪs] vt entwerten.

debatable [dɪ'beɪtəbl] a anfechtbar.

debate [dɪ'beɪt] n Debatte f, Diskussion f; vt debattieren, diskutieren; (consider) überlegen.

debauched [dɪ'bɔːtʃt] a ausschweifend.

debauchery [dɪ'bɔːtʃərɪ] n Ausschweifungen pl.

debit ['debɪt] n Schuldposten m; vt belasten.

debris ['debriː] n Trümmer pl.

debt [det] n Schuld f; **to be in** ~ verschuldet sein; ~**or** Schuldner m.

début ['deɪbuː] n Debüt nt.

decade [dekeɪd] n Jahrzehnt nt.

decadence ['dekədəns] n Verfall m, Dekadenz f.

decadent ['dekədənt] a dekadent.

decanter [dɪ'kæntə*] n Karaffe f.

decarbonize [diː'kɑːbənaɪz] vt entkohlen.

decay [dɪ'keɪ] n Verfall m; vi verfallen; teeth, meat etc faulen; leaves etc verrotten.

decease [dɪ'siːs] n Hinscheiden nt; ~**d** verstorben.

deceit [dɪ'siːt] n Betrug m; ~**ful** a falsch.

deceive [dɪ'siːv] vt täuschen.

decelerate [diː'seləreɪt] vti (sich) verlangsamen, die Geschwindigkeit verringern.

December [dɪ'sembə*] n Dezember m.

decency ['diːsənsɪ] n Anstand m.

decent [diːsənt] a (respectable) anständig; (pleasant) annehmbar.

decentralization [diːsentrəlaɪ'zeɪʃən] n Dezentralisierung f.

deception [dɪ'sepʃən] n Betrug m.

deceptive [dɪ'septɪv] a täuschend, irreführend.

decibel ['desɪbel] n Dezibel nt.

decide [dɪ'saɪd] vt entscheiden; vi sich entscheiden; **to** ~ **on sth** etw beschließen; ~**d** a bestimmt, entschieden; ~**dly** ad entschieden.

deciduous [dɪ'sɪdjuəs] a jedes Jahr abfallend, Laub-.

decimal ['desɪməl] a dezimal; n Dezimalzahl f; ~ **point** Komma nt (eines

Dezimalbruches); ~ **system** Dezimalsystem *nt.*

decimate ['desɪmeɪt] *vt* dezimieren.

decipher [dɪ'saɪfə*] *vt* entziffern.

decision [dɪ'sɪʒən] *n* Entscheidung *f*, Entschluß *m.*

decisive [dɪ'saɪsɪv] *a* entscheidend, ausschlaggebend.

deck [dek] *n* (*Naut*) Deck *nt*; (*of cards*) Pack *m*; ~**chair** Liegestuhl *m*; ~**hand** Matrose *m.*

declaration [deklə'reɪʃən] *n* Erklärung *f.*

declare [dɪ'klɛə*] *vt* (*state*) behaupten; *war* erklären; (*Customs*) verzollen.

decline [dɪ'klaɪn] *n* (*decay*) Verfall *m*; (*lessening*) Rückgang *m*, Niedergang *m*; *vt* *invitation* ausschlagen, ablehnen; *vi* (*of strength*) nachlassen; (*say no*) ablehnen.

declutch ['diː'klʌtʃ] *vi* auskuppeln.

decode ['diː'kəʊd] *vt* entschlüsseln.

decompose [diːkəm'pəʊz] *vi* (sich) zersetzen.

decomposition [diːkɒmpə'zɪʃən] *n* Zersetzung *f.*

decontaminate [diːkən'tæmɪneɪt] *vt* entgiften.

décor ['deɪkɔ:*] *n* Ausstattung *f.*

decorate ['dekəreɪt] *vt* *room* tapezieren; streichen; (*adorn*) (aus)schmücken; *cake* verzieren; (*honour*) auszeichnen.

decoration [dekə'reɪʃən] *n* (*of house*) (Wand)dekoration *f*; (*medal*) Orden *m.*

decorative [dekərətɪv] *a* dekorativ, Schmuck-.

decorator ['dekəreɪtə*] *n* Maler *m*, Anstreicher *m.*

decorum [dɪ'kɔ:rəm] *n* Anstand *m.*

decoy ['diːkɔɪ] *n* (*lit, fig*) Lockvogel *m.*

decrease [diː'kriːs] *n* Abnahme *f*; *vt* vermindern; *vi* abnehmen.

decree [dɪ'kriː] *n* Verfügung *f*, Erlaß *m.*

decrepit [dɪ'krepɪt] *a* hinfällig.

dedicate ['dedɪkeɪt] *vt* (*to God*) weihen; *book* widmen.

dedication [dedɪ'keɪʃən] *n* (*devotion*) Ergebenheit *f.*

deduce [dɪ'djuːs] *vt* ableiten, schließen (*from* aus).

deduct [dɪ'dʌkt] *vt* abziehen; ~**ion** [dɪ'dʌkʃən] *n* (*of money*) Abzug *m*; (*conclusion*) (Schluß)folgerung *f.*

deed [diːd] *n* Tat *f*; (*document*) Urkunde *f.*

deep [diːp] *a* tief; ~**en** *vt* vertiefen; ~**freeze** Tiefkühlung *f*; ~**seated** *a* tiefsitzend; ~**set** *a* tiefliegend.

deer [dɪə*] *n* Reh *nt*; (*with antlers*) Hirsch *m.*

deface [dɪ'feɪs] *vt* entstellen.

defamation [defə'meɪʃən] *n* Verleumdung *f.*

default [dɪ'fɔːlt] *n* Versäumnis *nt*; *vi* versäumen; **by** ~ durch Nichterscheinen *nt*; ~**er** Schuldner *m*, Zahlungsunfähige(r) *m.*

defeat [dɪ'fiːt] *n* (*overthrow*) Vernichtung *f*; (*battle*) Niederlage *f*; *vt* schlagen, zu Fall bringen; ~**ist** *a* defätistisch.

defect [dɪ'fekt] *n* Defekt *m*, Fehler *m*; [dɪ'fekt] *vi* überlaufen; ~**ive** [dɪ'fektɪv] *a* fehlerhaft, schadhaft.

defence [dɪ'fens] *n* (*Mil, Sport*) Verteidigung *f*; (*excuse*) Rechtfertigung *f*; ~**less** *a* wehrlos.

defend [dɪ'fend] *vt* verteidigen; ~**ant** Angeklagte(r) *m*; ~**er** Verteidiger *m.*

defensive [dɪ'fensɪv] *a* defensiv, Schutz-.

defer [dɪ'fɜ:*] *vt* verschieben; ~**ence** ['defərəns] Hochachtung *f*, Rücksichtnahme *f*; ~**ential** [defə'renʃəl] *a* ehrerbietig.

defiance [dɪ'faɪəns] *n* Trotz *m*, Unnachgiebigkeit *f*; **in** ~ **of the order** dem Befehl zum Trotz.

defiant [dɪ'faɪənt] *a* trotzig, unnachgiebig.

deficiency [dɪ'fɪʃənsɪ] *n* Unzulänglichkeit *f*, Mangel *m.*

deficient [dɪ'fɪʃənt] *a* unzureichend.

deficit ['defɪsɪt] *n* Defizit *nt*, Fehlbetrag *m.*

defile [dɪ'faɪl] *vt* beschmutzen; *n* ['diː'faɪl] Schlucht *f.*

define [dɪ'faɪn] *vt* bestimmen; (*explain*) definieren.

definite ['defɪnɪt] *a* bestimmt; (*clear*) klar, eindeutig; ~**ly** *ad* bestimmt.

definition [defɪ'nɪʃən] *n* Definition *f*; (*Phot*) Schärfe *f.*

definitive [dɪ'fɪnɪtɪv] *a* definitiv, endgültig.

deflate [diː'fleɪt] *vt* die Luft ablassen aus.

deflation [diː'fleɪʃən] *n* (*Fin*) Deflation *f.*

deflect [dɪ'flekt] *vt* ablenken.

deform [dɪ'fɔːm] *vt* deformieren, entstellen; ~**ed** *a* deformiert; ~**ity** Verunstaltung *f*, Mißbildung *f.*

defraud [dɪ'frɔːd] *vt* betrügen.

defray [dɪ'freɪ] *vt* bestreiten.

defrost [diː'frɒst] *vt* *fridge* abtauen; *food* auftauen.

deft [deft] *a* geschickt.

defunct [dɪ'fʌŋkt] *a* verstorben.

defy [dɪ'faɪ] *vt* (*challenge*) sich widersetzen (+*dat*); (*resist*) trotzen (+*dat*), sich stellen gegen.

degenerate [dɪ'dʒenəreɪt] *vi* degenerieren; [dɪ'dʒenərɪt] *a* degeneriert.

degradation [degrə'deɪʃən] *n* Erniedrigung *f.*

degrading [dɪ'greɪdɪŋ] *a* erniedrigend.

degree [dɪ'griː] *n* Grad *m*; (*Univ*) akademische(r) Grad *m*; **by** ~**s** allmählich; **to take one's** ~ sein Examen machen.

dehydrated [diː'haɪdreɪtɪd] *a* getrocknet, Trocken-.

de-ice [diː'aɪs] *vt* enteisen, auftauen.

deign [deɪn] *vi* sich herablassen.

deity ['diːɪtɪ] *n* Gottheit *f.*

dejected [dɪ'dʒektɪd] *a* niedergeschlagen.

dejection [dɪ'dʒekʃən] *n* Niedergeschlagenheit *f.*

delay [dɪ'leɪ] *vt* (*hold back*) aufschieben; **the flight was** ~**ed** die Maschine hatte Verspätung; *vi* (*linger*) sich aufhalten, zögern; *n* Aufschub *m*, Verzögerung *f*; **without** ~ unverzüglich; ~**ed** *a* action verzögert.

delegate ['delɪgɪt] *n* Delegierte(r) *mf*, Abgeordnete(r) *mf*; ['delɪgeɪt] *vt* delegieren.

delegation [delɪ'geɪʃən] n Abordnung f; (foreign) Delegation f.

delete [dɪ'liːt] vt (aus)streichen.

deliberate [dɪ'lɪbərɪt] a (intentional) bewußt, überlegt; (slow) bedächtig; [dɪ'lɪbəreɪt] vi (consider) überlegen; (debate) sich beraten; ~ly ad vorsätzlich.

deliberation [dɪlɪbə'reɪʃən] n Überlegung f, Beratung f.

delicacy ['delɪkəsɪ] n Zartheit f; (weakness) Anfälligkeit f; (tact) Zartgefühl nt; (food) Delikatesse f.

delicate ['delɪkɪt] a (fine) fein; (fragile) zart; (situation) heikel; (Med) empfindlich; ~ly ad bedenklich.

delicatessen [delɪkə'tesn] n Feinkostgeschäft nt.

delicious [dɪ'lɪʃəs] a köstlich, lecker, delikat.

delight [dɪ'laɪt] n Wonne f; vt entzücken; ~ful a entzückend, herrlich.

delinquency [dɪ'lɪŋkwənsɪ] n Straffälligkeit f, Delinquenz f.

delinquent [dɪ'lɪŋkwənt] n Straffällige(r) mf; a straffällig.

delirious [dɪ'lɪrɪəs] a irre, im Fieberwahn.

delirium [dɪ'lɪrɪəm] n Fieberwahn m, Delirium nt.

deliver [dɪ'lɪvə*] vt goods (ab)liefern; letter bringen, zustellen; verdict aussprechen; speech halten; ~y n (Ab)lieferung f; (of letter) Zustellung f; (of speech) Vortragsweise f; ~ van Lieferwagen m.

delouse ['diː'laus] vt entlausen.

delta ['deltə] n Delta nt.

delude [dɪ'luːd] vt täuschen.

deluge ['deljuːdʒ] n Überschwemmung f; (fig) Flut f; vt (fig) überfluten.

delusion [dɪ'luːʒən] n (Selbst)täuschung f.

de luxe [dɪ'lʌks] a Luxus-.

demand [dɪ'mɑːnd] vt verlangen; (request) Verlangen f; (Comm) Nachfrage f; in ~ begehrt, gesucht; on ~ auf Verlangen; ~ing a anspruchsvoll.

demarcation [diːmɑː'keɪʃən] n Abgrenzung f.

demeanour [dɪ'miːnə*] n Benehmen nt.

demented [dɪ'mentɪd] a wahnsinnig.

demi- ['demɪ] pref halb-.

demise [dɪ'maɪz] n Ableben nt.

demobilization ['diːməubɪlaɪ'zeɪʃən] n Demobilisierung f.

democracy [dɪ'mɔkrəsɪ] n Demokratie f.

democrat ['deməkræt] n Demokrat m; ~ic a, ~ically ad [demə'krætɪk, -lɪ] demokratisch.

demolish [dɪ'mɔlɪʃ] vt (lit) abreißen; (destroy) zerstören; (fig) vernichten.

demolition [demə'lɪʃən] n Abbruch m.

demon ['diːmən] n Dämon m.

demonstrate ['deménstreit] vti demonstrieren.

demonstration [demən'streiʃən] n Demonstration f; (proof) Beweisführung f.

demonstrative [dɪ'mɔnstrətɪv] a demonstrativ.

demonstrator ['deménstreitə*] n (Pol) Demonstrant(in f) m.

demoralize [dɪ'mɔrəlaɪz] vt demoralisieren.

demote [dɪ'məut] vt degradieren.

demure [dɪ'mjuə*] a ernst.

den [den] n (of animal) Höhle f, Bau m; Bude f; ~ of vice Lasterhöhle f.

denationalize [diː'næʃnəlaɪz] vt reprivatisieren.

denial [dɪ'naɪəl] n Leugnung f; official ~ Dementi nt.

denigrate ['denɪgreɪt] vt verunglimpfen.

denim ['denɪm] n Denim-; ~s pl Denim-Jeans.

denomination [dɪnɔmɪ'neɪʃən] n (Eccl) Bekenntnis nt; (type) Klasse f; (Fin) Wert m.

denominator [dɪ'nɔmɪneɪtə*] n Nenner; common ~ gemeinsame(r) Nenner m.

denote [dɪ'nəut] vt bedeuten.

denounce [dɪ'nauns] vt brandmarken.

dense [dens] a dicht, dick; (stupid) schwer von Begriff; ~ly ad dicht.

density ['densɪtɪ] n Dichte f.

dent [dent] n Delle f; vt einbeulen.

dental ['dentl] a Zahn-; ~ surgeon = dentist.

dentifrice ['dentɪfrɪs] n Zahnputzmittel nt.

dentist ['dentɪst] n Zahnarzt m/-ärztin f; ~ry Zahnmedizin f.

denture ['dentʃə*] n künstliche(s) Gebiß nt.

denude [dɪ'njuːd] vt entblößen.

deny [dɪ'naɪ] vt leugnen; rumour widersprechen (+dat); knowledge verweigern; help abschlagen; to ~ o.s. sth sich etw versagen.

deodorant [diː'əudərənt] n Desodorans nt.

depart [dɪ'pɑːt] vi abfahren.

department [dɪ'pɑːtmənt] n (Comm) Abteilung f, Sparte f; (Univ, Sch) Fachbereich m; (Pol) Ministerium nt, Ressort nt; ~al [-'mentl] a Fach-; ~ store Warenhaus nt.

departure [dɪ'pɑːtʃə*] n (of person) Weggang m; (on journey) Abreise f; (of train) Abfahrt f; (of plane) Abflug m; new ~ Neuerung f.

depend [dɪ'pend] vi: it ~s es kommt darauf an; ~ on abhängen von; parents etc angewiesen sein auf (+acc); ~able a zuverlässig; ~ence n Abhängigkeit f; ~ent n (person) Familienangehörige(r) mf; a bedingt (on durch).

depict [dɪ'pɪkt] vt schildern.

depleted [dɪ'pliːtɪd] a aufgebraucht.

deplorable [dɪ'plɔːrəbl] a bedauerlich.

deplore [dɪ'plɔː*] vt mißbilligen.

deploy [dɪ'plɔɪ] vt einsetzen.

depopulation [diːpɔpju'leɪʃən] n Entvölkerung f.

deport [dɪ'pɔːt] vt deportieren; ~ation [diːpɔː'teɪʃən] Abschiebung f; ~ation order Ausweisung f; ~ment Betragen nt.

depose [dɪ'pəuz] vt absetzen.

deposit [dɪ'pɔzɪt] n (in bank) Guthaben nt; (down payment) Anzahlung f; (security) Kaution f; (Chem) Niederschlag m; vt (in bank) deponieren; (put down) niederlegen;

~ **account** Sparkonto *nt*; ~**or** Konto-
inhaber *m*.
depot ['depəʊ] *n* Depot *nt*.
deprave [dɪ'preɪv] *vt* (moralisch)
verderben; ~**d** a verworfen.
depravity [dɪ'prævɪtɪ] *n* Verworfenheit *f*.
deprecate ['deprɪkeɪt] *vt* mißbilligen.
depreciate [dɪ'priːʃeɪt] *vi* im Wert sinken.
depreciation [dɪpriːʃɪ'eɪʃən] *n* Wert-
minderung *f*.
depress [dɪ'pres] *vt* (*press down*) niederdrücken; (*in mood*) deprimieren; ~**ed** a
person niedergeschlagen, deprimiert;
~**ed area** Notstandsgebiet *nt*; ~**ing** a
deprimierend; ~**ion** [dɪ'preʃən] (*mood*)
Depression *f*; (*in trade*) Wirtschaftskrise *f*;
(*hollow*) Vertiefung *f*; (*Met*) Tief(druck-
gebiet) *nt*.
deprivation [deprɪ'veɪʃən] *n* Entbehrung *f*,
Not *f*.
deprive [dɪ'praɪv] *vt* berauben (*of* +*gen*);
~**d** a *child* sozial benachteiligt; *area*
unterentwickelt.
depth [depθ] *n* Tiefe *f*; **in the** ~**s of**
despair in tiefster Verzweiflung; **to be**
out of one's ~ den Boden unter den
Füßen verloren haben; ~ **charge**
Wasserbombe *f*.
deputation [depjʊ'teɪʃən] *n* Abordnung *f*.
deputize ['depjʊtaɪz] *vi* vertreten (*for*
+*acc*).
deputy ['depjʊtɪ] a stellvertretend; *n*
(Stell)vertreter *m*.
derail [dɪ'reɪl] *vt* entgleisen lassen; **to be**
~**ed** entgleisen; ~**ment** Entgleisung *f*.
deranged [dɪ'reɪndʒd] a irr, verrückt.
derby ['dɑːbɪ] *n* (*US*) Melone *f*.
derelict ['derɪlɪkt] a verlassen; *building*
baufällig.
deride [dɪ'raɪd] *vt* auslachen.
derision [dɪ'rɪʒən] *n* Hohn *m*, Spott *m*.
derisory [dɪ'raɪsərɪ] a spöttisch.
derivation [derɪ'veɪʃən] *n* Ableitung *f*.
derivative [dɪ'rɪvətɪv] *n* Abgeleitete(s) *nt*;
a abgeleitet.
derive [dɪ'raɪv] *vt* (*get*) gewinnen;
(*deduce*) ableiten; *vi* (*come from*)
abstammen.
dermatitis [dɜːmə'taɪtɪs] *n* Hautent-
zündung *f*.
derogatory [dɪ'rogətərɪ] a geringschätzig.
derrick ['derɪk] *n* Drehkran *m*.
desalination [diːsælɪ'neɪʃən] *n* Entsalzung
f.
descend [dɪ'send] *vti* hinuntersteigen; **to**
~ **from** abstammen von; ~**ant** Nachkomme *m*.
descent [dɪ'sent] *n* (*coming down*) Abstieg
m; (*origin*) Abstammung *f*.
describe [dɪs'kraɪb] *vt* beschreiben.
description [dɪs'krɪpʃən] *n* Beschreibung
f; (*sort*) Art *f*.
descriptive [dɪs'krɪptɪv] a beschreibend;
word anschaulich.
desecrate ['desɪkreɪt] *vt* schänden.
desegregation [diːsegrə'geɪʃən] *n*
Aufhebung *f* der Rassentrennung.
desert[1] ['dezət] *n* Wüste *f*.
desert[2] [dɪ'zɜːt] *vt* verlassen; (*temporarily*)

im Stich lassen; *vi* (*Mil*) desertieren; ~**er**
Deserteur *m*; ~**ion** [dɪ'zɜːʃən] (*of wife*)
böswillige(s) Verlassen *nt*; (*Mil*) Fahnen-
flucht *f*.
deserve [dɪ'zɜːv] *vt* verdienen.
deserving [dɪ'zɜːvɪŋ] a *person* würdig;
action verdienstvoll.
design [dɪ'zaɪn] *n* (*plan*) Entwurf *m*; (*drawing*) Zeichnung *f*; (*planning*) Gestaltung *f*,
Design *nt*; *vt* entwerfen; (*intend*)
bezwecken; **to have** ~**s on** sb/sth es auf
jdn/etw abgesehen haben.
designate ['dezɪgneɪt] *vt* bestimmen;
['dezɪgnɪt] a designiert.
designation [dezɪg'neɪʃən] *n* Bezeichnung
f.
designer [dɪ'zaɪnə*] *n* Designer *m*; (*Theat*)
Bühnenbildner(in *f*) *m*.
desirability [dɪzaɪərə'bɪlɪtɪ] *n* Erwünscht-
heit *f*.
desirable [dɪ'zaɪərəbl] a wünschenswert;
woman begehrenswert.
desire [dɪ'zaɪə*] *n* Wunsch *m*, Verlangen
nt; *vt* (*lust*) begehren, wünschen; (*ask for*)
verlangen, wollen.
desirous [dɪ'zaɪərəs] a begierig (*of* auf
+*acc*).
desist [dɪ'zɪst] *vi* Abstand nehmen,
aufhören.
desk [desk] *n* Schreibtisch *m*.
desolate ['desəlɪt] a *öde*; (*sad*) trostlos.
desolation [desə'leɪʃən] *n* Trostlosigkeit *f*.
despair [dɪs'peə*] *n* Verzweiflung *f*; *vi*
verzweifeln (*of* an +*dat*).
despatch [dɪs'pætʃ] = **dispatch**.
desperate ['despərɪt] a verzweifelt;
situation hoffnungslos; **to be** ~ **for sth**
etw unbedingt brauchen; ~**ly** *ad* verzweifelt.
desperation [despə'reɪʃən] *n* Verzweiflung
f.
despicable [dɪs'pɪkəbl] a abscheulich.
despise [dɪs'paɪz] *vt* verachten.
despite [dɪs'paɪt] *prep* trotz (+*gen*).
despondent [dɪs'pondənt] a mutlos.
dessert [dɪ'zɜːt] *n* Nachtisch *m*; ~**spoon**
Dessertlöffel *m*.
destination [destɪ'neɪʃən] *n* (*of person*)
(Reise)ziel *nt*; (*of goods*) Bestimmungsort
m.
destine ['destɪn] *vt* (*set apart*) bestimmen.
destiny ['destɪnɪ] *n* Schicksal *nt*.
destitute ['destɪtjuːt] a notleidend.
destitution [destɪtjuːʃən] *n* Elend *f*.
destroy [dɪs'trɔɪ] *vt* zerstören; ~**er** (*Naut*)
Zerstörer *m*.
destruction [dɪs'trʌkʃən] *n* Zerstörung *f*.
destructive [dɪs'trʌktɪv] a zerstörend.
detach [dɪ'tætʃ] *vt* loslösen; ~**able** a
abtrennbar; ~**ed** a *attitude* distanziert,
objektiv; *house* Einzel-; ~**ment** (*Mil*)
Abteilung *f*, Sonderkommando *nt*; (*fig*)
Abstand *m*, Unvoreingenommenheit *f*.
detail ['diːteɪl] *n* Einzelheit *f*, Detail *nt*;
(*minor part*) unwichtige Einzelheit *f*; *vt*
(*relate*) ausführlich berichten; (*appoint*)
abkommandieren; **in** ~ ausführlich, bis
ins kleinste.

detain [dɪ'teɪn] vt aufhalten; (imprison) in Haft halten.

detect [dɪ'tekt] vt entdecken; ~**ion** [dɪ'tekʃən] Aufdeckung f; ~**ive** Detektiv m; ~**ive story** Krimi(nalgeschichte f) m; ~**or** Detektor m.

détente ['deɪtã:nt] n Entspannung f.

detention [dɪ'tenʃən] n Haft f; (Sch) Nachsitzen nt.

deter [dɪ'tɜ:*] vt abschrecken.

detergent [dɪ'tɜ:dʒənt] n Waschmittel nt; Reinigungsmittel nt.

deteriorate [dɪ'tɪərɪəreɪt] vi sich verschlechtern.

deterioration [dɪtɪərɪə'reɪʃən] n Verschlechterung f.

determination [dɪtɜ:mɪ'neɪʃən] n Entschlossenheit f.

determine [dɪ'tɜ:mɪn] vt bestimmen; ~**d** a entschlossen.

deterrent [dɪ'terənt] n Abschreckungsmittel nt; a abschreckend.

detest [dɪ'test] vt verabscheuen; ~**able** a abscheulich.

dethrone [di:'θrəʊn] vt entthronen.

detonate ['detəneɪt] vt detonieren.

detonator ['detəneɪtə*] n Sprengkapsel f.

detour ['deɪtʊə*] n Umweg m; (on road sign) Umleitung f.

detract [dɪ'trækt] vi schmälern (from acc.)

detriment ['detrɪmənt] n: to the ~ of zum Schaden (+gen); ~**al** [detrɪ'mentl] a schädlich.

deuce [dju:s] n (tennis) Einstand m.

devaluation [di:vælju'eɪʃən] n Abwertung f.

devalue ['di:'vælju:] vt abwerten.

devastate ['devəsteɪt] vt verwüsten.

devastating ['devəsteɪtɪŋ] a verheerend.

develop [dɪ'veləp] vt entwickeln; resources erschließen; vi sich entwickeln; ~**er** (Phot) Entwickler m; (of land) Bauunternehmer m; ~**ing** a country Entwicklungs-; ~**ment** Entwicklung f.

deviant ['di:vɪənt] a abweichend; n Abweichler m.

deviate ['di:vɪeɪt] vi abweichen.

deviation [di:vɪ'eɪʃən] n Abweichung f.

device [dɪ'vaɪs] n Vorrichtung f, Gerät nt.

devil ['devl] n Teufel m; ~**ish** a teuflisch.

devious ['di:vɪəs] a route gewunden; means krumm; person verschlagen.

devise [dɪ'vaɪz] vt entwickeln.

devoid [dɪ'vɔɪd] a: ~ **of** ohne, bar (+gen).

devolution [di:və'lu:ʃən] n Dezentralisierung f.

devote [dɪ'vəʊt] vt widmen (to dat); ~**d** a ergeben; ~**e** [devəʊ'ti:] Anhänger(in f) m, Verehrer(in f) m.

devotion [dɪ'vəʊʃən] n (piety) Andacht f; (loyalty) Ergebenheit f, Hingabe f.

devour [dɪ'vaʊə*] vt verschlingen.

devout [dɪ'vaʊt] a andächtig.

dew [dju:] n Tau m.

dexterity [deks'terɪtɪ] n Geschicklichkeit f.

diabetes [daɪə'bi:ti:z] n Zuckerkrankheit f.

diabetic [daɪə'betɪk] a zuckerkrank; n Diabetiker m.

diagnose ['daɪəgnəʊz] vt (Med) diagnostizieren; feststellen.

diagnosis [daɪəg'nəʊsɪs] n Diagnose f.

diagonal [daɪ'ægənl] a diagonal, schräg; n Diagonale f.

diagram ['daɪəgræm] n Diagramm nt, Schaubild nt.

dial ['daɪəl] n (Tel) Wählscheibe f; (of clock) Zifferblatt nt; vt wählen; ~**ling tone** Amtszeichen nt.

dialect ['daɪəlekt] n Dialekt m.

dialogue ['daɪəlɒg] n Gespräch nt; (Liter) Dialog m.

diameter [daɪ'æmɪtə*] n Durchmesser m.

diametrically [daɪə'metrɪkəlɪ] ad: ~ **opposed to** genau entgegengesetzt (+dat).

diamond ['daɪəmənd] n Diamant m; (Cards) Karo nt.

diaper ['daɪəpə*] n (US) Windel f.

diaphragm ['daɪəfræm] n Zwerchfell nt.

diarrhoea [daɪə'ri:ə] n Durchfall m.

diary ['daɪərɪ] n Taschenkalender m; (account) Tagebuch nt.

dice [daɪs] n Würfel pl; vt (Cook) in Würfel schneiden.

dicey ['daɪsɪ] a (col) riskant.

dichotomy [dɪ'kɒtəmɪ] n Kluft f.

dictate [dɪk'teɪt] vt diktieren; (of circumstances) gebieten; ['dɪkteɪt] n Mahnung f, Gebot nt.

dictation [dɪk'teɪʃən] n Diktat nt.

dictator [dɪk'teɪtə*] n Diktator m.

dictatorship [dɪk'teɪtəʃɪp] n Diktatur f.

diction ['dɪkʃən] n Ausdrucksweise f.

dictionary ['dɪkʃənrɪ] n Wörterbuch nt.

diddle ['dɪdl] vt (col) übers Ohr hauen.

didn't ['dɪdənt] = did not.

die [daɪ] vi sterben; (end) aufhören; ~ **away** vi schwächer werden; ~ **down** vi nachlassen; ~ **out** vi aussterben; (fig) nachlassen.

diesel ['di:zəl] ~ **engine** Dieselmotor m.

diet ['daɪət] n Nahrung f, Kost f; (special food) Diät f; (slimming) Abmagerungskur f; vi eine Abmagerungskur machen.

differ ['dɪfə*] vi sich unterscheiden; (disagree) anderer Meinung sein; **we** ~ wir sind unterschiedlicher Meinung; ~**ence** Unterschied m; (disagreement) (Meinungs)unterschied m; ~**ent** a verschieden; **that's** ~ das ist anders; ~**ential** [dɪfə'renʃəl] (Aut) Differentialgetriebe nt; (in wages) Lohnstufe f; ~**entiate** [dɪfə'renʃɪeɪt] vti unterscheiden; ~**ently** ad verschieden, unterschiedlich.

difficult ['dɪfɪkəlt] a schwierig; ~**y** Schwierigkeit f, **with** ~**y** nur schwer.

diffidence ['dɪfɪdəns] n mangelnde(s) Selbstvertrauen nt.

diffident ['dɪfɪdənt] a schüchtern.

diffuse [dɪ'fju:s] a langatmig; [dɪ'fju:z] vt verbreiten.

dig [dɪg] vti irreg hole graben; garden (um)graben; claws senken; n (prod) Stoß m; ~ **in** vi (Mil) sich eingraben; (to food) sich hermachen über (+acc); ~ **in!** greif zu!; ~ **up** vt ausgraben; (fig) aufgabeln.

digest [daɪ'dʒest] vt (lit, fig) verdauen;

['daɪdʒest] n Auslese f; ~**ible** a verdaulich; ~**ion** Verdauung f.

digit ['dɪdʒɪt] n einstellige Zahl f; (Anat) Finger m; Zehe f; ~**al computer** Einzahlencomputer m.

dignified ['dɪgnɪfaɪd] a würdevoll.

dignify ['dɪgnɪfaɪ] vt Würde verleihen (+dat).

dignitary ['dɪgnɪtərɪ] n Würdenträger m.

dignity ['dɪgnɪtɪ] n Würde f.

digress [daɪ'gres] vi abschweifen; ~**ion** [daɪ'grefən] Abschweifung f.

digs [dɪgz] npl (Brit col) Bude f.

dilapidated [dɪ'læpɪdeɪtɪd] a baufällig.

dilate [daɪ'leɪt] vti (sich) weiten.

dilatory ['dɪlətərɪ] a hinhaltend.

dilemma [daɪ'lemə] n Dilemma nt.

dilettante [dɪlɪ'tæntɪ] n Dilettant m.

diligence ['dɪlɪdʒəns] n Fleiß m.

diligent ['dɪlɪdʒənt] a fleißig.

dill [dɪl] n Dill m.

dilly-dally ['dɪlɪdælɪ] vi (col) herumtrödeln.

dilute [daɪ'lu:t] vt verdünnen; a verdünnt.

dim [dɪm] a trübe, matt; (stupid) schwer von Begriff; **to take a ~ view of sth** etw mißbilligen; vt verdunkeln.

dime [daɪm] (US) Zehncentstück nt.

dimension [dɪ'menfən] n Dimension f; ~**s** pl Maße pl.

diminish [dɪ'mɪnɪʃ] vti verringern.

diminutive [dɪ'mɪnjutɪv] a winzig; n Verkleinerungsform f.

dimly ['dɪmlɪ] ad trübe.

dimple ['dɪmpl] n Grübchen nt.

dim-witted ['dɪm'wɪtɪd] a (col) dämlich.

din [dɪn] n Getöse nt.

dine [daɪn] vi speisen; ~**r** Tischgast m; (Rail) Speisewagen m.

dinghy ['dɪŋgɪ] n kleine(s) Ruderboot nt; Dinghi nt.

dingy ['dɪndʒɪ] a armselig.

dining car ['daɪnɪŋka:*] n Speisewagen m.

dining room ['daɪnɪŋrum] n Eßzimmer nt; (in hotel) Speisezimmer nt.

dinner ['dɪnə*] n Mittagessen nt, Abendessen nt; (public) Festessen nt; ~ **jacket** Smoking m; ~ **party** Tischgesellschaft f; ~ **time** Tischzeit f.

dinosaur ['daɪnəsɔ:*] n Dinosaurier m.

diocese ['daɪəsɪs] n Diözese f, Sprengel m.

dip [dɪp] n (hollow) Senkung f; (bathe) kurze(s) Bad(en) nt; vt eintauchen; (Aut) abblenden; vi (slope) sich senken, abfallen.

diphtheria [dɪf'θɪərɪə] n Diphtherie f.

diphthong ['dɪfθɒŋ] n Diphthong m.

diploma [dɪ'pləumə] n Urkunde f, Diplom nt.

diplomat ['dɪpləmæt] n Diplomat(in f) m; ~**ic** [dɪplə'mætɪk] a diplomatisch; ~**ic corps** diplomatische(s) Korps nt.

dipstick ['dɪpstɪk] n Ölmeßstab m.

dire [daɪə*] a schrecklich.

direct [daɪ'rekt] a direkt; vt leiten; film die Regie führen (+gen); jury anweisen; (aim) richten, lenken; (tell way) den Weg erklären (+dat); (order) anweisen; ~ **current** Gleichstrom m; ~ **hit** Volltreffer m; ~**ion** [dɪ'rekfən] Führung f,

Leitung f; (course) Richtung f; (Cine) Regie f; ~**s** pl (for use) Gebrauchsanleitung f; (orders) Anweisungen pl; ~**ional** [dɪ'rekfənl] a Richt-; ~**ive** Direktive f; ~**ly** ad (in straight line) gerade, direkt; (at once) unmittelbar, sofort; ~**or** Direktor m, Leiter m; (of film) Regisseur m; ~**ory** Adreßbuch nt; (Tel) Telefonbuch nt.

dirt [dɜ:t] n Schmutz m, Dreck m; ~ **road** unbefestigte Straße; ~**y** a schmutzig, dreckig; gemein; vt beschmutzen; ~ **cheap** a spottbillig.

disability [dɪsə'bɪlɪtɪ] n Körperbehinderung f.

disabled [dɪs'eɪbld] a körperbehindert.

disabuse [dɪsə'bju:z] vt befreien.

disadvantage [dɪsəd'vɑ:ntɪdʒ] n Nachteil m; ~**ous** [dɪsædvɑ:n'teɪdʒəs] a ungünstig.

disagree [dɪsə'gri:] vi nicht übereinstimmen; (quarrel) sich streiten; (food) nicht bekommen (with dat); ~**able** a person widerlich; task unangenehm; ~**ment** (between persons) Streit m; (between things) Widerspruch m.

disallow [dɪsə'lau] vt nicht zulassen.

disappear [dɪsə'pɪə*] vi verschwinden; ~**ance** Verschwinden nt.

disappoint [dɪsə'pɔɪnt] vt enttäuschen; ~**ing** a enttäuschend; ~**ment** Enttäuschung f.

disapproval [dɪsə'pru:vəl] n Mißbilligung f.

disapprove [dɪsə'pru:v] vi mißbilligen (of acc); **she ~s** sie mißbilligt es.

disarm [dɪs'ɑ:m] vt entwaffnen; (Pol) abrüsten; ~**ament** Abrüstung f.

disaster [dɪ'zɑ:stə*] n Unglück nt; Katastrophe f.

disastrous [dɪ'zɑ:strəs] a verhängnisvoll.

disband [dɪs'bænd] vt auflösen.

disbelief ['dɪsbə'li:f] n Ungläubigkeit f.

disc [dɪsk] n Scheibe f; (record) (Schall)platte f.

discard [dɪs'kɑ:d] vt ablegen.

disc brake ['dɪsk breɪk] n Scheibenbremse f.

discern [dɪ'sɜ:n] vt unterscheiden (können), erkennen; ~**ing** a scharfsinnig.

discharge [dɪs'tʃɑ:dʒ] vt ship entladen; duties nachkommen (+dat); (dismiss) entlassen; gun abschießen; n (of ship) Entladung f, ['dɪstʃɑ:dʒ] (Med) Ausfluß m.

disciple [dɪ'saɪpl] n Jünger m.

disciplinary ['dɪsɪplɪnərɪ] a disziplinarisch.

discipline ['dɪsɪplɪn] n Disziplin f; vt (train) schulen; (punish) bestrafen.

disc jockey ['dɪskdʒɒkɪ] n Diskjockey m.

disclaim [dɪs'kleɪm] vt nicht anerkennen; (Pol) dementieren.

disclose [dɪs'kləuz] vt enthüllen.

disclosure [dɪs'kləuʒə*] n Enthüllung f.

disco ['dɪskəu] n abbr of discotheque.

discoloured [dɪs'kʌləd] a verfärbt, verschossen.

discomfort [dɪs'kʌmfət] n Unbehagen nt; (embarrassment) Verlegenheit f.

disconcert [dɪskən'sɜ:t] vt aus der

Fassung bringen; (*puzzle*) verstimmen.

disconnect [dɪskə'nekt] *vt* abtrennen.

discontent ['dɪskən'tent] *n* Unzufriedenheit *f*; ~ed *a* unzufrieden.

discontinue ['dɪskən'tɪnjuː] *vt* einstellen; *vi* aufhören.

discord ['dɪskɔːd] *n* Zwietracht *f*; (*noise*) Dissonanz *f*; ~ant [dɪs'kɔːdənt] *a* uneinig; *noise* mißtönend.

discotheque ['dɪskəʊtek] *n* Diskothek *f*.

discount ['dɪskaunt] *n* Rabatt *m*; [dɪs'kaunt] *vt* außer acht lassen.

discourage [dɪs'kʌrɪdʒ] *vt* entmutigen; (*prevent*) abraten, abhalten.

discouraging [dɪs'kʌrɪdʒɪŋ] *a* entmutigend.

discourteous [dɪs'kɜːtɪəs] *a* unhöflich.

discover [dɪs'kʌvə*] *vt* entdecken; ~y *n* Entdeckung *f*.

discredit [dɪs'kredɪt] *vt* in Verruf bringen.

discreet *a*, ~ly *ad* [dɪs'kriːt, -lɪ] taktvoll, diskret.

discrepancy [dɪs'krepənsɪ] *n* Unstimmigkeit *f*, Diskrepanz *f*.

discretion [dɪs'kreʃən] *n* Takt *m*, Diskretion *f*; (*decision*) Gutdünken *nt*; **to leave sth to sb's ~** etw jds Gutdünken überlassen.

discriminate [dɪs'krɪmɪneɪt] *vi* unterscheiden; **to ~ against** diskriminieren.

discriminating [dɪs'krɪmɪneɪtɪŋ] *a* klug; *taste* anspruchsvoll.

discrimination [dɪskrɪmɪ'neɪʃən] *n* Urteilsvermögen *nt*; (*pej*) Diskriminierung *f*.

discus ['dɪskəs] *n* Diskus *m*.

discuss [dɪs'kʌs] *vt* diskutieren, besprechen; ~ion [dɪs'kʌʃən] Diskussion *f*, Besprechung *f*.

disdain [dɪs'deɪn] *vt* verachten, für unter seiner Würde halten; *n* Verachtung *f*; ~ful *a* geringschätzig.

disease [dɪ'ziːz] *n* Krankheit *f*; ~d *a* erkrankt.

disembark [dɪsɪm'bɑːk] *vt* aussteigen lassen; *vi* von Bord gehen.

disenchanted ['dɪsɪn'tʃɑːntɪd] *a* desillusioniert.

disengage [dɪsɪn'geɪdʒ] *vt* (*Aut*) auskuppeln.

disentangle ['dɪsɪn'tæŋgl] *vt* entwirren.

disfavour [dɪs'feɪvə*] *n* Ungunst *f*.

disfigure [dɪs'fɪgə*] *vt* entstellen.

disgrace [dɪs'greɪs] *n* Schande *f*; (*thing*) Schandfleck *m*; *vt* Schande bringen über (+*acc*); (*less strong*) blamieren; ~ful *a* schändlich, unerhört; **it's ~ful** es ist eine Schande.

disgruntled [dɪs'grʌntld] *a* verärgert.

disguise [dɪs'gaɪz] *vt* verkleiden; *feelings* verhehlen; *voice* verstellen; *n* Verkleidung *f*; **in ~** verkleidet, maskiert.

disgust [dɪs'gʌst] *n* Abscheu *f*; *vt* anwidern; ~ing *a* abscheulich; (*terrible*) gemein.

dish [dɪʃ] *n* Schüssel *f*; (*food*) Gericht *nt*; ~ up *vt* auftischen; ~ cloth Spüllappen *m*.

dishearten [dɪs'hɑːtn] *vt* entmutigen.

dishevelled [dɪ'ʃevəld] *a* *hair* zerzaust; *clothing* ungepflegt.

dishonest [dɪs'ɒnɪst] *a* unehrlich; ~y Unehrlichkeit *f*.

dishonour [dɪs'ɒnə*] *n* Unehre *f*; *vt cheque* nicht einlösen; ~able *a* unehrenhaft.

dishwasher ['dɪʃwɒʃə*] *n* Geschirrspülmaschine *f*.

disillusion [dɪsɪ'luːʒən] *vt* enttäuschen, desillusionieren.

disinfect [dɪsɪn'fekt] *vt* desinfizieren; ~ant Desinfektionsmittel *nt*.

disingenuous [dɪsɪn'dʒenjʊəs] *a* unehrlich.

disinherit ['dɪsɪn'herɪt] *vt* enterben.

disintegrate [dɪs'ɪntɪgreɪt] *vi* sich auflösen.

disinterested [dɪs'ɪntrɪstɪd] *a* uneigennützig; (*col*) uninteressiert.

disjointed [dɪs'dʒɔɪntɪd] *a* unzusammenhängend.

disk [dɪsk] *n* = **disc**.

dislike [dɪs'laɪk] *n* Abneigung *f*; *vt* nicht leiden können.

dislocate ['dɪsləʊkeɪt] *vt* auskugeln; (*upset*) in Verwirrung bringen.

dislodge [dɪs'lɒdʒ] *vt* verschieben; (*Mil*) aus der Stellung werfen.

disloyal ['dɪs'lɔɪəl] *a* treulos.

dismal ['dɪzməl] *a* trostlos, trübe.

dismantle [dɪs'mæntl] *vt* demontieren.

dismay [dɪs'meɪ] *n* Bestürzung *f*; *vt* bestürzen.

dismiss [dɪs'mɪs] *vt employee* entlassen; *idea* von sich weisen; (*send away*) wegschicken; (*Jur*) *complaint* abweisen; ~al Entlassung *f*.

disobedience [dɪsə'biːdɪəns] *n* Ungehorsam *m*.

disobedient [dɪsə'biːdɪənt] *a* ungehorsam.

disobey ['dɪsə'beɪ] *vt* nicht gehorchen (+*dat*).

disorder [dɪs'ɔːdə*] *n* (*confusion*) Verwirrung *f*; (*commotion*) Aufruhr *m*; (*Med*) Erkrankung *f*.

disorderly [dɪs'ɔːdəlɪ] *a* (*untidy*) unordentlich; (*unruly*) ordnungswidrig.

disorganized [dɪs'ɔːgənaɪzd] *a* unordentlich.

disown [dɪs'əʊn] *vt son* verstoßen; **I ~ you** ich will nichts mehr mit dir zu tun haben.

disparaging [dɪs'pærɪdʒɪŋ] *a* geringschätzig.

disparity [dɪs'pærɪtɪ] *n* Verschiedenheit *f*.

dispassionate [dɪs'pæʃnɪt] *a* gelassen, unparteiisch.

dispatch [dɪs'pætʃ] *vt goods* abschicken, abfertigen; *n* Absendung *f*; (*esp Mil*) Meldung *f*.

dispel [dɪs'pel] *vt* zerstreuen.

dispensable [dɪs'pensəbl] *a* entbehrlich.

dispensary [dɪs'pensərɪ] *n* Apotheke *f*.

dispensation [dɪspen'seɪʃən] *n* (*Eccl*) Befreiung *f*.

dispense [dɪs'pens] ~ **with** *vt* verzichten auf (+*acc*); ~r (*container*) Spender *m*.

dispensing [dɪs'pensɪŋ] *a*: ~ **chemist** Apotheker *m*.

dispersal [dɪs'pɜːsəl] *n* Zerstreuung *f*.

disperse [dɪs'pɜːs] *vt* zerstreuen; *vi* sich verteilen.

dispirited [dɪsˈpɪrɪtɪd] a niedergeschlagen.

displace [dɪsˈpleɪs] vt verschieben; ~d a: ~ **person** Verschleppte(r) mf.

display [dɪsˈpleɪ] n (of goods) Auslage f; (of feeling) Zurschaustellung f; (Mil) Entfaltung f; vt zeigen, entfalten.

displease [dɪsˈpliːz] vt mißfallen (+dat).

displeasure [dɪsˈpleʒə*] n Mißfallen.

disposable [dɪsˈpəʊzəbl] a container etc Wegwerf-.

disposal [dɪsˈpəʊzəl] n (of property) Verkauf m; (throwing away) Beseitigung f; **to be at one's** ~ einem zur Verfügung stehen.

dispose [dɪsˈpəʊz]: ~ **of** loswerden.

disposed [dɪsˈpəʊzd] a geneigt.

disposition [dɪspəˈzɪʃən] n Wesen nt, Natur f.

disproportionate [dɪsprəˈpɔːʃnɪt] a unverhältnismäßig.

disprove [dɪsˈpruːv] vt widerlegen.

dispute [dɪsˈpjuːt] n Streit m; vt bestreiten.

disqualification [dɪskwɒlɪfɪˈkeɪʃən] n Disqualifizierung f.

disqualify [dɪsˈkwɒlɪfaɪ] vt disqualifizieren.

disquiet [dɪsˈkwaɪət] n Unruhe f.

disregard [dɪsrɪˈgɑːd] vt nicht (be)achten.

disreputable [dɪsˈrepjʊtəbl] a verrufen.

disrepute [ˈdɪsrɪˈpjuːt] n Verruf m.

disrespectful [dɪsrɪsˈpektfʊl] a respektlos.

disrupt [dɪsˈrʌpt] vt stören; programme unterbrechen; ~**ion** [dɪsˈrʌpʃən] Störung f, Unterbrechung f.

dissatisfaction [ˈdɪssætɪsˈfækʃən] n Unzufriedenheit f.

dissatisfied [ˈdɪsˈsætɪsfaɪd] a unzufrieden.

dissect [dɪˈsekt] vt zerlegen, sezieren.

disseminate [dɪˈsemɪneɪt] vt verbreiten.

dissent [dɪˈsent] n abweichende Meinung f; vi nicht übereinstimmen.

dissident [ˈdɪsɪdənt] a andersdenkend; n Dissident m.

dissimilar [ˈdɪˈsɪmɪlə*] a unähnlich (to dat).

dissipate [ˈdɪsɪpeɪt] vt (waste) verschwenden; (scatter) zerstreuen; ~d a ausschweifend.

dissipation [dɪsɪˈpeɪʃən] n Ausschweifung f.

dissociate [dɪˈsəʊʃɪeɪt] vt trennen.

dissolute [ˈdɪsəluːt] a liederlich.

dissolve [dɪˈzɒlv] vt auflösen; vi sich auflösen.

dissuade [dɪˈsweɪd] vt abraten (+dat).

distance [ˈdɪstəns] n Entfernung f; **in the** ~ in der Ferne.

distant [ˈdɪstənt] a entfernt, fern; (with time) fern; (formal) distanziert.

distaste [ˈdɪsˈteɪst] n Abneigung f; ~**ful** a widerlich.

distemper [dɪsˈtempə*] n (paint) Temperafarbe f; (Med) Staupe f.

distend [dɪsˈtend] vti (sich) ausdehnen.

distil [dɪsˈtɪl] vt destillieren; ~**lery** n Brennerei f.

distinct [dɪsˈtɪŋkt] a (separate) getrennt; (clear) klar, deutlich; ~**ion** [dɪsˈtɪŋkʃən]

Unterscheidung f; (eminence) Berühmtheit f; (in exam) Auszeichnung f; ~**ive** a bezeichnend; ~**ly** ad deutlich.

distinguish [dɪsˈtɪŋgwɪʃ] vt unterscheiden; ~**ed** a (eminent) berühmt; ~**ing** a unterscheidend, bezeichnend.

distort [dɪsˈtɔːt] vt verdrehen; (misrepresent) entstellen; ~**ion** [dɪsˈtɔːʃən] Verzerrung f.

distract [dɪsˈtrækt] vt ablenken; (bewilder) verwirren; ~**ing** a verwirrend; ~**ion** [dɪsˈtrækʃən] Zerstreutheit f; (distress) Raserei f; (diversion) Zerstreuung f.

distraught [dɪsˈtrɔːt] a bestürzt.

distress [dɪsˈtres] n Not f; (suffering) Qual f; vt quälen; ~**ing** a erschütternd; ~ **signal** Notsignal nt.

distribute [dɪsˈtrɪbjuːt] vt verteilen.

distribution [dɪstrɪˈbjuːʃən] n Verteilung f.

distributor [dɪsˈtrɪbjʊtə*] n Verteiler m.

district [ˈdɪstrɪkt] n (of country) Kreis m; (of town) Bezirk m; ~ **attorney** (US) Oberstaatsanwalt m; ~ **nurse** (Brit) Kreiskrankenschwester f.

distrust [dɪsˈtrʌst] n Mißtrauen nt; vt mißtrauen (+dat).

disturb [dɪsˈtɜːb] vt stören; (agitate) erregen; ~**ance** Störung f; ~**ing** a beunruhigend.

disuse [dɪsˈjuːs] n Nichtgebrauch m; **to fall into** ~ außer Gebrauch kommen.

disused [ˈdɪsˈjuːzd] a aufgegeben, außer Gebrauch.

ditch [dɪtʃ] n Graben m; vt im Stich lassen.

dither [ˈdɪðə*] vi verdattert sein.

ditto [ˈdɪtəʊ] n dito, ebenfalls.

divan [dɪˈvæn] n Liegesofa nt.

dive [daɪv] n (into water) Kopfsprung m; (Aviat) Sturzflug m; vi tauchen; ~**r** Taucher m.

diverge [daɪˈvɜːdʒ] vi auseinandergehen.

diverse [daɪˈvɜːs] a verschieden.

diversification [daɪvɜːsɪfɪˈkeɪʃən] n Verzweigung f.

diversify [daɪˈvɜːsɪfaɪ] vt (ver)ändern; vi variieren.

diversion [daɪˈvɜːʃən] n Ablenkung f; (traffic) Umleitung f.

diversity [daɪˈvɜːsɪtɪ] n Verschiedenheit f; (variety) Mannigfaltigkeit f.

divert [daɪˈvɜːt] vt ablenken; traffic umleiten.

divide [dɪˈvaɪd] vt teilen; vi sich teilen.

dividend [ˈdɪvɪdend] n Dividende f; (fig) Gewinn m.

divine [dɪˈvaɪn] a göttlich; vt erraten.

diving board [ˈdaɪvɪŋbɔːd] n Sprungbrett nt.

divinity [dɪˈvɪnɪtɪ] n Gottheit f, Gott m; (subject) Religion f.

divisible [dɪˈvɪzəbl] a teilbar.

division [dɪˈvɪʒən] n Teilung f; (Math) Division f, Teilung f; (Mil) Division f; (part) Teil m, Abteilung f; (in opinion) Uneinigkeit f.

divorce [dɪˈvɔːs] n (Ehe)scheidung f; vt scheiden; ~**d** a geschieden; **to get** ~**d** sich scheiden lassen; ~**e** [dɪvɔːˈsiː] Geschiedene(r) mf.

divulge [daɪˈvʌldʒ] vt preisgeben.

dizziness [ˈdɪzɪnəs] n Schwindelgefühl nt.

dizzy [ˈdɪzɪ] a schwindlig.

do [duː] irreg vt tun, machen; vi (proceed) vorangehen; (be suitable) passen; (be enough) genügen; n (party) Party f; **how ~ you ~?** guten Tag! etc.

docile [ˈdəʊsaɪl] a gefügig; dog gutmütig.

dock [dɒk] n Dock nt; (Jur) Anklagebank f; vi ins Dock gehen; **~er** Hafenarbeiter m.

docket [ˈdɒkɪt] n Inhaltsvermerk m.

dockyard [ˈdɒkjɑːd] n Werft f.

doctor [ˈdɒktə*] n Arzt m, Ärztin f; (Univ) Doktor m.

doctrinaire [dɒktrɪˈnɛə*] a doktrinär.

doctrine [ˈdɒktrɪn] n Doktrin f.

document [ˈdɒkjəmənt] n Dokument nt; **~ary** [dɒkjʊˈmentərɪ] Dokumentarbericht m; (film) Dokumentarfilm m; a dokumentarisch; **~ation** [dɒkjumenˈteɪʃən] dokumentarische(r) Nachweis m.

doddering [ˈdɒdərɪŋ], **doddery** [ˈdɒdərɪ] a zittrig.

dodge [dɒdʒ] n Kniff m; vt umgehen; ausweichen (+dat); **~m** Boxauto nt.

dodo [ˈdəʊdəʊ] n Dronte f: **as dead as the ~** von Anno dazumal.

dog [dɒg] n Hund m; **~ biscuit** Hundekuchen m; **~ collar** Hundehalsband nt; (Eccl) Kragen m des Geistlichen; **~-eared** a mit Eselsohren; **~fish** Hundsfisch m; **~ food** Hundefutter nt.

dogged [ˈdɒgɪd] a hartnäckig.

dogma [ˈdɒgmə] n Dogma nt; **~tic** [dɒgˈmætɪk] a dogmatisch.

doings [ˈduːɪŋz] npl (activities) Treiben nt.

do-it-yourself [ˈduːɪtjəˈself] n Do-it-yourself nt; a zum Selbermachen.

doldrums [ˈdɒldrəmz] npl: **to be in the ~** Flaute haben; (person) deprimiert sein.

dole [dəʊl] n (Brit) Stempelgeld nt; **to be on the ~** stempeln gehen; **~ out** vt ausgeben, austeilen.

doleful [ˈdəʊlfʊl] a traurig.

doll [dɒl] n Puppe f; vt: **~ o.s. up** sich aufdonnern.

dollar [ˈdɒlə*] n Dollar m.

dollop [ˈdɒləp] n Brocken m.

dolphin [ˈdɒlfɪn] n Delphin m, Tümmler m.

domain [dəˈmeɪn] n Sphäre f, Bereich m.

dome [dəʊm] n Kuppel f.

domestic [dəˈmestɪk] a häuslich; (within country) Innen-, Binnen-; animal Haus-; **~ated** a person häuslich; animal zahm.

domicile [ˈdɒmɪsaɪl] n (ständiger) Wohnsitz m.

dominant [ˈdɒmɪnənt] a vorherrschend.

dominate [ˈdɒmɪneɪt] vt beherrschen.

domination [dɒmɪˈneɪʃən] n (Vor)herrschaft f.

domineering [dɒmɪˈnɪərɪŋ] a herrisch, überheblich.

dominion [dəˈmɪnɪən] n (rule) Regierungsgewalt f; (land) Staatsgebiet nt mit Selbstverwaltung.

dominoes [ˈdɒmɪnəʊz] n Domino(spiel) nt.

don [dɒn] n akademische(r) Lehrer m.

donate [dəʊˈneɪt] vt (blood, little money) spenden; (lot of money) stiften.

donation [dəʊˈneɪʃən] n Spende f.

donkey [ˈdɒŋkɪ] n Esel m.

donor [ˈdəʊnə*] n Spender m.

don't [dəʊnt] = **do not**.

doom [duːm] n böse(s) Geschick nt; (downfall) Verderben nt; vt: **to be ~ed** zum Untergang verurteilt sein.

door [dɔː*] n Tür f; **~bell** Türklingel f; **~handle** Türklinke f; **~man** Türsteher m; **~mat** Fußmatte f; **~step** Türstufe f; **~way** Türöffnung f.

dope [dəʊp] n (drug) Aufputschmittel nt.

dopey [ˈdəʊpɪ] a (col) bekloppt.

dormant [ˈdɔːmənt] a schlafend, latent.

dormitory [ˈdɔːmɪtrɪ] n Schlafsaal m.

dormouse [ˈdɔːmaʊs] n Haselmaus f.

dosage [ˈdəʊsɪdʒ] n Dosierung f.

dose [dəʊs] n Dosis f; vt dosieren.

dossier [ˈdɒsɪeɪ] n Dossier m, Aktenbündel nt.

dot [dɒt] n Punkt m; **on the ~** pünktlich.

dote [dəʊt]: **~ on** vt vernarrt sein in (+acc).

double [ˈdʌbl] a, ad doppelt; n Doppelgänger m; vt verdoppeln; (fold) zusammenfalten; vi (in amount) sich verdoppeln; **at the ~** im Laufschritt; **~s** (tennis) Doppel nt; **~ bass** Kontrabaß m; **~ bed** Doppelbett nt; **~-breasted** a zweireihig; **~cross** n Betrug m; vt hintergehen; **~decker** Doppeldecker m; **~room** Doppelzimmer nt.

doubly [ˈdʌblɪ] ad doppelt.

doubt [daʊt] n Zweifel m; vi zweifeln; vt bezweifeln; **without ~** zweifellos; **~ful** a zweifelhaft, fraglich; **~less** ad ohne Zweifel, sicherlich.

dough [dəʊ] n Teig m; **~nut** Krapfen m, Pfannkuchen m.

dove [dʌv] n Taube f; **~tail** n Schwalbenschwanz m, Zinke f; vt verzahnen, verzinken.

dowdy [ˈdaʊdɪ] a unmodern, schlampig.

down [daʊn] n (fluff) Flaum m; (hill) Hügel m; ad unten; (motion) herunter; hinunter; prep **he came ~ the street** er kam die Straße herunter; **to go ~ the street** die Straße hinuntergehen; **he lives ~ the street** er wohnt unten an der Straße; vt niederschlagen; **~ with X!** nieder mit X!; **~-and-out** a abgerissen; n Tramp m; **~-at-heel** a schäbig; **~cast** a niedergeschlagen; **~fall** Sturz m; **~hearted** a niedergeschlagen, mutlos; **~hill** ad bergab; **~pour** Platzregen m; **~right** a völlig, ausgesprochen; (motion) nach unten; a untere(r, s); **~stream** ad flußabwärts; **~town** ad in die/der Innenstadt; a (US) im Geschäftsviertel, City-; **~ward** a sinkend, Abwärts-; **~wards** ad abwärts, nach unten.

dowry [ˈdaʊrɪ] n Mitgift f.

doze [dəʊz] vi dösen; n Schläfchen nt, Nickerchen nt.

dozen [ˈdʌzn] n Dutzend nt.

drab [dræb] a düster, eintönig.

draft [drɑːft] n Skizze f, Entwurf m; (Fin) Wechsel m; (US Mil) Einberufung f; vt skizzieren.

drag [dræg] vt schleifen, schleppen; river

mit einem Schleppnetz absuchen; *vi* sich (dahin)schleppen; *n* (*bore*) etwas Blödes; (*hindrance*) Klotz *m* am Bein; **in ~** als Tunte; **~ on** *vi* sich in die Länge ziehen.

dragon ['drægən] *n* Drache *m*; **~fly** Libelle *f*.

drain [dreɪn] *n* (*lit*) Abfluß *m*; (*ditch*) Abflußgraben *m*; (*fig: burden*) Belastung *f*; *vt* ableiten; (*exhaust*) erschöpfen; *vi* (*of water*) abfließen; **~age** Kanalisation *f*; **~pipe** Abflußrohr *nt*.

drama ['drɑːmə] *n* (*lit, fig*) Drama *nt*; **~tic** [drəˈmætɪk] *a* dramatisch; **~tist** Dramatiker *m*.

drape [dreɪp] *vt* drapieren; *npl*: **~s** (*US*) Vorhänge *pl*; **~r** Tuchhändler *m*.

drastic ['dræstɪk] *a* drastisch.

draught [drɑːft] *n* Zug *m*; (*Naut*) Tiefgang *m*; **~s** Damespiel *nt*; (*beer*) **on ~** vom Faß; **~board** Zeichenbrett *nt*; **~sman** technische(r) Zeichner *m*; **~y** a zugig.

draw [drɔː] *irreg vt* ziehen; *crowd* anlocken; *picture* zeichnen; *money* abheben; *water* schöpfen; *vi* (*Sport*) unentschieden spielen; *n* (*Sport*) Unentschieden *nt*; (*lottery*) Ziehung *f*; **to ~ to a close** (*speech*) zu Ende kommen; (*year*) zu Ende gehen; **~ out** *vi* (*train*) ausfahren; (*lengthen*) sich hinziehen; *vt money* abheben; **~ up** *vi* (*stop*) halten; *vt document* aufsetzen; **~back** (*disadvantage*) Nachteil *m*; (*obstacle*) Haken *m*; **~bridge** Zugbrücke *f*; **~er** Schublade *f*; **~ing** Zeichnung *f*, Zeichnen *nt*; **~ing pin** Reißzwecke *f*; **~ing room** Salon *m*.

drawl [drɔːl] *n* schleppende Sprechweise *f*; *vi* gedehnt sprechen.

drawn [drɔːn] *a game* unentschieden; *face* besorgt.

dread [dred] *n* Furcht *f*, Grauen *nt*; *vt* fürchten; sich grauen vor (+*dat*); **~ful** a furchtbar.

dream [driːm] *n* Traum *m*; (*fancy*) Wunschtraum *m*; *vti irreg* träumen (*about* von); *a house etc* Traum-; **~er** Träumer *m*; **~ world** Traumwelt *f*; **~y** a verträumt.

dreary ['drɪərɪ] *a* trostlos, öde.

dredge [dredʒ] *vt* ausbaggern; (*with flour etc*) mit Mehl *etc* bestreuen; **~r** Baggerschiff *nt*; (*for flour etc*) (Mehl *etc*)streuer *m*.

dregs [dregz] *npl* Bodensatz *m*; (*fig*) Abschaum *m*.

drench [drentʃ] *vt* durchnässen.

dress [dres] *n* Kleidung *f*; (*garment*) Kleid *nt*; *vt* anziehen; (*Med*) verbinden; (*Agr*) düngen; *food* anrichten; **to get ~ed** sich anziehen; **~ up** *vi* sich fein machen; **~ circle** erste(r) Rang *m*; **~er** (*furniture*) Anrichte *f*, Geschirrschrank *m*; **she's a smart ~er** sie zieht sich elegant an; **~ing** (*Med*) Verband *m*; (*Cook*) Soße *f*; **~ing gown** Morgenrock *m*; **~ing room** (*Theat*) Garderobe *f*; (*Sport*) Umkleideraum *m*; **~ing table** Toilettentisch *m*; **~maker** Schneiderin *f*; **~making** Schneidern *nt*; **~ rehearsal** Generalprobe *f*; **~ shirt** Frackhemd *nt*.

dribble ['drɪbl] *vi* tröpfeln; *vt* sabbern.

drift [drɪft] *n* Trift *f*, Strömung *f*; (*snow—*) Schneewehe *f*; (*fig*) Richtung *f*; *vi* getrieben werden; (*aimlessly*) sich treiben lassen; **~wood** Treibholz *nt*.

drill [drɪl] *n* Bohrer *m*; (*Mil*) Drill *m*; *vt* bohren; (*Mil*) ausbilden; *vi* (*Mil*) exerzieren; bohren (*for* nach); **~ing** Bohren *nt*; (*hole*) Bohrloch *nt*; (*Mil*) Exerzieren *nt*.

drink [drɪŋk] *n* Getränk *nt*; (*spirits*) Drink *m*; *vti irreg* trinken; **~able** a trinkbar; **~er** Trinker *m*; **~ing water** Trinkwasser *nt*.

drip [drɪp] *n* Tropfen *m*; (*dripping*) Tröpfeln *nt*; *vi* tropfen; **~-dry** a bügelfrei; **~ping** Bratenfett *nt*; **~ping wet** a triefend.

drive [draɪv] *n* Fahrt *f*; (*road*) Einfahrt *f*; (*campaign*) Aktion *f*; (*energy*) Schwung *m*, Tatkraft *f*; (*Sport*) Schlag *m*; *irreg vt car* fahren; *animals* treiben; *nail* einschlagen; *ball* schlagen; (*power*) antreiben; (*force*) treiben; *vi* fahren; **to ~ sb mad** jdn verrückt machen; **what are you driving at?** worauf willst du hinaus?; **~-in** *a* Drive-in-.

drivel ['drɪvl] *n* Faselei *f*.

driver ['draɪvəʳ] *n* Fahrer *m*; **~'s license** (*US*) Führerschein *m*.

driving ['draɪvɪŋ] *a rain* stürmisch; **~ instructor** Fahrlehrer *m*; **~ lesson** Fahrstunde *f*; **~ licence** (*Brit*) Führerschein *m*; **~ school** Fahrschule *f*; **~ test** Fahrprüfung *f*.

drizzle ['drɪzl] *n* Nieselregen *m*; *vi* nieseln.

droll [drəʊl] *a* drollig.

dromedary ['drɒmɪdərɪ] *n* Dromedar *nt*.

drone [drəʊn] *n* (*sound*) Brummen *nt*; (*bee*) Drohne *f*.

drool [druːl] *vi* sabbern.

droop [druːp] *vi* (*schlaff*) herabhängen.

drop [drɒp] *n* (*of liquid*) Tropfen *m*; (*fall*) Fall *m*; *vt* fallen lassen; (*lower*) senken; (*abandon*) fallenlassen; *vi* (*fall*) herunterfallen; **~ off** *vi* (*sleep*) einschlafen; **~ out** *vi* (*withdraw*) ausscheiden; **~out** Ausgeflippte(r) *mf*, Drop-out *mf*.

dross [drɒs] *n* Unrat *m*.

drought [draʊt] *n* Dürre *f*.

drove [drəʊv] *n* (*crowd*) Herde *f*.

drown [draʊn] *vt* ertränken; *sound* übertönen; *vi* ertrinken.

drowsy ['draʊzɪ] *a* schläfrig.

drudge [drʌdʒ] *n* Kuli *m*; **~ry** ['drʌdʒərɪ] Plackerei *f*.

drug [drʌg] *n* (*Med*) Arznei *f*; (*narcotic*) Rauschgift *nt*; *vt* betäuben; **~ addict** Rauschgiftsüchtige(r) *mf*; **~gist** (*US*) Drogist *m*; **~store** (*US*) Drogerie *f*.

drum [drʌm] *n* Trommel *f*; **~mer** Trommler *m*.

drunk [drʌŋk] *a* betrunken; *n* Betrunkene(r) *m*; Trinker(in *f*) *m*; **~ard** Trunkenbold *m*; **~en** a betrunken; **~enness** Betrunkenheit *f*.

dry [draɪ] *a* trocken; *vt* (ab)trocknen; *vi* trocknen, trocken werden; **~ up** *vi* austrocknen; (*dishes*) abtrocknen; **~-clean** *vt* chemisch reinigen; **~-cleaning** chemische Reinigung *f*; **~er** Trockner *m*;

~**ness** Trockenheit *f*; ~ **rot** Hausschwamm *m*.

dual ['djʊəl] *a* doppelt; ~ **carriageway** zweispurige Fahrbahn *f*; ~ **nationality** doppelte Staatsangehörigkeit *f*; ~-**purpose** *a* Mehrzweck-.

dubbed [dʌbd] *a film* synchronisiert.

dubious ['dju:bɪəs] *a* zweifelhaft.

duchess ['dʌtʃɪs] *n* Herzogin *f*.

duck [dʌk] *n* Ente *f*; *vt* (ein)tauchen; *vi* sich ducken; ~**ling** Entchen *nt*.

duct [dʌkt] *n* Röhre *f*.

dud [dʌd] *n* Niete *f*; *a* wertlos, miserabel; *cheque* ungedeckt.

due [dju:] *a* fällig; *(fitting)* angemessen; **the train is** ~ der Zug soll ankommen; *n* Gebühr *f*, *(right)* Recht *nt*; *ad south etc* genau, gerade; ~ **to** infolge (+*gen*), wegen (+*gen*).

duel ['djʊəl] *n* Duell *nt*.

duet [dju:'et] *n* Duett *nt*.

duke [dju:k] *n* Herzog *m*.

dull [dʌl] *a colour, weather* trübe; *(stupid)* schwer von Begriff; *(boring)* langweilig; *vt (soften, weaken)* abstumpfen.

duly ['dju:lɪ] *ad* ordnungsgemäß, richtig; *(on time)* pünktlich.

dumb [dʌm] *a (lit)* stumm; *(col: stupid)* doof, blöde.

dummy ['dʌmɪ] *n* Schneiderpuppe *f*; *(substitute)* Attrappe *f*; *(teat)* Schnuller *m*; *a* Schein-.

dump [dʌmp] *n* Abfallhaufen *m*; *(Mil)* Stapelplatz *m*; *(col: place)* Nest *nt*; *vt* abladen, auskippen; ~**ing** *(Comm)* Schleuderexport *m*; *(of rubbish)* Schuttabladen *nt*.

dumpling ['dʌmplɪŋ] *n* Kloß *m*, Knödel *m*.

dunce [dʌns] *n* Dummkopf *m*.

dune [dju:n] *n* Düne *f*.

dung [dʌŋ] *n* Mist *m*; *(Agr)* Dünger *m*.

dungarees [dʌŋgə'ri:z] *npl* Arbeitsanzug *m*, Arbeitskleidung *f*.

dungeon ['dʌndʒən] *n* Kerker *m*.

dupe [dju:p] *n* Gefoppte(r) *m*; *vt* hintergehen, anführen.

duplicate ['dju:plɪkɪt] *a* doppelt; *n* Duplikat *nt*, ['dju:plɪkeɪt] *vt* verdoppeln; *(make copies)* kopieren; **in** ~ in doppelter Ausführung.

duplicator ['dju:plɪkeɪtə*] *n* Vervielfältigungsapparat *m*.

durability [djʊərə'bɪlɪtɪ] *n* Haltbarkeit *f*.

durable ['djʊərəbl] *a* haltbar.

duration [djʊə'reɪʃən] *n* Dauer *f*.

during ['djʊərɪŋ] *prep* während (+*gen*).

dusk [dʌsk] *n* Abenddämmerung *f*.

dust [dʌst] *n* Staub *m*; *vt* abstauben; *(sprinkle)* bestäuben; ~**bin** *(Brit)* Mülleimer *m*; ~**er** Staubtuch *nt*; ~**man** *(Brit)* Müllmann *m*; ~ **storm** Staubsturm *m*; ~**y** *a* staubig.

dutiable ['dju:tɪəbl] *a* zollpflichtig.

duty ['dju:tɪ] *n* Pflicht *f*; *(job)* Aufgabe *f*; *(tax)* Einfuhrzoll *m*; **on** ~ im Dienst, diensthabend; ~-**free** *a* zollfrei; ~-**free articles** zollfreie Waren *pl*.

dwarf [dwɔ:f] *n* Zwerg *m*.

dwell [dwel] *vi irreg* wohnen; ~ **on** *vt* ver-

weilen bei; ~**ing** Wohnung *f*.

dwindle ['dwɪndl] *vi* schwinden.

dye [daɪ] *n* Farbstoff *m*; *vt* färben.

dying ['daɪɪŋ] *a person* sterbend; *moments* letzt.

dynamic [daɪ'næmɪk] *a* dynamisch; ~**s** Dynamik *f*.

dynamite ['daɪnəmaɪt] *n* Dynamit *nt*.

dynamo ['daɪnəməʊ] *n* Dynamo *m*.

dynasty ['dɪnəstɪ] *n* Dynastie *f*.

dysentery ['dɪsntrɪ] *n* Ruhr *f*.

dyspepsia [dɪs'pepsɪə] *n* Verdauungsstörung *f*.

E

E, e [i:] *n* E *nt*, e *nt*.

each [i:tʃ] *a* jeder/jede/jedes; *pron* (ein) jeder/(eine) jede/(ein) jedes; ~ **other** einander, sich.

eager *a*, ~**ly** *ad* ['i:gə*, -lɪ] eifrig; ~**ness** Eifer *m*; Ungeduld *f*.

eagle ['i:gl] *n* Adler *m*.

ear [ɪə*] *n* Ohr *nt*; *(of corn)* Ähre *f*; ~**ache** Ohrenschmerzen *pl*; ~**drum** Trommelfell *nt*.

earl [ɜ:l] *n* Graf *m*.

early ['ɜ:lɪ] *a, ad* früh; **you're** ~ du bist früh dran.

earmark ['ɪəmɑ:k] *vt* vorsehen.

earn [ɜ:n] *vt* verdienen.

earnest ['ɜ:nɪst] *a* ernst; **in** ~ im Ernst.

earnings ['ɜ:nɪŋz] *npl* Verdienst *m*.

earphones ['ɪəfəʊnz] *npl* Kopfhörer *pl*.

earplug ['ɪəplʌg] *n* Ohropax *"* *nt*.

earring ['ɪərɪŋ] *n* Ohrring *m*.

earshot ['ɪəʃɒt] *n* Hörweite *f*.

earth [ɜ:θ] *n* Erde *f*; *(Elec)* Erdung *f*; *vt* erden; ~**enware** Steingut *nt*; ~**quake** Erdbeben *nt*.

earthy ['ɜ:θɪ] *a* roh; *(sensual)* sinnlich.

earwig ['ɪəwɪg] *n* Ohrwurm *m*.

ease [i:z] *n (simplicity)* Leichtigkeit *f*; *(social)* Ungezwungenheit *f*; *vt pain* lindern; *burden* erleichtern; **at** ~ ungezwungen; *(Mil)* rührt euch!; **to feel at** ~ sich wohl fühlen; ~ **off** *or* **up** *vi* nachlassen.

easel ['i:zl] *n* Staffelei *f*.

easily ['i:zɪlɪ] *ad* leicht.

east [i:st] *n* Osten *m*; *a* östlich; *ad* nach Osten.

Easter ['i:stə*] *n* Ostern *nt*.

eastern ['i:stən] *a* östlich; orientalisch.

eastward(s) ['i:stwəd(z)] *ad* ostwärts.

easy ['i:zɪ] *a task* einfach; *life* bequem; *manner* ungezwungen, natürlich; *ad* leicht.

eat [i:t] *vt irreg* essen; *(animals)* fressen; *(destroy)* (zer)fressen; ~ **away** *vt (corrode)* zerfressen; ~**able** *a* genießbar.

eaves [i:vz] *npl* (überstehender) Dachrand *m*.

eavesdrop ['i:vzdrɒp] *vi* horchen, lauschen; ~ **on sb** jdn belauschen.

ebb [eb] *n* Ebbe *f*; *vi* ebben.

ebony ['ebənɪ] *n* Ebenholz *nt*.

ebullient [ɪ'bʌlɪənt] *a* sprudelnd, temperamentvoll.

eccentric [ɪk'sentrɪk] *a* exzentrisch, überspannt; *n* exzentrische(r) Mensch *m*.

ecclesiastical [ɪklɪːzɪˈæstɪkəl] *a* kirchlich, geistlich.

echo [ˈekəʊ] *n* Echo *nt*; *vt* zurückwerfen; (*fig*) nachbeten; *vi* widerhallen.

eclipse [ɪˈklɪps] *n* Verfinsterung *f*, Finsternis *f*; *vt* verfinstern.

ecology [ɪˈkɒlədʒɪ] *n* Ökologie *f*.

economic [iːkəˈnɒmɪk] *a* (volks)wirtschaftlich, ökonomisch; ~**al** *a* wirtschaftlich; *person* sparsam; ~**s** Volkswirtschaft *f*.

economist [ɪˈkɒnəmɪst] *n* Volkswirt- (schaftler) *m*.

economize [ɪˈkɒnəmaɪz] *vi* sparen (*on* an +*dat*).

economy [ɪˈkɒnəmɪ] *n* (*thrift*) Sparsamkeit *f*; (*of country*) Wirtschaft *f*.

ecstasy [ˈekstəsɪ] *n* Ekstase *f*.

ecstatic [eksˈtætɪk] *a* hingerissen.

ecumenical [iːkjuˈmenɪkəl] *a* ökumenisch.

eczema [ˈeksɪmə] *n* Ekzem *nt*.

Eden [ˈiːdn] *n* (Garten *m*) Eden *nt*.

edge [edʒ] *n* Rand *m*; (*of knife*) Schneide *f*; **on ~** nervös; (*nerves*) überreizt.

edging [ˈedʒɪŋ] *n* Einfassung *f*.

edgy [ˈedʒɪ] *a* nervös.

edible [ˈedɪbl] *a* eßbar.

edict [ˈiːdɪkt] *n* Erlaß *m*.

edifice [ˈedɪfɪs] *n* Gebäude *nt*.

edit [ˈedɪt] *vt* edieren, redigieren; ~**ion** [ɪˈdɪʃən] Ausgabe *f*; ~**or** (*of newspaper*) Redakteur *m*; (*of book*) Lektor *m*; ~**orial** [edɪˈtɔːrɪəl] *a* Redaktions-; *n* Leitartikel *m*.

educate [ˈedjukeɪt] *vt* erziehen, (aus)-bilden.

education [edjuˈkeɪʃən] *n* (*teaching*) Unterricht *m*; (*system*) Schulwesen *nt*; (*schooling*) Erziehung *f*; Bildung *f*; ~**al** *a* pädagogisch.

eel [iːl] *n* Aal *m*.

eerie [ˈɪərɪ] *a* unheimlich.

efface [ɪˈfeɪs] *vt* auslöschen.

effect [ɪˈfekt] *n* Wirkung *f*; *vt* bewirken; **in ~** in der Tat; ~**s** *pl* (*sound, visual*) Effekte *pl*; ~**ive** *a* wirksam, effektiv.

effeminate [ɪˈfemɪnɪt] *a* weibisch.

effervescent [efəˈvesnt] *a* (*lit*, *fig*) sprudelnd.

efficiency [ɪˈfɪʃənsɪ] *n* Leistungsfähigkeit *f*.

efficient *a*, ~**ly** *ad* [ɪˈfɪʃənt, -lɪ] tüchtig; (*Tech*) leistungsfähig; *method* wirksam.

effigy [ˈefɪdʒɪ] *n* Abbild *nt*.

effort [ˈefət] *n* Anstrengung *f*; **to make an ~** sich anstrengen; ~**less** *a* mühelos.

effrontery [ɪˈfrʌntərɪ] *n* Unverfrorenheit *f*.

egalitarian [ɪgælɪˈtɛərɪən] *a* Gleichheits-, egalitär.

egg [eg] *n* Ei *nt*; ~ **on** *vt* anstacheln; ~**cup** Eierbecher *m*; ~**plant** Aubergine *f*; ~**shell** Eierschale *f*.

ego [ˈiːgəʊ] *n* Ich *nt*, Selbst *nt*.

egotism [ˈegəʊtɪzəm] *n* Ichbezogenheit *f*.

egotist [ˈegəʊtɪst] *n* Egozentriker *m*.

eiderdown [ˈaɪdədaʊn] *n* Daunendecke *f*.

eight [eɪt] *num* acht; ~**een** *num* achtzehn; ~**h** [eɪtθ] *a* achte(r,s); *n* Achtel *nt*; ~**y** *num* achtzig.

either [ˈaɪðə*] *cj* ~ ... **or** entweder ... oder;

pron ~ **of the two** eine(r,s) von beiden; **I don't want ~** ich will keins von beiden; *a* **on ~ side** auf beiden Seiten; *ad* **I don't ~** ich auch nicht.

eject [ɪˈdʒekt] *vt* ausstoßen, vertreiben; ~**or seat** Schleudersitz *m*.

elaborate [ɪˈlæbərɪt] *a* sorgfältig ausgearbeitet, ausführlich; [ɪˈlæbəreɪt] *vt* sorgfältig ausarbeiten; ~**ly** *ad* genau, ausführlich.

elaboration [ɪlæbəˈreɪʃən] *n* Ausarbeitung *f*.

elapse [ɪˈlæps] *vi* vergehen.

elastic [ɪˈlæstɪk] *n* Gummiband *nt*; *a* elastisch; ~ **band** Gummiband *nt*.

elated [ɪˈleɪtɪd] *a* froh, in gehobener Stimmung.

elation [ɪˈleɪʃən] *n* gehobene Stimmung *f*.

elbow [ˈelbəʊ] *n* Ellbogen *m*.

elder [ˈeldə*] *a* älter; *n* Ältere(r) *mf*; ~**ly** *a* ältere(r,s).

elect [ɪˈlekt] *vt* wählen; *a* zukünftig; ~**ion** Wahl *f*; ~**ioneering** [ɪlekʃəˈnɪərɪŋ] Wahlpropaganda *f*; ~**or** Wähler *m*; ~**oral** *a* Wahl-; ~**orate** Wähler *pl*, Wählerschaft *f*.

electric [ɪˈlektrɪk] *a* elektrisch, Elektro-; ~**al** *a* elektrisch; ~ **blanket** Heizdecke *f*; ~ **chair** elektrische(r) Stuhl *m*; ~ **cooker** Elektroherd *m*; ~ **current** elektrische(r) Strom *m*; ~ **fire** elektrische(r) Heizofen *m*; ~**ian** [ɪlekˈtrɪʃən] Elektriker *m*; ~**ity** [ɪlekˈtrɪsɪtɪ] Elektrizität *f*.

electrification [ɪlektrɪfɪˈkeɪʃən] *n* Elektrifizierung *f*.

electrify [ɪˈlektrɪfaɪ] *vt* elektrifizieren; (*fig*) elektrisieren.

electro- [ɪˈlektrəʊ] *pref* Elektro-.

electrocute [ɪˈlektrəʊkjuːt] *vt* elektrisieren; durch elektrischen Strom töten.

electrode [ɪˈlektrəʊd] *n* Elektrode *f*.

electron [ɪˈlektrɒn] *n* Elektron *nt*.

electronic [ɪlekˈtrɒnɪk] *a* elektronisch, Elektronen-; ~**s** Elektronik *f*.

elegance [ˈelɪgəns] *n* Eleganz *f*.

elegant [ˈelɪgənt] *a* elegant.

elegy [ˈelɪdʒɪ] *n* Elegie *f*.

element [ˈelɪmənt] *n* Element *nt*; (*fig*) Körnchen *nt*; ~**ary** [elɪˈmentərɪ] *a* einfach; (*primary*) grundlegend, Anfangs-.

elephant [ˈelɪfənt] *n* Elefant *m*.

elevate [ˈelɪveɪt] *vt* emporheben.

elevation [elɪˈveɪʃən] *n* (*height*) Erhebung *f*; (*of style*) Niveau *nt*; (*Archit*) (Quer)-schnitt *m*.

elevator [ˈelɪveɪtə*] *n* (*US*) Fahrstuhl *m*, Aufzug *m*.

eleven [ɪˈlevn] *num* elf; *n* (*team*) Elf *f*.

elf [elf] *n* Elfe *f*.

elicit [ɪˈlɪsɪt] *vt* herausbekommen.

eligible [ˈelɪdʒəbl] *a* wählbar; **he's not ~** er kommt nicht in Frage; **to be ~ for a pension/competition** pensions-/teilnahmeberechtigt sein; ~ **bachelor** gute Partie *f*.

eliminate [ɪˈlɪmɪneɪt] *vt* ausschalten; beseitigen.

elimination [ɪlɪmɪˈneɪʃən] *n* Ausschaltung *f*; Beseitigung *f*.

elite [eɪˈliːt] *n* Elite *f*.

elm [elm] *n* Ulme *f*.

elocution [eləˈkjuːʃən] n Sprecherziehung f; (clarity) Artikulation f.

elongated [ˈiːlɒŋgeɪtɪd] a verlängert.

elope [ɪˈloʊp] vi entlaufen; ~ment Entlaufen nt.

eloquence [ˈeləkwəns] n Beredsamkeit f.

eloquent a. ~ly ad [ˈeləkwənt, -lɪ] redegewandt.

else [els] ad sonst; ~where ad anderswo, woanders; who ~? wer sonst?; sb ~ jd anders; or ~ sonst.

elucidate [ɪˈluːsɪdeɪt] vt erläutern.

elude [ɪˈluːd] vt entgehen (+dat).

elusive [ɪˈluːsɪv] a schwer faßbar.

emaciated [ɪˈmeɪsɪeɪtɪd] a abgezehrt.

emanate [ˈeməneɪt] vi ausströmen (from aus).

emancipate [ɪˈmænsɪpeɪt] vt emanzipieren; slave freilassen.

emancipation [ɪmænsɪˈpeɪʃən] n Emanzipation f; Freilassung f.

embalm [ɪmˈbɑːm] vt einbalsamieren.

embankment [ɪmˈbæŋkmənt] n (of river) Uferböschung f; (of road) Straßendamm m.

embargo [ɪmˈbɑːgoʊ] n Embargo nt.

embark [ɪmˈbɑːk] vi sich einschiffen; ~ on vt unternehmen; ~ation [embɑːˈkeɪʃən] Einschiffung f.

embarrass [ɪmˈbærəs] vt in Verlegenheit bringen; ~ed a verlegen; ~ing a peinlich; ~ment Verlegenheit f.

embassy [ˈembəsɪ] n Botschaft f.

embed [ɪmˈbed] vt einbetten.

embellish [ɪmˈbelɪʃ] vt verschönern.

embers [ˈembəz] npl Glut(asche) f.

embezzle [ɪmˈbezl] vt unterschlagen; ~ment Unterschlagung f.

embitter [ɪmˈbɪtə*] vt verbittern.

emblem [ˈembləm] n Emblem nt, Abzeichen nt.

embodiment [ɪmˈbɒdɪmənt] n Verkörperung f.

embody [ɪmˈbɒdɪ] vt ideas verkörpern; new features (in sich) vereinigen.

emboss [ɪmˈbɒs] vt prägen.

embrace [ɪmˈbreɪs] vt umarmen; (include) einschließen; n Umarmung f.

embroider [ɪmˈbrɔɪdə*] vt (be)sticken; story ausschmücken; ~y Stickerei f.

embryo [ˈembrɪoʊ] n (lit) Embryo m; (fig) Keim m.

emerald [ˈemərəld] n Smaragd m; a smaragdgrün.

emerge [ɪˈmɜːdʒ] vi auftauchen; (truth) herauskommen; ~nce Erscheinen nt; ~ncy n Notfall m; a action Not-; ~ncy exit Notausgang m.

emery [ˈemərɪ] n: ~ paper Schmirgelpapier nt.

emetic [ɪˈmetɪk] n Brechmittel nt.

emigrant [ˈemɪgrənt] n Auswanderer m, Emigrant m; a Auswanderungs-.

emigrate [ˈemɪgreɪt] vi auswandern, emigrieren.

emigration [emɪˈgreɪʃən] n Auswanderung f, Emigration f.

eminence [ˈemɪnəns] n hohe(r) Rang m; E~ Eminenz f.

eminent [ˈemɪnənt] a bedeutend.

emission [ɪˈmɪʃən] n (of gases) Ausströmen nt.

emit [ɪˈmɪt] vt von sich (dat) geben.

emotion [ɪˈmoʊʃən] n Emotion f, Gefühl nt; ~al a person emotional; scene ergreifend; ~ally ad gefühlsmäßig; behave emotional; sing ergreifend.

emotive [ɪˈmoʊtɪv] a gefühlsbetont.

emperor [ˈempərə*] n Kaiser m.

emphasis [ˈemfəsɪs] n (Ling) Betonung f; (fig) Nachdruck m.

emphasize [ˈemfəsaɪz] vt betonen.

emphatic a, ~ally ad [ɪmˈfætɪk, -əlɪ] nachdrücklich; to be ~ about sth etw nachdrücklich betonen.

empire [ˈempaɪə*] n Reich nt.

empirical [emˈpɪrɪkəl] a empirisch.

employ [ɪmˈplɔɪ] vt (hire) anstellen; (use) verwenden; ~ee [emplɔɪˈiː] Angestellte(r) mf; ~er Arbeitgeber(in f) m; ~ment Beschäftigung f; in ~ment beschäftigt.

empress [ˈemprɪs] n Kaiserin f.

emptiness [ˈemptɪnɪs] n Leere f.

empty [ˈemptɪ] a leer; vt contents leeren; container ausleeren; ~-handed a mit leeren Händen.

emu [ˈiːmjuː] n Emu m.

emulate [ˈemjʊleɪt] vt nacheifern (+dat).

enable [ɪˈneɪbl] vt ermöglichen; it ~s us to ... das ermöglicht es uns, zu . . .

enamel [ɪˈnæməl] n Email nt; (of teeth) (Zahn)schmelz m.

enamoured [ɪˈnæməd] a verliebt sein (of in +dat).

encase [ɪnˈkeɪs] vt einschließen; (Tech) verschalen.

enchant [ɪnˈtʃɑːnt] vt bezaubern; ~ing a entzückend.

encircle [ɪnˈsɜːkl] vt umringen.

enclose [ɪnˈkloʊz] vt einschließen; (in letter) beilegen (in, with dat); ~d (in letter) beiliegend, anbei.

enclosure [ɪnˈkloʊʒə*] n Einfriedung f; (in letter) Anlage f.

encore [ˈɒŋkɔː*] n Zugabe f; ~! da capo!

encounter [ɪnˈkaʊntə*] n Begegnung f; (Mil) Zusammenstoß m; vt treffen; resistance stoßen auf (+acc).

encourage [ɪnˈkʌrɪdʒ] vt ermutigen; ~ment Ermutigung f, Förderung f.

encouraging [ɪnˈkʌrɪdʒɪŋ] a ermutigend, vielversprechend.

encroach [ɪnˈkroʊtʃ] vi eindringen ((up)on in +acc), überschreiten ((up)on acc).

encyclop(a)edia [ensaɪkloʊˈpiːdɪə] n Konversationslexikon nt.

end [end] n Ende nt, Schluß m; (purpose) Zweck m; a End-; vt beenden; vi zu Ende gehen; ~ up vi landen.

endanger [ɪnˈdeɪndʒə*] vt gefährden.

endeavour [ɪnˈdevə*] n Bestrebung f; vi sich bemühen.

ending [ˈendɪŋ] n Ende nt.

endless [ˈendlɪs] a endlos; plain unendlich.

endorse [ɪnˈdɔːs] vt unterzeichnen; (approve) unterstützen; ~ment Bestätigung f; (of document) Unterzeichnung f; (on licence) Eintrag m.

endow [ɪn'daʊ] vt: ~ **sb with sth** jdm etw verleihen; (with money) jdm etw stiften.

end product ['endprɒdʌkt] n Endprodukt nt.

endurable [ɪn'djʊərəbl] a erträglich.

endurance [ɪn'djʊərəns] n Ausdauer f; (suffering) Ertragen nt.

endure [ɪn'djʊə*] vt ertragen; vi (last) (fort)dauern.

enemy ['enɪmɪ] n Feind m; a feindlich.

energetic [enə'dʒetɪk] a tatkräftig.

energy ['enədʒɪ] n (of person) Energie f, Tatkraft f; (Phys) Energie f.

enervating ['enɜ:veɪtɪŋ] a nervenaufreibend.

enforce [ɪn'fɔ:s] vt durchsetzen; obedience erzwingen.

engage [ɪn'geɪdʒ] vt (employ) einstellen; (in conversation) verwickeln; (Mil) angreifen; (Tech) einrasten lassen, einschalten; ~**d** a verlobt; (Tel, toilet) besetzt; (busy) beschäftigt, unabkömmlich; **to get** ~**d** sich verloben; (appointment) Verabredung f; (to marry) Verlobung f; (Mil) Gefecht nt; ~**ment ring** Verlobungsring m.

engaging [ɪn'geɪdʒɪŋ] a gewinnend.

engender [ɪn'dʒendə*] vt hervorrufen.

engine ['endʒɪn] n (Aut) Motor m; (Rail) Lokomotive f; ~**er** [endʒɪnɪə*] Ingenieur m; (US Rail) Lokomotivführer m; ~**ering** [endʒɪˈnɪərɪŋ] Technik f; Maschinenbau m; ~ **failure**, ~ **trouble** Maschinenschaden m; (Aut) Motorschaden m.

engrave [ɪn'greɪv] vt (carve) einschneiden; (fig) tief einprägen; (print) gravieren.

engraving [ɪn'greɪvɪŋ] n Stich m.

engrossed [ɪn'grəʊst] a vertieft.

engulf [ɪn'gʌlf] vt verschlingen.

enhance [ɪn'hɑ:ns] vt steigern, heben.

enigma [ɪ'nɪgmə] n Rätsel nt; ~**tic** [enɪg'mætɪk] a rätselhaft.

enjoy [ɪn'dʒɔɪ] vt genießen; privilege besitzen; ~**able** a erfreulich; ~**ment** Genuß m, Freude f.

enlarge [ɪn'lɑ:dʒ] vt erweitern; (Phot) vergrößern; **to** ~ **on sth** etw weiter ausführen; ~**ment** Vergrößerung f.

enlighten [ɪn'laɪtn] vt aufklären; ~**ment** Aufklärung f.

enlist [ɪn'lɪst] vt gewinnen; vi (Mil) sich melden.

enmity ['enmɪtɪ] n Feindschaft f.

enormity [ɪ'nɔ:mɪtɪ] n Ungeheuerlichkeit f.

enormous a, ~**ly** ad [ɪ'nɔ:məs, -lɪ] ungeheuer.

enough [ɪ'nʌf] a genug; ad genug, genügend; ~**!** genug!; **that's** ~**!** das reicht!

enquire [ɪn'kwaɪə*] = **inquire**.

enrich [ɪn'rɪtʃ] vt bereichern.

enrol [ɪn'rəʊl] vt (Mil) anwerben; vi (register) sich anmelden; ~**ment** (for course) Anmeldung f; (Univ) Einschreibung f.

en route [ɑ:n'ru:t] ad unterwegs.

ensign ['ensaɪn] n (Naut) Flagge f; (Mil) Fähnrich m.

enslave [ɪn'sleɪv] vt versklaven.

ensue [ɪn'sju:] vi folgen, sich ergeben.

ensuing [ɪn'sju:ɪŋ] a (nach)folgend.

ensure [ɪn'ʃʊə*] vt garantieren.

entail [ɪn'teɪl] vt mit sich bringen.

enter ['entə*] vt eintreten in (+dat), betreten; club beitreten (+dat); (in book) eintragen; vi hereinkommen, hineingehen; ~ **for** vt sich beteiligen an (+dat); ~ **into** vt agreement eingehen; argument sich einlassen auf (+acc); ~ **upon** vt beginnen.

enterprise ['entəpraɪz] n (in person) Initiative f, Unternehmungsgeist m; (Comm) Unternehmen nt, Betrieb m.

enterprising ['entəpraɪzɪŋ] a unternehmungslustig.

entertain [entə'teɪn] vt guest bewirten; (amuse) unterhalten; ~**er** Unterhaltungskünstler(in f) m; ~**ing** a unterhaltend, amüsant; ~**ment** (amusement) Unterhaltung f; (show) Veranstaltung f.

enthralled [ɪn'θrɔ:ld] a gefesselt.

enthusiasm [ɪn'θu:zɪæzəm] n Begeisterung f.

enthusiast [ɪn'θu:zɪæst] n Enthusiast m, Schwärmer(in f) m; ~**ic** [ɪnθu:zɪ'æstɪk] a begeistert.

entice [ɪn'taɪs] vt verleiten, locken.

entire [ɪn'taɪə*] a ganz; ~**ly** ad ganz, völlig; ~**ty** [ɪn'taɪərətɪ] n: **in its** ~**ty** in seiner Gesamtheit.

entitle [ɪn'taɪtl] vt (allow) berechtigen; (name) betiteln.

entity ['entɪtɪ] n Ding nt, Wesen nt.

entrance ['entrəns] n Eingang m; (entering) Eintritt m; [ɪn'trɑ:ns] vt hinreißen; ~ **examination** Aufnahmeprüfung f; ~ **fee** Eintrittsgeld nt.

entrancing [ɪn'trɑ:nsɪŋ] a bezaubernd.

entrant ['entrənt] n (for exam) Kandidat m; (into job) Anfänger m; (Mil) Rekrut m; (in race) Teilnehmer m.

entreat [ɪn'tri:t] vt anflehen, beschwören; ~**y** flehende Bitte f, Beschwörung f.

entrée ['ɒntreɪ] n Zwischengang m.

entrenched [ɪn'trentʃt] a (fig) verwurzelt.

entrust [ɪn'trʌst] vt anvertrauen (sb with sth jdm etw).

entry ['entrɪ] n Eingang m; (Theat) Auftritt m; (in account) Eintragung f; (in dictionary) Eintrag m; **'no** ~**'** 'Eintritt verboten'; (for cars) 'Einfahrt verboten'; ~ **form** Anmeldeformular nt.

enunciate [ɪ'nʌnsɪeɪt] vt (deutlich) aussprechen.

envelop [ɪn'veləp] vt einhüllen; ~**e** ['envələʊp] n Umschlag m.

enviable ['envɪəbl] a beneidenswert.

envious ['envɪəs] a neidisch.

environment [ɪn'vaɪərənmənt] n Umgebung f; (ecology) Umwelt f; ~**al** [ɪnvaɪərən'mentl] a Umwelt-.

envisage [ɪn'vɪzɪdʒ] vt sich (dat) vorstellen; (plan) ins Auge fassen.

envoy ['envɔɪ] n Gesandte(r) mf.

envy ['envɪ] n Neid m; (object) Gegenstand m des Neides; vt beneiden (sb sth jdn um etw).

enzyme ['enzaɪm] n Enzym nt.

ephemeral [ɪ'femərəl] a kurzlebig, vorübergehend.

epic ['epɪk] n Epos nt; (film) Großfilm m; a episch; (fig) heldenhaft.

epidemic [epɪ'demɪk] n Epidemie f.

epigram ['epɪgræm] n Epigramm nt.

epilepsy ['epɪlepsɪ] n Epilepsie f.

epileptic [epɪ'leptɪk] a epileptisch; n Epileptiker(in f) m.

epilogue ['epɪlog] n (of drama) Epilog m; (of book) Nachwort nt.

episode ['epɪsəʊd] n (incident) Vorfall m; (story) Episode f.

epistle [ɪ'pɪsl] n Brief m.

epitaph ['epɪtɑːf] n Grab(in)schrift f.

epitome [ɪ'pɪtəmɪ] n Inbegriff m.

epitomize [ɪ'pɪtəmaɪz] vt verkörpern.

epoch ['iːpok] n Epoche f.

equable ['ekwəbl] a ausgeglichen.

equal ['iːkwl] a gleich; ~ **to the task** der Aufgabe gewachsen; n Gleichgestellte(r) mf; vt gleichkommen (+dat); **two times two ~s four** zwei mal zwei ist (gleich) vier; **without ~** ohne seinesgleichen; **~ity** [ɪ'kwolɪtɪ] Gleichheit f; (equal rights) Gleichberechtigung f; **~ize** vt gleichmachen; vi (Sport) ausgleichen; **~izer** (Sport) Ausgleich(streffer) m; **~ly** ad gleich; **~s sign** Gleichheitszeichen nt.

equanimity [ekwə'nɪmɪtɪ] n Gleichmut m.

equate [ɪ'kweɪt] vt gleichsetzen.

equation [ɪ'kweɪʒən] n Gleichung f.

equator [ɪ'kweɪtə*] n Äquator m; **~ial** [ekwə'tɔːrɪəl] a Äquator-.

equilibrium [iːkwɪ'lɪbrɪəm] n Gleichgewicht nt.

equinox ['iːkwɪnoks] n Tag- und Nachtgleiche f.

equip [ɪ'kwɪp] vt ausrüsten; **~ment** Ausrüstung f; (Tech) Gerät nt.

equitable ['ekwɪtəbl] a gerecht, billig.

equity ['ekwɪtɪ] n Billigkeit f, Gerechtigkeit f.

equivalent [ɪ'kwɪvələnt] a gleichwertig (to dat), entsprechend (to dat); n (amount) gleiche Menge f; (in money) Gegenwert m; Äquivalent nt.

equivocal [ɪ'kwɪvəkəl] a zweideutig; (suspect) fragwürdig.

era ['ɪərə] n Epoche f, Ära f.

eradicate [ɪ'rædɪkeɪt] vt ausrotten.

erase [ɪ'reɪz] vt ausradieren; tape löschen; **~r** Radiergummi m.

erect [ɪ'rekt] a aufrecht; vt errichten; **~ion** Errichtung f; (Physiol) Erektion f.

ermine ['ɜːmɪn] n Hermelin(pelz) m.

erode [ɪ'rəʊd] vt zerfressen; land auswaschen.

erosion [ɪ'rəʊʒən] n Auswaschen nt, Erosion f.

erotic [ɪ'rotɪk] a erotisch; **~ism** [ɪ'rotɪsɪzəm] Erotik f.

err [ɜː*] vi sich irren.

errand ['erənd] n Besorgung f; **~ boy** Laufbursche m.

erratic [ɪ'rætɪk] a sprunghaft; driving unausgeglichen.

erroneous [ɪ'rəʊnɪəs] a irrig, irrtümlich.

error ['erə*] n Fehler m.

erudite ['eruːdaɪt] a gelehrt.

erudition [eru'dɪʃən] n Gelehrsamkeit f.

erupt [ɪ'rʌpt] vi ausbrechen; **~ion** Ausbruch m.

escalate ['eskəleɪt] vt steigern; vi sich steigern.

escalator ['eskəleɪtə*] n Rolltreppe f.

escapade [eskə'peɪd] n Eskapade f, Streich m.

escape [ɪs'keɪp] n Flucht f; (of gas) Entweichen nt; vti entkommen (+dat); (prisoners) fliehen; (leak) entweichen; **to ~ notice** unbemerkt bleiben; **the word ~s me** das Wort ist mir entfallen.

escapism [ɪs'keɪpɪzəm] n Flucht f (vor der Wirklichkeit).

escort ['eskɔːt] n (person accompanying) Begleiter m; (guard) Eskorte f; [ɪs'kɔːt] vt lady begleiten; (Mil) eskortieren.

especially [ɪs'peʃəlɪ] ad besonders.

espionage ['espɪənɑːʒ] n Spionage f.

esplanade ['espləneɪd] n Esplanade f, Promenade f.

Esquire [ɪs'kwaɪə*] n (in address) **J. Brown, Esq** Herrn J. Brown.

essay ['eseɪ] n Aufsatz m; (Liter) Essay m.

essence ['esəns] n (quality) Wesen nt; (extract) Essenz f, Extrakt m.

essential [ɪ'senʃəl] a (necessary) unentbehrlich; (basic) wesentlich; n Hauptbestandteil m, Allernötigste(s) nt; **~ly** ad in der Hauptsache, eigentlich.

establish [ɪs'tæblɪʃ] vt (set up) gründen, einrichten; (prove) nachweisen; **~ment** (setting up) Einrichtung f; (business) Unternehmen nt; **the E~ment** das Establishment.

estate [ɪs'teɪt] n Gut nt; (housing ~) Siedlung f; (will) Nachlaß m; **~ agent** Grundstücksmakler m; **~ car** (Brit) Kombiwagen m.

esteem [ɪs'tiːm] n Wertschätzung f.

estimate ['estɪmət] n (opinion) Meinung f; (of price) (Kosten)voranschlag m; ['estɪmeɪt] vt schätzen.

estimation [estɪ'meɪʃən] n Einschätzung f; (esteem) Achtung f.

estuary ['estjʊərɪ] n Mündung f.

etching ['etʃɪŋ] n Kupferstich m.

eternal a, **~ly** ad [ɪ'tɜːnl, -nəlɪ] ewig.

eternity [ɪ'tɜːnɪtɪ] n Ewigkeit f.

ether ['iːθə*] n (Med) Äther m.

ethical ['eθɪkəl] a ethisch.

ethics ['eθɪks] npl Ethik f.

ethnic ['eθnɪk] a Volks-, ethnisch.

etiquette ['etɪket] n Etikette f.

Eucharist ['juːkərɪst] n heilige(s) Abendmahl nt.

eulogy ['juːlədʒɪ] n Lobrede f.

eunuch ['juːnək] n Eunuch m.

euphemism ['juːfɪmɪzəm] n Euphemismus m.

euphoria [juː'fɔːrɪə] n Taumel m, Euphorie f.

euthanasia [juːθə'neɪzɪə] n Euthanasie f.

evacuate [ɪ'vækjueɪt] vt place räumen; people evakuieren; (Med) entleeren.

evacuation [ɪˌvækjuˈeɪʃən] n Evakuierung f; Räumung f; Entleerung f.

evade [ɪˈveɪd] vt (escape) entkommen (+dat); (avoid) meiden; duty sich entziehen (+dat).

evaluate [ɪˈvæljueɪt] vt bewerten; information auswerten.

evangelical [iːvænˈdʒelɪkəl] a evangelisch.

evangelist [ɪˈvændʒəlɪst] n Evangelist m.

evaporate [ɪˈvæpəreɪt] vi verdampfen; vt verdampfen lassen; ~d milk Kondensmilch f.

evaporation [ɪˌvæpəˈreɪʃən] n Verdunstung f.

evasion [ɪˈveɪʒən] n Umgehung f; (excuse) Ausflucht f.

evasive [ɪˈveɪzɪv] a ausweichend.

even [ˈiːvən] a eben; gleichmäßig; score etc unentschieden; number gerade; vt (ein)ebnen, glätten; ad ~ **you** selbst or sogar du; **he** ~ **said** ... er hat sogar gesagt ...; ~ **as he spoke** (gerade) da er sprach; ~ **if** sogar or selbst wenn, wenn auch; ~ **so** dennoch; ~ **out** or **up** vi sich ausgleichen; vt ausgleichen; **get** ~ sich revanchieren.

evening [ˈiːvnɪŋ] n Abend m; **in the** ~ abends, am Abend; ~ **class** Abendschule f; ~ **dress** (man's) Gesellschaftsanzug m; (woman's) Abendkleid nt.

evenly [ˈiːvənlɪ] ad gleichmäßig.

evensong [ˈiːvənsɒŋ] n (Rel) Abendandacht f.

event [ɪˈvent] n (happening) Ereignis nt; (Sport) Disziplin f; (horses) Rennen nt; **the next** ~ der nächste Wettkampf; **in the** ~ **of** im Falle (+gen); ~**ful** a ereignisreich.

eventual [ɪˈventʃuəl] a (final) schließlich; ~**ity** [ɪventʃuˈælɪtɪ] Möglichkeit f; ~**ly** ad (at last) am Ende; (given time) schließlich.

ever [ˈevə*] ad (always) immer; (at any time) je(mals); ~ **so big** sehr groß; ~ **so many** sehr viele; ~**green** a immergrün; n Immergrün nt; ~**-lasting** a immerwährend.

every [ˈevrɪ] a jeder/jede/jedes; ~ **day** jeden Tag; ~ **other day** jeden zweiten Tag; ~**body** pron jeder, alle pl; ~**day** a (daily) täglich; (commonplace) alltäglich, Alltags-; ~**one** = ~**body**; ~ **so often** hin und wieder; ~**thing** pron alles; ~**where** ad überall.

evict [ɪˈvɪkt] vt ausweisen; ~**ion** Ausweisung f.

evidence [ˈevɪdəns] n (sign) Spur f; (proof) Beweis m; (testimony) Aussage f; **in** ~ (obvious) zu sehen.

evident [ˈevɪdənt] a augenscheinlich; ~**ly** ad offensichtlich.

evil [ˈiːvl] a böse, übel; n Übel nt; Unheil nt; (sin) Böse(s) nt.

evocative [ɪˈvɒkətɪv] a **to be** ~ **of sth** an etw (acc) erinnern.

evoke [ɪˈvəʊk] vt hervorrufen.

evolution [ˌiːvəˈluːʃən] n Entwicklung f; (of life) Evolution f.

evolve [ɪˈvɒlv] vt entwickeln; vi sich entwickeln.

ewe [juː] n Mutterschaf nt.

ex- [eks] a Ex-, Alt-, ehemalig.

exact a, ~**ly** ad [ɪgˈzækt, -lɪ] genau; vt (demand) verlangen; (compel) erzwingen; money, fine einziehen; punishment vollziehen; ~**ing** a anspruchsvoll; ~**itude** Genauigkeit f; ~**ness** Genauigkeit f, Richtigkeit f.

exaggerate [ɪgˈzædʒəreɪt] vti übertreiben; ~**d** a übertrieben.

exaggeration [ɪgzædʒəˈreɪʃən] n Übertreibung f.

exalt [ɪgˈzɔːlt] vt (praise) verherrlichen.

exam [ɪgˈzæm] n Prüfung f.

examination [ɪgzæmɪˈneɪʃən] n Untersuchung f; (Sch, Univ) Prüfung f, Examen nt; (customs) Kontrolle f.

examine [ɪgˈzæmɪn] vt untersuchen; (Sch) prüfen; (consider) erwägen; ~**r** Prüfer m.

example [ɪgˈzɑːmpl] n Beispiel nt; **for** ~ zum Beispiel.

exasperate [ɪgˈzɑːspəreɪt] vt zum Verzweifeln bringen.

exasperating [ɪgˈzɑːspəreɪtɪŋ] a ärgerlich, zum Verzweifeln bringend.

exasperation [ɪgzɑːspəˈreɪʃən] n Verzweiflung f.

excavate [ˈekskəveɪt] vt (hollow out) aushöhlen; (unearth) ausgraben.

excavation [ekskəˈveɪʃən] n Ausgrabung f.

excavator [ˈekskəveɪtə*] n Bagger m.

exceed [ɪkˈsiːd] vt überschreiten; hopes übertreffen; ~**ingly** ad in höchstem Maße.

excel [ɪkˈsel] vi sich auszeichnen; vt übertreffen; ~**lence** [ˈeksələns] Vortrefflichkeit f; **His E~lency** [ˈeksələnsɪ] Seine Exzellenz f; ~**lent** [ˈeksələnt] a ausgezeichnet.

except [ɪkˈsept] prep (also ~ **for**) außer (+dat); vt ausnehmen; ~**ing** prep = **except**; ~**ion** [ɪkˈsepʃən] Ausnahme f; **to take** ~**ion to** Anstoß nehmen an (+dat); ~**ional** a, ~**ionally** ad [ɪkˈsepʃənl, -nlɪ] außergewöhnlich.

excerpt [ˈeksəːpt] n Auszug m.

excess [ekˈses] n Übermaß nt (of an +dat); Exzeß m; a money Nach-; baggage Mehr-; ~**es** pl Ausschweifungen pl, Exzesse pl; (violent) Ausschreitungen pl; ~ **weight** (of thing) Mehrgewicht nt; (of person) Übergewicht nt; ~**ive** a, ~**ively** ad übermäßig.

exchange [ɪksˈtʃeɪndʒ] n Austausch m; (Fin) Wechselstube f; (Tel) Vermittlung f, Zentrale f; (Post Office) (Fernsprech)amt nt; vt goods tauschen; greetings austauschen; money, blows wechseln; see **rate**.

exchequer [ɪksˈtʃekə*] n Schatzamt nt.

excisable [ekˈsaɪzbl] a (verbrauchs)-steuerpflichtig.

excise [ˈeksaɪz] n Verbrauchssteuer f; [ekˈsaɪz] vt (Med) herausschneiden.

excitable [ɪkˈsaɪtəbl] a erregbar, nervös.

excite [ɪkˈsaɪt] vt erregen; ~**d** a aufgeregt; **to get** ~**d** sich aufregen; ~**ment** Aufgeregtheit f, Erregung f.

exciting [ɪkˈsaɪtɪŋ] a aufregend; book, film spannend.

exclaim [ɪksˈkleɪm] vi ausrufen.

exclamation [ekskləˈmeɪʃən] n Ausruf m;

~ **mark** Ausrufezeichen *nt*.

exclude [ɪksˈkluːd] *vt* ausschließen.

exclusion [ɪksˈkluːʒən] *n* Ausschluß *m*.

exclusive [ɪksˈkluːsɪv] *a* (*select*) exklusiv; (*sole*) ausschließlich, Allein-; ~ **of** exklusive (+*gen*); ~**ly** *ad* nur, ausschließlich.

excommunicate [ekskəˈmjuːnɪkeɪt] *vt* exkommunizieren.

excrement [ˈekskrɪmənt] *n* Kot *m*.

excruciating [ɪksˈkruːʃɪeɪtɪŋ] *a* qualvoll.

excursion [ɪksˈkɜːʃən] *n* Ausflug *m*.

excusable [ɪksˈkjuːzəbl] *a* entschuldbar.

excuse [ɪksˈkjuːs] *n* Entschuldigung *f*; [ɪksˈkjuːz] *vt* entschuldigen; ~ **me!** entschuldigen Sie!

execute [ˈeksɪkjuːt] *vt* (*carry out*) ausführen; (*kill*) hinrichten.

execution [eksɪˈkjuːʃən] *n* Ausführung *f*; (*killing*) Hinrichtung *f*; ~**er** Scharfrichter *m*.

executive [ɪgˈzekjʊtɪv] *n* (*Comm*) leitende(r) Angestellte(r) *m*, Geschäftsführer *m*; (*Pol*) Exekutive *f*; *a* Exekutiv-, ausführend.

executor [ɪgˈzekjʊtə*] *n* Testamentsvollstrecker *m*.

exemplary [ɪgˈzemplərɪ] *a* musterhaft.

exemplify [ɪgˈzemplɪfaɪ] *vt* veranschaulichen.

exempt [ɪgˈzempt] *a* befreit; *vt* befreien; ~**ion** [ɪgˈzempʃən] Befreiung *f*.

exercise [ˈeksəsaɪz] *n* Übung *f*; *vt power* ausüben; *muscle, patience* üben; *dog* ausführen; ~ **book** (Schul)heft *nt*.

exert [ɪgˈzɜːt] *vt influence* ausüben; ~ **o.s.** sich anstrengen; ~**ion** Anstrengung *f*.

exhaust [ɪgˈzɔːst] *n* (*fumes*) Abgase *pl*; (*pipe*) Auspuffrohr *nt*; *vt* (*weary*) ermüden; (*use up*) erschöpfen; ~**ed** *a* erschöpft; ~**ing** *a* anstrengend; ~**ion** Erschöpfung *f*; ~**ive** *a* erschöpfend.

exhibit [ɪgˈzɪbɪt] *n* (*Art*) Ausstellungsstück *nt*; (*Jur*) Beweisstück *nt*; *vt* ausstellen; ~**ion** [eksɪˈbɪʃən] (*Art*) Ausstellung *f*; (*of temper etc*) Zurschaustellung *f*; ~**ionist** [eksɪˈbɪʃənɪst] Exhibitionist *m*; ~**or** Aussteller *m*.

exhilarating [ɪgˈzɪləreɪtɪŋ] *a* erhebend.

exhilaration [ɪgzɪləˈreɪʃən] *n* erhebende(s) Gefühl *nt*.

exhort [ɪgˈzɔːt] *vt* ermahnen; beschwören.

exile [ˈeksaɪl] *n* Exil *nt*; (*person*) im Exil Lebende(r) *mf*; *vt* verbannen; **in** ~ im Exil.

exist [ɪgˈzɪst] *vi* existieren; (*live*) leben; ~**ence** Existenz *f*; (*way of life*) Leben *nt*, Existenz *f*; ~**ing** *a* vorhanden, bestehend.

exit [ˈeksɪt] *n* Ausgang *m*; (*Theat*) Abgang *m*.

exonerate [ɪgˈzɒnəreɪt] *vt* entlasten.

exorbitant [ɪgˈzɔːbɪtənt] *a* übermäßig; *price* Phantasie-.

exotic [ɪgˈzɒtɪk] *a* exotisch.

expand [ɪksˈpænd] *vt* (*spread*) ausspannen; *operations* ausdehnen; *vi* sich ausdehnen.

expanse [ɪksˈpæns] *n* weite Fläche *f*, Weite *f*.

expansion [ɪksˈpænʃən] *n* Erweiterung *f*.

expatriate [eksˈpætrɪeɪt] *a* Exil-; *n* im Exil Lebende(r) *mf*; *vt* ausbürgern.

expect [ɪksˈpekt] *vt* erwarten; (*suppose*) annehmen; *vi*: **to be** ~**ing** ein Kind erwarten; ~**ant** *a* (*hopeful*) erwartungsvoll; *mother* werdend; ~**ation** [ekspekˈteɪʃən] (*hope*) Hoffnung *f*; ~**ations** *pl* Erwartungen *pl*; (*prospects*) Aussicht *f*.

expedience [ɪksˈpiːdɪəns], **expediency** [ɪksˈpiːdɪənsɪ] *n* Zweckdienlichkeit *f*.

expedient [ɪksˈpiːdɪənt] *a* zweckdienlich; *n* (Hilfs)mittel *nt*.

expedite [ˈekspɪdaɪt] *vt* beschleunigen.

expedition [ekspɪˈdɪʃən] *n* Expedition *f*.

expel [ɪksˈpel] *vt* ausweisen; *student* (ver)-weisen.

expend [ɪksˈpend] *vt money* ausgeben; *effort* aufwenden; ~**able** *a* entbehrlich; ~**iture** Kosten *pl*, Ausgaben *pl*.

expense [ɪksˈpens] *n* (*cost*) Auslage *f*, Ausgabe *f*; (*high cost*) Aufwand *m*; ~**s** *pl* Spesen *pl*; **at the** ~ **of** auf Kosten von; ~ **account** Spesenkonto *nt*.

expensive [ɪksˈpensɪv] *a* teuer.

experience [ɪksˈpɪərɪəns] *n* (*incident*) Erlebnis *nt*; (*practice*) Erfahrung *f*; *vt* erfahren, erleben; *hardship* durchmachen; ~**d** *a* erfahren.

experiment [ɪksˈperɪmənt] *n* Versuch *m*, Experiment *nt*; [ɪksˈperɪment] *vi* experimentieren; ~**al** [ɪksperɪˈmentl] *a* versuchsweise, experimentell.

expert [ˈekspɜːt] *n* Fachmann *m*, (*official*) Sachverständige(r) *m*; *a* erfahren; (*practised*) gewandt; ~**ise** [ekspɜːˈtiːz] Sachkenntnis *f*.

expiration [ekspaɪəˈreɪʃən] *n* (*breathing*) Ausatmen *nt*; (*fig*) Ablauf *m*.

expire [ɪksˈpaɪə*] *vi* (*end*) ablaufen; (*die*) sterben; (*ticket*) verfallen.

expiry [ɪksˈpaɪərɪ] *n* Ablauf *m*.

explain [ɪksˈpleɪn] *vt* (*make clear*) erklären; (*account for*) begründen; ~ **away** *vt* wegerklären.

explanation [ekspləˈneɪʃən] *n* Erklärung *f*.

explanatory [ɪksˈplænətərɪ] *a* erklärend.

explicable [eksˈplɪkəbl] *a* erklärlich.

explicit [ɪksˈplɪsɪt] *a* (*clear*) ausdrücklich; (*outspoken*) deutlich; ~**ly** *ad* deutlich.

explode [ɪksˈpləʊd] *vi* explodieren; *vt bomb* zur Explosion bringen; *theory* platzen lassen.

exploit [ˈeksplɔɪt] *n* (Helden)tat *f*; [ɪksˈplɔɪt] *vt* ausbeuten; ~**ation** [eksplɔɪˈteɪʃən] Ausbeutung *f*.

exploration [eksplɔːˈreɪʃən] *n* Erforschung *f*.

exploratory [eksˈplɔːrətərɪ] *a* sondierend, Probe-.

explore [ɪksˈplɔː*] *vt* (*travel*) erforschen; (*search*) untersuchen; ~**r** Forschungsreisende(r) *mf*, Erforscher(in *f*) *m*.

explosion [ɪksˈpləʊʒən] *n* (*lit*) Explosion *f*; (*fig*) Ausbruch *m*.

explosive [ɪksˈpləʊzɪv] *a* explosiv, Spreng-; *n* Sprengstoff *m*.

exponent [eksˈpəʊnənt] *n* Exponent *m*.

export [eksˈpɔːt] *vt* exportieren; [ˈekspɔːt] *n* Export *m*; *a trade* Export-; ~**ation**

[ekspɔ:'teɪʃən] Ausfuhr f; ~er Exporteur m.

expose [ɪks'pəuz] vt (to danger etc) aussetzen (to dat); imposter entlarven; lie aufdecken.

exposé [eks'pəuzeɪ] n (of scandal) Enthüllung f.

exposed [ɪks'pəuzd] a position exponiert.

exposure [ɪks'pəuʒə*] m (Med) Unterkühlung f; (Phot) Belichtung f; ~ **meter** Belichtungsmesser m.

expound [ɪks'paund] vt entwickeln.

express [ɪks'pres] a ausdrücklich; (speedy) Expreß-, Eil-; n (Rail) Zug m; vt ausdrücken; **to** ~ **o.s.** sich ausdrücken; ~**ion** [ɪks'preʃən] (phrase) Ausdruck m; (look) (Gesichts)ausdruck m; ~**ive** a ausdrucksvoll; ~**ly** ad ausdrücklich, extra.

expropriate [eks'prəuprieɪt] vt enteignen.

expulsion [ɪks'pʌlʃən] n Ausweisung f.

exquisite [eks'kwɪzɪt] a erlesen; ~**ly** ad ausgezeichnet.

extend [ɪks'tend] vt visit etc verlängern; building vergrößern, ausbauen; hand ausstrecken; welcome bieten.

extension [ɪks'tenʃən] n Erweiterung f; (of building) Anbau m; (Tel) Nebenanschluß m, Apparat m.

extensive [ɪks'tensɪv] a knowledge umfassend; use weitgehend.

extent [ɪks'tent] n Ausdehnung f; (fig) Ausmaß nt.

extenuating [eks'tenjueɪtɪŋ] a mildernd.

exterior [eks'tɪərɪə*] a äußere(r,s), Außen-; n Äußere(s) nt.

exterminate [eks'tɜ:mɪneɪt] vt ausrotten.

extermination [ekstɜ:mɪ'neɪʃən] n Ausrottung f.

external [eks'tɜ:nl] a äußere(r,s), Außen-; ~**ly** ad äußerlich.

extinct [ɪks'tɪŋkt] a ausgestorben; ~**ion** [ɪks'tɪŋkʃən] Aussterben nt.

extinguish [ɪks'tɪŋgwɪʃ] vt (aus)löschen; ~**er** Löschgerät nt.

extort [ɪks'tɔ:t] vt erpressen (sth from sb jdn um etw); ~**ion** [ɪks'tɔ:ʃən] Erpressung f; ~**ionate** [ɪks'tɔ:ʃənɪt] a überhöht, erpresserisch.

extra [ˈekstrə] a zusätzlich; ad besonders; n (work) Sonderarbeit f; (benefit) Sonderleistung f; (charge) Zuschlag m; (Theat) Statist m.

extract [ɪks'trækt] vt (heraus)ziehen; (select) auswählen; [ˈekstrækt] n (from book etc) Auszug m; (Cook) Extrakt m; ~**ion** (Heraus)ziehen nt; (origin) Abstammung f.

extradite [ˈekstrədaɪt] vt ausliefern.

extradition [ekstrə'dɪʃən] n Auslieferung f.

extraneous [eks'treɪnɪəs] a unwesentlich; influence äußere(r,s).

extraordinary [ɪks'trɔ:dnrɪ] a außerordentlich; (amazing) erstaunlich.

extravagance [ɪks'trævəgəns] n Verschwendung f; (lack of restraint) Zügellosigkeit f; (an —) Extravaganz f.

extravagant [ɪks'trævəgənt] a extravagant.

extreme [ɪks'tri:m] a edge äußerste(r,s), hinterste(r,s); cold äußerste(r,s); behaviour

außergewöhnlich, übertrieben; n Extrem nt, das Äußerste; ~**s** pl (excesses) Ausschreitungen pl; (opposites) Extreme pl; ~**ly** ad äußerst, höchst.

extremist [ɪks'tri:mɪst] a extremistisch; n Extremist(in f) m.

extremity [ɪks'tremɪtɪ] n (end) Spitze f, äußerste(s) Ende nt; (hardship) bitterste Not f; (Anat) Hand f; Fuß m.

extricate [ˈekstrɪkeɪt] vt losmachen, befreien.

extrovert [ˈekstrəuvɜ:t] n Extravertierte(r) mf; a extravertiert.

exuberance [ɪg'zu:bərəns] n Überschwang m.

exuberant [ɪg'zu:bərənt] a ausgelassen.

exude [ɪg'zju:d] vt absondern; vi sich absondern.

exult [ɪg'zʌlt] vi frohlocken; ~**ation** [egzʌl'teɪʃən] Jubel m.

eye [aɪ] n Auge nt; (of needle) Öhr nt; vt betrachten; (up and down) mustern; **to keep an** ~ **on** aufpassen auf (+acc); **in the** ~**s of** in den Augen (+gen); **up to the** ~**s** in bis zum Hals in; ~**ball** Augapfel m; ~**bath** Augenbad nt; ~**brow** Augenbraue f; ~**lash** Augenwimper f; ~**lid** Augenlid nt; **that was an** ~**opener** das hat mir die Augen geöffnet; ~**shadow** Lidschatten m; ~**sight** Sehkraft f; ~**sore** Schandfleck m; ~**wash** (lit) Augenwasser nt; (fig) Schwindel m; Quatsch m; ~ **witness** Augenzeuge m.

F

F,f [ef] n F nt, f nt.

fable [ˈfeɪbl] n Fabel f.

fabric [ˈfæbrɪk] n Stoff m, Gewebe nt; (fig) Gefüge m.

fabricate [ˈfæbrɪkeɪt] vt fabrizieren.

fabulous [ˈfæbjuləs] a (imaginary) legendär, sagenhaft; (unbelievable) unglaublich; (wonderful) fabelhaft, unglaublich.

façade [fə'sɑ:d] n (lit, fig) Fassade f.

face [feɪs] n Gesicht nt; (grimace) Grimasse f; (surface) Oberfläche f; (of clock) Zifferblatt nt; vt (point towards) liegen nach; situation sich gegenübersehen (+dat); difficulty mutig entgegentreten (+dat); **in the** ~ **of** angesichts (+gen); **to** ~ **up to sth** einer Sache ins Auge sehen; ~ **cream** Gesichtscreme f; ~ **powder** (Gesichts)puder m.

facet [ˈfæsɪt] n Seite f, Aspekt m; (of gem) Kristallfläche f, Schliff m.

facetious [fə'si:ʃəs] a schalkhaft; (humorous) witzig; ~**ly** ad spaßhaft, witzig.

face to face [feɪstə'feɪs] ad Auge in Auge, direkt.

face value [feɪs 'vælju:] n Nennwert m; (fig) **to take sth at its** ~ etw für bare Münze nehmen.

facial [ˈfeɪʃl] a Gesichts-.

facile [ˈfæsaɪl] a oberflächlich; (US: easy) leicht.

facilitate [fə'sɪlɪteɪt] vt erleichtern.

facility [fə'sɪlɪtɪ] n (ease) Leichtigkeit f;

(*skill*) Gewandtheit f; **facilities** pl Einrichtungen pl.

facing ['feɪsɪŋ] a zugekehrt; prep gegenüber.

facsimile [fæk'sɪmɪlɪ] n Faksimile nt.

fact [fækt] n Tatsache f; **in** ~ in der Tat.

faction ['fækʃən] n Splittergruppe f.

factor ['fæktə*] n Faktor m.

factory ['fæktərɪ] n Fabrik f.

factual ['fæktjuəl] a Tatsachen-, sachlich.

faculty ['fækəltɪ] n Fähigkeit f; (*Univ*) Fakultät f; (*US: teaching staff*) Lehrpersonal nt.

fade [feɪd] vi (*lose colour*) verschießen, verblassen; (*grow dim*) nachlassen, schwinden; (*sound, memory*) schwächer werden; (*wither*) verwelken; vt material verblassen lassen; ~**d** a verwelkt; *colour* verblichen; **to** ~ **in/out** (*Cine*) ein-/ausblenden.

fag [fæg] n Plackerei f; (*col: cigarette*) Kippe f; ~**ged** a (*exhausted*) erschöpft.

Fahrenheit ['færənhaɪt] n Fahrenheit.

fail [feɪl] vt exam nicht bestehen; *student* durchfallen lassen; (*courage*) verlassen; (*memory*) im Stich lassen; vi (*supplies*) zu Ende gehen; (*student*) durchfallen; (*eyesight*) nachlassen; (*light*) schwächer werden; (*crop*) fehlschlagen; (*remedy*) nicht wirken; ~ **to do sth** (*neglect*) es unterlassen, etw zu tun; (*be unable*) es nicht schaffen, etw zu tun; **without** ~ ganz bestimmt, unbedingt; ~**ing** n Fehler m, Schwäche f; prep in Ermangelung (+gen); ~**ing this** falls nicht, sonst; ~**ure** (*person*) Versager m; (*act*) Versagen nt; (*Tech*) Defekt m.

faint [feɪnt] a schwach, matt; n Ohnmacht f; vi ohnmächtig werden; ~**hearted** a mutlos, kleinmütig; ~**ly** ad schwach; ~**ness** Schwäche f; (*Med*) Schwächegefühl nt.

fair [fɛə*] a schön; *hair* blond; *skin* hell; *weather* schön, trocken; (*just*) gerecht, fair; (*not very good*) leidlich, mittelmäßig; *conditions* günstig, gut; (*sizeable*) ansehnlich; ad *play* ehrlich, fair; n (*Comm*) Messe f; (*fun* ~) Jahrmarkt m; ~**ly** ad (*honestly*) gerecht, fair; (*rather*) ziemlich; ~**ness** Schönheit f; (*of hair*) Blondheit f; (*of game*) Ehrlichkeit f, Fairneß f; ~**way** (*Naut*) Fahrrinne f.

fairy ['fɛərɪ] n Fee f; ~**land** Märchenland nt; ~ **tale** Märchen nt.

faith [feɪθ] n Glaube m; (*trust*) Vertrauen nt; (*sect*) Bekenntnis nt, Religion f; ~**ful** a, ~**fully** ad treu; yours ~**fully** hochachtungsvoll.

fake [feɪk] n (*thing*) Fälschung f; (*person*) Schwindler m; a vorgetäuscht; vt fälschen.

falcon ['fɔːlkən] n Falke m.

fall [fɔːl] n Fall m, Sturz m; (*decrease*) Fallen nt; (*of snow*) (Schnee)fall m; (*US: autumn*) Herbst m; vi irreg (lit, fig) fallen; (*night*) hereinbrechen; ~**s** pl (*waterfall*) Fälle pl; ~ **back on** vt in Reserve haben; ~ **down** vi (*person*) hinfallen; (*building*) einstürzen; ~ **flat** vi (lit) glatt hinfallen; (*joke*) nicht ankommen; **the plan fell flat** aus dem Plan wurde nichts; ~ **for** vt trick

hereinfallen auf (+acc); *person* sich verknallen in (+acc); ~ **off** vi herunterfallen (von); (*diminish*) sich vermindern; ~ **out** vi sich streiten; ~ **through** vi (*plan*) ins Wasser fallen.

fallacy ['fæləsɪ] n Trugschluß m.

fallible ['fæləbl] a fehlbar.

fallout ['fɔːlaʊt] n radioaktive(r) Niederschlag m.

fallow ['fæləʊ] a brach(liegend).

false [fɔːls] a falsch; (*artificial*) gefälscht, künstlich; **under** ~ **pretences** unter Vorspiegelung falscher Tatsachen; ~ **alarm** Fehlalarm m; ~**ly** ad fälschlicherweise; ~ **teeth** pl Gebiß nt.

falter ['fɔːltə*] vi schwanken; (*in speech*) stocken.

fame [feɪm] n Ruhm m.

familiar [fə'mɪlɪə*] a vertraut, bekannt; (*intimate*) familiär; **to be** ~ **with** vertraut sein mit, gut kennen; ~**ity** [fəmɪlɪ'ærɪtɪ] Vertrautheit f; ~**ize** vt vertraut machen.

family ['fæmɪlɪ] n Familie f; (*relations*) Verwandtschaft f; ~ **allowance** Kindergeld nt; ~ **business** Familienunternehmen nt; ~ **doctor** Hausarzt m; ~ **life** Familienleben nt; ~ **planning** Geburtenkontrolle f.

famine ['fæmɪn] n Hungersnot f.

famished ['fæmɪʃt] a ausgehungert.

famous ['feɪməs] a berühmt.

fan [fæn] n (*folding*) Fächer m; (*Elec*) Ventilator m; (*admirer*) begeisterte(r) Anhänger m; Fan m; vt fächeln; ~ **out** vi sich (fächerförmig) ausbreiten.

fanatic [fə'nætɪk] n Fanatiker(in f) m; ~**al** a fanatisch.

fan belt ['fænbelt] n Keilriemen m.

fancied ['fænsɪd] a beliebt, populär.

fanciful ['fænsɪful] a (*odd*) seltsam; (*imaginative*) phantasievoll.

fancy ['fænsɪ] n (*liking*) Neigung f; (*imagination*) Phantasie f, Einbildung f; a schick, ausgefallen; vt (*like*) gern haben, wollen; (*imagine*) sich einbilden; (**just**) ~ **(that)!** stellen Sie sich (das nur) vor!; ~ **dress** Verkleidung f, Maskenkostüm nt; ~-**dress ball** Maskenball m.

fanfare ['fænfɛə*] n Fanfare f.

fang [fæŋ] n Fangzahn m; (*snake's*) Giftzahn m.

fanlight ['fænlaɪt] n Oberlicht nt.

fantastic [fæn'tæstɪk] a phantastisch.

fantasy ['fæntəzɪ] n Phantasie f.

far [fɑː*] a weit; ad weit entfernt; (*very much*) weitaus, (sehr) viel; ~ **away**, ~ **off** weit weg; **by** ~ bei weitem; **so** ~ soweit; bis jetzt; ~**away** a weit entfernt; **the F~ East** der Ferne Osten.

farce [fɑːs] n Schwank m, Posse f; (fig) Farce f.

farcical ['fɑːsɪkəl] a possenhaft; (fig) lächerlich.

fare [fɛə*] n Fahrpreis m; Fahrgeld nt; (*food*) Kost f; vi: **he is faring well** es ergeht ihm gut; ~ **well** Abschied(sgruß) m; interj lebe wohl!; a Abschieds-.

far-fetched ['fɑː'fetʃt] a weit hergeholt.

farm [fɑːm] n Bauernhof m, Farm f; vt

bewirtschaften; vi Landwirt m sein; ~**er** Bauer m, Landwirt m; ~**hand** Landarbeiter m; ~**house** Bauernhaus nt; ~**ing** Landwirtschaft f; ~**land** Ackerland nt; ~**yard** Hof m.

far-reaching ['fɑː'riːtʃɪŋ] a weitgehend.

far-sighted ['fɑː'saɪtɪd] a weitblickend.

fart [fɑːt] n (col) Furz m; vi (col) furzen.

farther ['fɑːðə*] a, ad weiter.

farthest ['fɑːðɪst] a weiteste(r,s), fernste(r,s); ad am weitesten.

fascinate ['fæsɪneɪt] vt faszinieren, bezaubern.

fascinating ['fæsɪneɪtɪŋ] a faszinierend, spannend.

fascination [fæsɪ'neɪʃən] n Faszination f, Zauber m.

fascism ['fæʃɪzəm] n Faschismus m.

fascist ['fæʃɪst] n Faschist m; a faschistisch.

fashion ['fæʃən] n (of clothes) Mode f; (manner) Art f (und Weise f); vt machen, gestalten; **in** ~ in Mode; **out of** ~ unmodisch; ~**able** a clothes modern, modisch; place elegant; ~ **show** Mode(n)-schau f.

fast [fɑːst] a schnell; (firm) fest; (of clock) vorgehen; ad schnell; (firmly) fest; n Fasten nt; vi fasten.

fasten ['fɑːsn] vt (attach) befestigen; seat belt festmachen; (with rope) zuschnüren; vi sich schließen lassen; ~**er**, ~**ing** Verschluß m.

fastidious [fæs'tɪdɪəs] a wählerisch.

fat [fæt] a dick, fett; n (on person) Fett nt, Speck m (col); (on meat) Fett nt; (for cooking) (Braten)fett nt.

fatal ['feɪtl] a tödlich; (disastrous) verhängnisvoll; ~**ism** Fatalismus m, Schicksalsglaube m; ~**ity** [fə'tælɪtɪ] (road death etc) Todesopfer nt; ~**ly** ad tödlich.

fate [feɪt] n Schicksal nt; ~**ful** a (prophetic) schicksalsschwer; (important) schicksalhaft.

father ['fɑːðə*] n Vater m; (Rel) Pater m; ~**-in-law** Schwiegervater m; ~**ly** a väterlich.

fathom ['fæðəm] n Klafter m; vt ausloten; (fig) ergründen.

fatigue [fə'tiːg] n Ermüdung f; vt ermüden.

fatness ['fætnɪs] n Dicke f.

fatten ['fætn] vt dick machen; animals mästen; vi dick werden.

fatty ['fætɪ] a food fettig.

fatuous ['fætjuəs] a albern, affig.

faucet ['fɔːsɪt] n (US) Wasserhahn m.

fault [fɔːlt] n (defect) Defekt m; (Elec) Störung f; (blame) Fehler m, Schuld f; (Geog) Verwerfung f; **it's your** ~ du bist daran schuld; **at** ~ schuldig, im Unrecht; vt: ~ **sth** etwas an etw (dat) auszusetzen haben; ~**less** a fehlerfrei, tadellos; ~**y** a fehlerhaft, defekt.

fauna ['fɔːnɔ] n Fauna f.

favour, (US) **favor** ['feɪvə*] n (approval) Wohlwollen nt; (kindness) Gefallen m; vt (prefer) vorziehen; **in** ~ **of** für; zugunsten (+gen); ~**able** a, ~**ably** ad günstig; ~**ite** ['feɪvərɪt] a Lieblings-; n Günstling m; (child) Liebling m; (Sport) Favorit m;

~**itism** (Sch) Bevorzugung f; (Pol) Günstlingswirtschaft f.

fawn [fɔːn] a rehbraun; n (colour) Rehbraun nt; (animal) (Reh)kitz nt.

fawning ['fɔːnɪŋ] a kriecherisch.

fear [fɪə*] n Furcht f; vt fürchten; **no** ~! keine Angst!; ~**ful** a (timid) furchtsam; (terrible) fürchterlich; ~**less** a, ~**lessly** ad furchtlos; ~**lessness** Furchtlosigkeit f.

feasibility [fiːzə'bɪlɪtɪ] n Durchführbarkeit f.

feasible ['fiːzəbl] a durchführbar, machbar.

feast [fiːst] n Festmahl nt; (Rel) Kirchenfest nt; vi sich gütlich tun (on an +dat); ~ **day** kirchliche(r) Feiertag m.

feat [fiːt] n Leistung f.

feather ['feðə*] n Feder f.

feature ['fiːtʃə*] n (Gesichts)zug m; (important part) Grundzug m; (Cine, Press) Feature nt; vt darstellen; (advertising etc) groß herausbringen; **featuring X** mit X; vi vorkommen; ~ **film** Spielfilm m; ~**less** a nichtssagend.

February ['februərɪ] n Februar m.

federal ['fedərəl] a Bundes-.

federation [fedə'reɪʃən] n (society) Verband m; (of states) Staatenbund m.

fed-up [fed'ʌp] a: **to be** ~ **with sth** etw satt haben; **I'm** ~ ich habe die Nase voll.

fee [fiː] n Gebühr f.

feeble ['fiːbl] a person schwach; excuse lahm; ~**-minded** a geistesschwach.

feed [fiːd] n (for baby) Essen nt; (for animals) Futter nt; vt irreg füttern; (support) ernähren; **to** ~ **on** leben von, fressen; ~**back** (Tech) Rückkopplung f; (information) Feedback nt.

feel [fiːl] n: **it has a soft** ~ es fühlt sich weich an; **to get the** ~ **of sth** sich an etw (acc) gewöhnen; irreg vt (sense) fühlen; (touch) anfassen; (think) meinen; vi (person) sich fühlen; (thing) sich anfühlen; **I** ~ **cold** mir ist kalt; **I** ~ **like a cup of tea** ich habe Lust auf eine Tasse Tee; ~**er** Fühler m; ~**ing** Gefühl nt; (opinion) Meinung f.

feet [fiːt] npl of **foot.**

feign [feɪn] vt vortäuschen; ~**ed** a vorgetäuscht, Schein-.

feint [feɪnt] n Täuschungsmanöver nt.

feline ['fiːlaɪn] a Katzen-, katzenartig.

fell [fel] vt tree fällen; n (hill) kahle(r) Berg m; a: **with one** ~ **swoop** mit einem Schlag; auf einen Streich.

fellow ['feləʊ] n (companion) Gefährte m, Kamerad m; (man) Kerl m; ~ **citizen** Mitbürger(in f) m; ~ **countryman** Landsmann m; ~ **feeling** Mitgefühl nt; ~ **men** pl Mitmenschen pl; ~**ship** (group) Körperschaft f; (friendliness) Gemeinschaft f, Kameradschaft f; (scholarship) Forschungsstipendium nt; ~ **worker** Mitarbeiter(in f) m.

felony ['felənɪ] n schwere(s) Verbrechen nt.

felt [felt] n Filz m.

female ['fiːmeɪl] n (of animals) Weibchen nt; a weiblich.

feminine ['feminin] a (Gram) weiblich; qualities fraulich.

femininity [femɪ'nɪnɪtɪ] n Weiblichkeit f; (quality) Fraulichkeit f.

feminist ['feminist] n Feminist(in f) m.

fence [fens] n Zaun m; (crook) Hehler m; vi fechten; ~ **in** vt einzäunen; ~ **off** vt absperren.

fencing ['fensɪŋ] n Zaun m; (Sport) Fechten nt.

fend [fend] vi: ~ **for o.s.** sich (allein) durchschlagen.

fender ['fendə*] n Kaminvorsetzer m; (US Aut) Kotflügel m.

ferment [fə'ment] vi (Chem) gären; ['fɜːment] n (excitement) Unruhe f; ~**ation** [fɜːmen'teɪʃən] Gärung f.

fern [fɜːn] n Farn m.

ferocious [fə'rəʊʃəs] a wild, grausam; ~**ly** ad wild.

ferocity [fə'rɒsɪtɪ] n Wildheit f, Grimmigkeit f.

ferry ['feri] n Fähre f; vt übersetzen.

fertile ['fɜːtaɪl] a fruchtbar.

fertility [fə'tɪlɪtɪ] n Fruchtbarkeit f.

fertilization [fɜːtɪlaɪ'zeɪʃən] n Befruchtung f.

fertilize ['fɜːtɪlaɪz] vt (Agr) düngen; (Biol) befruchten; ~**r** (Kunst)dünger m.

fervent ['fɜːvənt] a admirer glühend; hope innig.

festival ['festivəl] n (Rel etc) Fest nt; (Art, Mus) Festspiele pl; Festival nt.

festive ['festɪv] a festlich; **the** ~ **season** (Christmas) die Festzeit f.

festivity [fes'tɪvɪtɪ] n Festlichkeit f.

fetch [fetʃ] vt holen; (in sale) einbringen, erzielen.

fetching ['fetʃɪŋ] a einnehmend, reizend.

fête [feɪt] n Fest nt.

fetish ['fi:tɪʃ] n Fetisch m.

fetters ['fetəz] npl (lit, fig) Fesseln pl.

fetus ['fi:təs] n (US) = **foetus**.

feud [fju:d] n Fehde f; vi sich befehden; ~**al** a lehnsherrlich, Feudal-; ~**alism** Lehnswesen nt, Feudalismus m.

fever ['fi:və*] n Fieber nt; ~**ish** a (Med) fiebrig, Fieber-; (fig) fieberhaft; ~**ishly** ad (fig) fieberhaft.

few [fju:] a wenig; pron wenige; **a** ~ a, pron einige; ~**er** weniger; ~**est** wenigste(r,s); **a good** ~ ziemlich viele.

fiancé [fɪ'ɑːnseɪ] n Verlobte(r) m; ~**e** Verlobte f.

fiasco [fɪ'æskəʊ] n Fiasko nt, Reinfall m.

fib [fɪb] n Flunkerei f; vi flunkern.

fibre, (US) **fiber** ['faɪbə*] n Faser f, Fiber f; (material) Faserstoff m; ~**glass** Glaswolle f.

fickle ['fɪkl] a unbeständig, wankelmütig; ~**ness** Unbeständigkeit f, Wankelmut m.

fiction ['fɪkʃən] n (novels) Romanliteratur f; (story) Erdichtung f; ~**al** a erfunden.

fictitious [fɪk'tɪʃəs] a erfunden, fingiert.

fiddle ['fɪdl] n Geige f, Fiedel f; (trick) Schwindelei f; vt accounts frisieren; ~ **with** vi herumfummeln an (+dat); ~**r** Geiger m.

fidelity [fɪ'delɪtɪ] n Treue f.

fidget ['fɪdʒɪt] vi zappeln; n Zappelphilipp m; ~**y** a nervös, zappelig.

field [fi:ld] n Feld nt; (range) Gebiet nt; ~ **day** (gala) Paradetag m; ~ **marshal** Feldmarschall m; ~**work** (Mil) Schanze f; (Univ) Feldforschung f.

fiend [fi:nd] n Teufel m; (beast) Unhold m; Fanatiker(in f) m; ~**ish** a teuflisch.

fierce a, ~**ly** ad [fɪəs, -lɪ] wild; ~**ness** Wildheit f.

fiery ['faɪərɪ] a glühend; (blazing) brennend; (hot-tempered) hitzig, heftig.

fifteen [fɪf'ti:n] num fünfzehn.

fifth [fɪfθ] a fünfte(r,s); n Fünftel nt.

fifty ['fɪftɪ] num fünfzig; ~-~ halbe halbe, fifty fifty (col).

fig [fɪg] n Feige f.

fight [faɪt] n Kampf m; (brawl) Schlägerei f; (argument) Streit m; irreg vt kämpfen gegen; sich schlagen mit; (fig) bekämpfen; vi kämpfen; sich schlagen; streiten; ~**er** Kämpfer(in f) m; (plane) Jagdflugzeug nt; ~**ing** Kämpfen nt; (war) Kampfhandlungen pl.

figment ['fɪgmənt] n ~ **of imagination** reine Einbildung f.

figurative ['fɪgərətɪv] a bildlich.

figure ['fɪgə*] n Form f; (of person) Figur f; (person) Gestalt f; (illustration) Zeichnung f; (number) Ziffer f; vt (US: imagine) glauben; vi (appear) eine Rolle spielen, erscheinen; (US: make sense) stimmen; ~ **out** vt verstehen, herausbekommen; ~**head** (Naut, fig) Galionsfigur f; ~ **skating** Eiskunstlauf m.

filament ['fɪləmənt] n Faden m; (Elec) Glühfaden m.

file [faɪl] n (tool) Feile f; (dossier) Akte f; (folder) Aktenordner m; (row) Reihe f; vt metal, nails feilen; papers abheften; claim einreichen; vi: ~ **in/out** hintereinander hereinkommen/hinausgehen; **in single** ~ einer hinter dem anderen.

filing ['faɪlɪŋ] n Feilen nt; ~**s** pl Feilspäne pl; ~ **cabinet** Aktenschrank m.

fill [fɪl] vt füllen; (occupy) ausfüllen; (satisfy) sättigen; n: **to eat one's** ~ sich richtig satt essen; **to have had one's** ~ genug haben; **to** ~ **the bill** (fig) allen Anforderungen genügen; ~ **in** vt hole (auf)füllen; form ausfüllen; ~ **up** vt container auffüllen; form ausfüllen.

fillet ['fɪlɪt] n Filet nt; vt als Filet herrichten.

filling ['fɪlɪŋ] n (Cook) Füllung f; (for tooth) (Zahn)plombe f; ~ **station** Tankstelle f.

fillip ['fɪlɪp] n Anstoß m, Auftrieb m.

film [fɪlm] n Film m; (layer) Häutchen nt, Film m; vt scene filmen; ~ **star** Filmstar m; ~**strip** Filmstreifen m.

filter ['fɪltə*] n Filter m; (for traffic) Verkehrsfilter m; vt filtern; vi durchsickern; ~ **tip** Filter m, Filtermundstück nt; ~-**tipped cigarette** Filterzigarette f.

filth [fɪlθ] n (lit) Dreck m; (fig) Unflat m; ~**y** a dreckig; (behaviour) gemein; weather scheußlich.

fin [fɪn] n Flosse f.

final ['faɪnl] a letzte(r,s); End-; (conclusive) endgültig; n (Ftbl etc) Endspiel nt; ~**s** pl

(*Univ*) Abschlußexamen *nt*; (*Sport*) Schlußrunde *f*; ~**e** [fɪ'nɑːlɪ] (*Theat*) Schlußszene *f*; (*Mus*) Finale *nt*; ~**ist** (*Sport*) Schlußrundenteilnehmer *m*; ~**ize** *vt* endgültige Form geben (+*dat*); abschließen; ~**ly** *ad* (*lastly*) zuletzt; (*eventually*) endlich; (*irrevocably*) endgültig.

finance [faɪ'næns] *n* Finanzwesen *nt*; ~**s** *pl* Finanzen *pl*; (*income*) Einkünfte *pl*; *vt* finanzieren.

financial [faɪ'nænʃəl] *a* Finanz-; finanziell; ~**ly** *ad* finanziell.

financier [faɪ'nænsɪə*] *n* Finanzier *m*.

find [faɪnd] *irreg vt* finden; *vi* (*realize*) erkennen; *n* Fund *m*; **to** ~ **sb guilty** jdn für schuldig erklären; **to** ~ **out** herausfinden; ~**ings** *pl* (*Jur*) Ermittlungsergebnis *nt*; (*of report*) Feststellung *f*, Befund *m*.

fine [faɪn] *a* fein; (*thin*) dünn, fein; (*good*) gut; *clothes* elegant; *weather* schön; *ad* (*well*) gut; (*small*) klein; *n* (*Jur*) Geldstrafe *f*; *vt* (*Jur*) mit einer Geldstrafe belegen; **to cut it** ~ (*fig*) knapp rechnen; ~ **arts** *pl* die schönen Künste *pl*; ~**ness** *n* Feinheit *f*; ~**ry** ['faɪnərɪ] Putz *m*; ~**sse** [fɪ'nes] Finesse *f*.

finger ['fɪŋɡə*] *n* Finger *m*; *vt* befühlen; ~**nail** Fingernagel *m*; ~**print** Fingerabdruck *m*; (*small*) (*Jur*) Geldstrafe ~**stall** Fingerling *m*; ~**tip** Fingerspitze *f*; **to have sth at one's** ~ **tips** etw parat haben.

finicky ['fɪnɪkɪ] *a* pingelig.

finish ['fɪnɪʃ] *n* Ende *nt*; (*Sport*) Ziel *nt*; (*of object*) Verarbeitung *f*; (*of paint*) Oberflächenwirkung *f*; *vt* beenden; *book* zu Ende lesen; **to be** ~**ed with sth** fertig sein mit etw; *vi* aufhören; (*Sport*) ans Ziel kommen; ~**ing line** Ziellinie *f*; ~**ing school** Mädchenpensionat *nt*.

finite ['faɪnaɪt] *a* endlich, begrenzt; (*Gram*) finit.

fiord [fjɔːd] *n* Fjord *m*.

fir [fɜː*] *n* Tanne *f*, Fichte *f*.

fire [faɪə*] *n* (*lit, fig*) Feuer *nt*; (*damaging*) Brand *m*, Feuer *nt*; **to set** ~ **to sth** etw in Brand stecken; **to be on** ~ brennen; *vt* (*Aut*) zünden; *gun* abfeuern; (*fig*) *imagination* entzünden; (*dismiss*) hinauswerfen; *vi* (*Aut*) zünden; **to** ~ **at sb** auf jdn schießen; ~ **away!** schieß los!; ~ **alarm** Feueralarm *m*; ~**arm** Schußwaffe *f*; ~ **brigade** Feuerwehr *f*; ~ **engine** Feuerwehrauto *nt*; ~ **escape** Feuerleiter *f*; ~ **extinguisher** Löschgerät *nt*; ~**man** Feuerwehrmann *m*; ~**place** offene(r) Kamin *m*; ~**proof** *a* feuerfest; ~**side** Kamin *m*; ~ **station** Feuerwehrwache *f*; ~**wood** Brennholz *nt*; ~**works** *pl* Feuerwerk *nt*.

firing ['faɪərɪŋ] *n* Schießen *nt*; ~ **squad** Exekutionskommando *nt*.

firm *a*, ~**ly** [fɜːm,-lɪ] fest; (*determined*) entschlossen; *n* Firma *f*; ~**ness** Festigkeit *f*; Entschlossenheit *f*.

first [fɜːst] *a* erste(r,s); *ad* zuerst; *arrive* als erste(r); *happen* zum erstenmal; *n* (*person: in race*) Erste(r) *mf*; (*Univ*) Eins *f*; (*Aut*) erste(r) Gang *m*; **at** ~ zuerst, anfangs; ~

---

of all zu allererst; ~ **aid** Erste Hilfe *f*; ~-**aid kit** Verbandskasten *m*; ~-**class** *a* erstklassig; (*travel*) erste(r) Klasse; ~-**hand** *a* aus erster Hand; ~ **lady** (*US*) First Lady *f*; ~**ly** *ad* erstens; ~ **name** Vorname *m*; ~ **night** Premiere *f*; Erstaufführung *f*; ~-**rate** *a* erstklassig.

fiscal ['fɪskəl] *a* fiskalisch, Finanz-.

fish [fɪʃ] *n* Fisch *m*; *vt river* angeln in (+*dat*); *sea* fischen in (+*dat*); *vi* fischen; angeln; ~ **out** *vt* herausfischen; **to go** ~**ing** angeln gehen; (*in sea*) fischen gehen; ~**erman** Fischer *m*; ~**ery** Fischgrund *m*; ~ **finger** Fischstäbchen *nt*; ~ **hook** Angelhaken *m*; ~**ing boat** Fischerboot *nt*; ~**ing line** Angelschnur *f*; ~**ing rod** Angel(rute) *f*; ~**ing tackle** Angelzeug *nt*; ~ **market** Fischmarkt *m*; ~**monger** Fischhändler *m*; ~ **slice** Fischvorlegemesser *nt*; ~**y** *a* (*col: suspicious*) faul.

fission ['fɪʃən] *n* Spaltung *f*.

fissure ['fɪʃə*] *n* Riß *m*.

fist [fɪst] *n* Faust *f*.

fit [fɪt] *a* (*Med*) gesund; (*Sport*) in Form, fit; (*suitable*) geeignet; *vt* passen (+*dat*); (*insert, attach*) einsetzen; *vi* (*correspond*) passen (zu); (*clothes*) passen; (*in space, gap*) hineinpassen; *n* (*of clothes*) Sitz *m*; (*Med, of anger*) Anfall *m*; (*of laughter*) Krampf *m*; ~ **in** *vi* sich einfügen; *vt* einpassen; ~ **out** *vt*, ~ **up** *vt* ausstatten; ~**fully, by** ~**s and starts** *move* ruckweise; *work* unregelmäßig; ~**ment** Einrichtungsgegenstand *m*; ~**ness** (*suitability*) Eignung *f*; (*Med*) Gesundheit *f*; (*Sport*) Fitneß *f*; ~**ter** (*Tech*) Monteur *m*; ~**ting** *a* passend; *n* (*of dress*) Anprobe *f*; (*piece of equipment*) (Ersatz)teil *nt*; ~**tings** *pl* Zubehör *nt*.

five [faɪv] *num* fünf; ~**r** (*Brit*) Fünf-Pfund-Note *f*.

fix [fɪks] *vt* befestigen; (*settle*) festsetzen; (*repair*) richten, reparieren; *drink* zurechtmachen; *n*: **in a** ~ in der Klemme; ~**ed** *a* repariert; *time* abgemacht; **it was** ~**ed** (*dishonest*) das war Schiebung; ~**ture** ['fɪkstʃə*] Installationsteil *m*; (*Sport*) Spiel *nt*.

fizz [fɪz] *n* Sprudeln *nt*; *vi* sprudeln.

fizzle ['fɪzl] *vi* zischen; ~ **out** *vi* verpuffen.

fizzy ['fɪzɪ] *a* Sprudel-, sprudelnd.

fjord [fjɔːd] *n* = **fiord**.

flabbergasted ['flæbəɡɑːstɪd] *a* (*col*) platt.

flabby ['flæbɪ] *a* wabbelig.

flag [flæɡ] *n* Fahne *f*; *vi* (*strength*) nachlassen; (*spirit*) erlahmen; ~ **down** *vt* stoppen, abwinken.

flagon ['flæɡən] *n* bauchige (Wein)flasche *f*, Krug *m*.

flagpole ['flæɡpəʊl] *n* Fahnenstange *f*.

flagrant ['fleɪɡrənt] *a* offenkundig; *offence* schamlos; *violation* flagrant.

flagstone ['flæɡstəʊn] *n* Steinplatte *f*.

flair [fleə*] *n* (*talent*) Talent *nt*; (*of style*) Schick *m*.

flake [fleɪk] *n* (*of snow*) Flocke *f*; (*of rust*) Schuppe *f*; *vi* (*also* ~ **off**) abblättern.

flamboyant [flæm'bɔɪənt] *a* extravagant; *colours* brillant; *gesture* großartig.

flame [fleɪm] *n* Flamme *f.*

flaming ['fleɪmɪŋ] *a* (*col*) verdammt; *row* irre.

flamingo [flə'mɪŋgəʊ] *n* Flamingo *m.*

flan [flæn] *n* Obsttorte *f.*

flank [flæŋk] *n* Flanke *f*; *vt* flankieren.

flannel ['flænl] *n* Flanell *m*; (*face* —) Waschlappen *m*; (*col*) Geschwafel *nt*; ~**s** *pl* Flanellhose *f.*

flap [flæp] *n* Klappe *f*; (*col: crisis*) (helle) Aufregung *f*; *vt wings* schlagen mit; *vi* lose herabhängen; flattern; (*col: panic*) sich aufregen.

flare [flɛə*] *n* (*signal*) Leuchtsignal *nt*; (*in skirt etc*) Weite *f*; ~ **up** *vi* aufflammen; (*fig*) aufbrausen; (*revolt*) (plötzlich) aus-brechen.

flared [flɛəd] *a trousers* ausgestellt.

flash [flæʃ] *n* Blitz *m*; (*news* —) Kurzmeldung *f*; (*Phot*) Blitzlicht *nt*; *vt* auf-leuchten lassen; *message* durchgeben; *vi* aufleuchten; **in a** ~ im Nu; **to** ~ **by** *or* **past** vorbeirasen; ~**back** Rückblende *f*; ~ **bulb** Blitzlichtbirne *f*; ~**er** (*Aut*) Blinker *m.*

flashy ['flæʃi] *a* (*pej*) knallig.

flask [flɑːsk] *n* Reiseflasche *f*; (*Chem*) Kolben *m*; (*vacuum* —) Thermosflasche *f.*

flat [flæt] *a* flach; (*dull*) matt; (*Mus*) erniedrigt; *beer* schal; *tyre* platt; **A** ~ as; *ad* (*Mus*) zu tief; (*in rooms*) Wohnung *f*; (*Mus*) b *nt*; (*Aut*) Reifenpanne *f*, Platte(r) *m*; ~ **broke** *a* (*col*) völlig pleite; ~**footed** *a* plattfüßig; ~**ly** *ad* glatt; ~**ness** Flach-heit *f*; ~**ten** *vt* (*also* ~**ten out**) platt machen, (ein)ebnen.

flatter ['flætə*] *vt* schmeicheln (+*dat*); ~**er** Schmeichler(in *f*) *m*; ~**ing** *a* schmeichelhaft; ~**y** Schmeichelei *f.*

flatulence ['flætjʊləns] *n* Blähungen *pl.*

flaunt [flɔːnt] *vt* prunken mit.

flavour, (*US*) **flavor** ['fleɪvə*] *n* Ge-schmack *m*; *vt* würzen; ~**ing** Würze *f.*

flaw [flɔː] *n* Fehler *m*; (*in argument*) schwache(r) Punkt *m*; ~**less** *a* einwand-frei.

flax [flæks] *n* Flachs *m*; ~**en** *a* flachs-farben.

flea [fliː] *n* Floh *m.*

flee [fliː] *irreg vi* fliehen; *vt* fliehen vor (+*dat*); *country* fliehen aus.

fleece [fliːs] *n* Schaffell *nt*, Vlies *nt*; *vt* (*col*) schröpfen.

fleet [fliːt] *n* Flotte *f.*

fleeting ['fliːtɪŋ] *a* flüchtig.

flesh [fleʃ] *n* Fleisch *nt*; (*of fruit*) Frucht-fleisch *nt*; ~ **wound** Fleischwunde *f.*

flex [fleks] *n* (*Leitungs*)kabel *nt*; *vt* beugen, biegen; ~**ibility** [fleksɪ'bɪlɪtɪ] Biegsamkeit *f*; (*fig*) Flexibilität *f*; ~**ible** *a* biegsam; *plans* flexibel.

flick [flɪk] *n* Schnippen *nt*; (*blow*) leichte(r) Schlag *m*; *vt* leicht schlagen; ~ **through** *vt* durchblättern; **to** ~ **sth off** etw weg-schnippen.

flicker ['flɪkə*] *n* Flackern *nt*; (*of emotion*) Funken *m*; *vi* flackern.

flier ['flaɪə*] *n* Flieger *m.*

flight [flaɪt] *n* Fliegen *nt*; (*journey*) Flug *m*; (*fleeing*) Flucht *f*; ~ **of stairs** Treppe *f*;

to take ~ die Flucht ergreifen; **to put to** ~ in die Flucht schlagen; ~ **deck** Flug-deck *nt*; ~**y** *a* flatterhaft.

flimsy ['flɪmzɪ] *a* nicht stabil, windig; (*thin*) hauchdünn; *excuse* fadenscheinig.

flinch [flɪntʃ] *vi* zurückschrecken (*away from* vor +*dat*).

fling [flɪŋ] *vt irreg* schleudern.

flint [flɪnt] *n* (*in lighter*) Feuerstein *m.*

flip [flɪp] *vt* werfen; **he** ~**ped the lid off** er klappte den Deckel auf.

flippancy ['flɪpənsɪ] *n* Leichtfertigkeit *f.*

flippant ['flɪpənt] *a* schnippisch; **to be** ~ **about sth** etw nicht ernst nehmen.

flirt [flɜːt] *vi* flirten; *n* kokette(s) Mädchen *nt*; **he/she is a** ~ er/sie flirtet gern; ~**ation** [flɜː'teɪʃən] Flirt *m.*

flit [flɪt] *vi* flitzen.

float [fləʊt] *n* (*Fishing*) Schwimmer *m*; (*esp in procession*) Plattformwagen *m*; *vi* schwimmen; (*in air*) schweben; *vt* schwimmen lassen; (*Comm*) gründen; *currency* floaten; ~**ing** *a* (*lit*) schwimmend; (*fig*) *votes* unentschieden.

flock [flɒk] *n* (*of sheep, Rel*) Herde *f*; (*of birds*) Schwarm *m*; (*of people*) Schar *f.*

flog [flɒg] *vt* prügeln; peitschen; (*col: sell*) verkaufen.

flood [flʌd] *n* Überschwemmung *f*; (*fig*) Flut *f*; **the F**~ die Sintflut *f*; **to be in** ~ Hochwasser haben; *vt* (*lit, fig*) über-schwemmen; ~**ing** Überschwemmung *f*; ~**light** *n* Flutlicht *nt*; *vt* anstrahlen; ~**lighting** Beleuchtung *f.*

floor [flɔː*] *n* (Fuß)boden *m*; (*storey*) Stock *m*; *vt person* zu Boden schlagen; **ground** ~ (*Brit*), **first** ~ (*US*) Erdgeschoß *nt*; **first** ~ (*Brit*), **second** ~ (*US*) erste(r) Stock *m*; ~**board** Diele *f*; ~ **show** Kabarettvorstellung *f*; ~**walker** (*Comm*) Abteilungsaufseher *m.*

flop [flɒp] *n* Plumps *m*; (*failure*) Reinfall *m*; *vi* (*fail*) durchfallen; **the project** ~**ped** aus dem Plan wurde nichts.

floppy ['flɒpɪ] *a* hängend; ~ **hat** Schlapphut *m.*

flora ['flɔːrə] *n* Flora *f*; ~**l** *a* Blumen-.

florid ['flɒrɪd] *a style* blumig.

florist ['flɒrɪst] *n* Blumenhändler(in *f*) *m*; ~**'s** (**shop**) Blumengeschäft *nt.*

flotsam ['flɒtsəm] *n* Strandgut *nt.*

flounce [flaʊns] *n* (*on dress*) Besatz *m*; *vi*: ~ **in/out** hinein-/hinausstürmen.

flounder ['flaʊndə*] *vi* herumstrampeln; (*fig*) ins Schleudern kommen.

flour ['flaʊə*] *n* Mehl *nt.*

flourish ['flʌrɪʃ] *vi* blühen; gedeihen; *vt* (*wave*) schwingen; *n* (*waving*) Schwingen *nt*; (*of trumpets*) Tusch *m*, Fanfare *f*; ~**ing** *a* blühend.

flout [flaʊt] *vt* mißachten, sich hinwegset-zen über (+*acc*).

flow [fləʊ] *n* Fließen *nt*; (*of sea*) Flut *f*; *vi* fließen.

flower ['flaʊə*] *n* Blume *f*; *vi* blühen; ~ **bed** Blumenbeet *nt*; ~**pot** Blumentopf *m*; ~**y** *a style* blumenreich.

flowing ['fləʊɪŋ] *a* fließend; *hair* wallend; *style* flüssig.

flu [fluː] *n* Grippe *f.*

fluctuate ['flʌktjueit] vi schwanken.
fluctuation [flʌktju'eiʃən] n Schwankung f.
fluency ['flu:ənsi] n Flüssigkeit f; **his ~ in English** seine Fähigkeit, fließend Englisch zu sprechen.
fluent a **~ly** ad ['flu:ənt,-li] speech flüssig; **to be ~ in German** fließend Deutsch sprechen.
fluff [flʌf] n Fussel f; **~y** a flaumig; pastry flockig.
fluid ['flu:id] n Flüssigkeit f; a (lit) flüssig; (fig) plans veränderbar.
fluke [flu:k] n (col) Dusel m.
fluorescent [fluə'resnt] a fluoreszierend, Leucht-.
fluoride ['fluəraid] n Fluorid nt.
flurry ['flʌri] n (of activity) Aufregung f; (of snow) Gestöber nt.
flush [flʌʃ] n Erröten nt; (of excitement) Glühen nt; (Cards) Sequenz f; vt (aus-)spülen; vi erröten; a glatt; **~ed** a rot.
fluster ['flʌstə*] n Verwirrung f; **~ed** a verwirrt.
flute [flu:t] n Querflöte f.
fluted ['flu:tid] a gerillt.
flutter ['flʌtə*] n (of wings) Flattern nt; (of excitement) Beben nt; vi flattern; (person) rotieren.
flux [flʌks] n: **in a state of ~** im Fluß.
fly [flai] n (insect) Fliege f; (on trousers, also **flies**) (Hosen)schlitz m; irreg vt fliegen; vi fliegen; (flee) fliehen; (flag) wehen; **~ open** vi auffliegen; **let ~** vti (shoot) losschießen; (verbally) loswettern; insults loslassen; **~ing** n Fliegen nt; **with ~ing colours** mit fliegenden Fahnen; **~ing saucer** fliegende Untertasse f; **~ing start** gute(r) Start m; **~ing visit** Stippvisite f; **~over** (Brit) Überführung f; **~paper** Fliegenfänger m; **~past** Luftparade f; **~sheet** (for tent) Regendach nt; **~swatter** Fliegenwedel m; **~wheel** Schwungrad nt.
foal [fəul] n Fohlen nt.
foam [fəum] n Schaum m; (plastic etc) Schaumgummi m; vi schäumen.
fob [fɔb] n: **~ off** vt andrehen (sb with sth jdm etw); (with promise) abspeisen.
focal ['fəukəl] a im Brennpunkt (stehend), Brennpunkt-.
focus ['fəukəs] n Brennpunkt m; (fig) Mittelpunkt m; vt attention konzentrieren; camera scharf einstellen; vi sich konzentrieren (on auf +acc); **in ~** scharf eingestellt; **out of ~** unscharf (eingestellt).
fodder ['fɔdə*] n Futter nt.
foe [fəu] n (liter) Feind m, Gegner m.
foetus ['fi:təs] n Fötus m.
fog [fɔg] n Nebel m; vt issue verunklären, verwirren; **~gy** a neblig, trüb.
foible ['fɔibl] n Schwäche f, Faible nt.
foil [fɔil] vt vereiteln; n (metal, also fig) Folie f; (fencing) Florett nt.
fold [fəuld] n (bend, crease) Falte f; (Agr) Pferch m; (for sheep) Pferch m; vt falten; **~ up** vt map etc zusammenfalten; vi (business) eingehen; **~er** (pamphlet) Broschüre f; (portfolio) Schnellhefter m; **~ing** a chair etc zusammenklappbar, Klapp-.

foliage ['fəulidʒ] n Laubwerk nt.
folio ['fəuliəu] n Foliant m.
folk [fəuk] n Volk nt; a Volks-; **~s** pl Leute pl; **~lore** (study) Volkskunde f; (tradition) Folklore f; **~song** Volkslied nt; (modern) Folksong m.
follow ['fɔləu] vt folgen (+dat); (obey) befolgen; fashion mitmachen; profession nachgehen (+dat); (understand) folgen können (+dat); vi folgen; (result) sich ergeben; **as ~s** wie im folgenden; **~ up** vt (weiter) verfolgen; **~er** Anhänger(in f) m; **~ing** a folgend; n Folgende(s) nt; (people) Gefolgschaft f.
folly ['fɔli] n Torheit f.
fond [fɔnd] a: **to be ~ of** gern haben; **~ly** ad (with love) liebevoll; (foolishly) törichterweise; **~ness** Vorliebe f; (for people) Liebe f.
font [fɔnt] n Taufbecken nt.
food [fu:d] n Essen nt, Nahrung f; (for animals) Futter nt; **~ mixer** Küchenmixer m; **~ poisoning** Lebensmittelvergiftung f; **~stuffs** pl Lebensmittel pl.
fool [fu:l] n Narr m, Närrin f; (jester) (Hof-)narr m, Hanswurst m; (food) Mus nt; vt (deceive) hereinlegen; vi (behave like a ~) (herum)albern; **~hardy** a tollkühn; **~ish** a, **~ishly** ad dumm; albern; **~ishness** Dummheit f; **~proof** a idiotensicher.
foot [fut] n Fuß m; (of animal) Pfote f; **to put one's ~ in it** ins Fettnäpfchen treten; **on ~** zu Fuß; vt bill bezahlen; **~ball** Fußball m; **~baller** Fußballer m; **~brake** Fußbremse f; **~bridge** Fußgängerbrücke f; **~hills** pl Ausläufer pl; **~hold** Halt m; Stütze f; **~ing** (lit) Halt m; (fig) Verhältnis nt; **to get a ~ing in society** in der Gesellschaft Fuß fassen; **to be on a good ~ing with sb** mit jdm auf gutem Fuß stehen; **~light** Rampenlicht nt; **~man** Bediente(r) m; **~-and-mouth** (disease) Maul- und Klauenseuche f; **~note** Fußnote f; **~path** Fußweg m; **~rest** Fußstütze f; **~sore** a fußkrank; **~step** Schritt m; **in his father's ~steps** in den Fußstapfen seines Vaters; **~wear** Schuhzeug nt.
fop [fɔp] n Geck m.
for [fɔ:*] prep für; cj denn; **what ~?** wozu?
forage ['fɔridʒ] n (Vieh)futter nt; vi nach Nahrung suchen.
foray ['fɔrei] n Raubzug m.
forbearing [fɔ:'bɛəriŋ] a geduldig.
forbid [fə'bid] vt irreg verbieten; **~den** a verboten; **~ding** a einschüchternd, abschreckend.
force [fɔ:s] n Kraft f, Stärke f; (compulsion) Zwang m; (Mil) Truppen pl; vt zwingen; lock aufbrechen; plant hochzüchten; **in ~ rule** gültig; group in großer Stärke; **the F~s** pl die Armee; **~d** a smile gezwungen; landing Not-; **~ful** a speech kraftvoll; personality resolut.
forceps ['fɔ:seps] npl Zange f.
forcible ['fɔ:səbl] a (convincing) wirksam, überzeugend; (violent) gewaltsam.
forcibly ['fɔ:səbli] ad unter Zwang, zwangsweise.
ford [fɔ:d] n Furt f; vt durchwaten.

fore [fɔː*] a vorder, Vorder-; n: **to the ~** in den Vordergrund.

forearm ['fɔːrɑːm] n Unterarm m.

foreboding [fɔːˈbəʊdɪŋ] n Vorahnung f.

forecast ['fɔːkɑːst] n Vorhersage f; vt irreg voraussagen.

forecourt ['fɔːkɔːt] n (of garage) Vorplatz m.

forefathers ['fɔːfɑːðəz] npl Vorfahren pl.

forefinger ['fɔːfɪŋgə*] n Zeigefinger m.

forefront ['fɔːfrʌnt] n Spitze f.

forego [fɔːˈgəʊ] vt irreg verzichten auf (+acc); ~**ing** a vorangehend; ~**ne conclusion** ausgemachte Sache.

foreground ['fɔːgraʊnd] n Vordergrund m.

forehead ['fɔrɪd] n Stirn f.

foreign ['fɔrɪn] a Auslands-; country, accent ausländisch; trade Außen-; body Fremd-; ~**er** Ausländer(in f) m; ~ **exchange** Devisen pl; ~ **minister** Außenminister m.

foreman ['fɔːmən] n Vorarbeiter m.

foremost ['fɔːməʊst] a erste(r,s).

forensic [fəˈrensɪk] a gerichtsmedizinisch.

forerunner ['fɔːrʌnə*] n Vorläufer m.

foresee [fɔːˈsiː] vt irreg vorhersehen; ~**able** a absehbar.

foreshore ['fɔːʃɔː*] n Küste f, Küstenland nt.

foresight ['fɔːsaɪt] n Voraussicht f.

forest ['fɔrɪst] n Wald m.

forestall [fɔːˈstɔːl] vt zuvorkommen (+dat).

forestry ['fɔrɪstrɪ] n Forstwirtschaft f.

foretaste ['fɔːteɪst] n Vorgeschmack m.

foretell [fɔːˈtel] vt irreg vorhersagen.

forever [fəˈrevə*] ad für immer.

forewarn [fɔːˈwɔːn] vt vorherwarnen.

foreword ['fɔːwɜːd] n Vorwort nt.

forfeit ['fɔːfɪt] n Einbuße f; vt verwirken.

forge [fɔːdʒ] n Schmiede f; vt fälschen; iron schmieden; ~ **ahead** vi Fortschritte machen; ~**r** Fälscher m; ~**ry** Fälschung f.

forget [fəˈget] vti irreg vergessen; ~**ful** a vergeßlich; ~**fulness** Vergeßlichkeit f.

forgive [fəˈgɪv] vt irreg verzeihen (sb for sth jdm etw).

forgiveness [fəˈgɪvnəs] n Verzeihung f.

forgo [fɔːˈgəʊ] see **forego**.

fork [fɔːk] n Gabel f; (in road) Gabelung f; vi (road) sich gabeln; ~ **out** vti (col: pay) blechen; ~**ed** a gegabelt; lightning zickzackförmig.

forlorn [fəˈlɔːn] a person verlassen; hope vergeblich.

form [fɔːm] n Form f; (type) Art f; (figure) Gestalt f; (Sch) Klasse f; (bench) (Schul)bank f; (document) Formular nt; vt formen; (be part of) bilden.

formal ['fɔːməl] a förmlich, formell; occasion offiziell; ~**ity** [fɔːˈmælɪtɪ] Förmlichkeit f; (of occasion) offizielle(r) Charakter m; ~**ities** pl Formalitäten pl; ~**ly** ad (ceremoniously) formell; (officially) offiziell.

format ['fɔːmæt] n Format nt.

formation [fɔːˈmeɪʃən] n Bildung f; Gestaltung f; (Aviat) Formation f.

formative ['fɔːmətɪv] a years formend.

former ['fɔːmə*] a früher; (opposite of latter) erstere(r,s); ~**ly** ad früher.

Formica '[fɔːˈmaɪkə] n Resopal ⁽ⁿ⁾ nt.

formidable ['fɔːmɪdəbl] a furchtbar; gewaltig.

formula ['fɔːmjʊlə] n Formel f; ~**te** ['fɔːmjʊleɪt] vt formulieren.

forsake [fəˈseɪk] vt irreg im Stich lassen, verlassen; habit aufgeben.

fort [fɔːt] n Feste f, Fort nt.

forte ['fɔːtɪ] n Stärke f, starke Seite f.

forth [fɔːθ] ad: **and so ~** und so weiter; ~**coming** a kommend; character entgegenkommend; ~**right** a offen, gerade heraus.

fortification [fɔːtɪfɪˈkeɪʃən] n Befestigung f.

fortify ['fɔːtɪfaɪ] vt (ver)stärken; (protect) befestigen.

fortitude ['fɔːtɪtjuːd] n Seelenstärke f, Mut m.

fortnight ['fɔːtnaɪt] n zwei Wochen pl, vierzehn Tage pl; ~**ly** a zweiwöchentlich; ad alle vierzehn Tage.

fortress ['fɔːtrɪs] n Festung f.

fortuitous [fɔːˈtjuːɪtəs] a zufällig.

fortunate ['fɔːtʃənɪt] a glücklich; ~**ly** ad glücklicherweise, zum Glück.

fortune ['fɔːtʃən] n Glück nt; (money) Vermögen nt; ~**teller** Wahrsager(in f) m.

forty ['fɔːtɪ] num vierzig.

forum ['fɔːrəm] n Forum nt.

forward ['fɔːwəd] a vordere(r,s); movement vorwärts; person vorlaut; planning Voraus-; ad vorwärts; n (Sport) Stürmer m; vt (send) schicken; (help) fördern; ~**s** ad vorwärts.

fossil ['fɔsl] n Fossil nt, Versteinerung f.

foster ['fɔstə*] vt talent fördern; ~ **child** Pflegekind nt; ~ **mother** Pflegemutter f.

foul [faʊl] a schmutzig; language gemein; weather schlecht; n (Sport) Foul nt; vt mechanism blockieren; (Sport) foulen.

found [faʊnd] vt (establish) gründen; ~**ation** [faʊnˈdeɪʃən] (act) Gründung f; (fig) Fundament nt; ~**ations** pl Fundament nt.

founder ['faʊndə*] n Gründer(in f) m; vi sinken.

foundry ['faʊndrɪ] n Gießerei f, Eisenhütte f.

fount [faʊnt] n (liter) Quell m; ~**ain** (Spring)brunnen m; ~**ain pen** Füllfederhalter m.

four [fɔː*] num vier; ~**on all ~s** auf allen vieren; ~**some** Quartett nt; ~**teen** num vierzehn; ~**th** a vierte(r,s).

fowl [faʊl] n Huhn nt; (food) Geflügel nt.

fox [fɔks] n Fuchs m; ~**ed** a verblüfft; ~**hunting** Fuchsjagd f; ~**trot** Foxtrott m.

foyer ['fɔɪeɪ] n Foyer nt, Vorhalle f.

fracas ['fræːkɑː] n Radau m.

fraction ['frækʃən] n (Math) Bruch m; (part) Bruchteil m.

fracture ['fræktʃə*] n (Med) Bruch m; vt brechen.

fragile ['frædʒaɪl] a zerbrechlich.

fragment ['frægmənt] n Bruchstück nt, Fragment nt; (small part) Stück nt, Splitter m; ~ary [fræg'mentərɪ] a bruchstückhaft, fragmentarisch.

fragrance ['freɪgrəns] n Duft m.

fragrant ['freɪgrənt] a duftend.

frail [freɪl] a schwach, gebrechlich.

frame [freɪm] n Rahmen m; (body) Gestalt f; vt einrahmen; (make) gestalten, machen; (col: incriminate) **to ~ sb** jdm etw anhängen; ~ **of mind** Verfassung f; ~**work** Rahmen m; (of society) Gefüge nt.

franchise ['fræntʃaɪz] n (aktives) Wahlrecht nt.

frank [fræŋk] a offen; ~**furter** Saitenwürstchen nt; ~**ly** ad offen gesagt; ~**ness** Offenheit f.

frankincense ['fræŋkɪnsens] n Weihrauch m.

frantic ['fræntɪk] a effort verzweifelt; ~ **with worry** außer sich vor Sorge; ~**ally** ad außer sich; verzweifelt.

fraternal [frə'tɜːnl] a brüderlich.

fraternity [frə'tɜːnɪtɪ] n (club) Vereinigung f; (spirit) Brüderlichkeit f; (US Sch) Studentenverbindung f.

fraternization [frætənaɪ'zeɪʃən] n Verbrüderung f.

fraternize ['frætənaɪz] vi fraternisieren.

fraud [frɔːd] n (trickery) Betrug m; (trick) Schwindel m, Trick m; (person) Schwindler(in f) m.

fraudulent ['frɔːdjulənt] a betrügerisch.

fraught [frɔːt] a voller (with gen).

fray [freɪ] n Rauferei f; vti ausfransen.

freak [friːk] n Monstrosität f; (crazy person) Irre(r) mf; (storm etc) Ausnahmeerscheinung f; ~ **a storm, conditions** anormal; animal monströs; ~ **out** vi (col) durchdrehen.

freckle ['frekl] n Sommersprosse f; ~**d** a sommersprossig.

free [friː] a frei; (loose) lose; (liberal) freigebig; **to get sth ~** etw umsonst bekommen; **you're ~ to . . .** es steht dir frei zu . . .; vt (set free) befreien; (unblock) freimachen; ~**dom** Freiheit f; ~**-for-all** allgemeine(r) Wettbewerb m; (fight) allgemeine(s) Handgemenge nt; ~ **kick** Freistoß m; ~**lance** a frei; artist freischaffend; ~**ly** ad frei; lose; (generously) reichlich; admit offen; ~**mason** Freimaurer m; ~**masonry** Freimaurerei f; ~ **trade** Freihandel m; ~**way** (US) Autobahn f; ~**wheel** vi im Freilauf fahren.

freesia ['friːʒə] n Freesie f.

freeze [friːz] irreg vi gefrieren; (feel cold) frieren; vt (lit, fig) einfrieren; n (fig, Fin) Stopp m; ~**r** Tiefkühltruhe f; (in fridge) Gefrierfach nt.

freezing ['friːzɪŋ] a eisig; (~ cold) eiskalt; ~ **point** Gefrierpunkt m.

freight [freɪt] n (goods) Fracht f; (money charged) Fracht(gebühr) f; ~ **car** (US) Güterwagen m; ~**er** (Naut) Frachtschiff nt.

French [frentʃ] a: ~ **fried potatoes** pl Pommes frites pl; ~ **window** Verandatür f; see appendix.

frenzy ['frenzɪ] n Raserei f, wilde Aufregung f.

frequency ['friːkwənsɪ] n Häufigkeit f; (Phys) Frequenz f.

frequent a, ~**ly** ad ['friːkwənt,-lɪ] häufig; [friːkwent] vt (regelmäßig) besuchen.

fresco ['freskəu] n Fresko nt.

fresh [freʃ] a frisch; (new) neu; (cheeky) frech; ~**en** (also ~ **en up**) vi (also) auffrischen; (person) sich frisch machen; vt auffrischen; ~**ly** ad gerade; ~**ness** Frische f; ~**water** a fish Süßwasser-.

fret [fret] vi sich (dat) Sorgen machen (about über+acc).

friar ['fraɪə*] n Klosterbruder m.

friction ['frɪkʃən] n (lit, fig) Reibung f.

Friday ['fraɪdeɪ] n Freitag m; see **good**.

fridge [frɪdʒ] n Kühlschrank m.

fried [fraɪd] a gebraten.

friend [frend] n Bekannte(r) mf; (more intimate) Freund(in f) m; ~**liness** Freundlichkeit f; ~**ly** a freundlich; relations freundschaftlich; ~**ship** Freundschaft f.

frieze [friːz] n Fries m.

frigate ['frɪgɪt] n Fregatte f.

fright [fraɪt] n Schrecken m; **you look a ~** (col) du siehst unmöglich aus!; ~**en** vt erschrecken; **to be ~ened** Angst haben; ~**ening** a schrecklich; ängstigend; ~**ful** a, ~**fully** ad (col) schrecklich, furchtbar.

frigid ['frɪdʒɪd] a kalt, eisig; woman frigide; ~**ity** [frɪ'dʒɪdɪtɪ] Kälte f; Frigidität f.

frill [frɪl] n Rüsche f.

fringe [frɪndʒ] n Besatz m; (hair) Pony m; (fig) äußere(r) Rand m, Peripherie f.

frisky ['frɪskɪ] a lebendig, ausgelassen.

fritter ['frɪtə*] n: ~ **away** vt vertun, verplempern.

frivolity [frɪ'vɒlɪtɪ] n Leichtfertigkeit f, Frivolität f.

frivolous ['frɪvələs] a frivol, leichtsinnig.

frizzy ['frɪzɪ] a kraus.

fro [frəu] see **to**.

frock [frɒk] n Kleid nt.

frog [frɒg] n Frosch m; ~**man** Froschmann m.

frolic ['frɒlɪk] n lustige(r) Streich m; vi ausgelassen sein.

from [frɒm] prep von; (place) aus; (judging by) nach; (because of) wegen (+gen).

front [frʌnt] n Vorderseite f; (of house) Fassade f; (promenade) Strandpromenade f; (Mil, Pol, Met) Front f; (fig: appearances) Fassade f; a (forward) vordere(r,s), Vorder-; (first) vorderste(r,s); page erste(r,s); door Eingangs-, Haus-; **in ~** ad vorne; **in ~ of** prep vor; ~**age** Vorderfront f; ~**al** a frontal, Vorder-; ~**ier** [frʌntɪə*] Grenze f; ~ **room** (Brit) Vorderzimmer nt, Wohnzimmer nt; ~**-wheel drive** Vorderradantrieb m.

frost [frɒst] n Frost m; ~**bite** Erfrierung f; ~**ed** a glass Milch-; ~**y** a frostig.

froth [frɒθ] n Schaum m; ~**y** a schaumig.

frown [fraun] n Stirnrunzeln nt; vi die Stirn runzeln.

frozen ['frəuzn] a food gefroren; (Fin) assets festgelegt.

frugal ['fruːgəl] a sparsam, bescheiden.

fruit [fru:t] *n* (*particular*) Frucht *f*; **I like** ~ ich esse gern Obst; ~**erer** Obsthändler *m*; ~**ful** *a* fruchtbar; ~**ion** [fru:'ɪʃən] Verwirklichung *f*; **to come to** ~**ion** in Erfüllung gehen; ~ **machine** Spielautomat *m*; ~ **salad** Obstsalat *m*.

frustrate [frʌs'treit] *vt* vereiteln; ~**d** *a* gehemmt; (*Psych*) frustriert.

frustration [frʌs'treiʃən] *n* Behinderung *f*; Frustration *f*.

fry [frai] *vt* braten; **small** ~ *pl* kleine Leute *pl*; (*children*) Kleine(n) *pl*; ~**ing pan** Bratpfanne *f*.

fuchsia ['fju:ʃə] *n* Fuchsie *f*.

fuddy-duddy ['fʌdɪdʌdɪ] *n* altmodische(r) Kauz *m*.

fudge [fʌdʒ] *n* Karamellen *pl*.

fuel [fjʊəl] *n* Treibstoff *m*; (*for heating*) Brennstoff *m*; (*for cigarette lighter*) Benzin *nt*; ~ **oil** (*diesel fuel*) Heizöl *nt*; ~ **tank** Tank *m*.

fugitive ['fju:dʒɪtɪv] *n* Flüchtling *m*; (*from prison*) Flüchtige(r) *mf*.

fulfil [fʊl'fɪl] *vt* duty erfüllen; *promise* einhalten; ~**ment** Erfüllung *f*; Einhaltung *f*.

full [fʊl] *a* box, bottle, price voll; *person* (*satisfied*) satt; *member, power, employment, moon* Voll-; (*complete*) völlig, ~ *speed* höchste(r, s); *skirt* weit; **in** ~ vollständig, ungekürzt; ~**back** Verteidiger *m*; ~**ness** Fülle *f*; ~ **stop** Punkt *m*; ~-**time** *a job* Ganztags-; *ad work* hauptberuflich; ~**y** *ad* völlig; ~-**y-fledged** *a* (*lit, fig*) flügge; **a** ~**y-fledged teacher** ein vollausgebildeter Lehrer.

fumble ['fʌmbl] *vi* herumfummeln (*with, at* an + *dat*).

fume [fju:m] *vi* rauchen, qualmen; (*fig*) wütend sein, kochen (*col*); ~**s** *pl* Abgase *pl*; Qualm *m*.

fumigate ['fju:mɪgeɪt] *vt* ausräuchern.

fun [fʌn] *n* Spaß *m*; **to make** ~ **of** sich lustig machen über (+ *acc*).

function ['fʌŋkʃən] *n* Funktion *f*; (*occasion*) Veranstaltung *f*, Feier *f*; *vi* funktionieren; ~**al** *a* funktionell, praktisch.

fund [fʌnd] *n* (*money*) Geldmittel *pl*, Fonds *m*; (*store*) Schatz *m*, Vorrat *m*.

fundamental [fʌndə'mentl] *a* fundamental, grundlegend; ~**s** *pl* Grundbegriffe *pl*; ~**ly** *ad* im Grunde.

funeral ['fju:nərəl] *n* Beerdigung *f*, Beerdigungs-.

fungus ['fʌŋgəs] *n*, *pl* fungi *or* funguses Pilz *m*.

funicular [fju:'nɪkjʊlə*] *n* (Draht)seilbahn *f*.

funnel ['fʌnl] *n* Trichter *m*; (*Naut*) Schornstein *m*.

funnily ['fʌnɪlɪ] *ad* komisch; ~ **enough** merkwürdigerweise.

funny ['fʌnɪ] *a* komisch; ~ **bone** Musikantenknochen *m*.

fur [fɜ:*] *n* Pelz *m*; ~ **coat** Pelzmantel *m*.

furious *a*, ~**ly** *ad* ['fjʊərɪəs, -lɪ] wütend; *attempt* heftig.

furlong ['fɜ:lɔŋ] *n* = 220 yards.

furlough ['fɜ:ləʊ] *n* (*US*) Urlaub *m*.

furnace ['fɜ:nɪs] *n* (Brenn)ofen *m*.

furnish ['fɜ:nɪʃ] *vt* einrichten, möblieren;

(*supply*) versehen; ~**ings** *pl* Einrichtung *f*.

furniture ['fɜ:nɪtʃə*] *n* Möbel *pl*.

furrow ['fʌrəʊ] *n* Furche *f*.

furry ['fɜ:rɪ] *a* pelzartig; *tongue* pelzig; *animal* Pelz-.

further ['fɜ:ðə*] *comp of* **far**; *a* weitere(r,s); *ad* weiter; *vt* fördern; ~ **education** Weiterbildung *f*; Erwachsenenbildung *f*; ~**more** *ad* ferner.

furthest ['fɜ:ðɪst] *superl of* **far**.

furtive *a*, ~**ly** *ad* ['fɜ:tɪv, -lɪ] verstohlen.

fury ['fjʊərɪ] *n* Wut *f*, Zorn *m*.

fuse [fju:z] *n* (*Elec*) Sicherung *f*; (*of bomb*) Zünder *m*; *vt* verschmelzen; *vi* (*Elec*) durchbrennen; ~ **box** Sicherungskasten *m*.

fuselage ['fju:zəlɑ:ʒ] *n* Flugzeugrumpf *m*.

fusion ['fju:ʒən] *n* Verschmelzung *f*.

fuss [fʌs] *n* Theater *nt*; ~**y** *a* (*difficult*) heikel; (*attentive to detail*) kleinlich.

futile ['fju:tail] *a* zwecklos, sinnlos.

futility [fju:'tɪlɪtɪ] *n* Zwecklosigkeit *f*.

future ['fju:tʃə*] *a* zukünftig; *n* Zukunft *f*; **in** (**the**) ~ in Zukunft, zukünftig.

futuristic [fju:tʃə'rɪstɪk] *a* futuristisch.

fuze [fju:z] (*US*) = **fuse**.

fuzzy ['fʌzɪ] *a* (*indistinct*) verschwommen; *hair* kraus.

G

G, g [dʒi:] *n* G *nt*, g *nt*.

gabble ['gæbl] *vi* plappern.

gable ['geɪbl] *n* Giebel *m*.

gadget ['gædʒɪt] *n* Vorrichtung *f*; ~**ry** Kinkerlitzchen *pl*.

gaffe [gæf] *n* Fauxpas *m*.

gag [gæg] *n* Knebel *m*; (*Theat*) Gag *m*; *vt* knebeln; (*Pol*) mundtot machen.

gaiety ['geɪɪtɪ] *n* Fröhlichkeit *f*.

gaily ['geɪlɪ] *ad* lustig, fröhlich.

gain [geɪn] *vt* (*obtain*) erhalten; (*win*) gewinnen; *vi* (*improve*) gewinnen (*in* an + *dat*); (*make progress*) Vorsprung gewinnen; (*clock*) vorgehen; *n* Gewinn *m*; ~**ful employment** Erwerbstätigkeit *f*.

gala ['gɑ:lə] *n* Fest *nt*.

galaxy ['gæləksɪ] *n* Sternsystem *nt*.

gale [geɪl] *n* Sturm *m*.

gallant ['gælənt] *a* tapfer, ritterlich; (*polite*) galant; ~**ry** Tapferkeit *f*, Ritterlichkeit *f*; Galanterie *f*.

gall-bladder ['gɔ:lblædə*] *n* Gallenblase *f*.

gallery ['gælərɪ] *n* Galerie *f*.

galley ['gælɪ] *n* (*ship's kitchen*) Kombüse *f*; (*ship*) Galeere *f*.

gallon ['gælən] *n* Gallone *f*.

gallop ['gæləp] *n* Galopp *m*; *vi* galoppieren.

gallows ['gæləʊz] *npl* Galgen *m*.

gallstone ['gɔ:lstəʊn] *n* Gallenstein *m*.

gamble ['gæmbl] *vi* (um Geld) spielen; *vt* (*risk*) aufs Spiel setzen; *n* Risiko *nt*; ~**r** Spieler(in *f*) *m*.

gambling ['gæmblɪŋ] *n* Glücksspiel *nt*.

game [geɪm] *n* Spiel *nt*; (*hunting*) Wild *nt*; *a* bereit (*for* zu); (*brave*) mutig; ~**keeper** Wildhüter *m*.

gammon ['gæmən] *n* geräucherte(r) Schinken *m*.

gander ['gændə*] n Gänserich m.

gang [gæŋ] n (of criminals, youths) Bande f; (of workmen) Kolonne f.

gangrene ['gæŋgriːn] n Brand m.

gangster ['gæŋstə*] n Gangster m.

gangway ['gæŋweɪ] n (Naut) Laufplanke f.

gaol [dʒeɪl] n = **jail**.

gap [gæp] n (hole) Lücke f; (space) Zwischenraum m.

gape [geɪp] vi glotzen.

gaping ['geɪpɪŋ] a wound klaffend; hole gähnend.

garage ['gærɑːʒ] n Garage f; (for repair) (Auto)reparaturwerkstatt f; (for petrol) Tankstelle f; vt einstellen.

garbage ['gɑːbɪdʒ] n Abfall m; ~ can (US) Mülltonne f.

garbled ['gɑːbld] a story verdreht.

garden ['gɑːdn] n Garten m; vi gärtnern; ~er Gärtner(in f) m; ~ing Gärtnern nt; ~ party Gartenfest nt.

gargle ['gɑːgl] vi gurgeln; n Gurgelmittel nt.

gargoyle ['gɑːgɔɪl] n Wasserspeier m.

garish ['gɛərɪʃ] a grell.

garland ['gɑːlənd] n Girlande f.

garlic ['gɑːlɪk] n Knoblauch m.

garment ['gɑːmənt] n Kleidungsstück nt.

garnish ['gɑːnɪʃ] vt food garnieren; n Garnierung f.

garret ['gærɪt] n Dachkammer f, Mansarde f.

garrison ['gærɪsən] n Garnison f; vt besetzen.

garrulous ['gærʊləs] a geschwätzig.

garter ['gɑːtə*] n Strumpfband nt.

gas [gæs] n Gas nt; (Med) Betäubungsmittel nt; (esp US: petrol) Benzin nt; to step on the ~ Gas geben; vt vergasen; ~ cooker Gasherd m; ~ cylinder Gasflasche f; ~ fire Gasofen m, Gasheizung f.

gash [gæʃ] n klaffende Wunde f; vt tief verwunden.

gasket ['gæskɪt] n Dichtungsring m.

gasmask ['gæsmɑːsk] n Gasmaske f.

gas meter ['gæsmiːtə*] n Gaszähler m.

gasoline ['gæsəliːn] n (US) Benzin nt.

gasp [gɑːsp] vi keuchen; (in astonishment) tief Luft holen; n Keuchen nt.

gas ring ['gæsrɪŋ] n Gasring m.

gas station ['gæssteɪʃən] n (US) Tankstelle f.

gas stove ['gæsstəʊv] n Gaskocher m.

gassy ['gæsɪ] a drink sprudelnd.

gastric ['gæstrɪk] a Magen-; ~ ulcer Magengeschwür nt.

gastronomy [gæs'trɒnəmɪ] n Kochkunst f.

gate [geɪt] n Tor nt; (barrier) Schranke f; ~crash vt party platzen in (+acc); ~way Toreingang m.

gather ['gæðə*] vt people versammeln; things sammeln; vi (understand) annehmen; (deduce) schließen (from aus); (assemble) sich versammeln; ~ing Versammlung f.

gauche [gəʊʃ] a linkisch.

gaudy ['gɔːdɪ] a schreiend.

gauge [geɪdʒ] n Normalmaß nt; (Rail) Spurweite f; (dial) Anzeiger m; (measure) Maß nt; vt (lit) (ab)messen; (fig) abschätzen.

gaunt [gɔːnt] a hager.

gauntlet ['gɔːntlɪt] n (knight's) Fehdehandschuh m; Handschuh m.

gauze [gɔːz] n Mull m, Gaze f.

gawk [gɔːk] vi dumm (an)glotzen (at acc).

gay [geɪ] a lustig; (coloured) bunt; (col) schwul.

gaze [geɪz] n Blick m; vi (an)blicken (at acc).

gazelle [gə'zel] n Gazelle f.

gazetteer [gæzɪ'tɪə*] n geographische(s) Lexikon nt.

gear [gɪə*] n Getriebe nt; (equipment) Ausrüstung f; (Aut) Gang m; to be out of/in ~ aus-/eingekuppelt sein; ~box Getriebe(gehäuse) nt; ~-lever, ~shift (US) Schalthebel m.

geese [giːs] pl of **goose**.

gelatin(e) ['dʒelətiːn] n Gelatine f.

gem [dʒem] n Edelstein m; (fig) Juwel nt.

Gemini ['dʒemɪniː] n Zwillinge pl.

gen [dʒen] n (col: information) Infos pl (on über +acc).

gender ['dʒendə*] n (Gram) Geschlecht nt.

gene [dʒiːn] n Gen nt.

general ['dʒenərəl] n General m; a allgemein; ~ election allgemeine Wahlen pl; ~ization Verallgemeinerung f; ~ize vi verallgemeinern; ~ly ad allgemein, im allgemeinen.

generate ['dʒenəreɪt] vt erzeugen.

generation [dʒenə'reɪʃən] n Generation f; (act) Erzeugung f.

generator ['dʒenəreɪtə*] n Generator m.

generosity [dʒenə'rɒsɪtɪ] n Großzügigkeit f.

generous a, ~ly ad ['dʒenərəs, -lɪ] (noble-minded) hochherzig; (giving freely) großzügig.

genetics [dʒɪ'netɪks] n Genetik f, Vererbungslehre f.

genial ['dʒiːnɪəl] a freundlich, jovial.

genitals ['dʒenɪtlz] npl Geschlechtsteile pl, Genitalien pl.

genitive ['dʒenɪtɪv] n Genitiv m, Wesfall m.

genius ['dʒiːnɪəs] n Genie nt.

genocide ['dʒenəʊsaɪd] n Völkermord m.

genteel [dʒen'tiːl] a (polite) wohlanständig; (affected) affektiert.

gentile ['dʒentaɪl] n Nichtjude m.

gentle ['dʒentl] a sanft, zart; ~man Herr m; (polite) Gentleman m; ~ness Zartheit f, Milde f.

gently ['dʒentlɪ] ad zart, sanft.

gentry ['dʒentrɪ] n Landadel m.

gents [dʒents] n: 'G~' (lavatory) 'Herren'.

genuine ['dʒenjuɪn] a echt, wahr; ~ly ad wirklich, echt.

geographer [dʒɪ'ɒgrəfə*] n Geograph(in f) m.

geographical [dʒɪə'græfɪkəl] a geographisch.

geography [dʒɪ'ɒgrəfɪ] n Geographie f, Erdkunde f.

geological [dʒɪə'lɒdʒɪkəl] a geologisch.

geologist [dʒɪ'ɒlədʒɪst] n Geologe m, Geologin f.

geology [dʒɪ'ɒlədʒɪ] n Geologie f.
geometric(al) [dʒɪə'metrɪk(əl)] a geometrisch.
geometry [dʒɪ'ɒmɪtrɪ] n Geometrie f.
geranium [dʒɪ'reɪnɪəm] n Geranie f.
germ [dʒɜːm] n Keim m; (Med) Bazillus m.
germination [dʒɜːmɪ'neɪʃən] n Keimen nt.
gesticulate [dʒes'tɪkjuleɪt] vi gestikulieren.
gesticulation [dʒestɪkju'leɪʃən] n Gesten pl, Gestikulieren nt.
gesture ['dʒestʃəˀ] n Geste f.
get [get] vt irreg (receive) bekommen, kriegen; (become) werden; (go, travel) kommen; (arrive) ankommen; to ~ sb to do sth jdn dazu bringen, etw zu tun, jdn etw machen lassen; ~ along vi (people) (gut) zurechtkommen; (depart) sich (acc) auf den Weg machen; ~ at vt facts herausbekommen; to ~ at sb (nag) an jdm herumnörgeln; ~ away vi (leave) sich (acc) davonmachen; (escape) entkommen (from dat); ~ away with you! laß den Quatsch!; ~ down vi (her)untergehen; vt (depress) fertigmachen; ~ in vi (train) ankommen; (arrive from) heimkommen; ~ off vi (from train etc) aussteigen (aus); (from horse) absteigen (von); ~ on vi (progress) vorankommen; (be friends) auskommen; (age) alt werden; vt train etc einsteigen (in +acc); horse aufsteigen (auf +acc); ~ out vi (of house) herauskommen; (of vehicle) aussteigen; vt (take out) herausholen; ~ over vt illness sich (acc) erholen von; surprise verkraften; news fassen; loss sich abfinden mit; I couldn't ~ over her ich konnte sie nicht vergessen; ~ up vi aufstehen; ~away Flucht f.
geyser ['gizəˀ] n Geiser m; (heater) Durchlauferhitzer m.
ghastly ['gɑːstlɪ] a (horrible) gräßlich; (pale) totenbleich.
gherkin ['gɜːkɪn] n Gewürzgurke f.
ghetto ['getəʊ] n G(h)etto nt.
ghost [gəʊst] n Gespenst nt, Geist m; ~ly a gespenstisch; ~ story Gespenstergeschichte f.
giant ['dʒaɪənt] n Riese m; a riesig, Riesen-.
gibberish ['dʒɪbərɪʃ] n dumme(s) Geschwätz nt.
gibe [dʒaɪb] n spöttische Bemerkung f.
giblets ['dʒɪblɪts] npl Geflügelinnereien pl.
giddiness ['gɪdɪnəs] n Schwindelgefühl nt.
giddy ['gɪdɪ] a schwindlig; (frivolous) leichtsinnig.
gift [gɪft] n Geschenk nt; (ability) Begabung f; ~ed a begabt.
gigantic [dʒaɪ'gæntɪk] a riesenhaft, ungeheuer groß.
giggle ['gɪgl] vi kichern; n Gekicher nt.
gild [gɪld] vt vergolden.
gill[1] [dʒɪl] n (1/4 pint) Viertelpinte f.
gill[2] [gɪl] n (of fish) Kieme f.
gilt [gɪlt] n Vergoldung f; a vergoldet.
gimlet ['gɪmlɪt] n Handbohrer m.
gimmick ['gɪmɪk] n (for sales, publicity) Gag m; it's so ~y es ist alles nur ein Gag.

gin [dʒɪn] n Gin m.
ginger ['dʒɪndʒəˀ] n Ingwer m; ~ ale, ~ beer Ingwerbier nt; ~bread Pfefferkuchen m; ~-haired a rothaarig.
gingerly ['dʒɪndʒəlɪ] ad behutsam.
gipsy ['dʒɪpsɪ] n Zigeuner(in f) m.
giraffe [dʒɪ'rɑːf] n Giraffe f.
girder ['gɜːdəˀ] n (steel) Eisenträger m; (wood) Tragebalken m.
girdle ['gɜːdl] n (woman's) Hüftgürtel m; vt umgürten.
girl [gɜːl] n Mädchen nt; ~friend Freundin f; ~ish a mädchenhaft.
girth [gɜːθ] n (measure) Umfang m; (strap) Sattelgurt m.
gist [dʒɪst] n Wesentliche(s) nt, Quintessenz f.
give [gɪv] irreg vt geben; vi (break) nachgeben; ~ away vt (give free) verschenken; (betray) verraten; ~ back vt zurückgeben; ~ in vi (yield) aufgeben; (agree) nachgeben; vt (hand in) abgeben; ~ up vti aufgeben; ~ way vi (traffic) Vorfahrt lassen; (to feelings) nachgeben (+dat).
glacier ['glæsɪəˀ] n Gletscher m.
glad [glæd] a froh; I was ~ to hear ... ich habe mich gefreut, zu hören ...; ~den vt erfreuen.
gladiator ['glædɪeɪtəˀ] n Gladiator m.
gladioli [glædɪ'əʊlaɪ] npl Gladiolen pl.
gladly ['glædlɪ] ad gern(e).
glamorous ['glæmərəs] a bezaubernd; life reizvoll.
glamour ['glæməˀ] n Zauber m, Reiz m.
glance [glɑːns] n flüchtige(r) Blick m; vi schnell (hin)blicken (at auf +acc); ~ off vi (fly off) abprallen von.
glancing ['glɑːnsɪŋ] a blow abprallend, Streif-.
gland [glænd] n Drüse f; ~ular fever Drüsenentzündung f.
glare [glɛəˀ] n (light) grelle(s) Licht nt; (stare) wilde(r) Blick m; vi grell scheinen; (angrily) böse ansehen (at acc).
glaring ['glɛərɪŋ] a injustice schreiend; mistake kraß.
glass [glɑːs] n Glas nt; (mirror) Spiegel m; ~es pl Brille f; ~house Gewächshaus nt; ~ware Glaswaren pl; ~y a glasig.
glaze [gleɪz] vt verglasen; (finish with a —) glasieren; n Glasur f.
glazier ['gleɪzɪəˀ] n Glaser m.
gleam [gliːm] n Schimmer m; vi schimmern; ~ing a schimmernd.
glee [gliː] n Frohsinn m; ~ful a fröhlich.
glen [glen] n Bergtal nt.
glib [glɪb] a (rede)gewandt; (superficial) oberflächlich; ~ly ad glatt.
glide [glaɪd] vi gleiten; n Gleiten nt; (Aviat) Segelflug m; ~r (Aviat) Segelflugzeug nt.
gliding ['glaɪdɪŋ] n Segelfliegen nt.
glimmer ['glɪməˀ] n Schimmer m; ~ of hope Hoffnungsschimmer m.
glimpse [glɪmps] n flüchtige(r) Blick m; vt flüchtig erblicken.
glint [glɪnt] n Glitzern nt; vi glitzern.
glisten ['glɪsn] vi glänzen.

glitter ['glɪtə*] vi funkeln; n Funkeln nt; ~ing a glitzernd.

gloat over ['gləutʌuvə*] vt sich weiden an (+dat).

global ['gləubl] a global.

globe [gləub] n Erdball m; (sphere) Globus m; ~-trotter Weltenbummler(in f) m, Globetrotter(in f) m.

gloom [glu:m] n (also ~iness) (darkness) Dunkel nt, Dunkelheit f; (depression) düstere Stimmung f; ~ily ad, ~y a düster.

glorification [glɔːrɪfɪˈkeɪʃən] n Verherrlichung f.

glorify ['glɔːrɪfaɪ] vt verherrlichen; **just a glorified cafe** nur ein besseres Café.

glorious ['glɔːrɪəs] a glorreich; (splendid) prächtig.

glory ['glɔːrɪ] n Herrlichkeit f; (praise) Ruhm m; **to ~ in** sich sonnen in (+dat).

gloss [glɒs] n (shine) Glanz m; ~ **paint** Ölfarbe f; ~ **over** vt übertünchen.

glossary ['glɒsərɪ] n Glossar nt.

glossy ['glɒsɪ] a surface glänzend.

glove [glʌv] n Handschuh m.

glow [gləu] vi glühen, leuchten; n (heat) Glühen nt; (colour) Röte f; (feeling) Wärme f.

glower ['glauə*] vi: ~ **at** finster anblicken.

glucose ['glu:kəus] n Traubenzucker m.

glue [glu:] n Klebstoff m, Leim m; vt leimen, kleben.

glum [glʌm] a bedrückt.

glut [glʌt] n Überfluß m; vt überladen.

glutton ['glʌtn] n Vielfraß m; (fig) Unersättliche(r) mf; ~ous a gierig; ~y Völlerei f; Unersättlichkeit f.

glycerin(e) ['glɪsəriːn] n Glyzerin nt.

gnarled [nɑːld] a knorrig.

gnat [næt] n Stechmücke f.

gnaw [nɔː] vt nagen an (+dat).

gnome [nəum] n Gnom m.

go [gəu] vi irreg gehen; (travel) reisen, fahren; (depart: train) (ab)fahren; (money) ausgehen; (vision) verschwinden; (smell) verfliegen; (disappear) (fort)gehen; (be sold) kosten; (at auction) weggehen; (work) gehen, funktionieren; (fit, suit) passen (with zu); (become) werden; (break etc) nachgeben; n (energy) Schwung m; (attempt) Versuch m; **can I have another ~?** darf ich noch mal?; ~ **ahead** vi (proceed) weitergehen; ~ **along with** vt (agree to support) zustimmen (+dat), unterstützen; ~ **away** vi (depart) weggehen; ~ **back** vi (return) zurückgehen; ~ **back on** vt promise nicht halten; ~ **by** vi (years, time) vergehen; ~ **down** vi (sun) untergehen; ~ **for** vt (fetch) holen (gehen); (like) mögen; (attack) sich stürzen auf (+acc); ~ **in** vi hineingehen; ~ **into** vt (enter) hineingehen in (+acc); (study) sich befassen mit; ~ **off** vi (depart) weggehen; (lights) ausgehen; (milk etc) sauer werden; (col: explode) losgehen; vt (dislike) nicht mehr mögen; ~ **on** vi (continue) weitergehen; (col: complain) meckern; (lights) angehen; **to ~ on with sth** mit etw weitermachen; ~ **out** vi

(fire, light) ausgehen; (of house) hinausgehen; ~ **over** vt (examine, check) durchgehen; ~ **up** vi (price) steigen; ~ **without** vt sich behelfen ohne; food entbehren.

goad [gəud] vt anstacheln; n Treibstock m.

go-ahead ['gəuəhed] a zielstrebig; (progressive) fortschrittlich; n grünes Licht nt.

goal [gəul] n Ziel nt; (Sport) Tor nt; ~**keeper** Torwart m; ~-**post** Torpfosten m.

goat [gəut] n Ziege f.

gobble ['gɒbl] vt hinunterschlingen.

go-between ['gəubɪtwiːn] n Mittelsmann m.

goblet ['gɒblɪt] n Kelch(glas nt) m.

goblin ['gɒblɪn] n Kobold m.

god [gɒd] n Gott m; ~**child** Patenkind nt; ~**dess** Göttin f; ~**father** Pate m; ~**forsaken** a gottverlassen; ~**mother** Patin f; ~**send** Geschenk nt des Himmels.

goggle ['gɒgl] vi (stare) glotzen; **to ~ at** anglotzen; ~**s** pl Schutzbrille f.

going ['gəuɪŋ] n (condition of ground) Straßenzustand m; (horse-racing) Bahn f; **it's hard** ~ es ist schwierig; **a rate** gängig; concern gutgehend; ~**s-on** pl Vorgänge pl.

gold [gəuld] n Gold nt; ~**en** a golden, Gold-; ~**fish** Goldfisch m; ~ **mine** Goldgrube f.

golf [gɒlf] n Golf nt; ~ **club** (society) Golfklub m; (stick) Golfschläger m; ~ **course** Golfplatz m; ~**er** Golfspieler(in f) m.

gondola ['gɒndələ] n Gondel f.

gong [gɒŋ] n Gong m.

good [gud] n (benefit) Wohl nt; (moral excellence) Güte f; a gut; (suitable) passend; ~**s** pl Ware(n f) f, Güter pl; **a ~ deal of** ziemlich viel; **a ~ many** ziemlich viele; ~**bye!** auf Wiedersehen!; **G~ Friday** Karfreitag m; ~-**looking** gutaussehend; ~ **morning!** guten Morgen!; ~**ness** Güte f, (virtue) Tugend f; ~**will** (favour) Wohlwollen nt; (Comm) Firmenansehen nt.

goose [guːs] n Gans f; ~**berry** [guzbərɪ] Stachelbeere f; ~**flesh**, ~ **pimples** pl Gänsehaut f.

gore [gɔː*] vt durchbohren; aufspießen; n Blut nt.

gorge [gɔːdʒ] n Schlucht f; vti (sich voll)fressen.

gorgeous ['gɔːdʒəs] a prächtig; person bildhübsch.

gorilla [gəˈrɪlə] n Gorilla m.

gorse [gɔːs] n Stechginster m.

gory ['gɔːrɪ] a blutig.

go-slow ['gəu'sləu] n Bummelstreik m.

gospel ['gɒspl] n Evangelium nt.

gossamer ['gɒsəmə*] n Spinnfäden pl.

gossip ['gɒsɪp] n Klatsch m; (person) Klatschbase f; vi klatschen.

goulash ['guːlæʃ] n Gulasch nt or m.

gout [gaut] n Gicht f.

govern ['gʌvən] vt regieren; verwalten; (Gram) bestimmen; ~**ess** Gouvernante f; ~**ing** a leitend; (fig) bestimmend; ~**ment** Regierung f; a Regierungs-; ~**or** Gouverneur m.

gown [gaʊn] n Gewand nt; (Univ) Robe f.

grab [græb] vt packen; an sich reißen; n plötzliche(r) Griff m; (crane) Greifer m.

grace [greɪs] n Anmut f; (favour) Güte f, Gefälligkeit f; (blessing) Gnade f; (prayer) Tischgebet nt; (Comm) Zahlungsfrist f; vt (adorn) zieren; (honour) auszeichnen; **5 days'** ~ 5 Tage Aufschub m; ~**ful** a ~**fully** ad anmutig, graziös.

gracious ['greɪʃəs] a gnädig; (kind, courteous) wohlwollend, freundlich.

gradation [grə'deɪʃən] n (Ab)stufung f.

grade [greɪd] n Grad m; (slope) Gefälle nt; **to make the** ~ es schaffen; vt (classify) einstufen; ~ **crossing** (US) Bahnübergang m.

gradient ['greɪdɪənt] n Steigung f; Gefälle nt.

gradual a, ~**ly** ad ['grædjʊəl, -lɪ] allmählich.

graduate ['grædjʊɪt] n: **to be a** ~ das Staatsexamen haben; ['grædjʊeɪt] vi das Staatsexamen machen or bestehen.

graduation [grædjʊ'eɪʃən] n Erlangung f eines akademischen Grades.

graft [grɑːft] n (on plant) Pfropfreis nt; (hard work) Schufterei f; (Med) Verpflanzung f; (unfair self-advancement) Schiebung f; vt propfen; (fig) aufpfropfen; (Med) verpflanzen.

grain [greɪn] n Korn nt, Getreide nt; (particle) Körnchen nt, Korn nt; (in wood) Maserung f.

grammar ['græmə*] n Grammatik f.

grammatical [grə'mætɪkəl] a grammatisch.

gram(me) [græm] n Gramm nt.

gramophone ['græməfəʊn] n Grammophon nt.

granary ['grænərɪ] n Kornspeicher m.

grand [grænd] a großartig; ~**daughter** Enkelin f; ~**eur** ['grændjə*] Erhabenheit f; ~**father** Großvater m; ~**iose** a (imposing) großartig; (pompous) schwülstig; ~**mother** Großmutter f; ~ **piano** Flügel m; ~**son** Enkel m; ~**stand** Haupttribüne f; ~ **total** Gesamtsumme f.

granite ['grænɪt] n Granit m.

granny ['grænɪ] n Oma f.

grant [grɑːnt] vt gewähren; (allow) zugeben; n Unterstützung f; (Univ) Stipendium nt; **to take sb/sth for** ~**ed** jdn/etw als selbstverständlich (an)nehmen.

granulated ['grænjʊleɪtɪd] a: ~ **sugar** raffiniert.

granule ['grænjuːl] n Körnchen nt.

grape [greɪp] n (Wein)traube f; ~**fruit** Pampelmuse f, Grapefruit f; ~ **juice** Traubensaft m.

graph [grɑːf] n Schaubild nt; ~**ic** a (descriptive) anschaulich, lebendig; drawing graphisch.

grapple ['græpl] vi sich raufen; ~ **with** (lit, fig) kämpfen mit.

grasp [grɑːsp] vt ergreifen; (understand) begreifen; n Griff m; (possession) Gewalt f; (of subject) Beherrschung f; ~**ing** a habgierig.

grass [grɑːs] n Gras nt; ~**hopper** Heuschrecke f; ~**land** Weideland nt; ~

roots pl (fig) Basis f; ~ **snake** Ringelnatter f; ~**y** a grasig, Gras-.

grate [greɪt] n Feuerrost m, Kamin m; vi kratzen; (sound) knirschen; (on nerves) zerren (on an +dat); vt cheese reiben.

grateful a, ~**ly** ad ['greɪtful, -flɪ] dankbar.

grater ['greɪtə*] n (in kitchen) Reibe f.

gratification [grætɪfɪ'keɪʃən] n Befriedigung f.

gratify ['grætɪfaɪ] vt befriedigen.

gratifying ['grætɪfaɪɪŋ] a erfreulich.

grating ['greɪtɪŋ] n (iron bars) Gitter nt; a noise knirschend.

gratitude ['grætɪtjuːd] n Dankbarkeit f.

gratuitous [grə'tjuːɪtəs] a (uncalled-for) grundlos, überflüssig; (given free) unentgeltlich, gratis.

gratuity [grə'tjuːɪtɪ] n (Geld)geschenk nt; (Comm) Gratifikation f.

grave [greɪv] n Grab nt; a (serious) ernst, schwerwiegend; (solemn) ernst, feierlich; ~**digger** Totengräber m.

gravel ['grævəl] n Kies m.

gravely ['greɪvlɪ] ad schwer, ernstlich.

gravestone ['greɪvstəʊn] n Grabstein m.

graveyard ['greɪvjɑːd] n Friedhof m.

gravitate ['grævɪteɪt] vi streben; (fig) tendieren.

gravity ['grævɪtɪ] n Schwerkraft f; (seriousness) Schwere f, Ernst m.

gravy ['greɪvɪ] n (Braten)soße f.

gray [greɪ] a = **grey**.

graze [greɪz] vi grasen; vt (touch) streifen; (Med) abschürfen; n (Med) Abschürfung f.

grease [griːs] n (fat) Fett nt; (lubricant) Schmiere f; vt (ab)schmieren; einfetten; ~ **gun** Schmierspritze f; ~**proof** a paper Butterbrot-.

greasy ['griːsɪ] a fettig.

great [greɪt] a groß; (important) groß, bedeutend; (distinguished) groß, hochstehend; (col: good) prima; ~**grandfather** Urgroßvater m; ~**grandmother** Urgroßmutter f; ~**ly** ad sehr; ~**ness** Größe f.

greed [griːd] n (also ~**iness**) Gier f (for nach); (meanness) Geiz m; ~**ily** ad gierig; ~**y** a gefräßig, gierig; ~**y for money** geldgierig.

green [griːn] a grün; n (village ~) Dorfwiese f; ~**grocer** Obst- und Gemüsehändler m; ~**house** Gewächshaus nt; ~**ish** a grünlich; ~ **light** (lit, fig) grüne(s) Licht nt.

greet [griːt] vt grüßen; ~**ing** Gruß m, Begrüßung f.

gregarious [grɪ'gɛərɪəs] a gesellig.

grenade [grɪ'neɪd] n Granate f.

grey [greɪ] a grau; ~**haired** a grauhaarig; ~**hound** Windhund m; ~**ish** a gräulich.

grid [grɪd] n Gitter nt; (Elec) Leitungsnetz nt; (on map) Gitternetz nt; ~**iron** Bratrost m.

grief [griːf] n Gram m, Kummer m.

grievance ['griːvəns] n Beschwerde f.

grieve [griːv] vi sich grämen; vt betrüben.

grill [grɪl] n (on cooker) Grill m; vt grillen;

(*question*) in die Mangel nehmen.

grille [grɪl] *n* (*on car etc*) (Kühler)gitter *nt*.

grim [grɪm] *a* grimmig; *situation* düster.

grimace [grɪˈmeɪs] *n* Grimasse *f*; *vi* Grimassen schneiden.

grime [graɪm] *n* Schmutz *m*.

grimly [ˈgrɪmlɪ] *ad* grimmig, finster.

grimy [ˈgraɪmɪ] *a* schmutzig.

grin [grɪn] *n* Grinsen *nt*; *vi* grinsen.

grind [graɪnd] *vt irreg* mahlen; (*sharpen*) schleifen; *teeth* knirschen mit; *n* (*bore*) Plackerei *f*.

grip [grɪp] *n* Griff *m*; (*mastery*) Griff *m*, Gewalt *f*; (*suitcase*) kleine(r) Handkoffer *m*; *vt* packen.

gripes [graɪps] *npl* (*bowel pains*) Bauchschmerzen *pl*, Bauchweh *nt*.

gripping [ˈgrɪpɪŋ] *a* (*exciting*) spannend.

grisly [ˈgrɪzlɪ] *a* gräßlich.

gristle [ˈgrɪsl] *n* Knorpel *m*.

grit [grɪt] *n* Splitt *m*; (*courage*) Mut *m*, Mumm *m*; *vt teeth* knirschen mit; *road* (mit Splitt be)streuen.

groan [grəʊn] *n* Stöhnen *nt*; *vi* stöhnen.

grocer [ˈgrəʊsəˈ] *n* Lebensmittelhändler *m*; ~**ies** *pl* Lebensmittel *pl*.

grog [grɒg] *n* Grog *m*.

groggy [ˈgrɒgɪ] *a* benommen; (*boxing*) angeschlagen.

groin [grɔɪn] *n* Leistengegend *f*.

groom [gruːm] *n* Bräutigam *m*; (*for horses*) Pferdeknecht *m*; *to* ~ **o.s.** (*of man*) sich zurechtmachen, sich pflegen; (*well*) ~**ed** gepflegt; *to* ~ **sb for a career** jdn auf eine Laufbahn vorbereiten.

groove [gruːv] *n* Rille *f*, Furche *f*.

grope [grəʊp] *vi* tasten.

gross [grəʊs] *a* (*coarse*) dick, plump; (*bad*) grob, schwer; (*Comm*) brutto; Gesamt-; *n* Gros *nt*; ~**ly** *ad* höchst, ungeheuerlich.

grotesque [grəʊˈtesk] *a* grotesk.

grotto [ˈgrɒtəʊ] *n* Grotte *f*.

ground [graʊnd] *n* Boden *m*, Erde *f*; (*land*) Grundbesitz *m*; (*reason*) Grund *m*; ~**s** *pl* (*dregs*) Bodensatz *m*; (*around house*) (Garten)anlagen *pl*; *vt* (*run ashore*) auf Strand setzen; *aircraft* stillegen; (*instruct*) die Anfangsgründe beibringen (+*dat*); *vi* (*run ashore*) stranden, auflaufen; ~**floor** (*Brit*) Erdgeschoß *nt*, Parterre *nt*; ~**ing** (*instruction*) Anfangsunterricht *m*; ~**sheet** Zeltboden *m*; ~**work** Grundlage *f*.

group [gruːp] *n* Gruppe *f*; *vti* (sich) gruppieren.

grouse [graʊs] *n* (*bird*) schottische(s) Moorhuhn *nt*; (*complaint*) Nörgelei *f*; *vi* (*complain*) meckern.

grove [grəʊv] *n* Gehölz *nt*, Hain *m*.

grovel [ˈgrɒvl] *vi* auf dem Bauch kriechen; (*fig*) kriechen.

grow [grəʊ] *irreg vi* wachsen, größer werden; (*grass*) wachsen; (*become*) werden; **it** ~**s on you** man gewöhnt sich daran; *vt* (*raise*) anbauen, ziehen; ~ **up** vi aufwachsen; (*mature*) erwachsen werden; ~**er** Züchter *m*; ~**ing** *a* wachsend; (*fig*) zunehmend.

growl [graʊl] *vi* knurren; *n* Knurren *nt*.

grown-up [ˈgrəʊnˈʌp] *a* erwachsen; *n* Erwachsene(r) *mf*.

growth [grəʊθ] *n* Wachstum *nt*, Wachsen *nt*; (*increase*) Anwachsen *nt*, Zunahme *f*; (*of beard etc*) Wuchs *m*.

grub [grʌb] *n* Made *f*, Larve *f*; (*col: food*) Futter *nt*; ~**by** *a* schmutzig, schmuddelig.

grudge [grʌdʒ] *n* Groll *m*; *vt* mißgönnen (*sb sth etw*); **to bear sb a** ~ einen Groll gegen jdn hegen.

grudging [ˈgrʌdʒɪŋ] *a* neidisch; (*unwilling*) widerwillig.

gruelling [ˈgrʊəlɪŋ] *a climb, race* mörderisch.

gruesome [ˈgruːsəm] *a* grauenhaft.

gruff [grʌf] *a* barsch.

grumble [ˈgrʌmbl] *vi* murren, schimpfen; *n* Brummen *nt*, Murren *nt*.

grumpy [ˈgrʌmpɪ] *a* verdrießlich.

grunt [grʌnt] *vi* grunzen; *n* Grunzen *nt*.

guarantee [gærənˈtiː] *n* (*promise to pay*) Gewähr *f*; (*promise to replace*) Garantie *f*; *vt* gewährleisten; garantieren.

guarantor [gærənˈtɔːˈ] *n* Gewährsmann *m*, Bürge *m*.

guard [gɑːd] *n* (*defence*) Bewachung *f*; (*sentry*) Wache *f*; (*Rail*) Zugbegleiter *m*; **to be on** ~ Wache stehen; **to be on one's** ~ aufpassen; *vt* bewachen, beschützen; ~**ed** *a* vorsichtig, zurückhaltend; ~**ian** Vormund *m*; (*keeper*) Hüter *m*; ~**'s van** (*Brit Rail*) Dienstwagen *m*.

guerrilla [gəˈrɪlə] *n* Guerilla(kämpfer) *m*; ~ **warfare** Guerillakrieg *m*.

guess [ges] *vti* (er)raten, schätzen; *n* Vermutung *f*; ~**work** Raterei *f*; **good** ~ gut geraten.

guest [gest] *n* Gast *m*; ~-**house** Pension *f*; ~ **room** Gastzimmer *nt*.

guffaw [gʌˈfɔː] *n* schallende(s) Gelächter *nt*; *vi* schallend lachen.

guidance [ˈgaɪdəns] *n* (*control*) Leitung *f*; (*advice*) Rat *m*, Beratung *f*.

guide [gaɪd] *n* Führer *m*; *vt* führen; **girl** ~ Pfadfinderin *f*; ~**book** Reiseführer *m*; ~**d missile** Fernlenkgeschoß *nt*; ~**lines** *pl* Richtlinien *f*.

guild [gɪld] *n* (*Hist*) Gilde *f*; (*society*) Vereinigung *f*; ~-**hall** (*Brit*) Stadthalle *f*.

guile [gaɪl] *n* Arglist *f*; ~**less** *a* arglos.

guillotine [ˈgɪləˈtiːn] *n* Guillotine *f*.

guilt [gɪlt] *n* Schuld *f*; ~**y** *a* schuldig.

guise [gaɪz] *n* (*appearance*) Verkleidung *f*; **in the** ~ **of** (*things*) in der Form (+*gen*); (*people*) gekleidet als.

guitar [gɪˈtɑːˈ] *n* Gitarre *f*; ~**ist** Gitarrist(in *f*) *m*.

gulf [gʌlf] *n* Golf *m*; (*fig*) Abgrund *m*.

gull [gʌl] *n* Möwe *f*.

gullet [ˈgʌlɪt] *n* Schlund *m*.

gullible [ˈgʌlɪbl] *a* leichtgläubig.

gully [ˈgʌlɪ] *n* (Wasser)rinne *f*; (*gorge*) Schlucht *f*.

gulp [gʌlp] *vi* hinunterschlucken; (*gasp*) schlucken; *n* große(r) Schluck *m*.

gum [gʌm] *n* (*around teeth*) Zahnfleisch *nt*; (*glue*) Klebstoff *m*; (*chewing* —) Kaugummi *m*; *vt* gummieren, kleben; ~**boots** *pl* Gummistiefel *pl*.

gumption ['gʌmpʃən] n (col) Mumm m.

gum tree ['gʌmtri:] n Gummibaum m; **up a** ~ (col) in der Klemme.

gun [gʌn] n Schußwaffe f; ~**fire** Geschützfeuer nt; ~**man** bewaffnete(r) Verbrecher m; ~**ner** Kanonier m, Artillerist m; ~**powder** Schießpulver nt; ~**shot** Schuß m; ~ **down** vt niederknallen.

gurgle ['gɜːgl] n Gluckern nt; vi gluckern.

gush [gʌʃ] n Strom m, Erguß m; vi (rush out) hervorströmen; (fig) schwärmen.

gusset ['gʌsɪt] n Keil m, Zwickel m.

gust [gʌst] n Windstoß m, Bö f.

gusto ['gʌstəʊ] n Genuß m, Lust f.

gut [gʌt] n (Anat) Gedärme pl; (string) Darm m; ~**s** pl (fig) Schneid m.

gutter ['gʌtə*] n Dachrinne f; (in street) Gosse f.

guttural ['gʌtərəl] a guttural, Kehl-.

guy [gaɪ] n (rope) Halteseil nt; (man) Typ m, Kerl m.

guzzle ['gʌzl] vti (drink) saufen; (eat) fressen.

gym(nasium) [dʒɪm'neɪzɪəm] n Turnhalle f.

gymnast ['dʒɪmnæst] n Turner(in f) m; ~**ics** [dʒɪm'næstɪks] Turnen nt, Gymnastik f.

gyn(a)ecologist [gaɪnɪ'kɒlədʒɪst] n Frauenarzt m/-ärztin f, Gynäkologe m, Gynäkologin f.

gyn(a)ecology [gaɪnɪ'kɒlədʒɪ] n Gynäkologie f, Frauenheilkunde f.

gypsy ['dʒɪpsɪ] n = gipsy.

gyrate [dʒaɪ'reɪt] vi kreisen.

H

H, h [eɪtʃ] n H nt, h nt.

haberdashery [hæbə'dæʃərɪ] n Kurzwaren pl.

habit ['hæbɪt] n (An)gewohnheit f; (monk's) Habit nt or m.

habitable ['hæbɪtəbl] a bewohnbar.

habitat ['hæbɪtæt] n Lebensraum m.

habitation [hæbɪ'teɪʃən] n Bewohnen nt; (place) Wohnung f.

habitual [hə'bɪtjʊəl] a üblich, gewohnheitsmäßig; ~**ly** ad gewöhnlich.

hack [hæk] vt hacken; n Hieb m; (writer) Schreiberling m.

hackney cab ['hæknɪ'kæb] n Taxi nt.

hackneyed ['hæknɪd] a abgedroschen.

haddock ['hædək] n Schellfisch m.

hadn't ['hædnt] = **had not**.

haemorrhage, (US) **hemo**~ ['hemərɪdʒ] n Blutung f.

haemorrhoids, (US) **hemo**~ ['hemərɔɪdz] n Hämorrhoiden pl.

haggard ['hægəd] a abgekämpft.

haggle ['hægl] vi feilschen.

haggling ['hæglɪŋ] n Feilschen nt.

hail [heɪl] n Hagel m; vt umjubeln; **to** ~ **sb as emperor** jdn zum Kaiser ausrufen; vi hageln; ~**storm** Hagelschauer m.

hair [hɛə*] n Haar nt, Haare pl; (one ~) Haar nt; ~**brush** Haarbürste f; ~**cut** Haarschnitt m; **to get a** ~**cut** sich (dat) die Haare schneiden lassen; ~**do** Frisur f;

~**dresser** Friseur m, Friseuse f; ~**drier** Trockenhaube f; (hand) Fön m; ~**net** Haarnetz nt; ~ **oil** Haaröl nt; ~**piece** (lady's) Haarteil nt; (man's) Toupet nt; ~**pin** (lit) Haarnadel f; (bend) Haarnadelkurve f; ~**raising** a haarsträubend; ~**'s breadth** Haaresbreite f; ~**style** Frisur f; ~**y** a haarig.

hake [heɪk] n Seehecht m.

half [hɑːf] n Hälfte f; a halb; ad halb, zur Hälfte; ~**back** Läufer m; ~**breed**, ~**caste** Mischling m; ~**hearted** a lustlos, unlustig; ~**hour** halbe Stunde f; ~**penny** ['heɪpnɪ] halbe(r) Penny m; ~**price** halbe(r) Preis m; ~**time** Halbzeit f; ~**way** ad halbwegs, auf halbem Wege.

halibut ['hælɪbət] n Heilbutt m.

hall [hɔːl] n Saal m; (entrance ~) Hausflur m; (building) Halle f.

hallmark ['hɔːlmɑːk] n (lit, fig) Stempel m.

hallo [hʌ'ləʊ] see hello.

hallucination [həluːsɪ'neɪʃən] n Halluzination f.

halo ['heɪləʊ] n (of saint) Heiligenschein m; (of moon) Hof m.

halt [hɔːlt] n Halt m; vti anhalten.

halve [hɑːv] vt halbieren.

ham [hæm] n Schinken m; ~ **sandwich** Schinkenbrötchen nt; ~**burger** Frikadelle f.

hamlet ['hæmlɪt] n Weiler m.

hammer ['hæmə*] n Hammer m; vt hämmern.

hammock ['hæmək] n Hängematte f.

hamper ['hæmpə*] vt (be)hindern; n Picknickkorb m; Geschenkkorb m.

hand [hænd] n Hand f; (of clock) (Uhr)zeiger m; (worker) Arbeiter m; vt (pass) geben; **to give sb a** ~ jdm helfen; **at first** ~ aus erster Hand; **to** ~ zur Hand; **in** ~ (under control) in fester Hand, unter Kontrolle; (being done) im Gange; (extra) übrig; ~**bag** Handtasche f; ~**ball** Handball m; ~**book** Handbuch nt; ~**brake** Handbremse f; ~ **cream** Handcreme f; ~**cuffs** pl Handschellen pl; ~**ful** Handvoll f; (col: person) Plage f.

handicap ['hændɪkæp] n Handikap nt; vt benachteiligen.

handicraft ['hændɪkrɑːft] n Kunsthandwerk nt.

handkerchief ['hæŋkətʃɪf] n Taschentuch nt.

handle ['hændl] n (of door etc) Klinke f; (of cup etc) Henkel m; (for winding) Kurbel f; vt (touch) anfassen; (deal with) things sich befassen mit; people umgehen mit; ~**bars** pl Lenkstange f.

hand-luggage ['hændlʌgɪdʒ] Handgepäck nt.

handmade ['hændmeɪd] a handgefertigt.

handshake ['hændʃeɪk] n Händedruck f.

handsome ['hænsəm] a gutaussehend; (generous) großzügig.

handwriting ['hændraɪtɪŋ] n Handschrift f.

handy ['hændɪ] a praktisch; shops leicht erreichbar.

handyman ['hændɪmən] n Mädchen nt für

alles; (*do-it-yourself*) Bastler *m*; (*general —*) Gelegenheitsarbeiter *m*.

hang [hæŋ] *irreg vt* aufhängen; (*execute*) hängen; **to ~ sth on sth** etw an etw (*acc*) hängen; *vi* (*droop*) hängen; **~ about** *vi* sich herumtreiben.

hangar ['hæŋə*] *n* Hangar *m*, Flugzeughalle *f*.

hanger ['hæŋə*] *n* Kleiderbügel *m*.

hanger-on ['hæŋər'ɒn] *n* Anhänger(in *f*) *m*.

hangover ['hæŋəʊvə*] *n* Kater *m*.

hank [hæŋk] *n* Strang *m*.

hanker ['hæŋkə*] *vi* sich sehnen (*for, after* nach).

haphazard ['hæp'hæzəd] *a* wahllos, zufällig.

happen ['hæpən] *vi* sich ereignen, passieren; **~ing** *n* Ereignis *nt*; (*Art*) Happening *nt*.

happily ['hæpɪlɪ] *ad* glücklich; (*fortunately*) glücklicherweise.

happiness ['hæpɪnɪs] *n* Glück *nt*.

happy ['hæpɪ] *a* glücklich; **~-lucky** *a* sorglos.

harass ['hærəs] *vt* bedrängen, plagen.

harbour, (*US*) **harbor** ['hɑːbə*] *n* Hafen *m*.

hard [hɑːd] *a* (*firm*) hart, fest; (*difficult*) schwer, schwierig; (*physically*) schwer; (*harsh*) hart(herzig), gefühllos; *ad* work hart; *try* sehr; *push, hit* fest; **~ by** (*close*) dicht or nahe an(+*dat*); **he took it ~** er hat es schwer genommen; **~-back** *n* kartonierte Ausgabe; **~-boiled** *a* hartgekocht; **~en** *vt* erhärten; (*fig*) verhärten; *vi* hart werden; (*fig*) sich verhärten; **~-hearted** *a* hartherzig; **~ly** *ad* kaum; **~ship** Not *f*; (*injustice*) Unrecht *nt*; **~-up** *a* knapp bei Kasse; **~ware** Eisenwaren *pl*.

hardy ['hɑːdɪ] *a* (*strong*) widerstandsfähig; (*brave*) verwegen.

hare [hɛə*] *n* Hase *m*.

harem [hɑː'riːm] *n* Harem *m*.

harm [hɑːm] *n* Schaden *m*; Leid *nt*; *vt* schaden (+*dat*); **it won't do any ~** es kann nicht schaden; **~ful** *a* schädlich; **~less** *a* harmlos, unschädlich.

harmonica [hɑː'mɒnɪkə] *n* Mundharmonika *f*.

harmonious [hɑː'məʊnɪəs] *a* harmonisch.

harmonize ['hɑːmənaɪz] *vt* abstimmen; *vi* harmonieren.

harmony ['hɑːmənɪ] *n* Harmonie *f*; (*fig also*) Einklang *m*.

harness ['hɑːnɪs] *n* Geschirr *nt*; *vt horse* anschirren; (*fig*) nutzbar machen.

harp [hɑːp] *n* Harfe *f*; **to ~ on about sth** auf etw (*dat*) herumreiten; **~ist** Harfenspieler(in *f*) *m*.

harpoon [hɑː'puːn] *n* Harpune *f*.

harrow ['hærəʊ] *n* Egge *f*, *vt* eggen.

harrowing ['hærəʊɪŋ] *a* nervenaufreibend.

harsh [hɑːʃ] *a* (*rough*) rauh, grob; (*severe*) schroff, streng; **~ly** *ad* rauh, barsch; **~ness** Härte *f*.

harvest ['hɑːvɪst] *n* Ernte *f*; (*time*) Erntezeit *f*; *vt* ernten.

harvester ['hɑːvɪstə*] *n* Mähbinder *m*.

hash [hæʃ] *vt* kleinhacken; *n* (*mess*) Kuddelmuddel *m*; (*meat cooked*) Haschee *nt*; (*raw*) Gehackte(s) *nt*.

hashish ['hæʃɪʃ] *n* Haschisch *nt*.

haste [heɪst] *n* (*speed*) Eile *f*; (*hurry*) Hast *f*; **~n** ['heɪsn] *vt* beschleunigen; *vi* eilen, sich beeilen.

hasty *a*, **hastily** *ad* [heɪstɪ, -lɪ] hastig; (*rash*) vorschnell.

hat [hæt] *n* Hut *m*.

hatbox ['hætbɒks] *n* Hutschachtel *f*.

hatch [hætʃ] *n* (*Naut*) Luke *f*; (*in house*) Durchreiche *f*; *vi brüten*; (*young*) ausschlüpfen; *vt brood* ausbrüten; *plot* aushecken.

hatchet ['hætʃɪt] *n* Beil *nt*.

hate [heɪt] *vt* hassen; **I ~ queuing** ich stehe nicht gern Schlange; *n* Haß *m*; **~ful** *a* verhaßt.

hatred ['heɪtrɪd] *n* Haß *m*; (*dislike*) Abneigung *f*.

hat trick ['hættrɪk] *n* Hattrick *m*.

haughty *a*, **haughtily** *ad* [hɔːtɪ, -lɪ] hochnäsig, überheblich.

haul [hɔːl] *vt* ziehen, schleppen; *n* (*pull*) Zug *m*; (*catch*) Fang *m*; **~age** Transport *m*; (*Comm*) Spedition *f*; **~ier** Transportunternehmer *m*, Spediteur *m*.

haunch [hɔːntʃ] *n* Lende *f*; **to sit on one's ~es** hocken.

haunt [hɔːnt] *vt* (*ghost*) spuken in (+*dat*), umgehen in (+*dat*); (*memory*) verfolgen; *pub* häufig besuchen; **the castle is ~ed** in dem Schloß spukt es; *n* Lieblingsplatz *m*.

have [hæv] *vt irreg* haben; (*at meal*) essen, trinken; (*col: trick*) hereinlegen; **to ~ sth done** etw machen lassen; **to ~ to do sth** etw tun müssen; **to ~ sb on** jdn auf den Arm nehmen.

haven ['heɪvn] *n* Hafen *m*; (*fig*) Zufluchtsort *m*.

haversack ['hævəsæk] *n* Rucksack *m*.

havoc ['hævək] *n* Verwüstung *f*.

hawk [hɔːk] *n* Habicht *m*.

hay [heɪ] *n* Heu *nt*; **~ fever** Heuschnupfen *m*; **~stack** Heuschober *m*.

haywire ['heɪwaɪə*] *a* (*col*) durcheinander.

hazard ['hæzəd] *n* (*chance*) Zufall *m*; (*danger*) Wagnis *nt*, Risiko *nt*; *vt* aufs Spiel setzen; **~ous** *a* gefährlich, riskant.

haze [heɪz] *n* Dunst *m*; (*fig*) Unklarheit *f*.

hazelnut ['heɪzlnʌt] *n* Haselnuß *f*.

hazy ['heɪzɪ] *a* (*misty*) dunstig, diesig; (*vague*) verschwommen.

he [hiː] *pron* er.

head [hed] *n* Kopf *m*; (*top*) Spitze *f*; (*leader*) Leiter *m*; a Kopf-; (*leading*) Ober-; *vt* (an)führen, leiten; **~ for** Richtung nehmen auf (+*acc*), zugehen auf (+*acc*); **~ache** Kopfschmerzen *pl*, Kopfweh *nt*; **~ing** Überschrift *f*; **~lamp** Scheinwerfer *m*; **~land** Landspitze *f*; **~light** = **~lamp**; **~line** Schlagzeile *f*; **~long** *ad* kopfüber; **~master** (*of primary school*) Rektor *m*; (*of secondary school*) Direktor *m*; **~mistress** Rektorin *f*; Direktorin *f*; **~-on** Frontal-; **~quarters** *pl* Zentrale *f*; (*Mil*) Hauptquartier *nt*; **~rest**

Kopfstütze f; ~**room** (of bridges etc) lichte Höhe f; Platz m für den Kopf; ~**s** (on coin) Kopf m, Wappen nt; ~**scarf** Kopftuch nt; ~**strong** a eigenwillig; ~**waiter** Oberkellner m; ~**way** Fahrt f (voraus); (fig) Fortschritte pl; ~**wind** Gegenwind m; ~**y** a (rash) hitzig; (intoxicating) stark, berauschend.

heal [hi:l] vt heilen; vi verheilen.

health [helθ] n Gesundheit f; **your** ~! prost!; ~**y** a gesund.

heap [hi:p] n Haufen m; vt häufen.

hear [hɪə*] irreg vt hören; (listen to) anhören; vi hören; ~**ing** Gehör nt; (Jur) Verhandlung f; (of witnesses) Vernehmung f; **to give sb a** ~**ing** jdn anhören; ~**ing aid** Hörapparat m; ~**say** Hörensagen nt.

hearse [hɜ:s] n Leichenwagen m.

heart [hɑ:t] n Herz nt; (centre also) Zentrum nt; (courage) Mut m; **by** ~ auswendig; **the** ~ **of the matter** der Kern des Problems; ~ **attack** Herzanfall m; ~**beat** Herzschlag m; ~**breaking** a herzzerbrechend; ~**broken** a (ganz)-gebrochen; ~**burn** Sodbrennen nt; ~ **failure** Herzschlag m; ~**felt** a aufrichtig.

hearth [hɑ:θ] n Herd m.

heartily [ˈhɑ:tɪlɪ] ad herzlich; eat herzhaft.

heartless [ˈhɑ:tlɪs] a herzlos.

hearty [ˈhɑ:tɪ] a kräftig; (friendly) freundlich.

heat [hi:t] n Hitze f; (of food, water etc) Wärme f; (Sport) Ausscheidungsrunde f; (excitement) Feuer nt; **in the** ~ **of the moment** in der Hitze des Gefechts; vt house heizen; substance heiß machen, erhitzen; ~ **up** vi warm werden; vt aufwärmen; ~**ed** a erhitzt; (fig) hitzig; ~**er** (Heiz)ofen m.

heath [hi:θ] n (Brit) Heide f.

heathen [ˈhi:ðən] n Heide m; a heidnisch, Heiden-.

heather [ˈheðə*] n Heidekraut nt, Erika f.

heating [ˈhi:tɪŋ] n Heizung f.

heatstroke [ˈhi:tstrəʊk] n Hitzschlag m.

heatwave [ˈhi:tweɪv] n Hitzewelle f.

heave [hi:v] vt hochheben; sigh ausstoßen; vi wogen; (breast) sich heben; n Heben nt.

heaven [ˈhevn] n Himmel m; (bliss) (der siebte) Himmel m; ~**ly** a himmlisch; ~**ly body** Himmelskörper m.

heavy, a, heavily ad [ˈhevɪ, -lɪ] schwer.

heckle [ˈhekl] vt unterbrechen; vi dazwischenrufen, störende Fragen stellen.

hectic [ˈhektɪk] a hektisch.

he'd [hi:d] = he had; he would.

hedge [hedʒ] n Hecke f; vt einzäunen; **to** ~ **one's bets** sich absichern; vi (fig) ausweichen.

hedgehog [ˈhedʒhɒg] n Igel m.

heed [hi:d] vt beachten; n Beachtung f; ~**ful** a achtsam; ~**less** a achtlos.

heel [hi:l] n Ferse f; (of shoe) Absatz m; vt shoes mit Absätzen versehen.

hefty [ˈheftɪ] a person stämmig; portion reichlich; bite kräftig; weight schwer.

heifer [ˈhefə*] n Färse f.

height [haɪt] n (of person) Größe f; (of object) Höhe f; (high place) Gipfel m; ~**en** vt erhöhen.

heir [ɛə*] n Erbe m; ~**ess** [ˈɛərɪs] Erbin f; ~**loom** Erbstück nt.

helicopter [ˈhelɪkɒptə*] n Hubschrauber m.

hell [hel] n Hölle f; interj verdammt!

he'll [hi:l] = he will, he shall.

hellish [ˈhelɪʃ] a höllisch, verteufelt.

hello [hʌˈləʊ] interj (greeting) Hallo; (surprise) hallo, he.

helm [helm] n Ruder nt, Steuer nt.

helmet [ˈhelmɪt] n Helm m.

helmsman [ˈhelmzmən] n Steuermann m.

help [help] n Hilfe f; vt helfen (+dat); **I can't** ~ **it ich kann nichts dafür; I couldn't** ~ **laughing** ich mußte einfach lachen; ~ **yourself** bedienen Sie sich; ~**er** Helfer m; ~**ful** a hilfreich; ~**ing** Portion f; ~**less** a hilflos.

hem [hem] n Saum m; ~ **in** vt einschließen; (fig) einengen.

hemisphere [ˈhemɪsfɪə*] n Halbkugel f; Hemisphäre f.

hemline [ˈhemlaɪn] n Rocklänge f.

hemp [hemp] n Hanf m.

hen [hen] n Henne f.

hence [hens] ad von jetzt an; (therefore) daher.

henchman [ˈhentʃmən] n Anhänger m, Gefolgsmann m.

henpecked [ˈhenpekt] a: **to be** ~ unter dem Pantoffel stehen; ~ **husband** Pantoffelheld m.

her [hɜ:*] pron (acc) sie; (dat) ihr; a ihr.

herald [ˈherəld] n Herold m; (fig) (Vor)-bote m; vt verkünden, anzeigen.

heraldry [ˈherəldrɪ] n Wappenkunde f.

herb [hɜ:b] n Kraut n.

herd [hɜ:d] n Herde f.

here [hɪə*] ad hier; (to this place) hierher; ~**after** ad hernach, künftig; n Jenseits nt; ~**by** ad hiermit.

hereditary [hɪˈredɪtərɪ] a erblich.

heredity [hɪˈredɪtɪ] n Vererbung f.

heresy [ˈherəsɪ] n Ketzerei f.

heretic [ˈherətɪk] n Ketzer m; ~**al** [hɪˈretɪkəl] a ketzerisch.

herewith [hɪəˈwɪð] ad hiermit; (Comm) anbei.

heritage [ˈherɪtɪdʒ] n Erbe nt.

hermetically [hɜːˈmetɪkəlɪ] ad luftdicht, hermetisch.

hermit [ˈhɜːmɪt] n Einsiedler m.

hernia [ˈhɜːnɪə] n Bruch m.

hero [ˈhɪərəʊ] n Held m; ~**ic** [hɪˈrəʊɪk] a heroisch.

heroin [ˈherəʊɪn] n Heroin n.

heroine [ˈherəʊɪn] n Heldin f.

heroism [ˈherəʊɪzəm] n Heldentum nt.

heron [ˈherən] n Reiher m.

herring [ˈherɪŋ] n Hering m.

hers [hɜ:z] pron ihre(r,s).

herself [hɜːˈself] pron sich (selbst); (emphatic) selbst; **she's not** ~ mit ihr ist etwas los or nicht in Ordnung.

he's [hi:z] = he is, he has.

hesitant [ˈhezɪtənt] a zögernd; speech stockend.

hesitate [ˈhezɪteɪt] vi zögern; (feel doubtful) unschlüssig sein.

hesitation [hezɪ'teɪʃən] n Zögern nt, Schwanken nt.

het up [het'ʌp] a (col) aufgeregt.

hew [hju:] vt irreg hauen, hacken.

hexagon ['heksəgən] n Sechseck nt; ~al [hek'sægənəl] a sechseckig.

heyday ['heɪdeɪ] n Blüte f, Höhepunkt m.

hi [haɪ] interj he, hallo.

hibernate ['haɪbəneɪt] vi Winterschlaf halten.

hibernation [haɪbə'neɪʃən] n Winterschlaf m.

hiccough, hiccup ['hɪkʌp] vi den Schluckauf haben; ~s pl Schluckauf m.

hide [haɪd] n (skin) Haut f, Fell nt; irreg vt verstecken; (keep secret) verbergen; vi sich verstecken; ~-and-seek Versteckspiel nt.

hideous ['hɪdɪəs] a abscheulich; ~ly ad scheußlich.

hiding ['haɪdɪŋ] n (beating) Tracht f Prügel; **to be in** ~ sich versteckt halten; ~ **place** Versteck nt.

hierarchy ['haɪərɑːkɪ] n Hierarchie f.

high [haɪ] a hoch; importance groß; spirits Hoch-; wind stark; living extravagant, üppig; ad hoch; ~**brow** n Intellektuelle(r) mf; a (betont) intellektuell; (pej) hochgestochen; ~**chair** Hochstuhl m, Sitzer m; ~-**handed** a eigenmächtig; ~-**heeled** a hochhackig; ~**jack** = hijack; ~-**level** a meeting wichtig, Spitzen-; ~-**light** (fig) Höhepunkt m; ~**ly** ad in hohem Maße, höchst; praise in hohen Tönen; ~**ly strung** a überempfindlich, reizbar; **H**~ **Mass** Hochamt nt; ~**ness** Höhe f; **H**~**ness** Hoheit f; ~-**pitched** a voice hoch, schrill, hell; ~ **school** Oberschule f; ~-**speed** a Schnell-; ~ **tide** Flut f; ~**way** Landstraße f.

hijack ['haɪdʒæk] vt hijacken, entführen.

hike [haɪk] vi wandern; n Wanderung f; ~r Wanderer m.

hiking ['haɪkɪŋ] n Wandern nt.

hilarious [hɪ'lɛərɪəs] a lustig; zum Schreien komisch.

hilarity [hɪ'lærɪtɪ] n Lustigkeit f.

hill [hɪl] n Berg m; ~**side** (Berg)hang m; ~**top** Bergspitze f; ~**y** a hügelig.

hilt [hɪlt] n Heft nt; **up to the** ~ ganz und gar.

him [hɪm] pron (acc) ihn; (dat) ihm.

himself [hɪm'self] pron sich (selbst); (emphatic) selbst; **he's not** ~ mit ihm ist etwas los or nicht in Ordnung.

hind [haɪnd] a hinter, Hinter-; n Hirschkuh f.

hinder ['hɪndə*] vt (stop) hindern; (delay) behindern.

hindrance ['hɪndrəns] n (delay) Behinderung f; (obstacle) Hindernis nt.

hinge [hɪndʒ] n Scharnier nt; (on door) Türangel f; vt mit Scharnieren versehen; vi (fig) abhängen (on von).

hint [hɪnt] n Tip m, Andeutung f; (trace) Anflug m; vi andeuten (at acc), anspielen (at auf +acc).

hip [hɪp] n Hüfte f.

hippopotamus [hɪpə'pɒtəməs] n Nilpferd nt.

hire ['haɪə*] vt worker anstellen; car mieten; n Miete f; **for** ~ taxi frei; **to have for** ~ verleihen; ~ **purchase** Teilzahlungskauf m.

his [hɪz] poss a sein; poss pron seine(r,s).

hiss [hɪs] vi zischen; n Zischen nt.

historian [hɪs'tɔːrɪən] n Geschichtsschreiber m; Historiker m.

historic [hɪs'tɒrɪk] a historisch.

historical [hɪs'tɒrɪkəl] a historisch, geschichtlich.

history ['hɪstərɪ] n Geschichte f; (personal) Entwicklung f, Werdegang m.

hit [hɪt] vt irreg schlagen; (injure) treffen, verletzen; n (blow) Schlag m, Stoß m; (success) Erfolg m, Treffer m; (Mus) Hit m.

hitch [hɪtʃ] vt festbinden; (pull up) hochziehen; (loop) Knoten m; (difficulty) Schwierigkeit f, Haken m.

hitch-hike ['hɪtʃhaɪk] vi trampen, per Anhalter fahren; ~r Tramper m.

hitherto ['hɪðə'tu:] ad bislang.

hive [haɪv] n Bienenkorb m.

hoard [hɔːd] n Schatz m; vt horten, hamstern.

hoarding ['hɔːdɪŋ] n Bretterzaun m; (for advertising) Reklamewand f.

hoarfrost ['hɔː'frɒst] n (Rauh)reif m.

hoarse [hɔːs] a heiser, rauh.

hoax [həʊks] n Streich m.

hobble ['hɒbl] vi humpeln.

hobby ['hɒbɪ] n Steckenpferd nt, Hobby nt.

hobo ['həʊbəʊ] n (US) Tippelbruder m.

hock [hɒk] n (wine) weiße(r) Rheinwein m.

hockey ['hɒkɪ] n Hockey nt.

hoe [həʊ] n Hacke f; vt hacken.

hog [hɒg] n Schlachtschwein nt; vt mit Beschlag belegen.

hoist [hɔɪst] n Winde f; vt hochziehen.

hold [həʊld] irreg vt halten; (keep) behalten; (contain) enthalten; (be able to contain) fassen; (keep back) zurück(be)-halten; breath anhalten; meeting abhalten; vi (withstand pressure) standhalten, aushalten; n (grasp) Halt m; (claim) Anspruch m; (Naut) Schiffsraum m; ~ **back** vt zurückhalten; ~ **down** vt niederhalten; job behalten; ~ **out** vt hinhalten, bieten; vi aushalten; ~ **up** vt (delay) aufhalten; (rob) überfallen; ~**all** Reisetasche f; ~**er** Behälter m; ~**ing** (share) (Aktien)anteil m; ~**up** (in traffic) Stockung f; (robbery) Überfall m.

hole [həʊl] n Loch nt; vt durchlöchern.

holiday ['hɒlədɪ] n (day) Feiertag m; freie(r) Tag m; (vacation) Urlaub m; (Sch) Ferien pl; ~**maker** Feriengast m, Urlauber(in) f m.

holiness ['həʊlɪnɪs] n Heiligkeit f.

hollow ['hɒləʊ] a hohl; (fig) leer; n Vertiefung f; (in rock) Höhle f; ~ **out** vt aushöhlen.

holly ['hɒlɪ] n Stechpalme f.

holster ['həʊlstə*] n Pistolenhalfter m.

holy ['həʊlɪ] a heilig; (religious) fromm.

homage ['hɒmɪdʒ] n Huldigung f; **to pay** ~ **to** huldigen (+dat).

home [həʊm] n Heim nt, Zuhause nt; (insti-

tution) Heim *nt*, Anstalt *f*; *a* einheimisch;
(*Pol*) inner; *ad* heim, nach Hause; **at** ~ zu
Hause; ~**coming** Heimkehr *f*; ~**less** *a*
obdachlos; ~**ly** *a* häuslich; (*US:* ugly)
unscheinbar; ~-**made** *a* selbstgemacht;
~**sick** *a*: **to be** ~**sick** Heimweh haben;
~**ward(s)** *a* heimwärts; ~**work** Hausaufgaben *pl*.

homicide ['hɒmɪsaɪd] *n* (*US*) Totschlag *m*,
Mord *m*.

homoeopathy [hɔʊmɪ'ɒpɔθɪ] *n*
Homöopathie *f*.

homogeneous [hɒmɔ'dʒi:nɪəs] *a* homogen,
gleichartig.

homosexual ['hɒmɔʊ'seksjʊəl] *a* homosexuell; *n* Homosexuelle(r) *m*.

hone [hɔʊn] *n* Schleifstein *m*; *vt* fein-
schleifen.

honest ['ɒnɪst] *a* ehrlich; (*upright*) aufrichtig; ~**ly** *ad* ehrlich; ~**y** Ehrlichkeit *f*.

honey ['hʌnɪ] *n* Honig *m*; ~**comb**
Honigwabe *f*, ~**moon** Flitterwochen *pl*,
Hochzeitsreise *f*.

honk [hɒŋk] *n* (*Aut*) Hupensignal *nt*; *vi*
hupen.

honorary ['ɒnərərɪ] *a* Ehren-.

honour, (*US*) **honor** ['ɒnə*] *vt* ehren;
cheque einlösen; *debts* begleichen; *contract*
einhalten; *n* (*respect*) Ehre *f*; (*reputation*)
Ansehen *nt*, gute(r) Ruf *m*; (*sense of right*)
Ehrgefühl *nt*; ~**s** *pl* (*titles*) Auszeich-
nungen *pl*; ~**able** *a* ehrenwert, rechtschaffen; *intention* ehrenhaft.

hood [hʊd] *n* Kapuze *f*; (*Aut*) Verdeck *nt*;
(*US Aut*) Kühlerhaube *f*; ~**wink** *vt*
reinlegen.

hoof [hu:f] *n* Huf *m*.

hook [hʊk] *n* Haken *m*; *vt* einhaken; ~-**up**
Gemeinschaftssendung *f*.

hooligan ['hu:lɪgən] *n* Rowdy *m*.

hoop [hu:p] *n* Reifen *m*.

hoot [hu:t] *vi* (*Aut*) hupen; **to** ~ **with
laughter** schallend lachen; *n* (*shout*)
Johlen *nt*; (*Aut*) Hupen *nt*; ~**er** (*Naut*)
Dampfpfeife *f*; (*Aut*) (Auto)hupe *f*.

hop¹ [hɒp] *vi* hüpfen, hopsen; *n* (*jump*)
Hopser *m*.

hop² [hɒp] *n* (*Bot*) Hopfen *m*.

hope [hɔʊp] *vi* hoffen; **I** ~ **that** ... hoffent-
lich ...; *n* Hoffnung *f*; ~**ful** *a* hoffnungs-
voll; (*promising*) vielversprechend; ~**less**
a hoffnungslos; (*useless*) unmöglich.

horde [hɔ:d] *n* Horde *f*.

horizon [hə'raɪzn] *n* Horizont *m*; ~**tal**
[hɒrɪ'zɒntl] *a* horizontal.

hormone ['hɔ:mɔʊn] *n* Hormon *nt*.

horn [hɔ:n] *n* Horn *nt*; (*Aut*) Hupe *f*; ~**ed** *a*
gehörnt, Horn-.

hornet ['hɔ:nɪt] *n* Hornisse *f*.

horny ['hɔ:nɪ] *a* schwielig; (*US*) scharf.

horoscope ['hɒrəskəʊp] *n* Horoskop *nt*.

horrible *a*, **horribly** *ad* ['hɒrɪbl, -blɪ]
fürchterlich.

horrid *a*, ~**ly** *ad* ['hɒrɪd, -lɪ] abscheulich,
scheußlich.

horrify ['hɒrɪfaɪ] *vt* entsetzen.

horror ['hɒrə*] *n* Schrecken *m*; (*great dislike*) Abscheu *m* (*of* vor +*dat*).

hors d'oeuvre [ɔ:'dɜ:vr] *n* Vorspeise *f*.

horse [hɔ:s] *n* Pferd *nt*; **on** ~**back**
beritten; ~ **chestnut** Roßkastanie *f*;
~-**drawn** *a* von Pferden gezogen,
Pferde-; ~**power** Pferdestärke *f*, PS *nt*;
~-**racing** Pferderennen *nt*; ~**shoe**
Hufeisen *nt*.

horsy ['hɔ:sɪ] *a* pferdenärrisch.

horticulture ['hɔ:tɪkʌltʃə*] *n* Gartenbau *m*.

hose(pipe) ['hɒʊz(paɪp)] *n* Schlauch *m*.

hosiery ['hɒʊzɪərɪ] *n* Strumpfwaren *pl*.

hospitable [hɒs'pɪtəbl] *a* gastfreundlich.

hospital ['hɒspɪtl] *n* Krankenhaus *nt*.

hospitality [hɒspɪ'tælɪtɪ] *n* Gastlichkeit *f*,
Gastfreundschaft *f*.

host [həʊst] *n* Gastgeber *m*; (*innkeeper*)
(Gast)wirt *m*; (*large number*) Heerschar *f*;
(*Eccl*) Hostie *f*.

hostage ['hɒstɪdʒ] *n* Geisel *f*.

hostel ['hɒstəl] *n* Herberge *f*.

hostess ['həʊstes] *n* Gastgeberin *f*.

hostile ['hɒstaɪl] *a* feindlich.

hostility [hɒs'tɪlɪtɪ] *n* Feindschaft *f*; **hos-
tilities** *pl* Feindseligkeiten *pl*.

hot [hɒt] *a* heiß; *drink, food, water* warm;
(*spiced*) scharf; (*angry*) hitzig; ~ **air** (*col*)
Gewäsch *nt*; ~ **bed** (*lit*) Mistbeet *nt*; (*fig*)
Nährboden *m*; ~-**blooded** *a* heißblütig;
~ **dog** heiße(s) Würstchen *nt*.

hotel [hɒʊ'tel] *n* Hotel *nt*; ~**ier** Hotelier *m*.

hotheaded ['hɒt'hedɪd] *a* hitzig, auf-
brausend.

hothouse ['hɒthaʊs] *n* (*lit, fig*) Treibhaus
nt.

hot line ['hɒtlaɪn] *n* (*Pol*) heiße(r) Draht
m.

hotly ['hɒtlɪ] *ad argue* hitzig; *pursue* dicht.

hot news ['hɒt'nju:z] *n* das Neueste vom
Neuen.

hotplate ['hɒtpleɪt] *n* Kochplatte *f*.

hot-water bottle [hɒt'wɔ:təbɒtl] *n* Wärm-
flasche *f*.

hound [haʊnd] *n* Jagdhund *m*; *vt* jagen,
hetzen.

hour ['aʊə*] *n* Stunde *f*; (*time of day*)
(Tages)zeit *f*; ~**ly** *a* stündlich.

house [haʊs] *n* Haus *nt*; [haʊz] *vt* (*accommodate*) unterbringen; (*shelter*) aufnehmen; ~**boat** Hausboot *nt*; ~**breaking** Einbruch *m*; ~**hold** Haushalt *m*;
~**keeper** Haushälterin *f*; ~**keeping**
Haushaltung *f*; ~**wife** Hausfrau *f*;
~**work** Hausarbeit *f*.

housing ['haʊzɪŋ] *n* (*act*) Unterbringung *f*;
(*houses*) Wohnungen *pl*; (*Pol*)
Wohnungsbau *m*; (*covering*) Gehäuse *nt*;
~ **estate** (Wohn)siedlung *f*.

hovel ['hɒvəl] *n* elende Hütte *f*; Loch *nt*.

hover ['hɒvə*] *vi* (*bird*) schweben; (*person*)
wartend herumstehen; ~**craft** Luft-
kissenfahrzeug *nt*.

how [haʊ] *ad* wie; ~ **many** wie viele; ~
much wieviel; ~**ever** *ad* (*but*) (je)doch,
aber; ~**ever you phrase it** wie Sie es
auch ausdrücken.

howl [haʊl] *n* Heulen *nt*; *vi* heulen.

howler ['haʊlə*] *n* grobe(r) Schnitzer *m*.

hub [hʌb] *n* Radnabe *f*; (*of the world*)
Mittelpunkt *m*; (*of commerce*) Zentrum *nt*.

hubbub ['hʌbʌb] *n* Tumult *m*.

hub cap ['hʌbkæp] n Radkappe f.

huddle ['hʌdl] vi sich zusammendrängen; n Grüppchen nt.

hue [hju:] n Färbung f, Farbton m; ~ **and cry** Zetergeschrei nt.

huff [hʌf] n Eingeschnapptsein nt; **to go into a** ~ einschnappen.

hug [hʌg] vt umarmen; (fig) sich dicht halten an (+acc); n Umarmung f.

huge [hju:dʒ] a groß, riesig.

hulk [hʌlk] n (ship) abgetakelte(s) Schiff nt; (person) Koloß m; ~**ing** a ungeschlacht.

hull [hʌl] n Schiffsrumpf m.

hullo [hʌ'ləu] see **hello**.

hum [hʌm] vi summen; (bumblebee) brummen; vt summen; n Summen nt.

human ['hju:mən] a menschlich; n (also ~ **being**) Mensch m.

humane [hju:'meɪn] a human.

humanity [hju:'mænɪtɪ] n Menschheit f; (kindliness) Menschlichkeit f.

humble ['hʌmbl] a demütig; (modest) bescheiden; vt demütigen.

humbly ['hʌmblɪ] ad demütig.

humdrum ['hʌmdrʌm] a eintönig, langweilig.

humid ['hju:mɪd] a feucht; ~**ity** [hju:'mɪdɪtɪ] Feuchtigkeit f.

humiliate [hju:'mɪlɪeɪt] vt demütigen.

humiliation [hju:mɪlɪ'eɪʃən] n Demütigung f.

humility [hju:'mɪlɪtɪ] n Demut f.

humorist ['hju:mərɪst] n Humorist m.

humorous ['hju:mərəs] a humorvoll, komisch.

humour, (US) **humor** ['hju:mə*] n (fun) Humor m; (mood) Stimmung f; vt nachgeben (+dat); bei Stimmung halten.

hump [hʌmp] n Buckel m.

hunch [hʌntʃ] n (presentiment) (Vor)-ahnung f; vt shoulders hochziehen; ~**back** Bucklige(r) m.

hundred ['hʌndrɪd] num, a, n hundert; ~**weight** Zentner m.

hunger ['hʌŋgə*] n Hunger m; (fig) Verlangen nt (for nach); vi hungern.

hungry a, **hungrily** ad ['hʌŋgrɪ, -lɪ] hungrig; **to be** ~ Hunger haben.

hunt [hʌnt] vt jagen; (search) suchen (for acc); vi jagen; n Jagd f; ~**er** Jäger m; ~**ing** Jagen nt, Jagd f.

hurdle ['hɜ:dl] n (lit, fig) Hürde f.

hurl [hɜ:l] vt schleudern.

hurrah [hu'rɑ:], **hurray** [hu'reɪ] n Hurra nt.

hurricane ['hʌrɪkən] n Orkan m.

hurried ['hʌrɪd] a eilig; (hasty) übereilt; ~**ly** ad übereilt, hastig.

hurry ['hʌrɪ] n Eile f; **to be in a** ~ es eilig haben; vi sich beeilen; ~**!** mach schnell!; vt (an)treiben; job übereilen.

hurt [hɜ:t] irreg vt weh tun (+dat); (injure, fig) verletzen; vi weh tun; ~**ful** a schädlich; remark verletzend.

hurtle ['hɜ:tl] vt schleudern; vi sausen.

husband ['hʌzbənd] n (Ehe)mann m, Gatte m.

hush [hʌʃ] n Stille f; vt zur Ruhe bringen; vi still sein; ~ interj pst, still.

husk [hʌsk] n Spelze f.

husky ['hʌskɪ] a voice rauh; figure stämmig; n Eskimohund m.

hustle ['hʌsl] vt (push) stoßen; (hurry) antreiben, drängen; n (Hoch)betrieb m; ~ **and bustle** Geschäftigkeit f.

hut [hʌt] n Hütte f.

hutch [hʌtʃ] n (Kaninchen)stall m.

hyacinth ['haɪəsɪnθ] n Hyazinthe f.

hybrid ['haɪbrɪd] n Kreuzung f; a Misch-.

hydrant ['haɪdrənt] n Hydrant m.

hydraulic [haɪ'drɔlɪk] a hydraulisch.

hydroelectric ['haɪdrəu'lektrɪk] a hydroelektrisch.

hydrofoil ['haɪdrəufɔɪl] n Tragflügel m; Tragflügelboot nt.

hydrogen ['haɪdrɪdʒən] n Wasserstoff m.

hyena [haɪ'i:nə] n Hyäne f.

hygiene ['haɪdʒi:n] n Hygiene f.

hygienic [haɪ'dʒi:nɪk] a hygienisch.

hymn [hɪm] n Kirchenlied nt.

hyphen ['haɪfən] n Bindestrich m; Trennungszeichen nt.

hypnosis [hɪp'nəusɪs] n Hypnose f.

hypnotism ['hɪpnətɪzəm] n Hypnotismus m.

hypnotist ['hɪpnətɪst] n Hypnotiseur m.

hypnotize ['hɪpnətaɪz] vt hypnotisieren.

hypochondriac [haɪpəu'kɒndrɪæk] n eingebildete(r) Kranke(r) mf.

hypocrisy [hɪ'pɒkrɪsɪ] n Heuchelei f, Scheinheiligkeit f.

hypocrite ['hɪpəkrɪt] n Heuchler m, Scheinheilige(r) m.

hypocritical [hɪpə'krɪtɪkəl] a scheinheilig, heuchlerisch.

hypothesis [haɪ'pɒθɪsɪs] n Hypothese f.

hypothetic(al) [haɪpəu'θetɪk(əl)] a hypothetisch.

hysteria [hɪs'tɪərɪə] n Hysterie f.

hysterical [hɪs'terɪkəl] a hysterisch.

hysterics [hɪs'terɪks] npl hysterische(r) Anfall m.

I

I, i [aɪ] n I nt, i nt; **I** pron ich.

ice [aɪs] n Eis nt; vt (Cook) mit Zuckerguß überziehen; vi (also ~ **up**) vereisen; ~**-axe** Eispickel m; ~**berg** Eisberg m; ~**box** (US) Kühlschrank m; ~**-cream** Eis nt; ~**-cold** a eiskalt; ~**-cube** Eiswürfel m; ~ **hockey** Eishockey nt; ~**rink** (Kunst)eisbahn f.

icicle ['aɪsɪkl] n Eiszapfen m.

icing ['aɪsɪŋ] n (on cake) Zuckerguß m; (on window) Vereisung f.

icon ['aɪkɒn] n Ikone f.

icy ['aɪsɪ] a (slippery) vereist; (cold) eisig.

I'd [aɪd] = **I would; I had.**

idea [aɪ'dɪə] n Idee f; **no** ~ keine Ahnung; **my** ~ **of a holiday** wie ich mir einen Urlaub vorstelle.

ideal [aɪ'dɪəl] n Ideal nt; a ideal; ~**ism** Idealismus m; ~**ist** Idealist m; ~**ly** ad ideal(erweise).

identical [aɪ'dentɪkəl] a identisch; *twins* eineiig.
identification [aɪdentɪfɪ'keɪʃən] n Identifizierung f.
identify [aɪ'dentɪfaɪ] vt identifizieren; (*regard as the same*) gleichsetzen.
identity [aɪ'dentɪtɪ] n Identität f; ~ **card** Personalausweis m; ~ **papers** pl (Ausweis)papiere pl.
ideology [aɪdɪ'ɒlədʒɪ] n Ideologie f.
idiocy ['ɪdɪəsɪ] n Idiotie f.
idiom ['ɪdɪəm] n (*expression*) Redewendung f; (*dialect*) Idiom nt.
idiosyncrasy [ɪdɪə'sɪŋkrəsɪ] n Eigenart f.
idiot ['ɪdɪət] n Idiot(in f) m; ~**ic** [ɪdɪ'ɒtɪk] a idiotisch.
idle ['aɪdl] a (*doing nothing*) untätig, müßig; (*lazy*) faul; (*useless*) vergeblich, nutzlos; *machine* still(stehend); *threat, talk* leer; ~**ness** Müßiggang m; Faulheit f; ~**r** Faulenzer m.
idol ['aɪdl] n Idol nt; ~**ize** vt vergöttern.
idyllic [ɪ'dɪlɪk] a idyllisch.
if [ɪf] cj wenn, falls; (*whether*) ob; ~ **only** ... wenn ... doch nur; ~ **not** falls nicht.
igloo ['ɪglu:] n Iglu m or nt.
ignite [ɪg'naɪt] vt (an)zünden.
ignition [ɪg'nɪʃən] n Zündung f; ~ **key** (*Aut*) Zündschlüssel m.
ignoramus [ɪgnə'reɪməs] n Ignorant m.
ignorance ['ɪgnərəns] n Unwissenheit f, Ignoranz f.
ignorant ['ɪgnərənt] a unwissend.
ignore [ɪg'nɔ:*] vt ignorieren.
ikon ['aɪkɒn] n = **icon.**
I'll [aɪl] = **I will, I shall.**
ill [ɪl] a krank; (*evil*) schlecht, böse; n Übel nt; ~**advised** a schlecht beraten, unklug; ~**at-ease** a unbehaglich.
illegal a, ~**ly** ad [ɪ'li:gl, -ɪ] illegal.
illegible [ɪ'ledʒəbl] a unleserlich.
illegitimate [ɪlɪ'dʒɪtɪmət] a unzulässig; *child* unehelich.
ill-fated [ɪl'feɪtɪd] a unselig.
ill-feeling [ɪl'fi:lɪŋ] n Verstimmung f.
illicit [ɪ'lɪsɪt] a verboten.
illiterate [ɪ'lɪtərət] a ungebildet.
ill-mannered [ɪl'mænəd] a ungehobelt.
illness ['ɪlnəs] n Krankheit f.
illogical [ɪ'lɒdʒɪkəl] a unlogisch.
ill-treat [ɪl'tri:t] vt mißhandeln.
illuminate [ɪ'lu:mɪneɪt] vt beleuchten.
illumination [ɪlu:mɪ'neɪʃən] n Beleuchtung f.
illusion [ɪ'lu:ʒən] n Illusion f.
illusive [ɪ'lu:sɪv], **illusory** [ɪ'lu:sərɪ] a illusorisch, trügerisch.
illustrate ['ɪləstreɪt] vt *book* illustrieren; (*explain*) veranschaulichen.
illustration [ɪləs'treɪʃən] n Illustration f; (*explanation*) Veranschaulichung f.
illustrious [ɪ'lʌstrɪəs] a berühmt.
ill will ['ɪl'wɪl] n Groll m.
I'm [aɪm] = **I am.**
image ['ɪmɪdʒ] n Bild nt; (*likeness*) Abbild nt; (*public* ~) Image nt; ~**ry** Symbolik f.
imaginable [ɪ'mædʒɪnəbl] a vorstellbar.

imaginary [ɪ'mædʒɪnərɪ] a eingebildet; *world* Phantasie-.
imagination [ɪmædʒɪ'neɪʃən] n Einbildung f; (*creative*) Phantasie f.
imaginative [ɪ'mædʒɪnətɪv] a phantasiereich, einfallsreich.
imagine [ɪ'mædʒɪn] vt sich vorstellen; (*wrongly*) sich einbilden.
imbalance [ɪm'bæləns] n Unausgeglichenheit f.
imbecile ['ɪmbəsi:l] n Schwachsinnige(r) m/f.
imbue [ɪm'bju:] vt durchdringen.
imitate ['ɪmɪteɪt] vt nachmachen, imitieren.
imitation [ɪmɪ'teɪʃən] n Nachahmung f, Imitation f.
imitator ['ɪmɪteɪtə*] n Nachahmer m.
immaculate [ɪ'mækjulɪt] a makellos; *dress* tadellos; (*Eccl*) unbefleckt.
immaterial [ɪmə'tɪərɪəl] a unwesentlich.
immature [ɪmə'tjuə*] a unreif.
immaturity [ɪmə'tjuərɪtɪ] n Unreife f.
immediate [ɪ'mi:dɪət] a (*instant*) sofortig; (*near*) unmittelbar; *relatives* nächste(r, s); *needs* dringlich; ~**ly** ad sofort; (*in position*) unmittelbar.
immense [ɪ'mens] a unermeßlich; ~**ly** ad ungeheuerlich; *grateful* unheimlich.
immerse [ɪ'mɜ:s] vt eintauchen.
immersion heater [ɪ'mɜ:ʃənhi:tə*] n Heißwassergerät nt.
immigrant ['ɪmɪgrənt] n Einwanderer m.
immigration [ɪmɪ'greɪʃən] n Einwanderung f.
imminent ['ɪmɪnənt] a bevorstehend; *danger* drohend.
immobilize [ɪ'məubɪlaɪz] vt lähmen.
immoderate [ɪ'mɒdərət] a maßlos, übertrieben.
immoral [ɪ'mɒrəl] a unmoralisch; (*sexually*) unsittlich; ~**ity** [ɪmə'rælɪtɪ] Verderbtheit f.
immortal [ɪ'mɔ:tl] a unsterblich; n Unsterbliche(r) m/f; ~**ity** [ɪmɔ:'tælɪtɪ] Unsterblichkeit f; (*of book etc*) Unvergänglichkeit f; ~**ize** vt unsterblich machen.
immune [ɪ'mju:n] a (*secure*) geschützt (*from gegen*), sicher (*from vor* +*dat*); (*Med*) immun.
immunity [ɪ'mju:nɪtɪ] n (*Med, Jur*) Immunität f; (*fig*) Freiheit f.
immunization [ɪmjunaɪ'zeɪʃən] n Immunisierung f.
immunize ['ɪmjunaɪz] vt immunisieren.
impact ['ɪmpækt] n (*lit*) Aufprall m; (*force*) Wucht f; (*fig*) Wirkung f.
impair [ɪm'peə*] vt beeinträchtigen.
impale [ɪm'peɪl] vt aufspießen.
impartial [ɪm'pɑ:ʃəl] a unparteiisch; ~**ity** [ɪmpɑ:ʃɪ'ælɪtɪ] Unparteilichkeit f.
impassable [ɪm'pɑ:səbl] a unpassierbar.
impassioned [ɪm'pæʃnd] a leidenschaftlich.
impatience [ɪm'peɪʃəns] n Ungeduld f.
impatient a, ~**ly** ad [ɪm'peɪʃənt, -lɪ] ungeduldig; **to be** ~ **to do sth** es nicht erwarten können, etw zu tun.

impeccable [ɪmˈpekəbl] a tadellos.
impede [ɪmˈpiːd] vt (be)hindern.
impediment [ɪmˈpedɪmənt] n Hindernis nt; (in speech) Sprachfehler m.
impending [ɪmˈpendɪŋ] a bevorstehend.
impenetrable [ɪmˈpenɪtrəbl] a (lit, fig) undurchdringlich; forest unwegsam; theory undurchsichtig; mystery unerforschlich.
imperative [ɪmˈperətɪv] a (necessary) unbedingt erforderlich; n (Gram) Imperativ m, Befehlsform f.
imperceptible [ɪmpəˈseptəbl] a nicht wahrnehmbar.
imperfect [ɪmˈpɜːfɪkt] a (faulty) fehlerhaft; (incomplete) unvollständig; ~ion [ɪmpəˈfekʃən] Unvollkommenheit f; (fault) Fehler m; (faultiness) Fehlerhaftigkeit f.
imperial [ɪmˈpɪərɪəl] a kaiserlich; ~ism Imperialismus m.
imperil [ɪmˈperɪl] vt gefährden.
impersonal [ɪmˈpɜːsnl] a unpersönlich.
impersonate [ɪmˈpɜːsəneɪt] vt sich ausgeben als; (for amusement) imitieren.
impersonation [ɪmpɜːsəˈneɪʃən] n Verkörperung f; (Theat) Imitation f.
impertinence [ɪmˈpɜːtɪnəns] n Unverschämtheit f.
impertinent [ɪmˈpɜːtɪnənt] a unverschämt, frech.
imperturbable [ɪmpəˈtɜːbəbl] a unerschütterlich, gelassen.
impervious [ɪmˈpɜːvɪəs] a undurchlässig; (fig) unempfänglich (to für).
impetuous [ɪmˈpetjuəs] a heftig, ungestüm.
impetus [ˈɪmpɪtəs] n Triebkraft f; (fig) Auftrieb m.
impinge [ɪmˈpɪndʒ] ~ on vt beeinträchtigen; (light) fallen auf (+acc).
implausible [ɪmˈplɔːzəbl] a unglaubwürdig, nicht überzeugend.
implement [ˈɪmplɪmənt] n Werkzeug nt, Gerät nt; [ˈɪmplɪment] vt ausführen.
implicate [ˈɪmplɪkeɪt] vt verwickeln, hineinziehen.
implication [ɪmplɪˈkeɪʃən] n (meaning) Bedeutung f; (effect) Auswirkung f; (hint) Andeutung f; (in crime) Verwicklung f; by ~ folglich.
implicit [ɪmˈplɪsɪt] a (suggested) unausgesprochen; (utter) vorbehaltlos.
implore [ɪmˈplɔː*] vt anflehen.
imply [ɪmˈplaɪ] vt (hint) andeuten; (be evidence for) schließen lassen auf (+acc); what does that ~? was bedeutet das?
impolite [ɪmpəˈlaɪt] a unhöflich.
impolitic [ɪmˈpɒlɪtɪk] a undiplomatisch.
imponderable [ɪmˈpɒndərəbl] a unwägbar.
import [ɪmˈpɔːt] vt einführen, importieren; [ˈɪmpɔːt] n Einfuhr f, Import m; (meaning) Bedeutung f, Tragweite f.
importance [ɪmˈpɔːtəns] n Bedeutung f; (influence) Einfluß m.
important [ɪmˈpɔːtənt] a wichtig; (influential) bedeutend, einflußreich.
import duty [ˈɪmpɔːtdjuːtɪ] n Einfuhrzoll m.

imported [ɪmˈpɔːtɪd] a eingeführt, importiert.
importer [ɪmˈpɔːtə*] n Importeur m.
import licence [ˈɪmpɔːtlaɪsəns] n Einfuhrgenehmigung f.
impose [ɪmˈpəʊz] vti auferlegen (on dat); penalty, sanctions verhängen (on gegen); to ~ (o.s.) on sb sich jdm aufdrängen; to ~ on sb's kindness jds Liebenswürdigkeit ausnützen.
imposing [ɪmˈpəʊzɪŋ] a eindrucksvoll.
imposition [ɪmpəˈzɪʃən] n (of burden, fine) Auferlegung f; (Sch) Strafarbeit f.
impossibility [ɪmpɒsəˈbɪlɪtɪ] n Unmöglichkeit f.
impossible a, **impossibly** ad [ɪmˈpɒsəbl, -blɪ] unmöglich.
impostor [ɪmˈpɒstə*] n Betrüger m; Hochstapler m.
impotence [ˈɪmpətəns] Impotenz f.
impotent [ˈɪmpətənt] a machtlos; (sexually) impotent.
impound [ɪmˈpaʊnd] vt beschlagnahmen.
impoverished [ɪmˈpɒvərɪʃt] a verarmt.
impracticable [ɪmˈpræktɪkəbl] a undurchführbar.
impractical [ɪmˈpræktɪkəl] a unpraktisch.
imprecise [ɪmprəˈsaɪs] a ungenau.
impregnable [ɪmˈpregnəbl] a castle uneinnehmbar.
impregnate [ˈɪmpregneɪt] vt (saturate) sättigen; (fertilize) befruchten; (fig) durchdringen.
impresario [ɪmpreˈsɑːrɪəʊ] n Impresario m.
impress [ɪmˈpres] vt (influence) beeindrucken; (imprint) (auf)drücken; to ~ sth on sb jdm etw einschärfen; ~ion Eindruck m; (on wax, footprint) Abdruck m; (of stamp) Aufdruck m; (of book) Auflage f; (take-off) Nachahmung f; I was under the ~ion ich hatte den Eindruck; ~ionable a leicht zu beeindrucken(d); ~ionist n Impressionist m; ~ive a eindrucksvoll.
imprison [ɪmˈprɪzn] vt ins Gefängnis schicken; ~ment Inhaftierung f; Gefangenschaft f; 3 years' ~ment eine Gefängnisstrafe von 3 Jahren.
improbable [ɪmˈprɒbəbl] a unwahrscheinlich.
impromptu [ɪmˈprɒmptjuː] a, ad aus dem Stegreif, improvisiert.
improper [ɪmˈprɒpə*] a (indecent) unanständig; (wrong) unrichtig, falsch; (unsuitable) unpassend.
impropriety [ɪmprəˈpraɪətɪ] n Ungehörigkeit f.
improve [ɪmˈpruːv] vt verbessern; vi besser werden; ~ment (Ver)besserung f; (of appearance) Verschönerung f.
improvisation [ɪmprəvaɪˈzeɪʃən] n Improvisation f.
improvise [ˈɪmprəvaɪz] vti improvisieren.
imprudence [ɪmˈpruːdəns] n Unklugheit f.
imprudent [ɪmˈpruːdənt] a unklug.
impudent [ˈɪmpjʊdənt] a unverschämt.
impulse [ˈɪmpʌls] n (desire) Drang m; (driving force) Antrieb m, Impuls m; my first ~ was to ... ich wollte zuerst ...

impulsive [ɪmˈpʌlsɪv] a impulsiv.

impunity [ɪmˈpjuːnɪtɪ] n Straflosigkeit f.

impure [ɪmˈpjuə*] a (dirty) unrein; (mixed) gemischt; (bad) schmutzig, unanständig.

impurity [ɪmˈpjuərɪtɪ] n Unreinheit f; (Tech) Verunreinigung f.

in [ɪn] prep in; (made of) aus; ~ Dickens/a child bei Dickens/einem Kind; ~ him you'll have ... an ihm hast du ...; ~ doing this he has ... dadurch, daß er das tat, hat er ...; ~ saying that I mean ... wenn ich das sage, meine ich ...; I haven't seen him ~ years ich habe ihn seit Jahren nicht mehr gesehen; 15 pence ~ the £ 15 Pence per Pfund; blind ~ the left eye auf dem linken Auge or links blind; ~ itself an sich; ~ that, ~ so or as far as insofern als; ad hinein; to be ~ zuhause sein; (train) da sein; (in fashion) in (Mode) sein; to have it ~ for sb es auf jdn abgesehen haben; ~s and outs pl Einzelheiten pl; to know the ~s and outs sich auskennen.

inability [ɪnəˈbɪlɪtɪ] n Unfähigkeit f.

inaccessible [ɪnækˈsesəbl] a unzugänglich.

inaccuracy [ɪnˈækjurəsɪ] n Ungenauigkeit f.

inaccurate [ɪnˈækjurɪt] a ungenau; (wrong) unrichtig.

inaction [ɪnˈækʃən] n Untätigkeit f.

inactive [ɪnˈæktɪv] a untätig.

inactivity [ɪnækˈtɪvɪtɪ] n Untätigkeit f.

inadequacy [ɪnˈædɪkwəsɪ] n Unzulänglichkeit f; (of punishment) Unangemessenheit f.

inadequate [ɪnˈædɪkwət] a unzulänglich; punishment unangemessen.

inadvertently [ɪnədˈvɜːtəntlɪ] ad unabsichtlich.

inadvisable [ɪnədˈvaɪzəbl] a nicht ratsam.

inane [ɪˈneɪn] a dumm, albern.

inanimate [ɪnˈænɪmət] a leblos.

inapplicable [ɪnəˈplɪkəbl] a unzutreffend.

inappropriate [ɪnəˈprəuprɪət] a clothing ungeeignet; remark unangebracht.

inapt [ɪnˈæpt] a unpassend; (clumsy) ungeschickt; ~itude Untauglichkeit f.

inarticulate [ɪnɑːˈtɪkjulət] a unklar; to be ~ sich nicht ausdrücken können.

inartistic [ɪnɑːˈtɪstɪk] a unkünstlerisch.

inasmuch as [ɪnəzˈmʌtʃəz] ad da, weil; (in so far as) soweit.

inattention [ɪnəˈtenʃən] n Unaufmerksamkeit f.

inattentive [ɪnəˈtentɪv] a unaufmerksam.

inaudible [ɪnˈɔːdəbl] a unhörbar.

inaugural [ɪnˈɔːgjurəl] a Eröffnungs-; (Univ) Antritts-.

inaugurate [ɪnˈɔːgjureɪt] vt (open) einweihen; (admit to office) (feierlich) einführen.

inauguration [ɪnɔːgjuˈreɪʃən] n Eröffnung f; (feierliche) Amtseinführung f.

inborn [ˈɪnˈbɔːn] a angeboren.

inbred [ˈɪnˈbred] a quality angeboren; they are ~ bei ihnen herrscht Inzucht.

inbreeding [ˈɪnˈbriːdɪŋ] n Inzucht f.

incalculable [ɪnˈkælkjuləbl] a person

unberechenbar; consequences unabsehbar.

incapability [ɪnkeɪpəˈbɪlɪtɪ] n Unfähigkeit f.

incapable [ɪnˈkeɪpəbl] a unfähig (of doing sth etw zu tun); (not able) nicht einsatzfähig.

incapacitate [ɪnkəˈpæsɪteɪt] vt untauglich machen; ~d behindert; machine nicht gebrauchsfähig.

incapacity [ɪnkəˈpæsɪtɪ] n Unfähigkeit f.

incarcerate [ɪnˈkɑːsəreɪt] vt einkerkern.

incarnate [ɪnˈkɑːnɪt] a menschgeworden; (fig) leibhaftig.

incarnation [ɪnkɑːˈneɪʃən] n (Eccl) Menschwerdung f; (fig) Inbegriff m.

incendiary [ɪnˈsendɪərɪ] a brandstifterisch, Brand-; (fig) aufrührerisch; n Brandstifter m; (bomb) Brandbombe f.

incense [ˈɪnsens] n Weihrauch m; [ɪnˈsens] vt erzürnen.

incentive [ɪnˈsentɪv] n Anreiz m.

incessant a, ~ly ad [ɪnˈsesnt, -lɪ] unaufhörlich.

incest [ˈɪnsest] n Inzest m.

inch [ɪntʃ] n Zoll m.

incidence [ˈɪnsɪdəns] n Auftreten nt; (of crime) Quote f.

incident [ˈɪnsɪdənt] n Vorfall m; (disturbance) Zwischenfall m; ~al [ɪnsɪˈdentl] a music Begleit-; expenses Neben-; (unplanned) zufällig; (unimportant) nebensächlich; remark beiläufig; ~al to sth mit etw verbunden; ~ally [ɪnsɪˈdentlɪ] ad (by chance) nebenbei; (by the way) nebenbei bemerkt, übrigens.

incinerator [ɪnˈsɪnəreɪtə*] n Verbrennungsofen m.

incision [ɪnˈsɪʒən] n Einschnitt m.

incisive [ɪnˈsaɪsɪv] a style treffend; person scharfsinnig.

incite [ɪnˈsaɪt] vt anstacheln.

inclement [ɪnˈklemənt] a weather rauh.

inclination [ɪnklɪˈneɪʃən] n Neigung f.

incline [ˈɪnklaɪn] n Abhang m; [ɪnˈklaɪn] vt neigen; (fig) veranlassen; to be ~d to do sth Lust haben, etw zu tun; (have tendency) dazu neigen, etw zu tun; vi sich neigen.

include [ɪnˈkluːd] vt einschließen; (on list, in group) aufnehmen.

including [ɪnˈkluːdɪŋ] prep: ~ X X inbegriffen.

inclusion [ɪnˈkluːʒən] n Aufnahme f, Einbeziehung f.

inclusive [ɪnˈkluːsɪv] a einschließlich; (Comm) inklusive.

incognito [ɪnkɒgˈniːtəu] ad inkognito.

incoherent [ɪnkəuˈhɪərənt] a zusammenhanglos.

income [ˈɪnkʌm] n Einkommen nt; (from business) Einkünfte pl; ~ tax Lohnsteuer f; (of self-employed) Einkommenssteuer f.

incoming [ˈɪnkʌmɪŋ] a ankommend; (succeeding) folgend; mail eingehend; tide steigend.

incomparable [ɪnˈkɒmpərəbl] a unvergleichlich.

incompatible [ɪnkəmˈpætəbl] a unvereinbar; people unverträglich.

incompetence [ɪnˈkɒmpɪtəns] *n* Unfähigkeit *f*.

incompetent [ɪnˈkɒmpɪtənt] *a* unfähig; *(not qualified)* nicht berechtigt.

incomplete [ɪnkəmˈpliːt] *a* unvollständig.

incomprehensible [ɪnkɒmprɪˈhensəbl] *a* unverständlich.

inconceivable [ɪnkənˈsiːvəbl] *a* unvorstellbar.

inconclusive [ɪnkənˈkluːsɪv] *a* nicht schlüssig.

incongruity [ɪnkɒŋˈgruːɪtɪ] *n* Seltsamkeit *f*; *(of remark etc)* Unangebrachtsein *nt*.

incongruous [ɪnˈkɒŋgruəs] *a* seltsam; *remark* unangebracht.

inconsequential [ɪnkɒnsɪˈkwenʃəl] *a* belanglos.

inconsiderable [ɪnkənˈsɪdərəbl] *a* unerheblich.

inconsiderate [ɪnkənˈsɪdərət] *a* rücksichtslos; *(hasty)* unüberlegt.

inconsistency [ɪnkənˈsɪstənsɪ] *n* innere(r) Widerspruch *m*; *(state)* Unbeständigkeit *f*.

inconsistent [ɪnkənˈsɪstənt] *a* unvereinbar; *behaviour* inkonsequent; *action, speech* widersprüchlich; *person, work* unbeständig.

inconspicuous [ɪnkənˈspɪkjuəs] *a* unauffällig.

inconstancy [ɪnˈkɒnstənsɪ] *n* Unbeständigkeit *f*.

inconstant [ɪnˈkɒnstənt] *a* unbeständig.

incontinence [ɪnˈkɒntɪnəns] *n* *(Med)* Unfähigkeit *f*, Stuhl und Harn zurückzuhalten; *(fig)* Zügellosigkeit *f*.

incontinent [ɪnˈkɒntɪnənt] *a* *(Med)* nicht fähig, Stuhl und Harn zurückzuhalten; *(fig)* zügellos.

inconvenience [ɪnkənˈviːnɪəns] *n* Unbequemlichkeit *f*; *(trouble to others)* Unannehmlichkeiten *pl*.

inconvenient [ɪnkənˈviːnɪənt] *a* ungelegen; *journey* unbequem.

incorporate [ɪnˈkɔːpəreɪt] *vt* *(include)* aufnehmen; *(unite)* vereinigen.

incorporated [ɪnˈkɔːpəreɪtɪd] *a* eingetragen; *(US)* GmbH.

incorrect [ɪnkəˈrekt] *a* unrichtig; *behaviour* inkorrekt.

incorrigible [ɪnˈkɒrɪdʒəbl] *a* unverbesserlich.

incorruptible [ɪnkəˈrʌptəbl] *a* unzerstörbar; *person* unbestechlich.

increase [ˈɪnkriːs] *n* Zunahme *f*, Erhöhung *f*; *(pay —)* Gehaltserhöhung *f*; *(in size)* Vergrößerung *f*; [ɪnˈkriːs] *vt* erhöhen; *wealth, rage* vermehren; *business* erweitern; *vi* zunehmen; *(prices)* steigen; *(in size)* größer werden; *(in number)* sich vermehren.

increasingly [ɪnˈkriːsɪŋlɪ] *ad* zunehmend.

incredible *a*, **incredibly** *ad* [ɪnˈkredəbl, -blɪ] unglaublich.

incredulity [ɪnkrɪˈdjuːlɪtɪ] *n* Ungläubigkeit *f*.

incredulous [ɪnˈkredjuləs] *a* ungläubig.

increment [ˈɪnkrɪmənt] *n* Zulage *f*.

incriminate [ɪnˈkrɪmɪneɪt] *vt* belasten.

incubation [ɪnkjuˈbeɪʃən] *n* Ausbrüten *nt*; **~ period** Inkubationszeit *f*.

incubator [ˈɪnkjubeɪtə*] *n* Brutkasten *m*.

incur [ɪnˈkɜː*] *vt* sich zuziehen; *debts* machen.

incurable [ɪnˈkjuərəbl] *a* unheilbar; *(fig)* unverbesserlich.

incursion [ɪnˈkɜːʃən] *n* (feindlicher) Einfall *m*.

indebted [ɪnˈdetɪd] *a* *(obliged)* verpflichtet *(to sb* jdm); *(owing)* verschuldet.

indecency [ɪnˈdiːsnsɪ] *n* Unanständigkeit *f*.

indecent [ɪnˈdiːsnt] *a* unanständig.

indecision [ɪndɪˈsɪʒən] *n* Unschlüssigkeit *f*.

indecisive [ɪndɪˈsaɪsɪv] *a* *battle* nicht entscheidend; *result* unentschieden; *person* unentschlossen.

indeed [ɪnˈdiːd] *ad* tatsächlich, in der Tat.

indefinable [ɪndɪˈfaɪnəbl] *a* undefinierbar; *(vague)* unbestimmt.

indefinite [ɪnˈdefɪnɪt] *a* unbestimmt; **~ly** *ad* auf unbestimmte Zeit; *wait* unbegrenzt lange.

indelible [ɪnˈdeləbl] *a* unauslöschlich; **~ pencil** Tintenstift *m*.

indemnify [ɪnˈdemnɪfaɪ] *vt* entschädigen; *(safeguard)* versichern.

indentation [ɪndenˈteɪʃən] *n* Einbuchtung *f*; *(Print)* Einrückung *f*.

independence [ɪndɪˈpendəns] *n* Unabhängigkeit *f*.

independent [ɪndɪˈpendənt] *a* *(free)* unabhängig; *(unconnected)* unabhängig von.

indescribable [ɪndɪsˈkraɪbəbl] *a* unbeschreiblich.

index [ˈɪndeks] *n* Index *m* *(also Eccl)*, Verzeichnis *nt*; **~ finger** Zeigefinger *m*.

indicate [ˈɪndɪkeɪt] *vt* anzeigen; *(hint)* andeuten.

indication [ɪndɪˈkeɪʃən] *n* Anzeichen *nt*; *(information)* Angabe *f*.

indicative [ɪnˈdɪkətɪv] *n* *(Gram)* Indikativ *m*.

indicator [ˈɪndɪkeɪtə*] *n* *(sign)* (An)zeichen *nt*; *(Aut)* Richtungsanzeiger *m*.

indict [ɪnˈdaɪt] *vt* anklagen; **~able** *a* *person* strafrechtlich verfolgbar; *offence* strafbar; **~ment** Anklage *f*.

indifference [ɪnˈdɪfrəns] *n* *(lack of interest)* Gleichgültigkeit *f*; *(unimportance)* Unwichtigkeit *f*.

indifferent [ɪnˈdɪfrənt] *a* *(not caring)* gleichgültig; *(unimportant)* unwichtig; *(mediocre)* mäßig.

indigenous [ɪnˈdɪdʒɪnəs] *a* einheimisch; **a plant ~ to X** eine in X vorkommende Pflanze.

indigestible [ɪndɪˈdʒestəbl] *a* unverdaulich.

indigestion [ɪndɪˈdʒestʃən] *n* Verdauungsstörung *f*, verdorbene(r) Magen *m*.

indignant [ɪnˈdɪgnənt] *a* ungehalten, entrüstet.

indignation [ɪndɪgˈneɪʃən] *n* Entrüstung *f*.

indignity [ɪnˈdɪgnɪtɪ] *n* Demütigung *f*.

indigo [ˈɪndɪgəʊ] *n* Indigo *m* or *nt*; *a* indigoblau.

indirect *a*, **~ly** *ad* [ɪndɪˈrekt, -lɪ] indirekt; *answer* nicht direkt; **by ~ means** auf Umwegen.

indiscernible [ɪndɪˈsɜːnəbl] *a* nicht wahrnehmbar.

indiscreet [ɪndɪsˈkriːt] *a* (*insensitive*) unbedacht; (*improper*) taktlos; (*telling secrets*) indiskret.

indiscretion [ɪndɪsˈkreʃən] *n* Taktlosigkeit *f*; Indiskretion *f*.

indiscriminate [ɪndɪsˈkrɪmɪnət] *a* wahllos; kritiklos.

indispensable [ɪndɪsˈpensəbl] *a* unentbehrlich.

indisposed [ɪndɪsˈpəʊzd] *a* unpäßlich.

indisposition [ɪndɪspəˈzɪʃən] *n* Unpäßlichkeit *f*.

indisputable [ɪndɪsˈpjuːtəbl] *a* unbestreitbar; *evidence* unanfechtbar.

indistinct [ɪndɪsˈtɪŋkt] *a* undeutlich.

indistinguishable [ɪndɪsˈtɪŋgwɪʃəbl] *a* nicht unterscheidbar; *difference* unmerklich.

individual [ɪndɪˈvɪdjʊəl] *n* Einzelne(r) *mf*, Individuum *nt*; *a* individuell; *case* Einzel-; (*of, for one person*) eigen, individuell; (*characteristic*) eigentümlich; **~ist** Individualist *m*; **~ity** [ɪndɪvɪdjʊˈælɪtɪ] Individualität *f*; **~ly** *ad* einzeln, individuell.

indoctrinate [ɪnˈdɒktrɪneɪt] *vt* indoktrinieren.

indoctrination [ɪndɒktrɪˈneɪʃən] *n* Indoktrination *f*.

indolence [ˈɪndələns] *n* Trägheit *f*.

indolent [ˈɪndələnt] *a* träge.

indoor [ˈɪndɔː*] *a* Haus-; Zimmer-; Innen-; (*Sport*) Hallen-; **~s** *ad* drinnen, im Haus; **to go ~s** hinein or ins Haus gehen.

indubitable [ɪnˈdjuːbɪtəbl] *a* unzweifelhaft.

indubitably [ɪnˈdjuːbɪtəblɪ] *ad* zweifellos.

induce [ɪnˈdjuːs] *vt* dazu bewegen, veranlassen; *reaction* herbeiführen; **~ment** Veranlassung *f*; (*incentive*) Anreiz *m*.

induct [ɪnˈdʌkt] *vt* in sein Amt einführen.

indulge [ɪnˈdʌldʒ] *vt* (*give way*) nachgeben (+*dat*); (*gratify*) frönen (+*dat*); **to ~ o.s. in sth** sich (*dat*) etw gönnen; *vi* frönen (*in dat*), sich gönnen (*in acc*); **~nce** Nachsicht *f*; (*enjoyment*) (übermäßiger) Genuß *m*; **~nt** *a* nachsichtig, (*pej*) nachgiebig.

industrial [ɪnˈdʌstrɪəl] *a* Industrie-, industriell; *dispute, injury* Arbeits-; **~ist** Industrielle(r) *mf*; **~ize** *vt* industrialisieren.

industrious [ɪnˈdʌstrɪəs] *a* fleißig.

industry [ˈɪndəstrɪ] *n* Industrie *f*; (*diligence*) Fleiß *m*; **hotel ~** Hotelgewerbe *nt*.

inebriated [ɪˈniːbrɪeɪtɪd] *a* betrunken, berauscht.

inedible [ɪnˈedɪbl] *a* ungenießbar.

ineffective [ɪnɪˈfektɪv], **ineffectual** [ɪnɪˈfektjʊəl] *a* unwirksam, wirkungslos; *person* untauglich.

inefficiency [ɪnɪˈfɪʃənsɪ] *n* Ineffizienz *f*.

inefficient [ɪnɪˈfɪʃənt] *a* ineffizient; (*in-effective*) unwirksam.

inelegant [ɪnˈelɪgənt] *a* unelegant.

ineligible [ɪnˈelɪdʒəbl] *a* nicht berechtigt; *candidate* nicht wählbar.

ineluctable [ɪnɪˈlʌktəbl] *a* unausweichlich.

inept [ɪˈnept] *a* *remark* unpassend; *person* ungeeignet.

inequality [ɪnɪˈkwɒlɪtɪ] *n* Ungleichheit *f*.

ineradicable [ɪnɪˈrædɪkəbl] *a* unausrottbar; *mistake* unabänderlich; *guilt* tiefsitzend.

inert [ɪˈnɜːt] *a* träge; (*Chem*) inaktiv; (*motionless*) unbeweglich.

inertia [ɪˈnɜːʃə] *n* Trägheit *f*.

inescapable [ɪnɪsˈkeɪpəbl] *a* unvermeidbar.

inessential [ɪnɪˈsenʃəl] *a* unwesentlich.

inestimable [ɪnˈestɪməbl] *a* unschätzbar.

inevitability [ɪnevɪtəˈbɪlɪtɪ] *n* Unvermeidlichkeit *f*.

inevitable [ɪnˈevɪtəbl] *a* unvermeidlich.

inexact [ɪnɪgˈzækt] *a* ungenau.

inexcusable [ɪnɪksˈkjuːzəbl] *a* unverzeihlich.

inexhaustible [ɪnɪgˈzɔːstəbl] *a* *wealth* unerschöpflich; *talker* unermüdlich; *curiosity* unstillbar.

inexorable [ɪnˈeksərəbl] *a* unerbittlich.

inexpensive [ɪnɪksˈpensɪv] *a* preiswert.

inexperience [ɪnɪksˈpɪərɪəns] *n* Unerfahrenheit *f*; **~d** *a* unerfahren.

inexplicable [ɪnɪksˈplɪkəbl] *a* unerklärlich.

inexpressible [ɪnɪksˈpresəbl] *a* *pain, joy* unbeschreiblich; *thoughts* nicht ausdrückbar.

inextricable [ɪnɪksˈtrɪkəbl] *a* un(auf)lösbar.

infallibility [ɪnfælɪˈbɪlɪtɪ] *n* Unfehlbarkeit *f*.

infallible [ɪnˈfæləbl] *a* unfehlbar.

infamous [ˈɪnfəməs] *a* *place* verrufen; *deed* schändlich; *person* niederträchtig.

infamy [ˈɪnfemɪ] *n* Verrufenheit *f*; Niedertracht *f*; (*disgrace*) Schande *f*.

infancy [ˈɪnfənsɪ] *n* frühe Kindheit *f*; (*fig*) Anfangsstadium *nt*.

infant [ˈɪnfənt] *n* kleine(s) Kind *nt*, Säugling *m*; **~ile** *a* kindisch, infantil; **~ school** Vorschule *f*.

infantry [ˈɪnfəntrɪ] *n* Infanterie *f*; **~man** Infanterist *m*.

infatuated [ɪnˈfætjʊeɪtɪd] *a* vernarrt; **to become ~ with** sich vernarren in (+*acc*).

infatuation [ɪnfætjʊˈeɪʃən] *n* Vernarrtheit *f* (*with* in +*acc*).

infect [ɪnˈfekt] *vt* anstecken (*also fig*), infizieren; **~ion** Ansteckung *f*, Infektion *f*; **~ious** [ɪnˈfekʃəs] *a* ansteckend.

infer [ɪnˈfɜː*] *vt* schließen; **~ence** [ɪnfərəns] *a* Schlußfolgerung *n*.

inferior [ɪnˈfɪərɪə*] *a* *rank* untergeordnet, niedriger; *quality* minderwertig; *n* Untergebene(r) *mf*; **~ity** [ɪnfɪərɪˈɒrɪtɪ] Minderwertigkeit *f*; (*in rank*) untergeordnete Stellung *f*; **~ity complex** Minderwertigkeitskomplex *m*.

infernal [ɪnˈfɜːnl] *a* höllisch.

inferno [ɪnˈfɜːnəʊ] *n* Hölle *f*, Inferno *nt*.

infertile [ɪnˈfɜːtaɪl] *a* unfruchtbar.

infertility [ɪnfɜːˈtɪlɪtɪ] *n* Unfruchtbarkeit *f*.

infest [ɪnˈfest] *vt* plagen, heimsuchen; **to be ~ed with** wimmeln von.

infidel ['ɪnfɪdəl] n Ungläubige(r) mf.

infidelity [ɪnfɪ'delɪtɪ] n Untreue f.

in-fighting ['ɪnfaɪtɪŋ] n Nahkampf m.

infiltrate ['ɪnfɪltreɪt] vt infiltrieren; spies einschleusen; (liquid) durchdringen; vi (Mil, liquid) einsickern; (Pol) unterwandern (into acc).

infinite ['ɪnfɪnɪt] a unendlich.

infinitive [ɪn'fɪnɪtɪv] n Infinitiv m, Nennform f.

infinity [ɪn'fɪnɪtɪ] n Unendlichkeit f.

infirm [ɪn'fɜːm] a schwach, gebrechlich; (irresolute) willensschwach.

infirmary [ɪn'fɜːmərɪ] n Krankenhaus nt.

infirmity [ɪn'fɜːmɪtɪ] n Schwäche f, Gebrechlichkeit f.

inflame [ɪn'fleɪm] vt (Med) entzünden; person reizen; anger erregen.

inflammable [ɪn'flæməbl] a feuergefährlich.

inflammation [ɪnflə'meɪʃən] n Entzündung f.

inflate [ɪn'fleɪt] vt aufblasen; tyre aufpumpen; prices hochtreiben.

inflation [ɪn'fleɪʃən] n Inflation f; ~ary a increase inflationistisch; situation inflationär.

inflexible [ɪn'fleksəbl] a person nicht flexibel; opinion starr; thing unbiegsam.

inflict [ɪn'flɪkt] vt zufügen (sth on sb jdm etw); punishment auferlegen (on dat); wound beibringen (on dat); ~ion [ɪn'flɪkʃən] n Zufügung f; Auferlegung f; (suffering) Heimsuchung f.

inflow ['ɪnfləʊ] n Einfließen nt, Zustrom m.

influence ['ɪnfluəns] n Einfluß m; vt beeinflussen.

influential [ɪnflu'enʃəl] a einflußreich.

influenza [ɪnflu'enzə] n Grippe f.

influx ['ɪnflʌks] n (of water) Einfluß m; (of people) Zustrom m; (of ideas) Eindringen nt.

inform [ɪn'fɔːm] vt informieren; to keep sb ~ed jdn auf dem laufenden halten.

informal [ɪn'fɔːməl] a zwanglos; ~ity [ɪnfɔː'mælɪtɪ] n Ungezwungenheit f.

information [ɪnfə'meɪʃən] n Auskunft f, Information f.

informative [ɪn'fɔːmətɪv] a informativ; person mitteilsam.

informer [ɪn'fɔːmə*] n Denunziant(in f) m.

infra-red ['ɪnfrə'red] a infrarot.

infrequent [ɪn'friːkwənt] a selten.

infringe [ɪn'frɪndʒ] vt law verstoßen gegen; ~ upon vt verletzen; ~ment n Verstoß m, Verletzung f.

infuriate [ɪn'fjʊərɪeɪt] vt wütend machen.

infuriating [ɪn'fjʊərɪeɪtɪŋ] a ärgerlich.

ingenious [ɪn'dʒiːnɪəs] a genial; thing raffiniert.

ingenuity [ɪndʒɪ'njuːɪtɪ] n Findigkeit f, Genialität f; Raffiniertheit f.

ingot ['ɪŋgət] n Barren m.

ingratiate [ɪn'greɪʃɪeɪt] vt einschmeicheln (o.s. with sb sich bei jdm).

ingratitude [ɪn'grætɪtjuːd] n Undankbarkeit f.

ingredient [ɪn'griːdɪənt] n Bestandteil m; (Cook) Zutat f.

inhabit [ɪn'hæbɪt] vt bewohnen; ~ant Bewohner(in f) m; (of island, town) Einwohner(in f) m.

inhale [ɪn'heɪl] vt einatmen; (Med, cigarettes) inhalieren.

inherent [ɪn'hɪərənt] a innewohnend (in dat).

inherit [ɪn'herɪt] vt erben; ~ance Erbe nt, Erbschaft f.

inhibit [ɪn'hɪbɪt] vt hemmen; (restrain) hindern; ~ion [ɪnhɪ'bɪʃən] n Hemmung f.

inhospitable [ɪnhɒs'pɪtəbl] a person ungastlich; country unwirtlich.

inhuman [ɪn'hjuːmən] a unmenschlich.

inimitable [ɪ'nɪmɪtəbl] a unnachahmlich.

iniquity [ɪ'nɪkwɪtɪ] n Ungerechtigkeit f.

initial [ɪ'nɪʃəl] a anfänglich, Anfangs-; n Anfangsbuchstabe m, Initiale f; vt abzeichnen; (Pol) paraphieren; ~ly ad anfangs.

initiate [ɪ'nɪʃɪeɪt] vt einführen; negotiations einleiten; (instruct) einweihen.

initiation [ɪnɪʃɪ'eɪʃən] n Einführung f; Einleitung f.

initiative [ɪ'nɪʃɪətɪv] n Initiative f.

inject [ɪn'dʒekt] vt einspritzen; (fig) einflößen; ~ion Spritze f, Injektion f.

injure ['ɪndʒə*] vt verletzen; (fig) schaden (+dat).

injury ['ɪndʒərɪ] n Verletzung f.

injustice [ɪn'dʒʌstɪs] n Ungerechtigkeit f.

ink [ɪŋk] n Tinte f.

inkling ['ɪŋklɪŋ] n (dunkle) Ahnung f.

inlaid ['ɪn'leɪd] a eingelegt, Einlege-.

inland ['ɪnlænd] a Binnen-; (domestic) Inlands-; ad landeinwärts; ~ revenue (Brit) Fiskus m.

in-law ['ɪnlɔː] n angeheiratete(r) Verwandte(r) mf.

inlet ['ɪnlet] n Öffnung f, Einlaß m; (bay) kleine Bucht f.

inmate ['ɪnmeɪt] n Insasse m.

inn [ɪn] n Gasthaus m, Wirtshaus nt.

innate [ɪ'neɪt] a angeboren, eigen (+dat).

inner ['ɪnə*] a inner, Innen-; (fig) verborgen, innerste(r,s).

innocence ['ɪnəsns] n Unschuld f; (ignorance) Unkenntnis f.

innocent ['ɪnəsnt] a unschuldig.

innocuous [ɪ'nɒkjuəs] a harmlos.

innovation [ɪnəʊ'veɪʃən] n Neuerung f.

innuendo [ɪnju'endəʊ] n (versteckte) Anspielung f.

innumerable [ɪ'njuːmərəbl] a unzählig.

inoculation [ɪnɒkju'leɪʃən] n Impfung f.

inopportune [ɪn'ɒpətjuːn] a remark unangebracht; visit ungelegen.

inordinately [ɪ'nɔːdɪnɪtlɪ] ad unmäßig.

inorganic [ɪnɔː'gænɪk] a unorganisch; (Chem) anorganisch.

in-patient ['ɪnpeɪʃənt] n stationäre(r) Patient(in f) m.

input ['ɪnpʊt] n (Elec) (Auf)ladung f; (Tech) zugeführte Menge f; (labour) angewandte Arbeitsleistung f; (money) Investitionssumme f.

inquest ['ɪnkwest] n gerichtliche Untersuchung f.

inquire [ɪn'kwaɪə*] vi sich erkundigen; vt

price sich erkundigen nach; ~ **into** vt untersuchen.

inquiring [ɪn'kwaɪərɪŋ] a mind wissensdurstig.

inquiry [ɪn'kwaɪərɪ] n (question) Erkundigung f, Nachfrage f; (investigation) Untersuchung f; ~ **office** Auskunft(sbüro nt) f.

inquisitive [ɪn'kwɪzɪtɪv] a neugierig; look forschend.

inroad ['ɪnrəʊd] n (Mil) Einfall m; (fig) Eingriff m.

insane [ɪn'seɪn] a wahnsinnig; (Med) geisteskrank.

insanitary [ɪn'sænɪtərɪ] a unhygienisch, gesundheitsschädlich.

insanity [ɪn'sænɪtɪ] n Wahnsinn m.

insatiable [ɪn'seɪʃəbl] a unersättlich.

inscription [ɪn'skrɪpʃən] n (on stone) Inschrift f; (in book) Widmung f.

inscrutable [ɪn'skruːtəbl] a unergründlich.

insect ['ɪnsekt] n Insekt nt; ~**icide** [ɪn'sektɪsaɪd] Insektenvertilgungsmittel nt.

insecure [ɪnsɪ'kjʊə*] a person unsicher; thing nicht fest or sicher.

insecurity [ɪnsɪ'kjʊərɪtɪ] n Unsicherheit f.

insensible [ɪn'sensɪbl] a gefühllos; (unconscious) bewußtlos; (imperceptible) unmerklich; ~ **of** or **to sth** unempfänglich für etw.

insensitive [ɪn'sensɪtɪv] a (to pain) unempfindlich; (without feelings) gefühllos.

inseparable [ɪn'sepərəbl] a people unzertrennlich; word untrennbar.

insert [ɪn'sɜːt] vt einfügen; coin einwerfen; (stick into) hineinstecken; advert aufgeben; ['ɪnsɜːt] n Beifügung f; (in book) Einlage f; (in magazine) Beilage f; ~**ion** Einfügung f; (Press) Inserat nt.

inshore ['ɪnʃɔː*] n Küsten-; ['ɪn'ʃɔː*] ad an der Küste.

inside ['ɪn'saɪd] n Innenseite f, Innere(s) nt; a innere(r,s), Innen-; ad (place) innen; (direction) nach innen, hinein; prep (place) in (+dat); (direction) in (+acc) . . . hinein; (time) innerhalb (+gen); ~ **forward** (Sport) Halbstürmer m; ~ **out** ad linksherum; know in- und auswendig; ~**r** Eingeweihte(r) mf; (member) Mitglied nt.

insidious [ɪn'sɪdɪəs] a heimtückisch.

insight ['ɪnsaɪt] n Einsicht f; Einblick m (into in +acc).

insignificant [ɪnsɪg'nɪfɪkənt] a unbedeutend.

insincere [ɪnsɪn'sɪə*] a unaufrichtig, falsch.

insincerity [ɪnsɪn'serɪtɪ] n Unaufrichtigkeit f.

insinuate [ɪn'sɪnjʊeɪt] vt (hint) andeuten; **to** ~ **o.s. into sth** sich in etw (acc) einschleichen.

insinuation [ɪnsɪnjʊ'eɪʃən] n Anspielung f.

insipid [ɪn'sɪpɪd] a fad(e).

insist [ɪn'sɪst] vi bestehen (on auf +acc); ~**ence** Bestehen nt; ~**ent** a hartnäckig; (urgent) dringend.

insolence ['ɪnsələns] n Frechheit f.

insolent ['ɪnsələnt] a frech.

insoluble [ɪn'sɒljʊbl] a unlösbar; (Chem) unlöslich.

insolvent [ɪn'sɒlvənt] a zahlungsunfähig.

insomnia [ɪn'sɒmnɪə] n Schlaflosigkeit f.

inspect [ɪn'spekt] vt besichtigen, prüfen; (officially) inspizieren; ~**ion** Besichtigung f, Inspektion f; ~**or** (official) Aufsichtsbeamte(r) m, Inspektor m; (police) Polizeikommissar m; (Rail) Kontrolleur m.

inspiration [ɪnspɪ'reɪʃən] n Inspiration f.

inspire [ɪn'spaɪə*] vt respect einflößen (in dat); hope wecken (in in +dat); person inspirieren; **to** ~ **sb to do sth** jdn dazu anregen, etw zu tun; ~**d** a begabt, einfallsreich.

inspiring [ɪn'spaɪərɪŋ] a begeisternd.

instability [ɪnstə'bɪlɪtɪ] n Unbeständigkeit f, Labilität f.

install [ɪn'stɔːl] vt (put in) einbauen, installieren; telephone anschließen; (establish) einsetzen; ~**ation** [ɪnstə'leɪʃən] (of person) (Amts)einsetzung f; (of machinery) Einbau m, Installierung f; (machines etc) Anlage f.

instalment, (US) **installment** [ɪn'stɔːlmənt] n Rate f; (of story) Fortsetzung f; **to pay in** ~**s** auf Raten zahlen.

instance ['ɪnstəns] n Fall m; (example) Beispiel nt; **for** ~ zum Beispiel.

instant ['ɪnstənt] n Augenblick m; a augenblicklich, sofortig; ~ **coffee** Pulverkaffee m; ~**ly** ad sofort.

instead [ɪn'sted] ad stattdessen; ~ **of** prep anstatt (+gen).

instigation [ɪnstɪ'geɪʃən] n Veranlassung f; (of crime etc) Anstiftung f.

instil [ɪn'stɪl] vt (fig) beibringen (in sb jdm).

instinct ['ɪnstɪŋkt] n Instinkt m; ~**ive** a, ~**ively** ad [ɪn'stɪŋktɪv, -lɪ] instinktiv.

institute ['ɪnstɪtjuːt] n Institut nt; (society also) Gesellschaft f; vt einführen; search einleiten.

institution [ɪnstɪ'tjuːʃən] n (custom) Einrichtung f, Brauch m; (society) Institution f; (home) Anstalt f; (beginning) Einführung f, Einleitung f.

instruct [ɪn'strʌkt] vt anweisen; (officially) instruieren; ~**ion** [ɪn'strʌkʃən] Unterricht m; ~**ions** pl Anweisungen pl; (for use) Gebrauchsanweisung f; ~**ive** a lehrreich; ~**or** Lehrer m; (Mil) Ausbilder m.

instrument ['ɪnstrəmənt] n (tool) Instrument nt, Werkzeug nt; (Mus) (Musik)instrument nt; ~**al** [ɪnstrʊ'mentl] a (Mus) Instrumental-; (helpful) behilflich (in bei); ~**alist** [ɪnstrʊ'mentəlɪst] Instrumentalist m; ~ **panel** Armaturenbrett nt.

insubordinate [ɪnsə'bɔːdənət] a aufsässig, widersetzlich.

insubordination ['ɪnsəbɔːdɪ'neɪʃən] n Gehorsamsverweigerung f.

insufferable [ɪn'sʌfərəbl] a unerträglich.

insufficient a, ~**ly** ad [ɪnsə'fɪʃənt, -lɪ] ungenügend.

insular ['ɪnsjələ*] a (fig) engstirnig; ~**ity** [ɪnsjʊ'lærɪtɪ] (fig) Engstirnigkeit f.

insulate ['ɪnsjʊleɪt] vt (Elec) isolieren; (fig) abschirmen (from vor +dat).

insulating tape ['insjuleitiŋteip] n Isolierband nt.

insulation [insju'leiʃən] n Isolierung f.

insulator ['insjuleitə*] n Isolator m.

insulin ['insjulin] n Insulin nt.

insult ['insʌlt] n Beleidigung f; [in'sʌlt] vt beleidigen; ~**ing** [in'sʌltiŋ] a beleidigend.

insuperable [in'su:pərəbl] a unüberwindlich.

insurance [in'ʃuərəns] n Versicherung f; ~ **agent** Versicherungsvertreter m; ~ **policy** Versicherungspolice f.

insure [in'ʃuə*] vt versichern.

insurmountable [insə'mauntəbl] a unüberwindlich.

insurrection [insə'rekʃən] n Aufstand m.

intact [in'tækt] a intakt, unangetastet, ganz.

intake ['inteik] n (place) Einlaßöffnung f; (act) Aufnahme f; (amount) aufgenommene Menge f; (Sch) Neuaufnahme f.

intangible [in'tændʒəbl] a unfaßbar; thing nicht greifbar.

integer ['intidʒə*] n ganze Zahl f.

integral ['intigrəl] a (essential) wesentlich; (complete) vollständig; (Math) Integral-.

integrate ['intigreit] vt vereinigen; people eingliedern, integrieren.

integration [inti'greiʃən] n Eingliederung f, Integration f.

integrity [in'tegriti] n (honesty) Redlichkeit f, Integrität f.

intellect ['intilekt] n Intellekt m; ~**ual** [inti'lektjuəl] a geistig, intellektuell; n Intellektuelle(r) mf.

intelligence [in'telidʒəns] n (understanding) Intelligenz f; (news) Information f; (Mil) Geheimdienst m.

intelligent [in'telidʒənt] a intelligent; beings vernunftbegabt; ~**ly** ad klug; write, speak verständlich.

intelligible [in'telidʒəbl] a verständlich.

intemperate [in'tempərət] a unmäßig.

intend [in'tend] vt beabsichtigen; that was ~**ed for you** das war für dich gedacht.

intense [in'tens] a stark, intensiv; person ernsthaft; ~**ly** ad äußerst; study intensiv.

intensify [in'tensifai] vt verstärken, intensivieren.

intensity [in'tensiti] n Intensität f, Stärke f.

intensive a, ~**ly** ad [in'tensiv, -li] intensiv.

intent [in'tent] n Absicht f; to all ~**s** and **purposes** praktisch; ~**ly** ad aufmerksam; look forschend; to be ~ **on doing sth** fest entschlossen sein, etw zu tun.

intention [in'tenʃən] n Absicht f; with good ~**s** mit guten Vorsätzen; ~**al** a, ~**ally** ad absichtlich.

inter [in't3:*] vt beerdigen.

inter- ['intə*] pref zwischen-, Zwischen-.

interact [intər'ækt] vi aufeinander einwirken; ~**ion** Wechselwirkung f.

intercede [intə'si:d] vi sich verwenden; (in argument) vermitteln.

intercept [intə'sept] vt abfangen; ~**ion** Abfangen nt.

interchange ['intə'tʃeindʒ] n (exchange) Austausch m; (on roads) Verkehrskreuz nt; [intə'tʃeindʒ] vt austauschen; ~**able** [intə'tʃeindʒəbl] a austauschbar.

intercom ['intəkəm] n (Gegen)sprechanlage f.

interconnect [intəkə'nekt] vt miteinander verbinden; vi miteinander verbunden sein; (roads) zusammenführen.

intercontinental ['intəkɔnti'nentl] a interkontinental.

intercourse ['intəkɔ:s] n (exchange) Verkehr m, Beziehungen pl; (sexual) Geschlechtsverkehr m.

interdependence [intədi'pendəns] n gegenseitige Abhängigkeit f.

interest ['intrest] n Interesse nt; (Fin) Zinsen pl; (Comm: share) Anteil m; (group) Interessengruppe f; to be ~ **of** von Interesse sein; vt interessieren; ~**ed** a (having claims) beteiligt; (attentive) interessiert; to be ~**ed** in sich interessieren für; ~**ing** a interessant.

interfere [intə'fiə*] vi (meddle) sich einmischen (with in + acc) stören (with acc); (with an object) sich zu schaffen machen (with an +dat); ~**nce** Einmischung f; (TV) Störung f.

interim ['intərim] a vorläufig; n: in the ~ zwischen.

interior [in'tiəriə*] n Innere(s) nt; a innere(r,s), Innen-.

interjection [intə'dʒekʃən] n Ausruf m; (Gram) Interjektion f.

interlock [intə'lɔk] vi ineinandergreifen; vt zusammenschließen, verzahnen.

interloper ['intələupə*] n Eindringling m.

interlude [in'təlu:d] n Pause f; (in entertainment) Zwischenspiel nt.

intermarriage [intə'mæridʒ] n Mischehe f.

intermarry [intə'mæri] vi untereinander heiraten.

intermediary [intə'mi:diəri] n Vermittler m.

intermediate [intə'mi:diət] a Zwischen-, Mittel-.

interminable [in't3:minəbl] a endlos.

intermission [intə'miʃən] n Pause f.

intermittent [intə'mitənt] a periodisch, stoßweise; ~**ly** ad mit Unterbrechungen.

intern [in't3:n] vt internieren; ['int3:n] n (US) Assistenzarzt m/-ärztin f.

internal [in't3:nl] a (inside) innere(r,s); (domestic) Inlands-; ~**ly** ad innen; (Med) innerlich; intern; ~ **revenue** (US) Sozialprodukt nt.

international [intə'næʃnl] a international; n (Sport) Nationalspieler m; (match) internationale(s) Spiel nt.

internment [in't3:nmənt] n Internierung f.

interplanetary [intə'plænitəri] a interplanetar.

interplay ['intəplei] n Wechselspiel nt.

Interpol ['intəpɔl] n Interpol f.

interpret [in't3:prit] vt (explain) auslegen, interpretieren; (translate) verdolmetschen; (represent) darstellen; ~**ation** Deutung f, Interpretation f; (translation)

Dolmetschen *nt*; ~**er** Dolmetscher(in *f*) *m*.

interrelated [ɪntərɪ'leɪtɪd] *a* untereinander zusammenhängend.

interrogate [ɪn'terəgeɪt] *vt* befragen; *(Jur)* verhören.

interrogation [ɪntərə'geɪʃən] *n* Verhör *nt*.

interrogative [ɪntə'rɒgətɪv] *a* fragend, Frage-.

interrogator [ɪn'terəgeɪtə*] *n* Vernehmungsbeamte(r) *m*.

interrupt [ɪntə'rʌpt] *vt* unterbrechen; ~**ion** Unterbrechung *f*.

intersect [ɪntə'sekt] *vt* (durch)schneiden; *vi* sich schneiden; ~**ion** *(of roads)* Kreuzung *f*; *(of lines)* Schnittpunkt *m*.

intersperse [ɪntə'spɜːs] *vt* *(scatter)* verstreuen; **to** ~ **sth with sth** etw mit etw durchsetzen.

intertwine [ɪntə'twaɪn] *vti* (sich) verflechten.

interval ['ɪntəvəl] *n* Abstand *m*; *(break)* Pause *f*; *(Mus)* Intervall *nt*; **at** ~**s** hier und da; *(time)* dann und wann.

intervene [ɪntə'viːn] *vi* dazwischenliegen; *(act)* einschreiten *(in* gegen*)*, eingreifen *(in* in +*acc)*.

intervening [ɪntə'viːnɪŋ] *a* dazwischenliegend.

intervention [ɪntə'venʃən] *n* Eingreifen *nt*, Intervention *f*.

interview ['ɪntəvjuː] *n* *(Press etc)* Interview *nt*; *(for job)* Vorstellungsgespräch *nt*; *vt* interviewen; ~**er** Interviewer *m*.

intestate [ɪn'testeɪt] *a* ohne Hinterlassung eines Testaments.

intestinal [ɪn'testɪnl] *a* Darm-.

intestine [ɪn'testɪn] *n* Darm *m*; ~**s** *pl* Eingeweide *nt*.

intimacy ['ɪntɪməsɪ] *n* vertraute(r) Umgang *m*, Intimität *f*.

intimate ['ɪntɪmət] *a* *(inmost)* innerste(r,s); *knowledge* eingehend; *(familiar)* vertraut; *friends* eng; ['ɪntɪmeɪt] *vt* andeuten; ~**ly** *ad* vertraut, eng.

intimidate [ɪn'tɪmɪdeɪt] *vt* einschüchtern.

intimidation [ɪntɪmɪ'deɪʃən] *n* Einschüchterung *f*.

into ['ɪntu] *prep* *(motion)* in (+*acc*) . . . hinein; **5** ~ **25 25** durch 5.

intolerable [ɪn'tɒlərəbl] *a* unerträglich.

intolerance [ɪn'tɒlərəns] *n* Intoleranz *f*.

intolerant [ɪn'tɒlərənt] *a* intolerant.

intonation [ɪntə'neɪʃən] *n* Intonation *f*.

intoxicate [ɪn'tɒksɪkeɪt] *vt* betrunken machen; *(fig)* berauschen; ~**d** *a* betrunken; *(fig)* trunken.

intoxication [ɪntɒksɪ'keɪʃən] *n* Rausch *m*.

intractable [ɪn'træktəbl] *a* *character* schwer zu handhaben(d); *problem* schwer lösbar.

intransigent [ɪn'trænsɪdʒənt] *a* unnachgiebig.

intransitive [ɪn'trænsɪtɪv] *a* intransitiv.

intravenous [ɪntrə'viːnəs] *a* intravenös.

intrepid [ɪn'trepɪd] *a* unerschrocken.

intricacy ['ɪntrɪkəsɪ] *n* Kompliziertheit *f*.

intricate ['ɪntrɪkət] *a* kompliziert.

intrigue [ɪn'triːg] *n* Intrige *f*; *vt* faszinieren.

intriguing [ɪn'triːgɪŋ] *a* faszinierend.

intrinsic [ɪn'trɪnsɪk] *a* innere(r,s); *difference* wesentlich.

introduce [ɪntrə'djuːs] *vt* *person* vorstellen *(to sb* jdm*)*; *sth new* einführen; *subject* anschneiden; **to** ~ **sb to sth** jdn in etw *(acc)* einführen.

introduction [ɪntrə'dʌkʃən] *n* Einführung *f*; *(to book)* Einleitung *f*.

introductory [ɪntrə'dʌktərɪ] *a* Einführungs-, Vor-.

introspective [ɪntrəu'spektɪv] *a* nach innen gekehrt.

introvert ['ɪntrəuvɜːt] *n* Introvertierte(r) *mf*; *a* introvertiert.

intrude [ɪn'truːd] *vi* stören *(on* acc*)*; ~**r** Eindringling *m*.

intrusion [ɪn'truːʒən] *n* Störung *f*; *(coming into)* Eindringen *nt*.

intrusive [ɪn'truːsɪv] *a* aufdringlich.

intuition [ɪntjuː'ɪʃən] *n* Intuition *f*.

intuitive *a*, ~**ly** *ad* [ɪn'tjuːɪtɪv, -lɪ] intuitiv.

inundate ['ɪnʌndeɪt] *vt* *(lit, fig)* überschwemmen.

invade [ɪn'veɪd] *vt* einfallen in (+*acc*); ~**r** Eindringling *m*.

invalid ['ɪnvəlɪd] *n* *(disabled)* Kranke(r) *mf*; Invalide *m*; *a* *(ill)* krank; *(disabled)* invalide; [ɪn'vælɪd] *(not valid)* ungültig; ~**ate** [ɪn'vælɪdeɪt] *vt* passport *(für)* ungültig erklären; *(fig)* entkräften.

invaluable [ɪn'væljuəbl] *a* unschätzbar.

invariable [ɪn'veərɪəbl] *a* unveränderlich.

invariably [ɪn'veərɪəblɪ] *ad* ausnahmslos.

invasion [ɪn'veɪʒən] *n* Invasion *f*, Einfall *m*.

invective [ɪn'vektɪv] *n* Beschimpfung *f*.

invent [ɪn'vent] *vt* erfinden; ~**ion** [ɪn'venʃən] Erfindung *f*; ~**ive** *a* erfinderisch; ~**iveness** Erfindungsgabe *f*; ~**or** Erfinder *m*.

inventory ['ɪnvəntrɪ] *n* *(Bestands)*-verzeichnis *nt*, Inventar *nt*.

inverse ['ɪn'vɜːs] *n* Umkehrung *f*; *a*, ~**ly** [ɪn'vɜːs, -lɪ] *ad* umgekehrt.

invert [ɪn'vɜːt] *vt* umdrehen; ~**ed commas** *pl* Anführungsstriche *pl*.

invertebrate [ɪn'vɜːtɪbrət] *n* wirbellose(s) Tier *nt*.

invest [ɪn'vest] *vt* *(Fin)* anlegen, investieren; *(endue)* ausstatten.

investigate [ɪn'vestɪgeɪt] *vt* untersuchen.

investigation [ɪnvestɪ'geɪʃən] *n* Untersuchung *f*.

investigator [ɪn'vestɪgeɪtə*] *n* Untersuchungsbeamte(r) *m*.

investiture [ɪn'vestɪtʃə*] *n* Amtseinsetzung *f*.

investment [ɪn'vestmənt] *n* Investition *f*.

investor [ɪn'vestə*] *n* *(Geld)*anleger *m*.

inveterate [ɪn'vetərət] *a* unverbesserlich.

invigorating [ɪn'vɪgəreɪtɪŋ] *a* stärkend.

invincible [ɪn'vɪnsəbl] *a* unbesiegbar.

inviolate [ɪn'vaɪələt] *a* unverletzt.

invisible [ɪn'vɪzəbl] *a* unsichtbar; *ink* Geheim-.

invitation [ɪnvɪ'teɪʃən] *n* Einladung *f*.

invite [ɪn'vaɪt] *vt* einladen; *criticism, discussion* herausfordern.

inviting [ɪn'vaɪtɪŋ] *a* einladend.

invoice ['invɔis] n Rechnung f,
Lieferschein m; vt goods in Rechnung
stellen (sth for sb jdm etw acc).

invoke [in'vəʊk] vt anrufen.

involuntary a, **involuntarily** ad
[in'vɒləntəri, -li] (unwilling) unfreiwillig;
(unintentional) unabsichtlich.

involve [in'vɒlv] vt (entangle) verwickeln;
(entail) mit sich bringen; ~d a verwickelt;
the person ~d die betreffende Person;
~ment Verwicklung f.

invulnerable [in'vʌlnərəbl] a unverwund-
bar; (fig) unangreifbar.

inward ['inwəd] a innere(r,s); curve Innen-;
~(s) ad nach innen; ~ly ad im Innern.

iodine ['aiədi:n] n Jod nt.

iota [ai'əʊtə] n (fig) bißchen nt.

irascible [i'ræsibl] a reizbar.

irate [ai'reit] a zornig.

iris ['aiəris] n Iris f.

irk [ɜ:k] vt verdrießen.

irksome ['ɜ:ksəm] a lästig.

iron ['aiən] n Eisen nt; (for ironing)
Bügeleisen nt; (golf club) Golfschläger m,
Metallschläger m; a eisern; vt bügeln; ~s
pl (chains) Hand-/Fußschellen pl; ~ out
vt (lit, fig) ausbügeln; differences ausgleichen; **I~ Curtain** Eiserne(r)
Vorhang m.

ironic(al) [ai'rɒnik(əl)] a ironisch;
coincidence etc witzig; ~ally ad ironisch;
witzigerweise.

ironing ['aiəniŋ] n Bügeln nt; (laundry)
Bügelwäsche f; ~ **board** Bügelbrett nt.

ironmonger ['aiənmʌŋgə*] n Eisen-
warenhändler m; ~'s **(shop)** Eisen-
warenhandlung f.

iron ore [aiən'ɔ:*] n Eisenerz nt.

ironworks ['aiənwɜ:ks] n Eisenhütte f.

irony ['aiərəni] n Ironie f; **the ~ of it was**
... das Witzige daran war ...

irrational [i'ræʃənl] a unvernünftig,
irrational.

irreconcilable [irekən'sailəbl] a
unvereinbar.

irredeemable [iri'di:məbl] a (Comm)
money nicht einlösbar; loan unkündbar;
(fig) rettungslos.

irrefutable [iri'fju:təbl] a unwiderlegbar.

irregular [i'regjʊlə*] a unregelmäßig;
shape ungleich(mäßig); (fig) unüblich;
behaviour ungehörig; ~ity [iregjʊ'læriti]
Unregelmäßigkeit f; Ungleichmäßigkeit f;
(fig) Vergehen nt.

irrelevance [i'reləvəns] n Belanglosigkeit
f.

irrelevant [i'reləvənt] a belanglos,
irrelevant.

irreligious [iri'lidʒəs] a ungläubig.

irreparable [i'repərəbl] a nicht
gutzumachen(d).

irreplaceable [iri'pleisəbl] a unersetzlich.

irrepressible [iri'presəbl] a nicht zu
unterdrücken(d); joy unbändig.

irreproachable [iri'prəʊtʃəbl] a untadelig.

irresistible [iri'zistəbl] a unwiderstehlich.

irresolute [i'rezəlu:t] a unentschlossen.

irrespective [iri'spektiv] : ~ **of** prep
ungeachtet (+gen).

irresponsibility ['irispɒnsə'biliti] n
Verantwortungslosigkeit f.

irresponsible [iris'pɒnsəbl] a
verantwortungslos.

irretrievably [iri'tri:vəbli] ad unwieder-
bringlich; lost unrettbar.

irreverence [i'revərəns] n Mißachtung f.

irreverent [i'revərənt] a respektlos.

irrevocable [i'revəkəbl] a unwiderrufbar.

irrigate ['irigeit] vt bewässern.

irrigation [iri'geiʃən] n Bewässerung f.

irritability [iritə'biliti] n Reizbarkeit f.

irritable ['iritəbl] a reizbar.

irritant ['iritənt] n Reizmittel nt.

irritate ['iriteit] vt irritieren, reizen (also
Med).

irritating ['iriteitiŋ] a irritierend, auf-
reizend.

irritation [iri'teiʃən] n (anger) Ärger m;
(Med) Reizung f.

is [iz] see **be**.

Islam ['izla:m] n Islam m.

island ['ailənd] n Insel f; ~**er** Insel-
bewohner(in f) m.

isle [ail] n (kleine) Insel f.

isn't ['iznt] = **is not**.

isobar ['aisəʊbɑ:*] n Isobare f.

isolate ['aisəʊleit] vt isolieren; ~**d** a
isoliert; case Einzel-.

isolation [aisəʊ'leiʃən] n Isolierung f; **to
treat sth in ~** etw vereinzelt or isoliert
behandeln.

isolationism [aisəʊ'leiʃənizəm] n
Isolationismus m.

isotope ['aisətəʊp] n Isotop nt.

issue ['iʃu:] n (matter) Problem nt, Frage f;
(outcome) Resultat nt, Ausgang m; (of
newspaper, shares) Ausgabe f; (offspring)
Nachkommenschaft f; (of river) Mündung
f; **that's not at ~** das steht nicht zur
Debatte; **to make an ~ out of sth** ein
Theater machen wegen etw (dat); vt
ausgeben; warrant erlassen; documents
ausstellen; orders erteilen; books
herausgeben; verdict aussprechen; **to ~
sb with sth** etw (acc) an jdn ausgeben.

isthmus ['isməs] n Landenge f.

it [it] pron (nom, acc) es; (dat) ihm.

italic [i'tælik] a kursiv; ~**s** pl Kursivschrift
f; **in ~s** kursiv gedruckt.

itch [itʃ] n Juckreiz m; (fig) brennende(s)
Verlangen nt; vi jucken; **to be ~ing to do
sth** darauf brennen, etw zu tun; ~**ing**
Jucken nt; ~**y** a juckend.

it'd ['itd] = **it would; it had.**

item ['aitəm] n Gegenstand m; (on list)
Posten m; (in programme) Nummer f; (in
agenda) (Programm)punkt m; (in newspaper) (Zeitungs)notiz f; ~**ize** vt
verzeichnen.

itinerant [i'tinərənt] a person
umherreisend.

itinerary [ai'tinərəri] n Reiseroute f;
(records) Reisebericht m.

it'll ['itl] = **it will, it shall.**

its [its] poss a (masculine, neuter) sein;
(feminine) ihr; poss pron seine(r,s),
ihre(r,s).

it's [its] = **it is; it has.**

itself [ɪt'self] *pron* sich (selbst); (*emphatic*) selbst.
I've [aɪv] = **I have**.
ivory ['aɪvərɪ] *n* Elfenbein *nt*; ~ **tower** (*fig*) Elfenbeinturm *m*.
ivy ['aɪvɪ] *n* Efeu *m*.

J

J, j [dʒeɪ] *n* J *nt*, j *nt*.
jab [dʒæb] *vti* (hinein)stechen; *n* Stich *m*, Stoß *m*; (*col*) Spritze *f*.
jabber ['dʒæbə*] *vi* plappern.
jack [dʒæk] *n* (Wagen)heber *m*; (*Cards*) Bube *m*; ~ **up** *vt* aufbocken.
jackdaw [dʒækdɔ:] *n* Dohle *f*.
jacket ['dʒækɪt] *n* Jacke *f*, Jackett *nt*; (*of book*) Schutzumschlag *m*; (*Tech*) Ummantelung *f*.
jack-knife ['dʒæknaɪf] *n* Klappmesser *nt*; *vi* (*truck*) sich zusammenschieben.
jackpot ['dʒækpɒt] *n* Haupttreffer *m*.
jade [dʒeɪd] *n* (*stone*) Jade *m*.
jaded ['dʒeɪdɪd] *a* ermattet.
jagged ['dʒægɪd] *a* zackig; *blade* scharfig.
jail [dʒeɪl] *n* Gefängnis *nt*; *vt* einsperren; ~**break** Gefängnisausbruch *m*; ~**er** Gefängniswärter *m*.
jam [dʒæm] *n* Marmelade *f*; (*crowd*) Gedränge *nt*; (*col: trouble*) Klemme *f*; see **traffic**; *vt people* zusammendrängen; (*wedge*) einklemmen; (*cram*) hineinzwängen; (*obstruct*) blockieren; **to ~ on the brakes** auf die Bremse treten.
jamboree [dʒæmbə'ri:] *n* (*Pfadfinder*)treffen *nt*.
jangle ['dʒæŋgl] *vti* klimpern; (*bells*) bimmeln.
janitor ['dʒænɪtə*] *n* Hausmeister *m*.
January ['dʒænjuərɪ] *n* Januar *m*.
jar [dʒɑ:*] *n* Glas *nt*; *vi* kreischen; (*colours etc*) nicht harmonieren.
jargon ['dʒɑ:gən] *n* Fachsprache *f*, Jargon *m*.
jarring ['dʒɑ:rɪŋ] *a sound* kreischend; *colour* unharmonisch.
jasmin(e) ['dʒæzmɪn] *n* Jasmin *m*.
jaundice ['dʒɔ:ndɪs] *n* Gelbsucht *f*; ~**d** *a* (*fig*) mißgünstig.
jaunt [dʒɔ:nt] *n* Spritztour *f*; ~**y** *a* (*lively*) munter; (*brisk*) flott; *attitude* unbekümmert.
javelin ['dʒævlɪn] *n* Speer *m*.
jaw [dʒɔ:] *n* Kiefer *m*; ~**s** *pl* (*fig*) Rachen *m*.
jaywalker ['dʒeɪwɔ:kə*] *n* unvorsichtige(r) Fußgänger *m*, Verkehrssünder *m*.
jazz [dʒæz] *n* Jazz *m*; ~ **up** *vt* (*Mus*) verjazzen; (*enliven*) aufpolieren; ~ **band** Jazzkapelle *f*; ~**y** *a colour* schreiend, auffallend.
jealous ['dʒeləs] *a* (*envious*) mißgünstig; *husband* eifersüchtig; (*watchful*) bedacht (*of auf +acc*); ~**ly** *ad* mißgünstig, eifersüchtig; sorgsam; ~**y** Mißgunst *f*; Eifersucht *f*.
jeans [dʒi:nz] *npl* Jeans *pl*.
jeep [dʒi:p] *n* Jeep *m*.

jeer [dʒɪə*] *vi* höhnisch lachen (*at über +acc*), verspotten (*at sb jdn*); *n* Hohn *m*; (*remark*) höhnische Bemerkung *f*; ~**ing** *a* höhnisch.
jelly ['dʒelɪ] *n* Gelee *nt*; (*on meat*) Gallert *nt*; (*dessert*) Grütze *f*; ~**fish** Qualle *f*.
jemmy ['dʒemɪ] *n* Brecheisen *nt*.
jeopardize ['dʒepədaɪz] *vt* gefährden.
jeopardy ['dʒepədɪ] *n* Gefahr *f*.
jerk [dʒɜ:k] *n* Ruck *m*; (*col: idiot*) Trottel *m*; *vt* ruckartig bewegen; *vi* sich ruckartig bewegen; (*muscles*) zucken.
jerkin ['dʒɜ:kɪn] *n* Wams *m*.
jerky ['dʒɜ:kɪ] *a movement* ruckartig; *writing* zitterig; *ride* rüttelnd.
jersey ['dʒɜ:zɪ] *n* Pullover *m*.
jest [dʒest] *n* Scherz *m*; **in** ~ im Spaß; *vi* spaßen.
jet [dʒet] *n* (*stream: of water etc*) Strahl *m*; (*spout*) Düse *f*; (*Aviat*) Düsenflugzeug *nt*; ~**-black** *a* rabenschwarz; ~ **engine** Düsenmotor *m*.
jetsam ['dʒetsəm] *n* Strandgut *nt*.
jettison ['dʒetɪsn] *vt* über Bord werfen.
jetty ['dʒetɪ] *n* Landesteg *m*, Mole *f*.
Jew [dʒu:] *n* Jude *m*.
jewel ['dʒu:əl] *n* (*lit, fig*) Juwel *nt*; (*stone*) Edelstein *m*; ~**(l)er** Juwelier *m*; ~**(l)er's (shop)** Schmuckwarengeschäft *nt*, Juwelier *m*; ~**(l)ery** Schmuck *m*, Juwelen *pl*.
Jewess ['dʒu:ɪs] *n* Jüdin *f*.
Jewish ['dʒu:ɪʃ] *a* jüdisch.
jib [dʒɪb] *n* (*Naut*) Klüver *m*; *vi* sich scheuen (*at vor +dat*).
jibe [dʒaɪb] *n* spöttische Bemerkung *f*.
jiffy ['dʒɪfɪ] *n* (*col*) **in a** ~ sofort.
jigsaw (puzzle) ['dʒɪgsɔ:(pʌzl)] *n* Puzzle-(spiel) *nt*.
jilt [dʒɪlt] *vt* den Laufpaß geben (*+dat*).
jingle ['dʒɪŋgl] *n* (*advertisement*) Werbesong *m*; (*verse*) Reim *m*; *vti* klimpern; (*bells*) bimmeln.
jinx [dʒɪŋks] *n* Fluch *m*; **to put a** ~ **on sth** etw verhexen.
jitters ['dʒɪtəz] *npl* (*col*) **to get the** ~ einen Bammel kriegen.
jittery ['dʒɪtərɪ] *a* (*col*) nervös.
jiujitsu [dʒu:'dʒɪtsu:] *n* Jiu-Jitsu *nt*.
job [dʒɒb] *n* (*piece of work*) Arbeit *f*; (*occupation*) Stellung *f*, Arbeit *f*; (*duty*) Aufgabe *f*; (*difficulty*) Mühe *f*; **what's your** ~? was machen Sie von Beruf?; **it's a good** ~ **he . . .** es ist ein Glück, daß er . . .; **just the** ~ genau das Richtige; ~**bing** *a* (*in factory*) Akkord-; (*freelance*) Gelegenheits-; ~**less** *a* arbeitslos.
jockey ['dʒɒkɪ] *n* Jockei *m*; *vi:* **to** ~ **for position** sich in eine gute Position drängeln.
jocular ['dʒɒkjʊlə*] *a* scherzhaft, witzig.
jodhpurs ['dʒɒdpɜ:z] *npl* Reithose *f*.
jog [dʒɒg] *vt* (an)stoßen; *vi* (*run*) einen Dauerlauf machen.
john [dʒɒn] *n* (*US col*) Klo *nt*.
join [dʒɔɪn] *vt* (*put together*) verbinden (*to mit*); *club* beitreten (*+dat*); *person* sich anschließen (*+dat*); *vi* (*unite*) vereinigen; (*bones*) zusammenwachsen; *n*

Verbindungsstelle *f*, Naht *f*; ~ **in** *vi* mitmachen; ~ **up** *vi* (*Mil*) zur Armee gehen; ~**er** Schreiner *m*; ~**ery** Schreinerei *f*; ~**t** *n* (*Tech*) Fuge *f*; (*of bones*) Gelenk *nt*; (*of meat*) Braten *m*; (*col: place*) Lokal *nt*; *a*, ~**tly** *ad* gemeinsam.

joist [dʒɔɪst] *n* Träger *m*.

joke [dʒəʊk] *n* Witz *m*; **it's no** ~ es ist nicht zum Lachen; *vi* spaßen, Witze machen; **you must be joking** das ist doch wohl nicht dein Ernst; ~**r** Witzbold *m*; (*Cards*) Joker *m*.

joking [dʒəʊkɪŋ] *a* scherzhaft; ~**ly** *ad* zum Spaß; *talk* im Spaß, scherzhaft.

jollity [dʒɒlɪtɪ] *n* Fröhlichkeit *f*.

jolly [dʒɒlɪ] *a* lustig, vergnügt; *ad* (*col*) ganz schön; ~ **good!** prima!; **to** ~ **sb along** jdn ermuntern.

jolt [dʒəʊlt] *n* (*shock*) Schock *m*; (*jerk*) Stoß *m*, Rütteln *nt*; *vt* (*push*) stoßen; (*shake*) durchschütteln; (*fig*) aufrütteln; *vi* holpern.

jostle [dʒɒsl] *vt* anrempeln.

jot [dʒɒt] *n*: **not one** ~ kein Jota *nt*; ~ **down** *vt* schnell aufschreiben, notieren; ~**ter** Notizbuch *nt*; (*Sch*) Schulheft *nt*.

journal [dʒɜːnl] *n* (*diary*) Tagebuch *nt*; (*magazine*) Zeitschrift *f*; ~**ese** [dʒɜːnə'liːz] Zeitungsstil *m*; ~**ism** Journalismus *m*; ~**ist** Journalist(in *f*) *m*.

journey [dʒɜːnɪ] *n* Reise *f*.

jovial [dʒəʊvɪəl] *a* jovial.

joy* [dʒɔɪ] *n* Freude *f*; ~**ful** *a* freudig; (*gladdening*) erfreulich; ~**fully** *ad* freudig; ~**ous** *a* freudig; ~ **ride** Schwarzfahrt *f*; ~**stick** Steuerknüppel *m*.

jubilant [dʒuːbɪlənt] *a* triumphierend.

jubilation [dʒuːbɪ'leɪʃən] *n* Jubel *m*.

jubilee [dʒuːbɪliː] *n* Jubiläum *nt*.

judge [dʒʌdʒ] *n* Richter *m*; (*fig*) Kenner *m*; *vt* (*Jur*) *person* die Verhandlung führen über (+*acc*); *case* verhandeln; (*assess*) beurteilen; (*criticize*) verurteilen; *vi* ein Urteil abgeben; **as far as I can** ~ soweit ich das beurteilen kann; **judging by sth** nach etw zu urteilen; ~**ment** (*Jur*) Urteil *nt*; (*Eccl*) Gericht *nt*; (*opinion*) Ansicht *f*; (*ability*) Urteilsvermögen *nt*.

judicial [dʒuː'dɪʃəl] *a* gerichtlich, Justiz-.

judicious [dʒuː'dɪʃəs] *a* weis(e).

judo [dʒuːdəʊ] *n* Judo *nt*.

jug [dʒʌg] *n* Krug *m*.

juggernaut [dʒʌgənɔːt] *n* (*truck*) Fernlastwagen *m*.

juggle [dʒʌgl] *vi* jonglieren; *vt facts* verdrehen; *figures* frisieren; ~**r** Jongleur *m*.

jugular [dʒʌgjʊlə*] *a vein* Hals-.

juice [dʒuːs] *n* Saft *m*.

juiciness [dʒuːsɪnɪs] *n* Saftigkeit *f*.

juicy [dʒuːsɪ] *a* (*lit*, *fig*) saftig; *story* schlüpfrig.

jukebox [dʒuːkbɒks] *n* Musikautomat *m*.

July [dʒuː'laɪ] *n* Juli *m*.

jumble [dʒʌmbl] *n* Durcheinander *nt*; *vt* (*also* ~ **up**) durcheinanderwerfen; *facts* durcheinanderbringen; ~ **sale** (*Brit*) Basar *m*, Flohmarkt *m*.

jumbo (jet) [dʒʌmbəʊ(dʒet)] *n* Jumbo(-Jet) *m*.

jump [dʒʌmp] *vi* springen; (*nervously*) zusammenzucken; **to** ~ **to conclusions** voreilige Schlüsse ziehen; *vt* überspringen; **to** ~ **the gun** (*fig*) voreilig handeln; **to** ~ **the queue** sich vordrängeln; *n* Sprung *m*; **to give sb a** ~ jdn erschrecken; ~**ed-up** *a* (*col*) eingebildet; ~**er** Pullover *m*; ~**y** *a* nervös.

junction [dʒʌŋkʃən] *n* (*of roads*) (Straßen)kreuzung *f*; (*Rail*) Knotenpunkt *m*.

juncture [dʒʌŋktʃə*] *n*: **at this** ~ in diesem Augenblick.

June [dʒuːn] *n* Juni *m*.

jungle [dʒʌŋgl] *n* Dschungel *m*, Urwald *m*.

junior [dʒuːnɪə*] *a* (*younger*) jünger; (*after name*) junior; (*Sport*) Junioren-; (*lower position*) untergeordnet; (*for young people*) Junioren-; *n* Jüngere(r) *m*.

junk [dʒʌŋk] *n* (*rubbish*) Plunder *m*; (*ship*) Dschunke *f*; ~**shop** Ramschladen *m*.

junta [dʒʌntə] *n* Junta *f*.

jurisdiction [dʒʊərɪs'dɪkʃən] *n* Gerichtsbarkeit *f*; (*range of authority*) Zuständigkeit(sbereich *m*) *f*.

jurisprudence [dʒʊərɪs'pruːdəns] *n* Rechtswissenschaft *f*, Jura no art.

juror [dʒʊərə*] *n* Geschworene(r) *mf*; Schöffe *m*, Schöffin *f*; (*in competition*) Preisrichter *m*.

jury [dʒʊərɪ] *n* (*court*) Geschworene *pl*; (*in competition*) Jury *f*, Preisgericht *nt*; ~**man** = **juror**.

just [dʒʌst] *a* gerecht; *ad* (*recently*, *now*) gerade, eben; (*barely*) gerade noch; (*exactly*) genau, gerade; (*only*) nur, bloß; (*a small distance*) gleich; (*absolutely*) einfach; ~ **as I arrived** gerade als ich ankam; ~ **as nice** genauso nett; ~ **as well** um so besser; ~ **about** so etwa; ~ **now** soeben, gerade; **not** ~ **now** nicht im Moment; ~ **try** versuch es bloß mal.

justice [dʒʌstɪs] *n* (*fairness*) Gerechtigkeit *f*; (*magistrate*) Richter *m*; ~ **of the peace** Friedensrichter *m*.

justifiable [dʒʌstɪfaɪəbl] *a* berechtigt.

justifiably [dʒʌstɪfaɪəblɪ] *ad* berechtigterweise, zu Recht.

justification [dʒʌstɪfɪ'keɪʃən] *n* Rechtfertigung *f*.

justify [dʒʌstɪfaɪ] *vt* rechtfertigen.

justly [dʒʌstlɪ] *ad* say mit Recht; *condemn* gerecht.

justness [dʒʌstnəs] *n* Gerechtigkeit *f*.

jut [dʒʌt] *vi* (*also* ~ **out**) herausragen, vorstehen.

juvenile [dʒuːvənaɪl] *a* (*young*) jugendlich; (*for the young*) Jugend-; *n* Jugendliche(r) *mf*; ~ **delinquency** Jugendkriminalität *f*; ~ **delinquent** jugendliche(r) Straftäter(in *f*) *m*.

juxtapose [dʒʌkstəpəʊz] *vt* nebeneinanderstellen.

juxtaposition [dʒʌkstəpə'zɪʃən] *n* Nebeneinanderstellung *f*.

K

K, k [keɪ] n K nt, k nt.

kaleidoscope [kə'laɪdəskəʊp] n Kaleidoskop nt.

kangaroo [kæŋgə'ru:] n Känguruh nt.

kayak ['kaɪæk] n Kajak m or nt.

keel [ki:l] n Kiel m; **on an even ~** (fig) im Lot.

keen [ki:n] a eifrig, begeistert; intelligence, wind, blade scharf; sight, hearing gut; price günstig; **~ly** ad leidenschaftlich; (sharply) scharf; **~ness** Schärfe f; (eagerness) Begeisterung f.

keep [ki:p] irreg vt (retain) behalten; (have) haben; animals, one's word halten; (support) versorgen; (maintain in state) halten; (preserve) aufbewahren; (restrain) abhalten; vi (continue in direction) sich halten; (food) sich halten; (remain: quiet etc) sein, bleiben; **it ~s happening** es passiert immer wieder; n Unterhalt m; (tower) Burgfried m; **~ back** vt fernhalten; secret verschweigen; **~ on** vi: **~ on doing sth** etw immer weiter tun; vt anbehalten; hat aufbehalten; **~ out** vt draußen lassen, nicht hereinlassen; '**~ out!**' 'Eintritt verboten!'; **~ up** vi Schritt halten; vt weitermachen; **~ing** (care) Obhut f; **in ~ing (with)** in Übereinstimmung (mit).

keg [keg] n Faß nt.

kennel ['kenl] n Hundehütte f.

kerb(stone) ['kɜːbstəʊn] n Bordstein m.

kernel ['kɜːnl] n Kern m.

kerosene ['kerəsiːn] n Kerosin nt.

kestrel ['kestrəl] n Turmfalke f.

ketchup ['ketʃəp] n Ketchup nt or m.

kettle ['ketl] n Kessel m; **~drum** Pauke f.

key [ki:] n Schlüssel m; (solution, answers) Schlüssel m, Lösung f; (of piano, typewriter) Taste f; (Mus) Tonart f; (explanatory note) Zeichenerklärung f; a position etc Schlüssel-; **~board** (of piano, typewriter) Tastatur f; **~hole** Schlüsselloch nt; **~note** Grundton m; **~ ring** Schlüsselring m.

khaki ['kɑːkɪ] n K(h)aki nt; a k(h)aki-(farben).

kick [kɪk] vt einen Fußtritt geben (+dat), treten; vi treten; (baby) strampeln; (horse) ausschlagen; n (Fuß)tritt m; (thrill) Spaß m; **~ around** vt person herumstoßen; **~ off** vi (Sport) anstoßen; **~ up** vt (col) schlagen; **~-off** (Sport) Anstoß m.

kid [kɪd] n (child) Kind nt; (goat) Zicklein nt; (leather) Glacéleder nt; vt auf den Arm nehmen; vi Witze machen.

kidnap ['kɪdnæp] vt entführen, kidnappen; **~per** Kidnapper m, Entführer m; **~ping** Entführung f, Kidnapping nt.

kidney ['kɪdnɪ] n Niere f.

kill [kɪl] vt töten, umbringen; chances ruinieren; vi töten; n Tötung f; (hunting) (Jagd)beute f; **~er** Mörder m.

kiln [kɪln] n Brennofen m.

kilo ['ki:ləʊ] n Kilo nt; **~gram(me)** Kilogramm nt; **~metre**, (US) **~meter** Kilometer m; **~watt** Kilowatt nt.

kilt [kɪlt] n Schottenrock m.

kimono [kɪ'məʊnəʊ] n Kimono m.

kin [kɪn] n Verwandtschaft f, Verwandte(n) pl.

kind [kaɪnd] a freundlich, gütig; n Art f; a **~ of** eine Art von; **(two) of a ~** (zwei) von der gleichen Art; **in ~** auf dieselbe Art; (in goods) in Naturalien.

kindergarten ['kɪndəgɑːtn] n Kindergarten m.

kind-hearted ['kaɪnd'hɑːtɪd] a gutherzig.

kindle ['kɪndl] vt (set on fire) anzünden; (rouse) reizen, (er)wecken.

kindliness ['kaɪndlɪnəs] n Freundlichkeit f, Güte f.

kindly ['kaɪndlɪ] a freundlich; ad liebenswürdig(erweise); **would you ~ ...?** wären Sie so freundlich und ...?

kindness ['kaɪndnəs] n Freundlichkeit f.

kindred ['kɪndrɪd] a verwandt; **~ spirit** Gleichgesinnte(r) mf.

kinetic [kɪ'netɪk] a kinetisch.

king [kɪŋ] n König m; **~dom** Königreich nt; **~fisher** Eisvogel m; **~pin** (Tech) Bolzen m; (Aut) Achsschenkelbolzen m; (fig) Stütze f; **~-size** a cigarette Kingsize.

kink [kɪŋk] n Knick m; **~y** a (fig) exzentrisch.

kiosk ['ki:ɒsk] n (Tel) Telefonhäuschen nt.

kipper ['kɪpə*] n Räucherhering m.

kiss [kɪs] n Kuß m; vt küssen; vi: **they ~ed** sie küßten sich.

kit [kɪt] n Ausrüstung f; (tools) Werkzeug nt; **~bag** Seesack m.

kitchen ['kɪtʃɪn] n Küche f; **~ garden** Gemüsegarten m; **~ sink** Spülbecken nt; **~ware** Küchengeschirr nt.

kite [kaɪt] n Drachen m.

kith [kɪθ] n: **~ and kin** Blutsverwandte pl; **with ~ and kin** mit Kind und Kegel.

kitten ['kɪtn] n Kätzchen nt.

kitty ['kɪtɪ] n (money) (gemeinsame) Kasse f.

kleptomaniac [kleptəʊ'meɪnɪæk] n Kleptomane m, Kleptomanin f.

knack [næk] n Dreh m, Trick m.

knapsack ['næpsæk] n Rucksack m; (Mil) Tornister m.

knave [neɪv] n (old) Schurke m.

knead [ni:d] vt kneten.

knee [ni:] n Knie nt; **~cap** Kniescheibe f; **~-deep** a knietief.

kneel [ni:l] vi irreg knien.

knell [nel] n Grabgeläute nt.

knickers ['nɪkəz] npl Schlüpfer m.

knife [naɪf] n Messer nt; vt erstechen.

knight [naɪt] n Ritter m; (chess) Springer m, Pferd nt; **~hood** Ritterwürde f.

knit [nɪt] vti stricken; vi (bones) zusammenwachsen; (people) harmonieren; **~ting** (occupation) Stricken nt; (work) Strickzeug nt; **~ting machine** Strickmaschine f; **~ting needle** Stricknadel f; **~wear** Strickwaren pl.

knob [nɒb] n Knauf m; (on instrument) Knopf m; (of butter etc) kleine(s) Stück nt.

knock [nɒk] vt schlagen; (criticize) heruntermachen; vi klopfen; (knees) zittern; n Schlag m; (on door) Klopfen nt;

~ **off** vt (do quickly) hinhauen; (col: steal) klauen; vi (finish) Feierabend machen; ~ **out** vt ausschlagen; (boxing) k.o. schlagen; ~**er** (on door) Türklopfer m; ~**-kneed** a x-beinig; ~**out** (lit) K.o.-Schlag m; (fig) Sensation f.

knot [nɒt] n Knoten m; (in wood) Astloch nt; (group) Knäuel nt or m; vt (ver)knoten; ~**ted** a verknotet.

knotty ['nɒtɪ] a knorrig; problem kompliziert.

know [nəu] vti irreg wissen; (be able to) können; (be acquainted with) kennen; (recognize) erkennen; **to ~ how to do sth** wissen, wie man etw macht, etw tun können; **you** ~ nicht (wahr); **to be well ~n** bekannt sein; ~**all** Alleswisser m; ~**-how** Kenntnis f, Know-how nt; ~**ing** a schlau; look, smile wissend; ~**ingly** ad wissend; (intentionally) wissentlich.

knowledge ['nɒlɪdʒ] n Wissen nt, Kenntnis f; ~**able** a informiert.

knuckle ['nʌkl] n Fingerknöchel m.

kudos ['kjuːdɒs] n Ehre f.

L

L, l [el] n L nt, l nt.

lab [læb] n (col) Labor nt.

label ['leɪbl] n Etikett nt, Schild nt; vt mit einer Aufschrift versehen, etikettieren.

laboratory [lə'bɒrətərɪ] n Laboratorium nt.

laborious a, ~**ly** ad [lə'bɔːrɪəs, -lɪ] mühsam.

labour, (US) **labor** ['leɪbə*] n Arbeit f; (workmen) Arbeitskräfte pl; (Med) Wehen pl; a (Pol) Labour-; **hard** ~ Zwangsarbeit f; ~**er** Arbeiter m; ~**-saving** a arbeitssparend.

laburnum [lə'bɜːnəm] n Goldregen m.

labyrinth ['læbərɪnθ] n (lit, fig) Labyrinth nt.

lace [leɪs] n (fabric) Spitze f; (of shoe) Schnürsenkel m; (braid) Litze f; vt (also ~ **up**) (zu)schnüren.

lacerate ['læsəreɪt] vt zerschneiden, tief verwunden.

lack [læk] vt nicht haben; **sb** ~**s sth** jdm fehlt etw (nom); vi: **to be** ~**ing** fehlen; **sb is** ~**ing in sth** es fehlt jdm an etw (dat); n Mangel m; **for** ~ **of** aus Mangel an (+dat).

lackadaisical [lækə'deɪzɪkəl] a lasch.

lackey ['lækɪ] n Lakei m.

lacklustre, (US) **lackluster** ['læklʌstə*] a glanzlos, matt.

laconic [lə'kɒnɪk] a lakonisch.

lacquer ['lækə*] n Lack m.

lacrosse [lə'krɒs] n Lacrosse nt.

lacy ['leɪsɪ] a spitzenartig, Spitzen-.

lad [læd] n (boy) Junge m; (young man) Bursche m.

ladder ['lædə*] n (lit) Leiter f; (fig) Stufenleiter f; (Brit: in stocking) Laufmasche f; vt Laufmaschen bekommen in (+dat).

laden ['leɪdn] a beladen, voll.

ladle ['leɪdl] n Schöpfkelle f.

lady ['leɪdɪ] n Dame f; (title) Lady f; **'Ladies'** (lavatory) 'Damen'; ~**bird**, (US)

~**bug** Marienkäfer m; ~**-in-waiting** Hofdame f; ~**like** a damenhaft, vornehm.

lag [læg] n (delay) Verzug m; (time –) Zeitabstand m; vi (also ~ **behind**) zurückbleiben; vt pipes verkleiden.

lager ['lɑːgə*] n Lagerbier nt, helles Bier nt.

lagging ['lægɪŋ] n Isolierung f.

lagoon [lə'guːn] n Lagune f.

laid [leɪd]: **to be ~ up** ans Bett gefesselt sein.

lair [lɛə*] n Lager nt.

laissez-faire ['leɪsɪ'fɛə*] n Laisser-faire nt.

laity ['leɪɪtɪ] n Laien pl.

lake [leɪk] n See m.

lamb [læm] n Lamm nt; (meat) Lammfleisch nt; ~ **chop** Lammkotelett nt; ~**'s wool** Lammwolle f.

lame [leɪm] a lahm; person also gelähmt; excuse faul.

lament [lə'ment] n Klage f; vt beklagen; ~**able** ['læməntəbl] a bedauerlich; (bad) erbärmlich; ~**ation** [læmən'teɪʃən] n Wehklage f.

laminated ['læmɪneɪtɪd] a beschichtet.

lamp [læmp] n Lampe f; (in street) Straßenlaterne f; ~**post** Laternenpfahl m; ~**shade** Lampenschirm m.

lance [lɑːns] n Lanze f; vt (Med) aufschneiden; ~ **corporal** Obergefreite(r) m.

lancet ['lɑːnsɪt] n Lanzette f.

land [lænd] n Land nt; vi (from ship) an Land gehen; (Aviat, end up) landen; vt (obtain) gewinnen, kriegen; passengers absetzen; goods abladen; troops, space probe landen; ~**ed a** Land-; ~**ing** Landung f; (on stairs) (Treppen)absatz m; ~**ing craft** Landungsboot nt; ~**ing stage** Landesteg m; ~**ing strip** Landebahn f; ~**lady** (Haus)wirtin f; ~**locked** a landumschlossen, Binnen-; ~**lord** (of house) Hauswirt m, Besitzer m; (of pub) Gastwirt m; (of land) Grundbesitzer m; ~**lubber** Landratte f; ~**mark** Wahrzeichen nt; (fig) Meilenstein m; ~**owner** Grundbesitzer m; ~**scape** Landschaft f; ~**slide** (Geog) Erdrutsch m; (Pol) überwältigende(r) Sieg m.

lane [leɪn] n (in town) Gasse f; (in country) Weg m; Sträßchen nt; (of motorway) Fahrbahn f, Spur f; (Sport) Bahn f.

language ['læŋgwɪdʒ] n Sprache f; (style) Ausdrucksweise f.

languid ['læŋgwɪd] a schlaff, matt.

languish ['læŋgwɪʃ] vi schmachten; (pine) sich sehnen (for nach).

languor ['læŋgə*] n Mattigkeit f.

languorous ['læŋgərəs] a schlaff, träge.

lank [læŋk] a dürr; ~**y** a schlacksig.

lantern ['læntən] n Laterne f.

lanyard ['lænjəd] n (Naut) Taljereep nt; (Mil) Kordel f.

lap [læp] n Schoß m; (Sport) Runde f; vt auflecken; vi (water) plätschern; ~**dog** Schoßhund m.

lapel [lə'pel] n Rockaufschlag m, Revers nt or m.

lapse [læps] n (mistake) Irrtum m; (moral) Fehltritt m; (time) Zeitspanne f.

larceny ['lɑːsənɪ] *n* Diebstahl *m*.

lard [lɑːd] *n* Schweineschmalz *nt*.

larder ['lɑːdə*] *n* Speisekammer *f*.

large [lɑːdʒ] *a* groß; **at ~** auf freiem Fuß; **by and ~** im großen und ganzen; **~ly** *ad* zum größten Teil; **~-scale** *a* groß angelegt, Groß-; **~sse** [lɑː'ʒes] Freigebigkeit *f*.

lark [lɑːk] *n* (*bird*) Lerche *f*; (*joke*) Jux *m*; **~ about** *vi* (*col*) herumalbern.

larva ['lɑːvə] *n* Larve *f*.

laryngitis [lærɪn'dʒaɪtɪs] *n* Kehlkopfentzündung *f*.

larynx ['lærɪŋks] *n* Kehlkopf *m*.

lascivious *a*, **~ly** *ad* [lə'sɪvɪəs, -lɪ] wollüstig.

lash [læʃ] *n* Peitschenhieb *m*; *vt* (*beat against*) schlagen an (*+acc*); (*rain*) schlagen gegen; (*whip*) peitschen; (*bind*) festbinden; **~ out** *vi* (*with fists*) um sich schlagen; (*spend money*) sich in Unkosten stürzen; *vt money etc* springen lassen; **~ing** (*beating*) Tracht *f* Prügel; (*tie*) Schleife *f*; **~ings of** (*col*) massenhaft.

lass [læs] *n* Mädchen *nt*.

lassitude ['læsɪtjuːd] *n* Abgespanntheit *f*.

lasso [læ'suː] *n* Lasso *nt*; *vt* mit einem Lasso fangen.

last [lɑːst] *a* letzte(r, s); *ad* zuletzt; (*last time*) das letztemal; *n* (*person*) Letzte(r) *mf*; (*thing*) Letzte(s) *nt*; (*for shoe*) (Schuh)leisten *m*; *vi* (*continue*) dauern; (*remain good*) sich halten; (*money*) ausreichen; **at ~** endlich; **~ night** gestern abend; **~ing** *a* dauerhaft, haltbar; *shame etc* andauernd; **~-minute** *a* in letzter Minute.

latch [lætʃ] *n* Riegel *m*; **~key** Hausschlüssel *m*.

late [leɪt] *a* spät; *zu* spät; (*recent*) jüngste(r, s); (*former*) frühere(r,s); (*dead*) verstorben; *ad* spät; (*after proper time*) zu spät; **to be ~** zu spät kommen; **of ~** in letzter Zeit; **~ in the day** (*lit*) spät; (*fig*) reichlich spät; **~comer** Nachzügler *m*; **~ly** *ad* in letzter Zeit.

lateness ['leɪtnəs] *n* (*of person*) Zuspätkommen *nt*; (*of train*) Verspätung *f*; **~ of the hour** die vorgerückte Stunde.

latent ['leɪtənt] *a* latent.

lateral ['lætərəl] *a* seitlich.

latest ['leɪtɪst] *n* (*news*) Neu(e)ste(s) *nt*; **at the ~** spätestens.

latex ['leɪteks] *n* Milchsaft *m*.

lath [læθ] *n* Latte *f*, Leiste *f*.

lathe [leɪð] *n* Drehbank *f*.

lather ['lɑːðə*] *n* (Seifen)schaum *m*; *vt* einschäumen; *vi* schäumen.

latitude ['lætɪtjuːd] *n* (*Geog*) Breite *f*; (*freedom*) Spielraum *m*.

latrine [lə'triːn] *n* Latrine *f*.

latter ['lætə*] *a* (*second of two*) letztere; (*coming at end*) letzte(r, s), später; **~ly** *ad* in letzter Zeit; **~-day** *a* modern.

lattice work ['lætɪswɜːk] *n* Lattenwerk *nt*, Gitterwerk *nt*.

laudable ['lɔːdəbl] *a* löblich.

laugh [lɑːf] *n* Lachen *nt*; *vi* lachen; **~ at** *vt* lachen über (*+acc*); **~ off** *vt* lachend abtun; **~able** *a* lachhaft; **~ing** *a* lachend;

~ing stock Zielscheibe *f* des Spottes; **~ter** Lachen *nt*, Gelächter *nt*.

launch [lɔːntʃ] *n* (*of ship*) Stapellauf *m*; (*of rocket*) Raketenabschuß *m*; (*boat*) Barkasse *f*; (*pleasure boat*) Vergnügungsboot *nt*; *vt* (*set afloat*) vom Stapel laufen lassen; *rocket* (ab)schießen; (*set going*) in Gang setzen, starten; **~ing** Stapellauf *m*; **~(ing) pad** Abschußrampe *f*.

launder ['lɔːndə*] *vt* waschen und bügeln; **~ette** [lɔːn'dret] Waschsalon *m*.

laundry ['lɔːndrɪ] *n* (*place*) Wäscherei *f*; (*clothes*) Wäsche *f*.

laureate ['lɔːrɪət] *a see* **poet.**

laurel ['lɒrəl] *n* Lorbeer *m*.

lava ['lɑːvə] *n* Lava *f*.

lavatory ['lævətrɪ] *n* Toilette *f*.

lavender ['lævəndə*] *n* Lavendel *m*.

lavish ['lævɪʃ] *a* (*extravagant*) verschwenderisch; (*generous*) großzügig; *vt money* verschwenden (*on* *sb* *+acc*): *attentions, gifts* überschütten mit (*on sb* jdn.); **~ly** *ad* verschwenderisch.

law [lɔː] *n* Gesetz *nt*; (*system*) Recht *nt*; (*of game etc*) Regel *f*; (*as studies*) Jura *no art*; **~-abiding** *a* gesetzestreu; **~breaker** Gesetzesübertreter *m*; **~ court** Gerichtshof *m*; **~ful** *a* gesetzlich, rechtmäßig; **~fully** *ad* rechtmäßig; **~less** *a* gesetzlos.

lawn [lɔːn] *n* Rasen *m*; **~mower** Rasenmäher *m*; **~ tennis** Rasentennis *m*.

law school ['lɔːskuːl] *n* Rechtsakademie *f*.

law student ['lɔːstjuːdənt] *n* Jurastudent *m*.

lawsuit ['lɔːsuːt] *n* Prozeß *m*.

lawyer ['lɔːjə*] *n* Rechtsanwalt *m* Rechtsanwältin *f*.

lax [læks] *a* lax.

laxative ['læksətɪv] *n* Abführmittel *nt*.

laxity ['læksɪtɪ] *n* Laxheit *f*.

lay [leɪ] *a* Laien-; *vt irreg* (*place*) legen; *table* decken; *fire* anrichten; *egg* legen; *trap* stellen; *money* wetten; **~ aside** *vt* zurücklegen; **~ by** *vt* (*set aside*) beiseite legen; **~ down** *vt* hinlegen; *rules* vorschreiben; *arms* strecken; **~ off** *vt workers* (vorübergehend) entlassen; **~ on** *vt* auftragen; *concert etc* veranstalten; **~ out** *vt* (her)auslegen; *money* ausgeben; *corpse* aufbahren; **~ up** *vt* (*store*) aufspeichern; *supplies* anlegen, (*save*) zurücklegen; **~about** Faulenzer *m*; **~-by** Parkbucht *f*; (*bigger*) Rastplatz *m*; **~er** Schicht *f*; **~ette** [leɪ'et] Babyausstattung *f*; **~man** Laie *m*; **~out** Anlage *f*; (*Art*) Layout *nt*.

laze [leɪz] *vi* faulenzen.

lazily ['leɪzɪlɪ] *ad* träge, faul.

laziness ['leɪzɪnəs] *n* Faulheit *f*.

lazy ['leɪzɪ] *a* faul; (*slow-moving*) träge.

lead¹ [led] *n* Blei *nt*; (*of pencil*) (Blei)stift)mine *f*; *a* bleiern, Blei-.

lead² [liːd] *n* (*front position*) Führung *f*; (*distance, time ahead*) Vorsprung *m*; (*example*) Vorbild *nt*; (*clue*) Tip *m*; (*of police*) Spur *f*; (*Theat*) Hauptrolle *f*; (*dog's*) Leine *f*; *irreg vt* (*guide*) führen; *group etc* leiten; *vi* (*be first*) führen; **~ astray** *vt* irreführen; **~ away** *vt* wegführen; *prisoner* abführen; **~ back** *vi* zurückführen; ~ **on** vt anführen; ~ **to** vt (street) (hin)führen nach; (result in) führen zu; ~ **up to** vt (drive) führen zu; (speaker etc) hinführen auf (+ acc); ~**er** Führer m, Leiter m; (of party) Vorsitzende(r) m; (Press) Leitartikel m; ~**ership** (office) Leitung f, (quality) Führerschaft f; ~**ing** a führend; ~**ing lady** (Theat) Hauptdarstellerin f; ~**ing light** (person) führende(r) Geist m; ~**ing man** (Theat) Hauptdarsteller m.

leaf [li:f] n Blatt nt; (of table) Ausziehplatte; ~**let** Blättchen nt; (advertisement) Prospekt m; (pamphlet) Flugblatt nt; (for information) Merkblatt nt; ~**y** a belaubt.

league [li:g] n (union) Bund m, Liga f; (Sport) Liga f, Tabelle f; (measure) 3 englische Meilen.

leak [li:k] n undichte Stelle f; (in ship) Leck nt; vt liquid etc durchlassen; vi (pipe etc) undicht sein; (liquid etc) auslaufen; ~ **out** vi (liquid etc) auslaufen; (information) durchsickern.

leaky ['li:kɪ] a undicht.

lean [li:n] a mager; n Magere(s) nt; irreg vi sich neigen; **to ~ against sth** an etw (dat) angelehnt sein; sich an etw (acc) anlehnen; vt (an)lehnen; ~ **back** vi sich zurücklehnen; ~ **forward** vi sich vorbeugen; ~ **on** vi sich stützen auf (+acc); ~ **over** vi sich hinüberbeugen; ~ **towards** vi neigen zu; ~**ing** Neigung f; ~**-to** Anbau m.

leap [li:p] n Sprung m; vi irreg springen; by ~**s and bounds** schnell; ~**frog** Bockspringen nt; ~ **year** Schaltjahr nt.

learn [lɜːn] vti irreg lernen; (find out) erfahren, hören; ~**ed** ['lɜːnɪd] a gelehrt; ~**er** Anfänger(in f) m; (Aut) Fahrschüler(in f) m; ~**ing** Gelehrsamkeit f.

lease [li:s] n (of property) Mietvertrag m; (of land) Pachtvertrag m; vt mieten; pachten.

leash [li:ʃ] n Leine f.

least [li:st] a kleinste(r, s); (slightest) geringste(r, s); n Mindeste(s) nt; **at ~** zumindest; **not in the ~!** durchaus nicht!

leather ['leðə*] n Leder nt; a ledern, Leder-; ~**y** a zäh, ledern.

leave [li:v] irreg vt verlassen; (— behind) zurücklassen; (forget) vergessen; (allow to remain) lassen; (after death) hinterlassen; (entrust) überlassen (to sb jdm); **to be left** (remain) übrigbleiben; vi weggehen, wegfahren; (for journey) abreisen; (bus, train) abfahren; n Erlaubnis f; (Mil) Urlaub m; **on ~** auf Urlaub; **to take one's ~ of** Abschied nehmen von; ~ **off** vi aufhören; ~ **out** vt auslassen.

lecherous ['letʃərəs] a lüstern.

lectern ['lektɜːn] n Lesepult nt.

lecture ['lektʃə*] n Vortrag m; (Univ) Vorlesung f; vi einen Vortrag halten; (Univ) lesen; ~**r** Vortragende(r) mf; (Univ) Dozent(in f) m.

ledge [ledʒ] n Leiste f; (window —) Sims m or nt; (of mountain) (Fels)vorsprung m.

ledger ['ledʒə*] n Hauptbuch nt.

lee [li:] n Windschatten m; (Naut) Lee f.

leech [li:tʃ] n Blutegel m.

leek [li:k] n Lauch m.

leer [lɪə*] n schiefe(r) Blick m; vi schielen (at nach).

leeway ['li:weɪ] n (fig) Rückstand m; (freedom) Spielraum m.

left [left] a link(s); ad links; nach links; n (side) linke Seite f; **the L~** (Pol) die Linke f; ~**-hand drive** Linkssteuerung f; ~**-handed** a linkshändig; ~**-hand side** linke Seite f; ~**-luggage (office)** Gepäckaufbewahrung f; ~**-overs** pl Reste pl, Überbleibsel pl; ~ **wing** linke(r) Flügel m; ~**-wing** a linke(r, s).

leg [leg] n Bein nt; (of meat) Keule f, (stage) Etappe f.

legacy ['legəsɪ] n Erbe nt, Erbschaft f.

legal ['li:gəl] a gesetzlich, rechtlich; (allowed) legal, rechtsgültig; **to take ~ action** prozessieren; ~**ize** vt legalisieren; ~**ly** ad gesetzlich; legal; ~ **tender** gesetzliche(s) Zahlungsmittel nt.

legation [lɪ'geɪʃən] n Gesandtschaft f.

legend ['ledʒənd] n Legende f; ~**ary** a legendär.

-legged ['legɪd] a -beinig.

leggings ['legɪŋz] npl (hohe) Gamaschen pl; (for baby) Gamaschenhose f.

legibility [ledʒɪ'bɪlɪtɪ] n Leserlichkeit f.

legible a, **legibly** ad ['ledʒəbl, -blɪ] leserlich.

legion ['li:dʒən] n Legion f.

legislate ['ledʒɪsleɪt] vi Gesetze geben.

legislation [ledʒɪs'leɪʃən] n Gesetzgebung f.

legislative ['ledʒɪslətɪv] a gesetzgebend.

legislator ['ledʒɪsleɪtə*] n Gesetzgeber m.

legislature ['ledʒɪslətʃə*] n Legislative f.

legitimacy [lɪ'dʒɪtɪməsɪ] n Rechtmäßigkeit f; (of birth) Ehelichkeit f.

legitimate [lɪ'dʒɪtɪmət] a rechtmäßig, legitim; child ehelich.

legroom ['legrum] n Platz m für die Beine.

leisure ['leʒə*] n Freizeit f, Freizeit-; **to be at ~** Zeit haben; ~**ly** a gemächlich.

lemming ['lemɪŋ] n Lemming m.

lemon ['lemən] n Zitrone f; (colour) Zitronengelb nt; ~**ade** [lemə'neɪd] Limonade f.

lend [lend] vt irreg leihen; **to ~ sb sth** jdm etw leihen; **it ~s itself to** es eignet sich zu; ~**er** Verleiher m; ~**ing library** Leihbibliothek f.

length [leŋθ] n Länge f; (section of road, pipe etc) Strecke f; (of material) Stück nt; ~ **of time** Zeitdauer f; **at ~** (lengthily) ausführlich; (at last) schließlich; ~**en** vt verlängern; vi länger werden; ~**ways** ad längs; ~**y** a sehr lang; langatmig.

leniency ['li:nɪənsɪ] n Nachsicht f.

lenient ['li:nɪənt] a nachsichtig; ~**ly** ad milde.

lens [lenz] n Linse f; (Phot) Objektiv nt.

Lent [lent] n Fastenzeit f.

lentil ['lentɪl] n Linse f.

Leo ['li:əʊ] n Löwe m.

leopard ['lepəd] n Leopard m.

leotard ['li:əta:d] n Trikot nt, Gymnastikanzug m.

leper ['lepə*] n Leprakranke(r) mf.

leprosy ['leprəsɪ] n Lepra f.

lesbian ['lezbɪən] a lesbisch; n Lesbierin f.

less [les] a, ad, n weniger.

lessen ['lesn] vi abnehmen; vt verringern, verkleinern.

lesser ['lesə*] a kleiner, geringer.

lesson ['lesn] n (Sch) Stunde f; (unit of study) Lektion f; (fig) Lehre f; (Eccl) Lesung f; ~**s start at 9** der Unterricht beginnt um 9.

lest [lest] cj damit ... nicht.

let [let] n: **without ~ or hindrance** völlig unbehindert; vt irreg lassen; (lease) vermieten; ~**'s go!** gehen wir!; ~ **down** vt hinunterlassen; (disappoint) enttäuschen; ~ **go** vi loslassen; vt things loslassen; person gehen lassen; ~ **off** vt gun abfeuern; steam ablassen; (forgive) laufen lassen; ~ **out** vt herauslassen; scream fahren lassen; ~ **up** vi nachlassen; (stop) aufhören; ~**down** Enttäuschung f.

lethal ['li:θəl] a tödlich.

lethargic [le'θɑːdʒɪk] a lethargisch, träge.

lethargy ['leθədʒɪ] n Lethargie f, Teilnahmslosigkeit f.

letter ['letə*] n (of alphabet) Buchstabe m; (message) Brief m; ~**s** pl (literature) (schöne) Literatur f; ~**box** Briefkasten m; ~**ing** Beschriftung f.

lettuce ['letɪs] n (Kopf)salat m.

let-up ['letʌp] n (col) Nachlassen nt.

leukaemia, (US) **leukemia** [luː'kiːmɪə] n Leukämie f.

level ['levl] n a ground eben; (of same height) auf gleicher Höhe; (equal) gleich gut; head kühl; **to do one's ~ best** sein möglichstes tun; ad auf gleicher Höhe; **to draw ~ with** gleichziehen mit; n (instrument) Wasserwaage f; (altitude) Höhe f; (flat place) ebene Fläche f; (position on scale) Niveau nt; (amount, degree) Grad m; **talks on a high ~** Gespräche auf hoher Ebene; **profits keep on the same ~** Gewinne halten sich auf dem gleichen Stand; **on the moral ~** aus moralischer Sicht; **on the ~** (lit) auf gleicher Höhe; (fig: honest) ehrlich; vt ground einebnen; building abreißen; town dem Erdboden gleichmachen; blow versetzen (at sb jdm.); remark richten (at gegen); ~ **off** or **out** vi flach or eben werden; (fig) sich ausgleichen; (plane) horizontal fliegen; vt ground planieren; differences ausgleichen; ~ **crossing** Bahnübergang m; ~**headed** a vernünftig.

lever ['liːvə*], (US) ['levə*] n Hebel m; (fig) Druckmittel nt; vt (hoch)stemmen; ~**age** Hebelkraft f; (fig) Einfluß m.

levity ['levɪtɪ] n Leichtfertigkeit f.

levy ['levɪ] n (of taxes) Erhebung f; (tax) Abgaben pl; (Mil) Aushebung f; vt erheben; (Mil) ausheben.

lewd [luːd] a unzüchtig, unanständig.

liability [laɪə'bɪlɪtɪ] n (burden) Belastung f; (duty) Pflicht f; (debt) Verpflichtung f; (proneness) Anfälligkeit f; (responsibility) Haftung f.

liable ['laɪəbl] a (responsible) haftbar; (prone) anfällig; **to be ~ for** etw (dat) unterliegen; **it's ~ to happen** es kann leicht vorkommen.

liaison [liː'eɪzɒn] n Verbindung f.

liar ['laɪə*] n Lügner m.

libel ['laɪbəl] n Verleumdung f; vt verleumden; ~**(l)ous** a verleumderisch.

liberal ['lɪbərəl] a (generous) großzügig; (open-minded) aufgeschlossen; (Pol) liberal; n liberal denkende(r) Mensch m; **L~** (Pol) Liberale(r) mf; ~**ly** ad (abundantly) reichlich.

liberate ['lɪbəreɪt] vt befreien.

liberation [lɪbə'reɪʃən] n Befreiung f.

liberty ['lɪbətɪ] n Freiheit f; (permission) Erlaubnis f; **to be at ~ to do sth** etw tun dürfen; **to take liberties with** sich (dat) Freiheiten herausnehmen gegenüber (+dat).

Libra ['liːbrə] n Waage f.

librarian [laɪ'breərɪən] n Bibliothekar(in f) m.

library ['laɪbrərɪ] n Bibliothek f; (lending ~) Bücherei f.

libretto [lɪ'bretəʊ] n Libretto nt.

lice [laɪs] npl of **louse**.

licence, (US) **license** ['laɪsəns] n (permit) Erlaubnis f, amtliche Zulassung f; (driving ~) Führerschein m; (excess) Zügellosigkeit f; ~ **plate** (US Aut) Nummernschild nt.

license ['laɪsəns] vt genehmigen, konzessionieren; ~**e** [laɪsən'siː] n Konzessionsinhaber m.

licentious [laɪ'senʃəs] a ausschweifend.

lichen ['laɪkən] n Flechte f.

lick [lɪk] vt lecken; vi (flames) züngeln; n Lecken nt; (small amount) Spur f.

licorice ['lɪkərɪs] n Lakritze f.

lid [lɪd] n Deckel m; (eye~) Lid nt.

lido ['liːdəʊ] n Freibad nt.

lie [laɪ] n Lüge f; vi lügen; irreg (rest, be situated) liegen; (put o.s. in position) sich legen; **to ~ idle** stillstehen; ~ **detector** Lügendetektor m.

lieu [luː] n: **in ~ of** anstatt (+gen).

lieutenant [lef'tenənt], (US) [luː'tenənt] n Leutnant m.

life [laɪf] n Leben nt; (story) Lebensgeschichte f; (energy) Lebendigkeit f; ~ **assurance** Lebensversicherung f; ~**belt** Rettungsring m; ~**boat** Rettungsboot nt; ~**guard** Badewärter m; Rettungsschwimmer m; ~ **jacket** Schwimmweste f; ~**less** a (dead) leblos, tot; (dull) langweilig; ~**like** a lebenswahr, naturgetreu; ~**line** (lit) Rettungsleine f; (fig) Rettungsanker m; ~**long** a lebenslang; ~ **preserver** Totschläger m; ~**raft** Rettungsfloß nt; ~**-sized** a in Lebensgröße; ~ **span** Lebensspanne f; ~**time** Lebenszeit f.

lift [lɪft] vt hochheben; vi sich heben; n (raising) (Hoch)heben nt; (elevator) Aufzug m, Lift m; **to give sb a ~** jdn mitnehmen; ~**-off** Abheben nt (vom Boden).

ligament ['lɪgəmənt] n Sehne f, Band nt.

light [laɪt] n Licht nt; (lamp) Lampe f; (flame) Feuer nt; ~**s** pl (Aut) Beleuchtung f; **in the ~ of** angesichts (+gen); vt irreg beleuchten; lamp anmachen; fire, cigarette anzünden; (brighten) erleuchten, erhellen; a (bright) hell, licht; (pale) hell-; (not heavy, easy) leicht; punishment milde; taxes niedrig; touch leicht; ~ **up** vi (lamp) angehen; (face) aufleuchten; vt (illuminate)

beleuchten; *lights* anmachen; ~ **bulb**
Glühbirne *f;* ~**en** *vi (brighten)* hell
werden; *(lightning)* blitzen; *vt (give light to)*
erhellen; *hair* aufhellen; *gloom* aufheitern;
(make less heavy) leichter machen; *(fig)*
erleichtern; ~**er** *(cigarette —)* Feuerzeug
nt; (boat) Leichter *m;* ~-**headed** *a*
(thoughtless) leichtsinnig; *(giddy)*
schwindlig; ~-**hearted** *a* leichtherzig,
fröhlich; ~-**house** Leuchtturm *m;* ~**ing**
Beleuchtung *f;* ~**ing-up time** Zeit *f* des
Einschaltens der Straßen-/Auto-
beleuchtung; ~**ly** *ad* leicht; *(irresponsibly)*
leichtfertig; ~ **meter** *(Phot)* Belichtungsmesser *m;* ~**ness** *(of weight)* Leichtigkeit
f; (of colour) Helle *f; (light)* Helligkeit *f;*
~**ning** Blitz *m;* ~**ning conductor** Blitz-
ableiter *m;* ~**weight** *a suit* leicht;
~**weight boxer** Leichtgewicht *nt;*
~**year** Lichtjahr *nt.*

lignite ['lıgnaıt] *n* Lignit *m.*

like [laık] *vt* mögen, gernhaben; **would**
you ~ ...? hatten Sie gern ...?; **would you**
~ **to ...?** möchten Sie gern...?; *prep* wie;
what's it/he ~? wie ist es/er?; **that's**
just ~ **him** das sieht ihm ähnlich; ~
that/this so; *a (similar)* ähnlich; *(equal)*
gleich; *n* Gleiche(s) *nt;* ~**able** *a*
sympathisch; ~**lihood** Wahrscheinlichkeit *f;* ~**ly** *a (probable)* wahrscheinlich; *(suitable)* geeignet; *ad* wahrscheinlich;
~-**minded** *a* gleichgesinnt; ~**n** *vt*
vergleichen *(to* mit;*)* ~**wise** *ad* ebenfalls.

liking ['laıkıŋ] *n* Zuneigung *f; (taste for)*
Vorliebe *f.*

lilac ['laılək] *n* Flieder *m.*

lilting [lıltıŋ] *a accent* singend; *tune*
munter.

lily ['lılı] *n* Lilie *f;* ~ **of the valley** Mai-
glöckchen *nt.*

limb [lım] *n* Glied *nt.*

limber ['lımbə*]:* ~ **up** *vi* sich auflockern;
(fig) sich vorbereiten.

limbo ['lımbəʊ] *n:* **to be in** ~ *(fig)* in der
Schwebe sein.

lime [laım] *n (tree)* Linde *f; (fruit)* Limone *f;*
(substance) Kalk *m;* ~ **juice** Limonensaft
m; ~**light** *(fig)* Rampenlicht *nt.*

limerick ['lımərık] *n* Limerick *m.*

limestone ['laımstəʊn] *n* Kalkstein *m.*

limit ['lımıt] *n* Grenze *f; (col)* Höhe *f; vt*
begrenzen, einschränken; ~**ation**
Grenzen *pl,* Einschränkung *f;* ~**ed** *a*
beschränkt; ~**ed company** Gesellschaft *f*
mit beschränkter Haftung, GmbH *f.*

limousine ['lıməzi:n] *n* Limousine *f.*

limp [lımp] *n* Hinken *nt; vi* hinken; *a*
(without firmness) schlaff.

limpet ['lımpıt] *n (lit)* Napfschnecke *f; (fig)*
Klette *f.*

limpid ['lımpıd] *a* klar.

limply ['lımplı] *ad* schlaff.

line [laın] *n* Linie *f; (rope)* Leine *f,* Schnur *f;*
(on face) Falte *f; (row)* Reihe *f; (of hills)*
Kette *f; (US: queue)* Schlange *f; (of goods)*
Linie *f,* Gesellschaft *f; (Rail)* Strecke *f; (pl)*
Geleise *pl; (Tel)* Leitung *f; (written)* Zeile *f;*
(direction) Richtung *f; (fig: business)*
Branche *f;* Beruf *m; (range of items)* Kollek-
tion *f;* **it's a bad** ~ *(Tel)* die Verbindung

ist schlecht; **hold the** ~ bleiben Sie am
Apparat; **in** ~ **with** in Übereinstimmung
mit; *vt coat* füttern; *(border)* säumen; ~ **up**
vi sich aufstellen; *vt* aufstellen; *(prepare)*
sorgen für; *support* mobilisieren; *surprise*
planen.

linear ['lınıə*] *a* gerade; *(measure)*
Längen-.

linen ['lının] *n* Leinen *nt; (sheets etc)*
Wäsche *f.*

liner ['laınə*] *n* Überseedampfer *m.*

linesman ['laınzmən] *n (Sport)* Linien-
richter *m.*

line-up ['laınʌp] *n* Aufstellung *f.*

linger ['lıŋgə*] *vi (remain long)* verweilen;
(taste) (zurück)bleiben; *(delay)* zögern,
verharren.

lingerie ['læ̃ʒɔri:] *n* Damenunterwäsche
f.

lingering ['lıŋgərıŋ] *a* lang; *doubt* zurück-
bleibend; *disease* langwierig; *taste* nach-
haltend; *look* lang.

lingo ['lıŋgəʊ] *n (col)* Sprache *f.*

linguist ['lıŋgwıst] *n* Sprachkundige(r) *mf;*
(Univ) Sprachwissenschaftler(in *f) m.*

linguistic [lıŋ'gwıstıc] *a* sprachlich;
sprachwissenschaftlich; ~**s** Sprach-
wissenschaft *f,* Linguistik *f.*

liniment ['lınımənt] *n* Einreibemittel *nt.*

lining ['laınıŋ] *n (of clothes)* Futter *nt.*

link [lıŋk] *n (of chain)* Glied *nt; (connection)* Verbindung *f; vt* verbinden; ~**s** *pl* Golfplatz *m;*
~-**up** *(Tel)* Verbindung *f; (of spaceships)*
Kopplung *f.*

lino ['laınəʊ] *n,* **linoleum** [lı'nəʊlıəm] *n*
Linoleum *nt.*

linseed oil ['lınsi:d'ɔıl] *n* Leinöl *nt.*

lint [lınt] *n* Verbandstoff *m.*

lintel ['lıntl] *n (Archit)* Sturz *m.*

lion ['laıən] *n* Löwe *m;* ~**ess** Löwin *f.*

lip [lıp] *n* Lippe *f; (of jug)* Tülle *f,* Schnabel
m; ~**read** *vi irreg* von den Lippen
ablesen; **to pay** ~ **service (to)** ein
Lippenbekenntnis ablegen (zu); ~**stick**
Lippenstift *m.*

liquefy ['lıkwıfaı] *vt* verflüssigen.

liqueur [lı'kjʊə*] *n* Likör *m.*

liquid ['lıkwıd] *n* Flüßigkeit *f;* ~
~**ate** *vt* liquidieren; ~**ation** Liquidation
f.

liquor ['lıkə*] *n* Alkohol *m,* Spirituosen *pl.*

lisp [lısp] *n* Lispeln *nt; vti* lispeln.

list [lıst] *n* Liste *f,* Verzeichnis *nt; (of ship)*
Schlagseite *f; vt (write down)* eine Liste
machen von; *(verbally)* aufzählen; *vi (ship)*
Schlagseite haben.

listen ['lısn] *vi* hören, horchen; ~ **to** *vt*
zuhören (+ *dat);* ~**er** (Zu)hörer(in *f) m.*

listless *a,* ~**ly** *ad* ['lıstləs, -lı] lustlos, teilnahmslos; ~**ness** Lustlosigkeit *f,* Teilnahmslosigkeit *f.*

litany ['lıtənı] *n* Litanei *f.*

literacy ['lıtərəsı] *n* Fähigkeit *f* zu lesen
und zu schreiben.

literal ['lıtərəl] *a* eigentlich, buchstäblich;
translation wortwörtlich; ~**ly** *ad* wörtlich;
buchstäblich.

literary ['lıtərərı] *a* literarisch, Literatur-.

literate ['lɪtərət] a des Lesens und Schreibens kundig.

literature ['lɪtrətʃə*] n Literatur f.

lithograph ['lɪθəʊgrɑːf] n Lithographie f.

litigate ['lɪtɪgeɪt] vi prozessieren.

litmus ['lɪtməs] n: ~ **paper** Lackmuspapier nt.

litre, (US) **liter** ['liːtə*] n Liter m.

litter ['lɪtə*] n (rubbish) Abfall m; (of animals) Wurf m; vt in Unordnung bringen; **to be** ~**ed with** übersät sein mit.

little ['lɪtl] a klein; (unimportant) unbedeutend; ad, n wenig; **a** ~ ein bißchen; **the** ~ das wenige.

liturgy ['lɪtədʒɪ] n Liturgie f.

live¹ [lɪv] vi leben; (last) fortleben; (dwell) wohnen; vt life führen; ~ **down** vt Gras wachsen lassen über (+acc); **I'll never** ~ **it down** das wird man mir nie vergessen; ~ **on** vi weiterleben; ~ **on sth** von etw leben; ~ **up to** vt standards gerecht werden (+dat); principles anstreben; hopes entsprechen (+dat).

live² [laɪv] a lebendig; (burning) glühend; (Mil) scharf; (Elec) geladen; broadcast live.

livelihood ['laɪvlɪhʊd] n Lebensunterhalt m.

liveliness ['laɪvlɪnəs] n Lebendigkeit f.

lively ['laɪvlɪ] a lebhaft, lebendig.

liver ['lɪvə*] n (Anat) Leber f; ~**ish** a (badtempered) gallig.

livery ['lɪvərɪ] n Livree f.

livestock ['laɪvstɒk] n Vieh nt, Viehbestand m.

livid ['lɪvɪd] a (lit) bläulich; (furious) fuchsteufelswild.

living ['lɪvɪŋ] n (Lebens)unterhalt m; a lebendig; language etc lebend; wage ausreichend; ~ **room** n Wohnzimmer nt.

lizard ['lɪzəd] n Eidechse f.

llama ['lɑːmə] n Lama nt.

load [ləʊd] n (burden) Last f; (amount) Ladung f, Fuhre f; ~**s of** (col) massenhaft; vt (be)laden; (fig) überhäufen; camera Film einlegen in (+acc); gun laden.

loaf [ləʊf] n Brot nt, Laib m; vi herumlungern, faulenzen.

loam [ləʊm] n Lehmboden m.

loan [ləʊn] n Leihgabe f; (Fin) Darlehen nt; vt leihen; **on** ~ geliehen.

loathe [ləʊð] vt verabscheuen.

loathing ['ləʊðɪŋ] n Abscheu f.

lobby ['lɒbɪ] n Vorhalle f; (Pol) Lobby f; vt politisch beeinflussen (wollen).

lobe [ləʊb] n Ohrläppchen nt.

lobster ['lɒbstə*] n Hummer m.

local ['ləʊkəl] a ortsansässig, hiesig, Orts-; anaesthetic örtlich; n (pub) Stammwirtschaft f; **the** ~**s** pl die Ortsansässigen pl; ~ **colour** Lokalkolorit nt; ~**ity** [ləʊ'kælɪtɪ] n Ort m; ~**ly** ad örtlich, am Ort.

locate [ləʊ'keɪt] vt ausfindig machen; (establish) errichten.

location [ləʊ'keɪʃən] n Platz m, Lage f; **on** ~ (Cine) auf Außenaufnahme.

loch [lɒx] n (Scot) See m.

lock [lɒk] n Schloß nt; (Naut) Schleuse f; (of hair) Locke f; vt (fasten) (ver)schließen; vi

(door etc) sich schließen (lassen); (wheels) blockieren.

locker ['lɒkə*] n Spind m.

locket ['lɒkɪt] n Medaillon nt.

locomotive [ləʊkə'məʊtɪv] n Lokomotive f.

locust ['ləʊkəst] n Heuschrecke f.

lodge [lɒdʒ] n (gatehouse) Pförtnerhaus nt; (freemasons') Loge f; vi (in Untermiete) wohnen (with bei); (get stuck) stecken(bleiben); vt protest einreichen; ~**r** (Unter)mieter m.

lodgings ['lɒdʒɪŋz] n (Miet)wohnung f; Zimmer nt.

loft [lɒft] n (Dach)boden m.

lofty ['lɒftɪ] a hoch(ragend); (proud) hochmütig.

log [lɒg] n Klotz m; (Naut) Log nt.

logarithm ['lɒgərɪθəm] n Logarithmus m.

logbook ['lɒgbʊk] n Bordbuch nt, Logbuch nt; (for lorry) Fahrtenschreiber m; (Aut) Kraftfahrzeugbrief m.

loggerheads ['lɒgəhedz] n: **to be at** ~ sich im Haaren liegen.

logic ['lɒdʒɪk] n Logik f; ~**al** a logisch; ~**ally** ad logisch(erweise).

logistics [lɒ'dʒɪstɪks] npl Logistik f.

loin [lɔɪn] n Lende f.

loiter ['lɔɪtə*] vi herumstehen, sich herumtreiben.

loll [lɒl] vi sich rekeln.

lollipop ['lɒlɪpɒp] n (Dauer)lutscher m.

lone [ləʊn] a einsam.

loneliness ['ləʊnlɪnəs] n Einsamkeit f.

lonely ['ləʊnlɪ] a einsam.

long [lɒŋ] a lang; distance weit; ad lange; **two-day-** ~ zwei Tage lang; vi sich sehnen (for nach); ~ **ago** vor langer Zeit; **before** ~ bald; **as** ~ **as** solange; **in the** ~ **run** auf die Dauer; ~**-distance** a Fern-; ~**-haired** a langhaarig; ~**hand** Langschrift f; ~**ing** Verlangen nt, Sehnsucht f; a sehnsüchtig; ~**ish** a ziemlich lang; ~**itude** Längengrad m; ~**jump** Weitsprung m; ~**-lost** a längst verloren geglaubt; ~**-playing** record Langspielplatte f; ~**-range** a Langstrecken-, Fern-; ~**-sighted** a weitsichtig; ~**-standing** a alt, seit langer Zeit bestehend; ~**-suffering** a schwer geprüft; ~**-term** a langfristig; ~ **wave** Langwelle f; ~**-winded** a langatmig.

loo [luː] n (col) Klo nt.

loofah ['luːfə*] n (plant) Luffa f; (sponge) Luffa(schwamm) m.

look [lʊk] vi schauen, blicken; (seem) aussehen; (face) liegen nach, gerichtet sein nach; n Blick m; ~**s** pl Aussehen nt; ~ **after** vt (care for) sorgen für; (watch) aufpassen auf (+acc); ~ **down on** vt (fig) herabsehen auf (+acc); ~ **for** vt (seek) suchen (nach); (expect) erwarten; ~ **forward to** vt sich freuen auf (+acc); ~ **out for** vt Ausschau halten nach; (be careful) achtgeben auf (+acc); ~ **to** vt (take care of) achtgeben auf (+acc); (rely on) sich verlassen auf (+acc); ~ **up** vi aufblicken; (improve) sich bessern; vt word nachschlagen; person besuchen; ~ **up to** vt aufsehen zu; ~**-out** (watch) Ausschau f;

(person) Wachposten *m; (place)* Ausguck *m; (prospect)* Aussichten *pl.*

loom [lu:m] *n* Webstuhl *m; vi* sich abzeichnen.

loop [lu:p] *n* Schlaufe *f,* Schleife *f; vt* schlingen; ~**hole** *(fig)* Hintertürchen *nt.*

loose [lu:s] *a* lose, locker; *(free)* frei; *(inexact)* unpräzise; *vt* lösen, losbinden; **to be at a ~ end** nicht wissen, was man tun soll; ~**ly** *ad* locker, lose; ~**ly speaking** grob gesagt; ~**n** *vt* lockern, losmachen; ~**ness** Lockerheit *f.*

loot [lu:t] *n* Beute *f; vt* plündern; ~**ing** Plünderung *f.*

lop [lɒp]: ~ **off** *vt* abhacken.

lop-sided ['lɒp'saidid] *a* schief.

lord [lɔ:d] *n (ruler)* Herr *m,* Gebieter *m; (Brit, title)* Lord *m;* **the L~** *(Gott)* der Herr *m;* ~**ly** *a* vornehm; *(proud)* stolz.

lore [lɔ:*] *n* Überlieferung *f.*

lorry ['lɒri] *n* Lastwagen *m.*

lose [lu:z] *irreg vt* verlieren; *chance* verpassen; ~ **out** on zu kurz kommen bei; *vi* verlieren; ~**r** Verlierer *m.*

losing ['lu:ziŋ] *a* Verlierer-; *(Comm)* verlustbringend.

loss [lɒs] *n* Verlust *m;* **at a ~** *(Comm)* mit Verlust; *(unable)* außerstande; **I am at a ~ for words** mir fehlen die Worte.

lost [lɒst] *a* verloren; ~ **cause** aussichtslose Sache *f;* ~ **property** Fundsachen *pl.*

lot [lɒt] *n (quantity)* Menge *f; (fate, at auction)* Los *nt; (col: people, things)* Haufen *m;* the ~ alles; *(people)* alle; a ~ of viel; *pl* viele; ~**s of** massenhaft, viel(e).

lotion ['ləʊʃən] *n* Lotion *f.*

lottery ['lɒtəri] *n* Lotterie *f.*

loud [laʊd] *a* laut; *(showy)* schreiend; *ad* laut; ~**ly** *ad* laut; ~**ness** Lautheit *f;* ~**speaker** Lautsprecher *m.*

lounge [laʊndʒ] *n (in hotel)* Gesellschaftsraum *m; (in house)* Wohnzimmer *nt; (on ship)* Salon *m; vi* sich herumlümmeln; ~**suit** Straßenanzug *m.*

louse [laʊs] *n* Laus *f.*

lousy ['laʊzi] *a (lit)* verlaust; *(fig)* lausig, miserabel.

lout [laʊt] *n* Lümmel *m.*

lovable ['lʌvəbl] *a* liebenswert.

love [lʌv] *n* Liebe *f; (person)* Liebling *m,* Schatz *m; (Sport)* null; *vt person* lieben; *activity* gerne mögen; **to ~ to do sth** etw *(sehr)* gerne tun; **to make ~** sich lieben; **to make ~ to/with sb** jdn lieben; ~ **affair** (Liebes)verhältnis *nt;* ~ **letter** Liebesbrief *m;* ~ **life** Liebesleben *nt;* ~**ly** *a* schön; *person, object also* entzückend, reizend; ~**-making** Liebe *f;* ~**r** Liebhaber *m;* Geliebte *f; (of books etc)* Liebhaber *m;* **the** ~**rs** die Liebenden, das Liebespaar; ~**song** Liebeslied *nt.*

loving ['lʌviŋ] *a* liebend, liebevoll; ~**ly** *ad* liebevoll.

low [ləʊ] *a* niedrig; *rank* niedere(r, s); *level, note, neckline* tief; *intelligence, density* gering; *(vulgar)* ordinär; *(not loud)* leise; *(depressed)* gedrückt; *ad (not high)* niedrig; *(not loudly)* leise; *n (low point)* Tiefstand *m;*

(Met) Tief *nt;* ~**-cut** *a dress* tiefausgeschnitten.

lower ['ləʊə*] *vt* herunterlassen; *eyes, gun* senken; *(reduce)* herabsetzen, senken.

lowly ['ləʊli] *a* bescheiden.

loyal ['lɔɪəl] *a (true)* treu; *(to king)* loyal, treu; ~**ly** *ad* treu; loyal; ~**ty** Treue *f;* Loyalität *f.*

lozenge ['lɒzɪndʒ] *n* Pastille *f.*

lubricant ['lu:brɪkənt] *n* Schmiermittel *nt.*

lubricate ['lu:brɪkeɪt] *vt* (ab)schmieren, ölen.

lubrication [lu:brɪ'keɪʃən] *n* (Ein- or Ab)schmierung *f.*

lucid ['lu:sɪd] *a* klar; *(sane)* bei klarem Verstand; *moment* licht; ~**ity** [lu:'sɪdɪtɪ] Klarheit *f;* ~**ly** *ad* klar.

luck [lʌk] *n* Glück *nt;* **bad ~** Pech *nt;* ~**ily** *ad* glücklicherweise, zum Glück; ~**y** *a* glücklich, Glücks-; **to be ~** Glück haben.

lucrative ['lu:krətɪv] *a* einträglich.

ludicrous ['lu:dɪkrəs] *a* grotesk.

ludo ['lu:dəʊ] *n* Mensch ärgere dich nicht *nt.*

lug [lʌg] *vt* schleppen.

luggage ['lʌgɪdʒ] *n* Gepäck *nt;* ~ **rack** Gepäcknetz *nt.*

lugubrious [lu:'gu:brɪəs] *a* traurig.

lukewarm ['lu:kwɔ:m] *a* lauwarm; *(indifferent)* lau.

lull [lʌl] *n* Flaute *f; vt* einlullen; *(calm)* beruhigen; ~**aby** ['lʌləbaɪ] Schlaflied *nt.*

lumbago [lʌm'beɪgəʊ] *n* Hexenschuß *m.*

lumber ['lʌmbə*] *n* Plunder *m; (wood)* Holz *nt;* ~**jack** Holzfäller *m.*

luminous ['lu:mɪnəs] *a* leuchtend, Leucht-.

lump [lʌmp] *n* Klumpen *m; (Med)* Schwellung *f; (in breast)* Knoten *m; (of sugar)* Stück *nt; vt* zusammentun; *(judge together)* in einen Topf werfen; ~ **sum** Pauschalsumme *f;* ~**y** klumpig; **to go ~y** klumpen.

lunacy ['lu:nəsɪ] *n* Irrsinn *m.*

lunar ['lu:nə*] *a* Mond-.

lunatic ['lu:nətɪk] *n* Wahnsinnige(r) *mf; a* wahnsinnig, irr.

lunch [lʌntʃ] *n (also* ~**eon** [-ən]) Mittagessen *nt;* ~ **hour** Mittagspause *f;* ~**time** Mittagszeit *f;* ~**eon meat** Frühstücksfleisch *nt.*

lung [lʌŋ] *n* Lunge *f;* ~ **cancer** Lungenkrebs *m.*

lunge [lʌndʒ] *vi* (los)stürzen.

lupin ['lu:pɪn] *n* Lupine *f.*

lurch [lɜ:tʃ] *vi* taumeln; *(Naut)* schlingern; *n* Taumeln *nt; (Naut)* plötzliche(s) Schlingern *nt.*

lure [ljʊə*] *n* Köder *m; (fig)* Lockung *f; vt* (ver)locken.

lurid ['ljʊərɪd] *a (shocking)* grausig, widerlich; *colour* grell.

lurk [lɜ:k] *vi* lauern.

luscious ['lʌʃəs] *a* köstlich; *colour* satt.

lush [lʌʃ] *a* satt; *vegetation* üppig.

lust [lʌst] *n* sinnliche Begierde *f (for* nach); *(sensation)* Wollust *f; (greed)* Gier *f; vi* gieren *(after* nach); ~**ful** *a* wollüstig, lüstern.

lustre, *(US)* **luster** ['lʌstə*] *n* Glanz *m.*

lusty ['lʌstɪ] a gesund und munter; *old person* rüstig.

lute [luːt] n Laute f.

luxuriant [lʌg'zjuərɪənt] a üppig.

luxurious [lʌg'zjuərɪəs] a luxuriös, Luxus-.

luxury ['lʌkʃərɪ] n Luxus m; **the little luxuries** die kleinen Genüsse.

lying ['laɪɪŋ] n Lügen nt; a verlogen.

lynch [lɪntʃ] vt lynchen.

lynx [lɪŋks] n Luchs m.

lyre ['laɪə*] n Leier f.

lyric ['lɪrɪk] n Lyrik f; (pl: words for song) (Lied)text m; a lyrisch; ~al a lyrisch, gefühlvoll.

M

M, m [em] n M nt, m nt.

mac [mæk] n (Brit col) Regenmantel m.

macabre [mə'kɑːbr] a makaber.

macaroni [mækə'rəʊnɪ] n Makkaroni pl.

mace [meɪs] n Amtsstab m; (spice) Muskat m.

machine [mə'ʃiːn] n Maschine f; vt dress etc mit der Maschine nähen; maschinell herstellen/bearbeiten; ~**gun** Maschinengewehr nt; ~**ry** [mə'ʃiːnərɪ] Maschinerie f, Maschinen pl; ~ **tool** Werkzeugmaschine f.

machinist [mə'ʃiːnɪst] n Machinist m.

mackerel ['mækrəl] n Makrele f.

mackintosh ['mækɪntɒʃ] n Regenmantel m.

macro- ['mækrəʊ] pref Makro-, makro-.

mad [mæd] a verrückt; dog tollwütig; (angry) wütend; ~ **about** (fond of) verrückt nach, versessen auf (+acc).

madam ['mædəm] n gnädige Frau f.

madden ['mædn] vt verrückt machen; (make angry) ärgern; ~**ing** a ärgerlich.

made-to-measure ['meɪdtə'meʒə*] a Maß-.

made-up ['meɪd'ʌp] a story erfunden.

madly ['mædlɪ] ad wahnsinnig.

madman ['mædmən] n Verrückte(r) m, Irre(r) m.

madness ['mædnəs] n Wahnsinn m.

Madonna [mə'dɒnə] n Madonna f.

madrigal ['mædrɪgəl] n Madrigal nt.

magazine ['mægəziːn] n Zeitschrift f; (in gun) Magazin nt.

maggot ['mægət] n Made f.

magic ['mædʒɪk] n Zauberei f, Magie f; (fig) Zauber m; a magisch, Zauber-; ~**al** a magisch; ~**ian** [mə'dʒɪʃən] Zauberer m.

magistrate ['mædʒɪstreɪt] n (Friedens)richter m.

magnanimity [mægnə'nɪmɪtɪ] n Großmut f.

magnanimous [mæg'nænɪməs] a großmütig.

magnate ['mægneɪt] n Magnat m.

magnet ['mægnɪt] n Magnet m; ~**ic** [mæg'netɪk] a magnetisch; (fig) anziehend, unwiderstehlich; ~**ism** Magnetismus m; (fig) Ausstrahlungskraft f.

magnification [mægnɪfɪ'keɪʃən] n Vergrößerung f.

magnificence [mæg'nɪfɪsəns] n Großartigkeit f.

magnificent a, ~**ly** ad [mæg'nɪfɪsənt, -lɪ] großartig.

magnify ['mægnɪfaɪ] vt vergrößern; ~**ing glass** Vergrößerungsglas nt, Lupe f.

magnitude ['mægnɪtjuːd] n (size) Größe f; (importance) Ausmaß nt.

magnolia [mæg'nəʊlɪə] n Magnolie f.

magpie ['mægpaɪ] n Elster f.

maharajah [mɑːhə'rɑːdʒə] n Maharadscha m.

mahogany [mə'hɒgənɪ] n Mahagoni nt; a Mahagoni-.

maid [meɪd] n Dienstmädchen nt; old ~ alte Jungfer f; ~**en** (liter) Maid f; a flight, speech Jungfern-; ~**en name** Mädchenname m.

mail [meɪl] n Post f; vt aufgeben; ~ **box** (US) Briefkasten m; ~**ing list** Anschreibeliste f; ~ **order** Bestellung f durch die Post; ~ **order firm** Versandhaus nt.

maim [meɪm] vt verstümmeln.

main [meɪn] a hauptsächlich, Haupt-; n (pipe) Hauptleitung f; **in the** ~ im großen und ganzen; ~**land** Festland nt; ~ **road** Hauptstraße f; ~**stay** (fig) Hauptstütze f.

maintain [meɪn'teɪn] vt machine, roads instand halten; (support) unterhalten; (keep up) aufrechterhalten; (claim) behaupten; innocence beteuern.

maintenance ['meɪntənəns] n (Tech) Wartung f; (of family) Unterhalt m.

maisonette [meɪzə'net] n kleine(s) Eigenheim nt; Wohnung f.

maize [meɪz] n Mais m.

majestic [mə'dʒestɪk] a majestätisch.

majesty ['mædʒɪstɪ] n Majestät f.

major ['meɪdʒə*] n Major m; a (Mus) Dur; (more important) Haupt-; (bigger) größer.

majority [mə'dʒɒrɪtɪ] n Mehrheit f; (Jur) Volljährigkeit f.

make [meɪk] vt irreg machen; (appoint) ernennen (zu); (cause to do sth) veranlassen; (reach) erreichen; (in time) schaffen; (earn) verdienen; **to** ~ **sth happen** etw geschehen lassen; n Marke f, Fabrikat nt; ~ **for** vi gehen/fahren nach; ~ **out** vi zurechtkommen; vt (write out) ausstellen; (understand) verstehen; (pretend) (so) tun (als ob); ~ **up** vt (make) machen, herstellen; face schminken; quarrel beilegen; story etc erfinden; vi sich versöhnen; ~ **up for** vt wiedergutmachen; (Comm) vergüten; ~**believe** n it's ~-**believe** es ist nicht wirklich; a Phantasie-, ersonnen; ~**r** (Comm) Hersteller m; ~**shift** a behelfsmäßig, Not-; ~-**up** Schminke f, Make-up nt.

making ['meɪkɪŋ] n: **in the** ~ im Entstehen; **to have the** ~**s of** das Zeug haben zu.

maladjusted ['mælə'dʒʌstɪd] a fehlangepaßt, umweltgestört.

malaise [mæ'leɪz] n Unbehagen nt.

malaria [mə'lɛərɪə] n Malaria f.

male [meɪl] n Mann m; (animal) Männchen nt; a männlich.

malevolence [mə'levələns] n Böswilligkeit f.

malevolent [mə'levələnt] a übelwollend.

malfunction [mæl'fʌŋkʃən] vi versagen, nicht funktionieren.

malice ['mælɪs] n Bosheit f.

malicious a, ~**ly** ad [mə'lɪʃəs, -lɪ] böswillig, gehässig.

malign [mə'laɪn] vt verleumden.

malignant [mə'lɪgnənt] a bösartig.

malinger [mə'lɪŋgə*] vi simulieren; ~**er** Drückeberger m, Simulant m.

malleable ['mælɪəbl] a formbar.

mallet ['mælɪt] n Holzhammer m.

malnutrition ['mælnju'trɪʃən] n Unterernährung f.

malpractice ['mæl'præktɪs] n Amtsvergehen nt.

malt [mɔːlt] n Malz nt.

maltreat [mæl'triːt] vt mißhandeln.

mammal ['mæməl] n Säugetier nt.

mammoth ['mæməθ] a Mammut-, Riesen-.

man [mæn] n, pl **men** Mann m; (human race) der Mensch, die Menschen pl; vt bemannen.

manage ['mænɪdʒ] vi zurechtkommen; vt (control) führen, leiten; (cope with) fertigwerden mit; **to ~ to do sth** etw schaffen; ~**able** a person, animal lenksam, fügsam; object handlich; ~**ment** (control) Führung f, Leitung f; (directors) Management nt; ~**r** Geschäftsführer m, (Betriebs)leiter m; ~**ress** ['mænɪdʒə'res] Geschäftsführerin f; ~**rial** [mænə'dʒɪərɪəl] a leitend; problem etc Management-.

managing ['mænɪdʒɪŋ] a: ~ **director** Betriebsleiter m.

mandarin ['mændərɪn] n (fruit) Mandarine f; (Chinese official) Mandarin m.

mandate ['mændeɪt] n Mandat nt.

mandatory ['mændətərɪ] a obligatorisch.

mandolin(e) ['mændəlɪn] n Mandoline f.

mane [meɪn] n Mähne f.

maneuver [mə'nuːvə*] (US) =**manoeuvre**.

manful a, ~**ly** ad ['mænfʊl, -fəlɪ] beherzt; mannhaft.

mangle ['mæŋgl] vt verstümmeln.

mango ['mæŋgəʊ] n Mango(pflaume) f.

mangrove ['mæŋgrəʊv] n Mangrove f.

mangy ['meɪndʒɪ] a dog räudig.

manhandle ['mænhændl] vt grob behandeln.

manhole ['mænhəʊl] n (Straßen)schacht m.

manhood ['mænhʊd] n Mannesalter nt; (manliness) Männlichkeit f.

man-hour ['mæn'aʊə*] n Arbeitsstunde f.

manhunt ['mænhʌnt] n Fahndung f.

mania ['meɪnɪə] n (craze) Sucht f, Manie f; (madness) Wahn(sinn) m; ~**c** ['meɪnɪæk] Wahnsinnige(r) mf, Verrückte(r) mf.

manicure ['mænɪkjʊə*] n Maniküre f; vt maniküren; ~ **set** Necessaire nt.

manifest ['mænɪfest] vt offenbaren; a offenkundig; ~**ation** (showing) Ausdruck m, Bekundung f; (sign) Anzeichen nt; ~**ly** ad offenkundig; ~**o** [mænɪ'festəʊ] Manifest nt.

manipulate [mə'nɪpjʊleɪt] vt handhaben; (fig) manipulieren.

manipulation [mənɪpjʊ'leɪʃən] n Manipulation f.

mankind [mæn'kaɪnd] n Menschheit f.

manliness ['mænlɪnəs] n Männlichkeit f.

manly ['mænlɪ] a männlich; mannhaft.

man-made ['mæn'meɪd] a fibre künstlich.

manner ['mænə*] n Art f, Weise f; (style) Stil m; **in such a ~** so; **in a ~ of speaking** sozusagen; ~**s** pl Manieren pl; ~**ism** (of person) Angewohnheit f; (of style) Manieriertheit f.

manoeuvrable [mə'nuːvrəbl] a manövrierfähig.

manoeuvre [mə'nuːvə*] vti manövrieren; n (Mil) Feldzug m; (general) Manöver nt, Schachzug m; ~**s** pl Truppenübungen pl, Manöver nt.

manor ['mænə*] n Landgut nt; ~ **house** Herrenhaus nt.

manpower ['mænpaʊə*] n Arbeitskräfte pl.

manservant ['mænsɜːvənt] n Diener m.

mansion ['mænʃən] n Herrenhaus nt, Landhaus nt.

manslaughter ['mænslɔːtə*] n Totschlag m.

mantelpiece ['mæntlpiːs] n Kaminsims m.

mantle ['mæntl] n (cloak) lange(r) Umhang m.

manual ['mænjʊəl] a manuell, Hand-; n Handbuch nt.

manufacture [mænjʊ'fæktʃə*] vt herstellen; n Herstellung f; ~**r** Hersteller m.

manure [mə'njʊə*] n Dünger m.

manuscript ['mænjʊskrɪpt] n Manuskript nt.

many ['menɪ] a viele; **as ~ as 20** sage und schreibe 20; ~ **a good soldier** so mancher gute Soldat; ~**'s the time** oft.

map [mæp] n (Land)karte f; (of town) Stadtplan m; vt eine Karte machen von; ~ **out** (fig) ausarbeiten.

maple ['meɪpl] n Ahorn m.

mar [mɑː*] vt verderben, beeinträchtigen.

marathon ['mærəθən] n (Sport) Marathonlauf m; (fig) Marathon m.

marauder [mə'rɔːdə*] n Plünderer m.

marble ['mɑːbl] n Marmor m; (for game) Murmel f.

March [mɑːtʃ] n März m.

march [mɑːtʃ] vi marschieren; n Marsch m; ~-**past** Vorbeimarsch m.

mare [mɛə*] n Stute f; ~**'s nest** Windei nt.

margarine [mɑːdʒə'riːn] n Margarine f.

margin ['mɑːdʒɪn] n Rand m; (extra amount) Spielraum m; (Comm) Spanne f; ~**al** a note Rand-; difference etc geringfügig; ~**ally** ad nur wenig.

marigold ['mærɪgəʊld] n Ringelblume f.

marijuana [mærɪ'hwɑːnə] n Marihuana nt.

marina [mə'riːnə] n Yachthafen m.

marine [mə'riːn] a Meeres-, See-; n (Mil) Marineinfanterist m; (fleet) Marine f; ~**r** ['mærɪnə*] Seemann m.

marionette [mærɪə'net] n Marionette f.

marital ['mærɪtl] a ehelich, Ehe-.

maritime ['mærɪtaɪm] a See-.

marjoram ['mɑːdʒərəm] n Majoran m.

mark [mɑːk] n (coin) Mark f; (spot) Fleck m; (scar) Kratzer m; (sign) Zeichen nt; (target) Ziel nt; (Sch) Note f; **quick off the ~** blitzschnell; **on your ~s** auf die Plätze; vt (make mark) Flecken/Kratzer machen auf (+acc); (indicate) markieren, bezeichnen; (note) sich (dat) merken; exam korrigieren; **to ~ time** (lit, fig) auf der Stelle treten; **~ out** vt bestimmen; area abstecken; **~ed** a deutlich; **~edly** ['mɑːkɪdlɪ] ad merklich; **~er** (in book) (Lese)zeichen nt; (on road) Schild nt.

market ['mɑːkɪt] n Markt m; (stock —) Börse f; vt (Comm: new product) auf den Markt bringen; (sell) vertreiben; **~ day** Markttag m; **~ garden** (Brit) Handelsgärtnerei f; **~ing** Marketing nt; **~ place** Marktplatz m.

marksman ['mɑːksmən] n Scharfschütze m; **~ship** Treffsicherheit f.

marmalade ['mɑːməleɪd] n Orangenmarmelade f.

maroon [mə'ruːn] vt aussetzen; a (colour) kastanienbraun.

marquee [mɑː'kiː] n große(s) Zelt nt.

marquess, marquis ['mɑːkwɪs] n Marquis m.

marriage ['mærɪdʒ] n Ehe f; (wedding) Heirat f; (fig) Verbindung f.

married ['mærɪd] a person verheiratet; couple, life Ehe-.

marrow ['mærəʊ] n (Knochen)mark nt; (vegetable) Kürbis m.

marry ['mærɪ] vt (join) trauen; (take as husband, wife) heiraten; vi (also **get married**) heiraten.

marsh [mɑːʃ] n Marsch f, Sumpfland nt.

marshal ['mɑːʃəl] n (US) Bezirkspolizeichef m; vt (an)ordnen, arrangieren.

marshy ['mɑːʃɪ] a sumpfig.

martial ['mɑːʃəl] a kriegerisch; **~ law** Kriegsrecht nt.

martyr ['mɑːtə*] n (lit, fig) Märtyrer(in f) m; vt zum Märtyrer machen; **~dom** Martyrium nt.

marvel ['mɑːvəl] n Wunder nt; vi sich wundern (at über +acc); **~lous**, (US) **~ous** a, **~lously**, (US) **~ously** ad wunderbar.

Marxism ['mɑːksɪzəm] n Marxismus m.

Marxist ['mɑːksɪst] n Marxist(in f) m.

marzipan [mɑːzɪ'pæn] n Marzipan nt.

mascara [mæs'kɑːrə] n Wimperntusche f.

mascot ['mæskət] n Maskottchen nt.

masculine ['mæskjʊlɪn] a männlich; n Maskulinum nt.

masculinity [mæskjʊ'lɪnɪtɪ] n Männlichkeit f.

mashed [mæʃt] a: **~ potatoes** pl Kartoffelbrei m or -püree nt.

mask [mɑːsk] n (lit, fig) Maske f; vt maskieren, verdecken.

masochist ['mæzəʊkɪst] n Masochist(in f) m.

mason ['meɪsn] n (stone—) Steinmetz m; (free—) Freimaurer m; **~ic** [mə'sɒnɪk] a Freimaurer-; **~ry** Mauerwerk nt.

masquerade [mæskə'reɪd] n Maskerade f; vi sich maskieren, sich verkleiden; **to ~ as** sich ausgeben als.

mass [mæs] n Masse f; (greater part) Mehrheit f; (Rel) Messe f; **~es of** massenhaft; vt sammeln, anhäufen; vi sich sammeln.

massacre ['mæsəkə*] n Blutbad nt; vt niedermetzeln, massakrieren.

massage ['mæsɑːʒ] n Massage f; vt massieren.

masseur [mæ'sɜː*] n Masseur m.

masseuse [mæ'sɜːz] n Masseuse f.

massive ['mæsɪv] a gewaltig, massiv.

mass media ['mæs'miːdɪə] npl Massenmedien pl.

mass-produce ['mæsprə'djuːs] vt serienmäßig herstellen.

mass production ['mæsprə'dʌkʃən] n Serienproduktion f, Massenproduktion f.

mast [mɑːst] n Mast m.

master ['mɑːstə*] n Herr m; (Naut) Kapitän m; (teacher) Lehrer m; (artist) Meister m; vt meistern; language etc beherrschen; **~ly** a meisterhaft; **~mind** n Kapazität f; vt geschickt lenken; **M~ of Arts** Magister Artium m; **~piece** Meisterstück nt; (Art) Meisterwerk nt; **~ stroke** Glanzstück nt; **~y** Können nt; **to gain ~y over sb** die Oberhand gewinnen über jdn.

masturbate ['mæstəbeɪt] vi masturbieren, onanieren.

masturbation [mæstə'beɪʃən] n Masturbation f, Onanie f.

mat [mæt] n Matte f; (for table) Untersetzer m; vi sich verfilzen; vt verfilzen.

match [mætʃ] n Streichholz nt; (sth corresponding) Pendant nt; (Sport) Wettkampf m; (ball games) Spiel nt; **it's a good ~** es paßt gut (for zu); **to be a ~ for sb** sich mit jdm messen können; jdm gewachsen sein; **he's a good ~** er ist eine gute Partie; vt (be alike, suit) passen zu; (equal) gleichkommen (+dat); (Sport) antreten lassen; vi zusammenpassen; **~box** Streichholzschachtel f; **~ing** a passend; **~less** a unvergleichlich; **~maker** Kuppler(in f) m.

mate [meɪt] n (companion) Kamerad m; (spouse) Lebensgefährte m; (of animal) Weibchen nt/Männchen nt; (Naut) Schiffsoffizier m; vi (chess) (schach)matt sein; (animals) sich paaren; vt (chess) matt setzen.

material [mə'tɪərɪəl] n Material nt; (for book, cloth) Material nt, Stoff m; a (important) wesentlich; damage Sach-; comforts etc materiell; **~s** pl Materialien pl; **~istic** a materialistisch; **~ize** vi sich verwirklichen, zustande kommen; **~ly** ad grundlegend.

maternal [mə'tɜːnl] a mütterlich, Mutter-; **~ grandmother** Großmutter mütterlicherseits.

maternity [mə'tɜːnɪtɪ] a Schwangeren-; dress Umstands-; benefit Wochen-.

matey ['meɪtɪ] a (Brit col) kameradschaftlich.

mathematical a, **~ly** ad [mæθə'mætɪkəl, -ɪ] mathematisch.

mathematician [mæθəmə'tɪʃən] n Mathematiker m.

mathematics [mæθə'mætɪks] n Mathematik f.

maths [mæθs] n Mathe f.

matinée ['mætɪneɪ] n Matinee f.

mating ['meɪtɪŋ] n Paarung f; ~ **call** Lockruf m.

matins ['mætɪnz] n (Früh)mette f.

matriarchal [meɪtrɪ'ɑːkl] a matriarchalisch.

matrimonial [mætrɪ'məʊnɪəl] a ehelich, Ehe-.

matrimony ['mætrɪmənɪ] n Ehestand m.

matron ['meɪtrən] n (Med) Oberin f; (Sch) Hausmutter f; ~**ly** a matronenhaft.

matt [mæt] a paint matt.

matter ['mætə*] n (substance) Materie f; (affair) Sache f, Angelegenheit f; (content) Inhalt m; (Med) Eiter m; vi darauf ankommen; **it doesn't** ~ es macht nichts; **no** ~ **how/what** egal wie/was; **what is the** ~? was ist los?; **as a** ~ **of fact** eigentlich; ~**-of-fact** a sachlich, nüchtern.

mattress ['mætrəs] n Matratze f.

mature [mə'tjʊə*] a reif; vi reif werden.

maturity [mə'tjʊərɪtɪ] n Reife f.

maudlin ['mɔːdlɪn] a weinerlich; gefühlsduselig.

maul [mɔːl] vt übel zurichten.

mausoleum [mɔːsə'lɪəm] n Mausoleum nt.

mauve [məʊv] a mauve.

mawkish ['mɔːkɪʃ] a kitschig; taste süßlich.

maxi ['mæksɪ] pref Maxi-.

maxim ['mæksɪm] n Maxime f.

maximize ['mæksɪmaɪz] vt maximieren.

maximum ['mæksɪməm] a höchste(r, s), Höchst-, Maximal-; n Höchstgrenze f, Maximum nt.

May [meɪ] n Mai m.

may [meɪ] v aux (be possible) können; (have permission) dürfen; **I** ~ **come** ich komme vielleicht, es kann sein, daß ich komme; **we** ~ **as well go** wir können ruhig gehen; ~ **you be very happy** ich hoffe, ihr seid glücklich; ~**be** ad vielleicht.

Mayday ['meɪdeɪ] n (message) SOS nt.

mayonnaise [meɪə'neɪz] n Mayonnaise f.

mayor [mɛə*] n Bürgermeister m; ~**ess** (wife) (die) Frau f Bürgermeister; (lady —) Bürgermeisterin f.

maypole ['meɪpəʊl] n Maibaum m.

maze [meɪz] n (lit) Irrgarten m; (fig) Wirrwarr nt; **to be in a** ~ (fig) durcheinander sein.

me [miː] pron (acc) mich; (dat) mir; **it's** ~ ich bin's.

meadow ['medəʊ] n Wiese f.

meagre, (US) **meager** ['miːgə*] a dürftig, spärlich.

meal [miːl] n Essen nt, Mahlzeit f; (grain) Schrotmehl nt; **to have a** ~ essen (gehen); ~**time** Essenszeit f; ~**y-mouthed** a: **to be** ~**y-mouthed** d(a)rum herumreden.

mean [miːn] a (stingy) geizig; (spiteful) gemein; (shabby) armselig, schäbig; (average) durchschnittlich, Durchschnitts-; irreg vt (signify) bedeuten; vi (intend) vorhaben, beabsichtigen; (be resolved) entschlossen sein; **he** ~**s well** er meint es gut; **I** ~ **it!** ich meine das ernst!; **do you**

~ **me?** meinen Sie mich?; **it** ~**s nothing to me** es sagt mir nichts; n (average) Durchschnitt m; ~**s** pl Mittel pl; (wealth) Vermögen nt; **by** ~**s of** durch; **by all** ~**s** selbstverständlich; **by no** ~**s** keineswegs.

meander [mɪ'ændə*] vi sich schlängeln.

meaning ['miːnɪŋ] n Bedeutung f; (of life) Sinn m; ~**ful** a bedeutungsvoll; life sinnvoll; ~**less** a sinnlos.

meanness ['miːnnəs] n (stinginess) Geiz m; (spitefulness) Gemeinheit f; (shabbiness) Schäbigkeit f.

meantime ['miːn'taɪm] ad, **meanwhile** ['miːn'waɪl] ad inzwischen, mittlerweile; **for the** ~ vorerst.

measles ['miːzlz] n Masern pl; **German** ~ Röteln pl.

measly ['miːzlɪ] a (col) poplig.

measurable ['meʒərəbl] a meßbar.

measure ['meʒə*] vti messen; n Maß nt; (step) Maßnahme f; **to be a** ~ **of** sth etw erkennen lassen; ~**d** a (slow) gemessen; ~**ment** (way of measuring) Messung f; (amount measured) Maß nt.

meat [miːt] n Fleisch nt; ~**y** a (lit) fleischig; (fig) gehaltvoll.

mechanic [mɪ'kænɪk] n Mechaniker m; ~**s** Mechanik f; ~**al** a mechanisch.

mechanism ['mekənɪzəm] n Mechanismus m.

mechanization [mekənaɪ'zeɪʃən] n Mechanisierung f.

mechanize ['mekənaɪz] vt mechanisieren.

medal ['medl] n Medaille f; (decoration) Orden m; ~**lion** [mɪ'dælɪən] n Medaillon nt; ~**list,** (US) ~**ist** Medaillengewinner(in f) m.

meddle ['medl] vi sich einmischen (in in +acc); (tamper) hantieren (with an +dat); ~ **with** sb sich mit jdm einlassen.

media ['miːdɪə] npl Medien pl.

mediate ['miːdɪeɪt] vi vermitteln.

mediation [miːdɪ'eɪʃən] n Vermittlung f.

mediator ['miːdɪeɪtə*] n Vermittler m.

medical ['medɪkəl] a medizinisch; Medizin-; ärztlich; n (ärztliche) Untersuchung f.

medicated ['medɪkeɪtɪd] a medizinisch.

medicinal [me'dɪsɪnl] a medizinisch, Heil-.

medicine ['medsɪn] n Medizin f; (drugs) Arznei f; ~ **chest** Hausapotheke f.

medieval [medɪ'iːvəl] a mittelalterlich.

mediocre [miːdɪ'əʊkə*] a mittelmäßig.

mediocrity [miːdɪ'ɒkrɪtɪ] n Mittelmäßigkeit f; (person also) kleine(r) Geist m.

meditate ['medɪteɪt] vi nachdenken (on über +acc); meditieren (on über +acc).

meditation [medɪ'teɪʃən] n Nachsinnen nt; Meditation f.

medium ['miːdɪəm] a mittlere(r, s), Mittel-, mittel-; n Mitte f; (means) Mittel nt; (person) Medium nt.

medley ['medlɪ] n Gemisch nt.

meek a, ~**ly** ad [miːk, -lɪ] sanft(mütig); (pej) duckmäuserisch.

meet [miːt] irreg vt (encounter) treffen, begegnen (+dat); (by arrangement) sich treffen mit; difficulties stoßen auf (+acc);

(become acquainted with) kennenlernen; *(fetch)* abholen; *(join)* zusammentreffen mit; *(river)* fließen in *(+acc)*; *(satisfy)* entsprechen *(+dat)*; *debt* bezahlen; **pleased to ~ you!** angenehm!; *vi* sich treffen; *(become acquainted)* sich kennenlernen; *(join)* sich treffen; *(rivers)* ineinanderfließen; *(roads)* zusammenlaufen; **~ with** *vt problems* stoßen auf *(+acc); (US: people)* zusammentreffen mit; **~ing** Treffen *nt; (business ~)* Besprechung *f,* Konferenz *f; (discussion)* Sitzung *f; (assembly)* Versammlung *f;* **~ing place** Treffpunkt *m.*

megaphone ['megəfəun] *n* Megaphon *nt.*

melancholy ['melənkəlɪ] *n* Melancholie *f; a person* melancholisch, schwermütig; *sight, event* traurig.

mellow ['meləu] *a* mild, weich; *fruit* reif, weich; *(fig)* gesetzt; *vi* reif werden.

melodious [mɪ'ləudɪəs] *a* wohlklingend.

melodrama ['meləudrɑ:mə] *n* Melodrama *nt;* **~tic** [meləudrə'mætɪk] *a* melodramatisch.

melody ['melədɪ] *n* Melodie *f.*

melon ['melən] *n* Melone *f.*

melt [melt] *vi* schmelzen; *(anger)* verfliegen; *vt* schmelzen; **~ away** *vi* dahinschmelzen; **~ down** *vt* einschmelzen; **~ing point** Schmelzpunkt *m;* **~ing pot** *(fig)* Schmelztiegel *m;* **to be in the ~ing pot** in der Schwebe sein.

member ['membə*] *n* Mitglied *nt; (of tribe, species)* Angehörige(r) *m; (Anat)* Glied *nt;* **~ship** Mitgliedschaft *f.*

membrane ['membreɪn] *n* Membrane *f.*

memento [mə'mentəu] *n* Andenken *nt.*

memo ['meməu] *n* Notiz *f,* Mitteilung *f.*

memoirs ['memwɑ:*z] *npl* Memoiren *pl.*

memorable ['memərəbl] *a* denkwürdig.

memorandum ['memə'rændəm] *n* Notiz *f,* Mitteilung *f; (Pol)* Memorandum *nt.*

memorial [mɪ'mɔ:rɪəl] *n* Denkmal *nt; a* Gedenk-.

memorize ['meməraɪz] *vt* sich einprägen.

memory ['memərɪ] *n* Gedächtnis *nt; (of computer)* Speicher *m; (sth recalled)* Erinnerung *f;* **in ~ of** zur Erinnerung an *(+acc);* **from ~** aus dem Kopf.

men [men] *npl of* **man.**

menace ['menɪs] *n* Drohung *f;* Gefahr *f; vt* bedrohen.

menacing *a,* **~ly** *ad* ['menɪsɪŋ, -lɪ] drohend.

ménage [me'nɑ:ʒ] *n* Haushalt *m.*

menagerie [mɪ'nædʒərɪ] *n* Tierschau *f.*

mend [mend] *vt* reparieren, flicken; *n* ausgebesserte Stelle *f;* **on the ~** auf dem Wege der Besserung.

menial ['mi:nɪəl] *a* niedrig, untergeordnet.

meningitis [menɪn'dʒaɪtɪs] *n* Hirnhautentzündung *f,* Meningitis *f.*

menopause ['menəupɔ:z] *n* Wechseljahre *pl,* Menopause *f.*

menstrual ['menstruəl] *a* Monats-, Menstruations-.

menstruate ['menstrueɪt] *vi* menstruieren.

menstruation [menstru'eɪʃən] *n* Menstruation *f.*

mental ['mentl] *a* geistig, Geistes-; *arithmetic* Kopf-; *hospital* Nerven-; *cruelty* seelisch; *(col: abnormal)* verrückt; **~ity** [men'tælɪtɪ] Mentalität *f;* **~ly** *ad* geistig; **~ly ill** geisteskrank.

mentholated ['menθəleɪtɪd] *a* Menthol-.

mention ['menʃən] *n* Erwähnung *f; vt* erwähnen; *names* nennen; **don't ~ it!** bitte (sehr), gern geschehen.

menu ['menju:] *n* Speisekarte *f; (food)* Speisen *pl.*

mercantile ['mɜ:kəntaɪl] *a* Handels-.

mercenary ['mɜ:sɪnərɪ] *a person* geldgierig; *(Mil)* Söldner-; *n* Söldner *m.*

merchandise ['mɜ:tʃəndaɪz] *n* (Handels)ware *f.*

merchant ['mɜ:tʃənt] *n* Kaufmann *m; a* Handels-; **~ navy** Handelsmarine *f.*

merciful ['mɜ:sɪful] *a* gnädig, barmherzig; **~ly** ['mɜ:sɪfəlɪ] *ad* gnädig; *(fortunately)* glücklicherweise.

merciless *a,* **~ly** *ad* ['mɜ:sɪləs, -lɪ] erbarmunglos.

mercurial [mɜ:'kjuərɪəl] *a* quecksilbrig, Quecksilber-.

mercury ['mɜ:kjurɪ] *n* Quecksilber *nt.*

mercy ['mɜ:sɪ] *n* Erbarmen *nt;* Gnade *f; (blessing)* Segen *m;* **at the ~ of** ausgeliefert *(+dat).*

mere *a,* **~ly** *ad* [mɪə*, 'mɪəlɪ] bloß.

merge [mɜ:dʒ] *vt* verbinden; *(Comm)* fusionieren; *vi* verschmelzen; *(roads)* zusammenlaufen; *(Comm)* fusionieren; **to ~ into** übergehen in *(+acc);* **~r** *(Comm)* Fusion *f.*

meridian [mə'rɪdɪən] *n* Meridian *m.*

meringue [mə'ræŋ] *n* Baiser *nt,* Schaumgebäck *nt.*

merit ['merɪt] *n* Verdienst *nt; (advantage)* Vorzug *m;* **to judge on ~** nach Leistung beurteilen; *vt* verdienen.

mermaid ['mɜ:meɪd] *n* Wassernixe *f,* Meerjungfrau *f.*

merrily ['merɪlɪ] *ad* lustig.

merriment ['merɪmənt] *n* Fröhlichkeit *f; (laughter)* Gelächter *nt.*

merry ['merɪ] *a* fröhlich; *(col)* angeheitert; **~-go-round** Karussell *nt.*

mesh [meʃ] *n* Masche *f; vi (gears)* ineinandergreifen.

mesmerize ['mezməraɪz] *vt* hypnotisieren; *(fig)* faszinieren.

mess [mes] *n* Unordnung *f; (dirt)* Schmutz *m; (trouble)* Schwierigkeiten *pl; (Mil)* Messe *f;* **to look a ~** fürchterlich aussehen; **to make a ~ of sth** etw verpfuschen; **to ~ about** *vi (tinker with)* herummurksen *(with* an *+dat); (play fool)* herumalbern; **to ~ nothing in particular)** herumgammeln; **~ up** *vt* verpfuschen; *(make untidy)* in Unordnung bringen.

message ['mesɪdʒ] *n* Mitteilung *f,* Nachricht *f;* **to get the ~** kapieren.

messenger ['mesɪndʒə*] *n* Bote *m.*

messy ['mesɪ] *a* schmutzig; *(untidy)* unordentlich.

metabolism [me'tæbəlɪzəm] *n* Stoffwechsel *m.*

metal ['metl] *n* Metall *nt;* **~lic** [mɪ'tælɪk] *a*

metallisch; ~**lurgy** [me'tælədʒɪ] Metallurgie f.

metamorphosis [metə'mɔːfəsɪs] n Metamorphose f.

metaphor ['metəfɔː*] n Metapher f; ~**ical** [metə'fɔrɪkəl] a bildlich, metaphorisch.

metaphysics [metə'fɪzɪks] n Metaphysik f.

meteor ['miːtɪə*] n Meteor m; ~**ic** [miːtɪ'ɒrɪk] a meteorisch, Meteor-; ~**ite** Meteorit m; ~**ological** [miːtɪərə'lɒdʒɪkəl] a meteorologisch; ~**ology** [miːtɪə'rolədʒɪ] Meteorologie f.

meter ['miːtə*] n Zähler m; (US) = **metre**.

method ['meθəd] n Methode f; ~**ical** [mɪ'θɒdɪkəl] a methodisch; ~**ology** [meθə'dɒlədʒɪ] Methodik f.

methylated spirit ['meθɪleɪtɪd' spɪrɪt] n (also **meths**) (Brenn)spiritus m.

meticulous [mɪ'tɪkjʊləs] a (über)genau.

metre ['miːtə*] n Meter m or nt; (verse) Metrum nt.

metric ['metrɪk] a (also ~**al**) metrisch; ~**ation** Umstellung f auf das Dezimalsystem; ~ **system** Dezimalsystem nt.

metronome ['metrənəum] n Metronom nt.

metropolis [me'trɒpəlɪs] n Metropole f.

mettle ['metl] n Mut m.

mezzanine ['mezəniːn] n Hochparterre nt.

miaow [miː'aʊ] vi miauen.

mice [maɪs] npl of **mouse**.

mickey ['mɪkɪ] n: **to take the ~ out of sb** (col) jdn auf den Arm nehmen.

microbe ['maɪkrəʊb] n Mikrobe f.

microfilm ['maɪkrəʊfɪlm] n Mikrofilm m; vt auf Mikrofilm aufnehmen.

microphone ['maɪkrəfəʊn] n Mikrophon nt.

microscope ['maɪkrəskəʊp] n Mikroskop nt.

microscopic [maɪkrə'skɒpɪk] a mikroskopisch.

mid [mɪd] a mitten in (+dat); **in the ~ eighties** Mitte der achtziger Jahre; **in ~ course** mittendrin.

midday ['mɪd'deɪ] n Mittag m.

middle ['mɪdl] n Mitte f; (waist) Taille f; **in the ~ of** mitten in (+dat); a mittlere(r, s), Mittel-; ~**-aged** a mittleren Alters; **the M~ Ages** pl das Mittelalter; ~**class** Mittelstand m or -klasse f; a Mittelstands-, Mittelklassen-; **the M~ East** der Nahe Osten; ~**man** (Comm) Zwischenhändler m; ~ **name** zweiter Vorname m; ~**-of-the-road** a gemäßigt.

middling ['mɪdlɪŋ] a mittelmäßig.

midge [mɪdʒ] n Mücke f.

midget ['mɪdʒɪt] n Liliputaner(in f) m; a Kleinst-.

midnight ['mɪdnaɪt] n Mitternacht f.

midriff ['mɪdrɪf] n Taille f.

midst [mɪdst] n **in the ~ of** persons mitten unter (+dat); things mitten in (+dat); **in our ~** unter uns.

midsummer ['mɪd'sʌmə*] n Hochsommer m; **M~'s Day** Sommersonnenwende f.

midway ['mɪd'weɪ] ad auf halbem Wege; a Mittel-.

midweek ['mɪd'wiːk] a, ad in der Mitte der Woche.

midwife ['mɪdwaɪf] n Hebamme f; ~**ry** ['mɪdwɪfərɪ] Geburtshilfe f.

midwinter ['mɪd'wɪntə*] n tiefste(r) Winter m.

might [maɪt] n Macht f, Kraft f; pt of **may**; **I ~ come** ich komme vielleicht; ~**ily** ad mächtig; ~**n't = might not**; ~**y** a, ad mächtig.

migraine ['miːgreɪn] n Migräne f.

migrant ['maɪgrənt] n (bird) Zugvogel m; (worker) Saison- or Wanderarbeiter m; a Wander-; bird Zug-.

migrate [maɪ'greɪt] vi (ab)wandern; (birds) (fort)ziehen.

migration [maɪ'greɪʃən] n Wanderung f, Zug m.

mike [maɪk] n = **microphone**.

mild [maɪld] a mild; medicine, interest leicht; person sanft.

mildew ['mɪldjuː] n (on plants) Mehltau m; (on food) Schimmel m.

mildly ['maɪldlɪ] ad leicht; **to put it ~** gelinde gesagt.

mildness ['maɪldnəs] n Milde f.

mile [maɪl] n Meile f; ~**age** Meilenzahl f; ~**stone** (lit, fig) Meilenstein m.

milieu ['miːljɜː] n Milieu nt.

militant ['mɪlɪtənt] n Militante(r) mf; a militant.

militarism ['mɪlɪtərɪzəm] n Militarismus m.

military ['mɪlɪtərɪ] a militärisch, Militär-, Wehr-; n Militär nt.

militate ['mɪlɪteɪt] vi sprechen; entgegenwirken (against dat).

militia [mɪ'lɪʃə] n Miliz f, Bürgerwehr f.

milk [mɪlk] n Milch f; vt (lit, fig) melken; ~ **chocolate** Milchschokolade f; ~**ing** Melken nt; ~**man** Milchmann m; ~ **shake** Milchmixgetränk nt; **M~y Way** Milchstraße f.

mill [mɪl] n Mühle f; (factory) Fabrik f; vt mahlen; vi (move around) umherlaufen; ~**ed** a gemahlen.

millennium [mɪ'lenɪəm] n Jahrtausend nt.

miller ['mɪlə*] n Müller m.

millet ['mɪlɪt] n Hirse f.

milligram(me) ['mɪlɪgræm] n Milligramm nt.

millilitre, (US) ~**liter** ['mɪlɪliːtə*] n Milliliter m.

millimetre, (US) ~**meter** ['mɪlɪmiːtə*] n Millimeter m.

milliner ['mɪlɪnə*] n Hutmacher(in f) m; ~**y** (hats) Hüte pl, Modewaren pl; (business) Hutgeschäft nt.

million ['mɪljən] n Million f; ~**aire** [mɪljə'nɛə*] Millionär(in f) m.

millwheel ['mɪlwiːl] n Mühlrad nt.

milometer [maɪ'lomɪtə*] n Kilometerzähler m.

mime [maɪm] n Pantomime f; (actor) Mime m, Mimin f; vti mimen.

mimic ['mɪmɪk] n Mimiker m; vti nachahmen; ~**ry** ['mɪmɪkrɪ] Nachahmung f; (Biol) Mimikry f.

mince [mɪns] vt (zer)hacken; vi (walk)

trippeln; n (meat) Hackfleisch nt; ~meat
süße Pastetenfüllung f; ~ pie gefüllte
(süße) Pastete f.
mincing ['mɪnsɪŋ] a manner affektiert.
mind [maɪnd] n Verstand m, Geist m;
(opinion) Meinung f; on my ~ auf dem
Herzen; to my ~ meiner Meinung nach;
to be out of one's ~ wahnsinnig sein; to
bear or keep in ~ bedenken, nicht vergessen; to change one's ~ es sich (dat)
anders überlegen; to make up one's ~
sich entschließen; to have sth in ~ an
etw (acc) denken; etw beabsichtigen; to
have a good ~ to do sth große Lust
haben, etw zu tun; vt aufpassen auf (+acc);
(object to) etwas haben gegen; vi etwas
dagegen haben; I don't ~ the rain der
Regen macht mir nichts aus; do you ~ if
I ... macht es Ihnen etwas aus, wenn ich ...;
do you ~! na hören Sie mal!; never ~!
macht nichts!; '~ the step' 'Vorsicht
Stufe'; ~ your own business kümmern
Sie sich um Ihre eigenen Angelegen-
heiten; ~ful a achtsam (of auf +acc);
~less a achtlos, dumm.
mine [maɪn] poss pron meine(r, s); n
(coal—) Bergwerk nt; (Mil) Mine f; (source)
Fundgrube f; vt abbauen; (Mil) verminen;
vi Bergbau betreiben; to ~ for sth etw
gewinnen; ~ detector Minensuchgerät
nt; ~field Minenfeld nt; ~er Bergarbeiter m.
mineral ['mɪnərəl] a mineralisch,
Mineral-; n Mineral nt; ~ water Mineralwasser nt.
minesweeper ['maɪnswiːpə*] n Minen-
suchboot nt.
mingle ['mɪŋgl] vt vermischen; vi sich
mischen (with unter +acc).
mingy ['mɪndʒɪ] a (col) knickerig.
mini ['mɪnɪ] pref Mini-, Klein-.
miniature ['mɪnɪtʃə*] a Miniatur-, Klein-; n
Miniatur f; in ~ en miniature.
minibus ['mɪnɪbʌs] n Kleinbus m, Minibus
m.
minicab ['mɪnɪkæb] n Kleintaxi nt.
minim ['mɪnɪm] n halbe Note f.
minimal ['mɪnɪml] a kleinste(r, s),
minimal, Mindest-.
minimize ['mɪnɪmaɪz] vt auf das
Mindestmaß beschränken; (belittle) herabsetzen.
minimum ['mɪnɪməm] n Minimum nt; a
Mindest-.
mining ['maɪnɪŋ] n Bergbau m; a Bergbau-,
Berg-.
minion ['mɪnjən] n (pej) Trabant m.
miniskirt ['mɪnɪskɜːt] n Minirock m.
minister ['mɪnɪstə*] n (Pol) Minister m;
(Eccl) Geistliche(r) m, Pfarrer m; ~ial
[mɪnɪs'tɪərɪəl] a ministeriell, Minister-.
ministry ['mɪnɪstrɪ] n (government body)
Ministerium nt; (Eccl) (office) geistliche(s)
Amt nt; (all ministers) Geistlichkeit f.
mink [mɪŋk] n Nerz m.
minnow ['mɪnəʊ] n Elritze f.
minor ['maɪnə*] a kleiner; operation leicht;
problem, poet unbedeutend; (Mus) Moll;
Smith ~ Smith der Jüngere; n (Brit: under

18) Minderjährige(r) mf; ~ity [maɪ'nɒrɪtɪ]
Minderheit f.
minster ['mɪnstə*] n Münster nt,
Kathedrale f.
minstrel ['mɪnstrəl] n (Hist) Spielmann m,
Minnesänger m.
mint [mɪnt] n Minze f; (sweet) Pfefferminz-
bonbon nt; (place) Münzstätte f; a condition
(wie) neu; stamp ungestempelt; ~ sauce
Minzsoße f.
minuet [mɪnjʊ'et] n Menuett nt.
minus ['maɪnəs] n Minuszeichen nt;
(amount) Minusbetrag m; prep minus,
weniger.
minute [maɪ'njuːt] a winzig, sehr klein;
(detailed) minuziös; ['mɪnɪt] n Minute f;
(moment) Augenblick m; ~s pl Protokoll
nt; ~ly [maɪ'njuːtlɪ] ad (in detail) genau.
miracle ['mɪrəkl] n Wunder nt; ~ play
geistliche(s) Drama nt.
miraculous [mɪ'rækjʊləs] a wunderbar;
~ly ad auf wunderbare Weise.
mirage ['mɪrɑːʒ] n Luftspiegelung f, Fata
Morgana f.
mirror ['mɪrə*] n Spiegel m; vt
(wider)spiegeln.
mirth [mɜːθ] n Freude f; Heiterkeit f.
misadventure [mɪsəd'ventʃə*] n Mißgeschick nt, Unfall m.
misanthropist [mɪ'zænθrəpɪst] n
Menschenfeind m.
misapprehension ['mɪsæprɪ'henʃən] n
Mißverständnis nt; to be under the ~
that . . . irrtümlicherweise annehmen,
daß. . .
misappropriate ['mɪsə'prəʊprɪeɪt] vt
funds veruntreuen.
misappropriation ['mɪsəprəʊprɪ'eɪʃən] n
Veruntreuung f.
misbehave ['mɪsbɪ'heɪv] vi sich schlecht
benehmen.
miscalculate ['mɪs'kælkjʊleɪt] vt falsch
berechnen.
miscalculation ['mɪskælkjʊ'leɪʃən] n
Rechenfehler m.
miscarriage ['mɪskærɪdʒ] n (Med)
Fehlgeburt f; ~ of justice Fehlurteil nt.
miscellaneous [mɪsɪ'leɪnɪəs] a verschieden.
miscellany [mɪsɪ'tʃɑːns] n (bunte) Sammlung f.
mischance [mɪs'tʃɑːns] n Mißgeschick nt.
mischief ['mɪstʃɪf] n Unfug m; (harm)
Schaden m.
mischievous a, ~ly ad ['mɪstʃɪvəs, -lɪ]
person durchtrieben; glance verschmitzt;
rumour bösartig.
misconception ['mɪskən'sepʃən] n fälsch-
liche Annahme f.
misconduct [mɪs'kɒndʌkt] n Vergehen nt.
misconstrue ['mɪskən'struː] vt mißverstehen.
miscount ['mɪs'kaʊnt] vt falsch
(be)rechnen.
misdemeanour, (US) **misdemeanor**
[mɪsdɪ'miːnə*] n Vergehen nt.
misdirect ['mɪsdɪ'rekt] vt person
irreleiten; letter fehlleiten.
miser ['maɪzə*] n Geizhals m.

miserable ['mɪzərəbl] a (unhappy) unglücklich; headache, weather fürchterlich; (poor) elend; (contemptible) erbärmlich.

miserably ['mɪzərəblɪ] ad unglücklich; fail kläglich.

miserly ['maɪzəlɪ] a geizig.

misery ['mɪzərɪ] n Elend nt, Qual f.

misfire ['mɪs'faɪə*] vi (gun) versagen; (engine) fehlzünden; (plan) fehlgehen.

misfit ['mɪsfɪt] n Außenseiter m.

misfortune [mɪs'fɔːtʃən] n Unglück nt.

misgiving [mɪs'gɪvɪŋ] n (often pl) Befürchtung f, Bedenken pl.

misguided ['mɪs'gaɪdɪd] a fehlgeleitet; opinions irrig.

mishandle ['mɪs'hændl] vt falsch handhaben.

mishap ['mɪshæp] n Unglück nt; (slight) Panne f.

mishear ['mɪs'hɪə*] vt irreg mißverstehen.

misinform ['mɪsɪn'fɔːm] vt falsch unterrichten.

misinterpret ['mɪsɪn'tɜːprɪt] vt falsch auffassen; ~ation ['mɪsɪntɜːprɪ'teɪʃən] falsche Auslegung f.

misjudge ['mɪs'dʒʌdʒ] vt falsch beurteilen.

mislay [mɪs'leɪ] vt irreg verlegen.

mislead [mɪs'liːd] vt irreg (deceive) irreführen; ~ing a irreführend.

mismanage ['mɪs'mænɪdʒ] vt schlecht verwalten; ~ment Mißwirtschaft f.

misnomer ['mɪs'nəʊmə*] n falsche Bezeichnung f.

misogynist [mɪ'sɒdʒɪnɪst] n Weiberfeind m.

misplace ['mɪs'pleɪs] vt verlegen.

misprint ['mɪsprɪnt] n Druckfehler m.

mispronounce ['mɪsprə'naʊns] vt falsch aussprechen.

misread ['mɪs'riːd] vt irreg falsch lesen.

misrepresent ['mɪsreprɪ'zent] vt falsch darstellen.

miss [mɪs] vt (fail to hit, catch) verfehlen; (not notice) verpassen; (be too late) versäumen, verpassen; (omit) auslassen; (regret the absence of) vermissen; **I ~ you** du fehlst mir; vi fehlen; n (shot) Fehlschuß m; (failure) Fehlschlag m; (title) Fräulein nt.

missal ['mɪsəl] n Meßbuch nt.

misshapen ['mɪs'ʃeɪpən] a mißgestaltet.

missile ['mɪsaɪl] n Geschoß nt, Rakete f.

missing ['mɪsɪŋ] a person vermißt; thing fehlend; **to be ~** fehlen.

mission ['mɪʃən] n (work) Auftrag n, Mission f; (people) Delegation f; (Rel) Mission f; **~ary** Missionar(in f) m.

misspent ['mɪs'spent] a youth vergeudet.

mist [mɪst] n Dunst m, Nebel m; vi (also ~ over, ~ up) sich beschlagen.

mistake [mɪs'teɪk] n Fehler m; vt irreg (misunderstand) mißverstehen; (mix up) verwechseln (for mit); ~n a idea falsch; ~n identity Verwechslung f; **to be ~n** sich irren.

mister ['mɪstə*] n (abbr **Mr**) Herr m.

mistletoe ['mɪsltəʊ] n Mistel f.

mistranslation ['mɪstræns'leɪʃən] n falsche Übersetzung f.

mistreat [mɪs'triːt] vt schlecht behandeln.

mistress ['mɪstrɪs] n (teacher) Lehrerin f; (in house) Herrin f; (lover) Geliebte f; (abbr **Mrs**) Frau f.

mistrust ['mɪs'trʌst] vt mißtrauen (+dat).

misty ['mɪstɪ] a neblig.

misunderstand ['mɪsʌndə'stænd] vti irreg mißverstehen, falsch verstehen; ~ing Mißverständnis nt; (disagreement) Meinungsverschiedenheit f.

misunderstood ['mɪsʌndə'stʊd] a person unverstanden.

misuse ['mɪs'juːs] n falsche(r) Gebrauch m; ['mɪs'juːz] vt falsch gebrauchen.

mite [maɪt] n Milbe f; (fig) bißchen nt.

mitigate ['mɪtɪgeɪt] vt pain lindern; punishment mildern.

mitre, (US) **miter** ['maɪtə*] n (Eccl) Mitra f.

mitt(en) ['mɪt(n)] n Fausthandschuh m.

mix [mɪks] vt (blend) (ver)mischen; vi (liquids) sich (ver)mischen lassen; (people) (get on) sich vertragen; (associate) Kontakt haben; **he ~es well** er ist kontaktfreudig; n (mixture) Mischung f; ~ed a gemischt; ~er (for food) Mixer m; (Tech) Mischmaschine f; ~ture Mischung f; (Med) Saft m; ~up Durcheinander nt, Verwechslung f; ~ up vt (mix) zusammenmischen; (confuse) verwechseln; **to be ~ed up in sth** in etw (dat) verwickelt sein; ~-ed-up a papers, person durcheinander.

moan [məʊn] n Stöhnen nt; (complaint) Klage f; vi stöhnen; (complain) maulen; ~ing nt; Gemaule f.

moat [məʊt] n (Burg)graben m.

mob [mɒb] n Mob m; (the masses) Pöbel m; vt star herfallen über (+acc).

mobile ['məʊbaɪl] a beweglich; library etc fahrbar; n (decoration) Mobile nt; ~ home Wohnwagen m.

mobility [məʊ'bɪlɪtɪ] n Beweglichkeit f.

moccasin ['mɒkəsɪn] n Mokassin m.

mock [mɒk] vt verspotten; (defy) trotzen (+dat); a Schein-; ~ery Spott m; (person) Gespött nt; ~ing a tone spöttisch; ~ing bird Spottdrossel f; ~-up Modell nt.

mode [məʊd] n (Art fund) Weise f.

model ['mɒdl] n Modell nt; (example) Vorbild nt; (in fashion) Mannequin nt; vt (make) formen, modellieren, bilden; (clothes) vorführen; a railway Modell-; (perfect) Muster-; vorbildlich; ~ling, (US) ~ing ['mɒdlɪŋ] (~ making) Basteln nt.

moderate ['mɒdərət] a gemäßigt; (fairly good) mittelmäßig; n (Pol) Gemäßigte(r) mf; ['mɒdəreɪt] vi sich mäßigen; vt mäßigen; ~ly ['mɒdərətlɪ] ad mäßig.

moderation [mɒdə'reɪʃən] n Mäßigung f; **in ~** mit Maßen.

modern ['mɒdən] a modern; history, languages neuere(r, s); (etc Neu-; ~ity [mɒ'dɜːnɪtɪ] Modernität f; ~ization [mɒdənaɪ'zeɪʃən] Modernisierung f; ~ize vt modernisieren.

modest a, ~ly ad ['mɒdɪst, -lɪ] attitude bescheiden; meal, home einfach; (chaste) schamhaft; ~y Bescheidenheit f; (chastity) Schamgefühl nt.

modicum ['mɒdɪkəm] n bißchen nt.

modification [mɒdɪfɪ'keɪʃən] n (Ab)änderung f.

modify ['mɒdɪfaɪ] vt abändern; (Gram) modifizieren.

modulation [mɒdju'leɪʃən] n Modulation f.

module ['mɒdjul] n (Raum)kapsel f.

mohair ['məʊhɛə*] n Mohair m; a Mohair-.

moist [mɔɪst] a feucht; ~en ['mɔɪsn] vt befeuchten; ~ure Feuchtigkeit f; ~urizer Feuchtigkeitscreme f.

molar ['məʊlə*] n Backenzahn m.

molasses [mə'læsɪz] npl Melasse f.

mold [məʊld] (US) = **mould**.

mole [məʊl] n (spot) Leberfleck m; (animal) Maulwurf m; (pier) Mole f.

molecular [məʊ'lekjʊlə*] a molekular, Molekular-.

molecule ['mɒlɪkju:l] n Molekül nt.

molest [məʊ'lest] vt belästigen.

mollusc ['mɒləsk] n Molluske f, Weichtier nt.

mollycoddle ['mɒlɪkɒdl] vt verhätscheln.

molt [məʊlt] (US) = **moult**.

molten ['məʊltən] a geschmolzen.

moment ['məʊmənt] n Moment m, Augenblick m; (importance) Tragweite f; ~ of truth Stunde f der Wahrheit; any ~ jeden Augenblick; ~arily ['məʊmən-'tærəlɪ] ad momentan; ~ary a kurz; ~ous [məʊ'mentəs] a folgenschwer; ~um [məʊ'mentəm] Schwung m.

monarch ['mɒnək] n Herrscher(in f) m; ~ist Monarchist(in f) m; ~y Monarchie f.

monastery ['mɒnəstrɪ] n Kloster nt.

monastic [mə'næstɪk] a klösterlich, Kloster-.

Monday ['mʌndeɪ] n Montag m.

monetary ['mʌnɪtərɪ] a geldlich, Geld-; (of currency) Währungs-, monetär.

money ['mʌnɪ] n Geld nt; ~ed a vermögend; ~lender Geldverleiher m; ~making a einträglich, lukrativ; ~ order Postanweisung f.

mongol ['mɒngəl] n (Med) mongoloide(s) Kind nt; a mongolisch; (Med) mongoloid.

mongoose ['mɒngu:s] n Mungo m.

mongrel ['mʌngrəl] n Promenadenmischung f, a Misch-.

monitor ['mɒnɪtə*] n (Sch) Klassenordner m; (television —) Monitor m; vt broadcasts abhören; (control) überwachen.

monk [mʌŋk] n Mönch m.

monkey ['mʌŋkɪ] n Affe m; ~ nut Erdnuß f; ~ wrench (Tech) Engländer m, Franzose m.

mono- ['mɒnəʊ] pref Mono-.

monochrome ['mɒnəkrəʊm] a schwarzweiß.

monocle ['mɒnəkl] n Monokel nt.

monogram ['mɒnəgræm] n Monogramm nt.

monolithic [mɒnəʊ'lɪθɪk] a monolithisch.

monologue ['mɒnəlɒg] n Monolog m.

monopolize [mə'nɒpəlaɪz] vt beherrschen.

monopoly [mə'nɒpəlɪ] n Monopol nt.

monorail ['mɒnəʊreɪl] n Einschienenbahn f.

monosyllabic ['mɒnəʊsɪ'læbɪk] a einsilbig.

monotone ['mɒnətəʊn] n gleichbleibende(r) Ton(fall) m.

monotonous [mə'nɒtənəs] a eintönig, monoton.

monotony [mə'nɒtənɪ] n Eintönigkeit f, Monotonie f.

monseigneur [mɒnsen'jɜ:*], **monsignor** [mɒn'si:njə*] n Monsignore m.

monsoon [mɒn'su:n] n Monsun m.

monster ['mɒnstə*] n Ungeheuer nt; (person) Scheusal nt; a (col) Riesen-.

monstrosity [mɒns'trɒsɪtɪ] n Ungeheuerlichkeit f; (thing) Monstrosität f.

monstrous ['mɒnstrəs] a (shocking) gräßlich, ungeheuerlich; (huge) riesig.

montage [mɒn'tɑ:ʒ] n Montage f.

month [mʌnθ] n Monat m; ~ly a monatlich, Monats-; ad einmal im Monat; n (magazine) Monatsschrift f.

monument ['mɒnjʊmənt] n Denkmal nt; ~al [mɒnjʊ'mentl] a (huge) gewaltig; ignorance ungeheuer.

moo [mu:] vi muhen.

mood [mu:d] n Stimmung f, Laune f; to be in the ~ for aufgelegt sein zu; I am not in the ~ for laughing mir ist nicht zum Lachen zumute; ~ily ad launisch; ~iness Launenhaftigkeit f; ~y a launisch.

moon [mu:n] n Mond m; ~beam Mondstrahl m; ~less a mondlos; ~light Mondlicht nt; ~lit a mondhell; ~shot Mondflug m.

moor [mʊə*] n Heide f, Hochmoor nt; vt ship festmachen, verankern; vi anlegen; ~ings pl Liegeplatz m; ~land Heidemoor nt.

moose [mu:s] n Elch m.

moot [mu:t] vt aufwerfen; a: ~ point strittige(r) Punkt m.

mop [mɒp] n Mop m; vt (auf)wischen; ~ of hair Mähne f.

mope [məʊp] vi Trübsal blasen.

moped ['məʊped] n (Brit) Moped nt.

moping ['məʊpɪŋ] a trübselig.

moquette [mə'ket] n Plüschgewebe nt.

moral ['mɒrəl] a moralisch; values sittlich; (virtuous) tugendhaft; n Moral f; ~s pl Moral f; ~e [mɒ'rɑ:l] Moral f, Stimmung f; ~ity [mə'rælɪtɪ] Sittlichkeit f; ~ly ad moralisch.

morass [mə'ræs] n Sumpf m.

morbid ['mɔ:bɪd] a morbid, krankhaft; jokes makaber.

more [mɔ:*] a, n, pron, ad mehr; ~ or less mehr oder weniger; ~ than ever mehr denn je; a few ~ noch ein paar; ~ beautiful schöner; ~over ad überdies.

morgue [mɔ:g] n Leichenschauhaus nt.

moribund ['mɒrɪbʌnd] a aussterbend.

morning ['mɔ:nɪŋ] n Morgen m; a morgendlich, Morgen-, Früh-; in the ~ am Morgen; ~ sickness (Schwangerschafts)erbrechen nt.

moron ['mɔ:rɒn] n Schwachsinnige(r) m; ~ic [mə'rɒnɪk] a schwachsinnig.

morose [mə'rəus] a mürrisch.
morphine ['mɔːfiːn] n Morphium nt.
Morse [mɔːs] n (also ~ **code**) Morsealphabet nt.
morsel ['mɔːsl] n Stückchen nt, bißchen nt.
mortal ['mɔːtl] a sterblich; (deadly) tödlich; (very great) Todes-; n (human being) Sterbliche(r) mf; ~**ity** [mɔː'tælɪtɪ] Sterblichkeit f; (death rate) Sterblichkeitsziffer f; ~**ly** ad tödlich.
mortar ['mɔːtə*] n (for building) Mörtel m; (bowl) Mörser m; (Mil) Granatwerfer m.
mortgage ['mɔːgɪdʒ] n Hypothek f; vt eine Hypothek aufnehmen (+acc).
mortification [mɔːtɪfɪ'keɪʃən] n Beschämung f.
mortified ['mɔːtɪfaɪd] a: **I was** ~ es war mir schrecklich peinlich.
mortuary ['mɔːtjuərɪ] n Leichenhalle f.
mosaic [məu'zeɪɪk] n Mosaik nt.
mosque [mɔsk] n Moschee f.
mosquito [mɔs'kiːtəu] n Moskito m.
moss [mɔs] n Moos nt; ~**y** a bemoost.
most [məust] a meiste(r, s); ~ **men** die meisten Männer; ad am meisten; (very) höchst; n das meiste, der größte Teil; (people) die meisten; ~ **of the time** meistens, die meiste Zeit; ~ **of the winter** fast den ganzen Winter über; the ~ **beautiful** der/die/das Schönste; **at the (very)** ~ allerhöchstens; **to make the** ~ **of** das Beste machen aus; ~**ly** ad größtenteils.
motel [məu'tel] n Motel nt.
moth [mɔθ] n Nachtfalter m; (wool-eating) Motte f; ~**ball** Mottenkugel f; ~-**eaten** a mottenzerfressen.
mother ['mʌðə*] n Mutter f; vt bemuttern; a tongue Mutter-; country Heimat-; ~**hood** Mutterschaft f; ~-**in-law** Schwiegermutter f; ~**ly** a mütterlich; ~-**to-be** werdende Mutter f.
mothproof ['mɔθpruːf] a mottenfest.
motif [məu'tiːf] n Motiv nt.
motion ['məuʃən] n Bewegung f; (in meeting) Antrag m; vti winken (+dat), zu verstehen geben (+dat); ~**less** a regungslos; ~ **picture** Film m.
motivated ['məutɪveɪtɪd] a motiviert.
motivation [məutɪ'veɪʃən] n Motivierung f.
motive ['məutɪv] n Motiv nt, Beweggrund m; a treibend.
motley ['mɔtlɪ] a bunt.
motor ['məutə*] n Motor m; (car) Auto nt; vi (im Auto) fahren; a Motor-; ~**bike** Motorrad nt; ~**boat** Motorboot nt; ~**car** Auto nt; ~**cycle** Motorrad nt; ~**cyclist** Motorradfahrer(in f) m; ~**ing** n Autofahren nt; a Auto-; ~**ist** ['məutərɪst] Autofahrer(in f) m; ~ **oil** Motorenöl nt; ~ **racing** Autorennen nt; ~ **scooter** Motorroller m; ~ **vehicle** Kraftfahrzeug nt; ~**way** (Brit) Autobahn f.
mottled ['mɔtld] a gesprenkelt.
motto ['mɔtəu] n Motto nt, Wahlspruch m.
mould [məuld] n Form f; (mildew) Schimmel m; vt (lit, fig) formen; ~**er** vi (decay) vermodern; ~**ing** Formen nt; ~**y** a schimmelig.
moult [məult] vi sich mausern.

mound [maund] n (Erd)hügel m.
mount [maunt] n (liter: hill) Berg m; (horse) Pferd nt; (for jewel etc) Fassung f; vt horse steigen auf (+acc); (put in setting) fassen; exhibition veranstalten; attack unternehmen; vi (also ~ **up**) sich häufen; (on horse) aufsitzen; ~**ain** ['mauntɪn] Berg m; ~**aineer** [mauntɪ'nɪə*] Bergsteiger(in f) m; ~**aineering** Bergsteigen nt; **to go** ~**aineering** klettern gehen; ~**ainous** a bergig; ~**ainside** Berg(ab)hang m.
mourn [mɔːn] vt betrauern, beklagen; vi trauern (for um); ~**er** Trauernde(r) mf; ~**ful** a traurig; ~**ing** (grief) Trauer f; **in** ~**ing** (period etc) in Trauer; (dress) in Trauerkleidung f.
mouse [maus] n, pl **mice** Maus f; ~**trap** Mausefalle f.
moustache [məs'tɑːʃ] n Schnurrbart m.
mousy ['mausɪ] a colour mausgrau; person schüchtern.
mouth [mauθ] n Mund m; (general) Öffnung f; (of river) Mündung f; (of harbour) Einfahrt f; [mauð] vt words affektiert sprechen; **down in the** ~ niedergeschlagen; ~**ful** Mundvoll m; ~**organ** Mundharmonika f; ~**piece** (lit) Mundstück nt; (fig) Sprachrohr nt; ~**wash** Mundwasser nt; ~**watering** a lecker, appetitlich.
movable ['muːvəbl] a beweglich.
move [muːv] n (movement) Bewegung f; (in game) Zug m; (step) Schritt m; (of house) Umzug m; vt bewegen; object rücken; people transportieren; (in job) versetzen; (emotionally) bewegen, ergreifen; **to** ~ **sb to do sth** jdn veranlassen, etw zu tun; vi sich bewegen; (change place) gehen; (vehicle, ship) fahren; (take action) etwas unternehmen; (go to another house) umziehen; **to get a** ~ **on** sich beeilen; **on the** ~ in Bewegung; **to** ~ **house** umziehen; **to** ~ **closer to or towards sth** sich etw (dat) nähern; ~ **about** vi sich hin- und herbewegen; (travel) unterwegs sein; ~ **away** vi weggehen; ~ **back** vi zurückgehen; (to the rear) zurückweichen; ~ **forward** vi vorwärtsgehen, sich vorwärtsbewegen; vt vorschieben; time vorverlegen; ~ **in** vi (to house) einziehen; (troops) einrücken; ~ **on** vi weitergehen; vt weitergehen lassen; ~ **out** vi (of house) ausziehen; (troops) abziehen; ~ **up** vi aufsteigen; (in job) befördert werden; vt nach oben bewegen; (in job) befördern; (Sch) versetzen; ~**ment** Bewegung f; (Mus) Satz m; (of clock) Uhrwerk nt.
movie ['muːvɪ] n Film m; **the** ~**s** (the cinema) das Kino; ~ **camera** Filmkamera f.
moving ['muːvɪŋ] a beweglich; force treibend; (touching) ergreifend.
mow [məu] vt irreg mähen; ~ **down** vt (fig) niedermähen; ~**er** (machine) Mähmaschine f; (lawn-) Rasenmäher m.
Mr [mɪstə*] Herr m.
Mrs ['mɪsɪz] Frau f.
Ms [mɪz] n Frau f.
much [mʌtʃ] a viel; ad sehr; viel; n viel, eine Menge f; ~ **better** viel besser; ~

the same size so ziemlich gleich groß; **how ~?** wieviel?; **too ~** zuviel; **~ to my surprise** zu meiner großen Überraschung; **~ as I should like to** so gern ich möchte.

muck [mʌk] n (lit) Mist m; (fig) Schmutz m; **~ about** (col) vi herumlungern; (meddle) herumalbern (with an +dat); vt **~ sb about** um jdn treiben, was man will; **~ up** vt (col: ruin) vermasseln; (dirty) dreckig machen; **~y** a (dirty) dreckig.

mucus ['mjuːkəs] n Schleim m.

mud [mʌd] n Schlamm m; (fig) Schmutz m.

muddle ['mʌdl] n Durcheinander nt; vt (also **~ up**) durcheinanderbringen; **~ through** vi sich durchwursteln.

muddy ['mʌdɪ] a schlammig.

mudguard ['mʌdgɑːd] n Schutzblech nt.

mudpack ['mʌdpæk] n Moorpackung f.

mud-slinging ['mʌdslɪŋɪŋ] n (col) Verleumdung f.

muff [mʌf] n Muff m.

muffin ['mʌfɪn] n süße(s) Teilchen nt.

muffle ['mʌfl] vt sound dämpfen; (wrap up) einhüllen.

mufti ['mʌftɪ] n: **in ~** in Zivil.

mug [mʌg] n (cup) Becher m; (col: face) Visage f; (col: fool) Trottel m; vt überfallen und ausrauben; **~ging** Überfall m.

muggy ['mʌgɪ] a weather schwül.

mulatto [mjuːˈlætəʊ] n Mulatte m, Mulattin f.

mule [mjuːl] n Maulesel m.

mull [mʌl]: **~ over** vt nachdenken über (+acc).

mulled [mʌld] a wine Glüh-.

multi- ['mʌltɪ] pref Multi-, multi-.

multicoloured, (US) **multicolored** ['mʌltɪˈkʌləd] a mehrfarbig.

multifarious [mʌltɪˈfɛərɪəs] a mannigfaltig.

multilateral ['mʌltɪˈlætərəl] a multilateral.

multiple ['mʌltɪpl] n Vielfache(s) nt; a mehrfach; (many) mehrere; **~ sclerosis** multiple Sklerose f; **~ store** Kaufhauskette f.

multiplication [mʌltɪplɪˈkeɪʃən] n Multiplikation f.

multiply ['mʌltɪplaɪ] vt multiplizieren (by mit); vi (Biol) sich vermehren.

multiracial ['mʌltɪˈreɪʃəl] a gemischtrassig; **~ policy** Rassenintegration f.

multitude ['mʌltɪtjuːd] n Menge f.

mum¹ [mʌm] a: **to keep ~** den Mund halten (about über +acc).

mum² [mʌm] n (col) Mutti f.

mumble ['mʌmbl] vti murmeln; n Gemurmel nt.

mummy ['mʌmɪ] n (dead body) Mumie f; (col) Mami f.

mumps [mʌmps] n Mumps m.

munch [mʌntʃ] vti mampfen.

mundane ['mʌnˈdeɪn] a weltlich; (fig) profan.

municipal [mjuːˈnɪsɪpəl] a städtisch, Stadt-; **~ity** [mjuːnɪsɪˈpælɪtɪ] Stadt f mit Selbstverwaltung.

munificence [mjuːˈnɪfɪsns] n Freigebigkeit f.

munitions [mjuːˈnɪʃənz] npl Munition f.

mural ['mjʊərəl] n Wandgemälde nt.

murder ['mɜːdə*] n Mord m; **it was ~** (fig) es war mörderisch; **to get away with ~** (fig) sich alles erlauben können; vt ermorden; **~er** Mörder m; **~ess** Mörderin f; **~ous** a Mord-; (fig) mörderisch.

murk [mɜːk] n Dunkelheit f **~y** a finster.

murmur ['mɜːmə*] n Murmeln nt; (of water, wind) Rauschen nt; **without a ~** ohne zu murren; vti murmeln.

muscle ['mʌsl] n Muskel m.

muscular ['mʌskjʊlə*] a Muskel-; (strong) muskulös.

muse [mjuːz] vi (nach)sinnen; **M~** Muse f.

museum [mjuːˈzɪəm] n Museum nt.

mushroom ['mʌʃruːm] n Champignon m; Pilz m; vi (fig) emporschießen.

mushy [mʌʃɪ] a breiig; (sentimental) gefühlsduselig.

music ['mjuːzɪk] n Musik f; (printed) Noten pl; **~al** a sound melodisch; person musikalisch; n (show) Musical nt; **~al box** Spieldose f; **~al instrument** Musikinstrument nt; **~ally** ad musikalisch; sing melodisch; **~ hall** (Brit) Varieté nt; **~ian** [mjuːˈzɪʃən] Musiker(in f) m.

muslin ['mʌzlɪn] n Musselin m.

mussel ['mʌsl] n Miesmuschel f.

must [mʌst] v aux müssen; (in negation) dürfen; n Muß nt; **the film is a ~** den Film muß man einfach gesehen haben.

mustache ['mʌstæʃ] (US) = **moustache.**

mustard ['mʌstəd] n Senf m.

muster ['mʌstə*] vt (Mil) antreten lassen; courage zusammennehmen.

mustiness ['mʌstɪnəs] n Muffigkeit f.

mustn't ['mʌsnt] = **must not.**

musty ['mʌstɪ] a muffig.

mute [mjuːt] a stumm; n (person) Stumme(r) mf; (Mus) Dämpfer m.

mutilate ['mjuːtɪleɪt] vt verstümmeln.

mutilation [mjuːtɪˈleɪʃən] n Verstümmelung f.

mutinous ['mjuːtɪnəs] a meuterisch.

mutiny ['mjuːtɪnɪ] n Meuterei f; vi meutern.

mutter ['mʌtə*] vti murmeln.

mutton ['mʌtn] n Hammelfleisch nt.

mutual ['mjuːtʃʊəl] a gegenseitig; beiderseitig; **~ly** ad gegenseitig; auf beiden Seiten; für beide Seiten.

muzzle ['mʌzl] n (of animal) Schnauze f; (for animal) Maulkorb m; (of gun) Mündung f; vt einen Maulkorb anlegen (+dat).

my [maɪ] poss a mein.

myopic [maɪˈɒpɪk] a kurzsichtig.

myrrh [mɜː*] n Myrrhe f.

myself [maɪˈself] pron mich (acc); mir (dat); (emphatic) selbst; **I'm not ~** mit mir ist etwas nicht in Ordnung.

mysterious [mɪsˈtɪərɪəs] a geheimnisvoll, mysteriös; **~ly** ad auf unerklärliche Weise.

mystery ['mɪstərɪ] n (secret) Geheimnis nt;

(sth difficult) Rätsel *nt;* ~ **play** Mysterienspiel *nt.*

mystic ['mɪstɪk] *n* Mystiker *m; a* mystisch; ~**al** *a* mystisch; ~**ism** ['mɪstɪsɪzəm] Mystizismus *m.*

mystification [mɪstɪfɪ'keɪʃən] *n* Verblüffung *f.*

mystify ['mɪstɪfaɪ] *vt* ein Rätsel sein *(+dat);* verblüffen.

mystique [mɪs'tiːk] *n* geheimnisvolle Natur *f.*

myth [mɪθ] *n* Mythos *m; (fig)* Erfindung *f;* ~**ical** *a* mythisch, Sagen-; ~**ological** [mɪθə'lɒdʒɪkəl] *a* mythologisch; ~**ology** [mɪ'θɒlədʒɪ] Mythologie *f.*

N

N, n [en] *n* N *nt,* n *nt.*

nab [næb] *vt (col)* schnappen.

nadir ['neɪdɪə*] *n* Tiefpunkt *m.*

nag [næg] *n (horse)* Gaul *m; (person)* Nörgler(in *f) m; vti* herumnörgeln *(sb* an jdm);* ~**ging** *a doubt* nagend; *n* Nörgelei *f.*

nail [neɪl] *n* Nagel *m; vt* nageln; ~ **down** *vt (lit, fig)* festnageln; ~**brush** Nagelbürste *f;* ~**file** Nagelfeile *f;* ~ **polish** Nagellack *m;* ~ **scissors** *pl* Nagelschere *f.*

naive *a,* ~**ly** *ad* [naɪ'iːv, -lɪ] naiv.

naked ['neɪkɪd] *a* nackt; ~**ness** Nacktheit *f.*

name [neɪm] *n* Name *m; (reputation)* Ruf *m; vt* nennen; *sth new* benennen; *(appoint)* ernennen; **what's your** ~? wie heißen Sie?; **in the** ~ **of** im Namen *(+gen); (for the sake of)* um *(+gen)* willen; ~ **dropping: he's always** ~ **dropping** er wirft immer mit großen Namen um sich; ~**less** *a* namenlos; ~**ly** *ad* nämlich; ~**sake** Namensvetter *m.*

nanny ['nænɪ] *n* Kindermädchen *nt.*

nap [næp] *n (sleep)* Nickerchen *nt; (on cloth)* Strich *m;* **to have a** ~ ein Nickerchen machen.

napalm ['neɪpɑːm] *n* Napalm *m.*

nape [neɪp] *n* Nacken *m.*

napkin ['næpkɪn] *n (at table)* Serviette *f; (Brit: for baby)* Windel *f.*

nappy ['næpɪ] *n (Brit: for baby)* Windel *f.*

narcissism [nɑː'sɪsɪzəm] *n* Narzißmus *m.*

narcotic [nɑː'kɒtɪk] *n* Betäubungsmittel *nt.*

narrate [nə'reɪt] *vt* erzählen.

narration [nə'reɪʃən] *n* Erzählung *f.*

narrative ['nærətɪv] *n* Erzählung *f; a* erzählend.

narrator [nə'reɪtə*] *n* Erzähler(in *f) m.*

narrow ['nærəʊ] *a* eng, schmal; *(limited)* beschränkt; *vi* sich verengen; **to** ~ **sth down to sth** etw auf etw *(acc)* einschränken; ~**ly** *ad miss* knapp; *escape* mit knapper Not; ~**-minded** *a* engstirnig; ~**-mindedness** Engstirnigkeit *f.*

nasal ['neɪzəl] *a* Nasal-.

nastily ['nɑːstɪlɪ] *ad* böse, gehässig.

nastiness ['nɑːstɪnəs] *n* Ekligkeit *f.*

nasty ['nɑːstɪ] *a* ekelhaft, fies; *business, wound* schlimm; **to turn** ~ gemein werden.

nation ['neɪʃən] *n* Nation *f,* Volk *nt;* ~**al** ['næʃənl] *a* national, National-, Landes-; *n* Staatsangehörige(r) *mf;* ~**al anthem** Nationalhymne *f;* ~**alism** ['næʃnəlɪzəm] Nationalismus *m;* ~**alist** ['næʃnəlɪst] *n* Nationalist(in *f) m; a* nationalistisch; ~**ality** [næʃə'nælɪtɪ] Staatsangehörigkeit *f;* Nationalität *f;* ~**alization** [næʃnəlaɪ'zeɪʃən] Verstaatlichung *f;* ~**alize** ['næʃnəlaɪz] *vt* verstaatlichen; ~**ally** ['næʃnəlɪ] *ad* national, auf Staatsebene; ~**-wide** *a,* ad* allgemein, landesweit.

native ['neɪtɪv] *n (born in)* Einheimische(r) *mf; (original inhabitant)* Eingeborene(r) *mf; a (coming from a certain place)* einheimisch; *(of the original inhabitants)* Eingeborenen-; *(belonging to birth)* heimatlich, Heimat-; *(inborn)* angeboren, natürlich; **a** ~ **of Germany** ein gebürtiger Deutscher; ~ **language** Muttersprache *f.*

natter ['nætə*] *vi (col: chat)* quatschen; *n* Gequatsche *nt.*

natural ['nætʃrəl] *a* natürlich; Natur-; *(inborn)* (an)geboren; ~**ist** Naturkundler(in *f) m;* ~**ize** *vt foreigner* einbürgern, naturalisieren; *plant etc* einführen; ~**ly** *ad* natürlich; ~**ness** Natürlichkeit *f.*

nature ['neɪtʃə*] *n* Natur *f;* **by** ~ von Natur (aus).

naught [nɔːt] *n* Null *f.*

naughtily ['nɔːtɪlɪ] *ad* unartig.

naughtiness ['nɔːtɪnəs] *n* Unartigkeit *f.*

naughty ['nɔːtɪ] *a child* unartig, ungezogen; *action* ungehörig.

nausea ['nɔːsɪə] *n (sickness)* Übelkeit *f; (disgust)* Ekel *m;* ~**te** ['nɔːsɪeɪt] *vt* anekeln.

nauseating ['nɔːsɪeɪtɪŋ] *a* ekelerregend; *job* widerlich.

nautical ['nɔːtɪkəl] *a* nautisch; See-; *expression* seemännisch.

naval ['neɪvəl] *a* Marine-, Flotten-.

nave [neɪv] *n* Kirchen(haupt)schiff *nt.*

navel ['neɪvəl] *n* Nabel *m.*

navigable ['nævɪgəbl] *a* schiffbar.

navigate ['nævɪgeɪt] *vt ship etc* steuern; *vi (sail)* (zu Schiff) fahren.

navigation [nævɪ'geɪʃən] *n* Navigation *f.*

navigator ['nævɪgeɪtə*] *n* Steuermann *m; (explorer)* Seefahrer *m; (Aviat)* Navigator *m; (Aut)* Beifahrer(in *f) m.*

navvy ['nævɪ] *n* Straßenarbeiter *m; (on railway)* Streckenarbeiter *m.*

navy ['neɪvɪ] *n* Marine *f,* Flotte *f; (warships etc)* (Kriegs)flotte *f;* ~**-blue** Marineblau *nt; a* marineblau.

nay [neɪ] *ad (old) (no)* nein; *(even)* ja sogar.

neap [niːp] *a:* ~ **tide** Nippflut *f.*

near [nɪə*] *a* nah; **the holidays are** ~ es sind bald Ferien; *ad in der* Nähe; **to come** ~**er** näher kommen; *(time)* näher rücken; *prep (also* ~ **to)** *(space)* in der Nähe *(+gen); (time)* um *(+acc)* ... herum; *vt* sich nähern *(+dat);* ~ **at hand** nicht weit weg; ~**by** *a* nahe (gelegen); *ad* in der Nähe; ~**ly** *ad* fast; **a** ~ **miss** knapp daneben; ~**ness** Nähe *f;* ~**-side** *(Aut)* Beifahrerseite *f; a* auf der Beifahrerseite; **a** ~ **thing** knapp.

neat *a,* ~**ly** *ad* ['niːt, -lɪ] *(tidy)* ordentlich; *(clever)* treffend; *solution* sauber; *(pure)* unverdünnt, rein; ~**ness** Ordentlichkeit *f,* Sauberkeit *f.*

nebulous ['nebjʊləs] *a* nebelhaft, verschwommen.

necessarily ['nesɪsərɪlɪ] *ad* unbedingt; notwendigerweise.

necessary ['nesɪsərɪ] *a* notwendig, nötig.

necessitate [nɪ'sesɪteɪt] *vt* erforderlich machen.

necessity [nɪ'sesɪtɪ] *n (need)* Not *f; (compulsion)* Notwendigkeit *f;* **in case of** ~ im Notfall; **necessities of life** Bedürfnisse *pl* des Lebens.

neck [nek] *n* Hals *m;* ~ **and** ~ Kopf an Kopf; ~**lace** ['neklɪs] Halskette *f;* ~**line** Ausschnitt *m;* ~**tie** *(US)* Krawatte *f.*

nectar ['nektə*] *n* Nektar *m.*

née [neɪ] *a* geborene.

need [ni:d] *n* Bedarf *m no pl (for an* +*dat);* Bedürfnis *nt (for* für*); (want)* Mangel *m; (necessity)* Notwendigkeit *f; (poverty)* Not *f; vt* brauchen; **to** ~ **to do** tun müssen; **if** ~ **be** wenn nötig; **to be in** ~ **of** brauchen; **there is no** ~ **for you to come** du brauchst nicht zu kommen; **there's no** ~ es ist nicht nötig.

needle ['ni:dl] *n* Nadel *f.*

needless *a,* ~**ly** *ad* ['ni:dlɪs, -lɪ] unnötig.

needlework ['ni:dlwɜ:k] *n* Handarbeit *f.*

needy ['ni:dɪ] *a* bedürftig.

negation [nɪ'geɪʃən] *n* Verneinung *f.*

negative ['negətɪv] *n (Phot)* Negativ *nt; a* negativ; *answer* abschlägig.

neglect [nɪ'glekt] *vt (leave undone)* versäumen; *(take no care of)* vernachlässigen; *n* Vernachlässigung *f.*

negligée ['neglɪʒeɪ] *n* Negligé *nt.*

negligence ['neglɪdʒəns] *n* Nachlässigkeit *f.*

negligent *a,* ~**ly** *ad* ['neglɪdʒənt, -lɪ] nachlässig, unachtsam.

negligible ['neglɪdʒəbl] *a* unbedeutend, geringfügig.

negotiable [nɪ'gəʊʃɪəbl] *a cheque* übertragbar, einlösbar.

negotiate [nɪ'gəʊʃɪeɪt] *vi* verhandeln; *vt treaty* abschließen, aushandeln; *difficulty* überwinden; *corner* nehmen.

negotiation [nɪgəʊʃɪ'eɪʃən] *n* Verhandlung *f.*

negotiator [nɪ'gəʊʃɪeɪtə*] *n* Unterhändler *m.*

Negress ['ni:gres] *n* Negerin *f.*

Negro ['ni:grəʊ] *n* Neger *m; a* Neger-.

neighbour, *(US)* **neighbor** ['neɪbə*] *n* Nachbar(in *f) m;* ~**hood** Nachbarschaft *f;* Umgebung *f;* ~**ing** *a* benachbart, angrenzend; ~**ly** *a* freundlich.

neither ['naɪðə*] *a, pron* keine(r, s) (von beiden); *cj* weder; **he can't do it, and** ~ **can I** er kann es nicht und ich auch nicht.

neo- ['ni:əʊ] *pref* neo-.

neon ['ni:ɒn] *n* Neon *nt;* ~ **light** Neonlicht *nt.*

nephew ['nefju:] *n* Neffe *m.*

nerve [nɜ:v] *n* Nerv *m; (courage)* Mut *m; (impudence)* Frechheit *f;* ~-**racking** *a* nervenaufreibend.

nervous ['nɜ:vəs] *a (of the nerves)* Nerven-;

(timid) nervös, ängstlich; ~ **breakdown** Nervenzusammenbruch *m;* ~**ly** *ad* nervös; ~**ness** Nervosität *f.*

nest [nest] *n* Nest *nt.*

nestle ['nesl] *vi* sich kuscheln; *(village)* sich schmiegen.

net [net] *n* Netz *nt; a:* ~(**t**) netto, Netto-, Rein-; ~**ball** Netzball *m.*

netting ['netɪŋ] *n* Netz(werk) *nt,* Drahtgeflecht *nt.*

network ['netwɜ:k] *n* Netz *nt.*

neurosis [njʊə'rəʊsɪs] *n* Neurose *f.*

neurotic [njʊə'rɒtɪk] *a* neurotisch; *n* Neurotiker(in *f) m.*

neuter ['nju:tə*] *a (Biol)* geschlechtslos; *(Gram)* sächlich; *n (Biol)* kastrierte(s) Tier *nt; (Gram)* Neutrum *nt.*

neutral ['nju:trəl] *a* neutral; ~**ity** [nju:'trælɪtɪ] Neutralität *f.*

never ['nevə*] *ad* nie(mals); **well I** ~ na so was!; ~-**ending** *a* endlos; ~**theless** [nevəðə'les] *ad* trotzdem, dennoch.

new [nju:] *a* neu; **they are still** ~ **to the work** die Arbeit ist ihnen noch neu; ~ **from** frisch aus *or* von; ~-**born** *a* neugeboren; ~**comer** Neuankömmling *m;* ~**ly** *ad* frisch, neu; ~ **moon** Neumond *m;* ~**ness** Neuheit *f.*

news [nju:z] *n* Nachricht *f; (Rad, TV)* Nachrichten *pl;* ~**agent** Zeitungshändler *m;* ~**flash** Kurzmeldung *f;* ~**letter** Rundschreiben *nt;* ~**paper** Zeitung *f;* ~**reel** Wochenschau *f.*

New Year ['nju:'jɪə*] *n* Neujahr *nt;* ~'**s Day** Neujahrstag *m;* ~'**s Eve** Silvester(abend *m) nt.*

next [nekst] *a* nächste(r, s); *ad (after)* dann, darauf; *(next time)* das nächstemal; *prep:* ~ **to** (gleich) neben (+*dat);* ~ **to nothing** so gut wie nichts; **to do sth** ~ etw als nächstes tun; **what** ~! was denn noch (alles)?; **the** ~ **day** am nächsten *or* folgenden Tag; ~ **door** *ad* nebenan; ~ **year** nächstes Jahr; ~ **of kin** Familienangehörige(r) *mf.*

nib [nɪb] *n* Spitze *f.*

nibble ['nɪbl] *vt* knabbern an (+*dat).*

nice [naɪs] *a* hübsch, nett, schön; *(subtle)* fein; ~-**looking** *a* hübsch, gutaussehend; ~**ly** *ad* gut, fein, nett.

nick [nɪk] *n* Einkerbung *f;* **in the** ~ **of time** gerade rechtzeitig.

nickel ['nɪkl] *n* Nickel *nt; (US)* Nickel *m (5 cents).*

nickname ['nɪkneɪm] *n* Spitzname *m.*

nicotine ['nɪkəti:n] *n* Nikotin *nt.*

niece [ni:s] *n* Nichte *f.*

niggardly ['nɪgədlɪ] *a* schäbig; *person* geizig.

niggling ['nɪglɪŋ] *a* pedantisch; *doubt, worry* quälend; *detail* kleinlich.

night [naɪt] *n* Nacht *f; (evening)* Abend *m;* **good** ~! gute Nacht!; **at** *or* **by** ~ nachts; abends; ~**cap** *(drink)* Schlummertrunk *m;* ~**club** Nachtlokal *nt;* ~**dress** Nachthemd *nt;* ~**fall** Einbruch *m* der Nacht; ~**ie** *(col)* Nachthemd *nt;* ~**ingale** Nachtigall *f;* ~**life** Nachtleben *nt;* ~**ly** *a, ad* jeden Abend; jede Nacht; ~**mare** Alptraum *m;* ~ **school** Abendschule *f;*

~**time** Nacht f; **at ~ time** nachts; ~
watchman Nachtwächter m.
nil [nɪl] n Nichts nt, Null f (also Sport).
nimble ['nɪmbl] a behend(e), flink; mind
beweglich.
nimbly ['nɪmblɪ] ad flink.
nine [naɪn] n Neun f; a neun; ~**teen**
Neunzehn f; a neunzehn; ~**ty** n Neunzig f;
a neunzig.
ninth [naɪnθ] a neunte(r, s); n Neuntel nt.
nip [nɪp] vt kneifen; n Kneifen nt.
nipple ['nɪpl] n Brustwarze f.
nippy ['nɪpɪ] a (col) person flink; car flott;
(cold) frisch.
nit [nɪt] n Nisse f.
nitrogen ['naɪtrədʒən] n Stickstoff m.
no [nəʊ] a kein; ad nein; n Nein nt; ~
further nicht weiter; ~ **more time**
keine Zeit mehr; **in ~ time** schnell.
nobility [nəʊ'bɪlɪtɪ] n Adel m; **the ~ of**
this deed diese edle Tat.
noble ['nəʊbl] a rank adlig; (splendid) nobel,
edel; n Adlige(r) mf; ~**man** Edelmann m,
Adlige(r) m.
nobly ['nəʊblɪ] ad edel, großmütig.
nobody ['nəʊbədɪ] pron niemand, keiner; n
Niemand m.
nod [nɒd] vi nicken; ~ **off** einnicken; n
Nicken nt.
noise [nɔɪz] n (sound) Geräusch nt; (unpleasant, loud) Lärm m.
noisily ['nɔɪzɪlɪ] ad lärmend, laut.
noisy ['nɔɪzɪ] a laut; crowd lärmend.
nomad ['nəʊmæd] n Nomade m; ~**ic**
[nəʊ'mædɪk] a nomadisch.
no-man's land ['nəʊmænzlænd] n (lit, fig)
Niemandsland nt.
nominal ['nɒmɪnl] a nominell; (Gram)
Nominal-.
nominate ['nɒmɪneɪt] vt (suggest) vorschlagen; (in election) aufstellen; (appoint)
ernennen.
nomination [nɒmɪ'neɪʃən] n (election)
Nominierung f; (appointment) Ernennung f.
nominee [nɒmɪ'niː] n Kandidat(in f) m.
non- [nɒn] pref Nicht-, un-; ~-**alcoholic** a
alkoholfrei.
nonchalant ['nɒnʃələnt] a lässig.
nondescript ['nɒndɪskrɪpt] a mittelmäßig.
none [nʌn] a, pron kein(e, r, s); ad: ~ **the**
wiser keineswegs klüger; ~ **of your**
cheek! sei nicht so frech!
nonentity [nɒ'nentɪtɪ] n Null f (col).
nonetheless ['nʌnðə'les] ad nichtsdesto-
weniger.
non-fiction [nɒn'fɪkʃən] n Sachbücher pl.
nonplussed [nɒn'plʌst] a verdutzt.
nonsense ['nɒnsəns] n Unsinn m.
non-stop [nɒn'stɒp] a pausenlos, Nonstop-.
noodles ['nuːdlz] npl Nudeln pl.
nook [nʊk] n Winkel m, Eckchen nt.
noon [nuːn] n (12 Uhr) Mittag m.
no one ['nəʊwʌn] pron = **nobody.**
noose [nuːs] n Schlinge f.
norm [nɔːm] n Norm f, Regel f.
normal ['nɔːml] a normal; ~**ly** ad
normal; (usually) normalerweise.
north [nɔːθ] n Norden m; a nördlich, Nord-;
ad nördlich, nach or im Norden; ~-**east**

Nordosten m; ~**ern** ['nɔːðən] a nördlich,
Nord-; ~**ward(s)** ad nach Norden;
~-**west** Nordwesten m.
nose [nəʊz] n Nase f; ~**bleed** Nasenbluten
nt; ~-**dive** Sturzflug m; ~**y** a neugierig.
nostalgia [nɒs'tældʒɪə] n Sehnsucht f,
Nostalgie f.
nostalgic [nɒs'tældʒɪk] a wehmütig,
nostalgisch.
nostril ['nɒstrɪl] n Nasenloch nt; (of animal)
Nüster f.
not [nɒt] ad nicht; **he is ~ an expert** er
ist kein Experte; ~ **at all** keineswegs;
(don't mention it) gern geschehen.
notable ['nəʊtəbl] a bemerkenswert.
notably ['nəʊtəblɪ] ad (especially)
besonders; (noticeably) bemerkenswert.
notch [nɒtʃ] n Kerbe f, Einschnitt m.
note [nəʊt] n (Mus) Note f, Ton m; (short
letter) Nachricht f; (Pol) Note f; (comment,
attention) Notiz f; (of lecture etc) Aufzeichnung f; (bank—) Schein m; (fame) Ruf
m, Ansehen nt; vt (observe) bemerken;
(write down) notieren; **to take ~s of** sich
Notizen machen über (+acc); ~**book**
Notizbuch nt; ~-**case** Brieftasche f; ~**d** a
bekannt; ~**paper** Briefpapier nt.
nothing ['nʌθɪŋ] n nichts; **for ~** umsonst;
it is ~ to me es bedeutet mir nichts.
notice ['nəʊtɪs] n (announcement) Anzeige f,
Bekanntmachung f; (attention) Beachtung
f; (warning) Ankündigung f; (dismissal)
Kündigung f; vt bemerken; **to take ~ of**
beachten; **to bring sth to sb's ~** jdn auf
etw (acc) aufmerksam machen; **take no
~!** kümmere dich nicht darum!; ~**able** a
merklich; ~ **board** Anschlagtafel f.
notification [nəʊtɪfɪ'keɪʃən] n Benachrichtigung f.
notify ['nəʊtɪfaɪ] vt benachrichtigen.
notion ['nəʊʃən] n (idea) Vorstellung f, Idee
f; (fancy) Lust f.
notorious [nəʊ'tɔːrɪəs] a berüchtigt.
notwithstanding [nɒtwɪð'stændɪŋ] ad
trotzdem; prep trotz.
nougat ['nuːgɑː] n weiße(r) Nougat m.
nought [nɔːt] n Null f.
noun [naʊn] n Hauptwort nt, Substantiv nt.
nourish ['nʌrɪʃ] vt nähren; ~**ing** a nahrhaft; ~**ment** Nahrung f.
novel ['nɒvəl] n Roman m; a neu(artig);
~**ist** Schriftsteller(in f) m; ~**ty** Neuheit f.
November [nəʊ'vembə*] n November m.
novice ['nɒvɪs] n Neuling m; (Eccl) Novize
m.
now [naʊ] ad jetzt; **right ~** jetzt, gerade;
do it right ~ tun Sie es sofort; ~ **and
then,** ~ **and again** ab und zu, manchmal; ~, ~ na, na; ~ ... or ~ ... then bald ...
bald, mal ... mal; ~**adays** ad heutzutage.
nowhere ['nəʊwɛə*] ad nirgends.
nozzle ['nɒzl] n Düse f.
nuance ['njuːɑːns] n Nuance f.
nuclear ['njuːklɪə*] a energy etc Atom-,
Kern-.
nucleus ['njuːklɪəs] n Kern m.
nude [njuːd] a neu; n (person) Nackte(r)
mf; (Art) Akt m; **in the ~** nackt.
nudge [nʌdʒ] vt leicht anstoßen.

nudist ['nju:dɪst] n Nudist(in f) m.

nudity ['nju:dɪtɪ] n Nacktheit f.

nuisance ['nju:sns] n Ärgernis nt; **that's a ~** das ist ärgerlich; **he's a ~** er geht einem auf die Nerven.

null [nʌl] a: **~ and void** null und nichtig; **~ify** vt für null und nichtig erklären.

numb [nʌm] a taub, gefühllos; vt betäuben.

number ['nʌmbə*] n Nummer f; (numeral also) Zahl f; (quantity) (An)zahl f; (Gram) Numerus m; (of magazine also) Ausgabe f; vt (give a number to) numerieren; (amount to) sein; **his days are ~ed** seine Tage sind gezählt; **~ plate** (Brit Aut) Nummernschild nt.

numbness ['nʌmnəs] n Gefühllosigkeit f.

numbskull ['nʌmskʌl] n Idiot m.

numeral ['nju:mərəl] n Ziffer f.

numerical [nju:'merɪkəl] a order zahlenmäßig.

numerous ['nju:mərəs] a zahlreich.

nun [nʌn] n Nonne f.

nurse [nɜ:s] n Krankenschwester f; (for children) Kindermädchen nt; vt patient pflegen; doubt etc hegen; **~ry** (for children) Kinderzimmer nt; (for plants) Gärtnerei f; (for trees) Baumschule f; **~ry rhyme** Kinderreim m; **~ry school** Kindergarten m.

nursing ['nɜ:sɪŋ] n (profession) Krankenpflege f; **~ home** Privatklinik f.

nut [nʌt] n Nuß f; (screw) Schraubenmutter f; (col) Verrückte(r) mf; **~s** a (col: crazy) verrückt.

nutcase ['nʌtkeɪs] n (col) Verrückte(r) mf.

nutcrackers ['nʌtkrækəz] npl Nußknacker m.

nutmeg ['nʌtmeg] n Muskat(nuß f) m.

nutrient ['nju:trɪənt] n Nährstoff m.

nutrition [nju:'trɪʃən] n Nahrung f.

nutritious [nju:'trɪʃəs] a nahrhaft.

nutshell ['nʌtʃel] n: **in a ~** in aller Kürze.

nylon ['naɪlɒn] n Nylon nt; a Nylon-.

O

O, o [əʊ] n O nt, o nt; (Tel) Null f; see **oh**.

oaf [əʊf] n Trottel m.

oak [əʊk] n Eiche f; a Eichen(holz)-.

oar [ɔ:*] n Ruder nt.

oasis [əʊ'eɪsɪs] n Oase f.

oath [əʊθ] n (statement) Eid m, Schwur m; (swearword) Fluch m.

oatmeal ['əʊtmi:l] n Haferschrot m.

oats [əʊts] n pl Hafer m; (Cook) Haferflocken pl.

obedience [ə'bi:dɪəns] n Gehorsam m.

obedient [ə'bi:dɪənt] a gehorsam, folgsam.

obelisk ['ɒbɪlɪsk] n Obelisk m.

obesity [əʊ'bi:sɪtɪ] n Korpulenz f, Fettleibigkeit f.

obey [ə'beɪ] vti gehorchen (+dat), folgen (+dat).

obituary [ə'bɪtjʊərɪ] n Nachruf m.

object ['ɒbdʒɪkt] n (thing) Gegenstand m, Objekt nt; (of feeling etc) Gegenstand m; (purpose) Ziel nt; (Gram) Objekt nt; [əb'dʒekt] vi dagegen sein, Einwände haben (to gegen); (morally) Anstoß nehmen (to an +acc); **~ion** [əb'dʒekʃən] (reason against) Einwand m, Einspruch m; (dislike) Abneigung f; **~ionable** [əb'dʒekʃnəbl] a nicht einwandfrei; language anstößig; **~ive** [əb'dʒektɪv] n Ziel nt; a objektiv; **~ively** [əb'dʒektɪvlɪ] ad objektiv; **~ivity** [ɒbdʒɪk'tɪvɪtɪ] Objektivität f; **~or** [əb'dʒektə*] Gegner(in f) m.

obligation [ɒblɪ'geɪʃən] n (duty) Pflicht f; (promise) Verpflichtung f; **no ~** unverbindlich; **be under an ~** verpflichtet sein.

obligatory [ɒ'blɪgətərɪ] a bindend, obligatorisch; **it is ~ to . . .** es ist Pflicht, zu . . .

oblige [ə'blaɪdʒ] vt (compel) zwingen; (do a favour) einen Gefallen tun (+dat); **you are not ~d to do it** Sie sind nicht verpflichtet, es zu tun; **much ~d** herzlichen Dank.

obliging [ə'blaɪdʒɪŋ] a entgegenkommend.

oblique [ə'bli:k] a schräg, schief; n Schrägstrich m.

obliterate [ə'blɪtəreɪt] vt auslöschen.

oblivion [ə'blɪvɪən] n Vergessenheit f.

oblivious [ə'blɪvɪəs] a nicht bewußt (of gen); **he was ~ of it** er hatte es nicht bemerkt.

oblong ['ɒblɒŋ] n Rechteck nt; a länglich.

obnoxious [əb'nɒkʃəs] a abscheulich, widerlich.

oboe ['əʊbəʊ] n Oboe f.

obscene [əb'si:n] a obszön, unanständig.

obscenity [əb'senɪtɪ] n Obszönität f; **obscenities** Zoten pl.

obscure [əb'skjʊə*] a unklar; (indistinct) undeutlich; (unknown) unbekannt, obskur; (dark) düster; vt verdunkeln; view verbergen; (confuse) verwirren.

obscurity [əb'skjʊərɪtɪ] n Unklarheit f; (being unknown) Verborgenheit f; (darkness) Dunkelheit f.

obsequious [əb'si:kwɪəs] a servil.

observable [əb'zɜ:vəbl] a wahrnehmbar, sichtlich.

observance [əb'zɜ:vəns] n Befolgung f.

observant [əb'zɜ:vənt] a aufmerksam.

observation [ɒbzə'veɪʃən] n (noticing) Beobachtung f; (surveillance) Überwachung f; (remark) Bemerkung f.

observatory [əb'zɜ:vətrɪ] n Sternwarte f, Observatorium nt.

observe [əb'zɜ:v] vt (notice) bemerken; (watch) beobachten; customs einhalten; **~er** Beobachter(in f) m.

obsess [əb'ses] vt verfolgen, quälen; **to be ~ed with an idea** von einem Gedanken besessen sein; **~ion** [əb'seʃən] Besessenheit f, Wahn m; **~ive** a krankhaft.

obsolescence [ɒbsə'lesns] n Veralten nt.

obsolescent [ɒbsə'lesnt] a veraltend.

obsolete ['ɒbsəli:t] a überholt, veraltet.

obstacle ['ɒbstəkl] n Hindernis nt; **~ race** Hindernisrennen nt.

obstetrics [ɒb'stetrɪks] n Geburtshilfe f.

obstinacy ['ɒbstɪnəsɪ] n Hartnäckigkeit f, Sturheit f.

obstinate a, **~ly** ad ['ɒbstɪnət, -lɪ] hartnäckig, stur.

obstreperous [əb'strepərəs] a aufmüpfig.

obstruct [əb'strʌkt] vt versperren; pipe verstopfen; (hinder) hemmen; ~ion [əb'strʌkʃən] Versperrung f; Verstopfung f; (obstacle) Hindernis nt; ~ive a hemmend.

obtain [əb'teɪn] vt erhalten, bekommen; result erzielen; ~able a erhältlich.

obtrusive [əb'tru:sɪv] a aufdringlich.

obtuse [əb'tju:s] a begriffsstutzig; angle stumpf.

obviate ['ɒbvɪeɪt] vt beseitigen; danger abwenden.

obvious ['ɒbvɪəs] a offenbar, offensichtlich; ~ly ad offensichtlich.

occasion [ə'keɪʒən] n Gelegenheit f; (special event) große(s) Ereignis nt; (reason) Grund m, Anlaß m; on ~ gelegentlich; vt veranlassen; ~al a, ~ally ad gelegentlich; very ~ally sehr selten.

occult [ɒ'kʌlt] n the ~ der Okkultismus; a okkult.

occupant ['ɒkjupənt] n Inhaber(in f) m; (of house etc) Bewohner(in f) m.

occupation [ɒkju'peɪʃən] n (employment) Tätigkeit f, Beruf m; (pastime) Beschäftigung f; (of country) Besetzung f, Okkupation f; ~al a hazard Berufs-; therapy Beschäftigungs-.

occupier ['ɒkjupaɪə*] n Bewohner(in f) m.

occupy ['ɒkjupaɪ] vt (take possession of) besetzen; seat belegen; (live in) bewohnen; position, office bekleiden; position in sb's life einnehmen; time beanspruchen; mind beschäftigen.

occur [ə'kɜ:*] vi (happen) vorkommen, geschehen; (appear) vorkommen; (come to mind) einfallen (to dat); ~rence (event) Ereignis nt; (appearing) Auftreten nt.

ocean ['əuʃən] n Ozean m, Meer nt; ~-going a Hochsee-.

ochre ['əukə*] n Ocker m or nt.

o'clock [ə'klɒk] ad: it is 5 ~ es ist 5 Uhr.

octagonal [ɒk'tægənl] a achteckig.

octane ['ɒkteɪn] n Oktan nt.

octave ['ɒktɪv] n Oktave f.

October [ɒk'təubə*] n Oktober m.

octopus ['ɒktəpəs] n Krake f; (small) Tintenfisch m.

oculist ['ɒkjulɪst] n Augenarzt m/-ärztin f.

odd [ɒd] a (strange) sonderbar; (not even) ungerade; (the other part missing) einzeln; (about) ungefähr; (surplus) übrig; (casual) Gelegenheits-, zeitweilig; ~ity (strangeness) Merkwürdigkeit f; (queer person) seltsame(r) Kauz m; (thing) Kuriosität f; ~ly ad seltsam; ~ly enough merkwürdigerweise; ~ment Rest m, Einzelstück nt; ~s pl Chancen pl; (betting) Gewinnchancen pl; it makes no ~s es spielt keine Rolle; at ~s uneinig; ~s and ends pl Reste pl; Krimskrams m.

ode [əud] n Ode f.

odious ['əudɪəs] a verhaßt; action abscheulich.

odour, (US) **odor** ['əudə*] n Geruch m; ~less a geruchlos.

of [ɒv, əv] prep von; (indicating material) aus; the first ~ May der erste Mai; within a month ~ his death einen Monat nach seinem Tod; a girl ~ ten ein zehnjähriges Mädchen; fear ~ God Gottesfurcht f; love ~ money Liebe f zum Geld; the six ~ us wir sechs.

off [ɒf] ad (absent) weg, fort; (switch) aus(geschaltet), ab(geschaltet); (milk) sauer; I'm ~ ich gehe jetzt; the button's ~, der Knopf ist ab; to be well-/badly ~ reich/arm sein; prep von; (distant from) ab(gelegen) von; 3% ~ 3% Nachlaß or Abzug; just ~ Piccadilly gleich bei Piccadilly; I'm ~ smoking ich rauche nicht mehr.

offal ['ɒfəl] n Innereien pl.

off-colour ['ɒf'kʌlə*] a nicht wohl.

offence, (US) **offense** [ə'fens] n (crime) Vergehen nt, Straftat f; (insult) Beleidigung f.

offend [ə'fend] vt beleidigen; ~er Gesetzesübertreter m; ~ing a verletzend.

offensive [ə'fensɪv] a (unpleasant) übel, abstoßend; weapon Kampf-; remark verletzend; n Angriff m, Offensive f.

offer ['ɒfə*] n Angebot f; on ~ zum Verkauf angeboten; vt anbieten; reward aussetzen; opinion äußern; resistance leisten; ~ing Gabe f; (collection) Kollekte f.

offhand ['ɒf'hænd] a lässig; ad ohne weiteres.

office ['ɒfɪs] n Büro nt; (position) Amt nt; (duty) Aufgabe f; (Eccl) Gottesdienst m; ~ block Büro(hoch)haus nt; ~ boy Laufjunge m; ~r (Mil) Offizier m; (public ~) Beamte(r) m im öffentlichen Dienst; ~ work Büroarbeit f; ~ worker Büroangestellte(r) mf.

official [ə'fɪʃəl] a offiziell, amtlich; n Beamte(r) m; (Pol) amtliche(r) Sprecher m; (of club etc) Funktionär m, Offizielle(r) m; ~ly ad offiziell.

officious [ə'fɪʃəs] a aufdringlich.

offing ['ɒfɪŋ] n: in the ~ in (Aus)sicht.

off-licence ['ɒflaɪsəns] n Wein- und Spirituosenhandlung f.

off-peak ['ɒfpi:k] a heating Speicher-; charges verbilligt.

off-season ['ɒfsi:zn] a außer Saison.

offset ['ɒfset] vt irreg ausgleichen.

offshore ['ɒf'ʃɔ:*] ad in einiger Entfernung von der Küste; a küstennah, Küsten-.

offside ['ɒf'saɪd] a (Sport) im Abseits (stehend); ad abseits; n (Aut) Fahrerseite f.

offspring ['ɒfsprɪŋ] n Nachkommenschaft f; (one) Sprößling m.

offstage ['ɒf'steɪdʒ] ad hinter den Kulissen.

off-the-cuff ['ɒfðəkʌf] a unvorbereitet, aus dem Stegreif.

often ['ɒfn] ad oft.

ogle ['əugl] vt liebäugeln mit.

oh [əu] interj oh, ach.

oil [ɔɪl] n Öl nt; vt ölen; ~can Ölkännchen nt; ~field Ölfeld nt; ~fired a Öl-; ~level Ölstand m; ~ painting Ölgemälde nt; ~ refinery Ölraffinerie f; ~rig Ölplattform f; ~skins pl Ölzeug nt; ~tanker (Öl)tanker m; ~ well Ölquelle f; ~y a ölig; (dirty) ölbeschmiert; manners schleimig.

ointment ['ɔɪntmənt] n Salbe f.

O.K., okay ['əu'keɪ] interj in Ordnung, O.K.;

a in Ordnung; **that's ~ with** or **by me** ich bin damit einverstanden; *n* Zustimmung *f*; *vt* genehmigen.

old [əʊld] *a* alt; *(former also)* ehemalig; **in the ~ days** früher; **any ~ thing** irgend etwas; **~ age** Alter *nt*; **~en** *a (liter)* alt, vergangen; **~-fashioned** *a* altmodisch; **~ maid** alte Jungfer *f*.

olive ['ɒlɪv] *n (fruit)* Olive *f*; *(colour)* Olive *nt*; *a* Oliven-; *(coloured)* olivenfarbig; **~ branch** Olzweig *m*; **~ oil** Olivenöl *nt*.

Olympic [əʊ'lɪmpɪk] *a* olympisch; **~ Games, ~s** *pl* Olympische Spiele *pl*.

omelet(te) ['ɒmlət] *n* Omelett *nt*.

omen ['əʊmən] *n* Zeichen *nt*, Omen *nt*.

ominous ['ɒmɪnəs] *a* bedrohlich.

omission [əʊ'mɪʃən] *n* Auslassung *f*; *(neglect)* Versäumnis *nt*.

omit [əʊ'mɪt] *vt* auslassen; *(fail to do)* versäumen.

on [ɒn] *prep* auf; **~ TV** im Fernsehen; **I have it ~** me ich habe es bei mir; **a ring ~ his finger** ein Ring am Finger; **~ the main road/the bank of the river** an der Hauptstraße/dem Flußufer; **~ foot** zu Fuß; **a lecture ~ Dante** eine Vorlesung über Dante; **~ the left** links; **~ the right** rechts; **~ Sunday** am Sonntag; **~ Sundays** sonntags; **~ hearing this, he left** als er das hörte, ging er; *ad* (dar)auf; **she had nothing ~** sie hatte nichts an; *(no plans)* sie hatte nichts vor; **what's ~ at the cinema?** was läuft im Kino?; **move ~** weitergehen; **go ~** mach weiter; **the light is ~** das Licht ist an; **you're ~** *(col)* akzeptiert; **it's not ~** *(col)* das ist nicht drin; **~ and off** hin und wieder.

once [wʌns] *ad* einmal; *cj* wenn ... einmal; **~ you've seen him** wenn du ihn erst einmal gesehen hast; **~ she had seen him** sobald sie ihn gesehen hatte; **at ~** sofort; *(at the same time)* gleichzeitig; **all at ~** plötzlich; **~ more** noch einmal; **more than ~** mehr als einmal; **~ in a while** ab und zu; **~ and for all** ein für allemal; **~ upon a time** es war einmal.

oncoming ['ɒnkʌmɪŋ] *a traffic* Gegen-, entgegenkommend.

one [wʌn] *a* ein; *(only)* einzig; *n* Eins *f*; *pron* eine(r, s); *(people, you)* man; **this ~, that ~** das; dieser/diese/dieses; **~ day** eines Tages; **the blue ~** der/die/das blaue; **which ~** welche(r, s); **he is ~ of us** er ist einer von uns; **~ by ~** einzeln; **~ another** einander; **~-man** *a* Einmann-; **~self** *pron* sich (selber); **~-way** *a street* Einbahn-.

ongoing ['ɒngəʊɪŋ] *a* stattfindend, momentan; *(progressing)* sich entwickelnd.

onion ['ʌnjən] *n* Zwiebel *f*.

onlooker ['ɒnlʊkə*] *n* Zuschauer(in *f*) *m*.

only ['əʊnlɪ] *ad* nur, bloß; *a* einzige(r, s); **~ yesterday** erst gestern; **~ just arrived** gerade erst angekommen.

onset ['ɒnset] *n (beginning)* Beginn *m*.

onshore ['ɒnʃɔ:*] *a* an Land; *a* Küsten-.

onslaught ['ɒnslɔ:t] *n* Angriff *m*.

onto ['ɒntu] *prep* **= on to.**

onus ['əʊnəs] *n* Last *f*, Pflicht *f*.

onwards ['ɒnwədz] *ad (place)* voran, vorwärts; **from that day ~** von dem Tag an; **from today ~** ab heute.

onyx ['ɒnɪks] *n* Onyx *m*.

ooze [u:z] *vi* sickern.

opacity [əʊ'pæsɪtɪ] *n* Undurchsichtigkeit *f*.

opal ['əʊpəl] *n* Opal *m*.

opaque [əʊ'peɪk] *a* undurchsichtig.

open ['əʊpən] *a* offen; *(public)* öffentlich; *mind* aufgeschlossen; *sandwich* belegt; **in the ~ (air)** im Freien; **to keep a day ~** einen Tag freihalten; *vt* öffnen, aufmachen; *trial, motorway, account* eröffnen; *vi (begin)* anfangen; *(shop)* aufmachen; *(door, flower)* aufgehen; *(play)* Premiere haben; **~ out** *vt* ausbreiten; *hole, business* erweitern; *vi (person)* aus sich herausgehen; **~ up** *vt* route erschließen; *shop, prospects* eröffnen; **~-air** *a* Frei(luft)-; **~er** Öffner *m*; **~ing** *(hole)* Öffnung *f*, Loch *nt*; *(beginning)* Eröffnung *f*, Anfang *m*; *(good chance)* Gelegenheit *f*; **~ly** *ad* offen; *(publicly)* öffentlich; **~-minded** *a* aufgeschlossen; **~-necked** *a* offen.

opera ['ɒpərə] *n* Oper *f*; **~ glasses** *pl* Opernglas *nt*; **~ house** Opernhaus *nt*.

operate ['ɒpəreɪt] *vt machine* bedienen; *brakes, light* betätigen; *vi (machine)* laufen, in Betrieb sein; *(person)* arbeiten; *(Med)* **to ~ on** operieren.

operatic [ɒpə'rætɪk] *a* Opern-.

operation [ɒpə'reɪʃən] *n (working)* Betrieb *m*, Tätigkeit *f*; *(Med)* Operation *f*; *(undertaking)* Unternehmen *nt*; *(Mil)* Einsatz *m*; **in full ~** in vollem Gang; **to be in ~** *(Jur)* in Kraft sein; *(machine)* in Betrieb sein; **~al** *a* einsatzbereit.

operative ['ɒpərətɪv] *a* wirksam; *law* rechtsgültig; *(Med)* operativ; *n* Mechaniker *m*; Agent *m*.

operator ['ɒpəreɪtə*] *n (of machine)* Arbeiter *m*; *(Tel)* Telefonist(in *f*) *m*; **phone the ~** rufen Sie die Vermittlung or das Fernamt an.

operetta [ɒpə'retə] *n* Operette *f*.

opinion [ə'pɪnjən] *n* Meinung *f*; **in my ~** meiner Meinung nach; **a matter of ~** Ansichtssache; **~ated** *a* starrsinnig.

opium ['əʊpɪəm] *n* Opium *nt*.

opponent [ə'pəʊnənt] *n* Gegner *m*.

opportune ['ɒpətju:n] *a* günstig; *remark* passend.

opportunist [ɒpə'tju:nɪst] *n* Opportunist *m*.

opportunity [ɒpə'tju:nɪtɪ] *n* Gelegenheit *f*, Möglichkeit *f*.

oppose [ə'pəʊz] *vt* entgegentreten *(+dat)*; *argument, idea* ablehnen; *plan* bekämpfen; **~d a: to be ~d** sich gegen etw sein; **as ~d to** im Gegensatz zu.

opposing [ə'pəʊzɪŋ] *a* gegnerisch; *points of view* entgegengesetzt.

opposite ['ɒpəzɪt] *a house* gegenüberliegend; *direction* entgegengesetzt; *ad* gegenüber; *prep* gegenüber; **~ me** mir gegenüber; *n* Gegenteil *nt*; **~ number** *(person)* Pendant *nt*; *(Sport)* Gegenspieler *m*.

opposition [ɒpə'zɪʃən] *n (resistance)* Widerstand *m*; *(Pol)* Opposition *f*; *(contrast)* Gegensatz *m*.

oppress [ə'pres] *vt* unterdrücken; *(heat etc)* bedrücken; **~ion** [ə'preʃən] Unterdrückung *f*; **~ive** *a* authority, law ungerecht; *burden, thought* bedrückend; *heat* drückend.

opt [ɒpt] *vi*: **~ for** sth sich entscheiden für etw; **to ~ to do** sth sich entscheiden, etw zu tun; **~ out of** vi sich drücken vor *(+dat)*; *(of society)* ausflippen aus *(+dat)*.

optical ['ɒptɪkəl] *a* optisch.

optician [ɒp'tɪʃən] *n* Optiker *m*.

optimism ['ɒptɪmɪzəm] *n* Optimismus *m*.

optimist ['ɒptɪmɪst] *n* Optimist *m*; **~ic** ['ɒptɪ'mɪstɪk] *a* optimistisch.

optimum ['ɒptɪməm] *a* optimal.

option ['ɒpʃən] *n* Wahl *f*; *(Comm)* Vorkaufsrecht *m*, Option *f*; **~al** *a* freiwillig; *subject* wahlfrei; **~al extras** Extras auf Wunsch.

opulence ['ɒpjʊləns] *n* Reichtum *m*.

opulent ['ɒpjʊlənt] *a* sehr reich.

opus ['əʊpəs] *n* Werk *nt*, Opus *nt*.

or [ɔː*] *cj* oder; **he could not read ~ write** er konnte weder lesen noch schreiben.

oracle ['ɒrəkl] *n* Orakel *nt*.

oral ['ɔːrəl] *a* mündlich; *n (exam)* mündliche Prüfung *f*, Mündliche(s) *nt*.

orange ['ɒrɪndʒ] *n (fruit)* Apfelsine *f*, Orange *f*; *(colour)* Orange *nt*; *a* orange.

orang-outang, orang-utan [ɔː'ræŋuːˈtæn] *n* Orang-Utan *m*.

oration [ɔː'reɪʃən] *n* feierliche Rede *f*.

orator ['ɒrətə*] *n* Redner(in *f*) *m*.

oratorio [ɒrə'tɔːrɪəʊ] *n* Oratorium *nt*.

orbit ['ɔːbɪt] *n* Umlaufbahn *f*; **2 ~s 2** Umkreisungen; **to be in ~** (die Erde/den Mond *etc*) umkreisen; *vt* umkreisen.

orchard ['ɔːtʃəd] *n* Obstgarten *m*.

orchestra ['ɔːkɪstrə] *n* Orchester *nt*; **~l** [ɔː'kestrəl] *a* Orchester-, orchestral; **~te** ['ɔːkɪstreɪt] *vt* orchestrieren.

orchid ['ɔːkɪd] *n* Orchidee *f*.

ordain [ɔː'deɪn] *vt (Eccl)* weihen; *(decide)* verfügen.

ordeal [ɔː'diːl] *n* schwere Prüfung *f*, Qual *f*.

order ['ɔːdə*] *n (sequence)* Reihenfolge *f*; *(good arrangement)* Ordnung *f*; *(command)* Befehl *m*; *(Jur)* Anordnung *f*; *(peace)* Ordnung *f*, Ruhe *f*; *(condition)* Zustand *m*; *(rank)* Klasse *f*; *(Comm)* Bestellung *f*; *(Eccl, honour)* Orden *m*; **out of ~** außer Betrieb; **in ~ to do** sth um etw zu tun; **in ~** that damit; **holy ~s** Priesterweihe *f*; *vt (arrange)* ordnen; *(command)* befehlen *(sth etw acc, sb jdm)*; *(Comm)* bestellen; **~form** Bestellschein *m*; **~ly** *n (Mil)* Offiziersbursche *m*; *(Mil Med)* Sanitäter *m*; *(Med)* Pfleger *m*; *a (tidy)* ordentlich; *(well-behaved)* ruhig; **~ly officer** diensthabender Offizier.

ordinal ['ɔːdɪnl] *a* Ordnungs-, Ordinal-.

ordinarily ['ɔːdnrɪlɪ] *ad* gewöhnlich.

ordinary ['ɔːdnrɪ] *a (usual)* gewöhnlich, normal; *(commonplace)* gewöhnlich, alltäglich.

ordination [ɔːdɪ'neɪʃən] *n* Priesterweihe *f*; *(Protestant)* Ordination *f*.

ordnance ['ɔːdnəns] *n* Artillerie *f*; Munition *f*; **~ factory** Munitionsfabrik *f*.

ore [ɔː*] *n* Erz *nt*.

organ ['ɔːgən] *n (Mus)* Orgel *f*; *(Biol, fig)* Organ *nt*; **~ic** [ɔː'gænɪk] *a* organisch; **~ism** ['ɔːgənɪzm] Organismus *m*; **~ist** Organist(in *f*) *m*.

organization [ɔːgənaɪ'zeɪʃən] *n* Organisation *f*; *(make-up)* Struktur *f*.

organize ['ɔːgənaɪz] *vt* organisieren; **~r** Organisator *m*, Veranstalter *m*.

orgasm ['ɔːgæzəm] *n* Orgasmus *m*.

orgy ['ɔːdʒɪ] *n* Orgie *f*.

Orient ['ɔːrɪənt] *n* Orient *m*.

oriental [ɔːrɪ'entəl] *a* orientalisch; *n* Orientale *m*, Orientalin *f*.

orientate ['ɔːrɪenteɪt] *vt* orientieren.

orifice ['ɒrɪfɪs] *n* Öffnung *f*.

origin ['ɒrɪdʒɪn] *n* Ursprung *m*; *(of the world)* Anfang *m*, Entstehung *f*.

original [ə'rɪdʒɪnl] *a (first)* ursprünglich; *painting* original; *idea* originell; *n* Original *nt*; **~ity** [ərɪdʒɪ'nælɪtɪ] Originalität *f*; **~ly** *ad* ursprünglich; originell.

originate [ə'rɪdʒɪneɪt] *vi* entstehen; **to ~ from** stammen aus; *vt* ins Leben rufen.

originator [ə'rɪdʒɪneɪtə*] *n (of movement)* Begründer *m*; *(of invention)* Erfinder *m*.

ornament ['ɔːnəmənt] *n* Schmuck *m*; *(on mantelpiece)* Nippesfigur *f*; *(fig)* Zierde *f*; **~al** [ɔːnə'mentl] *a* schmückend, Zier-; **~ation** Verzierung *f*.

ornate [ɔː'neɪt] *a* reich verziert; *style* überladen.

ornithologist [ɔːnɪ'θɒlədʒɪst] *n* Ornithologe *m*, Ornithologin *f*.

ornithology [ɔːnɪ'θɒlədʒɪ] *n* Vogelkunde *f*, Ornithologie *f*.

orphan ['ɔːfən] *n* Waise *f*, Waisenkind *nt*; *vt* zur Waise machen; **~age** Waisenhaus *nt*.

orthodox ['ɔːθədɒks] *a* orthodox.

orthopaedic, *(US)* **orthopedic** [ɔːθəʊ'piːdɪk] *a* orthopädisch.

oscillation [ɒsɪ'leɪʃən] *n* Schwingung *f*, Oszillation *f*.

ostensible *a*, **ostensibly** *ad* [ɒs'tensəbl, -blɪ] vorgeblich, angeblich.

ostentation [ɒsten'teɪʃən] *n* Zurschaustellen *nt*.

ostentatious [ɒsten'teɪʃəs] *a* großtuerisch, protzig.

ostracize ['ɒstrəsaɪz] *vt* ausstoßen.

ostrich ['ɒstrɪtʃ] *n* Strauß *m*.

other ['ʌðə*] *a* andere(r, s); **the ~ day** neulich; **every ~ day** jeden zweiten Tag; **any person ~ than him** alle außer ihm; **there are 6 ~s** da sind noch 6; *pron* andere(r, s); *ad*: **~ than** anders als; **~wise** *ad (in a different way)* anders; *(in other ways)* sonst, im übrigen; *(or else)* sonst.

otter ['ɒtə*] *n* Otter *m*.

ought [ɔːt] *v aux* sollen; **he behaves as he ~** er benimmt sich, wie es sich gehört; **you ~ to do that** Sie sollten das tun; **he ~ to win** er müßte gewinnen; **that ~ to do** das müßte *or* dürfte reichen.

ounce [aʊns] *n* Unze *f*.

our [aʊə*] *poss a* unser; **~s** *poss pron* unsere(r, s); **~selves** *pron* uns (selbst); *(emphatic)* (wir) selbst.

oust [aʊst] vt verdrängen.

out [aʊt] ad hinaus/heraus; (not indoors) draußen; (not alight) aus; (unconscious) bewußtlos; (results) bekanntgegeben; **to eat/go** ~ auswärts essen/ausgehen; **that fashion's** ~ das ist nicht mehr Mode; **the ball was** ~ der Ball war aus; **the flowers are** ~ die Blumen blühen; **he was** ~ **in his calculations** seine Berechnungen waren nicht richtig; **to be** ~ **for sth** auf etw (acc) aus sein; ~ **loud** ad laut; ~ **of** prep aus; (away from) außerhalb (+gen); **to be** ~ **of milk** etc keine Milch etc mehr haben; **made** ~ **of wood** aus Holz gemacht; ~ **of danger** außer Gefahr; ~ **of place** fehl am Platz; ~ **of curiosity** aus Neugier; ~ **of ten** neun von zehn; ~ **and** ~ durch und durch; ~**-of-bounds** a verboten; ~**-of-date** a veraltet; ~**-of-doors** ad im Freien; ~**-of-the-way** a (off the general route) abgelegen; (unusual) ungewöhnlich.

outback ['aʊtbæk] n Hinterland nt.

outboard (motor) ['aʊtbɔːd ('mɔʊtə*)] n Außenbordmotor m.

outbreak ['aʊtbreɪk] n Ausbruch m.

outbuilding ['aʊtbɪldɪŋ] n Nebengebäude nt.

outburst ['aʊtbɜːst] n Ausbruch m.

outcast ['aʊtkɑːst] n Ausgestoßene(r) mf.

outclass [aʊt'klɑːs] vt übertreffen.

outcome ['aʊtkʌm] n Ergebnis nt.

outcry ['aʊtkraɪ] n Protest m.

outdated [aʊt'deɪtɪd] a veraltet, überholt.

outdo [aʊt'duː] vt irreg übertrumpfen.

outdoor ['aʊtdɔː*] a Außen-; (Sport) im Freien.

outdoors [aʊt'dɔːz] ad draußen, im Freien; **to go** ~ ins Freie or nach draußen gehen.

outer ['aʊtə*] a äußere(r, s); ~ **space** Weltraum m.

outfit ['aʊtfɪt] n Ausrüstung f; (set of clothes) Kleidung f; ~**ters** (for men's clothes) Herrenausstatter m.

outgoings ['aʊtgɔʊɪŋz] npl Ausgaben pl.

outgrow [aʊt'grɔʊ] vt irreg clothes herauswachsen aus; habit ablegen.

outing ['aʊtɪŋ] n Ausflug m.

outlandish [aʊt'lændɪʃ] a eigenartig.

outlaw ['aʊtlɔː] n Geächtete(r) m; vt ächten; (thing) verbieten.

outlay ['aʊtleɪ] n Auslage f.

outlet ['aʊtlet] n Auslaß m, Abfluß m; (Comm) Absatzmarkt m; (for emotions) Ventil nt.

outline ['aʊtlaɪn] n Umriß m.

outlive [aʊt'lɪv] vt überleben.

outlook ['aʊtlʊk] n (lit, fig) Aussicht f; (attitude) Einstellung f.

outlying ['aʊtlaɪɪŋ] a entlegen; district Außen-.

outmoded [aʊt'mɔʊdɪd] a veraltet.

outnumber [aʊt'nʌmbə*] vt zahlenmäßig überlegen sein (+dat).

outpatient ['aʊtpeɪʃənt] n ambulante(r) Patient(in f) m.

outpost ['aʊtpɔʊst] n (Mil, fig) Vorposten m.

output ['aʊtpʊt] n Leistung f, Produktion f.

outrage ['aʊtreɪdʒ] n (cruel deed) Aus-

schreitung f, Verbrechen nt; (indecency) Skandal m; vt morals verstoßen gegen; person empören; ~**ous** [aʊt'reɪdʒəs] a unerhört, empörend.

outright ['aʊtraɪt] ad (at once) sofort; (openly) ohne Umschweife; **to refuse** ~ rundweg ablehnen; a denial völlig; sale Total-; winner unbestritten.

outset ['aʊtset] n Beginn m.

outside ['aʊt'saɪd] n Außenseite f; **on the** ~ außen; **at the very** ~ höchstens; a äußere(r, s), Außen-; price Höchst-; chance gering; ad außen; **to go** ~ nach draußen or hinaus gehen; prep außerhalb (+gen); ~**r** Außenseiter(in f) m.

outsize ['aʊtsaɪz] a übergroß.

outskirts ['aʊtskɜːts] npl Stadtrand m.

outspoken [aʊt'spəʊkən] a offen, freimütig.

outstanding [aʊt'stændɪŋ] a hervorragend; debts etc ausstehend.

outstay [aʊt'steɪ] vt: ~ **one's welcome** länger bleiben als erwünscht.

outstretched ['aʊtstretʃt] a ausgestreckt.

outward ['aʊtwəd] a äußere(r, s); journey Hin-; freight ausgehend; ad nach außen; ~**ly** ad äußerlich.

outweigh [aʊt'weɪ] vt (fig) überwiegen.

outwit [aʊt'wɪt] vt überlisten.

outworn [aʊt'wɔːn] a expression abgedroschen.

oval ['əʊvəl] a oval; n Oval nt.

ovary ['əʊvərɪ] n Eierstock m.

ovation [əʊ'veɪʃən] n Beifallssturm m.

oven ['ʌvn] n Backofen m.

over ['əʊvə*] ad (across) hinüber/herüber; (finished) vorbei; (left) übrig; (again) wieder, noch einmal; prep über; (in every part of) in; pref (excessively) übermäßig; **famous the world** ~ in der ganzen Welt berühmt; **five times** ~ fünfmal; ~ **the weekend** übers Wochenende; ~ **coffee** bei einer Tasse Kaffee; ~ **the phone** am Telephon; **all** ~ (everywhere) überall; (finished) vorbei; ~ **and** ~ wieder; ~ **and above** darüber hinaus.

over- ['əʊvə*] pref über-.

overact ['əʊvər'ækt] vi übertreiben.

overall ['əʊvərɔːl] n (Brit) (for woman) Kittelschürze f; a situation allgemein; length Gesamt-; ad insgesamt; ~**s** pl (for man) Overall m.

overawe [əʊvər'ɔː] vt (frighten) einschüchtern; (make impression) überwältigen.

overbalance [əʊvə'bæləns] vi Übergewicht bekommen.

overbearing [əʊvə'bɛərɪŋ] a aufdringlich.

overboard ['əʊvəbɔːd] ad über Bord.

overcast ['əʊvəkɑːst] a bedeckt.

overcharge ['əʊvə'tʃɑːdʒ] vt zuviel verlangen von.

overcoat ['əʊvəkəʊt] n Mantel m.

overcome [əʊvə'kʌm] vt irreg überwinden; (sleep, emotion) übermannen; ~ **by the song** vom Lied übermannt.

overcrowded [əʊvə'kraʊdɪd] a überfüllt.

overcrowding [əʊvə'kraʊdɪŋ] n Überfüllung f.

overdo [əʊvəˈduː] vt irreg (cook too much) verkochen; (exaggerate) übertreiben.

overdose [ˈəʊvədəʊs] n Überdosis f.

overdraft [ˈəʊvədrɑːft] n (Konto)Überziehung f; **to have an ~** sein Konto überzogen haben.

overdrawn [ˈəʊvəˈdrɔːn] a account überzogen.

overdrive [ˈəʊvədraɪv] n (Aut) Schnellgang m.

overdue [ˈəʊvəˈdjuː] a überfällig.

overenthusiastic [ˈəʊvərɪnθjuːzɪˈæstɪk] a zu begeistert.

overestimate [ˈəʊvərˈestɪmeɪt] vt überschätzen.

overexcited [ˈəʊvərɪkˈsaɪtɪd] a überreizt; children aufgeregt.

overexertion [ˈəʊvərɪgˈzɜːʃən] n Überanstrengung f.

overexpose [ˈəʊvərɪksˈpəʊz] vt (Phot) überbelichten.

overflow [əʊvəˈfləʊ] vi überfließen; [ˈəʊvəfləʊ] n (excess) Überschuß m; (outlet) Überlauf m.

overgrown [ˈəʊvəˈgrəʊn] a garden verwildert.

overhaul [əʊvəˈhɔːl] vt car überholen; plans überprüfen; [ˈəʊvəhɔːl] n Überholung f.

overhead [ˈəʊvəhed] a Hoch-; wire oberirdisch; lighting Decken-; [ˈəʊvəˈhed] ad oben; **~s** pl allgemeine Unkosten pl.

overhear [əʊvəˈhɪə*] vt irreg (mit an)hören.

overjoyed [əʊvəˈdʒɔɪd] a überglücklich.

overland [ˈəʊvəlænd] a Überland-; [ˈəʊvəˈlænd] ad travel über Land.

overlap [əʊvəˈlæp] vi sich überschneiden; (objects) sich teilweise decken; [ˈəʊvəlæp] n Überschneidung f.

overload [əʊvəˈləʊd] vt überladen.

overlook [əʊvəˈlʊk] vt (view from above) überblicken; (not to notice) übersehen; (pardon) hinwegsehen über (+acc).

overlord [ˈəʊvəlɔːd] n Lehnsherr m.

overnight [ˈəʊvəˈnaɪt] a journey Nacht-; ad über Nacht; **~ bag** Reisetasche f; **~ stay** Übernachtung f.

overpass [ˈəʊvəpɑːs] n Überführung f.

overpower [əʊvəˈpaʊə*] vt überwältigen; **~ing** a überwältigend.

overrate [əʊvəˈreɪt] vt überschätzen.

override [əʊvəˈraɪd] vt irreg order, decision aufheben; objection übergehen.

overriding [əʊvəˈraɪdɪŋ] a Haupt-, vorherrschend.

overrule [əʊvəˈruːl] vt verwerfen; **we were ~d** unser Vorschlag wurde verworfen.

overseas [ˈəʊvəˈsiːz] ad nach/in Übersee; a überseeisch, Übersee-.

overseer [ˈəʊvəsɪə*] n Aufseher m.

overshadow [əʊvəˈʃædəʊ] vt überschatten.

overshoot [əʊvəˈʃuːt] vt irreg runway hinausschießen über (+acc).

oversight [ˈəʊvəsaɪt] n (mistake) Versehen nt.

oversimplify [ˈəʊvəˈsɪmplɪfaɪ] vt zu sehr vereinfachen.

oversleep [ˈəʊvəˈsliːp] vi irreg verschlafen.

overspill [ˈəʊvəspɪl] n (Bevölkerungs)Überschuß m.

overstate [əʊvəˈsteɪt] vt übertreiben; **~ment** Übertreibung f.

overt [əʊˈvɜːt] a offen(kundig).

overtake [əʊvəˈteɪk] vti irreg überholen.

overthrow [əʊvəˈθrəʊ] vt irreg (Pol) stürzen.

overtime [ˈəʊvətaɪm] n Überstunden pl.

overtone [ˈəʊvətəʊn] n (fig) Note f.

overture [ˈəʊvətjʊə*] n Ouvertüre f; **~s** pl (fig) Angebot nt.

overturn [əʊvəˈtɜːn] vti umkippen.

overweight [ˈəʊvəˈweɪt] a zu dick, zu schwer.

overwhelm [əʊvəˈwelm] vt überwältigen; **~ing** a überwältigend.

overwork [ˈəʊvəˈwɜːk] n Überarbeitung f; vt überlasten; vi sich überarbeiten.

overwrought [ˈəʊvəˈrɔːt] a überreizt.

owe [əʊ] vt schulden; **to ~ sth to sb** money jdm etw schulden; favour etc jdm etw verdanken.

owing to [ˈəʊɪŋˈtuː] prep wegen (+gen).

owl [aʊl] n Eule f.

own [əʊn] vt besitzen; (admit) zugeben; **who ~s that?** wem gehört das?; a eigen; **I have money of my ~** ich habe selbst Geld; n Eigentum nt; **all my ~** mein Eigentum; **on one's ~** allein; **~ up** vi zugeben (to sth etw acc); **~er** Besitzer(in f) m, Eigentümer(in f) m; **~ership** Besitz m.

ox [ɒks] n Ochse m.

oxide [ˈɒksaɪd] n Oxyd nt.

oxtail [ˈɒksteɪl] n: **~ soup** Ochsenschwanzsuppe f.

oxyacetylene [ˈɒksɪəˈsetɪliːn] a Azetylensauerstoff-.

oxygen [ˈɒksɪdʒən] n Sauerstoff m; **~ mask** Sauerstoffmaske f; **~ tent** Sauerstoffzelt nt.

oyster [ˈɔɪstə*] n Auster f.

ozone [ˈəʊzəʊn] n Ozon nt.

P

P, p [piː] n P nt, p nt.

pa [pɑː] n (col) Papa m.

pace [peɪs] n Schritt m; (speed) Geschwindigkeit f, Tempo nt; vi schreiten; **to keep ~ with** Schritt halten mit; **~-maker** Schrittmacher m.

pacification [pæsɪfɪˈkeɪʃən] n Befriedung f.

pacifism [ˈpæsɪfɪzəm] n Pazifismus m.

pacifist [ˈpæsɪfɪst] n Pazifist m.

pacify [ˈpæsɪfaɪ] vt befrieden; (calm) beruhigen.

pack [pæk] n Packen m; (of wolves) Rudel nt; (of hounds) Meute f; (of cards) Spiel nt; (gang) Bande f; vti case packen; clothes einpacken; **~age** Paket nt; **~age tour** Pauschalreise; f ; **~et** Päckchen nt; **~horse** Packpferd nt; **~ ice** Packeis nt; **~ing** (action) Packen nt; (material) Verpackung f, **~ing case** (Pack)kiste f.

pact [pækt] n Pakt m, Vertrag m.

pad [pæd] n (of paper) (Schreib)block m;

(for inking) Stempelkissen *nt; (padding)* Polster *nt; vt* polstern.

paddle ['pædl] *n* Paddel *nt; vt boat* paddeln; *vi (in sea)* plantschen.

paddling pool ['pædliŋ pu:l] *n* Plantschbecken *nt*.

paddock ['pædɔk] *n* Koppel *f*.

paddy ['pædɪ] *n* → **field** Reisfeld *nt*.

padlock ['pædlɔk] *n* Vorhängeschloß *nt*.

padre ['pɑ:drɪ] *n* Militärgeistliche(r) *m*.

paediatrics [pi:dɪ'ætrɪks] *n* Kinderheilkunde *f*.

pagan ['peɪgən] *a* heidnisch.

page [peɪdʒ] *n* Seite *f; (person)* Page *m; vt (in hotel etc)* ausrufen lassen.

pageant ['pædʒənt] *n* Festzug *m; ~ry* Gepränge *nt*.

pagoda [pə'gəʊdə] *n* Pagode *f*.

pail [peɪl] *n* Eimer *m*.

pain [peɪn] *n* Schmerz *m*, Schmerzen *pl; ~s pl (efforts)* große Mühe *f*, große Anstrengungen *pl;* **to be at ~s to do sth** sich *(dat)* Mühe geben, etw zu tun; **~ed** *a expression* gequält; **~ful** *a (physically)* schmerzhaft; *(embarrassing)* peinlich; *(difficult)* mühsam; **~-killing drug** schmerzstillende(s) Mittel *nt;* **~less** *a* schmerzlos; **~staking** *a* gewissenhaft.

paint [peɪnt] *n* Farbe *f; vt* anstreichen; *picture* malen; **~brush** Pinsel *m;* **~er** Maler *m; (decorator)* Maler *m*, Anstreicher *m;* **~ing** *(act)* Malen *nt; (Art)* Malerei *f; (picture)* Bild *nt*, Gemälde *nt*.

pair [pɛə*] *n* Paar *nt; ~ of scissors* Schere *f; ~ of trousers* Hose *f*.

pajamas *(US)* [pə'dʒɑ:məz] *npl* Schlafanzug *m*.

pal [pæl] *n (col)* Kumpel *m; (woman)* (gute) Freundin *f*.

palace ['pæləs] *n* Palast *m*, Schloß *nt*.

palatable ['pælətəbl] *a* schmackhaft.

palate ['pælɪt] *n* Gaumen *m; (taste)* Geschmack *m*.

palaver [pə'lɑ:və*] *n (col)* Theater *nt*.

pale [peɪl] *a face* blaß, bleich; *colour* hell, blaß; **~ness** Blässe *f*.

palette ['pælɪt] *n* Palette *f*.

palisade [pælɪ'seɪd] *n* Palisade *f*.

pall [pɔ:l] *n* Bahr- or Leichentuch *nt; (of smoke)* (Rauch)wolke *f; vi* jeden Reiz verlieren, verblassen; **~bearer** Sargträger *m*.

pallid ['pælɪd] *a* blaß, bleich.

pally ['pælɪ] *a (col)* befreundet.

palm [pɑ:m] *n (of hand)* Handfläche *f; (also ~ tree)* Palme *f; ~ist* Handleserin *f;* **P~ Sunday** Palmsonntag *m*.

palpable ['pælpəbl] *a (lit, fig)* greifbar.

palpably ['pælpəblɪ] *ad* offensichtlich.

palpitation [pælpɪ'teɪʃən] *n* Herzklopfen *nt*.

paltry ['pɔ:ltrɪ] *a* armselig.

pamper ['pæmpə*] *vt* verhätscheln.

pamphlet ['pæmflət] *n* Broschüre *f*.

pan [pæn] *n* Pfanne *f; vi (Cine)* schwenken.

pan- [pæn] *pref* Pan-, All-.

panacea [pænə'sɪə] *n (fig)* Allheilmittel *nt*.

panache [pə'næʃ] *n* Schwung *m*.

pancake ['pænkeɪk] *n* Pfannkuchen *m*.

panda ['pændə] *n* Panda *m*.

pandemonium [pændɪ'məʊnɪəm] *n* Hölle *f; (noise)* Höllenlärm *m*.

pander ['pændə*] *vi* sich richten *(to* nach*)*.

pane [peɪn] *n* (Fenster)scheibe *f*.

panel ['pænl] *n (of wood)* Tafel *f; (TV)* Diskussionsteilnehmer *pl;* **~ing** *(US)*, **~ling** Täfelung *f*.

pang [pæŋ] *n* Stich *m*, Qual *f; ~s of conscience** Gewissensbisse *pl*.

panic ['pænɪk] *n* Panik *f; a* panisch; *vi* von panischem Schrecken erfaßt werden, durchdrehen; **don't ~** *(nur)* keine Panik; **~ky** *a person* überängstlich.

pannier ['pænɪə*] *n* (Trage)korb *m; (on bike)* Satteltasche *f*.

panorama [pænə'rɑ:mə] *n* Rundblick *m*, Panorama *nt*.

panoramic [pænə'ræmɪk] *a* Panorama-.

pansy ['pænzɪ] *n (flower)* Stiefmütterchen *nt; (col)* Schwule(r) *m*.

pant [pænt] *vi* keuchen; *(dog)* hecheln.

pantechnicon [pæn'teknɪkən] *n* Möbelwagen *m*.

panther ['pænθə*] *n* Panther *m*.

panties ['pæntɪz] *npl* (Damen)slip *m*.

pantomime ['pæntəmaɪm] *n* Märchenkomödie *f* um Weihnachten.

pantry ['pæntrɪ] *n* Vorratskammer *f*.

pants [pænts] *npl* Unterhose *f; (trousers)* Hose *f*.

papal ['peɪpəl] *a* päpstlich.

paper ['peɪpə*] *n* Papier *nt; (newspaper)* Zeitung *f; (essay)* Vortrag *m*, Referat *nt; a* Papier-, aus Papier; *vt wall* tapezieren; **~s** *pl (identity)* Ausweis(papiere *pl) m;* **~back** Taschenbuch *nt; ~ bag** Tüte *f; ~ clip** Büroklammer *f;* **~weight** Briefbeschwerer *m;* **~work** Schreibarbeit *f*.

papier-mâché ['pæpɪeɪ'mæʃeɪ] *n* Papiermaché *nt*.

paprika ['pæprɪkə] *n* Paprika *m*.

papyrus [pə'paɪərəs] *n* Papyrus *m*.

par [pɑ:*] *n (Comm)* Nennwert *m; (Golf)* Par *nt;* **on a ~ with** ebenbürtig *(+dat);* **to be on a ~ with sb** sich mit jdm messen können; **below ~** unter (jds) Niveau.

parable ['pærəbl] *n* Parabel *f; (Rel)* Gleichnis *nt*.

parachute ['pærəʃu:t] *n* Fallschirm *m; vi* (mit dem Fallschirm) abspringen.

parachutist ['pærəʃu:tɪst] *n* Fallschirmspringer *m*.

parade [pə'reɪd] *n* Parade *f; vt* aufmarschieren lassen; *vi* paradieren, vorbeimarschieren.

paradise ['pærədaɪs] *n* Paradies *nt*.

paradox ['pærədɔks] *n* Paradox *nt; ~ical* [pærə'dɔksɪkəl] *a* paradox, widersinnig; **~ically** [pærə'dɔksɪkəlɪ] *ad* paradoxerweise.

paraffin ['pærəfɪn] *n* Paraffin *nt*.

paragraph ['pærəgrɑ:f] *n* Absatz *m*, Paragraph *m*.

parallel ['pærəlel] *a* parallel; *n* Parallele *f*.

paralysis [pə'rælɪsɪs] *n* Lähmung *f*.

paralyze ['pærəlaɪz] *vt* lähmen.

paramount ['pærəmaʊnt] *a* höchste(r, s), oberste(r, s).

paranoia [pærə'nɔɪə] n Paranoia f.

parapet ['pærəpɪt] n Brüstung f.

paraphernalia ['pærəfə'neɪlɪə] n Zubehör nt, Utensilien pl.

paraphrase ['pærəfreɪz] vt umschreiben.

paraplegic [pærə'pliːdʒɪk] n Querschnittsgelähmte(r) mf.

parasite ['pærəsaɪt] n (lit, fig) Schmarotzer m, Parasit m.

parasol ['pærəsɒl] n Sonnenschirm m.

paratrooper ['pærətruːpə*] n Fallschirmjäger m.

parcel ['pɑːsl] n Paket nt; vt (also ~ up) einpacken.

parch [pɑːtʃ] vt (aus)dörren; **I'm ~ed** ich bin am Verdursten.

parchment ['pɑːtʃmənt] n Pergament nt.

pardon ['pɑːdn] n Verzeihung f; vt (Jur) begnadigen; ~ **me!**, **I beg your ~!** verzeihen Sie bitte!; (objection) aber ich bitte Sie!; ~ **me?** (US), (**I beg your**) ~? wie bitte?

parent ['peərənt] n Elternteil m; ~**al** [pə'rentl] a elterlich, Eltern-; ~**hood** Elternschaft f; ~**s** pl Eltern pl; ~ **ship** Mutterschiff nt.

parenthesis [pə'renθɪsɪs] n Klammer f; (sentence) Parenthese f.

parish ['pærɪʃ] n Gemeinde f; ~**ioner** [pə'rɪʃənə*] Gemeindemitglied nt.

parity ['pærɪtɪ] n (Fin) Umrechnungskurs m, Parität f.

park [pɑːk] n Park m; vti parken; ~**ing** Parken nt; **'no ~ing'** Parken verboten; ~**ing lot** (US) Parkplatz m; ~**ing meter** Parkuhr f; ~**ing place** Parkplatz m.

parliament ['pɑːləmənt] n Parlament nt; ~**ary** [pɑːlə'mentərɪ] a parlamentarisch, Parlaments-.

parlour, (US) **parlor** ['pɑːlə*] n Salon m, Wohnzimmer nt.

parlous ['pɑːləs] a state schlimm.

parochial [pə'rəʊkɪəl] a Gemeinde-, gemeindlich; (narrow-minded) eng(stirnig), Provinz-.

parody ['pærədɪ] n Parodie f; vt parodieren.

parole [pə'rəʊl] n: **on** ~ (prisoner) auf Bewährung.

parquet ['pɑːkeɪ] n Parkett(fußboden m) nt.

parrot ['pærət] n Papagei m; ~ **fashion** ad wie ein Papagei.

parry ['pærɪ] vt parieren, abwehren.

parsimonious a, ~**ly** ad [pɑːsɪ'məʊnɪəs, -lɪ] knauserig.

parsley ['pɑːslɪ] n Petersilie m.

parsnip ['pɑːsnɪp] n Pastinake f, Petersilienwurzel f.

parson ['pɑːsn] n Pfarrer m.

part [pɑːt] n (piece) Teil m; Stück nt; (Theat) Rolle f; (of machine) Teil nt; a Teil-; ad = **partly**; vt trennen; hair scheiteln; vi (people) sich trennen, Abschied nehmen; **for my** ~ ich für meinen Teil; **for the most** ~ meistens, größtenteils; ~ **with** vt hergeben; (renounce) aufgeben; **in ~ exchange** in Zahlung; ~**ial** ['pɑːʃəl] a (incomplete) teilweise, Teil-; (biased) ein-

genommen, parteiisch; eclipse partiell; **to be** ~**ial to** eine (besondere) Vorliebe haben für; ~**ially** ['pɑːʃəlɪ] ad teilweise, zum Teil.

participate [pɑː'tɪsɪpeɪt] vi teilnehmen (in an +dat).

participation [pɑːtɪsɪ'peɪʃən] n Teilnahme f; (sharing) Beteiligung f.

participle ['pɑːtɪsɪpl] n Partizip nt, Mittelwort nt.

particular [pə'tɪkjʊlə*] a bestimmt, speziell; (exact) genau; (fussy) eigen; in Einzelheit f; ~**s** pl (details) Einzelheiten pl; Personalien pl; ~**ly** ad besonders.

parting ['pɑːtɪŋ] n (separation) Abschied m, Trennung f; (of hair) Scheitel m; a Abschieds-.

partisan [pɑːtɪ'zæn] n Parteigänger m; (guerrilla) Partisan m; a Partei-; Partisanen-.

partition [pɑː'tɪʃən] n (wall) Trennwand f; (division) Teilung f.

partly ['pɑːtlɪ] ad zum Teil, teilweise.

partner ['pɑːtnə*] n Partner m; (Comm also) Gesellschafter m, Teilhaber m; vt der Partner sein von; ~**ship** Partnerschaft f, Gemeinschaft f; (Comm) Teilhaberschaft f.

partridge ['pɑːtrɪdʒ] n Rebhuhn nt.

part-time ['pɑːt'taɪm] a (half-day only) halbtägig, Halbtags-; (part of the week only) nebenberuflich; ad halbtags; nebenberuflich.

party ['pɑːtɪ] n (Pol, Jur) Partei f; (group) Gesellschaft f; (celebration) Party f; a dress Gesellschafts-, Party-; politics Partei-.

pass [pɑːs] vt vorbeikommen an (+dat); (on foot) vorbeigehen an (+dat); vorbeifahren an (+dat); (surpass) übersteigen; (hand on) weitergeben; (approve) gelten lassen, genehmigen; time verbringen; exam bestehen; vi (go by) vorbeigehen; vorbeifahren; (years) vergehen; (be successful) bestehen; n (in mountains) Paß m; (permission) Durchgangs- or Passierschein m; (Sport) Paß m, Abgabe f; (in exam) Bestehen nt; **to get a** ~ bestehen; ~ **away** vi (euph) verscheiden; ~ **by** vi vorbeigehen; vorbeifahren; (years) vergehen; ~ **for** vi gehalten werden für; ~ **out** vi (faint) ohnmächtig werden; ~**able** a road passierbar, befahrbar; (fairly good) passabel, leidlich; ~**ably** ad leidlich, ziemlich; ~**age** ['pæsɪdʒ] (corridor) Gang m, Korridor m; (in book) (Text)stelle f; (voyage) Überfahrt f; ~**ageway** Passage f, Durchgang m.

passenger ['pæsɪndʒə*] n Passagier m; (on bus) Fahrgast m; (in aeroplane also) Fluggast m.

passer-by ['pɑːsə'baɪ] n Passant(in f) m.

passing ['pɑːsɪŋ] n (death) Ableben nt; a car vorbeifahrend; thought, affair momentan; **in ~** en passant.

passion ['pæʃən] n Leidenschaft f; ~**ate** a, ~**ately** ad leidenschaftlich.

passive ['pæsɪv] n Passiv nt; a Passiv-, passiv.

Passover ['pɑːsəʊvə*] n Passahfest nt.

passport ['pɑːspɔːt] n (Reise)paß m.

password ['pɑːswɔːd] n Parole f, Kennwort nt, Losung f.

past [pɑːst] n Vergangenheit f; ad vorbei; prep **to go ~ sth** an etw (dat) vorbeigehen; **to be ~ 10** (with age) über 10 sein; (with time) nach 10 sein; **a years vergangen**; president etc ehemalig.

paste [peɪst] n (for pastry) Teig m; (fish — etc) Paste f; (glue) Kleister m; vt kleben; (put — on) mit Kleister bestreichen.

pastel ['pæstəl] a colour Pastell-.

pasteurized ['pæstəraɪzd] a pasteurisiert.

pastille ['pæstiːl] n Pastille f.

pastime ['pɑːstaɪm] n Hobby nt, Zeitvertreib m.

pastor ['pɑːstə*] n Pastor m, Pfarrer m.

pastoral ['pɑːstərəl] a literature Schäfer-, Pastoral-.

pastry ['peɪstrɪ] n Blätterteig m; (tarts etc) Stückchen pl; Tortengebäck nt.

pasture ['pɑːstʃə*] n Weide f.

pasty ['pæstɪ] n (Fleisch)pastete f; ['peɪstɪ] a bläßlich, käsig.

pat [pæt] n leichte(r) Schlag m, Klaps m; vt tätscheln.

patch [pætʃ] n Fleck m; vt flicken; **~ of fog** Nebelfeld nt; **a bad ~** eine Pechsträhne; **~work** Patchwork nt; **~y** a (irregular) ungleichmäßig.

pate [peɪt] n Schädel m.

patent ['peɪtənt] n Patent nt; vt patentieren lassen; (by authorities) patentieren; a offenkundig; **~ leather** Lackleder nt; **~ly** ad offensichtlich; **~ medicine** pharmazeutische(s) Präparat nt.

paternal [pə'tɜːnl] a väterlich; **his ~ grandmother** seine Großmutter väterlicherseits; **~istic** [pətɜːnə'lɪstɪk] a väterlich, onkelhaft.

paternity [pə'tɜːnɪtɪ] n Vaterschaft f.

path [pɑːθ] n Pfad m; Weg m; (of the sun) Bahn f.

pathetic a, **~ally** ad [pə'θetɪk, -lɪ] (very bad) kläglich; **it's ~** es ist zum Weinen.

pathological [pæθə'lɒdʒɪkəl] a krankhaft, pathologisch.

pathologist [pə'θɒlədʒɪst] n Pathologe m.

pathology [pə'θɒlədʒɪ] n Pathologie f.

pathos ['peɪθɒs] n Rührseligkeit f.

pathway ['pɑːθweɪ] n Pfad m, Weg m.

patience ['peɪʃəns] n Geduld f; (Cards) Patience f.

patient ['peɪʃənt] n Patient(in f) m, Kranke(r) mf; a, **~ly** ad geduldig.

patio ['pætɪəʊ] n Innenhof m; (outside) Terrasse f.

patriotic [pætrɪ'ɒtɪk] a patriotisch.

patriotism ['pætrɪətɪzəm] n Patriotismus m.

patrol [pə'trəʊl] n Patrouille f; (police) Streife f; vt patrouillieren in (+dat); vi (police) die Runde machen; (police) patrouillieren; **on ~** (police) auf Streife; **~ car** Streifenwagen m; **~man** (US) (Streifen)polizist m.

patron ['peɪtrən] n (in shop) (Stamm)kunde m; (in hotel) (Stamm)gast m; (supporter) Förderer m; **~age** ['pætrənɪdʒ] Förderung f; Schirmherrschaft f; (Comm) Kundschaft f; **~ize** also ['pætrənaɪz] (support) unterstützen; shop besuchen; ['pætrənaɪz] (treat condescendingly) von oben herab behandeln; **~izing a** attitude herablassend; **~ saint** Schutzheilige(r) mf, Schutzpatron(in f) m.

patter ['pætə*] n (sound) (of feet) Trappeln nt; (of rain) Prasseln nt; (sales talk) Art f zu reden, Gerede nt; vi (feet) trappeln; (rain) prasseln.

pattern ['pætən] n Muster nt; (sewing) Schnittmuster nt; (knitting) Strickanleitung f; vt **~ sth on sth** nach etw bilden.

paunch [pɔːntʃ] n dicke(r) Bauch m, Wanst m.

pauper ['pɔːpə*] n Arme(r) mf.

pause [pɔːz] n Pause f; vi innehalten.

pave [peɪv] vt pflastern; **to ~ the way for** den Weg bahnen für; **~ment** (Brit) Bürgersteig m.

pavilion [pə'vɪlɪən] n Pavillon m; (Sport) Klubhaus n.

paving ['peɪvɪŋ] n Straßenpflaster nt.

paw [pɔː] n Pfote f; (of big cats) Tatze f, Pranke f; vt (scrape) scharren; (handle) betatschen.

pawn [pɔːn] n Pfand nt; (chess) Bauer m; vt versetzen, verpfänden; **~broker** Pfandleiher m; **~shop** Pfandhaus nt.

pay [peɪ] n Erbse f, Lohn m; **to be in sb's ~** von jdm bezahlt werden; irreg vt bezahlen; **it would ~ you to ...** es würde sich für dich lohnen, zu ...; **to ~ attention** achtgeben (to auf +acc); vi zahlen; (be profitable) sich bezahlt machen; **it doesn't ~** es lohnt sich nicht; **~ for** vt bezahlen für; **~ up** vi bezahlen, seine Schulden begleichen; **~able** a zahlbar, fällig; **~day** Zahltag m; **~ee** [peɪ'iː] Zahlungsempfänger m; **~ing** a einträglich, rentabel; **~load** Nutzlast f; **~ment** Bezahlung f; **~ packet** Lohntüte f; **~roll** Lohnliste f.

pea [piː] n Erbse f; **~ souper** (col) Suppe f, Waschküche f.

peace [piːs] n Friede(n) m; **~able a, ~ably** ad friedlich; **~ful** a friedlich, ruhig; **~-keeping** a Friedens-; **~-keeping role** Vermittlerrolle f; **~ offering** Friedensangebot nt; **~time** Friede(n) m.

peach [piːtʃ] n Pfirsich m.

peacock ['piːkɒk] n Pfau m.

peak [piːk] n Spitze f; (of mountain) Gipfel m; (fig) Höhepunkt m; (of cap) (Mützen)schirm m; **~ period** Stoßzeit f, Hauptzeit f.

peal [piːl] n (Glocken)läuten nt.

peanut ['piːnʌt] n Erdnuß f; **~ butter** Erdnußbutter f.

pear [peə*] n Birne f.

pearl [pɜːl] n Perle f.

peasant ['pezənt] n Bauer m.

peat [piːt] n Torf m.

pebble ['pebl] n Kiesel m.

peck [pek] vti picken; n (with beak) Schnabelhieb m; (kiss) flüchtige(r) Kuß m; **~ish** a (col) ein bißchen hungrig.

peculiar [pɪ'kjuːlɪə*] a (odd) seltsam; **~ to** charakteristisch für; **~ity** [pɪkjulɪ'ærɪtɪ] (singular quality) Besonderheit f; (strange-

ness) Eigenartigkeit *f;* **~ly** *ad* seltsam; *(especially)* besonders.

pecuniary [pɪˈkjuːnɪərɪ] *a* Geld-, finanziell, pekuniär.

pedal [ˈpedl] *n* Pedal *nt; vti (cycle)* fahren, radfahren.

pedant [ˈpedənt] *n* Pedant *m.*

pedantic [pɪˈdæntɪk] *a* pedantisch.

pedantry [ˈpedəntrɪ] *n* Pedanterie *f.*

peddle [ˈpedl] *vt* hausieren gehen mit.

pedestal [ˈpedɪstl] *n* Sockel *m.*

pedestrian [pɪˈdestrɪən] *n* Fußgänger *m; a* Fußgänger-; *(humdrum)* langweilig; **~ crossing** Fußgängerüberweg *m;* **~ precinct** Fußgängerzone *f.*

pediatrics [piːdɪˈætrɪks] *n (US)* = **paediatrics.**

pedigree [ˈpedɪgriː] *n* Stammbaum *m; a animal* reinrassig, Zucht-.

pee [piː] *vi (col)* pissen, pinkeln.

peek [piːk] *n* flüchtige(r) Blick *m; vi* gucken.

peel [piːl] *n* Schale *f; vt* schälen; *vi (paint etc)* abblättern; *(skin)* sich schälen; **~ings** *pl* Schalen *pl.*

peep [piːp] *n (look)* neugierige(r) Blick *m; (sound)* Piepsen *nt; vi (look)* neugierig gucken; **~hole** Guckloch *nt.*

peer [pɪə*] *vi* spähen; angestrengt schauen *(at auf +acc); (peep)* gucken; *n (nobleman)* Peer *m; (equal)* Ebenbürtige(r) *m;* **his ~s** seinesgleichen; **~age** Peerswürde *f;* **~less** *a* unvergleichlich.

peeve [piːv] *vt (col)* verärgern; **~d** *a* ärgerlich; *person* sauer.

peevish [ˈpiːvɪʃ] *a* verdrießlich, brummig; **~ness** Verdrießlichkeit *f.*

peg [peg] *n* Stift *m; (hook)* Haken *m; (stake)* Pflock *m;* **clothes ~** Wäscheklammer *f;* **off the ~** von der Stange.

pejorative [prˈdʒɒrɪtɪv] *a* pejorativ, herabsetzend.

pekinese [piːkɪˈniːz] *n* Pekinese *m.*

pelican [ˈpelɪkən] *n* Pelikan *m.*

pellet [ˈpelɪt] *n* Kügelchen *nt.*

pelmet [ˈpelmɪt] *n* Blende *f,* Schabracke *f.*

pelt [pelt] *vt* bewerfen; *n* Pelz *m,* Fell *nt;* **~ down** *vi* niederprasseln.

pelvis [ˈpelvɪs] *n* Becken *nt.*

pen [pen] *n (fountain ~)* Federhalter *m; (ball-point)* Kuli *m; (for sheep)* Pferch *m;* **have you got a ~?** haben Sie etwas zum Schreiben?

penal [ˈpiːnl] *a* Straf-; **~ize** *vt (make punishable)* unter Strafe stellen; *(punish)* bestrafen; *(disadvantage)* benachteiligen; **~ty** [ˈpenltɪ] Strafe *f; (Ftbl)* Elfmeter *m;* **~ty area** Strafraum *m;* **~ty kick** Elfmeter *m.*

penance [ˈpenəns] *n* Buße *f.*

pence [pens] *npl (pl of penny)* Pence *pl.*

penchant [ˈpɑːŋʃɑːŋ] *n* Vorliebe *f,* Schwäche *f.*

pencil [ˈpensl] *n* Bleistift *m;* **~ sharpener** Bleistiftspitzer *m.*

pendant [ˈpendənt] *n* Anhänger *m.*

pending [ˈpendɪŋ] *prep* bis (zu); *a* unentschieden, noch offen.

pendulum [ˈpendjuləm] *n* Pendel *nt.*

penetrate [ˈpenɪtreɪt] *vt* durchdringen; *(enter into)* eindringen in *(+acc).*

penetrating [ˈpenɪtreɪtɪŋ] *a* durchdringend; *analysis* scharfsinnig.

penetration [penɪˈtreɪʃən] *n* Durchdringen *nt;* Eindringen *nt.*

penfriend [ˈpenfrend] *n* Brieffreund(in *f) m.*

penguin [ˈpeŋgwɪn] *n* Pinguin *m.*

penicillin [penɪˈsɪlɪn] *n* Penizillin *nt.*

peninsula [pɪˈnɪnsjulə] *n* Halbinsel *f.*

penis [ˈpiːnɪs] *n* Penis *m,* männliche(s) Glied *nt.*

penitence [ˈpenɪtəns] *n* Reue *f.*

penitent [ˈpenɪtənt] *a* reuig; **~iary** [penɪˈtenʃərɪ] *(US)* Zuchthaus *nt.*

penknife [ˈpennaɪf] *n* Federmesser *nt.*

pen name [ˈpenneɪm] *n* Pseudonym *nt.*

pennant [ˈpenənt] *n* Wimpel *m; (official ~)* Stander *m.*

penniless [ˈpenɪləs] *a* mittellos, ohne einen Pfennig.

penny [ˈpenɪ] *n* Penny *m.*

pension [ˈpenʃən] *n* Rente *f; (for civil servants, executives etc)* Ruhegehalt *nt,* Pension *f;* **~able** *a person* pensionsberechtigt; *job* mit Renten- or Pensionsanspruch; **~er** Rentner(in *f) m; (civil servant, executive)* Pensionär *m;* **~ fund** Rentenfonds *m.*

pensive [ˈpensɪv] *a* nachdenklich.

pentagon [ˈpentəgən] *n* Fünfeck *nt.*

Pentecost [ˈpentɪkɒst] *n* Pfingsten *pl or nt.*

penthouse [ˈpenthaus] *n* Dachterrassenwohnung *f.*

pent-up [ˈpentʌp] *a feelings* angestaut.

penultimate [pɪˈnʌltɪmət] *a* vorletzte(r, s).

people [ˈpiːpl] *n (nation)* Volk *nt; (inhabitants)* Bevölkerung *f; (persons)* Leute *pl;* **~ think** man glaubt; *vt* besiedeln.

pep [pep] *n (col)* Schwung *m,* Schmiß *m;* **~ up** *vt* aufmöbeln.

pepper [ˈpepə*] *n* Pfeffer *m; (vegetable)* Paprika *m; vt (pelt)* bombardieren; **~mint** *(plant)* Pfefferminze *f; (sweet)* Pfefferminz *nt.*

peptalk [ˈpeptɔːk] *n (col)* Anstachelung *f.*

per [pɜː*] *prep* pro; **~ annum** pro Jahr; **~ cent** Prozent *nt.*

perceive [pəˈsiːv] *vt (realize)* wahrnehmen, spüren; *(understand)* verstehen.

percentage [pəˈsentɪdʒ] *n* Prozentsatz *m.*

perceptible [pəˈseptəbl] *a* merklich, wahrnehmbar.

perception [pəˈsepʃən] *n* Wahrnehmung *f; (insight)* Einsicht *f.*

perceptive [pəˈseptɪv] *a person* aufmerksam; *analysis* tiefgehend.

perch [pɜːtʃ] *n* Stange *f; (fish)* Flußbarsch *m; vi* sitzen, hocken.

percolator [ˈpɜːkəleɪtə*] *n* Kaffeemaschine *f.*

percussion [pɜːˈkʌʃən] *n (Mus)* Schlagzeug *nt.*

peremptory [pəˈremptərɪ] *a* schroff.

perennial [pəˈrenɪəl] *a* wiederkehrend; *(everlasting)* unvergänglich; *n* perennierende Pflanze *f.*

perfect [ˈpɜːfɪkt] *a* vollkommen; *crime,*

solution perfekt; *(Gram)* vollendet; *n (Gram)* Perfekt *nt;* [pə'fekt] *vt* vervollkommnen; ~**ion** [pə'fekʃən] Vollkommenheit *f,* Perfektion *f;* ~**ionist** [pə'fekʃənist] Perfektionist *m;* ~**ly** *ad* vollkommen, perfekt; *(quite)* ganz, einfach.

perforate [pɜːfəreit] *vt* durchlöchern; ~**d** *a* durchlöchert, perforiert.

perforation [pɜːfə'reiʃən] *n* Perforation *f.*

perform [pə'fɔːm] *vt (carry out)* durch- or ausführen; *task verrichten; (Theat)* spielen, geben; *vi (Theat)* auftreten; ~**ance** Durchführung *f; (efficiency)* Leistung *f; (show)* Vorstellung *f;* ~**er** Künstler(in *f) m;* ~**ing** *a animal* dressiert.

perfume ['pɜːfjuːm] *n* Duft *m; (lady's)* Parfüm *nt.*

perfunctory [pə'fʌŋktəri] *a* oberflächlich, mechanisch.

perhaps [pə'hæps] *ad* vielleicht.

peril ['peril] *n* Gefahr *f;* ~**ous** *a,* ~**ously** *ad* gefährlich.

perimeter [pə'rimitə*] *n* Peripherie *f; (of circle etc)* Umfang *m.*

period ['piəriəd] *n* Periode *f,* Zeit *f; (Gram)* Punkt *m; (Med)* Periode *f; a costume* historisch; ~**ic(al)** [piəri'ɒdik(əl)] *a* periodisch; ~**ical** *n* Zeitschrift *f;* ~**ically** [piəri'ɒdikəli] *ad* periodisch.

peripheral [pə'rifərəl] *a* Rand-, peripher.

periphery [pə'rifəri] *n* Peripherie *f,* Rand *m.*

periscope ['periskəup] *n* Periskop *nt,* Sehrohr *nt.*

perish ['periʃ] *vi* umkommen; *(material)* unbrauchbar werden; *(fruit)* verderben; ~ **the thought!** daran wollen wir nicht denken; ~**able** *a fruit* leicht verderblich; ~**ing** *a (col: cold)* eisig.

perjure ['pɜːdʒə*] *vr:* ~ **o.s.** einen Meineid leisten.

perjury ['pɜːdʒəri] *n* Meineid *m.*

perk [pɜːk] *n (col: fringe benefit)* Vorteil *m,* Vergünstigung *f;* ~ **up** *vi* munter werden; *vt ears* spitzen; ~**y** *a (cheerful)* keck.

perm [pɜːm] *n* Dauerwelle *f.*

permanence ['pɜːmənəns] *n* Dauer(haftigkeit) *f,* Beständigkeit *f.*

permanent *a,* ~**ly** *ad* ['pɜːmənənt, -li] dauernd, ständig.

permissible [pə'misəbl] *a* zulässig.

permission [pə'miʃən] *n* Erlaubnis *f,* Genehmigung *f.*

permissive [pə'misiv] *a* nachgiebig; *society etc* permissiv.

permit ['pɜːmit] *n* Zulassung *f,* Erlaubnis(schein *m) f;* [pə'mit] *vt* erlauben, zulassen.

permutation [pɜːmju'teiʃən] *n* Veränderung *f; (Math)* Permutation *f.*

pernicious [pɜː'niʃəs] *a* schädlich.

perpendicular [pɜːpən'dikjulə*] *a* senkrecht.

perpetrate ['pɜːpitreit] *vt* begehen, verüben.

perpetual *a,* ~**ly** *ad* [pə'petjuəl, -i] dauernd, ständig.

perpetuate [pə'petjueit] *vt* verewigen, bewahren.

perpetuity [pɜːpi'tjuːiti] *n* Ewigkeit *f.*

perplex [pə'pleks] *vt* verblüffen; ~**ed** *a* verblüfft, perplex; ~**ing** *a* verblüffend; ~**ity** Verblüffung *f.*

persecute ['pɜːsikjuːt] *vt* verfolgen.

persecution [pɜːsi'kjuːʃən] *n* Verfolgung *f.*

perseverance [pɜːsi'viərəns] *n* Ausdauer *f.*

persevere [pɜːsi'viə*] *vi* beharren, durchhalten.

persist [pə'sist] *vi (in belief etc)* bleiben (in bei); *(rain, smell)* andauern; *(continue)* nicht aufhören; ~**ence** Beharrlichkeit *f;* ~**ent** *a,* ~**ently** *ad* beharrlich; *(unending)* ständig.

person ['pɜːsn] *n* Person *f,* Mensch *m; (Gram)* Person *f; on one's* ~ bei sich; **in** ~ persönlich; ~**able** *a* gut aussehend; ~**al** *a* persönlich; *(private)* privat; *(of body)* körperlich, Körper-; ~**ality** [pɜːsə'næliti] Persönlichkeit *f;* ~**ally** *ad* persönlich; ~**ification** [pɜːsɒnifi'keiʃən] Verkörperung *f;* ~**ify** [pɜː'sɒnifai] *vt* verkörpern, personifizieren.

personnel [pɜːsə'nel] *n* Personal *nt; (in factory)* Belegschaft *f;* ~ **manager** Personalchef *m.*

perspective [pə'spektiv] *n* Perspektive *f.*

Perspex ['pɜːspeks] *n* Plexiglas *nt.*

perspicacity [pɜːspi'kæsiti] *n* Scharfsinn *m.*

perspiration [pɜːspə'reiʃən] *n* Transpiration *f.*

perspire [pəs'paiə*] *vi* transpirieren.

persuade [pə'sweid] *vt* überreden; *(convince)* überzeugen.

persuasion [pə'sweiʒən] *n* Überredung *f;* Überzeugung *f.*

persuasive *a,* ~**ly** *ad* [pə'sweisiv, -li] überzeugend.

pert [pɜːt] *a* keck.

pertain [pɜː'tein] *vt* gehören (*to* zu).

pertaining [pɜː'teiniŋ]: ~ **to** betreffend (+*acc.*).

pertinent ['pɜːtinənt] *a* relevant.

perturb [pə'tɜːb] *vt* beunruhigen.

perusal [pə'ruːzəl] *n* Durchsicht *f.*

peruse [pə'ruːz] *vt* lesen.

pervade [pɜː'veid] *vt* erfüllen, durchziehen.

pervasive [pɜː'veisiv] *a* durchdringend; *influence etc* allgegenwärtig.

perverse *a,* ~**ly** *ad* [pə'vɜːs, -li] pervers; *(obstinate)* eigensinnig; ~**ness** Perversität *f;* Eigensinn *m.*

perversion [pə'vɜːʃən] *n* Perversion *f; (of justice)* Verdrehung *f.*

perversity [pə'vɜːsiti] *n* Perversität *f.*

pervert ['pɜːvɜːt] *n* perverse(r) Mensch *m;* [pə'vɜːt] *vt* verdrehen; *(morally)* verderben.

pessimism ['pesimizəm] *n* Pessimismus *m.*

pessimist ['pesimist] *n* Pessimist *m;* ~**ic** [pesi'mistik] *a* pessimistisch.

pest [pest] *n* Plage *f; (insect)* Schädling *m; (fig) (person)* Nervensäge *f; (thing)* Plage *f.*

pester ['pestə*] *vt* plagen.

pesticide ['pestisaid] *n* Insektenvertilgungsmittel *nt.*

pestle ['pesl] *n* Stößel *m.*

pet [pet] n (animal) Haustier nt; (person) Liebling m; vt liebkosen, streicheln.

petal ['petl] n Blütenblatt nt.

peter out ['pi:tə aut] vi allmählich zu Ende gehen.

petite [pə'ti:t] a zierlich.

petition [pə'tɪʃən] n Bittschrift f.

petrel ['petral] n Sturmvogel m.

petrified ['petrɪfaɪd] a versteinert; person starr (vor Schreck).

petrify ['petrɪfaɪ] vt versteinern; person erstarren lassen.

petrol ['petrəl] n (Brit) Benzin nt, Kraftstoff m; ~engine Benzinmotor m; ~eum [pɪ'trəuliəm] Petroleum nt; ~ pump (in car) Benzinpumpe f; (at garage) Zapfsäule f, Tanksäule f; ~ station Tankstelle f; ~tank Benzintank m.

petticoat ['petɪkəut] n Petticoat m.

pettifogging ['petɪfɒgɪŋ] a kleinlich.

pettiness ['petɪnəs] n Geringfügigkeit f; (meanness) Kleinlichkeit f.

petty ['petɪ] a (unimportant) geringfügig, unbedeutend; (mean) kleinlich; ~ cash Portokasse f; ~ officer Maat m.

petulant ['petjulənt] a leicht reizbar.

pew [pju:] n Kirchenbank f.

pewter ['pju:tə*] n Zinn nt.

phallic ['fælɪk] a phallisch, Phallus-.

phantom ['fæntəm] n Phantom nt, Geist m.

pharmacist ['fɑ:məsɪst] n Pharmazeut m; (druggist) Apotheker m.

pharmacy ['fɑ:məsɪ] n Pharmazie f; (shop) Apotheke f.

phase [feɪz] n Phase f; ~ out vt langsam abbauen; model auslaufen lassen; person absetzen.

pheasant ['feznt] n Fasan m.

phenomenal a, ~ly ad [fɪ'nɒmɪnl, -nəlɪ] phänomenal.

phenomenon [fɪ'nɒmɪnən] n Phänomen nt; common ~ häufige Erscheinung f.

phial ['faɪəl] n Fläschchen nt, Ampulle f.

philanderer [fɪ'lændərə*] n Schwerenöter m.

philanthropic [fɪlən'θrɒpɪk] a philanthropisch.

philanthropist [fɪ'lænθrəpɪst] n Philanthrop m, Menschenfreund m.

philatelist [fɪ'lætəlɪst] n Briefmarkensammler m, Philatelist m.

philately [fɪ'lætəlɪ] n Briefmarkensammeln nt, Philatelie f.

philosopher [fɪ'lɒsəfə*] n Philosoph m.

philosophical [fɪlə'sɒfɪkəl] a philosophisch.

philosophize [fɪ'lɒsəfaɪz] vi philosophieren.

philosophy [fɪ'lɒsəfɪ] n Philosophie f; Weltanschauung f.

phlegm [flem] n (Med) Schleim m; (calmness) Gelassenheit f; ~atic [fleg'mætɪk] a gelassen.

phobia ['fəubɪə] n krankhafte Furcht f, Phobie f.

phoenix ['fi:nɪks] n Phönix m.

phone [fəun] (abbr of telephone) n Telefon nt; vti telefonieren, anrufen.

phonetics [fəu'netɪks] n Phonetik f,

Laut(bildungs)lehre f; pl Lautschrift f.

phon(e)y ['fəunɪ] a (col) unecht; excuse faul; money gefälscht; n (person) Schwindler m; (thing) Fälschung f; (pound note) Blüte f.

phonograph ['fəunəgrɑ:f] n (US) Grammophon nt.

phonology [fəu'nɒlədʒɪ] n Phonologie f, Lautlehre f.

phosphate ['fɒsfeɪt] n Phosphat nt.

phosphorus ['fɒsfərəs] n Phosphor m.

photo ['fəutəu] n (abbr of **photograph**) Foto nt.

photocopier ['fəutəu'kɒpɪə*] n Kopiergerät nt.

photocopy ['fəutəukɒpɪ] n Fotokopie f; vt fotokopieren.

photoelectric ['fəutəuɪ'lektrɪk] a fotoelektrisch.

photo finish ['fəutəu'fɪnɪʃ] n Zielfotografie f.

photogenic [fəutəu'dʒenɪk] a fotogen.

photograph ['fəutəgrɑ:f] n Fotografie f, Aufnahme f; vt fotografieren, aufnehmen; ~er [fə'tɒgrəfə] Fotograf m; ~ic [ˌfəutə'græfɪk] a fotografisch; ~y [fə'tɒgrəfɪ] Fotografie f, Fotografieren nt; (of film, book) Aufnahmen pl.

photostat ['fəutəustæt] n Fotokopie f.

phrase [freɪz] n (kurzer) Satz m; (Gram) Phrase f; (expression) Redewendung f, Ausdruck m; vt ausdrücken, formulieren; ~book Sprachführer m.

physical a, ~ly ad [ˈfɪzɪkəl, -ɪ] physikalisch; (bodily) körperlich, physisch; ~ training Turnen nt.

physician [fɪ'zɪʃən] n Arzt m.

physicist ['fɪzɪsɪst] n Physiker(in f) m.

physics ['fɪzɪks] n Physik f.

physiology [fɪzɪ'ɒlədʒɪ] n Physiologie f.

physiotherapist [fɪzɪə'θerəpɪst] n Heilgymnast(in f) m.

physiotherapy [fɪzɪə'θerəpɪ] n Heilgymnastik f, Physiotherapie f.

physique [fɪ'zi:k] n Körperbau m; (in health) Konstitution f.

pianist ['pɪənɪst] n Pianist(in f) m.

piano ['pjɑ:nəu] n Klavier nt, Piano nt; ~-accordion Akkordeon nt.

piccolo ['pɪkələu] n Pikkoloflöte f.

pick [pɪk] n (tool) Pickel m; (choice) Auswahl f; **the ~ of** das Beste von; vt (gather) (auf)lesen, sammeln; fruit pflücken; (choose) aussuchen; (Mus) zupfen; **to ~ one's nose** in der Nase bohren; **to ~ sb's pocket** jdm bestehlen; **to ~ at one's food** im Essen herumstochern; ~ on vt person herumhacken auf (+dat); **why ~ on me?** warum ich?; ~ out vt auswählen; ~ up vi (improve) sich erholen; vt (lift up) aufheben; (learn) (schnell) mitbekommen; word aufschnappen; (collect) abholen; girl (sich dat) anlachen; speed gewinnen an (+dat); ~axe Pickel m.

picket ['pɪkɪt] n (stake) Pfahl m, Pflock m; (guard) Posten m; (striker) Streikposten m; vt factory (Streik)posten aufstellen vor (+dat); vi (Streik)posten stehen; ~ing Streikwache f; ~ line Streikpostenlinie f.

pickle ['pıkl] n (salty mixture) Pökel m; (col) Klemme f; vt (in Essig) einlegen; einpökeln.

pick-me-up ['pıkmi:ʌp] a Schnäpschen nt.

pickpocket ['pıkpɔkıt] n Taschendieb m.

pickup ['pıkʌp] n (on record player) Tonabnehmer m; (small truck) Lieferwagen m.

picnic ['pıknık] n Picknick nt; vi picknicken.

pictorial [pık'tɔ:rıəl] a in Bildern; n Illustrierte f.

picture ['pıktʃə*] n Bild nt; (likeness also) Abbild nt; (in words also) Darstellung f; **in the ~** (fig) im Bild; vt darstellen; (fig: paint) malen; (visualize) sich (dat) vorstellen; **the ~s** (Brit) Kino nt; **~ book** Bilderbuch nt; **~sque** [pıktʃə'resk] a malerisch.

piddling ['pıdlıŋ] a (col) lumpig; task pingelig.

pidgin ['pıdʒın] a: **~ English** Pidgin-Englisch nt.

pie [paı] n (meat) Pastete f; (fruit) Torte f.

piebald ['paıbɔ:ld] a gescheckt.

piece [pi:s] n Stück nt; **to go to ~s** (work, standard) wertlos werden; **he's gone to ~s** er ist vollkommen fertig; **in ~s** entzwei, kaputt; (taken apart) auseinandergenommen; **a ~ of cake** (col) ein Kinderspiel nt; **~meal** ad stückweise, Stück für Stück; **~work** Akkordarbeit f; **~ together** vt zusammensetzen.

pier [pıə*] n Pier m, Mole f.

pierce [pıəs] vt durchstechen, durchbohren (also look); durchdringen (also fig).

piercing ['pıəsıŋ] a durchdringend; cry also gellend; look also durchbohrend.

piety ['paıətı] n Frömmigkeit f.

pig [pıg] n Schwein nt.

pigeon ['pıdʒən] n Taube f; **~hole** (compartment) Ablegefach nt; vt ablegen; idea zu den Akten legen.

piggy bank ['pıgıbæŋk] n Sparschwein nt.

pigheaded ['pıg'hedıd] a dickköpfig.

piglet ['pıglət] n Ferkel nt, Schweinchen nt.

pigment ['pıgmənt] n Farbstoff m, Pigment nt (also Biol); **~ation** [pıgmən'teıʃən] Färbung f, Pigmentation f.

pigmy ['pıgmı] n = **pygmy.**

pigskin ['pıgskın] n Schweinsleder nt; a schweinsledern.

pigsty ['pıgstaı] n (lit, fig) Schweinestall m.

pigtail ['pıgteıl] n Zopf m.

pike [paık] n Pike f; (fish) Hecht m.

pilchard ['pıltʃəd] n Sardine f.

pile [paıl] n Haufen m; (of books, wood) Stapel m, Stoß m; (in ground) Pfahl m; (of bridge) Pfeiler m; (on carpet) Flausch m; vti (also ~ up) sich anhäufen.

piles [paılz] n Hämorrhoiden pl.

pile-up ['paılʌp] n (Aut) Massenzusammenstoß m.

pilfer ['pılfə*] vt stehlen, klauen; **~ing** Diebstahl m.

pilgrim ['pılgrım] n Wallfahrer(in f) m, Pilger(in f) m; **~age** Wallfahrt f, Pilgerfahrt f.

pill [pıl] n Tablette f, Pille f; **the P~** die (Antibaby)pille.

pillage ['pılıdʒ] vt plündern.

pillar ['pılə*] n Pfeiler m, Säule f (also fig); **~ box** (Brit) Briefkasten m.

pillion ['pıljən] n Soziussitz m; **~ passenger** Soziusfahrer m.

pillory ['pılərı] n Pranger m; vt an den Pranger stellen; (fig) anprangern.

pillow ['pıləu] n Kissen nt; **~case** Kissenbezug m.

pilot ['paılət] n Pilot m; (Naut) Lotse m; a scheme etc Versuchs-; vt führen; ship lotsen; **~ light** Zündflamme f.

pimp [pımp] n Zuhälter m.

pimple ['pımpl] n Pickel m.

pimply ['pımplı] a pick(e)lig.

pin [pın] n Nadel f; (sewing) Stecknadel f; (Tech) Stift m, Bolzen m; vt stecken, heften (to an +acc); (keep in one position) pressen, drücken; **~s and needles** Kribbeln m; **I have ~s and needles in my leg** mein Bein ist (mir) eingeschlafen; **~ down** vt (fig) person festnageln (to auf +acc).

pinafore ['pınəfɔ:*] n Schürze f; **~ dress** Kleiderrock m.

pincers ['pınsəz] npl Kneif- or Beißzange f; (Med) Pinzette f.

pinch [pıntʃ] n Zwicken, Kneifen nt; (of salt) Prise f; vti zwicken, kneifen; (shoe) drücken; vt (col) (steal) klauen; (arrest) schnappen; **at a ~** notfalls, zur Not; **to feel the ~** die Not or es zu spüren bekommen.

pincushion ['pınkuʃən] n Nadelkissen nt.

pine [paın] n (also ~ tree) Kiefer f, Föhre f, Pinie f; vi: **~ for** sich sehnen or verzehren nach; **~ away** sich zu Tode sehnen.

pineapple ['paınæpl] n Ananas f.

ping [pıŋ] n Peng nt; Kling nt; **~-pong** Pingpong nt.

pink [pıŋk] n (plant) Nelke f; (colour) Rosa nt; a rosa inv.

pinnacle ['pınəkl] n Spitze f.

pinpoint ['pınpɔınt] vt festlegen.

pinstripe ['pınstraıp] n Nadelstreifen m.

pint [paınt] n Pint nt.

pinup ['pınʌp] n Pin-up-girl nt.

pioneer [paıə'nıə*] n Pionier m; (fig also) Bahnbrecher m.

pious ['paıəs] a fromm; literature geistlich.

pip [pıp] n Kern m; (sound) Piepen nt; (on uniform) Stern m; **to give sb the ~** (col) jdn verrückt machen.

pipe [paıp] n (smoking) Pfeife f; (Mus) Flöte f; (tube) Rohr nt; (in house) (Rohr)leitung f; vti (durch Rohre) leiten; (Mus) blasen; **~ down** vi (be quiet) die Luft anhalten; **~-dream** Luftschloß nt; **~line** (for oil) Pipeline f; **~r** Pfeifer m; (bagpipes) Dudelsackbläser m; **~ tobacco** Pfeifentabak m.

piping ['paıpıŋ] n Leitungsnetz nt; (on cake) Dekoration f; (on uniform) Tresse f; ad: **~ hot** siedend heiß.

piquant ['pi:kənt] a pikant.

pique [pi:k] n gekränkte(r) Stolz m; **~d** a pikiert.

piracy ['paıərəsı] n Piraterie f, Seeräuberei f; (plagiarism) Plagiat nt.

pirate ['paɪərɪt] n Pirat m, Seeräuber m; (plagiarist) Plagiator m; ~ **radio** Schwarzsender m; (exterritorial) Piratensender m.

pirouette [pɪrʊ'et] n Pirouette f; vi pirouettieren, eine Pirouette drehen.

Pisces ['paɪsiːz] n Fische pl.

pissed [pɪst] a (col) blau, besoffen.

pistol ['pɪstl] n Pistole f.

piston ['pɪstən] n Kolben m.

pit [pɪt] n Grube f; (Theat) Parterre nt; (orchestra —) Orchestergraben m; vt (mark with scars) zerfressen; (compare) o.s. messen (against mit); sb/sth messen (against an +dat); **the** ~**s** pl (motor racing) die Boxen.

pitch [pɪtʃ] n Wurf m; (of trader) Stand m; (Sport) (Spiel)feld nt; (slope) Neigung f; (degree) Stufe f; (Mus) Tonlage f; (substance) Pech nt; **perfect** ~ absolute(s) Gehör nt; **to queer sb's** ~ (col) jdm alles verderben; vt werfen, schleudern; (set up) aufschlagen; song anstimmen; ~**ed too high** zu hoch; vi (fall) (längelang) hinschlagen; (Naut) rollen; ~**black** a pechschwarz; ~**ed battle** offene Schlacht f.

pitcher ['pɪtʃə*] n Krug m.

pitchfork ['pɪtʃfɔːk] n Heugabel f.

piteous ['pɪtɪəs] a kläglich, erbärmlich.

pitfall ['pɪtfɔːl] n (fig) Falle f.

pith [pɪθ] n Mark nt; (of speech) Kern m.

pithead ['pɪthed] n Schachtkopf m.

pithy ['pɪθɪ] a prägnant.

pitiable ['pɪtɪəbl] a bedauernswert; (contemptible) jämmerlich.

pitiful a, ~**ly** ad ['pɪtɪful, -fəlɪ] mitleidig; (deserving pity) bedauernswert; (contemptible) jämmerlich.

pitiless a, ~**ly** ad ['pɪtɪləs, -lɪ] erbarmungslos.

pittance ['pɪtəns] n Hungerlohn m.

pity ['pɪtɪ] n (sympathy) Mitleid nt; (shame) Jammer m; **to have** or **take** ~ **on sb** Mitleid mit jdm haben; **for** ~'**s sake** um Himmels willen; **what a** ~! wie schade!; **it's a** ~ es ist schade; vt Mitleid haben mit; **I** ~ **you** du tust mir leid; ~**ing** a mitleidig.

pivot ['pɪvət] n Drehpunkt m; (pin) (Dreh)zapfen m; (fig) Angelpunkt m; vi sich drehen (on um).

pixie ['pɪksɪ] n Elf(e f) m.

placard ['plækɑːd] n Plakat nt, Anschlag m; vt anschlagen.

placate [plə'keɪt] vt beschwichtigen, besänftigen.

place [pleɪs] n Platz m; (spot) Stelle f; (town etc) Ort m; vt setzen, stellen, legen; order aufgeben; (Sport) plazieren; (identify) unterbringen; **in** ~ am rechten Platz; **out of** ~ nicht am rechten Platz; (fig) remark unangebracht; **in** ~ **of** anstelle von; **in the first/second** etc ~ erstens/zweitens etc; **to give** ~ **to** Platz machen (+dat); **to invite sb to one's** ~ jdn zu sich (nach Hause) einladen; **to keep sb in his** ~ jdn in seinen Schranken halten; **to put sb in his** ~ jdn in seine Schranken (ver)weisen; ~ **of worship** Stätte f des Gebets; ~ **mat** Platzdeckchen nt.

placid ['plæsɪd] a gelassen, ruhig; ~**ity** [plə'sɪdɪtɪ] Gelassenheit f, Ruhe f.

plagiarism ['pleɪdʒɪərɪzəm] n Plagiat nt.

plagiarist ['pleɪdʒɪərɪst] n Plagiator m.

plagiarize ['pleɪdʒɪəraɪz] vt abschreiben, plagiieren.

plague [pleɪg] n Pest f; (fig) Plage f; vt plagen.

plaice [pleɪs] n Scholle f.

plaid [plæd] n Plaid nt.

plain a, ~**ly** ad [pleɪn, —lɪ] (clear) klar, deutlich; (simple) einfach, schlicht; (not beautiful) einfach, nicht attraktiv; (honest) offen, n Ebene f; **in** ~ **clothes** (police) in Zivil(kleidung); **it is** ~ **sailing** das ist ganz einfach; ~**ness** Einfachkeit f.

plaintiff ['pleɪntɪf] n Kläger m.

plait [plæt] n Zopf m; vt flechten.

plan [plæn] n Plan m; vt planen; (intend also) vorhaben; ~ **out** vt vorbereiten; **according to** ~ planmäßig.

plane [pleɪn] n Ebene f; (Aviat) Flugzeug nt; (tool) Hobel m; (tree) Platane f; a eben, flach; vt hobeln.

planet ['plænɪt] n Planet m.

planetarium [plænɪ'tɛərɪəm] n Planetarium nt.

planetary ['plænɪtərɪ] a planetarisch.

plank [plæŋk] n Planke f, Brett nt; (Pol) Programmpunkt m.

plankton ['plæŋktən] n Plankton nt.

planner ['plænə*] n Planer m.

planning ['plænɪŋ] n Planen nt, Planung f.

plant [plɑːnt] n Pflanze f; (Tech) (Maschinen)anlage f; (factory) Fabrik f, Werk nt; vt pflanzen; (set firmly) stellen.

plantain ['plæntɪn] n (Mehl)banane f.

plantation [plæn'teɪʃən] n Pflanzung f, Plantage f.

planter ['plɑːntə*] n Pflanzer m.

plaque [plæk] n Gedenktafel f.

plasma ['plæzmə] n Plasma nt.

plaster ['plɑːstə*] n Gips m; (whole surface) Verputz m; (Med) Pflaster nt; (for fracture: also ~ **of Paris**) Gipsverband m; **in** ~ (leg etc) in Gips; vt plastern; hole zugipsen; ceiling verputzen; (fig: with pictures etc) bekleben; ~**ed** a (col) besoffen; ~**er** Gipser m.

plastic ['plæstɪk] n Kunststoff m; a (made of plastic) Kunststoff-, Plastik-; (soft) formbar, plastisch; (Art) plastisch, bildend; **p**~**ine** ['plæstɪsiːn] Plastilin nt; ~ **surgery** plastische Chirurgie f; Schönheitsoperation f.

plate [pleɪt] n Teller m; (gold/silver) vergoldete(s)/versilberte(s) Tafelgeschirr nt; (flat sheet) Platte f; (in book) (Bild)tafel f; vt überziehen, plattieren; **to silver-/gold-**~ versilbern/vergolden.

plateau ['plætəʊ] n, pl ~**x** Hochebene f, Plateau nt.

plateful ['pleɪtful] n Teller(voll) m.

plate glass ['pleɪt'glɑːs] n Tafelglas nt.

platform ['plætfɔːm] n (at meeting) Plattform f, Podium nt; (stage) Bühne f; (Rail) Bahnsteig m; (Pol) Parteiprogramm nt; ~ **ticket** Bahnsteigkarte f.

platinum ['plætɪnəm] n Platin nt.

platitude ['plætɪtjuːd] *n* Gemeinplatz *m*, Platitüde *f.*

platoon [plə'tuːn] *n (Mil)* Zug *m.*

platter ['plætə*] *n* Platte *f.*

plausibility [plɔːzə'bɪlɪtɪ] *n* Plausibilität *f.*

plausible *a*, **plausibly** *ad* ['plɔːzəbl, -blɪ] plausibel, einleuchtend; *liar* überzeugend.

play [pleɪ] *n* Spiel *nt (also Tech); (Theat)* (Theater)stück *nt*, Schauspiel *nt; vti* spielen; *another team* spielen gegen; *(put sb in a team)* einsetzen, spielen lassen; **to ~ a joke on sb** jdm einen Streich spielen; **to ~ sb off against sb else** jdn gegen jdn anders ausspielen; **to ~ a part in** *(fig)* eine Rolle spielen bei; **~ down** *vt* bagatellisieren, herunterspielen; **~ up** *vi (cause trouble)* frech werden; *(bad leg etc)* weh tun; *vt person* plagen; **to ~ up to sb** jdm flattieren; **~acting** Schauspielerei *f;* **~boy** Playboy *m;* **~er** Spieler(in *f) m;* **~ful** *a* spielerisch, verspielt; **~goer** Theaterfreund *m;* **~ground** Spielplatz *m;* **~group** Kindergarten *m;* **~ing card** Spielkarte *f;* **~ing field** Sportplatz *m;* **~mate** Spielkamerad *m;* **~off** *(Sport)* Entscheidungsspiel *nt;* **~pen** Laufstall *m;* **~thing** Spielzeug *nt;* **~wright** Theaterschriftsteller *m.*

plea [pliː] *n (dringende)* Bitte *f*, Gesuch *nt; (Jur)* Antwort *f* des Angeklagten; *(excuse)* Ausrede *f*, Vorwand *m; (objection)* Einrede *f;* **~ of guilty** Geständnis *nt.*

plead [pliːd] *vt poverty* zur Entschuldigung anführen; *(Jur) sb's case* vertreten; *vi (beg)* dringend bitten *(with sb* jdn*); (Jur)* plädieren; **to ~ guilty** schuldig plädieren.

pleasant *a*, **~ly** *ad* ['plezt, -lɪ] angenehm; *freundlich;* **~ness** Angenehme(s) *nt; (of person)* angenehme(s) Wesen *nt*, Freundlichkeit *f;* **~ry** Scherz *m.*

please [pliːz] *vt (be agreeable to)* gefallen (*+dat)*; **~!** bitte!; **~ yourself!** wie du willst!; **do what you ~** mach' was du willst; **~d** *a* zufrieden; *(glad)* erfreut *(with* über *+acc).*

pleasing *a* ['pliːzɪŋ] *a* erfreulich.

pleasurable *a*, **pleasurably** *ad* ['pleʒərəbl, -blɪ] angenehm, erfreulich.

pleasure ['pleʒə*] *n* Vergnügen *nt*, Freude *f; (old: will)* Wünsche *pl;* **it's a** *~* gern geschehen; **they take (no/great) ~ in doing ...** es macht ihnen (keinen/ großen) Spaß zu...; **~ ground** Vergnügungspark *m;* **~-seeking** *a* vergnügungshungrig; **~ steamer** Vergnügungsdampfer *m.*

pleat [pliːt] *n* Falte *f.*

plebeian [plɪ'biːən] *n* Plebejer(in *f) m; a* plebejisch.

plebiscite ['plebɪsɪt] *n* Volksentscheid *m*, Plebiszit *nt.*

plebs [plebz] *npl* Plebs *m*, Pöbel *m.*

plectrum ['plektrəm] *n* Plektron *nt.*

pledge [pledʒ] *n* Pfand *nt; (promise)* Versprechen *nt; vt* verpfänden; *(promise)* geloben, versprechen; **to take the ~** dem Alkohol abschwören.

plenipotentiary [plenɪpə'tenʃərɪ] *m*

Bevollmächtiger *m; a* bevollmächtigt; **~ power** Vollmacht *f.*

plentiful ['plentɪful] *a* reichlich.

plenty ['plentɪ] *n* Fülle *f*, Überfluß *m; ad (col)* ganz schön; **~ of** eine Menge, viel; **in ~** reichlich, massenhaft; **to be ~** genug sein, reichen.

plethora ['pleθərə] *n* Überfülle *f.*

pleurisy ['pluərɪsɪ] *n* Rippenfellentzündung *f.*

pliability [plaɪə'bɪlɪtɪ] *n* Biegsamkeit *f; (of person)* Beeinflußbarkeit *f.*

pliable ['plaɪəbl] *a* biegsam; *person* beeinflußbar.

pliers ['plaɪəz] *npl* (Kneif)zange *f.*

plight [plaɪt] *n* (Not)lage *f; (schrecklicher)* Zustand *m.*

plimsolls ['plɪmsəlz] *npl* Turnschuhe *pl.*

plinth [plɪnθ] *n* Säulenplatte *f*, Plinthe *f.*

plod [plod] *vi (work)* sich abplagen; *(walk)* trotten; **~der** der Arbeitstier *nt; a* schwerfällig.

plonk [plonk] *n (col: wine)* billige(r) Wein *m; vt:* **~ sth down** etw hinknallen.

plot [plot] *n* Komplott *nt*, Verschwörung *f; (story)* Handlung *f; (of land)* Stück *nt* Land, Grundstück *nt; vt* markieren; *curve* zeichnen; *movements* nachzeichnen; *vi (plan secretly)* sich verschwören, ein Komplott schmieden; **~ter** Verschwörer *m;* **~ting** Intrigen *pl.*

plough, *(US)* plow [plau] *n* Pflug *m; vt* pflügen; *(col)* exam candidate durchfallen lassen; **~ back** *vt (Comm)* wieder in das Geschäft stecken; **~ through** *vt water* durchpflügen; *book* sich kämpfen durch; **~ing** Pflügen *nt.*

ploy [plɔɪ] *n* Masche *f.*

pluck [plʌk] *vt fruit* pflücken; *guitar* zupfen; *goose* rupfen; *n* Mut *m;* **to ~ up courage** all seinen Mut zusammennehmen; **~y** *a* beherzt.

plug [plʌg] *n* Stöpsel *m; (Elec)* Stecker *m; (of tobacco)* Pfriem *m; (col: publicity)* Schleichwerbung *f; (Aut)* Zündkerze *f; vt (zu)*stopfen; *(col: advertise)* Reklame machen für; **to ~ in a lamp** den Stecker einer Lampe einstecken.

plum [plʌm] *n* Pflaume *f*, Zwetschge *f; a job etc* Bomben-.

plumage ['pluːmɪdʒ] *n* Gefieder *nt.*

plumb [plʌm] *n* Lot *nt; out of* **~** nicht im Lot; *a* senkrecht; *ad (exactly)* genau; *vt* ausloten; *(fig)* sondieren; *mystery* ergründen.

plumber ['plʌmə*] *n* Klempner *m*, Installateur *m.*

plumbing ['plʌmɪŋ] *n (craft)* Installieren *nt; (fittings)* Leitungen *pl*, Installationen *pl.*

plumbline ['plʌmlaɪn] *n* Senkblei *nt.*

plume [pluːm] *n* Feder *f; (of smoke etc)* Fahne *f; vt (bird)* putzen.

plummet ['plʌmɪt] *n* Senkblei *nt; vi (ab)*stürzen.

plump [plʌmp] *a* rundlich, füllig; *vi* plumpsen, sich fallen lassen; *vt* plumpsen lassen; **to ~ for** *(col: choose)* wählen, sich entscheiden für; **~ness** Rundlichkeit *f.*

plunder ['plʌndə*] *n* Plünderung *f; (loot)* Beute *f; vt* plündern; *things* rauben.

plunge [plʌndʒ] n Sprung m, Stürzen nt; vt stoßen; vi (sich) stürzen; (ship) rollen; **a room ~d into darkness** ein in Dunkelheit getauchtes Zimmer.

plunging ['plʌndʒɪŋ] a neckline offenherzig.

pluperfect ['plu:'pə:fɪkt] n Plusquamperfekt nt, Vorvergangenheit f.

plural ['pluərəl] a Plural-, Mehrzahl-; n Plural m, Mehrzahl f; **~istic** [pluərə'lɪstɪk] a pluralistisch.

plus [plʌs] prep plus, und; a Plus-.

plush [plʌʃ] a (also **~y**: col: luxurious) feudal; n Plüsch m.

ply [plaɪ] n as in: **three-~** wood dreischichtig; **wool** Dreifach-; vt trade (be)treiben; (with questions) zusetzen (+dat); (ship, taxi) befahren; vi (ship, taxi) verkehren; **~wood** Sperrholz nt.

pneumatic [nju:'mætɪk] a pneumatisch; (Tech) Luft-; **~ drill** Preßlufthammer m; **~ tyre** Luftreifen m.

pneumonia [nju:'məʊnɪə] n Lungenentzündung f.

poach [pəʊtʃ] vt (Cook) pochieren; game stehlen; vi (steal) wildern (for nach); **~ed a egg** pochiert, verloren; **~er** Wilddieb m; **~ing** Wildern nt.

pocket ['pɒkɪt] n Tasche f; (of ore) Ader f; (of resistance) (Widerstands)nest nt; **air ~** Luftloch nt; vt einstecken, in die Tasche stecken; **to be out of ~** kein Geld haben; **~book** Taschenbuch nt; **~ful** Tasche(voll) f; **~ knife** Taschenmesser nt; **~ money** Taschengeld nt.

pockmarked ['pɒkmɑ:kt] a face pockennarbig.

pod [pɒd] Hülse f; (of peas also) Schote f.

podgy ['pɒdʒɪ] a pummelig.

poem ['pəʊəm] n Gedicht nt.

poet ['pəʊɪt] n Dichter m, Poet m; **~ic** [pəʊ'etɪk] a poetisch, dichterisch; beauty malerisch, stimmungsvoll; **~ laureate** Hofdichter m; **~ry** Poesie f; (poems) Gedichte pl.

poignant a, **~ly** ad ['pɔɪnjənt, -lɪ] scharf, stechend; (touching) ergreifend, quälend.

point [pɔɪnt] n Punkt m (also in discussion, scoring); (spot also) Stelle f; (sharpened tip) Spitze f; (moment) (Zeit)punkt m, Moment m; (purpose) Zweck m; (idea) Argument nt; (decimal) Dezimalstelle f; (personal characteristic) Seite f; vt zeigen mit; gun richten; vi zeigen; **~s** pl (Rail) Weichen pl; **~ of view** Stand- or Gesichtspunkt m; **what's the ~?** was soll das?; **you have a ~ there** da hast du recht; **three ~ two** drei Komma zwei, 3,2 nt; vt hinweisen auf (+acc); **~ to** vt zeigen auf (+acc); **~-blank** ad (at close range) aus nächster Entfernung; (fig) unverblümt; **~ duty** Verkehrsregelungsdienst m; **~ed a, ~edly ad** spitz, scharf; (fig) gezielt; **~er** Zeigestock m; (on dial) Zeiger m; **~less a, ~lessly ad** zwecklos, sinnlos; **~lessness** Zwecklosigkeit f, Sinnlosigkeit f.

poise [pɔɪz] n Haltung f; (fig also) Gelassenheit f, vt balancieren; knife, pen bereithalten; o.s. sich bereitmachen; **~d a** beherrscht.

poison ['pɔɪzn] n (lit, fig) Gift nt; vt vergiften; **~ing** Vergiftung f; **~ous** a giftig, Gift-.

poke [pəʊk] vt stoßen; (put) stecken; fire schüren; hole bohren; n Stoß m; **to ~ one's nose into** seine Nase stecken in (+acc); **to ~ fun at sb** sich über jdn lustig machen; **~ about** vi herumstochern; herumwühlen; **~r** Schürhaken m; (Cards) Poker nt; **~r-faced** a undurchdringlich.

poky ['pəʊkɪ] a eng.

polar ['pəʊlə*] a Polar-, polar; **~ bear** Eisbär m; **~ization** [pəʊləraɪ'zeɪʃən] n Polarisation f; **~ize** vt polarisieren; vi sich polarisieren.

pole [pəʊl] n Stange f, Pfosten m; (flag—, telegraph— also) Mast m; (Elec, Geog) Pol m; (Sport) (vaulting —) Stab m; (ski —) Stock m; **~s apart** durch Welten getrennt; **~cat** (US) Skunk m; **~ star** Polarstern m; **~ vault** Stabhochsprung m.

polemic [pɒ'lemɪk] n Polemik f.

police [pə'li:s] n Polizei f; vt polizeilich überwachen; kontrollieren; **~ car** Polizeiwagen m; **~man** Polizist m; **~ state** Polizeistaat m; **~ station** (Polizei)revier nt, Wache f; **~woman** Polizistin f.

policy ['pɒlɪsɪ] n Politik f; (of business also) Usus m; (insurance) (Versicherungs)police f; (prudence) Klugheit f; (principle) Grundsatz m; **~ decision/statement** Grundsatzentscheidung f/-erklärung f.

polio ['pəʊlɪəʊ] n (spinale) Kinderlähmung f, Polio f.

polish ['pɒlɪʃ] n Politur f; (for floor) Wachs nt; (for shoes) Creme f; (nail —) Lack m; (shine) Glanz m; (of furniture) Politur f; (fig) Schliff m; vt polieren; shoes putzen; (fig) den letzten Schliff geben (+dat), aufpolieren; **~ off** vt (col: work) erledigen; food wegputzen; drink hinunterschütten; **~ up** vt essay aufpolieren; knowledge auffrischen; **~ed** a glänzend (also fig); manners verfeinert.

polite a, **~ly** ad [pə'laɪt, -lɪ] höflich; society fein; **~ness** Höflichkeit f, Feinheit f.

politic ['pɒlɪtɪk] a (prudent) diplomatisch; **~al** a, **~ally** ad [pə'lɪtɪkəl, -ɪ] politisch; **~al science** Politologie f; **~ian** [pɒlɪ'tɪʃən] Politiker m, Staatsmann m; **~s** pl Politik f.

polka ['pɒlkə] n Polka f; **~ dot** Tupfen m.

poll [pəʊl] n Abstimmung f; (in election) Wahl f; (votes cast) Wahlbeteiligung f; (opinion —) Umfrage f; vt votes erhalten, auf sich vereinigen.

pollen ['pɒlən] n Blütenstaub m, Pollen m; **~ count** Pollenkonzentration f.

pollination [pɒlɪ'neɪʃən] n Befruchtung f.

polling booth ['pəʊlɪŋbu:ð] n Wahlkabine f.

polling day ['pəʊlɪŋ deɪ] n Wahltag m.

polling station ['pəʊlɪŋ steɪʃən] n Wahllokal nt.

pollute [pə'lu:t] vt verschmutzen, verunreinigen.

pollution [pə'lu:ʃən] n Verschmutzung f.

polo ['pəʊləʊ] n Polo nt.

poly- [pɒlɪ] pref Poly-.

polygamy [pɔ'lɪgəmɪ] n Polygamie f.

polytechnic [pɔlɪ'teknɪk] n technische Hochschule f.

polythene ['pɔlɪθiːn] n Plastik nt; ~ **bag** Plastiktüte f.

pomegranate ['pɔməgrænɪt] n Granatapfel m.

pommel ['pʌml] vt mit den Fäusten bearbeiten; n Sattelknopf m.

pomp [pɔmp] n Pomp m, Prunk m.

pompous a, ~**ly** ad ['pɔmpəs, -lɪ] aufgeblasen; language geschwollen.

ponce [pɔns] n (col) (pimp) Louis m; (queer) Schwule m.

pond [pɔnd] n Teich m, Weiher m.

ponder ['pɔndə*] vt nachdenken or nachgrübeln über (+acc); ~**ous** a schwerfällig.

pontiff ['pɔntɪf] n Pontifex m.

pontificate [pɔn'tɪfɪkeɪt] vi (fig) geschwollen reden.

pontoon [pɔn'tuːn] n Ponton m; (Cards) 17-und-4 nt.

pony ['pəʊnɪ] n Pony nt; ~**tail** Pferdeschwanz m.

poodle ['puːdl] n Pudel m.

pooh-pooh [puː'puː] vt die Nase rümpfen über (+acc).

pool [puːl] n (swimming —) Schwimmbad nt; (private) Swimming-pool m; (of spilt liquid, blood) Lache f; (fund) (gemeinsame) Kasse f; (billiards) Poolspiel nt; vt money etc zusammenlegen.

poor [pʊə*] a arm; (not good) schlecht, schwach; **the** ~ pl die Armen pl; ~**ly** ad schlecht, schwach; dressed ärmlich; a schlecht, elend.

pop [pɔp] n Knall m; (music) Popmusik f; (drink) Limo(nade) f; (US col) Pa m; vt (put) stecken; balloon platzen lassen; vi knallen; ~ **in/out** (person) vorbeikommen/hinausgehen; hinein-/hinausspringen; ~ **concert** Popkonzert nt; ~**corn** Puffmais m.

Pope [pəʊp] n Papst m.

poplar ['pɔplə*] n Pappel f.

poplin ['pɔplɪn] n Popelin m.

poppy ['pɔpɪ] n Mohn m; ~**cock** (col) Quatsch m.

populace ['pɔpjʊlɪs] n Volk nt.

popular ['pɔpjʊlə*] a beliebt, populär; (of the people) volkstümlich, Populär-; (widespread) allgemein; ~**ity** [pɔpjʊ'lærɪtɪ] Beliebtheit f, Popularität f; ~**ize** vt popularisieren; ~**ly** ad allgemein, überall.

populate ['pɔpjʊleɪt] vt bevölkern; town bewohnen.

population [pɔpjʊ'leɪʃən] n Bevölkerung f; (of town) Einwohner pl.

populous ['pɔpjʊləs] a dicht besiedelt.

porcelain ['pɔːslɪn] n Porzellan nt.

porch [pɔːtʃ] n Vorbau m, Veranda f; (in church) Vorhalle f.

porcupine ['pɔːkjʊpaɪn] n Stachelschwein nt.

pore [pɔː*] n Pore f; ~ **over** vt brüten or hocken über (+dat).

pork [pɔːk] n Schweinefleisch nt.

pornographic a, ~**ally** ad [pɔːnə'græfɪk, -əlɪ] pornographisch.

pornography [pɔː'nɔgrəfɪ] n Pornographie f.

porous ['pɔːrəs] a porös; skin porig.

porpoise ['pɔːpəs] n Tümmler m.

porridge ['pɔrɪdʒ] n Porridge m, Haferbrei m.

port [pɔːt] n Hafen m; (town) Hafenstadt f; (Naut: left side) Backbord nt; (opening for loads) Luke f; (wine) Portwein m.

portable ['pɔːtəbl] a tragbar; radio Koffer-; typewriter Reise-.

portal ['pɔːtl] n Portal nt.

portcullis [pɔːt'kʌlɪs] n Fallgitter nt.

portend [pɔː'tend] vt anzeigen, hindeuten auf (+acc).

portent ['pɔːtent] n schlimme(s) Vorzeichen nt; ~**ous** [pɔː'tentəs] a schlimm, ominös; (amazing) ungeheuer.

porter ['pɔːtə*] n Pförtner(in f) m; (for luggage) (Gepäck)träger m.

porthole ['pɔːthəʊl] n Bullauge nt.

portico ['pɔːtɪkəʊ] n Säulengang m.

portion ['pɔːʃən] n Teil m, Stück nt; (of food) Portion f.

portly ['pɔːtlɪ] a korpulent, beleibt.

portrait ['pɔːtrɪt] n Porträt nt, Bild(nis) nt.

portray [pɔː'treɪ] vt darstellen; (describe) schildern; ~**al** Darstellung f; Schilderung f.

pose [pəʊz] n Stellung f, Pose f (also affectation); vi posieren, sich in Positur setzen; vt stellen; **to** ~ **as** sich ausgeben als; ~**r** knifflige Frage f.

posh [pɔʃ] a (col) (piek)fein.

position [pə'zɪʃən] n Stellung f; (place) Position f, Lage f; (job) Stelle f; (attitude) Standpunkt m, Haltung f; **to be in a** ~ **to do sth** in der Lage sein, etw zu tun; vt aufstellen.

positive a, ~**ly** ad ['pɔzɪtɪv, -lɪ] positiv; (convinced) sicher; (definite) eindeutig.

posse ['pɔsɪ] n (US) Aufgebot nt.

possess [pə'zes] vt besitzen; **what** ~**ed you to . . .?** was ist in dich gefahren, daß...?; ~**ed** a besessen; ~**ion** [pə'zeʃən] Besitz m; ~**ive** a besitzergreifend, eigensüchtig; (Gram) Possessiv-, besitzanzeigend; ~**ively** ad besitzergreifend, eigensüchtig; ~**or** Besitzer m.

possibility [pɔsɪ'bɪlɪtɪ] n Möglichkeit f.

possible ['pɔsəbl] a möglich; **if** ~ wenn möglich, möglichst; **as big as** ~ so groß wie möglich, möglichst groß.

possibly ['pɔsəblɪ] ad möglicherweise, vielleicht; **as soon as I** ~ **can** sobald ich irgendwie kann.

post [pəʊst] n Post f; (pole) Pfosten m, Pfahl m; (place of duty) Posten m; (job) Stelle f; vt notice anschlagen; letters aufgeben; soldiers aufstellen; ~**age** Postgebühr f, Porto nt; ~**al** a Post-; ~**al order** Postanweisung f; ~**card** Postkarte f; ~**date** vt cheque nachdatieren; ~**er** Plakat nt, Poster m; ~**e restante** Aufbewahrungsstelle f für postlagernde Sendungen; **to send sth** ~**e restante** etw postlagernd schicken.

posterior [pɔs'tɪərɪə*] n (col) Hintern m.

posterity [pɔs'terɪtɪ] n Nachwelt f; (descendants) Nachkommenschaft f.

postgraduate ['pəust'grædjuit] n Weiter-
studierender(in f) m.

posthumous a, ~ly ad ['pɒstjuməs, -lı]
post(h)um.

postman ['pəustmən] n Briefträger m,
Postbote m.

postmark ['pəustmɑːk] n Poststempel m.

postmaster ['pəustmɑːstə*] n Postmeister
m; P~ **General** Postminister m.

post-mortem ['pəust'mɔːtəm] n Autopsie f.

post office ['pəustɒfɪs] n Postamt nt, Post f
(also organization).

postpone [pə'spəun] vt verschieben, aufschieben; ~**ment** Verschiebung f,
Aufschub m.

postscript ['pəusskrıpt] n Nachschrift f,
Postskript nt; (in book) Nachwort nt.

postulate ['pɒstjuleɪt] vt voraussetzen;
(maintain) behaupten.

postulation [pɒstju'leɪʃən] n Voraussetzung f, Behauptung f.

posture ['pɒstʃə*] n Haltung f; vi posieren.

postwar ['pəust'wɔː*] a Nachkriegs-.

posy ['pəuzı] n Blumenstrauß m.

pot [pɒt] n Topf m; (tea—) Kanne f; (col:
marijuana) Hasch m; vt plant eintopfen.

potash ['pɒtæʃ] n Pottasche f.

potato [pə'teɪtəu] n, pl ~**es** Kartoffel f.

potency ['pəutənsı] n Stärke f, Potenz f.

potent ['pəutənt] a stark; argument
zwingend.

potentate ['pəutənteɪt] n Machthaber m.

potential [pə'tenʃəl] a potentiell; **he is a
~ virtuoso** er hat das Zeug zum
Virtuosen; n Potential nt; ~**ly** ad
potentiell.

pothole ['pɒthəul] n Höhle f; (in road)
Schlagloch nt; ~**r** Höhlenforscher m.

potholing ['pɒthəulıŋ] n: **to go ~** Höhlen
erforschen.

potion ['pəuʃən] n Trank m.

potluck ['pɒt'lʌk] n: **to take ~ with sth**
etw auf gut Glück nehmen.

potpourri [pəu'purı] n Potpourri nt.

potshot ['pɒtʃɒt] n: **to take a ~ at sth** auf
etw (acc) ballern.

potted ['pɒtıd] a food eingelegt,
eingemacht; plant Topf-; (fig: book, version)
konzentriert.

potter ['pɒtə*] n Töpfer m; vi herum-
hantieren, herumwursteln; ~**y**
Töpferwaren pl, Steingut nt; (place)
Töpferei f.

potty ['pɒtı] a (col) verrückt; n Töpfchen nt.

pouch [pautʃ] n Beutel m; (under eyes)
Tränensack m; (for tobacco) Tabaksbeutel
m.

pouffe [puːf] n Sitzkissen nt.

poultice ['pəultıs] n Packung f.

poultry ['pəultrı] n Geflügel nt; ~ **farm**
Geflügelfarm f.

pounce [pauns] vi sich stürzen (on auf
+acc); n Sprung m, Satz m.

pound [paund] n (Fin, weight) Pfund nt; (for
cars, animals) Auslösestelle f; (for stray animals) (Tier)asyl nt; vi klopfen, hämmern;
vt (zer)stampfen; ~**ing** starke(s) Klopfen
nt, Hämmern nt, (Zer)stampfen nt.

pour [pɔː*] vt gießen, schütten; vi gießen;

(crowds etc) strömen; ~ **away** vt, ~ **off**
vt abgießen; ~**ing rain** strömende(r)
Regen m.

pout [paut] n Schnute f, Schmollmund m; vi
eine Schnute ziehen, schmollen.

poverty ['pɒvətı] n Armut f; ~-**stricken** a
verarmt, sehr arm.

powder ['paudə*] n Pulver nt; (cosmetic)
Puder m; vt pulverisieren; (sprinkle)
bestreuen; **to ~ one's nose** sich (dat) die
Nase pudern; ~ **room** Damentoilette f;
~**y** a pulverig, Pulver-.

power ['pauə*] n Macht f (also Pol); (ability)
Fähigkeit f; (strength) Stärke f; (authority)
Macht f, Befugnis f; (Math) Potenz f; (Elec)
Strom m; vt betreiben, antreiben; ~ **cut**
Stromausfall m; ~**ful** a person mächtig;
engine, government stark; ~**less** a
machtlos; ~ **line** (Haupt)stromleitung f;
~ **point** elektrische(r) Anschluß m; ~
station Elektrizitätswerk nt.

powwow ['pauwau] n Besprechung f; vi
eine Besprechung abhalten.

practicability [præktıkə'bılıtı] n Durchführbarkeit f.

practicable ['præktıkəbl] a durchführbar.

practical a, ~**ly** ad ['præktıkəl, -ı]
praktisch; ~ **joke** Streich m.

practice ['præktıs] n Übung f; (reality)
Praxis f; (custom) Brauch m; (in business)
Usus m; (doctor's, lawyer's) Praxis f; **in ~**
(in reality) in der Praxis; **out of ~** außer
Übung.

practise, **(US) practice** ['præktıs] vt
üben; profession ausüben; **to ~
law/medicine** als Rechtsanwalt/Arzt
arbeiten; vi (sich) üben; (doctor, lawyer)
praktizieren; ~**d** a erfahren.

practising, **(US) practicing** ['præktısıŋ]
a praktizierend; Christian etc aktiv.

practitioner [præk'tıʃənə*] n prak-
tische(r) Arzt m.

pragmatic [præg'mætık] a pragmatisch.

pragmatism ['prægmətızəm] n
Pragmatismus m.

pragmatist ['prægmətıst] n Pragmatiker m.

prairie ['prɛərı] n Prärie f, Steppe f.

praise [preız] n Lob nt, Preis m; vt loben;
(worship) (lob)preisen, loben; ~**worthy** a
lobenswert.

pram [præm] n Kinderwagen m.

prance [prɑːns] vi (horse) tänzeln; (person)
stolzieren; (gaily) herumhüpfen.

prank [præŋk] n Streich m.

prattle ['prætl] vi schwatzen, plappern.

prawn [prɔːn] n Garnele f, Krabbe f.

pray [preı] vi beten; ~**er** [prɛə*] Gebet nt;
~**er book** Gebetbuch nt.

pre- [priː] pref prä-, vor(her)-.

preach [priːtʃ] vi predigen; ~**er** Prediger
m.

preamble [priː'æmbl] n Einleitung f.

prearrange ['priːə'reındʒ] vt vereinbaren,
absprechen; ~**d** a vereinbart; ~**ment**
Vereinbarung f, vorherige Absprache f.

precarious a, ~**ly** ad [prı'kɛərıəs, -lı]
prekär, unsicher.

precaution [prı'kɔːʃən] n (Vor-
sichts)maßnahme f, Vorbeugung f; ~**ary**

a measure vorbeugend, Vorsichts-.

precede [prɪ'siːd] *vti* vorausgehen *(+dat); (be more important)* an Bedeutung übertreffen; **~nce** ['presɪdəns] Priorität *f,* Vorrang *m;* **to take ~nce over** den Vorrang haben vor *(+dat);* **~nt** ['presɪdənt] Präzedenzfall *m.*

preceding [prɪ'siːdɪŋ] *a* vorhergehend.

precept ['priːsept] *n* Gebot *nt,* Regel *f.*

precinct ['priːsɪŋkt] *n* Gelände *f; (district)* Bezirk *m; (shopping —)* Einkaufszone *f.*

precious ['preʃəs] *a* kostbar, wertvoll; *(affected)* preziös, geziert.

precipice ['presɪpɪs] *n* Abgrund *m.*

precipitate *a,* **~ly** *ad* [prɪ'sɪpɪtɪt, -lɪ] überstürzt, übereilt; [prɪ'sɪpɪteɪt] *vt* hinunterstürzen; *events* heraufbeschwören.

precipitation [prɪsɪpɪ'teɪʃən] *n* Niederschlag *m.*

precipitous *a,* **~ly** *ad* [prɪ'sɪpɪtəs, -lɪ] abschüssig; *action* überstürzt.

précis ['preɪsiː] *n* (kurze) Übersicht *f,* Zusammenfassung *f; (Sch)* Inhaltsangabe *f.*

precise *a,* **~ly** *ad* [prɪ'saɪs, -lɪ] genau, präzis.

preclude [prɪ'kluːd] *vt* ausschließen; *person* abhalten.

precocious [prɪ'kəʊʃəs] *a* frühreif.

preconceived ['priːkən'siːvd] *a idea* vorgefaßt.

precondition ['priːkən'dɪʃən] *n* Vorbedingung *f,* Voraussetzung *f.*

precursor [priː'kɜːsə*] *n* Vorläufer *m.*

predator ['predətə*] *n* Raubtier *nt;* **~y** *a* Raub-; räuberisch.

predecessor ['priːdɪsesə*] *n* Vorgänger *m.*

predestination [priːdestɪ'neɪʃən] *n* Vorherbestimmung *f,* Prädestination *f.*

predestine [priː'destɪn] *vt* vorherbestimmen.

predetermine ['priːdɪ'tɜːmɪn] *vt* vorherentscheiden, vorherbestimmen.

predicament [prɪ'dɪkəmənt] *n* mißliche Lage *f;* **to be in a ~** in der Klemme sitzen.

predicate ['predɪkət] *n* Prädikat *nt,* Satzaussage *f.*

predict [prɪ'dɪkt] *vt* voraussagen; **~ion** [prɪ'dɪkʃən] Voraussage *f.*

predominance [prɪ'dɒmɪnəns] *n (in power)* Vorherrschaft *f, (fig)* Vorherrschen *nt,* Überwiegen *nt.*

predominant [prɪ'dɒmɪnənt] *a* vorherrschend; *(fig also)* überwiegend; **~ly** *ad* überwiegend, hauptsächlich.

predominate [prɪ'dɒmɪneɪt] *vi* vorherrschen; *(fig also)* überwiegen.

pre-eminent [priː'emɪnənt] *a* hervorragend, herausragend.

pre-empt [priː'empt] *vt action, decision* vorwegnehmen.

preen [priːn] *vt* putzen; **to ~ o.s. on sth** sich *(dat)* etwas auf etw *(acc)* einbilden.

prefab ['priːfæb] *n* Fertighaus *nt.*

prefabricated ['priːfæbrɪkeɪtɪd] *a* vorgefertigt, Fertig-.

preface ['prefɪs] *n* Vorwort *nt,* Einleitung *f.*

prefect ['priːfekt] *n* Präfekt *m; (Sch)* Aufsichtsschüler(in *f) m.*

prefer [prɪ'fɜː*] *vt* vorziehen, lieber mögen; **to ~ to do sth** etw lieber tun; **~able** ['prefərəbl] *a* vorzuziehen(d) *(to dat);* **~ably** ['prefərəblɪ] *ad* vorzugsweise, am liebsten; **~ence** ['prefərəns] Präferenz *f,* Vorzug *m;* **~ential** [prefə'renʃəl] *a* bevorzugt, Vorzugs-.

prefix ['priːfɪks] *n* Vorsilbe *f,* Präfix *nt.*

pregnancy ['pregnənsɪ] *n* Schwangerschaft *f.*

pregnant ['pregnənt] *a* schwanger; **~ with meaning** *(fig)* bedeutungsschwer *or* -voll.

prehistoric ['priːhɪs'tɒrɪk] *a* prähistorisch, vorgeschichtlich.

prehistory [priː'hɪstərɪ] *n* Urgeschichte *f.*

prejudge ['priːdʒʌdʒ] *vt* vorschnell beurteilen.

prejudice ['predʒʊdɪs] *n* Vorurteil *nt;* Voreingenommenheit *f; (harm)* Schaden *m; vt* beeinträchtigen; **~d** *a person* voreingenommen.

prelate ['prelət] *n* Prälat *m.*

preliminary [prɪ'lɪmɪnərɪ] *a* einleitend, Vor-; **the preliminaries** *pl* die vorbereitenden Maßnahmen *pl.*

prelude ['preljuːd] *n* Vorspiel *nt; (Mus)* Präludium *nt; (fig also)* Auftakt *m.*

premarital ['priː'mærɪtl] *a* vorehelich.

premature ['premətʃʊə*] *a* vorzeitig, verfrüht; *birth* Früh-; *decision* voreilig; **~ly** *ad* vorzeitig; verfrüht; voreilig.

premeditate [priː'medɪteɪt] *vt* im voraus planen; **~d** *a* geplant; *murder* vorsätzlich.

premeditation [priː'medɪ'teɪʃən] *n* Planung *f.*

premier ['premɪə*] *a* erste(r, s), oberste(r, s), höchste(r, s); *n* Premier *m.*

premiere [premɪ'eə*] *n* Premiere *f;* Uraufführung *f.*

premise ['premɪs] *n* Voraussetzung *f,* Prämisse *f;* **~s** *pl* Räumlichkeiten *pl; (grounds)* Grundstück *nt.*

premium ['priːmɪəm] *n* Prämie *f;* **to sell at a ~** mit Gewinn verkaufen.

premonition [premə'nɪʃən] *n* Vorahnung *f.*

preoccupation [priːɒkjʊ'peɪʃən] *n* Sorge *f.*

preoccupied [priː'ɒkjupaɪd] *a look* geistesabwesend; **to be ~ with sth** mit dem Gedanken zu etw *(acc)* beschäftigt sein.

prep [prep] *n (Sch: study)* Hausaufgabe *f.*

prepaid [priː'peɪd] *a* vorausbezahlt; *letter* frankiert.

preparation ['prepə'reɪʃən] *n* Vorbereitung *f.*

preparatory [prɪ'pærətərɪ] *a* Vor-(bereitungs)-.

prepare [prɪ'peə*] *vt* vorbereiten *(for* auf *+acc);* vi sich vorbereiten; **to be ~d to ...** bereit sein zu ...

preponderance [prɪ'pɒndərəns] *n* Übergewicht *nt.*

preposition [prepə'zɪʃən] *n* Präposition *f,* Verhältniswort *nt.*

preposterous [prɪ'pɒstərəs] *a* absurd, widersinnig.

prerequisite ['pri:'rekwızıt] n (unerläßliche) Voraussetzung f.

prerogative [prı'rɒɡətıv] n Vorrecht nt, Privileg nt.

presbytery ['prezbıtərı] n (house) Presbyterium nt; (Catholic) Pfarrhaus nt.

prescribe [prıs'kraıb] vt vorschreiben, anordnen; (Med) verschreiben.

prescription [prıs'krıpʃən] n Vorschrift f; (Med) Rezept nt.

prescriptive [prıs'krıptıv] a normativ.

presence ['prezns] n Gegenwart f, Anwesenheit f; ~ of mind Geistesgegenwart f.

present ['preznt] a anwesend; (existing) gegenwärtig, augenblicklich; n Gegenwart f; at ~ im Augenblick; Präsens nt (Gram); (gift) Geschenk nt; [prı'zent] vt vorlegen; (introduce) vorstellen; (show) zeigen; (give) überreichen; to ~ sb with sth jdm etw überreichen; ~able [prı'zentəbl] a präsentabel; ~ation Überreichung f; ~-day a heutig, gegenwärtig, modern; ~ly ad bald; (at present) im Augenblick; ~ participle Partizip nt des Präsens, Mittelwort nt der Gegenwart; ~ tense Präsens nt, Gegenwart f.

preservation [prezə'veıʃən] n Erhaltung f.

preservative [prı'zɜ:vətıv] n Konservierungsmittel nt.

preserve [prı'zɜ:v] vt erhalten, schützen; food einmachen, konservieren; n (jam) Eingemachte(s) nt; (hunting) Schutzgebiet nt.

preside [prı'zaıd] vi den Vorsitz haben.

presidency ['prezıdənsı] n (Pol) Präsidentschaft f.

president ['prezıdənt] n Präsident m; ~ial [prezı'denʃəl] a Präsidenten-; election Präsidentschafts-; system Präsidial-.

press [pres] n Presse f; (printing house) Druckerei f; to give the clothes a ~ die Kleider bügeln; vt drücken, pressen; (iron) bügeln; (urge) (be)drängen; vi (push) drücken, pressen; to be ~ed for time unter Zeitdruck stehen; to be ~ed for money/space wenig Geld/Platz haben; to ~ for sth drängen auf etw (acc); ~ on vi vorwärtsdrängen; ~ agency Presseagentur f; ~ conference Pressekonferenz f; ~ cutting Zeitungsausschnitt m; ~ing a dringend; ~-stud Druckknopf m.

pressure [preʃə*] n Druck m; ~ cooker Schnellkochtopf m; ~ gauge Druckmesser m; ~ group Interessenverband m, Pressure Group f.

pressurized ['preʃəraızd] a Druck-.

prestige [pres'ti:ʒ] n Ansehen nt, Prestige nt.

prestigious [pres'tıdʒəs] a Prestige-.

presumably [prı'zju:məblı] ad vermutlich.

presume [prı'zju:m] vti annehmen; (dare) sich erlauben.

presumption [prı'zʌmpʃən] n Annahme f; (impudent behaviour) Anmaßung f.

presumptuous [prı'zʌmptjʊəs] a anmaßend.

presuppose [pri:sə'pəʊz] vt voraussetzen.

presupposition [pri:sʌpə'zıʃən] n Voraussetzung f.

pretence [prı'tens] n Vorgabe f, Vortäuschung f; (false claim) Vorwand m.

pretend [prı'tend] vt vorgeben, so tun als ob ...; vi so tun; to ~ to sth Anspruch erheben auf etw (acc).

pretense [prı'tens] n (US) = pretence.

pretension [prı'tenʃən] n Anspruch m; (impudent claim) Anmaßung f.

pretentious [prı'tenʃəs] a angeberisch.

pretext ['pri:tekst] n Vorwand m.

prettily ['prıtılı] ad hübsch, nett.

pretty ['prıtı] a hübsch, nett; ad (col) ganz schön.

prevail [prı'veıl] vi siegen (against, over über +acc); (custom) vorherrschen; to ~ upon sb to do sth jdn dazu bewegen, etw zu tun; ~ing a vorherrschend.

prevalent ['prevələnt] a vorherrschend.

prevarication [prıværı'keıʃən] n Ausflucht f.

prevent [prı'vent] vt (stop) verhindern, verhüten; to ~ sb from doing sth jdn (daran) hindern, etw zu tun; ~able a verhütbar; ~ative a Vorbeugungsmittel nt; ~ion [prı'venʃən] n Verhütung f, Schutz m (of gegen); ~ive a vorbeugend, Schutz-.

preview ['pri:vju:] n private Voraufführung f; (trailer) Vorschau f; vt film privat vorführen.

previous ['pri:vıəs] a früher, vorherig; ~ly ad früher.

prewar ['pri:'wɔ:*] a Vorkriegs-.

prey [preı] n Beute f; ~ on vt Jagd machen auf (+acc); mind nagen an (+dat); bird/beast of ~ Raubvogel m/Raubtier nt.

price [praıs] n Preis m; (value) Wert m; vt schätzen; (label) auszeichnen; ~less a (lit, fig) unbezahlbar; ~ list Preisliste f; ~y a (col) teuer.

prick [prık] n Stich m; vti stechen; to ~ up one's ears die Ohren spitzen.

prickle ['prıkl] n Stachel m, Dorn m; vi brennen.

prickly ['prıklı] a stachelig; (fig) person reizbar; ~ heat Hitzebläschen pl; ~ pear Feigenkaktus m; (fruit) Kaktusfeige f.

pride [praıd] n Stolz m; (arrogance) Hochmut m; to ~ o.s. on sth auf etw (acc) stolz sein.

priest [pri:st] n Priester m; ~ess Priesterin f; ~hood Priesteramt nt.

prig [prıg] n Selbstgefällige(r) mf.

prim a, ~ly ad [prım, -lı] prüde.

prima donna ['pri:mə 'dɒnə] n Primadonna f.

primarily ['praımərılı] ad vorwiegend, hauptsächlich.

primary ['praımərı] a Haupt-, Grund-, primär; ~ colour Grundfarbe f; ~ education Grundschul(aus)bildung f; ~ election Vorwahl f; ~ school Grundschule f, Volksschule f.

primate [praımıt] n (Eccl) Primas m; (Biol) Primat m.

prime [praım] a oberste(r, s), erste(r, s), wichtigste(r, s); (excellent) erstklassig, prima inv; vt vorbereiten; gun laden; n (of *life)* beste(s) Alter *nt;* ~ **minister** Premierminister *m,* Ministerpräsident *m;* ~r Elementarlehrbuch *nt,* Fibel *f.*

primeval [praɪˈmiːvəl] *a* vorzeitlich; *forests* Ur-.

primitive [ˈprɪmɪtɪv] *a* primitiv.

primrose [ˈprɪmrəʊz] *n* (gelbe) Primel *f.*

primula [ˈprɪmjʊlə] *n* Primel *f.*

primus (stove) " [ˈpraɪməs (stəʊv)] *n* Primuskocher *m.*

prince [prɪns] *n* Prinz *m; (ruler)* Fürst *m;* ~ss [prɪnˈses] Prinzessin *f;* Fürstin *f.*

principal [ˈprɪnsɪpəl] *a* Haupt-; wichtigste(r, s); *n (Sch)* (Schul)direktor *m,* Rektor *m; (money)* (Grund)kapital *nt;* ~ity [prɪnsɪˈpælɪtɪ] Fürstentum *nt;* ~ly *ad* hauptsächlich.

principle [ˈprɪnsəpl] *n* Grundsatz *m,* Prinzip *nt;* **in/on** ~ im/aus Prinzip, prinzipiell.

print [prɪnt] *n* Druck *m; (made by feet, fingers)* Abdruck *m; (Phot)* Abzug *m; (cotton)* Kattun *m; vt* drucken; *name* in Druckbuchstaben schreiben; *Photo* abziehen; ~**ed matter** Drucksache *f;* ~**er** Drucker *m;* ~**ing** Drucken *nt; (of photos)* Abziehen *nt;* ~**ing press** Druckerpresse *f;* **is the book still in ~?** wird das Buch noch gedruckt?; **out of** ~ vergriffen.

prior [ˈpraɪə*] *a* früher; ~ **to sth** vor etw *(dat);* ~ **to going abroad, she had** ... bevor sie ins Ausland ging, hatte sie ...; *n* Prior *m;* ~**ess** Priorin *f;* ~**ity** [praɪˈɒrɪtɪ] Vorrang *m;* Priorität *f;* ~**y** Kloster *nt.*

prise [praɪz] *vt:* ~ **open** aufbrechen.

prism [ˈprɪzəm] *n* Prisma *nt.*

prison [ˈprɪzn] *n* Gefängnis *nt;* ~**er** Gefangene(r) *mf;* ~**er of war** Kriegsgefangene(r) *m;* **to be taken** ~**er** in Gefangenschaft geraten.

prissy [ˈprɪsɪ] *a (col)* etepetete.

pristine [ˈprɪstiːn] *a* makellos.

privacy [ˈprɪvəsɪ] *n* Ungestörtheit *f,* Ruhe *f;* Privatleben *nt.*

private [ˈpraɪvɪt] *a* privat, Privat-; *(secret)* vertraulich, geheim; *soldier* einfach; *n* einfache(r) Soldat *m;* **in** ~ privat, unter vier Augen; ~ **eye** Privatdetektiv *m;* ~**ly** *ad* privat; vertraulich, geheim.

privet [ˈprɪvɪt] *n* Liguster *m.*

privilege [ˈprɪvɪlɪdʒ] *n* Vorrecht *nt,* Vergünstigung *f,* Privileg *nt;* ~**d** a bevorzugt, privilegiert.

privy [ˈprɪvɪ] *a* geheim, privat; ~ **council** Geheime(r) Staatsrat *m.*

prize [praɪz] *n* Preis *m; a example* erstklassig; *idiot* Voll-; *vt* (hoch)schätzen; ~ **fighting** Preisboxen *nt;* ~ **giving** Preisverteilung *f;* ~ **money** Geldpreis *m;* ~**winner** Preisträger(in *f*) *m; (of money)* Gewinner(in *f*) *m.*

pro- [prəʊ] *pref* pro-; *n:* **the** ~**s and cons** *pl* das Für und Wider.

pro [prəʊ] *n (professional)* Profi *m.*

probability [prɒbəˈbɪlɪtɪ] *n* Wahrscheinlichkeit *f;* **in all** ~ aller Wahrscheinlichkeit nach.

probable *a,* **probably** *ad* [ˈprɒbəbl, -blɪ] wahrscheinlich.

probation [prəˈbeɪʃən] *n* Probe(zeit) *f; (Jur)* Bewährung *f;* **on** ~ auf Probe; auf Bewährung; ~ **officer** Bewährungshelfer *m;* ~**ary** a Probe-; ~**er** *(nurse)* Lernschwester *f;* Pfleger *m* in der Ausbildung; *(Jur)* auf Bewährung freigelassene(r) Gefangene(r) *m.*

probe [prəʊb] *n* Sonde *f; (enquiry)* Untersuchung *f; vti* untersuchen, erforschen, sondieren.

probity [ˈprəʊbɪtɪ] *n* Rechtschaffenheit *f.*

problem [ˈprɒbləm] *n* Problem *nt;* ~**atic** [prɒblɪˈmætɪk] a problematisch.

procedural [prəˈsiːdjʊrəl] *a* verfahrensmäßig, Verfahrens-.

procedure [prəˈsiːdʒə*] *n* Verfahren *nt,* Vorgehen *nt.*

proceed [prəˈsiːd] *vi (advance)* vorrücken; *(start)* anfangen; *(carry on)* fortfahren; *(set about)* vorgehen; *(come from)* entstehen *(from aus); (Jur)* gerichtlich vorgehen; ~**ings** *pl* Verfahren *nt; (record of things)* Sitzungsbericht *m;* ~**s** [ˈprəʊsiːdz] *pl* Erlös *m,* Gewinn *m.*

process [ˈprəʊses] *n* Vorgang *m,* Prozeß *m; (method also)* Verfahren *nt; vt* bearbeiten; *food* verarbeiten; *film* entwickeln; ~**ing** *(Phot)* Entwickeln *nt.*

procession [prəˈseʃən] *n* Prozession *f,* Umzug *m.*

proclaim [prəˈkleɪm] *vt* verkünden, proklamieren; **to** ~ **sb king** jdn zum König ausrufen.

proclamation [prɒkləˈmeɪʃən] *n* Verkündung *f,* Proklamation *f;* Ausrufung *f.*

procrastination [prəʊkræstɪˈneɪʃən] *n* Hinausschieben *nt.*

procreation [prəʊkrɪˈeɪʃən] *n* (Er)zeugung *f.*

procure [prəˈkjʊə*] *vt* beschaffen.

prod [prɒd] *vt* stoßen; **to** ~ **sb** *(fig)* bohren; *n* Stoß *m.*

prodigal [ˈprɒdɪgəl] *a* verschwenderisch *(of mit);* **the** ~ **son** der verlorene Sohn.

prodigious [prəˈdɪdʒəs] *a* gewaltig, erstaunlich; *(wonderful)* wunderbar.

prodigy [ˈprɒdɪdʒɪ] *n* Wunder *nt;* **a child** ~ ein Wunderkind.

produce [ˈprɒdjuːs] *n (Agr)* (Boden)produkte *pl,* (Natur)erzeugnis *nt;* [prəˈdjuːs] *vt* herstellen, produzieren; *(cause)* hervorrufen; *(farmer)* erzeugen; *(yield)* liefern, bringen; *play* inszenieren; ~**r** Erzeuger *m,* Hersteller *m,* Produzent *m (also Cine.)*

product [ˈprɒdʌkt] *n* Produkt *nt,* Erzeugnis *nt;* ~**ion** [prəˈdʌkʃən] Produktion *f,* Herstellung *f; (thing)* Erzeugnis *nt,* Produkt *nt; (Theat)* Inszenierung *f;* ~**ion line** Fließband *nt;* ~**ive** a produktiv; *(fertile)* ertragreich, fruchtbar; **to be** ~**ive of** führen zu, erzeugen.

productivity [prɒdʌkˈtɪvɪtɪ] *n* Produktivität *f; (Comm)* Leistungsfähigkeit *f; (fig)* Fruchtbarkeit *f.*

prof [prɒf] *n (col)* Professor *m.*

profane [prəˈfeɪn] *a* weltlich, profan, Profan-.

profess [prəˈfes] *vt* bekennen; *(show)*

zeigen; *(claim to be)* vorgeben; ~**ion** [prə'feʃən] Beruf *m; (declaration)* Bekenntnis *nt;* ~**ional** [prə'feʃənl] Fachmann *m; (Sport)* Berufsspieler(in *f) m; a* Berufs-; *(expert)* fachlich; *player* professionell; ~**ionalism** [prə'feʃnəlizəm] (fachliches) Können *nt;* Berufssportlertum *nt;* ~**or** Professor *m.*

proficiency [prə'fiʃənsɪ] *n* Fertigkeit *f,* Können *nt.*

proficient [prə'fiʃənt] *a* fähig.

profile ['prəʊfail] *n* Profil *nt; (fig: report)* Kurzbiographie *f.*

profit ['prɒfit] *n* Gewinn *m,* Profit *m; vi* profitieren *(by, from* von), Nutzen *or* Gewinn ziehen *(by, from* aus); ~**ability** [prɒfitə'biliti] Rentabilität *f;* ~**able** *a* einträglich, rentabel; ~**ably** *ad* nützlich; ~**eering** [prɒfi'tɪərɪŋ] Profitmacherei *f.*

profound [prə'faʊnd] *a* tief; *knowledge* profund; *book, thinker* tiefschürfend; ~**ly** *ad* zutiefst.

profuse [prə'fjuːs] *a* überreich; **to be** ~ **in** überschwenglich sein bei; ~**ly** *ad* überschwenglich; *sweat* reichlich.

profusion [prə'fjuːʒən] *n* Überfülle *f,* Überfluß *m (of* an +*dat).*

progeny ['prɒdʒɪnɪ] *n* Nachkommenschaft *f.*

programme, *(US)* **program** ['prəʊgræm] *n* Programm *nt; vt* planen; *computer* programmieren.

programming, *(US)* **programing** ['prəʊgræmɪŋ] *n* Programmieren *nt,* Programmierung *f.*

progress ['prəʊgres] *n* Fortschritt *m;* **to be in** ~ im Gang sein; **to make** ~ Fortschritte machen; [prə'gres] *vi* fortschreiten, weitergehen; ~**ion** [prə'greʃən] Fortschritt *m,* Progression *f; (walking etc)* Fortbewegung *f;* ~**ive** [prə'gresɪv] *a* fortschrittlich, progressiv; ~**ively** [prə'gresɪvlɪ] *ad* zunehmend.

prohibit [prə'hibit] *vt* verbieten; ~**ion** [prəʊɪ'bɪʃən] Verbot *nt; (US)* Alkoholverbot *nt,* Prohibition *f;* ~**ive** *a price etc* unerschwinglich.

project ['prɒdʒekt] *n* Projekt *nt;* [prə'dʒekt] *vt* vorausplanen; *(Psych)* hineinprojizieren; *film etc* projizieren; *personality, voice* zum Tragen bringen; *vi (stick out)* hervorragen, (her)vorstehen; ~**ile** [prə'dʒektail] Geschoß *nt,* Projektil *nt;* ~**ion** [prə'dʒekʃən] Projektion *f; (sth prominent)* Vorsprung *m;* ~**or** [prə'dʒektə*] Projektor *m,* Vorführgerät *nt.*

proletarian [prəʊlɪ'teərɪən] *a* proletarisch, Proletarier-; *n* Proletarier(in *f) m.*

proletariat [prəʊlɪ'teərɪət] *n* Proletariat *nt.*

proliferate [prə'lɪfəreɪt] *vi* sich vermehren.

proliferation [prəlɪfə'reɪʃən] *n* Vermehrung *f.*

prolific [prə'lɪfɪk] *a* fruchtbar; *author etc* produktiv.

prologue ['prəʊlɒg] *n* Prolog *m; (event)* Vorspiel *nt.*

prolong [prə'lɒŋ] *vt* verlängern; ~**ed** *a* lang.

prom [prɒm] *n abbr of* **promenade** *and* **promenade concert;** *(US: college ball)* Studentenball *m.*

promenade [prɒmɪ'nɑːd] *n* Promenade *f;* ~ **concert** Promenadenkonzert *nt,* Stehkonzert *nt;* ~ **deck** Promenadendeck *nt.*

prominence ['prɒmɪnəns] *n* (große) Bedeutung *f,* Wichtigkeit *f; (sth standing out)* vorspringende(r) Teil *m.*

prominent ['prɒmɪnənt] *a* bedeutend; *politician* prominent; *(easily seen)* herausragend, auffallend.

promiscuity [prɒmɪs'kjuːɪtɪ] *n* Promiskuität *f.*

promiscuous [prə'mɪskjʊəs] *a* lose; *(mixed up)* wild.

promise ['prɒmɪs] *n* Versprechen *nt; (hope)* Aussicht *f (of auf* + *acc);* **to show** ~ vielversprechend sein; **a writer of** ~ ein vielversprechender Schriftsteller; *vti* versprechen; **the** ~**d land** das Gelobte Land.

promising ['prɒmɪsɪŋ] *a* vielversprechend.

promontory ['prɒməntrɪ] *n* Vorsprung *m.*

promote [prə'məʊt] *vt* befördern; *(help on)* fördern, unterstützen; ~**r** *(in sport, entertainment)* Veranstalter *m; (for charity etc)* Organisator *m.*

promotion [prə'məʊʃən] *n (in rank)* Beförderung *f; (furtherance)* Förderung *f; (Comm)* Werbung *f (of* für).

prompt [prɒmpt] *a* prompt, schnell; **to be** ~ **to do sth** etw sofort tun; *ad (punctually)* genau; **at two o'clock** ~ punkt zwei Uhr; *vt* veranlassen; *(Theat)* einsagen *(+dat),* soufflieren *(+dat);* ~**er** *(Theat)* Souffleur *m,* Souffleuse *f;* ~**ly** *ad* sofort; ~**ness** Schnelligkeit *f,* Promptheit *f.*

promulgate ['prɒməlgeɪt] *vt* (öffentlich) bekanntmachen, verkünden; *beliefs* verbreiten.

prone [prəʊn] *a* hingestreckt; **to be** ~ **to sth** zu etw neigen.

prong [prɒŋ] *n* Zinke *f.*

pronoun ['prəʊnaʊn] *n* Pronomen *nt,* Fürwort *nt.*

pronounce [prə'naʊns] *vt* aussprechen; *(Jur)* verkünden; *vi (give an opinion)* sich äußern *(on* zu); ~**d** *a* ausgesprochen; ~**ment** Erklärung *f.*

pronto ['prɒntəʊ] *ad (col)* fix, pronto.

pronunciation [prənʌnsɪ'eɪʃən] *n* Aussprache *f.*

proof [pruːf] *n* Beweis *m; (Print)* Korrekturfahne *f; (of alcohol)* Alkoholgehalt *m;* **to put to the** ~ unter Beweis stellen; *a* sicher; *alcohol* prozentig; **rain**~ regendicht.

prop [prɒp] *n* Stütze *f (also fig); (Min)* Stempel *m; (Theat)* Requisit *nt; vt (also* ~ **up)** (ab)stützen.

propaganda [prɒpə'gændə] *n* Propaganda *f.*

propagate ['prɒpəgeɪt] *vt* fortpflanzen; *news* propagieren, verbreiten.

propagation [prɒpə'geɪʃən] *n* Fortpflanzung f; (of knowledge also) Verbreitung f.

propel [prə'pel] vt (an)treiben; ~**ler** Propeller m; ~**ling pencil** Drehbleistift m.

propensity [prə'pensɪtɪ] n Tendenz f.

proper ['propə*] a richtig; (seemly) schicklich; ~**ly** ad richtig; ~**ly speaking** genau genommen; **it is not ~ to . . . es** schickt sich nicht, zu . . .; ~ **noun** Eigenname m.

property ['propətɪ] n Eigentum nt, Besitz m, Gut nt; (quality) Eigenschaft f; (land) Grundbesitz m; (Theat) **properties** pl Requisiten pl; ~ **owner** Grundbesitzer m.

prophecy ['profɪsɪ] n Prophezeiung f.

prophesy ['profɪsaɪ] vt prophezeien, vorhersagen.

prophet ['profɪt] n Prophet m; ~**ic** [prə'fetɪk] a prophetisch.

proportion [prə'pɔ:ʃən] n Verhältnis nt, Proportion f; (share) Teil m; vt abstimmen (to auf +acc); ~**al** a, ~**ally** ad proportional, verhältnismäßig; **to be ~al to** entsprechen (+dat); ~**ate** a, ~**ately** ad verhältnismäßig; ~**ed** a proportioniert.

proposal [prə'pəuzl] n Vorschlag m, Antrag m; (of marriage) Heiratsantrag m.

propose [prə'pəuz] vt vorschlagen; toast ausbringen; vi (offer marriage) einen Heiratsantrag machen; ~**r** Antragsteller m.

proposition [propə'zɪʃən] n Angebot nt; (Math) Lehrsatz m; (statement) Satz m.

propound [prə'paund] vt theory vorlegen.

proprietary [prə'praɪətərɪ] a Eigentums-; medicine gesetzlich geschützt.

proprietor [prə'praɪətə*] n Besitzer m, Eigentümer m.

props [props] npl Requisiten pl.

propulsion [prə'pʌlʃən] n Antrieb m.

pro-rata [prəu'rɑ:tə] ad anteilmäßig.

prosaic [prə'zeɪɪk] a prosaisch, alltäglich.

prose [prəuz] n Prosa f.

prosecute ['prosɪkju:t] vt (strafrechtlich) verfolgen.

prosecution [prosɪ'kju:ʃən] n Durchführung f; (Jur) strafrechtliche Verfolgung f; (party) Anklage f; Staatsanwaltschaft f.

prosecutor ['prosɪkju:tə*] n Vertreter m der Anklage; **Public P~** Staatsanwalt m.

prospect ['prospekt] n Aussicht f; [prəs'pekt] vi suchen (for nach); ~**ing** [prəs'pektɪŋ] (for minerals) Suche f; ~**ive** [prəs'pektɪv] a möglich; ~**or** [prəs'pektə*] (Gold)sucher m; ~**us** [prəs'pektəs] (Werbe)prospekt m.

prosper ['prospə*] vi blühen, gedeihen; (person) erfolgreich sein; ~**ity** [pros'perɪtɪ] Wohlstand m; ~**ous** a wohlhabend, reich; business gutgehend, blühend.

prostitute [prostɪtju:t] n Prostituierte f.

prostrate ['prostreɪt] a ausgestreckt (liegend); ~ **with grief/exhaustion** von Schmerz/Erschöpfung übermannt.

protagonist [prəu'tægənɪst] n Hauptperson f, Held m.

protect [prə'tekt] vt (be)schützen; ~**ion** [prə'tekʃən] Schutz m; ~**ive** a Schutz-,

(be)schützend; ~**or** (Be)schützer m.

protégé ['proteʒeɪ] n Schützling m.

protein ['prəuti:n] n Protein nt, Eiweiß nt.

protest ['prəutest] n Protest m; [prə'test] vi protestieren (against gegen); **to ~ that ...** beteuern . . .; **P~ant** a protestantisch; n Protestant(in f) m.

protocol ['prəutəkol] n Protokoll nt.

prototype ['prəutəutaɪp] n Prototyp m.

protracted [prə'træktɪd] a sich hinziehend.

protractor [prə'træktə*] n Winkelmesser m.

protrude [prə'tru:d] vi (her)vorstehen.

protuberance [prə'tju:bərəns] n Auswuchs m.

protuberant [prə'tju:bərənt] a (her)vorstehend.

proud a, ~**ly** ad [praud, -lɪ] stolz (of auf +acc).

prove [pru:v] vt beweisen; vi sich herausstellen, sich zeigen.

proverb ['provɜ:b] n Sprichwort nt; ~**ial** a, ~**ially** ad [prə'vɜ:bɪəl, -ɪ] sprichwörtlich.

provide [prə'vaɪd] vt versehen; (supply) besorgen; person versorgen; ~ **for** vt sorgen für, sich kümmern um; emergency Vorkehrungen treffen für; **blankets will be ~d** Decken werden gestellt; ~**d (that)** cj vorausgesetzt (daß); **P~nce** ['provɪdəns] die Vorsehung.

providing [prə'vaɪdɪŋ] cj = **provided (that).**

province ['provɪns] n Provinz f; (division of work) Bereich m; **the ~s** die Provinz.

provincial [prə'vɪnʃəl] a provinziell, Provinz-; n Provinzler(in f) m.

provision [prə'vɪʒən] n Vorkehrung f, Maßnahme f; (condition) Bestimmung f; ~**s** pl (food) Vorräte pl, Proviant m; ~**al** a, ~**ally** ad vorläufig, provisorisch.

proviso [prə'vaɪzəu] n Vorbehalt m, Bedingung f.

provocation [provə'keɪʃən] n Provokation f, Herausforderung f.

provocative [prə'vokətɪv] a provokativ, herausfordernd.

provoke [prə'vəuk] vt provozieren; (cause) hervorrufen.

prow [prau] n Bug m; ~**ess** überragende(s) Können nt; (valour) Tapferkeit f.

prowl [praul] vt streets durchstreifen; vi herumstreichen; (animal) schleichen; n: **on the ~** umherstreifend; (police) auf der Streife; ~**er** Eindringling m.

proximity [prok'sɪmɪtɪ] n Nähe f.

proxy ['proksɪ] n (Stell)vertreter m, Bevollmächtigte(r) m; (document) Vollmacht f; **to vote by ~** Briefwahl machen.

prudence ['pru:dəns] n Klugheit f, Umsicht f.

prudent a, ~**ly** ad ['pru:dənt, -lɪ] klug, umsichtig.

prudish ['pru:dɪʃ] a prüde; ~**ness** Prüderie f.

prune [pru:n] n Backpflaume f; vt ausputzen; (fig) zurechtstutzen.

pry [praɪ] vi seine Nase stecken (into in +acc).

psalm [sɑːm] n Psalm m.

pseudo ['sjuːdəʊ] a Pseudo-; (false) falsch, unecht; ~**nym** ['sjuːdənɪm] Pseudonym nt, Deckname m.

psyche ['saɪkɪ] n Psyche f.

psychiatric [saɪkɪ'ætrɪk] a psychiatrisch.

psychiatrist [saɪ'kaɪətrɪst] n Psychiater m.

psychiatry [saɪ'kaɪətrɪ] n Psychiatrie f.

psychic(al) ['saɪkɪk(əl)] a übersinnlich; person paranormal begabt; **you must be ~** du kannst wohl hellsehen.

psychoanalyse, (US) **psychoanalyze** [saɪkəʊ'ænəlaɪz] vt psychoanalytisch behandeln.

psychoanalysis [saɪkəʊə'nælɪsɪs] n Psychoanalyse f.

psychoanalyst [saɪkəʊ'ænəlɪst] n Psychoanalytiker(in f) m.

psychological a, ~**ly** ad [saɪkə'lɒdʒɪkəl, -lɪ] psychologisch.

psychologist [saɪ'kɒlədʒɪst] n Psychologe m, Psychologin f.

psychology [saɪ'kɒlədʒɪ] n Psychologie f.

psychopath ['saɪkəʊpæθ] n Psychopath(in f) m.

psychosomatic ['saɪkəʊsəʊ'mætɪk] a psychosomatisch.

psychotherapy ['saɪkəʊ'θerəpɪ] n Psychotherapie f.

psychotic [saɪ'kɒtɪk] a psychotisch; n Psychotiker(in f) m.

pub [pʌb] n Wirtschaft f, Kneipe f.

puberty ['pjuːbətɪ] n Pubertät f.

pubic ['pjuːbɪk] a Scham-.

public a, ~**ly** ad ['pʌblɪk, -lɪ] öffentlich; n (also **general** ~) Öffentlichkeit f; ~**an** Wirt m; ~**ation** [pʌblɪ'keɪʃən] Publikation f, Veröffentlichung f; ~ **company** Aktiengesellschaft f; ~ **convenience** öffentliche Toiletten pl; ~ **house** Lokal nt, Kneipe f; ~**ity** [pʌb'lɪsɪtɪ] Publicity f, Werbung f; ~ **opinion** öffentliche Meinung f; ~ **relations** pl Public Relations pl; ~ **school** (Brit) Privatschule f, Internatsschule f; ~**-spirited** a mit Gemeinschaftssinn; **to be ~-spirited** Gemeinschaftssinn haben.

publish ['pʌblɪʃ] vt veröffentlichen, publizieren; event bekanntgeben; ~**er** Verleger m, Verlegerin f; ~**ing** Herausgabe f, Verlegen nt; (business) Verlagswesen nt.

puce [pjuːs] a violettbraun.

puck [pʌk] n Puck m, Scheibe f.

pucker ['pʌkə*] vt face verziehen; lips kräuseln.

pudding ['pʊdɪŋ] n (course) Nachtisch m; Pudding m.

puddle ['pʌdl] n Pfütze f.

puerile ['pjʊəraɪl] a kindisch.

puff [pʌf] n (of wind etc) Stoß m; (cosmetic) Puderquaste f; vt blasen, pusten; pipe paffen; vi keuchen, schnaufen; (smoke) paffen; ~**ed** a (col: out of breath) außer Puste.

puffin ['pʌfɪn] n Papageitaucher m.

puff pastry, (US) **puff paste** ['pʌfˌpeɪstrɪ, ˌpʌf'peɪst] n Blätterteig m.

puffy ['pʌfɪ] a aufgedunsen.

pull [pʊl] n Ruck m; Zug m; (influence) Beziehung f; vt ziehen; trigger abdrücken; vi ziehen; **to ~ a face** ein Gesicht schneiden; **to ~ sb's leg** jdn auf den Arm nehmen; **to ~ to pieces** (lit) in Stücke reißen; (fig) verreißen; **to ~ one's weight** sich in die Riemen legen; **to ~ o.s. together** sich zusammenreißen; ~ **apart** vt (break) zerreißen; (dismantle) auseinandernehmen; fighters trennen; ~ **down** vt house abreißen; ~ **in** vi hineinfahren; (stop) anhalten; (Rail) einfahren; ~ **off** vt deal etc abschließen; ~ **out** vi (car) herausfahren; (fig: partner) aussteigen; vt herausziehen; ~ **round**, ~ **through** vi durchkommen; ~ **up** vi anhalten.

pulley ['pʊlɪ] n Rolle f, Flaschenzug m.

pullover ['pʊləʊvə*] n Pullover m.

pulp [pʌlp] n Brei m; (of fruit) Fruchtfleisch nt.

pulpit ['pʊlpɪt] n Kanzel f.

pulsate [pʌl'seɪt] vi pulsieren.

pulse [pʌls] n Puls m.

pulverize ['pʌlvəraɪz] vt pulverisieren, in kleine Stücke zerlegen (also fig).

puma ['pjuːmə] n Puma m.

pummel ['pʌml] vt mit den Fäusten bearbeiten.

pump [pʌmp] n Pumpe f; (shoe) leichter (Tanz)schuh m; vt pumpen; ~ **up** vt tyre aufpumpen.

pumpkin ['pʌmpkɪn] n Kürbis m.

pun [pʌn] n Wortspiel nt.

punch [pʌntʃ] n (tool) Stanze f; Locher m; (blow) (Faust)schlag m; (drink) Punsch m, Bowle f; vt stanzen; lochen; (strike) schlagen, boxen; ~**-drunk** a benommen; ~**-up** (col) Keilerei f.

punctual ['pʌŋktjʊəl] a pünktlich; ~**ity** [pʌŋktjʊ'ælɪtɪ] Pünktlichkeit f.

punctuate ['pʌŋktjʊeɪt] vt mit Satzzeichen versehen, interpunktieren; (fig) unterbrechen.

punctuation [pʌŋktjʊ'eɪʃən] n Zeichensetzung f, Interpunktion f.

puncture ['pʌŋktʃə*] n Loch nt; (Aut) Reifenpanne f; vt durchbohren.

pundit ['pʌndɪt] n Gelehrte(r) m.

pungent ['pʌndʒənt] a scharf.

punish ['pʌnɪʃ] vt bestrafen; (in boxing etc) übel zurichten; ~**able** a strafbar; ~**ment** Strafe f; (action) Bestrafung f.

punitive ['pjuːnɪtɪv] a strafend.

punt [pʌnt] n Stechkahn m.

punter ['pʌntə*] n (better) Wetter m.

puny ['pjuːnɪ] a kümmerlich.

pup [pʌp] n = **puppy**.

pupil ['pjuːpl] n Schüler(in f) m; (in eye) Pupille f.

puppet ['pʌpɪt] n Puppe f; Marionette f.

puppy ['pʌpɪ] n junge(r) Hund m.

purchase ['pɜːtʃɪs] n Kauf m, Anschaffung f; (grip) Halt m; vt kaufen, erwerben; ~**r** Käufer(in f) m.

pure [pjʊə*] a pur; rein (also fig); ~**ly** ['pjʊəlɪ] ad rein; (only) nur; (with a also) rein.

purée ['pjʊəreɪ] n Püree nt.

purgatory ['pɜːgətərɪ] n Fegefeuer nt.

purge [pɜːdʒ] n Säuberung f (also Pol); (medicine) Abführmittel nt; vt reinigen; body entschlacken.

purification [pjʊərɪfɪ'keɪʃən] n Reinigung f.

purify ['pjʊərɪfaɪ] vt reinigen.

purist ['pjʊərɪst] n Purist m.

puritan ['pjʊərɪtən] n Puritaner m; ~ical [pjʊərɪ'tænɪkəl] a puritanisch.

purity ['pjʊərɪtɪ] n Reinheit f.

purl [pɜːl] n linke Masche f; vt links stricken.

purple ['pɜːpl] a violett; face dunkelrot; n Violett nt.

purpose ['pɜːpəs] n Zweck m, Ziel nt; (of person) Absicht f; on ~ absichtlich; ~ful a zielbewußt, entschlossen; ~ly ad absichtlich.

purr [pɜː*] n Schnurren nt; vi schnurren.

purse [pɜːs] n Portemonnaie nt, Geldbeutel m; vt lips zusammenpressen, schürzen.

purser ['pɜːsə*] n Zahlmeister m.

pursue [pə'sjuː] vt verfolgen, nachjagen (+dat); study nachgehen (+dat); ~r Verfolger m.

pursuit [pə'sjuːt] n Jagd f (of nach), Verfolgung f; (occupation) Beschäftigung f.

purveyor [pə'veɪə*] n Lieferant m.

pus [pʌs] n Eiter m.

push [pʊʃ] n Stoß m, Schub m; (energy) Schwung m; (Mil) Vorstoß m; vt stoßen, schieben; button drücken; idea durchsetzen; vi stoßen, schieben; at a ~ zur Not; ~ aside vt beiseiteschieben; ~ off vi (col) abschieben; ~ on vi weitermachen; ~ through vt durchdrücken; policy durchsetzen; ~ up vt total erhöhen; prices hochtreiben; ~chair (Kinder)sportwagen m; ~ing a aufdringlich; ~over (col) Kinderspiel nt; ~y a (col) aufdringlich.

puss [pʊs] n Mieze(katze) f.

put [pʊt] vt irreg setzen, stellen, legen; (express) ausdrücken, sagen; (write) schreiben; ~ about vi (turn back) wenden; vt (spread) verbreiten; ~ across vt (explain) erklären; ~ away vt weglegen; (store) beiseitelegen; ~ back vt zurückstellen or -legen; ~ by vt zurücklegen, sparen; ~ down vt hinstellen or -legen; (stop) niederschlagen; animal einschläfern; (in writing) niederschreiben; ~ forward vt idea vorbringen; clock vorstellen; ~ off vt verlegen, verschieben; (discourage) abbringen von; it ~ me off smoking das hat mir die Lust am Rauchen verdorben; ~ on vt clothes etc anziehen; light etc anschalten, anmachen; play etc aufführen; brake anziehen; ~ out vt hand etc (her)ausstrecken; news, rumour verbreiten; light etc ausschalten, ausmachen; ~ up vt tent aufstellen; building errichten; price erhöhen; person unterbringen; to ~ up with sich abfinden mit; I won't ~ up with it das laß ich mir nicht gefallen.

putrid ['pjuːtrɪd] a faul.

putsch [pʊtʃ] n Putsch m.

putt [pʌt] vt (golf) putten, einlochen; n (golf)

Putten nt, leichte(r) Schlag m; ~er Putter m.

putty ['pʌtɪ] n Kitt m; (fig) Wachs nt.

put-up ['pʊtʌp] a: ~ job abgekartete(s) Spiel nt.

puzzle ['pʌzl] n Rätsel nt; (toy) Geduldspiel nt; vt verwirren; vi sich den Kopf zerbrechen.

puzzling ['pʌzlɪŋ] a rätselhaft, verwirrend.

pygmy ['pɪgmɪ] n Pygmäe m; (fig) Zwerg m.

pyjamas [pɪ'dʒɑːməz] npl Schlafanzug m, Pyjama m.

pylon ['paɪlən] n Mast m.

pyramid ['pɪrəmɪd] n Pyramide f.

python ['paɪθən] n Pythonschlange f.

Q

Q, q [kjuː] n Q nt, q nt.

quack [kwæk] n Quacken nt; (doctor) Quacksalber m.

quad [kwɒd] abbr of **quadrangle, quadruple, quadruplet.**

quadrangle ['kwɒdræŋgl] n (court) Hof m; (Math) Viereck nt.

quadruped ['kwɒdrʊped] n Vierfüßler m.

quadruple ['kwɒ'drʊpl] a vierfach; vi sich vervierfachen; vt vervierfachen.

quadruplet [kwɒ'druːplət] n Vierling m.

quagmire ['kwægmaɪə*] n Morast m.

quaint [kweɪnt] a kurios; malerisch; ~ly ad kurios; ~ness malerischer Anblick m; Kuriosität f.

quake [kweɪk] vi beben, zittern; **Q~r** Quäker m.

qualification [kwɒlɪfɪ'keɪʃən] n Qualifikation f; (sth which limits) Einschränkung f.

qualified ['kwɒlɪfaɪd] a (competent) qualifiziert; (limited) bedingt.

qualify ['kwɒlɪfaɪ] vt (prepare) befähigen; (limit) einschränken; vi sich qualifizieren.

qualitative ['kwɒlɪtətɪv] a qualitativ.

quality ['kwɒlɪtɪ] n Qualität f; (characteristic) Eigenschaft f; a Qualitäts-.

qualm [kwɑːm] n Bedenken nt, Zweifel m.

quandary ['kwɒndərɪ] n Verlegenheit f; to be in a ~ in Verlegenheit sein.

quantitative ['kwɒntɪtətɪv] a quantitativ.

quantity ['kwɒntɪtɪ] n Menge f, Quantität f.

quarantine ['kwɒrəntiːn] n Quarantäne f.

quarrel ['kwɒrəl] n Streit m; vi sich streiten; ~some a streitsüchtig.

quarry ['kwɒrɪ] n Steinbruch m; (animal) Wild nt; (fig) Opfer nt.

quart [kwɔːt] n Quart nt.

quarter ['kwɔːtə*] n Viertel nt; (of year) Quartal nt, Vierteljahr nt; vt (divide) vierteln, in Viertel teilen; (Mil) einquartieren; ~s pl (esp Mil) Quartier nt; ~ of an hour Viertelstunde f; ~ past three viertel nach drei; ~ to three dreiviertel drei, viertel vor drei; ~deck Achterdeck nt; ~ final Viertelfinale nt; ~ly a vierteljährlich; ~master Quartiermeister m.

quartet(te) [kwɔː'tet] n Quartett nt.

quartz [kwɔːts] n Quarz m.

quash [kwɒʃ] vt verdict aufheben.

quasi ['kwɑːzɪ] *ad* quasi.

quaver ['kweɪvə*] *n* (*Mus*) Achtelnote *f; vi* (*tremble*) zittern *m*.

quay [kiː] *n* Kai *m*.

queasiness ['kwiːzɪnəs] *n* Übelkeit *f*.

queasy ['kwiːzɪ] *a* übel; **he feels** ~ ihm ist übel.

queen [kwiːn] *n* Königin *f;* ~ **mother** Königinmutter *f*.

queer [kwɪə*] *a* seltsam, sonderbar, kurios; ~ **fellow** komische(r) Kauz *m; n* (*col: homosexual*) Schwule(r) *m*.

quell [kwel] *vt* unterdrücken.

quench [kwentʃ] *vt thirst* löschen, stillen; (*extinguish*) löschen.

query ['kwɪərɪ] *n* (*question*) (An)frage *f;* (*question mark*) Fragezeichen *nt; vt* in Zweifel ziehen, in Frage stellen.

quest [kwest] *n* Suche *f*.

question ['kwestʃən] *n* Frage *f; vt* (*ask*) (be)fragen; *suspect* verhören; (*doubt*) in Frage stellen, bezweifeln; **beyond** ~ ohne Frage; ~ **out of the** ~ ausgeschlossen; ~**able** *a* zweifelhaft; ~**er** Fragesteller *m;* ~**ing** a fragend; ~ **mark** Fragezeichen *nt;* ~**naire** Fragebogen *m;* (*enquiry*) Umfrage *f*.

queue [kjuː] *n* Schlange *f; vi* (*also* ~ **up**) Schlange stehen.

quibble ['kwɪbl] *n* Spitzfindigkeit *f; vi* kleinlich sein.

quick [kwɪk] *a,* ~**ly** *ad* [kwɪk, -lɪ] *a* schnell; *n* (*of nail*) Nagelhaut *f;* (*old: the living*) die Lebenden; **to the** ~ (*fig*) bis ins Innerste; ~**en** *vt* (*hasten*) beschleunigen; (*stir*) anregen; *vi* sich beschleunigen; ~**-fire** *a questions etc* Schnellfeuer-; ~**ness** Schnelligkeit *f;* (*mental*) Scharfsinn *m;* ~**sand** Treibsand *m;* ~**step** Quickstep *m;* ~**-witted** *a* schlagfertig, hell.

quid [kwɪd] *n* (*Brit col: £1*) Pfund *nt*.

quiet ['kwaɪət] *a* (*without noise*) leise; (*peaceful, calm*) still, ruhig; *n* Stille *f,* Ruhe *f;* ~**en** (*also* ~**en down**) *vi* ruhig werden; *vt* beruhigen; ~**ly** *ad* leise, ruhig; ~**ness** Ruhe *f,* Stille *f*.

quill [kwɪl] *n* (*of porcupine*) Stachel *m;* (*pen*) Feder *f*.

quilt [kwɪlt] *n* Steppdecke *f;* ~**ing** Füllung *f,* Wattierung *f*.

quin [kwɪn] *abbr of* **quintuplet.**

quince [kwɪns] *n* Quitte *f*.

quinine [kwɪˈniːn] *n* Chinin *nt*.

quinsy ['kwɪnzɪ] *n* Mandelentzündung *f*.

quintet(te) [kwɪnˈtet] *n* Quintett *nt*.

quintuplet [kwɪnˈtjuːplət] *n* Fünfling *m*.

quip [kwɪp] *n* witzige Bemerkung *f; vi* witzeln.

quirk [kwɜːk] *n* (*oddity*) Eigenart *f*.

quit [kwɪt] *irreg vt* verlassen; *vi* aufhören.

quite [kwaɪt] *ad* (*completely*) ganz, völlig; (*fairly*) ziemlich; ~ (**so**)! richtig!

quits [kwɪts] *a* quitt.

quiver ['kwɪvə*] *vi* zittern; *n* (*for arrows*) Köcher *m*.

quiz [kwɪz] *n* (*competition*) Quiz *nt;* (*series of questions*) Befragung *f; vt* prüfen; ~**zical** *a* fragend, verdutzt.

quoit [kwɔɪt] *n* Wurfring *m*.

quorum ['kwɔːrəm] *n* beschlußfähige Anzahl *f*.

quota ['kwəʊtə] *n* Anteil *m;* (*Comm*) Quote *f*.

quotation [kwəʊˈteɪʃən] *n* Zitat *nt;* (*price*) Kostenvoranschlag *m;* ~ **marks** *pl* Anführungszeichen *pl*.

quote [kwəʊt] *n see* **quotation;** *vi* (*from book*) zitieren; *vt* (*from book*) zitieren; *price* angeben.

quotient ['kwəʊʃənt] *n* Quotient *m*.

R

R, r [ɑː*] *n* R *nt,* r *nt*.

rabbi ['ræbaɪ] *n* Rabbiner *m;* (*title*) Rabbi *m*.

rabbit ['ræbɪt] *n* Kaninchen *nt;* ~ **hutch** Kaninchenstall *m*.

rabble ['ræbl] *n* Pöbel *m*.

rabies ['reɪbiːz] *n* Tollwut *f*.

raccoon [rəˈkuːn] *n* Waschbär *m*.

race [reɪs] *n* (*species*) Rasse *f;* (*competition*) Rennen *nt;* (*on foot also*) Wettlauf *m;* (*rush*) Hetze *f; vt* um die Wette laufen mit; *horses* laufen lassen; *vi* (*run*) rennen; (*in contest*) am Rennen teilnehmen; ~**course** (*for horses*) Rennbahn *f;* ~**horse** Rennpferd *nt;* ~ **meeting** (*for horses*) (Pferde)rennen *nt;* ~ **relations** *pl* Beziehungen *pl* zwischen den Rassen; ~**track** (*for cars etc*) Rennstrecke *f*.

racial ['reɪʃəl] *a* Rassen-; ~ **discrimination** Rassendiskriminierung *f;* ~**ism** Rassismus *m;* ~**ist** *a* rassistisch; *n* Rassist *m*.

racing ['reɪsɪŋ] *n* Rennen *nt;* ~ **car** Rennwagen *m;* ~ **driver** Rennfahrer *m*.

racism ['reɪsɪzəm] *n* Rassismus *m*.

racist ['reɪsɪst] *n* Rassist *m; a* rassistisch.

rack [ræk] *n* Ständer *m,* Gestell *nt; vt* (zer)martern; **to go to** ~ **and ruin** verfallen.

racket ['rækɪt] *n* (*din*) Krach *m;* (*scheme*) (Schwindel)geschäft *nt;* (*tennis*) (Tennis)schläger *m*.

racquet ['rækɪt] *n* = **racket** (*tennis*).

racy ['reɪsɪ] *a* gewagt; *style* spritzig.

radar ['reɪdɑː*] *n* Radar *nt or m*.

radiance ['reɪdɪəns] *n* strahlende(r) Glanz *m*.

radiant ['reɪdɪənt] *a* (*bright*) strahlend; (*giving out rays*) Strahlungs-.

radiate ['reɪdɪeɪt] *vti* ausstrahlen; (*roads, lines*) strahlenförmig wegführen.

radiation [reɪdɪˈeɪʃən] *n* (Aus)strahlung *f*.

radiator ['reɪdɪeɪtə*] *n* (*for heating*) Heizkörper *m;* (*Aut*) Kühler *m;* ~ **cap** Kühlerdeckel *m*.

radical *a,* ~**ly** *ad* ['rædɪkəl, -lɪ] radikal.

radio ['reɪdɪəʊ] *n* Rundfunk *m,* Radio *nt;* (*set*) Radio *nt,* Radioapparat *m;* ~ **active** radioaktiv; ~**activity** Radioaktivität *f;* ~**grapher** [reɪdɪˈɒɡrəfə*] Röntgenassistent(in *f) m;* ~**graphy** [reɪdɪˈɒɡrəfɪ] Radiographie *f,* Röntgenphotographie *f;* ~**logy** [reɪdɪˈɒlədʒɪ] Strahlenkunde *f;* ~ **station** Rundfunkstation *f;* ~ **telephone** Funksprechanlage *f;* ~ **telescope** Radioteleskop *nt;* ~**therapist** Radiologie-assistent(in *f*) *m.*

radish ['rædɪʃ] *n (big)* Rettich *m; (small)* Radieschen *nt.*

radium ['reɪdɪəm] *n* Radium *nt.*

radius ['reɪdɪəs] *n* Radius *m,* Halbkreis *m; (area)* Umkreis *m.*

raffia ['ræfɪə] *n* (Raffia)bast *m.*

raffish ['ræfɪʃ] *a* liederlich; *clothes* gewagt.

raffle ['ræfl] *n* Verlosung *f,* Tombola *f.*

raft [rɑːft] *n* Floß *nt.*

rafter ['rɑːftə*] *n* Dachsparren *m.*

rag [ræg] *n (cloth)* Lumpen *m,* Lappen *m; (col: newspaper)* Käseblatt *nt; (Univ: for charity)* studentische Sammelaktion *f; vt* auf den Arm nehmen; ~**bag** *(fig)* Sammelsurium *nt.*

rage [reɪdʒ] *n* Wut *f; (desire)* Sucht *f; (fashion)* große Mode *f;* **to be in a** ~ wütend sein; *vi* wüten, toben.

ragged ['rægɪd] *a edge* gezackt; *clothes* zerlumpt.

raging ['reɪdʒɪŋ] *a* tobend; *thirst* Heiden-.

raid [reɪd] *n* Überfall *m; (Mil)* Angriff *m: (by police)* Razzia *f; vt* überfallen; ~**er** *(person)* (Bank)räuber *m; (Naut)* Kaperschiff *nt.*

rail [reɪl] *n* Schiene *f,* Querstange *f; (on stair)* Geländer *nt; (of ship)* Reling *f; (Rail)* Schiene *f;* **by** ~ per Bahn; ~**ing(s)** Geländer *nt;* ~**road** *(US),* ~**way** *(Brit)* Eisenbahn *f;* ~**road** or ~**way station** Bahnhof *m.*

rain [reɪn] *n* Regen *m; vti* regnen; **the** ~**s** *pl* die Regenzeit; ~**bow** Regenbogen *m;* ~**coat** Regenmantel *m;* ~**drop** Regentropfen *m;* ~**fall** Niederschlag *m;* ~**storm** heftige(r) Regenguß *m;* ~**y** *a region, season* Regen-; *day* regnerisch, verregnet.

raise [reɪz] *n (esp US: increase)* (Lohn- or Gehalts- or Preis)erhöhung *f; vt (lift)* (hoch)heben; *(increase)* erhöhen; *question* aufwerfen; *doubts* äußern; *funds* beschaffen; *family* großziehen; *livestock* züchten; *(build)* errichten.

raisin ['reɪzn] *n* Rosine *f.*

rajah ['rɑːdʒə] *n* Radscha *m.*

rake [reɪk] *n* Rechen *m,* Harke *f; (person)* Wüstling *m; vt* rechen, harken; *(with gun)* (mit Feuer) bestreichen; *(search)* (durch)suchen; **to** ~ **in** or **together** zusammenscharren.

rakish ['reɪkɪʃ] *a* verwegen.

rally ['rælɪ] *n (Pol etc)* Kundgebung *f; (Aut)* Sternfahrt *f,* Rallye *f; (improvement)* Erholung *f; vt (Mil)* sammeln; *vi* Kräfte sammeln; ~ **round** *vti* (sich) scharen um; *(help)* zu Hilfe kommen (+*dat*).

ram [ræm] *n* Widder *m; (instrument)* Ramme *f; vt (strike)* rammen; *(stuff)* (hinein)stopfen.

ramble ['ræmbl] *n* Wanderung *f,* Ausflug *m; vi (wander)* umherstreifen; *(talk)* schwafeln; ~**r** Wanderer *m; (plant)* Kletterrose *f.*

rambling ['ræmblɪŋ] *a plant* Kletter-; *speech* weitschweifig; *town* ausgedehnt.

ramification [ræmɪfɪ'keɪʃən] *n* Verästelung *f;* ~**s** *pl* Tragweite *f.*

ramp [ræmp] *n* Rampe *f.*

rampage [ræm'peɪdʒ] *n:* **to be on the** ~ *(also* ~ *vi)* randalieren.

rampant ['ræmpənt] *a (heraldry)* aufgerichtet; **to be** ~ überhandnehmen.

rampart ['ræmpɑːt] *n* (Schutz)wall *m.*

ramshackle ['ræmʃækl] *a* baufällig.

ranch [rɑːntʃ] *n* Ranch *f;* ~**er** Rancher *m.*

rancid ['rænsɪd] *a* ranzig.

rancour, *(US)* **rancor** ['ræŋkə*] *n* Verbitterung *f,* Groll *m.*

random ['rændəm] *a* ziellos, wahllos; *n:* **at** ~ aufs Geratewohl.

randy ['rændɪ] *a (Brit)* geil, scharf.

range [reɪndʒ] *n* Reihe *f; (of mountains)* Kette *f; (Comm)* Sortiment *nt; (selection)* (große) Auswahl *f (of an* +*dat); (reach)* (Reich)weite *f; (of gun)* Schußweite *f; (for shooting practice)* Schießplatz *m; (stove)* (großer) Herd *m; vt (set in row)* anordnen, aufstellen; *(roam)* durchstreifen; *vi (extend)* sich erstrecken; **prices ranging from £5 to £10** Preise, die sich zwischen 5£ und 10£ bewegen; ~**r** Förster *m.*

rank [ræŋk] *n (row)* Reihe *f; (for taxis)* Stand *m; (Mil)* Dienstgrad *m,* Rang *m; (social position)* Stand *m; vt* einschätzen; *vi (have* ~) gehören *(among zu); a (strong-smelling)* stinkend; *(extreme)* krass; **the** ~**s** *pl (Mil)* die Mannschaften *pl;* **the** ~ **and file** *(fig)* die breite Masse.

rankle ['ræŋkl] *vi* nagen.

ransack ['rænsæk] *vt (plunder)* plündern; *(search)* durchwühlen.

ransom ['rænsəm] *n* Lösegeld *nt;* **to hold sb to** ~ jdn gegen Lösegeld festhalten.

rant [rænt] *vi* hochtrabend reden; ~**ing** Wortschwall *m.*

rap [ræp] *n* Schlag *m; vt* klopfen.

rape [reɪp] *n* Vergewaltigung *f; vt* vergewaltigen.

rapid ['ræpɪd] *a* rasch, schnell; ~**s** *pl* Stromschnellen *pl;* ~**ity** [rə'pɪdɪtɪ] Schnelligkeit *f;* ~**ly** *ad* schnell.

rapier ['reɪpɪə*] *n* Florett *nt.*

rapist ['reɪpɪst] *n* Vergewaltiger *m.*

rapport [ræ'pɔː*] *n* gute(s) Verhältnis *nt.*

rapprochement [ræ'prɒʃmɑːŋ] *n* (Wieder)annäherung *f.*

rapt [ræpt] *a* hingerissen.

rapture ['ræptʃə*] *n* Entzücken *nt.*

rapturous ['ræptʃərəs] *a applause* stürmisch; *expression* verzückt.

rare [rɛə*] *a* selten, rar; *(especially good)* vortrefflich; *(underdone)* nicht durchgebraten; ~**fied** ['rɛərɪfaɪd] *a air, atmosphere* dünn; ~**ly** *ad* selten.

rarity ['rɛərɪtɪ] *n* Seltenheit *f.*

rascal ['rɑːskəl] *n* Schuft *m; (child)* Strick *m.*

rash [ræʃ] *a* übereilt; *(reckless)* unbesonnen; *n* (Haut)ausschlag *m.*

rasher ['ræʃə*] *n* Speckscheibe *f.*

rashly ['ræʃlɪ] *ad* vorschnell, unbesonnen.

rashness ['ræʃnəs] *n* Voreiligkeit *f; (reck-lessness)* Unbesonnenheit *f.*

rasp [rɑːsp] *n* Raspel *f.*

raspberry ['rɑːzbərɪ] *n* Himbeere *f.*

rasping ['rɑːspɪŋ] *a noise* kratzend.

rat [ræt] n (animal) Ratte f; (person) Halunke m.

ratable ['reɪtəbl] a: ~ **value** Grundsteuer f.

ratchet ['rætʃɪt] n Sperrad nt.

rate [reɪt] n (proportion) Ziffer f, Rate f; (price) Tarif m, Gebühr f; (speed) Geschwindigkeit f; vt (ein)schätzen; ~**s** pl (Brit) Grundsteuer f, Gemeindeabgaben pl; **at any** ~ jedenfalls; (at least) wenigstens; **at this** ~ wenn es so weitergeht; ~ **of exchange** (Wechsel)kurs m; ~**payer** Steuerzahler(in f) m; see **first.**

rather ['rɑːðə*] ad (in preference) lieber, eher; (to some extent) ziemlich; ~**!** und ob!

ratification [rætɪfɪ'keɪʃən] n Ratifikation f.

ratify ['rætɪfaɪ] vt bestätigen; (Pol) ratifizieren.

rating ['reɪtɪŋ] n Klasse f; (sailor) Matrose m.

ratio ['reɪʃɪəʊ] n Verhältnis nt.

ration ['ræʃən] n (usually pl) Ration f; vt rationieren.

rational a, ~**ly** ad ['ræʃənl, -nəlɪ] rational, vernünftig; ~**e** [ræʃə'nɑːl] Grundprinzip nt; ~**ization** [ræʃnəlaɪ'zeɪʃən] Rationalisierung f; ~**ize** ['ræʃnəlaɪz] vt rationalisieren.

rationing ['ræʃnɪŋ] n Rationierung f.

rat race ['rætreɪs] n Konkurrenzkampf m.

rattle ['rætl] n (sound) Rattern nt, Rasseln nt; (toy) Rassel f; vi ratteln, klappern; ~**snake** Klapperschlange f.

raucous a, ~**ly** ad ['rɔːkəs, -lɪ] heiser, rauh.

ravage ['rævɪdʒ] vt verheeren; ~**s** pl verheerende Wirkungen pl; **the** ~**s of time** der Zahn der Zeit.

rave [reɪv] vi (talk wildly) phantasieren; (rage) toben.

raven ['reɪvn] n Rabe m.

ravenous ['rævənəs] a heißhungrig; appetite unersättlich.

ravine [rə'viːn] n Schlucht f, Klamm f.

raving ['reɪvɪŋ] a tobend; ~ **mad** total verrückt.

ravioli [rævɪ'əʊlɪ] n Ravioli pl.

ravish ['rævɪʃ] vt (delight) entzücken; (Jur) woman vergewaltigen; ~**ing** a hinreißend.

raw [rɔː] a roh; (tender) wund(gerieben); wound offen; (inexperienced) unerfahren; ~ **material** Rohmaterial nt.

ray [reɪ] n (of light) (Licht)strahl m; (gleam) Schimmer m.

rayon ['reɪɒn] n Kunstseide f, Reyon nt or m.

raze [reɪz] vt dem Erdboden gleichmachen.

razor ['reɪzə*] n Rasierapparat m; ~ **blade** Rasierklinge f.

re- [riː] pref wieder-.

re [riː] prep (Comm) betreffs (+ gen).

reach [riːtʃ] n Reichweite f; (of river) Flußstrecke f; **within** ~ (shops etc) in erreichbarer Weite or Entfernung; vt erreichen; (pass on) reichen, geben; vi (try to get) langen (for nach); (stretch) sich erstrecken; ~ **out** vi die Hand ausstrecken.

react [riː'ækt] vi reagieren; ~**ion** [riː'ækʃən] Reaktion f; ~**ionary** [riː'ækʃənrɪ] a reaktionär; ~**or** Reaktor m.

read [riːd] vti irreg lesen; (aloud) vorlesen; **it** ~**s as follows** es lautet folgendermaßen; ~**able** a leserlich; (worth ~ing) lesenswert; ~**er** (person) Leser(in f) m; (book) Lesebuch nt; ~**ership** Leserschaft f.

readily ['redɪlɪ] ad (willingly) bereitwillig; (easily) prompt.

readiness ['redɪnəs] n (willingness) Bereitwilligkeit f; (being ready) Bereitschaft f.

reading ['riːdɪŋ] n Lesen nt; (interpretation) Deutung f, Auffassung f; ~ **lamp** Leselampe f; ~ **matter** Lesestoff m, Lektüre f; ~ **room** Lesezimmer nt, Lesesaal m.

readjust ['riːə'dʒʌst] vt wieder in Ordnung bringen; neu einstellen; **to** ~ **(o.s.) to sth** sich wieder anpassen an etw (acc); ~**ment** Wiederanpassung f.

ready ['redɪ] a (prepared) bereit, fertig; (willing) bereit, willens; (in condition to) reif; (quick) schlagfertig; money verfügbar, bar; ad bereit; n: **at the** ~ bereit; ~-**made** a gebrauchsfertig, Fertig-; clothes Konfektions-; ~ **reckoner** Rechentabelle f.

real [rɪəl] a wirklich; (actual) eigentlich; (true) wahr; (not fake) echt; ~ **estate** Grundbesitz m; ~**ism** Realismus m; ~**ist** Realist m; ~**istic** a, ~**istically** ad realistisch; ~**ity** [riː'ælɪtɪ] (real existence) Wirklichkeit f, Realität f; (facts) Tatsachen pl; ~**ization** (understanding) Erkenntnis f; (fulfilment) Verwirklichung f; ~**ize** vt (understand) begreifen; (make real) verwirklichen; money einbringen; **I didn't** ~**ize . . .** ich wußte nicht, . . .; ~**ly** ad wirklich.

realm [relm] n Reich nt.

ream [riːm] n Ries nt.

reap [riːp] vt ernten; ~**er** Mähmaschine f.

reappear ['riːə'pɪə*] vi wieder erscheinen; ~**ance** Wiedererscheinen nt.

reapply ['riːə'plaɪ] vi wiederholt beantragen (for acc); (for job) sich erneut bewerben (for um).

reappoint ['riːə'pɔɪnt] vt wieder anstellen; wiederernennen.

reappraisal ['riːə'preɪzəl] n Neubeurteilung f.

rear [rɪə*] a hintere(r, s), Rück-; n Rückseite f; (last part) Schluß m; vt (bring up) aufziehen; vi (horse) sich aufbäumen; ~-**engined** a mit Heckmotor; ~**guard** Nachhut f.

rearm ['riː'ɑːm] vt wiederbewaffnen; vi wiederaufrüsten; ~**ament** Wiederaufrüstung f.

rearrange ['riːə'reɪndʒ] vt umordnen; plans ändern.

rear-view ['rɪəvjuː] a: ~ **mirror** Rückspiegel m.

reason ['riːzn] n (cause) Grund m; (ability to think) Verstand m; (sensible thoughts) Vernunft f; vi (think) denken; (use arguments) argumentieren; **to** ~ **with sb** mit jdm diskutieren; ~**able** a vernünftig; ~**ably** ad vernünftig; (fairly) ziemlich;

one could ~ably suppose man könnte doch (mit gutem Grund) annehmen; **~ed a argument** durchdacht; **~ing** Urteilen *nt*; *(argumentation)* Beweisführung *f*.

reassemble ['ri:ə'sembl] *vt* wieder versammeln; *(Tech)* wieder zusammensetzen, wieder zusammenbauen; *vi* sich wieder versammeln.

reassert ['ri:ə'sə:t] *vt* wieder geltend machen.

reassurance ['ri:ə'ʃuərəns] *n* Beruhigung *f*; *(confirmation)* nochmalige Versicherung *f*.

reassure ['ri:ə'ʃuə*] *vt* beruhigen; *(confirm)* versichern *(sb* jdm).

reassuring ['ri:ə'ʃuərɪŋ] *a* beruhigend.

reawakening ['ri:ə'weɪknɪŋ] *n* Wiedererwachen *nt*.

rebate ['ri:beɪt] *n* Rabatt *m*; *(money back)* Rückzahlung *f*.

rebel ['rebl] *n* Rebell *m*; *a* Rebellen-; **~lion** [rɪ'beljən] rebellion *f*, Aufstand *m*; **~lious** [rɪ'beljəs] *a* rebellisch; *(fig)* widerspenstig.

rebirth ['ri:'bə:θ] *n* Wiedergeburt *f*.

rebound [rɪ'baund] *vi* zurückprallen; ['ri:baund] *n* Rückprall *m*; **on the ~** *(fig)* als Reaktion.

rebuff [rɪ'bʌf] *n* Abfuhr *f*; *vt* abblitzen lassen.

rebuild ['ri:'bɪld] *vt irreg* wiederaufbauen; *(fig)* wiederherstellen; **~ing** Wiederaufbau *m*.

rebuke [rɪ'bju:k] *n* Tadel *m*; *vt* tadeln, rügen.

rebut [rɪ'bʌt] *vt* widerlegen.

recalcitrant [rɪ'kælsɪtrənt] *a* widerspenstig.

recall [rɪ'kɔ:l] *vt (call back)* zurückrufen; *(remember)* sich erinnern an *(+acc)*.

recant [rɪ'kænt] *vi* (öffentlich) widerrufen.

recap ['ri:kæp] *n* kurze Zusammenfassung *f*; *vti* information wiederholen.

recapture ['ri:'kæptʃə*] *vt* wieder (ein)fangen.

recede [rɪ'si:d] *vi* zurückweichen.

receding [rɪ'si:dɪŋ] *a:* **~ hair** Stirnglatze *f*.

receipt [rɪ'si:t] *n (document)* Quittung *f*; *(receiving)* Empfang *m*; **~s** *pl* Einnahmen *pl*.

receive [rɪ'si:v] *vt* erhalten; *visitors etc* empfangen; **~r** *(Tel)* Hörer *m*.

recent [ri:snt] *a vor kurzem* (geschehen), neuerlich; *(modern)* neu; **~ly** *ad* kürzlich, neulich.

receptacle [rɪ'septəkl] *n* Behälter *m*.

reception [rɪ'sepʃən] *n* Empfang *m*; *(welcome)* Aufnahme *f*; *(in hotel)* Rezeption *f*; **~ist** *(in hotel)* Empfangschef *m*/-dame *f*; *(Med)* Sprechstundenhilfe *f*.

receptive [rɪ'septɪv] *a* aufnahmebereit.

recess [ri:'ses] *n (break)* Ferien *pl*; *(hollow)* Nische *f*; **~es** *pl* Winkel *m*; **~ion** [rɪ'seʃən] Rezession *f*.

recharge ['ri:'tʃɑ:dʒ] *vt battery* aufladen.

recipe ['resɪpɪ] *n* Rezept *nt*.

recipient [rɪ'sɪpɪənt] *n* Empfänger *m*.

reciprocal [rɪ'sɪprəkəl] *a* gegenseitig; *(mutual)* wechselseitig.

reciprocate [rɪ'sɪprəkeɪt] *vt* erwidern.

recital [rɪ'saɪtl] *n (Mus)* Konzert *nt*, Vortrag *m*.

recitation [resɪ'teɪʃən] *n* Rezitation *f*.

recite [rɪ'saɪt] *vt* vortragen, aufsagen; *(give list of also)* aufzählen.

reckless *a*, **~ly** *ad* ['rekləs, -lɪ] leichtsinnig; *driving* fahrlässig; **~ness** Rücksichtslosigkeit *f*.

reckon ['rekən] *vt (count)* (be- or er)rechnen; *(consider)* halten für; *vi (suppose)* annehmen; **~ on** *vt* rechnen mit; **~ing** *(calculation)* Rechnen *nt*.

reclaim [rɪ'kleɪm] *vt land* abgewinnen *(from dat)*; *expenses* zurückverlangen.

reclamation [reklə'meɪʃən] *n (of land)* Gewinnung *f*.

recline [rɪ'klaɪn] *vi* sich zurücklehnen.

reclining [rɪ'klaɪnɪŋ] *a* verstellbar, Liege-.

recluse [rɪ'klu:s] *n* Einsiedler *m*.

recognition [rekəg'nɪʃən] *n (recognizing)* Erkennen *nt*; *(acknowledgement)* Anerkennung *f*.

recognizable ['rekəgnaɪzəbl] *a* erkennbar.

recognize ['rekəgnaɪz] *vt* erkennen; *(Pol, approve)* anerkennen.

recoil [rɪ'kɔɪl] *n* Rückstoß *m*; *vi (in horror)* zurückschrecken; *(rebound)* zurückprallen.

recollect [rekə'lekt] *vt* sich erinnern an *(+acc)*; **~ion** Erinnerung *f*.

recommend [rekə'mend] *vt* empfehlen; **~ation** Empfehlung *f*.

recompense ['rekəmpens] *n (compensation)* Entschädigung *f*; *(reward)* Belohnung *f*; *vt* entschädigen; belohnen.

reconcilable ['rekənsaɪləbl] *a* vereinbar.

reconcile ['rekənsaɪl] *vt facts* vereinbaren, in Einklang bringen; *people* versöhnen.

reconciliation [rekənsɪlɪ'eɪʃən] *n* Versöhnung *f*.

reconditioned ['ri:kən'dɪʃənd] *a* überholt, erneuert.

reconnaissance [rɪ'kɒnɪsəns] *n* Aufklärung *f*.

reconnoitre, *(US)* **reconnoiter** [rekə'nɔɪtə*] *vt* erkunden; *vi* aufklären.

reconsider ['ri:kən'sɪdə*] *vti* von neuem erwägen, (es) überdenken.

reconstitute ['ri:'kɒnstɪtju:t] *vt* neu bilden.

reconstruct ['ri:kən'strʌkt] *vt* wiederaufbauen; *crime* rekonstruieren; **~ion** ['ri:kən'strʌkʃən] Rekonstruktion *f*.

record ['rekɔ:d] *n* Aufzeichnung *f*; *(Mus)* Schallplatte *f*; *(best performance)* Rekord *m*; *a time* Rekord-; [rɪ'kɔ:d] *vt* aufzeichnen; *(Mus etc)* aufnehmen; **~ card** *(in file)* Karteikarte *f*; **~ed music** Musikaufnahmen *pl*; **~er** [rɪ'kɔ:də*] *(officer)* Protokollführer *m*; *(Mus)* Blockflöte *f*; **~holder** *(Sport)* Rekordinhaber *m*; **~ing** [rɪ'kɔ:dɪŋ] *(Mus)* Aufnahme *f*; **~ library** Schallplattenarchiv *nt*; **~ player** Plattenspieler *m*.

recount ['ri:kaunt] *n* Nachzählung *f*; *vt (count again)* nachzählen; [rɪ'kaunt] *(tell)* berichten.

recoup [rɪ'ku:p] *vt* wettmachen.

recourse [rɪ'kɔ:s] *n* Zuflucht *f*.

recover [rɪ'kʌvə*] vt (get back) zurückerhalten; ['riː'kʌvə*] quilt etc neu überziehen; vi sich erholen; ~**y** Wiedererlangung f; (of health) Genesung f.

recreate ['riː'krɪ'eit] vt wiederherstellen.

recreation [rekrɪ'eɪʃən] n Erholung f; Freizeitbeschäftigung f; ~**al** a Erholungs-.

recrimination [rɪkrɪmɪ'neɪʃən] n Gegenbeschuldigung f.

recruit [rɪ'kruːt] n Rekrut m; vt rekrutieren; ~**ing office** Wehrmeldeamt nt; ~**ment** Rekrutierung f.

rectangle ['rektæŋgl] n Rechteck nt.

rectangular [rek'tæŋgjulə*] a rechteckig, rechtwinklig.

rectify ['rektɪfaɪ] vt berichtigen.

rectory ['rektəri] n Pfarrhaus nt.

recuperate [rɪ'kuːpəreɪt] vi sich erholen.

recur [rɪ'kɜː*] vi sich wiederholen; ~**rence** Wiederholung f; ~**rent** a wiederkehrend.

red [red] n Rot nt; (Pol) Rote(r) m; a rot; **in the** ~ in den roten Zahlen; **R~ Cross** Rote(s) Kreuz nt; ~**den** vti (sich) röten; (blush) erröten; ~**dish** a rötlich.

redecorate ['riː'dekəreɪt] vt renovieren.

redecoration [riː'dekə'reɪʃən] n Renovierung f.

redeem [rɪ'diːm] vt (Comm) einlösen; (set free) freikaufen; (compensate) retten; **to** ~ **sb from sin** jdn von seinen Sünden erlösen.

redeeming [rɪ'diːmɪŋ] a virtue, feature rettend.

redeploy ['riːdɪ'plɔɪ] vt resources umverteilen.

red-haired ['red'hɛəd] a rothaarig.

red-handed ['red'hændɪd] ad auf frischer Tat.

redhead ['redhed] n Rothaarige(r) mf.

red herring ['red'herɪŋ] n Ablenkungsmanöver nt.

red-hot ['red'hɒt] a rotglühend; (excited) hitzig; tip heiß.

redirect [riːdaɪ'rekt] vt umleiten.

rediscovery ['riːdɪs'kʌvəri] n Wiederentdeckung f.

redistribute ['riːdɪs'trɪbjuːt] vt neu verteilen.

red-letter day ['red'letədeɪ] n (lit, fig) Festtag m.

redness ['rednəs] n Röte f.

redo [riː'duː] vt irreg nochmals tun or machen.

redolent ['redəulənt] a: ~ **of** riechend nach; (fig) erinnernd an (+acc).

redouble [riː'dʌbl] vt verdoppeln.

red tape ['red'teɪp] n Bürokratismus m.

reduce [rɪ'djuːs] vt price herabsetzen (to auf +acc); speed, temperature vermindern; photo verkleinern; **to** ~ **sb to tears/silence** jdn zum Weinen/ Schweigen bringen.

reduction [rɪ'dʌkʃən] n Herabsetzung f; Verminderung f; Verkleinerung f; (amount of money) Nachlaß m.

redundancy [rɪ'dʌndənsɪ] n Überflüssigkeit f; (of workers) Entlassung f.

redundant [rɪ'dʌndənt] a überflüssig;

workers ohne Arbeitsplatz; **to be made** ~ arbeitslos werden.

reed [riːd] n Schilf nt; (Mus) Rohrblatt nt.

reef [riːf] n Riff nt.

reek [riːk] vi stinken (of nach).

reel [riːl] n Spule f, Rolle f; vt (wind) wickeln, spulen; (stagger) taumeln.

re-election ['riːɪ'lekʃən] n Wiederwahl f.

re-engage ['riːɪn'geɪdʒ] vt wieder einstellen.

re-enter ['riː'entə*] vti wieder eintreten (in +acc).

re-entry ['riː'entrɪ] n Wiedereintritt m.

re-examine ['riːɪg'zæmɪn] vt neu überprüfen.

ref [ref] n (col) Schiri m.

refectory [rɪ'fektərɪ] n (Univ) Mensa f; (Sch) Speisesaal m; (Eccl) Refektorium nt.

refer [rɪ'fɜː*] vt: ~ **sb to sb/sth** jdn an jdn/etw verweisen; vi: ~ **to** hinweisen auf (+acc); (to book) nachschlagen in (+dat); (mention) sich beziehen auf (+acc).

referee [refə'riː] n Schiedsrichter m; (for job) Referenz f; vt schiedsrichtern.

reference ['refrəns] n (mentioning) Hinweis m; (allusion) Anspielung f; (for job) Referenz f; (in book) Verweis m; (number, code) Aktenzeichen nt; Katalognummer f; **with** ~ **to** in bezug auf (+acc); ~ **book** Nachschlagewerk nt.

referendum [refə'rendəm] n Volksabstimmung f.

refill ['riː'fɪl] vt nachfüllen; ['riː'fɪl] n Nachfüllung f; (for pen) Ersatzpatrone f; Ersatzmine f.

refine [rɪ'faɪn] vt (purify) raffinieren, läutern; (fig) bilden, kultivieren; ~**d** a gebildet, kultiviert; ~**ment** Bildung f; Kultiviertheit f; ~**ry** Raffinerie f.

reflect [rɪ'flekt] vt light reflektieren; (fig) (wider)spiegeln, zeigen; vi (meditate) nachdenken (on über +acc); ~**ion** Reflexion f; (image) Spiegelbild nt; (thought) Überlegung f, Gedanke m; ~**or** Reflektor m.

reflex ['riːfleks] n Reflex m; ~**ive** [rɪ'fleksɪv] a (Gram) Reflexiv-, rückbezüglich, reflexiv.

reform [rɪ'fɔːm] n Reform f; vt person bessern; **the R~ation** [refə'meɪʃən] die Reformation; ~**er** Reformer m; (Eccl) Reformator m.

refrain [rɪ'freɪn] vi unterlassen (from acc).

refresh [rɪ'freʃ] vt erfrischen; ~ **course** Wiederholungskurs m; ~**ing** a erfrischend; ~**ments** pl Erfrischungen pl.

refrigeration [rɪfrɪdʒə'reɪʃən] n Kühlung f.

refrigerator [rɪ'frɪdʒəreɪtə*] n Kühlschrank m.

refuel ['riː'fjuəl] vti auftanken; ~**ling** Auftanken nt.

refuge ['refjuːdʒ] n Zuflucht f; ~**e** [refjuː'dʒiː] Flüchtling m.

refund ['riːfʌnd] n Rückvergütung f; [rɪ'fʌnd] vt zurückerstatten, rückvergüten.

refurbish ['riː'fɜːbɪʃ] vt aufpolieren.

refurnish ['riː'fɜːnɪʃ] vt neu möblieren.

refusal [rɪ'fjuːzəl] n (Ver)weigerung f; (official) abschlägige Antwort f.

refuse ['refjuːs] n Abfall m, Müll m; [rɪ'fjuːz] vt abschlagen; vi sich weigern.

refute [rɪ'fjuːt] vt widerlegen.

regain [rɪ'geɪn] vt wiedergewinnen; consciousness wiedererlangen.

regal ['riːgəl] a königlich; ~**ia** [rɪ'geɪlɪə] pl Insignien pl; (of mayor etc) Amtsornat m.

regard [rɪ'gɑːd] n Achtung f; vt ansehen; ~s pl Grüße pl; ~**ing, as ~s, with ~ to** bezüglich (+gen), in bezug auf (+acc); ~**less** a ohne Rücksicht (of auf +acc); ad unbekümmert, ohne Rücksicht auf die Folgen.

regatta [rɪ'gætə] n Regatta f.

regency ['riːdʒənsɪ] n Regentschaft f.

regent ['riːdʒənt] n Regent m.

régime [reɪ'ʒiːm] n Regime nt.

regiment ['redʒɪmənt] n Regiment nt; ~**al** [redʒɪ'mentl] a Regiments-; ~**ation** Reglementierung f.

region ['riːdʒən] n Gegend f, Bereich m; ~**al** a örtlich, regional.

register ['redʒɪstə*] n Register nt, Verzeichnis nt, Liste f; vt (list) registrieren, eintragen; emotion zeigen; (write down) eintragen; vi (at hotel) sich eintragen; (with police) sich melden (with bei); (make impression) wirken, ankommen; ~**ed** a design eingetragen; letter Einschreibe-, eingeschrieben.

registrar [redʒɪs'trɑː*] n Standesbeamte(r) m.

registration [redʒɪs'treɪʃən] n (act) Erfassung f, Registrierung f; (number) Autonummer f, polizeiliche(s) Kennzeichen nt.

registry office ['redʒɪstrɪɒfɪs] n Standesamt nt.

regret [rɪ'gret] n Bedauern nt; **to have no ~s** nichts bedauern; vt bedauern; **to be** traurig; **to be ~ful about sth** etw bedauern; ~**fully** ad mit Bedauern, ungern; ~**table** a bedauerlich.

regroup ['riːgruːp] vt umgruppieren; vi sich umgruppieren.

regular ['regjulə*] a regelmäßig; (usual) üblich; (fixed by rule) geregelt; (coll) regelrecht; n (client etc) Stammkunde m; (Mil) Berufssoldat m; ~**ity** [regjo'lærɪtɪ] Regelmäßigkeit f; ~**ly** ad regelmäßig.

regulate ['regjuleɪt] vt regeln, regulieren.

regulation [regju'leɪʃən] n (rule) Vorschrift f; (control) Regulierung f; (order) Anordnung f, Regelung f.

rehabilitation ['riːhəbɪlɪ'teɪʃən] n (of criminal) Resozialisierung f.

rehash [riː'hæʃ] vt (coll) aufwärmen.

rehearsal [rɪ'hɜːsəl] n Probe f.

rehearse [rɪ'hɜːs] vt proben.

reign [reɪn] n Herrschaft f; vi herrschen; ~**ing** a monarch herrschend; champion gegenwärtig.

reimburse [riːɪm'bɜːs] vt entschädigen, zurückzahlen (sb for sth jdm etw).

rein [reɪn] n Zügel m.

reincarnation ['riːɪnkɑː'neɪʃən] n Wiedergeburt f.

reindeer ['reɪndɪə*] n Ren nt.

reinforce [riːɪn'fɔːs] vt verstärken; ~**d** a verstärkt; concrete Eisen-; ~**ment**

Verstärkung f; ~**ments** pl (Mil) Verstärkungstruppen pl.

reinstate ['riːɪn'steɪt] vt wiedereinsetzen.

reissue ['riː'ɪʃuː] vt neu herausgeben.

reiterate [riː'ɪtəreɪt] vt wiederholen.

reject ['riːdʒekt] n (Comm) Ausschuß(artikel) m; [rɪ'dʒekt] vt ablehnen; (throw away) ausrangieren; ~**ion** [rɪ'dʒekʃən] Zurückweisung f.

rejoice [rɪ'dʒɔɪs] vi sich freuen.

rejuvenate [rɪ'dʒuːvɪneɪt] vt verjüngen.

rekindle [riː'kɪndl] vt wieder anfachen.

relapse [rɪ'læps] n Rückfall m.

relate [rɪ'leɪt] vt (tell) berichten, erzählen; (connect) verbinden; ~**d** a verwandt (to mit).

relating [rɪ'leɪtɪŋ] prep: ~ **to** bezüglich (+gen).

relation [rɪ'leɪʃən] n Verwandte(r) mf; (connection) Beziehung f; ~**ship** Verhältnis nt, Beziehung f.

relative ['relətɪv] n Verwandte(r) mf; a relativ, bedingt; ~**ly** ad verhältnismäßig; ~ **pronoun** Verhältniswort nt, Relativpronomen nt.

relax [rɪ'læks] vi (slacken) sich lockern; (muscles, person) sich entspannen; (be less strict) freundlicher werden; vt (ease) lockern, entspannen; ~**! reg'** dich nicht auf!; ~**ation** [riːlæk'seɪʃən] Entspannung f; ~**ed** a entspannt, locker; ~**ing** a entspannend.

relay ['riːleɪ] n (Sport) Staffel f; vt message weiterleiten; (Rad, TV) übertragen.

release [rɪ'liːs] n (freedom) Entlassung f; (Tech) Auslöser m; vt befreien; prisoner entlassen; report, news verlautbaren, bekanntgeben.

relent [rɪ'lent] vi nachgeben; ~**less** a, ~**lessly** ad unnachgiebig.

relevance ['reləvəns] n Bedeutung f, Relevanz f.

relevant ['reləvənt] a wichtig, relevant.

reliability [rɪlaɪə'bɪlɪtɪ] n Zuverlässigkeit f.

reliable a, **reliably** ad [rɪ'laɪəbl, -blɪ] zuverlässig.

reliance [rɪ'laɪəns] n Abhängigkeit f (on von).

relic ['relɪk] n (from past) Überbleibsel nt; (Rel) Reliquie f.

relief [rɪ'liːf] n Erleichterung f; (help) Hilfe f, Unterstützung f; (person) Ablösung f; (Art) Relief nt; (distinctness) Hervorhebung f.

relieve [rɪ'liːv] vt (ease) erleichtern; (bring help) entlasten; person ablösen; **to ~ sb of sth** jdm etw abnehmen.

religion [rɪ'lɪdʒən] n Religion f.

religious [rɪ'lɪdʒəs] a religiös; ~**ly** ad religiös; (conscientiously) gewissenhaft.

reline ['riː'laɪn] vt brakes neu beschuhen.

relinquish [rɪ'lɪŋkwɪʃ] vt aufgeben.

relish ['relɪʃ] n Würze f, pikante Beigabe f; vt genießen.

relive ['riː'lɪv] vt noch einmal durchleben.

reluctance [rɪ'lʌktəns] n Widerstreben nt, Abneigung f.

reluctant [rɪˈlʌktənt] a widerwillig; **~ly** ad ungern.

rely [rɪˈlaɪ]: **~ on** vt sich verlassen auf (+acc).

remain [rɪˈmeɪn] vi (be left) übrigbleiben; (stay) bleiben; **~der** Rest m; **~ing** a übrig(geblieben); **~s** pl Überreste pl; (dead body) sterbliche Überreste pl.

· **remand** [rɪˈmɑːnd] n: **on ~** in Untersuchungshaft; vt: **~ in custody** in Untersuchungshaft schicken.

remark [rɪˈmɑːk] n Bemerkung f; vt bemerken; **~able** a, **~ably** ad bemerkenswert.

remarry [ˈriːˈmærɪ] vi sich wieder verheiraten.

remedial [rɪˈmiːdɪəl] a Heil-; teaching Hilfsschul-.

remedy [ˈremədɪ] n Mittel nt; vt pain abhelfen (+dat); trouble in Ordnung bringen.

remember [rɪˈmembə*] vt sich erinnern an (+acc); **~ me to them** grüße sie von mir.

remembrance [rɪˈmembrəns] n Erinnerung f; (official) Gedenken nt.

remind [rɪˈmaɪnd] vt erinnern; **~er** Mahnung f.

reminisce [remɪˈnɪs] vi in Erinnerungen schwelgen; **~nces** [remɪˈnɪsənsɪz] pl Erinnerungen pl; **~nt** a erinnernd (of an +acc), Erinnerungen nachrufend (of an +acc).

remit [rɪˈmɪt] vt money überweisen (to an +acc); **~tance** Geldanweisung f.

remnant [ˈremnənt] n Rest m.

remorse [rɪˈmɔːs] n Gewissensbisse pl; **~ful** a reumütig; **~less** a, **~lessly** ad unbarmherzig.

remote [rɪˈməut] a abgelegen, entfernt; (slight) gering; **~ control** Fernsteuerung f; **~ly** ad entfernt; **~ness** Entlegenheit f.

removable [rɪˈmuːvəbl] a entfernbar.

removal [rɪˈmuːvəl] n Beseitigung f; (of furniture) Umzug m; (from office) Entlassung f; **~ van** Möbelwagen m.

remove [rɪˈmuːv] vt beseitigen, entfernen; (dismiss) entlassen; **~r** (for paint etc) Fleckenentferner m; **~rs** pl Möbelspedition f.

remuneration [rɪmjuːnəˈreɪʃən] n Vergütung f, Honorar nt.

Renaissance [rəˈneɪsɑːns]: **the ~** die Renaissance.

rename [ˈriːˈneɪm] vt umbenennen.

rend [rend] vt irreg zerreißen.

render [ˈrendə*] vt machen; (translate) übersetzen; **~ing** (Mus) Wiedergabe f.

rendezvous [ˈrɒndɪvuː] n Verabredung f, Rendezvous nt.

renegade [ˈrenɪgeɪd] n Überläufer m.

renew [rɪˈnjuː] vt erneuern; contract, licence verlängern; (replace) ersetzen; **~al** Erneuerung f; Verlängerung f.

renounce [rɪˈnauns] vt (give up) verzichten auf (+acc); (disown) verstoßen.

renovate [ˈrenəveɪt] vt renovieren; building restaurieren.

renovation [renəuˈveɪʃən] n Renovierung f; Restauration f.

renown [rɪˈnaun] n Ruf m; **~ed** a namhaft.

rent [rent] n Miete f; (for land) Pacht f; vt (hold as tenant) mieten; pachten; (let) vermieten; verpachten; car etc mieten; (firm) vermieten; **~al** Miete f; Pacht f, Pachtgeld nt.

renunciation [rɪnʌnsɪˈeɪʃən] n Verzicht m (of auf +acc).

reopen [ˈriːˈəupən] vt wiedereröffnen.

reorder [ˈriːˈɔːdə*] vt wieder bestellen.

reorganization [ˈriːɔːgənaɪˈzeɪʃən] n Neugestaltung f; (Comm etc) Umbildung f.

reorganize [ˈriːˈɔːgənaɪz] vt umgestalten, reorganisieren.

rep [rep] n (Comm) Vertreter m; (Theat) Repertoire nt.

repair [rɪˈpɛə*] n Reparatur f; **in good ~** in gutem Zustand; vt reparieren; damage wiedergutmachen; **~ kit** vt Werkzeugkasten m; **~ man** Mechaniker m; **~ shop** Reparaturwerkstatt f.

repartee [repɑːˈtiː] n Witzeleien pl.

repay [riːˈpeɪ] vt irreg zurückzahlen; (reward) vergelten; **~ment** Rückzahlung f; (fig) Vergelten nt.

repeal [rɪˈpiːl] n Aufhebung f; vt aufheben.

repeat [rɪˈpiːt] n (Rad, TV) Wiederholung(ssendung) f; vt wiederholen; **~edly** ad wiederholt.

repel [rɪˈpel] vt (drive back) zurückschlagen; (disgust) abstoßen; **~lent** a abstoßend; n: **insect ~lent** Insektenmittel nt.

repent [rɪˈpent] vti bereuen; **~ance** Reue f.

repercussion [riːpəˈkʌʃən] n Auswirkung f; (of rifle) Rückstoß m.

repertoire [ˈrepətwɑː*] n Repertoire nt.

repertory [ˈrepətərɪ] n Repertoire nt.

repetition [repɪˈtɪʃən] n Wiederholung f.

repetitive [rɪˈpetɪtɪv] a sich wiederholend.

rephrase [ˈriːˈfreɪz] vt anders formulieren.

replace [rɪˈpleɪs] vt ersetzen; (put back) zurückstellen; **~ment** Ersatz m.

replenish [rɪˈplenɪʃ] vt (wieder) auffüllen.

replete [rɪˈpliːt] a (zum Platzen) voll.

replica [ˈreplɪkə] n Kopie f.

reply [rɪˈplaɪ] n Antwort f, Erwiderung f; vi antworten, erwidern.

report [rɪˈpɔːt] n Bericht m; (Sch) Zeugnis nt; (of gun) Knall m; (tell) berichten; (give information against) melden; (to police) anzeigen; vi (make report) Bericht erstatten; (present o.s.) sich melden; **~er** Reporter m.

reprehensible [reprɪˈhensɪbl] a tadelnswert.

represent [reprɪˈzent] vt darstellen, zeigen; (act) darstellen; (speak for) vertreten; **~ation** Darstellung f, (being represented) Vertretung f; **~ative** n (person) Vertreter m; a räpresentativ.

repress [rɪˈpres] vt unterdrücken; **~ion** [rɪˈpreʃən] Unterdrückung f; **~ive** a Unterdrückungs-; (Psych) Hemmungs-.

reprieve [rɪˈpriːv] n Aufschub m; (cancellation) Begnadigung f; (fig) Atempause f; vt Gnadenfrist gewähren (+dat); begnadigen.

reprimand [ˈreprɪmɑːnd] n Verweis m; vt

einen Verweis erteilen (+dat).
reprint ['ri:prɪnt] n Neudruck m; ['ri:'prɪnt] vt wieder abdrucken.
reprisal [rɪ'praɪzəl] n Vergeltung f.
reproach [rɪ'prəʊtʃ] n (blame) Vorwurf m, Tadel m; (disgrace) Schande f; beyond ~ über jeden Vorwurf erhaben; vt Vorwürfe machen (+dat), tadeln; ~ful a vorwurfsvoll.
reproduce [ri:prə'dju:s] vt reproduzieren; vi (have offspring) sich vermehren.
reproduction [ri:prə'dʌkʃən] n Wiedergabe f; (Art, Phot) Reproduktion f; (breeding) Fortpflanzung f.
reproductive [ri:prə'dʌktɪv] a reproduktiv; (breeding) Fortpflanzungs-.
reprove [rɪ'pru:v] vt tadeln.
reptile ['reptaɪl] n Reptil nt.
republic [rɪ'pʌblɪk] n Republik f; ~an a republikanisch; n Republikaner m.
repudiate [rɪ'pju:dɪeɪt] vt zurückweisen, nicht anerkennen.
repugnance [rɪ'pʌgnəns] n Widerwille m.
repugnant [rɪ'pʌgnənt] a widerlich.
repulse [rɪ'pʌls] vt (drive back) zurückschlagen; (reject) abweisen.
repulsion [rɪ'pʌlʃən] n Abscheu m.
repulsive [rɪ'pʌlsɪv] a abstoßend.
repurchase [ri:'pɜ:tʃəs] vt zurückkaufen.
reputable ['repjʊtəbl] a angesehen.
reputation [repjʊ'teɪʃən] n Ruf m.
repute [rɪ'pju:t] n hohe(s) Ansehen nt; ~d a, ~dly ad angeblich.
request [rɪ'kwest] n (asking) Ansuchen nt; (demand) Wunsch m; at sb's ~ auf jds Wunsch; vt (firm) erbitten; person ersuchen.
requiem ['rekwɪəm] n Requiem nt.
require [rɪ'kwaɪə*] vt (need) brauchen; (wish) wünschen; to be ~d to do sth etw tun müssen; ~ment (condition) Anforderung f; (need) Bedarf m.
requisite ['rekwɪzɪt] n Erfordernis nt; a erforderlich.
requisition [rekwɪ'zɪʃən] n Anforderung f; vt beschlagnahmen; (order) anfordern.
reroute [ri:'ru:t] vt umleiten.
rescind [rɪ'sɪnd] vt aufheben.
rescue ['reskju:] n Rettung f; vt retten; ~party Rettungsmannschaft f; ~r Retter m.
research [rɪ'sɜ:tʃ] n Forschung f; vi Forschungen anstellen (into über +acc); vt erforschen; ~er Forscher m; ~ work Forschungsarbeit f; ~ worker wissenschaftliche(r) Mitarbeiter(in f) m.
resemblance [rɪ'zembləns] n Ähnlichkeit f.
resemble [rɪ'zembl] vt ähneln (+dat).
resent [rɪ'zent] vt übelnehmen; ~ful a nachtragend, empfindlich; ~ment Verstimmung f, Unwille m.
reservation [rezə'veɪʃən] n (of seat) Reservierung f; (Theat) Vorbestellung f; (doubt) Vorbehalt m; (land) Reservat nt.
reserve [rɪ'zɜ:v] n (store) Vorrat m, Reserve f; (manner) Zurückhaltung f; (game —) Naturschutzgebiet nt; (native —) Reservat nt; (Sport) Ersatzspieler(in f) m; vt reservieren; judgement sich (dat) vor-

behalten; ~s pl (Mil) Reserve f; in ~ in Reserve; ~d a reserviert; all rights ~d alle Rechte vorbehalten.
reservist [rɪ'zɜ:vɪst] n Reservist m.
reservoir ['rezəvwɑ:*] n Reservoir nt.
reshape [ri:'ʃeɪp] vt umformen.
reshuffle [ri:'ʃʌfl] vt (Pol) umbilden.
reside [rɪ'zaɪd] vi wohnen, ansässig sein; ~nce ['rezɪdəns] (house) Wohnung f, Wohnsitz m; (living) Wohnen nt, Aufenthalt m; ~nt ['rezɪdənt] (in house) Bewohner m; (in area) Einwohner m; a wohnhaft, ansässig; ~ntial [rezɪ'denʃəl] a Wohn-.
residue ['rezɪdju:] n Rest m; (Chem) Rückstand m; (fig) Bodensatz m.
resign [rɪ'zaɪn] vt office aufgeben, zurücktreten von; to be ~ed to sth, to ~ o.s. to sth sich mit etw abfinden; vi (from office) zurücktreten; ~ation [rezɪg'neɪʃən] (resigning) Aufgabe f; (Pol) Rücktritt m; (submission) Resignation f; ~ed a resigniert.
resilience [rɪ'zɪlɪəns] n Spannkraft f, Elastizität f; (of person) Unverwüstlichkeit f.
resilient [rɪ'zɪlɪənt] a unverwüstlich.
resin ['rezɪn] n Harz nt.
resist [rɪ'zɪst] vt widerstehen (+dat); ~ance Widerstand m; ~ant a widerstandsfähig (to gegen); (to stains etc) abstoßend.
resolute a, ~ly ad ['rezəlu:t, -lɪ] entschlossen, resolut.
resolution [rezə'lu:ʃən] n (firmness) Entschlossenheit f; (intention) Vorsatz m; (decision) Beschluß m; (personal) Entschluß m.
resolve [rɪ'zɒlv] n Vorsatz m, Entschluß m; vt (decide) beschließen; it ~d itself es löste sich; ~d a (fest) entschlossen.
resonant ['rezənənt] a widerhallend; voice volltönend.
resort [rɪ'zɔ:t] n (holiday place) Erholungsort m; (help) Zuflucht f; vi Zuflucht nehmen (to zu); as a last ~ als letzter Ausweg.
resound [rɪ'zaʊnd] vi widerhallen; ~ing a nachhallend; success groß.
resource [rɪ'sɔ:s] n Findigkeit f; ~s pl (of energy) Energiequellen pl; (of money) Quellen pl; (of a country etc) Bodenschätze pl; ~ful a findig; ~fulness Findigkeit f.
respect [rɪs'pekt] n Respekt m; (esteem) (Hoch)achtung f; vt achten, respektieren; ~s pl Grüße pl; with ~ to in bezug auf (+acc), hinsichtlich (+gen); in ~ of in bezug auf (+acc); in this ~ in dieser Hinsicht; ~ability [rɪspektə'bɪlɪtɪ] Anständigkeit f, Achtbarkeit f; ~able a (decent) angesehen, achtbar; (fairly good) leidlich; ~ed a angesehen; ~ful a höflich; ~fully ad ehrerbietig; (in letter) mit vorzüglicher Hochachtung; ~ing prep betreffend; ~ive a jeweilig; ~ively ad beziehungsweise.
respiration [respɪ'reɪʃən] n Atmung f, Atmen nt.
respiratory [rɪs'pɪrətərɪ] a Atmungs-.
respite ['respaɪt] n Ruhepause f; without ~ ohne Unterlaß.

resplendent [rɪs'plendənt] a strahlend.
respond [rɪs'pond] vi antworten; (react) reagieren (to auf +acc).
response [rɪs'pons] n Antwort f; Reaktion f; (to advert etc) Resonanz f.
responsibility [rɪsponsə'bɪlɪtɪ] n Verantwortung f.
responsible [rɪs'ponsəbl] a verantwortlich; (reliable) verantwortungsvoll.
responsibly [rɪs'ponsəblɪ] ad verantwortungsvoll.
responsive [rɪs'ponsɪv] a empfänglich.
rest [rest] n Ruhe f; (break) Pause f; (remainder) Rest m; **the ~ of them** die übrigen; vi sich ausruhen; (be supported) (auf)liegen; (remain) liegen (with bei).
restaurant ['restərɔːŋ] n Restaurant nt, Gaststätte f; ~ **car** Speisewagen m.
rest cure ['restkjuə*] n Erholung f.
restful ['restful] a erholsam, ruhig.
rest home ['resthəum] n Erholungsheim nt.
restitution [restɪ'tjuːʃən] n Rückgabe f, Entschädigung f.
restive ['restɪv] a unruhig; (disobedient) störrisch.
restless ['restləs] a unruhig; ~**ly** ad ruhelos; ~**ness** Ruhelosigkeit f.
restock ['riː'stok] vt auffüllen.
restoration [restə'reɪʃən] n Wiederherstellung f, Neueinführung f, Wiedereinsetzung f, Rückgabe f, Restauration f, **the R ~** die Restauration.
restore [rɪs'tɔː*] vt order wiederherstellen; customs wieder einführen; person to position wiedereinsetzen; (give back) zurückgeben; paintings restaurieren.
restrain [rɪs'treɪn] vt zurückhalten; curiosity etc beherrschen; ~**ed** a style etc gedämpft, verhalten; ~**t** (restraining) Einschränkung f; (being restrained) Beschränkung f; (self-control) Zurückhaltung f.
restrict [rɪs'trɪkt] vt einschränken; ~**ed** a beschränkt; ~**ion** [rɪs'trɪkʃən] Einschränkung f; ~**ive** a einschränkend.
rest room ['restrum] n (US) Toilette f.
result [rɪ'zʌlt] n Resultat nt, Folge f; (of exam, game) Ergebnis nt; vi zur Folge haben (in acc); ~**ant** a (daraus) entstehend or resultierend.
resume [rɪ'zjuːm] vt fortsetzen; (occupy again) wieder einnehmen.
résumé ['reɪzjuːmeɪ] n Zusammenfassung f.
resumption [rɪ'zʌmpʃən] n Wiederaufnahme f.
resurgence [rɪ'sɜːdʒəns] n Wiedererwachen nt.
resurrection [rezə'rekʃən] n Auferstehung f.
resuscitate [rɪ'sʌsɪteɪt] vt wiederbeleben.
resuscitation [rɪsʌsɪ'teɪʃən] n Wiederbelebung f.
retail ['riːteɪl] n Einzelhandel m; a Einzelhandels-, Laden-; [riː'teɪl] vt im kleinen verkaufen; vi im Einzelhandel kosten; ~**er** ['riːteɪlə*] Einzelhändler m, Kleinhändler m; ~ **price** Ladenpreis m.

retain [rɪ'teɪn] vt (keep) (zurück)behalten; (pay) unterhalten; ~**er** (servant) Gefolgsmann m; (fee) (Honorar)vorschuß m.
retaliate [rɪ'tælɪeɪt] vi zum Vergeltungsschlag ausholen.
retaliation [rɪtælɪ'eɪʃən] n Vergeltung f.
retarded [rɪ'tɑːdɪd] a zurückgeblieben.
retention [rɪ'tenʃən] n Behalten nt.
retentive [rɪ'tentɪv] a memory gut.
rethink ['riː'θɪŋk] vt irreg nochmals durchdenken.
reticence ['retɪsəns] n Schweigsamkeit f.
reticent ['retɪsənt] a schweigsam.
retina ['retɪnə] n Netzhaut f.
retinue ['retɪnjuː] n Gefolge nt.
retire [rɪ'taɪə*] vi (from work) in den Ruhestand treten; (withdraw) sich zurückziehen; (go to bed) schlafen gehen; ~**d** a person pensioniert, im Ruhestand; ~**ment** Ruhestand m.
retiring [rɪ'taɪərɪŋ] a zurückhaltend, schüchtern.
retort [rɪ'tɔːt] n (reply) Erwiderung f; (Sci) Retorte f; vi (scharf) erwidern.
retrace [rɪ'treɪs] vt zurückverfolgen.
retract [rɪ'trækt] vt statement zurücknehmen; claws einziehen; ~**able** a aerial ausziehbar.
retrain ['riː'treɪn] vt umschulen; ~**ing** Umschulung f.
retreat [rɪ'triːt] n Rückzug m; (place) Zufluchtsort m; vi sich zurückziehen.
retrial ['riː'traɪəl] n Wiederaufnahmeverfahren nt.
retribution [retrɪ'bjuːʃən] n Strafe f.
retrieval [rɪ'triːvəl] n Wiedergewinnung f.
retrieve [rɪ'triːv] vt wiederbekommen; (rescue) retten; ~**r** Apportierhund m.
retroactive [retrəʊ'æktɪv] a rückwirkend.
retrograde ['retrəʊgreɪd] a step Rück-; policy rückschrittlich.
retrospect ['retrəʊspekt] n: **in ~** im Rückblick, rückblickend; ~**ive** [retrəʊ'spektɪv] a rückwirkend; rückblickend.
return [rɪ'tɜːn] n Rückkehr f; (profits) Ertrag m, Gewinn m; (report) amtliche(r) Bericht m; (rail ticket etc) Rückfahrkarte f; (plane) Rückflugkarte f; (bus) Rückfahrschein m; a **by ~ of post** postwendend; journey, match Rück-; vi zurückkehren or -kommen; vt zurückgeben, zurücksenden; (pay back) zurückzahlen; (elect) wählen; verdict aussprechen; ~**able** a bottle etc mit Pfand.
reunion [riː'juːnjən] n Wiedervereinigung f; (Sch etc) Treffen nt.
reunite ['riːjuː'naɪt] vt wiedervereinigen.
rev [rev] n Drehzahl f; vti (also ~ **up**) (den Motor) auf Touren bringen.
revamp ['riː'væmp] vt aufpolieren.
reveal [rɪ'viːl] vt enthüllen; ~**ing** a aufschlußreich.
reveille [rɪ'vælɪ] n Wecken nt.
revel ['revl] vi genießen (in acc).
revelation [revə'leɪʃən] n Offenbarung f.
reveller ['revələ*] n Schwelger m.
revelry ['revlrɪ] n Rummel m.

revenge [rɪ'vendʒ] n Rache f; vt rächen; ~ful a rachsüchtig.

revenue ['revənjuː] n Einnahmen pl, Staatseinkünfte pl.

reverberate [rɪ'vɜːbəreɪt] vi widerhallen.

reverberation [rɪvɜːbə'reɪʃən] n Widerhall m.

revere [rɪ'vɪə*] vt (ver)ehren; ~nce ['revərəns] Ehrfurcht f; ['revərənd] R ~nd . . . Hochwürden . . .; ~nt ['revərənt] a ehrfurchtsvoll.

reverie ['revərɪ] n Träumerei f.

reversal [rɪ'vɜːsəl] n Umkehrung f.

reverse [rɪ'vɜːs] n Rückseite f; (Aut: gear) Rückwärtsgang m; a order, direction entgegengesetzt; vt umkehren; vi (Aut) rückwärts fahren.

reversion [rɪ'vɜːʃən] n Umkehrung f.

revert [rɪ'vɜːt] vi zurückkehren.

review [rɪ'vjuː] n (Mil) Truppenschau f; (of book) Besprechung f, Rezension f; (magazine) Zeitschrift f; to be under ~ untersucht werden; vt Rückschau halten auf (+acc); (Mil) mustern; book besprechen, rezensieren; (reexamine) von neuem untersuchen; ~er (critic) Rezensent m.

revise [rɪ'vaɪz] vt durchsehen, verbessern; book überarbeiten; (reconsider) ändern, revidieren.

revision [rɪvɪʒən] n Durchsicht f, Prüfung f; (Comm) Revision f; (of book) verbesserte Ausgabe f; (Sch) Wiederholung f.

revisit [riː'vɪzɪt] vt wieder besuchen.

revitalize [riː'vaɪtəlaɪz] vt neu beleben.

revival [rɪ'vaɪvəl] n Wiederbelebung f; (Rel) Erweckung f; (Theat) Wiederaufnahme f.

revive [rɪ'vaɪv] vt wiederbeleben; (fig) wieder auffrischen; vi wiedererwachen; (fig) wieder aufleben.

revoke [rɪ'vəʊk] vt aufheben.

revolt [rɪ'vəʊlt] n Aufstand m, Revolte f; vi sich auflehnen; vt entsetzen; ~ing a widerlich.

revolution [revə'luːʃən] n (turn) Umdrehung f; (change) Umwälzung f; (Pol) Revolution f; ~ary a revolutionär; n Revolutionär m; ~ize vt revolutionieren.

revolve [rɪ'vɒlv] vi kreisen; (on own axis) sich drehen; ~r Revolver m.

revue [rɪ'vjuː] n Revue f.

revulsion [rɪ'vʌlʃən] n (disgust) Ekel m.

reward [rɪ'wɔːd] n Belohnung f; vt belohnen; ~ing a lohnend.

reword ['riː'wɜːd] vt anders formulieren.

rewrite ['riː'raɪt] vt irreg umarbeiten, neu schreiben.

rhapsody ['ræpsədɪ] n Rhapsodie f; (fig) Schwärmerei f.

rhetoric ['retərɪk] n Rhetorik f, Redekunst f; ~al [rɪ'tɒrɪkəl] a rhetorisch.

rheumatic [ruː'mætɪk] a rheumatisch.

rheumatism ['ruːmətɪzəm] n Rheumatismus m, Rheuma nt.

rhinoceros [raɪ'nɒsərəs] n Nashorn nt, Rhinozeros nt.

rhododendron [rəʊdə'dendrən] n Rhododendron m.

rhubarb ['ruːbɑːb] n Rhabarber m.

rhyme [raɪm] n Reim m.

rhythm ['rɪðəm] n Rhythmus m; ~ic(al) a, ~ically ad ['rɪðmɪk(l), -ɪ] rhythmisch.

rib [rɪb] n Rippe f; vt (mock) hänseln, aufziehen.

ribald ['rɪbəld] a saftig.

ribbon ['rɪbən] n Band nt.

rice [raɪs] n Reis m; ~ pudding Milchreis m.

rich [rɪtʃ] a reich, wohlhabend; (fertile) fruchtbar; (splendid) kostbar; food reichhaltig; ~es pl Reichtum m, Reichtümer pl; ~ly ad reich; deserve völlig; ~ness Reichtum m; (of food) Reichhaltigkeit f; (of colours) Sattheit f.

rick [rɪk] n Schober m.

rickets ['rɪkɪts] n Rachitis f.

rickety ['rɪkɪtɪ] a wack(e)lig.

rickshaw ['rɪkʃɔː] n Rikscha f.

ricochet ['rɪkəʃeɪ] n Abprallen nt; (shot) Querschläger m; vi abprallen.

rid [rɪd] vt irreg befreien (of von); to get ~ of loswerden; good ~dance! den/die/das wären wir los!

riddle ['rɪdl] n Rätsel nt; vt (esp passive) durchlöchern.

ride [raɪd] n (in vehicle) Fahrt f; (on horse) Ritt m; vt irreg vi horse reiten; bicycle fahren; vi fahren; reiten; (ship) vor Anker liegen; ~r Reiter m; (addition) Zusatz m.

ridge [rɪdʒ] n (of hills) Bergkette f; (top) Grat m, Kamm m; (of roof) Dachfirst m.

ridicule ['rɪdɪkjuːl] n Spott m; vt lächerlich machen.

ridiculous a, ~ly ad [rɪ'dɪkjʊləs, -lɪ] lächerlich.

riding ['raɪdɪŋ] n Reiten nt; to go ~ reiten gehen; ~ habit Reitkleid nt; ~ school Reitschule f.

rife [raɪf] a weit verbreitet.

riffraff ['rɪfræf] n Gesindel nt, Pöbel m.

rifle ['raɪfl] n Gewehr nt; vt berauben; ~range Schießstand m.

rift [rɪft] n Ritze f, Spalte f; (fig) Bruch m.

rig [rɪg] n (outfit) Takelung f; (fig) Aufmachung f; (oil –) Bohrinsel f; vt election etc manipulieren; ~ging Takelage f; ~out vt ausstatten; ~ up vt zusammenbasteln, konstruieren.

right [raɪt] a (correct, just) richtig, recht; (right side) rechte(r, s); n Recht nt; (not left, Pol) Rechte f; ad (on the right) rechts; (to the right) nach rechts; look, work richtig, recht; (directly) gerade; (exactly) genau; vt in Ordnung bringen, korrigieren; interj gut; ~ away sofort; to be ~ recht haben; all ~! gut!, in Ordnung!, schön!; ~ now in diesem Augenblick, eben; by ~s von Rechts wegen; ~ to the end bis ans Ende; on the ~ rechts; ~ angle Rechteck nt; ~eous ['raɪtʃəs] a rechtschaffen; ~eousness Rechtschaffenheit f; ~ful a rechtmäßig; ~fully ad rechtmäßig; (justifiably) zu Recht; ~-hand drive: to have ~-hand drive das Steuer rechts haben; ~-handed a rechtshändig; ~-hand man rechte Hand f; ~-hand side rechte Seite f; ~-ly ad mit Recht; ~-minded a rechtschaffen; ~ of way Vorfahrt f; ~-wing rechte(r) Flügel m.

rigid ['rɪdʒɪd] a (stiff) starr, steif; (strict) streng; ~ity [rɪ'dʒɪdɪtɪ] Starrheit f, Steifheit f; Strenge f; ~ly starr, steif; (fig) hart, unbeugsam.

rigmarole ['rɪgmərəʊl] n Gewäsch nt.

rigor mortis ['rɪgə'mɔːtɪs] n Totenstarre f.

rigorous a, ~ly ad ['rɪgərəs, -lɪ] streng.

rigour, (US) **rigor** ['rɪgə*] n Strenge f, Härte f.

rig-out ['rɪgaʊt] n (col) Aufzug m.

rile [raɪl] vt ärgern.

rim [rɪm] n (edge) Rand m; (of wheel) Felge f; ~less a randlos; ~med a gerändert.

rind [raɪnd] n Rinde f.

ring [rɪŋ] n Ring m; (of people) Kreis m; (arena) Ring m, Manege f; (of telephone) Klingeln nt, Läuten nt; **to give sb a** ~ jdn anrufen; **it has a familiar** ~ es klingt bekannt; vti irreg bell läuten; (also ~ **up**) anrufen; ~ **off** vi aufhängen; ~ **binder** Ringbuch nt; ~**leader** Anführer m, Rädelsführer m; ~**lets** pl Ringellocken pl; ~ **road** Umgehungsstraße f.

rink [rɪŋk] n (ice ~) Eisbahn f.

rinse [rɪns] n Spülen nt; vt spülen.

riot ['raɪət] n Aufruhr m; vi randalieren; ~**er** Aufrührer m; ~**ous** a, ~**ously** ad aufrührerisch; (noisy) lärmend.

rip [rɪp] n Schlitz m, Riß m; vti (zer)reißen.

ripcord ['rɪpkɔːd] n Reißleine f.

ripe [raɪp] a fruit reif; cheese ausgereift; ~**n** vti reifen, reif werden (lassen); ~**ness** Reife f.

riposte [rɪ'pɒst] n Nachstoß m; (fig) schlagfertige Antwort f.

ripple ['rɪpl] n kleine Welle f; vt kräuseln; vi sich kräuseln.

rise [raɪz] n (slope) Steigung f; (esp in wages) Erhöhung f; (growth) Aufstieg m; vi irreg aufstehen; (sun) aufgehen; (smoke) aufsteigen; (mountain) sich erheben; (ground) ansteigen; (prices) steigen; (in revolt) sich erheben; **to give** ~ **to** Anlaß geben zu; **to** ~ **to the occasion** sich der Lage gewachsen zeigen.

risk [rɪsk] n Gefahr f, Risiko nt; vt (venture) wagen; (chance loss of) riskieren, aufs Spiel setzen; ~**y** a gewagt, gefährlich, riskant.

risqué ['riːskeɪ] a gewagt.

rissole ['rɪsəʊl] n Fleischklößchen nt.

rite [raɪt] n Ritus m; **last** ~**s** pl Letzte Ölung f.

ritual ['rɪtjʊəl] n Ritual nt; a ritual, Ritual-; (fig) rituell.

rival ['raɪvəl] n Rivale m, Konkurrent m; a rivalisierend; vt rivalisieren mit; (Comm) konkurrieren mit; ~**ry** Rivalität f, Konkurrenz f.

river ['rɪvə*] n Fluß m, Strom m; ~**bank** Flußufer nt; ~**bed** Flußbett nt; ~**side** n Flußufer nt; a am Ufer gelegen, Ufer-.

rivet ['rɪvɪt] n Niete f; vt (fasten) (ver)nieten.

road [rəʊd] n Straße f; ~**block** Straßensperre f; ~**hog** Verkehrsrowdy m; ~**map** Straßenkarte f; ~**side** n Straßenrand m; a an der Landstraße (gelegen); ~ **sign** Straßenschild nt; ~ **user** Verkehrsteilnehmer m; ~**way** Fahrbahn f; ~**worthy** a verkehrssicher.

roam [rəʊm] vi (umher)streifen; vt durchstreifen.

roar [rɔː*] n Brüllen nt, Gebrüll nt; vi brüllen; ~**ing** a fire Bomben-, prasselnd; trade schwunghaft, Bomben-.

roast [rəʊst] n Braten m; vt braten, rösten, schmoren.

rob [rɒb] vt bestehlen, berauben; bank ausrauben; ~**ber** Räuber m; ~**bery** Raub m.

robe [rəʊb] n (dress) Gewand nt; (US) Hauskleid nt; (judge's) Robe f; vt feierlich ankleiden.

robin ['rɒbɪn] n Rotkehlchen nt.

robot ['rəʊbɒt] n Roboter m.

robust [rəʊ'bʌst] a stark, robust.

rock [rɒk] n Felsen m; (piece) Stein m; (bigger) Fels(brocken) m; (sweet) Zuckerstange f; vti wiegen, schaukeln; **on the** ~**s** drink mit Eis(würfeln); marriage gescheitert; ship aufgelaufen; ~**-bottom** (fig) Tiefpunkt m; ~**climber** (Steil)kletterer m; **to go** ~ **climbing** (steil)klettern gehen; ~**ery** Steingarten m.

rocket ['rɒkɪt] n Rakete f.

rock face ['rɒkfeɪs] n Felswand f.

rocking chair [rɒkɪŋ'tʃeə*] n Schaukelstuhl m.

rocking horse ['rɒkɪŋhɔːs] n Schaukelpferd nt.

rocky ['rɒkɪ] a felsig.

rococo [rəʊ'kəʊkəʊ] a Rokoko-; n Rokoko nt.

rod [rɒd] n (bar) Stange f; (stick) Rute f.

rodent ['rəʊdənt] n Nagetier nt.

rodeo ['rəʊdɪəʊ] n Rodeo m or nt.

roe [rəʊ] n (deer) Reh nt; (of fish) Rogen m.

rogue [rəʊg] n Schurke m; (hum) Spitzbube m.

roguish ['rəʊgɪʃ] a schurkisch; hum schelmisch.

role [rəʊl] n Rolle f.

roll [rəʊl] n Rolle f; (bread) Brötchen nt, Semmel f; (list) (Namens)liste f, Verzeichnis nt; (of drum) Wirbel m; vt (turn) rollen, (herum)wälzen; grass etc walzen; vi (swing) schlingern; (sound) (g)rollen; ~ **by** vi (time) verfließen; ~ **in** vi (mail) hereinkommen; ~ **over** vi sich (herum)drehen; ~ **up** vi (arrive) kommen, auftauchen; vt carpet aufrollen; ~ **call** Namensaufruf m; ~**ed** a umbrella zusammengerollt; ~**er** Rolle f, Walze f; (road ~er) Straßenwalze f; ~**er skates** pl Rollschuhe pl.

rollicking ['rɒlɪkɪŋ] a ausgelassen.

rolling ['rəʊlɪŋ] a landscape wellig; ~ **pin** Nudel- or Wellholz nt; ~ **stock** Wagenmaterial nt.

Roman [rəʊmən] a römisch; n Römer(in f) m; ~ **Catholic** a römisch-katholisch; n Katholik(in f) m.

romance [rəʊ'mæns] n Romanze f; (story) (Liebes)roman m; vi aufschneiden, erfinden; ~**r** (storyteller) Aufschneider m.

romantic [rəʊ'mæntɪk] a romantisch; **R**~**ism** [rəʊ'mæntɪsɪzəm] Romantik f.

romp [rɒmp] n Tollen nt; vi (also ~ **about**) herumtollen; ~**ers** pl Spielanzug m.

rondo ['rɒndəʊ] n (Mus) Rondo nt.

roof [ru:f] n Dach nt; (of mouth) Gaumen nt; vt überdachen, überdecken; ~**ing** Deckmaterial nt.

rook [rok] n (bird) Saatkrähe f; (chess) Turm m; vt (cheat) betrügen.

room [rum] n Zimmer nt, Raum m; (space) Platz m; (fig) Spielraum m; ~**s** pl Wohnung f; ~**iness** Geräumigkeit f; ~**mate** Mitbewohner(in f) m; ~**service** Zimmerbedienung f; ~**y** a geräumig.

roost [ru:st] n Hühnerstange f; vi auf der Stange hocken.

root [ru:t] n (lit, fig) Wurzel f; vt einwurzeln; ~**ed** a (fig) verwurzelt; ~ **about** vi (fig) herumwühlen; ~ **for** vt Stimmung machen für; ~ **out** vt ausjäten; (fig) ausrotten.

rope [rəup] n Seil nt, Strick m; vt (tie) festschnüren; to ~ **sb in** jdn gewinnen; ~ **off** vt absperren; **to know the** ~**s** sich auskennen; ~ **ladder** Strickleiter f.

rosary ['reuzərɪ] n Rosenkranz m.

rose [rəuz] n Rose f; a Rosen-, rosenrot.

rosé ['rəuzeɪ] n Rosé m.

rosebed ['rəuzbed] n Rosenbeet nt.

rosebud ['rəuzbʌd] n Rosenknospe f.

rosebush ['rəuzbʊʃ] n Rosenstock m, Rosenstrauch m.

rosemary ['rəuzmərɪ] n Rosmarin m.

rosette [rəu'zet] n Rosette f.

roster ['rɒstə*] n Dienstplan m.

rostrum ['rɒstrəm] n Rednerbühne f.

rosy ['rəuzɪ] a rosig.

rot [rɒt] n Fäulnis f; (nonsense) Quatsch m, Blödsinn m; vti verfaulen (lassen).

rota ['rəutə] n Dienstliste f.

rotary ['rəutərɪ] a rotierend, sich drehend.

rotate [rəu'teɪt] vt rotieren lassen; (two or more things in order) turnusmäßig wechseln; vi rotieren.

rotating [rəu'teɪtɪŋ] a rotierend.

rotation [rəu'teɪʃən] n Umdrehung f, Rotation f; **in** ~ der Reihe nach, abwechselnd.

rotor ['rəutə*] n Rotor m.

rotten ['rɒtn] a faul, verfault; (fig) schlecht, gemein.

rotund [rəu'tʌnd] a rund; person rundlich.

rouge [ru:ʒ] n Rouge nt.

rough [rʌf] a (not smooth) rauh; path uneben; (violent) roh, grob; crossing stürmisch; wind rauh; (without comforts) hart, unbequem; (unfinished, makeshift) grob; (approximate) ungefähr; n (grass) unebene(r) Boden m; (person) Rowdy m, Rohling m; **to** ~ **it** primitiv leben; **to play** ~ (Sport) hart spielen; **to sleep** ~ im Freien schlafen; ~ **out** vt entwerfen, flüchtig skizzieren; ~**en** vt aufrauhen; ~**ly** ad grob; (about) ungefähr; ~**ness** Rauheit f; (of manner) Ungeschliffenheit f.

roulette [ru:'let] n Roulette nt.

round [raund] a rund; figures abgerundet, aufgerundet; ad (in a circle) rundherum; prep um ... herum; n Runde f; (of ammunition) Magazin nt; (song) Kanon m; **theatre in the** ~ Rundtheater nt; vt corner biegen um; ~ **off** vt abrunden; ~ **up** vt (end) abschließen; figures aufrunden; ~ **of**

applause Beifall m; ~**about** n (traffic) Kreisverkehr m; (merry-go-round) Karussell nt; a auf Umwegen; ~**ed** a gerundet; ~**ly** ad (fig) gründlich; ~**shouldered** a mit abfallenden Schultern; ~**sman** (general) Austräger m; (milk ~) Milchmann m; ~**up** Zusammentreiben nt, Sammeln nt.

rouse [rauz] vt (waken) (auf)wecken; (stir up) erregen.

rousing ['rauzɪŋ] a welcome stürmisch; speech zündend.

rout [raut] n wilde Flucht f; Überwältigung f; vt in die Flucht schlagen.

route [ru:t] n Weg m, Route f.

routine [ru:'ti:n] n Routine f; a Routine-.

rover ['rəuvə*] n Wanderer m.

roving ['rəuvɪŋ] a reporter im Außendienst.

row [rəu] n (line) Reihe f; vti boat rudern.

row [rau] n (noise) Lärm m, Krach m, Radau m; (dispute) Streit m; (scolding) Krach m; vi sich streiten.

rowboat ['rəubəut] n (US) Ruderboot nt.

rowdy ['raudɪ] a rüpelhaft; n (person) Rowdy m.

rowing ['rəuɪŋ] n Rudern nt; (Sport) Rudersport m; ~ **boat** Ruderboot nt.

rowlock ['rɒlək] n Rudergabel f.

royal ['rɔɪəl] a königlich, Königs-; ~**ist** n Royalist m; a königstreu; ~**ty** (family) königliche Familie f; (for invention) Patentgebühr f; (for book) Tantieme f.

rub [rʌb] n (problem) Haken m; **to give sb a** ~ etw (ab)reiben; vt reiben; ~ **off** vi (lit, fig) abfärben (on auf +acc); **to** ~ **it in** darauf herumreiten.

rubber ['rʌbə*] n Gummi m; (Brit) Radiergummi m; ~ **band** Gummiband nt; ~ **plant** Gummibaum m; ~**y** a gummiartig, wie Gummi.

rubbish ['rʌbɪʃ] n (waste) Abfall m; (nonsense) Blödsinn m, Quatsch m; ~ **dump** Müllabladeplatz m.

rubble ['rʌbl] n (Stein)schutt m.

ruby ['ru:bɪ] n Rubin m; a rubinrot.

rucksack ['rʌksæk] n Rucksack m.

rudder ['rʌdə*] n Steuerruder nt.

ruddy ['rʌdɪ] a (colour) rötlich; (col: bloody) verdammt.

rude a, ~**ly** [ru:d, -lɪ] unhöflich, unverschämt; shock hart; awakening unsanft; (unrefined, rough) grob; ~**ness** Unhöflichkeit f, Unverschämtheit f; Grobheit f.

rudiment ['ru:dɪmənt] n Grundlage f; ~**ary** [ru:dɪ'mentərɪ] a rudimentär.

ruff [rʌf] n Halskrause f.

ruffian ['rʌfɪən] n Rohling m.

ruffle ['rʌfl] vt kräuseln; durcheinanderbringen.

rug [rʌg] n Brücke f; (in bedroom) Bettvorleger m; (for knees) (Reise)decke f.

rugged ['rʌgɪd] a coastline zerklüftet; features markig.

ruin ['ru:ɪn] n Ruine f; (downfall) Ruin m; vt ruinieren; ~**s** pl Trümmer pl; ~**ation** Zerstörung f, Ruinierung f; ~**ous** a ruinierend.

rule [ru:l] n Regel f; (government) Herrschaft f, Regierung f; (for measuring) Lineal nt; vti (govern) herrschen über (+acc), regieren; (decide) anordnen, entscheiden; (make lines) linieren; **as a ~ in** der Regel; **~d** a paper liniert; **~r** Lineal nt; Herrscher m.

ruling ['ru:liŋ] a party Regierungs-; class herrschend.

rum [rʌm] n Rum m; a (col) komisch.

rumble ['rʌmbl] n Rumpeln nt; (of thunder) Rollen nt; vi rumpeln; grollen.

ruminate ['ru:mineit] vi grübeln; (cows) wiederkäuen.

rummage ['rʌmidʒ] n Durchsuchung f; vi durchstöbern.

rumour, (US) **rumor** ['ru:mə*] n Gerücht nt; vt: **it is ~ed** that man sagt or man munkelt, daß.

rump [rʌmp] n Hinterteil nt; (of fowl) Bürzel m; **~ steak** Rumpsteak nt.

rumpus ['rʌmpəs] n Spektakel m, Krach m.

run [rʌn] n Lauf m; (in car) (Spazier)fahrt f; (series) Serie f, Reihe f; (of play) Spielzeit f; (sudden demand) Ansturm m, starke Nachfrage f; (for animals) Auslauf m; (ski —) (Ski)abfahrt f; (in stocking) Laufmasche f; irreg vt (cause to run) laufen lassen; car, train, bus fahren; (pay for) unterhalten; race, distance laufen, rennen; (manage) leiten, verwalten, führen; knife stoßen m; (pass) hand, eye gleiten lassen; vi laufen; (move quickly also) rennen; (bus, train) fahren; (flow) fließen, laufen; (colours) (ab)färben; **on the ~** auf der Flucht; **in the long ~** auf die Dauer; **to ~ riot** Amok laufen; **to ~ a risk** ein Risiko eingehen; **~ about** vi (children) umherspringen; **~ across** vt (find) stoßen auf (+acc); **~ away** vi weglaufen; **~ down** vi (clock) ablaufen; vt (with car) überfahren; (talk against) heruntermachen; **to be ~ down** erschöpft or abgespannt sein; **to ~ for president** für die Präsidentschaft kandidieren; **~ off** vi fortlaufen; **~ out** vi (person) hinausrennen; (liquid) auslaufen; (lease) ablaufen; (money) ausgehen; **he ran out of money/petrol** ihm ging das Geld/Benzin aus; **~ over** vt (in accident) überfahren; (read quickly) überfliegen; **~ through** vt instructions durchgehen; **~ up** vt debt, bill machen; **~ up against** vt difficulties stoßen auf (+acc); **~about** (small car) kleine(r) Flitzer m; **~away** a horse ausgebrochen; person flüchtig.

rung [rʌŋ] n Sprosse f.

runner ['rʌnə*] n Läufer(in f) m; (messenger) Bote m; (for sleigh) Kufe f; **~-up** Zweite(r) mf.

running ['rʌniŋ] n (of business) Leitung f; (of machine) Laufen nt, Betrieb m; a water fließend; commentary laufend; **3 days ~ 3** Tage lang or hintereinander.

run-of-the-mill ['rʌnəvðə'mil] a gewöhnlich, alltäglich.

runny ['rʌni] a dünn.

runway ['rʌnwei] n Startbahn f, Landebahn f, Rollbahn f.

rupture ['rʌptʃə*] n (Med) Bruch m; vt: **o.s.** sich (dat) einen Bruch zuziehen.

rural ['ruərəl] a ländlich, Land-.

ruse [ru:z] n Kniff m, List f.

rush [rʌʃ] n Eile f, Hetze f; (Fin) starke Nachfrage f; vt (carry along) auf dem schnellsten Wege schaffen or transportieren; (attack) losstürmen auf (+acc); **don't ~ me** dräng mich nicht; vi (hurry) eilen, stürzen; **to ~ into sth** etw überstürzen; **~es** pl (Bot) Schilf(rohr) nt; **~ hour** Hauptverkehrszeit f.

rusk [rʌsk] n Zwieback m.

rust [rʌst] n Rost m; vi rosten.

rustic ['rʌstik] a bäuerlich, ländlich, Bauern-.

rustle ['rʌsl] n Rauschen nt, Rascheln nt; vi rauschen, rascheln; vt rascheln lassen; cattle stehlen.

rustproof ['rʌstpru:f] a nichtrostend, rostfrei.

rusty ['rʌsti] a rostig.

rut [rʌt] n (in track) Radspur f; (of deer) Brunst f; (fig) Trott m.

ruthless a, **~ly** ad ['ru:θləs, -li] erbarmungslos; rücksichtslos; **~ness** Unbarmherzigkeit f; Rücksichtslosigkeit f.

rye [rai] n Roggen m; **~ bread** Roggenbrot nt.

S

S, s [es] n S nt, s nt.

sabbath ['sæbəθ] n Sabbat m.

sabbatical [sə'bætikəl] a: **~ year** Beurlaubungs- or Forschungsjahr nt.

sabotage ['sæbətɑ:ʒ] n Sabotage f; vt sabotieren.

sabre, (US) **saber** ['seibə*] n Säbel m.

saccharin(e) ['sækərin] n Saccharin nt.

sachet ['sæʃei] n (of shampoo) Briefchen nt, Kissen nt.

sack [sæk] n Sack m; **to give sb the ~** (col) jdn hinauswerfen; vt (col) hinauswerfen; (pillage) plündern; **~ful** Sack(voll) m; **~ing** (material) Sackleinen nt; (col) Rausschmiß m.

sacrament ['sækrəmənt] n Sakrament nt.

sacred ['seikrid] a building, music etc geistlich, Kirchen-; altar, oath heilig.

sacrifice ['sækrifais] n Opfer nt; vt (lit, fig) opfern.

sacrilege ['sækrilidʒ] n Schändung f.

sacrosanct ['sækrəusæŋkt] a sakrosankt.

sad [sæd] a traurig; **~den** vt traurig machen, betrüben.

saddle ['sædl] n Sattel m; vt (burden) aufhalsen (sb with sth jdm etw); **~bag** Satteltasche f.

sadism ['seidizəm] n Sadismus m.

sadist ['seidist] n Sadist m; **~ic** [sə'distik] a sadistisch.

sadly ['sædli] ad betrübt, beklagenswert; (very) arg.

sadness ['sædnəs] n Traurigkeit f.

safari [sə'fɑ:ri] n Safari f.

safe [seif] a (free from danger) sicher; (careful) vorsichtig; **it's ~ to say** man kann ruhig behaupten; n Safe m, Tresor m, Geldschrank m; **~guard** n Sicherung f; vt sichern, schützen; **~keeping** sichere Verwahrung f; **~ly** ad sicher; arrive

wohlbehalten; ~ness Zuverlässigkeit f;
~ty Sicherheit f; ~ty belt Sicherheitsgurt m; ~ty curtain eiserne(r) Vorhang
m; ~ty first (slogan) Sicherheit geht vor;
~ty pin Sicherheitsnadel f.

sag [sæg] vi (durch)sacken, sich senken.

saga ['sɑːgə] n Sage f.

sage [seɪdʒ] n (herb) Salbei m; (man)
Weise(r) m.

Sagittarius [sadʒɪ'tɛərɪəs] n Schütze m.

sago ['seɪgəu] n Sago m.

said [sed] A besagt.

sail [seɪl] n Segel nt; (trip) Fahrt f; vt
segeln; vi segeln; mit dem Schiff fahren;
(begin voyage) (person) abfahren; (ship)
auslaufen; (fig: cloud etc) dahinsegeln;
~boat (US) Segelboot nt; ~ing Segeln
nt; to go ~ing segeln gehen; ~ing ship
Segelschiff nt; ~or Matrose m, Seemann
m.

saint [seɪnt] n Heilige(r) mf; ~liness
Heiligkeit f; ~ly a heilig, fromm.

sake [seɪk] n: for the ~ of um (+gen)
willen; for your ~ um deinetwillen,
deinetwegen, wegen dir.

salad ['sæləd] n Salat m; ~ cream
gewürzte Mayonnaise f; ~ dressing
Salatsoße f; ~ oil Speiseöl nt, Salatöl nt.

salami [sə'lɑːmɪ] n Salami f.

salaried ['sælərɪd] a: ~ staff
Gehaltsempfänger pl.

salary ['sælərɪ] n Gehalt nt.

sale [seɪl] n Verkauf m; (reduced prices)
Schlußverkauf m; ~room Verkaufsraum
m; ~sman Verkäufer m; (representative)
Vertreter m; ~smanship Geschäfts-
tüchtigkeit f; ~swoman Verkäuferin f.

salient ['seɪlɪənt] a hervorspringend,
bemerkenswert.

saliva [sə'laɪvə] n Speichel m.

sallow ['sæləu] a fahl; face bleich.

salmon ['sæmən] n Lachs m.

salon ['sælɔ̃ːŋ] n Salon m.

saloon [sə'luːn] n (Aut) Limousine f; (ship's
lounge) Salon m.

salt [sɔːlt] n Salz nt; vt (cure) einsalzen;
(flavour) salzen; ~cellar Salzfaß nt; ~
mine Salzbergwerk nt; ~y a salzig.

salubrious [sə'luːbrɪəs] a gesund; district
etc ersprießlich.

salutary ['sæljutərɪ] a gesund, heilsam.

salute [sə'luːt] n (Mil) Gruß m, Salut m;
(with guns) Salutschüsse pl; vt (Mil)
salutieren.

salvage ['sælvɪdʒ] n (from ship) Bergung f;
(property) Rettung f; vt bergen; retten.

salvation [sæl'veɪʃən] n Rettung f; S~
Army Heilsarmee f.

salver ['sælvə*] n Tablett nt.

salvo ['sælvəu] n Salve f.

same [seɪm] a (similar) gleiche(r,s);
(identical) derselbe/dieselbe/ dasselbe; all
or just the ~ trotzdem; it's all the ~ to
me das ist mir egal; they all look the ~
to me für mich sehen sie alle gleich aus;
the ~ to you gleichfalls; at the ~ time
zur gleichen Zeit, gleichzeitig; (however)
zugleich, andererseits.

sampan ['sæmpæn] n Sampan m.

sample ['sɑːmpl] n (specimen) Probe f;
(example of sth) Muster nt, Probe f; vt
probieren.

sanatorium [sænə'tɔːrɪəm] n Sanatorium
nt.

sanctify ['sæŋktɪfaɪ] vt weihen.

sanctimonious [sæŋktɪ'məunɪəs] a
scheinheilig.

sanction ['sæŋkʃən] n Sanktion f.

sanctity ['sæŋktɪtɪ] n Heiligkeit f; (fig)
Unverletzlichkeit f.

sanctuary ['sæŋktjuərɪ] n Heiligtum nt;
(for fugitive) Asyl nt; (refuge) Zufluchtsort
m; (for animals) Naturpark m, Schutzgebiet nt.

sand [sænd] n Sand m; vt mit Sand
bestreuen; furniture schmirgeln; ~s pl
Sand m.

sandal ['sændl] n Sandale f.

sandbag ['sændbæg] n Sandsack m.

sand dune ['sænddjuːn] n (Sand)düne f.

sandpaper ['sændpeɪpə*] n Sandpapier nt.

sandpit ['sændpɪt] n Sandkasten m.

sandstone ['sændstəun] n Sandstein m.

sandwich ['sænwɪdʒ] n Sandwich m or nt;
vt einklemmen.

sandy ['sændɪ] a sandig, Sand-; (colour)
sandfarben; hair rotblond.

sane [seɪn] a geistig gesund or normal;
(sensible) vernünftig, gescheit.

sanguine ['sæŋgwɪn] a (hopeful) zuver-
sichtlich.

sanitarium [sænɪ'tɛərɪəm] n (US) =
sanatorium.

sanitary ['sænɪtərɪ] a hygienisch (ein-
wandfrei); (against dirt) hygienisch,
Gesundheits-; ~ napkin (US), ~ towel
(Monats)binde f.

sanitation [sænɪ'teɪʃən] n sanitäre
Einrichtungen pl; Gesundheitswesen nt.

sanity ['sænɪtɪ] n geistige Gesundheit f;
(good sense) gesunde(r) Verstand m,
Vernunft f.

Santa Claus [sæntə'klɔːz] n Nikolaus m,
Weihnachtsmann m.

sap [sæp] n (of plants) Saft m; vt strength
schwächen; health untergraben.

sapling ['sæplɪŋ] n junge(r) Baum m.

sapphire ['sæfaɪə*] n Saphir m.

sarcasm ['sɑːkæzm] n Sarkasmus m.

sarcastic [sɑː'kæstɪk] a sarkastisch.

sarcophagus [sɑː'kɒfəgəs] n Sarkophag m.

sardine [sɑː'diːn] n Sardine f.

sardonic [sɑː'dɒnɪk] a zynisch.

sari ['sɑːrɪ] n Sari m.

sash [sæʃ] n Schärpe f.

Satan ['seɪtn] n Satan m, Teufel m; s~ic
[sə'tænɪk] a satanisch, teuflisch.

satchel ['sætʃəl] n (Sch) Schulranzen m,
Schulmappe f.

satellite ['sætəlaɪt] n Satellit m; (fig)
Trabant m; a Satelliten-.

satin ['sætɪn] n Satin m; a Satin-.

satire ['sætaɪə*] n Satire f.

satirical [sə'tɪrɪkəl] a satirisch.

satirize ['sætəraɪz] vt (durch Satire) verspotten.

satisfaction [sætɪs'fækʃən] n Befriedigung
f, Genugtuung f.

satisfactorily [sætɪsˈfæktərɪlɪ] *ad* zufriedenstellend.

satisfactory [sætɪsˈfæktərɪ] *a* zufriedenstellend, befriedigend.

satisfy [ˈsætɪsfaɪ] *vt* befriedigen, zufriedenstellen; (*convince*) überzeugen; *conditions* erfüllen; ∼**ing** *a* befriedigend; *meal* sättigend.

saturate [ˈsætʃəreɪt] *vt* (durch)tränken.

saturation [sætʃəˈreɪʃən] *n* Durchtränkung *f*; (*Chem, fig*) Sättigung *f*.

Saturday [ˈsætədeɪ] *n* Samstag *m*, Sonnabend *m*.

sauce [sɔːs] *n* Soße *f*, Sauce *f*; ∼**pan** Kasserolle *f*; ∼**r** Untertasse *f*.

saucily [ˈsɔːsɪlɪ] *ad* frech.

sauciness [ˈsɔːsɪnəs] *n* Frechheit *f*.

saucy [ˈsɔːsɪ] *a* frech, keck.

sauna [ˈsɔːnə] *n* Sauna *f*.

saunter [ˈsɔːntə*] *vi* schlendern; *n* Schlendern *nt*.

sausage [ˈsɒsɪdʒ] *n* Wurst *f*; ∼ **roll** Wurst *f* im Schlafrock, Wurstpastete *f*.

savage [ˈsævɪdʒ] *a* (*fierce*) wild, brutal, grausam; (*uncivilized*) wild, primitiv; *n* Wilde(r) *mf*; *vt* (*animals*) zerfleischen; ∼**ly** *ad* grausam; ∼**ry** Roheit *f*, Grausamkeit *f*.

save [seɪv] *vt* retten; *money, electricity etc* sparen; *strength etc* aufsparen; **to ∼ you the trouble** um dir Mühe zu ersparen; *n* (*Sport*) (Ball)abwehr *f*; *prep, cj* außer, ausgenommen.

saving [ˈseɪvɪŋ] *a* rettend; *n* Sparen *nt*, Ersparnis *f*; ∼**s** *pl* Ersparnisse *pl*; ∼**s bank** Sparkasse *f*.

saviour [ˈseɪvjə*] *n* Retter *m*; (*Eccl*) Heiland *m*, Erlöser *m*.

savoir-faire [ˈsævwɑːˈfɛə*] *n* Gewandtheit *f*.

savour, (*US*) **savor** [ˈseɪvə*] *n* Wohlgeschmack *m*; *vt* (*taste*) schmecken; (*fig*) genießen; *vi* schmecken (*of* nach), riechen (*of* nach); ∼**y** *a* schmackhaft; *food* pikant, würzig.

savvy [ˈsævɪ] *n* (*col*) Grips *m*.

saw [sɔː] *n* (*tool*) Säge *f*; *vti irreg* sägen; ∼**dust** Sägemehl *nt*; ∼**mill** Sägewerk *nt*.

saxophone [ˈsæksəfəʊn] *n* Saxophon *nt*.

say [seɪ] *n* Meinung *f*; (*right*) Mitspracherecht *nt*; **to have no/a ∼ in sth** (kein) Mitspracherecht bei etw haben; **let him have his ∼** laß ihn doch reden; *vti irreg* sagen; **I couldn't ∼** schwer zu sagen; **how old would you ∼ he is?** wie alt schätzt du ihn?; **you don't ∼!** was du nicht sagst!; **don't ∼ you forgot** sag bloß nicht, daß du es vergessen hast; **there are,** ∼**, 50** es sind, sagen wir mal, 50. . .; **that is to ∼** das heißt; (*more precisely*) beziehungsweise, mit anderen Worten; **to ∼ nothing of . . .** ganz zu schweigen von. . .; ∼**ing** Sprichwort *nt*; ∼**-so** (*col*) Ja *nt*, Zustimmung *f*.

scab [skæb] *n* Schorf *m*; (*of sheep*) Räude *f*; (*pej*) Streikbrecher *m*.

scabby [ˈskæbɪ] *a* *sheep* räudig; *skin* schorfig.

scaffold [ˈskæfəʊld] *n* (*for execution*) Schafott *nt*; ∼**ing** (Bau)gerüst *nt*.

scald [skɔːld] *n* Verbrühung *f*; *vt* (*burn*) verbrühen; (*clean*) (ab)brühen; ∼**ing** *a* brühheiß.

scale [skeɪl] *n* (*of fish*) Schuppe *f*; (*Mus*) Tonleiter *f*; (*dish for measuring*) Waagschale *f*; (*on map, size*) Maßstab *m*; (*gradation*) Skala *f*; *vt* (*climb*) erklimmen; ∼**s** *pl* (*balance*) Waage *f*; **on a large ∼** (*fig*) im großen, in großem Umfang; ∼ **drawing** maßstabgerechte Zeichnung *f*.

scallop [ˈskɒləp] *n* Kammuschel *f*.

scalp [skælp] *n* Kopfhaut *f*; *vt* skalpieren.

scalpel [ˈskælpəl] *n* Skalpell *nt*.

scamp [skæmp] *vt* schlud(e)rig machen, hinschlampen.

scamper [ˈskæmpə*] *vi* huschen.

scan [skæn] *vt* (*examine*) genau prüfen; (*quickly*) überfliegen; *horizon* absuchen; *poetry* skandieren.

scandal [ˈskændl] *n* (*disgrace*) Skandal *m*; (*gossip*) böswillige(r) Klatsch *m*; ∼**ize** *vt* schockieren; ∼**ous** *a* skandalös, schockierend.

scant [skænt] *a* knapp; ∼**ily** *ad* knapp, dürftig; ∼**iness** Knappheit *f*; ∼**y** *a* knapp, unzureichend.

scapegoat [ˈskeɪpgəʊt] *n* Sündenbock *m*.

scar [skɑː*] *n* Narbe *f*; *vt* durch Narben entstellen.

scarce [skɛəs] *a* selten, rar; *goods* knapp; ∼**ly** *ad* kaum; ∼**ness** Seltenheit *f*.

scarcity [ˈskɛəsɪtɪ] *n* Mangel *m*, Knappheit *f*.

scare [ˈskɛə*] *n* Schrecken *m*, Panik *f*; *vt* erschrecken; ängstigen; **to be ∼d** Angst haben; ∼**crow** Vogelscheuche *f*; ∼**monger** Bangemacher *m*.

scarf [skɑːf] *n* Schal *m*; (*on head*) Kopftuch *nt*.

scarlet [ˈskɑːlət] *a* scharlachrot; *n* Scharlachrot *nt*; ∼ **fever** Scharlach *m*.

scarred [skɑːd] *a* narbig.

scary [ˈskɛərɪ] *a* (*col*) schaurig.

scathing [ˈskeɪðɪŋ] *a* scharf, vernichtend.

scatter [ˈskætə*] *n* Streuung *f*; *vt* (*sprinkle*) (ver)streuen; (*disperse*) zerstreuen; *vi* sich zerstreuen; ∼**brained** *a* flatterhaft, schusselig; ∼**ing (of)** ein paar.

scavenger [ˈskævɪndʒə*] *n* (*animal*) Aasfresser *m*.

scene [siːn] *n* (*of happening*) Ort *m*; (*of play, incident*) Szene *f*; (*canvas etc*) Bühnenbild *nt*; (*view*) Anblick *m*; (*argument*) Szene *f*, Auftritt *m*; **on the ∼** am Ort, dabei; **behind the ∼s** hinter den Kulissen; ∼**ry** [ˈsiːnərɪ] (*Theat*) Bühnenbild *nt*; (*landscape*) Landschaft *f*.

scenic [ˈsiːnɪk] *a* landschaftlich, Landschafts-.

scent [sent] *n* Parfüm *nt*; (*smell*) Duft *m*; (*sense*) Geruchsinn *m*; *vt* parfümieren.

sceptic [ˈskeptɪk] *n* Skeptiker *m*; ∼**al** *a* skeptisch; ∼**ism** [ˈskeptɪsɪzəm] Skepsis *f*.

sceptre, (*US*) **scepter** [ˈseptə*] *n* Szepter *nt*.

schedule [ˈʃedjuːl] *n* (*list*) Liste *f*, Tabelle *f*; (*plan*) Programm *nt*; *vt*: **it is ∼d for 2** es soll um 2 abfahren/stattfinden *etc*; **on ∼** pünktlich, fahrplanmäßig; **behind ∼** mit Verspätung.

scheme 346 **scrupulous**

scheme [ski:m] n Schema nt; (dishonest) Intrige f; (plan of action) Plan m, Programm nt; vi sich verschwören, intrigieren; vt planen.

scheming ['ski:mɪŋ] a intrigierend, ränkevoll.

schism ['skɪzəm] n Spaltung f; (Eccl) Schisma nt, Kirchenspaltung f.

schizophrenic [skɪtsəʊ'frenɪk] a schizophren.

scholar ['skɔlə*] n Gelehrte(r) m; (holding scholarship) Stipendiat m; ~ly a gelehrt; ~ship Gelehrsamkeit f, Belesenheit f; (grant) Stipendium nt.

school [sku:l] n Schule f; (Univ) Fakultät f; vt schulen; dog trainieren; ~book Schulbuch nt; ~boy Schüler m, Schuljunge m; ~days pl (alte) Schulzeit f; ~girl Schülerin f, Schulmädchen nt; ~ing Schulung f, Ausbildung · f; ~master Lehrer m; ~mistress Lehrerin f; ~room Klassenzimmer nt; ~teacher Lehrer(in f) m.

schooner ['sku:nə*] n Schoner m; (glass) große(s) Sherryglas nt.

sciatica [saɪ'ætɪkə] n Ischias m or nt.

science ['saɪəns] n Wissenschaft f; (natural —) Naturwissenschaft f; ~ fiction Science-fiction f.

scientific [saɪən'tɪfɪk] a wissenschaftlich; (natural sciences) naturwissenschaftlich.

scientist ['saɪəntɪst] n Wissenschaftler(in f) m.

scintillating ['sɪntɪleɪtɪŋ] a sprühend.

scissors ['sɪzəz] npl Schere f; a pair of ~ eine Schere.

scoff [skɔf] vt (eat) fressen; vi (mock) spotten (at über +acc).

scold [skəʊld] vt schimpfen.

scone [skɔn] n weiche(s) Teegebäck nt.

scoop [sku:p] n Schaufel f; (news) sensationelle Erstmeldung f; vt (also ~ out or up) schaufeln.

scooter ['sku:tə*] n Motorroller m; (child's) Roller m.

scope [skəʊp] n Ausmaß nt; (opportunity) (Spiel)raum m, Bewegungsfreiheit f.

scorch [skɔːtʃ] n Brandstelle f; vt versengen, verbrennen; ~er (col) heiße(r) Tag m; ~ing a brennend, glühend.

score [skɔː*] n (in game) Punktzahl f; (Spiel)ergebnis nt; (Mus) Partitur f; (line) Kratzer m; (twenty) 20, 20 Stück; on that ~ in dieser Hinsicht; what's the ~? wie steht's?; vt (goal) schießen; points machen; (mark) einkerben; zerkratzen, einritzen; vi (keep record) Punkte zählen; ~board Anschreibetafel f, ~card (Sport) Punktliste f; ~r Torschütze m; (recorder) (Auf)schreiber m.

scorn ['skɔːn] n Verachtung f; vt verhöhnen; ~ful a, ~fully ad höhnisch, verächtlich.

Scorpio ['skɔːpɪəʊ] n Skorpion m.

scorpion ['skɔːpɪən] n Skorpion m.

scotch [skɔtʃ] vt (end) unterbinden.

scoundrel ['skaʊndrəl] n Schurke m, Schuft m.

scour ['skaʊə*] vt (search) absuchen;

(clean) schrubben; ~er Topfkratzer m.

scourge [skɜːdʒ] n (whip) Geißel f; (plague) Qual f.

scout [skaʊt] n (Mil) Späher m, Aufklärer m; vi (reconnoitre) auskundschaften; see boy.

scowl [skaʊl] n finstere(r) Blick m; vi finster blicken.

scraggy ['skrægɪ] a dürr, hager.

scram [skræm] vi (col) verschwinden, abhauen.

scramble ['skræmbl] n (climb) Kletterei f; (struggle) Kampf m; vi klettern; (fight) sich schlagen; ~d eggs pl Rührei nt.

scrap [skræp] n (bit) Stückchen nt; (fight) Keilerei f; a Abfall-; vt verwerfen; vi (fight) streiten, sich prügeln; ~book Einklebealbum nt; ~s pl (waste) Abfall m.

scrape [skreɪp] n Kratzen nt; (trouble) Klemme f; vt kratzen; car zerkratzen; (clean) abkratzen; vi (make harsh noise) kratzen; ~r Kratzer m.

scrap heap ['skræphi:p] n Abfallhaufen m; (for metal) Schrotthaufen m.

scrap iron ['skræp'aɪən] n Schrott m.

scrappy ['skræpɪ] a zusammengestoppelt.

scratch ['skrætʃ] n (wound) Kratzer m, Schramme f; to start from ~ ganz von vorne anfangen; a (improvised) zusammengewürfelt; vt kratzen; car zerkratzen; vi (sich) kratzen.

scrawl [skrɔːl] n Gekritzel nt; vti kritzeln.

scream [skri:m] n Schrei m; vi schreien.

scree ['skri:] n Geröll(halde f) nt.

screech [skri:tʃ] n Schrei m; vi kreischen.

screen [skri:n] n (protective) Schutzschirm m; (film) Leinwand f; (TV) Bildschirm m; (against insects) Fliegengitter nt; (Eccl) Lettner m; vt (shelter) (be)schirmen; film zeigen, vorführen.

screw [skru:] n Schraube f; (Naut) Schiffsschraube f; vt (fasten) schrauben; (vulgar) bumsen; to ~ money out of sb (col) jdm das Geld aus der Tasche ziehen; ~driver Schraubenzieher m; ~y a (col) verrückt.

scribble ['skrɪbl] n Gekritzel nt; vt kritzeln.

scribe [skraɪb] n Schreiber m; (Jewish) Schriftgelehrte(r) m.

script [skrɪpt] n (handwriting) Handschrift f; (for film) Drehbuch nt; (Theat) Manuskript nt, Text m.

Scripture ['skrɪptʃə*] n Heilige Schrift f.

scriptwriter ['skrɪptraɪtə*] n Textverfasser m.

scroll [skrəʊl] n Schriftrolle f.

scrounge [skraʊndʒ] vt schnorren; n: on the ~ beim Schnorren.

scrub [skrʌb] n (clean) Schrubben nt; (in countryside) Gestrüpp nt; vt (clean) schrubben; (reject) fallenlassen.

scruff [skrʌf] n Genick nt, Kragen m; ~y a unordentlich, vergammelt.

scrum(mage) ['skrʌm(ɪdʒ)] n Getümmel nt.

scruple ['skru:pl] n Skrupel m, Bedenken nt.

scrupulous a, ~ly ad ['skru:pjʊləs, -lɪ] peinlich genau, gewissenhaft.

scrutinize ['skru:tinaiz] vt genau prüfen or untersuchen.

scrutiny ['skru:tini] n genaue Untersuchung f.

scuff [skʌf] vt shoes abstoßen.

scuffle ['skʌfl] n Handgemenge nt.

scullery ['skʌlərɪ] n Spülküche f; Abstellraum m.

sculptor ['skʌlptə*] n Bildhauer m.

sculpture ['skʌlptʃə*] n (art) Bildhauerei f; (statue) Skulptur f.

scum [skʌm] n (lit, fig) Abschaum m.

scurrilous ['skʌrɪləs] a unflätig.

scurry ['skʌrɪ] vi huschen.

scurvy ['skɜːvɪ] n Skorbut m.

scuttle ['skʌtl] n Kohleneimer m; vt ship versenken; vi (scamper) (+ away, off) sich davonmachen.

scythe [saɪð] n Sense f.

sea [si:] n Meer nt (also fig), See f; a Meeres-, See-; ~ **bird** Meervogel m; ~**board** Küste f; ~ **breeze** Seewind m; ~**dog** Seebär m; ~**farer** Seefahrer m; ~**faring** a seefahrend; ~**food** Meeresfrüchte pl; ~**front** Strandpromenade f; ~**going** a seetüchtig, Hochsee-; ~**gull** Möwe f.

seal [si:l] n (animal) Robbe f, Seehund m; (stamp, impression) Siegel nt; vt versiegeln.

sea level ['si:levl] n Meeresspiegel m.

sealing wax ['si:lɪŋwæks] n Siegellack m.

sea lion ['si:laɪən] n Seelöwe m.

seam [si:m] n Saum m; (edges joining) Naht f; (layer) Schicht f; (of coal) Flöz nt.

seaman ['si:mən] n Seemann m.

seamless ['si:mlɪs] a nahtlos.

seamy ['si:mɪ] a people, café zwielichtig; life anrüchig; ~ **side of life** dunkle Seite f des Lebens.

seaport ['si:pɔ:t] n Seehafen m, Hafenstadt f.

search [sɜːtʃ] n Suche f (for nach); vi suchen; vt (examine) durchsuchen; ~**ing** a look forschend, durchdringend; ~**light** Scheinwerfer m; ~ **party** Suchmannschaft f.

seashore ['si:ʃɔ:*] n Meeresküste f.

seasick ['si:sɪk] a seekrank; ~**ness** Seekrankheit f.

seaside ['si:saɪd] n Küste f; **at the** ~ an der See; **to go to the** ~ an die See fahren.

season ['si:zn] n Jahreszeit f; (eg Christmas) Zeit f, Saison f; vt (flavour) würzen; ~**al** a Saison-; ~**ing** Gewürz nt, Würze f; ~ **ticket** (Rail) Zeitkarte f; (Theat) Abonnement nt.

seat [si:t] n Sitz m, Platz m; (in Parliament) Sitz m; (part of body) Gesäß nt; (part of garment) Sitzfläche f, Hosenboden m; vt (place) setzen; (have space for) Sitzplätze bieten für; ~ **belt** Sicherheitsgurt m; ~**ing** Anweisen m von Sitzplätzen.

sea water ['si:wɔ:tə*] n Meerwasser nt, Seewasser nt.

seaweed ['si:wi:d] n (See)tang m, Alge f.

seaworthy ['si:wɜ:ðɪ] a seetüchtig.

secede [sɪ'si:d] vi sich lossagen.

secluded [sɪ'klu:dɪd] a abgelegen, ruhig.

seclusion [sɪ'klu:ʒən] n Zurückgezogenheit f.

second ['sekənd] a zweite(r,s); ad (in — position) an zweiter Stelle; (Rail) zweite(r) Klasse; n Sekunde f; (person) Zweite(r) m; (Comm: imperfect) zweite Wahl f; (Sport) Sekundant m; vt (support) unterstützen; ~**ary** a zweitrangig; ~**ary education** Sekundarstufe f; ~**ary school** höhere Schule f, Mittelschule f; ~**er** Unterstützer m; ~**hand** a aus zweiter Hand; car etc gebraucht; ~**ly** ad zweitens; **it is** ~ **nature to him** es ist ihm zur zweiten Natur geworden; ~**rate** a mittelmäßig; **to have** ~ **thoughts** es sich (dat) anders überlegen.

secrecy ['si:krəsɪ] n Geheimhaltung f.

secret ['si:krət] n Geheimnis nt; a geheim, heimlich, Geheim-; **in** ~ geheim, heimlich.

secretarial [sekrə'tɛərɪəl] a Sekretärs-.

secretariat [sekrə'tɛərɪət] n Sekretariat nt.

secretary ['sekrətrɪ] n Sekretär(in f) m; (government) Staatssekretär(in f) m; Minister m.

secretive ['si:krətɪv] a geheimtuerisch.

secretly ['si:krətlɪ] ad heimlich.

sect [sekt] n Sekte f; ~**arian** [sek'tɛərɪən] a (belonging to a sect) Sekten-.

section ['sekʃən] n Teil m, Ausschnitt m; (department) Abteilung f; (of document) Abschnitt m, Paragraph m; ~**al** a (regional) partikularistisch.

sector ['sektə*] n Sektor m.

secular ['sekjulə*] a weltlich, profan.

secure [sɪ'kjuə*] a (safe) sicher; (firmly fixed) fest; vt (make firm) befestigen, sichern; (obtain) sichern; ~**ly** ad sicher, fest.

security [sɪ'kjuərɪtɪ] n Sicherheit f; (pledge) Pfand nt; (document) Sicherheiten pl; (national —) Staatssicherheit f; ~ **guard** Sicherheitsbeamte(r) m; see **social**.

sedate [sɪ'deɪt] a (calm) gelassen; (serious) gesetzt; vt (Med) ein Beruhigungsmittel geben (+dat).

sedation [sɪ'deɪʃən] n (Med) Einfluß m von Beruhigungsmitteln.

sedative ['sedətɪv] n Beruhigungsmittel nt; a beruhigend, einschläfernd.

sedentary ['sedntrɪ] a job sitzend.

sediment ['sedɪmənt] n (Boden)satz m; ~**ary** [sedɪ'mentərɪ] a (Geol) Sediment-.

seduce [sɪ'dju:s] vt verführen.

seduction [sɪ'dʌkʃən] n Verführung f.

seductive [sɪ'dʌktɪv] a verführerisch.

see [si:] irreg vt sehen; (understand) (ein)-sehen, erkennen; (find out) sehen, herausfinden; (make sure) dafür sorgen (daß); (accompany) begleiten, bringen; (visit) besuchen; **to** ~ **a doctor** zum Arzt gehen; vi (be aware) sehen; (find out) nachsehen; **I** ~ ach so, ich verstehe; **let me** ~ warte mal; **we'll** ~ werden (mal) sehen; n (Eccl) (R.C.) Bistum nt; (Protestant) Kirchenkreis m; **to** ~ **sth through** etw durchfechten; **to** ~ **through sb/sth** jdn/etw durchschauen; **to** ~ **to it** dafür sorgen; **to** ~ **sb off** jdn zum Zug etc begleiten.

seed [si:d] *n* Samen *m*, (Samen)korn *nt*; *vt* (*Tennis*) plazieren; ~**ling** Setzling *m*; ~**y** *a* (*ill*) flau, angeschlagen; *clothes* schäbig; *person* zweifelhaft.

seeing ['si:ɪŋ] *cj* da.

seek [si:k] *vt irreg* suchen.

seem [si:m] *vi* scheinen; ~**ingly** *ad* anscheinend; ~**ly** *a* geziemend.

seep [si:p] *vi* sickern.

seer [sɪə*] *n* Seher *m*.

seesaw ['si:sɔ:] *n* Wippe *f*.

seethe [si:ð] *vi* kochen; (*with crowds*) wimmeln von.

see-through ['si:θru:] *a dress* durchsichtig.

segment ['segmənt] *n* Teil *m*; (*of circle*) Ausschnitt *m*.

segregate ['segrɪgeɪt] *vt* trennen, absondern.

segregation [segrɪ'geɪʃən] *n* Rassentrennung *f*.

seismic ['saɪzmɪk] *a* seismisch, Erdbeben-.

seize [si:z] *vt* (*grasp*) (er)greifen, packen; *power* ergreifen; (*take legally*) beschlagnahmen; *point* erfassen, begreifen; ~ **up** *vi* (*Tech*) sich festfressen.

seizure ['si:ʒə*] *n* (*illness*) Anfall *m*.

seldom ['seldəm] *ad* selten.

select [sɪ'lekt] *a* ausgewählt; *vt* auswählen; ~**ion** [sɪ'lekʃən] Auswahl *f*; ~**ive** *a person* wählerisch.

self [self] *n* Selbst *nt*, Ich *nt*; ~**adhesive** *a* selbstklebend; ~**appointed** *a* selbsternannt; ~**assurance** Selbstsicherheit *f*; ~**assured** *a* selbstbewußt; ~**coloured**, (*US*) ~**colored** *a* einfarbig; ~**confidence** Selbstvertrauen *nt*, Selbstbewußtsein *nt*; ~**confident** *a* selbstsicher; ~**conscious** *a* gehemmt, befangen; ~**contained** *a* (*complete*) (in sich) geschlossen; *person* verschlossen; ~**defeating** *a*: to be ~**defeating** ein Widerspruch in sich sein; ~**defence** Selbstverteidigung *f*; (*Jur*) Notwehr *f*; ~**employed** *a* frei(schaffend); ~**evident** *a* offensichtlich; ~**explanatory** *a* für sich (selbst) sprechend; ~**indulgent** *a* zügellos; ~**interest** Eigennutz *m*; ~**ish** *a*, ~**ishly** *ad* egoistisch, selbstsüchtig; ~**ishness** Egoismus *m*, Selbstsucht *f*; ~**lessly** *ad* selbstlos; ~**made** *a* selbstgemacht; ~**pity** Selbstmitleid *nt*; ~**portrait** Selbstbildnis *nt*; ~**propelled** *a* mit Eigenantrieb; ~**reliant** *a* unabhängig; ~**respect** Selbstachtung *f*; ~**respecting** *a* mit Selbstachtung; ~**righteous** *a* selbstgerecht; ~**satisfied** *a* selbstzufrieden; ~**service** *a* Selbstbedienungs-; ~**sufficient** *a* selbstgenügsam; ~**supporting** *a* (*Fin*) Eigenfinanzierungs-; *person* eigenständig.

sell [sel] *irreg vt* verkaufen; *vi* verkaufen; (*goods*) sich verkaufen (lassen); ~**er** Verkäufer *m*; ~**ing price** Verkaufspreis *m*.

semantic [sɪ'mæntɪk] *a* semantisch; ~**s** Semantik *f*.

semaphore ['seməfɔ:*] *n* Winkzeichen *pl*.

semi ['semɪ] *n* = ~**detached house**;

~**circle** Halbkreis *m*; ~**colon** Semikolon *nt*; ~**conscious** *a* halbbewußt; ~**detached house** Zweifamilienhaus *nt*, Doppelhaus *nt*; ~**final** Halbfinale *nt*.

seminar ['semɪnɑ:*] *n* Seminar *nt*.

semiquaver ['semɪkweɪvə*] *n* Sechzehntel *nt*.

semiskilled ['semɪ'skɪld] *a* angelernt.

semitone ['semɪtəun] *n* Halbton *m*.

semolina [semə'li:nə] *n* Grieß *m*.

senate ['senət] *n* Senat *m*.

senator ['senətə*] *n* Senator *m*.

send [send] *vt irreg* senden, schicken; (*col: inspire*) hinreißen; ~ **away** *vt* wegschicken; ~ **away for** *vt* holen lassen; ~ **back** *vt* zurückschicken; ~ **for** *vt* holen lassen; ~ **off** *vt goods* abschicken; *player* vom Feld schicken; ~ **out** *vt invitation* aussenden; ~ **up** *vt* hinaufsenden; (*col*) verulken; ~**er** Absender *m*; ~**off** Verabschiedung *f*; ~**up** (*col*) Verulkung *f*.

senile ['si:naɪl] *a* senil, Alters-.

senility [sɪ'nɪlɪtɪ] *n* Altersschwachheit *f*.

senior ['si:nɪə*] *a* (*older*) älter; (*higher rank*) Ober-; *n* (*older person*) Altere(r) *m*; (*higher ranking*) Rangälteste(r) *m*; ~**ity** [si:nɪ'ɒrɪtɪ] (*of age*) höhere(s) Alter *nt*; (*in rank*) höhere(r) Dienstgrad *m*.

sensation [sen'seɪʃən] *n* Empfindung *f*, Gefühl *nt*; (*excitement*) Sensation *f*, Aufsehen *nt*; ~**al** *a* sensationell, Sensations-.

sense [sens] *n* Sinn *m*; (*understanding*) Verstand *m*, Vernunft *f*; (*meaning*) Sinn *m*, Bedeutung *f*; (*feeling*) Gefühl *nt*; **to make** ~ Sinn ergeben; *vt* fühlen, spüren; ~**less** *a* sinnlos; (*unconscious*) besinnungslos; ~**lessly** *ad* (*stupidly*) sinnlos.

sensibility [sensɪ'bɪlɪtɪ] *n* Empfindsamkeit *f*; (*feeling hurt*) Empfindlichkeit *f*.

sensible *a*, **sensibly** *ad* ['sensəbl, -blɪ] vernünftig.

sensitive ['sensɪtɪv] *a* empfindlich (*to* gegen); (*easily hurt*) sensibel, feinfühlig; *film* lichtempfindlich.

sensitivity [sensɪ'tɪvɪtɪ] *n* Empfindlichkeit *f*; (*artistic*) Feingefühl *nt*; (*tact*) Feinfühligkeit *f*.

sensual ['sensjuəl] *a* sinnlich.

sensuous ['sensjuəs] *a* sinnlich, sinnenfreudig.

sentence ['sentəns] *n* Satz *m*; (*Jur*) Strafe *f*; Urteil *nt*; *vt* verurteilen.

sentiment ['sentɪmənt] *n* Gefühl *nt*; (*thought*) Gedanke *m*, Gesinnung *f*; ~**al** [sentɪ'mentl] *a* sentimental; (*of feelings rather than reason*) gefühlsmäßig; ~**ality** [sentɪmen'tælɪtɪ] Sentimentalität *f*.

sentinel ['sentɪnl] *n* Wachtposten *m*.

sentry ['sentrɪ] *n* (*Schild*)wache *f*.

separable ['sepərəbl] *a* (ab)trennbar.

separate ['seprət] *a* getrennt, separat; ['separeɪt] *vt* trennen; *vi* sich trennen; ~**ly** *ad* getrennt.

separation [sepə'reɪʃən] *n* Trennung *f*.

sepia ['si:pɪə] *a* Sepia-.

September [sep'tembə*] *n* September *m*.

septic ['septɪk] *a* vereitert, septisch.

sequel ['si:kwəl] *n* Folge *f*.

sequence ['siːkwəns] n (Reihen)folge f.

sequin ['siːkwɪn] n Paillette f.

serenade [serə'neɪd] n Ständchen nt, Serenade f; vt ein Ständchen bringen (+dat).

serene a, ~ly ad [sə'riːn, -lɪ] heiter, gelassen, ruhig.

serenity [sɪ'renɪtɪ] n Heiterkeit f, Gelassenheit f, Ruhe f.

serf [sɜːf] n Leibeigene(r) mf.

serge [sɜːdʒ] n Serge f.

sergeant ['sɑːdʒənt] n Feldwebel m; (police) (Polizei)wachtmeister m.

serial ['sɪərɪəl] n Fortsetzungsroman m; (TV) Fernsehserie f; a number (fort)-laufend; ~ize vt in Fortsetzungen veröffentlichen/ senden.

series ['sɪərɪz] n Serie f, Reihe f.

serious ['sɪərɪəs] a ernst; injury schwer; development ernstzunehmend; I'm ~ das meine ich ernst; ~ly ad ernst(haft); hurt schwer; ~ness Ernst m, Ernsthaftigkeit f.

sermon ['sɜːmən] n Predigt f.

serpent ['sɜːpənt] n Schlange f.

serrated [se'reɪtɪd] a gezackt; ~ knife Sägemesser nt.

serum ['sɪərəm] n Serum nt.

servant ['sɜːvənt] n Bedienstete(r) mf, Diener(in f) m; see civil.

serve [sɜːv] vt dienen (+dat); guest, customer bedienen; food servieren; writ zustellen (on sb jdm); vi dienen, nützen; (at table) servieren; (tennis) geben, aufschlagen; it ~s him right das geschieht ihm recht; that'll ~ the purpose das reicht; that'll ~ as a table das geht als Tisch; ~ out or up vt food auftragen, servieren.

service ['sɜːvɪs] n (help) Dienst m; (trains etc) Verkehrsverbindungen pl; (hotel) Service m, Bedienung f; (set of dishes) Service nt; (Rel) Gottesdienst m; (Mil) Waffengattung f; (car) Inspektion f; (for TVs etc) Kundendienst m; (tennis) Aufschlag m; to be of ~ to sb jdm einen großen Dienst erweisen; can I be of ~? kann ich Ihnen behilflich sein?; vt (Aut, Tech) warten, überholen; the S~s pl (armed forces) Streitkräfte pl; ~able a brauchbar; ~ area (on motorway) Raststätte f; ~ charge Bedienung f; ~man (soldier etc) Soldat m; ~ station (Groß)-tankstelle f.

servicing ['sɜːvɪsɪŋ] n Wartung f.

serviette [sɜːvɪ'et] n Serviette f.

servile ['sɜːvaɪl] a sklavisch, unterwürfig.

session ['seʃən] n Sitzung f; (Pol) Sitzungsperiode f.

set [set] n (collection of things) Satz m, Set nt; (Rad, TV) Apparat m; (tennis) Satz m; (group of people) Kreis m; (Cine) Szene f; (Theat) Bühnenbild nt; a festgelegt; (ready) bereit; ~ phrase feststehende(r) Ausdruck m; ~ square Zeichendreieck nt; irreg vt (place) setzen, stellen, legen; (arrange) (an)ordnen; table decken; time, price festsetzen; alarm, watch stellen; jewels (ein)fassen; task stellen; exam ausarbeiten; to ~ one's hair die Haare eindrehen; vi (sun) untergehen; (become hard) fest

werden; (bone) zusammenwachsen; to ~ on fire anstecken; to ~ free freilassen; to ~ sth going etw in Gang bringen; to ~ sail losfahren; ~ about vt task anpacken; ~ aside vt beseitelegen; ~ back vt zurückwerfen; ~ down vt absetzen; ~ off vi ausbrechen; vt (explode) zur Explosion bringen; alarm losgehen lassen; (show up well) hervorheben; ~ out vi aufbrechen; vt (arrange) anlegen, arrangieren; (state) darlegen; ~ up vt organization aufziehen; record aufstellen; monument erstellen; ~back Rückschlag m.

settee [se'tiː] n Sofa nt.

setting ['setɪŋ] n (Mus) Vertonung f; (scenery) Hintergrund m.

settle ['setl] vt beruhigen; (pay) begleichen, bezahlen; (agree) regeln; vi (also ~ down) sich einleben; (come to rest) sich niederlassen; (sink) sich setzen; (calm down) sich beruhigen; ~ment Regelung f; (payment) Begleichung f; (colony) Siedlung f, Niederlassung f; ~r Siedler m.

setup ['setʌp] n (arrangement) Aufbau m, Gliederung f; (situation) Situation f, Lage f.

seven ['sevn] num sieben; ~teen num siebzehn; ~th a siebte(r,s); n Siebtel nt; ~ty num siebzig.

sever ['sevə*] vt abtrennen.

several ['sevrəl] a mehrere, verschiedene; pron mehrere.

severance ['sevərəns] n Abtrennung f; (fig) Abbruch m.

severe [sɪ'vɪə*] a (strict) streng; (serious) schwer; climate rauh; (plain) streng, schmucklos; ~ly ad (strictly) streng, strikt; (seriously) schwer, ernstlich.

severity [sɪ'verɪtɪ] n Strenge f; Schwere f; Ernst m.

sew [səʊ] vti irreg nähen; ~ up vt zunähen.

sewage ['sjuːɪdʒ] n Abwässer pl.

sewer ['sjuə*] n (Abwasser)kanal m.

sewing ['səʊɪŋ] n Näharbeit f; ~ machine Nähmaschine f.

sex [seks] n Sex m; (gender) Geschlecht nt; ~ act Geschlechtsakt m.

sextant ['sekstənt] n Sextant m.

sextet [seks'tet] n Sextett nt.

sexual ['seksjuəl] a sexuell, geschlechtlich, Geschlechts-; ~ly ad geschlechtlich, sexuell.

sexy ['seksɪ] a sexy.

shabbily ['ʃæbɪlɪ] ad schäbig.

shabbiness ['ʃæbɪnəs] n Schäbigkeit f.

shabby ['ʃæbɪ] a (lit, fig) schäbig.

shack [ʃæk] n Hütte f.

shackle ['ʃækl] vt fesseln; ~s pl (lit, fig) Fesseln pl, Ketten pl.

shade [ʃeɪd] n Schatten m; (for lamp) Lampenschirm m; (colour) Farbton m; (small quantity) Spur f, Idee f; vt abschirmen.

shadow ['ʃædəʊ] n Schatten m; vt (follow) beschatten; a ~ cabinet (Pol) Schattenkabinett nt; ~y a schattig.

shady ['ʃeɪdɪ] a schattig; (fig) zwielichtig.

shaft [ʃɑːft] n (of spear etc) Schaft m; (in

mine) Schacht *m*; (*Tech*) Welle *f*; (*of light*) Strahl *m*.

shaggy ['ʃægɪ] *a* struppig.

shake [ʃeɪk] *irreg vt* schütteln, rütteln; (*shock*) erschüttern; **to ~ hands** die Hand geben (*with dat*); **they shook hands** sie gaben sich die Hand; **to ~ one's head** den Kopf schütteln; *vi* (*move*) schwanken; (*tremble*) zittern, beben; *n* (*jerk*) Schütteln *nt*, Rütteln *nt*; **~ off** abschütteln; **~ up** *vt* (*lit*) aufschütteln; (*fig*) aufrütteln; **~-up** Aufrüttelung *f*; (*Pol*) Umgruppierung *f*.

shakily ['ʃeɪkɪlɪ] *ad* zitternd, unsicher.

shakiness ['ʃeɪkɪnəs] *n* Wackeligkeit *f*.

shaky ['ʃeɪkɪ] *a* zittrig; (*weak*) unsicher.

shale [ʃeɪl] *n* Schiefer(ton) *m*.

shall [ʃæl] *v aux irreg* werden; (*must*) sollen.

shallow ['ʃæləʊ] *a* flach, seicht (*also fig*); **~s** *pl* flache Stellen *pl*.

sham [ʃæm] *n* Täuschung *f*, Trug *m*, Schein *m*; *a* unecht, falsch.

shambles ['ʃæmblz] *n sing* Durcheinander *nt*.

shame [ʃeɪm] *n* Scham *f*; (*disgrace, pity*) Schande *f*; *vt* beschämen; **what a ~!** wie schade!; **~ on you!** schäm dich!; **~-faced** *a* beschämt; **~ful** *a*, **~fully** *ad* schändlich; **~less** *a* schamlos; (*immodest*) unverschämt.

shampoo [ʃæm'puː] *n* Schampoon *nt*; *vt* schampunieren; **~ and set** Waschen *nt* und Legen.

shamrock ['ʃæmrɒk] *n* Kleeblatt *nt*.

shandy ['ʃændɪ] *n* Radlermaß *f*.

shan't [ʃɑːnt] = **shall not**.

shanty ['ʃæntɪ] *n* (*cabin*) Hütte *f*, Baracke *f*; **~ town** Elendsviertel *nt*.

shape [ʃeɪp] *n* Form *f*, Gestalt *f*; *vt* formen, gestalten; **to take ~** Gestalt annehmen; **~less** *a* formlos; **~ly** *a* wohlgeformt, wohlproportioniert.

share [ʃɛə*] *n* (An)teil *m*; (*Fin*) Aktie *f*; *vt* teilen; **~holder** Aktionär *m*.

shark [ʃɑːk] *n* Hai(fisch) *m*; (*swindler*) Gauner *m*.

sharp [ʃɑːp] *a* scharf; *pin* spitz; *person* clever; *child* aufgeweckt; (*unscrupulous*) gerissen, raffiniert; (*Mus*) erhöht; **~ practices** *pl* Machenschaften *pl*; *n* (*Mus*) Kreuz *nt*; *ad* (*Mus*) zu hoch; **nine o'clock ~** Punkt neun; **look ~!** mach schnell!; **~en** *vt* schärfen; *pencil* spitzen; **~ener** Spitzer *m*; **~-eyed** *a* scharfsichtig; **~ness** Schärfe *f*; **~-witted** *a* scharfsinnig, aufgeweckt.

shatter ['ʃætə*] *vt* zerschmettern; (*fig*) zerstören; *vi* zerspringen; **~ed** *a* (*lit, fig*) kaputt; **~ing** *a experience* furchtbar.

shave [ʃeɪv] *n* Rasur *f*, Rasieren *nt*; **to have a ~** sich rasieren (lassen); *vt* rasieren; *vi* sich rasieren; **~n** *a head* geschoren; **~r** (*Elec*) Rasierapparat *m*, Rasierer *m*.

shaving ['ʃeɪvɪŋ] *n* (*action*) Rasieren *nt*; **~s** *pl* (*of wood etc*) Späne *pl*; **~ brush** Rasierpinsel *m*; **~ cream** Rasierkrem *f*; **~ point** Rasiersteckdose *f*; **~ soap** Rasierseife *f*.

shawl [ʃɔːl] *n* Schal *m*, Umhang *m*.

she [ʃiː] *pron* sie; *a* weiblich; **~-bear** Bärenweibchen *nt*.

sheaf [ʃiːf] *n* Garbe *f*.

shear [ʃɪə*] *vt irreg* scheren; **~ off** *vt* abscheren; **~s** *pl* Heckenschere *f*.

sheath [ʃiːθ] *n* Scheide *f*; **~e** [ʃiːð] *vt* einstecken; (*Tech*) verkleiden.

shed [ʃed] *n* Schuppen *m*; (*for animals*) Stall *m*; *vt irreg leaves etc* abwerfen, verlieren; *tears* vergießen.

she'd [ʃiːd] = **she had**; **she would**.

sheep [ʃiːp] *n* Schaf *nt*; **~dog** Schäferhund *m*; **~ish** *a* verschämt, betreten; **~skin** Schaffell *nt*.

sheer [ʃɪə*] *a* bloß, rein; (*steep*) steil, jäh; (*transparent*) (hauch)dünn, durchsichtig; *ad* (*directly*) direkt.

sheet [ʃiːt] *n* Bettuch *nt*, Bettlaken *nt*; (*of paper*) Blatt *nt*; (*of metal etc*) Platte *f*; (*of ice*) Fläche *f*; **~ lightning** Wetterleuchten *nt*.

sheik(h) [ʃeɪk] *n* Scheich *m*.

shelf [ʃelf] *n* Bord *nt*, Regal *nt*.

she'll [ʃiːl] = **she will**; **she shall**.

shell [ʃel] *n* Schale *f*; (*sea—*) Muschel *f*; (*explosive*) Granate *f*; (*of building*) Mauern *pl*; *vt peas* schälen; (*fire on*) beschießen; **~fish** Schalentier *nt*; (*as food*) Meeresfrüchte *pl*.

shelter ['ʃeltə*] *n* Schutz *m*; Bunker *m*; *vt* schützen, bedecken; *refugees* aufnehmen; *vi* sich unterstellen; **~ed** *a life* behütet; *spot* geschützt.

shelve [ʃelv] *vt* aufschieben; *vi* abfallen.

shelving ['ʃelvɪŋ] *n* Regale *pl*.

shepherd ['ʃepəd] *n* Schäfer *m*; *vt* treiben, führen; **~ess** Schäferin *f*.

sheriff ['ʃerɪf] *n* Sheriff *m*.

sherry ['ʃerɪ] *n* Sherry *m*.

she's [ʃiːz] = **she is**; **she has**.

shield [ʃiːld] *n* Schild *m*; (*fig*) Schirm *m*, Schutz *m*; *vt* (be)schirmen; (*Tech*) abschirmen.

shift [ʃɪft] *n* Veränderung *f*, Verschiebung *f*; (*work*) Schicht *f*; *vt* (ver)rücken, verschieben; *office* verlegen; *arm* wegnehmen; *vi* sich verschieben; (*col*) schnell fahren; **~ work** Schichtarbeit *f*; **~y** *a* verschlagen.

shilling ['ʃɪlɪŋ] *n* (*old*) Shilling *m*.

shilly-shally ['ʃɪlɪʃælɪ] *vi* zögern.

shimmer ['ʃɪmə*] *n* Schimmer *m*; *vi* schimmern.

shin [ʃɪn] *n* Schienbein *nt*.

shine [ʃaɪn] *n* Glanz *m*, Schein *m*; *irreg vt* polieren; **to ~ a torch on sb** jdn (mit einer Lampe) anleuchten; *vi* scheinen; (*fig*) glänzen.

shingle ['ʃɪŋgl] *n* Schindel *f*; (*on beach*) Strandkies *m*; **~s** *pl* (*Med*) Gürtelrose *f*.

shining ['ʃaɪnɪŋ] *a light* strahlend.

shiny ['ʃaɪnɪ] *a* glänzend.

ship [ʃɪp] *n* Schiff *nt*; *vt* an Bord bringen, verladen; (*transport as cargo*) verschiffen; **~-building** Schiffbau *m*; **~ canal** Seekanal *m*; **~ment** Verladung *f*; (*goods shipped*) Schiffsladung *f*; **~per** Verschiffer *m*; **~ping** (*act*) Verschiffung *f*; (*ships*) Schiffahrt *f*; **~shape** *a* in Ordnung;

~wreck Schiffbruch m; (destroyed ship) Wrack nt; **~yard** Werft f.

shirk [ʃɜːk] vt ausweichen (+dat).

shirt [ʃɜːt] n (Ober)hemd nt; **in ~-sleeves** in Hemdsärmeln; **~y** a (col) mürrisch.

shiver [ˈʃɪvə*] n Schauer m; vi frösteln, zittern.

shoal [ʃəʊl] n (Fisch)schwarm m.

shock [ʃɒk] n Stoß m, Erschütterung f; (mental) Schock m; (Elec) Schlag m; vt erschüttern; (offend) schockieren; **~ absorber** Stoßdämpfer m; **~ing** a unerhört, schockierend; **~proof** a watch stoßsicher.

shoddiness [ˈʃɒdɪnəs] n Schäbigkeit f.

shoddy [ˈʃɒdɪ] a schäbig.

shoe [ʃuː] n Schuh m; (of horse) Hufeisen nt; vt irreg horse beschlagen; **~brush** Schuhbürste f; **~horn** Schuhlöffel m; **~lace** Schnürsenkel m.

shoot [ʃuːt] n (branch) Schößling m; irreg vt gun abfeuern; goal, arrow schießen; (kill) erschießen; film drehen, filmen; **shot in the leg** ins Bein getroffen; vi (gun, move quickly) schießen; **don't ~!** nicht schießen!; **~ down** vt abschießen; **~ing** Schießerei f; **~ing star** Sternschnuppe f.

shop [ʃɒp] n Geschäft nt, Laden m; (workshop) Werkstatt f; vi (also **go ~ping**) einkaufen gehen; **~ assistant** Verkäufer(in f) m; **~keeper** Geschäftsinhaber m; **~lifter** Ladendieb m; **~lifting** Ladendiebstahl m; **~per** Käufer(in f) m; **~ping** Einkaufen nt, Einkauf m; **~ping bag** Einkaufstasche f; **~ping centre,** (US) **~ping center** Einkaufszentrum nt; **~-soiled** a angeschmutzt; **~ steward** Betriebsrat m; **~ window** Schaufenster nt; see talk.

shore [ʃɔː*] n Ufer nt; (of sea) Strand m, Küste f; vt: **~ up** abstützen.

short [ʃɔːt] a kurz; person klein; (curt) kurz angebunden; (measure) zu knapp; **to be ~ of** zu wenig . . . haben; **two ~** zwei zu wenig; n (Elec: **~-circuit**) Kurzschluß m; ad (suddenly) plötzlich; vi (Elec) einen Kurzschluß haben; **to cut ~** abkürzen; **to fall ~** nicht erreichen; **for ~** kurz; **~age** Knappheit f, Mangel m; **~bread** Mürbegebäck m, Heidesand m; **~-circuit** Kurzschluß m; vi einen Kurzschluß haben; **~coming** Fehler m, Mangel m; **~ cut** Abkürzung f; **~en** vt (ab)kürzen; clothes kürzer machen; **~hand** Stenographie f, Kurzschrift f; **~hand typist** Stenotypistin f; **~list** engere Wahl f; **~-lived** a kurzlebig; **~ly** ad bald; **~ness** Kürze f; **~s** pl Shorts pl; **~-sighted** a (lit, fig) kurzsichtig; **~-sightedness** Kurzsichtigkeit f; **~ story** Kurzgeschichte f; **~-tempered** a leicht aufbrausend; **~-term** a effect kurzfristig; **~ wave** (Rad) Kurzwelle f.

shot [ʃɒt] n (from gun) Schuß m; (person) Schütze m; (try) Versuch m; (injection) Spritze f; (Phot) Aufnahme f, Schnappschuß m; **like a ~** wie der Blitz; **~gun** Schrotflinte f.

should [ʃʊd] v aux: **I ~ go now** ich sollte jetzt gehen; **I ~ say** ich würde sagen; **I**

~ like to ich möchte gerne, ich würde gerne.

shoulder [ˈʃəʊldə*] n Schulter f; vt rifle schultern; (fig) auf sich nehmen; **~ blade** Schulterblatt nt.

shouldn't [ˈʃʊdnt] = should not.

shout [ʃaʊt] n Schrei m; (call) Ruf m; vt rufen; vi schreien, laut rufen; **to ~ at** anbrüllen; **~ing** Geschrei nt.

shove [ʃʌv] n Schubs m, Stoß m; vt schieben, stoßen, schubsen; **~ off** vi (Naut) abstoßen; (fig col) abhauen.

shovel [ˈʃʌvl] n Schaufel f; vt schaufeln.

show [ʃəʊ] n (display) Schau f; (exhibition) Ausstellung f; (Cine, Theat) Vorstellung f, Show f; irreg vt zeigen; kindness erweisen; vi zu sehen sein; **to ~ sb in** jdn hereinführen; **to ~ sb out** jdn hinausbegleiten; **~ off** vi (pej) angeben, protzen; vt (display) ausstellen; **~ up** vi (stand out) sich abheben; (arrive) erscheinen; vt aufzeigen; (unmask) bloßstellen; **~ business** Showbusineß nt; **~down** Kraftprobe f, endgültige Auseinandersetzung f.

shower [ˈʃaʊə*] n Schauer m; (of stones) (Stein)hagel m; (of sparks) (Funken)regen m; (~ bath) Dusche f; **to have a ~** duschen; vt (fig) überschütten; **~proof** a wasserabstoßend; **~y** a weather regnerisch.

showground [ˈʃəʊɡraʊnd] n Ausstellungsgelände nt.

showing [ˈʃəʊɪŋ] n (of film) Vorführung f.

show jumping [ˈʃəʊdʒʌmpɪŋ] n Turnierreiten nt.

showmanship [ˈʃəʊmənʃɪp] n Talent nt als Showman.

show-off [ˈʃəʊɒf] n Angeber m.

showpiece [ˈʃəʊpiːs] n Paradestück nt.

showroom [ˈʃəʊruːm] n Ausstellungsraum m.

shrapnel [ˈʃræpnl] n Schrapnell nt.

shred [ʃred] n Fetzen m; vt zerfetzen; (Cook) raspeln; **in ~s** in Fetzen.

shrewd a, **~ly** ad [ʃruːd, -lɪ] scharfsinnig, clever; **~ness** Scharfsinn m.

shriek [ʃriːk] n Schrei m; vti kreischen, schreien.

shrill [ʃrɪl] a schrill, gellend.

shrimp [ʃrɪmp] n Krabbe f, Garnele f.

shrine [ʃraɪn] n Schrein m.

shrink [ʃrɪŋk] irreg vi schrumpfen, eingehen; vt einschrumpfen lassen; **~age** Schrumpfung f; **~ away** vi zurückschrecken (from vor +dat).

shrivel [ˈʃrɪvl] vti (also **~ up**) schrumpfen, schrumpeln.

shroud [ʃraʊd] n Leichentuch nt; vt umhüllen, (ein)hüllen.

Shrove Tuesday [ˈʃrəʊvˈtjuːzdeɪ] n Fastnachtsdienstag m.

shrub [ʃrʌb] n Busch m, Strauch m; **~bery** Gebüsch nt.

shrug [ʃrʌɡ] n Achselzucken nt; vi die Achseln zucken; **~ off** vt auf die leichte Schulter nehmen.

shrunken [ˈʃrʌŋkən] a eingelaufen.

shudder [ˈʃʌdə*] n Schauder m; vi schaudern.

shuffle [ˈʃʌfl] n (Cards) (Karten)mischen

nt; *vt cards* mischen; *vi (walk)* schlurfen.

shun [ʃʌn] *vt* scheuen, (ver)meiden.

shunt [ʃʌnt] *vt* rangieren.

shut [ʃʌt] *irreg vt* schließen, zumachen; *vi* sich schließen (lassen); ~ **down** *vti* schließen; ~ **off** *vt supply* abdrehen; ~ **up** *vi (keep quiet)* den Mund halten; *vt (close)* zuschließen; *(silence)* zum Schweigen bringen; ~ **up!** halt den Mund!; ~**ter** Fensterladen *m*, Rolladen *m*; *(Phot)* Verschluß *m*.

shuttlecock [ʃʌtlkɒk] *n* Federball *m*; Federballspiel *nt*.

shuttle service [ʃʌtlsɜːvɪs] *n* Pendelverkehr *m*.

shy *a*, ~**ly** *ad* [ʃaɪ, -lɪ] schüchtern, scheu; ~**ness** Schüchternheit *f*, Zurückhaltung *f*.

Siamese [saɪəˈmiːz] *a*: ~ **cat** Siamkatze *f*; ~ **twins** *pl* siamesische Zwillinge *pl*.

sick [sɪk] *a* krank; *humour* schwarz; *joke* makaber; **I feel** ~ mir ist schlecht; **I was** ~ ich habe gebrochen; **to be** ~ **of sb/sth** jdn/etw satt haben; ~ **bay** (Schiffs)lazarett *nt*; ~**bed** Krankenbett *nt*; ~**en** *vt (disgust)* krankmachen; *vi* krank werden; ~**ening** *a sight* widerlich; *(annoying)* zum Weinen.

sickle [sɪkl] *n* Sichel *f*.

sick leave [sɪkliːv] *n*: **to be on** ~ krank geschrieben sein.

sick list [sɪklɪst] *n* Krankenliste *f*.

sickly [sɪklɪ] *a* kränklich, blaß; *(causing nausea)* widerlich.

sickness [sɪknəs] *n* Krankheit *f*; *(vomiting)* Übelkeit *f*, Erbrechen *nt*.

sick pay [sɪkpeɪ] *n* Krankengeld *nt*.

side [saɪd] *n* Seite *f*; *a door, entrance* Seiten-, Neben-; **by the** ~ **of** neben; **on all** ~**s** von allen Seiten; **to take** ~**s (with)** Partei nehmen (für); *vi*: ~ **with sb** es halten mit jdm; ~**board** Anrichte *f*, Sideboard *nt*; ~**boards**, ~**burns** *pl* Koteletten *pl*; ~ **effect** Nebenwirkung *f*; ~**light** *(Aut)* Parkleuchte *f*, Standlicht *nt*; ~**line** *(Sport)* Seitenlinie *f*; *(fig: hobby)* Nebenbeschäftigung *f*; ~ **road** Nebenstraße *f*; ~ **show** Nebenausstellung *f*; ~**track** *vt (fig)* ablenken; ~**walk** *(US)* Bürgersteig *m*; ~**ways** *ad* seitwärts.

siding [saɪdɪŋ] *n* Nebengleis *nt*.

sidle [saɪdl] *vi*: ~ **up** sich heranmachen *(to an +acc)*.

siege [siːdʒ] *n* Belagerung *f*.

siesta [sɪˈestə] *n* Siesta *f*.

sieve [sɪv] *n* Sieb *nt*; *vt* sieben.

sift [sɪft] *vt* sieben; *(fig)* sichten.

sigh [saɪ] *n* Seufzer *m*; *vi* seufzen.

sight [saɪt] *n* *(power of seeing)* Sehvermögen *nt*, Augenlicht *nt*; *(view)* (An)blick *m*; *(scene)* Aussicht *f*, Blick *m*; *(of gun)* Zielvorrichtung *f*, Korn *nt*; ~**s** *pl* *(of city etc)* Sehenswürdigkeiten *pl*; **in** ~ in Sicht; **out of** ~ außer Sicht; *vt* sichten; ~**seeing** Besuch *m* von Sehenswürdigkeiten; **to go** ~**seeing** Sehenswürdigkeiten besichtigen; ~**seer** Tourist *m*.

sign [saɪn] *n* Zeichen *nt*; *(notice, road – etc)* Schild *nt*; *vt* unterschreiben; ~ **out** *vi* sich austragen; ~ **up** *vi* *(Mil)* sich verpflichten; *vt* verpflichten.

signal [sɪgnl] *n* Signal *nt*; *vt* ein Zeichen geben *(+dat)*.

signatory [sɪgnətrɪ] *n* Signatar *m*.

signature [sɪgnətʃə*] *n* Unterschrift *f*; ~ **tune** Erkennungsmelodie *f*.

signet ring [sɪgnətrɪŋ] *n* Siegelring *m*.

significance [sɪgˈnɪfɪkəns] *n* Bedeutung *f*.

significant [sɪgˈnɪfɪkənt] *a* *(meaning sth)* bedeutsam; *(important)* bedeutend, wichtig; ~**ly** *ad* bezeichnenderweise.

signify [sɪgnɪfaɪ] *vt* bedeuten; *(show)* andeuten, zu verstehen geben.

sign language [saɪnˈlæŋgwɪdʒ] *n* Zeichensprache *f*, Fingersprache *f*.

signpost [saɪnpəʊst] *n* Wegweiser *m*, Schild *nt*.

silence [saɪləns] *n* Stille *f*, Ruhe *f*; *(of person)* Schweigen *nt*; *vt* zum Schweigen bringen; ~**r** *(on gun)* Schalldämpfer *m*; *(Aut)* Auspufftopf *m*.

silent [saɪlənt] *a still*; *person* schweigsam; ~**ly** *ad* schweigend, still.

silhouette [sɪluˈet] *n* Silhouette *f*, Umriß *m*; *(picture)* Schattenbild *nt*; *vt*: **to be** ~**d against sth** sich als Silhouette abheben gegen etw.

silk [sɪlk] *n* Seide *f*; *a* seiden, Seiden-; ~**y** *a* seidig.

silliness [sɪlɪnəs] *n* Albernheit *f*, Dummheit *f*.

silly [sɪlɪ] *a* dumm, albern.

silo [saɪləʊ] *n* Silo *m*.

silt [sɪlt] *n* Schlamm *m*, Schlick *m*.

silver [sɪlvə*] *n* Silber *nt*; *a* silbern, Silber-; ~ **paper** Silberpapier *nt*; ~**plate** Silber(geschirr) *nt*; ~~**plated** *a* versilbert; ~**smith** Silberschmied *m*; ~**ware** Silber *nt*; ~**y** *a* silbern.

similar [sɪmɪlə*] *a* ähnlich *(to dat)*; ~**ity** [sɪmɪˈlærɪt] Ähnlichkeit *f*; ~**ly** *ad* in ähnlicher Weise.

simile [sɪmɪlɪ] *n* Vergleich *m*.

simmer [sɪmə*] *vti* sieden (lassen).

simple [sɪmpl] *a* einfach; *dress also* schlicht; ~**(-minded)** *a* naiv, einfältig.

simplicity [sɪmˈplɪsɪtɪ] *n* Einfachheit *f*; *(of person)* Einfältigkeit *f*.

simplification [sɪmplɪfɪˈkeɪʃən] *n* Vereinfachung *f*.

simplify [sɪmplɪfaɪ] *vt* vereinfachen.

simply [sɪmplɪ] *ad* einfach; *(only)* bloß, nur.

simulate [sɪmjʊleɪt] *vt* simulieren.

simulation [sɪmjʊˈleɪʃən] *n* Simulieren *nt*.

simultaneous *a*, ~**ly** *ad* [sɪməlˈteɪnɪəs, -lɪ] gleichzeitig.

sin [sɪn] *n* Sünde *f*; *vi* sündigen.

since [sɪns] *ad* seither; *prep* seit, seitdem; *cj* *(time)* seit; *(because)* da, weil.

sincere [sɪnˈsɪə*] *a* aufrichtig, ehrlich, offen; ~**ly** aufrichtig; **yours** ~**ly** mit freundlichen Grüßen.

sincerity [sɪnˈserɪtɪ] *n* Aufrichtigkeit *f*.

sinecure [saɪnɪkjʊə*] *n* einträgliche(r) Ruheposten *m*.

sinew [sɪnjuː] *n* Sehne *f*; *(of animal)* Flechse *f*.

sinful [sɪnfʊl] *a* sündig, sündhaft.

sing [sɪŋ] *vti irreg* singen.

singe [sɪndʒ] vt versengen.
singer ['sɪŋə*] n Sänger(in f) m.
singing ['sɪŋɪŋ] n Singen nt, Gesang m.
single ['sɪŋgl] a (one only) einzig; bed, room Einzel-, einzeln; (unmarried) ledig; ticket einfach; (having one part only) einzeln; n (ticket) einfache Fahrkarte f; ~s (tennis) Einzel nt; ~ out vt aussuchen, auswählen; ~-breasted a einreihig; in ~ file hintereinander; ~-handed a allein; ~-minded a zielstrebig.
singlet ['sɪŋglət] n Unterhemd nt.
singly ['sɪŋgli] ad einzeln, allein.
singular ['sɪŋgjulə*] a (Gram) Singular-; (odd) merkwürdig, seltsam; n (Gram) Einzahl f, Singular m; ~ly ad besonders, höchst.
sinister ['sɪnɪstə*] a (evil) böse; (ghostly) unheimlich.
sink [sɪŋk] n Spülbecken nt, Ausguß m; irreg vt ship versenken; (dig) einsenken; vi sinken; ~ in (news etc) eingehen (+dat); ~ing a feeling flau.
sinner ['sɪnə*] n Sünder(in f) m.
sinuous ['sɪnjuəs] a gewunden, sich schlängelnd.
sinus ['saɪnəs] n (Anat) Nasenhöhle f, Sinus m.
sip [sɪp] n Schlückchen nt; vt nippen an (+dat).
siphon ['saɪfən] n Siphon(flasche f) m; ~ off vt absaugen; (fig) abschöpfen.
sir [sɜ:*] n (respect) Herr m; (knight) Sir m; yes S~ ja(wohl, mein Herr).
siren ['saɪərən] n Sirene f.
sirloin ['sɜ:lɔɪn] n Lendenstück nt.
sirocco [sɪ'rɒkəu] n Schirokko m.
sissy ['sɪsi] n = cissy.
sister ['sɪstə*] n Schwester f; (nurse) Oberschwester f; (nun) Ordensschwester f; ~-in-law Schwägerin f.
sit [sɪt] irreg vi sitzen; (hold session) tagen, Sitzung halten; vt exam machen; to ~ tight abwarten; ~ down vi sich hinsetzen; ~ up vi (after lying) sich aufsetzen; (straight) sich gerade setzen; (at night) aufbleiben.
site [saɪt] n Platz m; vt plazieren, legen.
sit-in ['sɪtɪn] n Sit-in nt.
siting ['saɪtɪŋ] n (location) Platz m, Lage f.
sitting ['sɪtɪŋ] n (meeting) Sitzung f, Tagung f; ~ room Wohnzimmer nt.
situated ['sɪtjueɪtɪd] a: to be ~ liegen.
situation [sɪtju'eɪʃən] n Situation f, Lage f; (place) Lage f; (employment) Stelle f.
six [sɪks] num sechs; ~teen num sechzehn; ~th a sechste(r,s); n Sechstel nt; ~ty num sechzig.
size [saɪz] n Größe f; (of project) Umfang m; (glue) Kleister m; ~ up vt (assess) abschätzen, einschätzen; ~able a ziemlich groß, ansehnlich.
sizzle ['sɪzl] n Zischen nt; vi zischen; (Cook) brutzeln.
skate [skeɪt] n Schlittschuh m; vi Schlittschuh laufen; ~r Schlittschuhläufer(in f) m.
skating ['skeɪtɪŋ] n Eislauf m; to go ~ Eislaufen gehen; ~ rink Eisbahn f.

skeleton ['skelɪtn] n Skelett nt; (fig) Gerüst nt; ~ key Dietrich m.
skeptic ['skeptɪk] n (US) = sceptic.
sketch [sketʃ] n Skizze f; (Theat) Sketch m; vt skizzieren, eine Skizze machen von; ~book Skizzenbuch nt; ~ing Skizzieren nt; ~ pad Skizzenblock m; ~y a skizzenhaft.
skewer ['skjuə*] n Fleischspieß m.
ski [ski:] n Ski m, Schi m; vi Ski or Schi laufen; ~ boot Skistiefel m.
skid [skɪd] n (Aut) Schleudern nt; vi rutschen; (Aut) schleudern.
skidmark ['skɪdmɑːk] n Rutschspur f.
skier ['ski:ə*] n Skiläufer(in f) m.
skiing ['ski:ɪŋ] n: to go ~ Skilaufen gehen.
ski-jump ['ski:dʒʌmp] n Sprungschanze f; vi Ski springen.
ski-lift ['ski:lɪft] n Skilift m.
skilful a, ~ly ad ['skɪlful, -fəli] geschickt.
skill [skɪl] n Können nt, Geschicklichkeit f; ~ed a geschickt; worker Fach-, gelernt.
skim [skɪm] vt liquid abschöpfen; milk entrahmen; (read) überfliegen; (glide over) gleiten über (+acc).
skimp [skɪmp] vt (do carelessly) oberflächlich tun; ~y a work schlecht gemacht; dress knapp.
skin [skɪn] n Haut f; (peel) Schale f; vt abhäuten; schälen; ~-deep a oberflächlich; ~ diving Schwimmtauchen nt; ~ny a dünn; ~tight a dress etc hauteng.
skip [skɪp] n Sprung m, Hopser m; vi hüpfen, springen; (with rope) Seil springen; vt (pass over) übergehen.
ski pants ['ski:pænts] npl Skihosen pl.
skipper ['skɪpə*] n (Naut) Schiffer m, Kapitän m; (Sport) Mannschaftskapitän m; vt führen.
skipping rope ['skɪpɪŋrəup] n Hüpfseil nt.
skirmish ['skɜ:mɪʃ] n Scharmützel nt.
skirt [skɜ:t] n Rock m; vt herumgehen um; (fig) umgehen.
ski run ['ski:rʌn] n Skiabfahrt f.
skit [skɪt] n Parodie f.
ski tow ['ski:təu] n Schlepplift m.
skittle ['skɪtl] n Kegel m; ~s (game) Kegeln nt.
skive [skaɪv] vi (Brit col) schwänzen.
skulk [skʌlk] vi sich herumdrücken.
skull [skʌl] n Schädel m; ~ and crossbones Totenkopf m.
skunk [skʌŋk] n Stinktier nt.
sky [skaɪ] n Himmel m; ~-blue a himmelblau; n Himmelblau nt; ~light Dachfenster nt, Oberlicht nt; ~scraper Wolkenkratzer m.
slab [slæb] n (of stone) Platte f; (of chocolate) Tafel f.
slack [slæk] a (loose) lose, schlaff, locker; business flau; (careless) nachlässig, lasch; vi nachlässig sein; n (in rope etc) durchhängende(s) Teil nt; to take up the ~ straffziehen; ~s pl Hose(n pl) f; ~en (also ~en off) vi schlaff/locker werden; (become slower) nachlassen, stocken; vt (loosen) lockern; ~ness n Schlaffheit f.
slag [slæg] n Schlacke f; ~ heap Halde f.
slalom ['slɑːləm] n Slalom m.

slam [slæm] *n* Knall *m*; *vt* door zuschlagen, zuknallen; (*throw down*) knallen; *vi* zuschlagen.

slander ['slɑːndə*] *n* Verleumdung *f*; *vt* verleumden; ~**ous** *a* verleumderisch.

slang [slæŋ] *n* Slang *m*; Jargon *m*.

slant [slɑːnt] *n* (*lit*) Schräge *f*; (*fig*) Tendenz *f*, Einstellung *f*; *vt* schräg legen; *vi* schräg liegen; ~**ing** *a* schräg.

slap [slæp] *n* Schlag *m*, Klaps *m*; *vt* schlagen, einen Klaps geben (+*dat*); *ad* (*directly*) geradewegs; ~**dash** *a* salopp; ~**stick** (*comedy*) Klamauk *m*; ~**-up** *a meal* erstklassig, prima.

slash [slæʃ] *n* Hieb *m*, Schnittwunde *f*; *vt* (auf)schlitzen; *expenditure* radikal kürzen.

slate [sleɪt] *n* (*stone*) Schiefer *m*; (*roofing*) Dachziegel *m*; *vt* (*criticize*) verreißen.

slaughter ['slɔːtə*] *n* (*of animals*) Schlachten *nt*; (*of people*) Gemetzel *nt*; *vt* schlachten; *people* niedermetzeln.

slave [sleɪv] *n* Sklave *m* Sklavin *f*; *vi* schuften, sich schinden; ~**ry** Sklaverei *f*; (*work*) Schinderei *f*.

slavish *a*, ~**ly** *ad* ['sleɪvɪʃ, -lɪ] sklavisch.

slay [sleɪ] *vt irreg* ermorden.

sleazy ['slɪːzɪ] *a place* schmierig.

sledge [sledʒ] *n* Schlitten *m*; ~**hammer** Schmiedehammer *m*.

sleek [slɪːk] *a* glatt, glänzend; *shape* rassig.

sleep [slɪːp] *n* Schlaf *m*; *vi irreg* schlafen; **to go to** ~ einschlafen; ~ **in** *vi* ausschlafen; (*oversleep*) verschlafen; ~**er** (*person*) Schläfer *m*; (*Rail*) Schlafwagen *m*; (*beam*) Schwelle *f*; ~**ily** *ad* schläfrig; ~**iness** Schläfrigkeit *f*; ~**ing bag** Schlafsack *m*; ~**ing car** Schlafwagen *m*; ~**ing pill** Schlaftablette *f*; ~**less** *a night* schlaflos; ~**lessness** Schlaflosigkeit *f*; ~**walker** Schlafwandler *m*; ~**y** *a* schläfrig.

sleet [slɪːt] *n* Schneeregen *m*.

sleeve [slɪːv] *n* Ärmel *m*; (*of record*) Umschlag *m*; ~**less** *a garment* ärmellos.

sleigh [sleɪ] *n* Pferdeschlitten *m*.

sleight [slaɪt] *n*: ~ **of hand** Fingerfertigkeit *f*.

slender ['slendə*] *a* schlank; (*fig*) gering.

slice [slaɪs] *n* Scheibe *f*; *vt* in Scheiben schneiden.

slick [slɪk] *a* (*clever*) raffiniert, aalglatt; *n* Ölteppich *m*.

slide [slaɪd] *n* Rutschbahn *f*; (*Phot*) Dia(positiv) *nt*; (*for hair*) (Haar-)spange *f*; (*fall in prices*) (Preis)rutsch *m*; *irreg vt* schieben; *vi* (*slip*) gleiten, rutschen; **to let things** ~ die Dinge schleifen lassen; ~**rule** Rechenschieber *m*.

sliding ['slaɪdɪŋ] *a door* Schiebe-.

slight [slaɪt] *a* zierlich; (*trivial*) geringfügig; (*small*) leicht, gering; *n* Kränkung *f*; *vt* (*offend*) kränken; ~**ly** *ad* etwas, ein bißchen.

slim [slɪm] *a* schlank; *book* dünn; *chance* gering; *vi* eine Schlankheitskur machen.

slime [slaɪm] *n* Schlamm *m*; Schleim *m*.

slimming ['slɪmɪŋ] *n* Schlankheitskur *f*.

slimness ['slɪmnəs] *n* Schlankheit *f*.

slimy ['slaɪmɪ] *a* glitschig; (*dirty*) schlammig; *person* schmierig.

sling [slɪŋ] *n* Schlinge *f*; (*weapon*) Schleuder *f*; *vt irreg* werfen; (*hurl*) schleudern.

slip [slɪp] *n* (*slipping*) Ausgleiten *nt*, Rutschen *nt*; (*mistake*) Flüchtigkeitsfehler *m*; (*petticoat*) Unterrock *m*; (*of paper*) Zettel *m*; **to give sb the** ~ jdn entwischen; ~ **of the tongue** Versprecher *m*; *vt* (*put*) stecken, schieben; **it** ~**ped my mind** das ist mir entfallen, ich habe es vergessen; *vi* (*lose balance*) ausrutschen; (*move*) gleiten, rutschen; (*make mistake*) einen Fehler machen; (*decline*) nachlassen; **to let things** ~ die Dinge schleifen lassen; ~ **away** *vi* sich wegstehlen; ~ **by** *vi* (*time*) verstreichen; ~ **in** *vt* hineingleiten lassen; *vi* (*errors*) sich einschleichen; ~ **out** *vi* hinausschlüpfen; ~**per** Hausschuh *m*; ~**pery** *a* glatt; (*tricky*) aalglatt, gerissen; ~**road** Auffahrt *f*/Ausfahrt *f*; ~**shod** *a* schlampig; ~**stream** Windschatten *m*; ~**-up** Panne *f*; ~**way** Auslaufbahn *f*.

slit [slɪt] *n* Schlitz *m*; *vt irreg* aufschlitzen.

slither ['slɪðə*] *vi* schlittern; (*snake*) sich schlängeln.

slob [slɒb] *n* (*col*) Klotz *m*.

slog [slɒg] *n* (*great effort*) Plackerei *f*; *vi* (*work hard*) schuften.

slogan ['sləʊgən] *n* Schlagwort *nt*; (*Comm*) Werbespruch *m*.

slop [slɒp] *vi* überschwappen; *vt* verschütten.

slope [sləʊp] *n* Neigung *f*, Schräge *f*; (*of mountains*) (Ab)hang *m*; *vi*: ~ **down** sich senken; ~ **up** ansteigen.

sloping ['sləʊpɪŋ] *a* schräg; *shoulders* abfallend; *ground* abschüssig.

sloppily ['slɒpɪlɪ] *ad* schlampig.

sloppiness ['slɒpɪnəs] *n* Matschigkeit *f*; (*of work*) Nachlässigkeit *f*.

sloppy ['slɒpɪ] *a* (*wet*) matschig; (*careless*) schlampig; (*silly*) rührselig.

slot [slɒt] *n* Schlitz *m*; *vt*: ~ **sth in** etw einlegen; ~ **machine** Automat *m*.

slouch [slaʊtʃ] *vi* krumm dasitzen *or* dastehen.

slovenly ['slʌvnlɪ] *a* schlampig; *speech* salopp.

slow [sləʊ] *a* langsam; **to be** ~ (*clock*) nachgehen; (*stupid*) begriffsstutzig sein; ~ **down** *vi* langsamer werden; ~ **down!** mach langsam!; *vt* aufhalten, langsamer machen, verlangsamen; ~ **up** *vi* sich verlangsamen, sich verzögern; *vt* aufhalten, langsamer machen; ~**ly** *ad* langsam; allmählich; **in** ~ **motion** in Zeitlupe.

sludge [slʌdʒ] *n* Schlamm *m*, Matsch *m*.

slug [slʌg] *n* Nacktschnecke *f*; (*col: bullet*) Kugel *f*; ~**gish** *a* träge; (*Comm*) schleppend; ~**gishly** *ad* träge; ~**gishness** Langsamkeit *f*, Trägheit *f*.

sluice [slɪːs] *n* Schleuse *f*.

slum [slʌm] *n* Elendsviertel *nt*, Slum *m*.

slumber ['slʌmbə*] *n* Schlummer *m*.

slump [slʌmp] *n* Rückgang *m*; *vi* fallen, stürzen.

slur [slɜː*] *n* Undeutlichkeit *f*; (*insult*) Verleumdung *f*; *vt* (*also* ~ **over**) hinweggehen über (+*acc*); ~**red** [slɜːd] *a pronunciation* undeutlich.

slush [slʌʃ] *n* (*snow*) Schneematsch *m*; (*mud*) Schlamm *m*; ~**y** *a* (*lit*) matschig; (*fig: sentimental*) schmalzig.

slut [slʌt] *n* Schlampe *f*.

sly *a*, ~**ly** [slaɪ, -lɪ] *ad* schlau, verschlagen; ~**ness** Schlauheit *f*.

smack [smæk] *n* Klaps *m*; *vt* einen Klaps geben (+*dat*); **to** ~ **one's lips** schmatzen, sich (*dat*) die Lippen lecken; *vi* ~ **of** riechen nach.

small [smɔːl] *a* klein; ~ **change** Kleingeld *nt*; ~**holding** Kleinlandbesitz *m*; ~ **hours** *pl* frühe Morgenstunden *pl*; ~**ish** *a* ziemlich klein; ~**ness** Kleinheit *f*; ~**pox** Pocken *pl*; ~**scale** *a* klein, in kleinem Maßstab; ~ **talk** Konversation *f*, Geplauder *nt*.

smarmy ['smɑːmɪ] *a* (*col*) schmierig.

smart *a*, ~**ly** *ad* [smɑːt, -lɪ] (*fashionable*) elegant, schick; (*neat*) adrett; (*clever*) clever; (*quick*) scharf; *vi* brennen, schmerzen; ~**en up** *vi* sich in Schale werfen; *vt* herausputzen; ~**ness** Gescheitheit *f*, Eleganz *f*.

smash [smæʃ] *n* Zusammenstoß *m*; (*tennis*) Schmetterball *m*; *vt* (*break*) zerschmettern; (*destroy*) vernichten; *vi* (*break*) zersplittern, zerspringen; ~**ing** *a* (*col*) toll, großartig.

smattering ['smætərɪŋ] *n* oberflächliche Kenntnis *f*.

smear [smɪə*] *n* Fleck *m*; *vt* beschmieren.

smell [smel] *n* Geruch *m*; (*sense*) Geruchssinn *m*; *vti irreg* riechen (*of* nach); ~**y** *a* übelriechend.

smile [smaɪl] *n* Lächeln *nt*; *vi* lächeln.

smirk [smɜːk] *n* blöde(s) Grinsen *nt*; *vi* blöde grinsen.

smith [smɪθ] *n* Schmied *m*; ~**y** ['smɪðɪ] Schmiede *f*.

smock [smɒk] *n* Kittel *m*.

smog [smɒg] *n* Smog *m*.

smoke [sməʊk] *n* Rauch *m*; *vt* rauchen; *food* räuchern; *vi* rauchen; ~**r** Raucher *m*; (*Rail*) Raucherabteil *nt*; ~ **screen** Rauchwand *f*.

smoking ['sməʊkɪŋ] *n* Rauchen *nt*; **'no** ~**'** 'Rauchen verboten'.

smoky ['sməʊkɪ] *a* rauchig; *room* verraucht; *taste* geräuchert.

smolder ['sməʊldə*] *vi US* = **smoulder**.

smooth [smuːð] *a* glatt; *movement* geschmeidig; *person* glatt, gewandt; *vt* (*also* ~ **out**) glätten, glattstreichen; ~**ly** *ad* glatt, eben; (*fig*) reibungslos; ~**ness** Glätte *f*.

smother ['smʌðə*] *vt* ersticken.

smoulder ['sməʊldə*] *vi* glimmen, schwelen.

smudge [smʌdʒ] *n* Schmutzfleck *m*; *vt* beschmieren.

smug [smʌg] *a* selbstgefällig.

smuggle ['smʌgl] *vt* schmuggeln; ~**r** Schmuggler *m*.

smuggling ['smʌglɪŋ] *n* Schmuggel *m*.

smugly ['smʌglɪ] *ad* selbstgefällig.

smugness ['smʌgnəs] *n* Selbstgefälligkeit *f*.

smutty ['smʌtɪ] *a* (*fig: obscene*) obszön, schmutzig.

snack [snæk] *n* Imbiß *m*; ~ **bar** Imbißstube *f*.

snag [snæg] *n* Haken *m*; (*in stocking*) gezogene(r) Faden *m*.

snail [sneɪl] *n* Schnecke *f*.

snake [sneɪk] *n* Schlange *f*.

snap [snæp] *n* Schnappen *nt*; (*photograph*) Schnappschuß *m*; *a decision* schnell; *vt* (*break*) zerbrechen; (*Phot*) knipsen; **to** ~ **one's fingers** mit den Fingern schnipsen; *vi* (*break*) brechen; (*bite*) schnappen; (*speak*) anfauchen; ~ **out of it!** laß den auf!; ~ **off** *vt* (*break*) abbrechen; ~ **up** *vt* aufschnappen; ~**py** *a* flott; ~**shot** Schnappschuß *m*.

snare [snɛə*] *n* Schlinge *f*; *vt* mit einer Schlinge fangen.

snarl [snɑːl] *n* Zähnefletschen *nt*; *vi* (*dog*) knurren; (*engine*) brummen, dröhnen.

snatch [snætʃ] *n* (*grab*) Schnappen *nt*; (*small amount*) Bruchteil *m*; *vt* schnappen, packen.

sneak [sniːk] *vi* schleichen.

sneakers ['sniːkəz] *npl* (*US*) Freizeitschuhe *pl*.

sneer [snɪə*] *n* Hohnlächeln *nt*; *vi* höhnisch grinsen, spötteln.

sneeze [sniːz] *n* Niesen *nt*; *vi* niesen.

snide [snaɪd] *a* (*col: sarcastic*) schneidend.

sniff [snɪf] *n* Schnüffeln *nt*; *vi* schnieben; (*smell*) schnüffeln; *vt* schnuppern.

snigger ['snɪgə*] *n* Kichern *nt*; *vi* hämisch kichern.

snip [snɪp] *n* Schnippel *m*, Schnipsel *m*; *vt* schnippeln.

sniper ['snaɪpə*] *n* Heckenschütze *m*.

snippet ['snɪpɪt] *n* Schnipsel *m*; (*of conversation*) Fetzen *m*.

snivelling ['snɪvlɪŋ] *a* weinerlich.

snob [snɒb] *n* Snob *m*; ~**bery** Snobismus *m*; ~**ish** *a* versnobt; ~**bishness** Versnobtheit *f*, Snobismus *m*.

snooker ['snuːkə*] *n* Snooker *nt*.

snoop [snuːp] *vi*: ~ **about** herumschnüffeln.

snooty ['snuːtɪ] *a* (*col*) hochnäsig; *restaurant* stinkfein.

snooze [snuːz] *n* Nickerchen *nt*; *vi* ein Nickerchen machen, dösen.

snore [snɔː*] *vi* schnarchen.

snoring ['snɔːrɪŋ] *n* Schnarchen *nt*.

snorkel ['snɔːkl] *n* Schnorchel *m*.

snort [snɔːt] *n* Schnauben *nt*; *vi* schnauben.

snotty ['snɒtɪ] *a* (*col*) rotzig.

snout [snaʊt] *n* Schnauze *f*; (*of pig*) Rüssel *m*.

snow [snəʊ] *n* Schnee *m*; *vi* schneien; ~**ball** Schneeball *m*; ~**blind** *a* schneeblind; ~**bound** *a* eingeschneit; ~**drift** Schneewehe *f*; ~**drop** Schneeglöckchen *nt*; ~**fall** Schneefall *m*; ~**flake** Schneeflocke *f*; ~**line** Schneegrenze *f*; ~**man** Schneemann *m*; ~**plough**, (*US*) ~**plow** Schneepflug *m*; ~**storm** Schneesturm *m*.

snub [snʌb] *vt* schroff abfertigen; *n* Verweis *m*, schroffe Abfertigung *f*; *a* ~**-nosed** stupsnasig.

snuff [snʌf] *n* Schnupftabak *m*; ~**box** Schnupftabakdose *f*.

snug [snʌg] *a* gemütlich, behaglich.

so [səu] *ad* so; *cj* daher, folglich, also; ~ **as to** um zu; **or** ~ so etwa; ~ **long!** (*goodbye*) tschüß!; ~ **many** so viele; ~ **much** soviel; ~ **that** damit.

soak [səuk] *vt* durchnässen; (*leave in liquid*) einweichen; ~ **in** *vi* einsickern in (+*acc*); ~**ing** Einweichen *nt*; ~**ing wet** *a* klatschnaß.

soap [səup] *n* Seife *f*; ~**flakes** *pl* Seifenflocken *pl*; ~ **powder** Waschpulver *nt*; ~**y** *a* seifig, Seifen-.

soar [sɔː*] *vi* aufsteigen; (*prices*) in die Höhe schnellen.

sob [sɔb] *n* Schluchzen *nt*; *vi* schluchzen.

sober ['səubə*] *a* (*lit, fig*) nüchtern; ~ **up** *vi* nüchtern werden; ~**ly** *ad* nüchtern.

so-called ['səu'kɔːld] *a* sogenannt.

soccer ['sɔkə*] *n* Fußball *m*.

sociability [səufə'bɪlɪtɪ] *n* Umgänglichkeit *f*.

sociable ['səufəbl] *a* umgänglich, gesellig.

social ['səufəl] *a* sozial; (*friendly, living with others*) gesellig; ~**ism** Sozialismus *m*; ~**ist** Sozialist(in *f*) *m*; *a* sozialistisch; ~**ly** *ad* gesellschaftlich, privat; ~ **science** Sozialwissenschaft *f*; ~ **security** Sozialversicherung *f*; ~ **welfare** Fürsorge *f*; ~ **work** Sozialarbeit *f*; ~ **worker** Sozialarbeiter(in *f*) *m*.

society [sə'saɪətɪ] *n* Gesellschaft *f*; (*fashionable world*) die große Welt.

sociological [səusɪə'lɒdʒɪkəl] *a* soziologisch.

sociologist [səusɪ'ɒlədʒɪst] *n* Soziologe *m*, Soziologin *f*.

sociology [səusɪ'ɒlədʒɪ] *n* Soziologie *f*.

sock [sɔk] *n* Socke *f*; *vt* (*col*) schlagen.

socket ['sɔkɪt] *n* (*Elec*) Steckdose *f*; (*of eye*) Augenhöhle *f*; (*Tech*) Rohransatz *m*.

sod [sɔd] *n* Rasenstück *nt*; (*col*) Saukerl *m*.

soda ['səudə] *n* Soda *f*; ~ **water** Mineralwasser *nt*, Soda(wasser) *nt*.

sodden ['sɔdn] *a* durchweicht.

sofa ['səufə] *n* Sofa *nt*.

soft [sɔft] *a* weich; (*not loud*) leise, gedämpft; (*kind*) weichherzig, gutmütig; (*weak*) weich, nachgiebig; ~ **drink** alkoholfreie(s) Getränk *nt*; ~ **in** [*n* sɔfn] *vt* weich machen; *blow* abschwächen, mildern; *vi* weich werden; ~**-hearted** *a* weichherzig; ~**ly** *ad* sanft; leise; ~**ness** Weichheit *f*; (*fig*) Sanftheit *f*.

soggy ['sɔgɪ] *a* ground sumpfig; *bread* aufgeweicht.

soil [sɔɪl] *n* Erde *f*, Boden *m*; *vt* beschmutzen; ~**ed** *a* beschmutzt, schmutzig.

solace ['sɔləs] *n* Trost *m*.

solar ['səulə*] *a* Sonnen-; ~ **system** Sonnensystem *nt*.

solder ['səuldə*] *vt* löten; *n* Lötmetall *nt*.

soldier ['səuldʒə*] *n* Soldat *m*.

sole [səul] *n* Sohle *f*; (*fish*) Seezunge *f*; *vt* besohlen; *a* alleinig, Allein-; ~**ly** *ad* ausschließlich, nur.

solemn ['sɔləm] *a* feierlich; (*serious*) feierlich, ernst.

solicitor [sə'lɪsɪtə*] *n* Rechtsanwalt *m*.

solid ['sɔlɪd] *a* (*hard*) fest; (*of same material*) rein, massiv; (*not hollow*) massiv, stabil; (*without break*) voll, ganz; (*reliable*) solide, zuverlässig; (*sensible*) solide, gut; (*united*) eins, einig; *meal* kräftig; *n* Feste(s) *nt*; ~**arity** [sɔlɪ'dærɪtɪ] Solidarität *f*, Zusammenhalt *m*; ~ **figure** (*Math*) Körper *m*; ~**ify** [sə'lɪdɪfaɪ] *vi* fest werden, sich verdichten, erstarren; *vt* fest machen; verdichten; ~**ity** [sə'lɪdɪtɪ] Festigkeit *f*; ~**ly** *ad* (*fig*) behind einmütig; *work* ununterbrochen.

soliloquy [sə'lɪləkwɪ] *n* Monolog *m*.

solitaire [sɔlɪ'tɛə*] *n* (*Cards*) Patience *f*; (*gem*) Solitär *m*.

solitary ['sɔlɪtərɪ] *a* einsam, einzeln.

solitude ['sɔlɪtjuːd] *n* Einsamkeit *f*.

solo ['səuləu] *n* Solo *nt*; ~**ist** Soloist(in *f*) *m*.

solstice ['sɔlstɪs] *n* Sonnenwende *f*.

soluble ['sɔljubl] *a* substance löslich; *problem* (auf)lösbar.

solution [sə'luːʃən] *n* (*lit, fig*) Lösung *f*; (*of mystery*) Erklärung *f*.

solve [sɔlv] *vt* (auf)lösen.

solvent ['sɔlvənt] *a* (*Fin*) zahlungsfähig.

sombre, (*US*) **somber** *a*, ~**ly** *ad* ['sɔmbə*, -əlɪ] düster.

some [sʌm] *a* people etc einige; water etc etwas; (*unspecified*) (irgend)ein; (*remarkable*) toll, enorm; **that's** ~ **house** das ist vielleicht ein Haus; *pron* (*amount*) etwas; (*number*) einige; ~**body** *pron* (irgend) jemand; **he is** ~**body** er ist jemand or wer; ~**day** *ad* irgendwann; ~**how** *ad* (in a certain way) irgendwie; (*for a certain reason*) aus irgendeinem Grunde; ~**one** *pron* = somebody; ~**place** *ad* (*US*) = somewhere.

somersault ['sʌməsɔːlt] *n* Purzelbaum *m*; Salto *m*; *vi* Purzelbäume schlagen; einen Salto machen.

something ['sʌmθɪŋ] *pron* (irgend) etwas.

sometime ['sʌmtaɪm] *ad* (irgend) einmal; ~**s** *ad* manchmal, gelegentlich.

somewhat ['sʌmwɔt] *ad* etwas, ein wenig, ein bißchen.

somewhere ['sʌmwɛə*] *ad* irgendwo; (*to a place*) irgendwohin.

son [sʌn] *n* Sohn *m*.

sonata [sə'nɑːtə] *n* Sonate *f*.

song [sɔŋ] *n* Lied *nt*; ~**writer** Texter *m*.

sonic ['sɔnɪk] *a* Schall-; ~ **boom** Überschallknall *m*.

son-in-law ['sʌnɪnlɔː] *n* Schwiegersohn *m*.

sonnet ['sɔnɪt] *n* Sonett *nt*.

sonny ['sʌnɪ] *n* (*col*) Kleine(r) *m*.

soon [suːn] *ad* bald; **too** ~ zu früh; **as** ~ **as possible** so bald wie möglich; ~**er** *ad* (*time*) eher, früher; (*for preference*) lieber; **no** ~**er** kaum.

soot [sut] *n* Ruß *m*.

soothe [suːð] *vt* person beruhigen; *pain* lindern.

soothing ['suːðɪŋ] *a* (*for person*) beruhigend; (*for pain*) lindernd.

sop [sɔp] *n* (*bribe*) Schmiergeld *nt*.

sophisticated [səˈfɪstɪkeɪtɪd] *a person* kultiviert, weltgewandt; *machinery* differenziert, hochentwickelt; *plan* ausgeklügelt.

sophistication [səfɪstɪˈkeɪʃən] *n* Weltgewandtheit *f*, Kultiviertheit *f*; *(Tech)* technische Verfeinerung *f*.

sophomore [ˈsɒfəmɔː*] *n* (US) College-Student *m* im 2. Jahr.

soporific [sɒpəˈrɪfɪk] *a* einschläfernd, Schlaf-.

sopping [ˈsɒpɪŋ] *a* (*very wet*) patschnaß, triefend.

soppy [ˈsɒpɪ] *a* (col) schmalzig.

soprano [səˈprɑːnəʊ] *n* Sopran *m*.

sordid [ˈsɔːdɪd] *a* (*dirty*) schmutzig; (*mean*) niederträchtig.

sore [sɔː*] *a* schmerzend; *point* wund; **to be ~** weh tun; (*angry*) böse sein; *n* Wunde *f*; **~ly** *ad tempted* stark, sehr; **~ness** Schmerzhaftigkeit *f*, Empfindlichkeit *f*.

sorrow [ˈsɒrəʊ] *n* Kummer *m*, Leid *nt*; **~ful** *a* sorgenvoll; **~fully** *ad* traurig, betrübt, kummervoll.

sorry [ˈsɒrɪ] *a* traurig, erbärmlich; (**I'm**) **~** es tut mir leid; **I feel ~ for him** er tut mir leid.

sort [sɔːt] *n* Art *f*, Sorte *f*; *vt* (*also* **~ out**) *papers* sortieren, sichten; *problems* in Ordnung bringen.

so-so [ˈsəʊˈsəʊ] *ad* so(-so) la-la, mäßig.

soufflé [ˈsuːfleɪ] *n* Auflauf *m*, Soufflé *nt*.

soul [səʊl] *n* Seele *f*; (*music*) Soul *m*; **~-destroying** *a* trostlos; **~ful** *a* seelenvoll; **~less** *a* seelenlos, gefühllos.

sound [saʊnd] *a* (*healthy*) gesund; (*safe*) sicher, solide; (*sensible*) vernünftig; *theory* stichhaltig; (*thorough*) tüchtig, gehörig; *n* (*noise*) Geräusch *nt*, Laut *m*; (*Geog*) Meerenge *f*, Sund *m*; *vt* erschallen lassen; *alarm* (Alarm) schlagen; (*Med*) abhorchen; **to ~ one's horn** hupen; *vi* (*make a sound*) schallen, tönen; (*seem*) klingen; **~ out** *vt opinion* erforschen; *person* auf den Zahn fühlen (+*dat*); **~barrier** Schallmauer *f*; **~ing** (*Naut etc*) Lotung *f*; **~ly** *ad sleep* fest, tief; *beat* tüchtig; **~proof** *a room* schalldicht; *vt* schalldicht machen; **~track** Tonstreifen *m*; Filmmusik *f*.

soup [suːp] *n* Suppe *f*; **in the ~** (col) in der Tinte; **~ spoon** Suppenlöffel *m*.

sour [ˈsaʊə*] *a* (*lit, fig*) sauer.

source [sɔːs] *n* (*lit, fig*) Quelle *f*.

sourness [ˈsaʊənəs] *n* Säure *f*; (*fig*) Bitterkeit *f*.

south [saʊθ] *n* Süden *m*; *a* Süd-, südlich; *ad* nach Süden, südwärts; **~east** Südosten *m*; **~erly** [ˈsʌðəlɪ] *a* südlich; **~ern** [ˈsʌðən] *a* südlich, Süd-; **~ward(s)** *ad* südwärts, nach Süden; **~west** Südwesten *m*.

souvenir [suːvəˈnɪə*] *n* Andenken *nt*, Souvenir *nt*.

sovereign [ˈsɒvrɪn] *n* (*ruler*) Herrscher *m*; *a* (*independent*) souverän; **~ty** Oberhoheit *f*, Souveränität *f*.

sow [saʊ] *n* Sau *f*; [səʊ] *vt irreg* (*lit, fig*) säen.

soya bean [ˈsɔɪəˈbiːn] *n* Sojabohne *f*.

spa [spɑː] *n* (*spring*) Mineralquelle *f*; (*place*) Kurort *m*, Bad *nt*.

space [speɪs] *n* Platz *m*, Raum *m*; (*universe*) Weltraum *m*, All *nt*; (*length of time*) Abstand *m*; **~ out** *vt* Platz lassen zwischen; (*typing*) gesperrt schreiben; **~craft** Raumschiff *nt*; **~man** Raumfahrer *m*.

spacious [ˈspeɪʃəs] *a* geräumig, weit.

spade [speɪd] *n* Spaten *m*; **~s** (*Cards*) Pik *nt*, Schippe *f*; **~work** (*fig*) Vorarbeit *f*.

spaghetti [spəˈgetɪ] *n* Spaghetti *pl*.

span [spæn] *n* Spanne *f*; Spannweite *f*; *vt* überspannen.

spaniel [ˈspænjəl] *n* Spaniel *m*.

spank [spæŋk] *vt* verhauen, versohlen.

spanner [ˈspænə*] *n* Schraubenschlüssel *m*.

spar [spɑː*] *n* (*Naut*) Sparren *m*; *vi* (*boxing*) einen Sparring machen.

spare [spɛə*] *a* Ersatz-; **~ part**; *vt lives, feelings* verschonen; *trouble* ersparen; **4 to ~** 4 übrig; **~ part** Ersatzteil *nt*; **~ time** Freizeit *f*.

spark [spɑːk] *n* Funken *m*; **~(ing) plug** Zündkerze *f*.

sparkle [ˈspɑːkl] *n* Funkeln *nt*, Glitzern *nt*; (*gaiety*) Lebhaftigkeit *f*, Schwung *m*; *vi* funkeln, glitzern.

sparkling [ˈspɑːklɪŋ] *a* funkelnd, sprühend; *wine* Schaum-; *conversation* spritzig, geistreich.

sparrow [ˈspærəʊ] *n* Spatz *m*.

sparse *a*, **~ly** *ad* [spɑːs, -lɪ] spärlich, dünn.

spasm [ˈspæzəm] *n* (*Med*) Krampf *m*; (*fig*) Anfall *m*; **~odic** [spæzˈmɒdɪk] *a* krampfartig, spasmodisch; (*fig*) sprunghaft.

spastic [ˈspæstɪk] *a* spastisch.

spate [speɪt] *n* (*fig*) Flut *f*, Schwall *m*; **in ~** *river* angeschwollen.

spatter [ˈspætə*] *n* Spritzer *m*; *vt* bespritzen, verspritzen; *vi* spritzen.

spatula [ˈspætjʊlə] *n* Spatel *m*; (*for building*) Spachtel *f*.

spawn [spɔːn] *vi* laichen.

speak [spiːk] *irreg vt* sprechen, reden; *truth* sagen; *language* sprechen; *vi* sprechen (*to* mit *or* zu); **~ for** *vt* sprechen *or* eintreten für; **~ up** *vi* lauter sprechen; **~er** Sprecher *m*, Redner *m*; *loud* **~** Lautsprecher *m*; **not to be on ~ing terms** nicht miteinander sprechen.

spear [spɪə*] *n* Speer *m*, Lanze *f*, Spieß *m*; *vt* aufspießen, durchbohren.

spec [spek] *n* (col) **on ~** auf gut Glück.

special [ˈspeʃəl] *a* besondere(r,s); speziell; *n* (*Rail*) Sonderzug *m*; **~ist** Spezialist *m*; (*Tech*) Fachmann *m*; (*Med*) Facharzt *m*; **~ity** [speʃɪˈælɪtɪ] Spezialität *f*; (*study*) Spezialgebiet *nt*; **~ize** *vi* sich spezialisieren (*in auf* +*acc*); **~ly** *ad* besonders; (*explicitly*) extra, ausdrücklich.

species [ˈspiːʃiːz] *n* Art *f*.

specific [spəˈsɪfɪk] *a* spezifisch, eigentümlich, besondere(r,s); **~ally** *ad* genau, spezifisch; **~ations** *pl* [spesɪfɪˈkeɪʃənz] genaue Angaben *pl*; (*Tech*) technische Daten *pl*.

specify [ˈspesɪfaɪ] *vt* genau angeben.

specimen ['spesɪmɪn] n Probe f, Muster nt.

speck [spek] n Fleckchen nt; ~**led** a gesprenkelt.

specs [speks] npl (col) Brille f.

spectacle ['spektəkl] n Schauspiel nt; ~**s** pl Brille f.

spectacular [spek'tækjulə*] a aufsehenerregend, spektakulär.

spectator [spek'teɪtə*] n Zuschauer m.

spectre, (US) **specter** ['spektə*] n Geist m, Gespenst nt.

spectrum ['spektrəm] n Spektrum nt.

speculate ['spekjuleɪt] vi vermuten, spekulieren (also Fin).

speculation [spekju'leɪʃən] n Vermutung f, Spekulation f (also Fin).

speculative ['spekjulətɪv] a spekulativ.

speech [spiːtʃ] n Sprache f; (address) Rede f, Ansprache f; (manner of speaking) Sprechweise f; ~ **day** (Sch) (Jahres)schlußfeier f; ~**less** a sprachlos; ~ **therapy** Sprachheilpflege f.

speed [spiːd] n Geschwindigkeit f; (gear) Gang m; vi irreg rasen; (Jur) (zu) schnell fahren; ~ **up** vt beschleunigen; vi schneller werden/ fahren; ~**boat** Schnellboot nt; ~**ily** ad schnell, schleunigst; ~**ing** zu schnelles Fahren; ~ **limit** Geschwindigkeitsbegrenzung f; ~**ometer** [spɪ'dɒmɪtə*] Tachometer m; ~**way** (bike racing) Motorradrennstrecke f; ~**y** a schnell, zügig.

spell [spel] n (magic) Bann m, Zauber m; (period of time) Zeit f, Zeitlang f, Weile f; **sunny** ~**s** pl Aufheiterungen pl; **rainy** ~**s** pl vereinzelte Schauer pl; vt irreg buchstabieren; (imply) bedeuten; **how do you** ~ **. . .?** wie schreibt man . . .?; ~**bound** a (wie) gebannt; ~**ing** Buchstabieren nt; **English** ~**ing** die englische Rechtschreibung f.

spend [spend] vt irreg money ausgeben; time verbringen; ~**ing** **money** Taschengeld nt.

spent [spent] a patience erschöpft.

sperm [spɜːm] n (Biol) Samenflüssigkeit f.

spew [spjuː] vt (er)brechen.

sphere [sfɪə*] n (globe) Kugel f; (fig) Sphäre f, Gebiet nt.

spherical ['sferɪkəl] a kugelförmig.

sphinx [sfɪŋks] n Sphinx f.

spice [spaɪs] n Gewürz nt; vt würzen.

spiciness ['spaɪsɪnəs] n Würze f.

spick-and-span ['spɪkən'spæn] a blitzblank.

spicy ['spaɪsɪ] a würzig, pikant (also fig).

spider ['spaɪdə*] n Spinne f; ~**y** a writing krakelig.

spike [spaɪk] n Dorn m, Spitze f; ~**s** pl Spikes pl.

spill [spɪl] irreg vt verschütten; vi sich ergießen.

spin [spɪn] n Umdrehung f; (trip in car) Spazierfahrt f; (Aviat) (Ab)trudeln nt; (on ball) Drall m; irreg vt thread spinnen; (like top) schnell drehen, (herum)wirbeln; vi sich drehen; ~ **out** vt in die Länge ziehen; story ausmalen.

spinach ['spɪnɪtʃ] n Spinat m.

spinal ['spaɪnl] a spinal, Rückgrat-, Rückenmark-; ~ **cord** Rückenmark nt.

spindly ['spɪndlɪ] a spindeldürr.

spin-drier ['spɪn'draɪə*] n Wäscheschleuder f.

spin-dry ['spɪn'draɪ] vt schleudern.

spine [spaɪn] n Rückgrat nt; (thorn) Stachel m; ~**less** a (lit, fig) rückgratlos.

spinet [spɪ'net] n Spinett nt.

spinner ['spɪnə*] n (of thread) Spinner m.

spinning ['spɪnɪŋ] n (of thread) (Faden)spinnen nt; ~ **wheel** Spinnrad nt.

spinster ['spɪnstə*] n unverheiratete Frau f; (pej) alte Jungfer f.

spiral ['spaɪərəl] n Spirale f; a gewunden, spiralförmig, Spiral-; vi sich ringeln; ~ **staircase** Wendeltreppe f.

spire ['spaɪə*] n Turm m.

spirit ['spɪrɪt] n Geist m; (humour, mood) Stimmung f; (courage) Mut m; (verve) Elan m; (alcohol) Alkohol m; ~**s** pl Spirituosen pl; **in good** ~**s** gut aufgelegt; ~**ed** a beherzt; ~ **level** Wasserwaage f; ~**ual** a geistig, seelisch; (Rel) geistlich; n Spiritual nt; ~**ualism** Spiritismus m.

spit [spɪt] n (for roasting) (Brat)spieß m; (saliva) Spucke f; vi irreg spucken; (rain) sprühen; (make a sound) zischen; (cat) fauchen.

spite [spaɪt] n Gehässigkeit f; vt ärgern, kränken; **in** ~ **of** trotz (+gen or dat); ~**ful** a gehässig.

splash [splæʃ] n Spritzer m; (of colour) (Farb)fleck m; vt bespritzen; vi spritzen; ~**down** Wasserlandung f.

spleen [spliːn] n (Anat) Milz f.

splendid a, ~**ly** ad ['splendɪd, -lɪ] glänzend, großartig.

splendour, (US) **splendor** ['splendə*] n Pracht f.

splice [splaɪs] vt spleißen.

splint [splɪnt] n Schiene f.

splinter ['splɪntə*] n Splitter m; vi (zer)splittern.

split [splɪt] n Spalte f; (fig) Spaltung f; (division) Trennung f; irreg vt spalten; vi (divide) reißen; sich spalten; (col: depart) abhauen; ~ **up** vi sich trennen; vt aufteilen, teilen; ~**ting** a headache rasend, wahnsinnig.

splutter ['splʌtə*] vi spritzen; (person, engine) stottern.

spoil [spɔɪl] irreg vt (ruin) verderben; child verwöhnen, verziehen; vi (food) verderben; ~**s** pl Beute f; ~**sport** Spielverderber m.

spoke [spəʊk] n Speiche f; ~**sman** Sprecher m, Vertreter m.

sponge [spʌndʒ] n Schwamm m; vt mit dem Schwamm abwaschen; vi auf Kosten leben (on gen); ~ **bag** Kulturbeutel m; ~ **cake** Rührkuchen m; ~**r** (col) Schmarotzer m.

spongy ['spʌndʒɪ] a schwammig.

sponsor ['spɒnsə*] n Bürge m; (in advertising) Sponsor m; vt bürgen für; fördern; ~**ship** Bürgschaft f; (public) Schirmherrschaft f.

spontaneity [spɒntə'neɪɪtɪ] n Spontanität f.

spontaneous a, **~ly** ad [spɒn'teɪnɪəs, -lɪ] spontan.

spooky ['spu:kɪ] a (col) gespenstisch.

spool [spu:l] n Spule f, Rolle f.

spoon [spu:n] n Löffel m; **~-feed** vt irreg (lit) mit dem Löffel füttern; (fig) hoch-päppeln; **~ful** Löffel(voll) m.

sporadic [spə'rædɪk] a vereinzelt, sporadisch.

sport [spɔ:t] n Sport m; (fun) Spaß m; (person) feine(r) Kerl m; **~ing** a (fair) sportlich, fair; **~s car** Sportwagen m; **~(s) coat**, **~(s) jacket** Sportjackett nt; **~sman** Sportler m; (fig) anständige(r) Kerl m; **~smanship** Sportlichkeit f; (fig) Anständigkeit f; **~s page** Sportseite f; **~swear** Sportkleidung f; **~swoman** Sportlerin f; **~y** a sportlich.

spot [spɒt] n Punkt m; (dirty) Fleck(en) m; (place) Stelle f, Platz m; (Med) Pickel m, Pustel f; (small amount) Schluck m, Tropfen m; vt erspähen; mistake bemerken; **~ check** Stichprobe f; **~less** a, **~ly** ad fleckenlos; **~light** Schein-werferlicht nt; (lamp) Scheinwerfer m; **~ted** a gefleckt; dress gepunktet; **~ty** a face pickelig.

spouse [spauz] n Gatte m/Gattin f.

spout [spaut] n (of pot) Tülle f; (jet) Wasserstrahl m; vi speien, spritzen.

sprain [spreɪn] n Verrenkung f; vt verrenken.

sprawl [sprɔ:l] n (of city) Ausbreitung f, vi sich strecken.

spray [spreɪ] n Spray m; (off sea) Gischt f; (instrument) Zerstäuber m, Spraydose f; (of flowers) Zweig m; vt besprühen, sprayen.

spread [spred] n (extent) Verbreitung f; (of wings) Spannweite f; (col: meal) Schmaus m; (for bread) Aufstrich m; vt irreg ausbreiten; (scatter) verbreiten; butter streichen.

spree [spri:] n lustige(r) Abend m; (shopping) Einkaufsbummel m; **to go out on a ~** einen draufmachen.

sprig [sprɪg] n kleine(r) Zweig m.

sprightly ['spraɪtlɪ] a munter, lebhaft.

spring [sprɪŋ] n (leap) Sprung m; (metal) Feder f; (season) Frühling m; (water) Quelle f; vi irreg (leap) springen; **~ up** vi (problem) entstehen, auftauchen; **~board** Sprungbrett nt; **~clean** vt Frühjahrsputz machen in (+dat); **~cleaning** Frühjahrsputz m; **~iness** Elastizität f; **~time** Frühling m; **~y** a federnd, elastisch.

sprinkle ['sprɪŋkl] n Prise f; vt salt streuen; liquid sprenkeln.

sprinkling ['sprɪŋklɪŋ] n Spur f, ein bißchen.

sprint [sprɪnt] n Kurzstreckenlauf m; Sprint m; vi sprinten; **~er** Sprinter m, Kurzstreckenläufer m.

sprite [spraɪt] n Elfe f, Kobold m.

sprout [spraut] vi sprießen; n see **Brussels ~**.

spruce [spru:s] n Fichte f; a schmuck, adrett.

spry [spraɪ] a flink, rege.

spud [spʌd] n (col) Kartoffel f.

spur [spɜ:*] n Sporn m; (fig) Ansporn m; vt (also ~ on) (fig) anspornen; **on the ~ of the moment** spontan.

spurious ['spjuərɪəs] a falsch, unecht, Pseudo-.

spurn [spɜ:n] vt verschmähen.

spurt [spɜ:t] n (jet) Strahl m; (acceleration) Spurt m; vt spritzen; vi (jet) steigen; (liquid) schießen; (run) spurten.

spy [spaɪ] n Spion m; vi spionieren; vt erspähen; **to ~ on sb** jdm nach-spionieren; **~ing** Spionage f.

squabble ['skwɒbl] n Zank m; vi sich zanken.

squabbling ['skwɒblɪŋ] n Zankerei f.

squad [skwɒd] n (Mil) Abteilung f; (police) Kommando nt.

squadron ['skwɒdrən] n (cavalry) Schwadron f; (Naut) Geschwader nt; (air force) Staffel f.

squalid ['skwɒlɪd] a schmutzig, ver-kommen.

squall [skwɔ:l] n Bö f, Windstoß m; **~y** a weather stürmisch; wind böig.

squalor ['skwɒlə*] n Verwahrlosung f, Schmutz m.

squander ['skwɒndə*] vt verschwenden.

square [skwɛə*] n (Math) Quadrat nt; (open space) Platz m; (instrument) Winkel m; (col: person) Spießer m; a viereckig, quadratisch; (fair) ehrlich, reell; (meal) reichlich; (col) ideas, tastes spießig; ad (exactly) direkt, gerade; vt (arrange) aus-machen, aushandeln; (Math) ins Quadrat erheben; (bribe) schmieren; vi (agree) übereinstimmen; **all ~** quitt; **2 metres ~** 2 Meter im Quadrat; **2 ~ metres** 2 Quadratmeter; **~ly** ad fest, gerade.

squash [skwɒʃ] n (drink) Saft m; vt zerquetschen.

squat [skwɒt] a untersetzt, gedrungen; vi hocken; **~ter** Squatter m, Siedler m ohne Rechtstitel; Hausbesetzer m.

squaw [skwɔ:] n Squaw f.

squawk [skwɔ:k] n Kreischen nt; vi kreischen.

squeak [skwi:k] n Gequiek(s)e nt; vi quiek(s)en; (spring, door etc) quietschen; **~y** a quiek(s)end, quietschend.

squeal [skwi:l] n schrille(r) Schrei m; (of brakes etc) Quietschen nt; vi schrill schreien.

squeamish ['skwi:mɪʃ] a empfindlich; **that made me ~** davon wurde mir übel; **~ness** Überempfindlichkeit f.

squeeze [skwi:z] n (jet) Pressen nt; (Pol) Geldknappheit f, wirtschaftliche(r) Engpaß m; vt pressen, drücken; orange auspressen; **~ out** vt ausquetschen.

squid [skwɪd] n Tintenfisch m.

squint [skwɪnt] n Schielen nt; vi schielen.

squire ['skwaɪə*] n Gutsherr m.

squirm [skwɜ:m] vi sich winden.

squirrel ['skwɪrəl] n Eichhörnchen nt.

squirt [skwɜ:t] n Spritzer m, Strahl m; vti spritzen.

stab [stæb] n (blow) Stoß m, Stich m; (col: try) Versuch m; vt erstechen; **~bing** Messerstecherei f.

stability [stə'bılıtı] n Festigkeit f, Stabilität f.

stabilization [steıbəlaı'zeıʃən] n Festigung f, Stabilisierung f.

stabilize ['steıbəlaız] vt festigen, stabilisieren; ~r Stabilisator m.

stable ['steıbl] n Stall m; vt im Stall unterbringen; a fest, stabil; person gefestigt.

staccato [stə'kɑːtəʊ] a stakkato.

stack [stæk] n Stoß m, Stapel m; vt (auf-)stapeln.

stadium ['steıdıəm] n Stadion nt.

staff [stɑːf] n (stick, Mil) Stab m; (personnel) Personal nt; (Sch) Lehrkräfte pl; vt (with people) besetzen.

stag [stæg] n Hirsch m.

stage [steıdʒ] n Bühne f; (of journey) Etappe f, (degree) Stufe f; (point) Stadium nt; vt (put on) aufführen; play inszenieren; demonstration veranstalten; in ~s etappenweise; ~coach Postkutsche f; ~door Bühneneingang m; ~ manager Spielleiter m, Intendant m.

stagger ['stægə*] vi wanken, taumeln; vt (amaze) verblüffen; hours staffeln; ~ing a unglaublich.

stagnant ['stægnənt] a stagnierend; water stehend.

stagnate [stæg'neıt] vi stagnieren.

stagnation [stæg'neıʃən] n Stillstand m, Stagnation f.

staid [steıd] a gesetzt.

stain [steın] n Fleck m; (colouring for wood) Beize f; vt beflecken, Flecken machen auf (+acc); beizen; ~ed glass window buntes Glasfenster nt; ~less a steel rostfrei, nichtrostend; ~ remover Fleckentferner m.

stair [steə*] n (Treppen)stufe f; ~case Treppenhaus nt, Treppe f; ~s pl Treppe f; ~way Treppenaufgang m.

stake [steık] n (post) Pfahl m, Pfosten m; (money) Einsatz m; vt (bet money) setzen; to be at ~ auf dem Spiel stehen.

stalactite ['stæləktaıt] n Stalaktit m.

stalagmite ['stæləgmaıt] n Stalagmit m.

stale [steıl] a alt; cheese schal; bread altbacken; ~mate (chess) Patt nt; (fig) Stillstand m.

stalk [stɔːk] n Stengel m, Stiel m; vt game sich anpirschen an (+acc), jagen; vi (walk) stolzieren.

stall [stɔːl] n (in stable) Stand m, Box f; (in market) (Verkaufs)stand m; vt (Aut) (den Motor) abwürgen; vi (Aut) stehenbleiben; (avoid) Ausflüchte machen, ausweichen; ~s pl (Theat) Parkett nt.

stallion ['stælıən] n Zuchthengst m.

stalwart ['stɔːlwət] a standhaft; n treue(r) Anhänger m.

stamina ['stæmınə] n Durchhaltevermögen nt, Zähigkeit f.

stammer ['stæmə*] n Stottern nt; vti stottern, stammeln.

stamp [stæmp] n Briefmarke f; (with foot) Stampfen nt; (for document) Stempel m; vi stampfen; vt (mark) stempeln; mail frankieren; foot stampfen mit; ~ album Briefmarkenalbum nt; ~ collecting Briefmarkensammeln nt.

stampede [stæm'piːd] n panische Flucht f.

stance [stæns] n (posture) Haltung f, Stellung f; (opinion) Einstellung f.

stand [stænd] n Standort m, Platz m; (for objects) Gestell m; (seats) Tribüne f; vi stehen; (rise) aufstehen; (decision) feststehen; to ~ still still stehen; vt setzen, stellen; (endure) aushalten; person ausstehen, leiden können; nonsense dulden; it ~s to reason es ist einleuchtend; ~ by vi (be ready) bereitstehen; vt opinion treu bleiben (+dat); ~ for vt (signify) stehen für; (permit, tolerate) hinnehmen; ~ in for vt einspringen für; ~ out vi (be prominent) hervorstechen; ~ up vi (rise) aufstehen; ~ up for vt sich einsetzen für.

standard ['stændəd] n (measure) Standard m, Norm f, (flag) Standarte f, Fahne f; a size etc Normal-, Durchschnitts-; ~ization Vereinheitlichung f; ~ize vt vereinheitlichen, normen; ~ lamp Stehlampe f; ~ of living Lebensstandard m; ~ time Ortszeit f.

stand-by ['stændbaı] n Reserve f; ~ flight Standby-Flug m.

stand-in ['stændın] n Ersatz(mann) m, Hilfskraft f.

standing ['stændıŋ] a (erect) stehend; (permanent) ständig, dauernd; invitation offen; n (duration) Dauer f; (reputation) Ansehen nt; ~ jump Sprung m aus dem Stand; ~ order (at bank) Dauerauftrag m; ~ orders pl (Mil) Vorschrift f; ~ room only nur Stehplatz.

stand-offish ['stænd'ɒfıʃ] a zurückhaltend, sehr reserviert.

standpoint ['stændpɔınt] n Standpunkt m.

standstill ['stændstıl] n: to be at a ~ stillstehen; to come to a ~ zum Stillstand kommen.

stanza ['stænzə] n (verse) Strophe f; (poem) Stanze f.

staple ['steıpl] n (clip) Krampe f; (in paper) Heftklammer f; (article) Haupterzeugnis nt; a Grund-; Haupt-; vt (fest-)klammern; ~r Heftmaschine f.

star [stɑː*] n Stern m; (person) Star m; vi die Hauptrolle spielen; vt actor in der Hauptrolle zeigen.

starboard ['stɑːbəd] n Steuerbord nt; a Steuerbord-.

starch [stɑːtʃ] n Stärke f; vt stärken; ~y a stärkehaltig; (formal) steif.

stardom ['stɑːdəm] n Berühmtheit f.

stare [steə*] n starre(r) Blick m; vi starren (at auf +acc); ~ at anstarren.

starfish ['stɑːfıʃ] n Seestern m.

staring ['steərıŋ] a eyes starrend.

stark [stɑːk] a öde; ad: ~ naked splitternackt.

starless ['stɑːləs] a sternlos.

starlight ['stɑːlaıt] n Sternenlicht nt.

starling ['stɑːlıŋ] n Star m.

starlit ['stɑːlıt] a sternklar.

starring ['stɑːrıŋ] a mit . . . in der Hauptrolle.

star-studded ['stɑːstʌdıd] a mit Spitzenstars.

starry ['stɑːrɪ] *a* Sternen-; **~-eyed** *a* (*innocent*) blauäugig.

start [stɑːt] *n* Beginn *m*, Anfang *m*, Start *m*; (*Sport*) Start *m*; (*lead*) Vorsprung *m*; **to give a** ~ zusammenfahren; **to give sb a** ~ jdn zusammenfahren lassen; *vt* in Gang setzen, anfangen; *car* anlassen; *vi* anfangen; (*car*) anspringen; (*on journey*) aufbrechen; (*Sport*) starten; ~ **over** *vi* (*US*) wieder anfangen; ~ **up** *vi* anfangen; (*startled*) auffahren; *vt* beginnen; *car* anlassen; *engine* starten; **~er** (*Aut*) Anlasser *m*; (*for race*) Starter *m*; **~ing handle** Anlaßkurbel *f*; **~ing point** Ausgangspunkt *m*.

startle ['stɑːtl] *vt* erschrecken.

startling ['stɑːtlɪŋ] *a* erschreckend.

starvation [stɑːˈveɪʃən] *n* Verhungern *nt*; **to die of** ~ verhungern.

starve [stɑːv] *vi* verhungern; *vt* verhungern lassen; **to be** ~**d of affection** unter Mangel an Liebe leiden; ~ **out** *vt* aushungern.

starving ['stɑːvɪŋ] *a* (ver)hungernd.

state [steɪt] *n* (*condition*) Zustand *m*; (*Pol*) Staat *m*; (*col: anxiety*) Verfassung *f*; *vt* erklären; *facts* angeben; ~ **control** staatliche Kontrolle *f*; ~**d** *a* festgesetzt; **~liness** Pracht *f*, Würde *f*; **~ly** *a* würdevoll, erhaben; **~ment** Aussage *f*, (*Pol*) Erklärung *f*; ~ **secret** Staatsgeheimnis *nt*; **~sman** Staatsmann *m*.

static ['stætɪk] *n* Statik *f*; *a* statisch.

station ['steɪʃən] *n* (*Rail etc*) Bahnhof *m*; (*police etc*) Station *f*, Wache *f*; (*in society*) gesellschaftliche Stellung *f*; *vt* aufstellen; **to be** ~**ed** stationiert sein.

stationary ['steɪʃənrɪ] *a* stillstehend; *car* parkend.

stationer ['steɪʃənə*] *n* Schreibwarenhändler *m*; ~**'s (shop)** Schreibwarengeschäft *nt*; ~**y** Schreibwaren *pl*.

station master ['steɪʃənmɑːstə*] *n* Bahnhofsvorsteher *m*.

station wagon ['steɪʃənwægən] *n* Kombiwagen *m*.

statistic [stəˈtɪstɪk] *n* Statistik *f*; ~**al** *a* statistisch; ~**s** *pl* Statistik *f*.

statue ['stætjuː] *n* Statue *f*.

statuesque [stætjʊˈesk] *a* statuenhaft.

stature ['stætʃə*] *n* Wuchs *m*, Statur *f*; (*fig*) Größe *f*.

status ['steɪtəs] *n* Stellung *f*, Status *m*; **the** ~ **quo** der Status quo; ~ **symbol** Statussymbol *nt*.

statute ['stætjuːt] *n* Gesetz *nt*.

statutory ['stætjʊtərɪ] *a* gesetzlich.

staunch *a*, ~**ly** *ad* [stɔːntʃ, -lɪ] treu, zuverlässig; *Catholic* standhaft, erz-.

stave [steɪv] *n*; ~ **off** *vt attack* abwehren; *threat* abwenden.

stay [steɪ] *n* Aufenthalt *m*; (*support*) Stütze *f*, (*for tent*) Schnur *f*; *vi* bleiben; (*reside*) wohnen; **to** ~ **put** an Ort und Stelle bleiben; **to** ~ **with friends** bei Freunden untergebracht sein; **to** ~ **the night** übernachten; ~ **behind** *vi* zurückbleiben; ~ **in** *vi* (*at home*) zu Hause bleiben; ~ **on** *vi* (*continue*) länger bleiben; ~ **up** *vi* (*at night*) aufbleiben.

steadfast ['stedfəst] *a* standhaft, treu.

steadily ['stedɪlɪ] *ad* stetig, regelmäßig.

steadiness ['stedɪnəs] *n* Festigkeit *f*; (*fig*) Beständigkeit *f*.

steady ['stedɪ] *a* (*firm*) fest, stabil; (*regular*) gleichmäßig; (*reliable*) zuverlässig, beständig; *hand ruhig*; *job, boyfriend* fest; *vt* festigen; **to** ~ **o.s.** sich stützen.

steak [steɪk] *n* Steak *nt*; (*fish*) Filet *nt*.

steal [stiːl] *irreg vti* stehlen; *vi* sich stehlen; ~**th** ['stelθ] Heimlichkeit *f*; ~**thy** ['stelθɪ] *a* verstohlen, heimlich.

steam [stiːm] *n* Dampf *m*; *vt* (*Cook*) im Dampfbad erhitzen; *vi* dampfen; (*ship*) dampfen, fahren; ~ **engine** Dampfmaschine *f*; ~**er** Dampfer *m*; ~**roller** Dampfwalze *f*; ~**y** *a* dampfig.

steel [stiːl] *n* Stahl *m*; *a* Stahl-; (*fig*) stählern; ~**works** Stahlwerke *pl*.

steep [stiːp] *a* steil; *price* gepfeffert; *vt* einweichen.

steeple ['stiːpl] *n* Kirchturm *m*; ~**chase** Hindernisrennen *nt*; ~**jack** Turmarbeiter *m*.

steeply ['stiːplɪ] *ad* steil.

steepness ['stiːpnəs] *n* Steilheit *f*.

steer [stɪə*] *n* Mastochse *m*; *vti* steuern; *car etc* lenken; ~**ing** (*Aut*) Steuerung *f*; ~**ing column** Lenksäule *f*; ~**ing wheel** Steuer- *or* Lenkrad *nt*.

stellar ['stelə*] *a* Stern(en)-.

stem [stem] *n* (*Biol*) Stengel *m*, Stiel *m*; (*of glass*) Stiel *m*; *vt* aufhalten; ~ **from** *vi* abstammen von.

stench [stentʃ] *n* Gestank *m*.

stencil ['stensl] *n* Schablone *f*; (*paper*) Matrize *f*; *vt* (auf)drucken.

stenographer [steˈnɒɡrəfə*] *n* Stenograph(in *f*) *m*.

step [step] *n* Schritt *m*; (*stair*) Stufe *f*; **to take** ~**s** Schritte unternehmen; *vi* treten, schreiten; ~**s** = **ladder**; ~ **down** *vi* (*fig*) abtreten; ~ **up** *vt* steigern; ~**brother** Stiefbruder *m*; ~**child** Stiefkind *nt*; ~**father** Stiefvater *m*; ~**ladder** Trittleiter *f*; ~**mother** Stiefmutter *f*.

steppe [step] *n* Steppe *f*.

stepping stone ['stepɪŋstəʊn] Stein *m*; (*fig*) Sprungbrett *nt*.

stereo ['stɪərɪəʊ] *n* Stereoanlage *f*; ~**phonic** *a* stereophonisch; ~**type** Prototyp *m*; *vt* stereotypieren; (*fig*) stereotyp machen.

sterile ['steraɪl] *a* steril, keimfrei; *person* unfruchtbar; (*after operation*) steril.

sterility [steˈrɪlɪtɪ] *n* Unfruchtbarkeit *f*, Sterilität *f*.

sterilization [sterɪlaɪˈzeɪʃən] *n* Sterilisation *f*.

sterilize ['sterɪlaɪz] *vt* (*make unproductive*) unfruchtbar machen; (*make germfree*) sterilisieren, keimfrei machen.

sterling ['stɜːlɪŋ] *a* (*Fin*) Sterling-; *silver* von Standardwert; *character* bewährt, gediegen; **£** ~ Pfund Sterling; ~ **area** Sterlingblock *m*.

stern *a*, ~**ly** *ad* [stɜːn, -lɪ] streng; *n* Heck *nt*, Achterschiff *nt*; ~**ness** Strenge *f*.

stethoscope ['steθəskəup] n Stethoskop nt, Hörrohr nt.

stevedore ['sti:vədɔ:*] n Schauermann m.

stew [stju:] n Eintopf m; vti schmoren.

steward ['stju:əd] n Steward m; (in club) Kellner m; (organizer) Verwalter m; ~ess Stewardess f.

stick [stɪk] n Stock m, Stecken m; (of chalk etc) Stück nt; irreg vt (stab) stechen; (fix) stecken; (put) stellen; (gum) (an)kleben; (col: tolerate) vertragen; vi (stop) steckenbleiben; (get stuck) klemmen; (hold fast) kleben, haften; ~ **out** vi (project) hervorstehen aus; ~ **up** vi (project) in die Höhe stehen; ~ **up for** vt (defend) eintreten für; ~**er** Klebezettel m, Aufkleber m.

stickleback ['stɪklbæk] n Stichling m.

stickler ['stɪklə*] n Pedant m (for in +acc).

stick-up ['stɪkʌp] n (col) (Raub)überfall m.

sticky ['stɪkɪ] a klebrig; atmosphere stickig.

stiff [stɪf] a steif; (difficult) schwierig, hart; paste dick, zäh; drink stark; ~**en** vt versteifen, (ver)stärken; vi sich versteifen; ~**ness** Steifheit f.

stifle ['staɪfl] vt yawn etc unterdrücken.

stifling ['staɪflɪŋ] a atmosphere drückend.

stigma ['stɪgmə] n (disgrace) Stigma nt.

stile [staɪl] n Steige f.

still [stɪl] a still; ad (immer) noch; (anyhow) immerhin; ~**born** a totgeboren; ~ **life** Stilleben nt; ~**ness** Stille f.

stilt [stɪlt] n Stelze f.

stilted ['stɪltɪd] a gestelzt.

stimulant ['stɪmjulənt] n Anregungsmittel nt, Stimulans nt.

stimulate ['stɪmjuleɪt] vt anregen, stimulieren.

stimulating ['stɪmjuleɪtɪŋ] a anregend, stimulierend.

stimulation [stɪmju'leɪʃən] n Anregung f, Stimulation f.

stimulus ['stɪmjuləs] n Anregung f, Reiz m.

sting [stɪŋ] n Stich m; (organ) Stachel m; vti irreg stechen; (on skin) brennen.

stingily ['stɪndʒɪlɪ] ad knickerig, geizig.

stinginess ['stɪndʒɪnəs] n Geiz m.

stinging nettle ['stɪŋɪŋnetl] n Brennessel f.

stingy ['stɪndʒɪ] a geizig, knauserig.

stink [stɪŋk] n Gestank m; vi irreg stinken; ~**er** (col) (person) gemeine(r) Hund m; (problem) böse Sache f; ~**ing** a (fig) widerlich; ~**ing rich** steinreich.

stint [stɪnt] n Pensum nt; (period) Betätigung f; vt einschränken, knapphalten.

stipend ['staɪpend] n Gehalt nt.

stipulate ['stɪpjuleɪt] vt festsetzen.

stipulation [stɪpju'leɪʃən] n Bedingung f.

stir [stɜ:*] n Bewegung f; (Cook) Rühren nt; (sensation) Aufsehen nt; vt (um)rühren; vi sich rühren; ~ **up** vt mob aufhetzen; fire entfachen; mixture umrühren; dust aufwirbeln; **to** ~ **things up** Ärger machen; ~**ring** a ergreifend.

stirrup ['stɪrəp] n Steigbügel m.

stitch [stɪtʃ] n (with needle) Stich m; (Med) Faden m; (of knitting) Masche f; (pain) Stich m, Stechen nt; vt nähen.

stoat [stəut] n Wiesel nt.

stock [stɔk] n Vorrat m; (Comm) (Waren)lager nt; (live—) Vieh nt; (Cook) Brühe f; (Fin) Grundkapital nt; a stets vorrätig; (standard) Normal-; vt versehen, versorgen; (in shop) führen; **in** ~ auf Vorrat; **to take** ~ Inventur machen; (fig) Bilanz ziehen; **to** ~ **up with** Reserven anlegen von; ~**ade** [stɔ'keɪd] Palisade f; ~**broker** Börsenmakler m; ~ **exchange** Börse f.

stocking ['stɔkɪŋ] n Strumpf m.

stockist ['stɔkɪst] n Händler m.

stock market ['stɔkmɑːkɪt] n Börse f, Effektenmarkt m.

stockpile ['stɔkpaɪl] n Vorrat m; **nuclear** ~ Kernwaffenvorräte pl; vt aufstapeln.

stocktaking ['stɔkteɪkɪŋ] n Inventur f, Bestandsaufnahme f.

stocky ['stɔkɪ] n untersetzt.

stodgy ['stɔdʒɪ] a füllend, stopfend; (fig) langweilig, trocken.

stoic ['stəuɪk] n Stoiker m; ~**al** a stoisch; ~**ism** ['stəuɪsɪzəm] Stoizismus m; (fig) Gelassenheit f.

stoke [stəuk] vt schüren; ~**r** Heizer m.

stole [stəul] n Stola f; ~**n** a gestohlen.

stolid ['stɔlɪd] a schwerfällig; silence stur.

stomach ['stʌmək] n Bauch m, Magen m; **I have no** ~ **for it** das ist nichts für mich; vt vertragen; ~-**ache** Magen- or Bauchschmerzen pl.

stone [stəun] n Stein m; (seed) Stein m, Kern m; (weight) Gewichtseinheit f = 6.35 kg; a steinern, Stein-; vt entkernen; (kill) steinigen; ~-**cold** a eiskalt; ~-**deaf** a stocktaub; ~-**mason** Steinmetz m; ~-**work** Mauerwerk nt.

stony ['stəunɪ] a steinig.

stool [stu:l] n Hocker m.

stoop [stu:p] vi sich bücken.

stop [stɔp] n Halt m; (bus—) Haltestelle f; (punctuation) Punkt m; vt stoppen, anhalten; (bring to end) aufhören (mit), sein lassen; vi aufhören; (clock) stehenbleiben; (remain) bleiben; **to** ~ **doing sth** aufhören, etw zu tun; ~ **it!** hör auf (damit)!; ~ **dead** vi plötzlich aufhören, innehalten; ~ **in** vi (at home) zu Hause bleiben; ~ **off** vi kurz haltmachen; ~ **out** vi (of house) ausbleiben; ~ **over** vi übernachten, die Nacht bleiben; ~ **up** vi (at night) aufbleiben; vt hole zustopfen, verstopfen; ~-**lights** pl (Aut) Bremslichter pl; ~-**over** (on journey) Zwischenaufenthalt m; ~-**page** f ['stɔpɪdʒ] (An)halten nt; (traffic) Verkehrsstockung f; (strike) Arbeitseinstellung f; ~-**per** Propfen m, Stöpsel m; ~-**press** letzte Meldung f; ~-**watch** Stoppuhr f.

storage ['stɔːrɪdʒ] n Lagerung f.

store [stɔː*] n Vorrat m; (place) Lager nt, Warenhaus nt; (large shop) Kaufhaus nt; vt lagern; ~ **up** vt sich eindecken mit; ~-**room** Lagerraum m, Vorratsraum m.

storey ['stɔːrɪ] n (Brit) Stock m, Stockwerk nt.

stork [stɔːk] n Storch m.

storm [stɔːm] n (lit, fig) Sturm m; vti stürmen; **to take by** ~ im Sturm nehmen; ~-**cloud** Gewitterwolke *f*; ~**y** *a* stürmisch.

story ['stɔːrɪ] *n* Geschichte *f*, Erzählung *f*; (*lie*) Märchen *nt*: (*US: storey*) Stock *m*, Stockwerk *nt*; ~**book** Geschichtenbuch *nt*; ~**teller** Geschichtenerzähler *m*.

stout [staʊt] *a* (*bold*) mannhaft, tapfer; (*too fat*) beleibt, korpulent; ~**ness** Festigkeit *f*; (*of body*) Korpulenz *f*.

stove [stəʊv] *n* (*Koch*)herd *m*; (*for heating*) Ofen *m*.

stow [stəʊ] *vt* verstauen; ~**away** blinde(r) Passagier *m*.

straddle ['strædl] *vt* *horse, fence* rittlings sitzen auf (+*dat*); (*fig*) überbrücken.

strafe [strɑːf] *vt* beschießen, bombardieren.

straggle ['strægl] *vi* (*branches etc*) wuchern; (*people*) nachhinken; ~**r** Nachzügler *m*.

straight [streɪt] *a* gerade; (*honest*) offen, ehrlich; (*in order*) in Ordnung; *drink* pur, unverdünnt; *ad* (*direct*) direkt, geradewegs; *n* (*Sport*) Gerade *f*; ~**away** *ad* sofort, unverzüglich; ~ **off** *ad* sofort; direkt nacheinander; ~ **on** *ad* geradeaus; ~**en** *vt* (*also* ~**en out**) (*lit*) gerade machen; (*fig*) in Ordnung bringen, klarstellen; ~**forward** *a* einfach, unkompliziert.

strain [streɪn] *n* Belastung *f*; (*streak, trace*) Zug *m*; (*of music*) Fetzen *m*; *vt* überanstrengen; (*stretch*) anspannen; *muscle* zerren; (*filter*) (durch)seihen; **don't** ~ **yourself** überanstrenge dich nicht; *vi* (*make effort*) sich anstrengen; ~**ed** *a laugh* gezwungen; *relations* gespannt; ~**er** Sieb *nt*.

strait [streɪt] *n* Straße *f*, Meerenge *f*; ~**ened** *a circumstances* beschränkt; ~-**jacket** Zwangsjacke *f*; ~-**laced** *a* engherzig, streng.

strand [strænd] *n* (*lit, fig*) Faden *m*; (*of hair*) Strähne *f*; **to be** ~**ed** (*lit, fig*) gestrandet sein.

strange [streɪndʒ] *a* fremd; (*unusual*) merkwürdig, seltsam; ~**ly** *ad* merkwürdig; fremd; ~**ly enough** merkwürdigerweise; ~**ness** Fremdheit *f*; ~**r** Fremde(r) *mf*; **I'm a** ~**r here** ich bin hier fremd.

strangle ['stræŋgl] *vt* erdrosseln, erwürgen; ~**hold** (*fig*) Unklammerung *f*.

strangulation [stræŋgjʊ'leɪʃən] *n* Erdrosseln *nt*.

strap [stræp] *n* Riemen *m*; (*on clothes*) Träger *m*; *vt* (*fasten*) festschnallen; ~**less** *a dress* trägerlos; ~**ping** *a* stramm.

stratagem ['strætədʒəm] *n* (Kriegs)list *f*.

strategic *a*, ~**ally** *ad* [strə'tiːdʒɪk, -əlɪ] strategisch.

strategist ['strætədʒɪst] *n* Stratege *m*.

strategy ['strætədʒɪ] *n* Kriegskunst *f*; (*fig*) Strategie *f*.

stratosphere ['strætəʊsfɪə*] *n* Stratosphäre *f*.

stratum ['strɑːtəm] *n* Schicht *f*.

straw [strɔː] *n* Stroh *nt*; (*single stalk, drinking* ~) Strohhalm *m*; *a* Stroh-; ~**berry** Erdbeere *f*.

stray [streɪ] *n* verirrte(s) Tier *nt*; *vi* herumstreunen; *a animal* verirrt; *thought* zufällig.

streak ['striːk] *n* Streifen *m*; (*in character*) Einschlag *m*; (*in hair*) Strähne *f*; ~ **of bad luck** Pechsträhne *f*; *vt* streifen; ~**y** *a* gestreift; *bacon* durchwachsen.

stream [striːm] *n* (*brook*) Bach *m*; (*fig*) Strom *m*; (*flow of liquid*) Strom *m*, Flut *f*; *vi* strömen, fluten; ~**er** (*pennon*) Wimpel *m*; (*of paper*) Luftschlange *f*; ~-**lined** *a* stromlinienförmig; (*effective*) rationell.

street [striːt] *n* Straße *f*; ~**car** (*US*) Straßenbahn *f*; ~ **lamp** Straßenlaterne *f*.

strength [streŋθ] *n* Stärke *f* (*also fig*); Kraft *f*; ~**en** *vt* (ver)stärken.

strenuous ['strenjʊəs] *a* anstrengend; ~**ly** *ad* angestrengt.

stress [stres] *n* Druck *m*; (*mental*) Streß *m*; (*Gram*) Betonung *f*; *vt* betonen.

stretch [stretʃ] *n* Stück *nt*, Strecke *f*; *vt* ausdehnen, strecken; *vi* sich erstrecken; (*person*) sich strecken; **at a** ~ (*continuously*) ununterbrochen; ~ **out** *vi* sich ausstrecken; *vt* ausstrecken; ~**er** Tragbahre *f*.

stricken ['strɪkən] *a person* befallen, ergriffen; *city, country* heimgesucht.

strict [strɪkt] *a* (*exact*) genau; (*severe*) streng; ~**ly** *ad* streng, genau; ~**ly speaking** streng *or* genau genommen; ~**ness** Strenge *f*.

stride [straɪd] *n* lange(r) Schritt *m*; *vi irreg* schreiten.

strident ['straɪdənt] *a* schneidend, durchdringend.

strife [straɪf] *n* Streit *m*.

strike [straɪk] *n* Streik *m*, Ausstand *m*; (*discovery*) Fund *m*; (*attack*) Schlag *m*; *irreg vt* (*hit*) schlagen; treffen; (*collide*) stoßen gegen; (*come to mind*) einfallen (+*dat*); (*stand out*) auffallen; (*find*) stoßen auf (+*acc*), finden; *vi* (*stop work*) streiken; (*attack*) zuschlagen; (*clock*) schlagen; ~ **down** *vt* (*lay low*) niederschlagen; ~ **out** *vt* (*cross out*) ausstreichen; ~ **up** *vt music* anstimmen; *friendship* schließen; ~ **pay** Streikgeld *nt*; ~**r** Streikende(r) *mf*.

striking *a*, ~**ly** *ad* ['straɪkɪŋ, -lɪ] auffallend, bemerkenswert.

string [strɪŋ] *n* Schnur *f*, Kordel *f*, Bindfaden *m*; (*row*) Reihe *f*; (*Mus*) Saite *f*; ~ **bean** grüne Bohne *f*.

stringency ['strɪndʒənsɪ] *n* Schärfe *f*.

stringent ['strɪndʒənt] *a* streng, scharf.

strip [strɪp] *n* Streifen *m*; *vt* (*uncover*) abstreifen, abziehen; *clothes* ausziehen; (*Tech*) auseinandernehmen; *vi* (*undress*) sich ausziehen; ~ **cartoon** Bildserie *f*.

stripe [straɪp] *n* Streifen *m*; ~**d** *a* gestreift.

strip light ['strɪplaɪt] *n* Leuchtröhre *f*.

stripper ['strɪpə*] *n* Stripteasetänzerin *f*.

striptease ['strɪptiːz] *n* Striptease *nt*.

strive [straɪv] *vi irreg* streben (*for* nach).

stroke [strəʊk] *n* Schlag *m*, Hieb *m*; (*swim, row*) Stoß *m*; (*Tech*) Hub *m*; (*Med*) Schlaganfall *m*; (*caress*) Streicheln *nt*; *vt* streicheln; **at a** ~ mit einem Schlag; **on the** ~ **of** 5 Schlag 5.

stroll [strəʊl] *n* Spaziergang *m*; *vi*

spazierengehen, schlendern.

strong [strɒŋ] a stark; (firm) fest; **they are 50** ~ sie sind 50 Mann stark; ~**hold** Hochburg f; ~**ly** ad stark; ~**room** Tresor m.

structural ['strʌktʃərəl] a strukturell.

structure ['strʌktʃə*] n Struktur f, Aufbau m; (building) Gebäude nt, Bau m.

struggle ['strʌgl] n Kampf m, Anstrengung f; vi (fight) kämpfen; **to** ~ **to do sth** sich (ab)mühen etw zu tun.

strum [strʌm] vt guitar klimpern auf (+dat).

strung [strʌŋ] see **string**.

strut [strʌt] n Strebe f, Stütze f; vi stolzieren.

strychnine ['strɪkni:n] n Strychnin nt.

stub [stʌb] n Stummel m; (of cigarette) Kippe f.

stubble ['stʌbl] n Stoppel f.

stubbly ['stʌblɪ] a stoppelig, Stoppel-.

stubborn a, ~**ly** ad ['stʌbən, -lɪ] stur, hartnäckig; ~**ness** Sturheit f, Hartnäckigkeit f.

stubby ['stʌbɪ] a untersetzt.

stucco ['stʌkəʊ] n Stuck m.

stuck-up [stʌk'ʌp] a hochnäsig.

stud [stʌd] n (nail) Beschlagnagel m; (button) Kragenknopf m; (number of horses) Stall m; (place) Gestüt m; ~**ded with** übersät mit.

student ['stju:dənt] n Student(in f) m; (US also) Schüler(in f) m; **fellow** ~ Kommilitone m; Kommilitonin f.

studied ['stʌdɪd] a absichtlich.

studio ['stju:dɪəʊ] n Studio nt; (for artist) Atelier nt.

studious a, ~**ly** ad ['stju:dɪəs, -lɪ] lernbegierig.

study ['stʌdɪ] n Studium nt; (investigation also) Untersuchung f; (room) Arbeitszimmer nt; (essay etc) Studie f; vt studieren; face erforschen; evidence prüfen; vi studieren; ~ **group** Arbeitsgruppe f.

stuff [stʌf] n Stoff m; (col) Zeug nt; **that's hot** ~! das ist Klasse!; vt stopfen, füllen; animal ausstopfen; **to** ~ **o.s.** sich vollstopfen; ~**ed full** vollgepfropft; ~**iness** Schwüle f; Spießigkeit f; ~**ing** Füllung f; ~**y** a room schwül; person spießig.

stumble ['stʌmbl] vi stolpern; **to** ~ **on** zufällig stoßen auf (+acc).

stumbling block ['stʌmblɪŋblɒk] n Hindernis nt, Stein m des Anstoßes.

stump [stʌmp] n Stumpf m; vt umwerfen.

stun [stʌn] vt betäuben; (shock) niederschmettern.

stunning ['stʌnɪŋ] a betäubend; news überwältigend, umwerfend; ~**ly beautiful** traumhaft schön.

stunt [stʌnt] n Kunststück nt, Trick m; vt verkümmern lassen; ~**ed** a verkümmert.

stupefy ['stju:pɪfaɪ] vt betäuben; (by news) bestürzen; ~**ing** a betäubend; bestürzend.

stupendous [stju'pendəs] a erstaunlich, enorm.

stupid a, ~**ly** ad ['stju:pɪd, -lɪ] dumm; ~**ity** [stju:'pɪdɪtɪ] Dummheit f.

stupor ['stju:pə*] n Betäubung f.

sturdily ['stɜ:dɪlɪ] ad kräftig, stabil.

sturdiness [ʃtɜ:dɪnəs] n Robustheit f.

sturdy ['stɜ:dɪ] a kräftig, robust.

stutter ['stʌtə*] n Stottern nt; vi stottern.

sty [staɪ] n Schweinestall m.

stye [staɪ] n Gerstenkorn nt.

style [staɪl] n Stil m; (fashion) Mode f; **hair** ~ Frisur f; **in** ~ mit Stil; vt hair frisieren.

styling ['staɪlɪŋ] n (of car etc) Formgebung f.

stylish a, ~**ly** ad ['staɪlɪʃ, -lɪ] modisch, schick, flott.

stylized ['staɪlaɪzd] a stilisiert.

stylus ['staɪləs] n (Grammophon)nadel f.

styptic ['stɪptɪk] a: ~ **pencil** blutstillende(r) Stift m.

suave [swɑ:v] a zuvorkommend.

sub- [sʌb] pref Unter-.

subconscious ['sʌb'kɒnʃəs] a unterbewußt; n: **the** ~ das Unterbewußte.

subdivide ['sʌbdɪ'vaɪd] vt unterteilen.

subdivision ['sʌbdɪvɪʒən] n Unterteilung f; (department) Unterabteilung f.

subdue [səb'dju:] vt unterwerfen; ~**d** a lighting gedämpft; person still.

subject ['sʌbdʒɪkt] n (of kingdom) Untertan m; (citizen) Staatsangehörige(r) mf; (topic) Thema nt; (Sch) Fach nt; (Gram) Subjekt nt, Satzgegenstand m; [səb'dʒekt] vt (subdue) unterwerfen, abhängig machen; (expose) aussetzen; **to be** ~ **to** unterworfen sein (+dat); (exposed) ausgesetzt sein (+dat); ~**ion** [səb'dʒekʃən] (conquering) Unterwerfung f; (being controlled) Abhängigkeit f; ~**ive** a, ~**ively** ad [səb'dʒektɪv, -lɪ] subjektiv; ~ **matter** Thema nt.

sub judice [sʌb'dju:dɪsɪ] a in gerichtliche(r) Untersuchung.

subjunctive [səb'dʒʌŋktɪv] n Konjunktiv m, Möglichkeitsform f; a Konjunktiv-, konjunktivisch.

sublet ['sʌb'let] vt irreg untervermieten.

sublime [sə'blaɪm] a erhaben.

submarine [sʌbmə'ri:n] n Unterseeboot nt, U-Boot nt.

submerge [səb'mɜ:dʒ] vt untertauchen; (flood) überschwemmen; vi untertauchen.

submission [səb'mɪʃən] n (obedience) Ergebenheit f, Gehorsam m; (claim) Behauptung f; (of plan) Unterbreitung f.

submit [səb'mɪt] vt behaupten; plan unterbreiten; vi (give in) sich ergeben.

subnormal ['sʌb'nɔ:məl] a minderbegabt.

subordinate [sə'bɔ:dɪnət] a untergeordnet; n Untergebene(r) mf.

subpoena [sə'pi:nə] n Vorladung f; vt vorladen.

subscribe [səb'skraɪb] vi spenden, Geld geben; (to view etc) unterstützen, beipflichten (+dat); (to newspaper) abonnieren (to acc); ~**r** (to periodical) Abonnent m; (Tel) Telefonteilnehmer m.

subscription [səb'skrɪpʃən] n Abonnement nt; (Mitglieds)beitrag m.

subsequent ['sʌbsɪkwənt] a folgend, später; ~**ly** ad später.

subside [səb'saɪd] *vi* sich senken; ~**nce** [sʌb'saɪdəns] Senkung *f.*

subsidiary [səb'sɪdɪərɪ] *n* Neben-; *n* (*company*) Zweig *m*, Tochtergesellschaft *f.*

subsidize ['sʌbsɪdaɪz] *vt* subventionieren.

subsidy ['sʌbsɪdɪ] *n* Subvention *f.*

subsistence [səb'sɪstəns] *n* Unterhalt *m*; ~ **level** Existenzminimum *nt.*

substance ['sʌbstəns] *n* Substanz *f*, Stoff *m*; (*most important part*) Hauptbestandteil *m.*

substandard ['sʌb'stændəd] *a* unterdurchschnittlich.

substantial [səb'stænʃl] *a* (*strong*) fest, kräftig; (*important*) wesentlich; ~**ly** *ad* erheblich.

substantiate [səb'stænʃɪeɪt] *vt* begründen, belegen.

substation ['sʌbsteɪʃən] *n* (*Elec*) Nebenwerk *nt.*

substitute ['sʌbstɪtjuːt] *n* Ersatz *m*; *vt* ersetzen.

substitution [sʌbstɪ'tjuːʃən] *n* Ersetzung *f.*

subterfuge ['sʌbtəfjuːdʒ] *n* Vorwand *m*; Tricks *pl.*

subterranean [sʌbtə'reɪnɪən] *a* unterirdisch.

subtitle ['sʌbtaɪtl] *n* Untertitel *m.*

subtle ['sʌtl] *a* fein; (*sly*) raffiniert; ~**ty** subtile Art *f*, Raffinesse *f.*

subtly ['sʌtlɪ] *ad* fein, raffiniert.

subtract [səb'trækt] *vt* abziehen, subtrahieren; ~**ion** [səb'trækʃən] Abziehen *nt*, Subtraktion *f.*

subtropical ['sʌb'trɒpɪkəl] *a* subtropisch.

suburb ['sʌbɜːb] *n* Vorort *m*; ~**an** [sə'bɜːbən] *a* Vorort(s)-, Stadtrand-; ~**ia** [sə'bɜːbɪə] Vorstadt *f.*

subvention [səb'venʃən] *n* (*US*) Unterstützung *f*, Subvention *f.*

subversive [səb'vɜːsɪv] *a* subversiv.

subway ['sʌbweɪ] *n* (*US*) U-Bahn *f*, Untergrundbahn *f*; (*Brit*) Unterführung *f.*

sub-zero ['sʌb'zɪərəʊ] *a* unter Null, unter dem Gefrierpunkt.

succeed [sək'siːd] *vi* gelingen (+*dat*), Erfolg haben; **he** ~**ed** es gelang ihm; *vt* (nach)folgen (+*dat*); ~**ing** *a* (nach)folgend.

success [sək'ses] *n* Erfolg *m*; ~**ful** *a.* ~**fully** *ad* erfolgreich; ~**ion** [sək'seʃən] (Aufeinander)folge *f*; (*to throne*) Nachfolge *f*; ~**ive** *a* [sək'sesɪv] aufeinanderfolgend; ~**or** Nachfolger(in *f*) *m.*

succinct [sək'sɪŋkt] *a* kurz und bündig, knapp.

succulent ['sʌkjʊlənt] *a* saftig.

succumb [sə'kʌm] *vi* zusammenbrechen (*to* unter +*dat*); (*yield*) nachgeben; (*die*) erliegen.

such [sʌtʃ] *a* solche(r, s); ~ **a** so ein; ~ **a lot** so viel; ~ **is life** so ist das Leben; ~ **is my wish** das ist mein Wunsch; ~ **as** wie; *pron* solch; ~ **as I have** die, die ich habe; ~**like** a derartig; *pron* dergleichen.

suck [sʌk] *vt* saugen; *ice cream etc* lecken; *toffee etc* lutschen; *vi* saugen; ~**er** (*col*) Idiot *m*, Dummkopf *m.*

suckle ['sʌkl] *vt* säugen; *child* stillen; *vi* saugen.

suction ['sʌkʃən] *n* Saugen *nt*, Saugkraft *f.*

sudden *a.* ~**ly** *ad* ['sʌdn, -lɪ] plötzlich; **all of a** ~ ganz plötzlich, auf einmal; ~**ness** Plötzlichkeit *f.*

sue [suː] *vt* verklagen.

suède [sweɪd] *n* Wildleder *nt*; *a* Wildleder-.

suet [suɪt] *n* Nierenfett *nt.*

suffer ['sʌfə*] *vt* (er)leiden; (*old: allow*) zulassen, dulden; *vi* leiden; ~**er** Leidende(r) *mf*; ~**ering** Leiden *nt.*

suffice [sə'faɪs] *vi* genügen.

sufficient *a.* ~**ly** *ad* [sə'fɪʃənt, -lɪ] ausreichend.

suffix ['sʌfɪks] *n* Nachsilbe *f.*

suffocate ['sʌfəkeɪt] *vti* ersticken.

suffocation [sʌfə'keɪʃən] *n* Ersticken *nt.*

suffragette [sʌfrə'dʒet] *n* Suffragette *f.*

sugar ['ʃʊgə*] *n* Zucker *m*; *vt* zuckern; ~ **beet** Zuckerrübe *f*; ~ **cane** Zuckerrohr *nt*; ~**y** *a* süß.

suggest [sə'dʒest] *vt* vorschlagen; (*show*) schließen lassen auf (+*acc*); **what does this painting** ~ **to you?** was drückt das Bild für dich aus?; ~**ion** [sə'dʒestʃən] Vorschlag *m*; ~**ive** *a* anregend; (*indecent*) zweideutig; **to be** ~**ive of sth** an etw (*acc*) erinnern.

suicidal [suɪ'saɪdl] *a* selbstmörderisch; **that's** ~ das ist Selbstmord.

suicide ['suɪsaɪd] *n* Selbstmord *m*; **to commit** ~ Selbstmord begehen.

suit [suːt] *n* Anzug *m*; (*Cards*) Farbe *f*; *vt* passen (+*dat*); *clothes* stehen (+*dat*); (*adapt*) anpassen; ~ **yourself** mach doch, was du willst; ~**ability** [suːtə'bɪlɪtɪ] Eignung *f*; ~**able** *a* geeignet, passend; ~**ably** *ad* passend, angemessen; ~**case** (Hand)koffer *m.*

suite [swiːt] *n* (*of rooms*) Zimmerflucht *f*; (*of furniture*) Einrichtung *f*; (*Mus*) Suite *f*; **three-piece** ~ Couchgarnitur *f.*

sulfur ['sʌlfə*] *n* (*US*) = **sulphur.**

sulk [sʌlk] *vi* schmollen; ~**y** *a* schmollend.

sullen ['sʌlən] *a* (*gloomy*) düster; (*bad-tempered*) mürrisch, verdrossen.

sulphur ['sʌlfə*] *n* Schwefel *m.*

sulphuric [sʌl'fjʊərɪk] *a*: ~ **acid** Schwefelsäure *f.*

sultan ['sʌltən] *n* Sultan *m*; ~**a** [sʌl'tɑːnə] (*woman*) Sultanin *f*; (*raisin*) Sultanine *f.*

sultry ['sʌltrɪ] *a* schwül.

sum [sʌm] *n* Summe *f*; (*money also*) Betrag *m*; (*arithmetic*) Rechenaufgabe *f*; ~**s** *pl* Rechnen *nt*; ~ **up** *vti* zusammenfassen; ~**marize** *vt* kurz zusammenfassen; ~**mary** Zusammenfassung *f*; (*of book etc*) Inhaltsangabe *f.*

summer ['sʌmə*] *n* Sommer *m*; *a* Sommer-; ~**house** (*in garden*) Gartenhaus *nt*; ~**time** Sommerzeit *f.*

summing-up ['sʌmɪŋ'ʌp] *n* Zusammenfassung *f.*

summit ['sʌmɪt] *n* Gipfel *m*; ~ **conference** Gipfelkonferenz *f.*

summon ['sʌmən] *vt* bestellen, kommen lassen; (*Jur*) vorladen; (*gather up*) aufbieten, aufbringen; ~**s** (*Jur*) Vorladung *f.*

sump [sʌmp] *n* Ölwanne *f.*

sumptuous ['sʌmptjuəs] a prächtig; ~ness Pracht f.

sun [sʌn] n Sonne f; ~bathe vi sich sonnen; ~bathing Sonnenbaden nt; ~burn Sonnenbrand m; to be ~burnt einen Sonnenbrand haben.

Sunday ['sʌndeɪ] n Sonntag m.

sundial ['sʌndaɪəl] n Sonnenuhr f.

sundown ['sʌndaʊn] n Sonnenuntergang m.

sundry ['sʌndrɪ] a verschieden; n: sundries pl Verschiedene(s) nt; all and ~ alle.

sunflower ['sʌnflaʊə*] n Sonnenblume f.

sunglasses ['sʌnglɑːsɪz] npl Sonnenbrille f.

sunken ['sʌŋkən] a versunken; eyes eingesunken.

sunlight ['sʌnlaɪt] n Sonnenlicht nt.

sunlit ['sʌnlɪt] a sonnenbeschienen.

sunny ['sʌnɪ] a sonnig.

sunrise ['sʌnraɪz] n Sonnenaufgang m.

sunset ['sʌnset] n Sonnenuntergang m.

sunshade ['sʌnʃeɪd] n Sonnenschirm m.

sunshine ['sʌnʃaɪn] n Sonnenschein m.

sunspot ['sʌnspɒt] n Sonnenfleck m.

sunstroke ['sʌnstrəʊk] n Hitzschlag m.

sun tan ['sʌntæn] n (Sonnen)bräune f; to get a ~ braun werden.

suntrap ['sʌntræp] n sonnige(r) Platz m.

sunup ['sʌnʌp] n (col) Sonnenaufgang m.

super ['suːpə*] a (col) prima, klasse; Super-, Über-.

superannuation [suːpərænjueɪʃən] n Pension f.

superb a, ~ly ad [suːˈpɜːb, -lɪ] ausgezeichnet, hervorragend.

supercilious [suːpəˈsɪlɪəs] a herablassend.

superficial a, ~ly ad [suːpəˈfɪʃəl, -ɪ] oberflächlich.

superfluous [suˈpɜːfluəs] a überflüssig.

superhuman [suːpəˈhjuːmən] a effort übermenschlich.

superimpose ['suːpərɪmˈpəʊz] vt übereinanderlegen.

superintendent [suːpərɪnˈtendənt] n Polizeichef m.

superior [suˈpɪərɪə*] a (higher) höher(stehend); (better) besser; (proud) überlegen; n Vorgesetzte(r) mf; ~ity [supɪərɪˈɒrɪtɪ] Überlegenheit f.

superlative [suˈpɜːlətɪv] a höchste(r,s); n (Gram) Superlativ m.

superman ['suːpəmæn] n Übermensch m.

supermarket ['suːpəmɑːkɪt] n Supermarkt m.

supernatural [suːpəˈnætʃərəl] a übernatürlich.

superpower ['suːpəpaʊə*] n Weltmacht f.

supersede [suːpəˈsiːd] vt ersetzen.

supersonic ['suːpəˈsɒnɪk] n Überschall-.

superstition [suːpəˈstɪʃən] n Aberglaube m.

superstitious [suːpəˈstɪʃəs] a abergläubisch.

supervise ['suːpəvaɪz] vt beaufsichtigen, kontrollieren.

supervision [suːpəˈvɪʒən] n Aufsicht f.

supervisor ['suːpəvaɪzə*] n Aufsichtsperson f; ~y a Aufsichts-.

supper ['sʌpə*] n Abendessen nt.

supple ['sʌpl] a gelenkig, geschmeidig; wire biegsam.

supplement ['sʌplɪmənt] n Ergänzung f; (in book) Nachtrag m; ['sʌplɪ'ment] vt ergänzen; ~ary [sʌplɪˈmentərɪ] a ergänzend, Ergänzungs-, Zusatz-.

supplier [səˈplaɪə*] n Lieferant m.

supply [səˈplaɪ] vt liefern; n Vorrat m; (supplying) Lieferung f; supplies pl (food) Vorräte pl; (Mil) Nachschub m; ~ and demand Angebot nt und Nachfrage.

support [səˈpɔːt] n Unterstützung f; (Tech) Stütze f; vt (hold up) stützen, tragen; (provide for) ernähren; (speak in favour of) befürworten, unterstützen; ~er Anhänger m; ~ing a programme Bei-; role Neben-.

suppose [səˈpəʊz] vti annehmen, denken, glauben; I ~ so ich glaube schon; ~ he comes . . . angenommen, er kommt . . .; ~dly [səˈpəʊzɪdlɪ] ad angeblich.

supposing [səˈpəʊzɪŋ] cj angenommen.

supposition [sʌpəˈzɪʃən] n Voraussetzung f.

suppress [səˈpres] vt unterdrücken; ~ion [səˈpreʃən] Unterdrückung f; ~or (Elec) Entstörungselement nt.

supra- ['suːprə] pref Über-.

supremacy [suˈpreməsɪ] n Vorherrschaft f, Oberhoheit f.

supreme a, ~ly ad [suˈpriːm, -lɪ] oberste(r,s), höchste(r,s).

surcharge ['sɜːtʃɑːdʒ] n Zuschlag m.

sure [ʃʊə*] a sicher, gewiß; to be ~ sicher sein; to be ~ about sth sich (dat) einer Sache sicher sein; we are ~ to win wir werden ganz sicher gewinnen; ad sicher; ~! (of course) ganz bestimmt!, natürlich!, klar!; to make ~ of sich vergewissern (+gen); ~-footed a sicher (auf den Füßen); ~ly ad (certainly) sicherlich, gewiß; ~ly it's wrong das ist doch wohl falsch; ~ly not! das ist doch wohl nicht wahr!; ~ty Sicherheit f; (person) Bürge m.

surf [sɜːf] n Brandung f.

surface ['sɜːfɪs] n Oberfläche f; vt roadway teeren; vi auftauchen; ~ mail gewöhnliche Post f, Post per Bahn f.

surfboard ['sɜːfbɔːd] n Wellenreiterbrett nt.

surfeit ['sɜːfɪt] n Übermaß nt.

surfing ['sɜːfɪŋ] n Wellenreiten nt, Surfing nt.

surge [sɜːdʒ] n Woge f; vi wogen.

surgeon ['sɜːdʒən] n Chirurg(in f) m.

surgery ['sɜːdʒərɪ] n Praxis f; (room) Sprechzimmer nt; (time) Sprechstunde f; (treatment) operative(r) Eingriff m, Operation f; he needs ~ er muß operiert werden.

surgical ['sɜːdʒɪkəl] a chirurgisch.

surly ['sɜːlɪ] a verdrießlich, grob.

surmise [sɜːˈmaɪz] vt vermuten.

surmount [sɜːˈmaʊnt] vt überwinden.

surname ['sɜːneɪm] n Zuname m.

surpass [sɜːˈpɑːs] vt übertreffen.

surplus ['sɜːpləs] n Überschuß m; a überschüssig, Über(schuß)-.

surprise [sə'praɪz] n Überraschung f; vt überraschen.

surprising [sə'praɪzɪŋ] a überraschend; ~ly ad überraschend(erweise).

surrealism [sə'rɪəlɪzəm] n Surrealismus m.

surrealist [sə'rɪəlɪst] a surrealistisch; n Surrealist m.

surrender [sə'rendə*] n Übergabe f; Kapitulation f; vi sich ergeben, kapitulieren; vt übergeben.

surreptitious a, ~ly ad [sʌrəp'tɪʃəs, -lɪ] verstohlen.

surround [sə'raund] vt umgeben; (come all round) umringen; ~ed by umgeben von; ~ing a countryside umliegend; n: ~ings pl Umgebung f, (environment) Umwelt f.

surveillance [sɜː'veɪləns] n Überwachung f.

survey ['sɜːveɪ] n Übersicht f; [sɜː'veɪ] vt überblicken; land vermessen; ~ing [sə'veɪɪŋ] (of land) (Land)vermessung f; ~or [sə'veɪə*] Land(ver)messer m.

survival [sə'vaɪvəl] n Überleben nt; (sth from earlier times) Überbleibsel nt.

survive [sə'vaɪv] vti überleben.

survivor [sə'vaɪvə*] n Überlebende(r) mf.

susceptible [sə'septəbl] a empfindlich (to gegen); empfänglich (to für).

suspect ['sʌspekt] n Verdächtige(r) mf; a verdächtig; [səs'pekt] vt verdächtigen; (think) vermuten.

suspend [səs'pend] vt verschieben; (from work) suspendieren; (hang up) aufhängen; (Sport) sperren; n: ~ers pl Strumpfhalter m; (men's) Sockenhalter m; (US) Hosenträger m.

suspense [səs'pens] n Spannung f.

suspension [səs'penʃən] n (hanging) (Auf-) hängen nt, Aufhängung f; (postponing) Aufschub m; (from work) Suspendierung f; (Sport) Sperrung f; (Aut) Federung f; ~ bridge Hängebrücke f.

suspicion [səs'pɪʃən] n Mißtrauen nt; Verdacht m.

suspicious a, ~ly ad [səs'pɪʃəs, -lɪ] mißtrauisch; (causing suspicion) verdächtig; ~ness Mißtrauen nt.

sustain [səs'teɪn] vt (hold up) stützen, tragen; (maintain) aufrechterhalten; (confirm) bestätigen; (Jur) anerkennen; injury davontragen; ~ed a effort anhaltend.

sustenance ['sʌstɪnəns] n Nahrung f.

swab [swɒb] n (Med) Tupfer m; vt decks schrubben; wound abtupfen.

swagger ['swægə*] vi stolzieren; (behave) prahlen, angeben.

swallow ['swɒləʊ] n (bird) Schwalbe f; (of food etc) Schluck m; vt (ver)schlucken; ~ up vt verschlingen.

swamp [swɒmp] n Sumpf m; vt überschwemmen; ~y a sumpfig.

swan [swɒn] n Schwan m; ~ song Schwanengesang m.

swap [swɒp] n Tausch m; vt (ein)tauschen (for gegen); vi tauschen.

swarm [swɔːm] n Schwarm m; vi wimmeln (with von).

swarthy ['swɔːðɪ] a dunkel, braun.

swastika ['swɒstɪkə] n Hakenkreuz nt.

swat [swɒt] vt totschlagen.

sway [sweɪ] vi schwanken; (branches) schaukeln, sich wiegen; vt schwenken; (influence) beeinflussen, umstimmen.

swear [sweə*] vi irreg (promise) schwören; (curse) fluchen; to ~ to sth schwören auf etw (acc); ~word Fluch m.

sweat [swet] n Schweiß m; vi schwitzen; ~er Pullover m; ~y a verschwitzt.

swede [swiːd] n Steckrübe f.

sweep [swiːp] n (cleaning) Kehren nt; (wide curve) Bogen m; (with arm) schwungvolle Bewegung f; (chimney —) Schornsteinfeger m; irreg vt fegen, kehren; vi (road) sich dahinziehen; (go quickly) rauschen; ~ away vt wegfegen; (river) wegspülen; ~ past vi vorbeisausen; ~ up vt zusammenkehren; ~ing a gesture schwungvoll; statement verallgemeinernd; ~stake Toto nt.

sweet [swiːt] n (course) Nachtisch m; (candy) Bonbon nt; a, ~ly ad süß; ~corn Zuckermais m; ~en vt süßen; (fig) versüßen; ~heart Liebste(r) mf; ~ness Süße f; ~ pea Gartenwicke f; to have a ~ tooth ein Leckermaul sein.

swell [swel] n Seegang m; a (col) todschick; irreg vt numbers vermehren; vi (also ~ up) (an)schwellen; ~ing Schwellung f.

sweltering ['sweltərɪŋ] a drückend.

swerve [swɜːv] n Ausschwenken nt; vti ausscheren, zur Seite schwenken.

swift [swɪft] n Mauersegler m; a, ~ly ad geschwind, schnell, rasch; ~ness Schnelligkeit f.

swig [swɪg] n Zug m.

swill [swɪl] n (for pigs) Schweinefutter nt; vt spülen.

swim [swɪm] n: to go for a ~ schwimmen gehen; irreg vi schwimmen; my head is ~ming mir dreht sich der Kopf; vt (cross) (durch)schwimmen; ~mer Schwimmer(in f) m; ~ming Schwimmen nt; to go ~ming schwimmen gehen; ~ming baths pl Schwimmbad nt; ~ming cap Badehaube f, Badekappe f; ~ming costume Badeanzug m; ~ming pool Schwimmbecken nt; (private) Swimming-Pool m; ~suit Badeanzug m.

swindle ['swɪndl] n Schwindel m, Betrug m; vt betrügen; ~r Schwindler m.

swine [swaɪn] n (lit, fig) Schwein nt.

swing [swɪŋ] n (child's) Schaukel f; (swinging) Schwingen nt, Schwung m; (Mus) Swing m; irreg vt schwingen, (herum-) schwenken; vi schwingen, pendeln, schaukeln; (turn quickly) schwenken; in full ~ in vollem Gange; ~ bridge Drehbrücke f; ~ door Schwingtür f.

swipe [swaɪp] n Hieb m; vt (col) (hit) hart schlagen; (steal) klauen.

swirl [swɜːl] n Wirbel m; vi wirbeln.

switch [swɪtʃ] n (Elec) Schalter m; (change) Wechsel m; vti (Elec) schalten; (change) wechseln; ~ off vt ab- or ausschalten; ~ on vt an- or einschalten; ~back Achterbahn f; ~board

Vermittlung f, Zentrale f; (board) Schalt-
brett nt.
swivel ['swɪvl] vti (also ~ **round**) (sich)
drehen.
swollen ['swəulən] a geschwollen.
swoon [swuːn] vi (old) in Ohnmacht fallen.
swoop [swuːp] n Sturzflug m; (esp by police)
Razzia f; vi (also ~ **down**) stürzen.
swop [swɒp] = **swap**.
sword [sɔːd] n Schwert nt; ~**fish** Schwert-
fisch m; ~**sman** Fechter m.
sworn [swɔːn] a: ~ **enemies** pl Todfeinde
pl.
sycamore ['sɪkəmɔː*] n (US) Platane f;
(Brit) Bergahorn m.
sycophantic [sɪkə'fæntɪk] a schmeich-
lerisch, kriecherisch.
syllable ['sɪləbl] n Silbe f.
syllabus ['sɪləbəs] n Lehrplan m.
symbol ['sɪmbəl] n Symbol nt; ~**ic(al)**
[sɪm'bɒlɪk(əl)] a symbolisch; ~**ism**
symbolische Bedeutung f; (Art)
Symbolismus m; ~**ize** vt versinnbild-
lichen, symbolisieren.
symmetrical a, ~**ly** ad [sɪ'metrɪkəl, -lɪ]
symmetrisch, gleichmäßig.
symmetry ['sɪmɪtrɪ] n Symmetrie f.
sympathetic a, ~**ally** ad [sɪmpə'θetɪk,
-əlɪ] mitfühlend.
sympathize ['sɪmpəθaɪz] vi sym-
pathisieren; mitfühlen; ~**r** Mitfühlende(r)
mf; (Pol) Sympathisant m.
sympathy ['sɪmpəθɪ] n Mitleid nt,
Mitgefühl nt; (condolence) Beileid nt.
symphonic [sɪm'fɒnɪk] a sinfonisch.
symphony ['sɪmfənɪ] n Sinfonie f; ~
orchestra Sinfonieorchester nt.
symposium [sɪm'pəʊzɪəm] n Tagung f.
symptom ['sɪmptəm] n Symptom nt,
Anzeichen nt; ~**atic** [sɪmptə'mætɪk] a
(fig) bezeichnend (of für).
synagogue ['sɪnəgɒg] n Synagoge f.
synchromesh ['sɪŋkrəʊmeʃ] n Synchron-
schaltung f.
synchronize ['sɪŋkrənaɪz] vt synchro-
nisieren; vi gleichzeitig sein or ablaufen.
syndicate ['sɪndɪkət] n Konsortium nt,
Verband m, Ring m.
syndrome ['sɪndrəʊm] n Syndrom nt.
synonym ['sɪnənɪm] n Synonym nt; ~**ous**
[sɪ'nɒnɪməs] a gleichbedeutend.
synopsis [sɪ'nɒpsɪs] n Abriß m,
Zusammenfassung f.
syntactic [sɪn'tæktɪk] a syntaktisch.
syntax ['sɪntæks] n Syntax f.
synthesis ['sɪnθəsɪs] n Synthese f.
synthetic a, ~**ally** ad [sɪn'θetɪk, -əlɪ]
synthetisch, künstlich.
syphilis ['sɪfɪlɪs] n Syphilis f.
syphon ['saɪfən] = **siphon**.
syringe [sɪ'rɪndʒ] n Spritze f.
syrup ['sɪrəp] n Sirup m; (of sugar) Melasse
f.
system ['sɪstəm] n System nt; ~**atic** a,
~**atically** ad [sɪstə'mætɪk, -əlɪ] syste-
matisch, planmäßig.

T

T, t [tiː] n T nt, t nt; **to a** ~ genau.
ta [tɑː] interj (Brit col) danke.
tab [tæb] n Schlaufe f, Aufhänger m; (name
~) Schild nt.
tabby ['tæbɪ] n (female cat) (weibliche)
Katze f; a (black-striped) getigert.
tabernacle ['tæbənækl] n Tabernakel nt or
m.
table ['teɪbl] n Tisch m; (list) Tabelle f,
Tafel f; **to lay sth on the** ~ (fig) etw zur
Diskussion stellen; vt (Parl: propose) vorlegen, einbringen.
tableau ['tæbləʊ] n lebende(s) Bild nt.
tablecloth ['teɪblklɒθ] n Tischtuch nt,
Tischdecke f.
table d'hôte ['tɑːbl'dəʊt] n Tagesmenu nt.
tablemat ['teɪblmæt] n Untersatz m.
tablespoon ['teɪblspuːn] n Eßlöffel m;
~**ful** Eßlöffel(voll) m.
tablet ['tæblət] n (Med) Tablette f; (for
writing) Täfelchen nt; (of paper)
Schreibblock m; (of soap) Riegel m.
table talk ['teɪbltɔːk] n Tischgespräch nt.
table tennis ['teɪbltenɪs] n Tischtennis nt.
table wine ['teɪblwaɪn] n Tafelwein m.
taboo [tə'buː] n Tabu nt; a tabu.
tabulate ['tæbjuleɪt] vt tabellarisch
ordnen.
tacit a, ~**ly** ad ['tæsɪt, -lɪ] stillschweigend;
~**urn** a schweigsam, wortkarg.
tack [tæk] n (small nail) Stift m; (US:
thumb~) Reißzwecke f; (stitch) Heftstich
m; (Naut) Lavieren nt; (course) Kurs m.
tackle ['tækl] n (for lifting) Flaschenzug m;
(Naut) Takelage f; (Sport) Tackling nt; vt
(deal with) anpacken, in Angriff nehmen;
person festhalten; player angehen; **he
couldn't** ~ **it** er hat es nicht bewältigt.
tacky ['tækɪ] a klebrig.
tact [tækt] n Takt m; ~**ful** a, ~**fully** ad
taktvoll.
tactical ['tæktɪkəl] a taktisch.
tactics ['tæktɪks] npl Taktik f.
tactless a, ~**ly** ad ['tæktləs, -lɪ] taktlos.
tadpole ['tædpəʊl] n Kaulquappe f.
taffeta ['tæfɪtə] n Taft m.
taffy ['tæfɪ] n (US) Sahnebonbon nt.
tag [tæg] n (label) Schild nt, Anhänger m;
(maker's name) Etikett nt; (phrase) Floskel
f, Spruch m; ~ **along** vi mitkommen; ~
question Bestätigungsfrage f.
tail [teɪl] n Schwanz m; (of list) Schluß m;
(of comet) Schweif m; ~**s** (of coin)
Zahl(seite) f; vt folgen (+dat); ~ **off** vi
abfallen, schwinden; ~ **end** Schluß m,
Ende nt.
tailor ['teɪlə*] n Schneider m; ~**ing**
Schneidern nt, Schneiderarbeit f;
~**-made** a (lit) maßgeschneidert; (fig)
wie auf den Leib geschnitten (for sb jdm).
tailwind ['teɪlwɪnd] n Rückenwind m.
tainted ['teɪntɪd] a verdorben.
take [teɪk] vt irreg nehmen; prize
entgegennehmen; trip, exam machen;
(capture) person fassen; town einnehmen;
disease bekommen; (carry to a place)

bringing; (*Math: subtract*) abziehen (*from von*); (*extract*) *quotation* entnehmen (*from dat*); (*get for o.s.*) sich (*dat*) nehmen; (*gain, obtain*) bekommen; (*Fin, Comm*) einnehmen; (*record*) aufnehmen; (*consume*) zu sich nehmen; (*Phot*) aufnehmen, machen; (*put up with*) hinnehmen; (*respond to*) aufnehmen; (*understand, interpret*) auffassen; (*assume*) annehmen; (*contain*) fassen, Platz haben für; (*Gram*) stehen mit; **it ~s 4 hours** man braucht 4 Stunden; **it ~s him 4 hours** er braucht 4 Stunden; **to ~ sth from sb** jdm etw wegnehmen; **to ~ part in** teilnehmen an (+*dat*); **to ~ place** stattfinden; **~ after** *vt* ähnlich sein (+*dat*); **~ back** *vt* (*return*) zurückbringen; (*retract*) zurücknehmen; (*remind*) zurückversetzen (*to in* +*acc*); **~ down** *vt* (*pull down*) abreißen; (*write down*) aufschreiben; **~ in** *vt* (*deceive*) hereinlegen; (*understand*) begreifen; (*include*) einschließen; **~ off** *vi* (*plane*) starten; *vt* (*remove*) wegnehmen, abmachen; *clothing* ausziehen; (*imitate*) nachmachen; **~ on** *vt* (*undertake*) übernehmen; (*engage*) einstellen; (*opponent*) antreten gegen; **~ out** *vt* *girl, dog* ausführen; (*extract*) herausnehmen; *insurance* abschließen; *licence* sich (*dat*) geben lassen; *book* ausleihen; (*remove*) entfernen; **to ~ sth out on sb** etw an jdm auslassen; **~ over** *vt* übernehmen; *vi* ablösen (*from acc*); **~ to** *vt* (*like*) mögen; (*adopt as practice*) sich (*dat*) angewöhnen; **~ up** *vt* (*raise*) aufnehmen; *hem* kürzer machen; (*occupy*) in Anspruch nehmen; (*absorb*) aufsaugen; (*engage in*) sich befassen mit; **to ~ sb up on sth** jdn beim Wort nehmen; **to be ~n with** begeistert sein von; **~off** (*Aviat*) Abflug *m*, Start *m*; (*imitation*) Nachahmung *f*; **~over** (*Comm*) Übernahme *f*; **~over bid** Übernahmeangebot *nt*.

takings ['teɪkɪŋz] *npl* (*Comm*) Einnahmen *pl*.

talc [tælk] *n* (*also* **~um powder**) Talkumpuder *m*.

tale [teɪl] *n* Geschichte *f*, Erzählung *f*.

talent ['tælənt] *n* Talent *nt*, Begabung *f*; **~ed** a talentiert, begabt.

talk [tɔːk] *n* (*conversation*) Gespräch *m*; (*rumour*) Gerede *nt*; (*speech*) Vortrag *m*; *vi* sprechen, reden; (*gossip*) klatschen, reden; **~ing of** ... da wir gerade von ... sprechen; **~ about impertinence!** so eine Frechheit!; **to ~ sb into doing sth** jdn überreden, etw zu tun; **to ~ shop** fachsimpeln; **~ over** *vt* besprechen; **~ative** a redselig, gesprächig; **~er** Schwätzer *m*.

tall [tɔːl] a groß; *building* hoch; **~boy** Kommode *f*; **~ness** *f*; **Größe** *f*; Höhe *f*; **~story** übertriebene Geschichte *f*.

tally ['tælɪ] *n* Abrechnung *f*; *vi* übereinstimmen.

talon ['tælən] *n* Kralle *f*.

tambourine [tæmbə'riːn] *n* Tamburin *nt*.

tame [teɪm] a zahm; (*fig*) fade, langweilig;

vt zähmen; **~ness** Zahmheit *f*; (*fig*) Langweiligkeit *f*.

tamper ['tæmpə*]: **~ with** *vt* herumpfuschen an (+*dat*); *documents* fälschen.

tampon ['tæmpɒn] *n* Tampon *m*.

tan [tæn] *n* (*on skin*) (Sonnen)bräune *f*; (*colour*) Gelbbraun *nt*; a (*colour*) (gelb)braun.

tandem ['tændəm] *n* Tandem *nt*.

tang [tæŋ] *n* Schärfe *f*, scharfe(r) Geschmack *m* or Geruch *m*.

tangent ['tændʒənt] *n* Tangente *f*.

tangerine [tændʒə'riːn] *n* Mandarine *f*.

tangible ['tændʒəbl] a (*lit*) greifbar; (*real*) handgreiflich.

tangle ['tæŋgl] *n* Durcheinander *nt*; (*trouble*) Schwierigkeiten *pl*; *vt* verwirren.

tango ['tæŋgəʊ] *n* Tango *m*.

tank [tæŋk] *n* (*container*) Tank *m*, Behälter *m*; (*Mil*) Panzer *m*.

tankard ['tæŋkəd] *n* Seidel *nt*, Deckelkrug *m*.

tanker ['tæŋkə*] *n* (*ship*) Tanker *m*; (*vehicle*) Tankwagen *m*.

tankful ['tæŋkfʊl] *n* volle(r) Tank *m*.

tanned [tænd] a *skin* gebräunt, sonnenverbrannt.

tantalizing ['tæntəlaɪzɪŋ] a verlockend; (*annoying*) quälend.

tantamount ['tæntəmaʊnt] a gleichbedeutend (*to* mit).

tantrum ['tæntrəm] *n* Wutanfall *m*.

tap [tæp] *n* Hahn *m*; (*gentle blow*) leichte(r) Schlag *m*, Klopfen *nt*; *vt* (*strike*) klopfen; *supply* anzapfen.

tap-dance ['tæpdɑːns] *vi* steppen.

tape [teɪp] *n* Band *nt*; (*magnetic*) (Ton)band *nt*; (*adhesive*) Klebstreifen *m*; *vt* (*record*) (auf Band) aufnehmen; **~measure** Maßband *nt*.

taper ['teɪpə*] *n* (dünne) Wachskerze *f*; *vi* spitz zulaufen.

tape recorder ['teɪprɪkɔːdə*] *n* Tonbandgerät *nt*.

tapered ['teɪpəd], **tapering** ['teɪpərɪŋ] a spitz zulaufend.

tapestry ['tæpɪstrɪ] *n* Wandteppich *m*, Gobelin *m*.

tapioca [tæpɪ'əʊkə] *n* Tapioka *f*.

tappet ['tæpɪt] *n* (*Aut*) Nocke *f*.

tar [tɑː*] *n* Teer *m*.

tarantula [tə'ræntjʊlə] *n* Tarantel *f*.

tardy ['tɑːdɪ] a langsam, spät.

target ['tɑːgɪt] *n* Ziel *nt*; (*board*) Zielscheibe *f*.

tariff ['tærɪf] *n* (*duty paid*) Zoll *m*; (*list*) Tarif *m*.

tarmac ['tɑːmæk] *n* (*Aviat*) Rollfeld *nt*.

tarn [tɑːn] *n* Gebirgsee *m*.

tarnish ['tɑːnɪʃ] *vt* (*lit*) matt machen; (*fig*) beflecken.

tarpaulin [tɑː'pɔːlɪn] *n* Plane *f*, Persenning *f*.

tarry ['tærɪ] *vi* (*liter*) bleiben; (*delay*) säumen.

tart [tɑːt] *n* (*Obst*)torte *f*; (*col*) Nutte *f*; a scharf, sauer; *remark* scharf, spitz.

tartan ['tɑːtən] *n* schottisch-karierte(r) Stoff *m*; Schottenkaro *nt*.

tartar ['tɑːtə*] n Zahnstein m; ~(e) sauce Remouladensoße f.

tartly ['tɑːtlɪ] ad spitz.

task [tɑːsk] n Aufgabe f; (duty) Pflicht f; ~ force Sondertrupp m.

tassel ['tæsəl] n Quaste f.

taste [teɪst] n Geschmack m; (sense) Geschmackssinn m; (small quantity) Kostprobe f; (liking) Vorliebe f; vt schmecken; (try) versuchen; vi schmecken (of nach); ~ful a, ~fully ad geschmackvoll; ~less a (insipid) ohne Geschmack, fade; (in bad taste) geschmacklos; ~lessly ad geschmacklos.

tastily ['teɪstɪlɪ] ad schmackhaft.

tastiness ['teɪstɪnəs] n Schmackhaftigkeit f.

tasty ['teɪstɪ] a schmackhaft.

tata ['tæ'tɑː] interj (Brit col) tschüß.

tattered ['tætəd] a zerrissen, zerlumpt.

tatters ['tætəz] npl: **in ~** in Fetzen.

tattoo [tə'tuː] n (Mil) Zapfenstreich m; (on skin) Tätowierung f; vt tätowieren.

tatty ['tætɪ] a (col) schäbig.

taunt [tɔːnt] n höhnische Bemerkung f; vt verhöhnen.

Taurus ['tɔːrəs] n Stier m.

taut [tɔːt] a straff.

tavern ['tævən] n Taverne f.

tawdry ['tɔːdrɪ] a (bunt und) billig.

tawny ['tɔːnɪ] a gelbbraun.

tax [tæks] n Steuer f; vt besteuern; (strain) strapazieren; strength angreifen; ~ation [tæk'seɪʃən] Besteuerung f; ~ collector Steuereinnehmer m; ~-free a steuerfrei.

taxi ['tæksɪ] n Taxi nt; vi (plane) rollen.

taxidermist ['tæksɪdɜːmɪst] n Tierausstopfer m.

taxi driver ['tæksɪ draɪvə*] n Taxifahrer m.

taxi rank ['tæksɪræŋk] n Taxistand m.

taxpayer ['tækspeɪə*] n Steuerzahler m.

tax return ['tæksrɪ'tɜːn] n Steuererklärung f.

tea [tiː] n Tee m; (meal) (frühes) Abendessen nt; ~ **bag** Tee(aufguß)beutel m; ~ **break** Teepause f; ~ **cake** Rosinenbrötchen nt.

teach [tiːtʃ] vti irreg lehren; (Sch also) unterrichten; (show) zeigen, beibringen (sb sth jdm etw); **that'll ~ him!** das hat er nun davon!; ~**er** Lehrer(in f) m; ~**-in** Teach-in nt; ~**ing** (teacher's work) Unterricht m, Lehren nt; (doctrine) Lehre f.

tea cosy ['tiːkəʊzɪ] n Teewärmer m.

teacup ['tiːkʌp] n Teetasse f.

teak [tiːk] n Teakbaum m; a Teak(holz)-.

tea leaves ['tiːliːvz] npl Teeblätter pl.

team [tiːm] n (workers) Team nt; (Sport) Mannschaft f; (animals) Gespann nt; ~ **spirit** Gemeinschaftsgeist m; (Sport) Mannschaftsgeist m; ~**work** Zusammenarbeit f, Teamwork nt.

tea party ['tiːpɑːtɪ] n Kaffeeklatsch m.

teapot ['tiːpɒt] n Teekanne f.

tear [teə*] n n Riß m; irreg vt zerreißen; muscle zerren; **I am torn between . . .** ich

schwanke zwischen . . .; vi (zer)reißen; (rush) rasen, sausen.

tear [tɪə*] n Träne f; **in ~s** in Tränen (aufgelöst); ~**ful** a weinend; voice weinerlich; ~ **gas** Tränengas nt.

tearing ['tɛərɪŋ] a: **to be in a ~ hurry** es schrecklich eilig haben.

tearoom ['tiːrʊm] n Teestube f.

tease [tiːz] n Hänsler m; vt necken, aufziehen; animal quälen; **I was only teasing** ich habe nur Spaß gemacht.

tea set ['tiːset] n Teeservice nt.

teashop ['tiːʃɒp] n Café nt.

teaspoon ['tiːspuːn] n Teelöffel m; ~**ful** Teelöffel(voll) m.

tea strainer ['tiːstreɪnə*] n Teesieb nt.

teat [tiːt] n (of woman) Brustwarze f; (of animal) Zitze f; (of bottle) Sauger m.

tea towel ['tiːtaʊəl] n Küchenhandtuch nt.

tea urn ['tiːɜːn] n Teemaschine f.

technical ['teknɪkəl] a technisch; knowledge, terms Fach-; ~**ity** [teknɪ'kælɪtɪ] technische Einzelheit f; (Jur) Formsache f; ~**ly** ad technisch; speak spezialisiert; (fig) genau genommen.

technician [tek'nɪʃən] n Techniker m.

technique [tek'niːk] n Technik f.

technological [teknə'lɒdʒɪkəl] a technologisch.

technologist [tek'nɒlədʒɪst] n Technologe m.

technology [tek'nɒlədʒɪ] n Technologie f.

teddy (bear) ['tedɪ(bɛə*)] n Teddybär m.

tedious a, ~**ly** ad ['tiːdɪəs, -lɪ] langweilig, ermüdend.

tedium ['tiːdɪəm] n Langweiligkeit f.

tee [tiː] n (golf) Abschlagstelle f; (object) Tee m.

teem [tiːm] vi (swarm) wimmeln (with von); (pour) gießen.

teenage ['tiːneɪdʒ] a fashions etc Teenager-, jugendlich; ~**r** Teenager m, Jugendliche(r) mf.

teens [tiːnz] npl Jugendjahre pl.

teeter ['tiːtə*] vi schwanken.

teeth [tiːθ] npl of **tooth**.

teethe [tiːð] vi zahnen.

teething ring ['tiːðɪŋrɪŋ] n Beißring m.

teetotal ['tiː'təʊtl] a abstinent; ~**ler**, (US) ~**er** Antialkoholiker m, Abstinenzler m.

telecommunications ['telɪkəmjuːnɪ'keɪʃənz] npl Fernmeldewesen nt.

telegram ['telɪgræm] n Telegramm nt.

telegraph ['telɪgrɑːf] n Telegraph m; ~**ic** [telɪ'græfɪk] a address Telegramm-; ~ **pole** Telegraphenmast m.

telepathic [telɪ'pæθɪk] a telepathisch.

telepathy [tə'lepəθɪ] n Telepathie f, Gedankenübertragung f.

telephone ['telɪfəʊn] n Telefon nt, Fernsprecher m; vi telefonieren; vt anrufen; message telefonisch mitteilen; ~ **booth**, ~ **box** Telefonhäuschen nt, Fernsprechzelle f; ~ **call** Telefongespräch nt, Anruf m; ~ **directory** Telefonbuch nt; ~ **exchange** Telefonvermittlung f, Telefonzentrale f; ~ **number** Telefonnummer f.

telephonist [tə'lefənɪst] n Telefonist(in f) m.

telephoto lens ['telɪ'fəʊtəʊ'lenz] n Tele-objektiv nt.

teleprinter ['telɪprɪntə*] n Fernschreiber m.

telescope ['telɪskəʊp] n Teleskop nt, Fernrohr nt; vt ineinanderschieben.

telescopic [telɪs'kɒpɪk] a teleskopisch; aerial etc ausziehbar.

televiewer ['telɪvjuːə*] n Fernsehteil-nehmer(in f) m.

televise ['telɪvaɪz] vt durch das Fernsehen übertragen.

television [telɪvɪʒən] n Fernsehen nt; to watch ~ fernsehen; ~ (set) Fern-sehapparat m, Fernseher m; on ~ im Fernsehen.

telex ['teleks] n Telex nt.

tell [tel] irreg vt story erzählen; secret ausplaudern; (say, make known) sagen (sth to sb jdm etw); (distinguish) erkennen (sb by sth jdn an etw dat); (be sure) wissen; (order) sagen, befehlen (sb jdm); to ~ a lie lügen; to ~ sb about sth jdm von etw erzählen; vi (be sure) wissen; (divulge) es verraten; (have effect) sich auswirken; ~ off vt schimpfen; ~ on vt verraten, ver-petzen; ~er Kassenbeamte(r) mf; ~ing verräterisch, aufschlußreich; moment der Wahrheit; ~tale a verräterisch.

telly ['telɪ] n (col) Fernseher m.

temerity [tɪ'merɪtɪ] n (Toll)kühnheit f.

temper ['tempə*] n (disposition) Tempera-ment nt, Gemütsart f; (anger) Gereiztheit f, Zorn m; to be in a (bad) ~ wütend or gereizt sein; vt (tone down) mildern; metal härten; quick ~ed jähzornig, auf-brausend; ~ament Temperament nt, Veranlagung f; ~amental [tempərə-'mentl] a (moody) launisch.

temperance ['tempərəns] n Mäßigung f; (abstinence) Enthaltsamkeit f; ~ hotel alkoholfreie(s) Hotel nt.

temperate ['tempərət] a gemäßigt.

temperature ['temprɪtʃə*] n Temperatur f; (Med: high —) Fieber nt.

tempered ['tempəd] a steel gehärtet.

tempest ['tempɪst] n (wilder) Sturm m; ~uous [tem'pestjuəs] a stürmisch; (fig) ungestüm.

template ['templət] n Schablone f.

temple ['templ] n Tempel m; (Anat) Schläfe f.

tempo ['tempəʊ] n Tempo nt.

temporal ['tempərəl] a (of time) zeitlich; (worldly) irdisch, weltlich.

temporarily ['tempərərɪlɪ] ad zeitweilig, vorübergehend.

temporary ['tempərərɪ] a vorläufig; road, building provisorisch.

tempt [tempt] vt (persuade) verleiten, in Versuchung führen; (attract) reizen, (ver)-locken; ~ation [temp'teɪʃən] Versuchung f; ~ing a person verführerisch; object, situation verlockend.

ten [ten] num zehn.

tenable ['tenəbl] a haltbar; to be ~ (post) vergeben werden.

tenacious a, ~ly ad [tə'neɪʃəs, -lɪ] zäh, hartnäckig.

tenacity [tə'næsɪtɪ] n Zähigkeit f, Hart-näckigkeit f.

tenancy ['tenənsɪ] n Mietverhältnis nt; Pachtverhältnis nt.

tenant ['tenənt] n Mieter m; (of larger property) Pächter m.

tend [tend] vt (look after) sich kümmern um; vi neigen, tendieren (to zu); to ~ to do sth (things) etw gewöhnlich tun; ~ency Tendenz f; (of person also) Neigung f.

tender ['tendə*] a (soft) weich, zart; (delicate) zart; (loving) liebevoll, zärtlich; n (Comm: offer) Kostenanschlag m; ~ize vt weich machen; ~ly ad liebevoll; touch also zart; ~ness Zartheit f; (being loving) Zärtlichkeit f.

tendon ['tendən] n Sehne f.

tenement ['tenəmənt] n Mietshaus nt.

tenet ['tenət] n Lehre f.

tennis ['tenɪs] n Tennis nt; ~ ball Tennis-ball m; ~ court Tennisplatz m; ~ racket Tennisschläger m.

tenor ['tenə*] n (voice) Tenor(stimme f) m; (singer) Tenor m; (meaning) Sinn m, wesentliche(r) Inhalt m.

tense [tens] a angespannt; (stretched tight) gespannt, straff; n Zeitform f; ~ly ad (an)gespannt; ~ness Spannung f; (strain) Angespanntheit f.

tension ['tenʃən] n Spannung f; (strain) (An)gespanntheit f.

tent [tent] n Zelt nt.

tentacle ['tentəkl] n Fühler m; (of sea animals) Fangarm m.

tentative ['tentətɪv] a movement unsicher; offer Probe-; arrangement vorläufig; suggestion unverbindlich; ~ly ad versuchsweise; try, move vorsichtig.

tenterhooks ['tentəhʊks] npl: to be on ~ auf die Folter gespannt sein.

tenth [tenθ] a zehnte(r,s); n Zehntel nt.

tent peg ['tentpeg] n Hering m.

tent pole ['tentpəʊl] n Zeltstange f.

tenuous ['tenjuəs] a fein; air dünn; con-nection, argument schwach.

tenure ['tenjuə*] n (of land) Besitz m; (of office) Amtszeit f.

tepid ['tepɪd] a lauwarm.

term [tɜːm] n (period of time) Zeit(raum m) f; (limit) Frist f; (Sch) Quartal nt; (Univ) Trimester nt; (expression) Aus-druck m; vt (be)nennen; ~s pl (con-ditions) Bedingungen pl; (relationship) Beziehungen pl; to be on good ~s with sb mit jdm gut auskommen; ~inal (Rail, bus —inal; also —inus) Endstation f; (Aviat) Terminal m; a Schluß-; (Med) unheilbar; ~inal cancer Krebs m im Endstadium; ~inate vt beenden; vi enden, aufhören (in auf +dat); ~ination [tɜːmɪ'neɪʃən] Ende nt; (act) Beendigung f; ~inology [tɜːmɪ'nɒlədʒɪ] Terminologie f.

termite ['tɜːmaɪt] n Termite f.

terrace ['terəs] n (of houses) Häuserreihe f; (in garden etc) Terrasse f; ~d a garden terrassenförmig angelegt; house Reihen-.

terracotta ['terə'kɒtə] n Terrakotta f.

terrain [te'reɪn] n Gelände nt, Terrain nt.

terrible ['terəbl] *a* schrecklich, entsetzlich, fürchterlich.

terribly ['terəblɪ] *ad* fürchterlich.

terrier ['terɪə*] *n* Terrier *m*.

terrific *a*, ~**ally** *ad* [tə'rɪfɪk, -lɪ] unwahrscheinlich; ~! klasse!

terrify ['terɪfaɪ] *vt* erschrecken; ~**ing** *a* erschreckend, grauenvoll.

territorial [terɪ'tɔ:rɪəl] *a* Gebiets-, territorial; ~ **waters** *pl* Hoheitsgewässer *pl*.

territory ['terɪtərɪ] *n* Gebiet *nt*.

terror ['terə*] *n* Schrecken *m*; (*Pol*) Terror *m*; ~**ism** Terrorismus *m*; ~**ist** Terrorist- (in *f*) *m*; ~**ize** *vt* terrorisieren.

terse [tɜ:s] *a* knapp, kurz, bündig.

Terylene " ['terəli:n] *n* Terylen(e) *nt*.

test [test] *n* Probe *f*; (*examination*) Prüfung *f*; (*Psych, Tech*) Test *m*; *vt* prüfen; (*Psych*) testen.

testament ['testəmənt] *n* Testament *nt*.

test card ['testka:d] *n* (*TV*) Testbild *nt*.

test case ['testkeɪs] *n* (*Jur*) Präzedenzfall *m*; (*fig*) Musterbeispiel *nt*.

test flight ['testflaɪt] *n* Probeflug *m*.

testicle ['testɪkl] *n* Hoden *m*.

testify ['testɪfaɪ] *vi* aussagen; bezeugen (*to acc*).

testimonial [testɪ'məunɪəl] *n* (*of character*) Referenz *f*.

testimony ['testɪmənɪ] *n* (*Jur*) Zeugenaussage *f*; (*fig*) Zeugnis *nt*.

test match ['testmætʃ] *n* (*Sport*) Länderkampf *m*.

test paper ['testpeɪpə*] *n* schriftliche (Klassen)arbeit *f*.

test pilot ['testpaɪlət] *n* Testpilot *m*.

test tube ['testtju:b] *n* Reagenzglas *nt*.

testy ['testɪ] *a* gereizt; reizbar.

tetanus ['tetənəs] *n* Wundstarrkrampf *m*, Tetanus *m*.

tether ['teðə*] *vt* anbinden; **to be at the end of one's** ~ völlig am Ende sein.

text [tekst] *n* Text *m*; (*of document*) Wortlaut *m*; ~**book** Lehrbuch *nt*.

textile ['tekstaɪl] *n* Gewebe *nt*; ~**s** *pl* Textilien *pl*.

texture ['tekstʃə*] *n* Beschaffenheit *f*, Struktur *f*.

than [ðæn] *prep*, *cj* als.

thank [θæŋk] *vt* danken (+*dat*); **you've him to** ~ **for your success** Sie haben Ihren Erfolg ihm zu verdanken; ~**ful** *a* dankbar; ~**fully** *ad* (*luckily*) zum Glück; ~**less** *a* undankbar; ~**s** *pl* Dank *m*; ~**s to** dank (+*gen*); ~ **you**, ~**s** *interj* danke, dankeschön; **T**~**sgiving** (*US*) (Ernte)dankfest *nt*.

that [ðæt] *a* der/die/das, jene(r,s); *pron* das; *cj* daß; **and** ~**'s** ~ und damit Schluß; ~ **is** das heißt; **after** ~ danach; at ~ dazu noch; ~ **big** so groß.

thatched [θætʃt] *a* strohgedeckt.

thaw [θɔ:] *n* Tauwetter *nt*; *vi* tauen; (*frozen foods, fig: people*) auftauen; *vt* (auf)tauen lassen.

the [ðɪ, ðə] *def art* der/die/das; **to play** ~ **piano** Klavier spielen; ~ **sooner** ~ **better** je eher desto besser.

theatre, (*US*) **theater** [θɪətə*] *n* Theater *nt*; (*for lectures etc*) Saal *m*; (*Med*) Operationssaal *m*; ~**goer** Theaterbesucher(in *f*) *m*.

theatrical [θɪ'ætrɪkəl] *a* Theater-; *career* Schauspieler-; (*showy*) theatralisch.

theft [θeft] *n* Diebstahl *m*.

their [ðɛə*] *poss a* ihr; ~**s** *poss pron* ihre(r,s).

them [ðem, ðəm] *pron* (*acc*) sie; (*dat*) ihnen.

theme [θi:m] *n* Thema *nt*; (*Mus*) Motiv *nt*; ~ **song** Titelmusik *f*.

themselves [ðəm'selvz] *pl pron* (*reflexive*) sich (selbst); (*emphatic*) selbst.

then [ðen] *ad* (*at that time*) damals; (*next*) dann; *cj* also, folglich; (*furthermore*) ferner; *a* damalig; **from** ~ **on** von da an; **before** ~ davor; **by** ~ bis dahin; **not till** ~ erst dann.

theologian [θɪə'ləudʒən] *n* Theologe *m*, Theologin *f*.

theological [θɪə'lɒdʒɪkəl] *a* theologisch.

theology [θɪ'ɒlədʒɪ] *n* Theologie *f*.

theorem ['θɪərəm] *n* Grundsatz *m*, Theorem *nt*.

theoretical *a*, ~**ly** *ad* [θɪə'retɪkəl, -lɪ] theoretisch.

theorize ['θɪəraɪz] *vi* theoretisieren.

theory ['θɪərɪ] *n* Theorie *f*.

therapeutic(al) [θerə'pju:tɪk(əl)] *a* (*Med*) therapeutisch; erholsam.

therapist ['θerəpɪst] *a* Therapeut(in *f*) *m*.

therapy ['θerəpɪ] *n* Therapie *f*, Behandlung *f*.

there [ðɛə*] *ad* dort; (*to a place*) dorthin; *interj* (*see*) na also; (*to child*) (sei) ruhig, na na; ~ **is** es gibt; ~ **are** es sind, es gibt; ~**abouts** *ad* so ungefähr; ~**after** [ðɛər'ɑ:ftə*] *ad* danach, später; ~**by** *ad* dadurch; ~**fore** *ad* daher, deshalb; ~**'s** = **there is**.

thermal ['θɜ:məl] *a* *springs* Thermal-; (*Phys*) thermisch.

thermodynamics ['θɜ:məudaɪ'næmɪks] *n* Thermodynamik *f*.

thermometer [θə'mɒmɪtə*] *n* Thermometer *nt*.

thermonuclear ['θɜ:məu'nju:klɪə*] *a* thermonuklear.

Thermos " ['θɜ:məs] *n* Thermosflasche *f*.

thermostat ['θɜ:məstæt] *n* Thermostat *m*.

thesaurus [θɪ'sɔ:rəs] *n* Synonymwörterbuch *nt*.

these [ði:z] *pl pron, a* diese.

thesis ['θi:sɪs] *n* (*for discussion*) These *f*; (*Univ*) Dissertation *f*, Doktorarbeit *f*.

they [ðeɪ] *pl pron* sie; (*people in general*) man; ~**'d** = **they had; they would**; ~**'ll** = **they shall, they will**; ~**'re** = **they are**; ~**'ve** = **they have**.

thick [θɪk] *a* dick; *forest* dicht; *liquid* dickflüssig; (*slow, stupid*) dumm, schwer von Begriff; *n*: **in the** ~ **of** mitten in (+*dat*); ~**en** *vi* (*fog*) dichter werden; *vt* sauce etc verdicken; ~**ness** (*of object*) Dicke *f*, Dichte *f*; Dickflüssigkeit *f*; (*of person*) Dummheit *f*; ~**set** *a* untersetzt; ~**skinned** *a* dickhäutig.

thief [θi:f] *n* Dieb(in *f*) *m*.

thieving [ˈθiːvɪŋ] n Stehlen nt; a diebisch.
thigh [θaɪ] n Oberschenkel m; ~bone Oberschenkelknochen m.
thimble [ˈθɪmbl] n Fingerhut m.
thin [θɪn] a dünn; person also mager; (not abundant) spärlich; fog, rain leicht; excuse schwach.
thing [θɪŋ] n Ding nt; (affair) Sache f; my ~s pl meine Sachen pl.
think [θɪŋk] vti irreg denken; (believe) meinen, denken; **to** ~ **of doing sth** vorhaben or beabsichtigen, etw zu tun; ~ **over** vt überdenken; **to** ~ **up** vt sich (dat) ausdenken; ~**ing** a denkend.
thinly [ˈθɪnlɪ] ad dünn; disguised kaum.
thinness [ˈθɪnnəs] n Dünnheit f; Magerkeit f; Spärlichkeit f.
third [θɜːd] a dritte(r,s); n (person) Dritte(r) mf; (part) Drittel nt; ~**ly** ad drittens; ~ **party insurance** Haftpflichtversicherung f; ~**-rate** a minderwertig.
thirst [θɜːst] n (lit, fig) Durst m; (fig) Verlangen nt; ~**y** a person durstig; work durstig machend; **to be** ~**y** Durst haben.
thirteen [ˈθɜːˈtiːn] num dreizehn.
thirty [ˈθɜːtɪ] num dreißig.
this [ðɪs] a diese(r,s); pron dies/das; **it was** ~ **long** es war so lang.
thistle [ˈθɪsl] n Distel f.
thong [θɒŋ] n (Leder)riemen m.
thorn [θɔːn] n Dorn m, Stachel m; (plant) Dornbusch m; ~**y** a dornig; problem schwierig.
thorough [ˈθʌrə] a gründlich; contempt tief; ~**bred** Vollblut nt; a reinrassig, Vollblut-; ~**fare** Straße f; ~**ly** ad gründlich; (extremely) vollkommen, äußerst; ~**ness** n Gründlichkeit f.
those [ðəʊz] pl pron die (da), jene; a die, jene; ~ **who** diejenigen, die.
though [ðəʊ] cj obwohl; ad trotzdem; **as** ~ als ob.
thought [θɔːt] n (idea) Gedanke m; (opinion) Auffassung f; (thinking) Denken nt, Denkvermögen nt; ~**ful** a (thinking) gedankenvoll, nachdenklich; (kind) rücksichtsvoll, aufmerksam; ~**less** a gedankenlos, unbesonnen; (unkind) rücksichtslos.
thousand [ˈθaʊzənd] num tausend.
thrash [θræʃ] vt (lit) verdreschen; (fig) (vernichtend) schlagen.
thread [θred] n Faden m, Garn nt; (on screw) Gewinde nt; (in story) Faden m, Zusammenhang m; vt needle einfädeln; vi: ~ **one's way** sich hindurchschlängeln; ~**bare** a (lit, fig) fadenscheinig.
threat [θret] n Drohung f; (danger) Bedrohung f, Gefahr f; ~**en** vt bedrohen; vi drohen; **to** ~ **sb with sth** jdm etw androhen; ~**ening** a drohend; letter Droh-.
three [θriː] num drei; ~**-dimensional** a dreidimensional; ~**fold** a dreifach; ~**-piece suit** dreiteilige(r) Anzug m; ~**-piece suite** dreiteilige Polstergarnitur f; ~**-ply** a wool dreifach; wood dreischichtig; ~**-quarter** [θriːˈkwɔːtə*] a dreiviertel; ~**-wheeler** Dreiradwagen m.

thresh [θreʃ] vti dreschen; ~**ing machine** Dreschmaschine f.
threshold [ˈθreʃhəʊld] n Schwelle f.
thrift [θrɪft] n Sparsamkeit f; ~**y** a sparsam.
thrill [θrɪl] n Reiz m, Erregung f; **it gave me quite a** ~ **to . . .** es war ein Erlebnis für mich, zu . . .; vt begeistern, packen; vi beben, zittern; ~**er** Krimi m; ~**ing** a spannend, packend; news aufregend.
thrive [θraɪv] vi gedeihen (on bei).
thriving [ˈθraɪvɪŋ] a blühend, gut gedeihend.
throat [θrəʊt] n Hals m, Kehle f.
throb [θrɒb] n Pochen nt, Schlagen nt; (Puls)schlag m; vi klopfen, pochen.
throes [θrəʊz] npl: **in the** ~ **of** mitten in (+dat).
thrombosis [θrɒmˈbəʊsɪs] n Thrombose f.
throne [θrəʊn] n Thron m; (Eccl) Stuhl m.
throttle [ˈθrɒtl] n Gashebel m; **to open the** ~ Gas geben; vt erdrosseln.
through [θruː] prep durch; (time) während (+gen); (because of) aus, durch; ad durch; **to put sb** ~ (Tel) jdn verbinden (to mit); a ticket, train durchgehend; (finished) fertig; ~**out** [θruːˈaʊt] prep (place) überall in (+dat); (time) während (+gen); ad überall; die ganze Zeit; **we're** ~ es ist aus zwischen uns.
throw [θrəʊ] n Wurf m; vt irreg werfen; ~ **out** vt hinauswerfen; rubbish wegwerfen; plan verwerfen; ~ **up** vti (vomit) speien; ~**away** a (disposable) Wegwerf-; bottle Einweg-; ~**-in** Einwurf m.
thru [θruː] (US) = **through**.
thrush [θrʌʃ] n Drossel f.
thrust [θrʌst] n (Tech) Schubkraft f; vti irreg (push) stoßen; (fig) sich drängen; **to** ~ **oneself on sb** sich jdm aufdrängen; ~**ing** a person aufdringlich, unverfroren.
thud [θʌd] n dumpfe(r) (Auf)schlag m.
thug [θʌg] n Schlägertyp m.
thumb [θʌm] n Daumen m; vt book durchblättern; **a well-**~**ed book** ein abgegriffenes Buch; **to** ~ **a lift** per Anhalter fahren (wollen); ~ **index** Daumenregister nt; ~**nail** Daumennagel m; ~**tack** (US) Reißzwecke f.
thump [θʌmp] n (blow) Schlag m; (noise) Bums m; vi hämmern, pochen; vt schlagen auf (+acc).
thunder [ˈθʌndə*] n Donner m; vi donnern; vt brüllen; ~**ous** a stürmisch; ~**storm** Gewitter nt, Unwetter nt; ~**struck** a wie vom Donner gerührt; ~**y** a gewitterschwül.
Thursday [ˈθɜːzdeɪ] n Donnerstag m.
thus [ðʌs] ad (in this way) so; (therefore) somit, also, folglich.
thwart [θwɔːt] vt vereiteln, durchkreuzen; person hindern.
thyme [taɪm] n Thymian m.
thyroid [ˈθaɪrɔɪd] n Schilddrüse f.
tiara [tɪˈɑːrə] n Diadem nt; (pope's) Tiara f.
tic [tɪk] n Tick m.
tick [tɪk] n (sound) Ticken nt; (mark) Häkchen nt; **in a** ~ (col) sofort; vi ticken; vt abhaken.

ticket ['tɪkɪt] n (for travel) Fahrkarte f; (for entrance) (Eintritts)karte f; (price —) Preisschild nt; (luggage —) (Gepäck)-schein m; (raffle —) Los nt; (parking —) Strafzettel m; (permission) Parkschein m; ~ **collector** Fahrkartenkontrolleur m; ~ **holder** Karteninhaber m; ~ **office** (Rail etc) Fahrkartenschalter m; (Theat etc) Kasse f.

ticking-off ['tɪkɪŋ'ɒf] n (col) Anschnauzer m.

tickle ['tɪkl] n Kitzeln nt; vt kitzeln; (amuse) amüsieren; **that ~d her fancy** das gefiel ihr.

ticklish ['tɪklɪʃ] a (lit, fig) kitzlig.

tidal ['taɪdl] a Flut-, Tide-.

tidbit ['tɪdbɪt] n (US) Leckerbissen m.

tiddlywinks ['tɪdlɪwɪŋks] n Floh-(hüpf)spiel nt.

tide [taɪd] n Gezeiten pl, Ebbe f und Flut; **the ~ is in/out** es ist Flut/Ebbe.

tidily ['taɪdɪlɪ] ad sauber, ordentlich.

tidiness ['taɪdɪnəs] n Ordnung f.

tidy ['taɪdɪ] a ordentlich; vt aufräumen, in Ordnung bringen.

tie [taɪ] n (necktie) Kravatte f, Schlips m; (sth connecting) Band nt; (Sport) Unentschieden nt; vt (fasten, restrict) binden; knot schnüren, festbinden; vi (Sport) unentschieden spielen; (in competition) punktgleich sein; ~ **down** vt (lit) festbinden; (fig) binden; ~ **up** vt dog anbinden; parcel verschnüren; boat festmachen; person fesseln; **I am ~d up right now** ich bin im Moment beschäftigt.

tier [tɪə*] n Reihe f, Rang m; (of cake) Etage f.

tiff [tɪf] n kleine Meinungsverschiedenheit f.

tiger ['taɪgə*] n Tiger m.

tight [taɪt] a (close) eng, knapp; schedule gedrängt; (firm) fest, dicht; screw festsitzend; control streng; (stretched) stramm, angespannt; (col) blau, stramm; ~**s** pl Strumpfhose f; ~**en** vt anziehen, anspannen; restrictions verschärfen; vi sich spannen; ~**-fisted** a knauserig; ~**ly** ad eng; fest, dicht; stretched straff; ~**ness** Enge f; Festigkeit f; Straffheit f; (of money) Knappheit f; ~**-rope** Seil nt.

tile [taɪl] n (in roof) Dachziegel m; (on wall or floor) Fliese f; ~**d** a roof gedeckt, Ziegel-; floor, wall mit Fliesen belegt.

till [tɪl] n Kasse f; vt bestellen; prep,cj bis; **not ~** (in future) nicht vor; (in past) erst.

tiller ['tɪlə*] n Ruderpinne f.

tilt [tɪlt] vt kippen, neigen; vi sich neigen.

timber ['tɪmbə*] n Holz nt; (trees) Baumbestand m.

time [taɪm] n Zeit f; (occasion) Mal nt; (rhythm) Takt m; vt zur rechten Zeit tun, zeitlich einrichten; (Sport) stoppen; **I have no ~ for** people like him für Leute wie ihn habe ich nichts übrig; **in 2 weeks' ~** in 2 Wochen; **for the ~ being** vorläufig; **at all ~s** immer; **at one ~** früher; **at no ~** nie; **at ~s** manchmal; **by the ~** bis; **this ~** diesmal, dieses Mal; **to have a good ~** viel Spaß haben, sich amüsieren; **in ~** (soon enough) rechtzeitig; (after some

time) mit der Zeit; (Mus) im Takt; **on ~** pünktlich, rechtzeitig; **five ~s** fünfmal; **local ~** Ortszeit f; **what ~ is it?** wieviel Uhr ist es?, wie spät ist es?; ~**keeper** Zeitnehmer m; ~**-lag** (in travel) Verzögerung f; (difference) Zeitunterschied m; ~**less** a beauty zeitlos; ~ **limit** Frist f; ~**ly** a rechtzeitig; günstig; ~**-saving** a zeitsparend; ~ **switch** Zeitschalter m; ~**-table** Fahrplan m; (Sch) Stundenplan m; ~ **zone** Zeitzone f.

timid ['tɪmɪd] a ängstlich, schüchtern; ~**ity** [tɪ'mɪdɪtɪ] Ängstlichkeit f; ~**ly** ad ängstlich.

timing ['taɪmɪŋ] n Wahl f des richtigen Zeitpunkts, Timing nt; (Aut) Einstellung f.

timpani ['tɪmpənɪ] npl Kesselpauken pl.

tin [tɪn] n (metal) Blech nt; (container) Büchse f, Dose f; ~**foil** Staniolpapier nt.

tinge [tɪndʒ] n (colour) Färbung f; (fig) Anflug m; vt färben, einen Anstrich geben (+dat).

tingle ['tɪŋgl] n Prickeln nt; vi prickeln.

tinker ['tɪŋkə*] n Kesselflicker m; ~ **with** vt herumpfuschen an (+dat).

tinkle ['tɪŋkl] n Klingeln nt; vi klingeln.

tinned [tɪnd] a food Dosen-, Büchsen-.

tinny ['tɪnɪ] a Blech-, blechern.

tin opener ['tɪnəʊpnə*] n Dosen- or Büchsenöffner m.

tinsel ['tɪnsəl] n Rauschgold nt; Lametta nt.

tint [tɪnt] n Farbton m; (slight colour) Anflug m; (hair) Tönung f.

tiny ['taɪnɪ] a winzig.

tip [tɪp] n (pointed end) Spitze f; (money) Trinkgeld nt; (hint) Wink m, Tip m; **it's on the ~ of my tongue** es liegt mir auf der Zunge; vt (slant) kippen; hat antippen; (—over) umkippen; waiter ein Trinkgeld geben (+dat); ~**off** Hinweis m, Tip m; ~**ped** a cigarette Filter-.

tipple ['tɪpl] n (drink) Schnäpschen nt.

tipsy ['tɪpsɪ] a beschwipst.

tiptoe ['tɪptəʊ] n: **on ~** auf Zehenspitzen.

tiptop ['tɪp'tɒp] a: **in ~ condition** tipptopp, erstklassig.

tire ['taɪə*] n (US) = **tyre**; vti ermüden, müde machen/werden; ~**d** a müde; **to be ~d of sth** etw satt haben; ~**dness** Müdigkeit f; ~**less** a, ~**lessly** ad unermüdlich; ~**some** a lästig.

tiring ['taɪərɪŋ] a ermüdend.

tissue ['tɪʃuː] n Gewebe nt; (paper handkerchief) Papiertaschentuch nt; ~ **paper** Seidenpapier nt.

tit [tɪt] n (bird) Meise f; (col: breast) Titte f; ~ **for tat** wie du mir, so ich dir.

titbit ['tɪtbɪt] n Leckerbissen m.

titillate ['tɪtɪleɪt] vt kitzeln.

titillation [tɪtɪ'leɪʃən] n Kitzeln nt.

titivate ['tɪtɪveɪt] vt schniegeln.

title ['taɪtl] n Titel m; (in law) Rechtstitel m, Eigentumsrecht nt; ~ **deed** Eigentumsurkunde f; ~ **role** Hauptrolle f.

tittle-tattle ['tɪtltætl] n Klatsch m.

titter ['tɪtə*] vi kichern.

titular ['tɪtjʊlə*] a Titular-, nominell; possessions Titel-.

to [tuː, tə] prep (towards) zu; (with countries,

towns) nach; (indir obj) dat; (as far as) bis; (next to, attached to) an (+dat); (per) pro; cj (in order to) um... zu; ad ~ **and fro** hin und her; **to go ~ school/the theatre/bed** in die Schule/ins Theater/ins Bett gehen; **I have never been ~ Germany** ich war noch nie in Deutschland; **to give sth ~ sb** jdm etw geben; ~ **this day** bis auf den heutigen Tag; **20 (minutes) ~ 4** 20 (Minuten) vor 4; **superior ~ sth** besser als etw; **they tied him ~ a tree** sie banden ihn an einen Baum.

toad [təud] n Kröte f; ~**stool** Giftpilz m; ~**y** Speichellecker m, Kriecher m; vi kriechen (vor +dat).

toast [təust] n (bread) Toast m; (drinking) Trinkspruch m; vt trinken auf (+acc); bread toasten; (warm) wärmen; ~**er** Toaster m; ~**master** Zeremonienmeister m; ~**rack** Toastständer m.

tobacco [tə'bækəu] n Tabak m; ~**nist** [tə'bækənɪst] Tabakhändler m; ~**nist's (shop)** Tabakladen m.

toboggan [tə'bogən] n (Rodel)schlitten m.

today [tə'deɪ] ad heute; (at the present time) heutzutage; n (day) heutige(r) Tag m; (time) Heute nt, heutige Zeit f.

toddle ['todl] vi watscheln.

toddler ['todlə*] n Kleinkind nt.

toddy ['todɪ] n (Whisky)grog m.

to-do [tə'du:] n Aufheben nt, Theater nt.

toe [təu] n Zehe f; (of sock, shoe) Spitze f; vt: ~ **the line** (fig) sich einfügen; **to hold** Halt .m für die Fußspitzen; ~**nail** Zehennagel m.

toffee ['tofɪ] n Sahnebonbon nt; ~ **apple** kandierte(r) Apfel m.

toga ['təugə] n Toga f.

together [tə'geðə*] ad zusammen; (at the same time) gleichzeitig; ~**ness** (company) Beisammensein nt; (feeling) Zusammengehörigkeitsgefühl nt.

toil [tɔɪl] n harte Arbeit f, Plackerei f; vi sich abmühen, sich plagen.

toilet ['tɔɪlɪt] n Toilette f; a Toiletten-; ~**bag** Waschbeutel m; ~ **paper** Toilettenpapier nt; ~**ries** ['tɔɪlɪtrɪz] pl Toilettenartikel pl; ~ **roll** Rolle f Toilettenpapier; ~ **soap** Toilettenseife f; ~ **water** Toilettenwasser nt.

token ['təukən] n Zeichen nt; (gift ~) Gutschein m.

tolerable ['tolərəbl] a (bearable) erträglich; (fairly good) leidlich.

tolerably ['tolərəblɪ] ad ziemlich, leidlich.

tolerance ['tolərəns] n Toleranz f.

tolerant a, ~**ly** ad ['tolərənt, -lɪ] tolerant; (patient) geduldig.

tolerate ['toləreɪt] vt dulden; noise ertragen.

toleration [tolə'reɪʃən] n Toleranz f.

toll [təul] n Gebühr f; **it took a heavy ~ of human life** es forderte or kostete viele Menschenleben; vi (bell) läuten; ~**bridge** gebührenpflichtige Brücke f; ~ **road** gebührenpflichtige Autostraße f.

tomato [tə'mɑːtəu] n, pl -**es** Tomate f.

tomb [tu:m] n Grab(mal) nt.

tombola [tom'bəulə] n Tombola f.

tomboy ['tombɔɪ] n Wildfang m; **she's a ~** sie ist sehr burschikos.

tombstone ['tu:mstəun] n Grabstein m.

tomcat ['tomkæt] n Kater m.

tome [təum] n (volume) Band m; (big book) Wälzer m.

tomorrow [tə'mɒrəu] n Morgen nt; ad morgen.

ton [tʌn] n Tonne f; ~**s of** (col) eine Unmenge von.

tonal ['təunl] a tonal; Klang-.

tone [təun] n Ton m; vi (harmonize) passen (zu), harmonisieren (mit); vt eine Färbung geben (+dat); ~ **down** vt criticism, demands mäßigen; colours abtönen; ~**deaf** a ohne musikalisches Gehör.

tongs [tonz] npl Zange f; (curling ~) Lockenstab m.

tongue [tʌŋ] n Zunge f; (language) Sprache f; **with ~ in cheek** ironisch, scherzhaft; ~**tied** a stumm, sprachlos; ~**twister** Zungenbrecher m.

tonic ['tonɪk] n (Med) Stärkungsmittel nt; (Mus) Grundton m, Tonika f; ~ **water** Tonic(water) nt.

tonight [tə'naɪt] n heutige(r) Abend m; diese Nacht f; ad heute abend; heute nacht.

tonnage ['tʌnɪdʒ] n Tonnage f.

tonsil ['tonsl] n Mandel f; ~**itis** [tonsɪ'laɪtɪs] Mandelentzündung f.

too [tu:] ad zu; (also) auch.

tool [tu:l] n (lit, fig) Werkzeug nt; ~**box** Werkzeugkasten m; ~**kit** Werkzeug nt.

toot [tu:t] n Hupen nt; vi tuten; (Aut) hupen.

tooth [tu:θ] n, pl **teeth** Zahn m; ~**ache** Zahnschmerzen pl, Zahnweh nt; ~**brush** Zahnbürste f; ~**paste** Zahnpasta f; ~**pick** Zahnstocher m; ~ **powder** Zahnpulver nt.

top [top] n Spitze f; (of mountain) Gipfel m; (of tree) Wipfel m; (toy) Kreisel m; (~ gear) vierte(r) Gang m; a oberste(r,s); vt list an erster Stelle stehen auf (+dat); **to ~ it all, he said . . .** und er setzte dem noch die Krone auf, indem er sagte . . .; **from ~ to toe** von Kopf bis Fuß; ~**coat** Mantel m; ~**flight** a erstklassig, prima; ~ **hat** Zylinder m; ~**heavy** a oben schwerer als unten, kopflastig.

topic ['topɪk] n Thema nt, Gesprächsgegenstand m; ~**al** a aktuell.

topless ['toplɪs] a dress oben ohne.

top-level ['top'levl] a auf höchster Ebene.

topmost ['topməust] a oberste(r,s), höchste(r,s).

topple ['topl] vti stürzen, kippen.

top-secret ['top'si:krət] a streng geheim.

topsy-turvy ['topsɪ'tɜːvɪ] ad durcheinander; a auf den Kopf gestellt.

torch [tɔːtʃ] n (Elec) Taschenlampe f; (with flame) Fackel f.

torment ['tɔːment] n Qual f; [tɔː'ment] vt (annoy) plagen; (distress) quälen.

torn [tɔːn] a hin- und hergerissen.

tornado [tɔː'neɪdəu] n Tornado m, Wirbelsturm m.

torpedo [tɔː'piːdəu] n Torpedo m.

torpor ['tɔːpə*] n Erstarrung f.

torrent ['tɔrənt] n Sturzbach m; ~ial [tə'renʃəl] a wolkenbruchartig.

torso ['tɔːsəʊ] n Torso m.

tortoise ['tɔːtəs] n Schildkröte f.

tortuous ['tɔːtjʊəs] a (winding) gewunden; (deceitful) krumm, unehrlich.

torture ['tɔːtʃə*] n Folter f; vt foltern.

Tory ['tɔːrɪ] n Tory m; a Tory-, konservativ.

toss [tɒs] vt werfen, schleudern; n (of coin) Hochwerfen nt; **to ~ a coin, to ~ up for sth** etw mit einer Münze entscheiden.

tot [tɒt] n (small quantity) bißchen nt; (small child) Knirps m.

total ['təʊtl] n Gesamtheit f, Ganze(s) nt; a ganz, gesamt, total; vt (add up) zusammenzählen; (amount to) sich belaufen auf; ~itarian [təʊtælɪ'tɛərɪən] a totalitär; ~ity [təʊ'tælɪtɪ] Gesamtheit f; ~ly ad gänzlich, total.

totem pole ['təʊtəmpəʊl] n Totempfahl m.

totter ['tɒtə*] vi wanken, schwanken, wackeln.

touch [tʌtʃ] n Berührung f; (sense of feeling) Tastsinn m; (small amount) Spur f; (style) Stil m; vt (feel) berühren; (come against) leicht anstoßen; (emotionally) bewegen, rühren; **in ~ with** in Verbindung mit; **~ on** vt topic berühren, erwähnen; **~ up** vt paint auffrischen; **~-and-go** a riskant, knapp; **~down** Landen nt, Niedergehen nt; **~iness** Empfindlichkeit f; **~ing** a rührend, ergreifend; **~line** Seitenlinie f; **~y** a empfindlich, reizbar.

tough [tʌf] a (strong) zäh, widerstandsfähig; (difficult) schwierig, hart; meat zäh; **~ luck** Pech nt; n Schläger(typ) m; **~en** vt zäh machen; (make strong) abhärten; vi zäh werden; **~ness** Zähigkeit f; Härte f.

toupée ['tuːpeɪ] n Toupet nt.

tour ['tʊə*] n Reise f, Tour f, Fahrt f; vi umherreisen; (Theat) auf Tour sein/gehen; **~ing** Umherreisen nt; (Theat) Tournee f; **~ism** Fremdenverkehr m, Tourismus m; **~ist** Tourist(in f); a (class) Touristen-; ad Touristenklasse; **~ist office** Verkehrsamt nt.

tournament ['tʊənəmənt] n Tournier nt.

tousled ['taʊzld] a zerzaust.

tow [təʊ] n Schleppen nt; vt (ab)schleppen.

toward(s) [tə'wɔːd(z)] prep (with time) gegen; (in direction of) nach; **he walked ~ me/the town** er kam auf mich zu/er ging auf die Stadt zu; **my feelings ~ him** meine Gefühle ihm gegenüber.

towel ['taʊəl] n Handtuch nt.

tower ['taʊə*] n Turm m; **~ over** vi (lit, fig) überragen; **~ing** a hochragend; rage rasend.

town [taʊn] n Stadt f; **~ clerk** Stadtdirektor m; **~ hall** Rathaus nt; **~ planner** Stadtplaner m.

towpath ['təʊpɑːθ] n Leinpfad m.

towrope ['təʊrəʊp] n Abschlepptau nt.

toxic ['tɒksɪk] a giftig, Gift-.

toy [tɔɪ] n Spielzeug nt; **~ with** vt spielen mit; **~shop** Spielwarengeschäft nt.

trace [treɪs] n Spur f; vt (follow a course) nachspüren (+dat); (find out) aufspüren; (copy) zeichnen, durchpausen.

track [træk] n (mark) Spur f; (path) Weg

m, Pfad m; (race—) Rennbahn f; (Rail) Gleis nt; vt verfolgen; **to keep ~ of sb** jdn im Auge behalten; **to keep ~ of an argument** einer Argumentation folgen können; **to keep ~ of the situation** die Lage verfolgen; **to make ~s (for)** gehen (nach); **~ down** vt aufspüren; **~er dog** Spürhund m; **~less** a pfadlos.

tract [trækt] n (of land) Gebiet nt; (booklet) Abhandlung f, Traktat nt.

tractor ['træktə*] n Traktor m.

trade [treɪd] n (commerce) Handel m; (business) Geschäft nt, Gewerbe nt; (people) Geschäftsleute pl; (skilled manual work) Handwerk nt; vi handeln (in mit); vt tauschen; **~ in** vt in Zahlung geben; **~mark** Warenzeichen nt; **~ name** Handelsbezeichnung f; **~r** Händler m; **~sman** (shopkeeper) Geschäftsmann m; (workman) Handwerker m; (delivery man) Lieferant m; **~ union** Gewerkschaft f; **~ unionist** Gewerkschaftler(in f) m.

trading ['treɪdɪŋ] n Handel m; **~ estate** Industriegelände nt; **~ stamp** Rabattmarke f.

tradition [trə'dɪʃən] n Tradition f; **~al** a traditionell, herkömmlich; **~ally** ad üblicherweise, schon immer.

traffic ['træfɪk] n Verkehr m; (esp in drugs) Handel m (in mit); vi esp drugs handeln; **~ circle** (US) Kreisverkehr m; **~ jam** Verkehrsstauung f; **~ lights** pl Verkehrsampeln pl.

tragedy ['trædʒədɪ] n (lit, fig) Tragödie f.

tragic ['trædʒɪk] a tragisch; **~ally** ad tragisch, auf tragische Weise.

trail [treɪl] n (track) Spur f, Fährte f; (of meteor) Schweif m; (of smoke) Rauchfahne f; (of dust) Staubwolke f; (road) Pfad m, Weg m; vt animal verfolgen; person folgen (+dat); (drag) schleppen; vi (hang loosely) schleifen; (plants) sich ranken; (be behind) hinterherhinken; (Sport) weit zurückliegen; (walk) zuckeln; **on the ~** auf der Spur; **~ behind** vi zurückbleiben; **~er** Anhänger m; (US: caravan) Wohnwagen m; (for film) Vorschau f.

train [treɪn] n Zug m; (of dress) Schleppe f; (series) Folge f, Kette f; vt (teach) person ausbilden; animal abrichten; mind schulen; (Sport) trainieren; (aim) richten (on auf +acc); plant wachsen lassen, ziehen; vi (exercise) trainieren; (study) ausgebildet werden; **~ed** a eye geschult; person, voice ausgebildet; **~ee** Anlernling m; Lehrling m; Praktikant(in f) m; **~er** (Sport) Trainer m; Ausbilder m; **~ing** (for occupation) Ausbildung f; (Sport) Training nt; **in ~ing** im Training; **~ing college** Pädagogische Hochschule f, Lehrerseminar nt; (for priests) Priesterseminar nt.

traipse [treɪps] vi latschen.

trait [treɪ(t)] n Zug m, Merkmal nt.

traitor ['treɪtə*] n Verräter m.

trajectory [trə'dʒektərɪ] n Flugbahn f.

tram(car) ['træm(kɑː*)] n Straßenbahn f; **~line** Straßenbahnschiene f; (route) Straßenbahnlinie f.

tramp [træmp] n Landstreicher m; vi

(*walk heavily*) stampfen, stapfen; (*travel on foot*) wandern; ~**le** ['træmpl] *vt* (nieder)-trampeln; *vi* (herum)trampeln; ~**oline** Trampolin *nt*.

trance [trɑːns] *n* Trance *f*.

tranquil ['træŋkwil] *a* ruhig, friedlich; ~**ity** [træŋ'kwiliti] Ruhe *f*; ~**izer** Beruhigungsmittel *nt*.

trans- [trænz] *pref* Trans-.

transact [træn'zækt] *vt* (durch)führen, abwickeln; ~**ion** Durchführung *f*, Abwicklung *f*; (*piece of business*) Geschäft *nt*, Transaktion *f*.

transatlantic ['trænzət'læntik] *a* transatlantisch.

transcend [træn'send] *vt* übersteigen.

transcendent [træn'sendənt] *a* transzendent.

transcript ['trænskript] *n* Abschrift *f*, Kopie *f*; (*Jur*) Protokoll *nt*; ~**ion** [træn'skripʃən] Transkription *f*; (*product*) Abschrift *f*.

transept ['trænsept] *n* Querschiff *nt*.

transfer ['trænsfə*] *n* (*transferring*) Übertragung *f*; (*of business*) Umzug *m*; (*being transferred*) Versetzung *f*; (*design*) Abziehbild *nt*; (*Sport*) Transfer *m*; (*player*) Transferspieler *m*; [træns'fɜː*] *vt business* verlegen; *person* versetzen; *prisoner* überführen; *drawing* übertragen; *money* überweisen; ~**able** [træns'fɜːrəbl] *a* übertragbar.

transform [træns'fɔːm] *vt* umwandeln, verändern; ~**ation** [trænsfə'meiʃən] Umwandlung *f*, Veränderung *f*, Verwandlung *f*; ~**er** (*Elec*) Transformator *m*.

transfusion [træns'fjuːʒən] *n* Blut-übertragung *f*, Transfusion *f*.

transient ['trænziənt] *a* kurz(lebig).

transistor [træn'zistə*] *n* (*Elec*) Transistor *m*; (*radio*) Transistorradio *nt*.

transit ['trænzit] *n*: **in** ~ unterwegs, auf dem Transport.

transition [træn'ziʃən] *n* Übergang *m*; ~**al** *a* Übergangs-.

transitive *a*, ~**ly** *ad* ['trænzitiv, -li] transitiv.

transitory ['trænzitəri] *a* vorübergehend.

translate [trænz'leit] *vti* übersetzen.

translation [trænz'leiʃən] *n* Übersetzung *f*.

translator [trænz'leitə*] *n* Übersetzer(in *f*) *m*.

transmission [trænz'miʃən] *n* (*of information*) Übermittlung *f*; (*Elec, Med, TV*) Übertragung *f*; (*Aut*) Getriebe *nt*; (*process*) Übersetzung *f*.

transmit [trænz'mit] *vt message* übermitteln; (*Elec, Med, TV*) übertragen; ~**ter** Sender *m*.

transparency [træns'pɛərənsi] *n* Durchsichtigkeit *f*, Transparenz *f*; (*Phot also* [-'pærənsi] Dia(positiv) *nt*.

transparent [træns'pærənt] *a* (*lit*) durchsichtig; (*fig*) offenkundig.

transplant [træns'plɑːnt] *vt* umpflanzen; (*Med*) verpflanzen; (*fig*) *person* verpflanzen; ['trænsplɑːnt] *n* (*Med*) Transplantation *f*; (*organ*) Transplantat *nt*.

transport ['trænspɔːt] *n* Transport *m*, Beförderung *f*; (*vehicle*) fahrbare(r)

Untersatz *m*; **means of** ~ Transportmittel *nt*; [træns'pɔːt] *vt* befördern; transportieren; ~**able** [træns'pɔːtəbl] *a* transportabel; ~**ation** [trænspɔː'teiʃən] Transport *m*, Beförderung *f*; (*means*) Beförderungsmittel *nt*; (*cost*) Transportkosten *pl*.

transverse ['trænzvɜːs] *a* Quer-; *position* horizontal; *engine* querliegend.

transvestite [trænz'vestait] *n* Transvestit *m*.

trap [træp] *n* (*carriage*) zweirädrige(r) Einspänner *m*; (*col: mouth*) Klappe *f*; *vt* fangen; *person* in eine Falle locken; **the miners were** ~**ed** die Bergleute waren eingeschlossen; ~**door** Falltür *f*.

trapeze [trə'piːz] *n* Trapez *nt*.

trapper ['træpə*] *n* Fallensteller *m*, Trapper *m*.

trappings ['træpiŋz] *npl* Aufmachung *f*.

trash [træʃ] *n* (*rubbish*) wertlose(s) Zeug *nt*, Plunder *m*; (*nonsense*) Mist *m*, Blech *nt*; ~ **can** (*US*) Mülleimer *m*; ~**y** *a* wertlos; *novel etc* Schund-.

trauma ['trɔːmə] *n* Trauma *nt*; ~**tic** [trɔː'mætik] *a* traumatisch.

travel ['trævl] *n* Reisen *nt*; *vi* reisen, eine Reise machen; *vt distance* zurücklegen; *country* bereisen; ~**ler**, (*US*) ~**er** Reisende(r) *mf*; (*salesman*) Handlungsreisende(r) *m*; ~**ler's cheque**, (*US*) ~**er's check** Reisescheck *m*; ~**ling**, (*US*) ~**ing** Reisen *nt*; ~**ling bag** Reisetasche *f*; ~ **sickness** Reisekrankheit *f*.

traverse [træ'vɜːs] *vt* (*cross*) durchqueren; (*lie across*) überspannen.

travesty ['trævəsti] *n* Zerrbild *nt*, Travestie *f*; **a** ~ **of justice** ein Hohn *m* auf die Gerechtigkeit.

trawler ['trɔːlə*] *n* Fischdampfer *m*, Trawler *m*.

tray [trei] *n* (*tea* —) Tablett *nt*; (*receptacle*) Schale *f*; (*for mail*) Ablage *f*.

treacherous ['tretʃərəs] *a* verräterisch; *memory* unzuverlässig; *road* tückisch.

treachery ['tretʃəri] *n* Verrat *m*; (*of road*) tückische(r) Zustand *m*.

treacle ['triːkl] *n* Sirup *m*, Melasse *f*.

tread [tred] *n* Schritt *m*, Tritt *m*; (*of stair*) Stufe *f*; (*on tyre*) Profil *nt*; *vi irreg* treten; (*walk*) gehen; ~ **on** *vt* treten auf (+*acc*).

treason ['triːzn] *n* Verrat *m* (*to* an +*dat*).

treasure ['treʒə*] *n* Schatz *m*; *vt* schätzen; ~ **hunt** Schatzsuche *f*; ~**r** Kassenverwalter *m*, Schatzmeister *m*.

treasury ['treʒəri] *n* (*Pol*) Finanzministerium *nt*.

treat [triːt] *n* besondere Freude *f*; (*school* — *etc*) Fest *nt*; (*outing*) Ausflug *m*; *vt* (*deal with*) behandeln; (*entertain*) bewirten; **to** ~ **sb to sth** jdn zu etw einladen, jdm etw spendieren.

treatise ['triːtiz] *n* Abhandlung *f*.

treatment ['triːtmənt] *n* Behandlung *f*.

treaty ['triːti] *n* Vertrag *m*.

treble ['trebl] *a* dreifach; *vt* verdreifachen; *n* (*voice*) Sopran *m*; (*music*) Diskant *m*; ~ **clef** Violinschlüssel *m*.

tree [tri:] *n* Baum *m*; **~-lined** *a* baumbestanden; **~ trunk** Baumstamm *m*.

trek [trek] *n* Treck *m*, Zug *m*; *vi* trecken.

trellis ['trelɪs] *n* Gitter *nt*; *(for gardening)* Spalier *nt*.

tremble ['trembl] *vi* zittern; *(ground)* beben.

trembling ['tremblɪŋ] *n* Zittern *nt*; *a* zitternd.

tremendous [trə'mendəs] *a* gewaltig, kolossal; *(col: very good)* prima; **~ly** *ad* ungeheuer, enorm; *(col)* unheimlich.

tremor ['tremə*] *n* Zittern *nt*; *(of earth)* Beben *nt*.

trench [trentʃ] *n* Graben *m*; *(Mil)* Schützengraben *m*.

trend [trend] *n* Richtung *f*, Tendenz *f*; *vi* sich neigen, tendieren; **~y** *a* *(col)* modisch.

trepidation [trepɪ'deɪʃən] *n* Beklommenheit *f*.

trespass ['trespəs] *vi* widerrechtlich betreten *(on acc)*; **'~ers will be prosecuted'** 'Betreten verboten.'

tress [tres] *n* Locke *f*.

trestle ['tresl] *n* Bock *m*; **~ table** Klapptisch *m*.

tri- [traɪ] *pref* Drei-, drei-.

trial ['traɪəl] *n* *(Jur)* Prozeß *m*, Verfahren *nt*; *(test)* Versuch *m*, Probe *f*; *(hardship)* Prüfung *f*; **by ~ and error** durch Ausprobieren.

triangle ['traɪæŋgl] *n* Dreieck *nt*; *(Mus)* Triangel *f*.

triangular [traɪ'æŋgjulə*] *a* dreieckig.

tribal ['traɪbəl] *a* Stammes-.

tribe [traɪb] *n* Stamm *m*; **~sman** Stammesangehörige(r) *m*.

tribulation [trɪbju'leɪʃən] *n* Not *f*, Mühsal *f*.

tribunal [traɪ'bju:nl] *n* Gericht *nt*; *(inquiry)* Untersuchungsausschuß *m*.

tributary ['trɪbjʊtəri] *n* Nebenfluß *m*.

tribute ['trɪbju:t] *n* *(admiration)* Zeichen *nt* der Hochachtung.

trice [traɪs] *n*: **in a ~** im Nu.

trick [trɪk] *n* Trick *m*; *(mischief)* Streich *m*; *(habit)* Angewohnheit *f*; *(Cards)* Stich *m*; *vt* überlisten, beschwindeln; **~ery** Betrügerei *f*, Tricks *pl*.

trickle ['trɪkl] *n* Tröpfeln *nt*; *(small river)* Rinnsal *nt*; *vi* tröpfeln; *(seep)* sickern.

tricky ['trɪki] *a* *problem* schwierig; *situation* kitzlig.

tricycle ['traɪsɪkl] *n* Dreirad *nt*.

tried [traɪd] *a* erprobt, bewährt.

trier ['traɪə*] *n*: **to be a ~** sich *(dat)* ernsthaft Mühe geben.

trifle ['traɪfl] *n* Kleinigkeit *f*; *(Cook)* Trifle *m*; *ad*: **a ~** ein bißchen.

trifling ['traɪflɪŋ] *a* geringfügig.

trigger ['trɪgə*] *n* Drücker *m*; **~ off** *vt* auslösen.

trigonometry [trɪgə'nɒmətri] *n* Trigonometrie *f*.

trilby ['trɪlbi] *n* weiche(r) Filzhut *m*.

trill [trɪl] *n* *(Mus)* Triller *m*.

trilogy ['trɪlədʒi] *n* Trilogie *f*.

trim [trɪm] *a* ordentlich, gepflegt; *figure*

schlank; *n* (gute) Verfassung *f*; *(embellishment, on car)* Verzierung *f*; **to give sb's hair a ~** jdm die Haare etwas schneiden; *vt* *(clip)* schneiden; *trees* stutzen; *(decorate)* besetzen; *sails* trimmen; **~mings** *pl* *(decorations)* Verzierung(en *pl*) *f*; *(extras)* Zubehör *nt*.

Trinity ['trɪnɪti] *n*: **the ~** die Dreieinigkeit.

trinket ['trɪŋkɪt] *n* kleine(s) Schmuckstück *nt*.

trio ['tri:əʊ] *n* Trio *nt*.

trip [trɪp] *n* (kurze) Reise *f*; *(outing)* Ausflug *m*; *(stumble)* Stolpern *nt*; *vi* *(walk quickly)* trippeln; *(stumble)* stolpern; **~ over** *vt* stolpern über (+*acc*); **~ up** *vi* stolpern; *(fig also)* einen Fehler machen; *vt* zu Fall bringen; *(fig)* hereinlegen.

tripe [traɪp] *n* *(food)* Kutteln *pl*; *(rubbish)* Mist *m*.

triple ['trɪpl] *a* dreifach; **~ts** ['trɪpləts] *pl* Drillinge *pl*.

triplicate ['trɪplɪkət] *n*: **in ~** in dreifacher Ausfertigung.

tripod ['traɪpɒd] *n* Dreifuß *m*; *(Phot)* Stativ *nt*.

tripper ['trɪpə*] *n* Ausflügler(in *f*) *m*.

trite [traɪt] *a* banal.

triumph ['traɪʌmf] *n* Triumph *m*; *vi* triumphieren; **~al** [traɪʌmfəl] *a* triumphal, Sieges-; **~ant** [traɪ'ʌmfənt] *a* triumphierend; *(victorious)* siegreich; **~antly** *ad* triumphierend; siegreich.

trivial ['trɪvɪəl] *a* gering(fügig), trivial; **~lity** [trɪvɪ'ælɪti] *n* Trivialität *f*, Nebensächlichkeit *f*.

trolley ['trɒli] *n* Handwagen *m*; *(in shop)* Einkaufswagen; *(for luggage)* Kofferkuli *m*; *(table)* Teewagen *m*; **~ bus** O(berleitungs)bus *m*.

trollop ['trɒləp] *n* Hure *f*; *(slut)* Schlampe *f*.

trombone [trɒm'bəʊn] *n* Posaune *f*.

troop [tru:p] *n* Schar *f*; *(Mil)* Trupp *m*; **~s** *pl* Truppen *pl*; **~ in/out** *vi* hinein-/hinausströmen; **~er** Kavallerist *m*; **~ship** Truppentransporter *m*.

trophy ['trəʊfi] *n* Trophäe *f*.

tropic ['trɒpɪk] *n* Wendekreis *m*; **the ~s** *pl* die Tropen *pl*; **~al** *a* tropisch.

trot [trɒt] *n* Trott *m*; *vi* trotten.

trouble ['trʌbl] *n* *(worry)* Sorge *f*, Kummer *m*; *(in country, industry)* Unruhen *pl*; *(effort)* Umstand *m*, Mühe *f*; *vt* *(disturb)* beunruhigen, stören, belästigen; **to ~ to do sth** sich bemühen, etw zu tun; **to make ~** Schwierigkeiten *or* Unannehmlichkeiten machen; **to have ~ with** Ärger haben mit; **to be in ~** Probleme *or* Ärger haben; **~d** *a person* beunruhigt; *country* geplagt; **~-free** *a* sorglos; **~maker** Unruhestifter *m*; **~shooter** Vermittler *m*; **~some** *a* lästig, unangenehm; *child* schwierig.

trough [trɒf] *n* *(vessel)* Trog *m*; *(channel)* Rinne *f*, Kanal *m*; *(Met)* Tief *nt*.

trounce [traʊns] *vt* *(esp Sport)* vernichtend schlagen.

troupe [tru:p] *n* Truppe *f*.

trousers ['traʊzəz] *npl* (lange) Hose *f*, Hosen *pl*.

trousseau ['tru:səʊ] n Aussteuer f.

trout [traʊt] n Forelle f.

trowel ['traʊəl] n Kelle f.

truant ['truənt] n: **to play ~** (die Schule) schwänzen.

truce [tru:s] n Waffenstillstand m.

truck [trʌk] n Lastwagen m, Lastauto nt; (Rail) offene(r) Güterwagen m; (barrow) Gepäckkarren m; **to have no ~ with sb** nichts zu tun haben wollen mit jdm; **~ driver** Lastwagenfahrer m; **~ farm** (US) Gemüsegärtnerei f.

truculent ['trʌkjʊlənt] a trotzig.

trudge [trʌdʒ] vi sich (mühselig) dahinschleppen.

true [tru:] a (exact) wahr; (genuine) echt; friend treu.

truffle ['trʌfl] n Trüffel f.

truly ['tru:lɪ] ad (really) wirklich; (exactly) genau; (faithfully) treu; **yours ~** Ihr sehr ergebener.

trump [trʌmp] n (Cards) Trumpf m; **~ed-up** e erfunden.

trumpet ['trʌmpɪt] n Trompete f; vt ausposaunen; vi trompeten.

truncated [trʌŋ'keɪtɪd] a verstümmelt.

truncheon ['trʌntʃən] n Gummiknüppel m.

trundle ['trʌndl] vt schieben; vi: **~ along** (person) dahinschlendern; (vehicle) entlangrollen.

trunk [trʌŋk] n (of tree) (Baum)stamm m; (Anat) Rumpf m; (box) Truhe f, Überseekoffer m; (of elephant) Rüssel m; **~s** pl Badehose f; **~ call** Ferngespräch nt.

truss [trʌs] n (Med) Bruchband nt.

trust [trʌst] n (confidence) Vertrauen nt; (for property etc) Treuhandvermögen nt; vt (rely on) vertrauen (+dat), sich verlassen auf (+acc); (hope) hoffen; **~ him to break it!** er muß es natürlich kaputt machen, typisch!; **to ~ sth to sb** jdm etw anvertrauen; **~ed** a treu; **~ee** [trʌs'ti:] Vermögensverwalter m; **~ful** a, **~ing** a vertrauensvoll; **~worthy** a vertrauenswürdig; account glaubwürdig; **~y** a treu, zuverlässig.

truth [tru:θ] n Wahrheit f; **~ful** a ehrlich; **~fully** ad wahrheitsgemäß; **~fulness** Ehrlichkeit f; (of statement) Wahrheit f.

try [traɪ] n Versuch m; **to have a ~** es versuchen; vt (attempt) versuchen; (test) (aus)probieren; (Jur) person unter Anklage stellen; case verhandeln; (strain) anstrengen; courage, patience auf die Probe stellen; vi (make effort) versuchen, sich bemühen; **~ on** vt dress anprobieren; hat aufprobieren; **~ out** vt ausprobieren; **~ing** a schwierig; **~ing for** anstrengend für.

tsar [zɑ:*] n Zar m.

T-shirt ['ti:ʃɜ:t] n T-shirt nt.

T-square ['ti:skweə*] n Reißschiene f.

tub [tʌb] n Wanne f, Kübel m; (for margarine etc) Becher m.

tuba ['tju:bə] n Tuba f.

tubby ['tʌbɪ] a rundlich, klein und dick.

tube [tju:b] n (pipe) Röhre f, Rohr nt; (for toothpaste etc) Tube f; (in London) U-Bahn

tuber ['tju:bə*] n Knolle f.

tuberculosis [tjʊbɜ:kjʊ'ləʊsɪs] n Tuberkulose f.

tube station ['tju:bsteɪʃən] n U-Bahnstation f.

tubular ['tju:bjʊlə*] a röhrenförmig.

tuck [tʌk] n (fold) Falte f, Einschlag m; vt (put) stecken; (gather) fälteln, einschlagen; **~ away** vt wegstecken; **~ in** vt hineinstecken; blanket etc feststecken; person zudecken; vi (eat) hineinhauen, zulangen; **~ up** vt child warm zudecken; **~ shop** Süßwarenladen m.

Tuesday ['tju:zdeɪ] n Dienstag m.

tuft [tʌft] n Büschel m.

tug [tʌg] n (jerk) Zerren nt, Ruck m; (Naut) Schleppdampfer m; vti zerren, ziehen; boat schleppen; **~-of-war** Tauziehen nt.

tuition [tju'ɪʃən] n Unterricht m.

tulip ['tju:lɪp] n Tulpe f.

tumble ['tʌmbl] n (fall) Sturz m; vi (fall) fallen, stürzen; **~ down** a baufällig; **~r** (glass) Trinkglas nt, Wasserglas nt; (for drying) Trockenautomat m.

tummy ['tʌmɪ] n (col) Bauch m.

tumour ['tju:mə*] n Tumor m, Geschwulst f.

tumult ['tju:mʌlt] n Tumult m; **~uous** [tju:'mʌltjʊəs] a lärmend, turbulent.

tumulus ['tju:mjʊləs] n Grabhügel m.

tuna ['tju:nə] n Thunfisch m.

tundra ['tʌndrə] n Tundra f.

tune [tju:n] n Melodie f; vt (put in tune) stimmen; (Aut) richtig einstellen; **to sing in ~/out of ~** richtig/falsch singen; **to be out of ~ with** nicht harmonieren mit; **~ in** vi einstellen (to acc); **~ up** vi (Mus) stimmen; **~r** (person) (Instrumenten)stimmer m; (radio set) Empfangsgerät nt, Steuergerät nt; (part) Tuner m, Kanalwähler m; **~ful** a melodisch.

tungsten ['tʌŋstən] n Wolfram m.

tunic ['tju:nɪk] n Waffenrock m; (loose garment) lange Bluse f.

tuning ['tju:nɪŋ] n (Rad, Aut) Einstellen nt; (Mus) Stimmen nt.

tunnel ['tʌnl] n Tunnel m, Unterführung f; vi einen Tunnel anlegen.

tunny ['tʌnɪ] n Thunfisch m.

turban ['tɜ:bən] n Turban m.

turbid ['tɜ:bɪd] a trübe; (fig) verworren.

turbine ['tɜ:baɪn] n Turbine f.

turbot ['tɜ:bət] n Steinbutt m.

turbulence ['tɜ:bjʊləns] n (Aviat) Turbulenz f.

turbulent ['tɜ:bjʊlənt] a stürmisch.

tureen [tjʊri:n] n Terrine f.

turf [tɜ:f] n Rasen m; (piece) Sode f.

turgid ['tɜ:dʒɪd] a geschwollen.

turkey ['tɜ:kɪ] n Puter m, Truthahn m.

turmoil ['tɜ:mɔɪl] n Aufruhr m, Tumult m.

turn [tɜ:n] n (rotation) (Um)drehung f; (performance) (Programm)nummer f; (Med) Schock m; vt (rotate) drehen; (change position of) umdrehen, wenden; page umblättern; (transform) verwandeln;

(direct) zuwenden; vi (rotate) sich drehen; (change direction) (in car) abbiegen; (wind) drehen; (— round) umdrehen, wenden; (become) werden; (leaves) sich verfärben; (milk) sauer werden; (weather) umschlagen; (become) werden; **to make a ~** to the left nach links abbiegen; **the ~ of the tide** der Gezeitenwechsel; **the ~ of the century** die Jahrhundertwende; **to take a ~ for the worse** sich zum Schlechten wenden; **it's your ~** du bist dran or an der Reihe; **in ~, by ~s** abwechselnd; **to take ~s** sich abwechseln; **to do sb a good/bad ~** jdm einen guten/schlechten Dienst erweisen; **it gave me quite a ~** das hat mich schön erschreckt; **to ~ sb loose** jdn los- or freilassen; **~ back** vt umdrehen; person zurückschicken; clock zurückstellen; vi umkehren; **~ down** vt (refuse) ablehnen; (fold down) umschlagen; **~ in** vi (go to bed) ins Bett gehen; vt (fold inwards) ein- wärts biegen; **~ into** vi sich verwandeln in (+acc); **~ off** vi abbiegen; vt aus- schalten; tap zudrehen; machine, electricity abstellen; **~ on** vt (light) anschalten, ein- schalten; tap aufdrehen; machine anstellen; **~ out** vi (prove to be) sich herausstellen, sich erweisen; (people) sich entwickeln; **how did the cake ~ out?** wie ist der Kuchen geworden?; vt light abstellen; gas abstellen; (produce) produzieren; **~ to** vt sich zuwenden (+dat); **~ up** vi auftauchen; (happen) passieren, sich ereignen; vt collar hochklappen, hoch- stellen; nose rümpfen; (increase) radio lauter stellen; heat höher drehen; **~about** Kehrtwendung f; **~ed-up a** nose Stups-; **~ing** (in road) Abzweigung f; **~ing point** Wendepunkt m.

turnip ['tɜːnɪp] n Steckrübe f.

turnout ['tɜːnaʊt] n (Besucher)zahl f; (Comm) Produktion f.

turnover ['tɜːnəʊvə*] n Umsatz m; (of staff) Wechsel m; (Cook) Tasche f.

turnpike ['tɜːnpaɪk] n (US) gebühren- pflichtige Straße f.

turnstile ['tɜːnstaɪl] n Drehkreuz nt.

turntable ['tɜːnteɪbl] n (of record-player) Plattenteller m; (Rail) Drehscheibe f.

turn-up ['tɜːnʌp] n (on trousers) Aufschlag m.

turpentine ['tɜːpəntaɪn] n Terpentin nt.

turquoise ['tɜːkwɔɪz] n (gem) Türkis m; (colour) Türkis nt; a türkisfarben.

turret ['tʌrɪt] n Turm m.

turtle ['tɜːtl] n Schildkröte f.

tusk [tʌsk] n Stoßzahn m.

tussle ['tʌsl] n Balgerei f.

tutor ['tjuːtə*] n (teacher) Privatlehrer m; (college instructor) Tutor m; **~ial** [tjuːˈtɔːrɪəl] (Univ) Kolloquium nt, Seminarübung f.

tuxedo [tʌkˈsiːdəʊ] n (US) Smoking m.

TV ['tiːˈviː] n Fernseher m; a Fernseh-.

twaddle ['twɒdl] n (col) Gewäsch nt.

twang [twæŋ] n scharfe(r) Ton m; (of voice) Näseln nt; vt zupfen; vi klingen; (talk) näseln.

tweed [twiːd] n Tweed m.

tweezers ['twiːzəz] npl Pinzette f.

twelfth [twelfθ] a zwölfte(r,s); **T~ Night** Dreikönigsabend m.

twelve [twelv] num a zwölf.

twenty ['twentɪ] num a zwanzig.

twerp [twɜːp] n (col) Knülch m.

twice [twaɪs] ad zweimal; **~ as much** doppelt soviel; **~ my age** doppelt so alt wie ich.

twig [twɪg] n dünne(r) Zweig m; vt (col) kapieren, merken.

twilight ['twaɪlaɪt] n Dämmerung f, Zwielicht nt.

twill [twɪl] n Köper m.

twin [twɪn] n Zwilling m; a Zwillings-; (very similar) Doppel-.

twine [twaɪn] n Bindfaden m; vi binden.

twinge [twɪndʒ] n stechende(r) Schmerz m, Stechen nt.

twinkle ['twɪŋkl] n Funkeln nt, Blitzen nt; vi funkeln.

twin town ['twɪntaʊn] n Partnerstadt f.

twirl [twɜːl] n Wirbel m; vti (herum)- wirbeln.

twist [twɪst] n (twisting) Biegen nt, Drehung f; (bend) Kurve f; vt (turn) drehen; (make crooked) verbiegen; (distort) verdrehen; vi (wind) sich drehen; (curve) sich winden.

twit [twɪt] n (col) Idiot m.

twitch [twɪtʃ] n Zucken nt; vi zucken.

two [tuː] num a zwei; **to break in ~** in zwei Teile brechen; **~ by ~** zu zweit; **to be in ~ minds** nicht genau wissen; **to put ~ and ~ together** seine Schlüsse ziehen; **~-door** a zweitürig; **~-faced** a falsch; **~-fold** a, ad zweifach, doppelt; **~-piece** a zweiteilig; **~-seater** (plane, car) Zweisitzer m; **~-some** Paar nt; **~-way** a traffic Gegen-.

tycoon [taɪˈkuːn] n (Industrie)magnat m.

type [taɪp] n Typ m, Art f; (Print) Type f; vti maschineschreiben, tippen; **~-cast** a (Theat, TV) auf eine Rolle festgelegt; **~script** maschinegeschriebene(r) Text m; **~writer** Schreibmaschine f; **~written** a maschinegeschrieben.

typhoid ['taɪfɔɪd] n Typhus m.

typhoon [taɪˈfuːn] n Taifun m.

typhus ['taɪfəs] n Flecktyphus m.

typical a, **~ly** ad ['tɪpɪkəl, -klɪ] typisch (of für).

typify ['tɪpɪfaɪ] vt typisch sein für.

typing ['taɪpɪŋ] n Maschineschreiben nt.

typist ['taɪpɪst] n Maschinenschreiber(in f) m, Tippse f (col).

tyranny ['tɪrənɪ] n Tyrannei f, Gewaltherr- schaft f.

tyrant ['taɪrənt] n Tyrann m.

tyre [taɪə*] n Reifen m.

U

U, u [juː] n U nt, u nt.

ubiquitous [juːˈbɪkwɪtəs] adj überall zu finden(d); allgegenwärtig.

udder ['ʌdə*] n Euter nt.

ugh [ɜːh] interj hu.

ugliness ['ʌglɪnəs] n Häßlichkeit f.

ugly ['ʌglɪ] *a* häßlich; (*bad*) böse, schlimm.
ukulele [juːkəˈleɪlɪ] *n* Ukulele *f.*
ulcer ['ʌlsə*] *n* Geschwür *nt.*
ulterior [ʌlˈtɪərɪə*] *a*: ~ motive Hintergedanke *m.*
ultimate ['ʌltɪmət] *a* äußerste(r,s), allerletzte(r,s); ~ly *ad* schließlich, letzten Endes.
ultimatum [ʌltɪˈmeɪtəm] *n* Ultimatum *nt.*
ultra- ['ʌltrə] *pref* ultra-.
ultraviolet ['ʌltrəˈvaɪələt] *a* ultraviolett.
umbilical cord [ʌmˈbɪklɪkl kɔːd] *n* Nabelschnur *f.*
umbrage ['ʌmbrɪdʒ] *n*: to take ~ Anstoß nehmen (*at* an +*dat*).
umbrella [ʌmˈbrelə] *n* Schirm *m.*
umpire ['ʌmpaɪə*] *n* Schiedsrichter *m; vti* schiedsrichtern.
umpteen ['ʌmptiːn] *num* (*col*) zig.
un- [ʌn] *pref* un-.
unabashed ['ʌnəˈbæʃt] *a* unerschrocken.
unabated ['ʌnəˈbeɪtɪd] *a* unvermindert.
unable ['ʌnˈeɪbl] *a* außerstande; to be ~ to do sth etw nicht tun können.
unaccompanied ['ʌnəˈkʌmpanɪd] *a* ohne Begleitung.
unaccountably ['ʌnəˈkauntəblɪ] *ad* unerklärlich.
unaccustomed ['ʌnəˈkʌstəmd] *a* nicht gewöhnt (*to* an +*acc*); (*unusual*) ungewohnt.
unadulterated ['ʌnəˈdʌltəreɪtəd] *a* rein, unverfälscht.
unaided ['ʌnˈeɪdɪd] *a* selbständig, ohne Hilfe.
unanimity [juːnəˈnɪmɪtɪ] *n* Einstimmigkeit *f.*
unanimous *a*, ~ly *ad* [juːˈnænɪməs, -lɪ] einmütig; *vote* einstimmig.
unattached ['ʌnəˈtætʃt] *a* ungebunden.
unattended ['ʌnəˈtendɪd] *a person* unbeaufsichtigt; *thing* unbewacht.
unattractive ['ʌnəˈtræktɪv] *a* unattraktiv.
unauthorized ['ʌnˈɔːθəraɪzd] *a* unbefugt.
unavoidable *a*, **unavoidably** *ad* ['ʌnəˈvɔɪdəbl, -blɪ] unvermeidlich.
unaware ['ʌnəˈweə*] *a*: to be ~ of sth sich (*dat*) einer Sache nicht bewußt sein; ~s *ad* unversehens.
unbalanced ['ʌnˈbælənst] *a* unausgeglichen; (*mentally*) gestört.
unbearable [ʌnˈbeərəbl] *a* unerträglich.
unbeatable [ʌnˈbiːtəbl] *a* unschlagbar.
unbeaten [ʌnˈbiːtn] *a* ungeschlagen.
unbecoming ['ʌnbɪˈkʌmɪŋ] *a dress* unkleidsam; *behaviour* unpassend, unschicklich.
unbeknown ['ʌnbɪˈnəʊn] *ad* ohne jedes Wissen (*to* gen).
unbelief [ʌnbɪˈliːf] *n* Unglaube *m.*
unbelievable [ʌnbɪˈliːvəbl] *a* unglaublich.
unbend [ʌnˈbend] *irreg vt* geradebiegen, gerademachen; *vi* aus sich herausgehen.
unbounded [ʌnˈbaʊndɪd] *a* unbegrenzt.
unbreakable [ʌnˈbreɪkəbl] *a* unzerbrechlich.
unbridled [ʌnˈbraɪdld] *a* ungezügelt.
unbroken ['ʌnˈbrəʊkən] *a period*

ununterbrochen; *spirit* ungebrochen; *record* unübertroffen.
unburden [ʌnˈbɜːdn] *vt*: ~ o.s. (jdm) sein Herz ausschütten.
unbutton ['ʌnˈbʌtn] *vt* aufknöpfen.
uncalled-for [ʌnˈkɔːldfɔː*] *a* unnötig.
uncanny [ʌnˈkænɪ] *a* unheimlich.
unceasing [ʌnˈsiːsɪŋ] *a* unaufhörlich.
uncertain [ʌnˈsɜːtn] *a* unsicher; (*doubtful*) ungewiß; (*unreliable*) unbeständig; (*vague*) undeutlich, vage; ~ty Ungewißheit *f.*
unchanged ['ʌnˈtʃeɪndʒd] *a* unverändert.
uncharitable [ʌnˈtʃærɪtəbl] *a* hartherzig; *remark* unfreundlich.
uncharted ['ʌnˈtʃɑːtɪd] *a* nicht verzeichnet.
unchecked ['ʌnˈtʃekt] *a* ungeprüft; (*not stopped*) *advance* ungehindert.
uncivil ['ʌnˈsɪvɪl] *a* unhöflich, grob.
uncle ['ʌŋkl] *n* Onkel *m.*
uncomfortable ['ʌnˈkʌmfətəbl] *a* unbequem, ungemütlich.
uncompromising [ʌnˈkɒmprəmaɪzɪŋ] *a* kompromißlos, unnachgiebig.
unconditional ['ʌnkənˈdɪʃənl] *a* bedingungslos.
uncongenial ['ʌnkənˈdʒiːnɪəl] *a* unangenehm.
unconscious [ʌnˈkɒnʃəs] *a* (*Med*) bewußtlos; (*not aware*) nicht bewußt; (*not meant*) unbeabsichtigt; the ~ das Unbewußte; ~ly *ad* unwissentlich, unbewußt; ~ness Bewußtlosigkeit *f.*
uncontrollable [ʌnkənˈtrəʊləbl] *a* unkontrollierbar, unbändig.
uncork ['ʌnˈkɔːk] *vt* entkorken.
uncouth [ʌnˈkuːθ] *a* grob, ungehobelt.
uncover [ʌnˈkʌvə*] *vt* aufdecken.
unctuous ['ʌŋktjʊəs] *a* salbungsvoll.
undaunted [ʌnˈdɔːntɪd] *a* unerschrocken.
undecided ['ʌndɪˈsaɪdɪd] *a* unschlüssig.
undeniable [ʌndɪˈnaɪəbl] *a* unleugbar.
undeniably [ʌndɪˈnaɪəblɪ] *ad* unbestreitbar.
under ['ʌndə*] *prep* unter; *ad* darunter; ~ repair in Reparatur; ~-age a minderjährig.
undercarriage ['ʌndəkærɪdʒ] *n* Fahrgestell *nt.*
underclothes ['ʌndəkləʊðz] *npl* Unterwäsche *f.*
undercoat ['ʌndəkəʊt] *n* (*paint*) Grundierung *f.*
undercover ['ʌndəkʌvə*] *a* Geheim-.
undercurrent ['ʌndəkʌrənt] *n* Unterströmung *f.*
undercut ['ʌndəkʌt] *vt irreg* unterbieten.
underdeveloped ['ʌndədɪˈveləpt] *a* Entwicklungs-, unterentwickelt.
underdog ['ʌndədɒg] *n* Unterlegene(r) *mf.*
underdone ['ʌndəˈdʌn] *a* (*Cook*) nicht gar, nicht durchgebraten.
underestimate ['ʌndərˈestɪmeɪt] *vt* unterschätzen.
underexposed ['ʌndərɪksˈpəʊzd] *a* unterbelichtet.
underfed ['ʌndəˈfed] *a* unterernährt.
underfoot ['ʌndəˈfʊt] *ad* unter den Füßen.
undergo ['ʌndəˈgəʊ] *vt irreg* experience

durchmachen; *operation, test* sich unter-
ziehen (+dat).
undergraduate [ˌʌndəˈgrædjuət] *n*
Student(in *f*) *m*.
underground [ˈʌndəgraund] *n* Untergrundbahn *f*, U-Bahn *f*; *a press etc* Unter-
grund-.
undergrowth [ˈʌndəgrəuθ] *n* Gestrüpp *nt*,
Unterholz *nt*.
underhand [ˈʌndəhænd] *a* hinterhältig.
underlie [ʌndəˈlaɪ] *vt irreg (form the basis
of)* zugrundeliegen (+dat).
underline [ʌndəˈlaɪn] *vt* unterstreichen;
(emphasize) betonen.
underling [ˈʌndəlɪŋ] *n* Handlanger *m*.
undermine [ʌndəˈmaɪn] *vt* unterhöhlen;
(fig) unterminieren, untergraben.
underneath [ˈʌndəˈniːθ] *ad* darunter; *prep*
unter.
underpaid [ˈʌndəˈpeɪd] *a* unterbezahlt.
underpants [ˈʌndəpænts] *npl* Unterhose *f*.
underpass [ˈʌndəpɑːs] *n* Unterführung *f*.
underplay [ʌndəˈpleɪ] *vt* herunterspielen.
underprice [ʌndəˈpraɪs] *vt* zu niedrig
ansetzen.
underprivileged [ˈʌndəˈprɪvɪlɪdʒd] *a*
benachteiligt, unterpriviligiert.
underrate [ʌndəˈreɪt] *vt* unterschätzen.
undershirt [ˈʌndəʃɜːt] *n (US)* Unterhemd
nt.
undershorts [ˈʌndəʃɔːts] *npl (US)* Unterhose *f*.
underside [ˈʌndəsaɪd] *n* Unterseite *f*.
underskirt [ˈʌndəskɜːt] *n* Unterrock *m*.
understand [ʌndəˈstænd] *vt   irreg*
verstehen; **I ~ that . . .** ich habe gehört,
daß . .; **am I to ~ that . . .?** soll das
(etwa) heißen, daß . . .?; **what do you ~
by that?** was verstehen Sie darunter?; **it
is understood that . . .** es wurde
vereinbart, daß . .; **to make o.s. understood** sich verständlich machen; **is that
understood?** is das klar?; **~able** *a* verständlich; **~ing** Verständnis *nt*; *a* ver-
ständnisvoll.
understatement [ˈʌndəsteɪtmənt] *n*
Untertreibung *f*, Understatement *nt*.
understudy [ˈʌndəstʌdɪ] *n* Ersatz(schau)-
spieler(in *f*) *m*.
undertake [ʌndəˈteɪk]   *irreg   vt*
unternehmen; *vi (promise)* sich
verpflichten; **~r** Leichenbestatter *m*;
~r's Beerdigungsinstitut *nt*.
undertaking [ʌndəˈteɪkɪŋ] *n (enterprise)*
Unternehmen *nt*; *(promise)* Verpflichtung
f.
underwater [ˈʌndəˈwɔːtə*] *ad* unter
Wasser; *a* Unterwasser-.
underwear [ˈʌndəweə*] *n* Unterwäsche *f*.
underweight [ʌndəˈweɪt] *a*: **to be ~**
Untergewicht haben.
underworld [ˈʌndəwɜːld] *n (of crime)*
Unterwelt *f*.
underwriter [ˈʌndəraɪtə*] *n* Assekurant
m.
undesirable   [ʌndɪˈzaɪərəbl]   *a*
unerwünscht.
undies [ˈʌndɪz] *npl (col)* (Damen)unter-
wäsche *f*.

undiscovered   [ʌndɪsˈkʌvəd]   *a*
unentdeckt.
undisputed [ʌndɪsˈpjuːtɪd] *a* unbestritten.
undistinguished [ʌndɪsˈtɪŋgwɪʃt] *a*
unbekannt, nicht ausgezeichnet.
undo [ʌnˈduː] *vt irreg (unfasten)* öffnen, aufmachen; *work* zunichte machen; **~ing**
Verderben *nt*.
undoubted [ʌnˈdautɪd] *a* unbezweifelt;
~ly *ad* zweifellos, ohne Zweifel.
undress [ʌnˈdres] *vti* (sich) ausziehen.
undue [ˈʌndjuː] *a* übermäßig.
undulating [ˈʌndjuleɪtɪŋ] *a* wellenförmig;
country wellig.
unduly [ˈʌnˈdjuːlɪ] *ad* übermäßig.
unearth [ʌnˈɜːθ] *vt (dig up)* ausgraben;
(discover) ans Licht bringen; **~ly** *a*
schauerlich.
unease [ʌnˈiːz] *n* Unbehagen *nt*; *(public)*
Unruhe *f*.
uneasy [ʌnˈiːzɪ] *a (worried)* unruhig; *feeling*
ungut; *(embarrassed)* unbequem; **I feel ~
about it** mir ist nicht wohl dabei.
uneconomic(al) [ˈʌniːkəˈnɒmɪk(əl)] *a*
unwirtschaftlich.
uneducated [ʌnˈedjukeɪtɪd] *a* ungebildet.
unemployed [ˈʌnɪmˈplɔɪd] *a* arbeitslos;
the ~ die Arbeitslosen *pl*.
unemployment   [ˈʌnɪmˈplɔɪmənt]   *n*
Arbeitslosigkeit *f*.
unending [ʌnˈendɪŋ] *a* endlos.
unenviable [ˈʌnˈenvɪəbl]   *a*   wenig
beneidenswert.
unerring [ˈʌnˈɜːrɪŋ] *a* unfehlbar.
uneven [ʌnˈiːvən] *a surface* uneben; *quality*
ungleichmäßig.
unexploded [ˈʌnɪksˈpləudɪd]   *a*   nicht
explodiert.
unfailing [ʌnˈfeɪlɪŋ] *a* nie versagend.
unfair *a*, **~ly** *ad* [ʌnˈfeə*, -əlɪ] ungerecht,
unfair.
unfaithful [ˈʌnˈfeɪθful] *a* untreu.
unfasten [ʌnˈfɑːsn] *vt* öffnen, aufmachen.
unfavourable,   (US)   unfavorable
[ˈʌnˈfeɪvərəbl] *a* ungünstig.
unfeeling [ʌnˈfiːlɪŋ] *a* gefühllos, kalt.
unfinished [ʌnˈfɪnɪʃt] *a* unvollendet.
unfit [ˈʌnˈfɪt] *a* ungeeignet *(for* zu, für); *(in
bad health)* nicht fit.
unflagging [ʌnˈflægɪŋ] *a* unermüdlich.
unflappable [ʌnˈflæpəbl] *a* unerschütterlich.
unflinching [ʌnˈflɪntʃɪŋ] *a* unerschrocken.
unfold [ʌnˈfəuld] *vt* entfalten; *paper*
auseinanderfalten; *vi (develop)* sich entfalten.
unforeseen [ˈʌnfɔːˈsiːn]   *a*   unvorher-
gesehen.
unforgivable [ʌnfəˈgɪvəbl]   *a*   unverzeihlich.
unfortunate [ʌnˈfɔːtʃnət] *a* unglücklich,
bedauerlich; **~ly** *ad* leider.
unfounded [ʌnˈfaundɪd] *a* unbegründet.
unfriendly [ˈʌnˈfrendlɪ] *a* unfreundlich.
unfurnished [ʌnˈfɜːnɪʃt] *a* unmöbliert.
ungainly [ʌnˈgeɪnlɪ] *a* linkisch.
ungodly [ʌnˈgɒdlɪ] *a hour* nachtschlafend;
row heillos.

unguarded [ʌn'gɑːdɪd] *a moment* unbewacht.

unhappiness [ʌn'hæpɪnəs] *n* Unglück *nt*, Unglückseligkeit *f*.

unhappy [ʌn'hæpɪ] *a* unglücklich.

unharmed ['ʌn'hɑːmd] *a* wohlbehalten, unversehrt.

unhealthy [ʌn'helθɪ] *a* ungesund.

unheard-of [ʌn'hɜːdɒv] *a* unerhört.

unhurt ['ʌn'hɜːt] *a* unverletzt.

unicorn ['juːnɪkɔːn] *n* Einhorn *nt*.

unidentified [ʌnaɪ'dentɪfaɪd] *a* unbekannt, nicht identifiziert.

unification [juːnɪfɪ'keɪʃən] *n* Vereinigung *f*.

uniform ['juːnɪfɔːm] *n* Uniform *f*; *a* einheitlich; **~ity** [juːnɪ'fɔːmɪtɪ] Einheitlichkeit *f*.

unify ['juːnɪfaɪ] *vt* vereinigen.

unilateral ['juːnɪ'lætərəl] *a* einseitig.

unimaginable [ʌnɪ'mædʒɪnəbl] *a* unvorstellbar.

uninjured [ʌn'ɪndʒəd] *a* unverletzt.

unintentional [ʌnɪn'tenʃənl] *a* unabsichtlich.

union ['juːnjən] *n* (*uniting*) Vereinigung *f*; (*alliance*) Bund *m*, Union *f*; (*trade* ~) Gewerkschaft *f*; **U ~ Jack** Union Jack *m*.

unique [juː'niːk] *a* einzig(artig).

unison ['juːnɪzn] *n* Einstimmigkeit *f*; **in ~** einstimmig.

unit ['juːnɪt] *n* Einheit *f*.

unite [juː'naɪt] *vt* ~vereinigen; *vi* sich vereinigen; **~d** *a* vereinigt; (*together*) vereint; **U~d Nations** Vereinte Nationen *pl*.

unit trust ['juːnɪt'trʌst] *n* (*Brit*) Treuhandgesellschaft *f*.

unity ['juːnɪtɪ] *n* Einheit *f*; (*agreement*) Einigkeit *f*.

universal *a*, **~ly** *ad* [juːnɪ'vɜːsəl, -ɪ] allgemein.

universe ['juːnɪvɜːs] *n* (Welt)all *nt*, Universum *nt*.

university [juːnɪ'vɜːsɪtɪ] *n* Universität *f*.

unjust ['ʌn'dʒʌst] *a* ungerecht.

unjustifiable [ʌn'dʒʌstɪfaɪəbl] *a* ungerechtfertigt.

unkempt ['ʌn'kempt] *a* ungepflegt, verwahrlost.

unkind [ʌn'kaɪnd] *a* unfreundlich.

unknown ['ʌn'nəʊn] *a* unbekannt (*to dat*).

unladen ['ʌn'leɪdn] *a weight* Leer-, unbeladen.

unleash ['ʌn'liːʃ] *vt* entfesseln.

unleavened ['ʌn'levnd] *a* ungesäuert.

unless [ən'les] *cj* wenn nicht, es sei denn . . .

unlicensed ['ʌn'laɪsənst] *a* (*to sell alcohol*) unkonzessioniert.

unlike ['ʌn'laɪk] *a* unähnlich; *prep* im Gegensatz zu.

unlimited [ʌn'lɪmɪtɪd] *a* unbegrenzt.

unload ['ʌn'ləʊd] *vt* entladen.

unlock ['ʌn'lɒk] *vt* aufschließen.

unmannerly [ʌn'mænəlɪ] *a* unmanierlich.

unmarried [ʌn'mærɪd] *a* unverheiratet, ledig.

unmask [ʌn'mɑːsk] *vt* demaskieren; (*fig*) entlarven.

unmistakable [ʌnmɪs'teɪkəbl] *a* unverkennbar.

unmistakably [ʌnmɪs'teɪkəblɪ] *ad* unverwechselbar, unverkennbar.

unmitigated [ʌn'mɪtɪgeɪtɪd] *a* ungemildert, ganz.

unnecessary ['ʌn'nesəsərɪ] *a* unnötig.

unobtainable ['ʌnəb'teɪnəbl] *a*: **this number is ~** kein Anschluß unter dieser Nummer.

unoccupied ['ʌn'ɒkjupaɪd] *a seat* frei.

unopened ['ʌn'əʊpənd] *a* ungeöffnet.

unorthodox ['ʌn'ɔːθədɒks] *a* unorthodox.

unpack ['ʌn'pæk] *vti* auspacken.

unpalatable [ʌn'pælətəbl] *a truth* bitter.

unparalleled [ʌn'pærəleld] *a* beispiellos.

unpleasant [ʌn'pleznt] *a* unangenehm.

unplug ['ʌn'plʌg] *vt* den Stecker herausziehen von.

unpopular ['ʌn'pɒpjulə*] *a* unbeliebt, unpopulär.

unprecedented [ʌn'presɪdəntɪd] *a* noch nie dagewesen; beispiellos.

unqualified ['ʌn'kwɒlɪfaɪd] *a success* uneingeschränkt, voll; *person* unqualifiziert.

unravel [ʌn'rævəl] *vt* (*disentangle*) auffasern, entwirren; (*solve*) lösen.

unreal ['ʌn'rɪəl] *a* unwirklich.

unreasonable [ʌn'riːznəbl] *a* unvernünftig; *demand* übertrieben; **that's ~** das ist zuviel verlangt.

unrelenting ['ʌnrɪ'lentɪŋ] *a* unerbittlich.

unrelieved ['ʌnrɪ'liːvd] *a monotony* ungemildert.

unrepeatable ['ʌnrɪ'piːtəbl] *a* nicht zu wiederholen(d).

unrest [ʌn'rest] *n* (*discontent*) Unruhe *f*; (*fighting*) Unruhen *pl*.

unroll ['ʌn'rəʊl] *vt* aufrollen.

unruly [ʌn'ruːlɪ] *a child* undiszipliniert; schwer lenkbar.

unsafe ['ʌn'seɪf] *a* nicht sicher.

unsaid ['ʌn'sed] *a*: **to leave sth ~** etw ungesagt sein lassen.

unsatisfactory ['ʌnsætɪs'fæktərɪ] *a* unbefriedigend; unzulänglich.

unsavoury, (*US*) **unsavory** ['ʌn'seɪvərɪ] *a* (*fig*) widerwärtig.

unscrew ['ʌn'skruː] *vt* aufschrauben.

unscrupulous [ʌn'skruːpjuləs] *a* skrupellos.

unselfish [ʌn'selfɪ] *a* selbstlos, uneigennützig.

unsettled ['ʌn'setld] *a* unstet; *person* rastlos; *weather* wechselhaft; *dispute* nicht beigelegt.

unshaven ['ʌn'ʃeɪvn] *a* unrasiert.

unsightly [ʌn'saɪtlɪ] *a* unansehnlich.

unskilled ['ʌn'skɪld] *a* ungelernt.

unsophisticated ['ʌnsə'fɪstɪkeɪtɪd] *a* einfach, natürlich.

unsound ['ʌn'saʊnd] *a ideas* anfechtbar.

unspeakable [ʌn'spiːkəbl] *a joy* unsagbar; *crime* scheußlich.

unstuck ['ʌn'stʌk] *a*: **to come ~** (*lit*) sich lösen; (*fig*) ins Wasser fallen.

unsuccessful [ˈʌnsəkˈsesful] a erfolglos.

unsuitable [ʌnˈsuːtəbl] a unpassend.

unsuspecting [ˈʌnsəsˈpektɪŋ] a nichtsahnend.

unswerving [ʌnˈswɜːvɪŋ] a loyalty unerschütterlich.

untangle [ʌnˈtæŋgl] vt entwirren.

untapped [ˈʌnˈtæpt] a resources ungenützt.

unthinkable [ʌnˈθɪŋkəbl] a unvorstellbar.

untidy [ʌnˈtaɪdɪ] a unordentlich.

untie [ˈʌnˈtaɪ] vt aufmachen, aufschnüren.

until [ənˈtɪl] prep, cj bis.

untimely [ʌnˈtaɪmlɪ] a death vorzeitig.

untold [ˈʌnˈtəʊld] a unermeßlich.

untoward [ʌntəˈwɔːd] a widrig, ungünstig.

untranslatable [ˈʌntrænsˈleɪtəbl] a unübersetzbar.

untried [ˈʌnˈtraɪd] a plan noch nicht ausprobiert.

unused [ˈʌnˈjuːzd] a unbenutzt.

unusual a, ~ly ad [ʌnˈjuːʒʊəl, -l] ungewöhnlich.

unveil [ʌnˈveɪl] vt enthüllen.

unwary [ʌnˈwɛərɪ] a unbedacht(sam).

unwavering [ʌnˈweɪvərɪŋ] a standhaft, unerschütterlich.

unwell [ˈʌnˈwel] a unpäßlich.

unwieldy [ʌnˈwiːldɪ] a unhandlich, sperrig.

unwilling [ˈʌnˈwɪlɪŋ] a unwillig.

unwind [ˈʌnˈwaɪnd] irreg vt (lit) abwickeln; vi (relax) sich entspannen.

unwitting [ʌnˈwɪtɪŋ] a unwissentlich.

unwrap [ˈʌnˈræp] vt aufwickeln, auspacken.

unwritten [ˈʌnˈrɪtn] a ungeschrieben.

up [ʌp] prep auf; ad nach oben, hinauf; (out of bed) auf; **it is ~ to you** es liegt bei Ihnen; **what is he ~ to?** was hat er vor?; **he is not ~ to it** er kann es nicht (tun); **what's ~ to** (temporally) bis; **~-and-coming** a im Aufstiege; **the ~s and downs** das Auf und Ab.

upbringing [ˈʌpˈbrɪŋɪŋ] n Erziehung f.

update [ʌpˈdeɪt] vt auf den neuesten Stand bringen.

upend [ʌpˈend] vt auf Kante stellen.

upgrade [ʌpˈgreɪd] vt höher einstufen.

upheaval [ʌpˈhiːvəl] n Umbruch m.

uphill [ˈʌpˈhɪl] a ansteigend; (fig) mühsam; ad bergauf.

uphold [ʌpˈhəʊld] vt irreg unterstützen.

upholstery [ʌpˈhəʊlstərɪ] n Polster nt; Polsterung f.

upkeep [ˈʌpkiːp] n Instandhaltung f.

upon [əˈpɒn] prep auf.

upper [ˈʌpə*] n (on shoe) Oberleder nt; a obere(r,s), höhere(r,s); **the ~ class** die Oberschicht; **~-class** a vornehm; **~most** a oberste(r,s), höchste(r,s).

upright [ˈʌpraɪt] a (erect) aufrecht; (honest) aufrecht, rechtschaffen; n Pfosten m.

uprising [ʌpˈraɪzɪŋ] n Aufstand m.

uproar [ˈʌprɔː*] n Aufruhr m.

uproot [ʌpˈruːt] vt ausreißen; tree entwurzeln.

upset [ˈʌpset] n Aufregung f; [ʌpˈset] vt irreg (overturn) umwerfen; (disturb) aufregen, bestürzen; plans durcheinander-

bringen; ~**ting** a bestürzend.

upshot [ˈʌpʃɒt] n (End)ergebnis nt, Ausgang m.

upside-down [ˈʌpsaɪdˈdaʊn] ad verkehrt herum; (fig) drunter und drüber.

upstairs [ˈʌpˈstɛəz] ad oben, im oberen Stockwerk; **go** nach oben; **a room** obere(r,s), Ober-; n obere(s) Stockwerk nt.

upstart [ˈʌpstɑːt] n Emporkömmling m.

upstream [ˈʌpˈstriːm] ad stromaufwärts.

uptake [ˈʌpteɪk] n: **to be quick on the ~** schnell begreifen; **to be slow on the ~** schwer von Begriff sein.

uptight [ˈʌpˈtaɪt] a (col) (nervous) nervös; (inhibited) verklemmt.

up-to-date [ˈʌptəˈdeɪt] a clothes modisch, modern; information neueste(r,s); **to bring sth up to date** etw auf den neuesten Stand bringen.

upturn [ˈʌptɜːn] n (in luck) Aufschwung m.

upward [ˈʌpwəd] a nach oben gerichtet; ~(**s**) ad aufwärts.

uranium [juəˈreɪnɪəm] n Uran nt.

urban [ˈɜːbən] a städtisch, Stadt-.

urbane [ɜːˈbeɪn] a höflich, weltgewandt.

urchin [ˈɜːtʃɪn] n (boy) Schlingel m; (sea ~) Seeigel m.

urge [ɜːdʒ] n Drang m; vt drängen, dringen in (+acc); ~ **on** vt antreiben.

urgency [ˈɜːdʒənsɪ] n Dringlichkeit f.

urgent a, ~**ly** ad [ˈɜːdʒənt, -lɪ] dringend.

urinal [ˈjuərɪnl] n (Med) Urinflasche f; (public) Pissoir nt.

urinate [ˈjuərɪneɪt] vi urinieren, Wasser lassen.

urine [ˈjuərɪn] n Urin m, Harn m.

urn [ɜːn] n Urne f; (tea ~) Teemaschine f.

us [ʌs] pron uns.

usage [ˈjuːzɪdʒ] n Gebrauch m; (esp Ling) Sprachgebrauch m.

use [juːs] n Verwendung f, (custom) Brauch m, Gewohnheit f; (employment) Gebrauch m; (point) Zweck m; **in ~** in Gebrauch; **out of ~** außer Gebrauch; **it's no ~** es hat keinen Zweck; **what's the ~?** was soll's?; [juːz] vt gebrauchen; ~**d to** [juːst] gewöhnt an (+acc); **she ~d to live here** sie hat früher mal hier gewohnt; ~ **up** [juːz] vt aufbrauchen, verbrauchen; ~**d** [juːzd] a car Gebraucht-; ~**ful** a nützlich; ~**fulness** Nützlichkeit f; ~**less** a nutzlos, unnütz; ~**lessly** ad nutzlos; ~**lessness** Nutzlosigkeit f; ~**r** [ˈjuːzə*] Benutzer m.

usher [ˈʌʃə*] n Platzanweiser m; ~**ette** [ʌʃəˈret] Platzanweiserin f.

usual [ˈjuːʒʊəl] a gewöhnlich, üblich; ~**ly** ad gewöhnlich.

usurp [juːˈzɜːp] vt an sich reißen; ~**er** Usurpator m.

usury [ˈjuːʒʊrɪ] n Wucher m.

utensil [juːˈtensl] n Gerät nt, Utensil nt.

uterus [ˈjuːtərəs] n Gebärmutter f, Uterus m.

utilitarian [juːtɪlɪˈtɛərɪən] a Nützlichkeits-.

utility [juːˈtɪlɪtɪ] n (usefulness) Nützlichkeit f; (also public ~) öffentliche(r) Versorgungsbetrieb m.

utilization [juːtɪlaɪˈzeɪʃən] n Nutzbarmachung f; Benutzung f.

utilize ['ju:tılaız] *vt* nutzbar machen; benützen.

utmost ['ʌtməust] *a* äußerste(r,s); *n*: **to do one's ~** sein möglichstes tun.

utter ['ʌtə*] *a* äußerste(r,s) höchste(r,s), völlig; *vt* äußern, aussprechen; **~ance** Äußerung *f*; **~ly** *ad* äußerst, absolut, völlig.

U-turn ['ju:'tɜːn] *n* (*Aut*) Kehrtwendung *f*.

V

V, v [vi:] *n* V *nt*, v *nt*.

vacancy ['veıkənsı] *n* (*job*) offene Stelle *f*; (*room*) freies Zimmer *nt*.

vacant ['veıkənt] *a* leer; (*unoccupied*) frei; *house* leerstehend, unbewohnt; (*stupid*) (gedanken)leer; '**~**' (*on door*) 'frei'.

vacate [və'keıt] *vt* seat frei machen; *room* räumen.

vacation [və'keıʃən] *n* Ferien *pl*, Urlaub *m*; **~ist** (*US*) Ferienreisende(r) *mf*.

vaccinate ['væksıneıt] *vt* impfen.

vaccination [væksı'neıʃən] *n* Impfung *f*.

vaccine ['væksi:n] *n* Impfstoff *m*.

vacuum ['vækjʊm] *n* luftleere(r) Raum *m*, Vakuum *nt*; **~ bottle** (*US*), **~ flask** (*Brit*) Thermosflasche *f*; **~ cleaner** Staubsauger *m*.

vagary ['veıgərı] *n* Laune *f*.

vagina [və'dʒaınə] *n* Scheide *f*, Vagina *f*.

vagrant ['veıgrənt] *n* Landstreicher *m*.

vague [veıg] *a* unbestimmt, vage; *outline* verschwommen; (*absent-minded*) geistesabwesend; **~ly** *ad* unbestimmt, vage; *understand, correct* ungefähr; **~ness** Unbestimmtheit *f*; Verschwommenheit *f*.

vain [veın] *a* (*worthless*) eitel, nichtig; *attempt* vergeblich; (*conceited*) eitel, eingebildet; **in ~** vergebens, umsonst; **~ly** *ad* vergebens, vergeblich; eitel, eingebildet.

valentine ['væləntaın] *n* Valentinsgruß *m*.

valiant *a*, **~ly** *ad* ['væljənt, -lı] tapfer.

valid ['vælıd] *a* gültig; *argument* stichhaltig; *objection* berechtigt; **~ity** [və'lıdıtı] Gültigkeit *f*; Stichhaltigkeit *f*.

valise [və'li:z] *n* Reisetasche *f*.

valley ['vælı] *n* Tal *nt*.

valuable ['væljʊəbl] *a* wertvoll; *time* kostbar; **~s** *pl* Wertsachen *pl*.

valuation [væljʊ'eıʃən] *n* (*Fin*) Schätzung *f*; Beurteilung *f*.

value ['vælju:] *n* Wert *m*; (*usefulness*) Nutzen *m*; *vt* (*prize*) (hoch)schätzen, werthalten; (*estimate*) schätzen; **~d** *a* (hoch)geschätzt; **~less** *a* wertlos; **~r** Schätzer *m*.

valve [vælv] *n* Ventil *nt*; (*Biol*) Klappe *f*; (*Rad*) Röhre *f*.

vampire ['væmpaıə*] *n* Vampir *m*.

van [væn] *n* Lieferwagen *m*; Kombiwagen *m*.

vandal ['vændəl] *n* Vandale *m*; **~ism** mutwillige Beschädigung *f*, Vandalismus *m*.

vanilla [və'nılə] *n* Vanille *f*.

vanish ['vænıʃ] *vi* verschwinden.

vanity ['vænıtı] *n* Eitelkeit *f*, Einbildung *f*; **~ case** Schminkkoffer *m*.

vantage ['vɑ:ntıdʒ] *n*: **~ point** gute(r) Aussichtspunkt *m*.

vapour, (*US*) **vapor** ['veıpə*] *n* (*mist*) Dunst *m*; (*gas*) Dampf *m*.

variable ['vɛərıəbl] *a* wechselhaft, veränderlich; *speed, height* regulierbar.

variance ['vɛərıəns] *n*: **to be at ~** uneinig sein.

variant ['vɛərıənt] *n* Variante *f*.

variation [vɛərı'eıʃən] *n* Variation *f*, Veränderung *f*; (*of temperature, prices*) Schwankung *f*.

varicose ['værıkəus] *a*: **~ veins** Krampfadern *pl*.

varied ['vɛərıd] *a* verschieden, unterschiedlich; *life* abwechslungsreich.

variety [və'raıətı] *n* (*difference*) Abwechslung *f*; (*varied collection*) Vielfalt *f*; (*Comm*) Auswahl *f*; (*sorte*) Sorte *f*, Art *f*; **~ show** Varieté *nt*.

various ['vɛərıəs] *a* verschieden; (*several*) mehrere.

varnish ['vɑ:nıʃ] *n* Lack *m*; (*on pottery*) Glasur *f*; *vt* lackieren; *truth* beschönigen.

vary ['vɛərı] *vt* (*alter*) verändern; (*give variety to*) abwechslungsreicher gestalten; *vi* sich (ver)ändern; (*prices*) schwanken; (*weather*) unterschiedlich sein; **to ~ from sth** sich von etw unterscheiden; **~ing** *a* unterschiedlich; veränderlich.

vase [vɑ:z] *n* Vase *f*.

vast [vɑ:st] *a* weit, groß, riesig; **~ly** *ad* wesentlich; *grateful, amused* äußerst; **~ness** Unermeßlichkeit *f*, Weite *f*.

vat [væt] *n* große(s) Faß *nt*.

Vatican ['vætıkən] *n*: **the ~** der Vatikan.

vaudeville ['vəudəvıl] *n* (*US*) Varieté *nt*.

vault [vɔ:lt] *n* (*of roof*) Gewölbe *nt*; (*tomb*) Gruft *f*; (*in bank*) Tresorraum *m*; (*leap*) Sprung *m*; *vt* überspringen.

vaunted ['vɔ:ntıd] *a* gerühmt, gepriesen.

veal [vi:l] *n* Kalbfleisch *nt*.

veer [vıə*] *vi* sich drehen; (*of car*) ausscheren.

vegetable ['vedʒətəbl] *n* Gemüse *nt*; (*plant*) Pflanze *f*.

vegetarian [vedʒı'tɛərıən] *n* Vegetarier(in *f*) *m*; *a* vegetarisch.

vegetate ['vedʒıteıt] *vi* (dahin)-vegetieren.

vegetation [vedʒı'teıʃən] *n* Vegetation *f*.

vehemence ['vi:ıməns] *n* Heftigkeit *f*.

vehement ['vi:ımənt] *a* heftig; *feelings* leidenschaftlich.

vehicle ['vi:ıkl] *n* Fahrzeug *nt*; (*fig*) Mittel *nt*.

vehicular [vı'hıkjʊlə*] *a* Fahrzeug-; *traffic* Kraft-.

veil [veıl] *n* (*lit, fig*) Schleier *m*; *vt* verschleiern.

vein [veın] *n* Ader *f*; (*Anat*) Vene *f*; (*mood*) Stimmung *f*.

velocity [vı'lɒsıtı] *n* Geschwindigkeit *f*.

velvet ['velvıt] *n* Samt *m*.

vendetta [ven'detə] *n* Fehde *f*; (*in family*) Blutrache *f*.

vending machine ['vendıŋməʃi:n] *n* Automat *m*.

vendor ['vendɔ:*] n Verkäufer m.

veneer [və'nɪə*] n (lit) Furnier(holz) nt; (fig) äußere(r) Anstrich m.

venerable ['venərəbl] a ehrwürdig.

venereal [vɪ'nɪərɪəl] a · disease Geschlechts-.

venetian [vɪ'ni:ʃən] a: ~ **blind** Jalousie f.

vengeance ['vendʒəns] n Rache f; **with a** ~ gewaltig.

venison ['venɪsn] n Reh(fleisch) nt.

venom ['venəm] n Gift nt; ~**ous** a, ~**ously** ad giftig, gehässig.

vent [vent] n Öffnung f; (in coat) Schlitz m; (fig) Ventil nt; vt emotion abreagieren.

ventilate ['ventɪleɪt] vt belüften; question erörtern.

ventilation [ventɪ'leɪʃən] n (Be)lüftung f, Ventilation f.

ventilator ['ventɪleɪtə*] n Ventilator m.

ventriloquist [ven'trɪləkwɪst] n Bauchredner m.

venture ['ventʃə*] n Unternehmung f, Projekt nt; vt wagen; life aufs Spiel setzen; vi sich wagen.

venue ['venju:] n Schauplatz m; Treffpunkt m.

veranda(h) [və'rændə] a Veranda f.

verb [vɜ:b] n Zeitwort nt, Verb nt; ~**al** a (spoken) mündlich; translation wörtlich; (of a verb) verbal, Verbal-; ~**ally** ad mündlich; (as a verb) verbal; ~**atim** [vɜ:'beɪtɪm] ad Wort für Wort; a wortwörtlich.

verbose [vɜ:'bəʊs] a wortreich.

verdict ['vɜ:dɪkt] n Urteil nt.

verge [vɜ:dʒ] n Rand m; **on the** ~ **of doing sth** im Begriff, etw zu tun; vi: ~ **on** grenzen an (+acc).

verger ['vɜ:dʒə*] n Kirchendiener m, Küster m.

verification [verɪfɪ'keɪʃən] n Bestätigung f; (checking) Überprüfung f; (proof) Beleg m.

verify ['verɪfaɪ] vt (über)prüfen; (confirm) bestätigen; theory beweisen.

vermin ['vɜ:mɪn] npl Ungeziefer nt.

vermouth ['vɜ:məθ] n Wermut m.

vernacular [və'nækjʊlə*] n Landessprache f; (dialect) Dialekt m, Mundart f; (jargon) Fachsprache f.

versatile ['vɜ:sətaɪl] a vielseitig.

versatility [vɜ:sə'tɪlɪtɪ] n Vielseitigkeit f.

verse [vɜ:s] n (poetry) Poesie f; (stanza) Strophe f; (of Bible) Vers m; **in** ~ in Versform; ~**d** a: ~**d in** bewandert in (+dat), beschlagen in (+dat).

version ['vɜ:ʃən] n Version f; (of car) Modell nt.

versus ['vɜ:səs] prep gegen.

vertebra ['vɜ:tɪbrə] n (Rücken)wirbel m.

vertebrate ['vɜ:tɪbrət] a animal Wirbel-.

vertical ['vɜ:tɪkəl] a senkrecht, vertikal; ~**ly** ad senkrecht, vertikal.

vertigo ['vɜ:tɪgəʊ] n Schwindel m, Schwindelgefühl nt.

verve [vɜ:v] n Schwung m.

very ['verɪ] ad sehr; a (extreme) äußerste(r,s); **the** ~ **book** genau das Buch; **at that** ~ **moment** gerade or

genau in dem Augenblick; **at the** ~ **latest** allerspätestens; **the** ~ **same day** noch am selben Tag; **the** ~ **thought** der Gedanke allein, der bloße Gedanke.

vespers ['vespəz] npl Vesper f.

vessel ['vesl] n (ship) Schiff nt; (container) Gefäß nt.

vest [vest] n Unterhemd nt; (US: waistcoat) Weste f; vt: ~ **sb with sth** or **sth in sb** jdm etw verleihen; ~**ed** a: ~**ed interests** pl finanzielle Beteiligung f; (people) finanziell Beteiligte pl; (fig) persönliche(s) Interesse nt.

vestibule ['vestɪbju:l] n Vorhalle f.

vestige ['vestɪdʒ] n Spur f.

vestry ['vestrɪ] n Sakristei f.

vet [vet] n Tierarzt m/-ärztin f; vt genau prüfen.

veteran ['vetərən] n Veteran m; a altgedient.

veterinary ['vetɪnərɪ] a Veterinär-; ~ **surgeon** Tierarzt m/-ärztin f.

veto ['vi:təʊ] n Veto nt; **power of** ~ Vetorecht nt; vt sein Veto einlegen gegen.

vex [veks] vt ärgern; theory a verärgert; ~**ed** question umstrittene Frage f; ~**ing** a ärgerlich.

via ['vaɪə] prep über (+acc).

viability [vaɪə'bɪlɪtɪ] n (of plan, scheme) Durchführbarkeit f; (of company) Rentabilität f; (of life forms) Lebensfähigkeit f.

viable ['vaɪəbl] a plan durchführbar; company rentabel; plant, economy lebensfähig.

viaduct ['vaɪədʌkt] n Viadukt m.

vibrate [vaɪ'breɪt] vi zittern, beben; (machine, string) vibrieren; (notes) schwingen.

vibration [vaɪ'breɪʃən] n Schwingung f; (of machine) Vibrieren nt; (of voice, ground) Beben nt.

vicar ['vɪkə*] n Pfarrer m; ~**age** Pfarrhaus nt.

vice [vaɪs] n (evil) Laster nt; (Tech) Schraubstock m; pref: ~-**chairman** stellvertretende(r) Vorsitzende(r) m; ~-**president** Vizepräsident m; ~ **versa** ad umgekehrt.

vicinity [vɪ'sɪnɪtɪ] n Umgebung f; (closeness) Nähe f.

vicious ['vɪʃəs] a gemein, böse; ~ **circle** Teufelskreis m; ~**ness** Bösartigkeit f, Gemeinheit f.

vicissitudes [vɪ'sɪsɪtju:dz] npl Wechselfälle pl.

victim ['vɪktɪm] n Opfer nt; ~**ization** [vɪktɪmaɪ'zeɪʃən] Benachteiligung f; ~**ize** vt benachteiligen.

victor ['vɪktə*] n Sieger m.

Victorian [vɪk'tɔ:rɪən] a viktorianisch; (fig) (sitten)streng.

victorious [vɪk'tɔ:rɪəs] a siegreich.

victory ['vɪktərɪ] n Sieg m.

video ['vɪdɪəʊ] a Fernseh-, Bild-.

vie [vaɪ] vi wetteifern.

view [vju:] n (sight) Sicht f, Blick m; (scene) Aussicht f; (opinion) Ansicht f, Meinung f; (intention) Absicht f; **to have sth in** ~ etw beabsichtigen; **in** ~ **of**

wegen (+gen), angesichts (+gen); vt situation betrachten; house besichtigen; ~er (viewfinder) Sucher m; (Phot: small projector) Gucki m; (TV) Fernsehteilnehmer(in f) m; ~finder Sucher m; ~point Standpunkt m.

vigil ['vɪdʒɪl] n (Nacht)wache f; ~ance Wachsamkeit f; ~ant a wachsam; ~antly ad aufmerksam.

vigorous a, ~ly ad ['vɪgərəs, -lɪ] kräftig; protest energisch, heftig.

vigour, (US) vigor ['vɪgə*] n Kraft f, Vitalität f; (of protest) Heftigkeit f.

vile [vaɪl] a (mean) gemein; (foul) abscheulich.

vilify ['vɪlɪfaɪ] vt verleumden.

villa ['vɪlə] n Villa f.

village ['vɪlɪdʒ] n Dorf nt; ~r Dorfbewohner(in f) m.

villain ['vɪlən] n Schurke m, Bösewicht m.

vindicate ['vɪndɪkeɪt] vt rechtfertigen; (clear) rehabilitieren.

vindication [vɪndɪ'keɪʃən] n Rechtfertigung f; Rehabilitation f.

vindictive [vɪn'dɪktɪv] a nachtragend, rachsüchtig.

vine [vaɪn] n Rebstock m, Rebe f.

vinegar ['vɪnɪgə*] n Essig m.

vineyard ['vɪnjəd] n Weinberg m.

vintage ['vɪntɪdʒ] n (of wine) Jahrgang m; ~ car Vorkriegsmodell nt; ~ wine edle(r) Wein m; ~ year besondere(s) Jahr nt.

viola [vɪ'əʊlə] n Bratsche f.

violate ['vaɪəleɪt] vt promise brechen; law übertreten; rights, rule, neutrality verletzen; sanctity, woman schänden.

violation [vaɪə'leɪʃən] n Verletzung f; Übertretung f.

violence ['vaɪələns] n (force) Heftigkeit f; (brutality) Gewalttätigkeit f.

violent a, ~ly ad ['vaɪələnt, -lɪ] (strong) heftig; (brutal) gewalttätig, brutal; contrast kraß; death gewaltsam.

violet ['vaɪələt] n Veilchen nt; a veilchenblau, violett.

violin [vaɪə'lɪn] n Geige f, Violine f.

viper ['vaɪpə*] n Viper f; (fig) Schlange f.

virgin ['vɜːdʒɪn] n Jungfrau f; a jungfräulich, unberührt; ~ity [vɜː'dʒɪnɪtɪ] Unschuld f.

Virgo ['vɜːgəʊ] n Jungfrau f.

virile ['vɪraɪl] a männlich; (fig) kraftvoll.

virility [vɪ'rɪlɪtɪ] n Männlichkeit f.

virtual ['vɜːtjʊəl] a eigentlich; it was a ~ disaster es war geradezu eine Katastrophe; ~ly ad praktisch, fast.

virtue ['vɜːtjuː] n (moral goodness) Tugend f; (good quality) Vorteil m, Vorzug m; by ~ of aufgrund (+gen).

virtuoso [vɜːtjʊ'əʊzəʊ] n Virtuose m.

virtuous ['vɜːtjʊəs] a tugendhaft.

virulence ['vɪrjʊləns] n Bösartigkeit f.

virulent ['vɪrjʊlənt] a (poisonous) bösartig; (bitter) scharf, geharnischt.

virus ['vaɪərəs] n Virus m.

visa ['viːzə] n Visum nt, Sichtvermerk m.

vis-à-vis ['viːzəviː] prep gegenüber.

visibility [vɪzɪ'bɪlɪtɪ] n Sichtbarkeit f; (Met) Sicht(weite) f.

visible ['vɪzəbl] a sichtbar.

visibly ['vɪzəblɪ] ad sichtlich.

vision ['vɪʒən] n (ability) Sehvermögen nt; (foresight) Weitblick m; (in dream, image) Vision f; ~ary Hellseher m; (dreamer) Phantast m; a phantastisch.

visit ['vɪzɪt] n Besuch m; vt besuchen; town, country fahren nach; ~ing a professor Gast-; ~ing card Visitenkarte f; ~or (in house) Besucher(in f) m; (in hotel) Gast m; ~or's book Gästebuch nt.

visor ['vaɪzə*] n Visier nt; (on cap) Schirm m; (Aut) Blende f.

vista ['vɪstə] n Aussicht f.

visual ['vɪzjʊəl] a Seh-, visuell; ~ aid Anschauungsmaterial nt; ~ize vt (imagine) sich (dat) vorstellen; (expect) erwarten; ~ly ad visuell.

vital ['vaɪtl] a (important) unerläßlich; (necessary for life) Lebens-, lebenswichtig; (lively) vital; ~ity [vaɪ'tælɪtɪ] Vitalität f, Lebendigkeit f; ~ly ad äußerst, ungeheuer.

vitamin ['vɪtəmɪn] n Vitamin nt.

vitiate ['vɪʃɪeɪt] vt verunreinigen; theory etc ungültig machen.

vivacious [vɪ'veɪʃəs] a lebhaft.

vivacity [vɪ'væsɪtɪ] n Lebhaftigkeit f, Lebendigkeit f.

vivid a, ~ly ad ['vɪvɪd, -lɪ] (graphic) lebendig, deutlich; memory lebhaft; (bright) leuchtend.

vivisection [vɪvɪ'sekʃən] n Vivisektion f.

vocabulary [vəʊ'kæbjʊlərɪ] n Wortschatz m, Vokabular nt.

vocal ['vəʊkəl] a Vokal-, Gesang-; (fig) lautstark; ~ cord Stimmband nt; ~ist Sänger(in f) m.

vocation [vəʊ'keɪʃən] n (calling) Berufung f; ~al a Berufs-.

vociferous a, ~ly ad [vəʊ'sɪfərəs, -lɪ] lautstark.

vodka ['vɒdkə] n Wodka m.

vogue [vəʊg] n Mode f.

voice [vɔɪs] n (lit) Stimme f; (fig) Mitspracherecht nt; (Gram) Aktionsart f; active/passive ~ Aktiv nt/Passiv nt; with one ~ einstimmig; vt äußern; ~d consonant stimmhafte(r) Konsonant m.

void [vɔɪd] n Leere f; a (empty) leer; (lacking) ohne (of acc), bar (of gen); (Jur) ungültig; see null.

volatile ['vɒlətaɪl] a gas flüchtig; person impulsiv; situation brisant.

volcanic [vɒl'kænɪk] a vulkanisch, Vulkan-.

volcano [vɒl'keɪnəʊ] n Vulkan m.

volition [və'lɪʃən] n Wille m; of one's own ~ aus freiem Willen.

volley ['vɒlɪ] n (of guns) Salve f; (of stones) Hagel m; (of words) Schwall m; (tennis) Flugball m; ~ball Volleyball m.

volt [vəʊlt] n Volt nt; ~age (Volt)spannung f.

volte-face [vɒlt'fɑːs] n (Kehrt)wendung f.

voluble ['vɒljʊbl] a redselig.

volume ['vɒljuːm] n (book) Band m; (size)

voluntary *a*, **voluntarily** *ad* ['vɔləntəri, -lɪ] freiwillig.

volunteer [vɔlən'tɪə*] *n* Freiwillige(r) *mf*; *vi* sich freiwillig melden; *vt* anbieten.

voluptuous [və'lʌptjuəs] *a* sinnlich, wollüstig.

vomit ['vɔmɪt] *n* Erbrochene(s) *nt*; (*act*) Erbrechen *nt*; *vt* speien; *vi* sich übergeben.

vote [vəut] *n* Stimme *f*; (*ballot*) Wahl *f*, Abstimmung *f*; (*result*) Wahl- or Abstimmungsergebnis *nt*; (*right to vote*) Wahlrecht *nt*; *vti* wählen; **~r** Wähler(in *f*) *m*.

voting ['vəutɪŋ] *n* Wahl *f*; **low ~** geringe Wahlbeteiligung *f*.

vouch [vautʃ]: **~ for** *vt* bürgen für.

voucher ['vautʃə*] *n* Gutschein *m*.

vow [vau] *n* Versprechen *nt*; (*Rel*) Gelübde *nt*; *vt* geloben; **vengeance** schwören.

vowel ['vauəl] *n* Vokal *m*, Selbstlaut *m*.

voyage ['vɔɪɪdʒ] *n* Reise *f*.

vulgar ['vʌlgə*] *a* (*rude*) vulgär; (*of common people*) allgemein, Volks-; **~ity** [vʌl'gærɪtɪ] Gewöhnlichkeit *f*, Vulgarität *f*.

vulnerability [vʌlnərə'bɪlɪtɪ] *n* Verletzlichkeit *f*.

vulnerable ['vʌlnərəbl] *a* (*easily injured*) verwundbar; (*sensitive*) verletzlich.

vulture ['vʌltʃə*] *n* Geier *m*.

W

W, w ['dʌblju:] *n* W *nt*, w *nt*.

wad [wɔd] *n* (*bundle*) Bündel *nt*; (*of paper*) Stoß *m*; (*of money*) Packen *m*.

wade [weɪd] *vi* waten.

wafer ['weɪfə*] *n* Waffel *f*; (*Eccl*) Hostie *f*.

waffle ['wɔfl] *n* Waffel *f*; (*col: empty talk*) Geschwafel *nt*; *vi* (*col*) schwafeln.

waft [wɑ:ft] *vti* wehen.

wag [wæg] *vt tail* wedeln mit; *vi* (*tail*) wedeln; **her tongue never stops ~ging** ihr Mund steht nie still.

wage [weɪdʒ] *n* (Arbeits)lohn *m*; *vt* führen; **~s** *pl* Lohn *m*; **~ claim** Lohnforderung *f*; **~ earner** Lohnempfänger(in *f*) *m*; **~ freeze** Lohnstopp *m*.

wager ['weɪdʒə*] *n* Wette *f*; *vti* wetten.

waggle ['wægl] *vt tail* wedeln mit; *vi* wedeln.

wag(g)on ['wægən] *n* (horse-drawn) Fuhrwerk *nt*; (US Aut) Wagen *m*; (Brit Rail) Waggon *m*.

wail [weɪl] *n* Wehgeschrei *nt*; *vi* wehklagen, jammern.

waist [weɪst] *n* Taille *f*; **~coat** Weste *f*; **~line** Taille *f*.

wait [weɪt] *n* Wartezeit *f*; *vi* warten (*for auf* +acc); **to ~ for sb to do sth** darauf warten, daß jd etw tut; **~ and see!** abwarten!; **to ~ at table** servieren; **~er** Kellner *m*; (as address) Herr Ober *m*; **~ing list** Warteliste *f*; **~ing room** (Med) Wartezimmer *nt*; (Rail) Wartesaal *m*; **~ress** Kellnerin *f*; (as address) Fräulein *nt*.

waive [weɪv] *vt* verzichten auf (+acc).

wake [weɪk] *irreg vt* wecken; *vi* aufwachen; **to ~ up to** (*fig*) sich bewußt werden (+gen); *n* (Naut) Kielwasser *nt*; (for dead) Totenwache *f*; **in the ~ of** unmittelbar nach; **~n** *vt* aufwecken.

walk [wɔ:k] *n* Spaziergang *m*; (way of walking) Gang *m*; (route) Weg *m*; **~s of life** *pl* Sphären *pl*; **to take sb for a ~** mit jdm einen Spaziergang machen; **a 10-minute ~** 10 Minuten zu Fuß; *vi* gehen; (stroll) spazierengehen; (longer) wandern; **~er** Spaziergänger *m*; (hiker) Wanderer *m*; **~ie-talkie** tragbares Sprechfunkgerät *nt*; **~ing** *n* Gehen *nt*; Spazieren(gehen) *nt*; Wandern *nt*; *a* Wander-; **~ing stick** Spazierstock *m*; **~out** Streik *m*; **~over** (*col*) leichter Sieg *m*.

wall [wɔ:l] *n* (inside) Wand *f*; (outside) Mauer *f*; **~ed** *a* von Mauern umgeben.

wallet ['wɔlɪt] *n* Brieftasche *f*.

wallow ['wɔləu] *vi* sich wälzen or suhlen.

wallpaper ['wɔ:lpeɪpə*] *n* Tapete *f*.

walnut ['wɔ:lnʌt] *n* Walnuß *f*; (tree) Walnußbaum *m*; (wood) Nußbaumholz *nt*.

walrus ['wɔ:lrəs] *n* Walroß *nt*.

waltz [wɔ:lts] *n* Walzer *m*; *vi* Walzer tanzen.

wan [wɔn] *a* bleich.

wand [wɔnd] *n* Stab *m*.

wander ['wɔndə*] *vi* (roam) (herum)wandern; (fig) abschweifen; **~er** Wanderer *m*; **~ing** *a* umherziehend; **thoughts** abschweifend.

wane [weɪn] *vi* abnehmen; (fig) schwinden.

want [wɔnt] *n* (lack) Mangel *m* (of an +dat); (need) Bedürfnis *nt*; **for ~ of** aus Mangel an (+dat); mangels (+gen); *vt* (need) brauchen; (desire) wollen; (lack) nicht haben; **I ~ to go** ich will gehen; **he ~s confidence** ihm fehlt das Selbstvertrauen.

wanton ['wɔntən] *a* mutwillig, zügellos.

war [wɔ:*] *n* Krieg *m*.

ward [wɔ:d] *n* (in hospital) Station *f*; (child) Mündel *nt*; (of city) Bezirk *m*; **to ~ off** abwenden, abwehren.

warden ['wɔ:dən] *n* (guard) Wächter *m*, Aufseher *m*; (in youth hostel) Herbergsvater *m*; (Univ) Heimleiter *m*.

warder ['wɔ:də*] *n* Gefängnis-wärter *m*.

wardrobe ['wɔ:drəub] *n* Kleiderschrank *m*; (clothes) Garderobe *f*.

ware [wɛə*] *n* Ware *f*; **~house** Lagerhaus *nt*.

warfare ['wɔ:fɛə*] *n* Krieg *m*; Kriegsführung *f*.

warhead ['wɔ:hed] *n* Sprengkopf *m*.

warily ['wɛərɪlɪ] *ad* vorsichtig.

warlike ['wɔ:laɪk] *a* kriegerisch.

warm [wɔ:m] *a* warm; welcome herzlich; *vti* wärmen; **~ up** *vt* aufwärmen; *vi* warm werden; **~-hearted** *a* warmherzig; **~ly** *ad* warm; herzlich; **~th** Wärme *f*; Herzlichkeit *f*.

warn [wɔ:n] *vt* warnen (of, against vor +dat); **~ing** Warnung *f*; **without ~ing** unerwartet; **~ing light** Warnlicht *nt*.

warp [wɔ:p] *vt* verziehen; **~ed** *a* (lit) wellig; (fig) pervers.

warrant ['wɒrənt] n Haftbefehl m.
warranty ['wɒrəntɪ] n Garantie f.
warrior ['wɒrɪə*] n Krieger m.
warship ['wɔːʃɪp] n Kriegsschiff nt.
wart [wɔːt] n Warze f.
wartime ['wɔːtaɪm] n Kriegszeit f, Krieg m.
wary ['wɛərɪ] a vorsichtig; mißtrauisch.
was [wɒz, wəz] pt of **be**.
wash [wɒʃ] n Wäsche f; **to give sth a ~** etw waschen; **to have a ~** sich waschen; vt waschen; dishes abwaschen; vi sich waschen; (do washing) waschen; **~ away** vt abwaschen, wegspülen; **~able** a waschbar; **~basin** Waschbecken nt; **~er** (Tech) Dichtungsring m; (machine) Wasch- or Spülmaschine f; **~ing** Wäsche f; **~ing machine** Waschmaschine f; **~ing powder** Waschpulver nt; **~ing-up** Abwasch m; **~ leather** Waschleder nt; **~-out** (col) (event) Reinfall m; (person) Niete f; **~room** Waschraum m.
wasn't ['wɒznt] = **was not**.
wasp [wɒsp] n Wespe f.
wastage ['weɪstɪdʒ] n Verlust m; **natural ~** Verschleiß m.
waste [weɪst] n (wasting) Verschwendung f; (what is wasted) Abfall m; **~s** pl Einöde f, a (useless) überschüssig, Abfall-; vt object verschwenden; time, life vergeuden; vi: **~ away** verfallen; **~ful** a, **~fully** ad verschwenderisch; process aufwendig; **~land** Ödland nt; **~paper basket** Papierkorb m.
watch [wɒtʃ] n Wache f; (for time) Uhr f; **to be on the ~ (for sth)** (auf etw acc) aufpassen; vt ansehen; (observe) beobachten; (be careful of) aufpassen auf (+acc); (guard) bewachen; **to ~ TV** fernsehen; **to ~ sb doing sth** jdm bei etw zuschauen; **~ it!** paß bloß auf!; vi zusehen; (guard) Wache halten; **to ~ for sb/sth** nach jdm/etw Ausschau halten; **~ out!** paß auf!; **~dog** (lit) Wachthund m; (fig) Wächter m; **~ful** a wachsam; **~maker** Uhrmacher m; **~man** (Nacht)wächter m; **~strap** Uhrarmband nt.
water ['wɔːtə*] n Wasser nt; **~s** pl Gewässer nt; vt (be)gießen; (river) bewässern; horses tränken; vi (eye) tränen; **my mouth is ~ing** mir läuft das Wasser im Mund zusammen; **~ down** vt verwässern; **~ closet** (Wasser)klosett nt; **~colour,** (US) **~color** (painting) Aquarell nt; (paint) Wasserfarbe f; **~cress** (Brunnen)kresse f; **~fall** Wasserfall m; **~ hole** Wasserloch nt; **~ing can** Gießkanne f; **~ level** Wasserstand m; **~lily** Seerose f; **~line** Wasserlinie f; **~logged** a ground voll Wasser; wood mit Wasser vollgesogen; **~melon** Wassermelone f; **~ polo** Wasserball(spiel) nt; **~proof** a wasserdicht; **~shed** Wasserscheide f; **~skiing** Wasserschilaufen nt; **to go ~skiing** wasserschilaufen gehen; **~tight** a wasserdicht; **~works** pl Wasserwerk nt; **~y** a wäss(e)rig.
watt [wɒt] n Watt nt.
wave [weɪv] n Welle f; (with hand) Winken nt; vt (move to and fro) schwenken; hand, flag winken mit; hair wellen; vi (person) winken; (flag) wehen; (hair) sich wellen; **to ~ to sb** jdm zuwinken; **to ~ sb goodbye** jdm zum Abschied winken; **~length** (lit, fig) Wellenlänge f.
waver ['weɪvə*] vi (hesitate) schwanken; (flicker) flackern.
wavy ['weɪvɪ] a wellig.
wax [wæks] n Wachs nt; (sealing —) Siegellack m; (in ear) Ohrenschmalz nt; vt floor (ein)wachsen; vi (moon) zunehmen; **~works** pl Wachsfigurenkabinett nt.
way [weɪ] n Weg m; (road also) Straße f; (method) Art und Weise f, Methode f; (direction) Richtung f; (habit) Eigenart f, Gewohnheit f; (distance) Entfernung f; (condition) Zustand m; **a long ~ away** or **off** weit weg; **to lose one's ~** sich verirren; **to make ~ for sb/sth** jdm/etw Platz machen; **to be in a bad ~** schlecht dransein; **do it this ~** machen Sie es so; **give ~** (Aut) Vorfahrt achten!; **~ of thinking** Meinung f; **to get one's own ~** seinen Willen bekommen; **one ~ or another** irgendwie; **under ~** im Gange; **in a ~** in gewisser Weise; **in the ~** im Wege; **by the ~** übrigens; **by ~ of** (via) über (+acc); (in order to) um . . . zu; (instead of) als; **'~ in'** 'Eingang'; **'~ out'** 'Ausgang'; **~lay** vt irreg auflauern (+dat); **~ward** a eigensinnig.
we [wiː] pl pron wir.
weak a, **~ly** ad [wiːk, -lɪ] schwach; **~en** vt schwächen, entkräften; vi schwächer werden; nachlassen; **~ling** Schwächling m; **~ness** Schwäche f.
wealth [welθ] n Reichtum m; (abundance) Fülle f; **~y** a reich.
wean [wiːn] vt entwöhnen.
weapon ['wepən] n Waffe f.
wear [wɛə*] n (clothing) Kleidung f; (use) Verschleiß m; irreg vt (have on) tragen; smile etc haben; (use) abnutzen; vi (last) halten; (become old) (sich) verschleißen; (clothes) sich abtragen; **~ and tear** Abnutzung f, Verschleiß m; **~ away** vt verbrauchen; vi schwinden; **~ down** vt people zermürben; **~ off** vi sich verlieren; **~ out** vt verschleißen; person erschöpfen; **~er** Träger(in f) m.
wearily ['wɪərɪlɪ] ad müde.
weariness ['wɪərɪnəs] n Müdigkeit f.
weary ['wɪərɪ] a (tired) müde; (tiring) ermüdend; vt ermüden; vi überdrüssig werden (of gen).
weasel ['wiːzl] n Wiesel nt.
weather ['weðə*] n Wetter nt; vt verwittern lassen; (resist) überstehen; **~-beaten** a verwittert; skin wettergegerbt; **~cock** Wetterhahn m; **~forecast** Wettervorhersage f.
weave [wiːv] vt irreg weben; **to ~ one's way through** sth sich durch etw durchschlängeln; **~r** Weber(in f) m.
weaving ['wiːvɪŋ] n Weben nt, Weberei f.
web [web] n Netz nt; (membrane) Schwimmhaut f; **~bed** a Schwimm-, schwimmhäutig; **~bing** Gewebe nt.
wed [wed] vt irreg (old) heiraten.

we'd [wi:d] = **we had**; **we would**.

wedding ['wedɪŋ] n Hochzeit f; ~ **day** Hochzeitstag m; ~ **present** Hochzeitsgeschenk nt; ~ **ring** Trau- or Ehering m.

wedge [wedʒ] n Keil m; (of cheese etc) Stück nt; vt (fasten) festklemmen; (pack tightly) einkeilen.

Wednesday ['wenzdeɪ] n Mittwoch m.

wee [wi:] a (esp Scot) klein, winzig.

weed [wi:d] n Unkraut nt; vt jäten; ~-**killer** Unkrautvertilgungsmittel nt.

week [wi:k] n Woche f; a ~ **today** heute in einer Woche; ~-**day** Wochentag m; ~-**end** Wochenende nt; ~-**ly** a ad wöchentlich; wages, magazine Wochen-.

weep [wi:p] vi irreg weinen.

weigh [weɪ] vti wiegen; ~ **down** vt niederdrücken; ~ **up** vt prüfen, abschätzen; ~-**bridge** Brückenwaage f.

weight [weɪt] n Gewicht nt; **to lose/put on** ~ abnehmen/ zunehmen; ~-**lessness** Schwerelosigkeit f; ~-**lifter** Gewichtheber m; ~-**y** a (heavy) gewichtig; (important) schwerwiegend.

weir [wɪə*] n (Stau)wehr nt.

weird [wɪəd] a seltsam.

welcome ['welkəm] n Willkommen nt, Empfang m; vt begrüßen.

welcoming ['welkəmɪŋ] a Begrüßungs-; freundlich.

weld [weld] n Schweißnaht f; vt schweißen; ~-**er** Schweißer m; ~-**ing** Schweißen nt.

welfare ['welfɛə*] n Wohl nt; (social) Fürsorge f; ~ **state** Wohlfahrtsstaat m.

well [wel] n Brunnen m; (oil ~) Quelle f; a (in good health) gesund; **are you** ~? geht es Ihnen gut?; interj nun, na schön; (starting conversation) nun, tja; ~, ~! na, na!; ad gut; ~ **over 40** weit über 40; **it may** ~ **be** es kann wohl sein; **it would be (as)** ~ **to . . .** es wäre wohl gut, zu . . .; **you did** ~ **(not) to . . .** Sie haben gut daran getan, (nicht) zu . . .; **very** ~ (O.K.) nun gut.

we'll [wi:l] = **we will**, **we shall**.

well-behaved ['welbɪ'heɪvd] a wohlerzogen.

well-being ['welbi:ɪŋ] n Wohl nt, Wohlergehen nt.

well-built ['wel'bɪlt] a kräftig gebaut.

well-developed ['weldɪ'veləpt] a girl gut entwickelt; economy hochentwickelt.

well-earned ['wel'ɜːnd] a rest wohlverdient.

well-heeled ['wel'hi:ld] a (col: wealthy) gut gepolstert.

wellingtons ['welɪŋtənz] npl Gummistiefel pl.

well-known ['wel'nəun] a person weithin bekannt.

well-meaning ['wel'mi:nɪŋ] a person wohlmeinend; action gutgemeint.

well-off ['wel'ɒf] a gut situiert.

well-read ['wel'red] a (sehr) belesen.

well-to-do ['weltə'du:] a wohlhabend.

well-wisher ['welwɪʃə*] n wohlwollende(r) Freund m, Gönner m.

wench [wentʃ] n (old) Maid f, Dirne f.

went [went] pt of **go**.

were [wɜː*] pt pl of **be**.

we're [wɪə*] = **we are**.

weren't [wɜːnt] = **were not**.

west [west] n Westen m; a West-, westlich; ad westwärts, nach Westen; ~-**erly** a westlich; ~-**ern** a westlich, West-; n (Cine) Western m; ~-**ward(s)** ad westwärts.

wet [wet] a naß; ~ **blanket** (fig) Triefel m; ~-**ness** Nässe f, Feuchtigkeit f; '~ **paint**' 'frisch gestrichen'.

we've [wi:v] = **we have**.

whack [wæk] n Schlag m; vt schlagen.

whale [weɪl] n Wal m.

wharf [wɔːf] n Kai m.

what [wɒt] pron, interj was; a welche(r,s); ~ **a hat!** was für ein Hut!; ~ **money I had** das Geld, das ich hatte; ~ **about . . .?** (suggestion) wie wär's mit . . .?; ~ **about it?, so** ~? na und?; **well,** ~ **about him?** was ist mit ihm?; **and** ~ **about me?** und ich?; ~ **for?** wozu?; ~**ever** a: ~**ever he says** egal, was er sagt; **no reason** ~**ever** überhaupt kein Grund.

wheat [wi:t] n Weizen m.

wheel [wi:l] n Rad nt; (steering ~) Lenkrad nt; (disc) Scheibe f; vt schieben; vi (revolve) sich drehen; ~-**barrow** Schubkarren m; ~-**chair** Rollstuhl m.

wheeze [wi:z] n Keuchen nt; vi keuchen.

when [wen] ad interrog wann; ad,cj (with present tense) wenn; (with past tense) als; (with indir question) wann; ~**ever** ad wann immer; immer wenn.

where [wɛə*] ad (place) wo; (direction) wohin; ~ **from** woher; ~**abouts** ['wɛərə'bauts] ad wo; n Aufenthalt m, Verbleib m; ~-**as** [wɛər'æz] cj während, wo . . . doch; ~**ever** [wɛər'evə*] ad wo (immer).

whet [wet] vt appetite anregen.

whether ['weðə*] cj ob.

which [wɪtʃ] a (from selection) welche(r,s); rel pron der/die/das; (rel: which fact) was; (interrog) welche(r,s); ~**ever (book) he takes** welches (Buch) er auch nimmt.

whiff [wɪf] n Hauch m.

while [waɪl] n Weile f; cj während; **for a** ~ eine Zeitlang.

whim [wɪm] n Laune f.

whimper ['wɪmpə*] n Wimmern nt; vi wimmern.

whimsical ['wɪmzɪkəl] a launisch.

whine [waɪn] n Gewinsel nt, Gejammer nt; vi heulen, winseln.

whip [wɪp] n Peitsche f; (Parl) Einpeitscher m; vt (beat) peitschen; (snatch) reißen; ~-**round** (col) Geldsammlung f.

whirl [wɜːl] n Wirbel m; vti (herum)-wirbeln; ~-**pool** Wirbel m; ~-**wind** Wirbelwind m.

whirr [wɜː*] vi schwirren, surren.

whisk [wɪsk] n Schneebesen m; vt cream etc schlagen.

whisker ['wɪskə*] n (of animal) Barthaare pl; ~**s** pl (of man) Backenbart m.

whisk(e)y ['wɪskɪ] n Whisky m.

whisper ['wɪspə*] n Flüstern nt; vi flüstern; (leaves) rascheln; vt flüstern, munkeln.

whist [wɪst] n Whist nt.

whistle ['wɪsl] n Pfiff m; (instrument) Pfeife f; vti pfeifen.

white [waɪt] n Weiß nt; (of egg) Eiweiß nt; (of eye) Weiße(s) nt; a weiß; (with fear) blaß; ~-**collar worker** Angestellte(r) m; ~ **lie** Notlüge f; ~**ness** Weiß nt; ~**wash** n (paint) Tünche f; (fig) Ehrenrettung f; vt weißen, tünchen; (fig) reinwaschen.

whiting ['waɪtɪŋ] n Weißfisch m.

Whitsun ['wɪtsn] n Pfingsten nt.

whittle ['wɪtl] vt: ~ **away** or **down** stutzen, verringern;

whizz [wɪz] vi sausen, zischen, schwirren; ~ **kid** (col) Kanone f.

who [hu:] pron (interrog) wer; (rel) der/die/das; ~**ever** [hu:'evə*] pron wer immer; jeder, der/jede, die/jedes, das.

whole [həʊl] a ganz; (uninjured) heil; n Ganze(s) nt; **the** ~ **of the year** das ganze Jahr; **on the** ~ im großen und ganzen; ~**hearted** a rückhaltlos; ~**heartedly** ad von ganzem Herzen; ~**sale** Großhandel m; a trade Großhandels-; (fig) destruction vollkommen, Massen,; ~**saler** Großhändler m; ~**some** a bekömmlich, gesund.

wholly ['həʊlɪ] ad ganz, völlig.

whom [hu:m] pron (interrog) wen; (rel) den/die/das/die pl.

whooping cough ['hu:pɪŋkɒf] n Keuchhusten m.

whopper ['wɒpə*] n (col) Mordsding nt; faustdicke Lüge f.

whopping ['wɒpɪŋ] a (col) kolossal, Riesen-.

whore ['hɔ:*] n Hure f.

whose [hu:z] pron (interrog) wessen; (rel) dessen/deren/ dessen/deren pl.

why [waɪ] ad warum; interj nanu; **that's** ~ deshalb.

wick [wɪk] n Docht m.

wicked ['wɪkɪd] a böse; ~**ness** Bosheit f, Schlechtigkeit f.

wicker ['wɪkə*] n Weidengeflecht nt, Korbgeflecht n.

wicket ['wɪkɪt] n Tor nt, Dreistab m; (playing pitch) Spielfeld nt.

wide [waɪd] a breit; plain weit; (in firing) daneben; ~ of weitab von; ad weit; daneben; ~-**angle** a lens Weitwinkel-; ~-**awake** a hellwach; ~**ly** ad weit; known allgemein; ~**n** vt erweitern; ~**ness** Breite f, Ausdehnung f; ~-**open** a weit geöffnet; ~**spread** a weitverbreitet.

widow ['wɪdəʊ] n Witwe f; ~**ed** a verwitwet; ~**er** Witwer m.

width [wɪdθ] n Breite f, Weite f.

wield [wi:ld] vt schwingen, handhaben.

wife [waɪf] n (Ehe)frau f, Gattin f.

wig [wɪg] n Perücke f.

wiggle ['wɪgl] n Wackeln nt; vt wackeln mit; vi wackeln.

wigwam ['wɪgwæm] n Wigwam m, Indianerzelt nt.

wild [waɪld] a wild; (violent) heftig; plan, idea verrückt; **the** ~**s** pl die Wildnis; ~**erness** ['wɪldənəs] Wildnis f, Wüste f; ~-**goose chase** fruchtlose(s) Unternehmen nt; ~**life** Tierwelt f; ~**ly** ad wild, ungestüm; exaggerated irrsinnig.

wilful ['wɪlful] a (intended) vorsätzlich; (obstinate) eigensinnig.

will [wɪl] v aux: **he** ~ **come** er wird kommen; **I** ~ **do it!** ich werde es tun; n (power to choose) Wille m; (wish) Wunsch m, Bestreben nt; (Jur) Testament nt; vt wollen; ~**ing** a gewillt, bereit; ~**ingly** ad bereitwillig, gern; ~**ingness** (Bereit)willigkeit f.

willow ['wɪləʊ] n Weide f.

will power ['wɪl'paʊə*] n Willenskraft f.

wilt [wɪlt] vi (ver)welken.

wily ['waɪlɪ] a gerissen.

win [wɪn] n Sieg m; irreg vt gewinnen; vi (be successful) siegen; **to** ~ **sb over** jdn gewinnen, jdn dazu bringen.

wince [wɪns] n Zusammenzucken nt; vi zusammenzucken, zurückfahren.

winch [wɪntʃ] n Winde f.

wind [waɪnd] irreg vt rope winden; bandage wickeln; **to** ~ **one's way** sich schlängeln; vi (turn) sich winden; (change direction) wenden; ~ **up** vt clock aufziehen; debate (ab)schließen.

wind [wɪnd] n Wind m; (Med) Blähungen pl; ~**break** Windschutz m; ~**fall** unverhoffte(r) Glücksfall m.

winding ['waɪndɪŋ] a road gewunden, sich schlängelnd.

wind instrument ['wɪndɪnstrumənt] n Blasinstrument nt.

windmill ['wɪndmɪl] n Windmühle f.

window ['wɪndəʊ] n Fenster nt; ~ **box** Blumenkasten m; ~ **cleaner** Fensterputzer m; ~ **ledge** Fenstersims m; ~-**pane** Fensterscheibe f; ~-**shopping** Schaufensterbummel m; ~-**sill** Fensterbank f.

windpipe ['wɪndpaɪp] n Luftröhre f.

windscreen ['wɪndskri:n], (US) **windshield** ['wɪndʃi:ld] n Windschutzscheibe f; ~ **wiper** Scheibenwischer m.

windswept ['wɪndswept] a vom Wind gepeitscht; person zersaust.

windy ['wɪndɪ] a windig.

wine [waɪn] n Wein m; ~**glass** Weinglas nt; ~ **list** Weinkarte f; ~ **merchant** Weinhändler m; ~ **tasting** Weinprobe f; ~ **waiter** Weinkellner m.

wing [wɪŋ] n Flügel m; (Mil) Gruppe f; ~**s** pl (Theat) Seitenkulisse f; ~**er** (Sport) Flügelstürmer m.

wink [wɪŋk] n Zwinkern nt; vi zwinkern, blinzeln; **to** ~ **at sb** jdm zublinzeln; **forty** ~**s** Nickerchen nt.

winner ['wɪnə*] n Gewinner m; (Sport) Sieger m.

winning ['wɪnɪŋ] a team siegreich, Sieger-; goal entscheidend; n: ~**s** pl Gewinn m; ~ **post** Ziel nt.

winter ['wɪntə*] n Winter m; a clothes Winter-; vi überwintern; ~ **sports** pl Wintersport m.

wintry ['wɪntrɪ] a Winter-, winterlich.

wipe [waɪp] n Wischen nt; vt wischen, abwischen; ~ **out** vt debt löschen; (destroy) auslöschen.

wire ['waɪə*] n Draht m; (telegram) Telegramm nt; vt telegrafieren (sb jdm, sth etw); ~**less** Radio(apparat m) nt.

wiry ['waɪərɪ] a drahtig.

wisdom ['wɪzdəm] n Weisheit f; (of decision) Klugheit f; ~ **tooth** Weisheitszahn m.

wise [waɪz] a klug, weise; ~**crack** Witzelei f; ~**ly** ad klug, weise.

wish [wɪʃ] n Wunsch m; vt wünschen; he ~**es us to do it** er möchte, daß wir es tun; **with best** ~**es** herzliche Grüße; **to** ~ **sb goodbye** jdn verabschieden; **to** ~ **to do sth** etw tun wollen; ~**ful thinking** Wunschdenken nt.

wisp [wɪsp] n (Haar)strähne f; (of smoke) Wölkchen nt.

wistful ['wɪstful] a sehnsüchtig.

wit [wɪt] n (also ~s) Verstand m no pl; (amusing ideas) Witz m; (person) Witzbold m; **at one's** ~**s' end** mit seinem Latein am Ende; **to have one's** ~**s about one** auf dem Posten sein.

witch [wɪtʃ] n Hexe f; ~**craft** Hexerei f.

with [wɪð, wɪθ] prep mit; (in spite of) trotz (+gen or dat); ~ **him it's ...** bei ihm ist es ...; **to stay** ~ **sb** bei jdm wohnen; **I have no money** ~ **me** ich habe kein Geld bei mir; **shaking** ~ **fright** vor Angst zitternd.

withdraw [wɪð'drɔ:] irreg vt zurückziehen; money abheben; remark zurücknehmen; vi sich zurückziehen; ~**al** Zurückziehung f; Abheben nt; Zurücknahme f; ~**al symptoms** pl Entzugserscheinungen pl.

wither ['wɪðə*] vi (ver)welken; ~**ed** a verwelkt, welk.

withhold [wɪð'həʊld] vt irreg vorenthalten (from sb jdm).

within [wɪð'ɪn] prep innerhalb (+gen).

without [wɪð'aʊt] prep ohne; **it goes** ~ **saying** es ist selbstverständlich.

withstand [wɪð'stænd] vt irreg widerstehen (+dat).

witness ['wɪtnəs] n Zeuge m; Zeugin f; vt (see) sehen, miterleben; (sign document) beglaubigen; vi aussagen; ~ **box**, (US) ~ **stand** Zeugenstand m.

witticism ['wɪtɪsɪzəm] n witzige Bemerkung f.

witty a, **wittily** ad ['wɪtɪ, -lɪ] witzig, geistreich.

wizard ['wɪzəd] n Zauberer m.

wobble ['wɒbl] vi wackeln.

woe [wəʊ] n Weh nt, Leid nt, Kummer m.

wolf [wʊlf] n Wolf m.

woman ['wʊmən] n, pl **women** Frau f; a ~ in f.

womb [wu:m] n Gebärmutter f.

women ['wɪmɪn] npl of **woman**.

wonder ['wʌndə*] n (marvel) Wunder nt; (surprise) Staunen nt, Verwunderung f; vi sich wundern; **I** ~ **whether ...** ich frage mich, ob ...; ~**ful** a wunderbar, herrlich; ~**fully** ad wunderbar.

won't [wəʊnt] = **will not**.

wood [wʊd] n Holz nt; (forest) Wald m; ~ **carving** Holzschnitzerei f; ~**ed** a bewaldet, waldig, Wald-; ~**en** a (lit, fig) hölzern; ~**pecker** Specht m; ~**wind** Blasinstrumente pl; ~**work** Holzwerk nt; (craft) Holzarbeiten pl; ~**worm** Holzwurm m.

wool [wʊl] n Wolle f; ~**len**, (US) ~**en** a Woll-; ~**ly**, (US) ~**y** a wollig; (fig) schwammig.

word [wɜ:d] n Wort nt; (news) Bescheid m; **to have a** ~ **with sb** mit jdm reden; **to have** ~**s with sb** Worte wechseln mit jdm; **by** ~ **of mouth** mündlich; vt formulieren; ~**ing** Wortlaut m, Formulierung f.

work [wɜ:k] n Arbeit f; (Art, Liter) Werk nt; vi arbeiten; machine funktionieren; (medicine) wirken; (succeed) klappen; ~**s** (factory) Fabrik f, Werk nt; (of watch) Werk nt; ~ **off** vt debt abarbeiten; anger abreagieren; ~ **on** vi weiterarbeiten; vt (be engaged in) arbeiten an (+dat); (influence) bearbeiten; ~ **out** vi (sum) aufgehen; (plan) klappen; vt problem lösen; plan ausarbeiten; ~ **up to** vt hinarbeiten auf (+acc); **to get** ~**ed up** sich aufregen; ~**able** a soil bearbeitbar; plan ausführbar; ~**er** Arbeiter(in f) m; ~**ing class** Arbeiterklasse f; ~**ing-class** a Arbeiter-; ~**ing man** Werktätige(r) m; ~**man** Arbeiter m; ~**manship** Arbeit f, Ausführung f; ~**shop** Werkstatt f.

world [wɜ:ld] n Welt f; (animal — etc) Reich nt; **out of this** ~ himmlisch; **to come into the** ~ auf die Welt kommen; **to do sb/sth the** ~ **of good** jdm/etw sehr gut tun; **to be the** ~ **to sb** jds ein und alles sein; **to think the** ~ **of sb** große Stücke auf jdn halten; ~**-famous** a weltberühmt; ~**ly** a weltlich, irdisch; ~**-wide** a weltweit.

worm [wɜ:m] n Wurm m.

worn [wɔ:n] a clothes abgetragen; ~**-out** a object abgenutzt; person völlig erschöpft.

worried ['wʌrɪd] a besorgt, beunruhigt.

worrier ['wʌrɪə*] n: **he is a** ~ er macht sich (dat) ewig Sorgen.

worry ['wʌrɪ] n Sorge f, Kummer m; vt quälen, beunruhigen; vi (feel uneasy) sich sorgen, sich (dat) Gedanken machen; ~**ing** a beunruhigend.

worse [wɜ:s] a comp of **bad** schlechter, schlimmer; ad comp of **badly** schlimmer, ärger; n Schlimmere(s) nt, Schlechtere(s) nt; ~**n** vt verschlimmern; vi sich verschlechtern.

worship ['wɜ:ʃɪp] n Anbetung f, Verehrung f; (religious service) Gottesdienst m; (title) Hochwürden m; vt anbeten; ~**per** Gottesdienstbesucher(in f) m.

worst [wɜ:st] a superl of **bad** schlimmste(r,s), schlechteste(r,s); ad superl of **badly** am schlimmsten, am ärgsten; n Schlimmste(s) nt, Ärgste(s) nt.

worsted ['wʊstɪd] n Kammgarn nt.

worth [wɜ:θ] n Wert m; **£10** ~ **of food** Essen für 10 £; a wert; ~ **seeing** sehenswert; **it's** ~ **£10** es ist 10 £ wert; ~**less** a wertlos; person nichtsnutzig; ~**while** a lohnend, der Mühe wert; ad: **it's not** ~**while going** es lohnt sich nicht, dahin zu gehen; ~**y** ['wɜ:ðɪ] a (having worth) wertvoll; wert (of gen), würdig (of gen).

would [wʊd] v aux: **she** ~ **come** sie würde kommen; **if you asked he** ~

come wenn Sie ihn fragten, würde er kommen; ~ **you like a drink?** möchten Sie etwas trinken?; ~**-be** a angeblich; ~**n't** = ~ **not**.

wound [wu:nd] n (lit, fig) Wunde f; vt verwunden, verletzen (also fig).

wrangle ['ræŋgl] n Streit m; vi sich zanken.

wrap [ræp] n (stole) Umhang m, Schal m; vt (also ~ **up**) einwickeln; deal abschließen; ~**per** Umschlag m, Schutzhülle f; ~**ping paper** Einwickelpapier nt.

wreath [ri:θ] n Kranz m.

wreck [rek] n Schiffbruch m; (ship) Wrack nt; (sth ruined) Ruine f, Trümmerhaufen m; a **nervous** ~ ein Nervenbündel nt; vt zerstören; ~**age** Wrack nt, Trümmer pl.

wren [ren] n Zaunkönig m.

wrench [rentʃ] n (spanner) Schraubenschlüssel m; (twist) Ruck m, heftige Drehung f; vt reißen, zerren.

wrestle ['resl] vi ringen.

wrestling ['resliŋ] n Ringen nt; ~ **match** Ringkampf m.

wretched ['retʃid] a hovel elend; (col) verflixt; **I feel** ~ mir ist elend.

wriggle ['rigl] n Schlängeln nt; vi sich winden.

wring [riŋ] vt irreg wringen.

wrinkle ['riŋkl] n Falte f, Runzel f; vt runzeln; vi sich runzeln; (material) knittern.

wrist [rist] n Handgelenk nt; ~**watch** Armbanduhr f.

writ [rit] n gerichtliche(r) Befehl m.

write [rait] vti irreg schreiben; ~ **down** vt niederschreiben, aufschreiben; ~ **off** vt (dismiss) abschreiben; ~ **out** vt essay abschreiben; cheque ausstellen; ~ **up** vt schreiben; ~**-off: it is a cdl that kann man abschreiben; ~**r** Verfasser m; (author) Schriftsteller m; ~**-up** Besprechung f.

writing ['raitiŋ] n (act) Schreiben nt; (hand—) (Hand)schrift f; ~**s** pl Schriften pl, Werke pl; ~ **paper** Schreibpapier.

wrong [roŋ] a (incorrect) falsch; (morally) unrecht; (out of order) nicht in Ordnung; **he was** ~ **in doing that** es war nicht recht von ihm, das zu tun; **what's** ~ **with your leg?** was ist mit deinem Bein los?; **to go** ~ (plan) schiefgehen; (person) einen Fehler machen; n Unrecht nt; vt Unrecht tun (+dat); ~**ful** a unrechtmäßig; ~**ly** ad falsch; accuse zu Unrecht.

wrought [rɔ:t] a: ~ **iron** Schmiedeeisen nt.

wry [rai] a schief, krumm; (ironical) trocken; **to make a** ~ **face** das Gesicht verziehen.

X

X, x [eks] n X nt, x nt.

Xmas ['eksməs] n (col) Weihnachten nt.

X-ray ['eks'rei] n Röntgenaufnahme f; vt röntgen.

xylophone ['zailəfəun] n Xylophon nt.

Y

Y, y [wai] n Y nt, y nt.

yacht [jɔt] n Jacht f; ~**ing** (Sport)segeln nt; ~**sman** Sportsegler m.

Yank [jæŋk] n (col) Ami m.

yap [jæp] vi (dog) kläffen; (people) quasseln.

yard [jɑ:d] n Hof m; (measure) (englische) Elle f, Yard nt, 0,91 m; ~**stick** (fig) Maßstab m.

yarn [jɑ:n] n (thread) Garn nt; (story) (Seemanns)garn nt.

yawn [jɔ:n] n Gähnen nt; vi gähnen.

year [jiə*] n Jahr nt; ~**ly** a, ad jährlich.

yearn [jɜ:n] vi sich sehnen (for nach); ~**ing** Verlangen nt, Sehnsucht f.

yeast [ji:st] n Hefe f.

yell [jel] n gellende(r) Schrei m; vi laut schreien.

yellow ['jeləu] a gelb; n Gelb nt; ~ **fever** Gelbfieber nt.

yelp [jelp] n Gekläff nt; vi kläffen.

yeoman ['jəumən] n: **Y**~ **of the Guard** Leibgardist m.

yes [jes] ad ja; n Ja nt, Jawort nt; ~**man** Jasager m.

yesterday ['jestədei] ad gestern; n Gestern nt; **the day before** ~ vorgestern.

yet [jet] ad noch; (in question) schon; (up to now) bis jetzt; **and** ~ aber immer wieder or noch einmal; **as** ~ bis jetzt; (in past) bis dahin; cj doch, dennoch.

yew [ju:] n Eibe f.

Yiddish ['jidiʃ] n Jiddisch nt.

yield [ji:ld] n Ertrag m; vt result, crop hervorbringen; interest, profit abwerfen; (concede) abtreten; vi nachgeben; (Mil) sich ergeben.

yodel ['jəudl] vi jodeln.

yoga ['jəugə] n Joga m.

yoghurt ['jɔgət] n Joghurt m.

yoke [jəuk] n (lit, fig) Joch nt.

yolk [jəuk] n Eidotter m, Eigelb nt.

yonder ['jɒndə*] ad dort drüben, da drüben; a jene(r, s) dort.

you [ju:] pron (sing) (nom) du; (acc) dich; (dat) dir; (pl) (nom) ihr; (acc, dat) euch; (polite) (nom, acc) Sie; (dat) Ihnen; (indef) (nom) man; (acc) einen; (dat) einem.

you'd [ju:d] = **you had; you would**.

you'll [ju:l] = **you will, you shall**.

young [jʌŋ] a jung; npl die Jungen; ~**ish** a ziemlich jung; ~**ster** Junge m, junge(r) Bursche m/junge(s) Mädchen nt.

your ['jɔ:*] poss a (familiar) (sing) dein; (pl) euer, eure pl; (polite) Ihr.

you're ['juə*] = **you are**.

yours ['jɔ:z] poss pron (familiar) (sing) deine(r, s); (pl) eure(r, s); (polite) Ihre(r, s).

yourself [jɔ:'self] pron (emphatic) selbst; (familiar) (sing) (acc) dich (selbst); (dat) dir (selbst); (pl) euch (selbst); (polite) sich (selbst); **you're not** ~ mit dir/Ihnen ist etwas nicht in Ordnung.

youth [ju:θ] n Jugend f; (young man)

junge(r) Mann *m*; (*young people*) Jugend *f*; ~**ful** *a* jugendlich; ~ **hostel** Jugendherberge *f*.

you've [ju:v] = **you have**.

Z

Z, z [zɛd] *n* Z *nt*, z *nt*.

zany ['zeɪnɪ] *a* komisch.

zeal [zi:l] *n* Eifer *m*; ~**ous** ['zeləs] *a* eifrig.

zebra ['zi:brə] *n* Zebra *nt*; ~ **crossing** ['zi:brə'krɒsɪŋ] Zebrastreifen *m*.

zenith ['zenɪθ] *n* Zenit *m*.

zero ['zɪərəʊ] *n* Null *f*; (*on scale*) Nullpunkt *m*; ~ **hour** die Stunde X.

zest [zest] *n* Begeisterung *f*.

zigzag ['zɪgzæg] *n* Zickzack *m*; *vi* im Zickzack laufen/fahren.

zinc [zɪŋk] *n* Zink *nt*.

Zionism ['zaɪənɪzəm] *n* Zionismus *m*.

zip [zɪp] *n* (*also* ~ **fastener,** ~**per**) Reißverschluß *m*; *vt* (*also* ~ **up**) den Reißverschluß zumachen (+*gen*).

zither ['zɪðə*] *n* Zither *f*.

zodiac ['zəʊdɪæk] *n* Tierkreis *m*.

zombie ['zɒmbɪ] *n* Trantüte *f*.

zone [zəʊn] *n* Zone *f*; (*area*) Gebiet *nt*.

zoo [zu:] *n* Zoo *m*; ~**logical** [zəʊə'lɒdʒɪkəl] *a* zoologisch; ~**logist** [zu:'ɒlədʒɪst] Zoologe *m*; ~**logy** [zu:'ɒlədʒɪ] Zoologie *f*.

zoom [zu:m] *vi* (*engine*) surren; (*plane*) aufsteigen; (*move fast*) brausen; (*prices*) hochschnellen; ~ **lens** Zoomobjektiv *nt*.

Länder, Völker und Sprachen

ich bin Deutscher/Engländer/Albanier I am German/English/Albanian

ein Deutscher/Engländer/Albanier a German/an Englishman/an Albanian; **eine Deutsche/Engländerin/Albanierin** a German (woman/girl)/an English woman/girl/an Albanian (woman/girl)

sprechen Sie Deutsch/Englisch/Albanisch? do you speak German/English/Albanian?

Adria (die), Adriatische(s) Meer the Adriatic.
Afrika Africa; **Afrikaner(in** *f***)** *m* African; **afrikanisch** *a* African.
Ägäis (die), Ägäische(s) Meer the Aegean.
Ägypten Egypt; **Ägypter(in** *f***)** *m* Egyptian; **ägyptisch** *a* Egyptian.
Albanien Albania; **Albanier(in** *f***)** *m* Albanian; **albanisch** *a* Albanian.
Algerien Algeria; **Algerier(in** *f***)** *m* Algerian; **algerisch** *a* Algerian.
Alpen *pl* **(die)** the Alps *pl*.
Amazonas (der) the Amazon.
Amerika America; **Amerikaner(in** *f***)** *m* American; **amerikanisch** *a* American.
Anden *pl* **(die)** the Andes *pl*.
Antarktis (die) the Antarctic.
Antillen *pl* **(die)** the Antilles *pl*.
Antwerpen Antwerp.
Arabien Arabia; **Araber** *m* Arab, Arabian; **arabisch** *a* Arab, Arabic, Arabian.
Argentinien Argentina, the Argentine; **Argentinier(in** *f***)** *m* Argentinian; **argentinisch** *a* Argentinian.
Ärmelkanal (der) the English Channel.
Armenien Armenia; **Armenier(in** *f***)** *m* Armenian; **armenisch** *a* Armenian.
Asien Asia; **Asiat(in** *f***)** *m* Asian; **asiatisch** *a* Asian, Asiatic.
Athen Athens; **Athener(in** *f***)** *m* Athenian; **athenisch** *a* Athenian.
Äthiopien Ethiopia; **Äthiopier(in** *f***)** *m* Ethiopian; **äthiopisch** *a* Ethiopian.
Atlantik (der), Atlantische(r) Ozean the Atlantic (Ocean).
Ätna (der) Mount Etna.
Australien Australia; **Australier(in** *f***)** *m* Australian; **australisch** *a* Australian.
Azoren *pl* **(die)** the Azores *pl*.
Balkan (der) the Balkans *pl*.
Basel Basle.
Bayern Bavaria; **Bayer(in** *f***)** *m* Bavarian; **bayerisch** *a* Bavarian.
Belgien Belgium; **Belgier(in** *f***)** *m* Belgian; **belgisch** *a* Belgian.
Belgrad Belgrade.
Birma Burma; **Birmane** *m*, **Birmanin** *f* Burmese; **Birmanisch** *a* Burmese.
Biskaya (die) the Bay of Biscay.
Bodensee (der) Lake Constance.
Böhmen Bohemia; **Böhme** *m*, **Böhmin** *f* Bohemian; **böhmisch** *a* Bohemian.
Bolivien Bolivia; **Bolivianer(in** *f***)** *m* Bolivian; **bolivianisch, bolvisch** *a* Bolivian.
Brasilien Brazil; **Brasilianer(in** *f***)** *m* Brazilian; **brasilianisch** *a* Brazilian.
Braunschweig Brunswick.
Brite *m*, **Britin** *f* Briton; **britisch** *a* British.
Brüssel Brussels.
Bulgarien Bulgaria; **Bulgare** *m*, **Bulgarin** *f* Bulgarian, Bulgar; **bulgarisch** *a* Bulgarian.
Burgund Burgundy; **burgundisch, Burgunder** *a* Burgundian.
Calais: Straße von Calais (die) the Straits of Dover *pl*.
Chile Chile; **Chilene** *m*, **Chilenin** *f* Chilean; **chilenisch** *a* Chilean.
China China; **Chinese** *m*, **Chinesin** *f* Chinese; **chinesisch** *a* Chinese.
Dänemark Denmark; **Däne** *m*, **Dänin** *f* Dane; **dänisch** *a* Danish.
Deutsche Demokratische Republik (die) German Democratic Republic, East Germany.
Deutschland Germany; **Deutsche(r)** *mf* German; **deutsch** *a* German.
Dolomiten *pl* **(die)** the Dolomites *pl*.
Donau (die) the Danube.
Dünkirchen Dunkirk.

Eismeer (das) the Arctic.
Elfenbeinküste (die) the Ivory Coast.
Elsaß (das) Alsace; **Elsässer(in** f**)** m Alsatian; **elsässisch** a Alsatian.
Engadin (das) the Engadine.
England England; **Engländer(in** f**)** m Englishman/-woman; **englisch** a English.
Estland Estonia; **Este** m, **Estin** f Estonian; **estnisch** a Estonian.
Etsch (die) the Adige.
Euphrat (der) the Euphrates.
Eurasien Eurasia.
Europa Europe; **Europäer(in** f**)** m European; **europäisch** a European.
Ferne(r) Osten (der) the Far East.
Finnland Finland; **Finne** m, **Finnin** f Finn; **finnisch** a Finnish.
Flandern Flanders; **Flame** m, **Flämin** or **Flamin** f Fleming; **flämisch** a Flemish.
Florenz Florence; **Florentiner(in** f**)** m Florentine; **florentinisch** a Florentine.
Frankreich France; **Franzose** m, **Französin** f Frenchman/-woman; **französisch** a French.
Friesland Frisia; **Friese** m, **Friesin** f Frisian; **friesisch** a Frisian.
Genf Geneva.
Genfer See Lake Geneva.
Genua Genoa; **Genuese** m, **Genuesin** f Genoan; **genuesisch** a Genoan.
Griechenland Greece; **Grieche** m, **Griechin** f Greek; **griechisch** a Greek.
Großbritannien Great Britain; **Brite** m, **Britin** f Briton; **britisch, großbritannisch** a British.
Guinea Guinea.
Haag (der), Den Haag the Hague.
Hannover Hanover; **Hannoveraner(in** f**)** m Hanoverian; **Hannoveraner, hannoversch** a Hanoverian.
Hebriden pl (**die**) the Hebrides pl.
Helgoland Heligoland.
Hessen Hesse; **Hesse** m, **Hessin** f Hessian; **hessisch** a Hessian.
Holland Holland; **Holländer(in** f**)** m Dutchman/-woman; **holländisch** a Dutch.
Iberische Halbinsel (die) the Iberian Peninsula.
Indien India; **Inder(in** f**)** m, **Indianer(in** f**)** m Indian; **indisch, indianisch** a Indian.
Indonesien Indonesia; **Indonesier(in** f**)** m Indonesian; **indonesisch** a Indonesian.
Irak (auch **der**) Iraq; **Iraker(in** f**)** m Iraqi; **irakisch** a Iraqi.
Iran (auch **der**) Iran; **Iraner(in** f**)** m Iranian; **iranisch** a Iranian.
Irland Ireland; **Ire** m, **Irin** f Irishman/-woman; **irisch** a Irish.
Island Iceland; **Isländer(in** f**)** m Icelander; **isländisch** a Icelandic.
Israel Israel; **Israeli** mf Israeli; **israelisch** a Israeli.
Italien Italy; **Italiener(in** f**)** m Italian; **italienisch** a Italian.
Japan Japan; **Japaner(in** f**)** m Japanese; **japanisch** a Japanese.
Jemen (auch **der**) the Yemen; **Jemenit(in** f**)** m Yemeni; **jemenitisch** a Yemeni.
Jordanien Jordan; **Jordanier(in** f**)** m Jordanian; **jordanisch** a Jordanian.
Jugoslawien Yugoslavia; **Jugoslawe** m, **Jugoslawin** f Yugoslavian; **jugoslawisch** a Yugoslavian.
Kanada Canada; **Kanadier(in** f**)** m Canadian; **kanadisch** a Canadian.
Kanalinseln pl (**die**) the Channel Islands pl.
Kanarische Inseln pl (**die**) the Canary Islands pl, the Canaries pl.
Kap der Guten Hoffnung (das) the Cape of Good Hope.
Kapstadt Cape Town.
Karibische Inseln pl (**die**) the Caribbean Islands pl.
Karpaten pl (**die**) the Carpathians pl.
Kaspische(s) Meer the Caspian Sea.
Kleinasien Asia Minor.
Köln Cologne.
Konstanz Constance.
Kreml (der) the Kremlin.
Kreta Crete; **Kreter(in** f**)** m Cretan; **kretisch** a Cretan.
Krim (die) the Crimea.
Kroatien Croatia; **Kroate** m, **Kroatin** f Croatian; **kroatisch** a Croatian.
Lappland Lapland; **Lappe** m, **Lappin** f Laplander; **lappisch** a Lapp.
Lateinamerika Latin America.
Lettland Latvia; **Lette** m, **Lettin** f Latvian; **lettisch** a Latvian.
Libanon the Lebanon; **Libanese** m, **Libanesin** f Lebanese; **libanesisch** a Lebanese.
Libyen Libya; **Libyer(in** f**)** m Libyan; **libyisch** a Libyan.
Lissabon Lisbon.
Litauen Lithuania; **Litauer(in** f**)** m Lithuanian; **litauisch** a Lithuanian.
Livland Livonia; **Livländer(in** f**)** m Livonian; **livländisch** a Livonian.
London London; **Londoner(in** f**)** m Londoner; **Londoner** a London.

Lothringen Lorraine.
Lüneburger Heide (die) the Lüneburg Heath.
Luxemburg Luxembourg.
Maas (die) the Meuse.
Mähren Moravia.
Mailand Milan; **Mailänder(in** f) m Milanese; **mailändisch** a Milanese.
Mallorca Majorca.
Mandschurei (die) Manchuria; **Mandschure** m, **Mandschurin** f Manchurian; **mandschurisch** a Manchurian.
Marokko Morocco; **Marokkaner(in** f) m Moroccan; **marokkanisch** a Moroccan.
Mazedonien Macedonia; **Mazedonier(in** f) m Macedonian; **mazedonisch** a Macedonian.
Mittelamerika Central America.
Mitteleuropa Central Europe.
Mittelmeer (das) the Mediterranean.
Moldau (die) Moldavia.
Mongolei (die) Mongolia; **Mongole** m, **Mongolin** f Mongol(ian); **mongolisch** a Mongol(ian).
Moskau Moscow; **Moskauer(in** f) m Muscovite; **moskauisch** a Muscovite.
München Munich.
Nahe(r) Osten (der) the Near East.
Neapel Naples; **Neapolitaner(in** f) m Neapolitan; **neapolitanisch** a Neapolitan.
Neufundland Newfoundland; **Neufundländer(in** f) m Newfoundlander; **neufundländisch** a Newfoundland.
Neuguinea New Guinea.
Neuseeland New Zealand; **Neuseeländer(in** f) m New Zealander; **neuseeländisch** a New Zealand.
Niederlande pl **(die)** the Netherlands; **Niederländer(in** f) m Dutchman/ -woman; **niederländisch** a Dutch.
Niedersachsen Lower Saxony.
Niederrhein Lower Rhine.
Nil (der) the Nile.
Nordirland Northern Ireland.
Nordsee (die) the North Sea.
Norwegen Norway; **Norweger(in** f) m Norwegian; **norwegisch** a Norwegian.
Nord-Ostsee-Kanal (der) the Kiel Canal.
Nordrhein-Westfalen North Rhine-Westphalia.
Nürnberg Nuremberg.
Oberbayern Upper Bavaria.
Ostasien Eastern Asia.
Ostende Ostend.
Ostsee (die) the Baltic.
Österreich Austria; **Österreicher(in** f) m Austrian; **österreichisch** a Austrian.
Palästina Palestine; **Palästinenser(in** f) m Palestinian; **palästinensisch** a Palestinian.
Paris Paris; **Pariser(in** f) m Parisian; **Pariser** a Parisian.
Pazifik (der), Pazifische(r) Ozean the Pacific.
Peloponnes (der or **die)** the Peloponnese.
Persien Persia; **Perser(in** f) m Persian; **persisch** a Persian.
Philippinen pl **(die)** the Philippines pl.
Polen Poland; **Pole** m, **Polin** f Pole; **polnisch** a Polish.
Pommern Pomerania; **Pommer(in** f) m Pomeranian; **pommerisch** a Pomeranian.
Portugal Portugal; **Portugiese** m, **Portugiesin** f Portuguese; **portugiesisch** a Portuguese.
Prag Prague.
Preußen Prussia; **Preuße** m, **Preußin** f Prussian; **preußisch** a Prussian.
Pyrenäen pl **(die)** the Pyrenees pl.
Rhein (der) the Rhine; **rheinisch** a Rhenish.
Rhodesien Rhodesia; **Rhodesier(in** f) m Rhodesian; **rhodesisch** a Rhodesian.
Rhodos Rhodes.
Rom Rome; **Römer(in** f) m Roman; **römisch** a Roman.
Rote(s) Meer the Red Sea.
Rumänien Ro(u)mania; **Rumäne** m, **Rumänin** f Ro(u)manian; **rumänisch** a Ro(u)manian.
Rußland Russia; **Russe** m, **Russin** f Russian; **russisch** a Russian.
Saarland the Saar.
Sachsen Saxony; **Sachse** m, **Sächsin** f Saxon; **sächsisch** a Saxon.
Sardinien Sardinia; **Sardinier(in** f) m, **Sarde** m, **Sardin** f Sardinian; **sardinisch, sardisch** a Sardinian.
Schlesien Silesia; **Schlesier(in** f) m Silesian; **schlesisch** a Silesian.

Schottland Scotland; **Schotte** *m*, **Schottin** *f* Scot, Scotsman/-woman; **schottisch** *a* Scottish, Scots, Scotch.
Schwaben Swabia; **Schwabe** *m*, **Schwäbin** *f* Swabian; **schwäbisch** *a* Swabian.
Schwarzwald (der) the Black Forest.
Schweden Sweden; **Schwede** *m*, **Schwedin** *f* Swede; **schwedisch** *a* Swedish.
Schweiz (die) Switzerland; **Schweizer(in** *f*) *m* Swiss; **schweizerisch** *a* Swiss.
Serbien Serbia; **Serbe** *m*, **Serbin** *f* Serbian; **serbisch** *a* Serbian.
Sibirien Siberia; **sibirisch** *a* Siberian.
Sizilien Sicily; **Sizilianer(in** *f*) *m*, **Sizilier(in** *f*) *m* Sicilian; **sizilisch, sizilianisch** *a* Sicilian.
Skandinavien Scandinavia; **Skandinavier(in** *f*) *m* Scandinavian; **skandinavisch** *a* Scandinavian.
Slowakei (die) Slovakia; **Slowake** *m*, **Slowakin** *f* Slovak; **slowakisch** *a* Slovak.
Sowjetunion (die) the Soviet Union; **Sowjetbürger(in** *f*) *m* Soviet; **sowjetisch** *a* Soviet.
Spanien Spain; **Spanier(in** *f*) *m* Spaniard; **spanisch** *a* Spanish.
Steiermark Styria; **Steiermärker(in** *f*) *m*, **Steirer** *m*, **Steierin** *f* Styrian; **steiermärkisch, steirisch** *a* Styrian.
Stille(r) Ozean the Pacific.
Syrien Syria; **Syrer(in** *f*) *m* Syrian; **syrisch** *a* Syrian.
Teneriffa Tenerife.
Themse (die) the Thames.
Thüringen Thuringia; **Thüringer(in** *f*) *m* Thuringian; **thüringisch** *a* Thuringian.
Tirol the Tyrol; **Tiroler(in** *f*) *m* Tyrolean; **tirolisch** *a* Tyrolean.
Tschechoslowakei (die) Czechoslovakia; **Tscheche** *m*, **Tschechin** *f*, **Tschechoslowake** *m*, **Tschechoslowakin** *f* Czech, Czechoslovak(ian); **tschechisch, tschechoslowakisch** *a* Czech, Czechoslovak(ian).
Toscana (die) Tuscany.
Trient Trent.
Tunesien Tunisia; **Tunesier(in** *f*) *m* Tunisian; **tunesisch** *a* Tunisian.
Türkei (die) Turkey; **Türke** *m*, **Türkin** *f* Turk; **türkisch** *a* Turkish.
Ungarn Hungary; **Ungar(in** *f*) *m* Hungarian; **ungarisch** *a* Hungarian.
Venedig Venice; **Venetianer(in** *f*) *m* Venetian; **venetianisch** *a* Venetian.
Vereinigte Staaten *pl* **(die)** the United States *pl*.
Vesuv (der) Vesuvius.
Vierwaldstättersee (der) Lake Lucerne.
Vogesen *pl* **(die)** the Vosges *pl*.
Volksrepublik China (die) the People's Republic of China.
Vorderasien the Near East.
Warschau Warsaw.
Weichsel (die) the Vistula.
Westfalen Westphalia; **Westfale** *m*, **Westfälin** *f* Westphalian; **westfälisch** *a* Westphalian.
Westindien the West Indies; **westindisch** *a* West Indian.
Wien Vienna; **Wiener(in** *f*) *m* Viennese; **Wiener** *a* Viennese.
Zypern Cyprus; **Zyprer(in** *f*) *m*, **Zyprier(in** *f*) *m*, **Zypriot(in** *f*) *m* Cypriot; **zyprisch, zypriotisch** *a* Cypriot.

Countries, nationalities and languages

I am German/English/Albanian ich bin Deutscher/Engländer/Albanier

a German/an Englishman/an Albanian ein Deutscher/Engländer/Albanier; **a German (woman/girl)/an English woman/girl/an Albanian (woman/girl)** eine Deutsche/Engländerin/Albanierin

do you speak German/English/Albanian? sprechen Sie Deutsch/Englisch/Albanisch?

the Adriatic die Adria.
the Aegean die Ägäis.
Afghanistan Afghanistan *nt*; **Afghan** *n* Afghane *m*, Afghanin *f*; *a* afghanisch.
Africa Afrika *nt*; **African** *n* Afrikaner(in *f*) *m*; *a* afrikanisch.
Albania Albanien *nt*; **Albanian** *n* Albanier(in *f*) *m*; *a* albanisch.

Algeria Algerien *nt*; **Algerian** *n* Algerier(in *f*) *m*; *a* algerisch.
the Alps *pl* die Alpen *pl*.
America Amerika *nt*; **American** *n* Amerikaner(in *f*) *m*; *a* amerikanisch.
the Andes *pl* die Anden *pl*.
Angola Angola *nt*; **Angolan** *n* Angolaner(in *f*) *m*; *a* angolanisch.
the Antarctic die Antarktis; **Antarctic** *a* antarktisch.
Arabia Arabien *nt*; **Arab, Arabian** *n* Araber(in *f*) *m*; *a* arabisch.
the Arctic die Arktis; **Arctic** *a* arktisch.
Argentina, the Argentine Argentinien *nt*; **Argentinian** *n* Argentinier(in *f*) *m*; *a* argentinisch.
Asia Asien *nt*; **Asian** *n* Asiat(in *f*) *m*; *a* asiatisch.
Asia Minor Kleinasien *nt*.
Athens Athen *nt*.
the Atlantic (Ocean) der Atlantik, der Atlantische Ozean.
Australia Australien *nt*; **Australian** *n* Australier(in *f*) *m*; *a* australisch.
Austria Österreich *nt*; **Austrian** *n* Österreicher(in *f*) *m*; *a* österreichisch.
the Baltic die Ostsee.
Bavaria Bayern *nt*; **Bavarian** *n* Bayer(in *f*) *m*; *a* bay(e)risch.
the Bay of Biscay (der Golf von) Biskaya *f*.
Belgium Belgien *nt*; **Belgian** *n* Belgier(in *f*) *m*; *a* belgisch.
the Black Forest der Schwarzwald.
Bolivia Bolivien *nt*; **Bolivian** *n* Bolivianer(in *f*) *m*, Bolivier(in *f*) *m*; *a* boliv(ian)isch.
Brazil Brasilien *nt*; **Brazilian** *n* Brasilianer(in *f*) *m*; *a* brasilianisch.
Britain Großbritannien *nt*; **Briton** *n* Brite *m*, Britin *f*; **British** *a* britisch.
Brittany die Bretagne; **Breton** *n* Bretone *m*, Bretonin *f*; *a* bretonisch.
Brussels Brüssel *nt*.
Bulgaria Bulgarien *nt*; **Bulgarian, Bulgar** *n* Bulgare *m*, Bulgarin *f*; **Bulgarian** *a* bulgarisch.
Burma Birma *nt*; **Burmese** *n* Birmane *m*, Birmanin *f*; *a* birmanisch.
California Kalifornien *nt*; **Californian** *n* Kalifornier(in *f*) *m*; *a* kalifornisch.
Cambodia Kambodscha *nt*; **Cambodian** *n* Kambodschaner(in *f*) *m*; *a* kambodschanisch.
Canada Kanada *nt*; **Canadian** *n* Kanadier(in *f*) *m*; *a* kanadisch.
the Canary Islands *pl* die Kanarischen Inseln *pl*.
the Caribbean die Karibik; **Caribbean** *a* karibisch.
Central America Zentralamerika *nt*.
the Channel Islands *pl* die Kanalinseln *pl*, die Normannischen Inseln *pl*.
Chile Chile *nt*; **Chilean** *n* Chilene *m*, Chilenin *f*; *a* chilenisch.
China China *nt*; **Chinese** *n* Chinese *m*, Chinesin *f*; *a* chinesisch.
Cologne Köln *nt*.
Colombia Kolumbien *nt*; **Colombian** *n* Kolumbianer(in *f*) *m*, Kolumbier(in *f*) *m*; *a* kolumb(ian)isch.
Lake Constance der Bodensee.
Cornish *a* von/aus Cornwall.
Corsica Korsika *nt*; **Corsican** *n* Korse *m*, Korsin *f*; *a* korsisch.
Crete Kreta *nt*; **Cretan** *n* Kreter(in *f*) *m*; *a* kretisch.
Cuba Kuba *nt*; **Cuban** *n* Kubaner(in *f*) *m*; *a* kubanisch.
Cyprus Zypern *nt*; **Cypriot** *n* Zypriot(in *f*) *m*; *a* zypriotisch.
Czechoslovakia die Tschechoslowakei; **Czech, Czechoslovak(ian)** *n* Tscheche *m*, Tschechin *f*; *a* tschechisch.
Denmark Dänemark *nt*; **Dane** *n* Däne *m*, Dänin *f*; **Danish** *a* dänisch.
Dutch *a see* **Holland.**
East Germany Deutsche Demokratische Republik *f*; **East German** *n* Staatsbürger(in *f*) *m* der Deutschen Demokratischen Republik; **he is an East German** er ist aus der DDR; *a* der DDR; **East German towns** Städte (in) der DDR.
Ecuador Ecuador *nt*; **Ecuadorian** *n* Ecuadorianer(in *f*) *m*; *a* ecuadorianisch.
Egypt Ägypten *nt*; **Egyptian** *n* Ägypter(in *f*) *m*; *a* ägyptisch.
Eire ['eərə] (Republik *f*) Irland *nt*.
England England *nt*; **Englishman/-woman** *n* Engländer(in *f*) *m*; **English** *a* englisch.
the English Channel der Ärmelkanal.
Ethiopia Äthiopien *nt*; **Ethiopian** *n* Äthiopier(in *f*) *m*; *a* äthiopisch.
Europe Europa *nt*; **European** *n* Europäer(in *f*) *m*; *a* europäisch.
Fiji (Islands *pl*) die Fidschiinseln *pl*; **Fijian** *n* Fidschianer(in *f*) *m*; *a* fidschianisch.
Filipino *n see* **the Philippines.**
Finland Finnland *nt*; **Finn** *n* Finne *m*, Finnin *f*; **Finnish** *a* finnisch.
Flanders Flandern *nt*; **Fleming** *n* Flame *m*, Flämin *f*; **Flemish** *a* flämisch.
Florence Florenz *nt*; **Florentine** *n* Florentiner(in *f*) *m*; *a* florentinisch.

France Frankreich *nt*; **Frenchman/-woman** *n* Franzose *m*, Französin *f*; **French** *a* französisch.

Geneva Genf *nt*; **Lake Geneva** der Genfer See.

Germany Deutschland *nt*; **German** *n* Deutsche(r) *m*, Deutsche *f*; *a* deutsch.

Ghana Ghana *nt*; **Ghanaian** *n* Ghanaer(in *f*) *m*; *a* ghanaisch.

Great Britain Großbritannien *nt*.

Greece Griechenland *nt*; **Greek** *n* Grieche *m*, Griechin *f*; *a* griechisch.

the Hague Den Haag.

Haiti Haiti *nt*; **Haitian** *n* Haitianer(in *f*) *m*, Haitier(in *f*) *m*; *a* haitianisch, haitisch.

Hawaii Hawaii *nt*; **Hawaiian** *n* Hawaiier(in *f*) *m*; *a* hawaiisch.

the Hebrides *pl* die Hebriden *pl*.

the Himalayas *pl* der Himalaja.

Holland Holland *nt*; **Dutchman/-woman** *n* Holländer(in *f*) *m*; **Dutch** *a* holländisch, niederländisch.

Hungary Ungarn *nt*; **Hungarian** *n* Ungar(in *f*) *m*; *a* ungarisch.

Iceland Island *nt*; **Icelander** *n* Isländer(in *f*) *m*; **Icelandic** *a* isländisch.

India Indien *nt*; **Indian** *n* Inder(in *f*) *m*; *a* indisch.

Indonesia Indonesien *nt*; **Indonesian** *n* Indonesier(in *f*) *m*; *a* indonesisch.

Iran (der) Iran; **Iranian** *n* Iraner(in *f*) *m*; *a* iranisch.

Iraq (der) Irak; **Iraqi** *n* Iraker(in *f*) *m*; *a* irakisch.

Ireland Irland *nt*; **Irishman/-woman** *n* Ire *m*, Irin *f*; **Irish** *a* irisch.

Israel Israel *nt*; **Israeli** *n* Israeli *mf*; *a* israelisch.

Italy Italien *nt*; **Italian** *n* Italiener(in *f*) *m*; *a* italienisch.

Jamaica Jamaika *nt*; **Jamaican** *n* Jamaikaner(in *f*) *m*, Jamaiker(in *f*) *m*; *a* jamaikanisch, jamaikisch.

Japan Japan *nt*; **Japanese** *n* Japaner(in *f*) *m*; *a* japanisch.

Jordan Jordanien *nt*; **Jordanian** *n* Jordanier(in *f*) *m*; *a* jordanisch.

Kenya Kenia *nt*; **Kenyan** *n* Kenianer(in *f*) *m*; *a* kenianisch.

the Kiel Canal der Nord-Ostsee-Kanal.

Korea Korea *nt*; **Korean** *n* Koreaner(in *f*) *m*; *a* koreanisch.

Laos Laos *nt*; **Laotian** *n* Laote *m*, Laotin *f*; *a* laotisch.

Lapland Lappland *nt*; **Lapp** *n* Lappe *m*, Lappin *f*; *a* lappisch.

Latin America Lateinamerika *nt*.

Lebanon (der) Libanon; **Lebanese** *n* Libanese *m*, Libanesin *f*; *a* libanesisch.

Liberia Liberia *nt*; **Liberian** *n* Liberianer(in *f*) *m*; *a* liberianisch.

Libya Libyen *nt*; **Libyan** *n* Libyer(in *f*) *m*; *a* libysch.

Lisbon Lissabon *nt*.

London London *nt*; **Londoner** *n* Londoner(in *f*) *m*; **London** *a* Londoner *inv*.

Luxembourg Luxemburg *nt*; **Luxembourger** *n* Luxemburger(in *f*) *m*.

Majorca Mallorca *nt*; **Majorcan** *n* Bewohner(in *f*) *m* Mallorcas; *a* mallorkinisch.

Malaysia Malaysia *nt*; **Malaysian** *n* Malaysier(in *f*) *m*; *a* malaysisch.

Malta Malta *nt*; **Maltese** *n* Malteser(in *f*) *m*; *a* maltesisch.

the Mediterranean (Sea) das Mittelmeer.

Mexico Mexiko *nt*; **Mexican** *n* Mexikaner(in *f*) *m*; *a* mexikanisch.

Milan Mailand *nt*; **Milanese** *n* Mailänder(in *f*) *m*; *a* mailändisch.

Mongolia die Mongolei; **Mongolian** *n* Mongole *m*, mongolin *f*; *a* mongolisch.

Morocco Marokko *nt*; **Moroccan** *n* Marokkaner(in *f*) *m*; *a* marrokkanisch.

Moscow Moskau *nt*; **Muscovite** *n* Moskauer(in *f*) *m*; *a* moskauisch.

Munich München *nt*.

Naples Neapel *nt*; **Neapolitan** *n* Neapolitaner(in *f*) *m*; *a* neapolitanisch.

the Netherlands *pl* die Niederlande *pl*.

New Zealand Neuseeland *nt*; **New Zealander** *n* Neuseeländer(in *f*) *m*; **New Zealand** *a* neuseeländisch.

Nigeria Nigeria *nt*; **Nigerian** *n* Nigerianer(in *f*) *m*; *a* nigerianisch.

Normandy die Normandie; **Norman** *n* Normanne *m*, Normannin *f*; *a* normannisch.

Northern Ireland Nordirland *nt*.

the North Sea die Nordsee.

Norway Norwegen *nt*; **Norwegian** *n* Norweger(in *f*) *m*; *a* norwegisch.

the Pacific (Ocean) der Pazifik, der Pazifische *or* Stille Ozean.

Pakistan Pakistan *nt*; **Pakistani** *n* Pakistaner(in *f*) *m*; *a* pakistanisch.

Palestine Palästina *nt*; **Palestinian** *n* Palästinenser(in *f*) *m*; *a* palästinensisch.

Paraguay Paraguay *nt*; **Paraguayan** *n* Paraguayer(in *f*) *m*; *a* paraguayisch.

Paris Paris *nt*; **Parisian** *n* Pariser(in *f*) *m*; *a* Pariser *inv*.

the People's Republic of China die Volksrepublik China.

Persia Persien *nt*; **Persian** *n* Perser(in *f*) *m*; *a* persisch.

Peru Peru *nt*; **Peruvian** *n* Peruaner(in *f*) *m*; *a* peruanisch.

the Philippines *pl* die Philippinen *pl*; **Filipino** *n* Philippiner(in *f*) *m*; *a*, **Philippine** *a* philippinisch.

Poland Polen *nt*; **Pole** *n* Pole *m*, Polin *f*; **Polish** *a* polnisch.

Portugal Portugal *nt*; **Portuguese** *n* Portugiese *m*, Portugiesin *f*; a portugiesisch.
Puerto Rico Puerto Rico *nt*; **Puerto-Rican** *n* Puertoricaner(in *f*) *m*; a puertoricanisch.
the Pyrenees *pl* die Pyrenäen *pl*; **Pyrenean** a pyrenäisch.
the Red Sea das Rote Meer.
Rhodes Rhodos *nt*.
Rhodesia Rhodesien *nt*; **Rhodesian** *n* Rhodesier(in *f*) *m*; a rhodesisch.
Rome Rom *nt*; **Roman** *n* Römer(in *f*) *m*; a römisch.
Ro(u)mania Rumänien *nt*; **Ro(u)manian** *n* Rumäne *m*, Rumänin *f*; a rumänisch.
Russia Rußland *nt*; **Russian** *n* Russe *m*, Russin *f*; a russisch.
the Sahara die Sahara.
Sardinia Sardinien *nt*; **Sardinian** *n* Sarde *m*, Sardin *f*; a sardisch.
Saudi Arabia Saudi-Arabien *nt*; **Saudi (Arabian)** *n* Saudiaraber(in *f*) *m*; a saudiarabisch.
Scandinavia Skandinavien *nt*; **Scandinavian** *n* Skandinave *m* Skandinavin *f*; a skandinavisch.
Scotland Schottland *nt*; **Scot, Scotsman/-woman** *n* Schotte *m*, Schottin *f*; **Scottish, Scots, Scotch** a schottisch.
Siberia Sibirien *nt*; **Siberian** *n* Sibirier(in *f*) *m*; a sibirisch.
Sicily Sizilien *nt*; **Sicilian** *n* Sizilianer(in *f*) *m*, Sizilier(in *f*) *m*; a sizilianisch, sizilisch.
South Africa Südafrika *nt*; **South African** *n* Südafrikaner(in *f*) *m*; a südafrikanisch.
the Soviet Union die Sowjetunion.
Spain Spanien *nt*; **Spaniard** *n* Spanier(in *f*) *m*; **Spanish** a spanisch.
Sri Lanka Sri Lanka *nt*; **Sri Lankan** *n* Ceylonese *m*, Ceylonesin *f*; a ceylonesisch.
the Sudan der Sudan; **Sudanese** *n* Sudanese *m*, Sudanesin *f*, Sudaner(in *f*) *m*; a sudanesisch.
the Suez Canal der Suez-Kanal.
Sweden Schweden *nt*; **Swede** *n* Schwede *m*, Schwedin *f*; **Swedish** a schwedisch.
Switzerland die Schweiz; **Swiss** *n* Schweizer(in *f*) *m*; a Schweizer *inv*, schweizerisch.
Syria Syrien *nt*; **Syrian** Syrer(in *f*) *m*, Syrier(in *f*) *m*; a syrisch.
Tahiti Tahiti *nt*; **Tahitian** *n* Tahitianer(in *f*) *m*; a tahitianisch.
Taiwan Taiwan *nt*; **Taiwanese** *n* Taiwanese(r) *m*, Taiwanesin *f*; a taiwanesisch.
Tanzania Tansania *nt*; **Tanzanian** *n* Tansanier(in *f*) *m*; a tansanisch.
Tenerife Teneriffa *nt*.
Thailand Thailand *nt*; **Thai** *n* Thailänder(in *f*) *m*; a thailändisch.
the Thames die Themse.
the Tyrol Tirol *nt*; **Tyrolean** *n* Tiroler(in *f*) *m*; a Tiroler *inv*.
Tunisia Tunesien *nt*; **Tunisian** *n* Tunesier(in *f*) *m*; a tunesisch.
Turkey die Türkei; **Turk** *n* Türke *m*, Türkin *f*; **Turkish** a türkisch.
Uganda Uganda *nt*; **Ugandan** *n* Ugander(in *f*) *m*; a ugandisch.
the United Kingdom das Vereinigte Königreich.
the United States *pl* (**of America**) die Vereinigten Staaten *pl* (von Amerika).
Uruguay Uruguay *nt*; **Uruguayan** *n* Uruguayer(in *f*) *m*; a uruguayisch.
Venezuela Venezuela *nt*; **Venezuelan** *n* Venezolaner(in *f*) *m*; a venezolanisch.
Venice Venedig *nt*; **Venetian** *n* Venezianer(in *f*) *m*; a venezianisch.
Vienna Wien *nt*; **Viennese** *n* Wiener(in *f*) *m*; a wienerisch, Wiener *inv*.
Vietnam Vietnam *nt*; **Vietnamese** *n* Vietnamese *m*, Vietnamesin *f*; a vietnamesisch.
Wales Wales *nt*; **Welshman/-woman** *n* Waliser(in *f*) *m*; **Welsh** a walisisch.
Warsaw Warschau *nt*.
West Germany die Bundesrepublik (Deutschland); **West German** *n* Bundesdeutsche(r) *m*, Bundesdeutsche *f*; a Bundes-, der Bundesrepublik.
the West Indies *pl* Westindien *nt*; **West Indian** *n* Westinder(in *f*) *m*; a westindisch.
the Yemen (der) Jemen; **Yemeni, Yemenite** *n* Jemenit(in *f*) *m*; a jemenitisch.
Yugoslavia Jugoslawien *nt*; **Yugoslav(ian)** *n* Jugoslawe *m*, Jugoslawin *f*; a jugoslawisch.
Zaire Zaire *nt*.
Zambia Sambia *nt*; **Zambian** *n* Sambier(in *f*) *m*; a sambisch.

Deutsche Abkürzungen

Abf.	Abfahrt *departure, dep*
Abk.	Abkürzung *abbreviation, abbr*
Abs.	Absatz *paragraph;* Absender *sender*
Abt.	Abteilung *department, dept*
AG	Aktiengesellschaft *(Brit) (public) limited company, Ltd, (US) corporation, inc*
Ank.	Ankunft *arrival, arr*
Anm.	Anmerkung *note*
b.a.w.	bis auf weiteres *until further notice*
Best. Nr.	Bestellnummer *order number*
Betr.	Betreff, betrifft *re*
Bhf.	Bahnhof *station*
BRD	Bundesrepublik Deutschland *Federal Republic of Germany*
b.w.	bitte wenden *please turn over, pto*
bzgl.	bezüglich *with reference to, re*
bzw.	beziehungsweise *(see text)*
ca.	circa, ungefähr *approximately, approx*
Cie., Co.	Kompanie *company, co*
DDR	Deutsche Demokratische Republik *German Democratic Republic, GDR*
d.h.	das heißt *that is, i.e.*
d.J.	dieses Jahres *of this year*
d.M.	dieses Monats *instant, inst*
DM	Deutsche Mark *German Mark, Deutschmark*
EDV	elektronische Datenverarbeitung *electronic data processing, EDP*
einschl.	einschließlich *inclusive, including, incl*
Einw.	Einwohner *inhabitant*
empf.	empfohlen(er Preis) *recommended (price)*
ev.	evangelisch *Protestant*
evtl.	eventuell *perhaps, possibly*
EWG	Europäische Wirtschaftsgemeinschaft *European Economic Community, EEC*
e. Wz.	eingetragenes Warenzeichen *registered trademark*
Expl.	Exemplar *sample, copy*
Fa.	Firma *firm;* in Briefen: *Messrs*
ff.	folgende Seiten *pages, pp*
Ffm.	Frankfurt am Main
fl. W.	fließendes Wasser *running water*
Forts.	Fortsetzung *continued, cont'd*
geb.	geboren *born;* geborene *née;* gebunden *bound.*
Gebr.	Gebrüder *Brothers, Bros*
ges. gesch.	gesetzlich geschützt *registered*
GmbH	Gesellschaft mit beschränkter Haftung *(Brit) (private) limited company, Ltd, (US) corporation, inc*
Hbf.	Hauptbahnhof *central station*
hl.	heilig *holy*
Hrsg.	Herausgeber *editor, ed*
i.A.	im Auftrag *for;* in Briefen auch: *pp*
Ing.	Ingenieur *engineer*
Inh.	Inhaber *proprietor, prop;* Inhalt *contents*
i.V.	in Vertretung *by proxy, on behalf of;* im Vorjahre *in the last or previous year;* in Vorbereitung *in preparation*
Jh.	Jahrhundert *century, cent*
jr., jun.	junior, der Jüngere *junior, jun, jr*
kath.	katholisch *Catholic, Cath*
kfm.	kaufmännisch *commercial*
Kfz.	*(see text)*
KG	Kommanditgesellschaft *limited partnership*
led.	ledig *single*
Lkw.	*(see text)*

402

lt.	laut *according to*
m. E.	meines Erachtens *in my opinion*
Mehrw. St.	Mehrwertsteuer *value-added tax, VAT*
Mrd.	Milliarde *thousand millions, (US) billion*
n. Chr.	nach Christus *AD*
Nr.	Numero, Nummer *number, no*
NS	Nachschrift *postscript, PS;* nationalsozialistisch *National Socialist*
OHG	Öffene Handelsgesellschaft *general partnership*
PKW, Pkw.	*(see text)*
Pl.	Platz *square*
Postf.	Postfach *post-office box, PO box*
PS	Pferdestärken *horsepower, HP;* Nachschrift *postscript, PS*
S.	Seite *page, p*
s.	siehe *see*
sen.	senior, der Ältere *senior, sen, sr*
s.o.	siehe oben *see above*
St.	Stück *piece;* Sankt *Saint, St*
Std., Stde.	Stunde *hour, hr*
stdl.	stündlich *every hour*
Str.	Straße *street, St*
s.u.	siehe unten *see below*
tägl.	täglich *daily, per day*
Tsd.	Tausend *thousand*
u.	und *and*
u.a.	und andere(s) *and others;* unter anderem/anderen *among other things, inter alia/among others*
U.A.w.g.	Um Antwort wird gebeten *an answer is requested;* auf Einladung: *RSVP*
UdSSR	Union der Sozialistischen Sowjetrepubliken *Union of Soviet Socialist Republics, USSR*
u.E.	unseres Erachtens *in our opinion*
USA	Vereinigte Staaten (von Amerika) *United States (of America), USA.*
usf.	und so fort *and so forth, etc*
usw.	und so weiter *etcetera, etc*
u.U.	unter Umständen *possibly*
v. Chr.	vor Christus *BC*
Verf., Vf.	Verfasser *author*
verh.	verheiratet *married*
Verl.	Verlag *publishing firm;* Verleger *publisher*
vgl.	vergleiche *compare, cf, cp*
v.H.	vom Hundert *per cent*
Wz.	Warenzeichen *registered trademark*
z.B.	zum Beispiel *for example or instance, eg*
z.H(d)	zu Händen *for the attention of*
z.T.	zum Teil *partly*
zw.	zwischen *between; among*
z.Z(t).	zur Zeit *at the time, at present, for the time being*

English abbreviations

AD	after (the birth of) Christ *Anno Domini, nach Christi, A.D., n. Chr.*
AGM	annual general meeting *Jahresvollversammlung*
am	before midday (ante meridiem) *vormittags, vorm.;* 1.00am. *1.00 Uhr*
arr	arrival, arrives *Ankunft, Ank.*
asst	assistant *Assistent, Mitarbeiter*
Ave	avenue *Straße, Str.*
BA	Bachelor of Arts *Bakkalaureus der Philosophischen Fakultät*
B and B	bed and breakfast *Zimmer mit Frühstück,* in catalogue: *Zi. m Fr.,* as sign: *Fremdenzimmer*
BAOR	British Army of the Rhine *(britische) Rheinarmee*
BC	before (the birth of) Christ *vor Christi Geburt, v. Chr.*
BO	body odour *Körpergeruch*
Bros	[brɔs] brothers *Gebrüder, Gebr.*
BSc	Bachelor of Science *Bakkalaureus der Naturwissenschaftlichen Fakultät*

Cantab	['kæntæb] Cambridge University (Cantabrigiensis) *Cambridge*
CBI	Confederation of British Industry *Bundesverband der britischen Industrie*
cc	cubic centimetres *Kubikzentimeter, ccm.*
CD	Diplomatic Corps (French: Corps Diplomatique) *Diplomatisches Corps, CD*
CIA	Central Intelligence Agency *CIA*
CID	Criminal Investigation Department *Kriminalpolizei*
cif	cost insurance and freight *Kosten, Versicherung und Fracht einbegriffen*
C-in-C	Commander-in-Chief *Oberkommandierender*
cm	centimetre(s) *Zentimeter, cm*
c/o	care of *bei, c/o*
COD	cash on delivery *gegen Nachnahme*
C of E	Church of England *anglikanische Kirche*
cwt	hundredweight ≈ *Zentner, ztr.*
DA	(*US*) District Attorney *Bezirksstaatsanwalt*
dep	depart(s) *Abfahrt, Abf.*
dept	department *Abteilung, Abt.*
DJ	dinner jacket *Smoking*; disc jockey *Diskjockey*
ed	edited by *herausgegeben, hrsg.*; editor *Herausgeber, Hrsg.*
EEC	European Economic Community *Europäische Wirtschaftsgemeinschaft, EWG*
eg	for example (exempli gratia) *zum Beispiel, z.B.*
ESP	extrasensory perception *übersinnliche Wahrnehmung*
ETA	estimated time of arrival *voraussichtliche Ankunft*
etc	etcetera, and so on *und so weiter, usw., etc.*
FBI	Federal Bureau of Investigation *FBI*
fig	figure, illustration *Abbildung, Abb.*
fob	free on board *frei Schiff*
gbh	grievous bodily harm *schwere Körperverletzung*
GI	(government issue) private in the American Army *amerikanischer Soldat, GI*
govt	government *Regierung*
GP	General Practitioner *praktischer Arzt*
GPO	General Post Office *Britische Post; Hauptpostamt*
HM	His/Her Majesty *Seine/Ihre Majestät*
HMS	His/Her Majesty's Ship *Schiff der Königlichen Marine*
hp	(*Brit*) hire purchase *Abzahlungskauf*; horsepower *Pferdestärke, PS*
HQ	headquarters *Hauptquartier*
hr(s)	hour(s) *Stunde(n), Std.*
HRH	His/Her Royal Highness *Seine/Ihre Hoheit*
ID	identification *Ausweis*
i.e.	that is (id est) *das heißt, d.h.*
IOU	I owe you *Schuldschein*
JP	Justice of the Peace *Friedensrichter*
km	kilometre(s) *Kilometer, km*
kph	kilometres per hour *Stundenkilometer, km/h*
LA	Los Angeles
lb	pound (weight) *Pfund, Pfd.*
LP	long-playing (record), long-player *Langspielplatte, LP*
Ltd	limited (in names of businesses) *Gesellschaft mit beschränkter Haftung, GmbH*
MA	Master of Arts *Magister Artium, M.A.*
max	maximum *maximal, max*
MI5	department of British Intelligence Service (originally Military Intelligence) *Britischer Geheimdienst*
min	minimum *minimal*
MIT	Massachusetts Institute of Technology
mm	millimetre(s) *Millimeter, mm*
mod cons	[mɔd'kɔnz] modern conveniences (cooker, lights, *etc*) *mit allem Komfort*
MOT	Ministry of Transport (used for the roadworthiness test of motor vehicles) *Technischer Überwachungsverein, TÜV*
MP	Member of Parliament *Abgeordneter*; military policeman *Militärpolizist, MP*
mpg	miles per gallon *Meilen pro Gallone, Benzinverbrauch*
mph	miles per hour *Meilen pro Stunde*
Mr	['mɪstə] Mister *Herr*
Mrs	['mɪsɪz] Mistress *Frau*
Ms	[mɔz] *Frau*

NAAFI	['næfɪ] (*Brit*) Navy, Army and Air Force Institutes (canteen services) *Kantine*
NATO	['neɪtəʊ] North Atlantic Treaty Organization *Nordatlantikpakt, NATO*
NB	note well (nota bene) *notabene, NB*
NCO	non-commissioned officer *Unteroffizier, Uffz.*
no(s)	number(s) *Nummer(n), Nr.*
o.n.o.	or nearest offer *oder höchstes Angebot*
Oxon	['ɔksən] Oxford University (Oxonia) *Oxford*
oz	ounce(s) (onza) *Unze*
p	page *Seite, S.*; (new) pence *Pence, p*
PA	public address (system) *Lautsprecheranlage*
pa	per year (per annum) *pro Jahr, jährlich, jhrl.*
PC	police constable *Polizeibeamter*; Privy Councillor *Mitglied des Geheimen Staatsrats*
PhD	Doctor of Philosophy *Doktor der Philosophie, Dr. phil.*
PM	Prime Minister *Premierminister*
pm	afternoon (post meridiem) *nachmittags, nachm.*; 10.00pm *22.00 Uhr*
pop	population *Einwohner, Einw.*
POW	prisoner of war *Kriegsgefangener*
pp	pages *Seiten, ff.*; pro persona, for *im Auftrag, i.A.*
PRO	public relations officer *PR-Chef*
PS	postscript *Nachschrift, PS*
pto	please turn over *bitte wenden, b.w.*
QC	Queen's Counsel *Anwalt der königlichen Anwaltskammer*
RADA	Royal Academy of Dramatic Art
RAF	Royal Air Force *britische Luftwaffe*
Rd	road *Straße, Str.*
Rev	Reverend *Herr Pfarrer*
RIP	rest in peace (requiescat in pace) *ruhe in Frieden, R.I.P.*
RSVP	please reply (written on invitations, French: répondez s'il vous plaît) *um Antwort wird gebeten, u.A.w.g.*
Rt Hon	Right Honourable *Anrede für Grafen etc, Abgeordnete und Minister*
s.a.e.	stamped addressed envelope *vorfrankierter Umschlag*
SOS	(save our souls) *SOS*
Sq	square (in town) *Platz, Pl.*
ss	steamship *Dampfer*
St	saint *Sankt, St.*; street *Straße, Str.*
st	stone (weight) *6,35 kg*
STD	subscriber trunk dialling *Selbstwählfernverkehr*
TB	tuberculosis *Tuberkulose, TB*
Tel	telephone *Telefon, Tel.*
TUC	Trades Union Congress *Gewerkschaftsbund*
UFO	['juːfəʊ] unidentified flying object *unbekanntes Flugobjekt, Ufo*
UK	United Kingdom *Vereinigtes Königreich*
UN	United Nations *Vereinte Nationen*
USA	United States of America *Vereinigte Staaten von Amerika, USA*; United States Army *Amerikanische Armee*
USAF	United States Air Force *Amerikanische Luftwaffe*
USN	United States Navy *Amerikanische Marine*
USSR	Union of Soviet Socialist Republics *Sowjetunion, UdSSR*
VAT	[*also* væt] value added tax *Mehrwertsteuer, Mehrw.St.*
VD	venereal disease *Geschlechtskrankheit*
VHF	very high frequency *Ultrakurzwelle, UKW*
VIP	very important person *wichtige Persönlichkeit, VIP*
viz	[vɪz] namely (videlicet) *nämlich*
VSO	voluntary service overseas *Entwicklungshilfe*
WASP	(*US*) White Anglo-Saxon Protestant
WC	water closet *Toilette, WC*
ZIP	[zɪp] (*US*) Zone Improvement Plan (postal code) *Postleitzahl, PLZ*

German irregular verbs
* with 'sein'

infinitive	present indicative (2nd, 3rd sing.)	preterite	past participle
aufschrecken*	schrickst auf, schrickt auf	schrak or schreckte auf	aufgeschreckt
ausbedingen	bedingst aus, bedingt aus	bedang or bedingte aus	ausbedungen
backen	bäckst, bäckt	backte or buk	gebacken
befehlen	befiehlst, befiehlt	befahl	befohlen
beginnen	beginnst, beginnt	begann	begonnen
beißen	beißt, beißt	biß	gebissen
bergen	birgst, birgt	barg	geborgen
bersten*	birst, birst	barst	geborsten
bescheißen*	bescheißt, bescheißt	beschiß	beschissen
bewegen	bewegst, bewegt	bewog	bewogen
biegen	biegst, biegt	bog	gebogen
bieten	bietest, bietet	bot	geboten
binden	bindest, bindet	band	gebunden
bitten	bittest, bittet	bat	gebeten
blasen	bläst, bläst	blies	geblasen
bleiben*	bleibst, bleibt	blieb	geblieben
braten	brätst, brät	briet	gebraten
brechen*	brichst, bricht	brach	gebrochen
brennen	brennst, brennt	brannte	gebrannt
bringen	bringst, bringt	brachte	gebracht
denken	denkst, denkt	dachte	gedacht
dreschen	drisch(e)st, drischt	drasch	gedroschen
dringen*	dringst, dringt	drang	gedrungen
dürfen	darfst, darf	durfte	gedurft
empfehlen	empfiehlst, empfiehlt	empfahl	empfohlen
erbleichen*	erbleichst, erbleicht	erbleichte	erblichen
erlöschen*	erlischst, erlischt	erlosch	erloschen
erschrecken*	erschrickst, erschrickt	erschrak	erschrocken
essen	ißt, ißt	aß	gegessen
fahren*	fährst, fährt	fuhr	gefahren
fallen*	fällst, fällt	fiel	gefallen
fangen	fängst, fängt	fing	gefangen
fechten	fichtst, ficht	focht	gefochten
finden	findest, findet	fand	gefunden
flechten	flichst, flicht	flocht	geflochten
fliegen*	fliegst, fliegt	flog	geflogen
fliehen*	fliehst, flieht	floh	geflohen
fließen*	fließt, fließt	floß	geflossen
fressen	frißt, frißt	fraß	gefressen
frieren	frierst, friert	fror	gefroren
gären*	gärst, gärt	gor	gegoren
gebären	gebierst, gebiert	gebar	geboren
geben	gibst, gibt	gab	gegeben
gedeihen*	gedeihst, gedeiht	gedieh	gediehen
gehen*	gehst, geht	ging	gegangen
gelingen*	——, gelingt	gelang	gelungen
gelten	giltst, gilt	galt	gegolten
genesen*	gene(se)st, genest	genas	genesen
genießen	genießt, genießt	genoß	genossen
geraten*	gerätst, gerät	geriet	geraten
geschehen*	——, geschieht	geschah	geschehen
gewinnen	gewinnst, gewinnt	gewann	gewonnen
gießen	gießt, gießt	goß	gegossen
gleichen	gleichst, gleicht	glich	geglichen

406

infinitive	present indicative (2nd, 3rd sing.)	preterite	past participle
gleiten*	gleitest, gleitet	glitt	geglitten
glimmen	glimmst, glimmt	glomm	geglommen
graben	gräbst, gräbt	grub	gegraben
greifen	greifst, greift	griff	gegriffen
haben	hast, hat	hatte	gehabt
halten	hältst, hält	hielt	gehalten
hängen	hängst, hängt	hing	gehangen
hauen	haust, haut	hieb	gehauen
heben	hebst, hebt	hob	gehoben
heißen	heißt, heißt	hieß	geheißen
helfen	hilfst, hilft	half	geholfen
kennen	kennst, kennt	kannte	gekannt
klimmen	klimmst, klimmt	klomm	geklommen
klingen	klingst, klingt	klang	geklungen
kneifen	kneifst, kneift	kniff	gekniffen
kommen*	kommst, kommt	kam	gekommen
können	kannst, kann	konnte	gekonnt
kriechen*	kriechst, kriecht	kroch	gekrochen
laden	lädst, lädt	lud	geladen
lassen	läßt, läßt	ließ	gelassen
laufen*	läufst, läuft	lief	gelaufen
leiden	leidest, leidet	litt	gelitten
leihen	leihst, leiht	lieh	geliehen
lesen	liest, liest	las	gelesen
liegen*	liegst, liegt	lag	gelegen
lügen	lügst, lügt	log	gelogen
mahlen	mahlst, mahlt	mahlte	gemahlen
meiden	meidest, meidet	mied	gemieden
melken	milkst, milkt	molk	gemolken
messen	mißt, mißt	maß	gemessen
mißlingen*	——, mißlingt	mißlang	mißlungen
mögen	magst, mag	mochte	gemocht
müssen	mußt, muß	mußte	gemußt
nehmen	nimmst, nimmt	nahm	genommen
nennen	nennst, nennt	nannte	genannt
pfeifen	pfeifst, pfeift	pfiff	gepfiffen
preisen	preist, preist	pries	gepriesen
quellen*	quillst, quillt	quoll	gequollen
raten	rätst, rät	riet	geraten
reiben	reibst, reibt	rieb	gerieben
reißen*	reißt, reißt	riß	gerissen
reiten*	reitest, reitet	ritt	geritten
rennen*	rennst, rennt	rannte	gerannt
riechen	riechst, riecht	roch	gerochen
ringen	ringst, ringt	rang	gerungen
rinnen*	rinnst, rinnt	rann	geronnen
rufen	rufst, ruft	rief	gerufen
salzen	salzt, salzt	salzte	gesalzen
saufen	säufst, säuft	soff	gesoffen
saugen	saugst, saugt	sog	gesogen
schaffen	schaffst, schafft	schuf	geschaffen
schallen	schallst, schallt	scholl	geschollen
scheiden*	scheidest, scheidet	schied	geschieden
scheinen	scheinst, scheint	schien	geschienen
schelten	schiltst, schilt	schalt	gescholten
scheren	scherst, schert	schor	geschoren
schieben	schiebst, schiebt	schob	geschoben
schießen	schießt, schießt	schoß	geschossen
schinden	schindest, schindet	schund	geschunden
schlafen	schläfst, schläft	schlief	geschlafen
schlagen	schlägst, schlägt	schlug	geschlagen
schleichen*	schleichst, schleicht	schlich	geschlichen
schleifen	schleifst, schleift	schliff	geschliffen
schließen	schließt, schließt	schloß	geschlossen
schlingen	schlingst, schlingt	schlang	geschlungen
schmeißen	schmeißt, schmeißt	schmiß	geschmissen
schmelzen*	schmilzt, schmilzt	schmolz	geschmolzen
schneiden	schneidest, schneidet	schnitt	geschnitten
schreiben	schreibst, schreibt	schrieb	geschrieben

infinitive	(2nd, 3rd sing.)	preterite	participle
schreien	schreist, schreit	schrie	geschrie(e)n
schreiten	schreitest, schreitet	schritt	geschritten
schweigen	schweigst, schweigt	schwieg	geschwiegen
schwellen*	schwillst, schwillt	schwoll	geschwollen
schwimmen*	schwimmst, schwimmt	schwamm	geschwommen
schwinden*	schwindest, schwindet	schwand	geschwunden
schwingen	schwingst, schwingt	schwang	geschwungen
schwören	schwörst, schwört	schwur	geschworen
sehen	siehst, sieht	sah	gesehen
sein*	bist, ist	war	gewesen
senden	sendest, sendet	sandte	gesandt
singen	singst, singt	sang	gesungen
sinken*	sinkst, sinkt	sank	gesunken
sinnen	sinnst, sinnt	sann	gesonnen
sitzen*	sitzt, sitzt	saß	gesessen
sollen	sollst, soll	sollte	gesollt
speien	speist, speit	spie	gespie(e)n
spinnen	spinnst, spinnt	spann	gesponnen
sprechen	sprichst, spricht	sprach	gesprochen
sprießen*	sprießt, sprießt	sproß	gesprossen
springen*	springst, springt	sprang	gesprungen
stechen	stichst, sticht	stach	gestochen
stecken	steckst, steckt	steckte *or* stak	gesteckt
stehen	stehst, steht	stand	gestanden
stehlen	stiehlst, stiehlt	stahl	gestohlen
steigen*	steigst, steigt	stieg	gestiegen
sterben*	stirbst, stirbt	starb	gestorben
stinken	stinkst, stinkt	stank	gestunken
stoßen	stößt, stößt	stieß	gestoßen
streichen	streichst, streicht	strich	gestrichen
streiten*	streitest, streitet	stritt	gestritten
tragen	trägst, trägt	trug	getragen
treffen	triffst, trifft	traf	getroffen
treiben*	treibst, treibt	trieb	getrieben
treten*	trittst, tritt	trat	getreten
trinken	trinkst, trinkt	trank	getrunken
trügen	trügst, trügt	trog	getrogen
tun	tust, tut	tat	getan
verderben	verdirbst, verdirbt	verdarb	verdorben
verdrießen	verdrießt, verdrießt	verdroß	verdrossen
vergessen	vergißt, vergißt	vergaß	vergessen
verlieren	verlierst, verliert	verlor	verloren
verschleißen	verschleißt, verschleißt	verschliß	verschlissen
wachsen*	wächst, wächst	wuchs	gewachsen
wägen	wägst, wägt	wog	gewogen
waschen	wäschst, wäscht	wusch	gewaschen
weben	webst, webt	wob	gewoben
weichen*	weichst, weicht	wich	gewichen
weisen	weist, weist	wies	gewiesen
wenden	wendest, wendet	wandte	gewandt
werben	wirbst, wirbt	warb	geworben
werden*	wirst, wird	wurde	geworden
werfen	wirfst, wirft	warf	geworfen
wiegen	wiegst, wiegt	wog	gewogen
winden	windest, windet	wand	gewunden
wissen	weißt, weiß	wußte	gewußt
wollen	willst, will	wollte	gewollt
wringen	wringst, wringt	wrang	gewrungen
zeihen	zeihst, zeiht	zieh	geziehen
ziehen*	ziehst, zieht	zog	gezogen
zwingen	zwingst, zwingt	zwang	gezwungen

English irregular verbs

present	pt	ptp	present	pt	ptp
arise (arising)	arose	arisen	fall	fell	fallen
			feed	fed	fed
awake (awaking)	awoke	awaked	feel	felt	felt
			fight	fought	fought
be (am, is, are; being)	was, were	been	find	found	found
			flee	fled	fled
bear	bore	born(e)	fling	flung	flung
beat	beat	beaten	fly (flies)	flew	flown
become (becoming)	became	become	forbid (forbidding)	forbade	forbidden
befall	befell	befallen	forecast	forecast	forecast
begin (beginning)	began	begun	forego	forewent	foregone
			foresee	foresaw	foreseen
behold	beheld	beheld	foretell	foretold	foretold
bend	bent	bent	forget (forgetting)	forgot	forgotten
beseech	besought	besought	forgive (forgiving)	forgave	forgiven
beset (besetting)	beset	beset	forsake (forsaking)	forsook	forsaken
bet (betting)	bet (also betted)	bet (also betted)	freeze (freezing)	froze	frozen
bid (bidding)	bid	bid	get (getting)	got	got, (US) gotten
bind	bound	bound			
bite (biting)	bit	bitten	give (giving)	gave	given
bleed	bled	bled	go (goes)	went	gone
blow	blew	blown	grind	ground	ground
break	broke	broken	grow	grew	grown
breed	bred	bred	hang	hung (also hanged)	hung (also hanged)
bring	brought	brought			
build	built	built			
burn	burnt or burned	burnt (also burned)	have (has; having)	had	had
burst	burst	burst	hear	heard	heard
buy	bought	bought	hide (hiding)	hid	hidden
can	could	(been able)	hit (hitting)	hit	hit
cast	cast	cast	hold	held	held
catch	caught	caught	hurt	hurt	hurt
choose (choosing)	chose	chosen	keep	kept	kept
			kneel	knelt (also kneeled)	knelt (also kneeled)
cling	clung	clung			
come (coming)	came	come	know	knew	known
cost	cost	cost	lay	laid	laid
creep	crept	crept	lead	led	led
cut (cutting)	cut	cut	lean	leant (also leaned)	leant (also leaned)
deal	dealt	dealt			
dig (digging)	dug	dug	leap	leapt (also leaped)	leapt (also leaped)
do (3rd person; he/she/it/does)	did	done	learn	learnt (also learned)	learnt (also learned)
draw	drew	drawn	leave (leaving)	left	left
dream	dreamed (dreamt)	dreamed (dreamt)	lend	lent	lent
drink	drank	drunk	let (letting)	let	let
drive (driving)	drove	driven	lie (lying)	lay	lain
			light	lit (also lighted)	lit (also lighted)
dwell	dwelt	dwelt			
eat	ate	eaten	lose (losing)	lost	lost

present	pt	ptp	present	pt	ptp
make (making)	made	made	spell	spelt (also spelled)	spelt (also spelled)
may	might	——	spend	spent	spent
mean	meant	meant	spill	spilt (also spilled)	spilt (also spilled)
meet	met	met	spin (spinning)	spun	spun
mistake (mistaking)	mistook	mistaken	spit (spitting)	spat	spat
mow	mowed	mown (also mowed)	split (splitting)	split	split
must	(had to)	(had to)	spoil	spoiled (also spoilt)	spoiled (also spoilt)
pay	paid	paid	spread	spread	spread
put (putting)	put	put	spring	sprang	sprung
quit (quitting)	quit (also quitted)	quit (also quitted)	stand	stood	stood
read	read	read	steal	stole	stolen
rend	rent	rent	stick	stuck	stuck
rid (ridding)	rid	rid	sting	stung	stung
ride (riding)	rode	ridden	stink	stank	stunk
ring	rang	rung	stride (striding)	strode	stridden
rise (rising)	rose	risen	strike (striking)	struck	struck (also stricken)
run (running)	ran	run	strive (striving)	strove	striven
saw	sawed	sawn	swear	swore	sworn
say	said	said	sweep	swept	swept
see	saw	seen	swell	swelled	swollen (also swelled)
seek	sought	sought	swim (swimming)	swam	swum
sell	sold	sold	swing	swung	swung
send	sent	sent	take (taking)	took	taken
set (setting)	set	set	teach	taught	taught
shake (shaking)	shook	shaken	tear	tore	torn
shall	should	——	tell	told	told
shear	sheared	shorn (also sheared)	think	thought	thought
shed (shedding)	shed	shed	throw	threw	thrown
shine (shining)	shone	shone	thrust	thrust	thrust
shoot	shot	shot	tread	trod	trodden
show	showed	shown	wake (waking)	woke (also waked)	woken (also waked)
shrink	shrank	shrunk	waylay	waylaid	waylaid
shut (shutting)	shut	shut	wear	wore	worn
sing	sang	sung	weave (weaving)	wove (also weaved)	woven (also weaved)
sink	sank	sunk	wed (wedding)	wedded (also wed)	wedded (also wed)
sit (sitting)	sat	sat	weep	wept	wept
slay	slew	slain	win (winning)	won	won
sleep	slept	slept	wind	wound	wound
slide (sliding)	slid	slid	withdraw	withdrew	withdrawn
sling	slung	slung	withhold	withheld	withheld
slit (slitting)	slit	slit	withstand	withstood	withstood
smell	smelt (also smelled)	smelt (also smelled)	wring	wrung	wrung
sow	sowed	sown (also sowed)	write (writing)	wrote	written
speak	spoke	spoken			
speed	sped (also speeded)	sped (also speeded)			